FUNDAMENTALS OF INVESTING

THE ADDISON-WESLEY SERIES IN FINANCE

FUNDAMENTALS OF
INVESTING
NINTH EDITION

LAWRENCE J. GITMAN, CFP®
SAN DIEGO STATE UNIVERSITY

MICHAEL D. JOEHNK, CFA
ARIZONA STATE UNIVERSITY

PEARSON

Addison
Wesley

Boston   San Francisco   New York
London   Toronto   Sydney   Tokyo   Singapore   Madrid
Mexico City   Munich   Paris   Cape Town   Hong Kong   Montreal

Editor-in-Chief: Denise Clinton
Senior Acquisitions Editor: Donna Battista
Senior Project Manager: Mary Clare McEwing
Senior Production Supervisor: Nancy Fenton
Marketing Manager: Deborah Meredith
Design Manager: Regina Hagen Kolenda
Cover Designer: Leslie Haimes
Executive Media Producer: Michelle Neil
Media Producer: Jennifer Pelland
Supplements Coordinator: Diane Theriault
Senior Manufacturing Buyer: Hugh Crawford
Project Coordination, Text Design, Art Studio, and Electronic Page Makeup: Thompson Steele, Inc.

Questions appearing in the Putting Your Investment Know-How to the Test sections at the end of each chapter are used with permission:

Library of Congress Cataloging-in-Publication Data

Gitman, Lawrence J.
    Fundamentals of investing / Lawrence J. Gitman, Michael D. Joehnk. — 9th ed.
      p.   cm.
    Includes bibliographical references and index.
    ISBN 0-321-23685-8 (alk. paper)
    1. Investments.   2. Investments--Problems, exercises, etc.   I. Joehnk, Michael D.   II. Title.

HG4521.G547   2004b
332.6--dc22   2004044395

3 4 5 6 7 8 9 10—QWT—08 07 06

BRIEF CONTENTS

CONTENTS

PART THREE   INVESTING IN COMMON STOCKS 233

CHAPTER 6   COMMON STOCKS 234

INVESTING IN ACTION

Anatomy of a Market
Meltdown   238

In International Investing,
Currencies Can Make or
Break You   268

CHAPTER 9

PART FOUR

CHAPTER 10

CHAPTER 11

BOND VALUATION 457

CHAPTER 14

INVESTING IN ACTION

Taming the Portfolio
Monster   554

ETHICS IN INVESTING

Retirement at Enron   603

MANAGING YOUR OWN PORTFOLIO 596

PART SIX

DERIVATIVE SECURITIES 639

CHAPTER 15

OPTIONS: PUTS, CALLS, AND WARRANTS 640

INVESTING IN ACTION

he Call of the Bull and
Bear Spreads   662

Using Index Options to
Protect a Whole Portfolio 668

CHAPTER 16

COMMODITIES AND FINANCIAL FUTURES 685

APPENDIX A   FINANCIAL TABLES A-1

PREFACE

"Making informed decisions about what to do with your money will help build a more stable financial future for you and your family." This axiom from Federal Reserve Chairman Alan Greenspan sums up quite well the goal of this text—to help you make informed decisions about what to do with your money.

Sounds simple, doesn't it? Well it's not! There are many decisions and challenges involved in the process of investing in today's constantly changing financial marketplace. For example, What are the best investment vehicles for me? What's the market outlook? How can I reduce commissions on my transactions? Should I buy individual securities or mutual funds? Do I need a professional money manager? Can I afford one? What about risk? What are the tax implications of a given investment strategy? Should I include bonds in my portfolio? What role can options or futures play in my investment program? Clearly, it is not easy to make informed investment decisions!

The language, concepts, vehicles, and strategies of investing are foreign to many. In order to become an informed investor you must first become conversant with the many aspects of investing. Then you will be prepared to make informed decisions in the highly dynamic investment environment. Markets move, prices fluctuate, tax laws change, and new investment vehicles and strategies are developed. By understanding the fundamentals of investing and developing, implementing, and monitoring your investment plans and strategies, you should be able to weather the frequent storms in the financial marketplace and arrive safely in port with your investment goals achieved. This book provides the information and guidance that is needed by individual investors to make informed decisions and achieve their goals.

The ninth edition of *Fundamentals of Investing* provides those wishing to become informed investors with the knowledge needed to actively develop and monitor their own investment portfolios. It meets the needs of professors and students in the first course in investments offered at colleges and universities, junior and community colleges, professional certification programs, and continuing education courses. Focusing on both individual securities and portfolios, *Fundamentals of Investing* explains how to develop, implement, and monitor investment goals after considering the risk and return of both investment vehicles and markets. A conversational tone and liberal use of examples guide students through the material and demonstrate important points.

Key Features of the Ninth Edition

Using information gathered from both academicians and practicing investment professionals, plus feedback from adopters, the ninth edition reflects the realities of today's investment environment. At the same time, it provides a structured framework for successful teaching and learning.

Clear Focus on the Individual Investor

Today, slightly more than half of all U.S. households own stock either directly or indirectly [through mutual funds or participation in 401(k)s]. The focus of *Fundamentals of Investing* has always been on the individual investor. This focus gives students the information they need to develop, implement, and monitor a successful investment program. It also provides students with a solid foundation of basic concepts, tools, and techniques. Subsequent courses can build on that foundation by presenting the advanced concepts, tools, and techniques used by institutional investors and money managers.

Comprehensive yet Flexible Organization

The text provides a firm foundation for learning by first describing the overall investment environment, including online investing. Next it presents conceptual tools needed by investors—the concepts of risk and return and the basics of portfolio construction. It then examines each of the popular investment vehicles—common stocks, bonds, preferred stocks, convertible securities, and mutual funds. Following this series of chapters on investment vehicles comes a chapter on how to administer one's own portfolio. The final section of the book focuses on derivative securities—options and futures—which require more expertise. Although the first two parts of the textbook are best covered at the start of the course, instructors can cover particular investment vehicles in just about any sequence. The comprehensive yet flexible nature of the book enables instructors to customize it to their own course structure and teaching objectives.

We have organized each chapter according to a decision-making perspective, and we have been careful always to point out the pros and cons of the various vehicles and strategies that we present. With this information, individual investors can select the investment actions that are most consistent with their objectives. In addition, we've illustrated investment vehicles and strategies in such a way that students learn the decision-making implications and consequences of each investment action they contemplate.

Timely Topics

Various issues and developments constantly reshape financial markets and investment vehicles. Virtually all topics in this book take into account changes in the investment environment. For example, the recent corporate scandals that have rocked the investments world in particular and the financial world in general are incorporated into the ninth edition via a new focus on ethics in the book. The bursting of the tech bubble, the post-9/11 investment environment, online investing, and a host of other timely topics also embellish this new edition.

Globalization

One issue that is reshaping investing is the growing globalization of securities markets. As a result, *Fundamentals of Investing* continues to stress the global aspects of investing. We initially look at the growing importance of international markets, investing in foreign securities (indirectly or directly), international investment performance, and the risks of investing internationally. In later chapters, popular international investment opportunities and strategies are described as part of the coverage of each specific type of investment vehicle. This integration of international topics helps students understand the importance of maintaining a global focus when planning, building, and managing an investment portfolio. Global topics are highlighted by inclusion of a globe icon.

Comprehensive and Integrated Learning System

Another feature of the ninth edition is its comprehensive and integrated learning system, discussed in detail in the feature Walkthrough later in the Preface.

Online Trading and Investment Simulator (OTIS)

A truly exciting addition to our teaching/learning assets is the use of OTIS, a powerful trading and investment simulator developed at the Alfred P. West, Jr., Learning Lab at the Wharton School of the University of Pennsylvania. This Web-based simulator makes the student a virtual fund manager. Students learn how to construct and manage portfolios; understand the mechanics, risks, and requirements of margin trading; appreciate the benefits of short selling; and grasp the concept of liquidity as it applies to meeting a portfolio's short- and long-term needs, among other skills. The simulator enables the student fund manager to make trades, view holdings, assess performance, and evaluate performance against that of fellow classmates. A true innovation to the art and science of trading and investment, OTIS will quickly propel students into a hands-on, interactive learning environment. Exercises using OTIS appear at the end of appropriate chapters.

Specific Content Changes

Our many adopters are interested first and foremost in how the content has changed from the eighth to the ninth edition. We hope that this same information will interest potential new adopters also, because it indicates our mandate to stay current with the field of investments and to continue to shape a book that will truly meet the needs of students and instructors .

The chart on pages xx-xxii outlines in detail the chapter-by-chapter revisions we have made to the ninth edition and the benefits that we think accrue as a result of these changes. Although we have made many changes to this edition and updated all data and statistics, we see the major changes as follows:

- Significant new discussion of the high-tech bubble of the late 1990s and the resulting bear market after the bubble burst

- New discussion of corporate scandals and subsequent steps to correct them

- Changes in the 2003 Tax Act and how they affect portfolio management

- New material on the online investments environment

- A four-chapter treatment of common stocks, *with the addition of a new chapter on market price behavior (Chapter 9)*. This chapter on technical analysis and other market-related issues features an all-new section on behavioral finance and the challenge it poses to the efficient markets hypothesis.

- Increased coverage of mutual funds, with the addition of material on hedge funds

	REVISIONS	BENEFITS
PART ONE Preparing to Invest	Chapters updated and streamlined to provide clear focus on the current structure and operations of the investment environment.	Provides a modern view of the investment environment in which individual investors will obtain information and make transactions helpful in achieving their investment goals.
Chapter 1 The Investment Environment	Introduced actual historical return data, streamlined the discussion of the investment process, updated text discussions to reflect changes in the 2003 Tax Act, added a brief discussion of tax-advantage retirement vehicles, significantly shortened and tabularized the discussion of popular short-term investment vehicles, and updated all other discussions.	Maintains stronger focus on the role of investing in achieving long-term goals.
Chapter 2 Markets and Transactions	Added new IPO data, updated security exchange statistics and discussions, clarified role of market makers, extended discussion of recent market behavior and international performance, introduced euros into the discussion of currency exchange risk, updated the discussion of trading hours, streamlined discussion of the Sarbanes-Oxley Act of 2002, and added a detailed example of margin requirements and short selling.	Provides a modern focus on the structure, operation, and regulation of the securities markets and the key types of securities transactions that should prepare the reader to participate effectively in the securities markets.
Chapter 3 Online Information and Investing	Significantly revised discussions of the online investment environment to fully capture the standardization and changes that have occurred, updated all site descriptions and URLs, updated stock market average and index discussions, and revised and streamlined the discussions of making online securities transactions through a full-service or a premium or basic discount broker.	Provides a clear description of the primary traditional and online sources of investment information and securities brokerage services available to the typical individual investor for use in executing his or her investment plans.
PART TWO Important Conceptual Tools	Added real data, clarified key conceptual discussions, and integrated the use of Excel spreadsheets where appropriate.	Allows reader to better grasp the concepts presented and anchor them to reality; also provides an appreciation for the role that electronic spreadsheets can play in streamlining routine financial calculations.
Chapter 4 Return and Risk	Added real historical return and related risk data to the return and risk discussions, included Excel spreadsheet clips with each time value of money calculation demonstration, and updated all examples and discussions.	Adds practical insights to the concepts and computations presented with regard to risk and return as they relate to securities investments.
Chapter 5 Modern Portfolio Concepts	Clarified the discussion of correlation and diversification by adding a new figure and related explanation, updated all statistics and data, added a discussion of risk premiums to improve the explanation of CAPM, and added some closing comments on CAPM that include a brief discussion of arbitrage pricing theory (APT).	Increases reader understanding of the key concepts underlying modern portfolio theory and provides better insight into the practical strengths and weaknesses of the tools that derive from it.
PART THREE: Investing in Common Stocks	Updated all the comparative return data to 2003, totally restructured the chapter on stock valuation to focus on fundamental analysis, and added an all-new chapter on technical analysis and market price behavior.	Provides a more focused view of security analysis and stock valuation, enabling readers to gain a better appreciation of the investment attributes of common stocks.
Chapter 6: Common Stocks	Added considerable discussion and market performance data on the high-tech bubble that developed in the late-90s and the subsequent bear market of 2000-02, including a new box on "The Anatomy of a Market Meltdown"; provided new data through mid-2003 of the comparative returns on the Dow, the S&P, and the Nasdaq Composite; updated the discussion of dividends to include the new (2003) preferential tax rates; updated through 2002 the comparative annual and holding period returns in the world's major equity markets; and substantially tightened up the discussion of alternative investment strategies.	Provides a clear perspective of the current investment environment, and an appreciation of the impact that the market and other issues—like dividends—can have on investor returns.

	REVISIONS	BENEFITS
Chapter 7 **Analyzing** **Common Stocks**	Updated the discussion of economic and industry analysis and the roles they play in the stock valuation process, added discussion on some of the corporate and accounting "scandals" that occurred in the market and steps taken to correct them, added discussion of Standard & Poor's new earnings figure ("core earnings from operations"), tightened up and clarified the discussion of financial ratios, including the use of EBITDA rather than EBIT and its impact on various financial ratios, and added a new ratio that looks at the quality of earnings—the "cash realization ratio."	Maintains a clear and well-defined focus on the role that the economy, the industry, and the company play in security analysis and stock valuation.
Chapter 8 **Stock Valuation**	This chapter has been totally restructured so that emphasis is now centered on the fundamental analysis of the company and its stock; as part of this, the material on forecasting revenues and other valuation variables is updated and streamlined, as is the discussion of the various forms of the dividend valuation model. Added more discussion on valuing growth and non-dividend paying stocks, significantly revised the discussion on the price/earnings approach to stock valuation, and added all-new material on other price relative procedures, including the price to cash flow, price to sales, and price to book value ratios.	Provides a clear and concise discussion of fundamental analysis and valuation, from the generation of the variables used in the valuation process to the various stock valuation models.
Chapter 9 **Market Price** **Behavior**	This all-new chapter deals with technical analysis and other market-related issues; the chapter kicks off with discussion of technical analysis—including a variety of technical / market measures—and how it fits into the stock valuation process. Attention then shifts to the efficient market hypothesis and the questions it raises for technical analysis and the security analysis process, and finally to behavioral finance and the challenges it poses to the concept of efficient markets and the investor security selection process.	Provides focused discussion of market behavior, the principles and procedures used to assess the market, and the major theories that describe how prices are set in the market and how investors select securities.
PART FOUR **Investing in Fixed-** **Income Securities**	Updated and streamlined discussion of the various facets of fixed-income securities, including comparative returns with stocks, the principles and properties of bond valuation, and the features and properties of preferred stocks and convertible securities.	Enhances reader appreciation of the role that fixed-income securities can play in a well-developed investment program, and the variables that drive the yield and return behavior of these securities.
Chapter 10 **Fixed-Income** **Securities**	Added material on the behavior of interest rates and bond returns through 2003 and showed how they performed relative to stocks, restructured the discussion of essential bond features to cover bond price behavior before call features and other issue characteristics, updated the effects that the new federal tax rates have on the taxable equivalent yields of municipal bonds, updated and clarified the discussion of the major segments of the bond market and the major types of issues found in the market, both domestically and globally, and updated the corporate and Treasury bond quotes.	Enhances the practical side of the bond market and puts more emphasis on the variables that drive bond price behavior and the wide array of different kinds of securities available in the bond market.
Chapter 11: **Bond Valuation**	Added material relating bond risks to required rates of return, updated Treasury yield curve data and discussion, added more discussion about the reinvestment assumptions embedded in bond yield measures, and updated all yield and duration calculations and discussions.	Increases reader understanding of the principles and properties of bond valuation, as well as the uses and limitations of the popular yield and price volatility measures.

REVISIONS		BENEFITS
Chapter 12 Preferred Stock and Convertible Securities	Added discussion of the tax treatment of preferred dividends, included material about the use of maturity dates on trust pre-ferreds, updated the market statistics on convertible preferreds and convertible notes and bonds, clarified the discussion about the impact that bond coupons can have on payback period, and added a box about "busted convertibles" and the potential return opportunities they offer.	Provides a more focused discussion of the features, properties, and investor uses of preferred stocks and convertible securities.
PART FIVE Portfolio Management	Increased the breadth of mutual fund coverage to include a brief discussion of hedge funds and updated and improved the discussion of individual portfolio management in light of the 2003 Tax Act.	Provides more modern and up-to-date coverage of portfolio management, both through professional mutual fund man-agers and by individuals managing their own portfolios.
Chapter 13 Mutual Funds: Professionally Managed Portfolios	Updated all mutual fund data and return statistics; added a new box dealing with late trading and market timing being allowed in some mutual fund families; updated the quotes used with closed- and open-end funds; streamlined the discussion of unit investment trusts and added material on hedge funds, including the similarities and differences between hedge funds and mutual funds; and added material on what kind of mutual fund dividends are eligible for preferential tax treatment.	Maintains the strong focus on mutual funds as investment vehicles, the roles that these securities can play in an investment program, and the mutual fund selection process.
Chapter 14 Managing Your Own Portfolio	Updated all after-tax return calculation demonstrations to reflect the change in tax treatment of dividends reflected in the 2003 Tax Act and updated and improved the demonstration portfolios that are presented.	Uses realistic portfolios to give the reader up-to-date insight into how to evaluate, monitor, and assess the perfor-mance of both individual investments and portfolios.
PART SIX Derivative Securites	Updated and streamlined the discussion of options and futures, including the use of these derivative securities as hedging vehi-cles to modify risk.	Provides a clearer and more focused look at the investment merits and uses of derivative securities.
Chapter 15 Options: Puts, Calls, and Warrants	Added discussion on American vs. European options and the International Securities (options) Exchange, enhanced the dis-cussion of using options as hedging vehicles to modify risk exposure, updated all market data and statistics, and added dis-cussion about options on exchange traded funds.	Increases understanding of the options market and the uses of options as invest-ment vehicles.
Chapter 16 Commodities and Financial Futures	Updated all futures market data and statistics, streamlined the discussion on investor uses of commodities and financial futures, and added a new box on single-stock futures contracts.	Maintains focus on the basic properties and investor uses of commodities and financial futures.

THE

GITMAN / JOEHNK

PROVEN

TEACHING/LEARNING/MOTIVATIONAL

SYSTEM

Users of *Fundamentals of Investing* have praised the effectiveness of the Gitman/Joehnk teaching and learning system, which has been hailed as one of its leading hallmarks. The system, driven by a set of carefully developed learning goals, has been retained and polished in the ninth edition. Users have also praised the rich motivational framework that underpins each chapter. Key elements of the pedagogical and motivational features are illustrated and described below.

THE LEARNING GOAL SYSTEM

The Learning Goal System begins each chapter with **six Learning Goals**, labeled with numbered icons—these goals anchor the most important concepts and techniques to be learned. The Learning Goal icons are then tied to key points in the chapter's structure, including

- First-level headings
- Summary
- Discussion Questions
- Problems
- Cases

This tightly knit structure provides a clear roadmap for students—they know what they need to learn, where they can find it, and whether they've mastered it by the end of the chapter.

An **opening story** sets the stage for the content that follows by focusing on an investment situation involving a real company or real event, which is in turn linked to the chapter topics. Students see the relevance of the vignette to the world of investments.

What drives a stock's value? Many factors come into play, from positive industry trends to favorable earnings reports to company developments such as new products. Take Krispy Kreme Doughnuts, for example, whose many customers buy more than 5 million Krispy Kreme doughnuts every day in the company's 292 stores in 37 states, Canada, and Australia. Or maybe you were lucky enough to recognize a promising growth stock and gobble up shares soon after the company went public in April 2000 at $21 per share (which, after adjusting for *two* 2-for-1 stock splits, was more like $5.25 a share). The company's timing was particularly good: Investors were looking for an alternative to dot-com high fliers, and the company's popular brand and product appealed to many different types of consumers.

Krispy Kreme's strong fundamentals continue to please investors: low debt to equity ratio, excellent liquidity, rising revenues and net income, and rapid growth as it expands beyond its southeastern U.S. roots. In early 2004, the stock price was hovering around $36 and had a 52-week high close to $50.

Yet some analysts consider the stock overvalued. For the quarter ending July 31, 2003, its 12-month trailing price/earnings (P/E) ratio was almost 60, and the 12-month forward P/E was about 35. "This is a stock that people will always say is too expensive," says John Glass, a CIBC restaurant analyst. Glass estimates that on a 2004 P/E basis, its price is comparable to peers like Starbucks (P/E = 30). Krispy Kreme's earnings per share are growing faster, though—about 25% per year. Even so, Standard & Poor's analysts, using a discounted cash flow model and annual revenue growth of at least 20% for five years, downgraded the stock to "avoid." They thought the stock was trading at a price that reflected a 20% premium to its intrinsic value.

What do all of these numbers mean in terms of the value of Krispy Kreme's stock? This chapter explains how to determine a stock's intrinsic value by using dividend valuation, dividend and earnings, price/earnings, and other models.

Sources: "Krispy Kreme Announces Strong Fourth Quarter and Fiscal Year 2003 Results," *PRNewswire-FirstCall*, March 18, 2003, downloaded from www.krispykreme.com; Andy Serwer, "The Hole Story," *Fortune*, July 7, 2003, pp. 53–62; David Shook and Scott Livengood, "His Doughnut Stores Are His 'Children'," *Business Week Online*, December 9, 2002, downloaded from www.business.com; and "S&P Cuts Krispy Kreme to Avoid," *Business Week Online*, July 6, 2003, downloaded from www.businessweek.com.

CHAPTER 8

STOCK VALUATION

LEARNING GOALS

After studying this chapter, you should be able to:

LG 1 Explain the role that a company's future plays in the stock valuation process.

LG 2 Develop a forecast of a stock's expected cash flow, starting with corporate sales and earnings, and then moving to expected dividends and share price.

LG 3 Discuss the concepts of intrinsic value and required rates of return, and note how they are used.

LG 4 Determine the underlying value of a stock using the zero-growth, constant-growth and variable-growth dividend valuation models.

LG 5 Use other types of present-value–based models to derive the value of a stock, as well as alternative price-relative procedures.

LG 6 Gain a basic appreciation of the procedures used to value different types of stocks, from traditional dividend-paying shares to more growth-oriented stocks.

331

⚖ ETHICS IN INVESTING

COOKING THE BOOKS: WHAT WERE THEY THINKING?

The scandals involving fraudulent accounting practices at Enron, WorldCom, Adelphia, Xerox, Global Crossing, and Tyco have resulted in widespread public outrage. It appears that creative and un- ethical accounting practices kept real costs and debts off the books of these companies and inflated their stock prices. When the reality finally caught up with the fantasy, tens of thousands of investors and employees lost their life savings; at the same time, many of the corporate executives who were responsible for the fraud reaped huge financial rewards. For example, cooking the books at Enron cost investors almost $67 billion, while the implosion of WorldCom wiped out $175 billion of shareholder value, the biggest corporate bankruptcy in U.S. history.

Just two months after the Enron debacle, Global Crossing sought Chapter 11 protection from its creditors after the SEC started an official inquiry into the collapse and subpoenaed documents relating to widespread claims that the company had used "creative accounting" to inflate its earnings. The investigation also implicated accounting firm Arthur Andersen, which had been the auditor for both Global Crossing and Enron. When Global Crossing filed for bankruptcy in January 2002, it listed $22.4 billion in assets and $12.3 billion in debt. However, much of its value appeared to result from less than ethical accounting practices approved by Arthur Andersen. Since the company went public in 1998, however, its founder and chairman Gary Winnick had profited handsomely, selling $734 million worth of Global Crossing stock.

Another telecom giant, Qwest Communications, was under investigation by the SEC for its accounting practices when it disclosed on July 28, 2002, that it had incorrectly accounted for more than $1 billion of revenue since 1999. Qwest had booked hundreds of millions of dollars of revenue at the end of its quarterly reporting period that should have been delayed until the next quarter. Qwest actually has $26 billion in debt, and like many other telecommunication companies, faces intense pressure to meet quarterly revenue and profit targets.

At WorldCom, internal audits revealed that $3.8 billion in operating expenses had been fraudulently disguised as capital expenditures over five quarters dating back to January 2001. The stock that had peaked around $65 currently trades at 2 cents on the OTC pink sheets. Arthur Andersen was again implicated as the corporate auditor in this scandal.

Xerox, a leading office machine supplier, had to restate $6.4 billion of revenues dating back to 1997. It reached agreement with the SEC over

continued on next page

New! Ethics boxes—a series of boxed "caselets" on real-life scenarios in the investments world that focus on the ethics of a given situation—appear in selected chapters and on the book's Web site. Among the many issues explored are WorldCom and the perils of margin trading, Martha Stewart and charges of securities fraud, "cooking the books" at such companies as Enron and Global Crossing, and abuses in the mutual funds industry. Each ethics box contains a Critical Thinking Question for class discussion, with suggested answers given in the Instructor's Manual.

Each chapter features boxed essays, called **Investing in Action**, which describe real-life investing situations or events. These high-interest boxes, which have been written specifically for this textbook, demonstrate the book's concepts at work in the world of investing. Among the many new topics explored are the anatomy of the market meltdown from "irrational exuberance" to bursting of the dot.com bubble; the effects of 9/11; the rash of corporate scandals; the basic steps to investing online; and a profile of "investment junkies," among others. These boxes contain a Critical Thinking Question for class discussion, with suggested answers given in the Instructor's Manual.

INVESTING IN ACTION

INVESTMENT JUNKIES

When Howard, a young investor, watched his friends strike it rich, he stepped gingerly into the waters of online investing for himself. He made $4,000 in a matter of minutes on his first trade, and soon he was deep into *day trading*—the practice of buying and selling stocks very quickly to make a few cents profit. After he met with some success, Howard opened a margin account to leverage his profits. Before long he was a confirmed "investaholic." Not until the market tanked and he was deep in debt did reality hit home for Howard. "I never noticed the sunshine," said another compulsive investor. "All I did was watch CNBC and stare at my computer." Yet even after he stopped trading, he wistfully recalls the extreme euphoria: " I've never felt a high like that. Nothing can replace it."

These investment junkies were not alone. As long as the markets were up and paper profits climbed, the apparent ease of gaining quick riches lured many naive investors eager for quick profits. The speed and simplicity of point-and-click stock online trading led to more impulse buying, as well as a significant increase in the number of stock market gamblers. "It gives gamblers the quick fix and constant action they crave," comments Marvin Steinberg, psychologist and director of the Connecticut Council on Problem Gambling.

Investing as gambling? Hard to accept, but at one point stock traders represented about half the attendees at Gamblers Anonymous meetings. And because it's not uncommon for investment addicts to bet as much as $25,000 on one trade—whereas few gamblers would wager that much on one hand at the casino—the stock market can take them on a quick ride to bankruptcy.

As with other addictions, it's difficult to determine when you cross the line from making occasional impulse stock purchases to becoming a full-fledged investment junkie. According to the Council on Compulsive Gambling of New Jersey, problem gambling affects approximately 10% of investors. These investors can stop gambling after a big loss or intervention from family members. The 5% who cross into compulsive gambler territory have more trouble controlling their addiction.

Here are some warning signs to help you recognize a stock market gambling problem:

- Trading stocks to ease worries
- Becoming irritable when unable to trade
- Making increasingly speculative investments
- Borrowing to be able to invest more
- Experiencing euphoria when you hit it big and depression when you don't
- Needing to raise the amount you invest to feel the thrill

CRITICAL THINKING QUESTION How might online trading and market conditions contribute to an investor's gambling problem?

Sources: Steven T. Goldberg, "He Never Saw the Sun," *Kiplinger's Personal Finance Magazine,* August 2001, downloaded from www.kiplingerspersonalfinance.com; Ruth Simon and E. S. Browning, "Some Online Investors Can't Say No to Playing the Market," *Wall Street Journal,* August 4, 2000, pp. A1, A4; and Paul Sloan, "Can't Stop Checking Your Quotes?" *U.S. News & World Report,* July 10, 2000, p. 40.

WITHIN THE CHAPTER

Each chapter contains two to three **Investor Facts**—brief sidebar items that give an interesting statistic or cite an unusual investment experience. These facts add a bit of seasoning to the concepts under review and capture a real-world flavor. Among the many snapshots provided by the Investor Facts are buying bonds secured by the work of stars like David Bowie and James Brown, a portrait of an average mutual funds shareholder, and reverse stock splits.

Key Equations are screened in green throughout the text to help readers identify the most important mathematical relationships.

$$\text{Future value at end of year 2} = \$1,080 \times (1 + 0.08) = \underline{\$1,166.40}$$

Calculator Keystrokes At appropriate spots in the text the student will find sections on the use of financial calculators, with marginal calculator graphics that show the inputs and functions to be used.

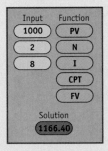

For help in study and review, **Key Terms** and their definitions appear in the margin when they are first introduced.

discount rate
the annual rate of return that could be earned currently on a similar investment; used when finding present value; also called *opportunity cost*.

Concepts in Review questions appear at the end of each section of the chapter. These review questions allow students to test their understanding of each section before moving on to the next section of the chapter.

Hot Links refer students to Web sites related to topics under discussion in the text and help to reinforce the use of the Internet in the investments world.

IN REVIEW

CONCEPTS

4.1 Explain what is meant by the *return* on an investment. Differentiate between the two components of return—current income and capital gains (or losses).

4.2 What role do historical performance data play in estimating the expected return from a given investment? Discuss the key factors affecting investment returns—internal characteristics and external forces.

STILL MORE LEARNING TOOLS

Each **Summary** lists the chapter's key concepts and ideas, which correspond directly to the numbered Learning Goals at the begining of the chapter. **Learning Goal** icons precede each summary item, which begins with a bold-faced restatement of the learning goal.

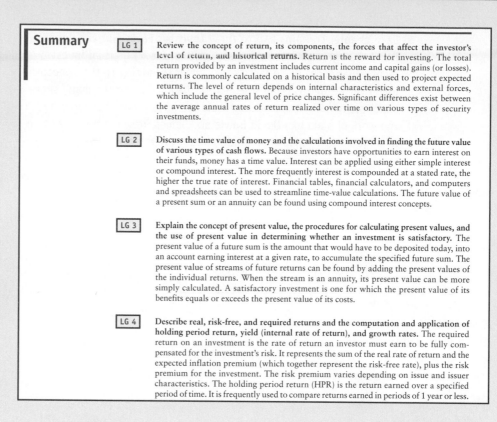

Summary

LG 1 Review the concept of return, its components, the forces that affect the investor's level of return, and historical returns. Return is the reward for investing. The total return provided by an investment includes current income and capital gains (or losses). Return is commonly calculated on a historical basis and then used to project expected returns. The level of return depends on internal characteristics and external forces, which include the general level of price changes. Significant differences exist between the average annual rates of return realized over time on various types of security investments.

LG 2 Discuss the time value of money and the calculations involved in finding the future value of various types of cash flows. Because investors have opportunities to earn interest on their funds, money has a time value. Interest can be applied using either simple interest or compound interest. The more frequently interest is compounded at a stated rate, the higher the true rate of interest. Financial tables, financial calculators, and computers and spreadsheets can be used to streamline time-value calculations. The future value of a present sum or an annuity can be found using compound interest concepts.

LG 3 Explain the concept of present value, the procedures for calculating present values, and the use of present value in determining whether an investment is satisfactory. The present value of a future sum is the amount that would have to be deposited today, into an account earning interest at a given rate, to accumulate the specified future sum. The present value of streams of future returns can be found by adding the present values of the individual returns. When the stream is an annuity, its present value can be more simply calculated. A satisfactory investment is one for which the present value of its benefits equals or exceeds the present value of its costs.

LG 4 Describe real, risk-free, and required returns and the computation and application of holding period return, yield (internal rate of return), and growth rates. The required return on an investment is the rate of return an investor must earn to be fully compensated for the investment's risk. It represents the sum of the real rate of return and the expected inflation premium (which together represent the risk-free rate), plus the risk premium for the investment. The risk premium varies depending on issue and issuer characteristics. The holding period return (HPR) is the return earned over a specified period of time. It is frequently used to compare returns earned in periods of 1 year or less.

Putting Your Investment Know-How to the Test

1. An investment of $231 will increase in value to $268 in 3 years. The annual compound growth rate in this case is closest to
   a. 3.0%.
   b. 4.0%.
   c. 5.0%.
   d. 6.0%.

2. What is the value in 5 years of $100 invested today at an interest rate of 8% per year, compounded quarterly?
   a. $144.50
   b. $146.02
   c. $148.02
   d. $148.59

3. All of the following statements about various types of risk are true *except*
   a. Business risk is the uncertainty of earnings caused by the nature of the firm's business.
   b. Financial risk is the uncertainty introduced by the method by which the firm finances its investments.
   c. Currency exchange rate risk is the uncertainty of returns caused by the possibility of a major change in the political or economic environment of a country.
   d. Liquidity risk is the uncertainty introduced by the secondary market for an investment.

4. An investor will receive a 5-year annuity of $2,500 per year. She will not receive the first payment until 3 years from today. If the annual rate is 8%, the present value of this annuity is closest to
   a. $8,105.
   b. $8,224.
   c. $8,558.
   d. $9,982.

5. An investor has a portfolio with a market value of $50,000 at the beginning of the year. The market value of the portfolio is $48,100 at the end of the year. During that period the investor collects $600 in dividends. The holding period return for this investor's portfolio for the year is
   a. −1.30%.
   b. −2.60%.
   c. −2.63%.
   d. −2.67%.

6. An investor holds a portfolio consisting of one share of each of the following stocks.

New! Putting Your Investment Know-How to the Test features a series of questions taken directly from the CFA® Level I exams, questions from the Schweser® Study Program, and multiple-choice questions that mimic the CFA and Schweser study materials. These questions will be an invaluable aid for those preparing to take the exam.

AT CHAPTER END

Discussion Questions, keyed to **Learning Goals**, guide students to integrate, investigate, and analyze the key concepts presented in the chapter. Many questions require that students apply the tools and techniques of the chapter to investment information they have obtained, and then make a recommendation with regard to a specific investment strategy or vehicle. These project-type questions are far broader than the Concepts in Review questions within the chapter. Answers to odd-numbered questions are at the end of the book.

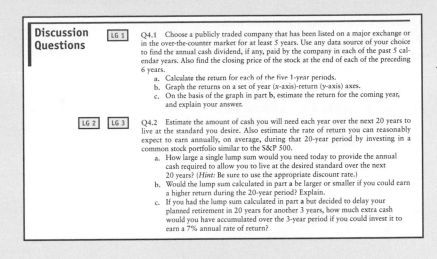

Discussion Questions

LG 1   **Q4.1**   Choose a publicly traded company that has been listed on a major exchange or in the over-the-counter market for at least 5 years. Use any data source of your choice to find the annual cash dividend, if any, paid by the company in each of the past 5 calendar years. Also find the closing price of the stock at the end of each of the preceding 6 years.
    a. Calculate the return for each of the five 1-year periods.
    b. Graph the returns on a set of year (x-axis)-return (y-axis) axes.
    c. On the basis of the graph in part **b**, estimate the return for the coming year, and explain your answer.

LG 2   **LG 3**   **Q4.2**   Estimate the amount of cash you will need each year over the next 20 years to live at the standard you desire. Also estimate the rate of return you can reasonably expect to earn annually, on average, during that 20-year period by investing in a common stock portfolio similar to the S&P 500.
    a. How large a single lump sum would you need today to provide the annual cash required to allow you to live at the desired standard over the next 20 years? (*Hint:* Be sure to use the appropriate discount rate.)
    b. Would the lump sum calculated in part **a** be larger or smaller if you could earn a higher return during the 20-year period? Explain.
    c. If you had the lump sum calculated in part **a** but decided to delay your planned retirement in 20 years for another 3 years, how much extra cash would you have accumulated over the 3-year period if you could invest it to earn a 7% annual rate of return?

Problems

LG 1   **P4.1**   How much would an investor earn on a stock purchased 1 year ago for $63 if it paid an annual cash dividend of $3.75 and had just been sold for $67.50? Would the investor have experienced a capital gain? Explain.

LG 1   **P4.2**   An investor buys a bond for $10,000. The bond pays $300 interest every 6 months. After 18 months, the investor sells the bond for $9,500. Describe the types of income and/or loss the investor had.

LG 1   **P4.3**   Assuming you purchased a share of stock for $50 one year ago, sold it today for $60, and during the year received three dividend payments totaling $2.70, calculate the following.
    a. Current income.
    b. Capital gain (or loss).
    c. Total return
       (1) In dollars.
       (2) As a percentage of the initial investment.

LG 1   **P4.4**   Assume you purchased a bond for $9,500. The bond pays $300 interest every 6 months. You sell the bond after 18 months for $10,000. Calculate the following:
    a. Current income.
    b. Capital gain or loss.
    c. Total return in dollars and as a percentage of the original investment.

New! Expanded Problem Sets—50% new—offer additional review and homework opportunities and are keyed to **Learning Goals**. Answers to odd-numbered Problems are found at the end of the book, while all answers/solutions are available in the Instructor's Manual. An icon appears next to those Problems and Discussion Questions that can be solved using the *Fundamentals of Investing* software, described in the section on supplementary materials.

Two **Case Problems**, keyed to the **Learning Goals**, encourage students to use higher-level critical thinking skills: to apply techniques presented in the chapter, to evaluate alternatives, and to recommend how an investor might solve a specific problem. Again, Learning Goals show the student the chapter topics on which the case problems focus.

Case Problem 9.1   *Rhett Runs Some Technical Measures on a Stock*

LG 2   **LG**

Case Problem 9.2   *Deb Takes Measure of the Market*

LG 2   **LG 3**   Several months ago, Deb Forrester received a substantial sum of money from the estate of her late aunt. Deb initially placed the money in a savings account because she was not sure what to do with it. Since then, however, she has taken a course in investments from a highly respected professor at the local university. The textbook for the course was, in fact, this one, and they just completed Chapter 9. Excited about what she has learned in class, Deb has decided that she definitely wants to invest in stocks. But before she does, she wants to use her newfound knowledge in technical analysis to determine whether now would be a good time to enter the market.

Deb has decided to use all five of the following measures to help her determine if now is, indeed, a good time to start putting money into the stock market:

- Dow theory
- Advance-decline line
- New highs-new lows (NH-NL) indicator (*Assume the current 10-day moving average is zero and the last 10 periods were each zero.*)
- Arms index
- Mutual fund cash ratio

Deb goes to the Internet and, after considerable effort, is able to put together the table of data shown on the next page.

New! Excel with Spreadsheets, appearing at the end of all chapters, challenge students to solve financial problems and make decisions through the creation of spreadsheets. In Chapter 1 students are directed to the Web site, www.aw-bc.com/gitman_joehnk, where they can complete a spreadsheet tutorial, if needed. In addition, selected tables within the text carrying a spreadsheet icon are available in spreadsheet form on the text Web site. Solutions to the end-of-chapter Excel with Spreadsheets exercises are also on the text Web site.

Excel with Spreadsheets

From her Investment Analysis class, Laura has been given an assignment to evaluate several securities on a risk-return tradeoff basis. The specific securities to be researched are International Business Machines, Helmerich & Payne, Inc., and the S&P 500 Index. The respective ticker symbols for the stocks are IBM and HP. She finds the following (assumed) data on the securities in question. It is as follows:

Year	2000	2001	2002	2003	2004	2005
Price$_{IBM}$	$ 49.38	$ 91.63	$112.25	$112.00	$107.89	$ 92.68
Dividend$_{IBM}$	$ .40	$ .44	$ .48	$ .52	$ .56	$ .64
Price$_{HP}$	$ 25.56	$ 17.56	$ 23.50	$ 47.81	$ 30.40	$ 27.93
Dividend$_{HP}$	$ .28	$ .28	$ .28	$ .30	$ .30	$ .32
Value$_{S\&P}$	980.3	1,279.6	1,394.6	1,366.0	1,130.2	1,121.8

Note: The value of the S&P 500 Index includes dividends.

Questions

Part One

a. Use the given data that Laura has found on the three securities and create a spreadsheet to calculate the holding period return (HPR) for each year and the average return over a 5-year period. Specifically, the HPR will be based upon five unique periods of 1 year (i.e., 2000 to 2001, 2001 to 2002, 2002 to 2003, 2003 to 2004, 2004 to 2005). Use the following formula:

$$HPR = [C + (V_n - V_o)] / V_o$$

Where

C = current income during period

V_n = ending investment value

V_o = beginning investment value

New! Trading Online with OTIS. The world of electronic investing comes alive with the addition of OTIS—the Online Trading and Investment Simulator, developed at the Alfred West, Jr. Learning Lab at the Wharton School of the University of Pennsylvania. OTIS, which can be bundled with the text, enables students to become "fund managers" and to buy and sell equities using real data from today's markets. A series of exercises, appearing in appropriate chapters and based on the OTIS materials, help students learn such key concepts as portfolio management, benchmarking, liquidity, and pricing in a hands-on environment.

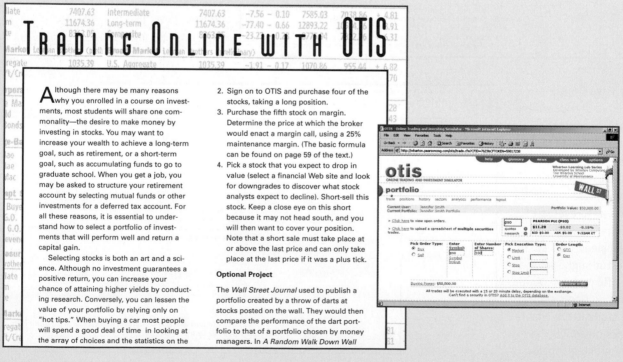

TRADING ONLINE WITH OTIS

Although there may be many reasons why you enrolled in a course on investments, most students will share one commonality—the desire to make money by investing in stocks. You may want to increase your wealth to achieve a long-term goal, such as retirement, or a short-term goal, such as accumulating funds to go to graduate school. When you get a job, you may be asked to structure your retirement account by selecting mutual funds or other investments for a deferred tax account. For all these reasons, it is essential to understand how to select a portfolio of investments that will perform well and return a capital gain.

Selecting stocks is both an art and a science. Although no investment guarantees a positive return, you can increase your chance of attaining higher yields by conducting research. Conversely, you can lessen the value of your portfolio by relying only on "hot tips." When buying a car most people will spend a good deal of time in looking at the array of choices and the statistics on the

2. Sign on to OTIS and purchase four of the stocks, taking a long position.
3. Purchase the fifth stock on margin. Determine the price at which the broker would enact a margin call, using a 25% maintenance margin. (The basic formula can be found on page 59 of the text.)
4. Pick a stock that you expect to drop in value (select a financial Web site and look for downgrades to discover what stock analysts expect to decline). Short-sell this stock. Keep a close eye on this short because it may not head south, and you will then want to cover your position. Note that a short sale must take place at or above the last price and can only take place at the last price if it was a plus tick.

Optional Project

The *Wall Street Journal* used to publish a portfolio created by a throw of darts at stocks posted on the wall. They would then compare the performance of the dart portfolio to that of a portfolio chosen by money managers. In *A Random Walk Down Wall*

Supplemental Materials

We recognize the key role of a complete and creative package of materials to supplement a basic textbook. We believe that the following materials, offered with the ninth edition, will enrich the investments course for both students and instructors.

Fundamentals of Investing Software

The *Fundamentals of Investing* software, programmed by Kathryn E. Coates and David Geis of KDC Software Solutions, can be downloaded from this text's Web site. The purpose of the software is to perform the calculations of virtually all of the formulas, ratios, and valuation procedures presented in the book. The software is very user-friendly and fully interactive. More than a problem solver, it also enhances the student's understanding of the investment process. The software is keyed to all applicable text discussions and end-of-chapter and ancillary materials with the icon shown to the left of the heading above. The software can be found on this text's Web site: www.aw-bc .com/gitman_joehnk.

Fundamentals of Investing Web Site

The book's Web site offers students and professors a rich, dynamic, and up-to-date source of supplemental materials. This resource is located at www.aw-bc.com/gitman_joehnk. Visitors will find links to the sites mentioned in the Hot Links boxes in each chapter; information on more investors' resources; a calculator keystrokes manual; *Fundamentals of Investing* software; Web exercises, enhanced for pedagogical value, to accompany each chapter of the book; additional *Investing in Action* and *Ethics in Investing* boxes on various topics; answers to odd-numbered Discussion Questions and Problems; and other material that is beyond the normal scope of the first-level investments course.

Also at the book's Web site are two complete chapters that appeared in the book in earlier editions: "Real Estate and Other Tangible Investments" and "Tax-Advantaged Investments." These highly informative chapters have been substantively updated and moved to the Web site in response to user, reviewer, and our own preference that the text focus solely on securities investing. In addition to its improved focus, moving these chapters to the Web site allows us both to tighten and improve a number of text discussions and to shorten the text's overall length. We feel this change improves the text's effectiveness in terms of both content and length.

Study Guide

The Study Guide to accompany *Fundamentals of Investing*, Ninth Edition, prepared by Karin B. Bonding, CFA, of the McIntire School at the University of Virginia and President of Capital Markets Institute, Inc., Ivy, Virginia, has been completely revised. Each chapter of the *Study Guide* contains a chapter summary, a chapter outline, and a programmed self-test that consists of true-false and multiple-choice questions. Following the self-test are problems with detailed solutions and, where appropriate, calculator key strokes showing use of the calculator to solve certain problems. All elements are similar in form and content to those found in the book.

Instructor's Manual

Revised by Thomas Krueger of the University of Wisconsin, La Crosse, the *Instructor's Manual* contains chapter outlines; lists of major topics discussed in each chapter; detailed chapter overviews; answers/suggested answers to all Concepts in Review questions, Discussion Questions, Problems, and Critical Thinking Questions to Investing in Action and Ethics in Investing boxes; solutions to the Case Problems; and ideas for outside projects.

Test Bank

Revised for the ninth edition by Kay Johnson of Pennsylvania State University, Erie, the *Test Bank* now includes a substantial number of new questions. Each chapter features true-false questions, multiple-choice questions, and several problems and short-essay questions. The *Test Bank* is also available in Test Generator Software (TestGen with QuizMaster). Fully networkable, this software is available for Windows and Macintosh. TestGen's graphical interface enables instructors to easily view, edit, and add questions; export questions to create tests; and print tests in a variety of fonts and forms. Search and sort features let the instructor quickly locate questions and arrange them in a preferred order. QuizMaster, working with your school's computer network, automatically grades the exams, stores results on disk, and allows the instructor to view or print a variety of reports.

PowerPoint Transparency Slides

To facilitate classroom presentations, PowerPoint slides of key text images are available for Windows and Macintosh. A PowerPoint viewer is provided for use by those who do not have the full software program. The slides were developed by Robert Maxwell, College of the Canyons.

Acknowledgments

Many people gave their generous assistance during the initial development and revisions of *Fundamentals of Investing*. The expertise, classroom experience, and general advice of both colleagues and practitioners have been invaluable. Reactions and suggestions from students throughout the country—comments we especially enjoy receiving—sustained our belief in the need for a fresh, informative, and teachable investments text.

A few individuals provided significant subject matter expertise in the initial development of the book. They are Terry S. Maness of Baylor University, Arthur L. Schwartz, Jr., of the University of South Florida at St. Petersburg, and Gary W. Eldred. Their contributions are greatly appreciated. In addition, Addison-Wesley obtained the advice of a large group of experienced reviewers. We appreciate their many suggestions and criticisms, which have had a strong influence on various aspects of this volume. Our special thanks go to the following people, who reviewed all or part of the manuscript for the previous eight editions of the book.

M. Fall Ainina
Gary Baker
Harisha Batra
Richard B. Bellinfante
Cecil C. Bigelow
Paul Bolster
A. David Brummett
Gary P. Cain
Gary Carman
Daniel J. Cartell
P. R. Chandy
David M. Cordell
Timothy Cowling
Robert M. Crowe
Richard F. DeMong
Clifford A. Diebold
James Dunn
Betty Marie Dyatt
Steven J. Elbert
Thomas Eyssell
Frank J. Fabozzi
Robert A. Ford

Albert J. Fredman
Chaim Ginsberg
Joel Gold
Frank Griggs
Brian Grinder
Harry P. Guenther
Mahboubul Hassan
Gay Hatfield
Robert D. Hollinger
Sue Beck Howard
Roland Hudson, Jr.
Ping Hsiao
Donald W. Johnson
Ravindra R. Kamath
Bill Kane
Daniel J. Kaufmann, Jr.
Nancy Kegelman
Phillip T. Kolbe
Sheri Kole
Christopher M. Korth
Thomas M. Krueger
George Kutner

Robert T. LeClair
Chun I. Lee
Larry A. Lynch
Weston A. McCormac
David J. McLaughlin
Keith Manko
Timothy Manuel
Kathy Milligan
Warren E. Moeller
Homer Mohr
Majed R. Muhtaseb
Joseph Newhouse
Joseph F. Ollivier
John Palffy
John Park
Thomas Patrick
Michael Polakoff
Barbara Poole
Ronald S. Pretekin
Stephen W. Pruitt
S. P. Umamaheswar Rao
William A. Richard

Linda R. Richardson
William A. Rini
Roy A. Roberson
Edward Rozalewicz
William J. Ruckstuhl
David Russo
Arthur L. Schwartz, Jr.
Keith V. Smith
Pat R. Stout
Nancy E. Strickler
Glenn T. Sweeney
Amir Tavakkol
Phillip D. Taylor
Wenyuh Tsay
Robert C. Tueting
Howard E. Van Auken
John R. Weigel
Peter M. Wichert
John C. Woods
Richard H. Yanow

The following people provided extremely useful reviews and input to the ninth edition:

Joan Anderssen, Arapahoe Community College
Steven P. Clark, University of North Carolina, Charlotte
John Gerlach, Sacred Heart University
Samuel Kyle Jones, Stephen F. Austin State University
Marie A. Kratochvil, Nassau Community College
James Lock, Northern Virginia Community College
Anne Macy, West Texas A&M University
James Mallett, Stetson University
Majed R. Muhtaseb, California State Polytechnic University
Michael Nugent, State University of New York, Stony Brook
Mark Palermo, State University of New York, Stony Brook
William Scroggins, Jacksonville State University
Daniel Singer, Towson University
P. V. Viswanath, Pace University
Ali E. Zadeh, California State University, Los Angeles
Edward Zajicek, Kalamazoo College

Because of the wide variety of topics covered in the book, we called upon many experts for advice. We thank them and their firms for allowing us to draw on their insights and awareness of recent developments, to ensure that the text is as current as possible. In particular, we want to mention Jeff Buetow, CFA, BFRC Services, Charlottesville, VA; Bill Bachrach, Bachrach & Associates, San Diego, CA; John Markese, President, American Association of Individual Investors, Chicago, IL; George Ebenhack, Oppenheimer & Co., Los Angeles, CA; Mark D. Erwin, LINSCO/Private Ledger, San Diego, CA; Andrew Temte, CFA, Schweser Study Program, La Crosse, WI; Martin P. Klitzer, Sunrise Capital Partners, Del Mar, CA; David M. Love, C.P. Eaton and Associates,

Rancho Santa Fe, CA; David H. McLaughlin, Chase Investment Counsel Corp., Charlottesville, VA; Michael R. Murphy, Sceptre Investment Counsel, Toronto, Ontario, Canada; Mark S. Nussbaum, UBS Financial Services, Inc., La Jolla, CA; John Richardson, Northern Trust Bank of Arizona, Phoenix, AZ; Pat Rupp, IDS, Inc., Dayton, OH; Richard Russell, Dow Theory Letters, La Jolla, CA; Mike Smith, Economic Analysis Corporation, Los Angeles, CA; Michael J. Steelman, Wachovia Securities, San Diego, CA; Fred Weaver, Washington Mutual, Phoenix, AZ; and Lynn Yturri, BancOne Arizona, Phoenix, AZ.

We greatly appreciate the support of our colleagues at San Diego State University and Arizona State University. Special thanks to attorney Robert J. Wright of Wright & Wrights, CPAs, San Diego, for his help in revising and updating the many tax discussions, and to Professor Edward Nelling of Drexel University for his help in preparing the material on tech stocks and tech-stock valuation and in updating and revising Discussion Questions. We also thank Mark Palermo of the State University of New York, Stony Brook, for his fine work on the Problems, Hot Links, Web exercises, and other text materials; Marie Kratochvil of Nassau Community College for her creativity in developing the exercises to accompany OTIS; Edward Zajicek of Kalamazoo College for his writing of the insightful and instructive Ethics in Investing boxes and the assembling of questions for Putting Your Investment Know-How to the Test; Steven Lifland of High Point University for his authoring of the Excel with Spreadsheet exercises; Karin Bonding of the University of Virginia for her useful feedback and for revising the *Study Guide;* Kay Johnson of Pennsylvania State University, Erie, for revising and updating the *Test Bank;* and Thomas Krueger of the University of Wisconsin, La Crosse, for the huge job of revising and updating the *Instructor's Manual.* Special thanks to Marlene Bellamy of Writeline Associates, La Jolla, California, for her work in preparing chapter vignettes, *Investing in Action* boxes, and *Investor Facts.* Our thanks also go to Kaye Coates and David Geis of KDC Software Solutions for developing the *Fundamentals of Investing* software.

The staff at Addison-Wesley, particularly Donna Battista and Denise Clinton, contributed their creativity, enthusiasm, and commitment to this textbook. Senior project manager Mary Clare McEwing of Addison-Wesley, Nancy Freihofer of Thompson Steele, Inc., and other dedicated Addison-Wesley staff, including senior production supervisor Nancy Fenton, senior designer Regina Hagen Kolenda, executive media producer Michelle Neil, media producer Jennifer Pelland, marketing manager Deborah Meredith, and supplements coordinator Diana Theriault warrant special thanks for shepherding the project through the development, production, marketing, and Web site construction stages. Without their care and concern, this text would not have evolved into the teachable and interesting text and package we believe it to be.

Finally, our wives, Robin and Charlene, and our children, Jessica and Zachary, and Chris and Terry and his wife, Sara, played important roles by providing support and understanding during the book's development, revision, and production. We are forever grateful to them, and we hope that this edition will justify the sacrifices required during the many hours we were away from them working on this book.

Lawrence J. Gitman
Michael D. Joehnk

PART ONE

PREPARING TO INVEST

CHAPTER 1
THE INVESTMENT ENVIRONMENT

CHAPTER 2
MARKETS AND TRANSACTIONS

CHAPTER 3
ONLINE INFORMATION AND INVESTING

CHAPTER 1

THE INVESTMENT ENVIRONMENT

LEARNING GOALS

After studying this chapter, you should be able to:

LG 1 Understand the meaning of the term *investment* and the factors commonly used to differentiate among types of investments.

LG 2 Describe the investment process and types of investors.

LG 3 Discuss the principal types of investment vehicles.

LG 4 Describe the steps in investing, particularly establishing investment goals, and cite fundamental personal tax considerations.

LG 5 Discuss investing over the life cycle and investing in different economic environments.

LG 6 Understand the popular types of short-term investment vehicles.

In just a few years, the world of investments has moved to center stage in American life. Twenty years ago, the only exposure to investment news that most people had came in the form of a 10-second announcement on the evening news about the change in the Dow Jones Industrial Average that day. Today, more than half of all Americans own stocks, and many of them have been investing only since 1996. Finding information about investing has become easier than ever. Cable TV stations like CNNfn specialize in business and financial news, and network newscasters feature business news more prominently. You can't pass a newsstand without seeing headlines that scream, "Ten Stocks to Buy Now!" or "The Hottest Mutual Funds," as well as advice on how to change your investment strategies as current market conditions change. Besides the *Wall Street Journal*, you can subscribe to *Investors Business Daily*, *Barron's*, *Kiplinger's Personal Finance Magazine*, *Money*, *Smart Money*, and dozens of other publications that focus on investing.

The Internet has played a major role in opening the world of investing to individual investors. By giving them access to tools formerly restricted to investment professionals, it creates a more level playing field. The Internet also makes enormous amounts of information readily available and puts a way to trade securities just a few mouse clicks away. In short, technology makes investing much easier—and at the same time can increase the risks for inexperienced investors.

Regardless of whether you conduct transactions online or use a traditional broker, the same investment fundamentals presented in this textbook apply. Chapter 1 introduces the various types of investments, the investment process, key investment vehicles, the role of investment plans, and the importance of meeting liquidity needs. Becoming familiar with investment alternatives and developing realistic investment plans should greatly increase your chance of achieving financial success.

2

Investments and the Investment Process

Note: The Learning Goals shown at the beginning of the chapter are keyed to text discussions using these icons.

investment
any vehicle into which funds can be placed with the expectation that it will generate positive income and/or preserve or increase its value.

returns
the rewards from investing, received as current income and/or increased value.

Note: Investing in Action boxes, which appear in each chapter, describe real-life investing situations or elaborate on innovative investment vehicles. These high-interest boxes have been written with student readers in mind and contain Critical Thinking Questions for discussion.

You are probably already an investor. If you have money in a savings account, you already have at least one investment to your name. An **investment** is simply any vehicle into which funds can be placed with the expectation that it will generate positive income and/or preserve or increase its value. The rewards, or **returns**, from investing are received in two basic forms: current income and increased value. For example, money invested in a savings account provides current income in the form of periodic interest payments. A share of common stock purchased as an investment is expected to increase in value between the time it is purchased and the time it is sold. Historically, since 1926 the average annual return on a savings account was about 3%, whereas the average annual return on the common stock of large companies was about 12.2%. Of course, during the major market downturn driven by the collapse of the high-flying tech stocks and an economic slowdown that started in 2000 and ran until late 2002, the returns on nearly all investment vehicles were well below these long-term historical averages. (We'll look more carefully at historical returns in Chapter 4.)

Is cash placed in a simple (no-interest) checking account an investment? No, because it fails both tests of the definition. It does not provide added income, nor does its value increase. (In fact, if the money kept in a checking account is in excess of the amount needed to pay bills or if the interest rate is high, its value is likely to decrease, because it is eroded over time by inflation.)

Before we proceed, you might want to establish a baseline on your investing "know-how" by testing your Investment IQ using the instrument given in the *Investing in Action* box on page 4. Studying this textbook should allow you to improve your Investment IQ. We now begin our study of investments by looking at types of investments and at the structure of the investment process.

Types of Investments

When you invest, the organization in which you invest—whether it is a company or a government entity—offers you an expected future benefit in exchange for the current use of your funds. Organizations compete for the use of your funds. The one that will get your investment dollars is the one that offers a benefit you judge to be better than any competitor offers. But, different investors judge benefits differently. As a result, investments of every type are available, from "sure things" such as earning 1% interest on your bank savings account, to the possibility of tripling your money fast by investing in a newly issued biotech stock. The investments you choose will depend on your resources, your goals, and your personality. We can differentiate types of investments on the basis of a number of factors.

securities
investments that represent debt or ownership or the legal right to acquire or sell an ownership interest.

Securities or Property Investments that represent debt or ownership or the legal right to acquire or sell an ownership interest are called **securities.** The most common types of securities are stocks, bonds, and options. The focus of this book is primarily on securities, particularly common stocks.

property
investments in real property or tangible personal property.

Property, on the other hand, consists of investments in real property or tangible personal property. *Real property* is land, buildings, and that which is permanently affixed to the land. *Tangible personal property* includes items such as gold, artwork, antiques, and other collectibles.

INVESTING IN ACTION

TEST YOUR INVESTMENT IQ

How much do you know about investing? Take this investor literacy quiz, developed by *Money* magazine and the Vanguard Group to test the investment savvy of 1,500 mutual fund investors.

The average score (for the full 20-question quiz) was only 37%. But don't despair if you, too, don't score well. You'll learn the answers to these and many other questions from this book.

1. Which type of investment has offered the best protection against inflation over long periods of time?
   a. Money market funds and bank accounts.
   b. Government National Mortgage Association securities (also known as Ginnie Maes or GNMAs).
   c. Stocks.
   d. Corporate bonds.

2. Common stocks always provide higher returns than bonds or money market investments.
   a. True.   b. False.

3. As an individual, the most you can contribute to an IRA each year is:
   a. $1,000.   b. $2,000.
   c. $5,000.   d. $10,000.

4. Interest earned by municipal bonds is exempt from federal income tax.
   a. True.   b. False.

5. If interest rates declined, the price of a bond or bond fund generally would:
   a. Increase.
   b. Decrease.
   c. Stay about the same.
   d. It is impossible to predict.

6. If you own only U.S. stocks in your investment portfolio, you will reduce your overall risk by adding international stocks.
   a. True.   b. False.

7. Which market benchmark or stock exchange is the best gauge of the performance of the entire U.S. stock market?
   a. S&P 500 Index.
   b. Wilshire 5000 Total Market Index.

   c. Dow Jones Industrial Average.
   d. Nasdaq Composite Index.

8. If you invest in a 401(k) plan at work, you are not eligible to contribute to an IRA.
   a. True.   b. False.

9. From 1926 to 2002, the return on U.S. stocks has averaged:
   a. 5% per year.
   b. 12% per year.
   c. 19% per year.
   d. 28% per year.

10. Which of the following is not an attribute of mutual funds?
    a. Diversification.
    b. Professional management.
    c. Guaranteed return.
    d. None of the above.

11. If your investment returned 10% last year and inflation was 3%, your "real" (i.e., adjusted for inflation) return was:
    a. 3.3%.   b. 7%.
    c. 13%.   d. 30%.

12. A mutual fund that invests in government securities is guaranteed not to lose money.
    a. True.   b. False.

Answers: 1 (c); 2 (b); 3 (b); 4 (a); 5 (a); 6 (a); 7 (b); 8 (b); 9 (b); 10 (c); 11 (b); 12 (b).

CRITICAL THINKING QUESTION How high is your investment IQ, as measured by the quiz? Make a note of your score so that you can impress yourself at the end of the course with how much you've learned.

Sources: Laura Lallos, "What's Your Investing IQ?" *Money,* August 2000, pp. 91–92; quiz downloaded from cgi.money.com/cgi-bin/money/polls/vanguard/ vanguard.plx.

Note: Theinvestingportal.com is one of many sites that provide extensive links to other Web sites for investors. The links are organized by popular search terms and "best of the Web". You will find links to many of the other sites discussed in this chapter, as well as many others, at www.theinvestingportal.com.

direct investment
investment in which an investor directly acquires a claim on a security or property.

indirect investment
investment made in a *portfolio,* or collection of securities or properties.

portfolio
collection of securities or properties, typically constructed to meet one or more investment goals.

debt
funds lent in exchange for interest income and the promised repayment of the loan at a given future date.

equity
ongoing ownership in a business or property.

derivative securities
securities that are structured to exhibit characteristics similar to those of an underlying security or asset and that derive their value from the underlying security or asset.

risk
the chance that actual investment returns will differ from those expected.

speculation
the purchase of high-risk investment vehicles that offer highly uncertain returns and future value.

short-term investments
investments that typically mature within one year

long-term investments
investments with maturities of longer than a year or with no maturity at all.

Direct or Indirect A **direct investment** is one in which an investor directly acquires a claim on a security or property. If you buy a stock or bond in order to earn income or preserve value, you have made a direct investment.

An **indirect investment** is an investment made in a **portfolio,** or collection of securities or properties, typically constructed to meet one or more investment goals. For example, you may purchase a share of a *mutual fund*. This share gives you a claim on a fraction of the entire portfolio rather than on the security of a single firm.

Debt, Equity, or Derivative Securities Usually, an investment represents either a debt or an equity interest. **Debt** represents funds lent in exchange for interest income and the promised repayment of the loan at a given future date. When you buy a debt instrument like a *bond*, in effect you lend money to the issuer. The issuer agrees to pay you a stated rate of interest over a specified period of time, at the end of which the original sum will be returned.

Equity represents ongoing ownership in a business or property. An equity investment may be held as a security or by title to a specific property. The most popular type of equity security is *common stock*.

Derivative securities are neither debt nor equity. They derive their value from, and have characteristics similar to those of, an underlying security or asset. *Options* are an example: An investor essentially buys the opportunity to sell or buy another security or asset at a specified price during a given period of time. Options and other derivative security investments, though not so common as debt and equity investments, have grown rapidly in popularity in recent years.

Low- or High-Risk Investments are sometimes differentiated on the basis of risk. As used in finance, **risk** is the chance that actual investment returns will differ from those expected. Of course, the actual return depends on the amount of the investment that is recouped. The broader the range of possible values or returns associated with an investment, the greater its risk.

Investors are confronted with a continuum of investments that range from low to high risk. Although each type of investment vehicle has a basic risk characteristic, the actual level of risk depends on the specific vehicle. For example, stocks are generally believed to be more risky than bonds. However, it is not difficult to find high-risk bonds that are more risky than the stock of a financially sound firm such as IBM or McDonald's.

Low-risk investments are those considered safe with regard to the receipt of a positive return. *High-risk investments* are considered speculative: Their levels of return are highly uncertain. **Speculation** offers highly uncertain returns and future value, so it is high-risk investment. Because of this greater risk, the returns associated with speculation are expected to be greater. Both investment and speculation differ from gambling, which involves playing games of chance. In this book we will use the term *investment* for both investment and speculation.

Short- or Long-Term The life of an investment can be described as either short- or long-term. **Short-term investments** typically mature within one year. **Long-term investments** are those with longer maturities or, like common stock, with no maturity at all. It is not unusual to find investors matching the maturity of an investment to the period of time over which they wish to invest their funds.

domestic investments
debt, equity, and derivative securities of U.S.-based companies.

foreign investments
debt, equity, and derivative securities of foreign-based companies.

financial institutions
organizations that channel the savings of governments, businesses, and individuals into loans or investments.

financial markets
forums in which suppliers and demanders of funds make financial transactions, often through intermediaries.

INVESTOR FACTS

AMERICANS LOVE STOCKS—
Even during the recent bear market, Americans continued to hold stocks. A recent survey showed that 52% of Americans now own stocks or stock mutual funds, compared to just 19% in 1983. Financial assets represent 42% of total assets. Stocks and mutual funds now account for about 34% of total household financial assets, up from 28% in 1995—and this figure does not include investments held in retirement accounts, which represent another 28% of financial assets.

Source: Ana M. Azicorbe, Arther B. Kennickell, and Kevin B. Moore, "Recent Changes in U.S. Family Finances: Results from the 1998 and 2001 Survey of Consumer Finances," *Federal Reserve Bulletin,* Board of Governors of the Federal Reserve System, Washington, D.C., January 2003, pp. 9, 15.

Domestic or Foreign As recently as 15 to 20 years ago, individuals invested almost exclusively in purely **domestic investments:** the debt, equity, and derivative securities of U.S.-based companies. Today, these same investors routinely also look for **foreign investments** (both direct and indirect) that might offer more attractive returns or lower risk than purely domestic investments. Information on foreign companies is now readily available, and it is now relatively easy to make foreign investments. As a result, many individuals now actively invest in foreign securities. All aspects of foreign investing are therefore routinely considered throughout this book.

The Structure of the Investment Process

The investment process brings together *suppliers* of extra funds with *demanders* who need funds. Suppliers and demanders of funds are most often brought together through a financial institution or a financial market. (Occasionally, especially in property transactions, buyers and sellers deal directly with one another.) **Financial institutions** are organizations that channel the savings of governments, businesses, and individuals into loans or investments. Banks and insurance companies are financial institutions. **Financial markets** are forums in which suppliers and demanders of funds make financial transactions, often through intermediaries. They include securities, commodities, and foreign exchange markets.

The dominant financial market in the United States is the *securities market.* It includes stock markets, bond markets, and options markets. Similar markets exist in most major economies throughout the world. Their common feature is that the price of an investment vehicle at any point in time results from an equilibrium between the forces of supply and demand. As new information about returns and risk becomes available, the changes in supply and demand may result in a new equilibrium or *market price.* Financial markets streamline the process of bringing together suppliers and demanders of funds, and they allow transactions to be made quickly and at a fair price. They also publicize security prices.

Figure 1.1 diagrams the investment process. Note that the suppliers of funds may transfer their resources to the demanders through financial institutions, through financial markets, or in direct transactions. As the broken lines show, financial institutions can participate in financial markets as either suppliers or demanders of funds.

Participants in the Investment Process Government, business, and individuals are the three key participants in the investment process. Each may act as a supplier and a demander of funds. For the economy to grow and prosper, funds must be available to qualified individuals and to government and business. If individuals began suddenly hiding their excess funds under floorboards rather than putting them in financial institutions or investing them in the financial markets, then government, business, and individuals in need of funds would have difficulty obtaining them. As a result, government spending, business expansion, and consumer purchases would decline, and economic activity would slow.

Government All levels of government—federal, state, and local—require vast sums of money to finance long-term projects related to the construction of

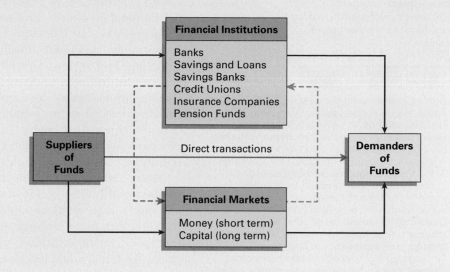

FIGURE 1.1

The Investment Process

Note that financial institutions participate in the financial markets as well as transfer funds between suppliers and demanders. Although the arrows go only from suppliers to demanders, for some transactions (e.g., the sale of a bond), the principal amount borrowed by the demander from the supplier (the lender) is eventually returned.

public facilities, such as schools, hospitals, public housing, and highways, and to meet operating needs—the money required to keep the government running. Occasionally, governments supply funds by making short-term investments to earn a positive return on temporarily idle funds. In general, though, government is a *net demander of funds*—it demands more funds than it supplies. The financial activities of governments, both as demanders and suppliers of funds, significantly affect the behavior of financial institutions and financial markets.

Business Most business firms require large sums of money to support operations. Like government, business has both long- and short-term financial needs. Businesses issue a wide variety of debt and equity securities to finance these needs. They also supply funds when they have excess cash. But like government, business firms in general are *net demanders of funds*.

Individuals You might be surprised to learn that the individual's role in the investment process is significant. Individuals frequently demand funds in the form of loans to finance the acquisition of property—typically automobiles and houses. Although the individual demand for funds seems great, individuals as a group are *net suppliers of funds:* They put more funds into the financial system than they take out.

Types of Investors When we refer to individuals in the investment process, we do so to differentiate households from government and business. We can further characterize the participation of individuals in the investment process in terms of who manages the funds. **Individual investors** manage their personal funds to achieve their financial goals. The individual investor usually concentrates on earning a return on idle funds, building a source of retirement income, and providing security for his or her family.

individual investors
investors who manage their own funds.

institutional investors
investment professionals who are
paid to manage other people's
money.

Note: Addresses of additional
information sources that can
be found on the Internet are
interspersed throughout the
chapters.

Note: The Concepts in Review
questions at the end of each text
section encourage you, before
you move on, to test your
understanding of the material
you've just read.

Individuals who lack the time or expertise to make investment decisions often employ **institutional investors**—investment professionals who are paid to manage other people's money. These professionals trade large volumes of securities for individuals, businesses, and governments. Sizable brokerage cost savings typically result from the large volumes traded. Institutional investors include financial institutions (banks, life insurance companies, mutual funds, and pension funds). Financial institutions invest large sums to earn a significant return for their customers. For example, a life insurance company invests its premium receipts to earn returns that will permit payments to policyholders or beneficiaries.

Both individual and institutional investors apply similar fundamental principles. However, institutional investors generally invest larger sums of money on behalf of others and therefore are often more sophisticated in investment knowledge and methods. The information presented in this textbook is aimed primarily at individual investors; it represents only the first step toward developing the expertise needed to qualify as an institutional investor.

I N   R E V I E W

CONCEPTS

1.1 Define the term *investment,* and explain why individuals invest.

1.2 Differentiate among the following types of investments, and cite an example of each: (a) securities and property investments; (b) direct and indirect investments; (c) debt, equity, and derivative securities; and (d) short-term and long-term investments.

1.3 Define the term *risk,* and explain how risk is used to differentiate among investments.

1.4 What are *foreign investments*, and what role do they play today for the individual investor?

1.5 Describe the structure of the overall investment process. Explain the role played by *financial institutions* and *financial markets.*

1.6 Classify the role of (a) government, (b) business, and (c) individuals as net suppliers or net demanders of funds.

1.7 Differentiate between *individual investors* and *institutional investors.*

Investment Vehicles

LG 3

A wide variety of investment vehicles are available to individual investors. Vehicles differ in terms of maturities or lives, costs, return and risk characteristics, and tax considerations. We devote the bulk of this book—Chapters 6 through 16—to describing the characteristics, special features, returns and risks, and possible investment strategies that can be used with vehicles available to the individual investor. Here we will introduce these investment vehicles. Table 1.1 summarizes the information presented in this section.

TABLE 1.1	Overview of Investment Vehicles		
Type	Description	Examples	Where Covered in This Book
Short-term vehicles	Savings instruments with lives of 1 year or less. Used to warehouse idle funds and to provide liquidity.	Deposit accounts Series EE savings bonds U.S. Treasury bills (T-bills) Certificates of deposit (CDs) Commercial paper Banker's acceptances Money market mutual funds	Ch. 1 Ch. 1 Ch. 1 Ch. 1 Ch. 1 Ch. 1 Ch. 1
Common stock	Equity investment vehicles that represent ownership in a corporation.		Chs. 6–9
Fixed-income securities	Investment vehicles that offer a fixed periodic return.	Bonds Preferred stock Convertible securities	Chs. 10, 11 Ch. 12 Ch. 12
Mutual funds	Companies that raise money from sale of shares and invest in and professionally manage a diversified portfolio of securities.		Ch. 13
Derivative securities	Securities that are neither debt nor equity but are structured to exhibit the characteristics of the underlying securities or assets from which they derive their value.	Options Futures	Ch. 15 Ch. 16
Other popular investment vehicles	Various other investment vehicles that are widely used by investors.	Real estate Tangibles Tax-advantaged investments	On text's Web site, www.aw-bc.com/gitman_joehnk

Short-Term Vehicles

short-term vehicles
savings instruments that usually have lives of 1 year or less.

liquidity
the ability of an investment to be converted into cash quickly and with little or no loss in value.

Short-term vehicles include savings instruments that usually have lives of 1 year or less. Short-term vehicles generally carry little or no risk. Often such instruments are used to "warehouse" idle funds and earn a return while long-term vehicles are being evaluated. They are also popular among conservative investors, who may use short-term vehicles as a primary investment outlet. Short-term vehicles also provide **liquidity.** That is, they can be converted into cash quickly and with little or no loss in value. Provision for liquidity is an important part of any financial plan. The role of short-term vehicles in financial planning and the key features of the most popular short-term vehicles are discussed later in this chapter.

Common Stock

common stock
equity investment that represents ownership in a corporation; each share represents a fractional ownership interest in the firm.

Common stock is an equity investment that represents ownership in a corporation. Each share of common stock represents a fractional ownership interest in the firm. For example, one share of common stock in a corporation that has 10,000 shares outstanding would represent 1/10,000 ownership interest. Next to short-term vehicles and home ownership, common stock is the most popular form of investment vehicle. Today more than half of all U.S. families own some common stock.

The return on investment in common stock comes from either of two sources: dividends or capital gains. **Dividends** are periodic payments made by the corporation to its shareholders from its current and past earnings. **Capital gains** result from selling the stock (or any asset) at a price that *exceeds* its original purchase price. For example, say you purchased a single share of One Tech Industries common stock for $40 per share. During the first year you owned it, you received $2.50 per share in cash dividends. At the end of the year, you sold the stock for $44 per share. If we ignore the costs associated with buying and selling the stock, you earned $2.50 in dividends and $4 in capital gains ($44 sale price—$40 purchase price). Since 1926, the average annual rate of return on common stocks of large firms has been about 12.2%, and the more risky common stocks of smaller firms have earned an average annual return of about 16.9%.

Fixed-Income Securities

Fixed-income securities are investment vehicles that offer a fixed periodic return. Some forms offer contractually guaranteed returns. Others have specified, but not guaranteed, returns. Because of their fixed returns, fixed-income securities tend to be popular during periods of high interest rates, when investors seek to "lock in" high returns. The key forms of fixed-income securities are bonds, preferred stock, and convertible securities.

Bonds **Bonds** are the long-term debt instruments (IOUs) issued by corporations and governments. A bondholder has a contractual right to receive a known interest return, plus return of the bond's *face value* (the stated value given on the certificate) at maturity (typically 20 to 40 years). If you purchased a $1,000 bond paying 9% interest in semiannual installments, you would expect to be paid $45 (9% × ½ year × $1,000) every 6 months. At maturity you would receive the $1,000 face value of the bond. An investor may be able to buy or sell a bond prior to maturity. Since 1926, the average annual rate of return on long-term corporate bonds has been about 6.2%, and the average annual return on less risky long-term government bonds has been about 5.8%.

Preferred Stock Like common stock, **preferred stock** represents an ownership interest in a corporation. Unlike common stock, preferred stock has a stated dividend rate. Payment of this dividend is given preference over common stock dividends of the same firm. Preferred stock has no maturity date. Investors typically purchase it for the dividends it pays, but it may also provide capital gains.

Convertible Securities A **convertible security** is a special type of fixed-income obligation (bond or preferred stock). It has a feature permitting the investor to convert it into a specified number of shares of common stock. Convertible bonds and convertible preferreds provide the fixed-income benefit of a bond (interest) or preferred stock (dividends) while offering the price-appreciation (capital gain) potential of common stock.

---

dividends
periodic payments made by firms to their shareholders.

capital gains
the amount by which the sale price of an asset *exceeds* its original purchase price.

fixed-income securities
investment vehicles that offer a fixed periodic return.

bonds
long-term debt instruments (IOUs), issued by corporations and governments, that offer a known interest return plus return of the bond's *face value* at maturity.

preferred stock
ownership interest in a corporation; has a stated dividend rate, payment of which is given preference over common stock dividends of the same firm.

convertible security
a fixed-income obligation (bond or preferred stock) with a feature permitting the investor to convert it into a specified number of shares of common stock.

mutual fund
a company that raises money from sale of its shares and invests in and professionally manages a diversified portfolio of securities.

money market mutual funds
mutual funds that invest solely in short-term investment vehicles.

options
securities that give the investor an opportunity to sell or buy another security at a specified price over a given period of time.

futures
legally binding obligations stipulating that the sellers of such contracts will make delivery and the buyers of the contracts will take delivery of a specified commodity or financial instrument at some specific date, at a price agreed on at the time the contract is sold.

real estate
entities such as residential homes, raw land, and income property.

tangibles
investment assets, other than real estate, that can be seen or touched.

Mutual Funds

A company that raises money from sale of its shares and invests in and professionally manages a diversified portfolio of securities is called a **mutual fund**. Investors in the fund own an interest in the fund's portfolio of securities. All mutual funds issue and repurchase shares of the fund at a price that reflects the value of the portfolio at the time the transaction is made. **Money market mutual funds** are mutual funds that invest solely in short-term investment vehicles.

Derivative Securities

As noted earlier, *derivative securities* derive their value from that of an underlying security or asset. They typically possess high levels of risk, because they usually have uncertain returns or unstable market values. But, because of their above-average risk, these vehicles also have high levels of expected return. The key derivative securities are options and futures.

Options Options are securities that give the investor an opportunity to sell or buy another security at a specified price over a given period of time. Most often, options are purchased to take advantage of an anticipated change in the price of common stock. However, the purchaser of an option is not guaranteed any return and could even lose the entire amount invested because the option does not become attractive enough to use. Aside from their speculative use, options are sometimes used to protect existing investment positions against losses. Three common types of options are *puts, calls,* and *warrants,* which we will discuss in detail in Chapter 15.

Futures Futures are legally binding obligations stipulating that the sellers of such contracts will make delivery and the buyers of the contracts will take delivery of a specified commodity or financial instrument at some specific date, at a price agreed on at the time the contract is sold. Examples of commodities sold by contract include soybeans, pork bellies, platinum, and cocoa. Examples of financial futures are contracts for Japanese yen, U.S. Treasury securities, interest rates, and stock indexes. Trading in commodity and financial futures is generally a highly specialized, high-risk proposition.

Other Popular Investment Vehicles

Various other investment vehicles are also used by investors. The most common are real estate, tangibles, and tax-advantaged investments.

Real estate consists of entities such as residential homes, raw land, and a variety of forms of income property, including warehouses, office and apartment buildings, and condominiums. The appeal of real estate investment is the potential returns in the form of rental income, tax write-offs, and capital gains. **Tangibles** are investment assets, other than real estate, that can be seen or touched. They include gold and other precious metals, gemstones, and collectibles such as coins, stamps, artwork, and antiques. These assets are purchased as investments in anticipation of price increases. Because the federal income tax rate for an individual can be as high as 35%, many investors look

tax-advantaged investments
investment vehicles and strategies for legally reducing one's tax liability.

for **tax-advantaged investments.** These are investment vehicles and strategies for legally reducing one's tax liability. With them, investors find that their after-tax rates of return can be far higher than with conventional investments.

IN REVIEW

CONCEPTS

1.8   What are *short-term vehicles?* How do they provide *liquidity?*

1.9   What is *common stock* and what are its two sources of potential return?

1.10   Briefly define and differentiate among the following investment vehicles. Which offer fixed returns? Which are derivative securities? Which offer professional investment management?

a. Bonds	b. Preferred stock
c. Convertible securities	d. Mutual funds
e. Options	f. Futures

Making Investment Plans

LG 4   LG 5

The process of investing can be carried out by following a logical progression of steps. It is important that your investment plans take into account the impact of taxes. Your plans also should be responsive to your stage in the life cycle and to the changing economic environment.

Steps in Investing

Investing can be conducted on a strictly intuitive basis or on the basis of plans carefully developed to achieve specific goals. Evidence favors the more logical approach that begins with establishing a set of overall financial goals and then developing and executing an investment program consistent with those goals. The following brief overview of the steps in investing provides a framework for discussion of the concepts, tools, and techniques presented throughout the book.

Step 1: Meeting Investment Prerequisites Before investing, you must make certain that the *necessities of life* are adequately provided for. This category includes funds for housing, food, transportation, taxes, and clothing. In addition, a pool of easily accessible funds should be established for meeting emergency cash needs. (Meeting liquidity needs is discussed later in this chapter.)

Another prerequisite is adequate protection against the losses that could result from death, illness or disability, damage to property, or a negligent act. Protection against such risks can be acquired through life, health, property, and liability insurance.

H O T

Detailed information on meeting life insurance needs is available on this text's Web site. Click on the Web chapter titled Tax-Advantaged Investments and then on Deferred Annuities.

www.aw-bc.com/gitman_joehnk

investment goals
the financial objectives that one wishes to achieve by investing.

Step 2: Establishing Investment Goals Once you have satisfied the prerequisites and set clearly defined financial goals, the next step is to establish *investment goals.* **Investment goals** are the financial objectives you wish to achieve by investing. Clearly, your investment goals will determine the types of investments you will make. Common investment goals include:

1. *Accumulating Retirement Funds.* Accumulating funds for retirement is the *single most important reason for investing.* Too often, people tend to rely heavily on Social Security and employers for retirement funds. It is of the utmost importance to review the amounts that can realistically be expected from these sources. You can then decide, on the basis of your retirement goals, *whether they will be adequate to meet your needs.* If they are not, they must be supplemented through your own investment program. The earlier in life you assess your retirement needs, the greater your chance of accumulating sufficient funds to meet them.

2. *Enhancing Current Income.* Investments enhance current income by earning dividends or interest. Retirees frequently choose investments offering *high current income at low risk.* The idea of a retired person "clipping coupons"—collecting interest—from high-grade bonds is a fair description of what most senior citizens should be doing at that point in their lives.

3. *Saving for Major Expenditures.* Families often put aside money over the years to accumulate the funds needed to make major expenditures. The most common of these are the down payment on a home, education, vacation travel, and capital to start a business. The appropriate types of investment vehicles depend on the purpose and the amount of money needed. For purposes such as the down payment on a home or a child's education, for example, much less risk should be tolerated than for other goals. The attainment of such basic goals should not, if possible, be placed in jeopardy.

4. *Sheltering Income from Taxes.* Federal income tax law allows certain noncash charges to be deducted from specified sources of income. Such deductions reduce the amount of final taxable income. Obviously, if a person can avoid (or defer) paying taxes on the income from an investment, he or she will have more funds left for reinvestment.

HOT

Tax-advantaged investments are discussed on the text's Web site. Click on the Web chapter titled Tax-Advantaged Investments.

www.aw-bc.com/gitman_joehnk

investment plan
a written document describing how funds will be invested and specifying the target date for achieving each investment goal and the amount of tolerable risk.

Step 3: Adopting an Investment Plan Once your general goals have been established, you should adopt an **investment plan**—a written document describing how funds will be invested. A series of supporting investment goals can be developed for each long-term goal. For each goal, specify the target date for achieving it and the amount of tolerable risk.

Generally, the more important the financial objective, the lower the risk that should be assumed. Suppose, for example, one long-run goal is to accumulate $80,000 in cash by the end of 10 years. That goal could be spelled out as a plan to accumulate $80,000 in cash by investing in a portfolio evenly divided between low-risk and speculative stocks providing a total return of 10% per year. The more specific you can be in your statement of investment goals, the easier it will be to establish an investment plan consistent with your goals.

Step 4: Evaluating Investment Vehicles Once you have your investment goals and plan laid out, you will want to evaluate investment vehicles by assessing each vehicle's potential return and risk. This process typically involves *valuation,* the use of measures of return and risk to estimate the worth of an investment vehicle. (Chapter 4 offers a general discussion of the procedures for measuring these key dimensions of potential investments. Subsequent chapters focus on the valuation of specific vehicles.)

diversification
the inclusion of a number of different investment vehicles in a portfolio to increase returns or reduce risk.

Step 5: Selecting Suitable Investments You now gather additional information and use it to select specific investment vehicles consistent with your goals. The best investments may not be those that simply maximize return. Other factors, such as risk and tax considerations, may also be crucial. For example, to receive maximum annual dividends, you might purchase the common stock of a firm expected to pay high dividends. However, if the firm whose stock you purchased goes bankrupt, you could lose the money. The stock of a firm that pays lower dividends but with less risk of bankruptcy might have been a better choice. Careful selection of investment vehicles is essential to successful investing. Vehicles should be consistent with established goals and offer acceptable levels of return, risk, and value.

Step 6: Constructing a Diversified Portfolio Selecting suitable investments involves choosing vehicles that enable you to achieve investment goals and that optimize return, risk, and investment values. To do this, you will assemble an investment *portfolio* that meets one or more investment goals. For example, your portfolio might contain common stock, government bonds, and short-term investments. **Diversification** is the inclusion of a number of different investment vehicles in a portfolio to increase returns or reduce risk. By *diversifying* in this way, investors are able to earn higher returns or be exposed to less risk than if they limit their investments to just one or two vehicles. Diversification is the financial term for the age-old advice "Don't put all your eggs in one basket." (Chapter 5 includes discussions of diversification and other modern portfolio concepts.)

Step 7: Managing the Portfolio Once you have constructed your portfolio, you should measure its actual behavior in relation to expected performance. If the investment results are not consistent with your objectives, you may need to take corrective action. Such action usually involves selling certain investments and using the proceeds to acquire other vehicles for the portfolio. *Portfolio management* involves monitoring the portfolio and restructuring it as dictated by the actual behavior of the investments. Many individual investors buy mutual funds to achieve diversification and receive the benefit of professional managements (see Chapter 13); others will construct and manage their own portfolios (see Chapter 14).

The *Investing in Action* box on page 15 summarizes some general tips for successful investing.

Considering Personal Taxes

Besides developing plans for achieving your specific investment goals, it's important to consider the tax consequences associated with various investments. A knowledge of the tax laws can help you reduce taxes. By doing so, you increase the amount of after-tax dollars available for achieving your investment goals. Because tax laws are complicated and subject to frequent revision, we present only the key concepts and how they apply to popular investment transactions.

INVESTING IN ACTION

LESSONS FOR INVESTMENT SUCCESS

The stock market has taken investors on a roller-coaster ride in recent years. Even in such volatile times, however, some basic rules still apply. Becoming a successful investor takes time and effort; there are no sure-fire schemes for beating the market. Here are some tips to help you get started on the road to financial security.

*   **Harness the power of compounding.** With compounding, time is your biggest ally. The longer you invest your money, the faster it will grow. If you earn a 9% annual return on your investment and reinvest your yearly earnings at the same rate for a 20-year period, your overall return is 460%, an average annual return of 23% (460%/20). Start now; waiting will cost you money. If you invest $2,000 per year for 10 years ($20,000 total) at 8% per year, in 35 years you'll have $198,422. But wait 10 years and invest $2,000 per year for 25 years at 8% per year, and your (considerably greater) $50,000 investment will be only $146,212 at the end of that same 35-year period. You can start small. Invest just $200 at 10% and you'll have almost $20,000 in 25 years. Make investing a habit now.
*   **Don't wait for the "right" time to invest.** There isn't one! The "best" time to invest is now. You can always find a reason to put off taking the plunge: It's an election year, the market is too high, there's a crisis somewhere in the world. Studies show that it's more important to invest than to pick the right time. In the short run, market activity is unpredictable, even for the experts. Don't make excuses, like you are too busy, investing is too hard, or you can't possibly save enough for college or retirement. Investing is one of the best uses of your time. Rethink your priorities: Is it more important to go to the movies or to plan for your financial future? And don't be intimidated by the investment process. Set realistic goals, learn the basics, and start with simple investments that you understand. Once you gain control of your finances, your confidence will increase.

*   **Diversify your portfolio.** Spreading your money among different types of investments is less risky than putting all your eggs in one investment basket. If some of your holdings go down, others go up, and vice versa. Diversify your portfolio by investing in several types of securities: short-term vehicles such as money market funds, intermediate-term bonds or bond funds, and, for the long-term, growth stocks or growth mutual funds. You should also have some international stocks or mutual funds. Don't concentrate too heavily in one industry or buy just one or two stocks. No one knows which sector will be hot tomorrow.
*   **Monitor your investments.** Don't just buy securities and hold them forever. Review your portfolio monthly to check your progress against your goals. Weed out your poor performers and evaluate current holdings relative to other investment opportunities. Don't be too quick to unload a stock or mutual fund or to chase after that hot stock tip, though. Do your homework and be sure you have a good reason to buy or sell.

CRITICAL THINKING QUESTIONS Why is it important to start investing now? Why is it a good idea to diversify?

Sources: Jonathan Clements, "Don't Ignore Luck's Role in Stock Picks," *Wall Street Journal,* September 26, 2000, p. C1; Jonathan Clements, "Lessons from the School of Hard Knocks, *Wall Street Journal,* March 14, 2000, p. C1; "Money 101: Basics of Investing," *Money.com,* downloaded from **money.cnn.com/pf/101**; Peter Psaras, "Ten Tips for Successful Investing," *The Motley Fool,* September 13, 2000, downloaded from **fool.com**; Linda Stern, "Post-traumatic Investing," *San Diego Union-Tribune,* April 27, 2003, p. H3.

Basic Sources of Taxation The two major types of taxes are those levied by the federal government and those levied by state and local governments. The federal *income tax* is the major form of personal taxation. Federal rates currently range from 10 to 35% of taxable income.

State and local taxes vary from area to area. Some states have income taxes that range as high as 15% or more of income. Some cities, especially large East Coast cities, also have local income taxes that typically range between 1% and 5% of income. In addition to income taxes, state and local governments rely heavily on sales and property taxes, which vary from community to community, as a source of revenue.

Income taxes at the federal, state, and local levels have the greatest impact on security investments, whose returns are in the form of dividends, interest, and increases in value. Property taxes can have a sizable impact on real estate and other forms of property investment.

Types of Income The income of individuals is classified into one of *three basic categories* defined below.

1. *Active income* consists of everything from wages and salaries to bonuses, tips, pension income, and alimony. Active income is made up of income earned on the job as well as most other forms of *noninvestment* income.
2. *Portfolio income* is earnings generated from various types of investment holdings. This category of income covers most (but not all) types of investments, from savings accounts, stocks, bonds, and mutual funds to options and futures. For the most part, portfolio income consists of interest, dividends, and capital gains (the profit on the sale of an investment).
3. *Passive income* is a special category of income, composed chiefly of income derived from real estate, limited partnerships, and other forms of tax-advantaged investments.

The key feature of these categories is that they limit the amount of deductions (write-offs) that can be taken, particularly for portfolio and passive income. The amount of allowable deductions for portfolio and passive income is *limited to the amount of income derived from these two sources*. For example, if you had a total of $380 in portfolio income for the year, you could deduct no more than $380 in investment-related interest expense. For deduction purposes, the portfolio and passive income categories cannot be mixed or combined with each other or with active income. *Investment-related expenses can be used only to offset portfolio income,* and (with a few exceptions) *passive investment expenses can be used only to offset the income from passive investments.*

Note: Key financial topics offer opportunities for additional study to enhance learning. A PC icon appears next to topics covered in the tutorials that are featured at the book's Web site.

Ordinary Income Regardless of whether it's classified as active, portfolio, or passive, ordinary income is taxed at one of six rates: 10, 15, 25, 28, 33, or 35%. There is one structure of tax rates for taxpayers who file *individual* returns and another for those who file *joint* returns with a spouse. Table 1.2 shows the tax rates and income brackets for these two categories. Note that the rates are *progressive*. That is, taxpayers with taxable income above a specified amount are taxed at a higher rate.

TABLE 1.2	Tax Rates and Income Brackets for Individual and Joint Returns (2003)	
	Taxable Income	
Tax Rates	Individual Returns	Joint Returns
10%	$0 to $7,000	$0 to $14,000
15%	$7,001 to $28,400	$14,001 to $56,800
25%	$28,401 to $68,800	$56,801 to $114,650
28%	$68,801 to $143,500	$114,651 to $174,700
33%	$143,501 to $311,950	$174,701 to $311,950
35%	Over $311,950	Over $311,950

An example will demonstrate how ordinary income is taxed. Consider the Ellis sisters, Joni and Cara. Both are single. Joni's taxable income is $25,000. Cara's is $50,000. Using Table 1.2, we can calculate their taxes as follows:

Joni:
$(0.10 \times \$7,000) + [0.15 \times (\$25,000 - \$7,000)] = \$700 + \$2,700 = \underline{\$3,400}$

Cara:
$(0.10 \times \$7,000) + [0.15 \times (\$28,400 - \$7,000)]$
$\quad + [0.25 \times (\$50,000 - \$28,400)] = \$700 + \$3,210 + \$5,400 = \underline{\$\ 9,310}$

The progressive nature of the federal income tax structure can be seen by the fact that although Cara's taxable income is twice that of Joni, her income tax is about 2.75 times Joni's.

Capital Gains and Losses A *capital asset* is property owned and used by the taxpayer for personal reasons, pleasure, or investment. The most common types are securities and real estate, including one's home. A *capital gain* represents the amount by which the proceeds from the sale of a capital asset *exceed* its original purchase price. Capital gains are taxed at two different rates depending on the holding period.

The capital gains tax rate is 15% if the asset is held for more than 12 months. This 15% capital gains tax rate assumes that you're in the 25%, 28%, 33%, or 35% tax bracket. If you're in the 10% or 15% tax bracket, then the capital gains tax rate on an asset held for more than 12 months is just 5%. If the asset is held for less than 12 months, then the amount of any capital gain realized is added to other sources of income, and the total is taxed at the rates given in Table 1.2.

For example, imagine that James McFail, a single person who has other taxable income totaling $75,000, sold 500 shares of stock at $12 per share. He originally purchased this stock at $10 per share. The total capital gain on this transaction was $1,000 [500 shares × ($12/share − $10/share)]. Thus James's taxable income would total $76,000, which puts him in the 28% tax bracket (see Table 1.2).

If the $1,000 capital gain resulted from an asset that was held for more than 12 months, and because James is in the 28% tax bracket, the capital gain would be taxed at the maximum rate of 15%. His total tax would be calculated as follows:

Ordinary income ($75,000)
$(0.10 \times \$7,000) + [0.15 \times (\$28,400 - \$7,000)]$
$+ [0.25 \times (\$68,800 - \$28,400)] + [0.28 \times (\$75,000 - \$68,800)]$
$= \$700 + \$3,210 + \$10,100 + \$1,736 = \$15,746$

Capital gain ($1,000)
$(0.15 \times \$1,000) =$ 150

                                    Total tax $15,896

James's total tax would be $15,896. Had his other taxable income been below $28,401 (i.e., in the 15% bracket), the $1,000 capital gain would have been taxed at 5% rather than 15%. Had James held the asset for less than 12 months, his $1,000 capital gain would have been taxed as ordinary income, which in James's case would result in a 28% rate.

Capital gains are appealing to investors because they are not taxed until actually realized. For example, if you own a stock originally purchased for $50 per share that at the end of the tax year has a market price of $60 per share, you have a "paper gain" of $10 per share. This *paper (unrealized) gain* is not taxable, because you still own the stock. *Only realized gains are taxed.* If you sold the stock for $60 per share during the tax year, you would have a realized—and therefore taxable—gain of $10 per share.

A **capital loss** results when a capital asset is sold for *less than* its original purchase price. Before taxes are calculated, all gains and losses must be netted out. Up to $3,000 of **net losses** can be applied against ordinary income in any year. Losses that cannot be applied in the current year may be carried forward and used to offset future income, subject to certain conditions.

Investments and Taxes   The opportunities created by the tax laws make tax planning important in the investment process. **Tax planning** involves looking at your earnings, both current and projected, and developing strategies that will defer and minimize the level of taxes. The tax plan should guide your investment activities so that over the long run you will achieve maximum after-tax returns for an acceptable level of risk. For example, the fact that capital gains are not taxed until actually realized allows you to defer tax payments on them as well as control the timing of these payments. However, investments that are likely to lead to capital gains income generally have higher risk than those that provide only current investment income. Therefore, the choice of investment vehicles cannot be made solely on the basis of the possible reduction of tax payments. The levels of both return and risk need to be viewed in light of their tax effects. *It is the after-tax return and associated risk that matter.*

Tax plans should also reflect the (1) form of returns—current income, capital gains, or tax-advantaged income—and (2) the timing of loss recognition and profit taking. One common strategy is to claim losses as soon as they occur and to delay profit taking. Such an approach allows you to benefit from the tax deductibility of a loss and to delay having to claim income from gains. Tax planning, which is usually done in coordination with an accountant, tax expert, or tax attorney, is most common among individuals with high levels of income ($200,000 or more annually). Yet sizable savings can result for investors with lower incomes as well.

capital loss
the amount by which the proceeds from the sale of a capital asset are *less than* its original purchase price.

net losses
the amount by which capital losses exceed capital gains; up to $3,000 of net losses can be applied against ordinary income in any year.

tax planning
the development of strategies that will defer and minimize an individual's level of taxes over the long run.

H O T L I N K S

The material on tax strategies and tax-advantaged investments available on this text's Web site provides more detailed information on this topic. Click on Chapter 18.

www.aw-bc.com/gitman_joehnk

Tax-Advantaged Retirement Vehicles The federal government over the years has established a number of types of retirement vehicles that can be used to either supplement an existing employer retirement plan or to provide self-directed retirement accounts for employed and self-employed individuals. Employer-sponsored plans include profit-sharing plans, thrift and savings plans, and 401(k) plans. These plans are often *voluntary* and allow employees to both increase the amount of money held for retirement and enjoy attractive tax deferral benefits. Individuals can also set up their own tax-sheltered retirement programs—for example, Keogh plans and SEP-IRAs for self-employed individuals. Individual retirement arrangements (IRAs), both deductible and nondeductible, and Roth IRAs, can be set up by just about anybody subject to certain qualifications. In general, these plans allow individuals to defer taxes, typically on both the contributions and the earnings on them, until some future date when retirement withdrawals take place. Because, as noted earlier, the single most important goal of investing is to accumulate retirement funds, the use of various tax-advantaged retirement vehicles allows the individual investor to supplement an employer-sponsored retirement plan and/or to develop his or her own plan under very favorable tax provisions. Although the details of the various tax-advantaged vehicles mentioned here are not covered in this text, the individual investor should take advantage of these vehicles when they are available and appropriate to achieving his or her investment goals.

Investing Over the Life Cycle

Investors tend to follow different investment philosophies as they move through different stages of the life cycle. Generally speaking, most investors tend to be more aggressive when they're young and more conservative as they grow older. Typically, investors move through the following investment stages.

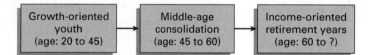

Most young investors, in their twenties and thirties, tend to prefer growth-oriented investments that stress *capital gains* rather than current income. Often young investors don't have much in the way of investable funds, so capital gains are viewed as the quickest (if not necessarily the surest) way to build capital. Young investors tend to favor growth-oriented and speculative vehicles, particularly high-risk common stocks, options, and futures.

As investors approach the middle-age consolidation stage of life (the mid-forties), family demands and responsibilities such as educational expenses and retirement contributions become more important. The whole portfolio goes through a transition to *higher-quality securities*. Low-risk growth and income stocks, high-grade bonds, preferred stocks, convertibles, and mutual funds are all widely used at this stage.

Finally, when investors approach their retirement years, preservation of capital and current income become the principal concerns. A secure, high level of income is paramount. Capital gains are viewed as merely a pleasant, occasional by-product of investing. The investment portfolio now becomes *highly conservative*. It consists of low-risk income stocks, high-yielding government bonds, quality corporate bonds, bank certificates of deposit (CDs), and other short-term vehicles. At this stage, investors reap the rewards of a lifetime of saving and investing.

Investing in Different Economic Environments

Despite the government's arsenal of weapons for moderating economic swings, numerous changes are sure to occur in the economy during your lifetime of investing. At all stages of the life cycle, your investment program must be flexible enough to allow you to recognize and react to changing economic conditions. The first rule of investing is to know *where* to put your money. The second is to know *when* to make your moves.

The first question is easier to deal with, because it involves matching the risk and return objectives of your investment plan with the available investment alternatives. For example, if you're a seasoned investor who can tolerate the risk, then speculative stocks may be right for you. If you're a novice who wants a fair return on your capital, perhaps you should consider a good growth-oriented mutual fund. Unfortunately, although stocks and growth funds may do well when the economy is expanding, they can turn out to be disasters at other times. This leads to the second, and more difficult, question: What effect do economic and market conditions have on investment returns?

The question of when to invest is difficult because it deals with *market timing*. The fact is that most economists and most professional money managers—not to mention most investors—cannot consistently predict the peaks and troughs in the economy or stock market. It's a lot easier to get a handle on the *current state* of the economy/market. That is, knowing whether the economy/market is in a state of expansion or decline is considerably different from being able to pinpoint when it's about to change course. Thus, for our purposes, we can define **market timing** as the process of identifying the current state of the economy/market and assessing the likelihood of its continuing on its present course.

market timing
the process of identifying the current state of the economy/market and assessing the likelihood of its continuing on its present course.

As an investor, it's best to confine your assessment of the economy to three distinct conditions: (1) a state of recovery or expansion, (2) a state of decline or recession, or (3) uncertainty as to the direction of its movement. These different stages are illustrated in Figure 1.2. It's easy to see when things are moving up (recovery/expansion) and when they're moving down (decline/ recession). The difficulty comes with the peaks and troughs. At those points, you don't know whether the economy will continue in its current direction, up or down, or whether it will change direction. That is why these areas in the figure are shaded, depicting *uncertainty*. How you will respond to these conditions depends on the types of investment vehicles you hold (for example, stocks or bonds).

Stocks and the Business Cycle Common stocks and other equity-related securities (convertible securities, stock mutual funds, stock options, and stock index futures) are highly responsive to conditions in the economy. Economic conditions are described generically as the *business cycle*. The business cycle reflects the current status of a variety of economic variables, including GDP (gross domestic product), industrial production, personal disposable income, the unemployment rate, and more.

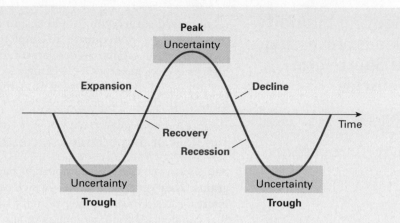

FIGURE 1.2

Different Stages of an Economic/Market Cycle

The economic/market cycle shows three different conditions: (1) a state of recovery/expansion, (2) a state of decline/recession, and (3) uncertainty as to the direction in which the economy/market is going to move (shown by the shaded areas).

A strong economy is reflected in an expanding business cycle. When business is good and profits are up, stocks react by increasing in value and return. Growth-oriented and speculative stocks tend to do especially well in strong markets. To a lesser extent, so do low-risk and income-oriented stocks. In contrast, when economic activity is declining, the values and returns on common stocks tend to be off as well.

Bonds and Interest Rates Bonds and other forms of fixed-income securities (preferred stocks and bond funds) are highly sensitive to movements in interest rates. In fact, interest rates are the single most important variable in determining bond price behavior and returns to investors. Interest rates and bond prices move in opposite directions (as will be explained in Chapters 10 and 11). Therefore, rising interest rates are unfavorable for bonds already held in an investor's portfolio. Of course, high interest rates enhance the attractiveness of new bonds because these bonds must offer high returns to attract investors.

IN REVIEW

CONCEPTS

1.11 What should an investor first establish before developing and executing an investment program? Briefly describe each of the seven steps involved in investing.

1.12 What are four common investment goals?

1.13 Define and differentiate among the following. Explain how each is related to federal income taxes.
- a. Active income
- b. Portfolio and passive income
- c. Capital gain
- d. Capital loss
- e. Tax planning
- f. Tax-advantaged retirement vehicles

1.14 Describe the differing investment philosophies typically applied during each of the following stages of an investor's life cycle.
- a. Youth (ages 20 to 45)
- b. Middle age (ages 45 to 60)
- c. Retirement years (age 60 on)

1.15 Describe the four stages of the economic/market cycle, and discuss the impact of this cycle on stock and bond investments.

Meeting Liquidity Needs: Investing in Short-Term Vehicles

LG 6

As discussed earlier, you should ensure that you have adequate liquidity. This provision is a prerequisite to implementing long-term investment goals. *Liquidity* is the ability to convert an investment into cash quickly and with little or no loss in value. A checking account is highly liquid. Stocks and bonds are not liquid, because there is no definite assurance that you will be able to quickly sell them at a price equal to or greater than their purchase price.

The Role of Short-Term Vehicles

Short-term vehicles are an important part of most savings and investment programs. They generate income—which can be quite high during periods of high interest rates. However, their primary function is to provide a pool of reserves that can be used for emergencies or simply to accumulate funds for some specific purpose. As a rule of thumb, financial planners often suggest that anywhere from 3 to 6 months' worth of after-tax income should be held in short-term vehicles to meet unexpected needs or to take advantage of attractive opportunities.

Investors usually hold short-term vehicles in their investment portfolios as a *temporary,* highly liquid investment until something better comes along. Some individuals choose to hold short-term vehicles because they simply are more comfortable with them. In fact, this approach has considerable merit during periods of economic and investment instability. Regardless of your motives for holding short-term vehicles, you should evaluate them in terms of their risk and return, just as you would longer-term investments.

Interest on Short-Term Investments Short-term investments earn interest in one of two ways. Some investments, such as savings accounts, pay a *stated rate of interest*. In this case, you can easily find the interest rate—it's the stated rate on the account.

Alternatively, interest is earned on short-term investments on a **discount basis.** This means that the security is purchased at a price below its redemption value, and the difference is the interest earned. U.S. Treasury bills (T-bills), for example, are issued on a discount basis.

discount basis
a method of earning interest on a security by purchasing it at a price below its redemption value; the difference is the interest earned.

Risk Characteristics Short-term investments are generally considered low in risk. Their primary risk results from the *loss of potential purchasing power* that occurs when the rate of return on these investments falls short of the inflation rate. This has often been the case with such vehicles as *passbook savings accounts,* the traditional bank savings accounts that generally pay a low rate of interest and have no minimum balance. Over long periods of time most other short-term investments have rates of return that are about equal to, or maybe slightly higher than, the average inflation rate.

The *risk of default*—nonpayment—is virtually nonexistent with short-term investment vehicles. The principal reason is that the primary issuers of most short-term vehicles are highly reputable institutions, such as the U.S. Treasury, large banks, and major corporations. Deposits in commercial banks, savings and loans, savings banks, and credit unions also are insured for up to $100,000 per account by government agencies. Finally, because the value of short-term investments does

H O T

A relatively simple formula can be applied when interest is earned on a discount basis in order to compare returns with vehicles earning a stated rate of interest. See this text's Web site for discussion of the formula.

www.aw-bc.com/gitman_joehnk

not change much in response to changing interest rates, exposure to capital loss is correspondingly low.

Advantages and Disadvantages of Short-Term Investments As noted, the major advantages of short-term investments are their high liquidity and low risk. Most are available from local financial institutions and can be readily converted to cash with minimal inconvenience. Finally, because the returns on most short-term investments vary with inflation and market interest rates, investors can readily capture higher returns as rates move up. On the negative side, when interest rates go down, returns drop as well.

Although a decline in market rates has undesirable effects on most short-term vehicles, perhaps their biggest disadvantage is their relatively low return. Because these securities are generally so low in risk, you can expect the returns on short-term investments to average less than the returns on long-term investments.

Popular Short-Term Investment Vehicles

Over the past 30 years or so, the number of short-term investment vehicles being offered has greatly expanded. Investing in short-term securities is no longer the easy task it once was, when the decision for most people amounted to whether to place funds in a passbook savings account or in U.S. savings bonds. Today, even some checking accounts pay interest on idle balances. Along with the increase in investment alternatives has come greater sophistication in short-term investment management. Investors now know they can use short-term vehicles as secure investment outlets for the long haul or as a place to hold cash until they find a longer-term outlet for the funds.

A variety of short-term investment vehicles are available to the individual investor. Some are deposit-type accounts in which an investor can place money, earn a relatively low rate of interest, and conveniently withdraw funds at his or her discretion. The popular deposit-type accounts are summarized in Part A of Table 1.3 on page 24. Another group of short-term investment vehicles are those issued by the federal government. The more popular of those vehicles are summarized in Part B of Table 1.3. The final group of short-term vehicles are nongovernment issues, typically issued by a financial institution, a corporation, or a professional money manager. Some of the more popular nongovernment issues are summarized in Part C of Table 1.3.

Investment Suitability

Individual investors use short-term vehicles for both savings and investment. They use short-term vehicles to maintain a desired level of savings that will be readily available if the need arises—in essence, to provide *safety and security*. For this purpose, high yield is less important than safety, liquidity, and convenience. Passbook savings accounts, NOW accounts, and Series EE savings bonds are the most popular savings vehicles.

When short-term vehicles are used for *investment purposes*, yield is often just as important as liquidity. However, because the objective is different, the short-term vehicles tend to be used much more aggressively. Most investors will hold at least a part of their portfolio in short-term, highly liquid securities,

TABLE 1.3	Popular Short-Term Investment Vehicles

Part A. Deposit-Type Accounts

Type of Account	Brief Description	Minimum Balance	Interest Rate	Federal Insurance
Passbook savings account	Savings accounts offered by banks.* Used primarily for convenience or if investors lack sufficient funds to purchase other short-term vehicles.	Typically none	0.5%–4% depending on economy	Yes, up to $100,000 per deposit.
NOW (negotiated order of withdrawal) account	Bank checking account that pays interest on balances.	No legal minimum, but often set at $500 to $1,000	At or near passbook rates	Yes, up to $100,000 per deposit.
Money market deposit account (MMDA)	Bank deposit account with limited check-writing privileges.	No legal minimum, but often set at about $2,500	Typically slightly above passbook rate	Yes, up to $100,000 per deposit.
Asset management account	Deposit account at bank, brokerage house, mutual fund, or insurance company that combines checking, investing, and borrowing. Automatically "sweeps" excess balances into short-term investments and borrows to meet shortages.	Typically $5,000 to $20,000	Similar to MMDAs	Yes, up to $100,000 per deposit in banks. Varies in other institutions.

Part B. Federal Government Issues

Security	Issuer	Description	Initial Maturity	Risk and Return
Series EE savings bonds	U.S. Treasury	Savings bonds issued by the U.S. Treasury and sold at banks and through payroll deduction plans, in varying denominations, at 50% of face value; pay a variable rate of interest tied to U.S. Treasury security market yields and calculated every six months in May and November.	None	Lowest, virtually risk-free
Treasury bills	U.S. Treasury	Issued weekly at auction; sold at a discount; strong secondary market; exempt from local and state income taxes	91 and 182 days	Lowest, virtually risk-free

Part C. Nongovernment Issues

Security	Issuer	Description	Initial Maturity	Risk and Return
Certificates of deposit (CDs)	Commercial banks	Represent specific cash deposits in commercial banks; amounts and maturities tailored to investor needs	1 month to 3 years or more	Higher than U.S. Treasury issues and comparable to commercial paper
Commercial paper	Corporation with a high credit standing	Unsecured note of issuer; large denominations	3 to 270 days	Higher than U.S. Treasury issues and comparable to negotiable CDs
Banker's acceptances	Banks	Results from a bank guarantee of a business transaction; sold at discount from maturity value	30 to 180 days	About the same as negotiable CDs and commercial paper but higher than U.S. Treasury issues
Money market mutual funds	Professional portfolio management companies	Professionally managed portfolios of marketable securities; provide instant liquidity	None—depends on wishes of investor	Vary, but generally higher than U.S. Treasury issues and comparable to negotiable CDs and commercial paper

*The term *bank* refers to commercial banks, savings and loans (S&Ls), savings banks, and credit unions.

if for no other reason than to be able to act on unanticipated investment opportunities. Some investors, in fact, devote all or most of their portfolios to such securities.

One of the most common uses of short-term securities as investment vehicles is as temporary outlets. In that use, investors buy short-term vehicles either to warehouse funds until an attractive permanent investment can be found or to sit on the sidelines in times of unsettled or undesirable market conditions. For example, if you have just sold some stock but do not have a suitable long-term investment alternative, you might place the proceeds in a money fund until you find a longer-term use for them. Or if you feel that interest rates are about to rise sharply, you might sell your long-term bonds and use the proceeds to buy T-bills. The higher-yielding securities—like MMDAs, CDs, commercial paper, banker's acceptances, and money funds—are generally preferred for use as part of an investment program, as are asset management accounts at major brokerage firms.

To decide which securities are most appropriate for a particular situation, you need to consider such issue characteristics as availability, safety, liquidity, and yield. Though all the investments we have discussed satisfy the basic liquidity demand, they do so to varying degrees. A NOW account is unquestionably the most liquid of all. You can write as many checks on the account as you wish and for any amount. A certificate of deposit, on the other hand, is not so liquid, because early redemption involves an interest penalty. Table 1.4 summarizes the key characteristics of the short-term investments described in Table 1.3. The letter grade assigned for each characteristic reflects an estimate of the investment's quality in that area. For example, MMMFs rate only a B+ on liquidity, because withdrawals must usually be made in a minimum amount of $250 to $500. NOW accounts are somewhat better in this respect, because a

TABLE 1.4   A Scorecard for Short-Term Investment Vehicles

Savings or Investment Vehicle	Availability	Safety	Liquidity	Yield (Average Rate)*
Passbook savings account	A+	A+	A	D (0.6%)
NOW account	A−	A+	A+	F (0.5%)
Money market deposit account (MMDA)	B	A+	A	B− (0.7%)
Asset management account	B−	A	A+	B (1.0%)
Series EE savings bond	A+	A++	C−	B+ (2.6%)
U.S. Treasury bill (91-day)	B−	A++	A−	A− (0.9%)
Certificate of deposit (3-month, large denomination)	B	A+	C	A (1.1%)
Commercial paper (90-day)	B−	A−	C	A− (1.1%)
Banker's acceptance (90-day)	B−	A	B	A− (1.1%)
Money market mutual fund (MMMF)	B	A/A+	B+	A− (0.5%)

*The average rates reflect representative or typical rates that existed in early 2004.

withdrawal can be for any amount. Yields are self-explanatory. You should note, though, that if an investment scores lower on availability, safety, or liquidity, it will generally offer a higher yield.

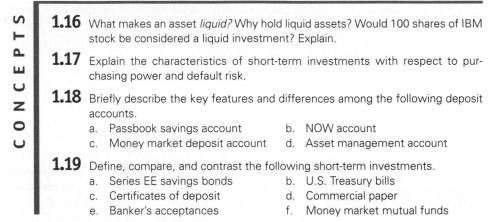

I N   R E V I E W

CONCEPTS

1.16 What makes an asset *liquid?* Why hold liquid assets? Would 100 shares of IBM stock be considered a liquid investment? Explain.

1.17 Explain the characteristics of short-term investments with respect to purchasing power and default risk.

1.18 Briefly describe the key features and differences among the following deposit accounts.
   a. Passbook savings account   b. NOW account
   c. Money market deposit account   d. Asset management account

1.19 Define, compare, and contrast the following short-term investments.
   a. Series EE savings bonds   b. U.S. Treasury bills
   c. Certificates of deposit   d. Commercial paper
   e. Banker's acceptances   f. Money market mutual funds

Summary

| LG 1 |

Note: The end-of-chapter Summaries restate the chapter's Learning Goals and review the key points of information related to each goal.

Understand the meaning of the term *investment* and the factors commonly used to differentiate among types of investments. An investment is any vehicle into which funds can be placed with the expectation that they will generate positive income and/or that their value will be preserved or will increase. The returns from investing are received either as current income or as increased value.

Some investment vehicles are securities; others are forms of property. Some investments are made directly, others indirectly. An investment can be a debt, an equity, or a derivative security such as an option. It can possess risk ranging from very low to extremely high. An individual can invest in either short-term or long-term vehicles. Today, individual investors have ready access to both domestic and foreign investments.

| LG 2 |

Describe the investment process and types of investors. The investment process is structured around financial institutions and financial markets that bring together suppliers and demanders of funds. The dominant financial market in the United States is the securities markets for stocks, bonds, and options. The participants in the investment process are government, business, and individuals. Of these groups, only individuals are net suppliers of funds. Investors can be either individual investors or institutional investors.

| LG 3 |

Discuss the principal types of investment vehicles. A broad range of investment vehicles is available. Short-term vehicles have low risk. They are used to earn a return on temporarily idle funds, to serve as a primary investment outlet of conservative investors, and to provide liquidity. Common stocks offer dividends and capital gains. Fixed-income securities—bonds, preferred stock, and convertible securities—offer fixed periodic returns with some potential for gain in value. Mutual funds allow investors conveniently to buy or sell interests in a professionally managed, diversified portfolio of securities.

Derivative securities are high-risk, high-expected-return vehicles. The key derivatives are options and futures. Options offer the investor an opportunity to buy or sell another security at a specified price over a given period of time. Futures are contracts between a seller and a buyer for delivery of a specified commodity or financial instrument, at a specified future date, at an agreed-on price. Other popular investment vehicles include real estate, tangibles, and tax-advantaged investments.

LG 4 **Describe the steps in investing, particularly establishing investment goals, and cite fundamental personal tax considerations.** Investing is a process that should be driven by well-developed plans established to achieve specific goals. It involves a logical set of steps: meeting investment prerequisites, establishing investment goals, adopting an investment plan, evaluating investment vehicles, selecting suitable investments, constructing a diversified portfolio, and managing the portfolio. Investment goals determine the types of investments made. Common investment goals include accumulating retirement funds, enhancing current income, saving for major expenditures, and sheltering income from taxes.

The tax consequences associated with various investment vehicles and strategies must also be considered. The key dimensions are ordinary income, capital gains and losses, tax planning, and the use of tax-advantaged retirement vehicles.

LG 5 **Discuss investing over the life cycle and investing in different economic environments.** The investment vehicles selected are affected by the investor's stage in the life cycle and by economic cycles. Younger investors tend to prefer growth-oriented investments that stress capital gains. As they age investors move to higher-quality securities. As they approach retirement they become even more conservative. The stage of the economy—(1) recovery or expansion, (2) decline or recession, or (3) uncertainty as to the direction of its movement—both current and expected, also affects investment choice.

LG 6 **Understand the popular types of short-term investment vehicles.** Investment plans must ensure adequate liquidity. Liquidity needs can be met by investing in various short-term vehicles, which can earn interest at a stated rate or on a discount basis. They typically have low risk. Numerous short-term investment vehicles are available from banks, the government, and brokerage firms. Their suitability depends on the investor's attitude toward availability, safety, liquidity, and yield.

Putting Your Investment Know-How to the Test

The Chartered Financial Analyst® designation is globally recognized as the highest professional designation you can receive in the field of professional money management. The CFA® charter is awarded to those candidates who successfully pass a series of three exams, with each exam lasting six hours and covering a full range of investment topics. The CFA Program is administered by the Association for Investment Management and Research (AIMR®) in Charlottesville, Virginia. For more information about the CFA program go to: www.aimr.org.

Many CFA candidates turn to the Schweser Study Program for high-quality exam preparation. The Schweser Study Program was founded in 1990 by Dr. Carl Schweser, whose goal was to write study materials that were effective and easy to understand. The Schweser Institute™ offers certificate programs in critical areas of advanced financial education. For more information go to: www.schweser.com.

Starting with Chapter 2 of the text and for every chapter thereafter, you will find a series of CFA questions taken from the Level 1 exam program and of Schweser questions for the same level. The CFA questions have actually appeared on past exams or in AIMR study materials, and the Schweser questions have also been published in their study materials. You will also find sprinkled throughout some multiple-choice questions that mimic the CFA and Schweser study materials, as here in Chapter 1, where the concepts under study are basic and introductory in nature.

1. What represents an ownership share in a corporation?
   a. Fixed-income security   b. Common stock
   c. Call option   d. Commercial paper

2. Money market securities are characterized by
   a. A very short term to maturity.
   b. Low risk.
   c. High liquidity.
   d. All of the above.

3. An example of a portfolio investment is a
   a. Stock.   b. Bond.
   c. Mutual fund.   d. All of the above.

4. Tangible assets include
   a. Residential homes.
   b. Gold and other precious metals.
   c. Certificates of deposit.
   d. Stocks and bonds.

5. You purchased ABC stock at $52 per share. The stock paid $2 in dividends and is
   currently selling at $48 per share. Your total return includes
   a. $4 in capital loss and $2 in dividend income.
   b. $2 in capital loss.
   c. $4 in capital gain and $2 in dividend income.
   d. $4 in investment loss.

6. A particularly attractive feature of T-bills is that
   a. They are exempt from local and state income taxes.
   b. They can be purchased from the U.S. government directly.
   c. They are default free.
   d. All of the above.

7. Three-month T-bill auctions are conducted
   a. Daily.   b. Weekly.
   c. Monthly.   d. Quarterly.

8. Commercial paper is a short-term security issued to raise funds by
   a. The United States Treasury.
   b. Commercial banks.
   c. The Federal Reserve.
   d. Large corporations.

9. Short-term investment vehicles, ranked in order of liquidity, are
   a. Commercial paper, certificates of deposit, T-bills, and NOW accounts.
   b. NOW accounts, passbook savings, T-bills, and EE-series savings bonds.
   c. Banker's acceptances, money market deposit accounts, T-bills,
      and commercial paper.
   d. Money market mutual funds, EE-series savings bonds, passbook savings,
      and certificates of deposit.

10. Which of the activities mentioned below are *not* part of investment planning?
    a. Evaluating suitable investment vehicles
    b. Constructing a diversified portfolio
    c. Performing tax analysis and sheltering income from taxes
    d. Timing the market

Answers: 1. b; 2. d; 3. c; 4. b; 5. a; 6. d; 7. b; 8. d; 9. b; 10. d

Discussion Questions

LG 4

LG 5

LG 6

Note: The Discussion Questions at the end of the chapter ask you to analyze and synthesize information presented in the chapter. These questions, like all other end-of-chapter assignment materials, are keyed to the chapter's learning goals.

Q1.1. Assume that you are 35 years old, are married with two young children, are renting a condo, and have an annual income of $90,000. Use the following questions to guide your preparation of a rough investment plan consistent with these facts.

   a. What are your key investment goals?

   b. How might personal taxes affect your investment plans? Use current tax rates to assess their impact.

   c. How might your stage in the life cycle affect the types of risk you might take?

Q1.2. What role, if any, will short-term vehicles play in your portfolio? Why? Complete the following table for the short-term investments listed. Find their yields in a current issue of the *Wall Street Journal,* and explain which, if any, you would include in your investment portfolio.

Savings or Investment Vehicle	Minimum Balance	Yield	Federal Insurance	Method and Ease of Withdrawing Funds
a. Passbook savings account	None		Yes	In person or through teller machines; very easy
b. NOW account				Unlimited check-writing privileges
c. Money market deposit account (MMDA)				
d. Asset management account				
e. Series EE savings bond	Virtually none			
f. U.S. Treasury bill				
g. Certificate of deposit (CD)				
h. Commercial paper				
i. Banker's acceptance				
j. Money market mutual fund (MMMF)				

Problems

LG 4

LG 5

Note: The Problems at the end of the chapter offer opportunities to perform calculations using the tools and techniques learned in the chapter. A Web icon appears next to problems that can be solved using the text's software accessible at its Web site: www.aw-bc.com/gitman_joehnk.

P1.1 Sonia Gomez, a 45-year-old widow, wishes to accumulate $250,000 over the next 15 years to supplement the retirement programs that are being funded by the federal government and her employer. She expects to earn an average annual return of about 8% by investing in a low-risk portfolio containing about 20% short-term securities, 30% common stock, and 50% bonds.

   Sonia currently has $31,500 that at an 8% annual rate of return will grow to about $100,000 at the end of 15 years (found using time-value techniques that will be described in Chapter 4). Her financial adviser indicated that for every $1,000 Sonia wishes to accumulate at the end of 15 years, she will have to make an annual investment of $36.83. (This amount is also calculated on the basis of an 8% annual rate of return using the time-value techniques that are described in Chapter 4.) Sonia plans to accumulate needed funds by making equal, annual, end-of-year investments over the next 15 years.

   a. How much money does Sonia need to accumulate by making equal, annual, end-of-year investments to reach her goal of $250,000?

   b. How much must Sonia deposit annually to accumulate at the end of year 15 the sum calculated in part **a**?

LG 4   **P1.2**   During 2003, the Allens and the Zells both filed joint tax returns. The Allens' taxable income was $130,000, and the Zells had total taxable income of $65,000 for the tax year ended December 31, 2003.
   a. Using the federal tax rates given in Table 1.2, calculate the taxes for both the Allens and the Zells.
   b. Calculate and compare the ratio of the Allens' to the Zells' taxable income and the ratio of the Allens' to the Zells' taxes. What does this demonstrate about the federal income tax structure?

LG 4   **P1.3**   Robert Pang, a 53-year-old software engineer, and his wife, Jean, have $50,000 to invest. They will need the money at retirement in 10 years. They are considering two investments. The first is a utility company common stock that costs $50 per share and pays dividends of $2 per share per year (a 4% dividend yield). They do not expect the value of this stock to increase. The other investment under consideration is a highly rated corporate bond that currently sells at par in $1,000 increments, and pays annual interest at a rate of 5%, or $50 per $1,000 invested. After 10 years, these bonds will be repaid at par, or $1,000 per $1,000 invested. Assume that the Pangs keep the income from their investments, but do not reinvest it (they keep the cash under a mattress). They will, however, need to pay income taxes on their investment income. They will sell the stock after 10 years if they buy it. If they buy the bonds, they will get the amount they invested back in 10 years. The Pangs are in the 33% tax bracket.
   a. How many shares of the stock can the Pangs buy?
   b. How much will they receive each year in dividend income if they buy the stock, after taxes?
   c. What is the total amount they would have from their original $50,000 if they purchased the stock and it all went as planned?
   d. How much will they receive each year in interest if they purchase the bonds, after taxes?
   e. What is the total amount they would have from their original $50,000 if they purchased the bonds and all went as planned?
   f. Based only on your calculations and ignoring other risk factors, should they buy the stock or the bonds?

LG 4   **P1.4**   Mike and Linda Smith are a working couple. They will file a joint income tax return. This year, they have the following taxable income:
   1. $125,000 from salary and wages (ordinary income).
   2. $1,000 in interest income.
   3. $3,000 in dividend income.
   4. $2,000 in profit from a stock they purchased two years ago.
   5. $2,000 in profit from a stock they purchased this year and sold this year.

Use the federal income tax rates given in Table 1.2 to work this problem.
   a. How much will Mike and Linda pay in federal income taxes on 2 above?
   b. How much will Mike and Linda pay in federal income taxes on 3 above?
   c. How much will Mike and Linda pay in federal income taxes on 4 above?
   d. How much will Mike and Linda pay in federal income taxes on 5 above?

**See the text Web site
(www.aw-bc.com/gitman_joehnk) for Web exercises
that deal with *the investment environment.***

Case Problem 1.1

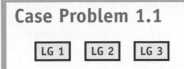

Note: Two Case Problems appear at the end of every chapter. They ask you to apply what you have learned in the chapter to a hypothetical investment situation.

Investments or Golf?

Judd Read and Judi Todd, senior accounting majors at a large midwestern university, have been good friends since high school. Each has already found a job that will begin after graduation. Judd has accepted a position as an internal auditor in a medium-sized manufacturing firm. Judi will be working for one of the major public accounting firms. Each is looking forward to the challenge of a new career and to the prospect of achieving success both professionally and financially.

Judd and Judi are preparing to register for their final semester. Each has one free elective to select. Judd is considering taking a golf course offered by the physical education department, which he says will help him socialize in his business career. Judi is planning to take a basic investments course. Judi has been trying to convince Judd to take investments instead of golf. Judd believes he doesn't need to take investments, because he already knows what common stock is. He believes that whenever he has accumulated excess funds, he can invest in the stock of a company that is doing well. Judi argues that there is much more to it than simply choosing common stock. She feels that exposure to the field of investments would be more beneficial than learning how to play golf.

Questions

a. Explain to Judd the structure of the investment process and the economic importance of investing.

b. List and discuss the other types of investment vehicles with which Judd is apparently unfamiliar.

c. Assuming that Judd already gets plenty of exercise, what arguments would you give to convince Judd to take investments rather than golf?

Case Problem 1.2

Preparing Carolyn Bowen's Investment Plan

Carolyn Bowen, who just turned 55, is a widow currently employed as a receptionist for the Xcon Corporation, where she has worked for the past 20 years. She is in good health, lives alone, and has two grown children. A few months ago, her husband died. Carolyn's husband left her with only their home and the proceeds from a $75,000 life insurance policy. After she paid medical and funeral expenses, $60,000 of the life insurance proceeds remained. In addition to the life insurance proceeds, Carolyn has $37,500 in a savings account, which she had secretly built over the past 10 years. Recognizing that she is within 10 years of retirement, Carolyn wishes to use her limited resources to develop an investment program that will allow her to live comfortably once she retires.

Carolyn is quite superstitious. After consulting with a number of psychics and studying her family tree, she feels certain she will not live past 80. She plans to retire at either 62 or 65, whichever will better allow her to meet her long-run financial goals. After talking with a number of knowledgeable individuals—including, of course, the psychics—Carolyn estimates that to live comfortably, she will need $45,000 per year, before taxes, once she retires. This amount will be required annually for each of 18 years if she retires at 62 or for each of 15 years if she retires at 65. As part of her financial plans, Carolyn intends to sell her home at retirement and rent an apartment. She has estimated that she will net $112,500 if she sells the house at 62 and $127,500 if she sells it at 65. Carolyn has no financial dependents and is not concerned about leaving a sizable estate to her heirs.

If Carolyn retires at age 62, she will receive from Social Security and an employer-sponsored pension plan a total of $1,359 per month ($16,308 annually); if she waits until age 65 to retire, her total retirement income will be $1,688 per month ($20,256 annually). For convenience, Carolyn has already decided that to convert all her assets at the time of retirement into a stream of annual income, she will at that time purchase an annuity by paying a single premium. The annuity will have a life just equal to the number of years remaining until her 80th birthday. Because Carolyn is uncertain as to the actual age at which she will retire, she obtained the following interest factors from her insurance agent to estimate the annual annuity benefit provided for a given purchase price.

Life of Annuity	Interest Factor
15 years	11.118
18 years	12.659

The yearly annuity benefit can be calculated by dividing the factors into the purchase price. Carolyn plans to place any funds currently available into a savings account paying 6% compounded annually until retirement. She does not expect to be able to save or invest any additional funds between now and retirement. To calculate the future value of her savings, she will need to multiply the amount of money currently available to her by one of the following factors, depending on the retirement age being considered.

Retirement Age	Time to Retirement	Future-Value Interest Factor
62	7 years	1.504
65	10 years	1.791

Questions

a. Assume that Carolyn places currently available funds in the savings account. Determine the amount of money Carolyn will have available at retirement once she sells her house if she retires at (1) age 62 and (2) age 65.

b. Using the results from question (a) and the interest factors given above, determine the level of annual income that will be provided to Carolyn through purchase of an annuity at (1) age 62 and (2) age 65.

c. With the results found in the preceding questions, determine the total annual retirement income Carolyn will have if she retires at (1) age 62 and (2) age 65.

d. From your findings, do you think Carolyn will be able to achieve her long-run financial goal by retiring at (1) age 62 or (2) age 65? Explain.

e. Evaluate Carolyn's investment plan in terms of her use of a savings account and an annuity rather than some other investment vehicles. Comment on the risk and return characteristics of her plan. What recommendations might you offer Carolyn? Be specific.

Excel with Spreadsheets

Note: Excel spreadsheet exercises at the end of each chapter will assist you in learning some useful applications of this tool in the personal investing process.

In the following chapters of this text, you will be asked to solve spreadsheet problems using Microsoft Excel®. While each person's skill and experience with Excel will vary, an assumption has been made that you understand the basics of Excel. This includes the entering of text and numbers, copying or moving a cell, moving and copying using "drag and drop," inserting and deleting rows and columns, and checking your spelling. The review in this chapter focuses on entering and editing data in the worksheet.

To complete the spreadsheet review, go to www.aw-bc.com/gitman_joehnk and go to "Student Resources." Click on "Spreadsheet Review." There you will be asked to create a spreadsheet and perform the following tasks.

Questions

a. Add and subtract data with a formula
b. Multiply and divide data with a formula
c. Total cells using the sum function and calculate an average
d. Use the average function
e. Copy a formula using the "drag and drop" method

TRADING ONLINE WITH OTIS

As noted at the beginning of the chapter, the Internet has played a major role in opening up the world of investing to individual investors. As an investor, you now have access to powerful tools and enormous amounts of information. Technology does make investing much easier—but at the same time riskier for the inexperienced.

We would like you to experience the world of electronic investing by making available the OTIS simulated stock trading and portfolio management program. OTIS—the Online Trading and Investment Simulator—takes financial education to a new level. Developed at the Alfred West, Jr., Learning Lab at the Wharton School of the University of Pennsylvania, OTIS enables you to become a "fund manager" and to buy and sell equities using real data from today's markets. Working with data in OTIS's hands-on learning environment, you will learn about such concepts as portfolio balancing and management, benchmarking, liquidity, and pricing—all issues to be discussed in future chapters. You will see how OTIS mirrors the sophisticated interface of many commercial trading applications used in the market today.

Because this program uses imaginary money, you have nothing to lose. At the same time you will gain a wealth of knowledge about how to trade stocks and structure a portfolio. At the end of selected chapters you will find exercises that will assist you in effectively utilizing this computerized trading system. The first of these exercises is designed to get you started by familiarizing yourself with the software.

Exercises

1. Register for the OTIS simulation following instructions from your teacher.
2. Explore your OTIS account by going to the following:
   a. *Positions,* which will help you to determine the cash value of your account.
   b. *Analytics,* where you can analyze and manage your portfolio.
3. Go to the "Trade" page and use the "symbol lookup" link to find the symbol for Nokia. To learn more about the stock, enter the ticker symbol in the "quotes/research" box and click the research link.

Note: At the end of selected chapters you will find exercises that will assist you in effectively utilizing the OTIS simulated stock trading and portfolio management program.

The market turmoil that rocked the global capital markets set the stage for major changes in the way U.S. securities markets and related financial institutions operate. Beset by scandals, from corporate wrongdoing to internal problems at the venerable New York Stock Exchange (NYSE), Wall Street's institutions are taking stock of how they operate and reassessing their own standards.

A few years ago Nasdaq, the pioneer of electronic trading systems that billed itself as "the market for the next 100 years," was grabbing market share from the NYSE. Its less stringent listing requirements and state-of-the-art technology made Nasdaq the preferred route for entrepreneurial companies to raise capital. Technology companies especially flocked to Nasdaq, and as their fortunes rose in the 1990s, so did Nasdaq's. When the technology bubble burst in 2000, contributing to the bear market that followed, Nasdaq was—not surprisingly—hit harder than the other exchanges. It retrenched, canceling its own initial public offering and curtailing the operations of Nasdaq Europe and other overseas ventures. Nevertheless, its automated matching system, which eliminates the middleman, remains popular with many customers.

The NYSE remains one of the few exchanges worldwide that is not wholly electronic. Criticized for its adherence to a traditional people-centered trading system, it managed to weather the bear market in better shape than its electronic counterparts. Even though its $0.078/share transaction fee is usually the lowest priced, high-speed electronic communications networks (ECNs) are coming close to that rate and beating it at times. Institutional investors are moving more of their trades from the exchange floor to ECNs such as Archipelago, Instinet, Posit, and the Internet-based Liquidnet. ECNs now handle about 15% of all NYSE trades.

The increasing competition among exchanges should benefit investors. It will promote better governance, encourage more innovation, and result in technological advances that improve the quality, fairness, and accuracy of securities transactions.

In this chapter, we will study the markets, the exchanges, the regulations, and the transactions that enable companies to raise money in the capital markets and institutions and individuals to invest in these companies.

Sources: Kim Clark, "Closing Bell for the NYSE?" *U.S. News & World Report*, June 9, 2003, p. 26; Mara Der Hovanesian, "The Big Board Risks Losing the Big Trades," *Business Week*, May 5, 2003, p. 40; Paula Dwyer and Amy Borrus, "Nasdaq, the Fight of Its Life," *Business Week*, August 11, 2003, p. 40; Gretchen Morgenson, "Is the Big Board Getting Creaky?" *The New York Times*, April 27, 2003, section 3, p. 1; and Andrei Postelni, "The Bull Market Hero at Bay," *Financial Times*, August 30, 2003, p. 13.

CHAPTER 2

MARKETS AND TRANSACTIONS

LEARNING GOALS

After studying this chapter, you should be able to:

LG 1 Identify the basic types of securities markets and describe the IPO process.

LG 2 Explain the characteristics of organized securities exchanges.

LG 3 Understand the over-the-counter markets, including Nasdaq and alternative trading systems, and the general conditions of securities markets.

LG 4 Review the importance of global securities markets, their performance, and the investment procedures and risks associated with foreign investments.

LG 5 Discuss trading hours and the regulation of securities markets.

LG 6 Explain long purchases and the motives, procedures, and calculations involved in making margin transactions and short sales.

Securities Markets

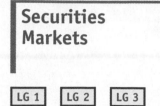

securities markets
forums that allow suppliers and demanders of *securities* to make financial transactions; they include both the *money market* and the *capital market*.

money market
market where *short-term* securities (with maturities less than one year) are bought and sold.

capital market
market in which *long-term* securities (with maturities greater than one year) such as stocks and bonds are bought and sold.

primary market
the market in which *new issues* of securities are sold to the public.

initial public offering (IPO)
the first public sale of a company's stock.

Securities and Exchange Commission (SEC)
federal agency that regulates securities offerings and markets.

public offering
the sale of a firm's securities to the general public.

rights offering
an offer of new shares of stock to existing stockholders on a pro rata basis.

private placement
the sale of new securities directly, without SEC registration, to selected groups of investors.

H O T

The SEC site, in addition to providing corporate documents such as annual reports, offers basic information and warnings to new investors.

www.sec.gov

Securities markets are forums that allow suppliers and demanders of *securities* to make financial transactions. They permit such transactions to be made quickly and at a fair price. In this section we will look at the various types of markets, their organization, and their general behavior.

Types of Securities Markets

Securities markets may be classified as either money markets or capital markets. The **money market** is the market where *short-term* securities (with maturities less than one year) are bought and sold. Investors turn to the **capital market** to make transactions involving *long-term* securities (with maturities greater than one year) such as stocks and bonds. In this book we will devote most of our attention to the capital market. There, investors can make stock, bond, mutual fund, options, and futures transactions. Capital markets can be classified as either *primary* or *secondary,* depending on whether securities are being sold initially by their issuing company or by intervening owners.

The Primary Market The market in which *new issues* of securities are sold to the public is the **primary market.** In the primary market, the issuer of the equity or debt securities receives the proceeds of sales. In 2003, only 79 companies offered their stock for sale in the primary market. This number compared miserably with the 452 companies that went public three years earlier. The main vehicle in the primary market is the **initial public offering (IPO),** the first public sale of a company's stock. The primary markets also provide a forum for the sale of new securities, called s*easoned new issues,* by companies that are already public.

Before offering its securities for public sale, the issuer must register them with and obtain approval from the **Securities and Exchange Commission (SEC).** This federal regulatory agency must confirm both the adequacy and the accuracy of the information provided to potential investors before a security is publicly offered for sale. In addition, the SEC regulates the securities markets.

To market its securities in the primary market, a firm has three choices. It may make (1) a **public offering,** in which the firm offers its securities for sale to the general public; (2) a **rights offering,** in which the firm offers new shares to existing stockholders on a pro rata basis; or (3) a **private placement,** in which the firm sells new securities directly, without SEC registration, to selected groups of investors such as insurance companies and pension funds.

Going Public: The IPO Process Most companies that go public are small, fast-growing companies that require additional capital to continue expanding. For example, credit and debit card processing company iPayment, Inc., raised almost $80 million when it went public in May 2003 at $16 per share. In addition, large companies may decide to spin off a unit into a separate public corporation. AT&T did this when it spun off its wireless operations into AT&T Wireless in April 2000, raising over $10 billion at $29.50 per share.

When a company decides to go public, it first must obtain the approval of its current shareholders, the investors who own its privately issued stock. Next, the company's auditors and lawyers must certify that all documents for the company are

prospectus
a portion of a security registration statement that describes the key aspects of the issue, the issuer, and its management and financial position.

red herring
a preliminary *prospectus* made available to prospective investors during the waiting period between the registration statement's filing with the SEC and its approval.

legitimate. The company then finds an investment bank willing to *underwrite* the offering. This underwriter is responsible for promoting the stock and facilitating the sale of the company's IPO shares. The underwriter often brings in other investment banking firms as participants. We'll discuss the role of the investment banker in more detail in the next section.

The company files a registration statement with the SEC. One portion of the registration statement is called the **prospectus.** It describes the key aspects of the issue, the issuer, and its management and financial position. During the waiting period between the statement's filing and its approval, prospective investors can receive a preliminary prospectus. This preliminary version is called a **red herring,** because a notice printed in red on the front cover indicates the tentative nature of the offer. The cover of the preliminary prospectus describing the 2003 stock issue of Hewitt Associates, Inc., a leading global provider of human resources outsourcing and consulting services, is shown in Figure 2.1 (on page 38). Note the red herring printed vertically on its left edge.

After the SEC approves the registration statement, the investment community can begin analyzing the company's prospects. However, from the time it files until at least one month after the IPO is complete, the company must observe a *quiet period,* during which there are restrictions on what company officials may say about the company. The purpose of the quiet period is to make sure that all potential investors have access to the same information about the company—that which is presented in the preliminary prospectus—and not to any unpublished data that might give them an unfair advantage.

The investment bankers and company executives promote the company's stock offering through a *road show,* a series of presentations to potential investors—typically institutional investors—around the country and sometimes overseas. In addition to providing investors with information about the new issue, road show sessions help the investment bankers gauge the demand for the offering and set an expected pricing range. After the underwriter sets terms and prices the issue, the SEC must approve the offering.

Table 2.1 (on page 39) shows, for each year between 1993 and 2002, the number of offerings, the average first-day return, and the gross proceeds of the given years' IPOs. Note the exceptionally high first-day returns and large number of offerings during 1999 and 2000 caused by the technology-stock-driven bull market that ended in late 2000. Since then, the number of offerings and the first-day returns have declined dramatically, consistent with the precipitous market decline that occurred in 2001 and 2002. During the boom of 1999 and 2000, it wasn't unusual for the price of an IPO to double on the first day. During that period many IPOs were underpriced, resulting in huge first-day gains. Some industry experts question whether the underwriters misjudge demand for an issue or set the price artificially low to please their institutional clients, who buy at the offering price and then resell the shares. Sometimes companies themselves support undervaluation so that their stock will generate excitement and additional investor interest when the price zooms upward on opening day.

The IPO markets haven't been particularly active in recent years. Their lack of activity has been a direct result of the weakness of the public equity markets. Investing in IPOs is risky business, particularly for individual investors who can't easily acquire shares at the offering

FIGURE 2.1

Cover of a Preliminary Prospectus for a Stock Issue

Some of the key factors related to the 2003 common stock issue by Hewitt Associates, Inc. are summarized on the cover of the prospectus. The type printed vertically on the left edge is normally red, which explains its name "red herring." (*Source:* Hewitt Associates, Inc., July 28, 2003, p. 1.)

Subject to Completion. Dated July 28, 2003.

9,850,000 Shares

Hewitt

Class A Common Stock

All of the shares of common stock of Hewitt Associates, Inc. in the offering are being sold by the selling stockholders identified in this prospectus. We will not receive any of the proceeds from the sale of the shares. We have agreed to pay for the expenses of the offering.

Our class A common stock is quoted on the New York Stock Exchange under the symbol "HEW". The last reported sale price of class A common stock on July 25, 2003 was $26.79 per share.

See "Risk Factors" beginning on page 10 to read about factors you should consider before buying shares of class A common stock.

Neither the Securities and Exchange Commission nor any other regulatory body has approved or disapproved of these securities or passed upon the adequacy or accuracy of this prospectus. Any representation to the contrary is a criminal offense.

	Per Share	Total
Initial price to public	$	$
Underwriting discount	$	$
Proceeds to the selling stockholders	$	$

To the extent that the underwriters sell more than 9,850,000 shares of class A common stock, the underwriters have the option to purchase up to an additional 1,477,500 shares from the selling stockholders at the initial price to public less the underwriting discount.

The underwriters expect to deliver the shares against payment in New York, New York on , 2003.

Goldman, Sachs & Co.

Banc of America Securities LLC

Citigroup

JPMorgan

UBS Investment Bank

Wachovia Securities

Prospectus dated , 2003.

The information in this preliminary prospectus is not complete and may be changed. These securities may not be sold until the registration statement filed with the Securities and Exchange Commission is effective. This preliminary prospectus is not an offer to sell nor does it seek an offer to buy these securities in any jurisdiction where the offer or sale is not permitted.

investment banker
financial intermediary that specializes in selling new security issues and advising firms with regard to major financial transactions.

underwriting
the role of the *investment banker* in bearing the risk of reselling, at a profit, the securities purchased from an issuing corporation at an agreed-on price.

price. Most of those shares go to institutional investors and brokerage firms' best clients. Although news stories may chronicle huge first-day gains, the stocks may not be good long-term investments.

The Investment Banker's Role Most public offerings are made with the assistance of an **investment banker.** The investment banker is a financial intermediary (such as Goldman, Sachs & Co. or Citigroup) that specializes in selling new security issues and advising firms with regard to major financial transactions. The main activity of the investment banker is **underwriting.** This process involves purchasing the security issue from the issuing corporation at an agreed-on price and bearing the risk of reselling it to the public at a profit.

1ˢᵗ Underwritten offering
2ⁿᵈ Best offering

TABLE 2.1	Annual IPO Data, 1993–2002		
Year	Number of Offerings	Average First-Day Return (%)	Gross Proceeds ($ million)
1993	507	12.7	29,257
1994	416	9.7	18,300
1995	465	21.0	28,872
1996	666	16.5	42.479
1997	484	13.9	33,218
1998	319	20.0	35,112
1999	490	69.1	65,460
2000	385	55.4	65,677
2001	81	13.7	34,368
2002	73	8.3	22,954

Source: Jay R. Ritter, "Some Factoids About the 2002 IPO Market," downloaded from Web site (**www.bearcba.ufl.edu/ritter/work_papers/IPOs2002.pdf**), January 14, 2003, Table 5.

underwriting syndicate
a group formed by an investment banker to share the financial risk associated with *underwriting* new securities.

selling group
a large number of brokerage firms that join the originating investment banker(s); each accepts responsibility for selling a certain portion of a new security issue and is paid a commission on the securities it sells.

The investment banker also provides the issuer with advice about pricing and other important aspects of the issue.

In the case of very large security issues, the investment banker brings in other bankers as partners to form an **underwriting syndicate.** The syndicate shares the financial risk associated with buying the entire issue from the issuer and reselling the new securities to the public. The originating investment banker and the syndicate members put together a **selling group,** normally made up of themselves and a large number of brokerage firms. Each member of the selling group accepts the responsibility for selling a certain portion of the issue and is paid a commission on the securities it sells. The selling process for a large security issue is depicted in Figure 2.2.

FIGURE 2.2

The Selling Process for a Large Security Issue

The investment banker hired by the issuing corporation may form an underwriting syndicate. The underwriting syndicate buys the entire security issue from the issuing corporation at an agreed-on price. The underwriter then has the opportunity (and bears the risk) of reselling the issue to the public at a profit. Both the originating investment banker and the other syndicate members put together a selling group to sell the issue on a commission basis to investors.

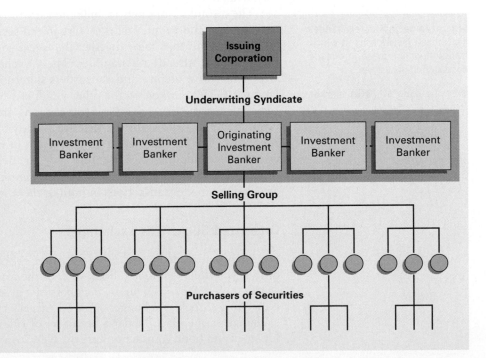

The relationships among the participants in this process can also be seen in the so-called *tombstone* for the July 2, 2003, common stock offering for White Electronic Designs shown in Figure 6.4 (on page 247). This layout of the announcement indicates the roles of the various participating firms. Isolated firm names or a larger typeface differentiates the underwriter and the underwriting syndicate from the selling group. (In the figure, the key participants in the offering are labeled in the margin at the right.)

Compensation for underwriting and selling services typically comes in the form of a discount on the sale price of the securities. For example, an investment banker may pay the issuing firm $24 per share for stock that will be sold for $26 per share. The investment banker may then sell the shares to members of the selling group for $25.25 per share. In this case, the original investment banker earns $1.25 per share ($25.25 sale price − $24 purchase price). The members of the selling group earn 75 cents for each share they sell ($26 sale price − $25.25 purchase price). Although some primary security offerings are directly placed by the issuer, the majority of new issues are sold through public offering via the mechanism just described.

secondary market
the market in which securities are traded *after they have been issued.*

Secondary Markets The market in which securities are traded *after they have been issued* is the **secondary market,** or the *aftermarket.* The secondary market provides a way for owners of securities that are already issued to sell them to others. In the secondary market, unlike the primary market, the transaction does not involve the corporation that issued the securities. Instead, money and securities are exchanged between investors; the seller exchanges securities for cash paid by the buyer. The secondary market gives security purchasers *liquidity.* It also provides a mechanism for continuous pricing of securities to reflect their value at each point in time, on the basis of the best information then available.

organized securities exchanges
centralized institutions in which transactions are made in already outstanding securities.

over-the-counter (OTC) market
widely scattered telecommunications network through which transactions are made in both *initial public offerings (IPOs)* and securities that are already outstanding.

The secondary markets include the various organized securities exchanges and the over-the-counter market. **Organized securities exchanges** are centralized institutions that bring together the forces of supply and demand for securities that are already outstanding. These exchanges are *auction markets* in which the flow of buy and sell orders determines the price. The **over-the-counter (OTC) market,** on the other hand, is a widely scattered telecommunications network through which transactions are made in both *initial public offerings (IPOs)* and securities that are already outstanding. The OTC market is a *dealer market* that uses a quote system in which negotiation and dealer quotes determine the price. Because popular investment vehicles trade on the organized exchanges and in the over-the-counter market, individual investors are likely to make transactions in both of these markets.

Organized Securities Exchanges

Securities that trade on *organized securities exchanges* account for about 62% of the total *dollar volume* (about 46% of the total *share volume*) of domestic shares traded. Persons who are members of a given exchange (for example, the New York Stock Exchange on Wall Street) conduct all trading for that exchange in one place, under a broad set of rules. The best-known exchanges for stock and bond transactions are the New York Stock Exchange (NYSE) and the American Stock Exchange (AMEX), both located in New York City. They account for approximately 90% and 4%, respectively, of the total annual dollar volume of shares traded on *organized* U.S. exchanges. Other domestic exchanges include *regional exchanges*, such as the Chicago Stock Exchange and the Pacific Exchange. Regional exchanges deal primarily in securities with regional or local appeal. Together, the regional exchanges account for about 6% of the annual dollar volume of shares traded on organized U.S. exchanges. In addition, foreign stock exchanges list and trade shares of firms in their own foreign markets. Separate domestic exchanges exist for options trading and for trading in futures. Here we will consider the basic structure, rules, and operations of each of these organized domestic securities exchanges. (We'll discuss foreign exchanges later.)

The New York Stock Exchange Most organized securities exchanges are modeled after the New York Stock Exchange (NYSE). It is the dominant organized exchange, often referred to as the "Big Board." To be a member, an individual or firm must own or lease a "seat" on the exchange. The word "seat" is used only figuratively, because its members trade securities standing up. The majority of seat holders are brokerage firms, and each typically owns more than one seat. The largest brokerage firm, Merrill Lynch, owns over 20 of the 1,366 seats on the NYSE.

Firms such as Merrill Lynch designate officers to occupy seats. Only such designated individuals can make transactions on the floor of the exchange. Although the majority of members make purchase and sale transactions on behalf of their customers, some members specialize in making transactions for other members or for their own account. There are two main types of floor brokers—commission brokers and independent brokers. *Commission brokers* execute orders for their firm's customers. An *independent broker* works for himself or herself and handles orders on a fee basis, typically for smaller brokerage firms or large firms that are too busy to handle their own orders.

Trading Activity Exchange members make all trades on the floor of the organized exchanges. The largest—the floor of the NYSE—is an area about the size of a football field. Its operation is typical of the various exchanges (though details vary). The NYSE floor has 20 trading posts. Certain stocks trade at each post. (Bonds and less active stocks are traded in an annex.) Around the perimeter are telephones and electronic equipment that transmit buy and sell orders from brokers' offices to the exchange floor and back again after members execute the orders.

All transactions on the floor of the exchange occur through an auction process. The goal is to fill all buy orders at the lowest price and to fill all sell orders at the highest price, with supply and demand determining the price. The actual auction takes place at the post where the particular security trades. Members interested in purchasing a given security publicly negotiate a transaction with members interested in selling that security. The job of the **specialist**—an exchange member who specializes in making transactions in one or more stocks—is to manage the auction process. The specialist buys or sells (at specified prices) to provide a continuous, fair, and orderly market in those securities assigned to her or him.

specialist
stock exchange member who specializes in making transactions in one or more stocks and manages the auction process.

Listing Policies To list its shares on an organized stock exchange, a firm must file an application and meet certain listing requirements. Currently, over 3,025 firms list their securities on the NYSE; they account for about 3,300 stocks (common and preferred) and 1,750 bond issues. Of these firms, almost 400 are non-U.S. corporations. Some firms have **dual listing,** or listings on more than one exchange.

The New York Stock Exchange has the strictest listing requirements. To be listed on the NYSE, a firm must have at least 2,200 stockholders owning 100 or more shares and a minimum of 1.1 million shares of publicly held stock outstanding; aggregate pretax earnings of at least $6.5 million over the previous 3 years, with no loss in the previous 2 years; and a minimum market value of public shares of $100 million. A foreign company must have aggregate pretax earnings of at least $100 million over the previous 3 years, with at least $25 million in each of the previous 2 years. The firm also must pay a listing fee of between $150,000 and $250,000. Once the NYSE accepts a firm's securities for listing, the company must continue to meet SEC requirements for exchange-listed securities. Listed firms that fail to meet specified requirements may be *de-listed* from the exchange.

The American Stock Exchange The American Stock Exchange (AMEX) is the second largest organized U.S. securities exchange in terms of number of listed companies. In terms of dollar volume of trading, the AMEX is actually smaller than the largest regional exchange—the Chicago. Its organization and its procedures are similar to those of the NYSE. Because its listing requirements are less stringent, many smaller and younger firms choose to list on the AMEX. In mid-1998 the AMEX merged with the National Association of Securities Dealers (NASD)—the backbone of the over-the-counter market—and, like the OTC, became a subsidiary of the NASD Market Holding Company. The AMEX has approximately 850 seats and about 800 listed stocks.

In recent years the AMEX has reinvented itself to focus on more specialized market instruments. Today about two-thirds of its daily volume comes from *exchange traded funds (ETFs)*, a security pioneered by AMEX about 10 years ago. These funds are baskets of securities that are designed to generally track an index of the broad stock or bond market, a stock industry sector, or an international stock, but trade like a single stock. Trading in stock options accounts for another large segment of the AMEX's business.

Regional Stock Exchanges Each of the regional exchanges typically lists the securities of 100–500 companies. As a group, these exchanges handle about 6% of the dollar volume of all shares traded on organized U.S. exchanges. The best-known regional exchanges are the Chicago, Pacific, Philadelphia, Boston, and Cincinnati exchanges. The Pacific Exchange's equity trading operations occur on the Archipelago Exchange, the first fully electronic national stock market in the United States. Most other regional exchanges are modeled after the NYSE, but their membership and listing requirements are considerably more lenient. Trading costs are also lower.

The majority of securities listed on regional exchanges are also listed on the NYSE or the AMEX. About 100 million NYSE shares pass through one of the regional exchanges on a typical trading day. This dual listing may enhance a security's trading activity. In addition, the *Intermarket Trading System (ITS)* links nine markets—five regional exchanges, the NYSE, the AMEX, the over-the-counter market, and the Chicago Board Options Exchange—through an electronic communications network that allows brokers and other traders to make transactions at the best prices.

Options Exchanges *Options* allow their holders to sell or to buy another security at a specified price over a given period of time. The dominant options exchange is the Chicago Board Options Exchange (CBOE). Options are also traded on the AMEX, the Pacific Exchange, the Philadelphia Stock Exchange, and the International Securities Exchange (ISE). Usually, an option to sell or buy a given security is listed on all five options exchanges. Options exchanges deal only in security options. Other types of options (not discussed in this text) result from private transactions made directly between sellers and buyers.

Futures Exchanges *Futures* are contracts that guarantee the delivery of a specified commodity or financial instrument at a specific future date at an agreed-on price. The dominant exchange for trading commodity and financial futures is the Chicago Board of Trade (CBT). There are a number of other futures exchanges, some of which specialize in certain commodities and financial instruments rather than handling the broad spectrum listed on the CBT. The largest of these exchanges are the New York Mercantile Exchange, the Chicago Mercantile Exchange, the Deutsche Terminboerse, the London International Financial Futures Exchange, the New York Coffee, Sugar & Cocoa Exchange, the New York Cotton Exchange, the Kansas City Board of Trade, and the Minneapolis Grain Exchange.

The Over-the-Counter Market

The *over-the-counter (OTC) market* is not a specific institution. It represents another way of trading securities. The OTC market is the result of an intangible relationship among sellers and purchasers of securities, who are linked by a telecommunications network. Nasdaq, the leading OTC market, accounts for about 38% of the total *dollar volume* (about 54% of the total *share volume*) of domestic shares traded, compared to approximately 56% for the NYSE, 2% for the AMEX, and 4% for regional exchanges. Instead of an auction system, the OTC market uses a quote system. This system relies on negotiation and dealer quotes to determine the prices at which securities trade in the OTC market. The actual process, which is described later, depends on the general activity of the security. Securities traded in this market are sometimes called *unlisted securities*.

About 35,000 stocks trade over the counter, as do most government and corporate bonds. The OTC market has three tiers. About 3,450 stocks have an active market in which transactions take place frequently, and another 3,600 trade on the OTC Bulletin Board. The rest are stocks of small, thinly traded companies. A majority of all corporate bonds, some of which are also listed on the NYSE, trade in the OTC market.

New Issues and Secondary Distributions To create a continuous market for unlisted securities, the OTC market also serves as a forum in which to sell both listed and unlisted *initial public offerings (IPOs)*. Subsequent transactions for listed securities then shift to the appropriate organized securities exchange;

secondary distributions
the public sales of large blocks of previously issued securities held by large investors.

unlisted securities continue to trade in the OTC market. **Secondary distributions**—the public sales of large blocks of previously issued securities held by large investors—are also made in the OTC market to minimize the potentially negative effects of such transactions on the price of listed securities. These transactions are forms of third- or fourth-market trades, which we will describe in a moment.

Market Makers The market price of OTC securities results from a matching of supply and demand for securities by dealers known as **market makers.** Each market maker "makes markets" in certain securities by offering to buy or sell them at stated prices. Unlike the organized exchanges, where a *broker* brings together the buyer and seller of a security, the OTC market links a buyer or seller with a *market maker*. That is, the second party to an OTC transaction is always a market maker.

market makers
dealers who "make markets" by offering to buy or sell certain over-the-counter securities at stated prices.

For example, a market maker in Raco Enterprises might offer to buy shares from investors at $29.50 and sell shares to other investors at $31. The **bid price** is the highest price the market maker offers to purchase a given security. The **ask price** is the lowest price at which the market maker is willing to sell a given security. Because more than one market maker frequently makes a market in a given security, they compete. Buyers and sellers attempt to find and negotiate the best price—lowest buy price or highest sell price—when making OTC market transactions. The market maker makes a profit from the spread between the bid price and the ask price.

bid price
the highest price offered by a market maker to purchase a given security.

ask price
the lowest price at which a market maker is willing to sell a given security.

Nasdaq OTC market makers connect with the sellers and purchasers of securities through the **Nasdaq (National Association of Securities Dealers Automated Quotation) system.** Nasdaq is the first electronic communications network for securities trading. Its automated system provides up-to-date bid and ask prices on about 7,000 selected, highly active OTC securities. It enables buyers and sellers to locate one another easily. Not all OTC securities are listed on Nasdaq, however. To trade in securities not quoted on Nasdaq, buyers and sellers must find each other through references or through known market makers in the securities involved.

Nasdaq (National Association of Securities Dealers Automated Quotation) system
an automated system that provides up-to-date bid and ask prices on certain selected, highly active OTC securities.

The Nasdaq Stock Market includes about 3,450 stocks divided into two groups. Included in the **Nasdaq National Market** are about 2,700 companies with a national or international shareholder base. These stocks meet certain qualification standards of financial size, performance, and trading activity. To list initially, companies must have significant net tangible assets or operating income, a minimum 1.1 million publicly held shares, at least 400 shareholders, and a minimum bid price of $5. Another 750 companies are part of the *Nasdaq SmallCap Market*. These companies too must also meet specified (but less stringent) requirements to list and trade their securities through Nasdaq's sophisticated electronic trading and surveillance system. Transactions in these two groups of stocks are reported quickly (immediately) and in detail similar to NYSE and AMEX trades in the financial press.

Nasdaq National Market
a list of national or international Nasdaq stocks that meet certain qualification standards of financial size, performance, and trading activity.

Alternative Trading Systems

third market
over-the-counter transactions made in securities listed on the NYSE, the AMEX, or one of the other organized exchanges.

Some individual and institutional traders now make direct transactions, without using brokers, securities exchanges, or Nasdaq, in the *third* and *fourth markets*. The **third market** consists of over-the-counter transactions made in securities listed on the NYSE, the AMEX, or one of the other organized exchanges. It allows large institutional investors, such as mutual funds, pension funds, and life insurance companies, to make large transactions at a reduced cost. These transactions are typically handled by firms or market makers that are not members of an organized securities exchange. Market makers charge lower commissions than the organized exchanges or Nasdaq would to bring together large buyers and sellers. Institutional investors are thus often able to realize sizable savings in brokerage commissions and to have minimal impact on the price of the transaction. Nasdaq also has third-market operations, called the Nasdaq InterMarket.

fourth market
transactions made directly between large institutional buyers and sellers of securities.

The **fourth market** consists of transactions made directly between large institutional buyers and sellers of securities. Unlike third-market transactions, fourth-market transactions bypass the market maker. The fourth market is a direct outgrowth of advanced computer technology. **Electronic communications networks (ECNs)** are at the heart of the fourth market. These privately owned electronic trading networks were formed in response to institutional investor frustration with the way organized exchanges handled large blocks of securities. Archipelago, Bloomberg Tradebook, Island, Instinet, and MarketXT are some of the many ECNs that handle these trades.

electronic communications networks (ECNs)
privately owned electronic trading networks that automatically match buy and sell orders that customers place electronically.

The ECNs' trading volume accounts for about a third of all Nasdaq transactions, as well as for an increasing share of New York Stock Exchange volume. They are most effective for high-volume, actively traded securities, and they play a key role in after-hours trading, discussed later in this chapter. They automatically match buy and sell orders that customers place electronically. If there is no immediate match, the ECN acts like a broker and posts its request on the Nasdaq under its own name. The trade will be executed if another trader is interested in making the transaction at the posted price.

ECNs can save customers money because they take only a transaction fee, either per share or based on order size. Money managers and institutions such as pension funds and mutual funds with large amounts of money to invest like ECNs for this reason. Many also use ECNs or trade directly with each other to find the best prices for their clients.

General Market Conditions: Bull or Bear

bull markets
favorable markets normally associated with rising prices, investor optimism, economic recovery, and government stimulus.

Conditions in the securities markets are commonly classified as "bull" or "bear," depending on whether securities prices are rising or falling over time. Changing market conditions generally stem from changes in investor attitudes, changes in economic activity, and government actions aimed at stimulating or slowing down economic activity. **Bull markets** are favorable markets normally associated with rising prices, investor optimism, economic recovery, and government stimulus. **Bear markets** are unfavorable markets normally associated with falling prices, investor pessimism, economic slowdown, and government restraint. From 1990 through 2000, the stock market was bullish primarily as a result of low inflation, improving trade balances, shrinking budget deficits, and economic recovery. Unfortunately, from then until late 2003, the market was bearish due to the bursting of the technology stock bubble, the September 11, 2001, terrorist attacks, a crisis in corporate accounting, and the Iraq war. Beginning in late 2003, there were signs that the bear market was ending and an expectation of a more bullish market.

bear markets
unfavorable markets normally associated with falling prices, investor pessimism, economic slowdown, and government restraint.

In general, investors experience higher (or positive) returns on common stock investments during a bull market. However, some securities are bullish in a bear market or bearish in a bull market. During bear markets, many investors invest in vehicles other than securities to obtain higher and less risky returns. Market conditions are difficult to predict and usually can be identified only after they exist. Sources of information that can be used to assess market conditions are described in Chapter 3 and are applied to the analysis and valuation of common stock price behavior in Chapters 7 through 9.

IN REVIEW

CONCEPTS

2.1 Differentiate between each of the following pairs of terms:

    a. *Money market* and *capital market*

    b. *Primary market* and *secondary market*

    c. *Organized securities* exchanges and *over-the-counter (OTC) market*

2.2 Briefly describe the *IPO* process and the role of the *investment banker* in underwriting a public offering. Differentiate among the terms *public offering, rights offering,* and *private placement*.

2.3 For each of the items in the left-hand column, select the most appropriate item in the right-hand column. Explain the relationship between the items matched.

a. AMEX	1. Trades unlisted securities
b. CBT	2. Futures exchange
c. NYSE	3. Options exchange
d. Boston Stock Exchange	4. Regional stock exchange
e. CBOE	5. Second largest organized U.S. exchange
f. OTC	6. Has the most stringent listing requirements

2.4 Explain how the *over-the-counter market* works. Be sure to mention *market makers, bid and ask prices, Nasdaq,* and the *Nasdaq National Market*. What role does this market play in initial public offerings (IPOs) and secondary distributions? What are the *third* and *fourth markets*?

2.5 Differentiate between a *bull market* and a *bear market*.

Globalization of Securities Markets

LG 4

diversification
the inclusion of a number of different investment vehicles in a portfolio to increase returns or reduce risk.

Today investors, issuers of securities, and securities firms look beyond the markets of their home countries to find the best returns, lowest costs, and best international business opportunities. The basic goal of most investors is to earn the highest return with the lowest risk. This outcome is achieved through **diversification**—the inclusion of a number of different investment vehicles in a portfolio to increase returns or reduce risk. The investor who includes foreign investments in a portfolio can greatly increase the potential for diversification by holding (1) a wider range of industries and securities, (2) securities traded in a larger number of markets, and (3) securities denominated in different currencies. The smaller and less diversified an investor's home market is, the greater the potential benefit from prudent international diversification. However, even investors from the United States and other highly developed markets can benefit from global diversification.

In short, globalization of the securities markets enables investors to seek out opportunities to profit from rapidly expanding economies throughout the world. Here we consider the growing importance of international markets, international investment performance, ways to invest in foreign securities, and the risks of investing internationally.

Growing Importance of International Markets

Securities exchanges now operate in over 100 countries worldwide. Both large (Tokyo) and small (Fiji), they are located not only in the major industrialized nations such as Japan, Great Britain, Canada, and Germany but also in emerging economies such as Brazil, Chile, India, South Korea, Malaysia, Mexico, Poland, Russia, and Thailand. The top four securities markets worldwide (based on dollar volume) are the New York, Nasdaq, London, and Tokyo stock exchanges. Other important foreign exchanges include Paris, Osaka, Toronto, Montreal, Sydney, Hong Kong, Zurich, and Taiwan.

The economic integration of the European Monetary Union (EMU), along with pressure from financial institutions that want an efficient process for trading shares across borders, is changing the European securities market environment. Instead of many small national exchanges, countries are banding together to create cross-border markets and compete more effectively in the pan-European equity-trading markets. The Paris, Amsterdam, and Brussels exchanges merged to form Euronext, and the Scandinavian markets formed Norex. Other stock exchanges are forming cooperative agreements—for example, Tokyo and Australia. The New York, Tokyo, Hong Kong, Australia, Mexico, Toronto, São Paulo, and Euronext exchanges are discussing the formation of a Global Equity Market (GEM). The exchanges would not merge but would form a 24-hour global market alliance, trading the stocks of selected large international companies via an electronic order-matching system. Nasdaq, with joint ventures in Japan, Hong Kong, Canada, and Australia, plans to expand into Latin America and the Middle East. As noted at the beginning of the chapter, these mergers and cooperative arrangements could be the first step toward a worldwide stock exchange.

Bond markets, too, have become global, and more investors than ever before regularly purchase government and corporate fixed-income securities in foreign markets. The United States dominates the international government bond market, followed by Japan, Germany, and Great Britain.

International Investment Performance

A primary motive for investing overseas is the lure of high returns. In fact, only once since 1980 did the United States finish first among the major stock markets of the world in terms of the rate of increase in its stock price index. For example, in 2003, an overall good year after three years of declines, investors would have earned higher returns in many foreign markets. During that year the Dow Jones Global Index in U.S. dollars for Thailand increased 139%; for

Germany increased 61%; for France increased 39%; for Japan increased 38%; for Mexico increased 32%; for the Netherlands increased 25%; and for Finland increased 17%. By comparison, the U.S. stock price index increased about 28%. Of course, foreign securities markets tend to be more risky than U.S. markets. A market with high returns in one year may not do so well in the next.

Investors can compare activity on U.S. and foreign exchanges by following market indexes that track the performance of those exchanges. For instance, the Dow Jones averages and the Standard & Poor's indexes are popular measures of the U.S. markets, and indexes for more than 20 different stock markets are available. (We'll discuss indexes in more detail in Chapter 3.) The *Wall Street Journal* publishes daily reports on most major indexes, trading activity in selected stocks on major foreign exchanges, and currency exchange rates. Other financial publications also include regular reports. Also, the *Wall Street Journal*'s "World Stock Markets" in Section C frequently compares the performance of the U.S. exchanges with that of selected foreign markets.

H O T L I N K S

Go to the Yahoo site and check the World Finance section for investment performance.

finance.yahoo.com/m2

Ways to Invest in Foreign Securities

Investors can make foreign security transactions either indirectly or directly. One form of *indirect* investment is purchasing shares of a U.S.-based multinational with substantial foreign operations. Many U.S.-based multinational firms, such as ExxonMobil, IBM, Citicorp, Dow Chemical, Coca-Cola, Colgate-Palmolive, and Hewlett-Packard, receive more than 50% of their revenues from overseas operations. By investing in the securities of such firms, an investor can achieve a degree of international diversification. Purchasing shares in a mutual fund that invests primarily in foreign securities is another way to invest indirectly. Investors can make both of these indirect foreign securities investment transactions in a conventional fashion through a stockbroker, as explained in Chapter 3 and in Chapter 13 (which is devoted to mutual funds).

H O T L I N K S

For information about ADRs, check out ADR.com, a joint project by JPMorgan Chase Bank ("JPMorgan") and Thomson Financial.

adr.com

To make *direct* investments in foreign companies, investors have three options: They can purchase securities on foreign exchanges, buy securities of foreign companies that trade on U.S. exchanges, or buy *American depositary receipts (ADRs)*.

The first way—purchasing securities on foreign exchanges—involves additional risks because the securities do not trade in U.S. dollars. This approach is not for the timid or inexperienced investor.

Because each country's exchange has its own regulations and procedures, investors must cope with currency exchange (dollars to pesos, for example). They also must cope with different securities exchange rules, transaction procedures, accounting standards, tax laws, and with language barriers. Direct transactions are best handled either through brokers at major Wall Street firms with large international operations or through major banks, such as JPMorgan Chase and Citibank, that have special units to handle foreign securities transactions. Alternatively, investors can deal with foreign broker-dealers, but such an approach is more complicated and more risky.

The second form of direct investment is to buy the securities of foreign companies that trade on both organized and over-the-counter U.S. exchanges.

Yankee bonds
dollar-denominated debt securities issued by foreign governments or corporations and traded in U.S. securities markets.

American depositary receipts (ADRs)
dollar-denominated negotiable receipts for the stocks of foreign companies that are held in the vaults of banks in the companies' home countries.

Transactions in foreign securities that trade on U.S. exchanges are handled in the same way as exchange-traded domestic securities. These securities are issued by large, well-known foreign companies. Stocks of companies such as Alcan (Canada), Gucci (Netherlands), National Westminster Bank (U.K.), and Unilever (Netherlands) trade directly on U.S. exchanges. In addition, **Yankee bonds**, dollar-denominated debt securities issued by foreign governments or corporations and traded in U.S. securities markets, trade on organized exchanges and in the over-the-counter market in the United States.

Finally, foreign stocks also trade on U.S. exchanges in the form of **American depositary receipts (ADRs)**. These are dollar-denominated negotiable receipts for the stocks of foreign companies that are held in the vaults of banks in the companies' home countries. Today, about 2,300 ADRs representing more than 50 different home countries are traded on U.S. exchanges. About one-fourth of them are actively traded. Included are ADRs of well-known companies such as DaimlerChrysler, Hitachi, Nokia, Philips Electronics, Sony, and Volvo. ADRs, which trade in the same way as standard domestic securities, are further discussed in Chapter 6.

Risks of Investing Internationally

Investing abroad is not without pitfalls. In addition to the usual risks involved in making any security transaction, investors must consider the risks associated with doing business in a particular foreign country. Changes in trade policies, labor laws, and taxation may affect operating conditions for the country's firms. The government itself may not be stable. When making investments in foreign markets, you must track similar environmental factors in each foreign country. This is clearly more difficult than following your home market, because you are less familiar with the foreign economic and political environments and may be following several countries.

U.S. securities markets are generally viewed as highly regulated and reliable. Foreign markets, on the other hand, may lag substantially behind the United States in both operations and regulation. Some countries place various restrictions on foreign investment. In Korea and Taiwan, for example, mutual funds are the only way for foreigners to invest. Mexico has a two-tier market, with some securities restricted to foreigners. Some countries make it difficult for foreigners to get their funds out, and many impose taxes on dividends. For example, Swiss taxes are about 20% on dividends paid to foreigners. In addition, accounting standards vary from country to country. Differences in accounting practices can affect a company's apparent profitability, conceal other attractive assets (such as the hidden reserves and undervalued assets that are permitted in many countries), and fail to disclose other risks. As a result, it is difficult to compare the financial performances and positions of firms operating in different foreign countries. Other difficulties include illiquid markets and an inability to obtain reliable investment information because of a lack of reporting requirements.

Furthermore, international investing involves securities denominated in foreign currencies. Trading profits and losses are affected not only by a security's price changes but also by changes in currency exchange rates. The values of the world's major currencies fluctuate with respect to each other on a daily basis. The relationship between two currencies at a specified date is called the

currency exchange rate
the relationship between two currencies on a specified date.

currency exchange rate. On May 12, 2003, the currency exchange rate for the European Monetary Union euro (€) and the U.S. dollar (US$) was expressed as follows:

$$US\$ = €\,0.8652 \qquad € = US\$\,1.1558$$

On that day, you would have received 0.8652 euros for every $1. Conversely, each euro was worth $1.1558.

Changes in the value of a particular foreign currency with respect to the U.S. dollar—or any other currency—are called *appreciation* and *depreciation*. For example, on August 11, 2003, the euro/US$ exchange rate was 0.8802. In the 3 months since May 12, 2003, the European Monetary Union euro had *depreciated* relative to the dollar (and the dollar had *appreciated* relative to the euro). On August 11 it took more euros to buy $1 (0.8802 versus 0.8652), so each euro was worth less in dollar terms ($1.1361 versus $1.1558). Had the European Monetary Union euro instead *appreciated* (and the dollar *depreciated* relative to the euro), each euro would have been worth more in dollar terms.

currency exchange risk
the risk caused by the varying exchange rates between the currencies of two countries.

Currency exchange risk is the risk caused by the varying exchange rates between the currencies of two countries. For example, assume that on May 12, 2003, you bought 100 shares of a French stock at 100 euros per share, held it for about 3 months, and then sold it for its original purchase price of 100 euros. The following table summarizes these transactions:

Date	Transaction	Number of Shares	Price in Euros	Value of Transaction Euros	Exchange Rate Euros/US$	Value in US$
5/12/03	Purchase	100	100	10,000	0.8652	$11,558.02
8/11/03	Sell	100	100	10,000	0.8802	$11,361.05

Although you realized the original purchase price in euros, in dollar terms the transaction resulted in a loss of $196.97 ($11,558.02 − $11,361.05). The value of the stock in dollars decreased because the European Monetary Union euro was worth less—had depreciated—relative to the dollar. Investors in foreign securities must be aware that the value of the foreign currency in relation to the dollar can have a profound effect on returns from foreign security transactions.

IN REVIEW

CONCEPTS

2.6 Why is globalization of securities markets an important issue today? How have international investments performed in recent years?

2.7 Describe how foreign security investments can be made, both indirectly and directly.

2.8 Describe the risks of investing internationally, particularly *currency exchange risk*.

Trading Hours and Regulation of Securities Markets

LG 5

crossing markets
after-hours trading in stocks that involve filling buy and sell orders by matching identical sell and buy orders at the desired price.

Understanding the structure of domestic and international securities markets is an important foundation for developing a sound investment program. Now let's look at market trading hours and the regulation of U.S. securities markets.

Trading Hours of Securities Markets

The regular trading session for organized U.S. exchanges and Nasdaq runs from 9:30 A.M. to 4:00 P.M. Eastern time. However, trading is no longer limited to these hours. The exchanges, Nasdaq, and ECNs offer extended trading sessions before and after regular hours. Most of the after-hours markets are **crossing markets** in which orders are filled only if they can be matched; that is, buy and sell orders are filled only if they can be matched with identical opposing sell and buy orders at the desired price. These allow U.S. securities markets to compete more effectively with foreign securities markets, in which investors can execute trades when U.S. markets are closed. The NYSE has two short electronic-trading sessions that begin after the 4:00 P.M. closing bell. One session, from 4:15 to 5:00 P.M., trades stocks at that day's closing prices via a computer matching system. Transactions occur only if a match can be made and are handled on a first-come, first-served basis. The other session lasts from 4:00 to 5:15 P.M. and allows institutional investors to trade large blocks of stock valued at $1 million or more. Since their inception, the NYSE has experienced increased volume in both sessions.

Nasdaq began its own extended-hours electronic-trading session in January 1992. Its Nasdaq International Market Session runs from 3:30 A.M. (when the London Exchange opens) to 9:00 A.M. Eastern Time, half an hour before the start of regular trading sessions in U.S. markets. Because it lists NYSE stocks as well as other U.S. equities and has less stringent disclosure requirements than other markets, Nasdaq International attracts traders from both the New York and the London exchanges. In addition, Nasdaq has an extended-hours session from 4:00 to 6:30 P.M. Eastern time, as well as two SelectNet trading sessions, from 8:00 to 9:30 A.M. Eastern time and from 4:00 to 5:15 P.M. Eastern time. Regional exchanges have also moved to after-hours trading sessions.

Until 1999, only large institutional investors could trade after hours. Most of this trading was through ECNs like Instinet and Market XT, which facilitated fourth-market transactions in thousands of U.S. and European stocks. Now individual investors, too, can participate in after-hours trading activity. Many large brokerage firms, both traditional and online, offer after-hours trading services for their individual clients.

It appears that after-hours trading will continue to expand and approximate a 24-hour market in the not too distant future. Many believe that the next big bull market will likely stimulate the development of a true 24-hour market. At the same time, it is important to recognize that the term "after-hours trading" is becoming obsolete because of the ability to trade major stocks on a variety of exchanges around the globe. For example, the stock of DaimlerChrysler, a major global automobile manufacturer, is traded in identical form on 11 worldwide exchanges in Asia, Europe, and the Americas. Clearly, by working through these exchanges you can effectively trade DaimlerChrysler on a 24-hour basis. The *Investing in Action* box on page 52 discusses the pros and cons of extended trading hours.

INVESTING IN ACTION

STOCK AROUND THE CLOCK

Trading 24/7—the idea sounds great. Pick up the phone or go to your computer at any hour and buy or sell stocks and mutual funds. While such round-the-clock live trading is not yet a reality, individual investors can trade securities before and after the close of regular trading sessions. Most of the after-hours trading currently takes place in the 90-minute periods before the NYSE and Nasdaq open at 9:30 A.M. and after these markets close at 4 P.M.

What's the appeal of extended trading hours? Some investors don't have time to reflect on market news during the day. Investors in the Pacific time zone (3 hours behind New York) want a longer trading day; their regular trading day ends at 1 P.M. Pacific time. Others want to act on company news that is released after the markets close or during the business day of companies headquartered outside the United States. Online trading and ECNs have made after-hours sessions accessible to individual investors, who have joined their institutional counterparts in trading about 70 million shares after the markets close. Although this traffic represents less than 6% of the NYSE's daily trading volume, investors who understand how to use these extended hours can profit or at least reduce losses. "The after-hours market allows you to beat everyone to the punch," says Mike Prus of MGP Capital Management in Boston.

Because companies often wait until after the closing bell to announce important news, stock prices in after-hours trading can exhibit more volatility than those during regular trading sessions. Savvy investors can use this extra time to get in or out of a stock ahead of other investors. For example, on February 5, 2003, scientific instrument manufacturer Agilent Technologies announced just after the market closed that its financial situation had taken a turn for the worse. Investors who sold in that day's after-hours market got out of the issue before the stock dropped 25% the following day. Similarly, early on February 6, 2003, Ericsson, a Swedish telecommunications equipment company, named a new chief executive. Early session investors bought Ericsson at $6.71, versus $7.42 after the bell sounded.

While still risky, after-hours trading has become less so since its introduction in 2000 and with the advent of higher volume. Like Agilent, most corporations continue to make their announcements after normal trading hours. If you want to benefit from extended-day trading, here are some basics to prepare you to enter this new arena:

- Understand how your brokerage firm handles after-hours trades—hours and methods to place orders. Each firm has different rules and may require separate orders for these trades.
- Learn how stock prices react to different types of company news, economic announcements, changes to major indexes, and new trading rules.
- Most extended-day trading is in blue-chip, large-cap stocks, so follow the after-hours trading patterns of the most active lists.
- To protect investors, most brokerages require limit orders (discussed in detail in Chapter 3) for after-hours trades, so that investors can set their highest buy/lowest sell price.

CRITICAL THINKING QUESTION What risks should individual investors consider before engaging in after-hours trading?

Sources: Mara der Hovanesian, "The Market's Closed—Wake Up," *Business Week,* March 3, 2003, pp. 132–133; and James McNair, "Happy-Hours Trading," *San Diego Union-Tribune,* July 2, 2000, pp. I–1, I–6.

Regulation of Securities Markets

Securities laws protect investors and participants in the financial marketplace. A number of state and federal laws require that investors receive adequate and accurate disclosure of information. Such laws also regulate the activities of participants in the securities markets. State laws that control the sale of securities

TABLE 2.2   Important Federal Securities Laws

Act	Brief Description
Securities Act of 1933	Passed to ensure full disclosure of information about new security issues. Requires the issuer of a new security to file with the Securities and Exchange Commission (SEC) a registration statement containing information about the new issue. The firm cannot sell the security until the SEC approves the registration statement, which usually takes about 20 days. Approval of the registration statement by the SEC merely indicates that the facts presented in the statement appear to reflect the firm's true position.
Securities Exchange Act of 1934	Formally established the SEC as the agency in charge of administering federal securities laws. The act gave the SEC the power to regulate the organized exchanges and the OTC market; their members, brokers, and dealers; and the securities traded in these markets. Each of these participants must file reports with the SEC and periodically update them. The 1934 act has been amended several times over the years.
Maloney Act of 1938	An amendment to the Securities Exchange Act of 1934, it provided for the establishment of trade associations to self-regulate the securities industry. Only one such trade association, the National Association of Securities Dealers (NASD), has been formed. NASD members include nearly all of the nation's securities firms that do business with the public. The NASD, operating under SEC supervision, establishes standardized procedures for securities trading and ethical behavior, monitors and enforces compliance with these procedures, and serves as the industry spokesperson. Today, any securities firms that are not members of the NASD must agree to direct SEC supervision.
Investment Company Act of 1940	Established rules and regulations for investment companies and formally authorized the SEC to regulate their practices and procedures. It required the investment companies to register with the SEC and to fulfill certain disclosure requirements. An *investment company* obtains funds by selling its shares to numerous investors and uses the proceeds to purchase securities. The dominant type of investment company is the *mutual fund* (discussed in detail in Chapter 13). A 1970 amendment prohibits investment companies from paying excessive fees to their advisers and from charging excessive commissions to purchasers of company shares.
Investment Advisers Act of 1940	To protect investors, it requires *investment advisers*, persons hired by investors to advise them about security investments, to disclose all relevant information about their backgrounds, conflicts of interest, and so on, as well as about any investments they recommend. Advisers must register and file periodic reports with the SEC. A 1960 amendment extended the SEC's powers to permit inspection of the records of investment advisers and to revoke the registration of advisers who violate the act's provisions.
Securities Acts Amendments of 1975	Amendment to the securities acts that requires the SEC and the securities industry to develop a competitive national system for trading securities. First the SEC abolished fixed-commission schedules, thereby providing for negotiated commissions. (Commissions are discussed in more detail in Chapter 3.) Second it established the *Intermarket Trading System (ITS),* an electronic communications network linking nine markets and trading over 4,000 eligible issues, that allows trades to be made across these markets wherever the network shows a better price for a given issue.
Insider Trading and Fraud Act of 1988	The economic prosperity and rapidly rising stock prices in the 1980s caused many speculators to operate without regard for the legality of their actions. Many of the illegal gains were achieved through *insider trading,* using *nonpublic* information to make profitable securities transactions. It is both illegal and unethical. The act established penalties for insider trading. Insiders include anyone who obtains nonpublic information, typically a company's directors, officers, major shareholders, bankers, investment bankers, accountants, or attorneys. To allow it to monitor insider trades, the SEC requires corporate insiders to file monthly reports detailing all transactions made in the company's stock. Recent legislation substantially increased the penalties for insider trading and gave the SEC greater power to investigate and prosecute claims of illegal insider-trading activity.
Sarbanes-Oxley Act of 2002	Passed to protect investors against corporate fraud, particularly accounting fraud. It created an oversight board to monitor the accounting industry, tightened audit regulations and controls, toughened penalties against executives who commit corporate fraud, strengthened accounting disclosure requirements and ethical guidelines for financial officers, established corporate board structure and membership guidelines, established guidelines for analyst conflicts of interest, and increased the SEC's authority and budgets for auditors and investigators. The act also mandated instant disclosure of stock sales by corporate executives.

within state borders are commonly called *blue sky laws* because they are intended to prevent investors from being sold nothing but "blue sky." These laws typically establish procedures for regulating both security issues and sellers of securities doing business within the state. Most states have a regulatory body, such as a state securities commission, that is charged with enforcing the related state statutes. The most important securities laws enacted by the federal government are listed (in chronological order) and briefly summarized in Table 2.2 on the previous page.

The intent of all of these federal securities laws is to protect investors. Most of these laws were passed in response to observed damaging abuses by certain market participants. The two most recent laws are the *Insider Trading and Fraud Act of 1988*, aimed at stopping **insider trading,** the use of *nonpublic* information about a company to make profitable securities transactions, and the *Sarbanes-Oxley Act of 2002*, which focused on eliminating corporate fraud related to accounting and other information releases. Both of these acts heightened the public's awareness of **ethics**—standards of conduct or moral judgment—in business. The financial community is continuing to develop and enforce ethical standards that will motivate market participants to adhere to laws and regulations. Although it is difficult to enforce ethical standards, it appears that opportunities for abuses in the financial markets are being reduced, thereby providing a more level playing field for all investors.

insider trading
the use of *nonpublic* information about a company to make profitable securities transactions.

ethics
standards of conduct or moral judgment.

IN REVIEW

CONCEPTS

2.9 How are after-hours trades typically handled? What role do ECNs play in after-hours trading?

2.10 Briefly describe the key requirements of the following federal securities laws:
a.   Securities Act of 1933.
b.   Securities Exchange Act of 1934.
c.   Maloney Act of 1938.
d.   Investment Company Act of 1940.
e.   Investment Advisers Act of 1940.
f.   Securities Acts Amendments of 1975.
g.   Insider Trading and Fraud Act of 1988.
h.   Sarbanes-Oxley Act of 2002.

Basic Types of Securities Transactions

LG 6

An investor can make a number of basic types of security transactions. Each type is available to those who meet certain requirements established by various government agencies as well as by brokerage firms. Although investors can use the various types of transactions in a number of ways to meet investment objectives, we describe only the most popular use of each transaction here, as we consider the long purchase, margin trading, and short selling.

long purchase
a transaction in which investors buy securities in the hope that they will increase in value and can be sold at a later date for profit.

Long Purchase

The **long purchase** is a transaction in which investors buy securities in the hope that they will increase in value and can be sold at a later date for profit. The object, then, is to *buy low and sell high*. A long purchase is the most common type of transaction. Because investors generally expect the price of a security to rise over the period of time they plan to hold it, their return comes from any dividends or interest received during the ownership period, *plus* the difference (capital gain or loss) between the price at which they sell the security and the price they paid to purchase it. This return, of course, is reduced by the transaction costs.

Ignoring any dividends (or interest) and transaction costs, we can illustrate the long purchase by a simple example. After studying various aspects of Varner Industries, you are convinced that its common stock, which currently sells for $20 per share, will increase in value over the next few years. On the basis of your analysis, you expect the stock price to rise to $30 per share within 2 years. You place an order and buy 100 shares of Varner for $20 per share. If the stock price rises to, say, $40 per share, you will profit from your long purchase. If it drops below $20 per share, you will experience a loss on the transaction. Obviously, one of the major motivating factors in making a long transaction is an expected rise in the price of the security.

Margin Trading

Security purchases do not have to be made on a cash basis; investors can use borrowed funds instead. This activity is referred to as **margin trading.** It is used for one basic reason: to magnify returns. As peculiar as it may sound, the term *margin* refers to the amount of equity (stated as a percentage) in an investment, or the amount that is *not* borrowed. If an investor uses 75% margin, for example, it means that 75% of the investment position is being financed with the person's own funds and the balance (25%) with borrowed money. Brokers must approve margin purchases. The brokerage firm then lends the purchaser the needed funds and retains the purchased securities as collateral. It is important to recognize that margin purchasers must pay a specified rate of interest on the amount they borrow.

The Federal Reserve Board (the "Fed"), which governs our banking system, sets the **margin requirement,** specifying the minimum amount of equity that must be the margin investor's own funds. The margin requirement for stocks has been at 50% for some time. By raising and lowering the margin requirement, the Fed can depress or stimulate activity in the securities markets.

A simple example will help to clarify the basic margin transaction. Assume that you wish to purchase 70 shares of common stock, which is currently selling for $63.50 per share. With the prevailing margin requirement of 50%, you need put up only $2,222.50 in cash ($63.50 per share × 70 shares × 0.50). The remaining $2,222.50 will be lent to you by your brokerage firm. You will, of course, have to pay interest on the amount you borrow, plus the applicable brokerage fees. With the use of margin, investors can purchase more securities than they could afford on a strictly cash basis. In this way, investors can magnify their returns (as demonstrated in a later section).

Although margin trading can lead to increased returns, it also presents substantial risks. One of the biggest is that the issue may not perform as expected. If this occurs, no amount of margin trading can correct matters. Margin trading can only magnify returns, not produce them. And if the security's return is negative, margin trading magnifies the loss. Because the security being margined is always the ultimate source of return, choosing the right securities is critical to this trading strategy.

margin trading
the use of borrowed funds to purchase securities; magnifies returns by reducing the amount of equity that the investor must put up.

margin requirement
the minimum amount of equity that must be a margin investor's own funds; set by the Federal Reserve Board (the "Fed").

INVESTOR FACTS

GOOD NEWS: MARGIN DEBT IS RISING—Rising levels of debt usually are not a reason to cheer. But increasing margin debt levels during the first half of 2003 gave investors hope that the recovery might be starting at last. Higher margin debt means that there is more liquidity in the markets—a positive sign for the stock markets, which tend to track margin debt trends closely. In July 2003, margin debt reached almost $148.5 billion, up from a four-year low of $130.2 billion in September 2002. Margin debt peaked in March 2000, the start of the market slide, at $278.5 billion.

Sources: Robin Goldwyn Blumenthal, "Summertime, and the Buying on Margin Is Easy," *Barron's*, July 21, 2003, p. 13; and "Margin Debt Fell Slightly in July to $148.5," *Wall Street Journal*, August 22, 2003, downloaded from www.wsj.com.

Essentials of Margin Trading Investors can use margin trading with most kinds of securities. It is regularly used, for example, with both common and preferred stocks, most types of bonds, mutual funds, options, warrants, and futures. It is not normally used with tax-exempt municipal bonds, because the interest paid on such margin loans is not deductible for income tax purposes. Since mid-1990, it has been possible to use margin on certain foreign stocks and bonds that meet prescribed criteria and appear on the Fed's "New List of Foreign Margin Stocks." For simplicity, we will use common stock as the vehicle in our discussion of margin trading.

financial leverage
the use of debt financing to magnify investment returns.

Magnified Profits and Losses With an investor's equity serving as a base, the idea of margin trading is to employ **financial leverage**—the use of debt financing to magnify investment returns. Here's is how it works: Suppose you have $5,000 to invest and are considering the purchase of 100 shares of stock at $50 per share. If you do not margin, you can buy outright 100 shares of the stock (ignoring brokerage commissions). If you margin the transaction—for example, at 50%—you can acquire the same $5,000 position with only $2,500 of your own money. This leaves you with $2,500 to use for other investments or to buy on margin another 100 shares of the same stock. Either way, by margining you will reap greater benefits from the stock's price appreciation.

The concept of margin trading is more fully illustrated in Table 2.3. It shows an unmargined (100% equity) transaction, along with the same transaction using various margins. Remember that the margin rates (e.g., 65%)

Read about margin trading at:
www.sec.gov/investor/pubs/margin.htm

EXCEL with
SPREADSHEETS

TABLE 2.3   **The Effect of Margin Trading on Security Returns**

	Without Margin (100% Equity)	With Margins of 80%	65%	50%
Number of $50 shares purchased	100	100	100	100
Cost of investment	$5,000	$5,000	$5,000	$5,000
Less: borrowed money	0	1,000	1,750	2,500
Equity in investment	$5,000	$4,000	$3,250	$2,500
A. Investor's position if price rises by $30 to $80/share				
Value of stock	$8,000	$8,000	$8,000	$8,000
Less: cost of investment	5,000	5,000	5,000	5,000
Capital gain	$3,000	$3,000	$3,000	$3,000
Return on investor's equity (capital gain/ equity in investment)	(60%)	(75%)	(92.3%)	(120%)
B. Investor's position if price falls by $30 to $20/share				
Value of stock	$2,000	$2,000	$2,000	$2,000
Less: cost of investment	5,000	5,000	5,000	5,000
Capital loss	$3,000	$3,000	$3,000	$3,000
Return on investor's equity (capital loss/ equity in investment)*	(60%)	(75%)	(92.3%)	(120%)

*With a capital loss, return on investor's equity is *negative*.

indicate the investor's equity in the investment. When the investment is unmargined and the price of the stock goes up by $30 per share (see Table 2.3, part A), the investor enjoys a very respectable 60% rate of return. However, observe what happens when margin is used: The rate of return shoots up as high as 120%, depending on the amount of equity in the investment. This occurs because the gain is the same ($3,000) *regardless of how the investor finances the transaction*. Clearly, as the investor's equity in the investment *declines* (with lower margins), the rate of return *increases* accordingly.

Three facets of margin trading become obvious from the table: (1) The price of the stock will move in whatever way it is going to, regardless of how the position is financed. (2) The lower the amount of the investor's equity in the position, the *greater the rate of return* the investor will enjoy when the price of the security rises. (3) The *loss is also magnified* (by the same rate) when the price of the security falls (see Table 2.3, part B).

Note that Table 2.3 has an "Excel with Spreadsheets" icon. Throughout the text, tables with this icon indicate that they are available as spreadsheets on the Web site, www.aw-bc.com/gitman_joehnk. The use of electronic spreadsheets in finance and investments, as well as in all functional areas of business, is pervasive. Excel makes managing numeric information much easier through its ability to create worksheets, databases, and charts. We use spreadsheets from time to time through-out the text to demonstrate how the content has been constructed or calculated. As you know from Chapter 1, we include Excel spreadsheet exercises at the end of most chapters. By working these exercises, you should develop the ability to clearly set out and visualize the logic needed to solve investment problems.

Advantages and Disadvantages of Margin Trading A magnified return is the major advantage of margin trading. The size of the magnified return depends on both the price behavior of the security that is margined and the amount of margin used. Another, more modest benefit of margin trading is that it allows for greater diversification of security holdings, because investors can spread their capital over a larger number of investments.

The major disadvantage of margin trading, of course, is the potential for magnified losses if the price of the security falls. Another disadvantage is the cost of the margin loans themselves. A **margin loan** is the official vehicle through which the borrowed funds are made available in a margin transaction. All margin loans are made at a stated interest rate, which depends on prevailing market rates and the amount of money being borrowed. This rate is usually 1% to 3% above the **prime rate**—the lowest interest rate charged the best business borrowers. For large accounts, it may be at the prime rate. The loan cost, which investors pay, will increase daily, reducing the level of profits (or increasing losses) accordingly.

Making Margin Transactions To execute a margin transaction, an investor must establish a **margin account** with a minimum of $2,000 in equity, in the form of either cash or securities. The broker will retain any securities purchased on margin as collateral for the loan.

The margin requirement established by the Federal Reserve Board sets the minimum amount of equity for margin transactions. Investors need not execute all margin transactions by using exactly the minimum amount of margin; they can use more than the minimum if they wish. Moreover, it is not unusual for brokerage firms and the major exchanges to establish their own margin

margin loan
vehicle through which borrowed funds are made available, at a stated interest rate, in a margin transaction.

prime rate
the lowest interest rate charged the best business borrowers.

margin account
a brokerage account for which margin trading is authorized.

TABLE 2.4   Initial Margin Requirements for Various Types of Securities

Security	Minimum Initial Margin (Equity) Required
Listed common and preferred stock	50%
OTC stocks traded on Nasdaq National Market	50%
Convertible bonds	50%
Corporate bonds	30%
U.S. government bills, notes, and bonds	10% of principal
U.S. government agencies	24% of principal
Options	Option premium plus 20% of market value of underlying stock
Futures	2% to 10% of the value of the contract

requirements, which are more restrictive than those of the Federal Reserve. In addition, brokerage firms may have their own lists of especially volatile stocks for which the margin requirements are higher. There are basically two types of margin requirements: initial margin and maintenance margin.

initial margin
the minimum amount of equity that must be provided by a margin investor *at the time of purchase.*

Initial Margin The minimum amount of equity that must be provided by the investor *at the time of purchase* is the **initial margin.** It prevents overtrading and excessive speculation. Generally, this is the margin requirement to which investors refer when discussing margin trading. All securities that can be margined have specific initial requirements, which the governing authorities can change at their discretion. Table 2.4 shows initial margin requirements for various types of securities. The more stable investment vehicles, such as U.S. government issues, generally have substantially lower margin requirements and therefore offer greater opportunities to magnify returns. OTC stocks traded on the Nasdaq National Market can be margined like listed securities; all other OTC stocks are considered to have no collateral value and therefore cannot be margined.

restricted account
a margin account whose equity is less than the initial margin requirement; the investor may not make further margin purchases and must bring the margin back to the initial level when securities are sold.

As long as the margin in an account remains at a level equal to or greater than prevailing initial requirements, the investor may use the account in any way he or she wants. However, if the value of the investor's holdings declines, the margin in his or her account will also drop. In this case, the investor will have what is known as a **restricted account,** one whose equity is less than the initial margin requirement. It does not mean that the investor must put up additional cash or equity. But as long as the account is restricted, the investor may not make further margin purchases and must bring the margin back to the initial level when securities are sold.

maintenance margin
the absolute minimum amount of margin (equity) that an investor must maintain in the margin account at all times.

margin call
notification of the need to bring the equity of an account whose margin is below the maintenance level up above the maintenance margin level or to have enough margined holdings sold to reach this standard.

Maintenance Margin The absolute minimum amount of margin (equity) that an investor must maintain in the margin account at all times is the **maintenance margin.** When an insufficient amount of maintenance margin exists, an investor will receive a **margin call.** This call gives the investor a short period of time (perhaps 72 hours) to bring the equity up above the maintenance margin. If this doesn't happen, the broker is authorized to sell enough of the investor's margined holdings to bring the equity in the account up to this standard.

Margin investors can be in for a surprise if markets are volatile. When the Nasdaq stock market fell 14% in one day in early April 2000, brokerages made many more margin calls than usual. Investors rushed to sell shares, often at a loss, to cover their margin calls—only to watch the market bounce back a few days later.

The maintenance margin protects both the brokerage house and investors: Brokers avoid having to absorb excessive investor losses, and investors avoid being wiped out. The maintenance margin on equity securities is currently 25%. It rarely changes, although it is often set slightly higher by brokerage firms for the added protection of brokers and customers. For straight debt securities such as government bonds, there is no official maintenance margin except that set by the brokerage firms themselves.

The Basic Margin Formula The amount of margin is always measured in terms of its relative amount of equity, which is considered the investor's collateral. A simple formula can be used with all types of long purchases to determine the amount of margin in the transaction at any given point. Basically, only two pieces of information are required: (1) the prevailing market value of the securities being margined and (2) the **debit balance,** which is the amount of money being borrowed in the margin loan. Given this information, we can compute margin according to Equation 2.1.

debit balance
the amount of money being borrowed in a margin loan.

Equation 2.1
$$\text{Margin} = \frac{\text{Value of securities} - \text{Debit balance}}{\text{Value of securities}}$$

Equation 2.1a
$$= \frac{V - D}{V}$$

To illustrate the use of this formula, consider the following example. Assume you want to purchase 100 shares of stock at $40 per share at a time when the initial margin requirement is 70%. Because 70% of the transaction must be financed with equity, the (30%) balance can be financed with a margin loan. Therefore, you will borrow $0.30 \times \$4,000$, or $1,200. This amount, of course, is the *debit balance.* The remainder ($4,000 − $1,200 = $2,800) represents your equity in the transaction. In other words, equity is represented by the numerator ($V - D$) in the margin formula.

What happens to the margin as the value of the security changes? If over time the price of the stock moves to $65, the margin is then

$$\text{Margin} = \frac{V - D}{V} = \frac{\$6,500 - \$1,200}{\$6,500} = 0.815 = \underline{81.5\%}$$

Note that the margin (equity) in this investment position has risen from 70% to 81.5%. *When the price of the security goes up, the investor's margin also increases.*

On the other hand, *when the price of the security goes down, so does the amount of margin.* For instance, if the price of the stock in our illustration drops to $30 per share, the new margin is only 60% [($3,000 − $1,200) ÷ $3,000]. In that case, we would be dealing with a *restricted account,* because the margin level would have dropped below the prevailing initial margin of 70%.

Finally, note that although our discussion has been couched largely in terms of individual transactions, the same margin formula applies to margin accounts. The only difference is that we would be dealing with input that applies to the account as a whole—the value of all securities held in the account and the total amount of margin loans.

Return on Invested Capital When assessing the return on margin transactions, you must take into account the fact that you put up only part of the funds. Therefore, you are concerned with the *rate of return* earned on only the portion of the funds that you provided. Using both current income received from dividends or interest and total interest paid on the margin loan, we can apply Equation 2.2 to determine the return on invested capital from a margin transaction.

Equation 2.2

$$\text{Return on invested capital from a margin transaction} = \frac{\begin{array}{c}\text{Total}\\\text{current}\\\text{income}\\\text{received}\end{array} - \begin{array}{c}\text{Total}\\\text{interest}\\\text{paid on}\\\text{margin loan}\end{array} + \begin{array}{c}\text{Market}\\\text{value of}\\\text{securities}\\\text{at sale}\end{array} - \begin{array}{c}\text{Market}\\\text{value of}\\\text{securities}\\\text{at purchase}\end{array}}{\text{Amount of equity at purchase}}$$

This equation can be used to compute either the expected or the actual return from a margin transaction. To illustrate: Assume you want to buy 100 shares of stock at $50 per share because you feel it will rise to $75 within 6 months. The stock pays $2 per share in annual dividends, and during your 6-month holding period you will be entitled to receive half of that amount, or $1 per share. You are going to buy the stock with 50% margin and will pay 10% interest on the margin loan. Therefore, you are going to put up $2,500 equity to buy $5,000 worth of stock that you hope will increase to $7,500 in 6 months. Because you will have a $2,500 margin loan outstanding at 10% for 6 months, you will pay $125 in total interest costs ($2,500 × 0.10 × 6/12 = $125). We can substitute this information into Equation 2.2 to find the expected return on invested capital from this margin transaction:

$$\text{Return on invested capital from a margin transaction} = \frac{\$100 - \$125 + \$7,500 - \$5,000}{\$2,500} = \frac{\$2,475}{\$2,500} = 0.99 = \underline{99\%}$$

Keep in mind that the 99% figure represents the rate of return earned over a 6-month holding period. If you wanted to compare this rate of return to other investment opportunities, you could determine the transaction's annualized rate of return by multiplying by 2 (the number of 6-month periods in a year). This would amount to an annual rate of return of 198% (99% × 2 = 198%).

pyramiding
the technique of using paper profits in margin accounts to partly or fully finance the acquisition of additional securities.

Uses of Margin Trading Investors most often use margin trading in one of two ways. As we have seen, one of its uses is to magnify transaction returns. The other major margin tactic is called pyramiding, which takes the concept of magnified returns to its limits. **Pyramiding** uses the paper profits in margin accounts to partly or fully finance the acquisition of additional securities. This allows investors to make such transactions at margins below prevailing initial margin levels, and sometimes substantially so. In fact, with this technique it is even possible to buy securities with no new cash at all. Rather, they can all be financed entirely with margin loans. The reason is that the paper profits in the account lead to **excess margin**—more equity in the account than required. For instance, if a margin account holds $60,000 worth of securities and has a debit balance of $20,000, it is at a margin level of 66⅔% [($60,000 − $20,000) ÷ $60,000]. This account would hold a substantial amount of excess margin if the prevailing initial margin requirement were only 50%.

The principle of pyramiding is to use the excess margin in the account to purchase additional securities. The only constraint—and the key to pyramiding—is that when the additional securities are purchased, the investor's margin account must be at or above the prevailing required initial margin level. Remember that it is the *account*, not the individual transactions, that must meet the minimum standards. If the account has excess margin, the investor can use it to build up security holdings. Pyramiding can continue as long as there are additional paper profits in the margin account and as long as the margin level exceeds the initial requirement that prevails when purchases are made. The tactic is somewhat complex but is also profitable, especially because it minimizes the amount of new capital required in the investor's account.

In general, margin trading is simple, but it is also risky. Risk is primarily associated with potential price declines in the margined securities. A decline in prices can result in a *restricted account*. If prices fall enough to cause the actual margin to drop below the maintenance margin, the resulting margin call will force the investor to deposit additional equity into the account almost immediately. In addition, losses (resulting from the price decline) are magnified in a fashion similar to that demonstrated in Table 2.3, part B. Clearly, the chance of a margin call and the magnification of losses make margin trading more risky than nonmargined transactions. Margin should be used only by investors who fully understand its operation and appreciate its pitfalls. The *Ethics* box on page 62 discusses the perilous side of margin trading in the story of one man's financial ruin through buying on margin.

Short Selling

In most cases, investors buy stock hoping that the price will rise. What if an investor expects the price of a particular security to fall? By using short selling, the investor may be able to profit from falling security prices. (Until 1997 investors could use short selling to *protect* themselves from falling security prices, a strategy called *shorting-against-the-box*.) Almost any type of security can be "shorted": common and preferred stocks, all types of bonds, convertible securities, listed mutual funds, options, and warrants. In practice, though, the short-selling activities of most investors are limited almost exclusively to common stocks and to options.

Essentials of Short Selling **Short selling** is generally defined as the practice of selling borrowed securities. Unusual as it may sound, selling borrowed securities is (in most cases) legal and quite common. Short sales start when securities that have been borrowed from a broker are sold in the marketplace. Later, when the price of the issue has declined, the short seller buys back the securities,

excess margin
more equity than is required in a margin account.

short selling
the sale of borrowed securities, their eventual repurchase by the short seller, and their return to the lender.

⚖ ETHICS IN INVESTING

THE PERILS OF MARGIN TRADING

The downfall of Bernard Ebbers, CEO of the global telecommunications giant, World-Com—a company he built from scratch—was about as spectacular as his meteoric rise to power. As a result of the biggest corporate bankruptcy in U.S. history, the former basketball coach, club bouncer, and Sunday school teacher emerged broke with a negative net worth approaching nine digits. However, what brought Ebbers down was less his greed and more his devotion and loyalty to the company: Ebbers simply owned too much of WorldCom stock that he bought on margin.

By investing his generous compensation and exercising the right to buy tens of millions of shares from his options package, Ebbers saw his holdings of company stock grow at a fast rate—much faster than he could afford. When his personal funds were insufficient, he would finance new purchases by using his existing holdings as collateral to borrow money, a practice known as *buying on margin*. This was not a problem as long as the stock of WorldCom was going up. In 1999, when its shares were trading close to $70, Ebbers' net worth—estimated to be $1.4 billion— put him on Forbes' list of richest Americans.

However, when WorldCom stock began its descent in 2000, Ebbers started receiving margin calls because the value of his initial collateral (WorldCom shares) was insufficient to maintain the loans from brokers that he had used to purchase additional shares. Because he could not meet tens of millions of dollars of margin calls, Ebbers faced difficult choices: either sell some of his vast holdings of stock and use the proceeds to pay the margin loans, or apply for personal loans to cover the calls. When WorldCom's board of directors learned about his margin calls, it rejected the first option on the grounds that the CEOs dumping of millions of WorldCom shares on the market would not only depress the price of the stock but also erode investor confidence in the company. Instead, the company granted Ebbers a low-interest loan for margin calls. However, as the bear market continued to unravel, prices of telecommunications companies took the hardest hit, and Ebbers faced new and bigger margin calls, which required new personal loans from the company. Borrowing money to cover margin calls may be a good idea if the stock recovers, but it may also result in financial ruin if the stock continues to fall.

In the end, WorldCom granted Ebbers $341 million in personal loans, the largest amount of money any publicly traded company has ever lent to one of its officers. WorldCom shares became worthless, and the company filed for Chapter 11 bankruptcy in July 2002 amidst allegation of accounting fraud. Although Ebbers so far has managed to escape federal indictments, he faces charges of violating state securities and tax laws associated with an $11 billion accounting fraud that brought WorldCom to its knees.

The policy of boards of directors regarding authorizing loans for senior executives raises important ethical questions. "A large loan to a senior executive epitomizes concerns about conflict of interest and breach of fiduciary duty," said former SEC enforcement official Seth Taube. The number of companies authorizing such loans has recently increased dramatically. In 2002, Congress addressed this issue by passing the Sarbanes-Oxley Act, which forbade companies from making such loans.

CRITICAL THINKING QUESTION Although it is legal to do so, in the wake of the WorldCom collapse, should executives be allowed to use margin accounts to trade the stocks of their companies?

Note: Ethics boxes, which appear in several chapters, focus on the ethical dimensions of particular situations and issues in the investments world. Each box includes a Critical Thinking Question for discussion.

which are then returned to the lender. A short seller must make an initial equity deposit with the broker, subject to rules similar to those for margin trading. The deposit plus the proceeds from sale of the borrowed shares assure the broker that sufficient funds are available to buy back the shorted securities at a later date, even if their price increases. Short sales, like margin transactions, require investors to work through a broker.

TABLE 2.5   The Mechanics of a Short Sale

Step 1—Short sale initiated:

100 shares of borrowed stock are *sold* at $50/share: Proceeds from sale to investor	$5,000

Step 2—Short sale covered:

Later, 100 shares of the stock are *purchased*
        at $30/share and returned to broker from
        whom stock was borrowed:
    Cost to investor
	3,000

Net profit	$2,000

SHORT INTEREST INDICATES?— Monitoring the short-selling levels can help you measure investor moods. Each month the *Wall Street Journal* reports the short interest, which reflects the number of shares that have not yet been repurchased to cover the short sales. A higher level tends to indicate a more pessimistic outlook and expectations of a downturn. For example, for the month ended August 15, 2003, the Nasdaq short interest fell 6% over the July level, while the NYSE level was 4.2% lower. These figures were in line with more positive investor attitudes resulting from stronger economic activity.

Source: Craig Karmin, "Short Interest Fell on Nasdaq in Latest Month," *Wall Street Journal,* August 27, 2003, p. B8.

Making Money When Prices Fall Making money when security prices fall is what short selling is all about. Like their colleagues in the rest of the investment world, short sellers are trying to make money by *buying low and selling high.* The only difference is that they reverse the investment process: *They start the transaction with a sale and end it with a purchase.*

Table 2.5 shows how a short sale works and how investors can profit from such transactions. (For simplicity, we ignore transaction costs.) The transaction results in a net profit of $2,000 as a result of an initial sale of 100 shares of stock at $50 per share (step 1) and subsequent covering (purchase) of the 100 shares for $30 per share (step 2). The amount of profit or loss generated in a short sale depends on the price at which the short seller can buy back the stock. Short sellers earn profit only when the proceeds from the sale of the stock are greater than the cost of buying it back.

Who Lends the Securities? Acting through their brokers, short sellers obtain securities from the brokerage firm or from other investors (brokers are the principal source of borrowed securities). As a service to their customers, they lend securities held in the brokers' portfolios or in *street name* accounts. It is important to recognize that when the brokerage firm lends street name securities, it is lending the short seller the securities of other investors. Individual investors typically do not pay fees to the broker for the privilege of borrowing the shares and, as a result, do not earn interest on the funds they leave on deposit with the broker.

Margin Requirements and Short Selling To make a short sale, the investor must make a deposit with the broker that is equal to the initial margin requirement (currently 50%) applied to the short sale proceeds. In addition, the broker retains the proceeds from the short sale. To demonstrate, assume that you sell short 100 shares of Smart, Inc., at $50 per share at a time when the initial margin requirement is 50% and the maintenance margin on short sales is 30%. The values in lines 1 through 4 under column A in Table 2.6 (on page 64) indicate that your broker would hold a total deposit of $7,500 on this transaction. Note in columns B and C that regardless of subsequent changes in Smart, Inc.'s stock price, your deposit with the broker would remain at $7,500 (line 4). By subtracting the cost of buying back the shorted stock at the given share price (line 5), your equity in the account under the current (column A) and two subsequent share prices (columns B and C) is shown in line 6. It can be seen that at the initial short sale price of $50 per share your equity would

TABLE 2.6		Margin Positions on Short Sales		
		A	B	C
Line	Item	Initial Short Sale Price	Subsequent Share Prices	
1	Price per share	$50	$30	$70
2	Proceeds from initial short sale [(1) × 100sh]	$5,000		
3	Initial margin deposit [.50 × (2)]	2,500		
4	Total deposit with broker [(2) + (3)]	$7,500	$7,500	$7,500
5	Current cost of buying back stock [(1) × 100sh]	5,000	3,000	7,000
6	Account equity [(4) − (5)]	$2,500	$4,500	$ 500
7	Actual margin [(6) ÷ (5)]	50%	150%	7.14%
8	Maintenance margin position [(7) > 30%?]	OK	OK	Margin call*

*Investor must either deposit at least an additional $1,600 with the broker to bring the total deposit to $9,100 ($7,500 + $1,600), which would equal the current value of the 100 shares of $7,000 plus a 30% maintenance margin deposit of $2,100 (.30 × $7,000), or buy back the 100 shares of stock and return them to the broker.

equal $2,500 (column A); if the share price subsequently drops to $30, your equity would rise to $4,500 (column B); and if the share price subsequently rises to $70, your equity would fall to $500 (column C). Dividing these account equity values (line 6) by the then-current cost of buying back the stock (line 5), the actual margins at each share price are calculated in line 7. It can be seen that at the current $50 price the actual margin is 50%, whereas at the $30 share price it is 150%, and at the $70 share price it is 7.14%.

As noted in line 8, given the 30% maintenance margin requirement, your margin would be okay at the current price of $50 (column A) or lower (column B), but at the $70 share price the 7.14% actual margin would be below the 30% maintenance margin, thereby resulting in a margin call. In that case (or whenever the actual margin on a short sale falls below the maintenance margin), the investor must respond to the margin call either by depositing additional funds with the broker or by buying the stock and covering (i.e., closing out) the short position.

If you wished to maintain the short position when the share price has risen to $70, you would have to deposit an additional $1,600 with the broker, which would increase your total deposit to $9,100 ($7,500 + $1,600)—an amount equal to the $7,000 value of the shorted stock plus the 30% maintenance margin, or $2,100 (.30 × $7,000). Buying back the stock to cover the short position would cost $7,000, thereby resulting in the return of the $500 of equity in your account from your broker. Clearly, margin requirements tend to complicate the short sale transaction and the impact of an increase in the shorted stock's share price on required deposits with the broker.

Advantages and Disadvantages The major advantage of selling short is, of course, the chance to profit from a price decline. The key disadvantage of many short-sale transactions is that the investor faces limited return opportunities, along with high risk exposure. The price of a security can fall only so far (to a value of or near zero), yet there is really no limit to how far such securities can rise in price. (Remember, a short seller is hoping for a price decline; when a security goes up in price, a short seller loses.) For example, note in Table 2.5 that the stock in question cannot possibly fall by more than $50, yet who is to say how high its price can go?

A less serious disadvantage is that short sellers never earn dividend (or interest) income. In fact, short sellers owe the lender of the shorted security any dividends (or interest) paid while the transaction is outstanding. That is, if a dividend is paid during the course of a short-sale transaction, the short seller must pay an equal amount to the lender of the stock. (The mechanics of these payments are taken care of automatically by the short seller's broker.)

Uses of Short Selling Investors short sell primarily to seek speculative profits when they expect the price of a security to drop. Because the short seller is betting against the market, this approach is subject to a considerable amount of risk. The actual procedure works as demonstrated in Table 2.5. Note that had you been able to sell the stock at $50 per share and later repurchase it at $30 per share, you would have generated a profit of $2,000 (ignoring dividends and brokerage commissions). However, if the market had instead moved against you, all or most of your $5,000 investment could have been lost.

IN REVIEW

CONCEPTS

2.11 What is a *long purchase?* What expectation underlies such a purchase? What is *margin trading,* and what is the key reason why it is sometimes used as part of a long purchase?

2.12 How does margin trading magnify profits and losses? What are the key advantages and disadvantages of margin trading?

2.13 Describe the procedures and regulations associated with margin trading. Be sure to explain *restricted accounts,* the *maintenance margin,* and the *margin call.* Define the term *debit balance,* and describe the common uses of margin trading.

2.14 What is the primary motive for *short selling?* Describe the basic short-sale procedure. Why must the short seller make an initial equity deposit?

2.15 What relevance do margin requirements have in the short-selling process? What would have to happen to experience a "margin call" on a short-sale transaction? What two actions could be used to remedy such a call?

2.16 Describe the key advantages and disadvantages of short selling. How are short sales used to earn speculative profits?

Summary

LG 1   **Identify the basic types of securities markets and describe the IPO process.** Short-term investment vehicles trade in the money market; longer-term securities, such as stocks and bonds, trade in the capital market. New security issues are sold in the primary market. Once securities are outstanding, investors buy and sell them in the secondary markets. The first public issue of a company's common stock is called an initial public offering (IPO). The company selects an investment banker to advise it and sell the securities. The lead investment banker may form a syndicate with other investment bankers and then create a selling group to sell the issue. The IPO process includes filing a registration statement with the Securities and Exchange Commission (SEC), getting SEC approval, promoting the offering to investors, pricing the issue, and selling the shares.

LG 2   **Explain the characteristics of organized securities exchanges.** The organized securities exchanges are auction markets. They include the New York Stock Exchange (NYSE), the American Stock Exchange (AMEX), regional stock exchanges, options exchanges, and futures exchanges. In these centralized markets, the forces of supply and demand determine prices. The organized exchanges act as secondary markets where existing securities trade.

LG 3   **Understand the over-the-counter markets, including Nasdaq and alternative trading systems, and the general conditions of securities markets.** The over-the-counter (OTC) market acts as a primary market in which initial public offerings are made. It also handles secondary trading in unlisted securities. It is a dealer market in which negotiation and market maker quotes, often obtained through its automated system, Nasdaq, determine price. Over-the-counter transactions in listed securities are made in the third market. Transactions directly between buyers and sellers are made in the fourth market. Electronic communications networks (ECNs) now offer an alternative to organized exchanges and Nasdaq. Market conditions are commonly classified as "bull" or "bear," depending on whether securities prices are generally rising or falling.

LG 4   **Review the importance of global securities markets, their performance, and the investment procedures and risks associated with foreign investments.** Today securities markets must be viewed globally. Securities exchanges operate in over 100 countries—both large and small. Foreign security investments can be made indirectly by buying shares of a U.S.-based multinational with substantial foreign operations or by purchasing shares of a mutual fund that invests primarily in foreign securities. Direct foreign investment can be achieved by purchasing securities on foreign exchanges, by buying securities of foreign companies that are traded on U.S. exchanges, or by buying American Depositary Receipts (ADRs). International investments can enhance returns, but they entail added risk, particularly currency exchange risk.

LG 5   **Discuss trading hours and the regulation of securities markets.** No longer are investors limited to trading securities during regular market hours (9:30 A.M. to 4:00 P.M., Eastern time). Pre- and post-market trading sessions are available to both individual and institutional investors. Most of these after-hours markets are crossing markets, in which orders are filled only if they can be matched. Trading activity during these sessions can be quite risky because of greater volatility and lack of centralized pricing data. The securities markets are regulated by the federal Securities and Exchange Commission (SEC) and by state commissions. The key federal laws regulating the securities industry are the Securities Act of 1933, the Securities Exchange Act of 1934, the Maloney Act of 1938, the Investment Company Act of 1940, the Investment Advisers Act of 1940, the Securities Acts Amendments of 1975, the Insider Trading and Fraud Act of 1988, and the Sarbanes-Oxley Act of 2002.

LG 6   **Explain long purchases and the motives, procedures, and calculations involved in making margin transactions and short sales.** Most investors make long purchases—buy low, sell high—in expectation of price increases. Many investors establish margin accounts to use borrowed funds to enhance their buying power. The Federal Reserve Board establishes the margin requirement—the minimum investor equity in a margin transaction, both initially and during the margin transaction. The return on invested capital in a margin transaction is magnified; positive returns *and* negative returns are larger than in a comparable unmargined transaction. Paper profits can be used to pyramid a margin account by investing its excess margin. The risks of margin trading are the chance of a restricted account or margin call and the consequences of magnification of losses due to price declines.

Short selling is used when a decline in security prices is anticipated. It involves selling securities, typically borrowed from the broker, with the expectation of earning a profit by repurchasing them at a lower price in the future. To execute a short sale, the investor must make an initial equity deposit with the broker, who also holds the initial sales proceeds. If the price of a shorted stock rises, the investor may receive a margin call from the broker, which can be remedied either by increasing the deposit with the broker or by buying back the stock to cover the short position. The major advantage of selling short is the chance to profit from a price decline. The disadvantages of selling short are that the return opportunities are limited in spite of the unlimited potential for loss, and that short sellers never earn dividend (or interest) income. Short selling is used primarily to seek speculative profits from an anticipated decline in share price.

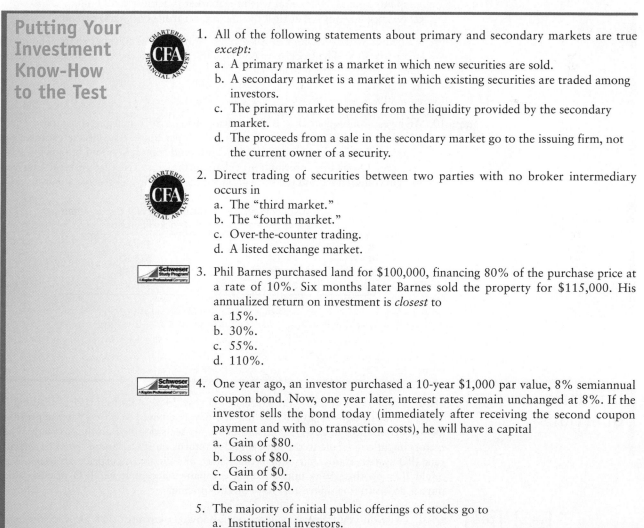

Putting Your Investment Know-How to the Test

1. All of the following statements about primary and secondary markets are true *except:*
   a. A primary market is a market in which new securities are sold.
   b. A secondary market is a market in which existing securities are traded among investors.
   c. The primary market benefits from the liquidity provided by the secondary market.
   d. The proceeds from a sale in the secondary market go to the issuing firm, not the current owner of a security.

2. Direct trading of securities between two parties with no broker intermediary occurs in
   a. The "third market."
   b. The "fourth market."
   c. Over-the-counter trading.
   d. A listed exchange market.

3. Phil Barnes purchased land for $100,000, financing 80% of the purchase price at a rate of 10%. Six months later Barnes sold the property for $115,000. His annualized return on investment is *closest* to
   a. 15%.
   b. 30%.
   c. 55%.
   d. 110%.

4. One year ago, an investor purchased a 10-year $1,000 par value, 8% semiannual coupon bond. Now, one year later, interest rates remain unchanged at 8%. If the investor sells the bond today (immediately after receiving the second coupon payment and with no transaction costs), he will have a capital
   a. Gain of $80.
   b. Loss of $80.
   c. Gain of $0.
   d. Gain of $50.

5. The majority of initial public offerings of stocks go to
   a. Institutional investors.
   b. Day traders.
   c. Market makers and specialists.
   d. The company's current stockholders.

6. The main reason for investing abroad is to
   a. Reduce currency fluctuations.
   b. Diversify portfolios and reduce risks.
   c. Increase returns.
   d. Provide capital to multinational corporations.

7. There are approximately _____ stocks listed on the New York Exchange.
   a. 2,500   b. 1,900
   c. 4,500   d. 3,300

8. To maintain a fair and orderly market, stock exchange specialists in the United States are expected to
   a. Buy against the market when the market is definitely declining and are expected to sell against the market when the market is definitely rising.
   b. Buy against the market when the market is definitely declining but are not expected to sell against the market when the market is definitely rising.
   c. Sell against the market when the market is definitely rising but are not expected to buy against the market when the market is definitely declining.
   d. Neither buy nor sell against the market, regardless of market trends.

9. You purchased 100 shares of XYZ stock on margin for $50 per share. The initial margin is 50%. The stock pays no dividend. If you sell the stock at $40 per share your investment return would be
   a. −20%.   b. −40%.
   c. −50%.   d. 25%.

10. An investor buys a stock at $32 per share, using a 50% margin; she hopes to hold the stock for a year and then sell it for $37.50 per share. Assume the maintenance margin is 25%, the stock pays no dividends, and transaction and borrowing costs are zero. Given this information, calculate the expected rate of return on this margin transaction, **and** the price at which the investor will receive a margin call.

	Expected Rate of return	Margin Call Will Occur When Stock Hits a Price of:
a.	17.2%	$16.00
b.	22.9%	$21.33
c.	34.4%	$21.33
d.	34.4%	$38.40

Answers: 1. d; 2. b; 3. d; 4. c; 5. a; 6. b; 7. d; 8. a; 9. b; 10. c

Discussion Questions

LG 1   Q2.1   From 1990 to 2003, the average IPO rose 24% in its first day of trading. In 1999, 117 deals doubled in price on the first day, compared to only 39 in the previous 24 years combined. In 2001, 2002, and 2003, no deals doubled on the first day. What factors might contribute to the huge first-day returns on IPOs? Some critics of the current IPO system claim that underwriters may knowingly underprice an issue. Why might they do this? Why might issuing companies accept lower IPO prices? What impact do institutional investors have on IPO pricing?

LG 2   LG 3   Q2.2   Why do you think some large, well-known companies such as Cisco Systems, Intel, and Microsoft prefer to trade on the Nasdaq National Market rather than on a major organized exchange such as the NYSE (for which they easily meet the listing requirements)? Discuss the pros and cons of listing on a major organized exchange.

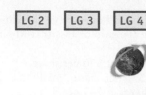

LG 2   **LG 3**   **LG 4**

Q2.3   On the basis of the current structure of the world's financial markets and your knowledge of the NYSE and OTC markets, describe the key features, functions, and problems that would be faced by a single global market (exchange) on which transactions can be made in all securities of all of the world's major companies. Discuss the likelihood of such a market developing.

LG 5

Q2.4   Critics of longer trading hours believe that expanded trading sessions turn the stock market into a casino and place the emphasis more on short-term gains than on long-term investment. Do you agree? Why or why not? Is it important to have a "breathing period" to reflect on the day's market activity? Why are smaller brokerages and ECNs, more than the NYSE and Nasdaq, pushing for longer trading hours?

LG 6

Q2.5   Describe how, if at all, conservative and aggressive investors might use each of the following types of transactions as part of their investment programs. Contrast these two types of investors in view of these preferences.
   a. Long purchase
   b. Margin trading
   c. Short selling

Problems

LG 4

P2.1   The current exchange rate between the U.S. dollar and the Japanese yen is 116.915 (Yen/$). How many dollars would you get for 1,000 Japanese yen?

LG 4

P2.2   An investor recently sold some stock that was a Eurodollar investment for 20,000 euros. The U.S.$/euro exchange rate is currently 1.1. How many U.S. dollars will the investor receive?

   LG 4

P2.3   In each of the following cases, calculate the price of one share of the foreign stock measured in United States dollars (US$).
   a. A Belgian stock priced at 103.2 euros (€) when the exchange rate is .8595 €/US$.
   b. A Swiss stock priced at 93.3 Swiss francs (Sf) when the exchange rate is 1.333 Sf/US$.
   c. A Japanese stock priced at 1,350 yen (¥) when the exchange rate is 110 ¥/US$.

   LG 4

P2.4   Lola Paretti purchased 50 shares of BMW, a German stock traded on the Frankfurt Exchange, for 64.5 euros (€) per share exactly 1 year ago, when the exchange rate was .78 €/US$. Today the stock is trading at 68.4 € per share, and the exchange rate is .86 €/US$.
   a. Did the € *depreciate* or *appreciate* relative to the US$ during the past year? Explain.
   b. How much in US$ did Lola pay for her 50 shares of BMW when she purchased them a year ago?
   c. For how much in US$ can Lola sell her BMW shares today?
   d. Ignoring brokerage fees and taxes, how much profit (or loss) in US$ will Lola realize on her BMW stock if she sells it today?

LG 4

P2.5   An investor believes that the U.S. dollar will rise in value relative to the Japanese yen. The same investor is considering two investments with identical risk and return characteristics: One is a Japanese yen investment and the other is a U.S. dollar investment. Should the investor purchase the Japanese yen investment?

LG 6

P2.6 Elmo Inc.'s stock is currently selling at $60 per share. For each of the following situations (ignoring brokerage commissions), calculate the gain or loss that Maureen Katz realizes if she makes a 100-share transaction.

    a. She sells short and repurchases the borrowed shares at $70 per share.

    b. She takes a long position and sells the stock at $75 per share.

    c. She sells short and repurchases the borrowed shares at $45 per share.

    d. She takes a long position and sells the stock at $60 per share.

LG 6

P2.7 Assume that an investor buys 100 shares of stock at $50 per share, putting up a 60% margin.

    a. What is the debit balance in this transaction?

    b. How much equity capital must the investor provide to make this margin transaction?

LG 6

P2.8 Assume that an investor buys 100 shares of stock at $50 per share, putting up a 60% margin. If the stock rises to $60 per share what is the investor's new margin position?

LG 6

Note: A PC icon appears next to problems and case questions that can be solved using the computation routines available at the book's Web site.

P2.9 Assume that an investor buys 100 shares of stock at $50 per share, putting up a 70% margin.

    a. What is the *debit balance* in this transaction?

    b. How much equity funds must the investor provide to make this margin transaction?

    c. If the stock rises to $80 per share, what is the investor's new margin position?

LG 6

P2.10 Doug purchased 100 shares of Can'tWin.com for $50 per share, using as little of his own money as he could. His broker has a 50% initial margin requirement and a 30% maintenance margin requirement. The price of the stock falls to $30 per share. What does Doug need to do?

 **LG 6**

P2.11 Jerri Kingston bought 100 shares of stock at $80 per share, using an *initial margin* of 60%. Given a *maintenance margin* of 25%, how far does the stock have to drop before Ms. Kingston faces a *margin call*? (Assume that there are no other securities in the margin account.)

 **LG 6**

P2.12 An investor buys 200 shares of stock selling at $80 per share, using a margin of 60%. The stock pays annual dividends of $1 per share. A margin loan can be obtained at an annual interest cost of 8%. Determine what return on invested capital the investor will realize if the price of the stock increases to $104 within 6 months. What is the *annualized* rate of return on this transaction?

 **LG 6**

P2.13 Marlene Bellamy purchased 300 shares of Writeline Communications stock at $55 per share, using the prevailing minimum *initial margin* requirement of 50%. She held the stock for exactly 4 months and sold it without any brokerage costs at the end of that period. During the 4-month holding period, the stock paid $1.50 per share in cash dividends. Marlene was charged 9% annual interest on the margin loan. The minimum *maintenance margin* was 25%.

    a. Calculate the initial value of the transaction, the *debit balance,* and the equity position on Marlene's transaction.

    b. For each of the following share prices, calculate the actual margin percentage, and indicate whether Marlene's margin account would have excess equity, would be restricted, or would be subject to a margin call.

       (1) $45

       (2) $70

       (3) $35

c. Calculate the dollar amount of (1) dividends received and (2) interest paid on the margin loan during the 4-month holding period.

d. Use each of the following sale prices at the end of the 4-month holding period to calculate Marlene's *annualized* rate of return on the Writeline Communications stock transaction.
  (1) $50
  (2) $60
  (3) $70

LG 6   **P2.14** Not long ago, Dave Edwards bought 200 shares of Almost Anything Inc. at $45 per share; he bought the stock on margin of 60%. The stock is now trading at $60 per share, and the Federal Reserve has recently lowered *initial margin* requirements to 50%. Dave now wants to do a little *pyramiding* and buy another 300 shares of the stock. What is the minimum amount of equity that he'll have to put up in this transaction?

LG 6   **P2.15** An investor short sells 100 shares of a stock for $20 per share. The initial margin is 50%. How much equity will be required in the account to complete this transaction?

LG 6   **P2.16** An investor short sells 100 shares of a stock for $20 per share. The initial margin is 50%. Ignoring transaction costs, how much will be in the investor's account after this transaction if this is the only transaction the investor has undertaken and the investor has deposited only the required amount?

LG 6   **P2.17** An investor short sells 100 shares of a stock for $20 per share. The initial margin is 50%, and the maintenance margin is 30%. The price of the stock falls to $12 per share. What is the margin, and will there be a margin call?

LG 6   **P2.18** An investor short sells 100 shares of a stock for $20 per share. The initial margin is 50% and the maintenance margin is 30%. The price of the stock rises to $28 per share. What is the margin, and will there be a margin call?

LG 6   **P2.19** Calculate the profit or loss per share realized on each of the following short-sale transactions.

Transaction	Stock Sold Short at Price/Share	Stock Purchased to Cover Short at Price/Share
A	$75	$83
B	30	24
C	18	15
D	27	32
E	53	45

LG 6   **P2.20** Charlene Hickman expected the price of Bio International shares to drop in the near future in response to the expected failure of its new drug to pass FDA tests. As a result, she sold short 200 shares of Bio International at $27.50. How much would Charlene earn or lose on this transaction if she repurchased the 200 shares 4 months later at each of the following prices per share?
  a. $24.75
  b. $25.13
  c. $31.25
  d. $27.00

See the text Web site
(www.aw-bc.com/gitman_joehnk) **for Web exercises**
that deal with *markets and transactions.*

Case Problem 2.1   *Dara's Dilemma: What to Buy?*

Dara Simmons, a 40-year-old financial analyst and divorced mother of two teenage children, considers herself a savvy investor. She has increased her investment portfolio considerably over the past 5 years. Although she has been fairly conservative with her investments, she now feels more confident in her investment knowledge and would like to branch out into some new areas that could bring higher returns. She has between $20,000 and $25,000 to invest.

Attracted to the hot market for technology stocks, Dara was interested in purchasing a tech IPO stock and identified "NewestHighTech.com," a company that makes sophisticated computer chips for wireless Internet connections, as a likely prospect. The 1-year-old company had received some favorable press when it got early-stage financing and again when its chip was accepted by a major cell phone manufacturer.

Dara also was considering an investment in 400 shares of Casinos International common stock, currently selling for $54 per share. After a discussion with a friend who is an economist with a major commercial bank, Dara believes that the long-running bull market is due to cool off and that economic activity will slow down. With the aid of her stockbroker, Dara researches Casinos International's current financial situation and finds that the future success of the company may hinge on the outcome of pending court proceedings on the firm's application to open a new floating casino on a nearby river. If the permit is granted, it seems likely that the firm's stock will experience a rapid increase in value, regardless of economic conditions. On the other hand, if the company fails to get the permit, the falling stock price will make it a good candidate for a short sale.

Dara felt that the following alternatives were open to her:

Alternative 1: Invest $20,000 in NewestHighTech.com when it goes public.

Alternative 2: Buy Casinos International now at $54 per share and follow the company closely.

Alternative 3: Sell Casinos short at $54 in anticipation that the company's fortunes will change for the worse.

Alternative 4: Wait to see what happens with the casino permit and then decide whether to buy or short the Casinos International stock.

Questions

a. Evaluate each of these alternatives. On the basis of the limited information presented, recommend the one you feel is best.

b. If Casinos International's stock price rises to $60, what will happen under alternatives 2 and 3? Evaluate the pros and cons of these outcomes.

c. If the stock price drops to $45, what will happen under alternatives 2 and 3? Evaluate the pros and cons of these outcomes.

Case Problem 2.2   *Ravi Dumar's High-Flying Margin Account*

LG 6

Ravi Dumar is a stockbroker who lives with his wife, Sasha, and their five children in Milwaukee, Wisconsin. Ravi firmly believes that the only way to make money in the market is to follow an aggressive investment posture—for example, to use margin trading. In fact, Ravi himself has built a substantial margin account over the years. He currently holds $75,000 worth of stock in his margin account, though the *debit balance* in the account amounts to only $30,000. Recently, Ravi uncovered a stock that, on the basis of extensive analysis, he feels is about to take off. The stock, Running Shoes (RS), currently trades at $20 per share. Ravi feels it should soar to at least $50 within a year. RS pays no dividends, the prevailing *initial margin* requirement is 50%, and margin loans are now carrying an annual interest charge of 10%. Because Ravi feels so strongly about RS, he wants to do some *pyramiding* by using his margin account to purchase 1,000 shares of the stock.

Questions

a. Discuss the concept of pyramiding as it applies to this investment situation.

b. What is the present margin position (in percent) of Ravi's account?

c. Ravi buys the 1,000 shares of RS through his margin account (bear in mind that this is a $20,000 transaction).
    1. What will the margin position of the account be after the RS transaction if Ravi follows the prevailing initial margin (50%) and uses $10,000 of his money to buy the stock?
    2. What if he uses only $2,500 equity and obtains a margin loan for the balance ($17,500)?
    3. How do you explain the fact that the stock can be purchased with only 12.5% margin when the prevailing initial margin requirement is 50%?

d. Assume that Ravi buys 1,000 shares of RS stock at $20 per share with a minimum cash investment of $2,500 and that the stock does take off and its price rises to $40 per share in 1 year.
    1. What is the *return on invested capital* for this transaction?
    2. What return would Ravi have earned if he had bought the stock without margin—that is, if he had used all his own money?

e. What do you think of Ravi's idea to pyramid? What are the risks and rewards of this strategy?

Excel with Spreadsheets

You have just learned about the mechanics of margin trading and want to take advantage of the potential benefits of financial leverage. You have decided to open a margin account with your broker and to secure a margin loan. The specifics of the account are as follows:

- Initial margin requirement is 70%.
- Maintenance margin is 30%.
- You are informed that if the value of your account falls below the maintenance margin, your account will be subject to a margin call.

You have been following the price movements of a stock over the past year and believe that it is currently undervalued and that the price will rise in the near future. You feel that the opening of a margin account is a good investment strategy. You have decided to purchase three round lots (i.e., 100 shares per round lot) of the stock at its current price of $25 per share.

Create a spreadsheet similar to the spreadsheet for Table 2.3, which can be viewed at www.aw-bc.com/gitman_joehnk, to model and analyze the following market transactions.

Questions

a. Calculate the value of the investment in the stock as if you did not make use of margin trading. In other words, what is the value of the investment if it is funded by 100% cash equity?

b. Calculate the debit balance and the cash equity in the investment at the time of opening a margin account, adhering to the initial margin requirement.

c. If you use margin and the price of the stock rises by $15 to $40/share, calculate the capital gain earned and the return on investor's equity.

d. What is the current margin percentage based on question **b**?

e. If you use margin and the price of the stock falls by $15 to $10/share, calculate the capital loss and the respective return on investor's equity.

f. What is the new margin percentage based on question **e**, and what is the implication for you, the investor?

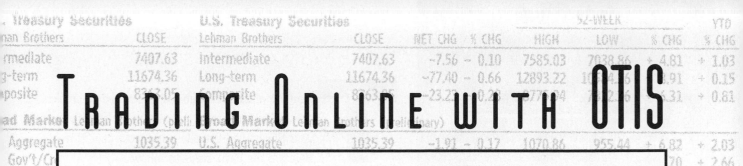

Trading Online with OTIS

Although there may be many reasons why you enrolled in a course on investments, most students will share one commonality—the desire to make money by investing in stocks. You may want to increase your wealth to achieve a long-term goal, such as retirement, or a short-term goal, such as accumulating funds to go to graduate school. When you get a job, you may be asked to structure your retirement account by selecting mutual funds or other investments for a deferred tax account. For all these reasons, it is essential to understand how to select a portfolio of investments that will perform well and return a capital gain.

Selecting stocks is both an art and a science. Although no investment guarantees a positive return, you can increase your chance of attaining higher yields by conducting research. Conversely, you can lessen the value of your portfolio by relying only on "hot tips." When buying a car most people will spend a good deal of time in looking at the array of choices and the statistics on the various models. Yet we sometimes fall prey to buying stocks by word of mouth. Such behavior is irrational because the return on stocks is greater than that on most consumer purchases, which usually depreciate the moment you buy them. To start you on your way in the basics of sound investing, we'll begin by asking you to select a portfolio of stocks utilizing the OTIS simulation.

Exercises

1. Go to Finance on www.yahoo.com or another financial site. Using the stock screener, select five stocks to purchase.

2. Sign on to OTIS and purchase four of the stocks, taking a long position.

3. Purchase the fifth stock on margin. Determine the price at which the broker would enact a margin call, using a 25% maintenance margin. (The basic formula can be found on page 59 of the text.)

4. Pick a stock that you expect to drop in value (select a financial Web site and look for downgrades to discover what stock analysts expect to decline). Short-sell this stock. Keep a close eye on this short because it may not head south, and you will then want to cover your position. Note that a short sale must take place at or above the last price and can only take place at the last price if it was a plus tick.

Optional Project

The *Wall Street Journal* used to publish a portfolio created by a throw of darts at stocks posted on the wall. They would then compare the performance of the dart portfolio to that of a portfolio chosen by money managers. In *A Random Walk Down Wall Street*, Burton G. Malkiel states that "a blindfolded chimpanzee throwing darts at the *Wall Street Journal* can select a portfolio that performs as well as those managed by the experts." It might be fun to test his theory.

Experiment Each student should select one stock and submit it, along with a firm profile, to the instructor. The instructor will create a class portfolio. At the end of the semester, compare the yield on this class portfolio to the average yield of the Standard and Poor's index portfolio.

CHAPTER 3

ONLINE INFORMATION AND INVESTING

LEARNING GOALS

After studying this chapter, you should
be able to:

LG 1 Discuss the growth in online
investing, including educational sites and
investment tools, and the pros and cons of
using the Internet as an investment tool.

LG 2 Identify the major types and sources
of traditional and online investment
information.

LG 3 Explain the characteristics,
interpretation, and uses of the commonly
cited stock and bond market averages
and indexes.

LG 4 Review the roles of full-service,
premium discount, and basic discount
stockbrokers, including the services they
provide, selection of a stockbroker, opening
an account, and transaction basics.

LG 5 Describe the basic types of orders
(market, limit, and stop-loss), online
transactions, transaction costs, and the legal
aspects of investor protection.

LG 6 Discuss the roles of investment
advisers and investment clubs.

There are millions of Web pages devoted to stocks and investment strategies that put everything at your fingertips—literally—and most of it is free. Here are the basic steps to follow.

First, determine your investment objectives and do some initial research to identify your risk tolerance, investing style (value and growth are two of several styles), and other criteria such as your time horizon. Then visit financial portal sites such as those offered by Yahoo! (finance.yahoo.com), Morningstar.com (www.morningstar.com), and CNN/Money (money.cnn.com). They can help you familiarize yourself with stocks and what's happening currently in the markets. Explore Yahoo!, for example, and you will find current and historical company data and industry comparisons.

Because you love to dine out, you might decide to look for promising restaurant stocks. Stock screening tools at sites like Quicken (www.quicken.com) and Morningstar will narrow the field. For example, you might define search criteria such as a price/earnings (P/E) ratio of less than 35, a debt-equity ratio of less than 1.0, and above-average earnings growth. In a few seconds, you'll have a list of stocks that meet these parameters. Then, head to each company's Web site to find the latest annual report, press releases, and other material. The more detailed Securities and Exchange Commission (SEC) filings are available online as well at www.sec.gov and www.freeedgar.com. Find out what the securities analysts say. If your broker doesn't offer free research reports on your top picks, you can buy individual stock research reports at Yahoo! or Reuters Investor (www.investor.reuters.com). Now evaluate your finalists and make your decisions—that's all there is to it!

Well, it's not quite that easy! Nevertheless, the power of the Internet enables you to access information in minutes that in the past was either unavailable to the average investor or would take weeks to accumulate. In Chapter 3, you'll learn more about the many sources of investment information, both online and offline, as well as how to make transactions.

Sources: Adapted from Carol Marie Cropper, "So How Well Does the Net Trawl for Stocks?" *Business Week*, May 27, 2002, pp. 103–104; Selena Maranjian, "Researching Companies Online," *Motley Fool*, May 29, 2003, downloaded from www.fool.com; and Susan Scherreik, "How to Dig Deep with a Few Mouse Clicks," *Business Week*, May 27, 2002, p. 101.

Online Investing

LG 1

Today the Internet is a major force in the investing environment. It has opened the world of investing to individual investors, creating a more level playing field and providing access to tools formerly restricted to professionals. You can trade many types of securities online and also find a wealth of information. This information ranges from real-time stock price quotes to securities analysts' research reports and tools for investment analysis. The savings from online investing in terms of time and money are huge. Instead of wading through mounds of paper, investors can quickly sort through vast databases to find appropriate investments, monitor their current investments, and make securities transactions—all without leaving their computers.

This chapter introduces you to online investing, types and sources of investment information, and the basics of making securities transactions. We will continue discussing online investing in subsequent chapters focused on analysis and selection of various types of securities. In addition, throughout the book you will find descriptions of useful investing Web sites that will help you become a more proficient and confident investor.

Because new Web sites appear every day and existing ones change constantly, it's impossible to describe all the good ones. Our intent is to give you a sampling of Web sites that will introduce you to the wealth of investing information available on the Internet. You'll find plenty of good sources to help you stay current.

The Growth of Online Investing

Online investing's popularity continues to grow at a rapid pace. It is expected to increase from about 14.3 million Internet users investing online in 2000 to 32.4 million in 2004, a 127% increase over a 5-year period. About 25 million households manage over $1 trillion in assets online. It's easy to see why online investing attracts new investors: The Internet makes buying and selling securities convenient, relatively simple, inexpensive, and fast. In today's rapidly changing stock markets, it provides the most current information, updated continuously. Even if you prefer to use a human broker, the Internet provides an abundance of resources to help you become a more informed investor.

To successfully navigate the cyberinvesting universe, open your Web browser and explore the multitude of investing sites. These sites typically include a combination of resources for novice and sophisticated investors alike. For example, look at brokerage firm TD Waterhouse's homepage (www.tdwaterhouse.com), shown in Figure 3.1 (on page 78). With a few mouse clicks you can learn about TD Waterhouse's services, open an account, and begin trading. In addition, you will find the day's and week's market activity, price quotes, news, analysts' research reports, and more. You can learn about various aspects of investing, including products, and make banking transactions through the TD Waterhouse Bank.

All this information can be overwhelming and intimidating. It takes time and effort to use the Internet wisely. But the Internet itself helps you sort through the maze. Educational sites are a good place to start. Then you can check out the many investment tools. In the following section, we'll discuss how to use the Internet wisely to become a smarter investor.

FIGURE 3.1

Investment Resources at the TD Waterhouse Web Site

TD Waterhouse's Web site presents a wealth of investment resources. You can open an account, assess market activity, obtain news, access analysts' research, and more. (*Source:* TD Waterhouse Investor Services, Inc., New York, www.tdwaterhouse.com.)

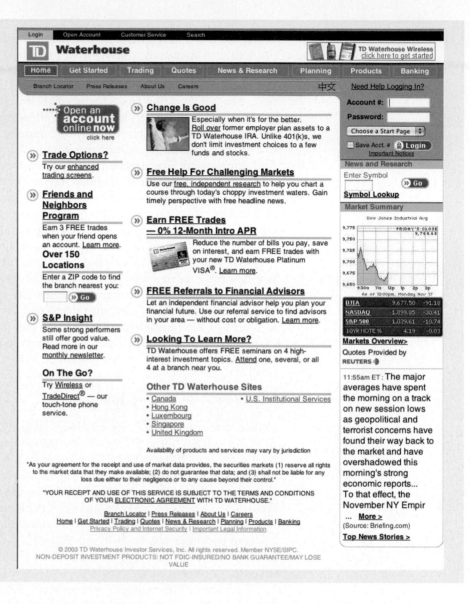

Investment Education Sites The Internet offers many tutorials, online classes, and articles to educate the novice investor. Even experienced investors will find sites that expand their investing knowledge. Although most investing-oriented Web sites and financial portals (described later) include many educational resources, here are a few good sites that feature investing fundamentals.

- *Investing Online Resource Center* (www.investingonline.org) is an educational site that provides a wealth of information for those getting started online as well as those already investing online. It includes an investment simulator that creates an online interactive learning experience that allows the user to "test drive" online trading.

- *Investor Guide.com* (www.investorguide.com) is a free educational site offering Investor Guide University, which is a collection of educational articles about investing and personal finance. In addition, the site provides access to quotes and charts, portfolio tracking software, research, news and commentary, and a glossary through Investor Words.com (www.investorwords.com).

- *The Motley Fool* (www.fool.com) has sections on investing basics, mutual fund investing, choosing a broker, and investment strategies and styles, as well as lively discussion boards and more.

- Investopedia (www.investopedia.com) is an educational site featuring tutorials on numerous basic and advanced investing and personal finance topics, a glossary of investing terms, and other useful investment aids.

- *WSJ.com* (www.wsj.com), a free site from the *Wall Street Journal,* is an excellent starting place to learn what the Internet can offer investors.

- Nasdaq (www.nasdaq.com) has an Education Initiatives section that provides links to a number of investment education resources.

Other good educational sites include leading personal finance magazines such as *Money* (money.cnn.com), *Kiplinger's Personal Finance Magazine* (www. kiplinger.com), and *Smart Money* (www.smartmoney.com).

Investment Tools Once you are familiar with investing basics, you can use the Internet to develop financial plans and set investment goals, find securities that meet your objectives, analyze potential investments, and organize your portfolio. Many of these tools, once used only by professional investment advisers, are free online. You'll find financial calculators and worksheets, screening and charting tools, and stock quotes and portfolio trackers at general financial sites (described in the later section on financial portals) and at the Web sites of larger brokerage firms. You can even set up a personal calendar that notifies you of forthcoming earnings announcements and can receive alerts when one of your stocks has hit a predetermined price target.

H O T

See NAIC, a not-for-profit organization site, for investment education of individuals and investment clubs.

www.better-investing.org

Planning Online calculators and worksheets help you find answers to your financial planning and investing questions. With them you can figure out how much to save each month for a particular goal, such as the down payment for your first home, a college education for your children, or retiring when you are 60. For example, the brokerage firm Fidelity (www.fidelity.com) has a wide selection of planning tools: life events, financial goals, retirement planning, estate planning, and college planning. It also makes a number of interactive tools and calculators available for use in investment planning, retirement, estate planing, college, tax, and annuity and life insurance. (Because not all calculators give the same answer, you may want to try out those at several sites.)

One of the best sites for financial calculators is FinanCenter.com (www.financenter.com). It includes over 140 calculators for financial planning, insurance, auto and home buying, and investing. Figure 3.2 (on page 80) lists, in question form, the 9 calculators specifically concerned with stocks. Other investment-related calculators focus on bonds, mutual funds, and retirement.

Screening With screening tools, you can quickly sort through huge databases of stocks, bonds, and mutual funds to find those that have specific characteristics. For stocks, you can specify low or high price/earnings ratios, small market

Financial Calculators Concerned with Stocks

At sites like FinanCenter, you'll find many calculators that can be used to solve specific problems. Below is the screen listing, in question form, of the 9 investment-related stock calculators available at FinanCenter. Input the variables for your situation, and the calculator will show you the selling price at which you will earn the desired return on your stock investment. (Source: FinanCenter, www.financenter.com/products/calculators/stock. Screenshot courtesy of FinanCenter. ©2003 FinanCenter)

value, high dividend return, specific revenue growth, and/or a low debt-to-equity ratio. For bonds, you can specify a given industry, maturity date, or yield. For mutual funds, you might specify low minimum investment, a particular industry or geographical sector, and low fees. Each screening tool uses a different method to sort. You answer a series of questions to specify the type of stock or fund, performance criteria, cost parameters, and so on. Then you can do more research on the stocks, bonds, or mutual funds that meet your requirements.

Quicken.com (www.quicken.com/investments) provides online brokerage and has some of the best free tools. Figure 3.3 shows the opening page for Quicken's "Brokerage Stock Search" screen that lists searches based on the most popular investment strategies. The full search lets you select industry, valuation, growth rates, analyst estimates, financial strength, and similar qualities. Morningstar (www.morningstar.com) offers some free tools but charges $11.95 a month or $109 a year for its premium tools. Wall Street City (www.wallstreetcity.com) offers some of the best screening tools. You can check out the site's prebuilt search strategies free—for example, "stocks with reversal potential" and "strong stocks/recently weak." More experienced investors can subscribe to its Wall Street City Pro for $9.95 a month and gain access to its ProSearch screening tool, which allows the creation of customized stock screens with over 300 criteria.

Charting *Charting* is a technique that plots the performance of stocks over a specified time period, from months to decades and beyond. Looking at the

FIGURE 3.3

Quicken's Brokerage Stock Search Tool

Search for stocks based on popular investment strategies. The full search allows selection from a list of variables, such as industry, valuation, growth rates, analyst estimates, financial strength, and similar qualities. Quicken's stock screening tool will give you a list of stocks that meet your specifications. (*Source:* Quicken.com, www.quicken.com/investments/stocks/search/popular/. Screenshot courtesy of Intuit. Copyright ©2003 Intuit.)

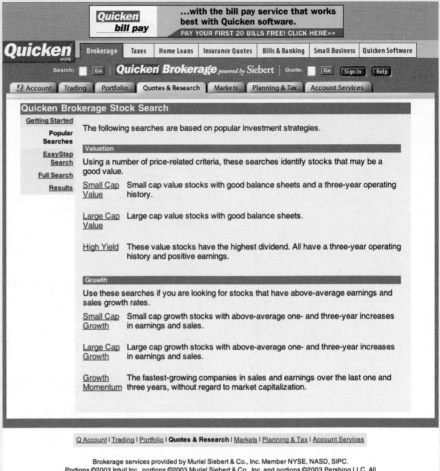

1-year stock chart for Qualcomm (QCOM) in Figure 3.4 (on page 82), it's obvious that charting can be tedious and expensive. But by going online, today you can see the chart for a selected stock in just seconds. With another click you can compare one company's price performance to that of other stocks, industries, sectors, or market indexes, choosing the type of chart, time frame, and indicators. Several good sites are Barchart.com (www.barchart.com), BigCharts (bigcharts.marketwatch.com), and Stock Charts (www.stockcharts.com). All have free charting features; Barchart.com charges a monthly fee for advanced capabilities. Another popular free site that offers good charting capabilities is Silicon Investor (siliconinvestor.com).

Stock Quotes and Portfolio Tracking Almost every investment-oriented Web site includes stock quotation and portfolio tracking tools. Simply enter the stock symbol to get the price, either in real time or delayed several minutes.

FIGURE 3.4

Stock Chart for Qualcomm

Specify the company's time frame and frequency (e.g., daily, weekly), and BigCharts will in seconds perform the tedious process of charting the selected stock's price (in this case, the price of Qualcomm) over the specified time frame (in this case, the year ended November 17, 2003). (*Source:* BigCharts Inc. is a service of MarketWatch.com, Inc., 825 Battery Street, San Francisco, CA 94111. bigcharts.marketwatch.com.)

Once you create a portfolio of stocks in a portfolio tracker, the tracker automatically updates your portfolio's value every time you check. You can usually link to more detailed information about each stock. Many sites let you set up multiple portfolios. The features, quality, and ease of use of stock and portfolio trackers varies, so check several to find the one that best meets your needs. Quicken.com/investments, MSN Money Investing (moneycentral.msn.com/investor), and E*Trade (www.etrade.com) have portfolio trackers that are easy to set up and customize.

Pros and Cons of Using the Internet as an Investment Tool

The power of the Internet as an investing tool is alluring. "Do-it-yourself" investing is readily available to the average investor, even novices who have never before bought stock. However, online investing also carries risks. Trading on the Internet requires that investors exercise the same—and possibly more—caution than they would if they were getting information from and placing orders with a human broker. You don't have the safety net of a live broker suggesting that you rethink your trade. The ease of point-and-click investing can be the financial downfall of inexperienced investors. Drawn by stories of others who have made lots of money, many novice investors take the plunge before they acquire the necessary skills and knowledge—often with disastrous results.

Online or off, the basic rules for smart investing are the same. Know what you are buying, from whom, and at what level of risk. Be skeptical. If it sounds too good to be true, it probably is! Always do your own research; don't accept someone else's word that a security is a good buy. Perform your own analysis before you buy, using the skills you will develop in later chapters of this book. Here is some additional advice:

- Don't let the speed and ease of making transactions blind you to the realities of online trading. More frequent trades mean high total transaction costs. Although some brokers advertise per-trade costs as low as $7, the average online transaction fee is higher (generally about $15 to $20). If you trade often, it will take longer to recoup your costs. Studies reveal that the more often you trade, the harder it is to beat the market. In addition, on short-term trades of less than one year, you'll pay taxes on profits at the higher, ordinary income tax rates, not the lower capital gains rate.

- Don't believe everything you read on the Internet. It's easy to be impressed with a screen full of data touting a stock's prospects or to act on a hot tip you find on a discussion board or in an online chat (more on this later). But what do you know about the person who posts the information? He or she could be a shill for a dealer, posing as an enthusiastic investor to push a stock. Stick to the sites of major brokerage firms, mutual funds, academic institutions, and well-known business and finance publications.

- If you get bitten by the online buying bug, don't be tempted to use margin debt to increase your stock holdings. You may instead be magnifying your losses, as noted in Chapter 2.

We will return to the subject of online investment fraud and scams and will discuss guidelines for online transactions in subsequent sections of this chapter.

IN REVIEW

CONCEPTS

3.1 Discuss the impact of the Internet on the individual investor, and summarize the types of resources it provides.

3.2 Identify the four main types of online investment tools. How can they help you become a better investor?

3.3 What are some of the pros and cons of using the Internet to choose and manage your investments?

Types and Sources of Investment Information

LG 2

As you learned in Chapter 1, becoming a successful investor starts with developing investment plans and meeting your liquidity needs. Once you have done that, you can search for the right investments to implement your investment plan and monitor your progress toward achieving your goals. Whether you use the Internet or print sources, you should examine various kinds of investment information to formulate expectations of the risk–return behaviors of potential investments and to monitor them once they are acquired. This section

descriptive information
factual data on the past behavior of the economy, the market, the industry, the company, or a given investment vehicle.

analytical information
available current data in conjunction with projections and recommendations about potential investments.

describes the key types and sources of investment information; the following section focuses on market averages and indexes.

Investment information can be either descriptive or analytical. **Descriptive information** presents factual data on the past behavior of the economy, the market, the industry, the company, or a given investment vehicle. **Analytical information** presents available current data in conjunction with projections and recommendations about potential investments. The sample page from *Value Line* included in Figure 3.5 provides both descriptive and analytical information on Wal-Mart Stores. Items that are primarily descriptive are marked with a D, analytical items with an A. Examples of descriptive information are the company's capital structure (7D) and monthly stock price ranges for the past 13 years (13D). Examples of analytical information are rank for timeliness (1A) and projected price range and associated annual total returns for the next 3 years (4A).

Some forms of investment information are free; others must be purchased individually or by annual subscription. You'll find free information on the Internet; in newspapers, in magazines, and at brokerage firms; and at public, university, and brokerage firm libraries. Alternatively, you can subscribe to free and paid services that provide periodic reports summarizing the investment outlook and recommending certain actions. Many Internet sites now offer free e-mail newsletters and alerts. You can even set up your own personalized home page at many financial Web sites so that stock quotes, portfolio tracking, current business news, and other information on stocks of interest to you appear whenever you visit the site. Other sites charge for premium content, such as brokerage research reports, whether in print or online form.

Although the Internet has increased the amount of free information, it may still make sense to pay for services that save you time and money by gathering material you need. But first consider the value of potential information: For example, paying $40 for information that increases your return by $27 would not be economically sound. The larger your investment portfolio, the easier it is to justify information purchases, because they are usually applicable to a number of investments.

Types of Information

Investment information can be divided into five types, each concerned with an important aspect of the investment process.

1. *Economic and current event information* includes background as well as forecast data related to economic, political, and social trends on a domestic as well as a global scale. Such information provides a basis for assessing the environment in which decisions are made.
2. *Industry and company information* includes background as well as forecast data on specific industries and companies. Investors use such information to assess the outlook in a given industry or a specific company. Because of its company orientation, it is most relevant to stock, bond, or options investments.
3. *Information on alternative investment vehicles* includes background and predictive data for securities other than stocks, bonds, and options, such as mutual funds and futures.

FIGURE 3.5 **A Report Containing Descriptive and Analytical Information**

Value Line's full-page report on Wal-Mart Stores from November 14, 2003, contains both descriptive (marked D) and analytical (marked A) information. (*Source:* Adapted from *The Value Line Investment Survey,* Ratings and Reports, November 14, 2003. ©Value Line Publishing, Inc., www.valueline.com. © 2003 Reproduced with the permission of Value Line Publishing, Inc.)

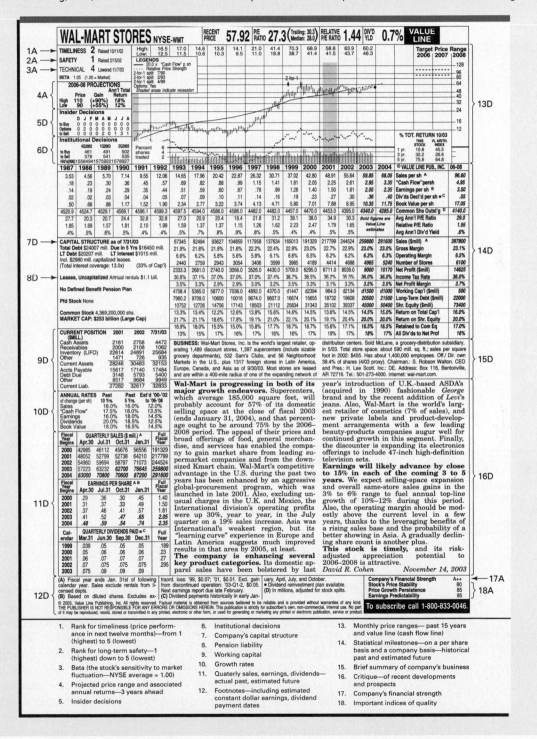

4. *Price information* includes current price quotations on certain investment vehicles, particularly securities. These quotations are commonly accompanied by statistics on the recent price behavior of the vehicle.

5. *Information on personal investment strategies* includes recommendations on investment strategies or specific purchase or sale actions. In general, this information tends to be educational or analytical rather than descriptive.

Sources of Information

A complete listing of the sources of each type of investment information is beyond the scope of this book. Our discussion focuses on the most common online and traditional sources of information on economic and current events, industries and companies, and prices, as well as other online sources.

Economic and Current Event Information   Investors who are aware of current economic, political, and business events tend to make better investment decisions. Popular sources of economic and current event information include financial journals, general newspapers, institutional news, business periodicals, government publications, and special subscription services. These are available in print and online versions; often the online versions are free but may have limited content. Most offer free searchable article archives and charge a nominal fee for each article downloaded.

Wall Street Journal
a daily business newspaper, published regionally; the most popular source of financial news.

Financial Journals   The *Wall Street Journal* is the most popular source of financial news. Published daily Monday through Friday in regional, European, and Asian editions, the *Journal* also has an online version called the *WSJ Online* (www.wsj.com), which is updated frequently throughout the day and on the weekends. In addition to giving daily price quotations on thousands of investment vehicles, it reports world, national, regional, and corporate news. The first page of the third section of the *Journal* usually contains a column called "Heard on the Street" that focuses on specific market and company events. In addition, a fourth section containing articles that address personal finance issues and topics is included in the Tuesday, Wednesday, and Thursday editions, and an Expanded version of that section, called "Weekend Journal," is included in Friday's edition. A print subscription to the *Wall Street Journal* costs $189 annually, compared to $79 per year for the online version; print subscribers pay $39 to add the online edition. *WSJ Online* includes features such as quotes and news that provides stock and mutual fund charting, company profiles, financials, and analyst ratings; article searches; special online-only articles; and access to the Dow Jones article archives.

HOT

Federal Reserve Economic Data (FRED) has a historical database of economic and financial statistics.

www.research.stlouisfed.org/fred2/

Barron's
a weekly business newspaper; a popular source of financial news.

A second popular source of financial news is *Barron's,* which is published weekly. *Barron's* generally offers lengthier articles on a variety of topics of interest to individual investors. Probably the most popular column in *Barron's* is "Up & Down Wall Street," which provides a critical and often humorous assessment of major developments affecting the stock market and business. *Barron's* also includes current price quotations and a summary of statistics on a range of investment vehicles. Subscribers to *WSJ Online* also have access to *Barron's* online edition (www.barrons.com) because both are published by Dow Jones & Company.

Investor's Business Daily is a third national business newspaper published Monday through Friday. It is similar to the *Wall Street Journal* but contains more detailed price and market data. Its Web site (www.investors.com) has limited free content. Another source of financial news is the *Financial Times* (www.ft.com), with U.S., U.K., European, and Asian editions.

General Newspapers Major metropolitan newspapers such as the *New York Times, Washington Post, Los Angeles Times,* and *Chicago Tribune* provide investors with a wealth of financial information in their print and online editions. Most major newspapers contain stock price quotations for major exchanges, price quotations on stocks of local interest, and a summary of the major stock market averages and indexes. Local newspapers are another convenient source of financial news. In most large cities, the daily newspaper devotes at least a few pages to financial and business news. Another popular source of financial news is *USA Today,* the national newspaper published daily Monday through Friday. It is available in print and online versions (usatoday.com). Each issue contains a "Money" section (Section B) devoted to business and personal financial news and to current security price quotations and summary statistics.

Institutional News The monthly economic letters of the nation's leading banks, such as Bank of America (based in Charlotte, North Carolina), Northern Trust (Chicago), and Wells Fargo (San Francisco), provide useful economic information. Wire services such as Dow Jones, Bloomberg Financial Services, AP (Associated Press), and UPI (United Press International) provide economic and business news feeds to brokerages, other financial institutions, and Web sites that subscribe to them. Bloomberg has its own comprehensive site (www.bloomberg.com). Business.com (www.business.com) offers industry-by-industry news, targeted business searches, and employment resources by industry. Web sites specializing in financial news include CNNMoney (money.cnn.com) and CBS MarketWatch (cbs.marketwatch.com).

Business Periodicals Business periodicals vary in scope. Some present general business and economic articles, others cover securities markets and related topics, and still others focus solely on specific industries. Regardless of the subject matter, most business periodicals present descriptive information, and some also include analytical information. They rarely offer recommendations.

The business sections of general-interest periodicals such as *Newsweek, Time,* and *U.S. News & World Report* cover business and economic news. Strictly business- and finance-oriented periodicals, including *Business Week, Fortune,* and *The Economist,* provide more in-depth articles. These magazines also have investing and personal finance articles.

Some financial periodicals specialize in securities and marketplace articles. The most basic, commonsense articles appear in *Forbes, Kiplinger's Personal Finance, Money, SmartMoney,* and *Worth. Forbes,* published every two weeks, is the most investment-oriented. *Kiplinger's Personal Finance, Money, SmartMoney,* and *Worth* are published monthly and contain articles on managing personal finances and on investments.

All these business and personal finance magazines have Web sites with free access to recent, if not all, content. Most include a number of other features. For example, *SmartMoney* has interactive investment tools, including a color-coded "Market Map 1000" that gives an aerial view of 1,000 U.S. and international stocks so that you can see which sectors and stocks are hot.

Government Publications A number of government agencies publish economic data and reports useful to investors. The annual *Economic Report of the President* (w3.access.gpo.gov/eop/) provides a broad view of the current and expected state of the economy. This document reviews and summarizes economic policy and conditions and includes data on important aspects of the economy. The *Federal Reserve Bulletin*, published monthly by the Board of Governors of the Federal Reserve System, and periodic reports published by each of the 12 Federal Reserve District Banks provide articles and data on various aspects of economic and business activity. (Visit www .federalreserve.gov to read many of these publications.) A useful Department of Commerce publication is the *Survey of Current Business* (www .bea.doc.gov/bea/pubs.htm). Published monthly, it includes indicators and data related to economic and business conditions. A good source of financial statement information on all manufacturers, broken down by industry and asset size, is the *Quarterly Financial Report for U.S. Manufacturing, Mining, and Trade Corporations* (www.census.gov/csd/qfr/view/qfr_mg.html), published by the Department of Commerce.

Special Subscription Services Investors who want additional insights into business and economic conditions can subscribe to special services. These reports include business and economic forecasts and give notice of new government policies, union plans and tactics, taxes, prices, wages, and so on. One popular service is the *Kiplinger Washington Letter,* a weekly publication that provides a wealth of economic information and analyses.

Industry and Company Information Of special interest to investors is information on particular industries and companies. Often, after choosing an industry in which to invest, an investor will want to analyze specific companies. A recent change in disclosure rules, discussed below, gives individual investors access to more company information than before. General business periodicals such as *Business Week, Forbes,* the *Wall Street Journal,* and *Fortune* carry articles on the activities of specific industries and individual companies. Trade publications such as *Chemical Week, American Banker, Computerworld, Industry Week, Oil and Gas Journal,* and *Public Utilities Fortnightly* provide more focused industry and company information. *Red Herring, PC Magazine, Business 2.0,* and *Fast Company* are magazines that can help you keep up with the high-tech world; all have good Web sites.

The Internet makes it easy to research specific industries and companies at the company's Web site, a publication's archive search, or database services such as the Dow Jones Publications Library. Company Web sites typically offer a wealth of information about the company, investor information—annual reports, filings, and financial releases, press releases, and more. Table 3.1 presents several free and subscription resources that emphasize industry and company information.

fair disclosure rule (Regulation FD)
rule requiring senior executives to disclose critical information simultaneously to investment professionals and the public via press releases or SEC filings.

Fair Disclosure Rules In August 2000, the SEC passed the **fair disclosure rule,** known as **Regulation FD,** a rule requiring senior executives to disclose

TABLE 3.1 Online Sources for Industry and Company Information

Web Site	Description	Cost
Hoover's Online (www.hoovers.com)	Reports and news on public and private companies with in-depth coverage of 21,000 of the world's top firms	$400 per year for individual accounts.
CNET (news.com.com)	One of the best sites for high-tech news, analysis, breaking news, great search capabilities, links.	Free.
Yahoo! Finance (finance.yahoo.com)	Provides information on companies from around the Web: stock quotes, news, investment ideas, research, financials, analyst ratings, insider trades, and more.	Free.
News Alert (www.newsalert.com)	Latest company news from various wire services. Searchable by industry or company. Good for earnings announcements and tech news.	Free.

critical information such as earnings forecasts and news of mergers and new products simultaneously to investment professionals and the public via press releases or SEC filings. Companies may limit contact with analysts if they are unsure whether the information requires a press release. However, Regulation FD does not apply to communications with journalists and securities ratings firms like Moody's Investor Service and Standard & Poor's. Violations of the rule carry injunctions and fines but are not considered fraud.

Stockholders' Reports An excellent source of data on an individual firm is the **stockholders' report,** or **annual report,** published yearly by publicly held corporations. These reports contain a wide range of information, including financial statements for the most recent period of operation, along with summarized statements for several prior years. These reports are free and may be obtained from the companies themselves, from brokers, or downloaded from the company's Web site. A sample page from Wal-Mart Stores, Inc. 2003 stockholders' report is shown in Figure 3.6 (on page 90). Most companies now place their annual reports on their Web sites. Report Gallery (www. reportgallery.com) provides links to more than 2,000 company reports.

In addition to the stockholders' report, many serious investors review a company's **Form 10-K.** This is a statement that firms with securities listed on an organized exchange or traded in the Nasdaq market must file annually with the SEC. Finding 10-K and other SEC filings is now a simple task, thanks to SEC/Edgar (Electronic Data Gathering and Analysis Retrieval), which has reports filed by all companies traded on a major exchange. You can read them free either at the SEC's Web site (www.sec.gov/edgar.shtml) or at EDGAR Online's FreeEdgar site (www.freeedgar.com).

Comparative Data Sources Sources of comparative data, typically broken down by industry and firm size, are a good tool for analyzing the financial condition of companies. Among these sources are Dun & Bradstreet's *Key Business Ratios,* Robert Morris and Associates' *Annual Statement Studies,* the *Quarterly Financial Report for U.S. Manufacturing, Mining, and Trade Corporations* (cited above), and the *Almanac of Business and Industrial*

stockholders' (annual) report
a report published yearly by a publicly held corporation; contains a wide range of information, including financial statements for the most recent period of operation.

Form 10-K
a statement that must be filed annually with the SEC by all firms having securities listed on an organized exchange or traded in the Nasdaq market.

FIGURE 3.6 Pages from a Stockholders' Report

The "Financial Highlights" on the right-hand page from the 2003 Annual Report of Wal-Mart Stores, Inc., quickly acquaints the investor with some key information on the firm's operations over the past year. The contents of the Annual Report are also shown. The actual Annual Report is available at Wal-Mart's Web site www.walmart.com. (*Source:* Wal-Mart Stores, Inc. 2003 Annual Report; Wal-Mart Stores, Inc., Investor Relations, 479-273-8446, Wal-Mart Stores, Inc., Bentonville, AR 72716-8611.)

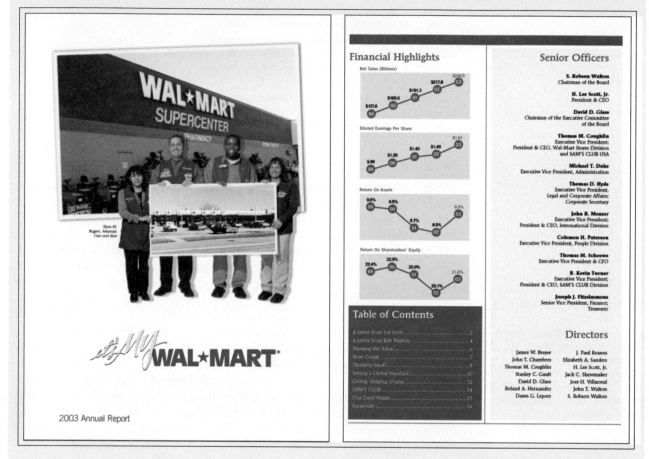

Financial Ratios. These sources, which are typically available in public and university libraries, are a useful benchmark for evaluating a company's financial condition.

Subscription Services A variety of subscription services provide data on specific industries and companies. Today, many of these services are available on the Internet. Generally, a subscriber pays a basic fee to access the service's information and can purchase premium services for greater depth or range. The major subscription services provide both descriptive and analytical information, but they generally do not make recommendations. Most investors, rather than subscribing to these services, access them through their stockbrokers or a large public or university library. The Web sites for most services offer some free information and charge for the rest.

TABLE 3.2	Popular Offerings of the Major Subscription Services	
Subscription Service/Offerings	Coverage	Frequency of Publication
Standard & Poor's Corporation (www.standardandpoors.com)		
Corporation Records	Detailed descriptions of publicly traded securities of over 12,000 public corporations.	Annually with updates throughout the year.
Stock Reports (sample shown in Figure 7.1, page 315)	Summary of financial history, current finances, and future prospects of about 5,000 companies.	Annually with updates throughout the year.
Stock Guide	Statistical data and analytical rankings of investment desirability for major stocks.	Monthly.
Bond Guide	Statistical data and analytical rankings of investment desirability of over 10,000 bonds.	Monthly.
The Outlook	Analytical articles with investment advice on the market, industries, and securities.	Weekly magazine.
Mergent (www.mergent.com)		
Mergent's Manuals	Eight reference manuals—*Bank and Finance, Industrial, International, Municipal and Government, OTC Industrial, OTC Unlisted, Public Utility,* and *Transportation*—with historical and current financial, organizational, and operational data on major firms.	Annually with monthly print updates (weekly online updates).
Handbook of Common Stocks	Common stock data.	Quarterly.
Dividend Record	Recent dividend announcements and payments.	Twice weekly, with annual summary.
Bond Record	Price and interest rate behavior of over 68,000 issues.	Monthly.
Value Line Investment Survey (www.valueline.com)		
Includes three reports:	A 40-page update listing about 1,700 of the most widely held stocks.	Weekly.
1. *Summary and Index*	Current ratings for each of the about 1,700 stocks.	
2. *Selection and Opinion*	A 12- to 16-page report featuring sample portfolios for different types of investors.	
3. *Ratings and Reports* (sample shown in Figure 3.5)	Full-page report including financial data, descriptions, analysis, and ratings for each of about 130 stocks.	

Standard & Poor's Corporation (S&P)
publisher of a large number of financial reports and services, including *Corporation Records* and *Stock Reports.*

Mergent
publisher of a variety of financial material, including *Mergent's Manuals.*

Value Line Investment Survey
one of the most popular subscription services used by individual investors; subscribers receive three basic reports weekly.

The dominant subscription services are those offered by Standard & Poor's, Mergent, and Value Line. Table 3.2 summarizes the most popular services of these companies. **Standard & Poor's Corporation (S&P)** (www. standardandpoors.com) offers a large number of different financial reports and services. Its Investing Web site, owned by *Business Week* (www. businessweek.com/investor), is geared toward individual investors. Although basic news and market commentary is free, *Business Week* subscribers obtain access to premium online services. **Mergent** (formerly Moody's Financial Information Services Division) (www.mergent.com) also publishes a variety of material, including its equity and bond portraits, corporate research, well-known reference manuals on eight industries, and numerous other products. The *Value Line Investment Survey* (www.valueline.com) is one of the most popular subscription services used by individual investors; it is available at most libraries and provides online access to additional services including data, graphing, portfolio tracking, and technical indicators.

Brokerage Reports Brokerage firms often make available to their clients reports from the various subscription services and research reports from their own securities analysts. They also provide clients with prospectuses for new security issues and *back-office research reports*. As noted in Chapter 2, a *prospectus* is a document that describes in detail the key aspects of the issue, the issuer, and its management and financial position. The cover of the preliminary prospectus describing the 2003 stock issue of Hewitt Associates, Inc., was shown in Figure 2.1 (on page 38). **Back-office research reports** include the brokerage firm's analyses of and recommendations on prospects for the securities markets, specific industries, or specific securities. Usually a brokerage firm publishes lists of securities classified by its research staff as either "buy," "hold," or "sell." Brokerage research reports are available on request at no cost to existing and potential clients.

Securities analysts' reports are now available on the Web, either from brokerage sites or from sites that consolidate research from many brokerages. At Multex Investor (www.multexinvestor.com), a leading research site, over 1.5 million reports on companies and industries from over 700 brokerage and research firms cost from zero to $150 each. Investors can use Zacks's (www.zacks.com) Brokerage Research Report Service to find and purchase reports from 3,200 analysts on 7,500 companies for $10 to $150 per report or to read free brokerage report abstracts with earnings revisions and recommendations.

back-office research reports
a brokerage firm's analyses of and recommendations on investment prospects; available on request at no cost to existing and potential clients or for purchase at some Web sites.

Investment Letters **Investment letters** are newsletters that provide, on a subscription basis, the analyses, conclusions, and recommendations of experts in securities investment. Some letters concentrate on specific types of securities; others are concerned solely with assessing the economy or securities markets. Among the more popular investment letters are *Blue Chip Advisor, Dick Davis Digest, The Dines Letter, Dow Theory Letters,* the *Growth Stock Outlook, Louis Rukeyser's Wall Street,* the *Prudent Speculator,* and *Zacks Advisor.* Most investment letters come out weekly or monthly and cost from $75 to $400 a year. Advertisements for many of these investment letters can be found in *Barron's* and in various business periodicals.

The *Hulbert Financial Digest* (cbs.marketwatch.com/hulbert) monitors the performance of investment letters. It is an excellent source of objective information on investment letters and a good place to check out those that interest you. Many investment letters now offer online subscriptions. Use a general search engine or Newsletter Access (www.newsletteraccess.com), a searchable database of newsletters that lists over 900 stock-investing newsletters!

investment letters
newsletters that provide, on a subscription basis, the analyses, conclusions, and recommendations of experts in securities investment.

Price Information Price information about various types of securities is contained in their **quotations**, which include current price data and statistics on recent price behavior. The Web makes it easy to find price quotes for actively traded securities, and many financially oriented sites include a stock price look-up feature or a stock ticker running across the screen, much like the ones that used to be found only in brokerage offices. The ticker consolidates and reports stock transactions made on the NYSE, AMEX, regional exchanges, and Nasdaq National Market as they occur. Cable TV subscribers in many areas can watch the ticker at the bottom of the screen on certain channels, including CNNfn, CNN Headline News, and MSNBC. The ticker symbols for some well-known companies are listed in Table 3.3.

quotations
price information about various types of securities, including current price data and statistics on recent price behavior.

TABLE 3.3   Symbols for Some Well-Known Companies

Company	Symbol	Company	Symbol
Amazon.com	AMZN	Microsoft	MSFT
Apple Computer	AAPL	Merrill Lynch	MER
AT&T	T	Nike	NKE
Cisco	CSCO	Oracle	ORCL
Dell	DELL	PepsiCo, Inc.	PEP
Eastman Kodak	EK	Reebok	RBK
ExxonMobil	XOM	Sears, Roebuck	S
Genentech	DNA	Starbucks	SBUX
General Electric	GE	Sun Microsystems	SUNW
Hewlett-Packard	HPQ	Texas Instruments	TXN
Intel	INTC	Time Warner	TWX
Int'l. Business Machines	IBM	United Parcel Service	UPS
Lucent Technologies	LU	Wal-Mart Stores	WMT
McDonald's Corporation	MCD	Yahoo!	YHOO

Investors can easily find the prior day's security price quotations in the published news media, both nonfinancial and financial. They also can find delayed or real-time quotations for free at numerous Web sites, including *financial portals* (described below), most business periodical Web sites, and brokerage sites. The Web sites for CNNfn and CNBC TV have real-time stock quotes, as do sites that subscribe to their news feed.

The major published source of security price quotations is the *Wall Street Journal,* which presents quotations for each previous business day's activities in all major markets. (We'll explain how to read and interpret actual price quotations in later chapters.)

Other Online Investment Information Sources Many other excellent Web sites provide information of all sorts to increase your investment skills and knowledge. Let's now look at financial portals, sites for bonds and mutual funds, international sites, and investment discussion forums. Table 3.4 (on page 94) lists some of the most popular financial portals, bond sites, and mutual fund sites. We'll look at online brokerage and investment adviser sites later in the chapter, and you'll find more specialized Web links in all chapters.

Financial Portals **Financial portals** are supersites that bring together a wide range of investing features, such as real-time quotes, stock and mutual fund screens, portfolio trackers, news, research, and transaction capabilities, along with other personal finance features. These sites want to be your investing home page. Some portals are general sites such as Yahoo! and Excite that offer a full range of investing features along with their other services, or they may be investing-oriented sites. You should check out several to see which best suits your needs, because their strengths and features vary greatly. Some portals, to motivate you to stay at their site, offer customization options so that your start page includes the data you want. Although finding one site where you can manage your investments is indeed appealing, you may not be able to find the

financial portals
supersites on the Web that bring together a wide range of investing features, such as real-time quotes, stock and mutual fund screens, portfolio trackers, news, research, and transaction capabilities, along with other personal finance features.

H O T

Superstar Investor provides descriptive summaries and more than 20,000 links to the best investing sites on the Internet. The Investsearch Directory guide for Online investing provides basic contact information for over 60,000 services and products of interest to investors and traders.

www.superstarinvestor.com
www.wallstreetdex.com

TABLE 3.4   **Popular Investment Web Sites**

The following Web sites are just a few of the thousands of sites that provide investing information. Unless otherwise mentioned, all are free.

Web Site	Description
Financial Portals	
America Online (proprietary portal)	Subscriber-only Personal Finance channel includes areas for business news, market and stock quotes, stocks, mutual funds, investment research, retirement, saving and planning, credit and debt, banking and loans, and more. Each area offers education, tools, and message boards. Ease of use is a big plus.
Excite (www.excite.com)	Offers an investing channel that provides news, market data, and research capabilities along with a variety of links for tracking stocks, portfolios, screening stocks, participating in conference calls, and obtaining SEC filings.
MSN MoneyCentral Investor (www.moneycentral.msn.com)	More editorial content than many sites; good research and interactive tools like Research Wizard; can consolidate accounts in portfolio tracker. (Many tools don't run on Macintosh.)
Motley Fool (www.fool.com)	Comprehensive and entertaining site with educational features, research, news, and message boards. Model portfolios cover a variety of investment strategies. Free but offers premium services such as Portfolio Trade Alerts for $25 a year.
Yahoo! Finance (http://finance.yahoo.com)	Simple design, content-rich; easy to find information quickly. Includes financial news, price quotes, portfolio trackers, bill paying, personalized home page, and a directory of other major sites.
Yodlee (www.yodlee.com)	Aggregation site that collects financial account data from banking, credit card, brokerage, mutual fund, mileage, and other sites. One-click access saves time and enables users to manage and interact with their accounts; offers e-mail accounts; easy to set up and track finances. Security issues concern potential users; few analytical tools.
Bond Sites	
Investing in Bonds (www.investinginbonds.com)	The Bond Market Association's Web site; good for novice investors. Investing guides, research reports, historical data, and links to other sites. Searchable database.
BondsOnline (www.bondsonline.com)	Comprehensive site for news, education, free research, ratings, and other bond information; strong emphasis on municipal bonds. Searchable database; Some charges for research.
CNNMoney Bonds & Rates (www.money.com/markets/bondcenter)	Individual investors can search for bond-related news, market data, and bond offerings.
Bureau of the Public Debt Online (www.publicdebt.treas.gov)	Run by U.S. Treasury Department; information about U.S. savings bonds and Treasury securities; can also buy Treasury securities online through Treasury Direct program.
Mutual Fund Sites	
Morningstar (www.morningstar.com)	Profiles of over 3,000 funds with ratings; screening tools, portfolio analysis and management; fund manager interviews, e-mail newsletters; educational sections. Advanced screening and analysis tools are $11.95 a month or $109 per year.
Mutual Fund Investor's Center (www.mfea.com)	Not-for-profit, easy-to-navigate site from the Mutual Fund Education Alliance with investor education, search feature, and links to profiles of funds, calculators for retirement, asset allocation, and college planning.
Fund Alarm (www.fundalarm.com)	Takes a different approach and identifies underperforming funds to help investors decide when to sell; alerts investors to fund manager changes. Lively commentary from the site founder, a CPA.
MAXfunds (www.maxfunds.com)	Offers several custom metrics and data points to help find the best funds and give investors tools other than past performance to choose funds. Covers more funds than any other on- or offline publication. MAXadvisor, a premium advisory service, costs $59.95 per year.
IndexFunds.com (www.indexfunds.com)	Comprehensive site covering only index funds.
Personal Fund (www.personalfund.com)	Especially popular for its fund cost calculator that shows the true cost of ownership, after fees, brokerage commissions, and taxes. Suggests lower-cost alternatives with similar investment objectives.

best of what you need at one portal. You'll want to explore several sites to find the ones that meet your needs. Table 3.4 includes a summary of the features of several popular financial portals.

Bond Sites Although many general investment sites include bond and mutual fund information, you can also visit sites that specialize in these investments. Because Internet bond-trading activity is fairly limited at the present time, there are fewer online resources for individuals. Some brokerage firms are starting to allow clients access to bond information that formerly was restricted to investment professionals. In addition to the sites listed in Table 3.4, other good sites for bond and interest rate information include Briefing.com (www.briefing.com) and WSJ.com (wsj.com).

The sites of the major bond ratings agencies—Moody's Investor Services (www.moodys.com), Standard & Poor's (www.standardandpoors.com), and Fitch (www.fitchibca.com)—provide ratings lists, recent ratings changes, and information about how they determine ratings.

Mutual Fund Sites With thousands of mutual funds, how do you find the ones that match your investment goals? The Internet makes this task much easier, offering many sites with screening tools and worksheets. Almost every major mutual fund family has its own Web site as well. Some allow visitors to hear interviews or participate in chats with fund managers. Fidelity (www.fidelity.com) is one of the most comprehensive sites, with educational articles, fund selection tools, fund profiles, and more. Portals and brokerage sites also offer these tools. Table 3.4 includes some independent mutual fund sites that are worth checking out.

International Sites The international reach of the Internet makes it a natural resource to help investors sort out the complexity of global investing, from country research to foreign currency exchange. Site-by-Site! International Investment Portal & Research Center (www.site-by-site.com/) is a comprehensive portal just for international investing. Free daily market data, news, economic insights, research, and analysis and commentary covering numerous countries and investment vehicles are among this site's features. For more localized coverage, check out Euroland European Investor (www.europeaninvestor.com), UK-Invest (www. uk-invest.com), LatinFocus (www.latin-focus.com), and similar sites for other countries and regions. J.P. Morgan's ADR site (www.adr.com) is a good place to research American depositary receipts and learn about their financial positions. For global business news, the *Financial Times* site (www.ft.com) gets high marks. CBS Marketwatch (cbs.marketwatch.com/news) has good technology and telecommunications news, as well as coverage of global markets.

Investment Discussion Forums Investors can exchange opinions about their favorite stocks and investing strategies at the *online discussion forums* (message boards and chat rooms) found at most major financial Web sites. However, remember that the key word here is opinion. You don't really know much about the qualifications of the person posting the information. *Always do your own research before acting on any hot tips!* The Motley Fool's (www.fool.com) boards are among the most popular, and Fool employees monitor the discussions. Message boards at Yahoo! Finance (http://messages.yahoo.com) are among the largest online, although many feel that the quality is not so good as at other sites. The Raging Bull (www.ragingbull.lycos.com) includes news along with its discussion groups. Technology investors flock to Silicon Investor (www.siliconinvestor.com), a portal site whose high-tech boards are considered among the best.

Avoiding Online Scams Just as the Internet increases the amount of information available to all investors, it also makes it easier for scam artists and others to spread false news and manipulate information. Anyone can sound like an investment expert online, posting stock tips with no underlying substance. As mentioned earlier, you may not know the identity of the person touting or panning a stock on the message boards. The person panning a stock could be a disgruntled former employee or a short seller. For example, the ousted former chief executive of San Diego's Avanir Pharmaceuticals posted negative remarks on stock message boards, adversely affecting share price. The company sued and won a court order prohibiting him from ever posting derogatory statements about the company on any Internet message boards.

In the fast-paced online environment, two types of scams turn up frequently: "pump-and-dump" schemes and get-rich-quick scams. In pump-and-dump schemes, promoters hype stocks, quickly send the prices sky-high, and then dump them at inflated prices. In get-rich-quick scams, promoters sell worthless investments to naïve buyers. One well-publicized pump-and-dump scheme demonstrates how easy it is to use the Internet to promote stocks. In September 2000, the SEC caught a 15-year-old boy who had made over $270,000 by promoting small-company stocks. The self-taught young investor would buy a block of a company's shares and then send out a barrage of false and/or misleading e-mail messages and message board postings singing the praises of that stock and the company's prospects. Once this misinformation pushed up the stock price, he sold and moved on to a new target company. His postings were so articulate that others at Silicon Investor's message boards thought he was a 40-year-old.

To crack down on cyber-fraud, in 1998 the SEC formed the Office of Internet Enforcement. Its staff members quickly investigate reports of suspected hoaxes and prosecute the offenders. Former SEC Chairman Arthur Levitt cautions investors to remember that the Internet is basically another way to send and receive information, one that has no controls for accuracy or truthfulness. The SEC Web site (www.sec.gov/investor/online/scams.htm) includes tips to avoid investment scams. Three key questions that investors should ask are:

- *Is the investment registered?* Check the SEC's EDGAR database (www.sec.gov/edgar.shtml) and with your state securities regulator (www.nasaa.org).

- *Who is making the sales pitch?* Make sure the seller is licensed in your state. Check with the NASD for any record of complaints or fraud.

- *Is it too good to be true?* Then it probably is. Just being on the Web doesn't mean it's legitimate.

Another place to check on online frauds is the "Online Fraud" link on the 123 Jump portal site (www.123jump.com) that provides links to recent news on online investment fraud.

IN REVIEW

CONCEPTS

3.4 Differentiate between *descriptive information* and *analytical information*. How might one logically assess whether the acquisition of investment information or advice is economically justified?

3.5 What popular financial business periodicals would you use to follow the financial news? General news? Business news? Would you prefer to get your news from print sources or online, and why?

3.6 Briefly describe the types of information that the following resources provide.
a. Stockholders' report.
b. Comparative data sources.
c. Standard & Poor's Corporation.
d. Mergent.
e. *Value Line Investment Survey.*

3.7 How would you access each of the following types of information, and how would the content help you make investment decisions?
a. Prospectuses.
b. Back-office research reports.
c. Investment letters.
d. Price quotations.

3.8 Briefly describe several types of information that are especially well suited to being made available on the Internet. What are the differences between the online and print versions, and when would you use each?

Understanding Market Averages and Indexes

 LG 3

averages
numbers used to measure the general behavior of stock prices by reflecting the arithmetic average price behavior of a representative group of stocks at a given point in time.

indexes
numbers used to measure the general behavior of stock prices by measuring the current price behavior of a representative group of stocks in relation to a base value set at an earlier point in time.

The investment information we have discussed in this chapter helps investors understand when the economy is moving up or down and how individual investments have performed. Investors can use this and other information to formulate expectations about future investment performance. It is also important to know whether market behavior is favorable or unfavorable. The ability to interpret various market measures should help you to select and time investment actions.

A widely used way to assess the behavior of securities markets is to study the performance of market averages and indexes. These measures allow you conveniently to (1) gauge general market conditions, (2) compare your portfolio's performance to that of a large, diversified (market) portfolio, and (3) study market cycles, trends, and behaviors in order to forecast future market behavior. Here we discuss key measures of stock and bond market activity. In later chapters, we will discuss averages and indexes associated with other investment vehicles. Like price quotations, these measures of market performance are available at many Web sites.

Stock Market Averages and Indexes

Stock market averages and indexes measure the general behavior of stock prices over time. Although the terms *average* and *index* tend to be used interchangeably when people discuss market behavior, technically they are different types of measures. **Averages** reflect the arithmetic average price behavior of a representative group of stocks at a given point in time. **Indexes** measure the current price behavior of a representative group of stocks in relation to a base value set at an earlier point in time.

FIGURE 3.7

Major Stock Market Averages and Indexes (August 25, 2003)

The "Major Stock Indexes" summarizes the key stock market averages and indexes. It includes statistics showing the change from the previous day, the 52-week change, and the year-to-date change. (*Source: Wall Street Journal*, August 26, 2003, p. C2. Reprinted by permission of the *Wall Street Journal*. ©Dow Jones & Company, Inc. All rights reserved.)

Major Stock Indexes

Dow Jones Averages	HIGH	LOW	CLOSE	NET CHG	% CHG	HIGH	LOW	% CHG	YTD % CHG
30 Industrials	9350.77	9280.94	9317.64	−31.23	−0.33	9428.90	7286.27	+ 4.47	+11.70
20 Transportations	2649.07	2624.08	2633.01	− 8.55	−0.32	2681.65	1942.19	+ 8.60	+13.99
15 Utilities	238.09	236.11	238.09	+ 1.79	+0.76	255.00	167.57	− 6.52	+10.65
65 Composite	2667.88	2651.33	2662.98	− 3.85	−0.14	2695.42	2033.44	+ 3.29	+12.13
Dow Jones Indexes									
US Total Market	233.91	232.51	233.79	− 0.09	−0.04	236.66	179.60	+ 6.12	+14.32
US Large-Cap	216.69	215.38	216.69	+ 0.20	+0.09	221.98	172.31	+ 2.96	+11.78
US Mid-Cap	273.84	271.74	272.91	− 0.91	−0.33	276.74	192.15	+14.19	+20.47
US Small-Cap	310.40	307.55	308.80	− 1.59	−0.51	314.87	209.81	+18.71	+25.03
US Growth	921.51	914.91	920.36	− 0.45	−0.05	926.66	687.99	+ 8.13	+18.69
US Value	1192.12	1185.39	1191.76	+ 0.48	+0.04	1235.14	938.11	+ 4.21	+10.30
Global Titans 50	162.65	162.00	162.46	− 0.20	−0.12	170.66	134.76	+ 1.19	+ 7.46
Asian Titans 50	94.69	93.62	93.87	− 0.81	−0.86	95.35	71.25	− 1.55	+13.77
DJ STOXX 50	2531.78	2507.89	2510.49	−20.66	−0.82	2852.49	1909.05	−10.12	+ 4.28
Nasdaq Stock Market									
Composite	1768.12	1752.12	1794.31	− 1.01	−0.06	1777.55	1114.11	+26.77	+32.11
Nasdaq 100	1307.85	1295.82	1306.64	+ 2.10	+0.16	1314.65	804.64	+28.51	+32.74
Biotech	715.81	708.89	712.61	− 2.32	−0.32	752.51	438.38	+35.54	+43.43
Computer	822.30	814.20	820.48	+ 0.74	+0.09	820.48	503.26	+24.59	+31.78
Telecommunications	150.18	148.08	150.11	+ 0.19	+0.13	160.42	81.43	+42.60	+37.98
Standard & Poor's Indexes									
500 Index	993.71	987.91	993.71	+ 0.65	+0.07	1011.66	776.76	+ 4.83	+12.94
MidCap 400	508.16	504.03	505.75	− 2.03	−0.40	514.00	372.88	+ 9.79	+17.67
SmallCap 600	238.77	237.00	238.19	− 0.58	−0.24	243.48	170.73	+14.60	+21.14
SuperComp 1500	220.59	219.36	220.58	+ 0.03	+0.01	223.12	171.10	+ 5.55	+13.60
New York Stock Exchange									
Composite	5594.93	5566.06	5585.64	− 9.29	−0.17	5722.85	4452.49	+ 3.66	+11.71
Industrials	654.95	651.84	654.68	− 0.20	−0.03	664.61	532.37	+ 3.38	+12.11
Finance	578.52	574.76	578.36	− 0.05	−0.01	599.39	437.72	+ 4.82	+13.30
Others									
Russell 2000	485.51	480.99	438.87	− 1.64	−0.34	494.82	327.04	+18.67	+26.31
Wilshire 5000	9613.36	9556.52	9588.68	−23.79	−0.25	9715.26	7342.84	+ 7.12	+14.93
Value Line	318.24	315.99	317.32	− 0.92	−0.29	322.47	219.50	+10.01	+20.21
Amex Composite	970.33	965.00	967.01	− 1.92	−0.20	977.57	771.88	+11.45	+17.30

DAILY (HIGH / LOW / CLOSE / NET CHG / % CHG); *52-WEEK* (HIGH / LOW / % CHG); *YTD % CHG*

Averages and indexes provide a convenient method of capturing the general mood of the market. They also can be compared at different points in time to assess the relative strength or weakness of the market. Current and recent values of the key averages and indexes are quoted daily in the financial news, in most local newspapers, and on many radio and television news programs. Figure 3.7, a version of which is published daily in the *Wall Street Journal*, provides a summary and statistics on the major stock market averages and indexes. Let's look at the key averages and indexes listed there.

The Dow Jones Averages Dow Jones & Company, publisher of the *Wall Street Journal*, prepares four stock averages. The most popular is the **Dow Jones Industrial Average (DJIA)**. This average is made up of 30 stocks selected for total market value and broad public ownership. The group consists of high-quality stocks whose behaviors are believed to reflect overall market activity. The box at the bottom of Figure 3.8 lists the stocks currently included in the DJIA.

Occasionally, a merger, bankruptcy, or extreme lack of activity causes a change in the makeup of the average. Citicorp's merger with Travelers moved

Dow Jones Industrial Average (DJIA)
a stock market average made up of 30 high-quality stocks selected for total market value and broad public ownership and believed to reflect overall market activity.

FIGURE 3.8

The DJIA from February 26, 2003, to August 25, 2003

During this 6-month period, the stock market remained mildly bullish beginning in April and continuing through August. (*Source: Wall Street Journal,* August 26, 2003, p. C2. Reprinted by permission of the *Wall Street Journal.* © Dow Jones & Company, Inc. All rights reserved.)

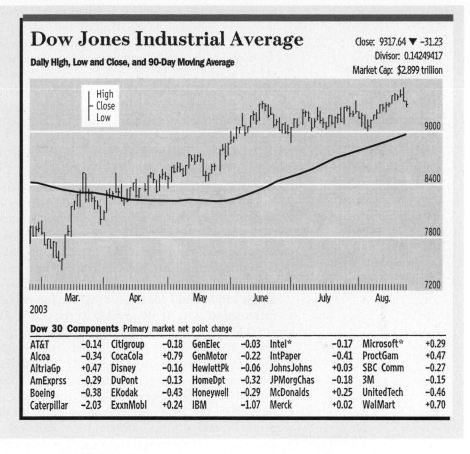

Dow Jones Industrial Average

Close: 9317.64 ▼ −31.23
Divisor: 0.14249417
Market Cap: $2.899 trillion

Daily High, Low and Close, and 90-Day Moving Average

| | High — Close — Low |

2003   Mar.   Apr.   May   June   July   Aug.

9000
8400
7800
7200

Dow 30 Components Primary market net point change

AT&T	−0.14	Citigroup	−0.18	GenElec	−0.03	Intel*	−0.17	Microsoft*	+0.29
Alcoa	−0.34	CocaCola	+0.79	GenMotor	−0.22	IntPaper	−0.41	ProctGam	+0.47
AltriaGp	+0.47	Disney	−0.16	HewlettPk	−0.06	JohnsJohns	+0.03	SBC Comm	−0.27
AmExprss	−0.29	DuPont	−0.13	HomeDpt	−0.32	JPMorgChas	−0.18	3M	−0.15
Boeing	−0.38	EKodak	−0.43	Honeywell	−0.29	McDonalds	+0.25	UnitedTech	−0.46
Caterpillar	−2.03	ExxnMobl	+0.24	IBM	−1.07	Merck	+0.02	WalMart	+0.70

it (Citigroup) to the DJIA. Changes to the 30 stocks also occur when Dow Jones believes that the average does not reflect the broader market. For example, in recent years technology companies such as Microsoft and Intel and financial services companies such as American Express replaced Allied Signal, Goodyear, and Union Carbide; Home Depot replaced Sears. When a new stock is added, the average is readjusted so that it continues to behave in a manner consistent with the immediate past.

The value of the DJIA is calculated each business day by substituting the *closing share prices* of each of the 30 stocks in the average into the following equation:

Equation 3.1

$$\text{DJIA} = \frac{\begin{array}{c}\text{Closing share price} \\ \text{of stock 1}\end{array} + \begin{array}{c}\text{Closing share price} \\ \text{of stock 2}\end{array} + \cdots + \begin{array}{c}\text{Closing share price} \\ \text{of stock 30}\end{array}}{\text{DJIA divisor}}$$

The value of the DJIA is merely the sum of the closing share prices of the 30 stocks included in it, divided by a "divisor." The purpose of the divisor is to adjust for any stock splits, company changes, or other events that have occurred over time. Without the divisor, whose calculation is very complex, the DJIA value would be totally distorted. The divisor makes it possible to use the DJIA to make time-series comparisons. On August 25, 2003, the sum of the closing prices of the 30 industrials was 1327.71, which, when divided by the divisor of 0.14249417, resulted in a DJIA value of 9317.64. The current divisor is included in the *Wall Street Journal* figure "Dow Jones Industrial Average" (printed in the upper-right corner, as seen in Figure 3.8).

Because the DJIA results from summing the prices of the 30 stocks, higher-priced stocks tend to affect the index more than do lower-priced stocks. For example, a 5% change in the price of a $50 stock (i.e., $2.50) has less impact on the index than a 5% change in a $100 stock (i.e., $5.00). In spite of this and other criticisms leveled at the DJIA, it remains the most widely cited stock market indicator.

The actual value of the DJIA is meaningful only when compared to earlier values. For example, the DJIA on August 25, 2003, closed at 9317. This value is meaningful only when compared to the previous day's closing value of 9349, a change of −0.33%. Many people mistakenly believe that one DJIA "point" equals $1 in the value of an average share. Actually, one point currently translates into about 0.47 cents in average share value. Figure 3.8 shows the DJIA over the 6-month period February 26, 2003, to August 25, 2003. During this 6-month period, the stock market remained mildly bullish, beginning in April and continuing through August. It started at about 7800 and dropped to about 7500 in mid-March. During the following 160 days, the market steadily increased to close at about 9320 at the end of August.

The three other Dow Jones averages are the transportation, utilities, and composite. The *Dow Jones Transportation Average* is based on 20 stocks, including railroads, airlines, freight forwarders, and mixed transportation companies. The *Dow Jones Utilities Average* is computed using 15 public utility stocks. The *Dow Jones 65 Stocks Composite Average* is made up of the 30 industrials, the 20 transportations, and the 15 utilities. Like the DJIA, each of the other Dow Jones averages is calculated using a divisor to allow for continuity of the average over time. The transportation, utilities, and 65-stocks composite are often cited in the financial news along with the DJIA, as shown in Figure 3.7.

Dow Jones also publishes numerous indexes as seen in the second section of Figure 3.7. The first one listed, the *Dow Jones U.S. Total Market Index,* is a market-weighted index. "Market-weighted" means that companies with large total market values have the most effect on the index's movement. The Dow Jones U.S. Total Market Index reflects 95% of the total market value for large-sized, medium-sized, and small-sized companies. The base value of the index is 100, which represents its value on June 30, 1997.

Standard & Poor's Indexes   Standard & Poor's Corporation, another leading financial publisher, publishes six major common stock indexes. One oft-cited S&P index is the 500-stock composite index. Unlike the Dow Jones averages, **Standard & Poor's indexes** are true indexes. They are calculated each business day by substituting the *closing market value of each stock* (closing price × number of shares outstanding) into the following equation:

Standard & Poor's indexes
true indexes that measure the current price of a group of stocks relative to a base (set in the 1941–1943 period) having an index value of 10.

Equation 3.2

$$\text{S\&P Index} = \frac{\substack{\text{Current closing} \\ \text{market value} \\ \text{of stock 1}} + \substack{\text{Current closing} \\ \text{market value} \\ \text{of stock 2}} + \cdots + \substack{\text{Current closing} \\ \text{market value} \\ \text{of last stock}}}{\substack{\text{Base period} \\ \text{closing market} \\ \text{value of stock 1}} + \substack{\text{Base period} \\ \text{closing market} \\ \text{value of stock 2}} + \cdots + \substack{\text{Base period} \\ \text{closing market} \\ \text{value of last stock}}} \times 10$$

The value of the S&P index is found by dividing the sum of the market values of all stocks included in the index by the market value of the stocks in the base period and then multiplying the resulting quotient by 10, the base value of the S&P indexes. Most S&P indexes are calculated in a similar fashion. The main differences lie in the stocks included in the index, the base period, and the base value of the index. For example, on August 25, 2003, the ratio of the closing market values of the S&P 500 composite stocks to the 1941–1943 base-period closing market values was 99.371, which, when multiplied by the base value of the S&P index of 10, results in an index value of 993.71 (as shown in Figure 3.7).

Certain of the S&P indexes contain many more shares than the Dow averages do, and all of them are based on *market values* rather than *share prices*. Therefore, many investors feel that the S&P indexes provide a more broad-based and representative measure of general market conditions than do the Dow averages. Although some technical computational problems exist with these indexes, they are widely used—frequently as a basis for estimating the "market return," an important concept that is introduced in Chapter 4.

Like the Dow averages, the S&P indexes are meaningful only when compared to values in other time periods or to the 1941–1943 base-period value of 10. For example, the August 25, 2003, value of the S&P 500 Stock Composite Index of 993.71 means that the market values of the stocks in the index increased by a factor of 99.371 (993.71 ÷ 10) since the 1941–1943 period. The August 25, 2003, market value of the stocks in the index was 1.28 times the lowest index value of 776.76 in the preceding 52-week period (993.71 ÷ 776.76), and hence represented an increase of 28%.

The eight major common stock indexes published by Standard & Poor's are

- The *industrials index,* made up of the common stock of 400 industrial firms.

- The *transportation index,* which includes the stock of 20 transportation companies.

- The *utilities index,* made up of 40 public utility stocks.

- The *financials index,* which contains 40 financial stocks.

- The *composite index* (described above), which consists of the total of 500 stocks that make up the industrials, transportation, utilities, and financials indexes.

- The *MidCap index,* made up of the stocks of 400 medium-sized companies.

- The *SmallCap index,* made up of 600 small-sized companies.

- The *1500 SuperComp index,* which includes all stocks in the composite, MidCap, and SmallCap indexes.

Like the Dow averages and indexes, many of the S&P indexes are frequently quoted in the financial news, as shown in Figure 3.7.

Although the Dow Jones averages and S&P indexes tend to behave in a similar fashion over time, their day-to-day magnitude and even direction (up or down) can differ significantly because the Dows are averages and the S&Ps are indexes.

NYSE, AMEX, and Nasdaq Indexes Three indexes measure the daily results of the New York Stock Exchange (NYSE), the American Stock Exchange (AMEX), and the National Association of Securities Dealers Automated Quotation (Nasdaq) system. Each reflects the movement of stocks listed on its exchange. The **NYSE composite index** includes about 2,100 or so stocks listed on the "Big Board." The index's base of 5000 reflects the December 31, 2002, value of stocks listed on the NYSE. In addition to the composite index, the NYSE publishes indexes for industrials and finance subgroups. The behavior of the NYSE industrial index is normally similar to that of the DJIA and the S&P 500 indexes.

NYSE composite index
measure of the current price behavior of stocks listed on the NYSE, relative to a base of 5000 set at December 31, 2002.

The **AMEX composite index** reflects the price of all shares traded on the American Stock Exchange, relative to a base of 550 set at December 29, 1995. Although it does not always closely follow the S&P and NYSE indexes, the AMEX index tends to move in the general direction they do.

AMEX composite index
measure of the current price behavior of all shares traded on the AMEX, relative to a base of 550 set at December 29, 1995.

The **Nasdaq Stock Market indexes** reflect over-the-counter market activity. The most comprehensive of the Nasdaq indexes is the *composite index*, which is calculated using the about 3,450 domestic common stocks traded on the Nasdaq system. It is based on a value of 100 set at February 5, 1971. Also important is the *Nasdaq 100*, which includes 100 of the largest domestic and international nonfinancial companies listed on Nasdaq. It is based on a value of 125, set on January 1, 1994. The other three commonly quoted Nasdaq indexes are the *biotech*, the *computer*, and the *telecommunications indexes*. Although their degrees of responsiveness may vary, the Nasdaq indexes tend to move in the same direction at the same time as the other major indexes.

Nasdaq Stock Market indexes
measures of current price behavior of securities sold OTC, relative to a base of 100 set at specified dates.

Value Line Indexes Value Line publishes a number of stock indexes constructed by equally weighting the price of each stock included. This is accomplished by considering only the percentage changes in stock prices. This approach eliminates the effects of differing market price and total market value on the relative importance of each stock in the index. The **Value Line composite index** includes the about 1,700 stocks in the *Value Line Investment Survey* that are traded on the NYSE, AMEX, and OTC markets. The base of 100 reflects the stock prices on June 30, 1961. In addition to its composite index, Value Line publishes other specialized indexes.

Value Line composite index
stock index that reflects the percentage changes in share price of about 1,700 stocks, relative to a base of 100 set at June 30, 1961.

Other Averages and Indexes A number of other indexes are available. The **Wilshire 5000 index,** published by Wilshire Associates, Inc., is reported daily in the *Wall Street Journal*. It represents the total dollar value (in billions of dollars) of more than 5,000 actively traded stocks, including all those on the NYSE and the AMEX in addition to active OTC stocks. Frank Russell Company, a pension advisory firm, publishes three primary indexes. The *Russell 1000* includes the 1,000 largest companies, the most widely quoted *Russell 2000* includes 2,000 small- to medium-sized companies, and the *Russell 3000* includes all 3,000 companies in the Russell 1000 and 2000.

Wilshire 5000 index
measure of the total dollar value (in billions of dollars) of more than 5,000 actively traded stocks, including all those on the NYSE and the AMEX in addition to active OTC stocks.

In addition, the *Wall Street Journal* publishes a number of global and foreign stock market indexes summarized in the "International Stocks & Indexes" section, normally in Section C. Included are Dow Jones indexes for countries in the Americas, Latin America, Europe, South Africa, and the Asia-Pacific region that are based on a value of 100 set at December 31, 1991. More than 30 foreign stock market indexes and the Morgan Stanley Capital International (MSCI) Indexes are also given for major countries, including a

World Index and the *Europe/Australia/ Far East (EAFE MSCI) Index*. Each of the MSCI Indexes is calculated in local currencies and based on a value of 100 set at December 31, 1969. Like the purely domestic averages and indexes, these international averages and indexes measure the general price behavior of the stocks that are listed and traded in the given market. Useful comparisons of the market averages and indexes over time and across markets are often made to assess both trends and relative strengths of foreign markets throughout the world.

Bond Market Indicators

A number of indicators are available for assessing the general behavior of the bond markets. A "Bond Market Data Bank" that includes a wealth of return and price index data for various types of bonds and various domestic and foreign markets is published daily in the *Wall Street Journal*. However, there are fewer indicators of overall bond market behavior than of stock market behavior. The key measures of overall U.S. bond market behavior are bond yields, the Dow Jones Corporate Bond Index, and the New York Stock Exchange bond diary.

bond yield
summary measure of the total return an investor would receive on a bond if it were purchased at its current price and held to maturity; reported as an annual rate of return.

Bond Yields A **bond yield** is a summary measure of the total return an investor would receive on a bond if it were purchased at its current price and held to maturity. Bond yields are reported as annual rates of return. For example, a bond with a yield of 5.50% would provide its owner with a total return from periodic interest and capital gain (or loss) that would be equivalent to a 5.50% annual rate of earnings on the amount invested, if the bond were purchased at its current price and held to maturity.

Typically, bond yields are quoted for a group of bonds that are similar with respect to type and quality. For example, *Barron's* quotes the yields on the Dow Jones bond averages of 10 high-grade corporate bonds, 10 medium-grade corporate bonds, and a confidence index that is calculated as a ratio of the high-grade to medium-grade indexes. In addition, like the *Wall Street Journal,* it quotes numerous other bond indexes and yields, including those for Treasury and municipal bonds. Similar bond yield data are available from S&P, Moody's, and the Federal Reserve. Like stock market averages and indexes, bond yield data are especially useful when viewed over time.

Dow Jones Corporate Bond Index
mathematical averages of the *closing prices* for 96 bonds— 32 industrial, 32 financial, and 32 utility/telecom.

Dow Jones Corporate Bond Index The **Dow Jones Corporate Bond Index** includes 96 bonds—32 industrial, 32 financial, and 32 utility/telecom bonds. It reflects the simple mathematical average of the *closing prices* for the bonds. It is based on a value of 100 set at December 31, 1996. The Index is published daily in the *Wall Street Journal* and summarized weekly in *Barron's*. A similar bond market index, prepared by investment banker Lehman Brothers, is also published daily in the *Wall Street Journal* and summarized weekly in *Barron's.*

NYSE Bond Diary The New York Stock Exchange is the dominant organized exchange on which bonds are traded. Thus certain summary statistics on daily bond-trading activity on the NYSE provide useful insight into the behavior of the bond markets in general. These statistics include the number of issues traded and the number that advanced, declined, remained unchanged, reached new highs, and reached new lows. For example, on August 22, 2003, 98 issues traded, 37 advanced, 47 declined, 14 remained unchanged, 3 achieved new highs, and 2 achieved new lows. Total sales volume was $5,911,000. The NYSE bond diary is published weekly, showing the past week's daily data, in *Barron's*.

IN REVIEW

CONCEPTS

3.9 Describe the basic philosophy and use of stock market averages and indexes. Explain how the behavior of an average or index can be used to classify general market conditions as bull or bear.

3.10 List each of the major averages or indexes prepared by (a) Dow Jones & Company and (b) Standard & Poor's Corporation. Indicate the number and source of the securities used in calculating each average or index.

3.11 Briefly describe the composition and general thrust of each of the following indexes.
  a. NYSE composite index.
  b. AMEX composite index.
  c. Nasdaq Stock Market indexes.
  d. Value Line composite index.
  e. Wilshire 5000 index.

3.12 Discuss each of the following as they are related to assessing bond market behavior.
  a. Bond yields.
  b. Dow Jones Corporate Bond Index.
  c. NYSE bond diary.

Making Securities Transactions

Now that you know how to find information to help you locate attractive security investments, you should understand how to make securities transactions. Whether you decide to start a self-directed online investment program or to use a traditional stockbroker, you must first open an account with a stockbroker to buy and sell securities. In this section we will look at the role stockbrokers play and how that role has changed with the growth in online investing. We will also explain the basic types of orders you can place, the procedures required to make regular and online securities transactions, the costs of investment transactions, and investor protection.

The Role of Stockbrokers

stockbrokers
individuals licensed by both the SEC and the securities exchanges to facilitate transactions between buyers and sellers of securities.

Stockbrokers—also called *account executives, investment executives,* and *financial consultants*—act as intermediaries between buyers and sellers of securities. They typically charge a commission to facilitate these securities transactions. Stockbrokers must be licensed by both the SEC and the securities exchanges on which they place orders and must follow the ethical guidelines of those bodies.

Although the procedure for executing orders on organized exchanges may differ from that in the OTC market, it starts the same way: An investor places an order with his or her stockbroker. The broker works for a brokerage firm

TOO MUCH PAPERWORK—
Wasn't the computer supposed to cut down on paperwork? Tell that to the stock brokerage firms and mutual fund companies that send you monthly and year-end statements, confirmations of buy and sell orders, newsletters, and so on. What can you throw away? Keep your most recent brokerage statements and the year-end documents (which you'll need to prepare your tax returns). Check over the monthly statements to make sure they're correct—and then toss them when the next month's statements arrive.

street name
security certificates issued in the brokerage firm's name but held in trust for its client, who actually owns them.

that owns seats on the organized securities exchanges, and members of the securities exchange execute orders that the brokers in the firm's various sales offices transmit to them. For example, the largest U.S. brokerage firm, Merrill Lynch, transmits orders for listed securities from its offices in most major cities throughout the country to the main office of Merrill Lynch and then to the floor of the stock exchanges (NYSE and AMEX), where Merrill Lynch exchange members execute them. Confirmation of the order goes back to the broker placing the order, who relays it to the customer. This process can take a matter of seconds with the use of sophisticated telecommunications networks and Internet trading.

For an over-the-counter securities transaction, brokerage firms transmit orders to market makers, who are dealers in the OTC market specializing in that security. As we learned in Chapter 2, the Nasdaq system, along with the available information on who makes markets in certain securities, enables brokers to execute orders in OTC securities. Normally, OTC transactions are executed rapidly, because market makers maintain inventories of the securities in which they deal.

Brokerage Services The primary activity of stockbrokers is to execute clients' purchase and sale transactions at the best possible price. Brokerage firms will hold the client's security certificates for safekeeping; the securities kept by the firm in this manner are said to be held in **street name**. Because the brokerage house issues the securities in its own name and holds them in trust for the client (rather than issuing them in the client's name), the firm can transfer the securities at the time of sale without the client's signature. Street name is actually a common way of buying securities, because most investors do not want to be bothered with the handling and safekeeping of stock certificates. In such cases, the brokerage firm records the details of the client's transaction and keeps track of his or her investments through a series of bookkeeping entries. Dividends and notices received by the broker are forwarded to the client who owns the securities.

Stockbrokers also offer clients a variety of other services. For example, the brokerage firm normally provides free information about investments. Quite often, the firm has a research staff that periodically issues analyses of economic, market, industry, or company behavior and makes recommendations to buy, sell, or hold certain securities. As a client of a large brokerage firm, you can expect to receive regular bulletins on market activity and possibly a recommended investment list. You will also receive a statement describing your transactions for the month and showing commission and interest charges, dividends and interest received, and detailed listings of your current holdings.

Today, most brokerage firms will invest surplus cash left in a client's account in a money market mutual fund, allowing the client to earn a reasonable rate of interest on these balances. Such arrangements help the investor earn as much as possible on temporarily idle funds.

Types of Brokerage Firms Just a few years ago, there were three distinct types of brokerage firms: full-service, premium discount, and basic discount. No longer are the lines between these categories clear-cut. Most brokerage firms, even the most traditional ones, now offer online services. And many discount brokers now offer services, like research reports for clients, that were once available only from a full-service broker.

full-service broker
broker who, in addition to executing clients' transactions, provides them with a full array of brokerage services.

premium discount broker
broker who charges low commissions to make transactions for customers but provides limited free research information and investment advice.

basic discount broker
typically a deep-discount broker through which investors can execute trades electronically online via a commercial service, on the Internet, or by phone. (Also called *online brokers* or *electronic brokers*.)

The traditional broker, or so-called **full-service broker,** in addition to executing clients' transactions, offers investors a full array of brokerage services: providing investment advice and information, holding securities in street name, offering online brokerage services, and extending margin loans. Investors who wish merely to make transactions and are not interested in taking advantage of other services should consider either a premium or basic discount broker.

Premium discount brokers focus primarily on making transactions for customers. They charge low commissions and provide limited free research information and investment advice. The investor visits the broker's office, calls a toll-free number, or accesses the broker's Web site to initiate a transaction, and the discount broker confirms the transaction in person or by phone, e-mail, or regular mail. However, brokers like Charles Schwab, the first discount broker, now offer many of the same services that you'd find at a full-service broker. Other premium discounters are similar.

Basic discount brokers, also called *online brokers* or *electronic brokers,* are typically deep-discount brokers through which investors can execute trades electronically online via a commercial service, on the Internet, or by phone. The investor accesses the basic discounter's Web site to open an account, review the commission schedule, or see a demonstration of the available transactional services and procedures. Confirmation of online trades can take as little as 10 seconds, and most trades occur within 1 minute. Some firms, such as Ameritrade, E*Trade, and TD Waterhouse, operate primarily online, but also provide telephone and live broker backup in case there are problems with the Web site or the customer is away from his or her computer. In response to the rapid growth of online investors, particularly among affluent young investors who enjoy surfing the Web, most brokerage firms now offer online trading. These firms usually charge higher commissions when live broker assistance is required.

The rapidly growing volume of business done by both premium and basic discount brokers attests to their success. Today, many full-service brokers, banks, and savings institutions are making discount and online brokerage services available to their customers and depositors who wish to buy stocks, bonds, mutual funds, and other investment vehicles. Some of the major full-service, premium discount, and basic discount brokers are listed in Table 3.5.

TABLE 3.5	**Major Full-Service, Premium Discount, and Basic Discount Brokers**	
	Type of Broker	
Full-Service	Premium Discount	Basic Discount
A.G. Edwards	Charles Schwab	Ameritrade
Merrill Lynch	Fidelity Investments	Brown Co
Morgan Stanley	Quick & Reilly	E* Trade
Smith Barney	T. Rowe Price	Harris Direct
UBS Financial Services	USAA	Scottrade
Wells Fargo	Vanguard	TD Waterhouse

⚖ ETHICS IN INVESTING

DID MARTHA STEWART CROSS THE LINE?

On June 4, 2003, the Securities and Exchange Commission filed securities fraud charges against Marth Stewart and her former stockbroker, Peter Bacanovic. According to the SEC, Martha Stewart committed illegal insider trading when she sold stock in a biotech company, ImClone Systems, Inc., on December 27, 2001, after receiving a tip from Bacanovic. The SEC also alleged that Stewart and Bacanovic created an alibi for her ImClone sales and attempted to obstruct justice during investigations into her trades. The homemaking queen, who has achieved financial success and celebrity status, has found herself tarred by a scandal, during which she resigned as Chairman and CEO of her company. In addition, the stock of her company dropped more than 20%, and her holdings took nearly a $200 million hit, wiping out more than a quarter of her net worth.

The government alleged that Bacanovic tipped off Stewart that two of his other clients, ImClone's CEO Samuel Waksal and Waksal's daughter, had just placed orders to sell all the ImClone stock they held in their Merrill Lynch accounts. Waksal, a long-time friend of Stewart, had secretly obtained information that the U.S. Food and Drug Administration (FDA) was about to reject ImClone's new key cancer product, Erbitux. Information about the Waksals' efforts to sell was confidential under Merrill Lynch policies, which prohibited employees from disclosing client transactions to third parties.

As a result of the tip, Stewart promptly sold all 3,928 shares of her ImClone stock, thus avoiding about $45,000 in losses. The very next day—December 28, 2001—ImClone announced that the FDA had rejected ImClone's application for Erbitux. By the close of the next trading day the price of ImClone stock dropped 16% to $46 per share. According to authorities, Stewart and Bacanovic fabricated an alibi for Stewart's trades, stating that she sold her ImClone stock because she and her broker had decided earlier that she would sell if the price fell below $60 per share. In addition, Stewart told the government that she did not recall anyone telling her that day that the Waksals were selling their ImClone stock.

It's for the courts to decide whether Martha Stewart broke the law. However, as Stephen M. Cutler, the SEC's Director of Enforcement, said, "It is fundamentally unfair for someone to have an edge on the market just because she has a stockbroker who is willing to break the rules and give her an illegal tip. It's worse still when the individual engaging in the insider trading is the Chairman and CEO of a public company."

CRITICAL THINKING QUESTION In light of the *Insider Trading and Fraud Act of 1988*, does Martha Stewart or any other investor have the right to sell stock every time a broker tells them to?

Selecting a Stockbroker If you decide to start your investing activities with the assistance of either a full-service or premium discount stockbroker, select the person you believe best understands your investment goals. Choosing a broker whose disposition toward investing is similar to yours is the best way to establish a solid working relationship. Your broker should also make you aware of investment possibilities that are consistent with your objectives and attitude toward risk.

You should also consider the cost and types of services available from the firm with which the broker is affiliated, to receive the best service at the lowest possible cost to you. The premium discount brokerage service is primarily transactional, and the basic discount brokerage service is *purely* transactional.

Contact with a broker, advice, and research assistance generally are available only at a higher price. Investors must weigh the added commissions they pay a full-service broker against the value of the advice they receive, because the amount of available advice is the only major difference among basic discount, premium discount, and full-service brokers.

Referrals from friends or business associates are a good way to begin your search for a stockbroker. Don't forget to consider the investing style and goals of the person making the recommendation. However, it is not important—and often not even advisable—to know your stockbroker personally. And in this age of online brokers, you may never meet your broker face to face! A strictly business relationship eliminates the possibility that social concerns will interfere with the achievement of your investment goals. This does not mean that your broker's sole interest should be commissions. Responsible brokers do not engage in **churning**—that is, causing excessive trading of their clients' accounts to increase commissions. Churning is both illegal and unethical under SEC and exchange rules. However, it is often difficult to prove. For an example of a stockbroker-client business relationship that may have crossed the line into illegal, see the *Ethics* box on page 107.

churning
an illegal and unethical practice engaged in by a broker to increase commissions by causing excessive trading of clients' accounts.

Opening an Account To open an account, the customer fills out various documents that establish a legal relationship between the customer and the brokerage firm. A signature card and a personal data card provide the information needed to identify the client's account. The stockbroker must also have a reasonable understanding of a client's personal financial situation to assess his or her investment goals—and to be sure that the client can pay for the securities purchased. The client also provides the broker with instructions regarding the transfer and custody of securities. Customers who wish to borrow money to make transactions must establish a margin account (described on page 109). If the customer is acting as a custodian, trustee, or executor or is a corporation, the brokerage firm will require additional documents. Today, all of this can be done online at most brokerage firms.

Investors may have accounts with more than one stockbroker. Many investors establish accounts at different types of firms to obtain the benefit and opinions of a diverse group of brokers and to reduce their overall cost of making purchase and sale transactions.

Next you must select the type of account best suited to your needs. We will briefly consider several of the more popular types.

Single or Joint A brokerage account may be either single or joint. Joint accounts are most common between husband and wife or parent and child. The account of a minor (a person younger than 18 years of age) is a **custodial account,** in which a parent or guardian must be part of all transactions. Regardless of the form of the account, the name(s) of the account holder(s) and an account number are used to identify it.

custodial account
the brokerage account of a minor; requires a parent or guardian to be part of all transactions.

Cash or Margin A **cash account,** the more common type, is one in which the customer can make only cash transactions. Customers can initiate cash transactions via phone or online and are given 3 business days in which to transmit the cash to the brokerage firm. The firm is likewise given 3 business days in which to deposit the proceeds from the sale of securities in the customer's cash account.

cash account
a brokerage account in which a customer can make only cash transactions.

margin account
a brokerage account in which the customer has been extended borrowing privileges by the brokerage firm.

A **margin account** is an account in which the brokerage firm extends borrowing privileges to a creditworthy customer. By leaving securities with the firm as collateral, the customer can borrow a prespecified proportion of the securities' purchase price. The brokerage firm will, of course, charge the customer a stated rate of interest on borrowings. (The mechanics of margin trading are covered in Chapter 2.)

wrap account
a brokerage account in which customers with large portfolios pay a flat annual fee that covers the cost of a money manager's services and the commissions on all trades. (Also called a *managed account*.)

Wrap The **wrap account** (also called a *managed account*) allows brokerage customers with large portfolios (generally $100,000 or more) to shift stock selection decisions conveniently to a professional money manager, either in-house or independent. In return for a flat annual fee equal to between 1% and 3% of the portfolio's total asset value, the brokerage firm helps the investor select a money manager, pays the manager's fee, and executes the money manager's trades. Initially the investor, broker, and/or manager discuss the client's overall goals. Wrap accounts are appealing for a number of reasons other than convenience. The annual fee in most cases covers commissions on all trades, virtually eliminating the chance of the broker churning the account. In addition, the broker monitors the manager's performance and provides the investor with detailed reports, typically quarterly.

Odd-Lot or Round-Lot Transactions Investors can buy stock in either odd or round lots. An **odd lot** consists of less than 100 shares of a stock. A **round lot** is a 100-share unit or a multiple thereof. You would be dealing in an odd lot if you bought, say, 25 shares of stock but in round lots if you bought 200 shares. A trade of 225 shares would be a combination of an odd lot and two round lots.

odd lot
less than 100 shares of stock.

round lot
100-share units of stock or multiples thereof.

Transactions in odd lots require either additional processing by the brokerage firm or the assistance of a specialist. For odd lots, an added fee—known as an *odd-lot differential*—is tacked on to the normal commission charge, driving up the costs of these small trades. Small investors in the early stages of their investment programs are primarily responsible for odd-lot transactions.

Basic Types of Orders

Investors can use different types of orders to make security transactions. The type placed normally depends on the investor's goals and expectations. The three basic types of orders are the market order, the limit order, and the stop-loss order.

market order
an order to buy or sell stock at the best price available when the order is placed.

Market Order An order to buy or sell stock at the best price available when the investor places the order is a **market order.** It is generally the quickest way to fill orders, because market orders are usually executed as soon as they reach the exchange floor or are received by the market maker. Because of the speed with which market orders are executed, the buyer or seller of a security can be sure that the price at which the order is transacted will be very close to the market price prevailing at the time the order was placed.

limit order
an order to buy at or below a specified price or to sell at or above a specified price.

Limit Order A **limit order** is an order to buy at or below a specified price or to sell at or above a specified price. When the investor places a limit order, the broker transmits it to a specialist dealing in the security. The specialist notes the number of shares and price of the limit order in his or her book and executes the order as soon as the specified market price (or better) exists. The specialist must first satisfy all other orders with precedence—similar orders received earlier, buy orders at a higher specified price, or sell orders at a lower specified price. Investors can place the limit order in one of the following forms:

1. A *fill-or-kill order,* which is canceled if not immediately executed.
2. A *day order,* which if not executed is automatically canceled at the end of the day.
3. A *good-'til-canceled (GTC) order,* which generally remains in effect for 6 months unless executed, canceled, or renewed.

Assume, for example, that you place a limit order to buy, at a limit price of $30, 100 shares of a stock currently selling at $30.50. Once the specialist clears all similar orders received before yours, and once the market price of the stock falls to $30 or less, he or she executes your order. It is possible, of course, that your order might expire (if it is not a GTC order) before the stock price drops to $30.

Although a limit order can be quite effective, it can also keep you from making a transaction. If, for instance, you wish to buy at $30 or less and the stock price moves from its current $30.50 price to $42 while you are waiting, you have missed the opportunity to make a profit of $11.50 per share ($42 − $30.50). If you had placed a *market order* to buy at the best available price ($30.50), the profit of $11.50 would have been yours. Limit orders for the sale of a stock are also disadvantageous when the stock price closely approaches, but does not attain, the minimum sale price limit before dropping substantially. Generally speaking, limit orders are most effective when the price of a stock fluctuates greatly, because there is then a better chance that the order will be executed.

stop-loss (stop) order
an order to sell a stock when its market price reaches or drops below a specified level; can also be used to buy stock when its market price reaches or rises above a specified level.

Stop-Loss Order When an investor places a **stop-loss order** or **stop order,** the broker tells the specialist to sell a stock when its market price reaches or drops below a specified level. Stop-loss orders are *suspended orders* placed on stocks; they are activated when and if the stock reaches a certain price. The stop-loss order is placed on the specialist's book and becomes active once the stock reaches the stop price. Like limit orders, stop-loss orders are typically day or GTC orders. When activated, the stop order becomes a *market order* to sell the security at the best price available. Thus it is possible for the actual price at which the sale is made to be well below the price at which the stop was initiated. Investors use these orders to protect themselves against the adverse effects of a rapid decline in share price.

For example, assume you own 100 shares of Ballard Industries, which is currently selling for $35 per share. Because you believe the stock price could decline rapidly at any time, you place a stop order to sell at $30. If the stock price does in fact drop to $30, the specialist will sell the 100 shares at the best price available at that time. If the market price declines to $28 by the time your stop-loss order comes up, you will receive less than $30 per share. Of course, if the market price stays above $30 per share, you will have lost nothing as a result of placing the order, because the stop order will never be initiated. Often investors raise the level of the stop as the price of the stock rises. Such action helps to lock in a higher profit when the price is increasing.

Investors can also place stop orders to buy a stock, although buy orders are far less common than sell orders. For example, an investor may place a stop order to buy 100 shares of MJ Enterprises, currently selling for $70 per share, once its price rises to, say, $75 (the stop price). These orders are commonly used either to limit losses on short sales (discussed in Chapter 2) or to buy a stock just as its price begins to rise.

To avoid the risk of the market moving against you when your stop order becomes a market order, you can place a *stop-limit order*, rather than a plain stop order. This is an order to buy or sell stock at a given price, or better, once a stipulated stop price has been met. For example, in the Ballard Industries example, had a stop-limit order been in effect, then when the market price of Ballard dropped to $30, the broker would have entered a limit order to sell your 100 shares at $30 a share or *better*. Thus you would have run no risk of getting less than $30 a share for your stock—unless the price of the stock kept right on falling. In that case, as is true for any limit order, you might miss the market altogether and end up with stock worth much less than $30. Even though the stop order to sell was triggered (at $30), the stock will not be sold, with a stop-limit order, if it keeps falling in price.

Online Transactions

The competition for your online business increases daily as more players enter an already crowded arena. Brokerage firms are encouraging customers to trade online and offering a variety of incentives to get their business, including free trades! However, low cost is not the only reason to choose a brokerage firm. As with any financial decision, you must consider your needs and find the firm that best matches them. One investor may want timely information, research, and quick, reliable trades from a full-service broker like Merrill Lynch or Smith Barney or a premium discounter like Charles Schwab or Quick & Reilly. Another, who is an active trader, will focus on cost and fast trades rather than research and so will sign up with a basic discounter like Ameritrade or Harris Direct. Ease of site navigation is a major factor in finding a basic discount broker to use in executing online transactions. Table 3.6 (on page 112) gives Smart Money's assessment of the features, services, and costs of a number of leading basic discount brokerage firms, all of which offer online trading of stocks. Some also offer online trading of bonds and mutual funds as well.

Day Trading For some investors, online stock trading is so compelling that they become day traders. The opposite of buy-and-hold investors with a long-term perspective, **day traders** buy and sell stocks quickly throughout the day. They hope that their stocks will continue to rise in value for the very short time they own them—sometimes just seconds or minutes—so they can make quick profits. Some also sell short, looking for small price decreases. True day traders do not own any stocks overnight—hence the term "day trader"— because they believe that the extreme risk of prices changing radically from day to day will lead to large losses. Day trading is not illegal or unethical, but it is highly risky. To compound their risk, day traders usually buy on margin to use leverage to earn higher profits. But as we saw in Chapter 2, margin trading also increases the risk of large losses.

day trader
an investor who buys and sells stocks quickly throughout the day in hopes of making quick profits.

TABLE 3.6 Smart Money's Assessment of the Features, Services, and Costs of Leading Basic Discount Brokerage Firms

Overall Rank	Broker	Notable Features	Minimum Opening Balance	Quality of service	Commissions and fees	Mutual Funds	Research Tools	Investment Products	Amenities	Commissions on Market Trades*	Average Phone Wait**	Trade* Execution Quality
1	TD Waterhouse www.tdwaterhouse.com	Widest range of products and services, and a strong showing on most every front.	None	6	7	1	2	1	2	$17.95	142	Good
2	Muriel Siebert www.siebertnet.com	Lots of research tools, plus no account fees.	None	5	8	8	1	2	3	$14.95	38	Good
3	Bidwell www.bidwell.com	Good customer service. Had the most-detailed account statements.	None	1	6	9	8ᵗ	3	11ᵗ	$12.75	16	Good
4	Scottrade www.scottrade.com	Few fees make it the cheapest broker, but the Web site is outdated.	$2,000	11	1	10	10	5	11ᵗ	$7.00	5	Good
5	Harris Direct www.harrisdirect.com	Wireless options galore. Cheap broker-assisted trades.	None	8	2	6	3	4	1	$20.00	59	Poor
6	BrownCo www.brownco.com	Easy-to-use online trading interface is a boon for active traders.	$15,000	3ᵗ	3	5	7	13	13	$5.00	47	Good
7	Firstrade www.firstrade.com	Cheap trades and great execution. But that's about it.	None	3ᵗ	4	11	13	10ᵗ	10	$6.95	22	Excellent
8	Ameritrade www.ameritrade.com	Least-detailed statements, but decent customer service.	$2,000	7	5	7	8ᵗ	9	7	$10.99	125	Excellent
9	E*Trade www.etrade.com	The highest fees of the bunch. At least the Web site is easy to navigate.	$1,000	10	10	13	5	6	8	$22.99	622	Poor
10	Wells Fargo www.wellsfargo.com	Great customer service; skimpy on the research.	$1,000	2	12	3	12	8	5ᵗ	$24.95	38	Excellent
11	Merrill Lynch Direct www.mldirect.com	Most expensive, with high trade commissions and lots of fees.	$2,000	9	13	2	4	10ᵗ	4	$29.95	143	Fair
12	Cititrade www.cititrade.com	Least-helpful phone and e-mail reps. One perk: low margin rates.	$2,000	12	9	12	6	10ᵗ	9	$24.95	85	Fair
13	Bank of America www.bankofamerica.com/investments	Frustrating site and poor customer service. No research reports.	None	13	11	4	11	7	5ᵗ	$24.95	161	Poor

t = Tie. *Trade costs are for 1,000 shares, with fees. **Phone wait is for customer service, in seconds. *Note:* Quality of service reflects customer service, trade execution, Web reliability.

Source: Anne Kadet and Eleanor Laise, "Basic Discount Brokers—Rankings," 2003 Broker Survey, *Smart Money,* August 5, 2003, p. 68, downloaded from smartmoney.com/brokers/index.cfm?story=2003-basic-table. Reprinted by permission of Smart Money. Copyright © 2003 Smart Money. Smart Money is a joint publishing venture of Dow Jones & Company, Inc. and Hearst Communications, Inc. All Rights Reserved Worldwide.

Because the Internet makes investment information and transactions accessible to the masses, day trading has grown in popularity. Day traders watch their computer screens continuously, trying to track numerous ticker quotes and price data to identify market trends. It's a very difficult task—essentially a very stressful, full-time job. Yet pitches for day trading make it seem like an easy route to quick riches. Quite the reverse is true. Day traders typically incur major financial losses when they start trading. Some never achieve profitability. Day traders also have high expenses for brokerage commissions, training, and computer equipment. They must earn sizable trading profits annually to break even on fees and commissions alone. The *Investing in Action* box on page 114 details an even darker side of day trading—how it can sometimes turn into compulsive investing.

Technical and Service Problems As the number of online investors increases, so do the problems that beset brokerage firms and their customers. During the past few years most brokerage firms have upgraded their systems to reduce the number of service outages. But the potential problems go beyond the brokerage sites. Once an investor places a trade at a firm's Web site, it goes through several other parties to be executed. Most online brokers don't have their own trading desks and have agreements with other trading firms to execute their orders on the *New York Stock Exchange* or *Nasdaq Stock Market*. Slowdowns at any point in the process can create problems confirming trades. Investors, thinking that their trades had not gone through, might place the order again—only to discover later that they have bought the same stock twice. Online investors who don't get immediate trade execution and confirmation use the telephone when they can't get through online or to solve other problems with their accounts, and they often face long waiting times on hold.

Tips for Successful Online Trades Successful online investors take additional precautions before submitting their orders. Here are some tips to protect yourself from common problems:

- *Know how to place and confirm your order before you begin trading.* This simple step can keep you from having problems later.

- *Verify the stock symbol of the security you wish to buy.* Two very different companies can have similar symbols. Some investors have bought the wrong stock because they didn't check before placing their order.

- *Use limit orders.* The order you see on your computer screen may not be the one you get. With a limit order, you avoid getting burned in fast-moving markets. Although limit orders cost more, they can save you thousands of dollars. For example, customers eager to get shares of a hot IPO stock placed market orders. Instead of buying the stock near the offering price of $9, some were shocked to find that their orders were filled at prices as high as $90 during the stock's first trading day. Investors who were aware of the price run-up tried to cancel orders but couldn't get through to brokers. Because of this, some brokers accept only limit orders for online IPO purchases on the first day of trading.

- *Don't ignore the online reminders that ask you to check and recheck.* It's easy to make a typo that adds an extra digit to a purchase amount.

INVESTING IN ACTION

INVESTMENT JUNKIES

When Howard, a young investor, watched his friends strike it rich, he stepped gingerly into the waters of online investing for himself. He made $4,000 in a matter of minutes on his first trade, and soon he was deep into *day trading*—the practice of buying and selling stocks very quickly to make a few cents profit. After he met with some success, Howard opened a margin account to leverage his profits. Before long he was a confirmed "investaholic." Not until the market tanked and he was deep in debt did reality hit home for Howard. "I never noticed the sunshine," said another compulsive investor. "All I did was watch CNBC and stare at my computer." Yet even after he stopped trading, he wistfully recalls the extreme euphoria: " I've never felt a high like that. Nothing can replace it."

These investment junkies were not alone. As long as the markets were up and paper profits climbed, the apparent ease of gaining quick riches lured many naive investors eager for quick profits. The speed and simplicity of point-and-click stock online trading led to more impulse buying, as well as a significant increase in the number of stock market gamblers. "It gives gamblers the quick fix and constant action they crave," comments Marvin Steinberg, psychologist and director of the Connecticut Council on Problem Gambling.

Investing as gambling? Hard to accept, but at one point stock traders represented about half the attendees at Gamblers Anonymous meetings. And because it's not uncommon for investment addicts to bet as much as $25,000 on one trade—whereas few gamblers would wager that much on one hand at the casino—the stock market can take them on a quick ride to bankruptcy.

As with other addictions, it's difficult to determine when you cross the line from making occasional impulse stock purchases to becoming a full-fledged investment junkie. According to the Council on Compulsive Gambling of New Jersey, problem gambling affects approximately 10% of investors. These investors can stop gambling after a big loss or intervention from family members. The 5% who cross into compulsive gambler territory have more trouble controlling their addiction.

Here are some warning signs to help you recognize a stock market gambling problem:

- Trading stocks to ease worries
- Becoming irritable when unable to trade
- Making increasingly speculative investments
- Borrowing to be able to invest more
- Experiencing euphoria when you hit it big and depression when you don't
- Needing to raise the amount you invest to feel the thrill

CRITICAL THINKING QUESTION How might online trading and market conditions contribute to an investor's gambling problem?

Sources: Steven T. Goldberg, "He Never Saw the Sun," *Kiplinger's Personal Finance Magazine,* August 2001, downloaded from www.kiplingerspersonalfinance.com; Ruth Simon and E. S. Browning, "Some Online Investors Can't Say No to Playing the Market," *Wall Street Journal,* August 4, 2000, pp. A1, A4; and Paul Sloan, "Can't Stop Checking Your Quotes?" *U.S. News & World Report,* July 10, 2000, p. 40.

- *Don't get carried away.* It's easy to churn your own account. In fact, new online investors trade about twice as much as they did before they went online. To control impulse trading, have a strategy and stick to it.

- *Open accounts with two brokers.* This protects you if your online brokerage's computer system crashes. It also gives you an alternative if one brokerage is blocked with heavy trading volume.

- *Double-check orders for accuracy.* Make sure each trade was completed according to your instructions. It's very easy to make typos or use the wrong stock symbol, so review the confirmation notice to verify that the right number of shares was bought or sold and that the price and commissions or fees are as quoted. Check your account for "unauthorized" trades.

Transaction Costs

Making transactions through brokers or market makers is considerably easier for investors than it would be to negotiate directly, trying to find someone who wants to buy that which they want to sell (or vice versa). To compensate the broker for executing the transaction, investors pay transaction costs, which are usually levied on both the purchase and the sale of securities. When making investment decisions, you must consider the structure and magnitude of transaction costs, because they affect returns.

Since the passage of the *Securities Acts Amendments of 1975*, brokers have been permitted to charge whatever brokerage commissions they deem appropriate. Most firms have established **fixed-commission schedules** that apply to small transactions, the ones most often made by individual investors. On large institutional transactions, the client and broker may arrange a **negotiated commission**—commissions to which both parties agree. Negotiated commissions are also available to individual investors who maintain large accounts, typically above $50,000.

The commission structure varies with the type of security and the type of broker. We'll describe the basic commission structures for various types of securities in subsequent chapters. Because of the way brokerage firms charge commissions on stock trades, it is difficult to compare prices precisely. Traditional brokers generally charge on the basis of number of shares and the price of the stock at the time of the transaction. Internet brokers usually charge flat rates, often for transactions up to 1,000 shares, with additional fees for larger or more complicated orders. However, many traditional brokerage firms have reduced their commissions on broker-assisted trades and have instituted annual flat fees (on wrap accounts) set as a specified percentage of the value of the assets in the account. Unless you are a very active trader, you will probably be better off paying commissions on a per-transaction basis.

Obviously, premium and basic discount brokers charge substantially less than full-service brokers for the same transaction. However, most discounters charge a minimum fee to discourage small orders. For example, one basic discounter, Harris Direct, charges a minimum fee of about $20 but adds a surcharge of $25 for broker-assisted trades. The savings from the discounter are substantial: Depending on the size and type of transaction, premium and basic discount brokers can typically save investors between 30% and 80% of the commission charged by the full-service broker.

Investor Protection: SIPC and Arbitration

Although most investment transactions take place safely, it is important for you to know what protection you have if things *don't* go smoothly. As a client, you are protected against the loss of the securities or cash held by your broker. The **Securities Investor Protection Corporation (SIPC)**, a nonprofit membership

fixed-commission schedules
fixed brokerage commissions that typically apply to the small transactions usually made by individual investors.

negotiated commissions
brokerage commissions agreed to by the client and the broker as a result of their negotiations; typically apply on large institutional transactions and to individual investors who maintain large accounts.

Securities Investor Protection Corporation (SIPC)
a nonprofit membership corporation, authorized by the federal government, that insures each brokerage customer's account for up to $500,000, with claims for cash limited to $100,000 per customer.

corporation, was authorized by the *Securities Investor Protection Act of 1970* to protect customer accounts against the consequences of financial failure of the brokerage firm. The SIPC currently insures each customer's account for up to $500,000, with claims for cash limited to $100,000 per customer. Note that SIPC insurance does not guarantee that the investor will recover the dollar value of the securities; it guarantees only that the securities themselves will be returned. Some brokerage firms also insure certain customer accounts for amounts in excess of $500,000. Certainly, in light of the diversity and quality of services available among brokerage firms, this may be an additional service you should consider when you select a firm and an individual broker.

The SIPC provides protection in case your brokerage firm fails. But what happens if your broker gave you bad advice and, as a result, you lost a lot of money on an investment? Or what if you feel your broker is *churning* your account, the illegal but difficult-to-prove practice of causing excessive trading to increase commissions? In either case, the SIPC won't help. It's not intended to insure you against bad investment advice or churning. Instead, if you have a dispute with your broker, the first thing you should do is discuss the situation with the managing officer at the branch where you do business. If that doesn't do any good, then contact the firm's compliance officer and the securities regulator in your home state.

If you still don't get any satisfaction, you can use litigation (judicial methods in the courts) to resolve the dispute. Alternative dispute resolution processes that may avoid litigation include *mediation* and *arbitration*. **Mediation** is an informal, voluntary approach in which you and the broker agree to a mediator, who facilitates negotiations between the two of you to resolve the case. The mediator does not impose a solution on you and the broker. The NASD and securities-related organizations encourage investors to mediate disputes rather than arbitrate them, because mediation can reduce costs and time for both investors and brokers.

If mediation is not pursued or if it fails, you may have no choice but to take the case to **arbitration,** a formal process whereby you and your broker present the two sides of the argument before an arbitration panel. The panel then decides the case. Many brokerage firms require you to resolve disputes by *binding arbitration;* in this case, you don't have the option to sue. You must accept the arbitrator's decision, and in most cases you cannot go to court to review your case. Before you open an account, check whether the brokerage agreement contains a binding-arbitration clause.

Settling securities disputes through mediation or arbitration rather than litigation has advantages and disadvantages. Mediation and arbitration proceedings typically cost less and are resolved more quickly than litigation. Recent legislation has given many investors the option of using either securities industry panels or independent arbitration panels such as those sponsored by the American Arbitration Association (AAA). Independent panels are considered more sympathetic toward investors. In addition, only one of the three arbitrators on a panel can be connected with the securities industry. However, in 2003, in about 55% of the arbitration cases the client was awarded damages.

Probably the best thing you can do to avoid the need to mediate, arbitrate, or litigate with your broker is to select him or her carefully, understand the

---

HOT LINKS

The Securities Investor Protection Corporation (SIPC) protects customers of broker-dealers registered with the U.S. Securities and Exchange Commission.

www.sipc.org

---

mediation
an informal, voluntary dispute resolution process in which a client and a broker agree to a mediator, who facilitates negotiations between them to resolve the case.

arbitration
a formal dispute resolution process in which a client and a broker present their argument before a panel, which then decides the case.

financial risks involved in the broker's recommendations, thoroughly evaluate the advice he or she offers, and continuously monitor the volume of transactions that he or she recommends and executes. Clearly, it is much less costly to choose the right broker initially than to incur later the financial and emotional costs of having chosen a bad one.

If you have a problem with an online trade, immediately file a written—not e-mail—complaint with the broker. Cite dates, times, and amounts of trades, and include all supporting documentation. File a copy with the NASD regulatory arm Web site (www.nasdr.com) and with your state securities regulator. If you can't resolve the problems with the broker, you can try mediation and then resort to arbitration, litigation being the last resort.

IN REVIEW

CONCEPTS

3.13 Describe the types of services offered by brokerage firms, and discuss the criteria for selecting a suitable stockbroker.

3.14 Briefly differentiate among the following types of brokerage accounts:
a. Single or joint   b. Custodial
c. Cash   d. Margin
e. Wrap

3.15 Differentiate among *market orders*, *limit orders*, and *stop-loss orders*. What is the rationale for using a stop-loss order rather than a limit order?

3.16 Differentiate between the services and costs associated with *full-service*, *premium discount*, and *basic discount* brokers. Be sure to discuss online transactions.

3.17 What is *day trading*, and why is it risky? How can you avoid problems as an online trader?

3.18 In what two ways, based on the number of shares transacted, do brokers typically charge for executing transactions? How are online transaction fees structured relative to the degree of broker involvement?

3.19 What protection does the *Securities Investor Protection Corporation (SIPC)* provide securities investors? How are mediation and arbitration procedures used to settle disputes between investors and their brokers?

Investment Advisers and Investment Clubs

LG 6

investment advisers
Individuals or firms that provide investment advice, typically for a fee.

Although financial information is available from numerous sources, many investors have neither the time nor the expertise to analyze it and make decisions on their own. Instead, they turn to an **investment adviser,** which is an individual or firm that provides investment advice, typically for a fee. Alternatively, some small investors join investment clubs. Here we will discuss using an investment adviser and then briefly cover the key aspects of investment clubs.

Using an Investment Adviser

The "product" provided by an investment adviser ranges from broad, general advice to detailed, specific analyses and recommendations. The most general form of advice is a newsletter published by the adviser. These letters comment on the economy, current events, market behavior, and specific securities. Investment advisers also provide complete individualized investment evaluation, recommendation, and management services.

Regulation of Advisers As we noted in Chapter 2, the *Investment Advisers Act of 1940* ensures that investment advisers make full disclosure of information about their backgrounds, about conflicts of interest, and so on. The act requires professional advisers to register and file periodic reports with the SEC. A 1960 amendment permits the SEC to inspect the records of investment advisers and to revoke the registration of those who violate the act's provisions. However, financial planners, stockbrokers, bankers, lawyers, and accountants who provide investment advice in addition to their main professional activity are not regulated by the act. Many states have also passed similar legislation, requiring investment advisers to register and to abide by the guidelines established by the state law.

Be aware that the federal and state laws regulating the activities of professional investment advisers do not guarantee competence. Rather, they are intended to protect the investor against fraudulent and unethical practices. It is important to recognize that, at present, no law or regulatory body controls entrance into the field. Therefore, investment advisers range from highly informed professionals to totally incompetent amateurs. Advisers who possess a professional designation are usually preferred because they have completed academic courses in areas directly or peripherally related to the investment process. Such designations include CFA (Chartered Financial Analyst), CIMA (Certified Investment Management Analyst), CIC (Chartered Investment Counselor), CFP® (Certified Financial Planner), ChFC (Chartered Financial Consultant), CLU (Chartered Life Underwriter), and CPA (Certified Public Accountant).

Online Investment Advice You can also find financial advice online. Whether it's a retirement planning tool or advice on how to diversify your assets, automated financial advisers may be able to help you. If your needs are specific rather than comprehensive, you can find good advice at other sites. For example, T. Rowe Price has an excellent college planning section (www. troweprice.com/college). Financial Engines (www.financialengines. com), AdviceAmerica (www.adviceamerica.com), and DirectAdvice (www. directadvice.com) are among several independent advice sites that offer broader planning capabilities. Many mutual fund family Web sites have online financial advisers. For example, The Vanguard Group (www.vanguard.com) has a personal investors section that helps you choose funds for specific investment objectives, such as retirement or financing a college education.

The Cost and Use of Investment Advice Professional investment advice typically costs, annually, between 0.25% and 3% of the dollar amount of money being managed. For large portfolios, the fee is typically in the range of 0.25% to 0.75%. For small portfolios (less than $100,000), an annual fee ranging from 2% to 3% of the dollar amount of funds managed would not be unusual. These fees generally cover complete management of a client's money, excluding any purchase or sale commissions. The cost of periodic investment advice not provided as part of a subscription service could be based on a fixed-fee schedule or quoted as an hourly charge for consultation. Online advisers are much less expensive; they either are free or charge an annual fee.

Whether you choose a traditional investment advisory service or decide to try an online service, some are better than others. More expensive services do not necessarily provide better advice. It is best to study carefully the track record and overall reputation of an investment adviser before purchasing his or her services. Not only should the adviser have a good performance record, but he or she also should be responsive to the investor's personal goals.

How good is the advice from online advisers? It's very hard to judge. Their suggested plans are only as good as the input. Beginning investors may not have sufficient knowledge to make wise assumptions on future savings, tax, or inflation rates or to analyze results thoroughly. A good personal financial planner will ask lots of questions to assess your investing expertise and explain what you don't know. These early-stage automated tools may take too narrow a focus and not consider other parts of your investment portfolio. For many investors, online advisers lack what leads them to get help in the first place—the human touch. They want hand-holding, reassurance, and gentle nudging to follow through on their plans.

Investment Clubs

investment club
a legal partnership through which a group of investors are bound to a specified organizational structure, operating procedures, and purpose, which is typically to earn favorable long-term returns from moderate-risk investments.

Another way to obtain investment advice and experience is to join an investment club. This route can be especially useful for those of moderate means who do not want to incur the cost of an investment adviser. An **investment club** is a legal partnership binding a group of investors (partners) to a specified organizational structure, operating procedures, and purpose. The goal of most clubs is to earn favorable long-term returns by making investments in vehicles of moderate risk.

Individuals with similar goals usually form investment clubs to pool their knowledge and money to create a jointly owned and managed portfolio. Certain members are responsible for obtaining and analyzing data on a specific investment vehicle or strategy. At periodic meetings, the members present their findings and recommendations for discussion and further analysis by the membership. The group decides whether to pursue the proposed vehicle or strategy. Most clubs require members to make scheduled contributions to the club's treasury, thereby regularly increasing the pool of investable funds. Although most clubs concentrate on investments in stocks and bonds, some may concentrate on specialized investments such as options or futures.

Membership in an investment club provides an excellent way for the novice investor to learn the key aspects of portfolio construction and investment management, while (one hopes) earning a favorable return on his or her funds. In fact, many investment clubs regularly earn returns above the market and even above professional money managers. The reason? Investment clubs typically buy stocks for the long term, rather than trying to make the quick buck.

As you might expect, investment clubs have also joined the online investing movement. By tapping into the Internet, clubs are freed from geographical restrictions. Now investors around the world, many who have never met, can form a club and discuss investing strategies and stock picks just as easily as if they gathered in person. Finding a time or place to meet is no longer

H O T

A good source of information about investment clubs can be found at fool.com. Go to:

www.fool.com/InvestmentClub/
InvestmentClubIntroduction.htm

an issue. Some clubs are formed by friends; others are strangers who have similar investing philosophies and may have met online. Online clubs conduct business via e-mail or set up a private Web site. Members of the *National Association of Investors Corporation (NAIC)*, a not-for-profit organization, qualify for a site at Yahoo! that includes meeting rooms, investment tools, and other investment features. Other portals offer sites for nonmembers.

NAIC, which has over 325,000 individual and club investors and 28,000 regular and online investment clubs, publishes a variety of useful materials and also sponsors regional and national meetings. (To learn how to start an investment club, visit the NAIC Web site at www.better-investing.org. Or order an information package by calling the toll-free number 877-ASK-NAIC (877-275-6242) or writing NAIC, P.O. Box 220, Royal Oak, MI 48068.)

IN REVIEW

CONCEPTS

3.20 Describe the services that professional investment advisers perform, the way in which they are regulated, online investment advisers, and the cost of investment advice.

3.21 What benefits does an *investment club* offer the small investor? Why do investment clubs regularly outperform the market and the pros? Would you prefer to join a regular or an online club, and why?

Summary

LG 1   **Discuss the growth in online investing, including educational sites and investment tools, and the pros and cons of using the Internet as an investment tool.** The Internet has empowered individual investors by providing information and tools formerly available only to investing professionals and by simplifying the investing process. The savings it provides in time and money are huge. Investors get the most current information, including real-time stock price quotes, market activity data, research reports, educational articles, and discussion forums. Tools such as financial planning calculators, stock-screening programs, charting, and stock quotes and portfolio tracking are free at many sites. Buying and selling securities online is convenient, relatively simple, inexpensive, and fast.

LG 2   **Identify the major types and sources of traditional and online investment information.** Investment information, descriptive or analytical, includes information about the economy and current events, industries and companies, and alternative investment vehicles, as well as price information and personal investment strategies. It can be obtained from financial journals, general newspapers, institutional news, business periodicals, government publications, special subscription services, stockholders' reports, comparative data sources, subscription services, brokerage reports, investment letters, price quotations, and electronic and online sources. Most print publications also have Web sites with access to all or part of their content. Financial portals bring together a variety of financial information online. Investors will also find specialized sites for bond, mutual fund, and international information, as well as discussion forums (message boards and chat rooms) that discuss individual securities and investment strategies. Because it is hard to know the qualifications of those who make postings on message boards, participants must do their own homework before acting on an online tip.

LG 3 Explain the characteristics, interpretation, and uses of the commonly cited stock and bond market averages and indexes. Investors commonly rely on stock market averages and indexes to stay abreast of market behavior. The most often cited are the Dow Jones averages, which include the Dow Jones Industrial Average (DJIA). Also widely followed are the Standard & Poor's indexes, the NYSE composite index, the AMEX composite index, the Nasdaq Stock Market indexes, and the Value Line indexes. Numerous other averages and indexes, including a number of global and foreign market indexes, are regularly reported in financial publications.

Bond market indicators are most often reported in terms of average bond yields and average prices. The Dow Jones Corporate Bond Index is among the most popular. A wealth of yield and price index data is also available for various types of bonds and various domestic and foreign markets. Both stock and bond market statistics are published daily in the *Wall Street Journal* and summarized weekly in *Barron's*.

LG 4 Review the roles of full-service, premium discount, and basic discount stockbrokers, including the services they provide, selection of a stockbroker, opening an account, and transaction basics. Stockbrokers facilitate transactions among buyers and sellers of securities, and they provide a variety of other client services. An investor should select a stockbroker who has a compatible disposition toward investing and whose firm offers the desired services at competitive costs. Today the distinctions among full-service, premium discount, and basic discount brokers is blurring. Most brokers now offer online trading capabilities, and many no-frills brokers are expanding their services to include research and advice. Investors can open a variety of types of brokerage accounts, such as single, joint, custodial, cash, margin, and wrap. An investor can make odd-lot transactions (less than 100 shares) or round-lot transactions (100 shares or multiples thereof). An added fee is typically charged on odd-lot transactions.

LG 5 Describe the basic types of orders (market, limit, and stop-loss), online transactions, transaction costs, and the legal aspects of investor protection. A market order is an order to buy or sell stock at the best price available. A limit order is an order to buy at a specified price or below or to sell at a specified price or above. Stop-loss orders become market orders as soon as the minimum sell price or the maximum buy price is hit. Limit and stop-loss orders can be placed as fill-or-kill orders, day orders, or good-'til-canceled (GTC) orders.

On small transactions, most brokers have fixed-commission schedules; on larger transactions, they will negotiate commissions. Commissions also vary by type of security and type of broker: full-service, premium discount, or basic discount. The Securities Investor Protection Corporation (SIPC) insures customers' accounts against the brokerage firm's failure. To avoid litigation, mediation and arbitration procedures are frequently employed to resolve disputes between investor and broker. These disputes typically concern the investor's belief that the broker either gave bad advice or churned the account.

LG 6 Discuss the roles of investment advisers and investment clubs. There are a variety of different types of investment advisers, who charge an annual fee ranging from 0.25% to 3% of the dollar amount being managed and are often regulated by federal and state law. Web sites that provide investment advice on topics such as retirement planning, asset diversification, and stock and mutual fund selection are now available as well. Investment clubs provide individual investors with investment advice and help them gain investing experience. Online clubs have members in various geographical areas and conduct business via e-mail or at a private Web site.

Putting Your Investment Know-How to the Test

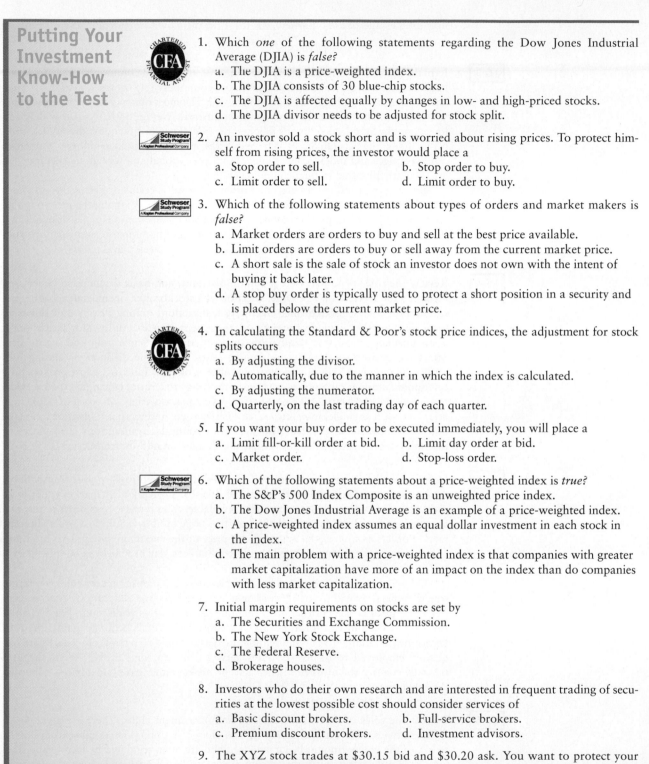

1. Which *one* of the following statements regarding the Dow Jones Industrial Average (DJIA) is *false*?
   a. The DJIA is a price-weighted index.
   b. The DJIA consists of 30 blue-chip stocks.
   c. The DJIA is affected equally by changes in low- and high-priced stocks.
   d. The DJIA divisor needs to be adjusted for stock split.

2. An investor sold a stock short and is worried about rising prices. To protect himself from rising prices, the investor would place a
   a. Stop order to sell.   b. Stop order to buy.
   c. Limit order to sell.   d. Limit order to buy.

3. Which of the following statements about types of orders and market makers is *false*?
   a. Market orders are orders to buy and sell at the best price available.
   b. Limit orders are orders to buy or sell away from the current market price.
   c. A short sale is the sale of stock an investor does not own with the intent of buying it back later.
   d. A stop buy order is typically used to protect a short position in a security and is placed below the current market price.

4. In calculating the Standard & Poor's stock price indices, the adjustment for stock splits occurs
   a. By adjusting the divisor.
   b. Automatically, due to the manner in which the index is calculated.
   c. By adjusting the numerator.
   d. Quarterly, on the last trading day of each quarter.

5. If you want your buy order to be executed immediately, you will place a
   a. Limit fill-or-kill order at bid.   b. Limit day order at bid.
   c. Market order.   d. Stop-loss order.

6. Which of the following statements about a price-weighted index is *true*?
   a. The S&P's 500 Index Composite is an unweighted price index.
   b. The Dow Jones Industrial Average is an example of a price-weighted index.
   c. A price-weighted index assumes an equal dollar investment in each stock in the index.
   d. The main problem with a price-weighted index is that companies with greater market capitalization have more of an impact on the index than do companies with less market capitalization.

7. Initial margin requirements on stocks are set by
   a. The Securities and Exchange Commission.
   b. The New York Stock Exchange.
   c. The Federal Reserve.
   d. Brokerage houses.

8. Investors who do their own research and are interested in frequent trading of securities at the lowest possible cost should consider services of
   a. Basic discount brokers.   b. Full-service brokers.
   c. Premium discount brokers.   d. Investment advisors.

9. The XYZ stock trades at $30.15 bid and $30.20 ask. You want to protect your investment by placing a $30 stop-limit order. When the bid price suddenly drops to $29.90, your order
   a. Automatically executes at $30.
   b. Becomes a market order.
   c. May not execute since the bid price has dropped to less than $30.
   d. Becomes a stop-loss order.

10. Which of the following is *true* about day trading?
    a. It is allowed only in OTC-listed stocks.
    b. It is less risky than buy-and-hold investing because it usually does not involve overnight holding of securities.
    c. It usually involves trading on margin.
    d. It permits investors to buy and sell stocks on credit as long as they buy and sell stocks on the same day.

Answers: 1. c; 2. b; 3. d; 4. b; 5. c; 6. b; 7. c; 8. a; 9. c; 10. c

Discussion Questions

LG 2 **Q3.1** Thomas Weisel, chief executive of a securities firm that bears his name, believes that individual investors already have too much information. "Many lose money by trading excessively on stray data," he says. Other industry professionals oppose the SEC's fair disclosure rule for the same reason. The Securities Industry Association's general counsel expressed concern that the rule will restrict rather than encourage the flow of information. Other securities professionals argue that individual investors aren't really capable of interpreting much of the information now available to them. Explain why you agree or disagree with these opinions.

LG 2 **Q3.2** Innovative Internet-based bookseller Amazon.com has now expanded into other retail categories. Gather appropriate information from relevant sources to assess the following with an eye toward investing in Amazon.com.
    a. Economic conditions and the key current events during the past 12 months.
    b. Information on the status and growth (past and future) of the bookselling industry and specific information on Amazon.com and its major competitors.
    c. Brokerage reports and analysts' recommendations with respect to Amazon.com.
    d. A history of the past and recent dividends and price behavior of Amazon.com, which is traded on the Nasdaq National Market.
    e. A recommendation with regard to the advisability of investing in Amazon.com.

LG 2 **LG 6** **Q3.3** Visit four financial portals or other financial information Web sites listed in Table 3.4. Compare them in terms of ease of use, investment information, investment tools, advisory services, and links to other services. Also catalog the costs, if any, of obtaining these services. Which would you recommend, and why?

LG 3 **Q3.4** Gather and evaluate relevant market averages and indexes over the past 6 months to assess recent stock and bond market conditions. Describe the conditions in each of these markets. Using recent history, coupled with relevant economic and current event data, forecast near-term market conditions. On the basis of your assessment of market conditions, would you recommend investing in stocks, in bonds, or in neither at this time? Explain the reasoning underlying your recommendation.

LG 4 **Q3.5** Prepare a checklist of questions and issues you would use when shopping for a stockbroker. Describe both the ideal broker and the ideal brokerage firm, given your investment goals and disposition. Discuss the pros and cons of using a full-service rather than a premium discount or basic discount broker. If you plan to trade online, what additional questions would you ask?

LG 4 **Q3.6** Visit the sites of two brokerages listed in Table 3.6 or any others you know. After exploring the sites, compare them for ease of use, quality of information, availability of investing tools, reliability, other services, and any other criteria important to you. Summarize your findings and explain which you would choose if you were to open an account, and why.

Q3.7 Describe how, if at all, a conservative and an aggressive investor might use each of the following types of orders as part of their investment programs. Contrast these two types of investors in view of these preferences.
  a. Market.
  b. Limit.
  c. Stop-loss.

Q3.8 Learn more about day trading at sites such as Edgetrade (www.edgetrade .com), Daytradingthemarkets.com (www.daytradingstocks.com), TrendVue (www.trendVUE. com), and The Rookie DayTrader (www.rookiedaytrader.com). On the basis of your research, summarize the way in which day trading works, some strategies for day traders, the risks, and the rewards. What type of person would make a good day trader?

Q3.9 Differentiate between the financial advice you would receive from a traditional investment adviser and one of the new online planning and advice sites. Which would you personally prefer to use, and why? How could membership in an investment club serve as an alternative to a paid investment adviser?

Problems

P3.1 Bill Shaffer estimates that if he does 10 hours of research using data that will cost $75, there is a good chance that he can improve his expected return on a $10,000, 1-year investment from 8% to 10%. Bill feels that he must earn at least $10 per hour on the time he devotes to his research.
  a. Find the cost of Bill's research.
  b. By how much (in dollars) will Bill's return increase as a result of the research?
  c. On a strict economic basis, should Bill perform the proposed research?

P3.2 Imagine that the Mini-Dow Average (MDA) is based on the closing prices of five stocks. The divisor used in the calculation of the MDA is currently 0.765. The closing prices for each of the five stocks in the MDA today and exactly a year ago, when the divisor was 0.790, are given in the accompanying table.

| | Closing Stock Price | |
Stock	Today	One Year Ago
Ace Computers	$ 65	$74
Coburn Motor Company	37	34
National Soap & Cosmetics	110	96
Ronto Foods	73	72
Wings Aircraft	96	87

  a. Calculate the MDA today and that of a year ago.
  b. Compare the values of the MDA calculated in part (a) and describe the apparent market behavior over the last year. Was it a bull or a bear market?

P3.3 The SP-6 index (a fictitious index) is used by many investors to monitor the general behavior of the stock market. It has a base value set equal to 100 at January 1, 1970. In the accompanying table, the closing market values for each of the six stocks included in the index are given for three dates.

	Closing Market Value of Stock		
Stock	June 30, 2005 (Thousands)	January 1, 2005 (Thousands)	January 1, 1970 (Thousands)
1	$ 430	$ 460	$240
2	1,150	1,120	630
3	980	990	450
4	360	420	150
5	650	700	320
6	290	320	80

a. Calculate the value of the SP-6 index on both January 1, 2005, and June 30, 2005, using the data presented here.

b. Compare the values of the SP-6 index calculated in part (a) and relate them to the base index value. Would you describe the general market condition during the 6-month period January 1 to June 30, 2005, as a bull or a bear market?

LG 3

P3.4 Carla Sanchez wishes to develop an average or index that can be used to measure the general behavior of stock prices over time. She has decided to include six closely followed, high-quality stocks in the average or index. She plans to use August 15, 1978, her birthday, as the base and is interested in measuring the value of the average or index on August 15, 2002, and August 15, 2005. She has found the closing prices for each of the six stocks, A through F, at each of the three dates and has calculated a divisor that can be used to adjust for any stock splits, company changes, and so on that have occurred since the base year, which has a divisor equal to 1.00.

	Closing Stock Price		
Stock	August 15, 2005	August 15, 2002	August 15, 1978
A	$46	$40	$50
B	37	36	10
C	20	23	7
D	59	61	26
E	82	70	45
F	32	30	32
Divisor	0.70	0.72	1.00

Note: The number of shares of each stock outstanding has remained unchanged at each of the three dates. Therefore, the closing stock prices will behave identically to the closing market values.

a. Using the data given in the table, calculate the market average, using the same methodology used to calculate the Dow averages, at each of the three dates—the 15th of August 1978, 2002, and 2005.

b. Using the data given in the table and assuming a base index value of 10 on August 15, 1978, calculate the market index, using the same methodology used to calculate the S&P indexes, at each of the three dates.

c. Use your findings in parts **a** and **b** to describe the general market condition—bull or bear—that existed between August 15, 2002, and August 15, 2005.

d. Calculate the percentage changes in the average and index values between August 15, 2002, and August 15, 2005. Why do they differ?

LG 5

P3.5 Al Cromwell places a *market order* to buy a round lot of Thomas, Inc., common stock, which is traded on the NYSE and is currently quoted at $50 per share. Ignoring brokerage commissions, how much money would Cromwell probably have to pay? If he had placed a market order to sell, how much money will he probably receive? Explain.

P3.6 Imagine that you have placed a *limit order* to buy 100 shares of Sallisaw Tool at a price of $38, though the stock is currently selling for $41. Discuss the consequences, if any, of each of the following.

    a. The stock price drops to $39 per share 2 months before cancellation of the limit order.

    b. The stock price drops to $38 per share.

    c. The minimum stock price achieved before cancellation of the limit order was $38.50. When the limit order was canceled, the stock was selling for $47.50 per share.

 P3.7 If you place a *stop-loss order* to sell at $23 on a stock currently selling for $26.50 per share, what is likely to be the minimum loss you will experience on 50 shares if the stock price rapidly declines to $20.50 per share? Explain. What if you had placed a *stop-limit order* to sell at $23, and the stock price tumbled to $20.50?

 P3.8 You sell 100 shares of a stock short for $40 per share. You want to limit your loss on this transaction to no more than $500. What order should you place?

LG 5 **P3.9** You have been researching a stock that you like, which is currently trading at $50 per share. You would like to buy the stock if it were a little less expensive—say, $47 per share. You believe that the stock price will go to $70 by year-end, and then level off or decline. You decide to place a limit order to buy 100 shares of the stock at $47, and a limit order to sell it at $70. It turns out that you were right about the direction of the stock price, and it goes straight to $75. What is your current position?

LG 5 **P3.10** You own 500 shares of Ups&Downs, Inc., stock. It is currently priced at $50. You are going on vacation, and you realize that the company will be reporting earnings while you are away. To protect yourself against a rapid drop in the price, you place a limit order to sell 500 shares at $40. It turns out the earnings report was not so good, and the stock price fell to $30 right after the announcement. It did, however, bounce back, and by the end of the day it was back to $42. What happened in your account?

LG 5 **P3.11** You have $5,000 in a 50% margin account. You have been following a stock that you think you want to buy. The stock is priced at $52. You decide that if the stock falls to $50, you would like to buy it. You place a limit order to buy 300 shares at $50. The stock falls to $50. What happens?

See the text Web site
(**www.aw-bc.com/gitman_joehnk**) **for Web exercises**
that deal with *online information and investing*.

Case Problem 3.1   *The Perezes' Good Fortune*

LG 2   **LG 4**   **LG 6**

Angel and Marie Perez own a small pool hall located in southern New Jersey. They enjoy running the business, which they have owned for nearly 3 years. Angel, a retired professional pool shooter, saved for nearly 10 years to buy this business, which he and his wife own free and clear. The income from the pool hall is adequate to allow Angel, Marie, and their two children, Mary (age 10) and José (age 4), to live comfortably.

Although he lacks formal education beyond the tenth grade, Angel has become an avid reader. He enjoys reading about current events and personal finance, particularly investing. He especially likes *Money* magazine, from which he has gained numerous ideas for better managing the family's finances. Because of the long hours required to run the business, Angel can devote 3 to 4 hours a day (on the job) to reading.

Recently, Angel and Marie were notified that Marie's uncle had died and left them a portfolio of stocks and bonds with a current market value of $300,000. They were elated to learn of their good fortune but decided it would be best not to change their lifestyle as a result of this inheritance. Instead, they want their newfound wealth to provide for their children's college education as well as their own retirement. They decided that, like their uncle, they would keep these funds invested in stocks and bonds. Angel felt that in view of this, he needed to acquaint himself with the securities currently in the portfolio. He knew that to manage the portfolio himself, he would have to stay abreast of the securities markets as well as the economy in general. He also realized that he would need to follow each security in the portfolio and continuously evaluate possible alternative securities that could be substituted as conditions warranted. Because Angel had plenty of time in which to follow the market, he strongly believed that with proper information, he could manage the portfolio. Given the amount of money involved, Angel was not too concerned with the information costs; rather, he wanted the best information he could get at a reasonable price.

Questions

a. Explain what role the *Wall Street Journal* and/or *Barron's* might play in meeting Angel's needs. What other general sources of economic and current event information would you recommend to Angel? Explain.

b. How might Angel be able to use the services of Standard & Poor's Corporation, Mergent, and the *Value Line Investment Survey* to learn about the securities in the portfolio? Indicate which, if any, of these services you would recommend, and why.

c. Recommend some specific online investment information sources and tools to help Angel and Marie manage their investments.

d. Explain to Angel the need to find a good stockbroker and the role the stockbroker could play in providing information and advice. Should he consider hiring a financial adviser to manage the portfolio?

e. Give Angel a summary prescription for obtaining information and advice that will help to ensure the preservation and growth of the family's newfound wealth.

Case Problem 3.2   *Peter and Deborah's Choices of Brokers and Advisers*

Peter Chang and Deborah Barry, friends who work for a large software company, decided to leave the relative security of their employer and join the staff of OnlineSpeed Inc., a 2-year-old company working on new broadband technology for fast Internet access. Peter will be a vice president for new-product development; Deborah will be treasurer. Although they are excited about the potential their new jobs offer, they recognize the need to consider the financial implications of the move. Of immediate concern are their 401(k) retirement plans. On leaving their current employer, each of them will receive a lump-sum settlement of about $75,000 that they must roll over into self-directed, tax-deferred retirement accounts. The friends met over lunch to discuss their options for investing these funds.

Peter is 30 years old and single, with a bachelor's degree in computer science. He rents an apartment and would like to buy a condominium fairly soon but is in no rush. For now, he is happy using his money on the luxuries of life. He considers himself a bit of a risk taker and has dabbled in the stock market from time to time, using his technology expertise to invest in software and Internet companies. Deborah's undergraduate degree was in English, followed by an M.B.A. in finance. She is 32, is married, and hopes to start a family very soon. Her husband is a physician in private practice.

Peter is very computer-savvy and likes to pick stocks on the basis of his own Internet research. Although Deborah's finance background gives her a solid understanding of investing fundamentals, she is more conservative and has thus far stayed with blue-chip stocks and mutual funds. Among the topics that come up during their lunchtime conversation are stockbrokers and financial planners. Peter is leaning toward a bare-bones basic discount broker with low cost per online trade that is offering free trades for a limited time. Deborah is also cost-conscious but warns Peter that the low costs can be deceptive if you have to pay for other services or find yourself trading more often. She also thinks Peter is too focused on the technology sector and encourages him to seek financial advice to balance his portfolio. They agree to research a number of brokerage firms and investment advisers and meet again to compare notes.

Questions

a.   Research at least four different full-service, premium discount, and basic discount stock brokerage firms, and compare the services and costs. What brokers would suit Peter's needs best, and why? What brokers would suit Deborah's needs best, and why? What are some key questions each should ask when interviewing potential brokers?

b.   What factors should Peter and Deborah consider before deciding to use a particular broker? Compare the pros and cons of getting the personal attention of a full-service broker with the services provided by the discount brokers.

c.   Do you think that a broker that assists in making transactions and focuses on personal attention would be a good choice for either Peter or Deborah?

d.   Peter mentioned to Deborah that he had read an article about *day trading* and wanted to try it. What would you advise Peter about the risks and rewards of this strategy?

e.   Prepare a brief overview of the traditional and online sources of investment advice that could help Peter and Deborah create suitable portfolios. Which type of adviser would you recommend for Peter? For Deborah? Explain your reasoning.

Excel with Spreadsheets

Peter Tanaka is interested in starting a stock portfolio. He has heard many financial reporters talk about the Dow Jones Industrial Average (DJIA) as being a proxy for the overall stock market. From visiting various online investment sites, Peter is able to track the variability in the Dow. Peter would like to develop an average or index that will measure the price performance of his selected portfolio over time. He has decided to create a price-weighted index, similar to the Dow where the stocks are held in proportion to their share prices. He wishes to form an index based on the following ten high quality stocks and has designated October 13, 1971, as the base year. The number of shares outstanding has remained constant over the time period 1971 through 2005. The implication is that the closing stock prices will behave just like the closing market values. Given the data below, **create a spreadsheet** to model and analyze the use of an index.

Stocks	Prices		
	10/13/2005	10/13/2001	10/13/1971
A	45	50	55
B	12	9	15
C	37	37	37
D	65	66	67
E	36	42	48
F	26	35	43
G	75	68	59
H	35	38	30
I	67	74	81
J	84	88	92

Questions

a. The divisor is 1.00 on October 13, 1971, .75 on October 13, 2001, and .85 on October 13, 2005. Using this information and the data supplied above, calculate the market average, using the same methodology used to calculate the Dow averages, on each of the three dates—the 13th of October 1971, 2001, and 2005.

b. The DJIA is the most widely cited stock market indicator, yet there are criticisms of the model. One criticism is that the higher-priced securities in the portfolio will impact the Dow more than the relatively lower-priced stocks. Assume that Stock J increases by 10%. Recalculate the market averages on each of the three dates.

c. Next, assume Stock J is back to its original level and Stock B increases by 10%. Recalculate the market averages on each of the three dates. Compare your findings in all three scenarios. Do you find support for the criticism of the Dow? Explain.

TRADING ONLINE WITH OTIS

There are fundamental differences among traded stocks. Organized exchanges such as the New York Stock Exchange (NYSE) are auction markets. In contrast, the over-the-counter (OTC) market is a dealers' market that involves a computerized network of market makers. The National Association of Securities Dealers Automated Quotation (Nasdaq) system is the most prominent dealers' market. In this electronic quotation system, the difference between the bid price and the asked price constitutes the *spread*, which represents the commission to the dealer in that stock.

On the NYSE, prices are set by supply and demand. Orders are directed to a specialist in the stock who works on the floor of the exchange either electronically or through a broker. The specialist matches the orders, and the stock is sold at one price. Specialists are required to make a fair and orderly market in securities assigned to them. They do not make a commission for matching orders but rather for filling special orders or buying and selling for their own account.

Although numerous special orders exist, the exercises here will be limited to the following:

Limit, Limit Order, or Limited Price Order
This order directs the specialist to buy a stock at a specified price or lower if obtainable when the order is given to the trading floor. It is an order to sell a security at the specified price or higher.

Stop Order A stop order to buy becomes a market order when a transaction in the security occurs at or above the stop price. A stop order to sell becomes a market order when a transaction in the security reaches or falls below the stop price.

Stop-Limit Order An order to buy becomes a limit order executable at the limit price or a better price, if a transaction in the stock occurs at or above the stop price. A stop-limit order to sell is executable at or above the limit price.

Exercises

1. Buy a stock and put in a limit order to sell it at a given price.
2. Place two stop orders to buy securities at a price close to where it is presently trading (above or below). If a stop price is reached and it becomes a market order, record the price at which it was purchased. Was it purchased at the stop price? Must it be purchased at the stop price?
3. Sell a stock with a stop-limit order.

PART TWO

IMPORTANT CONCEPTUAL TOOLS

CHAPTER 4
RETURN AND RISK

CHAPTER 5
MODERN PORTFOLIO CONCEPTS

CHAPTER 4

RETURN AND RISK

LEARNING GOALS

After studying this chapter, you should be able to:

LG 1 Review the concept of return, its components, the forces that affect the investor's level of return, and historical returns.

LG 2 Discuss the time value of money and the calculations involved in finding the future value of various types of cash flows.

LG 3 Explain the concept of present value, the procedures for calculating present values, and the use of present value in determining whether an investment is satisfactory.

LG 4 Describe real, risk-free, and required returns and the computation and application of holding period return, yield (internal rate of return), and growth rates.

LG 5 Discuss the key sources of risk and how they might affect potential investment vehicles.

LG 6 Understand the risk of a single asset, risk assessment, and the steps that combine return and risk.

 hen you go shopping for a stereo system, you go to the store, consult a catalog, or visit a Web site to examine the merchandise. When you invest in the stock of a company, you may be familiar with its products, but this information tells only part of the story. Suppose you are considering buying the stock of ChevronTexaco, a major global energy company. A visit to the company's Web site, www.chevrontexaco.com, would tell you that the company was on the upswing, with the first half of fiscal year 2003 (June 30, 2003) showing huge gains over the same period in 2002. For this 6-month period, revenues were up 30%, net income was up 218%, and earnings per share were up 210%. The company also reduced its debt from its December 31, 2002, levels and raised its dividend for the sixteenth consecutive year.

This promising picture might increase your desire to buy the stock. But before placing that buy order, you should investigate the risks associated with the stock by searching the business press and online investment sites for articles and investment research about ChevronTexaco. Your research would tell you that the higher 2003 revenues reflected product price increases, while the healthy jump in net income arose in part because 2002 earnings were low due to expenses of the Chevron–Texaco merger. The energy industry has risks specific to it, such as the potential for failure of costly exploration efforts. ChevronTexaco's presence in more than 180 countries exposes it to additional external risk. For example, a political coup in a country where ChevronTexaco has refineries or pipelines could disrupt operations. Changes in legislation in foreign countries could affect taxation. Currency exchange risk is another key factor for ChevronTexaco.

To use this information wisely, you need to understand the concepts of return and risk, which lie at the heart of any investment decision. In this chapter we'll explain which factors affect the level of investment return and consider how to assess the different types of risk.

Sources: "ChevronTexaco," Yahoo! Finance, downloaded from http://finance.yahoo.com, accessed September 29, 2003; "ChevronTexaco Reports Second Quarter Net Income of $1.6 Billion," ChevronTexaco Corporation press release, August 1, 2003, downloaded from the ChevronTexaco Web site, www.chevrontexaco.com.

The Concept of Return

return
the level of profit from an investment—that is, the reward for investing.

Investors are motivated to invest in a given vehicle by its expected return. The **return** is the level of profit from an investment—that is, the reward for investing. Suppose you have $1,000 in an insured savings account paying 5% annual interest, and a business associate asks you to lend her that much money. If you lend her the money for 1 year, at the end of which she pays you back, your return will depend on the amount of interest you charge. If you make an interest-free loan, your return will be zero. If you charge 5% interest, your return will be $50 (0.05 × $1,000). Because you are already earning a safe 5% on the $1,000, it seems clear that to equal that return you should charge your associate a minimum of 5% interest.

Some investment vehicles guarantee a return; others do not. The return earned on $1,000 deposited in an insured savings account at a large bank can be viewed as certain. The return earned on a $1,000 loan to your business associate might be less certain. What is your return if she runs into financial difficulty? If she can repay you only $850, your return will be minus $150 ($850 − $1,000), or minus 15% (−$150 ÷ $1,000). Thus the size of the expected return is one important factor in choosing a suitable investment.

Components of Return

The return on an investment may come from more than one source. The most common source is periodic payments, such as dividends or interest. The other source of return is appreciation in value, the gain from selling an investment vehicle for more than its original purchase price. We call these two sources of return *current income* and *capital gains* (or *capital losses*), respectively.

Current Income Current income may take the form of dividends from stocks, interest received on bonds, or dividends received from mutual funds. To be considered income, it must be in the form of cash or be readily convertible into cash. For our purposes, **current income** is usually cash or near-cash that is periodically received as a result of owning an investment.

Using the data in Table 4.1 (on page 134), we can calculate the current income from investments A and B, both purchased for $1,000, over a 1-year period of ownership. Investment A would provide current income of $80, investment B $120. Solely on the basis of the current income received over the 1-year period, investment B seems preferable.

Capital Gains (or Losses) The second dimension of return is concerned with the change, if any, in the market value of an investment. As noted in Chapter 1, the amount by which the proceeds from the sale of an investment exceed its original purchase price is called a *capital gain*. If an investment is sold for less than its original purchase price, a *capital loss* results.

We can calculate the capital gain or loss of the investments as shown in Table 4.1. For investment A, a capital gain of $100 ($1,100 sale price − $1,000 purchase price) is realized over the 1-year period. For investment B, a $40 capital loss results ($960 sale price − $1,000 purchase price).

Combining the capital gain (or loss) with the current income (calculated in the preceding section) gives the **total return** on each investment over the 1-year ownership period as shown in Table 4.2 (on page 134). In terms of the total return earned on the $1,000 investment over the 1-year period, investment A is superior to investment B.

current income
usually cash or near-cash that is periodically received as a result of owning an investment.

total return
the sum of the current income and the capital gain (or loss) earned on an investment over a specified period of time.

TABLE 4.1	Profiles of Two Investments		
		Investment	
		A	B
Purchase price (beginning of year)		$1,000	$1,000
Cash received			
1st quarter		$ 10	$ 0
2nd quarter		20	0
3rd quarter		20	0
4th quarter		30	120
Total current income (for year)		$ 80	$ 120
Sale price (end of year)		$1,100	$ 960

TABLE 4.2	Total Returns of Two Investments		
		Investment	
Return		A	B
Current income		$ 80	$120
Capital gain (loss)		100	(40)
Total return		$180	$ 80

The use of *percentage returns* is generally preferred to the use of dollar returns. Percentages allow direct comparison of different sizes and types of investments. Investment A earned an 18% return ($180 ÷ $1,000), whereas B yielded only an 8% return ($80 ÷ $1,000). At this point investment A appears preferable, but differences in risk might cause some investors to prefer B. (We will see why later in this chapter.)

Why Return Is Important

Return is a key variable in the investment decision: It allows us to compare the actual or expected gains of various investments with the levels of return we need. For example, you would be satisfied with an investment that earns 12% if you needed it to earn only 10%. You would not be satisfied with a 10% return if you needed a 14% return. Return can be measured historically, or it can be used to formulate future expectations.

Historical Performance Although most people recognize that future performance is not guaranteed by past performance, they would agree that past data often provide a meaningful basis for future expectations. A common practice in the investment world is to look closely at the historical performance of a given vehicle when formulating expectations about its future.

Interest rates and other measures of financial return are most often cited on an annual basis. Evaluation of past investment returns is typically done on the same basis. Consider the data for a hypothetical investment presented in Table 4.3. Two aspects of these data are important. First, we can determine the

TABLE 4.3   Historical Investment Data for a Hypothetical Investment

		Market Value (Price)			Total Return	
Year	(1) Income	(2) Beginning of Year	(3) End of Year	(4) (3) − (2) Capital Gain	(5) (1) + (4) ($)	(6) (5) ÷ (2) (%)*
1996	$4.00	$100	$ 95	− $ 5.00	− $ 1.00	− 1.00%
1997	3.00	95	99	4.00	7.00	7.37
1998	4.00	99	105	6.00	10.00	10.10
1999	5.00	105	115	10.00	15.00	14.29
2000	5.00	115	125	10.00	15.00	13.04
2001	3.00	125	120	− 5.00	− 2.00	− 1.60
2002	3.00	120	122	2.00	5.00	4.17
2003	4.00	122	130	8.00	12.00	9.84
2004	5.00	130	140	10.00	15.00	11.54
2005	5.00	140	155	15.00	20.00	14.29
Average	$4.10			$ 5.50	$ 9.60	8.20%

*Percent return on beginning-of-year market value of investment.

average level of return generated by this investment over the past 10 years. Second, we can analyze the trend in this return. As a percentage, the average total return (column 6) over the past 10 years was 8.20%. Looking at the yearly returns, we can see that after the negative return in 1996, 4 years of positive and generally increasing returns occurred before the negative return was repeated in 2001. From 2002 through 2005, positive and increasing returns were again realized.

Expected Return   In the final analysis, it's the future that matters when we make investment decisions. Therefore, **expected return** is a vital measure of performance. It's what you think the investment will earn in the future that determines what you should be willing to pay for it.

To demonstrate, let's return to the data in Table 4.3. Looking at the historical return figures in the table, an investor would note the increasing trend in returns from 2002 through 2005. But to project future returns, we need insights into the investment's prospects. If the trend in returns seems likely to continue, an expected return in the range of 12% to 15% for 2006 or 2007 would seem reasonable. On the other hand, if future prospects seem poor, or if the investment is subject to cycles, an expected return of 8% to 9% may be a more reasonable estimate. Over the past 10 years, the investment's returns have cycled from a poor year (1996 and 2001) to 4 years of increasing returns (1997–2000 and 2002–2005). We might therefore expect low returns in 2006 to be followed by increasing returns in the 2007–2010 period.

expected return
the return an investor thinks an investment will earn in the future.

Level of Return

The level of return achieved or expected from an investment will depend on a variety of factors. The key factors are internal characteristics and external forces.

Internal Characteristics Certain characteristics of an investment affect its level of return. Examples include the type of investment vehicle, the quality of management, how the investment is financed, and the customer base of the issuer. For example, the common stock of a large, well-managed, completely equity-financed plastics manufacturer whose major customer is IBM would be expected to provide a level of return different from that of a small, poorly managed, largely debt-financed clothing manufacturer whose customers are small specialty stores. As we will see in later chapters, assessing internal factors and their impact on return is one important step in analyzing potential investments.

External Forces External forces such as Federal Reserve actions, shortages, war, price controls, and political events may also affect the level of return. None of these are under the control of the issuer of the investment vehicle. Investment vehicles are affected differently by these forces. It is not unusual to find two vehicles with similar internal characteristics offering significantly different returns. As a result of the same external force, the expected return from one vehicle may increase, while that of another decreases. Likewise, the economies of various countries respond to external forces in different ways.

inflation
a period of generally rising prices.

deflation
a period of generally declining prices.

Another external force is the *general level of price changes,* either up—**inflation**—or down—**deflation**. Inflation tends to have a positive impact on investment vehicles such as real estate, and a negative impact on vehicles such as stocks and fixed-income securities. Rising interest rates, which normally accompany increasing rates of inflation, can significantly affect returns. The actions, if any, the federal government takes to control inflation can increase, decrease, or have no effect on investment returns. Furthermore, the return on each type of investment vehicle exhibits its own unique response to inflation. The *Investing in Action* box on page 137 looks at the returns in the stock market in recent years, and considers whether such returns are likely to continue and what to do if they do not.

Historical Returns

Investment returns vary both over time and between different types of investments. By averaging historical returns over a long period of time, it is possible to eliminate the impact of various types of risk. This enables the investor to focus on the differences in return that are attributable primarily to the types of investment. Table 4.4 shows the average annual rates of return for a number of

TABLE 4.4	Historical Returns for Popular Security Investments (1926–2002)
Investment	Average Annual Return
Large-company stocks	12.2%
Small-company stocks	16.9
Long-term corporate bonds	6.2
Long-term government bonds	5.8
U.S. Treasury bills	3.8
Inflation	3.1%

Source: Stocks, Bonds, Bills, and Inflation, 2003 Yearbook (Chicago: Ibbotson Associates, Inc., 2002), p. 33.

INVESTING IN ACTION

MANY HAPPY RETURNS . . . MAYBE

Until 2000, it was fairly easy to make money in the stock market. From April 1991 through December 2000, the economy continued to expand—for a record 117 months, compared to an average expansion of 35 months. Even novice investors have enjoyed stellar returns. For example, during the period 1990–1999 the average annual return on the S&P 500 stocks was 18.2%, and it climbed to a whopping 28.4% from 1995 through 1999. That return is considerably higher than the 1926–2002 average annual return of 12.2% per year, compared with 6.2% for long-term bonds over the same period. According to Jeremy Siegel, finance professor at the University of Pennsylvania's Wharton School, stocks outperformed bonds and cash in 80% of the 10-year periods dating back to 1802, when the first data became available.

Yet investors who started buying stocks during the past few years got a rude wake-up call in 2000, when the markets turned from bull to bear. No longer could they expect average returns of 15% to 30% and ignore the market's brief bear-like periods, saying, "It's just a minor correction. Stocks will bounce back." From 1998 to 2003, annual returns averaged a mere 1.7%; for the period January 1, 2000, to June 30, 2003, returns slid to −4.7% (based on the Dow Jones Industrial Average). Bond yields also tumbled to a four-decade low. If this kind of bear market coincides with your retirement, you could find yourself unable to afford the lifestyle you envisioned.

Many experts, including Warren Buffet and Wharton's Siegel, believe that lower returns will be the norm for at least the next decade as investors who saw their portfolios dwindle in the recent bear market hesitate to buy stocks again. Even with annual returns in the 5% to

7% range, however, stocks offer the best growth picture for the long term, outpacing bonds or cash after taking inflation into account. "That math isn't bad, but it is bad for people who expected long-term returns based on looking in the rear-view mirror," comments Buffett.

What can you do to ride out the market's twists and turns? Plan to invest for the long term, because you can't predict stock market gains in advance. They come in sudden clumps—a big month or two, followed by flat or down months. If you try to time the market, by selling when a price drop scares you and buying when prices are rising, you won't benefit from the market's successful long-term record. Focus on what share prices will be in the future, using analysis techniques like the ones we describe in Part Three of this book, not what they were 3 years ago. Invest as much as you can now, and let compounding work in your favor. Don't be dazzled by companies with rapid revenue growth but not profits. Finally, diversify your portfolio among asset classes (more on this in Chapter 5).

CRITICAL THINKING QUESTIONS What has history taught us about the stock market? What should you do to ride out the market's twists and turns?

Sources: Jeff Brown, "Even a Good January Doesn't Guarantee You Solid Returns This Year," *Knight Ridder Tribune News Service,* January 6, 2003, downloaded from ProQuest, proquest.umi.com; Jonathan Clements, "Why Baby Boomers Shouldn't Root for a Quick Stock-Market Rebound," *Wall Street Journal,* March 26, 2003, p. D.1; Terence Flanagan, "Buffett Tells Investors to Be Realistic About Stock Returns," *Washington Post,* May 4, 2003, p. A.7; and Kathy Kristof, "Bull Run Shouldn't Lead Expectations Astray," *Dallas Morning News,* May 5, 2000, p. 5H.

popular security investments (and inflation) over the 77-year period January 1, 1926, through December 31, 2002. Each rate represents the average annual rate of return an investor would have realized had he or she purchased the investment on January 1, 1926, and sold it on December 31, 2002. You can see that significant differences exist between the average annual rates of return realized on the various types of stocks, bonds, and bills shown. Later in this chapter, we will see how these differences in return can be linked to differences in the risk of each of these investments.

4.1 Explain what is meant by the *return* on an investment. Differentiate between the two components of return—current income and capital gains (or losses).

4.2 What role do historical performance data play in estimating the expected return from a given investment? Discuss the key factors affecting investment returns—internal characteristics and external forces.

The Time Value of Money*

LG 2   LG 3

time value of money
the fact that as long as an opportunity exists to earn interest, the value of money is affected by the point in time when the money is received.

Imagine that at age 25 you begin making annual cash deposits of $1,000 into a savings account that pays 5% annual interest. After 40 years, at age 65, you will have made deposits totaling $40,000 (40 years × $1,000 per year). Assuming you made no withdrawals, what do you think your account balance will be—$50,000? $75,000? $100,000? The answer is none of the above. Your $40,000 will have grown to nearly $121,000! Why? Because the time value of money allows the deposits to earn interest, and that interest also earns interest over the 40 years. **Time value of money** refers to the fact that as long as an opportunity exists to earn interest, the value of money is affected by the point in time when the money is received.

As a general rule, *the sooner you receive a return on a given investment, the better.* For example, two investments each requiring a $1,000 outlay and each expected to return $100 interest over a 2-year holding period are *not necessarily* equally desirable. If the first investment returns $100 at the end of the first year and the second investment returns the $100 at the end of the second year, the first investment is preferable (assuming that the base value of each remains at $1,000). Investment 1 is preferable because the $100 interest it earns could be *reinvested to earn more interest* while the $100 in interest from investment 2 is still accruing at the end of the first year. You should not fail to consider time value concepts when making investment decisions.

Interest: The Basic Return to Savers

A savings account at a bank is one of the most basic forms of investment. The saver receives interest in exchange for placing idle funds in an account. **Interest** can be viewed as the "rent" paid by a borrower for use of the lender's money. The saver will experience neither a capital gain nor a capital loss, because the value of the investment (the initial deposit) will change only by the amount of interest earned. For the saver, the interest earned over a given time frame is that period's current income.

interest
the "rent" paid by a borrower for use of the lender's money.

Simple Interest The income paid on investment vehicles that pay interest (such as CDs and bonds) is most often calculated using **simple interest**: Interest

simple interest
interest paid only on the initial deposit for the amount of time it is held.

---

* This section presents the fundamental concepts and techniques of time value of money. Those already familiar with these important ideas may wish to skip this discussion and continue at the heading "Determining a Satisfactory Investment" on page 149.

is paid only on the initial deposit for the amount of time it is held. For example, if you held a $100 initial deposit in an account paying 6% interest for 1½ years, you would earn $9 in interest (1½ × 0.06 × $100) over this period. Had you withdrawn $50 at the end of half a year, the total interest earned over the 1½ years would be $6. You would earn $3 interest on $100 for the first half year (½ × 0.06 × $100) and $3 interest on $50 for the next full year (1 × 0.06 × $50).

true rate of interest (return)
the actual rate of interest earned.

When an investment earns simple interest, the stated rate of interest is the **true rate of interest** (or **return**). This is the actual rate of interest earned. In the foregoing example, the true rate of interest is 6%. Because the interest rate reflects the rate at which current income is earned regardless of the size of the deposit, it is a useful measure of current income.

compound interest
interest paid not only on the initial deposit but also on any interest accumulated from one period to the next.

Compound Interest Compound interest is interest paid not only on the initial deposit but also on any interest accumulated from one period to the next. This is the method typically used by savings institutions. When interest is compounded annually over a single year, compound and simple interest calculations provide similar results. In such a case, the stated interest rate and the true interest rate are equal.

The data in Table 4.5 illustrate compound interest. In this case, the interest earned each year is left on deposit rather than withdrawn. The $50 of interest earned on the $1,000 initial deposit during 2004 becomes part of the beginning (initial) balance on which interest is paid in 2005, and so on. *Note that simple interest is used in the compounding process;* that is, interest is paid only on the initial balance held during the given time period.

When an investment earns compound interest, the stated and true interest rates are equal only when interest is compounded annually. In general, *the more frequently interest is compounded at a stated rate, the higher the true rate of interest.* The interest calculations for the deposit data in Table 4.5, assuming that interest is compounded semiannually (twice a year), are shown in Table 4.6 (on page 140). The interest for each 6-month period is found by multiplying the beginning (initial) balance for the 6 months by half of the stated 5% interest rate (see column 3 of Table 4.6). You can see that larger returns are associated with more frequent compounding: Compare the end-of-2006 account balance at 5% compounded annually with the end-of-2006 account balance at 5% compounded semiannually. The semiannual compounding results in a higher balance ($1,879.19 versus $1,876.88). Clearly, with semiannual compounding, the true rate of interest is greater than the 5%

EXCEL with
SPREADSHEETS

TABLE 4.5   Savings Account Balance Data
(5% interest compounded annually)

Date	(1) Deposit (Withdrawal)	(2) Beginning Account Balance	(3) 0.05 × (2) Interest for Year	(4) (2) + (3) Ending Account Balance
1/1/04	$1,000	$1,000.00	$50.00	$1,050.00
1/1/05	(300)	750.00	37.50	787.50
1/1/06	1,000	1,787.50	89.38	1,876.88

TABLE 4.6   Savings Account Balance Data
(5% interest compounded semiannually)

Date	(1) Deposit (Withdrawal)	(2) Beginning Account Balance	(3) 0.05 × 1/2 × (2) Interest for 6 Months	(4) (2) + (3) Ending Account Balance
1/1/04	$1,000	$1,000.00	$25.00	$1,025.00
7/1/04		1,025.00	25.63	1,050.63
1/1/05	(300)	750.63	18.77	769.40
7/1/05		769.40	19.24	788.64
1/1/06	1,000	1,788.64	44.72	1,833.36
7/1/06		1,833.36	45.83	1,879.19

TABLE 4.7   True Rate of Interest for Various Compounding Frequencies
(5% stated rate of interest)

Compounding Frequency	True Rate of Interest	Compounding Frequency	True Rate of Interest
Annually	5.000%	Monthly	5.120%
Semiannually	5.063	Weekly	5.125
Quarterly	5.094	Continuously	5.127

annually compounded rate. The true rates of interest associated with a 5% stated rate and various compounding frequencies are shown in Table 4.7.

continuous compounding
interest calculation in which interest is compounded over the smallest possible interval of time.

Continuous compounding calculates interest by compounding over the smallest possible interval of time. It results in the maximum true rate of interest that can be achieved with a given stated rate of interest. Table 4.7 shows that the more frequently interest is compounded, the higher the true rate of interest. Because of the impact that differences in compounding frequencies have on return, you should evaluate the true rate of interest associated with various alternatives before making a deposit.

Computational Aids for Use in Time Value Calculations

Time-consuming calculations are often involved in adjusting for the time value of money. Although you should understand the concepts and mathematics underlying these calculations, the application of time value techniques can be streamlined. We will demonstrate the use of financial tables, hand-held financial calculators, and computers and spreadsheets as computational aids.

Financial Tables Financial tables include various interest factors that simplify time value calculations. The values in these tables are easily developed from formulas, with various degrees of rounding. The tables are typically indexed by the interest rate (in columns) and the number of periods (in rows). Figure 4.1 shows this general layout. The interest factor at a 20% interest rate for 10 years would be found at the intersection of the 20% column and the 10-period row, as shown by the dark blue box. A full set of the four basic financial tables is included in Appendix A at the end of the book. These tables are described more fully later in this chapter.

FIGURE 4.1

Financial Tables

Layout and use of a
financial table

Period	1%	2%	⋯	10%	⋯	20%	⋯	50%
						Interest Rate ↓		
1			⋯		⋯	⋮	⋯	
2			⋯		⋯	⋮	⋯	
3			⋯		⋯	⋮	⋯	
⋮	⋮	⋮	⋯	⋮	⋯	⋮	⋯	⋮
→ 10	⋯	⋯	⋯	⋯	⋯	**X.XXX**	⋯	⋯
⋮	⋮	⋮	⋯	⋮	⋯	⋮	⋯	⋮
20			⋯		⋯	⋮	⋯	
⋮	⋮	⋮	⋯	⋮	⋯	⋮	⋯	⋮
50			⋯		⋯	⋮	⋯	

Financial Calculators Financial calculators also can be used for time value computations. Generally, *financial calculators* include numerous preprogrammed financial routines. In this and later chapters, we show the keystrokes for various financial computations.

We focus primarily on the keys pictured and defined in Figure 4.2. We typically use four of the five keys in the left column, plus the compute (CPT) key. One of the four keys represents the unknown value being calculated. (Occasionally, all five of the keys are used, with one representing the unknown value.) The keystrokes on some of the more sophisticated calculators are menu-driven: After you select the appropriate routine, the calculator prompts you to input each value; on these calculators, a compute key is not needed to obtain a solution. Regardless, any calculator with the basic time value functions can be used in lieu of financial tables. The keystrokes for other financial calculators are explained in the reference guides that accompany them.

Once you understand the basic underlying concepts, you probably will want to use a calculator to streamline routine financial calculations. With a little practice, you can increase both the speed and the accuracy of your financial computations. Note that because of a calculator's greater precision, slight differences are likely to exist between values calculated by using financial

FIGURE 4.2

Calculator Keys

Important financial keys on the typical calculator

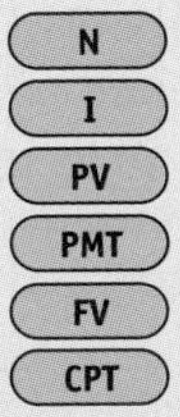

N	PMT	FV	CPT

N	—	Number of periods
I	—	Interest rate per period
PV	—	Present value
PMT	—	Amount of payment (used only for annuities)
FV	—	Future value
CPT	—	Compute key used to initiate financial calculation once all values are input

tables and those found with a financial calculator. Remember that *conceptual understanding of the material is the objective.* An ability to solve problems with the aid of a calculator does not necessarily reflect such an understanding, so don't just settle for answers. Work with the material until you are sure you also understand the concepts.

Computers and Spreadsheets Like financial calculators, computers and spreadsheets have built-in routines that simplify time value calculations. We provide in the text a number of spreadsheet solutions that identify the cell entries for calculating time values. The value for each variable is entered in a cell in the spreadsheet, and the calculation is programmed using an equation that links the individual cells. If values of the variables are changed, the solution automatically changes as a result of the equation linking the cells. In the spreadsheet solutions in this book, the equation that determines the calculation is shown at the bottom of the spreadsheet.

The ability to use spreadsheets has become a prime skill for today's investors. As the saying goes, "Get aboard the bandwagon, or get run over." The spreadsheet solutions we present in this book will help you climb up onto that bandwagon!

Future Value: An Extension of Compounding

future value
the amount to which a current deposit will grow over a period of time when it is placed in an account paying compound interest.

Future value is the amount to which a current deposit will grow over a period of time when it is placed in an account paying compound interest. Consider a deposit of $1,000 that is earning 8% (0.08 in decimal form) compounded annually. The following calculation yields the future value of this deposit at the end of 1 year.

Equation 4.1

$$\text{Future value at end of year 1} = \$1,000 \times (1 + 0.08) = \underline{\$1,080}$$

If the money were left on deposit for another year, 8% interest would be paid on the account balance of $1,080. Thus, at the end of the second year, there would be $1,166.40 in the account. This amount would represent the beginning-of-year balance of $1,080 plus 8% of the $1,080 ($86.40) in interest. The future value at the end of the second year would be calculated as follows.

Equation 4.2

$$\text{Future value at end of year 2} = \$1,080 \times (1 + 0.08) = \underline{\$1,166.40}$$

To find the future value of the $1,000 at the end of year n, the procedure illustrated above would be repeated n times. Future values can be determined either mathematically or by using a financial table, financial calculator, or a computer and spreadsheet. Here we demonstrate use of a table of future-value interest factors, use of a calculator, and use of an Excel spreadsheet.

TABLE USE The factors in Appendix A, Table A.1 represent the amount to which an initial $1 deposit would grow for various periods (typically years) and interest rates. For example, a dollar deposited in an account paying 8%

TIME IS ON YOUR SIDE—It's never too early to begin saving for retirement, even if it seems a long way off. The power of compounding—which Albert Einstein once called the "eighth wonder of the world"—will multiply your funds considerably. If you began today and socked away $2,000 per year for just the next 8 years into an account that earned 10% per year and left those funds on deposit until the end of 40 years, that $16,000 would grow to more than $480,000. You can wait, but it will cost you. Time is your biggest investment ally.

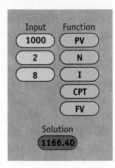

interest and left there for 2 years would accumulate to $1.166. Using the future-value interest factor for 8% and 2 years (1.166), we can find the future value of an investment that can earn 8% over 2 years: We would *multiply* the amount invested by the appropriate interest factor. In the case of $1,000 left on deposit for 2 years at 8%, the resulting future value is $1,166 (1.166 × $1,000). This agrees (except for a slight rounding difference) with the value calculated in Equation 4.2.

A few points with respect to Appendix A, Table A.1, Future-Value Interest Factors for One Dollar, should be emphasized.

1. The values in the table represent factors for determining the future value of one dollar at the *end* of the given year.
2. As the interest rate increases for any given year, the future-value interest factor also increases. The higher the interest rate, the greater the future value.
3. For a given interest rate, the future value of a dollar increases with the passage of time.
4. The future-value interest factor is always greater than 1. Only if the interest rate were zero would this factor equal 1, and the future value would therefore equal the initial deposit.

CALCULATOR USE* A financial calculator can be used to calculate the future value directly.** First punch in $1,000 and depress **PV**; next punch in 2 and depress **N**; then punch in 8 and depress **I**.† Finally, to calculate the future value, depress **CPT** and then **FV**. The future value of $1,166.40 should appear on the calculator display as shown in the art at the left. On many calculators, this value will be preceded by a minus sign (−1166.40). *If a minus sign appears on your calculator, ignore it here as well as in all other "Calculator Use" illustrations in this text.*‡

The calculator is more accurate than the future value factors, which have been rounded to the nearest 0.001. Therefore, a slight difference will frequently exist between the values found by these alternative methods. In this case, there is a $.40 difference. Clearly, the improved accuracy and ease of

---

* Many calculators allow the user to set the number of payments per year. Most of these calculators are preset for monthly payments—12 payments per year. Because we work primarily with annual payments—one payment per year—it is important *to be sure that your calculator is set for one payment per year.* And although most calculators are preset to recognize that all payments occur at the end of the period, it is important *to make sure that your calculator is correctly set on the END mode.* Consult the reference guide that accompanies your calculator for instructions for setting these values.

** To avoid including previous data in current calculations, *always clear all registers of your calculator before inputting values and making each computation.*

† The known values *can be punched into the calculator in any order.* The order specified in this as well as other demonstrations of calculator use included in this text merely reflects convenience and personal preference.

‡ The calculator differentiates inflows from outflows with a negative sign. For example, in the problem just demonstrated, the $1,000 present value (PV), because it was keyed as a positive number (1000) is considered an inflow or deposit. Therefore, the calculated future value (FV) of −1166.40 is preceded by a minus sign to show that it is the resulting outflow or withdrawal. Had the $1,000 present value been keyed in as a negative number (−1000), the future value of $1166.40 would have been displayed as a positive number (1166.40). Simply stated, *present value (PV) and future value (FV) cash flows will have opposite signs.*

calculation tend to favor the use of the calculator. (*Note:* In future examples of calculator use, we will use only a display similar to that shown on the previous page. If you need a reminder of the procedure involved, come back and review the preceding paragraph.)

SPREADSHEET USE The future value of the single amount also can be calculated as shown on the following Excel spreadsheet.

	A	B
1	**FUTURE VALUE OF A SINGLE AMOUNT**	
2	Present value	$1,000
3	Interest rate, pct per year compounded annually	8%
4	Number of years	2
5	Future value	$1,166.40
	Entry in Cell B5 is =FV(B3,B4,0,–B2,0). The minus sign appears before B2 because the present value is an outflow (i.e., the initial deposit).	

Future Value of an Annuity

annuity
a stream of equal cash flows that occur at equal intervals over time.

An **annuity** is a stream of equal cash flows that occur at equal intervals over time. Receiving $1,000 per year at the end of each of the next 8 years is an example of an annuity. The cash flows can be *inflows* of returns earned from an investment or *outflows* of funds invested (deposited) to earn future returns.

ordinary annuity
an annuity for which the cash flows occur at the *end* of each period.

Investors are sometimes interested in finding the future value of an annuity. Their concern is typically with what's called an **ordinary annuity**—one for which the cash flows occur at the *end* of each period. Here we can simplify our calculations by using either tables of the factors for an annuity, a financial calculator, or an Excel spreadsheet. (A complete set of these tables is included in Appendix A, Table A.2.)

TABLE USE The factors in Appendix A, Table A.2 represent the amount to which annual end-of-year deposits of $1 would grow for various periods (years) and interest rates. For example, a dollar deposited at the end of each year for 8 years into an account paying 6% interest would accumulate to $9.897. Using the future-value interest factor for an 8-year annuity earning 6% (9.897), we can find the future value of this cash flow: We would *multiply* the annual investment by the appropriate interest factor. In the case of $1,000 deposited at the end of each year for 8 years at 6%, the resulting future value is $9,897 (9.897 × $1,000).

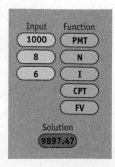

Input	Function
1000	PMT
8	N
6	I
	CPT
	FV
Solution	
9897.47	

CALCULATOR USE When a financial calculator is used to find the future value of an annuity, the annual deposit is input using the **PMT** key (rather than the **PV** key, which was used to find the future value of a single deposit). Use of the **PMT** key tells the calculator that a stream of **N** (the number of years input) end-of-year deposits in the amount of **PMT** dollars represents the deposit stream.

Using the calculator inputs shown at the left, we find the future value of the $1,000, 8-year ordinary annuity earning a 6% annual rate of interest to be $9,897.47. This is a slightly more precise answer than that found by using the table.

SPREADSHEET USE The future value of the ordinary annuity also can be calculated as shown on the following Excel spreadsheet.

	A	B
1	**FUTURE VALUE OF AN ORDINARY ANNUITY**	
2	Annual payment	$1,000
3	Annual rate of interest, compounded annually	6%
4	Number of years	8
5	Future value of an ordinary annuity	$9,897.47

Entry in Cell B5 is =FV(B3,B4,−B2)
The minus sign appears before B2 because
the annual payment is a cash outflow.

Present Value: An Extension of Future Value

present value
the *value today* of a sum to be received at some future date; the inverse of future value.

Present value is the inverse of future value. That is, rather than measuring the value of a present amount at some future date, **present value** expresses the *current value of a future sum*. By applying present-value techniques, we can calculate the *value today* of a sum to be received at some future date.

When determining the present value of a future sum, we are answering the basic question, "How much would have to be deposited today into an account paying $i\%$ interest in order to equal a specified sum to be received so many years in the future?" The applicable interest rate when we are finding present value is commonly called the **discount rate** (or *opportunity cost*). It represents the annual rate of return that could be earned currently on a similar investment.

discount rate
the annual rate of return that could be earned currently on a similar investment; used when finding present value; also called *opportunity cost*.

The basic present-value calculation is best illustrated using a simple example. Imagine that you are offered an opportunity that will provide you, 1 year from today, with exactly $1,000. If you could earn 8% on similar types of investments, how much is the most you would pay for this opportunity? In other words, what is the present value of $1,000 to be received 1 year from now, discounted at 8%? Letting *x* equal the present value, we can use Equation 4.3 to describe this situation.

Equation 4.3
$$x \times (1 + 0.08) = \$1,000$$

Solving Equation 4.3 for *x*, we get:

Equation 4.4
$$x = \frac{\$1,000}{(1 + 0.08)} = \underline{\underline{\$925.93}}$$

Thus the present value of $1,000 to be received 1 year from now, discounted at 8%, is $925.93. In other words, $925.93 deposited today into an account paying 8% interest will accumulate to $1,000 in 1 year. To check this conclusion, *multiply* the future-value interest factor for 8% and 1 year, or 1.080 (from Appendix A, Table A.1), by $925.93. The result is a future value of $1,000 (1.080 × $925.93).

The calculations involved in finding the present value of sums to be received in the distant future are more complex than those for a 1-year investment. Here we use either tables of present-value interest factors to simplify these calculations, a financial calculator, or an Excel spreadsheet. (A complete set of these tables is included in Appendix A, Table A.3.)

TABLE USE The factors in Appendix A, Table A.3 represent the present value of $1 associated with various combinations of periods (years) and discount (interest) rates. For example, the present value of $1 to be received 1 year from now discounted at 8% is $0.926. Using this factor (0.926), we can find the present value of $1,000 to be received 1 year from now at an 8% discount rate by *multiplying* it by $1,000. The resulting present value of $926 (0.926 × $1,000) agrees (except for a slight rounding difference) with the value calculated in Equation 4.4.

Another example may help clarify the use of present-value tables. The present value of $500 to be received 7 years from now, discounted at 6%, is calculated as follows:

Present value = 0.665 × $500 = $332.50

The 0.665 represents the present-value interest factor from Appendix A, Table A.3 for 7 years discounted at 6%.

A few points with respect to Appendix A, Table A.3, Present-Value Interest Factors for One Dollar, should be emphasized.

1. The present-value interest factor for a single sum is always less than 1. Only if the discount rate were zero would this factor equal 1.
2. The higher the discount rate for a given year, the smaller the present-value interest factor. In other words, the greater your opportunity cost, the less you have to invest today in order to have a given amount in the future.
3. The further in the future a sum is to be received, the less it is worth at present.
4. At a discount rate of 0%, the present-value interest factor always equals 1. Therefore, in such a case the future value of a sum equals its present value.

CALCULATOR USE Using the financial calculator inputs shown at the left, we find the present value of $500 to be received 7 years from now, discounted at 6%, to be $332.53. This value is slightly more precise than that found using the table, but for our purposes the difference is insignificant.

SPREADSHEET USE The present value of the single future amount also can be calculated as shown on the following Excel spreadsheet.

	A	B
1	**PRESENT VALUE OF A SINGLE FUTURE AMOUNT**	
2	Future value	$500
3	Interest rate, pct per year compounded annually	6%
4	Number of years	7
5	Present value	$332.53

Entry in Cell B5 is =−PV(B3,B4,0,B2).
The minus sign appears before PV to change
the present value to a positive amount.

The Present Value of a Stream of Returns

In the preceding paragraphs we illustrated the technique for finding the present value of a single sum to be received at some future date. Because the returns from a given investment are likely to be received at various future dates rather than as a single lump sum, we also need to be able to find the present value of a *stream of returns*. A stream of returns can be viewed as a package of single-sum returns; it may be classified as a mixed stream or an annuity. A **mixed stream** of returns is one that exhibits no special pattern. As noted earlier, an *annuity* is a stream of equal periodic returns. Table 4.8 shows the end-of-year returns illustrating each of these types of patterns. To find the present value of each of these streams (measured at the *beginning* of 2005), we must calculate the total of the present values of the individual annual returns. Because shortcuts can be used for an annuity, calculation of the present value of each type of return stream is illustrated separately.

mixed stream
a stream of returns that, unlike an annuity, exhibits no special pattern.

Present Value of a Mixed Stream To find the present value of the mixed stream of returns given in Table 4.8, we must find and then total the present values of the individual returns. Assuming a 9% discount rate, we can stream-line the calculation of the present value of the mixed stream using financial tables, a financial calculator, or an Excel spreadsheet.

TABLE USE Table A.3 in Appendix A can be used to find the appropriate present-value interest factors for each of the 5 years of the mixed stream's life at the 9% discount rate. Table 4.9 (on page 148) demonstrates the use of these factors, shown in column 2, with the corresponding year's return, shown in column 1, to calculate the present value of each year's return, shown in column 3. The total of the present values of the returns for each of the 5 years is found by summing column 3. The resulting present value of $187.77 represents the amount today (*beginning* of 2005) that, invested at 9%, would provide the same returns as those shown in column 1 of Table 4.9.

CALCULATOR USE You can use a financial calculator to find the present value of each individual return, as demonstrated on page 146. You then sum the present values to get the present value of the stream. However, most financial calculators have a function that allows you to punch in *all returns* (typically referred to as *cash flows*), specify the discount rate, and then directly calculate the present value of the entire return stream. Because calculators provide solutions

EXCEL with
SPREADSHEETS

TABLE 4.8	Mixed and Annuity Return Streams	
End of Year	**Returns**	
	Mixed Stream	**Annuity**
2005	$30	$50
2006	40	50
2007	50	50
2008	60	50
2009	70	50

TABLE 4.9   Mixed-Stream Present-Value Calculation

End of Year	(1) Return	(2) 9% Present-Value Interest Factor	(3) (1) × (2) Present Value
2005	$30	.917	$ 27.51
2006	40	.842	33.68
2007	50	.772	38.60
2008	60	.708	42.48
2009	70	.650	45.50
		Present value of stream	$187.77

Note: Column 1 values are from Table 4.8. Column 2 values are from Appendix A, Table A.3, for a 9% discount rate and 1 through 5 periods (years).

more precise than those based on rounded table factors, the present value of the mixed stream of returns in Table 4.8, found using a calculator, will be close to, but not precisely equal to, the $187.77 (see Table 4.9).

SPREADSHEET USE The present value of the mixed stream of returns also can be calculated as shown on the following Excel spreadsheet.

	A	B
1	**PRESENT VALUE OF A MIXED STREAM OF RETURNS**	
2	Discount Rate, pct/year	9%
3	Year	Year-End Return
4	1	$30
5	2	$40
6	3	$50
7	4	$60
8	5	$70
9	Present value	$187.80

Entry in Cell B9 is =NPV(B2,B4:B8).

Investing about $188 would provide exactly a 9% return.

Present Value of an Annuity The present value of an annuity can be found in the same way as the present value of a mixed stream. Fortunately, however, there are simpler approaches. Here we simplify our calculations by using either tables of these factors for an annuity, a financial calculator, or an Excel spreadsheet. (A complete set of these tables is included in Appendix A, Table A.4.)

TABLE USE The factors in Appendix A, Table A.4 represent the present value of a $1 annuity for various periods (years) and discount (interest) rates. For example, the present value of $1 to be received at the end of each year for the next 5 years discounted at 9% is $3.890. Using the present-value interest factor for a 5-year annuity discounted at 9% (3.890), we can find the present value of the $50, 5-year annuity (given in Table 4.8) at a 9% discount rate: We *multiply* the annual return by the appropriate interest factor. The resulting present value is $194.50 (3.890 × $50).

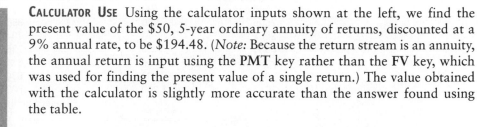

Input	Function
50	PMT
5	N
9	I
	CPT
	PV

Solution
194.48

CALCULATOR USE Using the calculator inputs shown at the left, we find the present value of the $50, 5-year ordinary annuity of returns, discounted at a 9% annual rate, to be $194.48. (*Note:* Because the return stream is an annuity, the annual return is input using the **PMT** key rather than the **FV** key, which was used for finding the present value of a single return.) The value obtained with the calculator is slightly more accurate than the answer found using the table.

SPREADSHEET USE The present value of the annuity of returns also can be calculated as shown on the following Excel spreadsheet.

	A	B
1	**PRESENT VALUE OF ANNUITY RETURNS**	
2	Annual return	$50
3	Annual discount rate, compounded annually	9%
4	Number of years	5
5	Present value of an ordinary annuity	$194.48

Entry in Cell B5 is =PV(B3,B4,–B2).
The minus sign appears before B2 because
the annual return is a cash outflow.

Determining a Satisfactory Investment

satisfactory investment
an investment whose present value of benefits (discounted at the appropriate rate) *equals* or *exceeds* the present value of its costs.

Time value of money techniques can be used to determine an acceptable investment. Ignoring risk at this point, a **satisfactory investment** would be one for which the present value of benefits (discounted at the appropriate rate) *equals* or *exceeds* the present value of its costs. Because the cost of the investment would be incurred initially (at time zero), the cost and its present value are viewed as one and the same. The three possible benefit–cost relationships and their interpretations follow:

1. If the present value of the benefits *just equals the cost,* you would earn a rate of return equal to the discount rate.
2. If the present value of benefits *exceeds the cost,* you would earn a rate of return greater than the discount rate.
3. If the present value of benefits is *less than the cost,* you would earn a rate of return less than the discount rate.

You would prefer only those investments for which the present value of benefits equals or exceeds its cost—situations 1 and 2. In these cases, the rate of return would be equal to or greater than the discount rate.

The information in Table 4.10 (on page 150) demonstrates the application of present value to investment decision making using a financial table. (*Note:* A financial calculator or an Excel spreadsheet could have been used, as described earlier, to find the present value of this mixed-stream investment.)

EXCEL with
SPREADSHEETS

TABLE 4.10   **Present Value Applied to an Investment**

End of Year	(1) Return	(2) 8% Present-Value Interest Factor*	(3) (1) × (2) Present Value
2005	$ 90	.926	$ 83.34
2006	100	.857	85.70
2007	110	.794	87.34
2008	120	.735	88.20
2009	100	.681	68.10
2010	100	.630	63.00
2011	1,200	.583	699.60
		Present value of returns	$1,175.28

* Column 2 values are from Appendix A, Table A.3, for an 8% discount rate and 1 through 7 periods (years).

Assuming an 8% discount rate, we can see that the present value (at the beginning of 2005) of the returns (benefits) to be received over the assumed 7-year period (year-end 2005 through year-end 2011) is $1,175.28. If the cost of the investment (beginning of 2005) were any amount less than or equal to the $1,175.28 present value, it would be acceptable. At that cost, a rate of return equal to at least 8% would be earned. At a cost above the $1,175.28 present value, the investment would not be acceptable. At that cost, the rate of return would be less than 8%. Clearly, in that case it would be preferable to find an alternative investment with a present value of benefits that equals or exceeds its cost.

IN REVIEW

CONCEPTS

4.3   What is the *time value of money?* Explain why an investor should be able to earn a positive return.

4.4   Define, discuss, and contrast the following terms.
a.   Interest
b.   Simple interest
c.   Compound interest
d.   True rate of interest (or return)

4.5   When interest is compounded more frequently than annually at a stated rate, what happens to the *true rate of interest?* Under what condition would the stated and true rates of interest be equal? What is *continuous compounding?*

4.6   Describe, compare, and contrast the concepts of *future value* and *present value.* Explain the role of the *discount rate* in calculating present value.

4.7   What is an *annuity?* How can calculation of the future value of an annuity be simplified? What about the present value of an annuity?

4.8   What is a *mixed stream* of returns? Describe the procedure used to find the present value of such a stream.

4.9   What is a *satisfactory investment?* When the present value of benefits exceeds the cost of an investment, what is true of the rate of return earned by the investor relative to the discount rate?

Measuring Return

Thus far, we have discussed the concept of return in terms of its two components (current income and capital gains) and the key factors that affect the level of return (internal characteristics and external forces). These discussions intentionally oversimplified the computations involved in determining the historical or expected return. To compare returns from different investment vehicles, we need to incorporate time value of money concepts that explicitly consider differences in the timing of investment income and capital gains. We must also be able to place a current value on future benefits. Here we will look at several measures that enable us to compare alternative investment vehicles. First, we must define and consider the relationships among various rates of return.

Real, Risk-Free, and Required Returns

Rational investors will choose investments that fully compensate them for the risk involved. The greater the risk, the greater the return required by investors. The return that fully compensates for an investment's risk is called the **required return.** To better understand required returns, it is helpful to consider their makeup. The required return on any investment j consists of three basic components: the real rate of return, an expected inflation premium, and a risk premium, as noted in Equation 4.5.

required return
the rate of return an investor must earn on an investment to be fully compensated for its risk.

Equation 4.5

$$\genfrac{}{}{0pt}{}{\text{Required return}}{\text{on investment } j} = \genfrac{}{}{0pt}{}{\text{Real rate}}{\text{of return}} + \genfrac{}{}{0pt}{}{\text{Expected inflation}}{\text{premium}} + \genfrac{}{}{0pt}{}{\text{Risk premium}}{\text{for investment } j}$$

Equation 4.5a

$$r_j = r^* + IP + RP_j$$

real rate of return
the rate of return that could be earned in a perfect world where all outcomes are known and certain—where there is no risk.

The **real rate of return** is the rate of return that could be earned in a perfect world where all outcomes were known and certain—where there is no risk. In such a world, the real rate of return would create an equilibrium between the supply of savings and the demand for funds. The real rate of return changes with changing economic conditions, tastes, and preferences. Historically, it has been relatively stable and in the range of 0.5% to 2%. For convenience, we'll assume a real rate of return of 2%.

expected inflation premium
the average rate of inflation expected in the future.

The **expected inflation premium** represents the average rate of inflation expected in the future. By adding the expected inflation premium to the real rate of return, we get the **risk-free rate.** This is the rate of return that can be earned on a risk-free investment, most commonly a 3-month U.S. Treasury bill. The formula for this rate is shown in Equation 4.6.

risk-free rate
the rate of return that can be earned on a risk-free investment; the sum of the real rate of return and the expected inflation premium.

Equation 4.6

$$\text{Risk-free rate} = \genfrac{}{}{0pt}{}{\text{Real rate}}{\text{of return}} + \genfrac{}{}{0pt}{}{\text{Expected inflation}}{\text{premium}}$$

Equation 4.6a

$$R_F = r^* + IP$$

To demonstrate, a real rate of return of 2% and an expected inflation premium of 4% would result in a risk-free rate of return of 6%.

risk premium
a return premium that reflects the issue and issuer characteristics associated with a given investment vehicle.

The required return can be found by adding to the risk-free rate a **risk premium,** which varies depending on specific issue and issuer characteristics. *Issue characteristics* are the type of vehicle (stock, bond, etc.), its maturity (2 years, 5 years, infinity, etc.), and its features (voting/nonvoting, callable/noncallable, etc.). *Issuer characteristics* are industry and company factors such as the line of business and financial condition of the issuer. Together, the issue and issuer factors cause investors to require a risk premium above the risk-free rate.

Substituting the risk-free rate, R_F, from Equation 4.6a, into Equation 4.5a for the first two terms to the right of the equals signs ($r^* + IP$), we get Equation 4.7.

Equation 4.7

$$\frac{\text{Required return}}{\text{on investment } j} = \frac{\text{Risk-free}}{\text{rate}} + \frac{\text{Risk premium}}{\text{for investment } j}$$

Equation 4.7a

$$r_j = R_F + RP_j$$

For example, if the required return on IBM common stock is 11% when the risk-free rate is 6%, investors require a 5% risk premium (11% − 6%) as compensation for the risk associated with common stock (the issue) and IBM (the issuer). Later in Chapter 5, we will explore further the relationship between the risk premium and required returns.

Next, we consider the specifics of return measurement.

Holding Period Return

The return to a *saver* is the amount of interest earned on a given deposit. Of course, the amount "invested" in a savings account is not subject to change in value, as is the amount invested in stocks, bonds, and mutual funds. Because we are concerned with a broad range of investment vehicles, we need a measure of return that captures both periodic benefits and changes in value. One such measure is *holding period return*.

holding period
the period of time over which one wishes to measure the return on an investment vehicle.

The **holding period** is the period of time over which one wishes to measure the return on an investment vehicle. When comparing returns, be sure to use holding periods of the same length. For example, comparing the return on a stock over the 6-month period ended December 31, 2004, with the return on a bond over the 1-year period ended June 30, 2004, could result in a poor investment decision. To avoid this problem, be sure you define the holding period. It is often best to annualize the holding period and use that as a standard. And when comparing the returns from alternative investment vehicles, you should use similar periods in time.

realized return
current income actually received by an investor during a given period.

Understanding Return Components Earlier in this chapter we identified the two components of investment return: current income and capital gains (or losses). The portion of current income received by the investor during the period is a **realized return.** Most but not all current income is realized. (Accrued interest on taxable zero-coupon bonds is treated as current income for tax purposes but is not a realized return until the bond is sold or matures.) Capital gains returns, on the other hand, are realized only when the invest-

paper return
a return that has been achieved but not yet realized by an investor during a given period.

ment vehicle is actually sold at the end of the holding period. Until the vehicle is sold, the capital gain is merely a **paper return.**

For example, the capital gain return on an investment that increases in market value from $50 to $70 during a year is $20. For that capital gain to be realized, you would have to have sold the investment for $70 at the end of that year. An investor who purchased the same investment but plans to hold it for another 3 years would also have experienced the $20 capital gain return during the year specified, but he or she *would not have realized the gain in terms of cash flow.* However, *even if the capital gains return is not realized during the period over which the total return is measured, it must be included in the return calculation.*

A second point to recognize about returns is that both the current income and the capital gains component can have a negative value. Occasionally, an investment may have negative current income. That is, you may be required to pay out cash to meet certain obligations. This situation is most likely to occur in various types of property investments. For example, assume you have purchased an apartment complex and the rental income is inadequate to meet the payments associated with its operation. In such a case, you would have to pay the deficit in operating costs, and that payment would represent negative current income. A capital loss can occur on *any* investment vehicle: Stocks, bonds, mutual funds, options, futures, real estate, and gold can all decline in market value over a given holding period.

holding period return (HPR)
the total return earned from holding an investment for a specified holding period (*usually 1 year or less*).

Computing the Holding Period Return (HPR) The **holding period return (HPR)** is the total return earned from holding an investment for a specified period of time (the holding period). The HPR is customarily used with holding periods of *1 year or less.* (We'll explain why later.) It represents the sum of current income and capital gains (or losses) achieved over the holding period, divided by the beginning investment value (market price). The equation for HPR is

Equation 4.8

$$\text{Holding period return} = \frac{\text{Current income during period} + \text{Capital gain (or loss) during period}}{\text{Beginning investment value}}$$

Equation 4.8a

$$\text{HPR} = \frac{C + CG}{V_0}$$

where

Equation 4.9

$$\text{Capital gain (or loss) during period} = \text{Ending investment value} - \text{Beginning investment value}$$

Equation 4.9a

$$CG = V_n - V_0$$

The HPR equation provides a convenient method for either measuring the total return realized or estimating the total return expected. For example, Table 4.11 (on page 154) summarizes the key financial variables for four investment vehicles over the past year. The total current income and capital

EXCEL with SPREADSHEETS

TABLE 4.11   Key Financial Variables for Four Investment Vehicles

| | Investment Vehicle | | | |
	Savings Account	Common Stock	Bond	Futures Contract
Cash received				
1st quarter	$15	$10	$ 0	$0
2nd quarter	15	10	70	0
3rd quarter	15	10	0	0
4th quarter	15	15	70	0
(1) Total current income	$60	$45	$140	$0
Investment value				
End-of-year	$1,000	$2,200	$ 970	$3,300
(2) Beginning-of-year	1,000	2,000	1,000	3,000
(3) Capital gain (loss)	$ 0	$ 200	($ 30)	$ 300
(4) Total return [(1) + (3)]	$ 60	$ 245	$ 110	$ 300
(5) Holding period return [(4) ÷ (2)]	6.00%	12.25%	11.00%	10.00%

gain or loss during the holding period are given in the lines labeled (1) and (3), respectively. The total return over the year is calculated, as shown in line (4), by adding these two sources of return. Dividing the total return value [line (4)] by the beginning-of-year investment value [line (2)], we find the holding period return, given in line (5). Over the 1-year holding period the common stock had the highest HPR (12.25%). The savings account had the lowest (6%).

As these calculations show, all we need to find the HPR is beginning- and end-of-period investment values, along with the value of current income received by the investor during the period. Note that if the current income and capital gain (or loss) values in lines (1) and (3) of Table 4.11 had been drawn from a 6-month rather than a 1-year period, the HPR values calculated in line 18 would have been *the same*.

Holding period return can be negative or positive. HPRs can be calculated with Equation 4.8 using either historical data (as in the preceding example) or forecast data.

Using the HPR in Investment Decisions The holding period return is easy to use in making investment decisions. Because it considers both current income and capital gains relative to the beginning investment value, it tends to overcome any problems that might be associated with comparing investments of different size. If we look only at the total returns calculated for each of the four investments in Table 4.11 [line (4)], the futures contract investment appears best, because it has the highest total return. However, the futures contract investment would require the largest dollar outlay ($3,000). The holding period return offers a *relative comparison,* by dividing the total return by the amount of the investment. Comparing HPRs [line (5)], we find the investment alternative with the *highest return per invested dollar* to be the common stock's HPR of 12.25%. Because the return per invested dollar reflects the efficiency of the investment, the HPR provides a logical method for evaluating and comparing investment returns, particularly for holding periods of 1 year or less.

Yield: The Internal Rate of Return

An alternative way to define a satisfactory investment is in terms of the compound annual rate of return it earns. Why do we need an alternative to the HPR? Because *HPR fails to consider the time value of money.* Although the holding period return is useful with investments held for 1 year or less, it is generally inappropriate for longer holding periods. Sophisticated investors typically do not use HPR when the time period is greater than 1 year. Instead, they use a present-value-based measure, called **yield** (or **internal rate of return**), to determine the compound annual rate of return earned on investments held for longer than 1 year. Yield can also be defined as the discount rate that produces a present value of benefits just equal to its cost.

yield (internal rate of return)
the compound annual rate of return earned by a long-term investment; the discount rate that produces a present value of the investment's benefits that just equals its cost.

Once you know the yield you can decide whether an investment is acceptable. If the yield on an investment *is equal to or greater than the required return,* then the investment is acceptable. An investment with a yield *below the required return* is unacceptable; it will not compensate you adequately for the risk involved.

The yield on an investment providing a single future cash flow is relatively easy to calculate. The yield on an investment providing a stream of future cash flows generally involves more time-consuming calculations. Many hand-held financial calculators and Excel spreadsheets are available for simplifying these calculations.

Yield for a Single Cash Flow Some investments, such as U.S. savings bonds, stocks paying no dividends, zero-coupon bonds, and futures contracts, are purchased by paying a fixed amount up front. The investor expects them to provide *no periodic income,* but to provide a single—and, the investor hopes, a large—future cash flow at maturity or when the investment is sold. The yield on investments expected to provide a single future cash flow can be estimated using financial tables, a financial calculator, or an Excel spreadsheet.

TABLE USE Assume you wish to find the yield on an investment costing $1,000 today that you expect will be worth $1,400 at the end of a 5-year holding period. We can find the yield on this investment by solving for the discount rate that causes the present value of the $1,400 to be received 5 years from now to equal the initial investment of $1,000.

The first step involves dividing the present value ($1,000) by the future value ($1,400), which results in a value of 0.714. The second step is to find in the table of present-value interest factors the 5-year factor that is closest to 0.714. Referring to the present-value table (Appendix A, Table A.3), we find that for 5 years the factor closest to 0.714 is 0.713, which occurs at a 7% discount rate. Therefore, the yield on this investment is about 7%. If you require a 6% return, this investment is acceptable (7% expected return ≥ 6% required return).

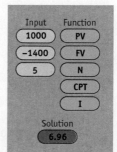

CALCULATOR USE Using a financial calculator to find the yield for the investment described above, we can treat the earliest value as a present value, **PV,** and the latest value as a future value, **FV.** (*Note:* Most calculators require *either* the **PV** or the **FV** value to be input as a negative number to calculate an unknown yield.) Using the inputs shown at the left, we find the yield to be 6.96%. This is consistent with, but more precise than, the value found using Appendix A, Table A.3.

SPREADSHEET USE The yield for the single cash flow also can be calculated as shown on the following Excel spreadsheet.

	A	B
1	**YIELD FOR A SINGLE CASH FLOW**	
2	Point in Time	Cash Flow
3	Future	$1,400
4	Present	$1,000
5	Number of Years	5
6	Yield	6.96%

Entry in Cell B6 is
= Rate((B5),0,–B4,B3,0),
The minus sign appears before B4
because the present investment
is treated as a cash outflow.

Yield for a Stream of Income Investment vehicles such as income-oriented stock and bonds typically provide the investor with a *stream of income*. The yield (or internal rate of return) for a stream of income (returns) is generally more difficult to estimate. The most accurate approach is based on searching for the discount rate that produces a present value of income just equal to the cost of the investment. It can be applied using financial tables, a financial calculator, or an Excel spreadsheet.

TABLE USE If we use the investment in Table 4.10 and assume that its cost is $1,100, we find that the yield must be greater than 8%. At an 8% discount rate, the present value of income (calculated in column 3 of Table 4.10) is greater than the cost ($1,175.28 versus $1,100). The present values at 9% and

EXCEL with
SPREADSHEETS

TABLE 4.12   Yield Calculation for an $1,100 Investment

Year	(1) Income	(2) 9% Present-Value Interest Factor	(3) (1) × (2) Present Value at 9%	(4) 10% Present-Value Interest Factor	(5) (1) × (4) Present Value at 10%
2005	$ 90	.917	$ 82.53	.909	$ 81.81
2006	100	.842	84.20	.826	82.60
2007	110	.772	84.92	.751	82.61
2008	120	.708	84.96	.683	81.96
2009	100	.650	65.00	.621	62.10
2010	100	.596	59.60	.564	56.40
2011	1,200	.547	656.40	.513	615.60
	Present value of income		$1,117.61		$1,063.08

10% discount rates are calculated in Table 4.12. If we look at the present values of income calculated at the 9% and 10% rates, we see that the yield on the investment must be somewhere between 9% and 10%. At 9% the present value ($1,117.61) is too high. At 10% the present value ($1,063.08) is too low. The discount rate that causes the present value of income to be closer to the $1,100 cost is 9%, because it is only $17.61 away from $1,100. Thus, if you require an 8% return, the investment is clearly acceptable.

CALCULATOR USE A financial calculator can be used to find the yield (or *internal rate of return*) on an investment that will produce a stream of income. This procedure typically involves punching in the cost of the investment (typically referred to as the *cash outflow* at time zero) and all of the income expected each period (typically referred to as the *cash inflow* at in year *x*) and then directly calculating the yield (typically referred to as the *internal rate of return, IRR*). Because calculators provide solutions that are more precise than those based on rounded table factors, the yield of 9.32% found for the investment in Table 4.10 using a financial calculator (keystrokes not shown) is close to, but not equal to, the 9% value estimated above using Table 4.12.

SPREADSHEET USE The yield for a stream of income also can be calculated as shown on the following Excel spreadsheet.

	A	B
1	YIELD FOR A STREAM OF INCOME	
2	Year	Cash Flow
3	2011	$1,200
4	2010	$100
5	2009	$100
6	2008	$120
7	2007	$110
8	2006	$100
9	2005	$90
10	Yield	9.32%

Entry in Cell B10 is
=RATE((A3–A9),0,B9,–B3,0).
The expression A3–A9 in the entry
calculates the number of years of growth.
The minus sign appears before B3 because
the investment in 2011
is treated as a cash outflow.

Interest on Interest: The Critical Assumption The critical assumption underlying the use of yield as a return measure is an ability to earn a return equal to the yield on *all income* received during the holding period. This concept can best be illustrated with a simple example. Suppose you buy a $1,000 U.S. Treasury bond that pays 8% annual interest ($80) over its 20-year maturity. Each year you receive $80, and at maturity the $1,000 in principal is repaid. There is no loss of capital, no default; all payments are made right on time. But you must be able to reinvest the $80 annual interest receipts in order to earn 8% on this investment.

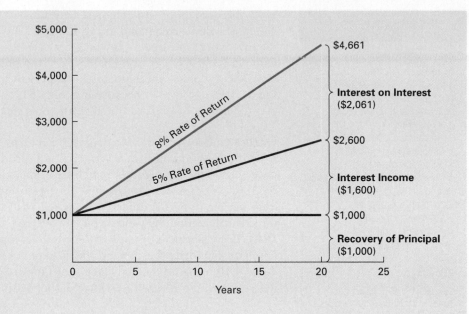

FIGURE 4.3

Earning Interest on Interest

If you invested in a $1,000, 20-year bond with an 8% coupon, you would have only $2,600 at the end of 20 years if you did not reinvest the $80 annual interest receipts—only about a 5% rate of return. If you reinvested the interest at the 8% interest rate, you would have $4,661 at the end of 20 years—an 8% rate of return. To achieve the calculated yield of 8%, you must therefore be able to earn interest on interest at that rate.

Figure 4.3 shows the elements of return on this investment to demonstrate the point. If you don't *reinvest* the interest income of $80 per year, you'll end up on the 5% line. You'll have $2,600—the $1,000 principal plus $1,600 interest income ($80/year × 20 years)—at the end of 20 years. (The yield on a single cash flow of $1,000 today that will be worth $2,600 in 20 years is about 5%.) To move to the 8% line, you have to earn 8% on the annual interest receipts. If you do, you'll have $4,661—the $1,000 principal plus the $3,661 future value of the 20-year $80 annuity of interest receipts invested at 8% [$80/year × 45.762 (the 8%, 20-year factor from Appendix A, Table A.2)]— at the end of 20 years. (The yield on a single cash flow of $1,000 today that will be worth $4,661 in 20 years is 8%.) The future value of the investment would be $2,061 greater ($4,661 − $2,600) with interest on interest than without reinvestment of the interest receipts.

It should be clear to you that if you start out with an 8% investment, *you have to earn that same rate of return when reinvesting your income.* The rate of return you start with is the required, or minimum, **reinvestment rate**—the rate of return earned on interest or other income received over the relevant investment horizon. By putting your current income to work at this rate, you'll earn the rate of return you set out to. If you fail to do so, your return will decline accordingly. Even though a bond was used in this illustration, the same principle applies to any other type of investment vehicle.

The earning of interest on interest is what the market refers to as a **fully compounded rate of return**. It's an important concept: You can't start reaping the full potential from your investments until you start earning a fully compounded rate of return on them.

Interest on interest is a particularly important element of return for investment programs that involve a lot of current income. You have to reinvest current income. (With capital gains, the investment vehicle itself is automatically doing the reinvesting.) It follows, therefore, that for investment programs that

reinvestment rate
the rate of return earned on interest or other income received from an investment over its investment horizon.

fully compounded rate of return
the rate of return that includes interest earned on interest.

			TABLE 4.13 Dividends Per Share			

TABLE 4.13   Dividends Per Share

Year	Year Number	Dividends per Share	Year	Year Number	Dividends per Share
1996	0	$2.45	2001	5	$3.15
1997	1	2.60	2002	6	3.20
1998	2	2.80	2003	7	3.20
1999	3	3.00	2004	8	3.40
2000	4	3.20	2005	9	3.50

lean toward income-oriented securities, the continued reinvestment of income plays an important role in investment success.

Finding Growth Rates

rate of growth
the compound annual rate of change in the value of a stream of income.

In addition to finding compound annual rates of return, we frequently need to find the **rate of growth.** This is the compound annual rate of change in the value of a stream of income, particularly dividends or earnings. Here we use an example to demonstrate a simple technique for estimating growth rates using a financial table, a financial calculator, or an Excel spreadsheet.

TABLE USE   Imagine that you wish to find the rate of growth for the dividends given in Table 4.13. The year numbers in the table show that 1996 is viewed as the base year (year 0); the subsequent years, 1997–2005, are considered years 1 through 9, respectively. Although 10 years of data are presented in Table 4.13, they represent only 9 years of growth, because the value for the earliest year must be viewed as the initial value at time zero.

   To find the growth rate, we first divide the dividend for the earliest year (1996) by the dividend for the latest year (2005). The resulting quotient is 0.700 ($2.45 ÷ $3.50). It represents the value of the present-value interest factor for 9 years. To estimate the compound annual dividend growth rate, we find the discount rate in Appendix A, Table A.3 associated with the factor closest to 0.700 for 9 years. Looking across year 9 in Table A.3 shows that the factor for 4% is 0.703—very close to the 0.700 value. Therefore, the growth rate of the dividends in Table 4.13 is approximately 4%.

CALCULATOR USE   Using a financial calculator to find the growth rate for the dividend stream shown in Table 4.13, we treat the earliest (1996) value as a present value, **PV,** and the latest (2005) value as a future value, **FV.** (*Note:* Most calculators require *either* the **PV** or the **FV** value to be input as a negative number to calculate an unknown growth rate.) As noted above, although 10 years of dividends are shown in Table 4.13, there are only 9 years of growth (**N** = 9) because the earliest year (1996) must be defined as the base year (year 0). Using the inputs shown at the left, we calculate the growth rate to be 4.04%. This rate is consistent with, but more precise than, the value found using the financial tables.

Input	Function
2.45	PV
−3.50	FV
9	N
	CPT
	I

Solution
4.04

SPREADSHEET USE   The growth rate for a dividend stream can also be calculated as shown on the Excel spreadsheet on page 160.

	A	B
1	**GROWTH RATE FOR A DIVIDEND STREAM**	
2	Year	Dividend/share
3	2005	$3.50
4	2004	$3.40
5	2003	$3.20
6	2002	$3.20
7	2001	$3.15
8	2000	$3.20
9	1999	$3.00
10	1998	$2.80
11	1997	$2.60
12	1996	$2.45
13	Annual growth rate	4.04%

Entry in Cell B13 is
=RATE((A3–A12),0,–B12,B3,0).
The expression A3–A12 in the entry
calculates the number of years of growth.
The minus sign appears before B12 because
the investment in 1996
is treated as a cash outflow.

The use of growth rates, which are often an important input to the common stock valuation process, is explored in greater detail in Chapter 8.

IN REVIEW

CONCEPTS

4.10 Define the following terms and explain how they are used to find the risk-free rate of return and the required rate of return for a given investment.
a. *Real rate of return.*
b. *Expected inflation premium.*
c. *Risk premium* for a given investment.

4.11 What is meant by the *holding period,* and why it is advisable to use holding periods of equal length when comparing alternative investment vehicles? Define the *holding period return (HPR),* and explain for what length holding periods it is typically used.

4.12 Define *yield* (or *internal rate of return*). When is it appropriate to use yield rather than the HPR to measure the return on an investment?

4.13 Explain why you must earn 10% on *all* income received from an investment during its holding period in order for its yield actually to equal the 10% value you've calculated.

4.14 Explain how either the present value (of benefits versus cost) or the yield measure can be used to find a *satisfactory investment.* Given the following data, indicate which, if any, of these investments is acceptable. Explain your findings.

	Investment		
	A	B	C
Cost	$200	$160	$500
Appropriate	7%	10%	9%
Present value of benefits	—	$150	—
Yield	8%	—	8%

Risk: The Other Side of the Coin

risk
the chance that the actual return from an investment may differ from what is expected.

risk-return tradeoff
the relationship between risk and return, in which investments with more risk should provide higher returns, and vice versa.

Thus far, our primary concern in this chapter has been return. However, we cannot consider return without also looking at risk. Expanding a bit on its definition in Chapter 1, **risk** is the chance that the actual return from an investment may differ from what is expected.

The risk associated with a given investment is directly related to its expected return. In general, the broader the range of possible returns, the greater the investment's risk, and vice versa. Put another way, riskier investments should provide higher levels of return. Otherwise, what incentive is there for an investor to risk his or her capital? In general, investors attempt to minimize risk for a given level of return or to maximize return for a given level of risk. This relationship between risk and return is called the **risk-return tradeoff**. It is introduced here and will be discussed in greater detail in Chapter 5. Here we begin by examining the key sources of risk. We then consider the measurement and assessment of risk: the risk of a single asset, the assessment of risk associated with a potential investment, and the steps by which return and risk can be combined in the decision process.

Sources of Risk

The risk associated with a given investment vehicle may result from a combination of possible sources. A prudent investor considers how the major sources of risk might affect potential investment vehicles. The combined impact of the presence of any of the sources of risk, discussed below, in a given investment vehicle would be reflected in its *risk premium*. As discussed earlier in the chapter and shown in Equation 4.7, the required return on an investment can be found by adding its risk premium to the risk-free rate. This premium in a broad sense results from the sources of risk, which derive from characteristics of both the issue (e.g., stock, bond) and issuer (e.g., voting/nonvoting, callable/noncallable). Of course, as discussed in Chapter 2, *currency exchange risk* is another source of risk that should also be considered when investing internationally.

business risk
the degree of uncertainty associated with an investment's earnings and the investment's ability to pay the returns owed investors.

Business Risk In general, **business risk** is the degree of uncertainty associated with an investment's earnings and the investment's ability to pay the returns (interest, principal, dividends) owed investors. For example, business owners may receive no return if the firm's earnings are not adequate to meet obligations. Debtholders, on the other hand, are likely to receive some (but not necessarily all) of the amount owed them, because of the preferential treatment legally accorded to debt.

Much of the business risk associated with a given investment vehicle is related to its kind of business. For example, the amount of business risk in a public utility common stock differs from the amount in the common stock of a high-fashion clothing manufacturer or an Internet start-up. Generally, investments in similar kinds of firms have similar business risk, although differences in management, costs, and location can cause varying levels of risk.

Financial Risk The degree of uncertainty of payment attributable to the mix of debt and equity used to finance a business is

financial risk
the degree of uncertainty of payment attributable to the mix of debt and equity used to finance a business; the larger the proportion of debt financing, the greater this risk.

purchasing power risk
the chance that changing price levels (inflation or deflation) will adversely affect investment returns.

interest rate risk
the chance that changes in interest rates will adversely affect a security's value.

financial risk. The larger the proportion of debt used to finance a firm, the greater its financial risk. Debt financing obligates the firm to make interest payments as well as to repay the debt, thus increasing risk. Inability to meet obligations associated with the use of debt could result in business failure and in losses for bondholders as well as stockholders and owners.

Purchasing Power Risk The chance that changing price levels (inflation or deflation) will adversely affect investment returns is **purchasing power risk.** Specifically, this risk is the chance that generally rising prices (inflation) will reduce *purchasing power* (the amount of a given commodity that can be purchased with a dollar). For example, if last year a dollar would buy three candy bars and today it can buy only two because candy bars now cost 50 cents each, the purchasing power of your dollar has decreased. In periods of declining price levels (deflation), the purchasing power of the dollar increases.

In general, investments whose values move with general price levels have low purchasing power risk and are most profitable during periods of rising prices. Those that provide fixed returns have high purchasing power risk, and they are most profitable during periods of low inflation or declining price levels. The returns on stocks of durable-goods manufacturers, for example, tend to move with the general price level, whereas returns from deposit accounts and bonds do not.

Interest Rate Risk Securities are especially affected by interest rate risk. This is particularly true for those securities that offer purchasers a fixed periodic return. **Interest rate risk** is the chance that changes in interest rates will adversely affect a security's value. The interest rate changes themselves result from changes in the general relationship between the supply of and the demand for money.

As interest rates change, the prices of many securities fluctuate: They typically decrease with increasing interest rates, and they increase with decreasing interest rates. As we will see in greater detail in Chapters 10, 11, and 12, the prices of fixed-income securities (bonds and preferred stock) drop when interest rates rise. They thus provide purchasers with the same rate of return that would be available at prevailing rates. The opposite occurs when interest rates fall: The return on a fixed-income security is adjusted downward to a competitive level by an upward adjustment in its market price.

A second, more subtle aspect of interest rate risk is associated with reinvestment of income. As noted in our earlier discussion of interest on interest, only if you can earn the initial rate of return on income received from an investment can you achieve a *fully compounded rate of return* equal to the initial rate of return. In other words, if a bond pays 8% annual interest, you must be able to earn 8% on the interest received during the bond's holding period in order to earn a fully compounded 8% rate of return over that period. This same aspect of interest rate risk applies to reinvestment of the proceeds received from an investment at its maturity or sale.

A final aspect of interest rate risk is related to investing in short-term securities such as U.S. Treasury bills and certificates of deposit (discussed in Chapter 1). Investors face the risk that when short-term securities mature, their proceeds may have to be invested in lower-yielding, new short-term securities. By initially making a long-term investment, you can lock in a return for a period of years, rather than face the risk of declines in short-term interest rates. Clearly, when interest rates are declining, the returns from a strategy of investing in short-term securities are adversely affected. On the other hand, interest rate increases have a positive impact on such a strategy. The chance that interest rates will decline is therefore the interest rate risk of a short-term security investment strategy.

Most investment vehicles are subject to interest rate risk. Although fixed-income securities are most directly affected by interest rate movements, they also affect other long-term vehicles such as common stock and mutual funds. *Generally, the higher the interest rate, the lower the value of an investment vehicle, and vice versa.*

liquidity risk
the risk of not being able to liquidate an investment conveniently and at a reasonable price.

Liquidity Risk The risk of not being able to liquidate an investment conveniently and at a reasonable price is called **liquidity risk**. The liquidity of a given investment vehicle is an important consideration. In general, investment vehicles traded in *thin markets*, where demand and supply are small, tend to be less liquid than those traded in *broad markets*.

One can generally sell an investment vehicle merely by significantly cutting its price. However, to be liquid, an investment must be easily sold *at a reasonable price*. For example, a security recently purchased for $1,000 would not be viewed as highly liquid if it could be quickly sold only at a greatly reduced price, such as $500. Vehicles such as stocks and bonds of major companies listed on the New York Stock Exchange are generally highly liquid; others, such as the stock of a small company in a declining industry, are not.

tax risk
the chance that Congress will make unfavorable changes in tax laws, driving down the after-tax returns and market values of certain investments.

Tax Risk The chance that Congress will make unfavorable changes in tax laws is known as **tax risk**. The greater the chance that such changes will drive down the after-tax returns and market values of certain investments, the greater the tax risk. Undesirable changes in tax laws include elimination of tax exemptions, limitation of deductions, and increases in tax rates.

In recent years, Congress has passed numerous changes in tax laws. One of the most significant was the *Tax Reform Act of 1986*, which contained provisions that reduced the attractiveness of many investment vehicles, particularly real estate and other tax shelters. More recently, the *Jobs and Growth Tax Relief Reconciliation Act of 2003* reduced tax rates, taxes on dividends, and taxes on capital gains. Clearly, this change benefits investors and does not represent the unfavorable consequences of tax risk.

Though virtually all investments are vulnerable to increases in tax rates, certain tax-advantaged investments, such as municipal and other bonds, real estate, and natural resources, generally have greater tax risk.

market risk
risk of decline in investment returns because of market factors independent of the given investment.

Market Risk **Market risk** is the risk that investment returns will decline because of market factors independent of the given investment. Examples include political, economic, and social events, as well as changes in investor tastes and preferences. Market risk actually embodies a number of different risks: purchasing power risk, interest rate risk, and tax risk.

The impact of market factors on investment returns is not uniform. Both the degree and the direction of change in return differ among investment vehicles. For example, legislation placing restrictive import quotas on Japanese goods may result in a significant increase in the value (and therefore the return) of domestic automobile and electronics stocks. Essentially, market risk is reflected in the *price volatility* of a security—the more volatile the price of a security, the greater its perceived market risk.

Event Risk Event risk occurs when something happens to a company that has a sudden and substantial impact on its financial condition. Event risk goes beyond business and financial risk. It does not necessarily mean the company or market is doing poorly. Instead, it involves an unexpected event that has a significant and usually immediate effect on the underlying value of an investment. An example of event risk is the August 2000 offer by Bridgestone/Firestone to replace 6.5 million tires, mainly on Ford light trucks and SUVs, based on 46 deaths and more than 300 incidents involving Firestone tires that were alleged to have shredded on the highway. The stock of Bridgestone Corporation—the Japanese parent company of Bridgestone/Firestone—was quickly and negatively affected. It dropped by about 20% on the Tokyo Exchange during the two days immediately following the announcement.

Event risk can take many forms and can affect all types of investment vehicles. Fortunately, its impact tends to be isolated in most cases. For instance, the stocks of only a small number of companies were directly affected by Bridgestone/Firestone's offer to replace tires.

Risk of a Single Asset

Most people have at some time in their lives asked themselves how risky some anticipated course of action is. In such cases, the answer is usually a subjective judgment, such as "not very" or "quite." Such a judgment may or may not help in decision making. In finance, we are able to quantify the measurement of risk, which improves comparisons between investments and enhances decision making.

The risk or variability of both single assets and portfolios of assets can be measured statistically. Here we focus solely on the risk of single assets. We first consider standard deviation, which is an absolute measure of risk. Then we consider the coefficient of variation, a relative measure of risk. We will consider the risk and return of portfolios of assets in Chapter 5.

Standard Deviation: An Absolute Measure of Risk The most common single indicator of an asset's risk is the **standard deviation, s.** It measures the dispersion (variation) of returns around an asset's average or expected return. The formula is

Equation 4.10

$$\text{Standard deviation} = \sqrt{\dfrac{\sum\limits_{j=1}^{n}\left(\begin{array}{c}\text{Return for} \\ \text{outcome } j\end{array} - \begin{array}{c}\text{Average or} \\ \text{expected return}\end{array}\right)^2}{\begin{array}{c}\text{Total number} \\ \text{of outcomes}\end{array} - 1}}$$

Equation 4.10a

$$s = \sqrt{\dfrac{\sum\limits_{j=1}^{n}(r_j - \bar{r})^2}{n - 1}}$$

Consider two competing investments—A and B—described in Table 4.14. Note that both investments earned an average return of 15% over the 6-year period shown. Reviewing the returns shown for each investment in light of

TABLE 4.14	Returns on Investments A and B	
	Rate of Return (r_j)	
Year (j)	Investment A	Investment B
2000	15.6%	8.4%
2001	12.7	12.9
2002	15.3	19.6
2003	16.2	17.5
2004	16.5	10.3
2005	13.7	21.3
Average ($\bar{r}$)	15.0%	15.0%

their 15% averages, we can see that the returns for investment B vary more from this average than do the returns for investment A.

The standard deviation provides a quantitative tool for comparing investment risk. Table 4.15 on page 166 demonstrates the calculation of the standard deviations, s_A and s_B, for investments A and B, respectively. Evaluating the calculations, we can see that the standard deviation of 1.49% for the returns on investment A is, as expected, considerably below the standard deviation of 5.24% for investment B. The greater absolute dispersion of investment B's return, reflected in its larger standard deviation, indicates that B is the more risky investment. Of course, these values are absolute measures based on *historical* data. There is no assurance that the risks of these two investments will remain the same in the future.

coefficient of variation, CV
a statistic used to measure the *relative* dispersion of an asset's returns; it is useful in comparing the risk of assets with differing average or expected returns.

Coefficient of Variation: A Relative Measure of Risk The **coefficient of variation, CV,** is a measure of the *relative* dispersion of an asset's returns. It is useful in comparing the risk of assets with differing average or expected returns. Equation 4.11 gives the formula for the coefficient of variation.

Equation 4.11
$$\text{Coefficient of variation} = \frac{\text{Standard deviation}}{\text{Average or expected return}}$$

Equation 4.11a
$$CV = \frac{s}{\bar{r}}$$

As was the case for the standard deviation, the higher the coefficient of variation, the greater the risk.

We can substitute into Equation 4.11a the standard deviation values (from Table 4.15) and the average returns (from Table 4.14) for investments A and B. We get a coefficient of variation for A of 0.099 (1.49% ÷ 15%) and for B of 0.349 (5.24% ÷ 15%). Investment B has the higher coefficient of variation and, as expected, has more relative risk than investment A. Because both investments have the same average return, the coefficient of variation in this case has not provided any more information than the standard deviation.

The real utility of the coefficient of variation is in comparing investments that have *different* expected returns. For example, assume you want to select the less risky of two alternative investments—X and Y. The average return, the

EXCEL with
SPREADSHEETS

TABLE 4.15 Calculation of Standard Deviations of Returns for Investments A and B

Investment A

Year (j)	(1) Return, r_j	(2) Average Return, $\bar{r}$	(3) (1) − (2) $r_j - \bar{r}$	(4) (3)^2 $(r_j - \bar{r})^2$
2000	15.6%	15.0%	.6%	0.36%
2001	12.7	15.0	−2.3	5.29
2002	15.3	15.0	.3	0.09
2003	16.2	15.0	1.2	1.44
2004	16.5	15.0	1.5	2.25
2005	13.7	15.0	−1.3	1.69

$$\sum_{j=1}^{6} (r_j - \bar{r})^2 = 11.12$$

$$s_A = \sqrt{\frac{\sum_{j=1}^{6} (r_j - \bar{r})^2}{n - 1}} = \sqrt{\frac{11.12}{6 - 1}} = \sqrt{2.224} = \underline{1.49\%}$$

Investment B

Year (j)	(1) Return, r_j	(2) Average Return, $\bar{r}$	(3) (1) − (2) $r_j - \bar{r}$	(4) (3)^2 $(r_j - \bar{r})^2$
2000	8.4%	15.0%	−6.6%	43.56%
2001	12.9	15.0	−2.1	4.41
2002	19.6	15.0	4.6	21.16
2003	17.5	15.0	2.5	6.25
2004	10.3	15.0	−4.7	22.09
2005	21.3	15.0	6.3	39.69

$$\sum_{j=1}^{6} (r_j - \bar{r})^2 = 137.16$$

$$s_B = \sqrt{\frac{\sum_{j=1}^{6} (r_j - \bar{r})^2}{n - 1}} = \sqrt{\frac{137.16}{6 - 1}} = \sqrt{27.432} = \underline{5.24\%}$$

standard deviation, and the coefficient of variation for each of these investments are as follows.

Statistics	Investment X	Investment Y
(1) Average return	12%	20%
(2) Standard deviation	9%*	10%
(3) Coefficient of variation [(2) ÷ (1)]	0.75	0.50*

*Preferred investment using the given risk measure.

If you compared the investments solely on the basis of their standard deviations, you would prefer investment X. It has a lower standard deviation than investment Y (9% versus 10%). But by comparing the coefficients of variation, you can see that you would be making a mistake in choosing X over Y. The *relative* dispersion, or risk, of the investments, as reflected in the coefficient of variation, is lower for Y than for X (0.50 versus 0.75). Clearly, the coefficient of variation considers the relative size, or average return, of each investment.

TABLE 4.16	Historical Returns, Standard Deviations, and Coefficients of Variation for Popular Security Investments (1926–2002)		
Investment	Average Annual Return	Standard Deviation	Coefficient of Variation*
Large-company stocks	12.2%	20.5%	1.68
Small-company stocks	16.9	33.2	1.96
Long-term corporate bonds	6.2	8.7	1.40
Long-term government bonds	5.8	9.4	1.62
U.S. Treasury bills	3.8	3.2	0.84
Inflation	3.1%	4.4%	1.42

*Calculated by dividing the standard deviation by the average annual return.

Source: *Stocks, Bonds, Bills, and Inflation, 2003 Yearbook* (Chicago: Ibbotson Associates, Inc., 2002), p. 33.

Historical Returns and Risk We can now use the standard deviation and coefficient of variation as a measure of risk to assess the historical (1926–2002) investment return data in Table 4.4. Table 4.16 repeats the historical returns and shows the standard deviations and coefficients of variation associated with each of them. A close relationship can be seen between the investment returns and the standard deviations and coefficients of variation: Investments with higher return have higher standard deviations and coefficients of variation. Because higher standard deviations and coefficients of variation are associated with greater risk, the historical data confirm the existence of a positive relationship between risk and return. That relationship reflects the fact that market participants require higher returns as compensation for greater risk. The historical data in Table 4.16 clearly show that during the 1926–2002 period investors were rewarded with higher returns on higher-risk investments.

HOT

Visit the Securities Industry Association site's Investing Essentials section. While there, click on [understanding risk], [understanding return], and [risk and return].

www.siainvestor.org/categories/ investingessentials/ie_intro.htm

Assessing Risk

Techniques for quantifying the risk of a given investment vehicle are quite useful. However, they will be of little use if you are unaware of your feelings toward risk. The individual investor typically tends to seek answers to these questions: "Is the amount of perceived risk worth taking to get the expected return?" "Can I get a higher return for the same level of risk or a lower risk for the same level of return?" A look at the general risk-return characteristics of alternative investment vehicles and at the question of an acceptable level of risk will help shed light on how to evaluate risk.

Risk-Return Characteristics of Alternative Investment Vehicles A wide variety of risk-return behaviors are associated with each type of investment vehicle. Some common stocks offer low returns and low risk. Others offer high returns and high risk. In general, ignoring differences in maturity, the risk-return characteristics of the major investment vehicles are as shown in Figure 4.4 (on page 168). Of course, a broad range of risk-return behaviors exists for specific investments of each type. In other words, once you have selected the appropriate type of vehicle, you must still decide which specific security to acquire.

FIGURE 4.4

Risk-Return Tradeoffs for Various Investment Vehicles

A risk-return tradeoff exists such that for a higher risk one expects a higher return, and vice versa. In general, ignoring differences in maturity, low-risk/low-return investment vehicles include U.S. government securities and deposit accounts. High-risk/high-return vehicles include real estate and other tangible investments, options, and futures.

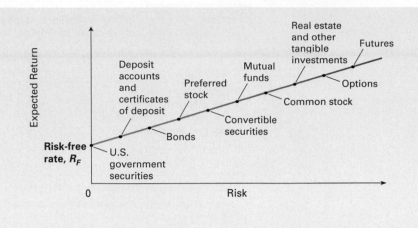

An Acceptable Level of Risk The three basic risk preferences (risk-indifferent, risk-averse, and risk-seeking) are depicted graphically in Figure 4.5.

- For the **risk-indifferent** investor, the required return does not change as risk goes from x_1 to x_2. In essence, no change in return would be required for the increase in risk.

- For the **risk-averse** investor, the required return increases for an increase in risk. Because they shy away from risk, these investors require higher expected returns to compensate them for taking greater risk.

- For the **risk-seeking** investor, the required return decreases for an increase in risk. Theoretically, because they enjoy risk, these investors are willing to give up some return to take more risk.

Most investors are risk-averse: For a given increase in risk, they require an increase in return. This risk-averse behavior is also depicted in Figure 4.4.

Of course, the amount of return required by each investor for a given increase in risk differs depending on the investor's degree of risk aversion (reflected in the slope of the line). Investors generally tend to be conservative when accepting risk. The more aggressive an investor you are (the farther to

risk-indifferent
describes an investor who does not require a change in return as compensation for greater risk.

risk-averse
describes an investor who requires greater return in exchange for greater risk.

risk-seeking
describes an investor who will accept a lower return in exchange for greater risk.

FIGURE 4.5

Risk Preferences

The risk-indifferent investor requires no change in return for a given increase in risk. The risk-averse investor requires an increase in return for a given risk increase. The risk-seeking investor gives up some return for more risk. The majority of investors are risk-averse.

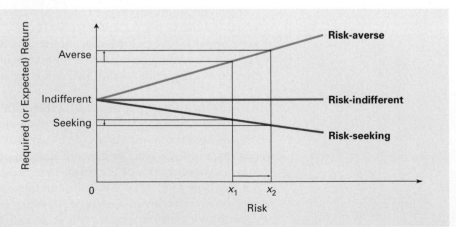

INVESTING IN ACTION

WHAT'S YOUR RISK TOLERANCE?

During the strong bull market of the 1990s and early 2000s, it seemed that investors couldn't lose. Even when the market took a nosedive, they rushed to buy at lower prices and assumed that their stocks would go up again. The lure of easy money pushed the idea of risk into the background for many investors, who assumed higher levels of risk without stopping to consider their personal risk tolerance. The rise of online, do-it-yourself investing also contributed to this new attitude toward risk.

The key to risk taking is to determine your personal level of risk tolerance—how comfortable you feel with the volatility of your investments. Understanding your risk tolerance will prevent you from taking on more risk than you can handle and will reduce the likelihood that you will panic and abandon your plan in midstream.

The following quiz can help you evaluate your personal capacity for risk. After you've taken it, you may want to check out a few other risk tolerance quizzes at these sites: Investor Education Fund's Risk quizzes, **www.investored. ca/en/interactive/games_quizzes_risk.htm**; MSN's Money Central, **moneycentral.msn.com/ articles/invest/prepare/risktol.asp**; and Rutgers Cooperative Extension, **www.rce.rutgers.edu/ money/riskquiz/default.asp**. With this information in hand, you can build a portfolio that will let you sleep better at night.

What is Your Investment Risk Tolerance?

1. Which best describes your feelings about investing?
   a. "Better safe than sorry."
   b. "Moderation in all things."
   c. "Nothing ventured, nothing gained."

2. Which is the most important to you as an investor?
   a. Steady income
   b. Steady income and growth
   c. Rapid price appreciation

3. You won! Which prize would you select?
   a. $4,000 in cash
   b. A 50% chance to win $10,000
   c. A 20% chance to win $100,000

4. The stocks in your retirement account have dropped 20% since last quarter. The market experts are optimistic. What would you do?
   a. Transfer out of stocks to avoid losing more.
   b. Stay in stocks and wait for them to come back.
   c. Shift more money into stocks. If they made sense before, they're a bargain now.

5. The stocks in your retirement account have suddenly gone up 20%. You have no more information. What would you do?
   a. Transfer out of stocks and lock in my gains.
   b. Stay in stocks, hoping for more gains.
   c. Transfer more money into stocks. They might go higher.

6. Would you borrow money to take advantage of a good investment opportunity?
   a. Never   b. Maybe   c. Yes

7. How would you characterize yourself as an investor?
   a. Conservative
   b. Moderate risk taker
   c. Aggressive

How to determine your score:

Each (a) answer is worth 1 point. Each (b) is worth 2 points. Each (c) is worth 3 points. Add them up to find your total score.

   7-11 points: a conservative investor
   12-16 points: a moderate risk taker
   17-21 points: an aggressive investor

CRITICAL THINKING QUESTION Judging by your quiz results, what is your personal tolerance for investment risk? Using the graph in Figure 4.4, determine what investment vehicles might be appropriate for your level of risk tolerance.

Sources: Maria Crawford Scott, "Life-Cycle Investing: Investment Decisions and Your Personal Investment Profile" *AAII Journal,* March 1993, pp. 16–19; Ann Perry, "Putting Stock in the Market," *San Diego Union-Tribune,* July 18, 1993, pp. 11–12; and Jeff D. Opdyke, "Bumpy Market Reminds Investors to Assess Their Risk Tolerance," *Wall Street Journal,* July 14, 2002, pp. C1, C11.

the right you operate on the risk-averse line), the greater your tolerance for risk, and the greater your required return. To get a feel for your own risk-taking orientation, read the *Investing in Action* box on page 169.

Steps in the Decision Process: Combining Return and Risk

When you are deciding among alternative investments, you should take the following steps to combine return and risk.

1. Using historical or projected return data, estimate the expected return over a given holding period. Use yield (or present-value) techniques to make sure you give the time value of money adequate consideration.
2. Using historical or projected return data, assess the risk associated with the investment. Subjective risk assessment, use of the standard deviation or coefficient of variation of returns, and use of more sophisticated measures, such as beta (developed in Chapter 5), are the primary approaches available to individual investors.
3. Evaluate the risk-return behavior of each alternative investment to make sure that the return expected is reasonable given the level of risk. If other vehicles with lower levels of risk provide equal or greater returns, the investment is not acceptable.
4. Select the investment vehicles that offer the highest returns associated with the level of risk you are willing to take. As long as you get the highest return for your acceptable level of risk, you have made a "good investment."

Probably the most difficult step in this process is assessing risk. Aside from return and risk considerations, other factors, such as portfolio considerations, taxes, and liquidity, affect the investment decision. We will develop portfolio concepts in Chapter 5 and, in later chapters, will look at all of these factors as they are related to specific investment vehicles.

IN REVIEW

CONCEPTS

4.15 Define *risk*. Explain what we mean by the *risk-return tradeoff*. What happens to the required return as risk increases? Explain.

4.16 Define and briefly discuss each of the following sources of risk.
  a. Business risk
  b. Financial risk
  c. Purchasing power risk
  d. Interest rate risk
  e. Liquidity risk
  f. Tax risk
  g. Market risk
  h. Event risk

4.17 Briefly describe each of the following measures of risk or variability, and explain their similarity. Under what circumstances is each preferred when comparing the risk of competing investments?
  a. Standard deviation
  b. Coefficient of variation

4.18 Differentiate among the three basic risk preferences: *risk-indifferent, risk-averse,* and *risk-seeking.* Which of these behaviors best describes most investors?

4.19 Describe the steps involved in the investment decision process. Be sure to mention how returns and risks can be evaluated together to determine acceptable investments.

Summary

LG 1   **Review the concept of return, its components, the forces that affect the investor's level of return, and historical returns.** Return is the reward for investing. The total return provided by an investment includes current income and capital gains (or losses). Return is commonly calculated on a historical basis and then used to project expected returns. The level of return depends on internal characteristics and external forces, which include the general level of price changes. Significant differences exist between the average annual rates of return realized over time on various types of security investments.

LG 2   **Discuss the time value of money and the calculations involved in finding the future value of various types of cash flows.** Because investors have opportunities to earn interest on their funds, money has a time value. Interest can be applied using either simple interest or compound interest. The more frequently interest is compounded at a stated rate, the higher the true rate of interest. Financial tables, financial calculators, and computers and spreadsheets can be used to streamline time-value calculations. The future value of a present sum or an annuity can be found using compound interest concepts.

LG 3   **Explain the concept of present value, the procedures for calculating present values, and the use of present value in determining whether an investment is satisfactory.** The present value of a future sum is the amount that would have to be deposited today, into an account earning interest at a given rate, to accumulate the specified future sum. The present value of streams of future returns can be found by adding the present values of the individual returns. When the stream is an annuity, its present value can be more simply calculated. A satisfactory investment is one for which the present value of its benefits equals or exceeds the present value of its costs.

LG 4   **Describe real, risk-free, and required returns and the computation and application of holding period return, yield (internal rate of return), and growth rates.** The required return on an investment is the rate of return an investor must earn to be fully compensated for the investment's risk. It represents the sum of the real rate of return and the expected inflation premium (which together represent the risk-free rate), plus the risk premium for the investment. The risk premium varies depending on issue and issuer characteristics. The holding period return (HPR) is the return earned over a specified period of time. It is frequently used to compare returns earned in periods of 1 year or less.

    Yield or internal rate of return is the compound annual rate of return earned on investments held for more than 1 year. If the yield is greater than or equal to the required return, the investment is acceptable. Implicit in the use of yield is an ability to earn a return equal to the calculated yield on all income received from the investment during the holding period. Present-value techniques can be used to find a rate of growth, which is the compound annual rate of change in the value of a stream of income, particularly dividends or earnings.

LG 5   **Discuss the key sources of risk and how they might affect potential investment vehicles.** Risk is the chance that the actual return from an investment will differ from what is expected. The total risk associated with a given investment vehicle may result from a combination of sources: business, financial, purchasing power, interest rate, liquidity, tax, market, and event risk. These risks typically have varying effects on different types of investment vehicles. The combined impact of any of the sources of risk in a given investment vehicle would be reflected in its risk premium.

LG 6   **Understand the risk of a single asset, risk assessment, and the steps that combine return and risk.** The risk of both single assets and portfolios of assets can be measured statistically on an absolute basis by the standard deviation and on a relative basis by the coefficient of variation. There is a tradeoff between risk and return. Historical return and risk data for popular security investments confirm that investors require higher returns as compensation for greater risk. Generally, each type of investment vehicle displays certain risk-return characteristics. Most investors are risk-averse: In exchange for a given increase in risk, they require an increase in return. The investment decision involves estimating the return and risk of each alternative and then selecting those investments that offer the highest returns for the level of risk the investor is willing to take.

Putting Your Investment Know-How to the Test

1. An investment of $231 will increase in value to $268 in 3 years. The annual compound growth rate in this case is closest to
   a. 3.0%.   b. 4.0%.
   c. 5.0%.   d. 6.0%.

2. What is the value in 5 years of $100 invested today at an interest rate of 8% per year, compounded quarterly?
   a. $144.50   b. $146.02
   c. $148.02   d. $148.59

3. All of the following statements about various types of risk are true *except*
   a. Business risk is the uncertainty of income flows caused by the nature of a firm's business.
   b. Financial risk is the uncertainty introduced by the method by which the firm finances its investments.
   c. Exchange rate risk is the uncertainty of returns caused by the possibility of a major change in the political or economic environment of a country.
   d. Liquidity risk is the uncertainty introduced by the secondary market for an investment.

4. An investor will receive a 5-year annuity of $2,500 per year. She will not receive the first payment until 3 years from today. If the annual rate is 8%, the present value of this annuity is *closest* to
   a. $8,105.   b. $8,224.
   c. $8,558.   d. $9,982.

5. An investor has a portfolio with a market value of $50,000 at the end of May. The market value of the portfolio is $48,700 at the end of June. The holding-period yield on the investor's portfolio for June is closest to
   a. −1.30%.   b. −2.60%.
   c. −2.63%.   d. −2.67%.

6. An investor holds a portfolio consisting of one share of each of the following stocks:

Stock	Price at the Beginning of the Year	Price at the End of the Year	Cash Dividend During the Year
A	$10	$20	$0
B	$50	$60	$1
C	$100	$110	$4

For the 1-year holding period, the portfolio return as a weighted investment is *closest* to
a. 15.79%.   b. 18.42%.
c. 18.75%.   d. 21.88%.

7. Rob Monroe buys a $150,000 house and puts $30,000 down. He finances the house with a 30-year, fixed-rate loan. The rate on the mortgage loan is a 2% spread above the yield on a 6%, 10-year Treasury bond. The monthly mortgage payment is *closest* to

   a. $333. b. $881.

   c. $966. d. $996.

8. Which of the following is the *least likely* to affect the required rate of return on an investment?

   a. Real risk free rate.

   b. Asset risk premium.

   c. Expected rate of inflation.

   d. Investor's composite propensity to consume.

9. A bank lends a company $2,000,000 to be repaid in three year-end installments. If the bank charges 9% interest, the annual installment payment will be *closest* to

   a. $666,667. b. $724,871.

   c. $726,667. d. $790,110.

10. An individual deposits $1,500 today and $1,500 one year from today into an interest-earning account. The deposits earn 12% compounded annually. The total amount in the account 2 years from today is closest to

    a. $3,180. b. $3,360.

    c. $3,382. d. $3,562.

Answers: 1. c; 2. d; 3. c; 4. d; 5. b; 6. d; 7. b; 8. d; 9. d; 10. d

---

Discussion Questions

LG 1

Q4.1 Choose a publicly traded company that has been listed on a major exchange or in the over-the-counter market for at least 5 years. Use any data source of your choice to find the annual cash dividend, if any, paid by the company in each of the past 5 calendar years. Also find the closing price of the stock at the end of each of the preceding 6 years.

    a. Calculate the return for each of the five 1-year periods.

    b. Graph the returns on a set of year (*x*-axis)-return (*y*-axis) axes.

    c. On the basis of the graph in part **b**, estimate the return for the coming year, and explain your answer.

LG 2   LG 3

Q4.2 Estimate the amount of cash you will need each year over the next 20 years to live at the standard you desire. Also estimate the rate of return you can reasonably expect to earn annually, on average, during that 20-year period by investing in a common stock portfolio similar to the S&P 500.

    a. How large a single lump sum would you need today to provide the annual cash required to allow you to live at the desired standard over the next 20 years? (*Hint:* Be sure to use the appropriate discount rate.)

    b. Would the lump sum calculated in part **a** be larger or smaller if you could earn a higher return during the 20-year period? Explain.

    c. If you had the lump sum calculated in part **a** but decided to delay your planned retirement in 20 years for another 3 years, how much extra cash would you have accumulated over the 3-year period if you could invest it to earn a 7% annual rate of return?

LG 4

Q4.3 Access appropriate estimates of the expected inflation rate over the next year, and the current yield on one-year risk-free securities (the yield on these securities is referred to as the *nominal* rate of interest). Use the data to estimate the current risk-free *real* rate of interest.

LG 4 **LG 5** **LG 6**

Q4.4 Choose three NYSE-listed stocks and maintain a record of their dividend payments, if any, and closing prices each week over the next 6 weeks.

  a. At the end of the 6-week period, calculate the 1-week holding period returns (HPRs) for each stock for each of the 6 weeks.

  b. For each stock, average the six weekly HPRs calculated in part **a** and compare them.

  c. Use the averages you computed in part **b** and compute the standard deviation of the six HPRs for each stock. Discuss the stocks' relative risk and return behavior. Did the stocks with the highest risk earn the greatest return?

Problems

LG 1

P4.1 How much would an investor earn on a stock purchased 1 year ago for $63 if it paid an annual cash dividend of $3.75 and had just been sold for $67.50? Would the investor have experienced a capital gain? Explain.

LG 1

P4.2 An investor buys a bond for $10,000. The bond pays $300 interest every 6 months. After 18 months, the investor sells the bond for $9,500. Describe the types of income and/or loss the investor had.

LG 1

P4.3 Assuming you purchased a share of stock for $50 one year ago, sold it today for $60, and during the year received three dividend payments totaling $2.70, calculate the following.

  a. Current income.

  b. Capital gain (or loss).

  c. Total return
  (1) In dollars.
  (2) As a percentage of the initial investment.

LG 1

P4.4 Assume you purchased a bond for $9,500. The bond pays $300 interest every 6 months. You sell the bond after 18 months for $10,000. Calculate the following:

  a. Current income.

  b. Capital gain or loss.

  c. Total return in dollars and as a percentage of the original investment.

LG 1

P4.5 Consider the historical data given in the accompanying table.

  a. Calculate the total return (in dollars) for each year.

  b. Indicate the level of return you would expect in 2006 and in 2007.

  c. Comment on your forecast.

Year	Income	Market Value (Price)	
		Beginning	Ending
2001	$1.00	$30.00	$32.50
2002	1.20	32.50	35.00
2003	1.30	35.00	33.00
2004	1.60	33.00	40.00
2005	1.75	40.00	45.00

LG 1   **P4.6**   Refer to the table in Problem 4.5. What is the total return in dollars and as a percentage of your original investment if you purchased 100 shares of the investment at the beginning of 2001 and sold it at the end of 2003?

LG 2   **P4.7**   For each of the savings account transactions in the accompanying table, calculate the following.
     a. End-of-year account balance. (Assume that the account balance at December 31, 2004, is zero.)
     b. Annual interest, using 6% simple interest and assuming all interest is withdrawn from the account as it is earned.
     c. True rate of interest, and compare it to the stated rate of interest. Discuss your finding.

Date	Deposit (Withdrawal)	Date	Deposit (Withdrawal)
1/1/05	$5,000	1/1/07	$2,000
1/1/06	(4,000)	1/1/08	3,000

LG 2   **P4.8**   Using the appropriate table of interest factors found in Appendix A or a financial calculator, calculate the following.
     a. The future value of a $300 deposit left in an account paying 7% annual interest for 12 years.
     b. The future value at the end of 6 years of an $800 *annual* end-of-year deposit into an account paying 7% annual interest.

LG 2   **P4.9**   For each of the following initial investment amounts, calculate the future value at the end of the given investment period if interest is compounded annually at the specified rate of return over the given investment period.

Investment	Investment Amount	Rate of Return	Investment Period
A	$ 200	5%	20 years
B	4,500	8	7
C	10,000	9	10
D	25,000	10	12
E	37,000	11	5

LG 2   **P4.10**   Using the appropriate table of interest factors found in Appendix A or a financial calculator, calculate the future value in 2 years of $10,000 invested today in an account that pays a stated annual interest rate of 12%, compounded monthly.

LG 2   **P4.11**   For each of the following annual deposits into an account paying the stated annual interest rate over the specified deposit period, calculate the future value of the *annuity* at the end of the given deposit period.

Deposit	Amount of Annual Deposit	Interest Rate	Deposit Period
A	$ 2,500	8%	10 years
B	500	12	6
C	1,000	20	5
D	12,000	6	8
E	4,000	14	30

LG 2 **P4.12** If you deposit $1,000 into an account at the end of each of the next 5 years, and the account pays an annual interest rate of 6%, how much will be in the account after 5 years?

LG 2 **P4.13** If you could earn 9% on similar-risk investments, what is the least you would accept at the end of a 6-year period, given the following amounts and timing of your investment?

a. Invest $5,000 as a lump sum today.
b. Invest $2,000 at the end of *each* of the next 5 years.
c. Invest a lump sum of $3,000 today and $1,000 at the end of *each* of the next 5 years.
d. Invest $900 at the end of years 1, 3, and 5.

LG 3 **P4.14** For each of the following investments, calculate the present value of the future sum, using the specified discount rate and assuming the sum will be received at the end of the given year.

Investment	Future Sum	Discount Rate	End of Year
A	$ 7,000	12%	4
B	28,000	8	20
C	10,000	14	12
D	150,000	11	6
E	45,000	20	8

LG 3 **P4.15** A Florida state savings bond can be converted to $1,000 at maturity 8 years from purchase. If the state bonds are to be competitive with U.S. savings bonds, which pay 6% interest compounded annually, at what price will the state's bonds sell, assuming they make no cash payments prior to maturity?

LG 3 **P4.16** Referring to Problem 4.15 above, at what price would the bond sell if U.S. savings bonds were paying 8% interest compounded annually? Compare your answer to your answer to the preceding problem.

LG 3 **P4.17** How much should you be willing to pay for a lump sum of $10,000 5 years from now if you can earn 3% every 6 months on other similar investments?

LG 3 **P4.18** Find the present value of each of the following streams of income, assuming a 12% discount rate.

A		B		C	
End of Year	Income	End of Year	Income	End of Year	Income
1	$2,200	1	$10,000	1-5	$10,000/yr
2	3,000	2-5	5,000/yr	6-10	8,000/yr
3	4,000	6	7,000		
4	6,000				
5	8,000				

LG 3 **P4.19** Consider the streams of income given in the following table.

a. Find the present value of each income stream, using a 15% discount rate.
b. Compare the calculated present values and discuss them in light of the fact that the undiscounted total income amounts to $10,000 in each case.

	Income Stream	
End of Year	A	B
1	$ 4,000	$ 1,000
2	3,000	2,000
3	2,000	3,000
4	1,000	4,000
Total	$10,000	$10,000

P4.20 For each of the investments below, calculate the present value of the *annual* end-of-year returns at the specified discount rate over the given period.

Investment	Annual Returns	Discount Rate	Period
A	$ 1,200	7%	3 years
B	5,500	12	15
C	700	20	9
D	14,000	5	7
E	2,200	10	5

P4.21 Congratulations! You have won the lottery! Would you rather have $1 million at the end of each of the next 20 years or $15 million today? (Assume an 8% discount rate.)

P4.22 Using the appropriate table of interest factors found in Appendix A, a financial calculator, or an Excel spreadsheet, calculate the following.
  a. The present value of $500 to be received 4 years from now, using an 11% discount rate.
  b. The present value of the following end-of-year income streams, using a 9% discount rate and assuming it is now the beginning of 2006.

End of Year	Income Stream A	Income Stream B
2006	$80	$140
2007	80	120
2008	80	100
2009	80	80
2010	80	60
2011	80	40
2012	80	20

P4.23 Terri Allessandro has an opportunity to make any of the following investments. The purchase price, the amount of its lump-sum future value, and its year of receipt are given below for each investment. Terri can earn a 10% rate of return on investments similar to those currently under consideration. Evaluate each investment to determine whether it is satisfactory, and make an investment recommendation to Terri.

Investment	Purchase Price	Future Value	Year of Receipt
A	$18,000	$30,000	5
B	600	3,000	20
C	3,500	10,000	10
D	1,000	15,000	40

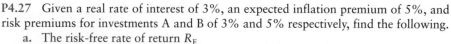

P4.24 Kent Weitz wishes to assess whether the following two investments are satisfactory. Use his required return (discount rate) of 17% to evaluate each investment. Make an investment recommendation to Kent.

	Investment	
	A	B
Purchase price	$13,000	$8,500
End of Year	Income Stream	
1	$ 2,500	$4,000
2	3,500	3,500
3	4,500	3,000
4	5,000	1,000
5	5,500	,500

LG 3

P4.25 You purchased a car using some cash and borrowing $15,000 (the present value) for fifty months at 12% per year. Calculate the monthly payment (annuity).

LG 3

P4.26 Referring to Problem 4.25 above, assume you have made 10 payments. What is the balance (present value) of your loan?

LG 4

P4.27 Given a real rate of interest of 3%, an expected inflation premium of 5%, and risk premiums for investments A and B of 3% and 5% respectively, find the following.
  a. The risk-free rate of return R_F
  b. The required returns for investments A and B.

LG 4

P4.28 The risk free rate is 7%, and expected inflation is 4.5%. If inflation expectations change such that future expected inflation rises to 5.5%, what will the new risk-free rate be?

LG 4

P4.29 Calculate the holding period return (HPR) for the following two investment alternatives. Which, if any, of the return components is likely not to be realized if you continue to hold each of the investments beyond 1 year? Which vehicle would you prefer, assuming they are of equal risk? Explain.

	Investment Vehicle	
	X	Y
Cash received		
1st quarter	$ 1.00	$ 0
2nd quarter	1.20	0
3rd quarter	0	0
4th quarter	2.30	2.00
Investment value		
End of year	$29.00	$56.00
Beginning of year	30.00	50.00

LG 4

P4.30 You are considering two investment alternatives. The first is a stock that pays quarterly dividends of $0.50 per share, is trading at $25 per share, and you expect to sell the stock in six months for $27. The second is a stock that pays quarterly dividends of $0.60 per share, is trading at $27 per share, and you expect to sell the stock in one year for $30. Which stock will provide the better annualized holding period return?

LG 4

P4.31 You are considering purchasing a bond that pays annual interest of $50 per $1,000 of par value. The bond matures in one year, when you will collect the par value and the interest payment. If you can purchase this bond for $950, what is the holding period return?

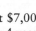

P4.32 Assume you invest $5,000 today in an investment vehicle that promises to return $9,000 in exactly 10 years.
  a. Use the present-value technique to estimate the yield on this investment.
  b. If a minimum return of 9% is required, would you recommend this investment?

P4.33 You invest $7,000 in stock and receive $65, $70, $70, and $65 in dividends over the following 4 years. At the end of the four years, you sell the stock for $7,900. What was the yield on this investment?

P4.34 Your friend asks you to invest $10,000 in a business venture. Based on your estimates, you would receive nothing for four years, at the end of year five you would receive interest on the investment compounded annually at 8%, and at the end of year six you would receive $14,500. If your estimates are correct, what would be the yield on this investment?

P4.35 Use the appropriate present-value interest factor table, a financial calculator, or an Excel spreadsheet to estimate the yield for each of the following investments.

Investment	Initial Investment	Future Value	End of Year
A	$ 1,000	$ 1,200	5
B	10,000	20,000	7
C	,400	2,000	20
D	3,000	4,000	6
E	5,500	25,000	30

P4.36 Rosemary Santos must earn a return of 10% on an investment that requires an initial outlay of $2,500 and promises to return $6,000 in 8 years.
  a. Use present-value techniques to estimate the yield on this investment.
  b. On the basis of your finding in part **a**, should Rosemary make the proposed investment? Explain.

P4.37 Use the appropriate present-value interest factors, a financial calculator, or an Excel spreadsheet to estimate the yield for each of the following two investments.

	Investment	
	A	B
Initial Investment	$8,500	$9,500
End of Year	Income	
1	$2,500	$2,000
2	2,500	2,500
3	2,500	3,000
4	2,500	3,500
5	2,500	4,000

P4.38 Elliott Dumack must earn a minimum rate of return of 11% to be adequately compensated for the risk of the following investment.

Initial Investment	$14,000
End of year	Income
1	$ 6,000
2	3,000
3	5,000
4	2,000
5	1,000

a. Use present-value techniques to estimate the yield on this investment.
b. On the basis of your finding in part **a**, should Elliott make the proposed investment? Explain.

 LG 4

P4.39 Assume the investment that generates income stream B in Problem 4.22 can be purchased at the beginning of 2006 for $1,000 and sold at the end of 2012 for $1,200. Estimate the yield for this investment. If a minimum return of 9% is required, would you recommend this investment? Explain.

 LG 4

P4.40 For each of the following streams of dividends, estimate the compound annual rate of growth between the earliest year for which a value is given and 2005.

	Dividend Stream		
Year	A	B	C
1996		$1.50	
1997		1.55	
1998		1.61	
1999		1.68	$2.50
2000		1.76	2.60
2001	$5.00	1.85	2.65
2002	5.60	1.95	2.65
2003	6.40	2.06	2.80
2004	7.20	2.17	2.85
2005	8.00	2.28	2.90

LG 4

P4.41 A company paid dividends of $1.00 per share in 1997, and just announced that it will pay $2.21 in 2004. Estimate the compound annual growth rate of the dividends.

LG 4

P4.42 A company reported net income in 2000 of $350 million. In 2004, the company expects net income to be $441.7 million. Estimate the annual compound growth rate of net income.

 **LG 6**

P4.43 The historical returns for two investments—A and B—are summarized in the table below for the period 2001 to 2005. Use the data to answer the questions that follow.

	Investment	
	A	B
Year	Rate of Return	
2001	19%	8%
2002	1	10
2003	10	12
2004	26	14
2005	4	16
Average	12%	12%

a. On the basis of a review of the return data, which investment appears to be more risky? Why?

b. Calculate the standard deviation and the coefficient of variation for each investment's returns.

c. On the basis of your calculations in part **b**, which investment is more risky? Compare this conclusion to your observation in part **a**.

d. Does the coefficient of variation provide better risk comparison than the standard deviation in the case? Why or why not?

 P4.44 Referring to Problem 4.43, if one investment's required return is 12% and the other is 14%, which one is 14%

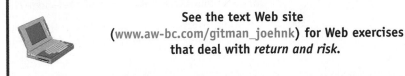

See the text Web site
(www.aw-bc.com/gitman_joehnk) **for Web exercises that deal with** *return and risk*.

Case Problem 4.1   *Solomon's Decision*

LG 2   **LG 3**   **LG 4**

Dave Solomon, a 23-year-old mathematics teacher at Xavier High School, recently received a tax refund of $1,100. Because Dave didn't need this money for his current living expenses, he decided to make a long-term investment. After surveying a number of alternative investments costing no more than $1,100, Dave isolated two that seemed most suitable to his needs.

Each of the investments cost $1,050 and was expected to provide income over a 10-year period. Investment A provided a relatively certain stream of income. Dave was a little less certain of the income provided by investment B. From his search for suitable alternatives, Dave found that the appropriate discount rate for a relatively certain investment was 12%. Because he felt a bit uncomfortable with an investment like B, he estimated that such an investment would have to provide a return at least 4% *higher* than investment A. Although Dave planned to reinvest funds returned from the investments in other vehicles providing similar returns, he wished to keep the extra $50 ($1,100 − $1,050) invested for the full 10 years in a savings account paying 5% interest compounded annually.

As he makes his investment decision, Dave has asked for your help in answering the questions that follow the expected return data for these investments.

Year	Expected Returns A	Expected Returns B	Year	Expected Returns A	Expected Returns B
2006	$150	$100	2011	$ 150	$350
2007	150	150	2012	150	300
2008	150	200	2013	150	250
2009	150	250	2014	150	200
2010	150	300	2015	1,150	150

Questions

a. Assuming that investments A and B are equally risky and using the 12% discount rate, apply the present-value technique to assess the acceptability of each investment and to determine the preferred investment. Explain your findings.

b. Recognizing that investment B is more risky than investment A, reassess the two alternatives, adding the 4% risk premium to the 12% discount rate for investment A and therefore applying a 16% discount rate to investment B. Compare your findings relative to acceptability and preference to those found for question **a.**

c. From your findings in questions **a** and **b**, indicate whether the yield for investment A is above or below 12% and whether that for investment B is above or below 16%. Explain.

d. Use the present-value technique to estimate the yield on each investment. Compare your findings and contrast them with your response to question **c.**

e. From the information given, which, if either, of the two investments would you recommend that Dave make? Explain your answer.

f. Indicate to Dave how much money the extra $50 will have grown to by the end of 2015, assuming he makes no withdrawals from the savings account.

Case Problem 4.2

The Risk-Return Tradeoff: Molly O'Rourke's Stock Purchase Decision

LG 4   LG 5   LG 6

Over the past 10 years, Molly O'Rourke has slowly built a diversified portfolio of common stock. Currently her portfolio includes 20 different common stock issues and has a total market value of $82,500.

Molly is at present considering the addition of 50 shares of one of two common stock issues—X or Y. To assess the return and risk of each of these issues, she has gathered dividend income and share price data for both over each of the last 10 years (1996 through 2005). Molly's investigation of the outlook for these issues suggests that each will, on average, tend to behave in the future just as it has in the past. She therefore believes that the expected return can be estimated by finding the average holding period return (HPR) over the past 10 years for each of the stocks. The historical dividend income and stock price data collected by Molly are given in the accompanying table.

| | Stock X | | | Stock Y | | |
| | Dividend | Share Price | | Dividend | Share Price | |
Year	Income	Beginning	Ending	Income	Beginning	Ending
1996	$1.00	$20.00	$22.00	$1.50	$20.00	$20.00
1997	1.50	22.00	21.00	1.60	20.00	20.00
1998	1.40	21.00	24.00	1.70	20.00	21.00
1999	1.70	24.00	22.00	1.80	21.00	21.00
2000	1.90	22.00	23.00	1.90	21.00	22.00
2001	1.60	23.00	26.00	2.00	22.00	23.00
2002	1.70	26.00	25.00	2.10	23.00	23.00
2003	2.00	25.00	24.00	2.20	23.00	24.00
2004	2.10	24.00	27.00	2.30	24.00	25.00
2005	2.20	27.00	30.00	2.40	25.00	25.00

Questions

a. Determine the holding period return (HPR) for each stock in each of the preceding 10 years. Find the expected return for each stock, using the approach specified by Molly.

b. Use the HPRs and expected return calculated in question **a** to find both the standard deviation and the coefficient of variation of the HPRs for each stock over the 10-year period 1996 to 2005.

c. Use your findings to evaluate and discuss the return and risk associated with stocks X and Y. Which stock seems preferable? Explain.

d. Ignoring her existing portfolio, what recommendations would you give Molly with regard to stocks X and Y?

Excel with Spreadsheets

From her Investment Analysis class, Laura has been given an assignment to evaluate several securities on a risk-return tradeoff basis. The specific securities to be researched are International Business Machines, Helmerich & Payne, Inc., and the S&P 500 Index. The respective ticker symbols for the stocks are IBM and HP. She finds the following (assumed) data on the securities in question. It is as follows:

Year	2000	2001	2002	2003	2004	2005
Price$_{IBM}$	$ 49.38	$ 91.63	$112.25	$112.00	$107.89	$ 92.68
Dividend$_{IBM}$	$ .40	$ .44	$ .48	$ .52	$ .56	$ .64
Price$_{HP}$	$ 25.56	$ 17.56	$ 23.50	$ 47.81	$ 30.40	$ 27.93
Dividend$_{HP}$	$ .28	$ .28	$ .28	$ .30	$ .30	$ .32
Value$_{S\&P}$	980.3	1,279.6	1,394.6	1,366.0	1,130.2	1,121.8

Note: The value of the S&P 500 Index includes dividends.

Questions

Part One

a. Use the given data that Laura has found on the three securities and create a spreadsheet to calculate the holding period return (HPR) for each year and the average return over a 5-year period. Specifically, the HPR will be based upon five unique periods of 1 year (i.e., 2000 to 2001, 2001 to 2002, 2002 to 2003, 2003 to 2004, 2004 to 2005). Use the following formula:

$$HPR = [C + (V_n - V_o)] / V_o$$

Where

C = current income during period
V_n = ending investment value
V_o = beginning investment value

Part Two

Create a spreadsheet similar to the spreadsheet for Table 4.15, which can be viewed at www.aw-bc.com/gitman_joehnk, in order to evaluate the risk-return tradeoff.

b. Calculate the standard deviations of the returns for IBM, HP, and the S&P 500 Index.

c. Calculate the coefficients of variation for IBM, HP, and the S&P 500 Index.

d. What industries are associated with IBM and HP?

e. Based on your answer in **d** and your results for the average return and the standard deviation and coefficient of variation, what conclusions can Laura make about investing in either IBM or HP?

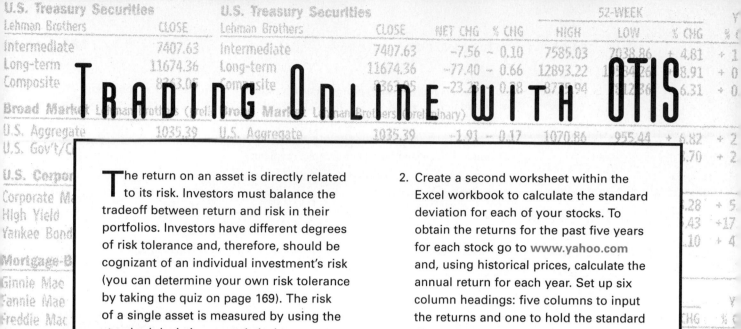

TRADING ONLINE WITH OTIS

The return on an asset is directly related to its risk. Investors must balance the tradeoff between return and risk in their portfolios. Investors have different degrees of risk tolerance and, therefore, should be cognizant of an individual investment's risk (you can determine your own risk tolerance by taking the quiz on page 169). The risk of a single asset is measured by using the standard deviation, a statistical process. These measures can easily be calculated and recorded in OTIS, which uploads a portfolio to an Excel spreadsheet.

Exercises

1. Using the OTIS investment simulation, upload your portfolio into an Excel spreadsheet. Create two additional columns on the worksheet to record the standard deviation and the coefficient of variation.

2. Create a second worksheet within the Excel workbook to calculate the standard deviation for each of your stocks. To obtain the returns for the past five years for each stock go to www.yahoo.com and, using historical prices, calculate the annual return for each year. Set up six column headings: five columns to input the returns and one to hold the standard deviation. Program the formula for the standard deviation into the sixth column. Transfer the standard deviation into the first worksheet by copying the data from the second worksheet.

3. To obtain the values for the coefficient of variation, program the formula in the column under that heading in the first worksheet. Examine the values for the coefficients of variation to compare the risks of your stocks and then restructure the portfolio on OTIS to reflect your risk tolerance.

Buffeted about by highly volatile markets of recent years, many investors watched their portfolio values plunge by 35% to 50% or more as they grappled with tough questions. Do I sell now or wait for a stock to recover? Should I stay with individual stocks or move into mutual finds to get professional management? How should I allocate my assets among fixed-income securities, equities, and cash? Is my portfolio diversified enough? What investment strategy or style should I follow?

Mutual fund managers face the same questions but on an even larger scale. Neil Hennessey, president of the fund family bearing his name, advocates a disciplined approach that removes emotion and leads to solid returns over time, as the results attained by his Hennessey Cornerstone Growth fund demonstrate. In the 12 months ending October 31, 2003, the fund returned 38%, compared to 21% for the S&P 500. Even going back 3 years, a period that included much of the bear market, fund owners earned an 11.6% return, while the S&P 500 lost 8.3%.

Each of Hennessey's four funds has a well-defined investment objective and disciplined strategy. For example, the growth fund buys the 50 stocks with the highest 1-year price appreciation as of the date of purchase. Unlike some other funds, which trade securities throughout the year, Hennessey funds hold their securities for one year. Once a year the fund managers rebalance the portfolio to make sure its holdings are still in line with the fund's objectives.

To reduce risk, Hennessey Cornerstone Growth is widely diversified across industry sectors. For example, a recent review of the fund's portfolio indicated that 92% of the holdings were spread across 10 sectors.

The investment strategies employed by Hennessey and other investment professionals provide good lessons for individual investors as well. He advises people to examine their portfolios regularly and ask, "Where am I and what am I trying to do?" As we'll see in Chapter 5, understanding your investment objectives and developing appropriate asset allocation strategies are the way to build your own portfolio.

Sources: "Growth Manager Likes Gateway, Hasbro," *CBS Marketwatch*, September 26, 2003, downloaded from **cbs.marketwatch.com**; "Hennessey Cornerstone Growth Fund Profile," *CBS Marketwatch*, downloaded from **cbs.marketwatch.com/tools/mutual funds**, accessed November 14, 2003; and Karyn McCormack and Neil Hennessey. "Emotion, Curse of the Investing Class," *Business Week Online*, August 27, 2003, downloaded from **www.businessweek.com**.

CHAPTER 5

MODERN PORTFOLIO CONCEPTS

LEARNING GOALS

After studying this chapter, you should be able to:

LG 1 Understand portfolio management objectives and the procedures used to calculate the return and standard deviation of a portfolio.

LG 2 Discuss the concepts of correlation and diversification, and the effectiveness, methods, and benefits of international diversification.

LG 3 Describe the two components of risk, beta, and the capital asset pricing model (CAPM).

LG 4 Review traditional and modern approaches to portfolio management and reconcile them.

LG 5 Describe the role of investor characteristics and objectives and of portfolio objectives and policies in constructing an investment portfolio.

LG 6 Summarize why and how investors use an asset allocation scheme to construct an investment portfolio.

Principles of Portfolio Planning

growth-oriented portfolio
a portfolio whose primary objective is long-term price appreciation.

income-oriented portfolio
a portfolio that stresses current dividend and interest returns.

efficient portfolio
a portfolio that provides the highest return for a given level of risk or that has the lowest risk for a given level of return.

Investors benefit from holding portfolios of investments rather than single investment vehicles. Without sacrificing returns, investors who hold portfolios can reduce risk, often to a level below that of any of the investments held in isolation. In other words, when it comes to risk, $1 + 1 < 1$.

As defined in Chapter 1, a *portfolio* is a collection of investment vehicles assembled to meet one or more investment goals. Of course, different investors have different objectives for their portfolios. The primary goal of a **growth-oriented portfolio** is long-term price appreciation. An **income-oriented portfolio** stresses current dividend and interest returns.

Portfolio Objectives

Setting portfolio objectives involves definite tradeoffs: tradeoffs between risk and return, between potential price appreciation and current income, and between varying risk levels in the portfolio. These will depend on your tax bracket, current income needs, and ability to bear risk. The key point is that the portfolio objectives must be established *before* beginning to invest.

The ultimate goal of an investor is an **efficient portfolio,** one that provides the highest return for a given level of risk or that has the lowest risk for a given level of return. Thus, given the choice between two equally risky investments offering different returns, the investor would be expected to choose the one with the higher return. Likewise, given two vehicles offering the same returns but differing in risk, the *risk-averse* investor would prefer the one with the lower risk. Efficient portfolios aren't necessarily obvious: Investors usually must search out investment alternatives to get the best combinations of risk and return.

Portfolio Return and Standard Deviation

The return on a portfolio is calculated as a weighted average of returns on the assets (investment vehicles) from which it is formed. The portfolio return, r_p, can be found by using Equation 5.1:

Equation 5.1

$$
\begin{pmatrix} \text{Return} \\ \text{on} \\ \text{portfolio} \end{pmatrix} = \begin{pmatrix} \text{Proportion of} \\ \text{portfolio's total} \\ \text{dollar value} \\ \text{represented by} \\ \text{asset 1} \end{pmatrix} \times \begin{pmatrix} \text{Return} \\ \text{on asset} \\ 1 \end{pmatrix} + \begin{pmatrix} \text{Proportion of} \\ \text{portfolio's total} \\ \text{dollar value} \\ \text{represented by} \\ \text{asset 2} \end{pmatrix} \times \begin{pmatrix} \text{Return} \\ \text{on asset} \\ 2 \end{pmatrix} + \cdots +
$$

$$
\begin{pmatrix} \text{Proportion of} \\ \text{portfolio's total} \\ \text{dollar value} \\ \text{represented by} \\ \text{asset } n \end{pmatrix} \times \begin{pmatrix} \text{Return} \\ \text{on asset} \\ n \end{pmatrix} = \sum_{j=1}^{n} \begin{pmatrix} \text{Proportion of} \\ \text{portfolio's total} \\ \text{dollar value} \\ \text{represented by} \\ \text{asset } j \end{pmatrix} \times \begin{pmatrix} \text{Return} \\ \text{on asset} \\ j \end{pmatrix}
$$

Equation 5.1a

$$
r_p = (w_1 \times r_1) + (w_2 \times r_2) + \cdots + (w_n \times r_n) = \sum_{j=1}^{n}(w_j \times r_j)
$$

Of course, $\sum_{j=1}^{n} w_j = 1$, which means that 100% of the portfolio's assets must be included in this computation.

TABLE 5.1   Expected Return, Average Return, and Standard Deviation of Returns for Portfolio XY

A. Expected Portfolio Returns

| | (1) | (2) | (3) | (4) |
| | Expected Return | | | Expected Portfolio |
Year	Asset X	Asset Y	Portfolio Return Calculation*	Return, r_p
2006	8%	16%	$(.50 \times 8\%) + (.50 \times 16\%) =$	12%
2007	10	14	$(.50 \times 10) + (.50 \times 14) =$	12
2008	12	12	$(.50 \times 12) + (.50 \times 12) =$	12
2009	14	10	$(.50 \times 14) + (.50 \times 10) =$	12
2010	16	8	$(.50 \times 16) + (.50 \times 8) =$	12

B. Average Expected Portfolio Return, 2006–2010

$$\bar{r}_p = \frac{12\% + 12\% + 12\% + 12\% + 12\%}{5} = \frac{60\%}{5} = \underline{12\%}$$

C. Standard Deviation of Expected Portfolio Returns**

$$s_p = \sqrt{\frac{(12\% - 12\%)^2 + (12\% - 12\%)^2 + (12\% - 12\%)^2 + (12\% - 12\%)^2 + (12\% - 12\%)^2}{5 - 1}}$$

$$= \sqrt{\frac{0\% + 0\% + 0\% + 0\% + 0\%}{4}} = \sqrt{\frac{0\%}{4}} = \underline{\underline{0\%}}$$

*Using Equation 5.1.
**Using Equation 4.10 presented in Chapter 4.

The *standard deviation of a portfolio's returns* is found by applying Equation 4.10, the formula we used to find the standard deviation of a single asset. Assume that we wish to determine the return and standard deviation of returns for Portfolio XY, created by combining equal portions (50%) of assets X and Y. The expected returns of assets X and Y for each of the next 5 years (2006–2010) are given in columns 1 and 2, in part A of Table 5.1. In columns 3 and 4, the weights of 50% for both assets X and Y, along with their respective returns from columns 1 and 2, are substituted into Equation 5.1 to get an expected portfolio return of 12% for each year, 2006 to 2010. As shown in part B of Table 5.1, the average expected portfolio return, $\bar{r}_p$, over the 5-year period is also 12%. Substituting into Equation 4.10, we calculate Portfolio XY's standard deviation, s_p, of 0% in part C of Table 5.1. This value should not be surprising. Because the expected return each year is the same (12%), no variability is exhibited in the expected returns from year to year shown in column 4 of part A of the table.

Correlation and Diversification

As noted in Chapter 2, *diversification* involves the inclusion of a number of different investment vehicles in a portfolio. It is an important aspect of creating an efficient portfolio. Underlying the intuitive appeal of diversification is the statistical concept of *correlation*. For effective portfolio planning, you need to understand the concepts of correlation and diversification and their relationship to a portfolio's total risk and return.

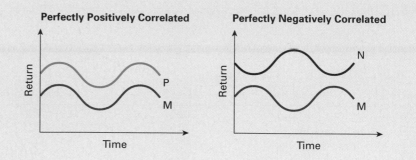

The Correlation Between Series M, N, and P

The perfectly positively correlated series M and P in the graph on the left move exactly together. The perfectly negatively correlated series M and N in the graph on the right move in exactly opposite directions.

correlation
a statistical measure of the relationship, if any, between series of numbers representing data of any kind.

positively correlated
describes two series that move in the same direction.

negatively correlated
describes two series that move in opposite directions.

correlation coefficient
a measure of the degree of correlation between two series.

perfectly positively correlated
describes two positively correlated series that have a correlation coefficient of +1.

perfectly negatively correlated
describes two negatively correlated series that have a correlation coefficient of −1.

uncorrelated
describes two series that lack any relationship or interaction and therefore have a correlation coefficient close to zero.

Correlation **Correlation** is a statistical measure of the relationship, if any, between series of numbers representing data of any kind. If two series move in the same direction, they are **positively correlated.** If the series move in opposite directions, they are **negatively correlated.**

The degree of correlation—whether positive or negative—is measured by the **correlation coefficient.** The coefficient ranges from +1 for **perfectly positively correlated** series to −1 for **perfectly negatively correlated** series. These two extremes are depicted in Figure 5.1 for series M, N, and P. The perfectly positively correlated series (M and P) move exactly together. The perfectly negatively correlated series (M and N) move in exactly opposite directions.

Diversification To reduce overall risk in a portfolio, it is best to combine assets that have a negative (or a low-positive) correlation. Combining negatively correlated assets can reduce the overall variability of returns, s, or risk. Figure 5.2 shows negatively correlated assets F and G, both having the same average expected return, $\bar{r}$. The portfolio that contains those negatively correlated assets also has the same return, $\bar{r}$, but has less risk (variability) than either of the individual assets. Even if assets are not negatively correlated, the lower the positive correlation between them, the lower the resulting risk.

Some assets are **uncorrelated:** They are completely unrelated, with no interaction between their returns. Combining uncorrelated assets can reduce risk—not as effectively as combining negatively correlated assets, but more effectively than combining positively correlated assets. The correlation coefficient for uncorrelated assets is close to zero and acts as the midpoint between perfect positive and perfect negative correlation.

Correlation is important to reducing risk, but it can do only so much. A portfolio of two assets that have perfectly positively correlated returns *cannot* reduce the portfolio's overall risk below the risk of the least risky asset. However, a portfolio combining two assets with less than perfectly positive correlation *can* reduce total risk to a level below that of either of the components, which in certain situations may be zero.

For example, assume you own the stock of a machine tool manufacturer that is very *cyclical*. This company has high earnings when the economy is expanding and low earnings during a recession. If you bought stock in another machine tool company, which would have earnings positively correlated with those of the stock you already own, the combined earnings would continue to be cyclical. The risk would remain the same.

As an alternative, however, you could buy stock in a sewing machine manufacturer, which is *countercyclical*. It typically has low earnings during eco-

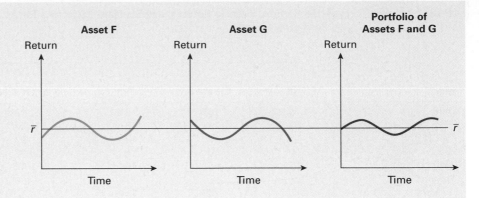

FIGURE 5.2

Combining Negatively Correlated Assets to Diversify Risk

The risk or variability of returns, resulting from combining negatively correlated assets F and G, both having the same expected return, $\bar{r}$, results in a portfolio (shown in the rightmost graph) with the same level of expected return but less risk.

nomic expansion and high earnings during recession. Combining the machine tool stock and the sewing machine stock should reduce risk: The low machine tool earnings during a recession would be balanced out by high sewing machine earnings, and vice versa.

A numeric example will provide an even better understanding. Table 5.2 (on page 190) presents the expected returns from three different assets—X, Y, and Z—over the next 5 years (2006–2010), along with their average returns and standard deviations. Each of the assets has an expected value of return of 12% and a standard deviation of 3.16%. The assets therefore have equal return and equal risk, although their return patterns are not identical. The returns of assets X and Y are perfectly negatively correlated, because they move in exactly opposite directions over time. The returns of assets X and Z are perfectly positively correlated: They move in precisely the same direction. (The returns for X and Z are identical, although it is not necessary for return streams to be identical for them to be perfectly positively correlated.)

Portfolio XY (shown in Table 5.2) combines equal portions of assets X and Y—the perfectly negatively correlated assets. Calculation of portfolio XY's annual expected returns, average expected return, and the standard deviation of expected portfolio returns was demonstrated in Table 5.1. The risk of the portfolio created by this combination, as reflected in the standard deviation, is reduced to 0%, while its average return remains at 12%. Because both assets have the same average return, are combined in the optimal proportions (a 50–50 mix in this case), and are perfectly negatively correlated, the combination results in the complete elimination of risk. Whenever assets are perfectly negatively correlated, an optimal combination (similar to this 50–50 mix of assets X and Y) exists for which the resulting standard deviation will equal 0.

Portfolio XZ (shown in Table 5.2) is created by combining equal portions of assets X and Z—the perfectly positively correlated assets. The risk of this portfolio, reflected by its standard deviation, which remains at 3.16%, is unaffected by this combination. Its average return remains at 12%. Whenever perfectly positively correlated assets such as X and Z are combined, the standard deviation of the resulting portfolio cannot be reduced below that of the least risky asset; the maximum portfolio standard deviation will be that of the riskiest asset. Because assets X and Z have the same standard deviation (3.16%), the minimum and maximum standard deviations are both

EXCEL with
SPREADSHEETS

| **TABLE 5.2** | Expected Returns, Average Returns, and Standard Deviations for Assets X, Y, and Z and Portfolios XY and XZ |

| | Assets | | | Portfolios | |
| | | | | XY* | XZ** |
Year	X	Y	Z	(50%X + 50%Y)	(50%X + 50%Z)
2006	8%	16%	8%	12%	8%
2007	10	14	10	12	10
2008	12	12	12	12	12
2009	14	10	14	12	14
2010	16	8	16	12	16
Statistics:					
Average return†	12%	12%	12%	12%	12%
Standard deviation‡	3.16%	3.16%	3.16%	0%	3.16%

*Portfolio XY illustrates *perfect negative correlation,* because these two return streams behave in completely opposite fashion over the 5-year period. The return values shown here were calculated in part A of Table 5.1.

**Portfolio XZ illustrates *perfect positive correlation,* because these two return streams behave identically over the 5-year period. These return values were calculated using the same method demonstrated for Portfolio XY in part A of Table 5.1.

†The average return for each asset is calculated as the arithmetic average found by dividing the sum of the returns for the years 2006–2010 by 5, the number of years considered.

‡Equation 4.10 was used to calculate the standard deviation. Calculation of the average return and standard deviation for portfolio XY is demonstrated in parts B and C, respectively, of Table 5.1. The portfolio standard deviation can be directly calculated from the standard deviation of the component assets using the following formula:

$$s_p = \sqrt{w_1^2 s_1^2 + w_2^2 s_2^2 + 2w_1 w_2 p_{1,2} s_1 s_2}$$

where w_1 and w_2 are the proportions of the component assets 1 and 2; s_1 and s_2 are the standard deviations of the component assets 1 and 2; and $p_{1,2}$ is the correlation coefficient between the returns of component assets 1 and 2.

3.16%, which is the only value that could be taken on by a combination of these assets.

Impact on Risk and Return In general, the lower (less positive and more negative) the correlation between asset returns, the greater the potential diversification of risk. For each pair of assets, there is a combination that will result in the lowest risk (standard deviation) possible. *The amount of potential risk reduction for this combination depends on the degree of correlation of the two assets.* Many potential combinations could be made, given the expected return of the two assets, the standard deviation for each, and the correlation coefficient. However, *only one combination* of the infinite number of possibilities will minimize risk.

Three possible correlations—perfect positive, uncorrelated, and perfect negative—illustrate the effect of correlation on the diversification of risk and return. Table 5.3 summarizes the impact of correlation on the range of return and risk. The table shows that as you move from perfect positive correlation to perfect negative correlation, you reduce risk. Note that in no case will a portfolio of assets have risk greater than that of the riskiest asset included in the portfolio.

To demonstrate, assume that a firm has carefully calculated the average return, $\bar{r}$, and risk, s, for each of two assets, A and B, as summarized below.

Asset	Average Return, $\bar{r}$	Risk (Standard Deviation), s
A	6%	3%
B	8%	8%

TABLE 5.3   Correlation, Return, and Risk for Various Two-Asset Portfolio Combinations

Correlation Coefficient	Range of Return	Range of Risk
+1 (perfect positive)	Between returns of two assets held in isolation	Between risk of two assets held in isolation
0 (uncorrelated)	Between returns of two assets held in isolation	Between risk of most risky asset and less than risk of least risky asset, but greater than 0
−1 (perfect negative)	Between returns of two assets held in isolation	Between risk of most risky asset and 0

From these data, we can see that asset A is clearly a lower-risk, lower-return asset than asset B.

To evaluate possible combinations, let's consider three possible correlations: perfect positive, uncorrelated, and perfect negative. The results are shown in Figure 5.3. The ranges of return and risk exhibited are consistent with those in Table 5.3. In all cases, the return will range between the 6% return of A and the 8% return of B. The risk, on the other hand, has a wider variability. That variability depends on the degree of correlation: In the case of perfect positive correlation, the risk ranges between the individual risks of A and B (from 3% to 8%). In the uncorrelated case, the risk ranges from below 3% (the risk of A) but greater than 0%, to 8% (the risk of B). In the case of perfect negative correlation, the risk ranges between 0% and 8%.

Note that *only in the case of perfect negative correlation can the risk be reduced to 0%.* As the correlation becomes less positive and more negative (moving from the top of Figure 5.3 down), the ability to reduce risk improves.

FIGURE 5.3

Range of Portfolio Return and Risk for Combinations of Assets A and B for Various Correlation Coefficients

The range of a portfolio's return (r_p) is between that of the lowest and highest component asset returns and is unaffected by the degree of asset correlation. Portfolio risk (s_p), on the other hand, can be reduced below the risk of the least risky asset as the asset correlation moves from perfectly positive to uncorrelated to perfectly negative, where it can be reduced to zero by combining assets in the proper proportion.

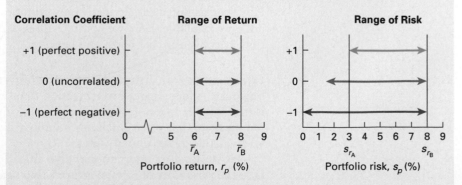

FIGURE 5.4

Risk and Return for All Combinations of Assets A and B for Various Correlation Coefficients

For each correlation coefficient there exist an infinite number of combinations of two assets A and B that result in many possible risk-return combinations, the ranges of which are consistent with those shown in Figure 5.3. The less positive and more negative the correlation, the greater the potential risk reduction.

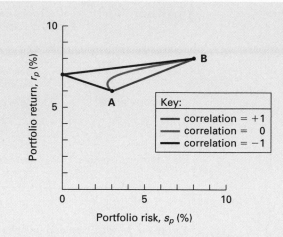

If we had numerous risk-return observations for each of the three correlations—perfect positive, uncorrelated, and perfect negative—all possible combinations of assets A and B could be plotted for each correlation on a set of risk (s_p)-return (r_p) axes as shown in Figure 5.4. For each correlation coefficient, there exist an infinite number of combinations of the two assets A and B that result in numerous risk-return combinations, the range of which is consistent with that shown in Figure 5.3. The less positive and more negative the correlation, the greater the potential risk reduction. Again, it should be clear that for any two-asset portfolio, the ability to reduce risk depends on both the degree of correlation and the proportions of each asset in the portfolio.

Although determining the risk-minimizing combination is beyond the scope of this discussion, you should know that it is an important issue in developing portfolios of assets. The *Investing in Action* box on page 193 describes the success of student-managed portfolios. Later in this chapter we use modern portfolio theory to explain the risk-return combinations available from all possible portfolios.

International Diversification

Diversification is clearly a primary consideration when constructing an investment portfolio. Thus far, our focus and examples have been basically domestic. However, as noted earlier, many opportunities for international diversification are now available. Here we consider three aspects of international diversification: effectiveness, methods, and benefits.

Effectiveness of International Diversification Investing internationally obviously offers greater diversification than investing only domestically. That is true for U.S. investors. It is even truer for investors from countries with capital markets that offer much more limited diversification opportunities than are available in the United States.

However, does international diversification actually reduce risk, particularly the variability of rates of return? Two studies overwhelmingly support the

INVESTING IN ACTION

STUDENT-MANAGED PORTFOLIOS EARN TOP GRADES

Imagine having $100,000 or more to invest while you are still in college—real money, not fantasy portfolios that are part of an investment game. According to the Association of Student-Managed Investment Programs at Florida's Stetson University, more than 110 colleges and universities allocate funds, often from endowment portfolios or alumni donations, to student portfolio managers. Some schools, including the University of Dayton, allocate at least $1 million for this purpose. Dayton's student investors manage more than $3 million as part of a formal class, while the Syracuse University Investment Club began in 1984 as a not-for-profit corporation that donates its proceeds to charitable causes. The club's initial $1,000 donation has grown to $95,000 today.

Undergraduate students at the University of Dayton's Center for Portfolio Management, which was founded in 1999, manage a portfolio of more than $3 million, one of the country's largest student-managed portfolios. To participate in the Center's programs, students are required to take classes in corporate finance, investments, and portfolio management and to participate in investment simulations. The Center offers a professional investment environment, complete with news feeds from cable financial and news channels, real-time stock quotes, opportunities to talk to securities analysts, and institutional-caliber portfolio management tools. As a result, explains David Sauer, associate professor of finance and founder of the Center, "[students get] the equivalent of two years or more of real work experience."

Dayton's students discuss potential investment decisions, with a two-thirds vote being required to take action. Portfolio assets are evenly divided between equities and fixed-income securities. The focus is typically mid-cap and large-cap companies, with each student following a particular industry.

At Syracuse, Dayton, and other student-managed investment groups, the chance to gain hands-on money management experience is an unparalleled opportunity. Students learn first-hand about the realities of investment management, including the considerable time and research needed to keep up with market trends, investigate new investment opportunities, and track portfolio holdings. "The added pressure makes people a lot more in tune with what's going on. You can't take a day off," Dayton's Rick Davis says.

Each school sets its own investment guidelines. For example, the students in Alaska Pacific University's (APU) global finance class manage $185,000 with the help of a professor who is also a professional portfolio manager. APU students must limit higher-risk, small-cap stocks to 10% of the portfolio, hold 10 of the top 15 largest-cap stocks, and adhere to specific growth and value criteria.

How have student managers done during the recent bear market? Dayton's teams have significantly outperformed the S&P 500, and other schools report similar results. "When you thrust responsibility on students, they rise to the occasion," says Doug North, APU president.

CRITICAL THINKING QUESTION After reading the rest of this chapter, develop a brief proposal for your school's new student-managed investment portfolio. Suggest an asset allocation strategy and two other parameters, and explain your reasoning.

Sources: Jim Bohman, "Executive to Donate $1M to UD," *Dayton Daily News*, May 13, 2003, p. D.1; Dee Klees, "Youthful Stocks and Bonds; Young Investors Study Market, Create Network," *The Post-Standard* (Syracuse), September 29, 2003, p. 5; Sarana Schell, "Analyze This: APU Students Master Global Finance by Investing Real Money," *Anchorage Daily News*, November 3, 2003, p. F1; and "Students Play the Market with Colleges' Money," *Houston Chronicle*, September 26, 2002, p. 2.

argument that well-structured international diversification does indeed reduce the risk of a portfolio and increase the return on portfolios of comparable risk. One study looked at diversification across 12 European countries in 7 different industries between 1978 and 1992. It demonstrated that an investor could actually reduce the risk of a portfolio much more by diversifying internationally *in the same industry* than by diversifying across industries within one country. If the investor diversified both across countries and across industries, the opportunities for risk reduction would be even greater.

Another study examined the risk-return performance between January 1984 and November 1994 of diversified stock portfolios: the S&P 500 in the United States and Morgan Stanley's Europe/Australia/Far East (EAFE) Index. It found that a 100% EAFE portfolio offered a much greater return than a 100% S&P 500 portfolio did—but at much greater risk. However, a portfolio composed of various combinations of the two indexes would have been better: It would have realized both lower risk and a higher return than did the 100% S&P 500 portfolio, and less risk and a moderately lower return than did the 100% EAFE portfolio. For the U.S. investor, a portfolio consisting of 70% S&P 500 coupled with 30% EAFE would have reduced risk by about 5% and increased return by about 7% (from around 14% to more than 15%). Or, for the same degree of risk, an investor could have increased return by about 18% (from around 14% to more than 16.5%).

Methods of International Diversification In later chapters we will examine a wide range of alternatives for international portfolio diversification. We will see that investments in bonds and other debt instruments can be made abroad in U.S. dollars or in foreign currencies—either directly or via foreign mutual funds. Foreign currency investment, however, brings currency exchange risk. This risk can be hedged using various contracts, most commonly currency forwards, futures, and options.

Investing abroad, even if there is little or no currency exchange risk, is generally less convenient, more expensive, and riskier than investing domestically. When making direct investments abroad, you must know what you're doing: You should have a clear idea of the benefits being sought and enough time to monitor foreign markets.

International diversification can also be achieved by U.S. domestic investments. Several hundred foreign companies list their stocks on U.S. exchanges or over the counter; most of them are Canadian companies. Also, many foreign issuers, both corporate and government, sell their bonds (called *Yankee bonds*) in the United States. The stocks of about 2,300 foreign companies, from more than 50 countries, trade in the United States in the form of American Depositary Receipts (ADRs). Finally, international mutual funds (such as the Fidelity Japan Fund and the AIM Global Trends Fund) provide investors with a broad range of foreign investment opportunities. These domestic alternatives offer the advantages of convenience and low cost, often with less risk than investments made directly abroad.

It is important to realize that international diversification typically cannot be achieved by investing in U.S. multinationals. In spite of the fact that U.S.-based firms with major foreign operations may generate sizable revenues and profits abroad, most of their costs and expenses—particularly labor costs—are incurred in the United States. The net result is that the firm's behavior tends to be more U.S.-driven than foreign-driven. The multinational firm's results tend to be positively correlated with those in the domestic market, thereby resulting in low diversification. The strategy of investing in domestic companies that have major foreign operations therefore is generally not as effective as investing directly in foreign companies in the given country.

Benefits of International Diversification Can greater returns be found overseas than in the United States? Yes! Can a portfolio's risk be reduced by including foreign investments? Yes! Is international diversification desirable for you? We don't know! A successful global investment strategy depends on many things, just as a purely domestic strategy does. Included are factors such as your resources, goals, sophistication, and psychology. What percentage of your portfolio you allocate to foreign investments depends on your overall investment goals and risk preferences. Commonly cited allocations to foreign investments are about 20% to 30%, with two-thirds of this allocation in established foreign markets and the other one-third in emerging markets.

In general, you should avoid investing directly in foreign-currency-denominated instruments. Unless the magnitude of each foreign investment is in hundreds of thousands of dollars, the transactions costs will tend to be high, not just when you are buying and selling but especially when dividends or interest are paid. Therefore, for most investors looking for international diversification, the optimal vehicles are available in the United States. International mutual funds offer diversified foreign investments, coupled with the professional investment expertise of fund managers. ADRs can be used by those who want to make foreign investments in individual stocks. With either mutual funds or ADRs, you can obtain international diversification along with low cost, convenience, transactions in U.S. dollars, protection under U.S. security laws, and (usually) attractive markets (although some ADRs have thin markets).

We shouldn't leave this topic without saying that some of the benefits of international diversification are diminishing over time. Technological advances in communication have greatly improved the quality of information on foreign companies. In addition, new markets and expanded trading hours have improved access to foreign investments. Participation by a growing number of better-informed investors in the foreign markets continues to reduce the opportunities to earn "excess" returns on the additional risk embodied in foreign investments, thereby leveling the playing field for global investors. Although the opportunities to earn excess returns on foreign investments are shrinking, the relatively low correlation of returns in Asian and emerging markets with U.S. returns continues to make international investments appealing as a way to diversify your portfolio. Foreign investments continue to provide greater risk reduction than domestic investments. Clearly, today an important motive for international investment is portfolio diversification rather than realizing sizable excess returns.

IN REVIEW

CONCEPTS

5.1 What is an *efficient portfolio*, and what role should such a portfolio play in investing?

5.2 How can the return and standard deviation of a portfolio be determined? Compare the portfolio standard deviation calculation to that for a single asset.

5.3 What is *correlation*, and why is it important with respect to asset returns? Describe the characteristics of returns that are (a) positively correlated, (b) negatively correlated, and (c) uncorrelated. Differentiate between *perfect positive correlation* and *perfect negative correlation*.

5.4 What is *diversification?* How does the diversification of risk affect the risk of the portfolio compared to the risk of the individual assets it contains?

5.5 Discuss how the correlation between asset returns affects the risk and return behavior of the resulting portfolio. Describe the potential range of risk and return when the correlation between two assets is (a) perfectly positive, (b) uncorrelated, and (c) perfectly negative.

5.6 What benefit, if any, does international diversification offer the individual investor? Compare and contrast the methods of achieving international diversification by investing abroad versus investing domestically.

The Capital Asset Pricing Model (CAPM)

LG 3

From an investor's perspective, the most important aspect of risk is the *overall risk* of the firm. This overall risk significantly affects the returns earned and the value of the firm in the financial marketplace. As we'll learn in Chapter 8, the firm's value is directly determined by its risk and the associated return. The basic theory that links return and risk for all assets is the *capital asset pricing model (CAPM)*.

Components of Risk

diversifiable (unsystematic) risk
the portion of an investment's risk that results from uncontrollable or random events that are firm-specific; can be eliminated through diversification.

The risk of an investment consists of two components: diversifiable and nondiversifiable risk. **Diversifiable risk,** sometimes called **unsystematic risk,** results from uncontrollable or random events that are firm-specific, such as labor strikes, lawsuits, and regulatory actions. It is the portion of an investment's risk that can be eliminated through diversification. **Nondiversifiable risk,** also called **systematic risk,** is the inescapable portion of an investment's risk. It is attributed to more general forces such as war, inflation, and political events that affect all investments and therefore are not unique to a given vehicle. The sum of nondiversifiable risk and diversifiable risk is called **total risk.**

Equation 5.2

Total risk = Nondiversifiable risk + Diversifiable risk

nondiversifiable (systematic) risk
the inescapable portion of an investment's risk attributable to forces that affect all investments and therefore are not unique to a given vehicle.

Any careful investor can reduce or virtually eliminate diversifiable risk by holding a diversified portfolio of securities. Studies have shown that investors can eliminate most diversifiable risk by carefully selecting a portfolio of 8 to 15 securities. Therefore, *the only relevant risk is nondiversifiable risk,* which is inescapable. Each security has its own unique level of nondiversifiable risk, which we can measure, as we'll show in the following section.

total risk
the sum of an investment's nondiversifiable risk and diversifiable risk.

Beta: A Popular Measure of Risk

During the past 40 years much theory has been developed on the measurement of risk and its use in assessing returns. The two key components of this theory are *beta,* which is a measure of risk, and the *capital asset pricing model (CAPM),* which uses beta to estimate return.

beta
a measure of *nondiversifiable, or market, risk* that indicates how the price of a security responds to market forces.

First we will look at **beta,** a number that measures *nondiversifiable, or market, risk.* Beta indicates how the price of a security responds to market forces. The more responsive the price of a security is to changes in the market, the higher that security's beta. Beta is found by relating the historical returns

market return
the average return on all (or a
large sample of) stocks, such as
those in the *Standard & Poor's
500-Stock Composite Index.*

for a security to the market return. **Market return** is the average return for all
(or a large sample of) stocks. The average return on all stocks in the *Standard
& Poor's 500-Stock Composite Index* or some other broad stock index is commonly used to measure market return. You don't have to calculate betas yourself; you can easily obtain them for actively traded securities from a variety of
published and online sources. But you should understand how betas are
derived, how to interpret them, and how to apply them to portfolios.

Deriving Beta The relationship between a security's return and the market
return, and its use in deriving beta, can be demonstrated graphically. Figure 5.5
plots the relationship between the returns of two securities, C and D, and the
market return. Note that the horizontal (*x*) axis measures the historical market
returns, and the vertical (*y*) axis measures the individual security's historical
returns.

The first step in deriving beta is plotting the coordinates for the market
return and the security return at various points in time. Such annual market-
return and security-return coordinates are shown *for security D only* in Figure 5.5 for the years 1998 through 2005 (the years are noted in parentheses).
For example, in 2005 security D's return was 20% when the market return
was 10%.

By use of statistical techniques, the "characteristic line" that best explains
the relationship between security-return and market-return coordinates is fit

FIGURE 5.5

**Graphical Derivation of Beta
for Securities C and D***

Betas can be derived graphically
by plotting the coordinates for
the market return and security
return at various points in time
and using statistical techniques
to fit the "characteristic line"
to the data points. The slope
of the characteristic line is beta.
For securities C and D, beta is
found to be 0.80 and 1.30,
respectively.

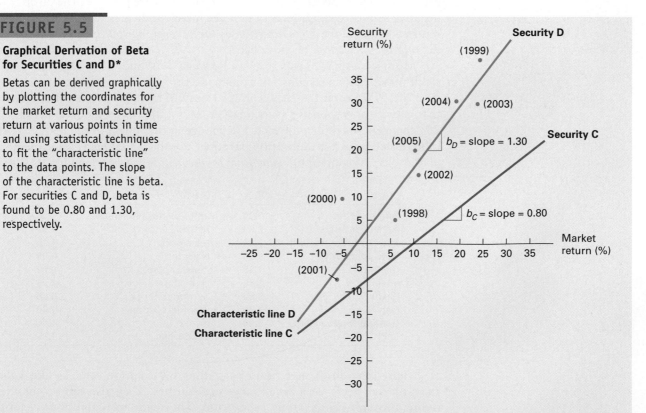

* All data points shown are associated with security D. No data points are shown for
security C.

TABLE 5.4	Selected Betas and Associated Interpretations	
Beta	Comment	Interpretation
2.00 ⎫		Twice as responsive as the market
1.00 ⎬ Move in same direction as the market		Same response as the market
0.50 ⎭		Only half as responsive as the market
0		Unaffected by market movement
−0.50 ⎫		Only half as responsive as the market
−1.00 ⎬ Move in opposite direction to the market		Same response as the market
−2.00 ⎭		Twice as responsive as the market

to the data points. *The slope of this line is beta.* The beta for security C is about 0.80; for security D it is about 1.30. Security D's higher beta (steeper characteristic line slope) indicates that its return is more responsive to changing market returns. *Therefore security D is more risky than security C.*

Interpreting Beta The beta for the overall market is considered to be 1.00. All other betas are viewed in relation to this value. Table 5.4 shows some selected beta values and their associated interpretations. As you can see, betas can be positive or negative, though nearly all betas are positive. The positive or negative sign preceding the beta number merely indicates whether the stock's return changes in the *same direction as the general market* (positive beta) or in the *opposite direction (*negative beta).

Most stocks have betas that fall between 0.50 and 1.75. The return of a stock that is half as responsive as the market ($b = 0.50$) is expected to change by ½ of 1% for each 1% change in the return of the market portfolio. A stock that is twice as responsive as the market ($b = 2.0$) is expected to experience a 2% change in its return for each 1% change in the return of the market portfolio. Listed here, for illustration purposes, are the actual betas for some popular stocks, as reported by *Value Line Investment Survey* on January 16, 2004:

Stock	Beta	Stock	Beta
Amazon.com	1.60	Int'l Business Machines	1.10
Anheuser-Busch	0.60	Merrill Lynch & Co.	1.60
Bank of America Corp.	1.25	Microsoft	1.15
Dow Jones & Co.	1.00	Nike, Inc.	0.90
Disney	1.25	PepsiCo, Inc.	0.65
eBay	1.55	Qualcomm	1.20
ExxonMobil Corp.	0.80	Sempra Energy	0.85
Gap (The), Inc.	1.35	Wal-Mart Stores	1.00
General Motors Corp.	1.20	Xerox	1.45
Intel	1.35	Yahoo! Inc.	1.85

Many large brokerage firms, as well as subscription services like *Value Line,* publish betas for a broad range of securities. They also can be obtained online through sites such as yahoo.com. The ready availability of security betas has enhanced their use in assessing investment risks. The importance of beta in planning and building portfolios of securities will be discussed later in this chapter.

Applying Beta Individual investors will find beta useful. It can help in assessing market risk and in understanding the impact the market can have on the return expected from a share of stock. In short, beta reveals how a security responds to market forces. For example, if the market is expected to experience a 10% *increase* in its rate of return over the next period, we would expect a stock with a beta of 1.50 to experience an *increase* in return of about 15% ($1.50 \times 10\%$). Because its beta is greater than 1.00, this stock is more volatile than the market as a whole.

For stocks with positive betas, increases in market returns result in increases in security returns. Unfortunately, decreases in market returns are translated into decreasing security returns. In the preceding example, if the market is expected to experience a 10% *decrease* in its rate of return, then a stock with a beta of 1.50 should experience a 15% *decrease* in its return. Because the stock has a beta greater than 1.00, it is more responsive than the market, either up or down.

Stocks that have betas less than 1.00 are, of course, less responsive to changing returns in the market. They are therefore considered less risky. For example, a stock with a beta of 0.50 will increase or decrease its return by about half that of the market as a whole. Thus, if the market return went down by 8%, such a stock's return would probably experience only about a 4% ($0.50 \times 8\%$) decline.

Here are some important points to remember about beta:

- Beta measures the nondiversifiable (or market) risk of a security.

- The beta for the market is 1.00.

- Stocks may have positive or negative betas. Nearly all are positive.

- Stocks with betas greater than 1.00 are more responsive to changes in the market return and therefore are more risky than the market. Stocks with betas less than 1.00 are less risky than the market.

- Because of its greater risk, the higher a stock's beta, the greater its level of expected return.

The CAPM: Using Beta to Estimate Return

About 40 years ago, finance professors William F. Sharpe and John Lintner developed a model that uses beta to formally link the notions of risk and return. Called the **capital asset pricing model (CAPM)**, it explains the behavior of security prices. It also provides a mechanism whereby investors can assess the impact of a proposed security investment on their portfolio's risk and return.

The CAPM can be viewed as an equation, in terms of historical risk premiums, and as a graph.

capital asset pricing model (CAPM)
model that formally links the notions of risk and return; it uses beta, the risk-free rate, and the market return to help investors define the required return on an investment.

The Equation With beta, b, as the measure of nondiversifiable risk, the capital asset pricing model defines the required return on an investment as follows.

Equation 5.3

$$\text{Required return on investment } j = \text{Risk-free rate} + \left[\text{Beta for investment } j \times \left(\text{Market return} - \text{Risk-free rate} \right) \right]$$

Equation 5.3a

$$r_j = R_F + [b_j \times (r_m - R_F)]$$

where

r_j = the required return on investment j, given its risk as measured by beta

R_F = the risk-free rate of return; the return that can be earned on a risk-free investment

b_j = beta coefficient or index of nondiversifiable risk for investment j

r_m = the market return; the average return on all securities (typically measured by the average return on all securities in the Standard & Poor's 500-Stock Composite Index or some other broad stock market index)

The CAPM can be divided into two parts: (1) the risk-free rate of return, R_F, and (2) the *risk premium*, $b_j \times (r_m - R_F)$, which is the amount of return investors demand beyond the risk-free rate to compensate for the investment's nondiversifiable risk as measured by beta. The equation shows that *as beta increases, the risk premium increases thereby causing the required return for the given investment to increase.*

Application of the CAPM can be demonstrated with the following example. Assume you are considering security Z with a beta (b_Z) of 1.25. The risk-free rate (R_F) is 6% and the market return (r_m) is 10%. Substituting these data into the CAPM equation, Equation 5.3a, we get:

$$r_z = 6\% + [1.25 \times (10\% - 6\%)] = 6\% + [1.25 \times 4\%]$$

$$= 6\% + 5\% = \underline{11\%}$$

You should therefore expect—indeed, require—an 11% return on this investment as compensation for the risk you have to assume, given the security's beta of 1.25.

If the beta were lower, say 1.00, the required return would be lower:

$$r_z = 6\% + [1.00 \times (10\% - 6\%)] = 6\% + 4\% = \underline{10\%}$$

If the beta were higher, say 1.50, the required return would be higher:

$$r_z = 6\% + [1.50 \times (10\% - 6\%)] = 6\% + 6\% = \underline{12\%}$$

Clearly, the CAPM reflects the positive mathematical relationship between risk and return, because the higher the risk (beta), the higher the risk premium, and therefore the higher the required return.

Historical Risk Premiums Using the historical return data for selected security investments for the 1926–2002 period shown in Chapter 4, Table 4.4 on page 136, we can calculate the risk premiums for each investment category. The calculation (consistent with Equation 5.3) involves merely subtracting the historical U.S. Treasury bill's average return (the assumed risk-free rate of return, R_F) from the historical average return for a given investment:

Investment	Risk Premium*
Large-company stocks	12.2% − 3.8% = 8.4%
Small-company stocks	16.9 − 3.8 = 13.1
Long-term corporate bonds	6.2 − 3.8 = 2.4
Long-term government bonds	5.8 − 3.8 = 2.0
U.S. Treasury bills	3.8 − 3.8 = 0.0

*Return values obtained from Chapter 4, Table 4.4 on page 136.

Reviewing the risk premiums calculated above, we can see that the risk premium is highest for small-company stocks, followed by large-company stocks, long-term corporate bonds, and long-term government bonds. This outcome makes sense intuitively because small-company stocks are riskier than large-company stocks, which are riskier than long-term corporate bonds (equity is riskier than debt investment). Long-term corporate bonds are riskier than long-term government bonds (because the government is less likely to renege on debt). And of course, U.S. Treasury bills, because of their lack of default risk and their very short maturity, are virtually risk free, as indicated by their lack of any risk premium.

The Graph: The Security Market Line (SML) When the capital asset pricing model is depicted graphically, it is called the **security market line (SML)**. Plotting the CAPM, we would find that the SML is, in fact, a straight line. For each level of nondiversifiable risk (beta), the SML reflects the required return the investor should earn in the marketplace.

The CAPM at a given point in time can be plotted by simply calculating the required return for a variety of betas. For example, as we saw earlier, using a 6% risk-free rate and a 10% market return, the required return is 11% when the beta is 1.25. Increase the beta to 2.00, and the required return equals 14% (6% + [2.00 × (10% − 6%)]). Similarly, we can find the required return for a number of betas and end up with the following combinations of risk (beta) and required return.

Risk (beta)	Required Return
0.0	6%
0.5	8
1.0	10
1.5	12
2.0	14
2.5	16

security market line (SML)
the graphical depiction of the capital asset pricing model; reflects the investor's required return for each level of nondiversifiable risk, measured by beta.

H O T

You can find the betas for companies at the Yahoo finance Web site. Enter a stock symbol, then choose [Key Statistics].

finance.yahoo.com

Plotting these values on a graph (with beta on the horizontal axis and required returns on the vertical axis) would yield a straight line like the one in Figure 5.6 (on page 202). The shaded area, the amount by which the required return exceeds the risk-free rate, represents the risk premiums. It is clear from the SML that as risk (beta) increases, so do the risk premium and required return, and vice versa.

Some Closing Comments The capital asset pricing model generally relies on historical data. The betas may or may not actually reflect the *future* variability of returns. Therefore, the required returns specified by the model can be viewed only as rough approximations. Analysts who use betas commonly make subjective adjustments to the historically determined betas to reflect their expectations of the future.

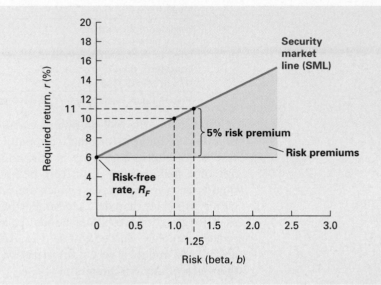

FIGURE 5.6

The Security Market Line (SML)

The security market line clearly depicts the tradeoff between risk and return. At a beta of 0, the required return is the risk-free rate of 6%. At a beta of 1.0, the required return is the market return of 10%. Given these data, the required return on an investment with a beta of 1.25 is 11% and its risk premium is 5% (11% − 6%).

arbitrage pricing theory (APT)
a theory that suggests that the market risk premium on securities may be better explained by a number of factors underlying and in some cases replacing the market return used in CAPM; the CAPM can be viewed as being derived from APT.

Is there a better model? Although CAPM has been widely accepted, a broader theory, **arbitrage pricing theory (APT)**, first described by Stephen A. Ross in 1976, has received a great deal of attention in the financial literature. APT suggests that the risk premium on securities may be better explained by a number of factors underlying and in some cases replacing the market return used in the CAPM. The CAPM, in effect, can be viewed as being derived from APT. As a result of APT's failure to identify other risk factors clearly, as well as APT's lack of practical acceptance and usage, attention remains focused on CAPM.

Despite its predictive limitations, the CAPM provides a useful conceptual framework for evaluating and linking risk and return. Its simplicity and practical appeal cause beta and CAPM to remain important tools for investors who seek to measure risk and link it to required returns in security markets.

IN REVIEW

CONCEPTS

5.7 Briefly define and give examples of each of the following components of total risk. Which is the relevant risk, and why?
a. Diversifiable risk   b. Nondiversifiable risk

5.8 Explain what is meant by *beta*. What is the relevant risk measured by beta? What is the *market return?* How is the interpretation of beta related to the market return?

5.9 What range of values does beta typically exhibit? Are positive or negative betas more common? Explain.

5.10 What is the *capital asset pricing model (CAPM)?* What role does beta play in it? What is the *risk premium?* How is the *security market line (SML)* related to the CAPM?

5.11 Is the CAPM a predictive model? How is the CAPM related to *arbitrage pricing theory (APT)?* Why do beta and the CAPM remain important to investors?

Traditional Versus Modern Portfolio Management

LG 4

Two approaches are currently used by individual and institutional investors to plan and construct their portfolios. The *traditional approach* refers to the less quantitative methods that investors have been using since the evolution of the public securities markets. *Modern portfolio theory (MPT)* is a more recent, more mathematical development that continues to grow in popularity and acceptance. Some MPT concepts are indirectly used by practitioners of the traditional approach, yet there are major differences between the two.

The Traditional Approach

traditional portfolio management
an approach to portfolio management that emphasizes "balancing" the portfolio by assembling a wide variety of stocks and/or bonds of companies from a broad range of industries.

Traditional portfolio management emphasizes "balancing" the portfolio by assembling a wide variety of stocks and/or bonds. The typical emphasis is *interindustry diversification.* This produces a portfolio with securities of companies from a broad range of industries. Traditional portfolios are constructed using the security analysis techniques discussed in Chapters 7 and 8.

Table 5.5 (on page 204) presents the industry groupings, number of issues held in each group (noted in parentheses), and the percentages invested in them by a typical mutual fund that is managed by professionals using the traditional approach. This fund, The Growth Fund of America (GFA), is an open-end mutual fund. The portfolio value at August 31, 2003, was approximately $54 billion. Its objective is to invest in a wide range of companies that appear to offer superior opportunities for growth of capital. The GFA holds shares of 211 different stocks from 21 industries, as well as short-term securities of 34 different issuers.

Analyzing the stock position of The Growth Fund of America, which accounts for about 90% of the fund's total assets, we observe the traditional approach to portfolio management at work. This fund holds numerous stocks from a broad cross section of the total universe of available stocks. The stocks are a mix of large and small companies. By far the largest industry group is semiconductors and semiconductor equipment, representing 12.78% of the total portfolio. The fund's largest individual holding is Time Warner, Inc., a media and entertainment company, which accounts for 3.3% of the total portfolio. Lowe's Companies, Inc., a retailer of home improvement products, ranks second at 2.5%. The third largest holding—2.3%—is American International Group, Inc., a holding company engaged in insurance and insurance-related activities. Although many of the fund's 211 stocks are those of large recognizable companies, its portfolio does include stocks of smaller, less-recognizable companies such as Xilinx, Inc., Amylin Pharmaceuticals, Inc., Arch Coal, Inc., and Monster Worldwide, Inc.

Those who manage traditional portfolios want to invest in well-known companies for three reasons. First, because these are known as successful business enterprises, investing in them is perceived as less risky than investing in lesser-known firms. Second, the securities of large firms are more liquid and are available in large quantities. Third, institutional investors prefer successful well-known companies because it is easier to convince clients to invest in them. Called *window dressing,* this practice of loading up a portfolio, particularly at the end of a reporting period, with successful well-known stocks makes it easier for institutional investors to sell their services.

TABLE 5.5   The Growth Fund of America, August 31, 2003

The Growth Fund of America (GFA) appears to adhere to the traditional approach to portfolio management. Its total portfolio value is about $54 billion, of which 90% ($48 billion) is common stock, including 211 different stocks in 21 broad industry groupings, plus about 10% ($6 billion) in short-term securities of 34 different issuers. In addition, the fund has a very small position in fixed-income securities that is offset by an equally small amount of net liabilities.

The Growth Fund of America Investments by Industry Group as of August 31, 2003			
Industry Group (# of issues)	Percentage	Industry Group (# of issues)	Percentage
Equity Securities	**89.72%**	Materials (11)	1.96
Semiconductors and semiconductor equipment (21)	12.78	Hotels, restaurants, and leisure (4)	1.45
Retailing (11)	9.70	Commercial services and supplies (7)	1.11
Media (12)	9.63	Food and staples retailing (3)	1.02
Pharmaceuticals and biotechnology (22)	8.82	Utilities (2)	0.36
Energy (21)	6.01	Household and personal products (1)	0.03
Software and services (15)	5.13	Miscellaneous	3.33
Telecommunication services (13)	4.24	**Fixed-Income Securities**	**0.02%**
Capital goods (9)	4.17	Media (1)	0.02
Banks and diversified financials (11)	4.12	**Short-Term Securities**	**10.47%**
Insurance (7)	4.05	Corporate short-term notes (27)	4.23
Food, beverage, and tobacco (8)	3.45	U.S. Treasuries (1)	3.23
Technology hardware and equipment (19)	3.28	Federal agency discount notes (4)	2.79
Transportation (5)	2.56	Certificates of deposit (2)	0.22
Health care equipment and services (9)	2.52	**Net Liabilities**	**−0.21%**

Source: The Growth Fund of America, *Annual Report for the Year Ended August 31, 2003*, pp. 13–26.

Modern Portfolio Theory

modern portfolio theory (MPT)
an approach to portfolio management that uses several basic statistical measures to develop a portfolio plan.

During the 1950s, Harry Markowitz, a trained mathematician, first developed the theories that form the basis of modern portfolio theory. Many other scholars and investment experts have contributed to the theory in the intervening years. **Modern portfolio theory (MPT)** utilizes several basic statistical measures to develop a portfolio plan. Included are *expected returns* and *standard deviations of returns* for both securities and portfolios, and the *correlation between returns*. According to MPT, diversification is achieved by combining securities in a portfolio *in such a way that individual securities have negative (or low-positive) correlations between each other's rates of return*. Thus the statistical diversification is the deciding factor in choosing securities for an MPT portfolio.

Two important aspects of MPT are the *efficient frontier* and *portfolio betas*.

The Efficient Frontier   At any point in time, you are faced with virtually hundreds of investment vehicles from which to choose. You can form any number of possible portfolios. In fact, using only, say, 10 of the vehicles, you could create hundreds of portfolios by changing the proportion of each asset in the portfolio.

If we were to create all possible portfolios, calculate the return and risk of each, and plot each risk-return combination on a set of risk-return axes, we would have the *feasible* or *attainable set* of all possible portfolios. This set is represented by the shaded area in Figure 5.7. It is the area bounded by

The Feasible or Attainable Set and the Efficient Frontier

The *feasible* or *attainable set* (shaded area) represents the risk-return combinations attainable with all possible portfolios; the *efficient frontier* is the locus of all efficient portfolios. The point 0 where the investor's highest possible indifference curve is tangent to the efficient frontier is the optimal portfolio. It represents the highest level of satisfaction the investor can achieve given the available set of portfolios.

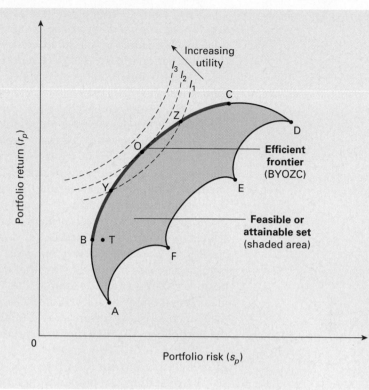

ABYOZCDEF. As defined earlier, an *efficient portfolio* is a portfolio that provides the highest return for a given level of risk or provides minimum risk for a given level of return. For example, let's compare portfolio T to portfolios B and Y shown in Figure 5.7. Portfolio Y appears preferable to portfolio T because it has a higher return for the same level of risk. Portfolio B also "dominates" portfolio T because it has lower risk for the same level of return.

The boundary BYOZC of the feasible set of portfolios represents *all efficient portfolios*—those portfolios that provide the best tradeoff between risk and return. This boundary is called the **efficient frontier.** *All portfolios on the efficient frontier are preferable to all other portfolios in the attainable set.* Any portfolios that would fall to the left of the efficient frontier are not available for investment, because they fall outside of the attainable set. Portfolios that fall to the right of the efficient frontier are *not desirable,* because their risk-return tradeoffs are inferior to those of portfolios on the efficient frontier.

The efficient frontier can, in theory, be used to find the highest level of satisfaction the investor can achieve given the available set of portfolios. To do this, we would plot on the risk-return axes an *investor's utility function* or *risk-indifference curves.* These curves indicate, for a given level of utility (satisfaction), the set of risk-return combinations among which an investor would be indifferent. These curves, labeled I_1, I_2, and I_3 in Figure 5.7, reflect increasing satisfaction as we move from I_1 to I_2 to I_3. The optimal portfolio, O, is the point at which indifference curve I_2 meets the efficient frontier. The higher utility provided by I_3 cannot be achieved given the best available portfolios represented by the efficient frontier.

efficient frontier
the leftmost boundary of the *feasible (attainable) set* of portfolios that includes all *efficient portfolios*—those providing the best attainable tradeoff between risk (measured by the standard deviation) and return.

When coupled with a risk-free asset, the efficient frontier can be used to develop the *capital asset pricing model* (introduced earlier) in terms of portfolio risk (measured by the standard deviation, s_p) and return (r_p). Rather than focus further on theory, let's shift our attention to the more practical aspects of the efficient frontier and its extensions. To do so, we consider the use of *portfolio betas*.

Portfolio Betas As we have noted, investors strive to diversify their portfolios by including a variety of noncomplementary investment vehicles so as to reduce risk while meeting return objectives. Remember that investment vehicles embody two basic types of risk: (1) *diversifiable risk,* the risk unique to a particular investment vehicle, and (2) *nondiversifiable risk,* the risk possessed by every investment vehicle.

A great deal of research has been conducted on the topic of risk as it relates to security investments. As we noted earlier, the results show that in general, *to earn more return, one must bear more risk.* More startling, however, are research results showing that only with nondiversifiable risk is there a positive risk-return relationship. High levels of *diversifiable risk* do not result in correspondingly high levels of return. Because there is no reward for bearing diversifiable risk, investors should minimize this form of risk by diversifying the portfolio so that only nondiversifiable risk remains.

Risk Diversification As we've seen, diversification minimizes diversifiable risk by offsetting the poor return on one vehicle with the good return on another. Minimizing diversifiable risk through careful selection of investment vehicles requires that the vehicles chosen for the portfolio come from a wide range of industries.

To understand better the effect of diversification on the basic types of risk, let's consider what happens when we begin with a single asset (security) in a portfolio and then expand the portfolio by randomly selecting additional securities. Using the standard deviation, s_p, to measure the portfolio's *total risk,* we can depict the behavior of the total portfolio risk as more securities are added, as done in Figure 5.8. As securities are added (*x*-axis) the total portfolio risk (*y*-axis) declines because of the effects of diversification (explained earlier), and it tends to approach a limit.

Research has shown that, on average, most of the benefits of diversification, in terms of risk reduction, can be gained by forming portfolios containing 8 to 15 randomly selected securities. Unfortunately, because an investor holds but one of a large number of possible *x*-security portfolios, it is unlikely that he or she will experience the average outcome. As a consequence, some researchers suggest that the individual investor needs to hold about 40 different stocks to achieve efficient diversification. This suggestion tends to support the popularity of investment in mutual funds.

Because any investor can create a portfolio of assets that will eliminate virtually all diversifiable risk, the only **relevant risk** is that which is nondiversifiable. You must therefore be concerned solely with nondiversifiable risk. The measurement of nondiversifiable risk is thus of primary importance.

relevant risk
risk that is nondiversifiable.

Calculating Portfolio Betas As we saw earlier, the *nondiversifiable* or *relevant risk* of a security can be measured using *beta.* The beta for the market is equal to 1.00. Securities with betas greater than 1.00 are more risky than the

Portfolio Risk and Diversification

As randomly selected securities are combined to create a portfolio, the total risk of the portfolio (measured by its standard deviation, s_p) declines. The portion of the risk eliminated is the *diversifiable risk;* the remaining portion is the *nondiversifiable* or *relevant risk.* On average, most of the benefits of diversification result from forming portfolios that contain 8 to 15 randomly selected securities.

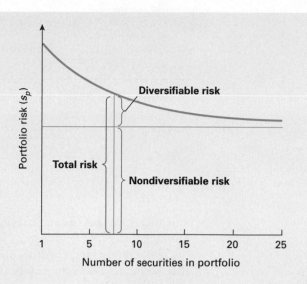

market, and those with betas less than 1.00 are less risky than the market. The beta for the risk-free asset is 0.

The **portfolio beta,** b_p, is merely the weighted average of the betas of the individual assets it includes. It can be easily estimated using the betas of the component assets. To find the portfolio beta, b_p, we can use Equation 5.4.

portfolio beta, b_p
the beta of a portfolio; calculated as the weighted average of the betas of the individual assets it includes.

Equation 5.4

$$\text{Portfolio beta} = \begin{pmatrix} \text{Proportion of} \\ \text{portfolio's total} & \text{Beta} \\ \text{dollar value} & \times & \text{for} \\ \text{represented by} & \text{asset 1} \\ \text{asset 1} \end{pmatrix} + \begin{pmatrix} \text{Proportion of} \\ \text{portfolio's total} & \text{Beta} \\ \text{dollar value} & \times & \text{for} \\ \text{represented by} & \text{asset 2} \\ \text{asset 2} \end{pmatrix} + \cdots +$$

$$\begin{pmatrix} \text{Proportion of} \\ \text{portfolio's total} & \text{Beta} \\ \text{dollar value} & \times & \text{for} \\ \text{represented by} & \text{asset } n \\ \text{asset } n \end{pmatrix} = \sum_{j=1}^{n} \begin{pmatrix} \text{Proportion of} \\ \text{portfolio's total} & \text{Beta} \\ \text{dollar value} & \times & \text{for} \\ \text{represented by} & \text{asset } j \\ \text{asset } j \end{pmatrix}$$

Equation 5.4a

$$b_p = (w_1 \times b_1) + (w_2 \times b_2) + \cdots + (w_n \times b_n) = \sum_{j=1}^{n} (w_j \times b_j)$$

Of course, $\sum_{j=1}^{n} w_j = 1$, which means that 100% of the portfolio's assets must be included in this computation.

Portfolio betas are interpreted in exactly the same way as individual asset betas. They indicate the degree of responsiveness of the *portfolio's* return to changes in the market return. For example, when the market return increases by 10%, a portfolio with a beta of 0.75 will experience a 7.5% increase in its return ($0.75 \times 10\%$). A portfolio with a beta of 1.25 will experience a 12.5% increase in its return ($1.25 \times 10\%$). Low-beta portfolios are less responsive,

TABLE 5.6	Austin Fund's Portfolios V and W			
	Portfolio V		**Portfolio W**	
Asset	Proportion	Beta	Proportion	Beta
1	0.10	1.65	0.10	0.80
2	0.30	1.00	0.10	1.00
3	0.20	1.30	0.20	0.65
4	0.20	1.10	0.10	0.75
5	0.20	1.25	0.50	1.05
Total	1.00		1.00	

and therefore less risky, than high-beta portfolios. Clearly, a portfolio containing mostly low-beta assets will have a low beta, and vice versa.

To demonstrate, consider the Austin Fund, a large investment company that wishes to assess the risk of two portfolios, V and W. Both portfolios contain five assets, with the proportions and betas shown in Table 5.6. The betas for portfolios V and W, b_v and b_w, can be calculated by substituting the appropriate data from the table into Equation 5.4, as follows.

$$b_v = (0.10 \times 1.65) + (0.30 \times 1.00) + (0.20 \times 1.30) + (0.20 \times 1.10) + (0.20 \times 1.25)$$

$$= 0.165 + 0.300 + 0.260 + 0.220 + 0.250 = 1.195 \approx \underline{1.20}$$

$$b_w = (0.10 \times 0.80) + (0.10 \times 1.00) + (0.20 \times 0.65) + (0.10 \times 0.75) + (0.50 \times 1.05)$$

$$= 0.080 + 0.100 + 0.130 + 0.075 + 0.525 = \underline{0.91}$$

Portfolio V's beta is 1.20, and portfolio W's is 0.91. These values make sense because portfolio V contains relatively high-beta assets and portfolio W contains relatively low-beta assets. Clearly, portfolio V's returns are more responsive to changes in market returns—and therefore more risky—than portfolio W's.

Using Portfolio Betas The usefulness of beta depends on how well it explains return fluctuations. We can use *the coefficient of determination* (R^2) to evaluate a beta coefficient statistically. This coefficient indicates the percentage of the change in an individual security's return that is explained by its relationship with the market return. R^2 can range from 0 to 1.0. If a regression equation has an R^2 of 0, then none (0%) of the variation in the security's return is explained by its relationship with the market. An R^2 of 1.0 indicates the existence of perfect correlation (100%) between a security and the market.

Beta is much more useful in explaining a portfolio's return fluctuations than a security's return fluctuations. A well-diversified stock portfolio will have a beta equation R^2 of around 0.90. This means that 90% of the stock portfolio's fluctuations are related to changes in the stock market as a whole. Individual security betas have a wide range of R^2s but tend to be in the 0.20 to 0.50 range. Other factors (diversifiable risk, in particular) also cause individual security prices to fluctuate. When securities are combined in a well-diversified portfolio, most of the fluctuation in that portfolio's return is caused by the movement of the entire stock market.

Interpreting Portfolio Betas If a portfolio has a beta of +1.00, the portfolio experiences changes in its rate of return equal to changes in the market's rate of return. The +1.00 beta portfolio would tend to experience a 10% increase in return if the stock market as a whole experienced a 10% increase in return. Conversely, if the market return fell by 6%, the return on the +1.00 beta portfolio would also fall by 6%.

Table 5.7 lists the expected returns for three portfolio betas in two situations: an increase in market return of 10% and a decrease in market return of 10%. The 2.00 beta portfolio is twice as volatile as the market. When the market return increases by 10%, the portfolio return increases by 20%. When the market return declines by 10%, the portfolio's return will fall by 20%. This portfolio would be considered a high-risk, high-return portfolio.

The middle, 0.50 beta portfolio is considered a low-risk, low-return portfolio. This would be a conservative portfolio for investors who wish to maintain a low-risk investment posture. The 0.50 beta portfolio is half as volatile as the market.

A portfolio with a beta of −1.00 moves in the opposite direction from the market. A bearish investor would probably want to own a negative-beta portfolio, because this type of investment tends to rise in value when the stock market declines, and vice versa. Finding securities with negative betas is difficult, however. Most securities have positive betas, because they tend to experience return movements in the same direction as changes in the stock market.

The Risk-Return Tradeoff: Some Closing Comments Another valuable outgrowth of modern portfolio theory is the specific link between nondiversifiable risk and investment return. The basic premise is that an investor must have a portfolio of relatively risky investments to earn a relatively high rate of return. That relationship is illustrated in Figure 5.9 (on page 210). The upward-sloping line shows the **risk-return tradeoff**. The point where the risk-return line crosses the return axis is called the **risk-free rate, R_F**. This is the return an investor can earn on a risk-free investment such as a U.S. Treasury bill or an insured money market deposit account.

As we proceed upward along the risk-return tradeoff line, portfolios of risky investments appear. For example, four investment portfolios, A through D, are depicted. Portfolios A and B are investment opportunities that provide a level of return commensurate with their respective risk levels. Portfolio C provides a high return at a relatively low risk level—and therefore would be an excellent investment. Portfolio D, in contrast, offers high risk but low return—an investment to avoid.

risk-return tradeoff
the positive relationship between the risk associated with a given investment and its expected return.

risk-free rate, R_F
the return an investor can earn on a risk-free investment such as a U.S. Treasury bill or an insured money market deposit account.

TABLE 5.7 Portfolio Betas and Associated Changes in Returns

Portfolio Beta	Change in Market Return	Change in Expected Portfolio Return
+2.00	+10.0%	+20.0%
	−10.0	−20.0
+0.50	+10.0	+5.0
	−10.0	−5.0
−1.00	+10.0	−10.0
	−10.0	+10.0

FIGURE 5.9

The Portfolio Risk-Return Tradeoff

As the risk of an investment portfolio increases from zero, the return provided should increase above the risk-free rate, R_F. Portfolios A and B offer returns commensurate with their risk, portfolio C provides a high return at a low-risk level, and portfolio D provides a low return for high risk. Portfolio C is highly desirable; portfolio D should be avoided.

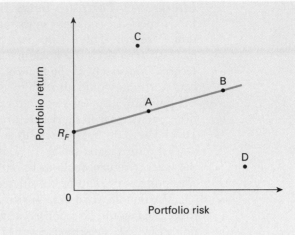

Reconciling the Traditional Approach and MPT

We have reviewed two fairly different approaches to portfolio management: the traditional approach and MPT. The question that naturally arises is which technique you should use. There is no definite answer; the question must be resolved by the judgment of each investor. However, we can offer a few useful ideas.

The average individual investor does not have the resources, computers, and mathematical acumen to implement a total MPT portfolio strategy. But most individual investors can extract and use ideas from *both* the traditional and MPT approaches. The traditional approach stresses security selection, which is discussed in Chapters 7 and 8. It also emphasizes diversification of the portfolio across industry lines. MPT stresses negative correlations between rates of return for the securities within the portfolio. This approach calls for diversification, to minimize diversifiable risk. Thus diversification must be accomplished to ensure satisfactory performance with either strategy. Also, beta is a useful tool for determining the level of a portfolio's nondiversifiable risk and should be part of the decision-making process.

We recommend the following portfolio management policy, which uses aspects of both approaches:

- Determine how much risk you are willing to bear.

- Seek diversification among different types of securities and across industry lines, and pay attention to how the return from one security is related to that from another.

- Consider how a security responds to the market, and use beta in diversifying your portfolio as a way to keep the portfolio in line with your acceptable level of risk.

- Evaluate alternative portfolios to make sure that the portfolio selected provides the highest return for the given level of acceptable risk.

CONCEPTS

IN REVIEW

5.12 Describe *traditional portfolio management*. Give three reasons why traditional portfolio managers like to invest in well-established companies.

5.13 What is *modern portfolio theory (MPT)?* What is the *feasible* or *attainable set* of all possible portfolios? How is it derived for a given group of investment vehicles?

5.14 What is the *efficient frontier?* How is it related to the attainable set of all possible portfolios? How can it be used with an investor's utility function to find the optimal portfolio?

5.15 Define and differentiate among the diversifiable, nondiversifiable, and total risk of a portfolio. Which is considered the *relevant risk?* How is it measured?

5.16 Define *beta*. How can you find the beta of a portfolio when you know the beta for each of the assets included within it?

5.17 What does the *coefficient of determination (R^2)* for the regression equation used to derive a beta coefficient indicate? Would this statistic indicate that beta is more useful in explaining the return fluctuations of individual assets than of portfolios?

5.18 Explain how the traditional and modern portfolio approaches can be reconciled.

Constructing a Portfolio Using an Asset Allocation Scheme

LG 5   LG 6

In this section we will examine the criteria for constructing a portfolio and then will use these factors to develop a plan for allocating assets in various investment categories. This plan provides a basic, useful framework for selecting individual investment vehicles for the portfolio. In attempting to weave the concepts of risk and diversification into a solid portfolio policy, we will rely on both traditional and modern approaches.

Investor Characteristics and Objectives

Your financial and family situations are important inputs in determining portfolio policy. Vital determinants include level and stability of income, family factors, net worth, investor experience and age, and disposition toward risk. The types of investments in your portfolio depend on relative income needs and ability to bear risk.

The size of your income and the certainty of your employment also bear on portfolio strategy. An investor with a secure job can handle more risk than one with a less secure position. And, the higher your income, the more important the tax ramifications of an investment program become. Your investment experience also influences your investment strategy. It normally is best to "get one's feet wet" in the investment market by slipping into it gradually rather than leaping in headfirst. A cautiously developed investment program is likely to provide more favorable long-run results than an impulsive one.

Once you have developed a personal financial profile, the next question is, "What do I want from my portfolio?" You must generally choose between earning a high current income or obtaining significant capital appreciation. It is difficult to have both. The price of having high appreciation potential in the portfolio is often low potential for current income.

Your needs may determine which avenue is chosen. A retired investor whose income depends on his or her portfolio will probably choose a lower-risk, current-income-oriented approach. In contrast, a high-income, financially secure investor (such as a physician) may be much more willing to take on risky investments in the hope of improving net worth. Thus it should be clear that a portfolio must be built around the individual's needs, which depend on income, responsibilities, financial resources, age, retirement plans, and ability to bear risk.

Portfolio Objectives and Policies

Constructing a portfolio is a logical activity that is best done after you have analyzed your needs and the available investment vehicles. You should consider these objectives when planning and constructing a portfolio: current income needs, capital preservation, capital growth, tax considerations, and risk.

Any one or more of these factors will play an influential role in defining the desirable type of portfolio. For convenience, these factors can be tied together as follows: The first two items, current income and capital preservation, are portfolio objectives consistent with a low-risk, conservative investment strategy. Normally, a portfolio with this orientation contains low-beta (low-risk) securities. The third item, a capital growth objective, implies increased risk and a reduced level of current income. Higher-risk growth stocks, options, futures, and other more speculative investments may be suitable for this investor. The fourth item, an investor's tax bracket, will influence investment strategy. A high-income investor probably wishes to defer taxes and earn investment returns in the form of capital gains. This implies a strategy of higher-risk investments and a longer holding period. Lower-bracket investors are less concerned with how they earn the income, and they may wish to invest in higher-current-income vehicles. The most important item, finally, is risk. The risk-return tradeoff should be considered *in all investment decisions*.

Developing an Asset Allocation Scheme

Once you have translated your needs into specific portfolio objectives, you can construct a portfolio designed to achieve these goals. Before buying any investment vehicles, however, you must develop an *asset allocation scheme*. **Asset allocation** involves dividing one's portfolio into various asset classes, such as U.S. stocks, U.S. bonds, foreign securities, short-term securities, and other vehicles like tangibles (especially gold) and real estate. The emphasis of asset allocation is on *preservation of capital*—protecting against negative developments while taking advantage of positive developments. Asset allocation, although similar to diversification in its objective, is a bit different: Its focus is on *investment in various asset classes*. Diversification, in contrast, tends to focus more on **security selection**—selecting the *specific* securities to be held *within* an asset class.

Asset allocation is based on the belief that the total return of a portfolio is influenced more by the division of investments into asset classes than by the actual investments. In fact, studies have shown that as much as 90% or more

asset allocation
a scheme that involves dividing one's portfolio into various asset classes to *preserve capital* by protecting against negative developments while taking advantage of positive ones.

security selection
the procedures used to select the *specific* securities to be held *within* an asset class.

of a portfolio's *return* comes from asset allocation. Therefore, less than 10% can be attributed to the actual security selection. Furthermore, researchers have found that asset allocation has a much greater impact on reducing *total risk* than does selecting the best investment vehicle in any single asset category. Clearly, asset allocation is a very important aspect of portfolio management.

Approaches to Asset Allocation There are three basic approaches to asset allocation: (1) fixed weightings, (2) flexible weightings, and (3) tactical asset allocation. The first two differ with respect to the proportions of each asset category maintained in the portfolio. The third is a more exotic technique used by institutional portfolio managers.

fixed-weightings approach
asset allocation plan in which a fixed percentage of the portfolio is allocated to each asset category.

Fixed Weightings The **fixed-weightings approach** allocates a fixed percentage of the portfolio to each of the asset categories, of which there typically are three to five. Assuming four categories—common stock, bonds, foreign securities, and short-term securities—a fixed allocation might be as follows.

Category	Allocation
Common stock	30%
Bonds	50
Foreign securities	15
Short-term securities	5
Total portfolio	100%

Generally, the fixed weightings do not change over time. When market values shift, the portfolio may have to be adjusted annually or after major market moves to maintain the desired fixed-percentage allocations.

Fixed weights may or may not represent equal percentage allocations to each category. One could, for example, allocate 25% to each of the four categories above. Research has shown that over a long period (1967–1988) equal (20%) allocations to U.S. stocks, foreign stocks, long-term bonds, cash, and real estate resulted in a portfolio that outperformed the S&P 500 in terms of both return and risk. These findings add further support to the importance of even a somewhat naive "buy and hold" asset allocation strategy.

H O T   L I N K S

The *Investing in Action* box at the book's Web site offers some basic portfolio-building tips for the novice investor.

www.aw-bc.com/gitman_joehnk

flexible-weightings approach
asset allocation plan in which weights for each asset category are adjusted periodically based on market analysis.

Flexible Weightings The **flexible-weightings approach** involves periodic adjustment of the weights for each asset category on the basis of market analysis. The use of a flexible weighting scheme is often called *strategic asset allocation*. For example, the initial and new allocation based on a flexible weighting scheme may be as follows.

Category	Initial Allocation	New Allocation
Common stock	30%	45%
Bonds	40	40
Foreign securities	15	10
Short-term securities	15	5
Total portfolio	100%	100%

A change from the initial to the new allocation would be triggered by shifts in market conditions or expectations. For example, the new allocation shown above

INVESTING IN ACTION

KEEP YOUR BALANCE

Despite numerous studies that indicate that asset allocation, rather than individual security selection, is a key determinant of a portfolio's return, most investors tend to buy hot stocks and mutual funds in a seemingly random fashion. By not developing and following an asset allocation strategy when adding securities, the investor ends up with a portfolio that may be too concentrated in one or two asset classes or industry sectors. This can be a big mistake, as many investors who jumped on the technology stock bandwagon in the late 1990s discovered. Their portfolios were overweighted in this high-risk area, and they suffered heavy losses when the tech bubble burst.

Begin by evaluating your investment goals and risk tolerance. Then you can determine how much to allocate to each asset class, developing a long-term strategy that should cover 5 to 10 years. If you are 30 years old and single, for example, you may choose to invest a larger percentage of your portfolio in growth stocks than would a 70-year-old retiree who focuses on fixed-income securities with the goal of preserving capital and generating income for living expenses.

Within each broad asset category, you should further refine your allocation. For example, you may decide to divide your equity allocation among growth stocks, income stocks, and foreign company stocks. "You want to select groups that don't move in lockstep with each other" such as domestic large-cap, small-cap, and foreign stocks, advises David Yeske, president of the Financial Planning Association (FPA). Your fixed-income securities might include Treasury bonds, municipal bonds, corporate bonds, and high-yield bonds. Don't overlook real-estate investment trusts and alternative securities such as commodities. Once your framework is in place, choose the individual securities and mutual funds for each category.

As hard as it may be to stick with your target percentages, resist the temptation to abandon your strategy. Otherwise, as Bryan Olson, vice president of the Schwab Center for Investment Research, explains, you let the market dictate your risk levels and asset allocations. About once a year, reexamine your portfolio and rebalance it as necessary to maintain your target percentages, thereby managing risk and maximizing return potential.

For example, tech investors who had rebalanced their portfolios would have sold some top performers and bought securities in an under-represented sector, lessening their overall risk through diversification. This requires firm discipline because you must "sell the things that have been making you happy recently and buy the things that have been making you sad," comments FPA's Yeske. Over time, however, biting the bullet will pay off. If in 1972 you had set up a portfolio of $10,000, split evenly into four categories—blue-chip U.S. stocks, small-cap stocks, foreign equities, and real-estate investment trusts—and left it alone for 30 years, in 2002 your portfolio would have grown to $305,000. Had you rebalanced each category to the 25% level each year, you would have lowered your risk and seen your portfolio grow to $323,000.

CRITICAL THINKING QUESTION Use the ideas presented above to develop an asset allocation strategy consistent with your investment goals.

Sources: Kathy Chu, "Time for Annual Investment Checkup," *Dow Jones Newswires*, October 22, 2003, downloaded from online.wsj.com; Jonathan Clements, "Make Sure to Stay the Course," *San Diego Union-Tribune*, September 21, 2003, p. H7; Humberto Cruz, "Study Ties Asset Allocation to Inflation Rate," *South Florida Sun–Sentinel*, November 12, 2003, p. 3D; and Cliff Pletschet, "Financial Planning All About the 'Right Mix'," *Oakland Tribune* (CA), October 20, 2003, p. 1.

may have resulted from an anticipated decline in inflation. That decline would be expected to result in increased domestic stock and bond prices and a decline in foreign and short-term security returns. The weightings were therefore changed to capture greater returns in a changing market.

tactical asset allocation
asset allocation plan that uses stock-index futures and bond futures to change a portfolio's asset allocation based on forecast market behavior.

Tactical Asset Allocation The third approach, **tactical asset allocation,** is a form of market timing that uses stock-index futures and bond futures (see Chapter 16) to change a portfolio's asset allocation. When stocks are forecast to be less attractive than bonds, this strategy involves selling stock-index futures and buying bond futures. Conversely, when bonds are forecast to be less attractive than stocks, the strategy results in buying stock-index futures and selling bond futures. Because this sophisticated technique relies on a large portfolio and the use of quantitative models for market timing, it is generally appropriate only for large institutional investors.

Asset Allocation Alternatives Assuming the use of a fixed-weight asset allocation plan and using, say, four asset categories, we can demonstrate three asset allocations. Table 5.8 shows allocations in each of four categories for conservative (low return/low risk), moderate (average return/average risk), and aggressive (high return/high risk) portfolios. The conservative allocation relies heavily on bonds and short-term securities to provide predictable returns. The moderate allocation consists largely of common stock and bonds and includes more foreign securities and fewer short-term securities than the conservative allocation. Its moderate risk-return behavior reflects a move away from safe, short-term securities to a larger dose of common stock and foreign securities. Finally, in the aggressive allocation, more dollars are invested in common stock, fewer in bonds, and more in foreign securities, thereby generally increasing the expected portfolio return and risk.

Applying Asset Allocation An asset allocation plan should consider the economic outlook and your investments, savings and spending patterns, tax situation, return expectations, and risk tolerance. Such plans must be formulated for the long run, must stress capital preservation, and must provide for periodic revision to maintain consistency with changing investment goals. Generally, to decide on the appropriate asset mix, you must evaluate each asset category in terms of current return, growth potential, safety, liquidity, transaction costs (brokerage fees), and potential tax savings.

Many investors use mutual funds (see Chapter 13) as part of their asset allocation activities, to diversify within each asset category. Or, as an alternative to constructing your own portfolio, you can buy shares in an **asset allocation fund**—a mutual fund that seeks to reduce variability of returns by investing in the right assets at the right time. These funds, like all asset allocation schemes, emphasize diversification. They perform at a relatively consistent

asset allocation fund
a mutual fund that seeks to reduce the variability of returns by investing in the right assets at the right time; emphasizes diversification and performs at a relatively consistent level by passing up the potential for spectacular gains.

TABLE 5.8   Alternative Asset Allocations

	Allocation Alternative		
Category	Conservative (low return/ low risk)	Moderate (average return/ average risk)	Aggressive (high return/ high risk)
Common stock	15%	30%	40%
Bonds	45	40	30
Foreign securities	5	15	25
Short-term securities	30	15	5
Total portfolio	100%	100%	100%

level by passing up the potential for spectacular gains in favor of predictability. Some asset allocation funds use fixed weightings, whereas others have flexible weights that change within prescribed limits. As a rule, investors with more than about $100,000 to invest and adequate time can justify do-it-yourself asset allocation. Those with between $25,000 and $100,000 and adequate time can use mutual funds to create a workable asset allocation. Those with less than $25,000 or with limited time may find asset allocation funds most attractive.

Most important, you should recognize that to be effective an asset allocation scheme *must be designed for the long haul.* Develop an asset allocation scheme you can live with for at least 7 to 10 years, and perhaps longer. Once you have it set, stick with it. The key to success is remaining faithful to your asset allocation; that means fighting the temptation to wander. The *Investing in Action* box on page 214 emphasizes this point by describing the importance of developing and following an asset allocation strategy.

IN REVIEW

CONCEPTS

5.19 What role, if any, do an investor's personal characteristics play in determining portfolio policy? Explain.

5.20 What role do an investor's portfolio objectives play in constructing a portfolio?

5.21 What is *asset allocation?* How does it differ from diversification? What role does asset allocation play in constructing an investment portfolio?

5.22 Briefly describe the three basic approaches to asset allocation: (a) fixed weightings, (b) flexible weightings, and (c) tactical asset allocation.

5.23 What role could an *asset allocation fund* play? What makes an asset allocation scheme effective?

Summary

 LG 1 Understand portfolio management objectives and the procedures used to calculate the return and standard deviation of a portfolio. A portfolio is a collection of investment vehicles assembled to achieve one or more investment goals. It involves a tradeoff between risk and return, potential price appreciation and current income, and varying risk levels. The return on a portfolio is calculated as a weighted average of the returns of the assets from which it is formed. The standard deviation of a portfolio's returns is found by applying the same formula that is used to find the standard deviation of a single asset.

LG 2 Discuss the concepts of correlation and diversification, and the effectiveness, methods, and benefits of international diversification. Correlation is a statistic used to measure the relationship, if any, between the returns on assets. To diversify, it is best to add assets with negatively correlated returns. In general, the less positive and more negative the correlation between asset returns, the more effectively a portfolio can be diversified

to reduce its risk. Through diversification, the risk (standard deviation) of a portfolio can be reduced below the risk of the least risky asset (sometimes to zero); however, the return of the resulting portfolio will be no lower than the smallest return of its component assets. For any two-asset portfolio, the ability to reduce risk depends on both the degree of correlation and proportion of each asset in the portfolio.

International diversification may allow an investor to reduce portfolio risk without a corresponding reduction in return. It can be achieved by investing abroad or through domestic investment in foreign companies or funds, but it typically cannot be achieved by investing in U.S. multinationals. The preferred method of international diversification for individual investors is the use of ADRs or international mutual funds available in the United States. Although opportunities to earn "excess" returns in international investments are diminishing over time, they continue to be effective diversification vehicles.

LG 3 **Describe the two components of risk, beta, and the capital asset pricing model (CAPM).** The two basic components of total risk are diversifiable (unsystematic) and nondiversifiable (systematic) risk; nondiversifiable risk is the relevant risk. Beta can be used to measure the nondiversifiable, or market, risk associated with a security investment. It is derived from the historical relationship between a security's return and the market return. The capital asset pricing model (CAPM) relates risk (as measured by beta) to return. It can be divided into two parts: (1) the risk-free rate of return, R_F, and (2) the risk premium, $b \times (r_m - R_F)$. The graphic depiction of the CAPM is the security market line (SML). The CAPM reflects increasing required returns for increasing risk. The CAPM relies on historical data, can be viewed as being derived from arbitrage pricing theory (APT), and provides a useful conceptual framework for linking risk and return.

LG 4 **Review traditional and modern approaches to portfolio management and reconcile them.** The traditional approach constructs portfolios by combining a large number of securities issued by companies from a broad cross section of industries. Modern portfolio theory (MPT) uses statistical diversification to develop efficient portfolios. To determine the optimal portfolio, MPT finds the efficient frontier and couples it with an investor's risk-indifference curves. In practice, portfolio betas can be used to develop efficient portfolios consistent with the investor's risk-return preferences. Generally, investors use elements of both the traditional approach and MPT to create portfolios.

LG 5 **Describe the role of investor characteristics and objectives and of portfolio objectives and policies in constructing an investment portfolio.** To construct a portfolio, the investor should consider characteristics such as level and stability of income, family factors, net worth, experience and age, and disposition toward risk. He or she should specify objectives and should plan and construct a portfolio consistent with them. Commonly considered portfolio objectives include current income, capital preservation, capital growth, tax considerations, and level of risk.

LG 6 **Summarize why and how investors use an asset allocation scheme to construct an investment portfolio.** Asset allocation is the key influence on the total return of a portfolio. It involves dividing one's portfolio into various asset classes, whereas diversification tends to focus more on security selection within an asset class. Like diversification, asset allocation aims to protect against negative developments while taking advantage of positive ones. The basic approaches to asset allocation involve the use of fixed weightings, flexible weightings, and tactical asset allocation. Asset allocation can be achieved on a do-it-yourself basis, with the use of mutual funds, or by merely buying shares in an asset allocation fund.

Putting Your Investment Know-How to the Test

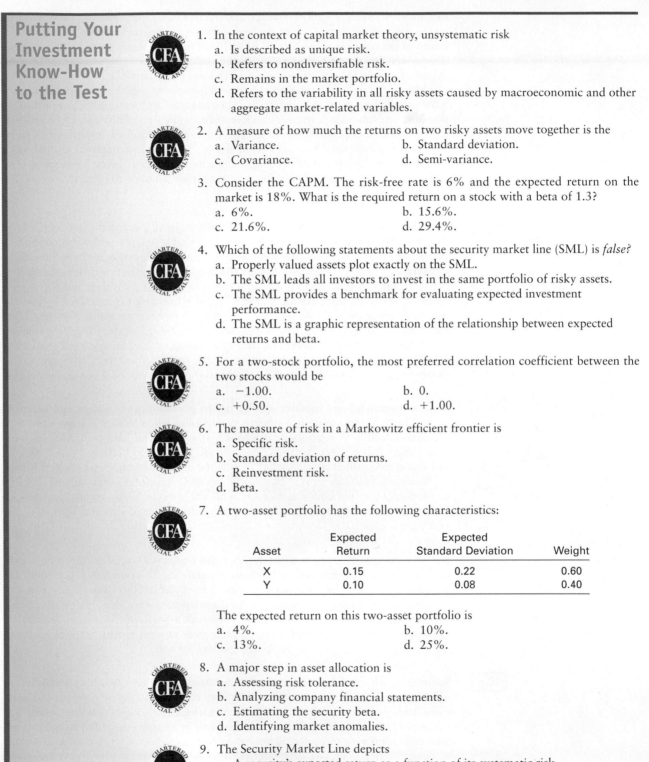

1. In the context of capital market theory, unsystematic risk
   a. Is described as unique risk.
   b. Refers to nondiversifiable risk.
   c. Remains in the market portfolio.
   d. Refers to the variability in all risky assets caused by macroeconomic and other aggregate market-related variables.

2. A measure of how much the returns on two risky assets move together is the
   a. Variance.   b. Standard deviation.
   c. Covariance.   d. Semi-variance.

3. Consider the CAPM. The risk-free rate is 6% and the expected return on the market is 18%. What is the required return on a stock with a beta of 1.3?
   a. 6%.   b. 15.6%.
   c. 21.6%.   d. 29.4%.

4. Which of the following statements about the security market line (SML) is *false*?
   a. Properly valued assets plot exactly on the SML.
   b. The SML leads all investors to invest in the same portfolio of risky assets.
   c. The SML provides a benchmark for evaluating expected investment performance.
   d. The SML is a graphic representation of the relationship between expected returns and beta.

5. For a two-stock portfolio, the most preferred correlation coefficient between the two stocks would be
   a. −1.00.   b. 0.
   c. +0.50.   d. +1.00.

6. The measure of risk in a Markowitz efficient frontier is
   a. Specific risk.
   b. Standard deviation of returns.
   c. Reinvestment risk.
   d. Beta.

7. A two-asset portfolio has the following characteristics:

Asset	Expected Return	Expected Standard Deviation	Weight
X	0.15	0.22	0.60
Y	0.10	0.08	0.40

The expected return on this two-asset portfolio is
   a. 4%.   b. 10%.
   c. 13%.   d. 25%.

8. A major step in asset allocation is
   a. Assessing risk tolerance.
   b. Analyzing company financial statements.
   c. Estimating the security beta.
   d. Identifying market anomalies.

9. The Security Market Line depicts
   a. A security's expected return as a function of its systematic risk.
   b. The market portfolio as the optimal portfolio of risky securities.
   c. The relationship between a security's return and the return on an index.
   d. The complete portfolio as a combination of the market portfolio and the risk-free asset.

10. According to the capital asset pricing model, the rate of return of a portfolio with a beta (B) of 1.0 and an alpha of 0 is
    a. Between R_m and R_f.
    b. The risk-free rate, R_f.
    c. $B(R_m - R_f)$.
    d. The return on the market, R_m.

Answers: 1. a; 2. c; 3. c; 4. b; 5. a; 6. b; 7. c; 8. a; 9. a; 10. d

Discussion Questions

Q5.1 State your portfolio objectives. Then construct a 10-stock portfolio that you feel is consistent with your objectives. (Use companies that have been public for at least 5 years.) Obtain annual dividend and price data for each of the past 5 years.
  a. Calculate the historical return for each stock for each year.
  b. Calculate the historical portfolio return for each of the 5 years, using your findings in part **a**.
  c. Use your findings in part **b** to calculate the average portfolio return over the 5 years.
  d. Use your findings in parts **b** and **c** to find the standard deviation of the portfolio's returns over the 5-year period.
  e. Use the historical average return from part **c** and the standard deviation from part **d** to evaluate the portfolio's return and risk in light of your stated portfolio objectives.

Q5.2 Using the following guidelines, choose the stocks—A, B, and C—of three firms that have been public for at least 10 years. Stock A should be one you are interested in buying. Stock B should be a stock, possibly in the same line of business or industry, that you feel will have high positive return correlation with stock A. Finally, stock C should be one you feel will have high negative return correlation with stock A.
  a. Calculate the annual rates of return for each of the past 10 years for each stock.
  b. Plot the 10 annual return values for each stock on the same set of axes, where the *x*-axis is the year and the *y*-axis is the annual return in percentage terms.
  c. Join the points for the returns for each stock on the graph. Evaluate and describe the returns of stocks A and B in the graph. Do they exhibit the expected positive correlation? Why or why not?
  d. Evaluate and describe the relationship between the returns of stocks A and C in the graph. Do they exhibit the expected negative correlation? Why or why not?
  e. Compare and contrast your findings in parts **c** and **d** to the expected relationships among stocks A, B, and C. Discuss your findings.

Q5.3 From the *Wall Street Journal*, a Web site such as Yahoo! Finance (finance. yahoo.com), or some other source, obtain a current estimate of the risk-free rate (use a 10-year Treasury bond). Use the *Value Line Investment Survey* or Yahoo! Finance to obtain the beta for each of the following stocks:

General Motors (autos)
Dell (computers)
Sempra Energy (utilities)
Kroger (groceries)
Merrill Lynch (financial services)

Use the information you gathered, along with the market risk premium on large stocks given in the chapter, to find the required return for each stock with the Capital Asset Pricing Model (CAPM).

LG 3   Q5.4   From the *Wall Street Journal*, a Web site such as Yahoo! Finance (finance. yahoo.com), or some other source, obtain a current estimate of the risk-free rate (use a 10-year Treasury bond). Use the *Value Line Investment Survey* or Yahoo! Finance to obtain the beta for each of the companies listed on page 198.

    a. Compare the current betas to the January 16, 2004 betas given in the chapter for each of the companies.

    b. What might cause betas to change over time, even in a stable economic environment?

    c. Use the current betas, along with the market risk premium on large stocks given in the chapter, to find the required return for each stock with the Capital Asset Pricing Model (CAPM).

    d. Compare and discuss your findings in part **c** with regard to the specific business that each company is in.

   LG 2 **LG 4**   Q5.5   Obtain a prospectus and an annual report for a major mutual fund that includes some international securities. Carefully read the prospectus and annual report and study the portfolio's composition in light of the fund's stated objectives.

    a. Evaluate the amount of diversification and the types of industries and companies held. Is the portfolio well diversified?

    b. Discuss the additional risks faced by an investor in this fund compared to an investor in a domestic stock portfolio such as the S&P 500.

LG 4   Q5.6   Use *Value Line Investment Survey* or some other source to select four stocks with betas ranging from about 0.50 to 1.50. Record the current market prices of each of these stocks. Assume you wish to create a portfolio that combines all four stocks in such a way that the resulting portfolio beta is about 1.10.

    a. Through trial and error, use all four stocks to create a portfolio with the target beta of 1.10.

    b. If you have $100,000 to invest in this portfolio, on the basis of the weightings determined in part **a**, how much in dollars would you invest in each stock?

    c. Approximately how many shares of each of the four stocks would you buy, given the dollar amounts calculated in part **b**?

    d. Repeat parts **a**, **b**, and **c** with a different set of weightings that still result in a portfolio beta of 1.10. Can only one unique portfolio with a given beta be created from a given set of stocks?

 LG 5 **LG 6**   Q5.7   List your personal characteristics and then state your investment objectives in light of them. Use these objectives as a basis for developing your portfolio objectives and policies. Assume that you plan to create a portfolio aimed at achieving your stated objectives. The portfolio will be constructed by allocating your money to any of the following asset classes: common stock, bonds, foreign securities, and short-term securities.

    a. Determine and justify an asset allocation to these four classes in light of your stated portfolio objectives and policies.

    b. Describe the types of investments you would choose for each of the asset classes.

    c. Assume that after making the asset allocations specified in part **a**, you receive a sizable inheritance that causes your portfolio objectives to change to a much more aggressive posture. Describe the changes that you would make in your asset allocations.

    d. Describe other asset classes you might consider when developing your asset allocation scheme.

Problems

P5.1 Your portfolio had the values in the following table for the four-year period listed. Calculate your average return over the four-year period.

	Beginning Value	Ending Value
2002	$50,000.00	$55,000.00
2003	$55,000.00	$58,000.00
2004	$58,000.00	$65,000.00
2005	$65,000.00	$70,000.00

P5.2 Using your data from Problem 5.1 above, calculate the portfolio standard deviation.

P5.3 Assume you are considering a portfolio containing two assets, L and M. Asset L will represent 40% of the dollar value of the portfolio, and asset M will account for the other 60%. The expected returns over the next 6 years, 2006–2011, for each of these assets are summarized in the following table.

	Expected Return (%)	
Year	Asset L	Asset M
2006	14	20
2007	14	18
2008	16	16
2009	17	14
2010	17	12
2011	19	10

a. Calculate the expected portfolio return, $\bar{r}_p$, for each of the 6 years.
b. Calculate the average expected portfolio return, $\bar{r}_p$, over the 6-year period.
c. Calculate the standard deviation of expected portfolio returns, s_p, over the 6-year period.
d. How would you characterize the correlation of returns of the two assets L and M?
e. Discuss any benefits of diversification achieved through creation of the portfolio.

P5.4 Refer to Problem 5.3 above. Assume that asset L represents 60% of the portfolio and asset M 40%. Calculate the average expected return and standard deviation of expected portfolio return over the 6-year period. Compare your answers to the answers from Problem 5.3.

P5.5 You have been given the following return data on three assets—F, G, and H—over the period 2006–2009.

	Expected Return (%)		
Year	Asset F	Asset G	Asset H
2006	16	17	14
2007	17	16	15
2008	18	15	16
2009	19	14	17

Using these assets, you have isolated three investment alternatives:

Alternative	Investment
1	100% of asset F
2	50% of asset F and 50% of asset G
3	50% of asset F and 50% of asset H

a. Calculate the portfolio return over the 4-year period for each of the three alternatives.
b. Calculate the standard deviation of returns over the 4-year period for each of the three alternatives.
c. On the basis of your findings in parts **a** and **b**, which of the three investment alternatives would you recommend? Why?

LG 1 **LG 2**   **P5.6** You have been asked for your advice in selecting a portfolio of assets and have been supplied with the following data.

	Expected Return (%)		
Year	Asset A	Asset B	Asset C
2006	12	16	12
2007	14	14	14
2008	16	12	16

You have been told that you can create two portfolios—one consisting of assets A and B and the other consisting of assets A and C—by investing equal proportions (50%) in each of the two component assets.
a. What is the average expected return, $\bar{r}$, for each asset over the 3-year period?
b. What is the standard deviation, s, for each asset's expected return?
c. What is the average expected return, $\bar{r}_p$, for each of the two portfolios?
d. How would you characterize the correlations of returns of the two assets making up each of the two portfolios identified in part **c**?
e. What is the standard deviation of expected returns, s_p, for each portfolio?
f. Which portfolio do you recommend? Why?

LG 1 **LG 2**   **P5.7** Referring to Problem 5.6 above, what would happen if you constructed a portfolio consisting of assets A, B, and C, equally weighted? Would this reduce risk or enhance return?

LG 1 **LG 2**   **P5.8** Assume you wish to evaluate the risk and return behaviors associated with various combinations of assets V and W under three assumed degrees of correlation: perfect positive, uncorrelated, and perfect negative. The following average return and risk values were calculated for these assets.

Asset	Average Return, $\bar{r}$ (%)	Risk (Standard Deviation), s (%)
V	8	5
W	13	10

a. If the returns of assets V and W are *perfectly positively correlated* (correlation coefficient = +1), describe the *range* of (1) return and (2) risk associated with all possible portfolio combinations.

b. If the returns of assets V and W are *uncorrelated* (correlation coefficient = 0), describe the *approximate range* of (1) return and (2) risk associated with all possible portfolio combinations.

c. If the returns of assets V and W are *perfectly negatively correlated* (correlation coefficient = −1), describe the *range* of (1) return and (2) risk associated with all possible portfolio combinations.

P5.9 Imagine you wish to estimate the betas for two investments, A and B. You have gathered the following return data for the market and for each of the investments over the past 10 years, 1996–2005.

		Historical Returns	
		Investment	
Year	Market	A	B
1996	6%	11%	16%
1997	2	8	11
1998	−13	−4	−10
1999	−4	3	3
2000	−8	0	−3
2001	16	19	30
2002	10	14	22
2003	15	18	29
2004	8	12	19
2005	13	17	26

a. On a set of market return (*x*-axis)–investment return (*y*-axis) axes, use the data to draw the characteristic lines for investments A and B on the same set of axes.

b. Use the characteristic lines from part **a** to estimate the betas for investments A and B.

c. Use the betas found in part **b** to comment on the relative risks of investments A and B.

P5.10 You are evaluating two possible stock investments, Buyme Co. and Getit Corp. Buyme Co. has an expected return of 14%, and a beta of 1. Getit Corp. has an expected return of 14%, and a beta of 1.2. Based only on this data, which stock should you buy and why?

P5.11 Referring to Problem 5.10 above, if you expected a significant market rally, would your decision be altered? Explain.

P5.12 A security has a beta of 1.20. Is this security more or less risky than the market? Explain. Assess the impact on the required return of this security in each of the following cases.

a. The market return increases by 15%.

b. The market return decreases by 8%.

c. The market return remains unchanged.

P5.13 Assume the betas for securities A, B, and C are as shown here.

Security	Beta
A	1.40
B	0.80
C	−0.90

a. Calculate the change in return for each security if the market experiences an increase in its rate of return of 13.2% over the next period.
b. Calculate the change in return for each security if the market experiences a decrease in its rate of return of 10.8% over the next period.
c. Rank and discuss the relative risk of each security on the basis of your findings. Which security might perform best during an economic downturn? Explain.

LG 3   **LG 4**   **P5.14** Referring to Problem 5.13 above, assume you have a portfolio with $20,000 invested in each of Investment A, B, and C. What is your portfolio beta?

LG 3   **P5.15** Referring to Problem 5.14 above, using the portfolio beta, what would you expect the value of your portfolio to be if the market rallied 20%? Declined 20%

LG 3   **P5.16** Use the capital asset pricing model (CAPM) to find the required return for each of the following securities in light of the data given.

Security	Risk-Free Rate	Market Return	Beta
A	5%	8%	1.30
B	8	13	0.90
C	9	12	−0.20
D	10	15	1.00
E	6	10	0.60

LG 3   **P5.17** Bob is reviewing his portfolio of investments, which include certain stocks and bonds. He has a large amount tied up in U.S. Treasury bills paying 3%. He is considering moving some of his funds from the T-bills into a stock. The stock has a beta of 1.25. If Bob expects a return of 14% from the stock (a little better than the current market return of 13%), should he buy the stock or leave his funds in the T-bill?

LG 3   **P5.18** The risk-free rate is currently 7%, and the market return is 12%. Assume you are considering the following investment vehicles.

Investment Vehicle	Beta
A	1.50
B	1.00
C	0.75
D	0
E	2.00

a. Which vehicle is most risky? Least risky?
b. Use the capital asset pricing model (CAPM) to find the required return on each of the investment vehicles.
c. Draw the security market line (SML), using your findings in part **b**.
d. On the basis of your findings in part **c**, what relationship exists between risk and return? Explain.

LG 4   **P5.19** Portfolios A through J, which are listed in the following table along with their returns (r_p) and risk (measured by the standard deviation, s_p), represent all currently available portfolios in the feasible or attainable set.

Portfolio	Return (r_p)	Risk (s_p)
A	9%	8%
B	3	3
C	14	10
D	12	14
E	7	11
F	11	6
G	10	12
H	16	16
I	5	7
J	8	4

a. Plot the *feasible* or *attainable set* represented by these data on a set of portfolio risk, s_p (*x*-axis)–portfolio return, r_p (*y*-axis) axes.

b. Draw the *efficient frontier* on the graph in part **a**.

c. Which portfolios lie on the efficient frontier? Why do these portfolios dominate all others in the feasible or attainable set?

d. How would an investor's *utility function* or *risk-indifference curves* be used with the efficient frontier to find the optimal portfolio?

P5.20 For his portfolio, David Finney randomly selected securities from all those listed on the New York Stock Exchange. He began with one security and added securities one by one until a total of 20 securities were held in the portfolio. After each security was added, David calculated the portfolio standard deviation, s_p. The calculated values follow.

Number of Securities	Portfolio Risk, s_p (%)	Number of Securities	Portfolio Risk, s_p (%)
1	14.50	11	7.00
2	13.30	12	6.80
3	12.20	13	6.70
4	11.20	14	6.65
5	10.30	15	6.60
6	9.50	16	6.56
7	8.80	17	6.52
8	8.20	18	6.50
9	7.70	19	6.48
10	7.30	20	6.47

a. On a set of axes showing the number of securities in the portfolio (*x*-axis) and portfolio risk, s_p (*y*-axis), plot the portfolio risk data given in the preceding table.

b. Divide the total portfolio risk in the graph into its *nondiversifiable* and *diversifiable* risk components, and label each of these on the graph.

c. Describe which of the two risk components is the *relevant risk*, and explain why it is relevant. How much of this risk exists in David Finney's portfolio?

P5.21 If portfolio A has a beta of $+1.50$ and portfolio Z has a beta of -1.50, what do the two values indicate? If the return on the market rises by 20%, what impact, if any, would this have on the returns from portfolios A and Z? Explain.

P5.22 Stock A has a beta of 0.80, stock B has a beta of 1.40, and stock C has a beta of -0.30.

a. Rank these stocks from the most risky to the least risky.

b. If the return on the market portfolio increases by 12%, what change in the return for each of the stocks would you expect?

c. If the return on the market portfolio declines by 5%, what change in the return for each of the stocks would you expect?

d. If you felt the stock market was about to experience a significant decline, which stock would you be most likely to add to your portfolio? Why?

e. If you anticipated a major stock market rally, which stock would you be most likely to add to your portfolio? Why?

LG 4

P5.23 Rose Berry is attempting to evaluate two possible portfolios consisting of the same five assets but held in different proportions. She is particularly interested in using beta to compare the risk of the portfolios and, in this regard, has gathered the following data:

		Portfolio Weights (%)	
Asset	Asset Beta	Portfolio A	Portfolio B
1	1.30	10	30
2	0.70	30	10
3	1.25	10	20
4	1.10	10	20
5	0.90	40	20
Total		100	100

a. Calculate the betas for portfolios A and B.

b. Compare the risk of each portfolio to the market as well as to each other. Which portfolio is more risky?

LG 3

P5.24 Referring to Problem 5.23 above, if the risk-free rate is 2% and the market return is 12%, calculate the required return for each portfolio using the CAPM.

LG 4

P5.25 Referring to Problem 5.24 above, assume you now have the following annual returns (r_j) for each investment.

Asset (j)	r_j
1	16.5%
2	12.0%
3	15.0%
4	13.0%
5	7.0%

Using your finding from Problem 5.24 and the additional return data, determine which portfolio you would choose and explain why.

**See the text Web site
(www.aw-bc.com/gitman_joehnk) for Web exercises
that deal with *modern portfolio concepts*.**

Case Problem 5.1

LG 3   LG 4

Traditional Versus Modern Portfolio Theory: Who's Right?

Walt Davies and Shane O'Brien are district managers for Lee, Inc. Over the years, as they moved through the firm's sales organization, they became (and still remain) close friends. Walt, who is 33 years old, currently lives in Princeton, New Jersey. Shane, who is 35, lives in Houston, Texas. Recently, at the national sales meeting, they were discussing various company matters, as well as bringing each other up to date on their families, when the subject of investments came up. Each had always been fascinated by the stock market, and now that they had achieved some degree of financial success, they had begun actively investing. As they discussed their investments, Walt said he felt the only way an individual who does not have hundreds of thousands of dollars can invest safely is to buy mutual fund shares. He emphasized that to be safe, a person needs to hold a broadly diversified portfolio and that only those with a lot of money and time can achieve independently the diversification that can be readily obtained by purchasing mutual fund shares.

Shane totally disagreed. He said, "Diversification! Who needs it?" He felt that what one must do is look carefully at stocks possessing desired risk-return characteristics and then invest all one's money in the single best stock. Walt told him he was crazy. He said, "There is no way to measure risk conveniently—you're just gambling." Shane disagreed. He explained how his stockbroker had acquainted him with beta, which is a measure of risk. Shane said that the higher the beta, the more risky the stock, and therefore the higher its return. By looking up the betas for potential stock investments on the Internet, he can pick stocks that have an acceptable risk level for him. Shane explained that with beta, one does not need to diversify; one merely needs to be willing to accept the risk reflected by beta and then hope for the best. The conversation continued, with Walt indicating that although he knew nothing about beta, he didn't believe one could safely invest in a single stock. Shane continued to argue that his broker had explained to him that betas can be calculated not just for a single stock but also for a portfolio of stocks, such as a mutual fund. He said, "What's the difference between a stock with a beta of, say, 1.20 and a mutual fund with a beta of 1.20? They both have the same risk and should therefore provide similar returns."

As Walt and Shane continued to discuss their differing opinions relative to investment strategy, they began to get angry with each other. Neither was able to convince the other that he was right. The level of their voices now raised, they attracted the attention of the company vice-president of finance, Elinor Green, who was standing nearby. She came over and indicated she had overheard their argument about investments and thought that, given her expertise on financial matters, she might be able to resolve their disagreement. She asked them to explain the crux of their disagreement, and each reviewed his own viewpoint. After hearing their views, Elinor responded, "I have some good news and some bad news for each of you. There is some validity to what each of you says, but there also are some errors in each of your explanations. Walt tends to support the traditional approach to portfolio management. Shane's views are more supportive of modern portfolio theory." Just then, the company president interrupted them, needing to talk to Elinor immediately. Elinor apologized for having to leave and offered to continue their discussion later that evening.

Questions

a. Analyze Walt's argument and explain why a mutual fund investment may be over-diversified. Also explain why one does not necessarily have to have hundreds of thousands of dollars to diversify adequately.

b. Analyze Shane's argument and explain the major error in his logic relative to the use of beta as a substitute for diversification. Explain the key assumption underlying the use of beta as a risk measure.

c. Briefly describe the traditional approach to portfolio management, and relate it to the approaches supported by Walt and Shane.

d. Briefly describe modern portfolio theory (MPT), and relate it to the approaches supported by Walt and Shane. Be sure to mention diversifiable risk, nondiversifiable risk, and total risk, along with the role of beta.

e. Explain how the traditional approach and modern portfolio theory can be blended into an approach to portfolio management that might prove useful to the individual investor. Relate this to reconciling Walt's and Shane's differing points of view.

Case Problem 5.2

LG 3   LG 4

LG 5   LG 6

Susan Lussier's Inherited Portfolio: Does It Meet Her Needs?

Susan Lussier is a 35-year-old divorcée currently employed as a tax attorney for a major oil and gas exploration company. She has no children and earns nearly $135,000 per year from her salary and from participation in the company's drilling activities. Divorced only a year, Susan has found being single quite exciting. An expert on oil and gas taxation, she is not worried about job security—she is content with her income and finds it adequate to allow her to buy and do whatever she wishes. Her current philosophy is to live each day to its fullest, not concerning herself with retirement, which is too far in the future to require her current attention.

A month ago, Susan's only surviving parent, her father, was killed in a sailing accident. He had retired in La Jolla, California, 2 years earlier and had spent most of his time sailing. Prior to retirement, he managed a children's clothing manufacturing firm in South Carolina. Upon retirement he sold his stock in the firm and invested the proceeds in a security portfolio that provided him with supplemental retirement income of over $30,000 per year. In his will, which incidentally had been drafted by Susan a number of years earlier, he left his entire estate to her. The estate was structured in such a way that in addition to a few family heirlooms, Susan received a security portfolio having a market value of nearly $350,000 and about $10,000 in cash.

Susan's father's portfolio contained 10 securities: 5 bonds, 2 common stocks, and 3 mutual funds. The accompanying table lists the securities and their key characteristics. The common stocks were issued by large, mature, well-known firms that had exhibited continuing patterns of dividend payment over the past 5 years. The stocks offered only moderate growth potential—probably no more than 2% to 3% appreciation per year. The mutual funds in the portfolio were income funds invested in diversified portfolios of income-oriented stocks and bonds. They provided stable streams of dividend income but offered little opportunity for capital appreciation.

Now that Susan owns the portfolio, she wishes to determine whether it is suitable for her situation. She realizes that the high level of income provided by the portfolio will be taxed at a rate (federal plus state) of about 40%. Because she does not currently need it, Susan plans to invest the after-tax income primarily in common stocks offering high capital gain potential. During the coming years she clearly needs to avoid generating taxable income. (Susan is already paying out a sizable portion of her current income in taxes.) She feels fortunate to have received the portfolio and wants to make certain it provides her with the maximum benefits, given her financial situation. The $10,000 cash left to her will be especially useful in paying broker's commissions associated with making portfolio adjustments.

Case 5.2 The Securities Portfolio That Susan Lussier Inherited

		Bonds				
Par Value	Issue	S&P Rating	Interest Income	Quoted Price	Total Cost	Current Yield
$40,000	Delta Power and Light 10.125% due 2023	AA	$ 4,050	98.000	$ 39,200	10.33%
30,000	Mountain Water 9.750% due 2015	A	2,925	102.000	30,600	9.56
50,000	California Gas 9.500% due 2010	AAA	4,750	97.000	48,500	9.79
20,000	Trans-Pacific Gas 10.000% due 2021	AAA	2,000	99.000	19,800	10.10
20,000	Public Service 9.875% due 2011	AA	1,975	100.000	20,000	9.88

		Common Stocks					
Number of Shares	Company	Dividend per Share	Dividend Income	Price per Share	Total Cost	Beta	Dividend Yield
2,000	International Supply	$2.40	$ 4,800	$ 22	$ 44,900	0.97	10.91%
3,000	Black Motor	1.50	4,500	17	52,000	0.85	8.82

		Mutual Funds					
Number of Shares	Fund	Dividend per Share	Dividend Income	Price per Share	Total Cost	Beta	Dividend Yield
2,000	International Capital Income A Fund	$ .80	$ 1,600	$ 10	$ 20,000	1.02	8.00%
1,000	Grimner Special Income Fund	2.00	2,000	15	15,000	1.10	7.50
4,000	Ellis Diversified Income Fund	1.20	4,800	12	48,000	0.90	10.00

Total annual income: $33,400   Portfolio value: $338,000   Portfolio current yield: 9.88%

Questions

a. Briefly assess Susan's financial situation and develop a portfolio objective for her that is consistent with her needs.

b. Evaluate the portfolio left to Susan by her father. Assess its apparent objective and evaluate how well it may be doing in fulfilling this objective. Use the total cost values to describe the asset allocation scheme reflected in the portfolio. Comment on the risk, return, and tax implications of this portfolio.

c. If Susan decided to invest in a security portfolio consistent with her needs—indicated in response to question **a**—describe the nature and mix, if any, of securities you would recommend she purchase. What asset allocation scheme would result from your recommendation? Discuss the risk, return, and tax implications of such a portfolio.

d. Compare the nature of the security portfolio inherited by Susan, from the response to question **b**, with what you believe would be an appropriate security portfolio for her, from the response to question **c**.

e. What recommendations would you give Susan about the inherited portfolio? Explain the steps she should take to adjust the portfolio to her needs.

Excel with Spreadsheets

In the previous chapter's spreadsheet problem, you helped Laura evaluate the risk-return tradeoff for three stand-alone securities. An alternative for Laura is to look at the investment as a portfolio of both IBM and HP and not as stand-alone situations. Laura's professor suggests that she use the capital asset pricing model to define the required returns for the two companies (refer to Equations 5.3 and 5.3a).

$$r_j = R_F + [b_j \times (r_m - R_F)]$$

Laura measures R_F using the current long-term Treasury bond return of 5% and measures r_m using the average return on the S&P 500 Index from her calculations in the Chapter 4 spreadsheet problem. She researches a source for the beta information and follows these steps:

- Go to moneycentral.msn.com.
- Within the "Get Quote" box, type IBM and press "Go."
- In the left column, look under "Research" and choose "Company Report."
- Under the heading of "Stock Activity," find the "Volatility (beta)" figure.
- Repeat the same steps for the HP stock.

Questions

a. What are the beta values for IBM and HP? Assume that the beta for the S&P 500 Index is 1.0. Using the CAPM, create a spreadsheet to determine the required rates of return for both IBM and HP.

b. Laura has decided that the portfolio will be distributed between IBM and HP in a 60% and 40% split, respectively. Hence, a weighted average can be calculated for both the returns and betas of the portfolio. This concept is shown in the spreadsheet for Table 5.2, which can be viewed at www.aw-bc.com/gitman_joehnk. **Create a spreadsheet** using the following models for the calculations:

$$\text{war} = w_i * r_i + w_j * r_j$$

where:

   war = weighted average required rate of return for the portfolio
   w_i = weight of security i in the portfolio
   r_i = required return of security i in the portfolio
   w_j = weight of security j in the portfolio
   r_j = required return of security j in the portfolio

$$\text{wab} = w_i * b_i + w_j * b_j$$

where:

   wab = weighted average beta for the portfolio
   w_i = weight of security i in the portfolio
   b_i = beta for security i
   w_j = weight of security j in the portfolio
   b_j = beta for security j

TRADING ONLINE WITH OTIS

To achieve the highest possible return with an acceptable level of risk, a portfolio should be well diversified. An efficiently diversified portfolio should include stocks selected from a broad range of sectors, including foreign markets, and an understanding of the roles that both non-diversifiable and diversifiable risk play. An investor can eliminate diversifiable risk through diversification. Nondiversifiable risk cannot be eliminated and, therefore, is of primary importance in managing the portfolio.

Exercises

1. Sign onto OTIS and select "sectors." Follow the directions for uploading sector assignments. Determine the portfolio's exposure to inter-industry diversification by assessing the sector for each of your stocks. If necessary, rebalance the portfolio to ensure that it represents a broad range of industries.

2. Obtain the beta for each of the equities in your portfolio by visiting a financial Web site such as www.esignal.com. In the appropriate row for each investment, record the beta. Can you make a statement about the risk and return of each of these securities based on its beta? (*Hint:* See page 199 in the text.)

3. Calculate the weight of each investment in the portfolio, being certain that the weights total 100%. Designate a column for the weights and list each investment's weight.

4. Generate another column for the portfolio beta and program a formula to determine the portfolio beta. Describe how sensitive your portfolio is to the market. (*Hint:* See page 209 in the text to see how to construct a portfolio beta.)

CHAPTER 6

COMMON STOCKS

ear or bull market? Lately, it's been hard to tell! One day the headlines proclaim, "Dow Industrials Surge." The next day, investors may read, "Stocks, Bonds Slip Back on Fed Move." Other articles discuss "Is the Rally Real?", as some analysts say "yes" while others call recent events a mere correction.

Take, for example, two seasoned mutual fund managers: Walter McCormick and John Rutledge. In March 2003, McCormick believed that the upward trend in the major market averages marked the beginning of a rally and pushed his firm to buy more stocks. Rutledge, in contrast, advised caution: "I am not sure we have seen the bottom; I think we could see new, lower lows."

The irony: Both fund managers work at Evergreen Investments. Their differing views were by no means unusual. "Do we have lots of positive economic reports signaling improvement? So far, no," said Clare Zempel, chief investment strategist at Robert W. Baird, a Milwaukee firm. "But I think the odds are extremely high . . . that this postwar rebound is sustainable." Through late summer 2003, McCormick and Zempel appeared to be right. In fact, both blue-chip stocks and technology issues hit new highs in August. Rutledge benefited from the gains—even as he held firm to his conviction that a decline was imminent—but saw his fund returns lag considerably behind those of his peers (his return from January 1 to August 22, 2003, was about 18%, compared to the category-average of 37.5%). McCormick's performance of 13.7% was just above his peer-group average, 13.4%.

How do you choose stocks during such confusing times? In boom times, it looked easy: Almost everything went up. During the bear market, investors wondered if they should still buy stocks. Regardless of market conditions, investors who place their money at risk must learn how to gather, analyze, and interpret information about each company they consider and the industry in which it operates. This chapter introduces you to common stocks and the key concepts and principles of investing in these complex but potentially rewarding securities.

Sources: E. S. Browning, "Dow Industrials Surge a Record 499.19," *The Wall Street Journal*, March 17, 2000, p. C1; E. S. Browning, "Experts Duel Over Fate of Bellwether Rally," *The Wall Street Journal*, June 16, 2003, pp. C1, C3; "Fund Returns," *Morningstar.com*, August 23, 2003, downloaded from www.morningstar.com; and James M. Pethokoukis, "Is the Rally Real?" *Newsweek*, July 7, 2003, pp. 16–17.

What Stocks Have to Offer

residual owners
owners/stockholders of a firm, who are entitled to dividend income and a prorated share of the firm's earnings only after all other obligations have been met.

The basic investment attribute of common stocks is that they enable investors to participate in the profits of the firm. Every shareholder is a part owner of the firm and, as such, is entitled to a piece of the firm's profits. This claim on income is not without limitations, however, because common stockholders are really the **residual owners** of the company. That is, they are entitled to dividend income and a share of the company's earnings only after all other corporate obligations have been met. Equally important, as residual owners, holders of common stock have no guarantee that they will ever receive any return on their investment. The challenge, of course, is to find stocks that will provide the kind of return you're looking for. That's no easy task, as there are literally thousands of actively traded stocks to choose from.

The Appeal of Common Stocks

Even in spite of the recent (2000–2002) bear market, common stocks remain a popular form of investing, used by literally millions of individual investors. They are popular, in part, because they offer investors the opportunity to tailor their investment programs to meet individual needs and preferences. Given the size and diversity of the stock market, it's safe to say that no matter what the investment objective, there are common stocks to fit the bill. For people living off their investment holdings, stocks provide a way of earning a steady stream of current income (from the dividends they produce). For investors less concerned about current income, common stocks can serve as the basis for long-run accumulation of wealth. With this strategy, stocks are used very much like a savings account: Investors buy stock for the long haul as a way to earn not only dividends but also a steady flow of capital gains. These investors recognize that stocks have a tendency to go up in price over time, and they simply position themselves to take advantage of that fact. Indeed, it is this potential for capital gains that is the real draw for most investors. Whereas dividends can provide a steady stream of income, the big returns—under normal, long-term market conditions—come from capital gains. And few securities can match common stocks when it comes to capital gains.

Putting Stock Price Behavior in Perspective

Given the underlying nature of common stocks, when the market is strong, investors can generally expect to benefit from steady price appreciation. A good example is the performance that took place in 1999, when the market, as measured by the Dow Jones Industrial Average (DJIA), went up by more than 25%. Unfortunately, when markets falter, so do investor returns. Just look what happened over the 3-year period from early 2000 through late 2002, when the market (again, as measured by the DJIA) fell some 38%. Excluding dividends, that means a $100,000 investment would have declined in value to a little over $60,000. That hurts!

Make no mistake about it: The market does have its bad days, and sometimes those bad days seem to go on for months. Even though it may not always appear to be so, those bad days *really are the exception rather than the rule*. That was certainly the case over the 54-year period from 1950 through mid-2003, when the Dow went down (for the year) just 16 times. That's less than 30% of the time; the other 70% the market was up—anywhere from 2% on the year to more than 40%! True, there is some risk and price volatility (even in good markets), but that's the price you pay for all the upside potential. Consider, for example, the behavior of the market from 1982 through early 2000. Starting in August 1982, when the Dow stood at 777, this market saw the DJIA climb nearly 11,000 points to a high of 11,723, reached in January 2000. This turned out to be one of the longest bull markets in history, as the DJIA grew (over 18 years) at an average annual rate of nearly 17%. Yet, even in this market, there were some off days, and even a few off years. But, clearly, they were the exception rather than the rule.

From Stock Prices to Stock Returns

Our discussion so far has centered on *stock prices*, but what are even more important to investors are *stock returns*, which take into account not only price behavior but also dividend income. Table 6.1 uses the DJIA to show annual market returns over the 54-year period from 1950 to 2003. In addition to total returns, the table breaks market performance down into the two basic sources of return: dividends and capital gains. These figures, of course, reflect

TABLE 6.1   Annual Returns in the Stock Market, 1950–2003 (returns based on performance of the DJIA)

Year	Rate of Return from Dividends	Rate of Return from Capital Gains	Total Rate of Return	Year	Rate of Return from Dividends	Rate of Return from Capital Gains	Total Rate of Return
2003	2.20%	8.72%	10.92%	1976	4.12%	17.86%	21.98%
2002	2.27	−16.76	−14.49	1975	4.39	38.32	42.71
2001	1.81	−7.10	−5.29	1974	6.12	−27.57	−21.45
2000	1.61	−6.18	−4.58	1973	4.15	−16.58	−12.43
1999	1.47	25.22	26.69	1972	3.16	14.58	17.74
1998	1.65	16.10	17.75	1971	3.47	6.11	9.58
1997	1.72	22.64	24.36	1970	3.76	4.82	8.58
1996	2.03	26.01	28.04	1969	4.24	−15.19	−10.95
1995	2.27	33.45	35.72	1968	3.32	4.27	7.59
1994	2.75	2.14	4.89	1967	3.33	15.20	18.53
1993	2.65	13.72	16.37	1966	4.06	−18.94	−14.88
1992	3.05	4.17	7.22	1965	2.95	10.88	13.83
1991	3.00	20.32	23.32	1964	3.57	14.57	18.14
1990	3.94	−4.34	−0.40	1963	3.07	17.00	20.07
1989	3.74	26.96	30.70	1962	3.57	−10.81	−7.24
1988	3.67	11.85	15.52	1961	3.11	18.71	21.82
1987	3.67	2.26	5.93	1960	3.47	−9.34	−5.87
1986	3.54	22.58	26.12	1959	3.05	16.40	19.45
1985	4.01	27.66	31.67	1958	3.43	33.96	37.39
1984	5.00	−3.74	1.26	1957	4.96	−12.77	−7.81
1983	4.47	20.27	24.74	1956	4.60	2.27	6.87
1982	5.17	19.60	24.77	1955	4.42	20.77	25.19
1981	6.42	−9.23	−2.81	1954	4.32	43.96	48.28
1980	5.64	14.93	20.57	1953	5.73	−3.77	1.96
1979	6.08	4.19	10.27	1952	5.29	8.42	13.71
1978	6.03	−3.15	2.88	1951	6.07	14.37	20.44
1977	5.51	−17.27	−11.76	1950	6.85	17.63	24.48

Note: Total return figures are based on both dividend income *and* capital gains (or losses); all figures are compiled from DJIA performance information, as obtained from *Barron's* and the *Wall Street Journal;* 2003 figures are through the second quarter (June 30) of the year.

the *general behavior of the market as a whole,* not necessarily that of *individual stocks.* Think of them as the return behavior on a well-balanced portfolio of common stocks.

The numbers show a market that, over the past 54 years, has provided annual returns ranging from a low of −21.45% (in 1974) to a high of +48.28% (in 1954). Breaking down the returns into dividends and capital gains reveals, not surprisingly, that the big returns (or losses) come from capital gains. Overall, as Table 6.2 shows, *stocks have provided average returns of around 11% over the 50-year period from 1953–2002.* But as can be seen in the table, the 1980s and 90s definitely were not average, especially not the last half of the nineties. Indeed, while the first 5 years of the decade produced below-average returns of "only" 10% per year, the second half turned in annual returns of over 26%. That all changed in 2000, however, when a bear market took hold, and the return on the Dow fell to a *minus* 4.3%. Factor that decline into the most recent 5-year holding period and you can see (in Table 6.2) what happened— from 1998 through mid-2003, the average annual return on the DJIA amounted to a measly 1.7%.

Keep in mind that the numbers here represent market performance; *individual* stocks can and often do perform quite differently. But at least the averages give us a benchmark against which we can assess current stock returns and our own expectations. For example, if a return of 10% to 12% can be considered a good long-term estimate for stocks, then *sustained* returns of 15% to 18% should definitely be viewed as extraordinary. (These higher returns are possible, of course, but to get them, investors must either take on more risk or hope for a continuation of the nineties bull market.) Likewise, long-run stock returns of only 6% to 8% should probably be viewed as substandard. If that's the best you think you can do, then you may want to consider sticking with bonds or CDs, where you'll earn almost as much, but with less risk.

TABLE 6.2	Holding Period Returns in the Stock Market 1950-2003		
Holding Periods	Average Annual Returns	Cumulative Returns	Amount to Which $10,000 Will Grow
5(+) years: 1998–2003	1.7%	8.6%	$ 10,859
3(+) years: 2000–2003	*−4.3*	*−14.3*	*8,572*
5 years: 1995–1999	26.4	222.4	32,238
5 years: 1990–1994	10.0	60.7	16,075
10 years: 1993–2002	11.8	204.0	30,399
15 years: 1988–2002	12.8	504.6	60,465
25 years: 1978–2002	13.2	2,128.4	222,841
50 years: 1953–2002	10.7	15,806.9	1,590,690
The 1990s: 1990–1999	18.3	438.9	53,897
The 1980s: 1980–1989	17.2	390.5	49,049
The 1970s: 1970–1979	5.3	67.9	16,792
The 1960s: 1960–1969	5.2	66.0	16,602
The 1950s: 1950–1959	18.0	421.7	52,171

Note: Average annual return figures are fully compounded returns and assume that all dividend income and capital gains are automatically reinvested. All figures compiled from DJIA performance information, as obtained from *Barron's* and the *Wall Street Journal*; 2003 data through the second quarter.

INVESTING IN ACTION

ANATOMY OF A MARKET MELTDOWN

It seemed like the bull market that would never end. Between August 1982 and January 2000, the Dow Jones Industrial Average (DJIA) rose an average of 17% per year. When the U.S. economy really took off in 1995, the stock markets of the late 1990s carried investors on a wild ride. Share prices moved sharply upward as the DJIA broke through successive 1,000-point barriers, peaking at 11,723 on January 14, 2000. Annual returns from 1995 to 1999 averaged about 26%. Technology stocks led the way, and investors cheered as on paper at least they made impressive gains—even as Alan Greenspan, chairman of the Federal Reserve Board, cautioned against the "irrational exuberance" in the markets.

Throughout the 5-year run-up, naysayers warned that the market euphoria couldn't last forever. Each year investors wondered when the bull market would stumble, and each year it continued to surge ahead, spurred on by a strong economy and a relatively peaceful world situation. Excited investors bought stock in technology and Internet companies, many only a year or two old with no track records, products, or profits. Novices and pros alike ignored warning signs along the way. "In the '90s, the public got sucked into that vortex of speculation where they thought that 'this time is different' and that we would never have another recession," commented Ned Riley, chief investment strategist at State Street Global Advisors in Boston.

The year 2000 began with the DJIA and Nasdaq Composite reaching all-time highs in January and March, respectively. The Federal Reserve increased the money supply to guard against possible year-2000 computer problems, which contributed to the still-growing tech bubble. When the market peaked, tech stocks accounted for more than 40% of the S&P 500's value. But under Wall Street's slick surface were rumblings that all was not well. In March 2000, the Fed raised interest rates to curb inflation, and businesses reported decreasing investment in technology.

In the weeks that followed, the Nasdaq Composite lost 33% of its value. Dot-com sensations suffered; Yahoo!, for example, lost 40% of its market value in just 3 weeks. But blue chips held firm, leading market strategists to speculate whether the decline was a warning sign or another brief setback. Money continued to flow into stocks as a rebound followed each sharp drop. This up-and-down pattern continued for the next 3 years. For example, the DJIA took a record 499.19-point (4.9%) leap in mid-March 2000, but then resumed its downward spiral.

In the same way that tech stocks had led the market to new heights, so they pulled it down when the dot-com bubble burst. A comeback in spring and summer 2000 drew investors back to tech mainstays, but bad news such as lower sales at Dell Computer and the antitrust suit against Microsoft soon made investors reconsider their tech stock positions. By year-end 2000, shares of Oracle and Cisco had dropped 40%, and Intel's stock price had plunged 60%.

Once again the blue chips rallied, and the DJIA ended the year down just 8% from its high, although the more tech-heavy S&P 500 was down 14% and the Nasdaq had declined by 51%. Investors began to abandon tech companies that offered promises rather than earnings, turning to sectors that seemed safer—for example, financial institutions and utilities. One exciting new area was energy, where natural gas trading companies like Enron and Dynegy were revitalizing the utility industry.

The first of a series of Federal Reserve interest rate cuts in January 2001 sent the markets soaring. Subsequent cuts did little to stimulate the economy, however, and the country entered into a recession. Unable to revive sales, companies cut costs to keep earnings from falling farther. A spring rally was again short-lived; even blue chips provided no safe haven for investors. The markets continued to bounce investors around through the summer months.

On September 11, 2001, the financial markets suffered another blow—a physical one—as terrorists struck the World Trade Center towers in the heart of New York's financial district. A stunned United States and world went into shock. The markets closed for about a week, amid great uncertainty and insecurity. When they reopened, the Dow dropped another 14%. By September 2001, investors had lost more than $6 trillion since the January 2000 market peak.

To bolster the financial markets, the Fed again poured money into the system, sparking a rally

continued on next page

INVESTING IN ACTION

continued from previous page

that amazed everyone in light of the shocking terrorist attacks. The Nasdaq jumped 45% between September 2001 and January 2002, and the DJIA and S&P 500 were also up considerably. Was the market finally going to turn bullish again?

Investors had little time to savor the latest rebound, however. The battered markets soon faced a very different setback: corporate scandals that severely undermined investor confidence. The first to erupt involved Enron, the new-breed energy company. Under its glittering façade Enron was manipulating accounting rules to create the illusion of growth and enhance its financial statements. As Enron's financial games and phantom earnings became public knowledge in late 2001, its financial house of cards tumbled down. Along with it came the demise of Arthur Andersen, its once prestigious auditor. In addition, several other financial institutions found themselves under investigation for their involvement in Enron's off-balance-sheet deals.

Alarmed at how Enron had obscured financial information in its published financial reports, investors began to question the reliability of corporate financial reporting in general. Before long executives from Adelphia, Qwest, Tyco, WorldCom, Xerox, and other companies joined the rogue's gallery of corporate financial wrongdoers. A crackdown on stock analyst malfeasance by New York State's attorney general further damaged investor confidence. Money drained out of the equity markets and into bonds and other investment vehicles.

Matters went downhill from there, as the DJIA slid to 7,286 on October 9, 2002—a 38% decline. Likewise, the S&P 500 and Nasdaq, with their larger numbers of technology stocks, dropped 49% and 77% from their peaks, respectively.

What or who is to blame for this bear market, which ranks among the worst in market history? Fingers now point in many directions, as events unrelated to fiscal or monetary policy—among them the September 11 and subsequent terrorist threats, corporate scandals, and the war in Iraq—joined with the more traditional causes to create a sense of financial insecurity that weakened investor faith in the financial system. From 1999 through 2002, the DJIA closed lower at year end—the first time since 1941 it had declined in three successive years. The total return on investment for stocks in the DJIA plummeted from 27.2% in 1999 to –15% in 2002.

Every sector, including the most solid blue chips, suffered greatly from the weakened economy, corporate scandals, and lower earnings. About 70% of stocks on major exchanges closed down for the year. Jaded investors looked to companies that paid dividends, not those promising astronomical growth rates.

In March 2003, after a few more false starts, the markets appeared to be moving steadily upward. By mid-September, the DJIA was up 16% for the year, while the S&P 500 posted an 18% gain and the Nasdaq composite saw growth of 39%. As noted in the chapter opener, however, experts remained divided on whether the bear market was over or the rebound represented a short-lived correction.

While investor mania is nothing new—in the seventeenth century, for example, Dutch investors speculated on tulips, not tech stocks—the recent boom-and-bust cycle has implications for important shifts in the workings of the economy and the capital markets. The stock market's meteoric rise brought individual investors, many of whom previously shunned equities as too risky, into the picture. Everyone wanted a piece of the tech stock action, as young companies went public to much acclaim; VA Linux Systems, for example, saw its share price rise an unbelievable 698% on its first day of trading. Have investors now learned their lessons, and realize that they should look for a solid track record and not empty promises? Only time will tell.

CRITICAL THINKING QUESTION Describe the major factors that contributed to the 2000 market meltdown. What steps can you take to protect yourself in the future?

Sources: Ken Brown, "Company Blowups Abound, Rebounds Rare," *The Wall Street Journal*, January 2, 2003, p. R2; E. S. Browning, "Investors Seek Ray of Hope," *The Wall Street Journal*, January 2, 2003, p. R1; E. S. Browning, "Stocks, Bonds Slip on Fed Move," *The Wall Street Journal*, June 26, 2003, p. C1; E. S. Browning and Ianthe Jeanne Dugan, "Aftermath of a Market Mania," *The Wall Street Journal*, December 16, 2002, pp. C1, C13; James M. Pethokoukis, "Is the Rally Real?" *Newsweek*, July 7, 2003, pp. 16–17; "2001 Investment Scoreboard," *The Wall Street Journal*, January 2, 2002, p. R2; "2002 Investment Scoreboard," *The Wall Street Journal*, January 2, 2003, p. R2; and Penelope Wang, Amy Feldman, Jon Birger, and Aravind Adiga, "How Bad Is It?" *Money*, September 2002, p. 78.

The Dow, the S&P, and the Nasdaq

Most of our discussion in this chapter has been in terms of the DJIA, in large part because the Dow is such a widely followed measure of market performance. However, the DJIA is just one measure of market behavior, and it doesn't always tell the whole story. Two other closely followed market indexes are the S&P (Standard & Poor's) 500 and the Nasdaq Composite.

The problem with the Dow is that it captures the performance of a small, very select group of (just 30) large-cap stocks. Thus, it does not always reflect what's happening in the broad market. In contrast, the *S&P 500* tracks the performance of 500 of the very biggest and most important firms in the market and as such, is felt to be far more representative of market behavior. The *Nasdaq Composite*, on the other hand, tracks the behavior of many of this country's *tech stocks*, from the very largest, like Microsoft and Intel, to most of the newest (and much smaller) dot-com firms.

Comparative Performance of the Three Market Measures To see how these market measures performed in the 1990s and beyond (through mid-2003), take a look at Figure 6.1. The upper panel shows the DJIA relative to the S&P 500, and the lower panel shows the Dow relative to the Nasdaq Composite. Starting with the upper panel, we can see very similar performances for the DJIA and S&P 500 at least through 1999. But the S&P was much harder hit by the bear market and, as a result, a noticeable gap between these two measures started to appear in early 2000, and it grew wider over time. The net result was a sharply lower return for the S&P 500. Indeed, as seen in Table 6.3 (on page 242), there was about a 1½-point spread in comparative returns over the full 13½-year period, from 1990 through mid-2003. The Dow ended up with an average annual return of 11.77%, while the S&P turned in a 10.20% return.

While you would expect some similarity in the behavior of the Dow and the S&P (after all, both track the performance of large-cap stocks), you wouldn't expect the same performance when you match the Dow with the Nasdaq Composite—and you don't get it. But look at the lower panel of Figure 6.1: There's probably more similarity between the two measures than you'd expect—especially in the first 5 or 6 years. Indeed, note in Table 6.3 that in the first half of the decade, the DJIA and the Nasdaq Composite had almost the same average annual returns (10.26% for the Dow versus 10.58% for the Nasdaq). In fact, these two measures tracked one another fairly closely through 1997. Then, in 1998, they went their separate ways. High-tech stocks and the Nasdaq moved up sharply, while large-cap "old economy" stocks continued up at a far more modest pace. Thus, by the end of the decade, whereas the Dow had a very respectable 10-year return of 18.35%, the Nasdaq registered an incredible 24.50% rate of return (see Table 6.3). But then along came the bear—and the Nasdaq Composite was hammered. In a little more than a year, the huge positive spread between the Nasdaq and the Dow totally disappeared, and suddenly it was the Nasdaq trailing the Dow. As a result, over the full 13½-year period ending mid-2003, the DJIA actually beat the Nasdaq Composite by almost two full percentage points.

Bulls, Bubbles, and Bears The bull market that began in August 1982 continued on through the 1980s and into the early 1990s. Except for the length of this market, it didn't appear to be out of the ordinary in any other way—at

FIGURE 6.1 **Thirteen Years of the Dow, the S&P, and the Nasdaq (1990 to 2002,** *plus the first half of 2003***)**

Here's how the DJIA performed relative to the S&P 500 (top) and the Nasdaq Composite (bottom) in the 1990s, through mid-2003. As it turns out, the Dow held its own against not only the S&P 500, but also the tech-heavy Nasdaq Composite.

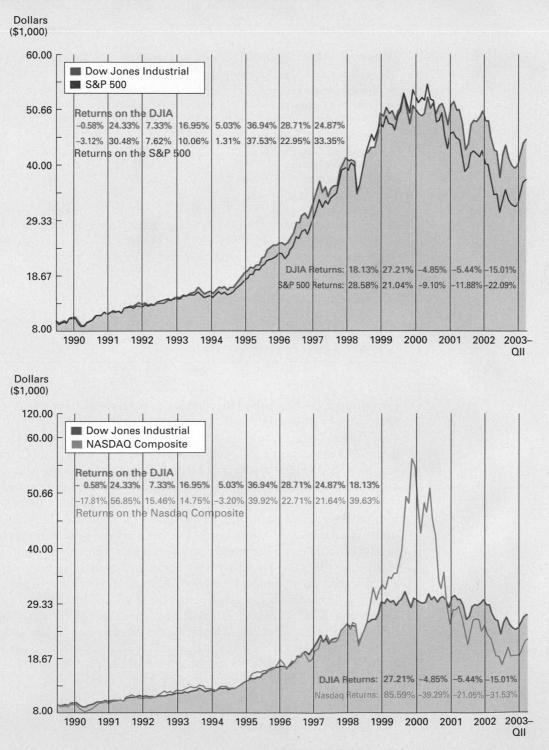

TABLE 6.3   Comparative Returns on the Dow, the S&P, and the Nasdaq

Holding Periods and Return Measures'	DJIA	S&P 500	Nasdaq Composite
Full 13½-Year Period: 1990 to Mid-2003			
• Average annual returns	11.77%	10.20%	9.88%
• Cumulative returns	349.28%	271.22%	256.82%
• Amount to which $10,000 will grow	$44,928	$37,122	$35,682
3½-Year Period: 2000 to Mid-2003			
• Average annual returns	−5.07%	−9.79%	−23.10%
• Cumulative returns	−16.64%	−30.26%	−60.12%
• Amount to which $10,000 will grow	$8,336	$6,974	$3,988
The Decade of the '90s: 1990–1999			
• Average annual returns	18.35%	18.20%	24.50%
• Cumulative returns	438.97%	432.33%	794.75%
• Amount to which $10,000 will grow	$53,897	$53,233	$89,475
Last Half of the Decade: 1995–1999			
• Average annual returns	27.03%	28.54%	40.71%
• Cumulative returns	230.75%	250.91%	441.16%
• Amount to which $10,000 will grow	$33,075	$35,091	$54,116
First Half of the Decade: 1990–1994			
• Average annual returns	10.26%	8.69%	10.58%
• Cumulative returns	62.96%	51.70%	65.34%
• Amount to which $10,000 will grow	$16,296	$15,170	$16,534

Note: Average annual return figures are fully compounded and assume that all dividends and capital gains are reinvested.
Source: Morningstar Principia Pro, June 2003.

least through the first half of the nineties. Indeed, the average rate of growth in share prices through 1994 was just 12 percent. But then in 1995, 1996, and 1997, things began to heat up, and the average rate of growth in share prices jumped to more than 27%. And by 1998, the *tech stock bubble* was in full bloom. This is readily apparent in Figure 6.2, which tracks the behavior of the DJIA and the Nasdaq Composite over the 10-year period ending mid-2003.

As can be seen, in August 1998, the tech-heavy Nasdaq Composite began to skyrocket, and over the next 18 months, went up an incredible 240%. Outright speculation was in firm control of the market—price/earnings multiples (a widely used measure of market sentiment) went through the roof. In fact, it really didn't seem to matter whether companies were generating earnings or not. These kinds of details, we were told, were no longer important; the only thing that seemed to matter was whether the stock had a technology or Internet connection. That, of course, all came to a screeching halt in early 2000. The three major market indexes—The DJIA, the Nasdaq Composite, and the S&P 500—all peaked in early 2000: the Dow at 11,722.98, the Nasdaq at 5,048.62, and the S&P at 1,527.46. Over the course of the next 32 months, through September 2002, these market measures performed as follows:

• The Dow fell 38%.

• The S&P dropped 49%.

• The Nasdaq fell 77%

FIGURE 6.2 | Bulls, Bubbles, and Bears

One of the greatest bull markets in history began on August 12, 1982, with the Dow at 777. It continued on through the 1980s and into the 1990s. But in late 1998, the bull turned into a bubble that lasted for about 18 months before it burst in early 2000, at which time the market went from a bubble to a full-fledged bear. (*Source:* Morningstar, Inc.)

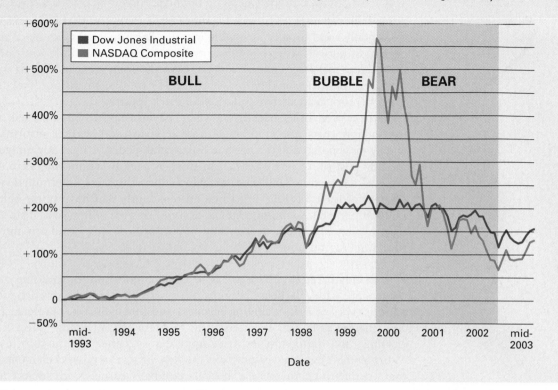

This period turned out to be one of the worst bear markets in recent history and clearly had a devastating effect on investor returns. All of the excesses that had built up over the last half of the 1990s were eliminated in a little more than 2½ years. But as the accompanying *Investing in Action* box (on pages 238–239) explains, this market was dealing with more than just old-fashioned speculation; it also had to cope with the September 11, 2001, terrorist attack on the United States, war, and various scandals, not to mention a weak economy.

The Pros and Cons of Stock Ownership

Investors own stocks for all sorts of reasons: They like the potential for capital gains that stocks offer, or their current income, or perhaps the high degree of market liquidity. But as with any investment vehicle, there is a good side to these securities and a bad side.

The Advantages of Stock Ownership Certainly one reason stocks are so appealing to investors is the substantial return opportunities they offer. As we just saw, stocks generally provide attractive, highly competitive returns over the long haul. Indeed, common stock returns compare very favorably to other investment outlets such as long-term corporate bonds and U.S. Treasury securities. For example, over the period from 1950 through 2003, high-grade corporate bonds averaged annual returns of around 6%—*about half that of common stocks.* Although long-term bonds sometimes outperform stocks on a year-by-year basis (as they did in the early to mid-1980s and again in 2001–2003, when interest rates were in a free fall), the opposite is true far more often than not; that is, stocks outperform bonds, and usually by a wide margin. Because stocks can be counted on over most periods to provide returns that exceed annual inflation rates, they make ideal inflation hedges. Indeed, over the long run, as long as inflation rates remain at reasonably low levels of 3% to 4%, stocks are likely to continue to produce attractive inflation-adjusted returns.

Stocks offer other benefits as well: They are easy to buy and sell, and the transaction costs are modest. Moreover, price and market information is widely disseminated in the news and financial media. A final advantage is that the unit cost of a share of common stock is usually within the reach of most individual investors. Unlike bonds, which normally carry minimum denominations of at least $1,000, and some mutual funds that have fairly hefty minimum investments, common stocks don't have such minimums. Instead, most stocks today are priced at less than $50 or $60 a share—and any number of shares, no matter how few, can be bought or sold.

The Disadvantages There are also some disadvantages to common stock ownership, with risk being perhaps the most significant. Stocks are subject to various types of risk, including business and financial risk, purchasing power risk, market risk, and event risk. All of these can adversely affect a stock's earnings and dividends, its price appreciation, and, of course, the rate of return earned by an investor. Even the best of stocks possess elements of risk that are difficult to overcome, because company earnings are subject to many factors, including government control and regulation, foreign competition,

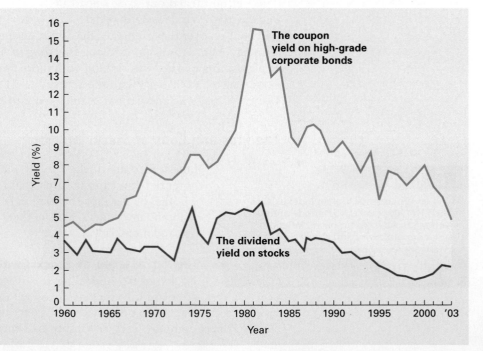

FIGURE 6.3

The Current Income of Stocks and Bonds

Clearly, the level of current income (dividends) paid to stockholders falls far short of the amount of interest income paid to bondholders. Note also that even though interest rates had fallen to 40-year lows by 2003, the dividend yield on stocks was still less than half the coupon yield on bonds.

and the state of the economy. Because such factors affect sales and profits, they also affect the price behavior of the stock and possibly even dividends. All of this leads to another disadvantage: The earnings and general performance of stocks are subject to wide swings, so it is difficult to value common stocks and consistently select top performers. The selection process is complex because so many elements go into formulating expectations of stock performance. In other words, not only is the future outcome of the company and its stock uncertain, but the evaluation and selection process itself is far from perfect.

A final disadvantage of stocks is the sacrifice in current income. Several types of investments—bonds, for instance—pay higher levels of current income and do so with much greater certainty. Figure 6.3 compares the dividend yield on common stocks with the coupon yield on high-grade corporate bonds. It shows the degree of sacrifice common stock investors make in terms of current income. Clearly, even though the yield gap has narrowed a great deal in the past few years, common stocks still have a long way to go before they catch up with the *current income levels* available from bonds and most other types of fixed-income securities.

IN REVIEW

CONCEPTS

6.1 What is a *common stock*? What is meant by the statement that holders of common stock are the *residual owners* of the firm?

6.2 What are two or three of the major investment attributes of common stocks?

6.3 Briefly describe the behavior of the U.S. stock market over the past 10 to 15 years, paying special attention to market behavior since the mid-1990s. Contrast the market's performance over the 1990s as measured by the DJIA with its performance as measured by the S&P 500 and by the Nasdaq Composite.

6.4 How important are dividends as a source of return? What about capital gains? Which is more important to total return? Which causes wider swings in total return?

6.5 What are some of the advantages *and* disadvantages of owning common stock? What are the major types of risk to which stockholders are exposed?

Basic Characteristics of Common Stock

equity capital
evidence of ownership position in a firm, in the form of shares of common stock.

Each share of common stock represents equity (ownership) in a company. It's this equity position that explains why common stocks are often referred to as *equity securities* or **equity capital**. Every share entitles the holder to an equal ownership position and participation in the corporation's earnings and dividends, an equal vote, and an equal voice in management. Together, the common stockholders own the company. The more shares an investor owns, the bigger his or her ownership position. Common stock has no maturity date—it remains outstanding indefinitely.

Common Stock as a Corporate Security

All corporations "issue" common stock of one type or another. But the shares of many, if not most, corporations are never traded, because the firms either are too small or are family controlled. The stocks of interest to us in this book

publicly traded issues
shares of stock that are readily available to the general public and are bought and sold in the open market.

public offering
an offering to sell to the investing public a set number of shares of a firm's stock at a specified price.

rights offering
an offering of a new issue of stock to existing stockholders, who may purchase new shares in proportion to their current ownership position.

stock spin-off
conversion of one of a firm's subsidiaries to a stand-alone company by distribution of stock in that new company to existing shareholders.

stock split
a maneuver in which a company increases the number of shares outstanding by exchanging a specified number of new shares of stock for each outstanding share.

HOT LINKS

Get the latest information on stock splits at:
biz.yahoo.com/c/s.html

are **publicly traded issues**—the shares that are readily available to the general public and which are bought and sold in the open market. The firms issuing such shares range from giants like AT&T and Microsoft to much smaller regional or local firms. The market for publicly traded stocks is enormous: The value of all actively traded listed and OTC stocks in mid-2003 was nearly $10 trillion.

Issuing New Shares Shares of common stock can be issued in several different ways. The most widely used procedure today is the **public offering.** In using this procedure, the corporation offers the investing public a certain number of shares of its stock at a certain price. Figure 6.4 shows an announcement for such an offering. Note in this case that *White Electronic Designs* is offering 5,175,000 shares of stock at a price of $10 per share, providing this Nasdaq-traded company with some $50 million in new capital.

New shares of stock can also be issued using what is known as a **rights offering.** In a rights offering, existing stockholders are given the first opportunity to buy the new issue. In essence, a stock right gives a shareholder the right (but not the obligation) to purchase new shares of the company's stock in proportion to his or her current ownership position. For instance, if a stockholder currently owns 1% of a firm's stock and the firm issues 10,000 additional shares, the rights offering will give that stockholder the opportunity to purchase 1% (100 shares) of the new issue. If the investor doesn't want to use the rights, he or she can sell them to someone who does. The net result of a rights offering is the same as that of a public offering: The firm ends up with more equity in its capital structure, and the number of shares outstanding increases.

Stock Spin-Offs Perhaps one of the most creative ways of bringing a new issue to the market is through a **stock spin-off.** Basically, a spin-off occurs when a company gets rid of one of its subsidiaries or divisions. For example, Ralston Purina did this when it spun off its Energizer subsidiary. The company doesn't just sell the subsidiary to some other firm. Rather, it creates a new stand-alone company and then distributes stock in that company to its existing stockholders. Thus every Ralston Purina shareholder received a certain (prorated) number of shares in the newly created, and now publicly traded, Energizer company. There have been hundreds of stock spin-offs in the last 10 to 15 years. Some of the more notable ones were the spin-off of Coach (the designer bag company) by Sara Lee, Carmax by Circuit City in February 2002, the spin-off of debit-card processor Global Payments from NDCHealth, and the Edwards Lifesciences spin-off by Baxter International. Normally, companies execute stock spin-offs if they believe the subsidiary is no longer a good fit, or if they feel they've become too diversified and want to focus on their core products. The good news is such spin-offs often work very well for investors, too.

Stock Splits Companies can also increase the number of shares outstanding by executing a **stock split.** In declaring a split, a firm merely announces that it will increase the number of shares outstanding by exchanging a specified number of new shares for each outstanding share of stock. For example, in a 2-for-1 stock split, two new shares of stock are exchanged for each old share. In a 3-for-2 split, three new shares are exchanged for every two old shares outstanding. Thus, a stockholder who owned 200 shares of stock before a 2-for-1

FIGURE 6.4 **An Announcement of a New Stock Issue**

This announcement indicates that the company—White Electronic Designs—is issuing over 5 million shares of stock at a price of $10 per share. For this manufacturer of specialty microelectronic memory products, the new issue will mean some $50,000,000 in new capital. (*Source: Wall Street Journal*, August 14, 2003.)

This announcement is neither an offer to sell nor a solicitation of an offer to buy these securities.
The offer is made only by the Prospectus.

July 2, 2003 ◄─── Date of issue

5,175,000 Shares ◄

Number of shares being offered

WHITE ELECTRONIC DESIGNS ◄───

Name of issuer

Common Stock

───────
Price $10 Per Share ◄───
───────

Price at which shares were being offered to the public

Copies of the Prospectus may be obtained in any State in which this
announcement is circulated only from such of the undersigned
as may legally offer these securities in such State.

Needham & Companny, Inc.

A.G. Edwards & Sons, Inc.

Raymond James

The under-writing group handling this new issue

split becomes the owner of 400 shares; the same investor would hold 300 shares if there had been a 3-for-2 split.

Stock splits are used when a firm wants to enhance its stock's trading appeal by lowering its market price. Normally, the firm gets the desired result: The price of the stock tends to fall in close relation to the terms of the split (unless the stock split is accompanied by a big increase in the level of dividends).

REDISCOVERING THE REVERSE STOCK SPLIT—The recent meltdown in the market has led to some incredibly low share prices. But companies don't like to see their stocks sell at bargain basement prices. So what do they do? One tactic is to improve profits and other fundamentals. A far easier way is to use a *reverse stock split*. This sleight of hand is guaranteed to raise share prices, but it won't change the overall value of the company or its fundamentals. In a normal stock split, you turn in 1 share of stock and get, say, 4 back; so the price of the stock *drops* from, say, $100 to $25 per share. A reverse stock split works in the opposite way: You turn in 4 shares and get 1 back, so the price of the stock goes *up* from, say, $5 to $20 per share. With so many stocks selling at such low prices, some market observers feel we're going to see a lot of these.

Source: Adapted from "Less Is Not More" by Michelle Deblasi, *Bloomberg Personal Finance*, July/August 2002, pp. 23–25.

treasury stock
shares of stock that have been sold and subsequently repurchased by the issuing firm.

classified common stock
common stock issued by a company in different classes, each of which offers different privileges and benefits to its holders.

For example, using the ratio of the number of old shares to new, we can expect a $100 stock to trade at or close to $50 a share after a 2-for-1 split. Specifically, we divide the original price per share by the ratio of new shares to old. That same $100 stock would trade at about $67 after a 3-for-2 split—that is, $100 ÷ 3/2 = $100 ÷ 1.5 = $67. (A variation of the stock split, known as a stock dividend, will be discussed later in this chapter.)

Treasury Stock Instead of increasing the number of outstanding shares, corporations sometimes find it desirable to *reduce* the number of shares in the hands of the investing public by buying back their own stock. Generally speaking, firms repurchase their own stock when they view it as undervalued in the marketplace. When that happens, the company's own stock becomes an attractive investment candidate. Those firms that can afford to do so will purchase their stock in the open market by becoming investors, like any other individual or institution. When these shares are acquired, they become known as **treasury stock**. Technically, treasury stocks are simply shares of stock that have been issued and subsequently repurchased by the issuing firm. Treasury stocks are kept by the corporation and can be used at a later date for any number of reasons. For example, they could be used for mergers and acquisitions, to meet employee stock option plans, or as a means of paying stock dividends. Or the shares can simply be held in treasury for an indefinite time.

The impact of these share repurchases—or *buybacks*, as they're sometimes called—is not clear. Generally, the feeling is that if the buyback is substantial (involving a significant number of shares), the stockholder's equity position and claim on income will increase. This result is likely to benefit stockholders to the extent that such action has a positive effect on the market price of the stock. However, it has also been suggested that buybacks are often used merely as a way to prop up the price of an overvalued stock.

Classified Common Stock For the most part, all the stockholders in a corporation enjoy the same benefits of ownership. Occasionally, however, a company will *issue different classes of common stock*, each of which entitles holders to different privileges and benefits. These issues are known as **classified common stock**. Hundreds of publicly traded firms have created such stock classes. Though issued by the same company, each class of common stock is different and has its own value.

Classified common stock is customarily used to denote either different voting rights or different dividend obligations. For instance, class A could designate nonvoting shares, and class B would carry normal voting rights. Or the class A stock would receive no dividends, and class B would receive regular cash dividends. Notable for its use of classified stock is Ford Motor Company, which has two classes of stock outstanding. Ford's class A stock is owned by the investing public, and class B stock is owned by the Ford family and their trusts or corporations. The two classes of stock share equally in the dividends. But class A stock has one vote per share, whereas the voting rights of the class B stock are structured to give the Ford family a 40% absolute control of the company. Similar types of classified stock are used at the Washington Post, Dillards Department Stores, Dow Jones & Co., Nike, and Berkshire Hathaway. Regardless of the specifics, whenever there is more than one class of common stock outstanding, investors should take the time to determine the privileges, benefits, and limitations of each class.

Buying and Selling Stocks

Whether buying or selling stocks, you should become familiar with how stocks are quoted and with the costs of executing common stock transactions. Certainly, keeping track of *current prices* is an essential element in the buy-and-sell decisions of investors. They are the link in the decision process that lets investors decide when to buy or sell a stock; they also help investors monitor the market performance of their security holdings. Similarly, *transaction costs* are important because of the impact they can have on investment returns. Indeed, the costs of executing stock transactions can sometimes consume most (or all) of the profits from an investment. These costs should not be taken lightly.

Reading the Quotes Investors in the stock market have come to rely on a highly efficient information system that quickly disseminates market prices to the public. The stock quotes that appear daily in the financial press are a vital part of that information system. To see how price quotations work and what they mean, consider the quotes that appear daily (Monday through Friday) in the *Wall Street Journal*. As we'll see, these quotes give not only the most recent price of each stock but also a great deal of additional information.

Some NYSE stock quotes are presented in Figure 6.5 (on page 250)—let's use the Disney quotations for purposes of illustration. These quotes were published in the *Wall Street Journal* on Tuesday, July 8, 2003, and describe the trading activity that occurred the day before, which in this case was Monday, July 7. A glance at the quotations shows that stocks, like most other securities, are quoted in dollars and cents. In addition to stock prices, a typical stock quote conveys an array of other information, including

- The stock's year-to-date change in price—see the first column ("YTD % CHG"); note that Disney stock has gone up a whopping 26.2% since the first of the year. The next two columns, labeled "Hi" and "Lo," show the highest and lowest prices at which the stock sold during the past 52 weeks—you can see that Disney has traded between $21.55 and $13.48 a share during the preceding 52-week period.

- Listed to the right of the company's name is its *stock symbol*; Disney goes by the three-letter abbreviation **DIS.** These symbols are the abbreviations used to identify specific companies; every common stock (and mutual fund) has a unique three- to five-letter symbol that distinguishes it from any other security and is used to execute market trades.

- The figure listed after the stock symbol is the annual cash dividend paid on each share of stock, which for Disney was 21 cents. This is followed by the stock's dividend yield (1.0% for Disney) and its price/earnings (P/E) ratio, which amounted to 39 times earnings for Disney.

- The daily share volume follows the P/E ratio. The sales numbers are listed in lots of 100 shares, so the figure 66186 means that 6,618,600 shares of Disney stock were traded on July 7.

- The next entry, the "Close" column, contains the closing (final) price, $20.58, at which the stock sold on the day in question.

- Finally, as the last ("Net Change") column shows, Disney closed up 51 cents. This means the stock closed $0.51 higher than the day before (which in this case was Thursday, July 3, when it closed at $20.07).

FIGURE 6.5 Stock Quotations

This figure shows the quotations for a small sample of stocks traded on the NYSE, providing a summary of the transactions that occurred on one day. (*Source: Wall Street Journal*, July 8, 2003.)

YTD %CHG	52-WEEK HI	LO	STOCK (SYM)	DIV	YLD %	PE	VOL 100s	CLOSE	NET CHG
16.4	13.86	7.75 ♣ DnbryRes DNR		...		12	2530	13.15	-0.29
19.9	15.69	8.95 Dept56 DFS		...		7	741	15.47	0.31
-3.3	10.11	5.21 DescSA ADS DES	.56e	8.6	...	25	6.53	0.14
45.7	72.23	35.26 DtscheBK DB	1.53e	2.3	...	540	66.18	0.60
18.8	15.64	8.10 ♣ DtscheTel ADS DT		...	...	5203	15.09	0.09
35.1	29.62	17.25 DevDivRlty DDR	1.64	5.5	24	2779	29.70	0.32
47.9	26.38	12.10 DeVry DV		...	26	2205	24.57	0.72
-0.5	53	37.55 Diageo ADS DEO	1.69e	3.9	...	7071	43.59	-1.21
4.9	47.64	30 DiagnstPdt DP	.24	.6	24	1208	40.50	-0.05
-3.0	22.45	17.12 DialCp DL	.16	.8	29	4377	19.75	0.14
-5.7	28.70	17.30 DmndOffshr DO	.50	2.4	cc	16969	20.60	-0.93
99.4	38.83	12.15 DicksSprtgGds DKS n		...	20	3509	38.28	0.99
10.6	45.90	30.30 Diebold DBD	.68	1.5	25	4706	45.60	1.00
-13.2	28.14	12.32 Dillards DDS	.16	1.2	11	5716	13.76	0.09
21.7	7.50	5.35 ♣ Dimon DMN	.30	4.1	12	1050	7.30	0.18
26.2	21.55	13.48 Disney DIS	.21	1.0	39	66186	20.58	0.51
8.9	27.48	23.70 Disney 6.875Corts KVJ n	1.72	6.3	...	14	27.18	0.23
27.0	13.05	7.50 Dist&Srv ADS DYS	.21e	1.7	...	540	12.70	-0.20
211.2	11.40	2.70 djOrthopedics DJO		...	dd	1703	11.70	0.69
58.4	19.95	9.50 DlrGenl DG	.14	.7	23	13925	18.93	0.27
-7.1	26.60	14.35 ♣ DlrThrfty DTG		...	14	575	19.65	0.15
24.9	27.30	17.55 DomResBlkWar DOM	2.56e	9.5	...	196	27.05	-0.01
15.5	66.15	35.40 ♣ DominRes D	2.58	4.1	13	8587	63.43	-0.19
11.0	55	36.77 ♣ Domin un	4.38	8.1	...	95	53.90	-0.07
8.8	11.73	8.60 Domtar DTC	.17fg	...	...	840	10.95	-0.07
27.8	45.68	29.91 ♣ Donaldson DCI	.36	.8	22	924	46.01	0.57
23.2	28.40	16.94 ♣ Donnelly DNY	1.00	3.7	24	5762	26.83	0.78

Annotations (right side):
- Year-to-date changes in price, in percentages
- High and low prices for previous 52 weeks
- Company name and stock symbol
- Annual dividends per share for past 12 months
- Dividend yield (dividends as percent of share price)
- Price/earnings ratio: $\left(\dfrac{\text{market price}}{\text{earnings per share}}\right)$
- Share volume, in hundreds
- Closing (final) price for the day—this is also the price used to compute dividend yield and the P/E ratio
- Net change in price from previous day

The same basic quotation system is used for *some* OTC stocks. Actually, for quotation purposes, OTC stocks are divided into two groups: Nasdaq National Market issues and other OTC stocks. The National Market stocks are those of major, actively traded companies; *they are quoted just like NYSE issues*. Other OTC stocks (i.e., Nasdaq Small Cap issues) and AMEX stocks are quoted in a highly abbreviated form that includes only stock name, symbol, volume, closing price, and price change.

Transaction Costs As explained in Chapter 3, common stock can be bought and sold in round or odd lots. A *round lot* is 100 shares of stock or multiples thereof. An *odd lot* is a transaction involving less than 100 shares. For example, the sale of 400 shares of stock would be a round-lot transaction, whereas the sale of 75 shares would be an odd-lot transaction. Trading 250 shares of stock would involve a combination of two round lots and an odd lot.

An investor incurs certain transaction costs when buying or selling stock. In addition to some modest transfer fees and taxes paid by the *seller*, the major cost is the brokerage fee paid—by both *buyer and seller*—at the time of the transaction. As a rule, brokerage fees amount to 1% to 5% of most transactions. But they can go much higher, particularly for very small trades. Higher fees are connected with the purchase or sale of odd lots, which requires a specialist known as an *odd-lot dealer*. This usually results in an *odd-lot differential* of 10 to 25 cents per share, which is tacked on to the normal commission charge, driving up the costs of these small trades. Indeed, the relatively high cost of an odd-lot trade makes it better to deal in round lots whenever possible.

Common Stock Values

The worth of a share of common stock can be described in a number of ways. Terms such as *par value*, *book value*, *market value*, and *investment value* are all found in the financial media. Each designates some accounting, investment, or monetary attribute of a stock.

par value
the stated, or face, value of a stock.

Par Value The term **par value** refers to the stated, or face, value of a stock. Except for accounting purposes, it is relatively useless. In many ways, par value is a throwback to the early days of corporate law, when it was used as a basis for assessing the extent of a stockholder's legal liability. Because the term has little or no significance for investors, many stocks today are issued as no-par or low-par stocks. That is, they may have par values of only a penny or two.

book value
the amount of stockholders' equity in a firm; equals the amount of the firm's assets minus the firm's liabilities and preferred stock.

Book Value Book value, another accounting measure, represents the amount of stockholders' equity in the firm. As we will see in the next chapter, it is commonly used in stock valuation. Book value indicates the amount of stockholder funds used to finance the firm. It is calculated by subtracting the firm's liabilities and preferred stock from its assets. Let's assume that a corporation has $10 million in assets, owes $5 million in various forms of short- and long-term debt, and has $1 million worth of preferred stock outstanding. The book value of this firm would be $4 million.

Book value can be converted to a per-share basis—*book value per share*—by dividing it by the number of common shares outstanding. For example, if the firm just described has 100,000 shares of common stock outstanding, then its book value per share is $40. As a rule, most stocks have market prices that are well above their book values.

market value
the prevailing market price of a security.

Market Value Market value is one of the easiest stock values to determine. It is simply *the prevailing market price of an issue*. In essence, market value indicates how the market participants as a whole have assessed the worth of a share of stock. By multiplying the market price of the stock by the number of shares outstanding, we can also find the market value of the firm itself—or what is known as the firm's *market capitalization*. For example, if a firm has 1 million shares outstanding and its stock trades at $50 per share, the company has a market value (or "market cap") of $50 million. For obvious reasons, the market value of a share of stock is generally of considerable importance to stockholders.

investment value
the amount that investors believe
a security should be trading for,
or what they think it's worth.

Investment Value **Investment value** is probably the most important measure for a stockholder. It indicates the worth investors place on the stock—in effect, what they think the stock *should* be trading for. Determining a security's investment value is a complex process based on expectations of the return and risk characteristics of a stock. Any stock has two potential sources of return: annual dividend payments and the capital gains that arise from appreciation in market price. In establishing investment value, investors try to determine how much money they will make from these two sources. They then use those estimates as the basis for formulating the return potential of the stock. At the same time, they try to assess the amount of risk to which they will be exposed by holding the stock. Such return and risk information helps them place an investment value on the stock. This value represents the *maximum* price an investor should be willing to pay for the issue. Investment value is the major topic in Chapter 8.

IN REVIEW

C O N C E P T S

6.6 What is a *stock split?* How does a stock split affect the market value of a share of stock? Do you think it would make any difference (in price behavior) if the company also changed the dividend rate on the stock? Explain.

6.7 What is a *stock spin-off?* In very general terms, explain how a stock spin-off works. Are these spin-offs of any value to investors? Explain.

6.8 Define and differentiate between the following pairs of terms.
a. *Treasury stock* versus *classified stock*.
b. *Round lot* versus *odd lot*.
c. *Par value* versus *market value*.
d. *Book value* versus *investment value*.

6.9 What is an *odd-lot differential* and what effect does it have on the cost of buying and selling stocks? How can you avoid odd-lot differentials? Which of the following transactions would involve an odd-lot differential?
a. Buy 90 shares of stock.
b. Sell 200 shares of stock.
c. Sell 125 shares of stock.

Common Stock Dividends

LG 5

In 2002, U.S. corporations paid out more than $400 billion in dividends. Yet, in spite of these numbers, dividends still don't get much respect. Many investors, particularly younger ones, often put very little value on dividends. To a large extent, that's because capital gains provide a much bigger source of return than dividends—at least over the long haul. But things are beginning to change. The protracted bear market of 2000–2002 revealed in a very painful fashion just how uncertain capital gains can be and, indeed, that all those potential profits can at times turn into substantial capital losses. At least with dividends, the cash flow is far more certain; plus, dividends provide a nice cushion when the market stumbles (or falls flat on its face). Moreover, recent changes in the (federal) tax laws put dividends on the same plane as capital

earnings per share (EPS)
the amount of annual earnings available to common stockholders, as stated on a per-share basis.

gains, as both are now taxed at the same (maximum 15%) tax rate. Thus, capital gains are no longer taxed at more attractive rates, making dividends just as attractive and perhaps even more so, as they're far less risky. Let's now take a closer look at this important source of income.

The Dividend Decision

By paying out dividends, typically on a quarterly basis, companies share with their stockholders some of the profits they've earned. Actually, the question of how much to pay in dividends is decided by a firm's board of directors. The directors evaluate the firm's operating results and financial condition to determine whether dividends should be paid and, if so, in what amount. If the directors decide to pay dividends, they also establish several important payment dates. In this section we'll look at the corporate and market factors that go into the dividend decision. Then we'll briefly examine some of the key payment dates.

Corporate Versus Market Factors When the board of directors assembles for its regular dividend meeting, it weighs a variety of factors in making the decision to pay out dividends. First, the board looks at the firm's earnings. Even though a company does not have to show a profit to pay dividends, profits are still considered a vital link in the dividend decision. With common stocks, the annual earnings of a firm are usually measured and reported in terms of **earnings per share (EPS)**. Basically, EPS translates aggregate corporate profits into profits on a per-share basis. It provides a convenient measure of the amount of earnings available to stockholders. Earnings per share is found by using the following formula:

Equation 6.1
$$EPS = \frac{\text{Net profit after taxes} - \text{Preferred dividends}}{\text{Number of shares of common stock outstanding}}$$

For example, if a firm reports a net profit of $1.25 million, pays $250,000 in dividends to preferred stockholders, and has 500,000 shares of common stock outstanding, it has an EPS of $2—that is, ($1,250,000 − $250,000)/500,000). Note in Equation 6.1 that preferred dividends are subtracted from profits, since they must be paid before any funds can be made available to common stockholders.

While assessing profits, the board also looks at the firm's growth prospects. It is very likely some of the firm's present earnings will be needed for investment purposes and to help finance expected growth. In addition, the board will take a close look at the firm's cash position. Depending on the company and the firm's current dividend rate, the payment of dividends can take up a large amount of cash, so board members will want to make sure plenty of this precious resource is available. Finally, the board will want to make sure that it is meeting all legal and contractual constraints. For example, the firm may be subject to a loan agreement that legally limits the amount of dividends it can pay.

After looking at internal matters, the board will consider certain market effects and responses. Most investors feel that if a company is going to retain earnings rather than pay them out in dividends, it should exhibit proportionately higher growth and profit levels. The market's message is clear: If the firm is investing the money wisely and at a high rate of return, fine; otherwise, pay a larger portion of earnings out in the form of dividends. Moreover, to the extent that different types of investors tend to be attracted to different types of firms, the board must make every effort to meet the dividend expectations of its shareholders. For example, income-oriented investors are attracted to firms that generally pay high dividends. Failure to meet those expectations can lead to disastrous results—a sell-off of the firm's stock—in the marketplace. Finally, the board cannot ignore the fact that investors today are placing a much higher value on dividends. Indeed, after being mothballed for the past decade or so, dividends definitely are now back in style.

HOT LINK

Boards of directors have come under scrutiny in recent years. For some insight on this issue, see the *Ethics* box for Chapter 6 on the book's Web site at

www.aw-bc.com/gitman_joehnk

Some Important Dates Let's assume the directors decide to declare a dividend. Once that's done, they must indicate the date of payment and other important dates associated with the dividend. Normally, the directors issue a statement to the press indicating their dividend decision, along with the pertinent dividend payment dates. These statements are widely quoted in the financial media. Typical of such releases are the dividend news captions depicted in Figure 6.6.

Three dates are particularly important to the stockholder: date of record, ex-dividend date, and payment date. The *date of record* is the date on which the investor must be a registered shareholder of the firm to be entitled to a dividend. All investors who are official stockholders as of the close of business on that date will receive the dividends that have just been declared. These stockholders are often referred to as *holders of record*. The **payment date**, also set by the board of directors, generally follows the date of record by a week or two. It is the actual date on which the company will mail dividend checks to holders of record. (Note that in the dividend news reported in Figure 6.6, this date is called the *payable date*.)

Because of the time needed to make bookkeeping entries after a stock is traded, the stock will sell without the dividend (ex-dividend) for three business days up to and including the date of record. The **ex-dividend date** will dictate whether you were an official shareholder and therefore eligible to receive the declared dividend. If you sell a stock *on or after* the ex-dividend date, you receive the dividend—the reason is that the buyer of the stock (the *new* shareholder) will not have held the stock on the date of record. Instead, you (the seller) will still be the holder of record. Just the opposite will occur if you sell the stock *before* the ex-dividend date. In this case, the new shareholder (the buyer of the stock) will receive the dividend because he or she will be the holder of record.

To see how this works, consider the following sequence of events. On June 3, the board of directors of Cash Cow, Inc., declares a quarterly dividend of 50 cents a share to holders of record on June 18. Checks will be mailed on the payment date, June 30. The calendar on the next page shows these various dividend dates. In this case, if you bought 200 shares of the stock on June 15, you'd receive a check in the mail sometime after June 30 in the amount of $100.

date of record
the date on which an investor must be a registered shareholder to be entitled to receive a dividend.

payment date
the actual date on which the company will mail dividend checks to shareholders (also known as the *payable date*).

ex-dividend date
three business days up to the date of record; determines whether one is an official shareholder and thus eligible to receive a declared dividend.

FIGURE 6.6

Important Dates and Data About Dividends

The dividend actions of corporations are big news in the financial community. This news release, taken from the *Wall Street Journal*, provides timely information about cash and stock dividends, as well as stocks that have gone ex-dividend. (*Source: Wall Street Journal*, July 9, 2003.)

Corporate Dividend News

Procter & Gamble Co.

CINCINNATI—Procter & Gamble Co.'s board declared an 11% increase in the quarterly dividend of its common stock and Series A ESOP convertible preferred stock.

The consumer-products company raised the dividend on both classes of stock to 45.5 cents from 41 cents, payable Aug. 15 to holders of record on July 18.

In 4 p.m. composite trading yesterday on the New York Stock Exchange, P&G was at $90.10, off 69 cents.

Dividends Reported July 8

COMPANY	PERIOD	AMT	PAYABLE DATE	RECORD DATE
REGULAR				
Bank of New York	Q	.19	7-31-03	7-18
Cummins Inc	Q	.30	9-02-03	8-15
FirstBncp MIPS pfB	M	.173958	7-31-03	7-29
FirstBncp pfC	M	.154167	7-31-03	7-29
FirstBncp pfD	M	.151042	7-31-03	7-29
Golden Enterprises	Q	.0313	7-30-03	7-18
Kerr-McGee Corp	Q	.45	10-01-03	9-05
Liberty Homes A	Q	.07	8-15-03	7-28
Liberty Homes B	Q	.07	8-15-03	7-28
Lone Star Stkhse	Q	.165	7-28-03	7-14
Oriental Fin'l A	M	.148438	7-30-03	7-15
Paccar Inc	Q	.22	9-05-03	8-18
PFS Bancorp	Q	.075	7-25-03	7-15
Puget Energy Inc	Q	.25	8-15-03	7-18
Puget Sound 7.45%	Q	.465625	10-01-03	9-12
SBI Capital Tr pf	Q	.58125	7-31-03	7-15
Summit Sec S-3 pf	M	.006458	8-20-03	8-05
Weyerhaeuser Co	Q	.40	9-02-03	8-01
IRREGULAR				
Metropol Mtg E-7pf	M	.007917	8-20-03	8-05
Popular pfA	–	.132812	7-31-03	7-15
Western United pfA	M	.007083	8-20-03	8-05
FUNDS, REITS, INVESTMENT COS, LPS				
Anthracite Cap pf	–	.410156	7-31-03	7-15
Century Realty Tr	Q	.12	8-18-03	7-25
Colonial Intmk Inc	M	.054	8-01-03	7-15
Colonial InvGr Mun	M	.0575	8-01-03	7-15
Hatteras Inco Secs	M	.065	7-31-03	7-17
ML RegBk Hldrs	–	.0432	7-28-03	7-11
Insured MuniInco	M	.07	7-31-03	7-17
Invest GrdMunIlnco	M	.08	7-31-03	7-17
NCE PetrofdTr	M	b.18	7-31-03	7-17
NCE PetrofdTr	M	b.18	8-29-03	8-15
NCE PetrofdTr	M	b.18	9-30-03	9-16

COMPANY	PERIOD	AMT	PAYABLE DATE	RECORD DATE
Pfd Inco Fd	M	.0915	7-31-03	7-24
Pfd Inco Oppy Fd	M	.073	7-31-03	7-24
Prudential RE A	–	.073	7-11-03	7-10
Prudential RE B	–	.052	7-11-03	7-10
Sabine Royalty Tr	M	r.20257	7-29-03	7-15
Scudder Intmdt Gvt	M	.03	7-31-03	7-17
Scudder Multi-Mkt	M	.0615	7-31-03	7-17
Scudder Muni Inco	M	.065	7-31-03	7-17
Scudder Strat Inco	M	.09	7-31-03	7-17
Scudder Strat Muni	M	.0725	7-31-03	7-17
Seligman Qlty Muni	M	.066	7-28-03	7-17
Seligman Sel Muni	M	.0575	7-28-03	7-17
Templeton China	A	h.1162	7-28-03	7-18
STOCKS				
GreenPoint Fin'l			s	8-20-03	8-08
s-3-for-2 stock split.				
Synergx Systems			s	t7-25-03	7-18
s-2-for-1 stock split.				
r-Revised to include payable date.				
FOREIGN				
ICICI Bank ADS	–	t.324	–	8-05
INCREASED				

		AMOUNTS			
		NEW	OLD		
Bank Mutual Corp	Q	.11	.10	9-03-03	8-20
GreenPoint Fin'l	Q	.36	.3125	8-20-03	8-08
Procter & Gamble	Q	.455	.41	8-15-03	7-18
Smith (A.O.) Corp	Q	.15	.14	8-15-03	7-31
Wels Markets	Q	.28	.27	8-22-03	8-08

EXTRA

FrprtMcMrnC&GcId	Q	m2.2645	8-01-03	7-15

m-Represents fifth mandatory partial redemption.
A-Annual. M-Monthly. Q-Quarterly. S-Semi-annual. b-Payable in Canadian funds. c-Corrected. h-From income. k-From capital gains. r-Revised. t-Approximate U.S. dollar amount per American Depositary Receipt/Share before adjustment for foreign taxes.

Stocks Ex-Dividend July 10

COMPANY	AMOUNT	COMPANY	AMOUNT
ABM Industries Inc	.095	Neubrgr Brm RE Inc	.115
AES Trlll 6.75pf	.84375	Neubrgr Brm Rltyln	.1125
Amer AnnGrpl TOPrS	.578125	OGE Energy Capl pf	.523438
AmerFinl ToprS	.570312	Pep Boys	.0675
BankOneCapVI7.2%pf	.45	MerLynDepPrfTRUpS	.95625
BellS Cp Corts7.12	.89	MerLynDep 8.15%P+	.379201
BremerCapTr 9%pf	.5625	MerLynDep8.5%TRUCs	1.0625
Citigo 7% Trups	.4375	MerLynP•PhilMoris	.753819
Fstlin Corts7.5	.9375	Provident Fin'l nt	.52344
FW Capl 9 3/8%pf	.234375	RPM Int'l	.13
Glacier WaterTr pf	.18875	Rotonics Mfg	.05
GBWCapTr1 10% TrupsA	.25	Sadia S/A ADS	t.7515
HartfordLfCaplpfA	.45	Safeco Corts8.375	1.046876
Hartford Lf TrupsB	.476562	Safeco II Corts8.7	1.0875
Europe 2001 HOLDRs	t.020702	Safeco Corts8.75	1.09375
Int'l Game Tech	.075	Safeco Corts8.072	1.009
LehmnCorts Safeco	1.09375	Shelbourne Propll	6.75
LehmnCorts6%BellSt	.691667	St Paul Capl 7.6%	.475
LehmnCorts Altria	.46875	TECO Energy un	.59375
LehmnCorts HSBC	.633681	Universal Corp	.36
LehmnCorts JPM1-1A	.98125	US Home&Grdn 9.4%	.1958
LehmnCorts1-7KeyCp	1.09375	t-Approximate U.S. dollar amount per	
LehmnCorts 7.2%JPM	.90	American Depositary Receipt/Share be-	
MerLyn STRIDES BAC	.701	fore adjustment for foreign taxes.	

On the other hand, if you purchased the stock on June 16, the *seller* of the stock would receive the check, because he or she will be recognized as the holder of record, not you.

June

S	M	T	W	T	F	S	
	1	2	3	4	5	6	— Declaration date
7	8	9	10	11	12	13	
14	15	16	17	18	19	20	— Date of record
21	22	23	24	25	26	27	— Ex-dividend date
28	29	30					— Payment date

Types of Dividends

cash dividend
payment of a dividend in the form of cash.

stock dividend
payment of a dividend in the form of additional shares of stock.

Normally, companies pay dividends in the form of cash, though sometimes they do so by issuing additional shares of stock. The first type of distribution is known as a **cash dividend**; the second is called a **stock dividend**. Occasionally, dividends are paid in still other forms, such as a *stock spin-off* (discussed earlier in this chapter) or perhaps even samples of the company's products. But dividends in the form of either cash or stock remain by far the most popular, so let's take a closer look at them.

Cash Dividends   More firms pay *cash dividends* than any other type of dividend. A nice by-product of cash dividends is that *they tend to increase over time, as companies' earnings grow*. In fact, for companies that pay cash dividends, the average annual increase in dividends is around 3% to 5%. That's down considerably from the rate of growth that existed 15 or 20 years ago, but at least it is starting to go back up again. This trend represents good news for investors, because *a steadily increasing stream of dividends tends to shore up stock returns in soft markets*.

dividend yield
a measure that relates dividends to share price and puts common stock dividends on a relative (percentage) rather than absolute (dollar) basis.

A convenient way of assessing the amount of dividends received is to measure the stock's **dividend yield**. Basically, this is a measure of dividends on a relative (percentage) basis, rather than on an absolute (dollar) basis. Dividend yield, in effect, indicates the rate of current income earned on the investment dollar. It is computed as follows:

Equation 6.2

$$\text{Dividend yield} = \frac{\text{Annual dividends received per share}}{\text{Current market price of the stock}}$$

Income Yield

Thus, a company that annually pays $2 per share in dividends to its stockholders, and whose stock is trading at $40, has a dividend yield of 5%.

dividend payout ratio
the portion of earnings per share (EPS) that a firm pays out as dividends.

To put dividend yield into perspective, it is helpful to look at a company's **dividend payout ratio**. The payout ratio describes that portion of earnings per share (EPS) that is paid out as dividends. It is computed as follows:

Equation 6.3

$$\text{Dividend payout ratio} = \frac{\text{Dividends per share}}{\text{Earnings per share}}$$

A company would have a payout ratio of 50% if it had earnings of $4 a share and paid annual dividends of $2 a share. Although stockholders like to receive dividends, they normally do not like to see payout ratios over 60% to 70%. Payout ratios that high are difficult to maintain and may lead the company into trouble.

The appeal of cash dividends took a giant leap forward in 2003, when the federal tax code was changed so as to reduce the tax on dividends. Prior to this time, cash dividends were taxed as ordinary income, meaning they could be taxed at rates as high as 39%. For that reason, many investors viewed cash dividends as a highly unattractive source of income, especially since capital gains (when realized) were taxed at much lower preferential rates. Now, *both dividends and capital gains are taxed at the same low, preferential rate* (of 15% or less). That, of course, makes dividend-paying stocks far more attractive, even to investors in higher tax brackets. Other things being equal, the tax change should have a positive effect on the price behavior of dividend-paying stocks and, in turn, motivate companies either to begin paying dividends or to increase their dividend payout rate.

Stock Dividends Occasionally, a firm may declare a *stock dividend*. A stock dividend simply means that the dividend is paid in additional shares of stock. For instance, if the board declares a 10% stock dividend, each shareholder receives 1 new share of stock for each 10 shares currently owned.

Although they seem to satisfy some investors, *stock dividends really have no value*, because they represent the receipt of something already owned. The market responds to such dividends by adjusting share prices according to the terms of the stock dividend. Thus, in the example above, a 10% stock dividend normally leads to a decline of around 10% in the stock's share price. The market value of your shareholdings after a stock dividend, therefore, is likely to be the same as it was before the stock dividend. For example, if you owned 200 shares of stock that were trading at $100 per share, the total market value of your investment would be $20,000. After a 10% stock dividend, you'd own 220 shares of stock (i.e., 200 shares × 1.10), but they'd be trading at around $90 or $91 per share. Thus, you'd own more shares but they would be trading at lower prices, so the total market value of your investment would remain about the same. There is, however, one bright spot in all this: Unlike cash dividends, stock dividends are not taxed until the stocks are actually sold.

Dividend Reinvestment Plans

dividend reinvestment plans (DRIPs)
plans in which shareholders have cash dividends automatically reinvested into additional shares of the firm's common stock.

Want to have your cake and eat it too? When it comes to dividends, there is a way to do just that. You can participate in a **dividend reinvestment plan (DRIP)**. In these corporate-sponsored programs, shareholders can have their cash dividends automatically reinvested into additional shares of the company's common stock. (Similar reinvestment programs are offered by mutual funds, which we'll discuss in Chapter 13, and by some brokerage houses, such as Merrill Lynch and Fidelity.) The basic investment philosophy is that *if the company is good enough to invest in, it's good enough to reinvest in.* As Table 6.4 (on page 258) demonstrates, such an approach can have a tremendous impact on your investment position over time.

HOT

Use the directory of online resources about dividend reinvestment plans (DRIPs) and direct purchase of stocks at

www.stock1.com

Today more than 1,000 companies (including most major corporations) offer dividend reinvestment plans. Each one provides investors with a convenient and inexpensive way to accumulate capital. Stocks in most DRIPs are acquired free of any brokerage commissions, and most plans allow *partial participation*. That is, participants may specify a portion of their shares for dividend reinvestment and receive cash dividends on the rest. Some plans even sell stocks to their DRIP investors at below-market prices—often at discounts of 3% to 5%. In addition, most plans will credit fractional shares to the investor's account, and many will even allow investors to buy additional shares of the company's stock. For example, once enrolled in the General Mills plan, investors can purchase up to $3,000 worth of the company's stock each quarter, free of commissions.

Shareholders can join dividend reinvestment plans by simply sending a completed authorization form to the company. (Generally, it takes about 30 to 45 days for all the paperwork to be processed.) Once you're in, the number of

TABLE 6.4   Cash or Reinvested Dividends?

Situation: You buy 100 shares of stock at $25 a share (total investment $2,500); the stock currently pays $1 a share in annual dividends. The price of the stock increases at 8% per year; dividends grow at 5% per year.

Investment Period	Number of Shares Held	Market Value of Stock Holdings	Total Cash Dividends Received
		Take Dividends in Cash	
5 years	100	$ 3,672	$ 552
10 years	100	5,397	1,258
15 years	100	7,930	2,158
20 years	100	11,652	3,307
		Full Participation in Dividend Reinvestment Plan (100% of cash dividends reinvested)	
5 years	115.59	$ 4,245	$ 0
10 years	135.66	7,322	0
15 years	155.92	12,364	0
20 years	176.00	20,508	0

shares you hold will begin to accumulate with each dividend date. There is a catch, however: Even though these dividends take the form of additional shares of stock, you must still pay taxes on them *as though they were cash dividends*. Don't confuse these dividends with stock dividends—*reinvested dividends are treated as taxable income in the year they're received*, just as though they had been received in cash. But at least with the new preferential tax rate, even this feature is much less of a burden than it used to be.

IN REVIEW

CONCEPTS

6.10 Briefly explain how the dividend decision is made. What corporate and market factors are important in deciding whether, and in what amount, to pay dividends?

6.11 Why is the *ex-dividend date* important to stockholders? If a stock is sold on the ex-dividend date, who receives the dividend—the buyer or the seller? Explain.

6.12 What is the difference between a *cash dividend* and a *stock dividend?* Which would be more valuable to you? How does a stock dividend compare to a stock split? Is a 200% stock dividend the same as a 2-for-1 stock split? Explain.

6.13 What are *dividend reinvestment plans*, and what benefits do they offer to investors? Are there any disadvantages?

Types and Uses of Common Stock

LG 6

Common stocks appeal to investors because they offer the potential for everything from current income and stability of capital to attractive capital gains. The market contains a wide range of stocks, from the most conservative to the highly speculative. Generally, the kinds of stocks that investors seek will depend on their investment objectives and investment programs. We will examine several of the more popular types of common stocks here, as well as the various ways such securities can be used in different types of investment programs.

Types of Stocks

As an investor, one of the things you'll want to understand is the market system used to classify common stock. That's because a stock's general classification reflects not only its fundamental source of return but also the quality of the company's earnings, the issue's susceptibility to market risks, the nature and stability of its earnings and dividends, and even its susceptibility to adverse economic conditions. Such insight is useful in selecting stocks that will best fit your overall investment objectives. Among the many different types of stocks, the following are the most common: blue chips, income stocks, growth stocks, tech stocks, speculative stocks, cyclical stocks, defensive stocks, mid-cap stocks, and small-cap stocks. We will now look at each of these to see what they are and how they might be used.

Blue-Chip Stocks Blue chips are the cream of the common stock crop. They are stocks that are unsurpassed in quality and have a long and stable record of earnings and dividends. **Blue-chip stocks** are issued by large, well-established firms that have impeccable financial credentials. These companies hold important, often leading positions in their industries and frequently set the standards by which other firms are measured.

Not all blue chips are alike, however. Some provide consistently high dividend yields; others are more growth oriented. Good examples of blue-chip growth stocks are Wal-Mart, Proctor & Gamble, Microsoft, United Parcel Service, Pfizer, and 3M Company. (Some basic operating and market information about 3M's stock, as obtained from the introductory part of a typical *S&P Stock Report*, is shown in Figure 6.7.) Examples of high-yielding blue chips include such companies as Eastman Kodak, General Motors, ChevronTexaco, SBC Communications, and Kimberly-Clark.

HOT LINKS

At this site, you can choose stocks by company size and type, and access growth and return rates. Lists show stock prices, quotes, and ratios.

screen.yahoo.com/stocks.html

---

blue-chip stocks
financially strong, high-quality stocks with long and stable records of earnings and dividends.

FIGURE 6.7

A Blue-Chip Stock

(*Source:* Standard & Poor's *Stock Reports,* July 12, 2003.)

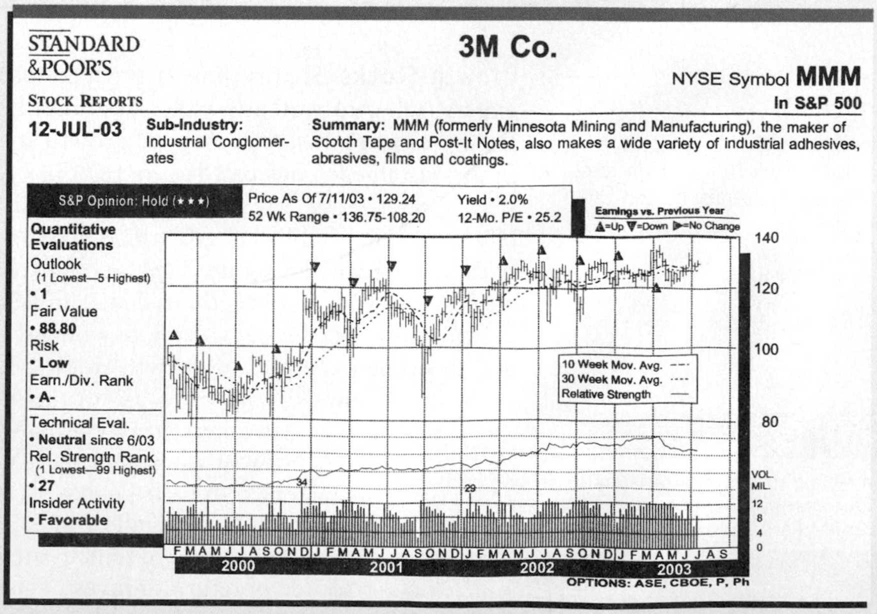

While blue-chip stocks (like most equity securities) are not immune from bear markets, they do nonetheless provide the potential for relatively attractive long-term returns. As such, they tend to appeal to investors who are looking for quality investment outlets that offer decent dividend yields and respectable growth potential. They're often used for long-term investment purposes and, because of their relatively low risk, as a way of obtaining modest but dependable rates of return.

income stocks
stocks with long and sustained records of paying higher-than-average dividends.

Income Stocks Some stocks are appealing simply because of the dividends they pay. This is the case with **income stocks.** These are issues that have a long and sustained record of regularly paying higher-than-average dividends. Income stocks are ideal for those who seek a relatively safe and high level of current income from their investment capital. But there's more: Holders of income stocks (unlike bonds and preferred stocks) can expect the dividends they receive to increase regularly over time. Thus, a company that paid, say, $1.00 a share in dividends in 1990 would be paying almost $1.50 a share in 2003, if dividends had been growing at just 3% per year. That's a big jump in dividends, and it's something that can have a definite impact on total return.

The major disadvantage of income stocks is that some of them may be paying high dividends because of limited growth potential. Indeed, it's not unusual for income securities to exhibit only low or modest rates of growth in earnings. This does not mean that such firms are unprofitable or lack future prospects. Quite the contrary: Most firms whose shares qualify as income stocks are highly profitable organizations with excellent future prospects. A number of income stocks are among the giants of U.S. industry, and many are also classified as quality blue chips. Many public utilities, such as FPL Group, Scana, DTE Energy, Dominion Resources, and Southern Company, are in this group. Also in this group are telecommunications stocks, such as Verizon and Alltel, and selected industrial and financial issues, such as Conagra Foods, Pitney Bowes, R. R. Donnelley, Bank of America, and AmSouth Bancorp. By their very nature, income stocks are not exposed to a great deal of business and market risk. They are, however, subject to a fair amount of interest rate risk.

growth stocks
stocks that experience high rates of growth in operations and earnings.

Growth Stocks Shares that have experienced, and are expected to continue experiencing, consistently high rates of growth in operations and earnings are known as **growth stocks.** A good growth stock might exhibit a *sustained* rate of growth in earnings of 15% to 18% per year over a period when common stocks, on average, are experiencing growth rates of only 6% to 8%. Generally speaking, established growth companies combine steady earnings growth with high returns on equity. They also have high operating margins and plenty of cash flow to service their debt. Lowe's, Boston Scientific, Progressive Corporation, Harley-Davidson, Starbucks, and Kohls (shown in Figure 6.8) are all prime examples of growth stocks. As this list suggests, some growth stocks also rate as blue chips and provide quality growth, whereas others represent higher levels of speculation.

Growth stocks normally pay little or nothing in the way of dividends, so their payout ratios seldom exceed 10% to 15% of earnings. Instead, all or most of the profits are reinvested in the company and used to help finance rapid growth. Thus the major source of return to investors is price appreciation—and that can have both a good side and a bad side. That is, with growth

H O T

To read about characteristics of growth and value companies and their performance in recent years, go to:

www.putnam.com
Click on "Individual Investor"
"Education" "Value and Growth"

FIGURE 6.8

A Growth Stock

(*Source:* Standard & Poor's *Stock Reports,* July 12, 2003.)

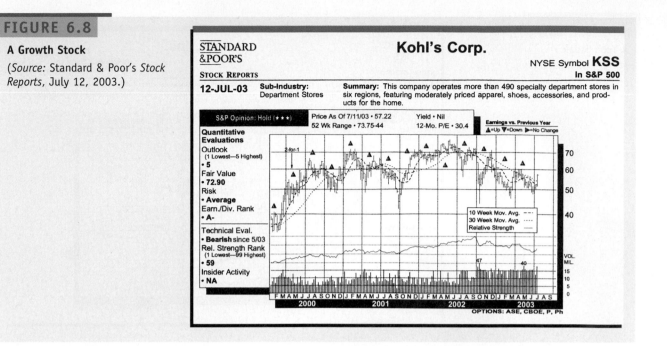

tech stocks
stocks that represent the technology sector of the market.

stocks, when the markets are good, these stocks are hot, but when the markets turn down, so do these stocks, often in a big way. Growth shares generally appeal to investors who are looking for attractive capital gains rather than dividends and who are willing to assume a higher element of risk.

Tech Stocks Over the past 15 years or so, *tech stocks* have become such a dominant force in the market (both positive and negative) that they deserve to be put in a class all their own. **Tech stocks** basically represent the technology sector of the market and include companies that produce or provide everything from computers, semiconductors, data storage, computer software, and computer hardware to peripherals, Internet services, content providers, networking, and wireless communications. These companies provide the high-tech equipment, networking systems, and online services to all lines of businesses, education, health care, communications, governmental agencies, and the home. Some of these stocks are listed on the NYSE and AMEX, though the vast majority are traded on the Nasdaq.

These stocks, in fact, dominate the Nasdaq market and, as such, the Nasdaq Composite Index and other Nasdaq measures of market performance. They were the ones that were hammered especially hard during the market fall of 2000–2002, when the tech-heavy Nasdaq Composite fell nearly 80%. Indeed, the value of many tech stocks fell to just pennies a share, as literally hundreds of these firms simply went out of business. The strongest did survive, however, and some even thrived.

These stocks would probably fall into either the *growth stock* category (see above) or the *speculative stock* class (see page 262), although some of them are legitimate *blue chips*. Tech stocks today may, indeed, offer the potential for attractive (and, in some cases, phenomenal) returns. But they also involve considerable risk, and are probably most suitable for the more risk-tolerant investor. Included in the tech-stock category you'll find some big

FIGURE 6.9

A Tech Stock

(*Source*: Standard & Poor's *Stock Reports*, November 1, 2003.)

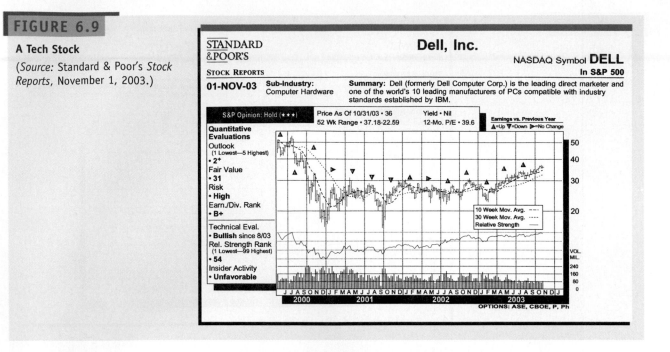

names, like Microsoft, Cisco Systems, Applied Materials, Qualcomm, and Dell (see Figure 6.9). You'll also find many not-so-big names, like BEA Systems, NVIDIA, KLA-Tencor, American Tower, Invitrogen, and Rambus.

speculative stocks
stocks that offer the potential for substantial price appreciation, usually because of some special situation, such as new management or the introduction of a promising new product.

Speculative Stocks Shares that lack sustained records of success but still offer the potential for substantial price appreciation are known as **speculative stocks.** Perhaps investors' hopes are spurred by a new management team that has taken over a troubled company or by the introduction of a promising new product. Other times, it's the hint that some new information, discovery, or production technique will favorably affect the growth prospects of the firm. Speculative stocks are a special breed of securities, and they enjoy a wide following, particularly when the market is bullish.

Generally speaking, the earnings of speculative stocks are uncertain and highly unstable. These stocks are subject to wide swings in price, and they usually pay little or nothing in dividends. On the plus side, speculative stocks such as P. F. Chang's China Bistro, Quicksilver, K-Swiss, Idexx Labs, Serena Software, and Dollar General offer attractive growth prospects and the chance to "hit it big" in the market. To be successful, however, an investor has to identify the big-money winners before the rest of the market does. Speculative stocks are highly risky; they require not only a strong stomach but also a considerable amount of investor know-how. They are used to seek capital gains, and investors will often aggressively trade in and out of these securities as the situation demands.

cyclical stocks
stocks whose earnings and overall market performance are closely linked to the general state of the economy.

Cyclical Stocks Cyclical stocks are issued by companies whose earnings are closely linked to the general level of business activity. They tend to reflect the general state of the economy and to move up and down with the business cycle. Companies that serve markets tied to capital equipment spending by business, or to consumer spending for big-ticket, durable items like houses and cars, typically head the list of cyclical stocks. Examples include Alcoa, Caterpillar, Genuine Parts, Maytag Corporation, Rohm & Haas, and Timken.

Cyclical stocks generally do well when the economy is moving ahead, but they tend to do *especially well* when the country is in the early stages of economic recovery. They are, however, perhaps best avoided when the economy begins to weaken. Cyclical stocks are probably most suitable for investors who are willing to trade in and out of these issues as the economic outlook dictates and who can tolerate the accompanying exposure to risk.

defensive stocks
stocks that tend to hold their own, and even do well, when the economy starts to falter.

Defensive Stocks Sometimes it is possible to find stocks whose prices remain stable or even increase when general economic activity is tapering off. These securities are known as **defensive stocks.** They tend to be less affected than the average issue by downswings in the business cycle. Defensive stocks include the shares of many public utilities, as well as industrial and consumer goods companies that produce or market such staples as beverages, foods, and drugs. An excellent example of a defensive stock is Bandag. This recession-resistant company is the world's leading manufacturer of rubber used to retread tires. Other examples are Checkpoint Systems, a manufacturer of antitheft clothing security clips, and WD-40, the maker of that famous all-purpose lubricant. Defensive shares are commonly used by more aggressive investors, who tend to "park" their funds temporarily in defensive stocks while the economy remains soft, or until the investment atmosphere improves.

Mid-Cap Stocks As explained earlier, a stock's size is based on its market value—or, more commonly, on what is known as its *market capitalization* (the market price of the stock times the number of shares outstanding). Generally speaking, the U.S. stock market can be broken into three segments, as measured by a stock's market "cap":

Small-cap   less than $1 billion

Mid-cap $1 billion to $4 or $5 billion

Large-cap   more than $4 or $5 billion

The large-cap stocks are the real biggies—the Wal-Marts, GMs, and Microsofts of the investment world. Although there are far fewer large-cap stocks than any other size, these companies account for about 80% to 90% of the total market value of all U.S. equities. But as the saying goes, bigger isn't necessarily better. Nowhere is that statement more accurate than in the stock market. Indeed, both the small-cap and mid-cap segments of the market tend to hold their own, or even to outperform large stocks over time.

mid-cap stocks
medium-sized stocks, generally with market values of less than $4 or $5 billion but more than $1 billion.

Mid-cap stocks are a special breed, and offer investors some attractive return opportunities. They provide much of the sizzle of small-stock returns, without as much price volatility. (We'll look at small-cap stocks soon.) At the same time, because mid-caps are fairly good-sized companies and many of them have been around for a long time, they offer some of the safety of the big, established stocks. Among the ranks of the mid-caps are such well-known companies as Wendy's International, Barnes & Noble, Petsmart (see Figure 6.10 on page 264), Outback Steakhouse, Lennar, and Cheesecake Factory. Although these securities offer a nice alternative to large stocks without the uncertainties of small-caps, they probably are most appropriate for investors who are willing to tolerate a bit more risk and price volatility.

FIGURE 6.10

A Mid-Cap Stock

(*Source:* Standard & Poor's *Stock Reports*, July 12, 2003.)

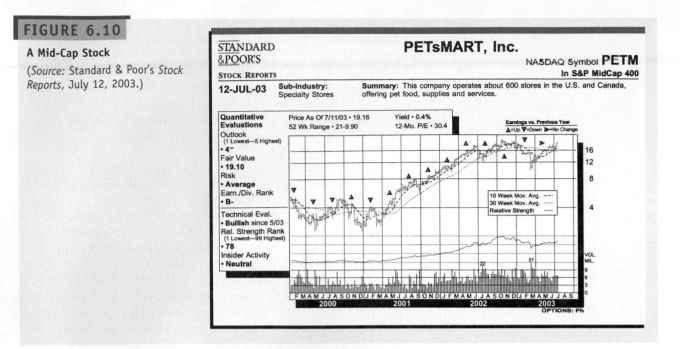

One type of mid-cap stock of particular interest is the so-called *baby blue chip*. Also known as "baby blues," these companies have all the characteristics of a regular blue chip *except size*. Like their larger counterparts, baby blues have rock-solid balance sheets, only modest levels of debt, and long histories of steady profit growth. Baby blues normally pay a modest level of dividends, but like most mid-caps, they tend to emphasize growth. Thus they're considered ideal for investors seeking quality long-term growth. Some well-known baby blues are Tootsie Roll, Reynolds & Reynolds, Hormel Foods, and Pall Corporation.

Small-Cap Stocks Some investors consider small companies to be in a class by themselves in terms of attractive return opportunities. And in many cases, this has turned out to be true. Known as **small-cap stocks,** these companies generally have annual revenues of less than $250 million. But because of their size, spurts of growth can have dramatic effects on their earnings and stock prices. Churchill Downs (where the Kentucky Derby is run), Green Mountain Power, Hancock Fabrics, Hot Topic, JoAnn Stores, and Sonic Corporation (see Figure 6.11) are some better-known small-cap stocks.

Although some small-caps (like Sonic) are solid companies with equally solid financials, that's not the case with most of them. Indeed, because many of these companies are so small, they don't have a lot of stock outstanding, and their shares are not widely traded. In addition, small-company stocks have a tendency to be "here today and gone tomorrow." Although some of these stocks may hold the potential for high returns, investors should also be aware of the very high risk exposure that comes with many of them.

A special category of small-cap stocks is the so-called *initial public offering (IPO)*. Most IPOs are small, relatively new companies that are going public for the first time. (Prior to their public offering, these stocks were pri-

small-cap stocks
stocks that generally have market values of less than $1 billion but can offer above-average returns.

FIGURE 6.11

A Small-Cap Stock

(*Source:* Standard & Poor's *Stock Reports*, July 12, 2003.)

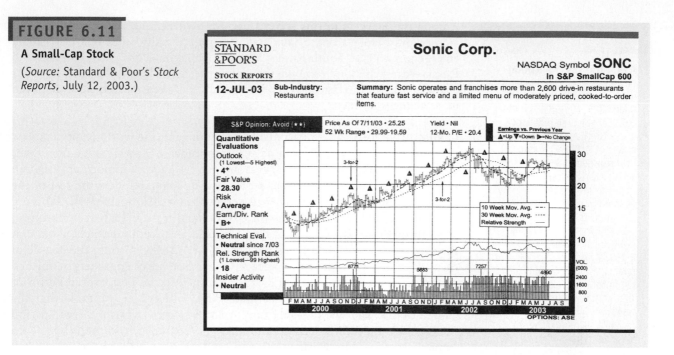

vately held and not publicly traded.) Like other small-company stocks, IPOs are attractive because of the substantial capital gains that investors can earn. Of course, there's a catch: To stand a chance of buying some of the better, more attractive IPOs, you need to be either an active trader or a preferred client of the broker. Otherwise, the only IPOs you're likely to hear of will be the ones these guys don't want. Without a doubt, IPOs are high-risk investments, with the odds stacked against the investor. Because there's no market record to rely on, these stocks should be used only by investors who know what to look for in a company and who can tolerate substantial exposure to risk.

Investing in Foreign Stocks

One of the most dramatic changes to occur in our financial markets in the 1980s and '90s was the trend toward globalization. Indeed, globalization became the buzzword of the 1990s, and nowhere was that more evident than in the world equity markets. Consider, for example, that in 1970 the U.S. stock market accounted for fully *two-thirds of the world market*. In essence, our stock market was twice as big as all the rest of the world's stock markets *combined*. That's no longer true: By 2002, the U.S. share of the world equity market had dropped to less than 50%.

Today the world equity markets are dominated by just six countries, which together account for about 80% of the total market. The United States, by far, has the biggest equity market, which in mid-2003 had a total market value of $10 *trillion*. In a distant second place was Japan (at about one-third the size of the U.S. market), closely followed by the United Kingdom. Rounding out the list were Germany, France and Canada. In addition to these six, another dozen or so markets are also regarded as major world players.

INVESTOR FACTS

A BAD DAY ON THE NIKKEI—
On February 1, 2002, Japan's most popular stock index, the Nikkei 225, closed below the DJIA for the first time since 1957. On that Friday, the Nikkei closed at 9,791.43, while the Dow finished at 9,907.26. So, what's the big deal?

Just this: On the final day of trading in 1989, the Nikkei closed at its all-time high of 38,915.87; in contrast, the DJIA finished the year at 2,753.20. A little over 12 years later, that 36,000-point differential totally disappeared! Over that period, while the Dow went *up* some 7,150 points (a 260% increase), the Nikkei went *down* more than 29,000 points (for a 75% decline).

Source: "Tokyo Stock Market Passes Dubious Milestone," *Wall Street Journal,*" February 4, 2002, pp. C1–2.

Among the markets in this second tier are Switzerland, Australia, Italy, the Netherlands, Hong Kong, Spain, and Singapore. Finally, some relatively small, emerging markets—South Korea, Mexico, Malaysia, Portugal, Thailand, and Russia—are beginning to make their presence felt. Clearly, the landscape has changed a lot in the last 20 years, and there's every reason to believe that even more changes lie ahead.

Comparative Returns The United States dominates the world equity markets in terms of sheer size, as well as in the number of listed companies (over 10,000 of them). But that still leaves unanswered a very important question: How has the U.S. equity market performed in comparison to the rest of the world's major stock markets? The answer: not too well, unfortunately. Table 6.5 summarizes total annual returns (in U.S. dollars) for the 23-year period from 1980 through 2002, for eight of the world's largest equity markets. Note that the United States finished first only once (in 1982). Even so, in the decade of the 1990s, and through 2002, because the U.S. market consistently finished near the top (in every year but 1993), it turned in the best overall performance, closely followed by Switzerland. Also, observe in the table that the United States was not the only one to suffer losses over the 3-year period 2000–2002. Indeed the negative returns showed up across the board, with some countries—like Germany, Japan, and France—suffering much deeper losses. Keep in mind that the returns shown in Table 6.5 *are in U.S. dollars*. But as the *Investing in Action* box on pages 268–269 reveals, a good deal of the performance of non-U.S. markets is due to the behavior of *currency exchange rates* and not the markets themselves. Indeed, the U.S. stock market is one of the strongest and best performing in the world! Still, the fact remains that when both markets and currencies are combined, some very rewarding opportunities are available to U.S. investors who are willing to invest in foreign securities.

Going Global: Direct Investments Basically, there are two ways to invest in foreign stocks: through direct investments or through ADRs. (We'll discuss a third way—international mutual funds—in Chapter 13.) Without a doubt, the most adventuresome way is to *buy shares directly in foreign markets*. Investing directly is *not* for the uninitiated, however. For you have to know what you're doing and be prepared to tolerate a good deal of market risk. Although most major U.S. brokerage houses are set up to accommodate investors interested in buying foreign securities, there are still many logistical problems to be faced. To begin with, you have to cope with currency fluctuations and changing foreign exchange rates, as these can have a dramatic impact on your returns. But that's just the start: You also have to deal with different regulatory and accounting standards. The fact is that most foreign markets, even the bigger ones, are not as closely regulated as U.S. exchanges. Investors in foreign markets, therefore, may have to put up with insider trading and other practices that can cause wild swings in market prices. Finally, there are the obvious language barriers, tax problems, and general "red tape" that all too often plague international transactions. There's no doubt that the returns from direct foreign investments can be substantial, but so can the obstacles placed in your way.

H O T

Visit the CNN financial network to find out which country's stock market has registered the highest percentage change and which registered the lowest percentage change from the previous trading day. Can you cite the reasons why?

money.cnn.com/markets/world_markets.html

TABLE 6.5 Comparative Annual Returns in the World's Major Equity Markets, 1980–2002

	Annual Total Returns (in U.S. dollars)								
	Australia	Canada	France	Germany	Japan	Switzerland	United Kingdom	United States	Rank*
2002	−0.3%	−12.8%	−20.8%	−32.9%	−10.1%	−10.0%	−15.2%	−14.5%	5th
2001	2.6	−20.0	−22.0	−21.9	−29.2	−21.0	−14.0	−5.3	2nd
2000	−9.1	5.6	−4.1	−15.3	−28.1	6.4	−11.5	−4.6	4th
1999	18.7	54.4	29.7	20.5	61.8	−6.6	12.4	26.7	4th
1998	7.1	−5.7	42.1	29.9	5.2	24.0	17.8	17.8	4th
1997	−9.5	13.3	12.4	25.0	−23.6	44.8	22.6	24.4	3rd
1996	17.7	29.0	21.6	14.0	−15.3	2.8	27.2	28.0	2nd
1995	12.5	19.1	14.8	17.0	0.9	45.0	21.3	35.7	2nd
1994	1.4	−5.1	−7.3	3.1	21.4	30.0	−4.4	4.9	3rd
1993	33.4	17.4	19.6	34.8	23.9	41.7	19.0	16.4	8th
1992	−6.1	−4.6	5.2	−2.1	−26.0	26.0	14.0	7.2	3rd
1991	35.8	12.1	18.6	8.7	9.0	16.8	16.0	23.3	2nd
1990	−16.2	−12.2	−13.3	−8.8	−35.9	−5.1	10.4	−0.4	2nd
1989	10.8	25.2	37.6	48.2	2.3	28.0	23.1	30.7	3rd
1988	38.2	17.9	37.1	19.8	35.4	5.8	4.1	15.5	6th
1987	9.5	14.8	−13.9	−24.6	41.0	−9.2	35.2	5.9	5th
1986	45.0	10.8	79.9	36.4	101.2	34.7	27.7	26.1	7th
1985	21.1	16.2	84.2	138.1	44.0	109.2	53.4	31.7	6th
1984	−12.4	−7.1	4.8	−5.2	17.2	−11.1	5.3	1.2	4th
1983	55.2	32.4	33.2	23.9	24.8	19.9	17.3	24.7	5th
1982	−22.2	2.6	−4.2	10.5	−0.6	2.9	9.0	24.8	1st
1981	−23.8	−10.1	−28.5	−10.3	15.7	−9.5	−10.2	−2.8	2nd
1980	54.7	21.6	−2.0	−10.7	30.4	−7.8	42.0	20.6	5th
	Average Annual Returns Over Extended Holding Periods								
5 years									
1998–2002	3.4%	1.4%	1.7%	−7.0%	−4.9%	−2.6%	−3.1%	2.9%	
1995–1999	8.8	20.5	23.7	21.2	2.1	20.1	20.2	26.4	
1990–1994	7.6	0.9	3.7	6.2	−4.9	20.8	10.7	9.9	
Decades									
1993–2002	7.5%	8.0%	7.1%	5.2%	−2.5%	11.2%	7.1%	11.8%	
1990s	8.6	9.8	13.5	12.8	−0.7	17.4	14.2	17.9	
1980s	13.9	11.6	17.6	16.3	28.6	12.2	19.3	17.2	
23 years									
1980–2002	9.2%	7.5%	10.7%	8.9%	7.2%	12.6%	12.7%	13.8%	

Note: Total return = coupon income + capital gain (or loss) + profit (or loss) from changes in currency exchange rates.

*"Rank" shows how U.S. returns ranked among the listed major markets (e.g., in 2002, the United States ranked fifth out of the eight markets listed in the table).

Source: International returns obtained from Morgan Stanley Capital International; U.S. returns based on DJIA.

Going Global with ADRs Fortunately, there is an easier way to invest in foreign stocks, and that is to buy *American Depositary Receipts (ADRs)*, or *American Depositary Shares (ADSs)* as they're sometimes called. As we saw in Chapter 2, ADRs are negotiable instruments, with each ADR representing a specific number of shares in a specific foreign company. (The number of shares can range from a fraction of a share to 20 shares or more.) ADRs are great for investors who want foreign stocks but don't want the hassles that often come with them. That's because American Depositary receipts are bought and sold

INVESTING IN ACTION

IN INTERNATIONAL INVESTING, CURRENCIES CAN MAKE OR BREAK YOU

Investing overseas can pay off in many ways: It offers not only attractive return opportunities, but also attractive portfolio diversification properties. Capitalism is spreading like wildfire around the globe, and the economic expansion in many developing areas dwarfs U.S. growth. Accounting practices have improved, as many foreign companies realize that they must make extensive financial disclosures—beyond their normal comfort levels—if they want to attract U.S. investors. In addition, investing overseas can help to diversify and strengthen a portfolio. You may have to look overseas to find industry leaders, and foreign markets may rise when the U.S. market stalls.

Even with these advantages and global opportunities, it's still difficult to believe that an investor in international stocks can consistently outperform one who invests only in U.S. stocks. But take a look at the accompanying graph: *When measured in U.S. dollars*, foreign stocks (as represented by the EAFE index) actually outperformed American equities between 1985 and 1996. What these numbers don't reveal, however, is the impact of a weakening U.S. dollar. To see how currencies can affect international returns, take another look at the behavior of the EAFE, but this time in *local currencies*. From 1990 to mid-2003, the returns on foreign stocks lagged far behind the returns on U.S. equities. Indeed, for the total period 1985 through mid-2003, *if you exclude the currency factor, U.S. stocks outperformed their overseas counterparts by a wide margin.* For example, in the 10-year

period ending June 30, 2003, the average annual total return for the Standard & Poor's 500 was approximately 10% per year, compared to just 3% for the EAFE in local currencies. Let's examine what this means for you as an investor.

A favorable currency movement for a U.S. investor in a foreign market is a *weakening* dollar. Money that is invested outside the domestic market is converted to a local currency and later converted back to dollars. If the dollar weakens between the time the investor buys and sells the stock, the local currency buys more dollars at the time of the sale. Such was the case during the first half of 2003, for example, as the dollar depreciated against the euro, boosting returns to investors in European equities.

In contrast, a *strengthening* dollar is bad news for U.S. investors buying overseas securities, because the local currency later buys fewer dollars. In the mid-1990s and again from 1997 to late 2002, the U.S. dollar strengthened against most currencies. To see the implications wrought by a stronger dollar, consider the Australian market: Over the 5-year period ending December 31, 2002, this market produced average returns of approximately 6.5% per year, when measured in Aussie dollars. When measured in U.S. dollars, however, the Australian market produced average annual returns of less than 3.5%. Why the big difference in returns? Just one reason: *changing currency exchange rates!* In other words, as the U.S. dollar strengthened relative to the Australian dollar, returns to U.S. investors declined. Under these conditions, U.S. investors

continued on next page

on U.S. markets just like stocks in U.S. companies. Their prices are quoted in U.S. dollars, not British pounds, Japanese yen, or euros. Furthermore, dividends are paid in dollars. Although there are about 400 foreign companies *whose shares are directly listed on U.S. exchanges* (over 200 of which are Canadian), most foreign companies are traded in this country as ADRs. Indeed, shares of about 1,000 companies, from more than 40 countries, are traded as ADRs on the NYSE, AMEX, and Nasdaq/OTC markets.

To see how ADRs are structured, take a look at Cadbury Schweppes, the British food and household products firm, whose ADRs are traded on the

INVESTING IN ACTION

continued from previous page

may have been in an appreciating market, but they were in a depreciating currency.

The fact is, when measured in local currencies, not many stock markets consistently outperform the U.S. markets, even in down years, like 2001–2002; it usually takes a weak dollar to achieve that goal. Even so, most of those markets that did outperform the U.S. market—among them, South Africa, Indonesia, South Korea, and Malaysia—carried significant risks beyond currency risk, such as political unrest and stability of their governments, that don't worry investors in U.S. stocks.

CRITICAL THINKING QUESTION Explain why a strengthening dollar erodes returns from non-U.S. investments. Is the dollar currently weak or strong, and what does this mean for investors?

Sources: Frederick Balfour, "Where to Strike as the Dollar Droops," *Business Week*, June 30, 2003, pp. 104–105; Craig Karmin, "A Year for Most Overseas Investors to Forget," *The Wall Street Journal*, January 3, 2003, pp. R16, R17; Julia Lichtblau, "Global Stocks: Make the World Your Oyster Again," *Business Week*, July 2, 2001, downloaded from www.businessweek.com; and "MSCI Index Returns," Morgan Stanley Capital International, downloaded from www.mscidata.com.

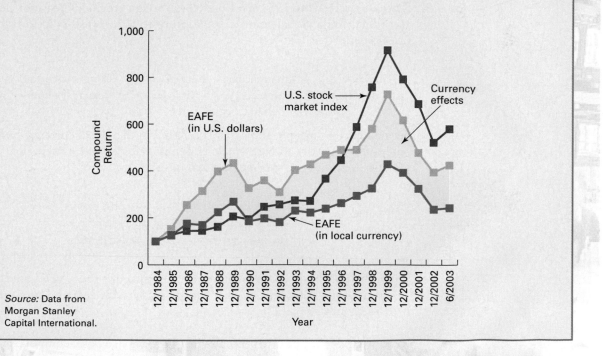

Source: Data from Morgan Stanley Capital International.

NYSE. Each Cadbury ADR represents ownership of four shares of Cadbury stock. These shares are held in a custodial account by a U.S. bank (or its foreign correspondent), which receives dividends, pays any foreign withholding taxes, and then converts the net proceeds to U.S. dollars, which it passes on to investors. Other foreign stocks that can be purchased as ADRs include Sony (a Japanese stock), Ericsson Telephone (from Sweden), Nokia (Finland), Vodafone Airtouch (U.K.), Royal Dutch Petroleum (Netherlands), Nestle's (Switzerland), Shanghai Petro-chemicals (China), Elan Corporation (Ireland), and Grupo Televisa (Mexico). You can even buy ADRs on Russian companies, such as Vimpel-Communications, a Moscow-based cellular phone company whose shares trade (as ADRs) on the NYSE.

Putting Global Returns in Perspective Whether you buy foreign stocks directly or through ADRs, the whole process of global investing is a bit more complex and more risky than domestic investing. The reason: when investing globally, *you have to pick both the right stock and the right market.* Basically, foreign stocks are valued much the same way as U.S. stocks. Indeed, the same variables that drive U.S. share prices (earnings, dividends, and so on) also drive stock values in foreign markets. On top of this, each market reacts to its own set of economic forces (inflation, interest rates, level of economic activity), which set the tone of the market. At any given time, therefore, some markets are performing better than others. The challenge facing global investors is to be in the right market at the right time. As with U.S. stocks, foreign shares produce the same two basic sources of returns: dividends and capital gains (or losses).

But with global investing, there is a third variable—*currency exchange rates*—that plays an important role in defining returns to U.S. investors. In particular, as the U.S. dollar weakens or strengthens relative to a foreign currency, the returns to U.S. investors from foreign stocks increase or decrease accordingly. In a global context, total return to U.S. investors in foreign securities is defined as follows:

Equation 6.4

$$\begin{array}{c}\text{Total return} \\ \text{(in U.S. dollars)}\end{array} = \begin{array}{c}\text{Current income} \\ \text{(dividends)}\end{array} + \begin{array}{c}\text{Current gains} \\ \text{(or losses)}\end{array} \pm \begin{array}{c}\text{Changes in currency} \\ \text{exchange rates}\end{array}$$

Because current income and capital gains are in the "local currency" (the currency in which the foreign stock is denominated, such as the euro or the Japanese yen), we can shorten the total return formula to:

Equation 6.5

$$\begin{array}{c}\text{Total return} \\ \text{(in U.S. dollars)}\end{array} = \begin{array}{c}\text{Returns from current} \\ \text{income and capital gains} \\ \text{(in local currency)}\end{array} \pm \begin{array}{c}\text{Returns from} \\ \text{changes in currency} \\ \text{exchange rates}\end{array}$$

Thus, the two basic components of total return are *those generated by the stocks themselves* (dividends plus change in share prices) and *those derived from movements in currency exchange rates.*

Measuring Global Returns Employing the same two basic components noted in Equation 6.5, above, we can compute total return in U.S. dollars by using the following holding period return (HPR) formula, as modified for changes in currency exchange rates.

Equation 6.6

$$\begin{array}{c}\text{Total return} \\ \text{(in U.S. dollars)}\end{array} = \left[\frac{\begin{array}{c}\text{Ending value of} \\ \text{stock in foreign} \\ \text{currency}\end{array} + \begin{array}{c}\text{Amount of dividends} \\ \text{received in} \\ \text{foreign currency}\end{array}}{\begin{array}{c}\text{Beginning value of stock} \\ \text{in foreign currency}\end{array}} \times \frac{\begin{array}{c}\text{Exchange rate} \\ \text{at end of} \\ \text{holding period}\end{array}}{\begin{array}{c}\text{Exchange rate} \\ \text{at beginning of} \\ \text{holding period}\end{array}} \right] - 1.00$$

In Equation 6.6, the "exchange rate" represents the *value of the foreign currency in U.S. dollars*—that is, how much one unit of the foreign currency is worth in U.S. money.

This modified HPR formula is best used over investment periods of one year or less. Also, because it is assumed that dividends are received at the same exchange rate as the ending price of the stock, this equation provides only an approximate (though fairly close) measure of return. Essentially, the first component of Equation 6.6 provides returns on the stock in local currency, and the second element accounts for the impact of changes in currency exchange rates.

To see how this formula works, consider a U.S. investor who buys several hundred shares of Gucci, the luxury goods company that trades on the Amsterdam Stock Exchange. Since the Netherlands is part of the European Common Market, its currency is the *euro*. Now, assume the investor paid a price *per share* of 90.48 euros for the stock, at a time when the exchange rate between the U.S. dollar and the euro (U.S. $/€) was $0.945, meaning a euro was worth almost 95 (U.S.) cents. The stock paid *annual* dividends of 5 euros per share. Twelve months later, the stock was trading at 94.00 euros, when the U.S. $/€ exchange rate was $1.083. Clearly, the stock went up in price and so did the euro, so the investor must have done all right. To find out just what kind of return this investment generated (in U.S. dollars), we'll have to use Equation 6.6.

$$\text{Total return (in U.S. dollars)} = \left[\frac{94.00 + 5.00}{90.48} \times \frac{\$1.083}{\$0.945} \right] - 1.00$$

$$= [1.0942 \times 1.1460] - 1.00$$

$$= [1.2540] - 1.00$$

$$= \underline{25.4\%}$$

With a return of 25.4%, the investor obviously did quite well. However, *most of this return was due to currency movements, not to the behavior of the stock*. Look at just the first part of the equation, which shows the return (in local currency) *earned on the stock* from dividends and capital gains: 1.0942 − 1.00 = 9.42%. Thus, the stock itself produced a return of less than 9½%. All the rest of the return—about 16% (i.e., 25.40 − 9.42)—came from the change in currency values. In this case, the value of the U.S. dollar went down relative to the euro and thus added to the return.

Currency Exchange Rates As we've just seen, exchange rates can have a dramatic impact on investor returns. They can convert mediocre returns or even losses into very attractive returns—and vice versa. Only one thing determines whether the so-called *currency effect* is going to be positive or negative: the behavior of the U.S. dollar relative to the currency in which the security is denominated. In essence, *a stronger dollar has a negative impact on total returns to U.S. investors, and a weaker dollar has a positive impact*. Thus, other things being equal, the best time to be in foreign securities is when the dollar is *falling*.

Of course, the greater the amount of fluctuation in the currency exchange rate, the greater the impact on total returns. The challenge facing global investors is to find not only the best-performing foreign stock(s) but also the best-performing foreign currencies. You want the *value of both the foreign stock and the foreign currency to go up over your investment horizon*. And note that this rule applies *both* to direct investment in foreign stocks and to the purchase of ADRs. (Even though ADRs are denominated in dollars, their quoted prices vary with ongoing changes in currency exchange rates.)

Alternative Investment Strategies

Basically, common stocks can be used (1) as a "storehouse" of value, (2) as a way to accumulate capital, and (3) as a source of income. Storage of value is important to all investors, as nobody likes to lose money. However, some investors are more concerned about it than others and, therefore, rank safety of principal as their most important stock selection criteria. These investors are more quality-conscious and tend to gravitate toward blue chips and other nonspeculative shares. Accumulation of capital, in contrast, is generally an important goal to those with long-term investment horizons. These investors use the capital gains and/or dividends that stocks provide to build up their wealth. Some use growth stocks for this purpose, others do it with income shares, and still others use a little of both. Finally, some investors use stocks as a source of income. To them, a dependable flow of dividends is essential. High-yielding, good-quality income shares are usually the preferred investment vehicle for these people.

Individual investors can use various *investment strategies* to reach their investment goals. These include buy-and-hold, current income, quality long-term growth, aggressive stock management, and speculation and short-term trading. The first three strategies appeal to investors who consider storage of value important. Depending on the temperament of the investor and the time he or she has to devote to an investment program, any of the strategies might be used to accumulate capital. In contrast, the current-income strategy is the logical choice for those using stocks as a source of income.

Buy-and-Hold Buy-and-hold is the most basic of all investment strategies, and is certainly one of the most conservative. The objective is to place money in a secure investment outlet (safety of principal is vital) and watch it grow over time. In this strategy, investors select high-quality stocks that offer attractive current income and/or capital gains and hold them for extended periods—perhaps as long as 10 to 15 years. This strategy is often used to finance future retirement plans, to meet the educational needs of children, or simply to accumulate capital over the long haul. Generally, investors pick out a few good stocks and then invest in them on a regular basis for long periods of time—until either the investment climate or corporate conditions change dramatically.

Buy-and-hold investors regularly add fresh capital to their portfolios (many treat them like savings plans). Most also plow the income from annual dividends back into the portfolio and reinvest in additional shares (often through dividend reinvestment plans). Long popular with so-called *value-oriented investors*, this approach is used by quality-conscious individuals who are looking for competitive returns over the long haul.

Current Income Some investors use common stocks to seek high levels of current income. Common stocks are desirable for this purpose not so much for their high dividend yields but because their *dividend levels tend to increase over time*. In this strategy, safety of principal and stability of income are vital, while capital gains are of secondary importance. Quality income shares are the obvious medium of choice for this strategy. Some investors adopt it simply as a way of earning high (and relatively safe) returns on their investment capital. More often, however, the current-income strategy is used by those who are trying to supplement their income. Indeed, many of these investors plan to use the added income for consumption purposes, such as a retired couple supplementing their retirement benefits with income from stocks.

Quality Long-Term Growth This strategy is *less conservative* than either of the first two in that it *seeks capital gains as the primary source of return*. A fair amount of trading takes place with this approach. Most of the trading is confined to *quality growth stocks* (including some of the better tech stocks, as well as baby blues and other mid-caps) that offer attractive growth prospects and the chance for considerable price appreciation. A number of growth stocks also pay dividends, which many growth-oriented investors consider *an added source of return*. But even so, this strategy still emphasizes capital gains as the principal way to earn big returns. The approach involves a greater element of risk, because of its heavy reliance on capital gains. Therefore, a good deal of diversification is often used. Long-term accumulation of capital is the most common reason for using this approach, but compared to the buy-and-hold tactic, the investor aggressively seeks a bigger payoff by doing considerably more trading and assuming more market risk.

A variation of this investment strategy combines quality long-term growth with high income. This is the so-called *total-return approach* to investing. Though solidly anchored in long-term growth, this approach also considers dividend income as a source of return that should be sought after, rather than relegated to an after-thought or treated as merely a pleasant by-product. In essence, with the total return approach, investors seek attractive long-term returns from *both* dividend income *and* capital gains. These investors hold both income stocks and growth stocks in their portfolios. Or they may hold stocks that provide both dividends and capital gains. In the latter case, the investor doesn't necessarily look for high-yielding stocks, but rather for stocks that offer the potential for *high rates of growth in their dividend streams*. Like their counterparts who employ current-income or quality long-term growth strategies, total-return investors are very concerned about quality. Indeed, about the only thing that separates these investors from current-income and quality long-term growth investors is that to them, what matters is not so much the *source of return* as *the amount of return*. For this reason, total-return investors seek the most attractive returns wherever they can find them— be it from a growing stream of dividends or from appreciation in the price of a stock.

Aggressive Stock Management Aggressive stock management also uses quality issues but seeks attractive rates of return through a fully managed portfolio. Such a portfolio would be one in which the investor aggressively trades in and out of stocks to achieve eye-catching returns, primarily from capital gains. Blue chips, growth stocks, big-name tech stocks, mid-caps, and cyclical issues are the primary investment vehicles. More aggressive investors might even consider small-cap stocks, including some of the more speculative tech stocks, foreign shares, and ADRs.

This approach is similar to the quality long-term growth strategy. However, it involves considerably more trading, and the investment horizon is generally much shorter. For example, rather than waiting 2 or 3 years for a stock to move, an aggressive stock trader would go after the same investment payoff in 6 months to a year. Timing security transactions and turning investment capital over fairly rapidly are both key elements of this strategy. These investors try to stay fully invested in stocks when the market is bullish. When it weakens, they shift to a more defensive posture by putting a big chunk of their money into defensive stocks or even into cash and other short-term debt instruments. This strategy has substantial risks. It also places real demands on the individual's time and investment skills. But the rewards can be equally substantial.

Speculation and Short-Term Trading Speculation and short-term trading characterize the least conservative of all investment strategies. The sole objective of this strategy is capital gains. And the shorter the time in which the objective can be achieved, the better. Although such investors confine most of their attention to speculative or small-cap stocks and tech stocks, they are not averse to using foreign shares (especially those in so-called *emerging markets*) or other forms of common stock if they offer attractive short-term opportunities. Many speculators feel that information about the industry or company is less important than market psychology or the general tone of the market. It is a process of constantly switching from one position to another as new opportunities unfold. Because the strategy involves so much risk, many transactions yield little or no profit, or even substantial losses. The hope is, of course, that when one does hit, it will be in a big way, and returns will be more than sufficient to offset losses. This strategy obviously requires considerable knowledge and time. Perhaps most important, it also requires the psychological and financial fortitude to withstand the shock of financial losses.

IN REVIEW

CONCEPTS

6.14 Define and briefly discuss the investment merits of each of the following.
a. *Blue chips.*
b. *Income stocks.*
c. *Mid-cap stocks.*
d. *American Depositary Receipts.*
e. *IPOs.*
f. *Tech stocks.*

6.15 Why do most income stocks offer only limited capital gains potential? Does this mean the outlook for continued profitability is also limited? Explain.

6.16 With all the securities available in this country, why would a U.S. investor want to buy foreign stocks? Briefly describe the two ways in which a U.S. investor can buy stocks in a foreign company. As a U.S. investor, which approach would you prefer? Explain.

6.17 Which *investment approach (or approaches)* do you feel would be most appropriate for a quality-conscious investor? What kind of investment approach do you think you'd be most comfortable with? Explain.

Summary

LG 1 **Explain the investment appeal of common stocks and why individuals like to invest in them.** Common stocks have long been a popular investment vehicle, largely because of the attractive return opportunities they provide. From current income to capital gains, there are common stocks available to fit just about any investment need.

LG 2 **Describe stock returns from a historical perspective and understand how current returns measure up to historical standards of performance.** Stock returns consist of both dividends and capital gains, though price appreciation is the key component. Over the long haul, stocks have provided investors with annual returns of around 10% to 12%. The decade of the 1990s was especially rewarding, as stocks generated returns of anywhere from around 20% (on the Dow and S&P 500) to nearly 30% in the tech-heavy Nasdaq market. That situation changed in early 2000, when one of the biggest bull markets in history came to an abrupt end. In fact, the next 3 years, from 2000 through late 2002, saw the DJIA fall some 35% and the S&P 500 nearly 50%. But that was nothing compared to the Nasdaq, which fell an eye-popping 77% from its all-time high.

LG 3 **Discuss the basic features of common stocks, including issue characteristics, stock quotations, and transaction costs.** Common stocks are a form of equity capital and, as such, each share represents partial ownership of a company. Publicly traded stock can be issued via a public offering or through a rights offering to existing stockholders. Companies can also increase the number of shares outstanding through a stock split. To reduce the number of shares of stock in circulation, companies can buy back shares, which are then held as treasury stock. Occasionally, a company issues different classes of common stock, known as classified common stock.

LG 4 **Understand the different kinds of common stock values.** There are several ways to calculate the value of a share of stock. Book value represents accounting value. Market and investment values, which are most important to investors, represent what the stock is or should be worth.

LG 5 **Discuss common stock dividends, types of dividends, and dividend reinvestment plans.** Companies often share their profits by paying out cash dividends to stockholders. Such actions are normally taken only after carefully considering a variety of corporate and market factors. Sometimes companies declare stock dividends rather than, or in addition to, cash dividends. Many firms that pay cash dividends have dividend reinvestment plans, through which shareholders can have cash dividends automatically reinvested in the company's stock.

LG 6 **Describe various types of common stocks, including foreign stocks, and note how stocks can be used as investment vehicles.** The type of stock selected depends on an investor's needs and preferences. In today's market, investors can choose blue chips, income stocks, growth stocks, tech stocks, speculative issues, cyclicals, defensive shares, mid-cap stocks, small-cap stocks, and initial public offerings. In addition, U.S. investors can buy the common stocks of foreign companies either directly on foreign exchanges or on U.S. markets as American Depositary Receipts (ADRs). Generally speaking, common stocks can be used as a storehouse of value, as a way to accumulate capital, and as a source of income. Different investment strategies (buy-and-hold, current income, quality long-term growth, aggressive stock management, and speculation and short-term trading) can be followed to achieve these objectives.

Putting Your Investment Know-How to the Test

1. A Japanese investor buys stock in a New Zealand company for 70 New Zealand dollars (NZD), holds it for a year, and then sells the stock for 65 NZD. The stock paid a 2 NZD dividend. During the year, the NZD appreciated 6% relative to the yen. The investor's approximate yen return over the investment holding period is
   a. Equal to – 4.3%.
   b. Less than – 4.3% because of the currency appreciation.
   c. Greater than – 4.3%, because each NZD bought more yen over the period.
   d. Greater than – 4.3%, because each NZD bought fewer yen over the period.

2. The holding period return on a stock is equal to
   a. The capital gain during the period plus the inflation rate.
   b. The capital gain during the period plus the dividend yield.
   c. The current yield plus the dividend yield.
   d. The dividend yield plus the risk premium.

3. Growth stocks usually exhibit
   a. High dividend yields.
   b. Low price-to-book ratios.
   c. High P/E ratios.
   d. None of the above.

4. A firm's earnings per share increased from $4 to $6, its dividends increased from $3.00 to 3.60, and its share price increased $40 to $50. Based upon this information, we can say that:
   a. the firm increased the number of shares outstanding.
   b. the stock's P/E ration has increased.
   c. the company's dividend payout ratio has decreased.
   d. the company's market capitalization has decreased.

5. The worth of a share of common stock for a stockholder can be best described as its
   a. Market value.   b. Par value.
   c. Book value.   d. Investment value.

6. The main reason for investing in stocks is
   a. They are easy to buy and sell.
   b. They have outperformed inflation in the long run.
   c. They provide superior returns compared to many other investment vehicles.
   d. All of the above.

7. Which of the following is true about various types of stocks?
   a. Income stocks have a record of consistent above-average earnings growth.
   b. Cyclical stocks provide superior returns during recessions.
   c. Small-cap stocks often have a lot of price volatility.
   d. Most defensive stocks are related to the aerospace and defense sectors.

8. You are considering purchasing shares of ABC company. You expect to collect $2 in dividends and sell the stock for $40 a year from now. What is the maximum price you would pay for a share of ABC today if you wanted to earn a 15% return?
   a. $34.78   b. $36.52
   c. $37.50   d. $46.00

9. Provided below and on the next page is information about the financial structure of AXZ Enterprises. (All information is for the fiscal year just ended).

   Number of common shares at the beginning of the year: 5,000,000
   Common stock dividend declared on July 1: 20%
   Net (after-tax) income: $2,500,000

Dividend paid on common stock for the year: $1,100,000
Preferred dividends for the year: $300,000

Given this information, the company's EPS is closest to
a. $0.40.   b. $0.50.
c. $0.30.   d. $0.24.

10. Assuming that the common stock of AXZ currently trades at $10, its dividend yield is
a. 2.50%.   b. 2.00%.
c. 2.20%.   d. 2.55%.

Answers: 1. c; 2. b; 3. c; 4. c; 5. d; 6. d; 7. c; 8. b; 9. a; 10. b

Discussion Questions

LG 2 **Q6.1** Look at the record of stock returns in Tables 6.1 and 6.2, particularly the return performance during the 1970s, 1980s, 1990s, and 2000–2003.

    a. How would you compare the returns during the 1970s with those produced in the 1980s? How would you characterize market returns in the 1990s? Is there anything that stands out about this market? How does it compare with the market that existed from early 2000 through mid-2003?

    b. Now look at Figure 6.2 and Table 6.3. On the basis of the information in these exhibits, how would you describe the market's performance during the 1990s and through the first half of 2003?

    c. Considering the average annual returns that have been generated over holding periods of 5 years or more, what rate of return do you feel is typical for the stock market in general? Is it unreasonable to expect this kind of return, on average, in the future? Explain.

LG 3 **Q6.2** Assume that the following quote for the Alpha Beta Corporation (a NYSE stock) was obtained from the Thursday, April 10, issue of the *Wall Street Journal*.

| +6.8 | 254.00 | 150.50 | AlphaBet | ALF | 6.00 | 3.1 | 15 | 755 | 189.12 | −3.88 |

Given this information, answer the following questions.

    a. On what day did the trading activity occur?

    b. At what price did the stock sell at the end of the day on Wednesday, April 9?

    c. How much (in percentage terms) has the price of this stock gone up or down since the first of the year?

    d. What is the firm's price/earnings ratio? What does that indicate?

    e. What is the last price at which the stock traded on the date quoted?

    f. How large a dividend is expected in the current year?

    g. What are the highest and lowest prices at which the stock traded during the latest 52-week period?

    h. How many shares of stock were traded on the day quoted?

    i. How much, if any, of a change in price took place between the day quoted and the immediately preceding day? At what price did the stock close on the immediately preceding day?

LG 4 **Q6.3** Listed below are three pairs of stocks. Look at each pair and select the security you would like to own, given that you want to *select the one that's worth more money.* Then, *after* you make all three of your selections, use the *Wall Street Journal* or some other source to find the latest market value of the two securities in each pair.

    a. 50 shares of Berkshire Hathaway (stock symbol BRKA) or 150 shares of Coca-Cola (stock symbol KO). (Both are listed on the NYSE.)

    b. 100 shares of WD-40 (symbol WDFC—a Nasdaq National Market issue) or 100 shares of Nike (symbol NKE—a NYSE stock).

    c. 150 shares of Wal-Mart (symbol WMT) or 50 shares of Sears (symbol S). (Both are listed on the NYSE.)

How many times did you pick the one that was worth more money? Did the price of any of these stocks surprise you? If so, which one(s)? Does the price of a stock represent its value? Explain.

LG 6

Q6.4   Assume that a wealthy individual comes to you looking for some investment advice. She is in her early forties and has $250,000 to put into stocks. She wants to build up as much capital as she can over a 15-year period and is willing to tolerate a "fair amount" of risk.

    a. What types of stocks do you think would be most suitable for this investor? Come up with at least three different types of stocks, and briefly explain the rationale for each.

    b. Would your recommendations change if you were dealing with a smaller amount of money—say, $50,000? What if the investor were more risk-averse? Explain.

LG 6

Q6.5   Identify and briefly describe the three sources of return to U.S. investors in foreign stocks. How important are currency exchange rates? With regard to currency exchange rates, when is the best time to be in foreign securities?

    a. Listed below are exchange rates (for the beginning and end of a hypothetical 1-year investment horizon) for three currencies: the British pound (B£), Australian dollar (A$), and Mexican peso (Mp).

| | Currency Exchange Rates at | |
Currency	Beginning of Investment Horizon	End of One-Year Investment Horizon
British pound (B£)	1.55 U.S.$ per B£	1.75 U.S.$ per B£
Australian dollar (A$)	1.35 A$ per U.S.$	1.25 A$ per U.S.$
Mexican peso (Mp)	0.10 U.S.$ per Mp	0.08 U.S.$ per Mp

    From the perspective of a U.S. investor holding a foreign (British, Australian, or Mexican) stock, which of the above changes in currency exchange rates would have a positive effect on returns (in U.S. dollars)? Which would have a negative effect?

    b. ADRs are denominated in U.S. dollars. Are their returns affected by currency exchange rates? Explain.

LG 6

Q6.6   Briefly define each of the following types of investment programs, and note the kinds of stock (blue chips, speculative stocks, etc.) that would best fit with each.

    a. A buy-and-hold strategy.

    b. A current-income portfolio.

    c. Long-term total return.

    d. Aggressive stock management.

Problems

LG 3

P6.1   An investor owns some stock in General Refrigeration & Cooling. The stock recently underwent a 5-for-2 stock split. If the stock was trading at $50 per share just before the split, how much is each share most likely selling for after the split? If the investor owned 200 shares of the stock before the split, how many shares would she own afterward?

P6.2 An investor deposits $20,000 in a new brokerage account. The investor buys 1,000 shares of Tipco stock for $19 per share. Two weeks later, the investor sells the Tipco stock for $20 per share. When the investor receives his brokerage account statement, he sees that there is a balance of $20,900 in his account:

Item	Number	Price per Share	Total Transaction	Account Balance
1. Deposit			$20,000	$20,000
2. Tipco purchase	1,000 shares	$19	($19,000)	$20,000
3. Tipco sale	1,000 shares	$20	$20,000	$21,000
4.				
5. Balance				$20,900

What belongs in item 4 on this statement?

P6.3 The Kracked Pottery Company has total assets of $2.5 million, total short- and long-term debt of $1.8 million, and $200,000 worth of 8% preferred stock outstanding. What is the firm's total book value? What would its book value per share be if the firm had 50,000 shares of common stock outstanding?

P6.4 Lots ov' Profit, Inc., is trading at $25 per share. There are 250 million shares outstanding. What is the market capitalization of this company?

P6.5 The MedTech Company recently reported net profits after taxes of $15.8 million. It has 2.5 million shares of common stock outstanding and pays preferred dividends of $1 million per year.
   a. Compute the firm's earnings per share (EPS).
   b. Assuming that the stock currently trades at $60 per share, determine what the firm's dividend yield would be if it paid $2 per share to common stockholders.
   c. What would the firm's dividend payout ratio be if it paid $2 per share in dividends?

P6.6 On January 1, 2002, an investor bought 200 shares of Gottahavit, Inc., for $50 per share. On January 3, 2003, the investor sold the stock for $55 per share. The stock paid a quarterly dividend of $0.25 per share. How much (in $) did the investor earn on this investment, and, assuming the investor is in the 33% tax bracket, how much will she pay in income taxes on this transaction?

P6.7 Consider the following information about Truly Good Coffee, Inc.

Total assets	$240 million
Total debt	$115 million
Preferred stock	$25 million
Common stockholders' equity	$100 million
Net profits after taxes	$22.5 million
Number of preferred stock outstanding	1 million shares
Number of common stock outstanding	10 million shares
Preferred dividends paid	$2/share
Common dividends paid	$0.75/share
Market price of the preferred stock	$30.75/share
Market price of the common stock	$25.00/share

Use the information above to find the following.
   a. The company's book value.
   b. Its book value per share.
   c. The stock's earnings per share (EPS).
   d. The dividend payout ratio.

e. The dividend yield on the common stock.

f. The dividend yield on the preferred stock.

 P6.8   East Coast Utilities is currently trading at $28 per share. The company pays a quarterly dividend of $0.28 per share. What is the dividend yield?

 P.6.9   West Coast Utilities had net profit of $900 million. It has 900 million shares outstanding, and paid annual dividends of $0.90 per share. What is the dividend payout ratio?

P6.10   Collin Smythies owns 200 shares of Consolidated Glue. The company's board of directors recently declared a cash dividend of 50 cents a share payable April 18 (a Wednesday) to shareholders of record on March 22 (a Thursday).

a. How much in dividends, if any, will Collin receive if he *sells* his stock on March 20?

b. Assume Collin decides to hold on to the stock rather than sell it. If he belongs to the company's dividend reinvestment plan, how many new shares of stock will he receive if the stock is currently trading at $40 and the plan offers a 5% discount on the share price of the stock? (Assume that all of Collin's dividends are diverted to the plan.) Will Collin have to pay any taxes on these dividends, given that he is taking them in stock rather than cash?

P6.11   Southern Cities Trucking Company has the following 5-year record of earnings per share.

Year	EPS
2000	$1.40
2001	2.10
2002	1.00
2003	3.25
2004	0.80

Which of the following procedures would produce the greater amount of dividends to stockholders over this 5-year period?

a. Paying out dividends at a fixed ratio of 40% of EPS.

b. Paying out dividends at a fixed rate of $1 per share.

 P6.12   Using the resources available at your campus or public library, or on the Internet, select any three common stocks you like, and determine the latest book value per share, earnings per share, dividend payout ratio, and dividend yield for each. (Show all your calculations.)

P6.13   In January 2000, an investor purchased 800 shares of Engulf & Devour, a rapidly growing high-tech conglomerate. Over the 5-year period from 2000 through 2004, the stock turned in the following dividend and share price performance.

Year	Share Price at Beginning of Year	Dividends Paid During Year	Share Price at End of Year
2000	$42.50*	$0.82	$ 54.00
2001	54.00	1.28	74.25
2002	74.25	1.64	81.00
2003	81.00	1.91	91.25
2004	91.25	2.30	128.75

*Investor purchased stock in 2000 at this price.

On the basis of this information, find the annual holding period returns for 2000 through 2004. (*Hint:* See Chapter 4 for the HPR formula.)

LG 6   P6.14   George Robbins considers himself to be an aggressive investor. At the present time, he's thinking about investing in some foreign securities. In particular, he's looking at two stocks: (1) Siemens AG, the big German electronics firm, and (2) Swisscom AG, the Swiss telecommunications company.

Siemens, which trades on the Frankfurt Exchange, is currently priced at 53.25 euros per share. It pays annual dividends of 1.5 euros per share. Robbins expects the stock to climb to 60.00 euros per share over the next 12 months. The current exchange rate is 0.9025 €/U.S. $, but that's expected to rise to 1.015 €/U.S. $.

The other company, Swisscom, trades on the Zurich Exchange and is currently priced at 715 Swiss francs (Sf) per share. The stock pays annual dividends of 15 Sf per share. Its share price is expected to go up to 760 Sf within a year. At current exchange rates, one Sf is worth $0.75 U.S., but that's expected to go to $0.85 by the end of the 1-year holding period.

     a. *Ignoring the currency effect*, which of the two stocks promises the higher total return (in its local currency)? Based on this information, which of the two stocks looks like the better investment?

     b. Which of the two stocks has the better total return *in U.S. dollars*? Did currency exchange rates affect their returns in any way? Do you still want to stick with the same stock you selected in part (a)? Explain.

LG 6   P6.15   Bob buys $25,000 of UH-OH Corporation stock. Unfortunately, a major newspaper reveals the very next day that the company is being investigated for accounting fraud, and the stock price falls by 50%. What is the percentage increase now required for Bob to get back to $25,000 of value?

LG 6   P6.16   The euro is currently trading at a ratio of 1.02 relative to the dollar. You expect this to change such that the euro will be trading at 0.8941 to the dollar in 6 months.

     a. If you are correct, what currency transaction would you execute to profit from this move?

     b. If you had $10,000 and you executed the transaction, how much would you make before taxes, assuming your prediction was correct?

See the text Web site
(www.aw-bc.com/gitman_joehnk) for Web exercises
that deal with *common stocks*.

Case Problem 6.1   *Sara Decides to Take the Plunge*

LG 1   **LG 6**

Sara Thomas is a child psychologist who has built up a thriving practice in her hometown of Boise, Idaho. Over the past several years she has been able to accumulate a substantial sum of money. She has worked long and hard to be successful, but she never imagined anything like this. Success has not spoiled Sara. Still single, she keeps to her old circle of friends. One of her closest friends is Terry Jenkins, who happens to be a stockbroker, and who acts as Sara's financial adviser.

Not long ago, Sara attended a seminar on investing in the stock market and since then she's been doing some reading about the market. She has concluded that keeping all of her money in low-yielding savings accounts doesn't make any sense. As a result, Sara has decided to move part of her money to stocks. One evening, Sara told Terry about her decision and explained that she had found several stocks that she thought looked "sort of interesting." She described them as follows:

- *North Atlantic Swim Suit Company.* This highly speculative stock pays no dividends. Although the earnings of NASS have been a bit erratic, Sara feels that its growth prospects have never been brighter—"what with more people than ever going to the beaches the way they are these days," she says.

- *Town and Country Computer.* This is a long-established computer firm that pays a modest dividend yield (of about 1½%). It is considered a quality growth stock. From one of the stock reports she read, Sara understands that T&C offers excellent long-term growth and capital gains potential.

- *Southeastern Public Utility Company.* This income stock pays a dividend yield of around 5%. Although it's a solid company, it has limited growth prospects because of its location.

- *International Gold Mines, Inc.* This stock has performed quite well in the past, especially when inflation has become a problem. Sara feels that if it can do so well in inflationary times, it will do even better in a strong economy. Unfortunately, the stock has experienced wide price swings in the past. It pays almost no dividends.

Questions

a.   What do you think of the idea of Sara keeping "substantial sums" of money in savings accounts? Would common stocks make better investments for her than savings accounts? Explain.

b.   What is your opinion of the four stocks Sara has described? Do you think they are suitable for her investment needs? Explain.

c.   What kind of common stock investment program would you recommend for Sara? What investment objectives do you think she should set for herself, and how can common stocks help her achieve her goals?

Case Problem 6.2

LG 5   LG 6

Wally Wonders Whether There's a Place for Dividends

Wally Wilson is a commercial artist who makes a good living by doing freelance work—mostly layouts and illustrations for local ad agencies and major institutional clients (such as large department stores). Wally has been investing in the stock market for some time, buying mostly high-quality growth stocks as a way to achieve long-term growth and capital appreciation. He feels that with the limited time he has to devote to his security holdings, high-quality issues are his best bet. He has become a bit perplexed lately with the market, disturbed that some of his growth stocks aren't doing even as well as many good-grade income shares. He therefore decides to have a chat with his broker, Al Fried.

During the course of their conversation, it becomes clear that both Al and Wally are thinking along the same lines. Al points out that dividend yields on income shares are indeed way up and that, because of the state of the economy, the outlook for growth stocks is not particularly bright. He suggests that Wally seriously consider putting some of his money into income shares to capture the high dividend yields that are available. After all, as Al says, "the bottom line is not so much where the payoff comes from as how much it amounts to!" They then talk about a high-yield public utility stock, Hydro-Electric Light and Power. Al digs up some forecast information about Hydro-Electric and presents it to Wally for his consideration:

Year	Expected EPS	Expected Dividend Payout Ratio
2004	$3.25	40%
2005	3.40	40
2006	3.90	45
2007	4.40	45
2008	5.00	45

The stock currently trades at $60 per share. Al thinks that within 5 years it should be trading at around $75 to $80 a share. Wally realizes that to buy the Hydro-Electric stock, he will have to sell his holdings of CapCo Industries—a highly regarded growth stock that Wally is disenchanted with because of recent substandard performance.

Questions

a.   How would you describe Wally's present investment program? How do you think it fits him and his investment objectives?

b.   Consider the Hydro-Electric stock.
1.   Determine the amount of annual dividends Hydro-Electric can be expected to pay over the years 2004 to 2008.
2.   Compute the total dollar return that Wally will make from Hydro-Electric if he invests $6,000 in the stock and all the dividend and price expectations are realized.
3.   If Wally participates in the company's dividend reinvestment plan, how many shares of stock will he have by the end of 2008? What will they be worth if the stock trades at $80 on December 31, 2008? Assume that the stock can be purchased through the dividend reinvestment plan at a net price of $50 a share in 2004, $55 in 2005, $60 in 2006, $65 in 2007, and $70 in 2008. Use fractional shares, to two decimals, in your computations. Also, assume that, as in part (b), Wally starts with 100 shares of stock and all dividend expectations are realized.

c.   Would Wally be going to a different investment strategy if he decided to buy shares in Hydro-Electric? If the switch is made, how would you describe his new investment program? What do you think of this new approach? Is it likely to lead to more trading on Wally's behalf? If so, can you reconcile that with the limited amount of time he has to devote to his portfolio?

Excel with Spreadsheets

Efficient information that quickly disseminates market prices is imperative for investors in the stock market. A major component of the information system is the stock quote that appears daily in the financial press.

You found the following stock quote (on page 284) for City National Corporation (CYN) in the January 12, 2004 edition of the *Wall Street Journal*. Refer to Figure 6.5 "Stock Quotations" for an explanation of the array of information related to the listed stock. Given the respective quote, create a spreadsheet to answer the following questions concerning the common stock investment.

	A	B	C	D	E	F	G	H	I	J	K	L
1					**New York Stock Exchange Composite Transactions**							
2		YTD	52	WEEKS				YLD		VOL		NET
3		%CHG	HI	LO	STOCK (SYM)		DIV	%	PE	100S	LAST	CHG
4	[1]	−0.03	64.49	38.7	CityNtl CYN		1.117	18%	16.16	4887	?	−1.89
5												
6												
7												
8												

Questions

a. What was the closing price for this stock yesterday?

b. How many round lots of stock were traded yesterday? How many individual stocks does that translate into?

c. What are the current earnings per share (EPS) for this stock based on the data presented?

d. What is the current net income for this stock? (*Hint*: You must find out the number of shares outstanding.) Using the Internet, follow these steps:

- Go to www.moneycentral.msn.com.
- Place "CYN" in quote box and click "Go."
- Look on the left side for "Financial Results."
- Click on "Statements."
- Choose "Balance Sheet" from the pull-down financial statement menu and "annual" from the view box pull-down menu.
- At the bottom of the statement, look for "Total Common Shares Outstanding."

e. Calculate the dividend payout ratio for City National.

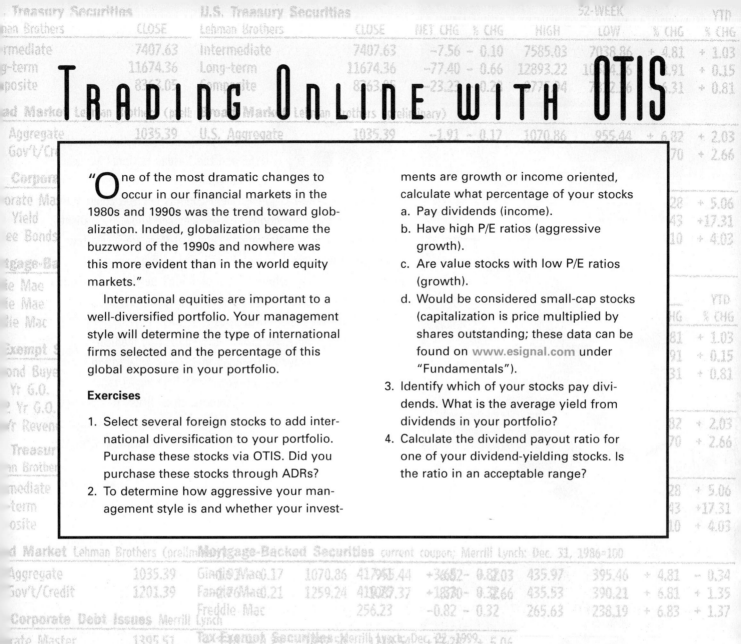

TRADING ONLINE WITH OTIS

"One of the most dramatic changes to occur in our financial markets in the 1980s and 1990s was the trend toward globalization. Indeed, globalization became the buzzword of the 1990s and nowhere was this more evident than in the world equity markets."

International equities are important to a well-diversified portfolio. Your management style will determine the type of international firms selected and the percentage of this global exposure in your portfolio.

Exercises

1. Select several foreign stocks to add international diversification to your portfolio. Purchase these stocks via OTIS. Did you purchase these stocks through ADRs?
2. To determine how aggressive your management style is and whether your investments are growth or income oriented, calculate what percentage of your stocks
   a. Pay dividends (income).
   b. Have high P/E ratios (aggressive growth).
   c. Are value stocks with low P/E ratios (growth).
   d. Would be considered small-cap stocks (capitalization is price multiplied by shares outstanding; these data can be found on www.esignal.com under "Fundamentals").
3. Identify which of your stocks pay dividends. What is the average yield from dividends in your portfolio?
4. Calculate the dividend payout ratio for one of your dividend-yielding stocks. Is the ratio in an acceptable range?

CHAPTER 7

ANALYZING COMMON STOCKS

With over 7,000 companies listed on the NYSE and the Nasdaq National Market, how do you decide which ones are good investment candidates? You could start with companies whose goods and services you know. Dell, Disney, Ford, General Electric, McDonald's, and Wal-Mart are just a few companies that come to mind. Familiarity with a company's products is certainly helpful. But it shouldn't be the only criterion for buying securities. You would very likely eliminate a lot of attractive investment opportunities that way.

Take, for example, Medtronic, Inc., a leading medical instrumentation company. Founded in 1949 in a garage in Minneapolis, the company developed the first implantable pacemaker for cardiac-rhythm disorders. In addition to devices that control irregular heartbeats, Medtronic's product line now includes a wide array of implantable and intervention devices for cardiac, neurological, and other disorders.

In addition to the product lineup, you'd want to know more about Medtronic's market share, patents on its products, and new products under development. Evaluating this company's products tells you only part of the story, however. After researching the company's stock price history, you'd learn that in the 10 years from mid-1993 through mid-2003 (which, by the way, includes the bear market of 2000–2002), Medtronic's stock price grew at a compound rate of nearly 28%, compared to the 8.2% annual growth rate of the S&P 500 index over the same period. Put another way, if you had invested $10,000 in Medtronic stock a decade ago, you'd have more than $115,000 as of mid-year 2003; by contrast, the same amount invested in the stock market as a whole would have been worth only $22,000.

Why did Medtronic's stock perform so much better than the market in general? The answer may lie in analyses of the economy, the medical-device industry, or the company's fundamentals (its financial and operating characteristics). This chapter, the first of two on security analysis, introduces some of the techniques and procedures you can use to evaluate the future of the economy, of industries, and of specific companies, such as Medtronic.

Security Analysis

security analysis
the process of gathering and organizing information and then using it to determine the intrinsic value of a share of common stock.

intrinsic value
the underlying or inherent value of a stock, as determined through fundamental analysis.

The obvious motivation for investing in stocks is to watch your money grow. Consider, for example, the case of Kohl's Corporation, one of the fastest-growing family-oriented department store chains in the country. If you had purchased $5,000 worth of Kohl's stock in June 1992, that investment would have grown to nearly $145,000 by mid-2003. That works out to an average annual return of nearly 36%, as compared to the 8% or 9% return that was generated over the same period by the average large-cap stock, as measured by the S&P 500. Unfortunately, for every story of great success in the market, there are dozens more that don't end so well. Certainly, the nasty bear market we've just experienced has taken its toll; but in addition to that, most investment flops can be traced to bad timing, greed, poor planning, or failure to use common sense in making investment decisions. Although these chapters on stock investments cannot offer the keys to sudden wealth, they do provide sound principles for formulating a successful long-range investment program. The techniques described are quite traditional; they are the same proven methods that have been used by millions of investors to achieve attractive rates of return on their capital.

Principles of Security Analysis

Security analysis consists of gathering information, organizing it into a logical framework, and then using the information to determine the intrinsic value of common stock. That is, given a rate of return that's compatible with the amount of risk involved in a proposed transaction, **intrinsic value** provides a measure of the underlying worth of a share of stock. It provides a standard for helping you judge whether a particular stock is undervalued, fairly priced, or overvalued. The entire concept of stock valuation is based on the belief that all securities possess an intrinsic value that their market value will approach over time.

In investments, the question of value centers on return. In particular, a satisfactory investment candidate is one *that offers a level of expected return commensurate with the amount of risk involved.* That is, the *minimum rate of return* that you should be able to earn on an investment varies with the amount of risk you have to assume. As a result, not only must an investment candidate be profitable, but it also must be *sufficiently* profitable—in the sense that you'd expect it to generate a return that's high enough to offset the perceived exposure to risk.

If you could have your way, you'd probably like to invest in something that offers complete preservation of capital, along with sizable helpings of current income and capital gains. The problem, of course, is finding such a security. One approach is to buy whatever strikes your fancy. A more rational approach is to use security analysis to look for promising investment candidates. Security analysis addresses the question of *what to buy* by determining what a stock *ought to be worth.* Presumably, an investor will buy a stock *only if its prevailing market price does not exceed its worth*—its intrinsic value. Ultimately, intrinsic value depends on several factors:

1. Estimates of the stock's future cash flows (the amount of dividends you expect to receive over the holding period and the estimated price of the stock at time of sale).

2. The discount rate used to translate these future cash flows into a present value.
3. The amount of risk embedded in achieving the forecasted level of performance.

The Top-Down Approach to Security Analysis Traditional security analysis usually takes a "top-down" approach, in that it begins with economic analysis, then moves to industry analysis, and finally to fundamental analysis. *Economic analysis* assesses the general state of the economy and its potential effects on security returns. *Industry analysis* deals with the industry within which a particular company operates. It looks at how the company stacks up against the major competitors in the industry, and the general outlook for that industry. *Fundamental analysis* looks in depth at the financial condition and operating results of a specific company and the underlying behavior of its common stock. In essence, it looks at the "fundamentals of the company." These fundamentals include the company's investment decisions, the liquidity of its assets, its use of debt, its profit margins and earnings growth, and ultimately the future prospects of the company and its stock.

Fundamental analysis is closely linked to the notion of intrinsic value, because it *provides the basis for projecting a stock's future cash flows.* A key part of this analytical process is *company analysis,* which takes a close look at the actual financial performance of the company. Such analysis is not meant simply to provide interesting tidbits of information about how the company has performed in the past. Rather, company analysis is done to *help investors formulate expectations about the future performance of the company and its stock.* Make no mistake about it: In investments, it's the future that matters. But to understand the future prospects of the firm, an investor should have a good handle on the company's current condition and its ability to produce earnings. That's just what company analysis does: It helps investors predict the future by looking at the past and determining how well the company is situated to meet the challenges that lie ahead.

Who Needs Security Analysis in an Efficient Market?

The concept of security analysis in general and fundamental analysis in particular is based on the assumption that investors are capable of formulating reliable estimates of a stock's future behavior. Fundamental analysis operates on the broad premise that some securities may be mispriced in the marketplace at any given point in time. Further, it assumes that, by undertaking a careful analysis of the inherent characteristics of each of the firms in question, it is possible to distinguish those securities that are correctly priced from those that are not.

To many, those two assumptions of fundamental analysis seem reasonable. However, there are others who just don't accept the assumptions of fundamental analysis. These so-called *efficient market* advocates who believe that the market is so efficient in processing new information that securities trade very close to or at their correct values at all times. Thus, they argue, it is virtually impossible to consistently outperform the market. In its strongest form, the *efficient market hypothesis* asserts the following: (1) Securities are rarely, if ever, substantially mispriced in the marketplace; and (2) No security analysis, however detailed, is capable of identifying mispriced securities with a frequency greater than that which might be expected by random chance alone. Is the efficient market hypothesis correct? Is there a place for fundamental analysis in modern investment theory? Interestingly, most financial theorists and practitioners would answer "yes" to both questions.

The solution to this apparent paradox is quite simple. Basically, fundamental analysis is of value in the selection of alternative investment vehicles for two important reasons. First, financial markets are as efficient as they are because a large number of people and powerful financial institutions invest a great deal of time and money in analyzing the fundamentals of most widely held investments. In other words, markets tend to be efficient, and securities tend to trade at or near their intrinsic values, simply because a great many people have done the research to determine just what their intrinsic values should be. Second, although the financial markets are generally quite efficient, they are by no means perfectly efficient. Pricing errors are inevitable. Those individuals who have conducted the most thorough studies of the fundamentals of a given security are the most likely to profit when errors do occur. We will study the ideas and implications of efficient markets in some detail in Chapter 9. For now, however, we will assume that traditional security analysis is useful in identifying attractive equity investments.

IN REVIEW

CONCEPTS

7.1 Identify the three major parts of security analysis, and explain why security analysis is important to the stock selection process.

7.2 What is *intrinsic value?* How does it fit into the security analysis process?

7.3 How would you describe a satisfactory investment vehicle? How does security analysis help in identifying investment candidates?

7.4 Would there be any need for security analysis if we operated in an efficient market environment? Explain.

Economic Analysis

LG 2

If we lived in a world where economic activity had absolutely no effect on the stock market or on security prices, we would not need to study the economy. The fact is, of course, that we do not live in such a world. Rather, stock prices are heavily influenced by the state of the economy and by economic events. As a rule, stock prices tend to move up when the economy is strong, and they retreat when the economy starts to soften. It's not a perfect relationship, but it is a fairly powerful one.

The reason why the economy is so important to the market is simple: The overall performance of the economy has a significant bearing on the performance and profitability of the companies that issue common stock. As the fortunes of the issuing firms change with economic conditions, so do the prices of their stocks. Of course, not all stocks are affected in the same way or to the same extent. Some sectors of the economy, like food retailing, may be only

economic analysis
a study of general economic conditions that is used in the valuation of common stock.

H O T **L I N K S**

Check out Economics Network, U.S. business cycle dates, at

www.prudential.com/yardeni

business cycle
an indication of the current state of the economy, reflecting changes in total economic activity over time.

mildly affected by the economy. Others, like the construction and auto industries, are often hard hit when times get rough.

Economic analysis consists of a general study of the prevailing economic environment. It is meant to help investors gain insight into the underlying condition of the economy and the potential impact it might have on the behavior of share prices. It can go so far as to include a detailed examination of each sector of the economy, or it may be done on a very informal basis. However, from a security analysis perspective, its purpose is always the same: to establish a sound foundation for the valuation of common stock.

Economic Analysis and the Business Cycle

Economic analysis is the first step in the top-down approach and, as such, sets the tone for the entire security analysis process. Thus, if the economic future looks bleak, you can probably expect most stock returns to be equally dismal. If the economy looks strong, stocks should do well. As we saw in Chapter 2, the behavior of the economy is captured in the **business cycle**, which reflects changes in total economic activity over time. Two widely followed measures of the business cycle are gross domestic product and industrial production. *Gross domestic product* (GDP) represents the market value of all goods and services produced in a country over the period of a year. *Industrial production* is a measure (it's really an index) of the activity/output in the industrial or productive segment of the economy. Normally, GDP and the index of industrial production move up and down with the business cycle.

Key Economic Factors

Financial and market decisions are made by economic units at all levels, from individual consumers and households to business firms and governments. These various decisions together have an impact on the direction of economic activity. Particularly important in this regard are the following:

> *Government fiscal policy*
> Taxes
> Government spending
> Debt management
>
> *Monetary policy*
> Money supply
> Interest rates
>
> *Other factors*
> Inflation
> Consumer spending
> Business investments
> Foreign trade and foreign exchange rates

Government fiscal policy tends to be expansive when it encourages spending—when the government reduces taxes and/or increases the size of the budget. Similarly, monetary policy is said to be expansive when money is readily available and interest rates are relatively low. An expansive economy also depends on a generous level of spending by consumers and business concerns. These same variables moving in a reverse direction can have a contractionary (recessionary) impact on the economy, as, for example, when taxes and interest rates increase or when spending by consumers and businesses falls off.

The impact of these major forces filters through the system and affects several key dimensions of the economy. The most important of these are industrial production, corporate profits, retail sales, personal income, the unemployment rate, and inflation. For example, a strong economy exists when industrial production, corporate profits, retail sales, and personal income are moving up and unemployment is down. Thus, when conducting an economic analysis, an investor should keep an eye on fiscal and monetary policies, consumer and business spending, and foreign trade *for the potential impact they have on the economy*. At the same time, he or she must stay abreast of the level of industrial production, corporate profits, retail sales, personal income, unemployment, and inflation *in order to assess the state of the business cycle*.

To help you keep track of the economy, Table 7.1 (on page 292) provides a brief description of some key economic measures. These economic statistics are compiled by various government agencies and are widely reported in the financial media. (Most of the reports are released monthly.) Take the time to carefully read about the various economic measures and reports cited in Table 7.1. When you understand the behavior of these statistics, you can make your own educated guess as to the current state of the economy and where it's headed.

H O T

To keep up with the status of the economy, you can view the monthly leading index of economic indicators computed by the Conference Board in New York.

At the White House site, you can visit the economic statistics briefing room. *The Economist* also provides data useful for keeping track of the economy. See the following sites:

www.conference-board.org/
www.whitehouse.gov/fsbr/esbr.html
www.economist.com

Developing an Economic Outlook

Conducting an economic analysis involves studying fiscal and monetary policies, inflationary expectations, consumer and business spending, and the state of the business cycle. Often, investors do this on a fairly informal basis. As they form their economic judgments, many rely on one or more of the popular published sources (e.g., the *Wall Street Journal, Barron's, Fortune,* and *Business Week*) as well as on periodic reports from major brokerage houses. These sources provide a convenient summary of economic activity and give investors a general feel for the condition of the economy.

H O T

At this site, choose from the left side of the box Today's Economy, and from the categories, select [Especially for Students]. Read an article that interests you.

www.dismal.com

Once you have developed a general economic outlook, you can use the information in one of two ways. One approach is to construct an economic outlook and then consider where it leads in terms of possible areas for further analysis. For example, suppose you uncover information that strongly suggests the outlook for business spending is very positive. On the basis of such an analysis, you might want to look more closely at capital goods producers, such as office equipment manufacturers. Similarly, if you feel that because of sweeping changes in world politics, U.S. government defense spending is likely to drop off, you might want to avoid the stocks of major defense contractors.

A second way to use information about the economy is to consider specific industries or companies and ask, "How will they be affected by expected developments in the economy?" Take, for example, an investor with an interest in *business equipment stocks*. This industry category includes companies involved in the production of everything from business machines and electronic

TABLE 7.1   Keeping Track of the Economy

To help you sort out the confusing array of figures that flow almost daily from Washington, D.C., and keep track of what's happening in the economy, here are some of the most important economic measures and reports to watch.

- **Gross domestic product (GDP).** This is the broadest measure of the economy's performance. Issued every 3 months by the Commerce Department, it is an estimate of the total dollar value of all the goods and services produced in this country. Movements in many areas of the economy are closely related to changes in GDP, so it is a good analytic tool. In particular, watch the annual rate of growth or decline in "real" or "constant" dollars. This number eliminates the effects of inflation and thus measures the actual volume of production. Remember, though, that frequent revisions of GDP figures sometimes change the picture of the economy.

- **Industrial production.** Issued monthly by the Federal Reserve Board, this index shows changes in the physical output of U.S. factories, mines, and electric and gas utilities. The index tends to move in the same direction as the economy; it is thus a good guide to business conditions between reports on GDP. Detailed breakdowns of the index give a reading on how individual industries are faring.

- **The index of leading indicators.** This boils down to one number, which summarizes the movement of a dozen statistics that tend to predict—or "lead"—changes in the GDP. This monthly index, issued by the Commerce Department, includes such things as layoffs of workers, new orders placed by manufacturers, changes in the money supply, and the prices of raw materials. If the index moves in the same direction for several months, it's a fairly good sign that total output will move the same way in the near future.

- **Personal income.** A monthly report from the Commerce Department, this shows the before-tax income received in the form of wages and salaries, interest and dividends, rents, and other payments, such as Social Security, unemployment compensation, and pensions. As a measure of individuals' spending power, the report helps explain trends in consumer buying habits, a major part of total GDP. When personal income rises, people often increase their buying. But note a big loophole: Excluded are the billions of dollars that change hands in the so-called underground economy—cash transactions that are never reported to tax or other officials.

- **Retail sales.** The Commerce Department's monthly estimate of total sales at the retail level includes everything from cars to groceries. Based on a sample of retail establishments, the figure gives a rough clue to consumer attitudes. It can also indicate future conditions: A long slowdown in sales can lead to cuts in production.

- **Money supply.** The Federal Reserve reports weekly this measure of the amount of money in circulation. Actually, there are three measures of the money supply: *M1* is basically currency, demand deposits, and NOW accounts. *M2,* the most widely followed measure, equals M1 plus savings deposits, money market deposit accounts, and money market mutual funds. *M3* is M2 plus large CDs and a few other less significant types of deposits/transactions. Reasonable growth in the money supply, as measured by M2, is thought to be necessary for an expanding economy. However, too rapid a rate of growth in money is considered inflationary; in contrast, a sharp slowdown in the growth rate is viewed as recessionary.

- **Consumer prices.** Issued monthly by the Labor Department, this index shows changes in prices for a fixed market basket of goods and services. The most widely publicized figure is for all urban consumers. A second figure, used in labor contracts and some government programs, covers urban wage earners and clerical workers. Both are watched as a measure of inflation, but many economists believe that flaws cause them to be inaccurate.

- **Producer prices.** This monthly indicator from the Labor Department shows price changes of goods at various stages of production, from crude materials such as raw cotton to finished goods like clothing and furniture. An upward surge may mean higher consumer prices later. However, the index can miss discounts and may exaggerate rising price trends. Watch particularly changes in the prices of finished goods. These do not fluctuate as widely as the prices of crude materials and thus are a better measure of inflationary pressures.

- **Employment.** The percentage of the workforce that is involuntarily out of work (*unemployment*) is a broad indicator of economic health. But another monthly figure issued by the Labor Department—the number of payroll jobs—may be better for spotting changes in business. A decreasing number of jobs is a sign that firms are cutting production.

- **Housing starts.** A pickup in the pace of housing starts usually follows an easing in the availability and cost of money and is an indicator of improving economic health. This monthly report from the Commerce Department also includes the number of new building permits issued across the country, an even earlier indicator of the pace of future construction.

systems to work lockers and high-fashion office furnishings. In this industry, you'll find companies like Pitney Bowes, Diebold, Herman Miller, Hon Industries, and Steelcase. These stocks are highly susceptible to changing economic conditions. That's because when the economy starts slowing down, companies can put off purchases of durable equipment and fixtures. Especially important to this industry, therefore, is the outlook for corporate profits and business investments. So long as these economic factors look good, the prospects for business equipment stocks should be positive.

Assessing the Potential Impact on Share Prices In this instance, our imaginary investor would first want to assess the current state of the business cycle. Using that insight, he could then formulate some expectations about the future of the economy and the potential impact it holds for the stock market in general and business equipment stocks in particular. (Table 7.2 on page 294, shows how some of the more important economic variables can affect the behavior of the stock market.) To see how this might be done, let's assume that the economy has just gone through a year-long recession and is now in the recovery stage of the business cycle: Employment is starting to pick up. Inflation and interest rates have come back down. Both GDP and industrial production have experienced sharp increases in the past two quarters. And Congress is putting the finishing touches on a major piece of legislation that will lead to reduced taxes. More important, although the economy is now in the early stages of a recovery, things are expected to get even better in the future. The economy is definitely starting to build steam, and all indications are that both corporate profits and business spending should undergo a sharp increase. All of these predictions should be good news for the producers of business equipment and office furnishings, as a good deal of their sales and an even larger portion of their profits depend on the level of corporate profits and business spending. In short, our investor sees an economy that's in good shape and set to become even stronger—the consequences of which are favorable not only for the market but for business equipment stocks as well.

Note that these conclusions could have been reached by relying on sources no more sophisticated than *Barron's* or *Business Week*. In fact, about the only "special thing" this investor would have to do is pay careful attention to those economic forces that are particularly important to the business equipment industry (e.g., corporate profits and capital spending). The economic portion of the analysis has set the stage for further evaluation by indicating the type of economic environment to expect in the near future. The next step is to narrow the focus a bit and conduct the industry phase of the analysis.

The Market as a Leading Indicator Before we continue our analysis, however, it is vital to clarify a bit the relationship that normally exists between the stock market and the economy. As we just saw, the economic outlook is used to get a handle on the market and to direct investors to developing industry sectors. Yet it is important to note that changes in stock prices normally occur *before* the actual forecasted changes become apparent in the economy. Indeed, the current trend of stock prices is frequently used to help *predict* the course of the economy itself. The apparent conflict here can be resolved somewhat by noting that because of this relationship, it is even more important to derive a reliable economic outlook and to be sensitive to underlying economic changes that may mean the current outlook is becoming dated. Investors in the stock

TABLE 7.2   Economic Variables and the Stock Market

Economic Variable	Potential Effect on the Stock Market
Real growth in GDP	Positive impact—it's good for the market.
Industrial production	Continued increases are a sign of strength, which is good for the market.
Inflation	Detrimental to stock prices. Higher inflation leads to higher interest rates and lower price/earnings multiples, and generally makes equity securities less attractive.
Corporate profits	Strong corporate earnings are good for the market.
Unemployment	A downer—an increase in unemployment means business is starting to slow down.
Federal budget surplus or deficit	Budget surpluses are good for interest rates and stock prices. Budget deficits, in contrast, may be a positive sign for a depressed economy but can lead to inflation in a stronger economic environment and therefore have a negative impact.
Weak dollar	Often the result of big trade imbalances, a weak dollar has a negative effect on the market. It makes our markets less attractive to foreign investors. However, it also makes our products more affordable in overseas markets and therefore can have a positive impact on our economy.
Interest rates	Another downer—rising rates tend to have a negative effect on the market for stocks.
Money supply	Moderate growth can have a positive impact on the economy and the market. Rapid growth, however, is inflationary and therefore detrimental to the stock market.

market tend to look into the future to justify the purchase or sale of stock. If their perception of the future is changing, stock prices are also likely to be changing. Therefore, watching the course of stock prices as well as the course of the general economy can make for more accurate investment forecasting.

IN REVIEW

CONCEPTS

7.5 Describe the general concept of *economic analysis*. Is this type of analysis necessary, and can it really help the individual investor make a decision about a stock? Explain.

7.6 Why is the business cycle so important to economic analysis? Does the business cycle have any bearing on the stock market?

7.7 Briefly describe each of the following:
   a. Gross domestic product.   b. Leading indicators.
   c. Money supply.   d. Producer prices.

7.8 What effect, if any, does inflation have on common stocks?

Industry Analysis

LG 3

Have you ever thought about buying oil stocks, or autos, or chemicals? How about computer stocks or telecommunications stocks? Looking at securities in terms of industry groupings is widely used by both individual and institutional investors. And it makes a lot of sense, too, because stock prices are influenced, to one degree or another, by industry conditions. Indeed, various industry forces, including the level of demand within an industry, can have a real impact on individual companies. Thus, if the outlook is good for an industry, then the prospects are likely to be strong for many of the companies that make up that industry.

Key Issues

industry analysis
study of industry groupings that looks at the competitive position of a particular industry in relation to others and identifies companies that show particular promise within an industry.

H O T

Go to the following site and click [ProSearch], [Industry Groups], [Best and Worst Industries]. Select [1, 6, 18, or 26 week], and 1-, 3-, or 5-year periods to see how the industries fared on returns.

www.wallstreetcity.com

The first step in **industry analysis** is to establish the competitive position of a particular industry *in relation to others,* for as Table 7.3 (on page 296) indicates, not all industries perform alike. The next step is to identify companies *within the industry* that hold particular promise. This sets the stage for a more thorough analysis of individual companies and securities. Analyzing an industry means looking at such things as its makeup and basic characteristics, the key economic and operating variables that drive industry performance, and the outlook for the industry. The investor will also want to keep an eye out for specific companies that appear well situated to take advantage of industry conditions. Companies with strong market positions should be favored over those with less secure positions. Such dominance is indicative of an ability to maintain pricing leadership and suggests that the firm will be in a position to enjoy economies of scale and low-cost production. Market dominance also enables a company to support a strong research and development effort, thereby helping it secure its leadership position for the future.

Normally, an investor can gain valuable insight about an industry by seeking answers to the following questions:

1. *What is the nature of the industry?* Is it monopolistic, or are there many competitors? Do a few set the trend for the rest, and if so, who are those few?
2. *To what extent is the industry regulated?* Is it regulated (e.g., public utilities)? If so, how "friendly" are the regulatory bodies?
3. *What role does labor play in the industry?* How important are labor unions? Are there good labor relations within the industry? When is the next round of contract talks?
4. *How important are technological developments?* Are any new developments taking place? What impact are potential breakthroughs likely to have?
5. *Which economic forces are especially important to the industry?* Is demand for the industry's goods and services related to key economic variables? If so, what is the outlook for those variables? How important is foreign competition to the health of the industry?
6. *What are the important financial and operating considerations?* Is there an adequate supply of labor, material, and capital? What are the capital spending plans and needs of the industry?

growth cycle
a reflection of the amount of business vitality that occurs within an industry (or company) over time.

The Industry Growth Cycle Questions like these can sometimes be answered in terms of an industry's **growth cycle,** which reflects the vitality of the industry over time. In the first phase—*initial development*—investment opportunities are usually not available to most investors. The industry is new and untried, and the risks are very high. The second stage is *rapid expansion,* during which product acceptance is spreading and investors can foresee the industry's future more clearly. At this stage, economic and financial variables have little to do with the industry's overall performance (sound a bit like some Internet stocks?). Investors will be interested in investing almost regardless of the economic climate. This is the phase that is of substantial interest to investors, and a good deal of work is done to find such opportunities.

TABLE 7.3	A Look at the Stock Performance of Key Industry Groups

In searching for value, an early step is to look at the big picture: *industry-group trends*. One source for such information is Standard & Poor's, which tracks the performance of over 100 industries that it breaks into 10 major industrial groups. Shown here is the performance of all 10 of those major industrial groups, plus a wide-ranging sample of 30 separate industries. Each of these groups or industries, in effect, has its own market index (much like, say, the S&P 500) that measures the performance of stocks within that group or industry. As is apparent in the numbers below, some industries simply do much better than others, at least over certain time periods. (*Source: S&P Sector Scorecard* as reported on www.businessweek.com, June 27, 2003.)

	Industry Performance (% Price Change)		
	Year to date (through 2nd Qtr. 2003)	2002	5 years
Major Industry Groups			
Consumer Discretionary (1)	16.4%	−22.3%	−1.8%
Consumer Staples (2)	1.1	−6.0	−3.0
Energy (3)	7.3	−11.4	1.0
Financials (4)	11.4	−15.5	0.4
Health Care (5)	12.1	−20.0	1.9
Industrials (6)	8.3	−25.5	−1.5
Information Technology (7)	17.9	−37.7	−3.9
Materials (8)	3.5	−9.5	−3.6
Telecommunications (9)	−1.6	−32.6	−11.8
Electric Utilities (10)	12.3	−18.2	−1.2
Individual Industries			
Apparel Retail (1)	12.6%	−1.2%	−1.0%
Auto Parts & Equipment (1)	8.5	−10.5	−9.0
Consumer Electronics (1)	33.7	31.9	N/A
Home Furnishings (1)	−1.8	−5.4	−2.6
Movies & Entertainment (1)	14.0	−37.8	−7.5
Brewers (2)	4.0	7.4	14.3
Food Distributors (2)	3.6	2.7	13.4
Personal Products (2)	7.1	−1.6	−5.8
Oil & Gas Drilling (3)	3.1	−3.6	1.8
Oil & Gas Exploration & Production (3)	8.8	0.4	3.2
Consumer Finance (4)	28.3	−32.9	−0.1
Insurance Brokers (4)	11.8	−20.1	4.2
Multi-line Insurance (4)	−1.5	−27.1	0.2
Property & Casualty Insurance (4)	13.0	−10.6	−1.8
Biotechnology (5)	31.0	−28.0	25.6
Health Care Supplies (5)	22.1	−8.5	11.5
Managed Health Care (5)	25.5	5.2	5.7
Pharmaceuticals (5)	9.5	−21.7	−0.2
Aerospace & Defense (6)	16.2	−7.2	−3.3
Airlines (6)	18.5	−39.8	−10.0
Environmental Services (6)	3.1	−23.6	−9.5
Trucking (6)	−2.4	13.4	2.8
Application Software (7)	21.4	−38.9	−6.3
Computer Hardware (7)	14.9	−29.9	1.1
Internet Software & Services (7)	69.9	−24.2	13.5
Semiconductor Equipment (7)	24.8	−39.3	14.9
Forest Products (8)	10.8	−8.5	2.5
Metal & Glass Containers (8)	−6.6	22.0	−16.6
Electric Utilities (10)	12.3	−18.2	−1.2
Water Utilities (10)	21.2	3.9	16.9

Note: The parenthetical number behind the industry name represents the industry group to which it belongs. For example, the first five industries are identified with a (1), meaning they belong to the "Consumer Discretionary" industry group, which is also identified with a (1).

Unfortunately, most industries do not experience rapid growth for long. Instead, they eventually slip into the next category in the growth cycle, *mature growth,* which is the one most influenced by economic developments. In this stage, expansion comes from growth of the economy. It is a slower source of overall growth than that experienced in stage 2. In stage 3, the long-term nature of the industry becomes apparent. Industries in this category include defensive ones, like food and apparel, and cyclical industries, like autos and heavy equipment.

The last phase is either *stability* or *decline.* In the decline phase, demand for the industry's products is diminishing, and companies are leaving the industry. Investment opportunities at this stage are almost nonexistent, unless you are seeking only dividend income. Investors want to avoid this stage. However, few really good companies ever reach this final stage because they continually bring new products to the market and, in so doing, remain at least in the mature growth phase.

Developing an Industry Outlook

Industry analysis can be conducted by individual investors themselves. Or, as is more often the case, it can be done with the help of published industry reports, such as the popular *S&P Industry Surveys.* These surveys cover all the important economic, market, and financial aspects of an industry, providing commentary as well as vital statistics. Other widely used sources of industry information include brokerage house reports and articles in the popular financial media.

Let's resume our example of the imaginary investor who is thinking about buying business equipment stocks. Recall from our prior discussion that the economic phase of the analysis suggested a strong economy for the foreseeable future—one in which corporate profits and business spending will be expanding. Now the investor is ready to focus on the industry. A logical starting point is to assess the expected industry response to forecasted economic developments. Demand for the product and industry sales would be especially important. The industry is made up of many large and small competitors, and although it is labor-intensive, labor unions are not an important force. Thus, our investor may want to look closely at the potential effect of these factors on the industry's cost structure. Also worth a look is the work being done in research and development (R&D), and in industrial design within the industry. You would want to know which firms are coming out with the new products and fresh ideas, because these firms are likely to be the industry leaders (or potential industry leaders).

Industry analysis yields an understanding of the nature and operating characteristics of an industry, which can then be used to form judgments about the prospects for industry growth. Let's assume that our investor, by using various types of published reports, has examined the key elements of the office equipment industry and has concluded that the industry, *particularly the office furnishings segment,* is well positioned to take advantage of the rapidly improving economy. Many new and exciting products have come out in the last couple of years, and more are on the drawing board or in the R&D stage. Even more compelling is the current emphasis on new products that will contribute to the long-term productivity of businesses and other institutions. Thus the demand for office furniture and fixtures should increase, and although profit margins may tighten a bit, the level of profits should move up smartly, providing a healthy outlook for growth.

In the course of researching the industry, our investor has noticed several companies that stand out, but one looks particularly attractive: Universal Office Furnishings. Long regarded as one of the top design firms in the industry, Universal designs, manufactures, and sells to commercial and institutional users a full line of high-end office furniture and fixtures (desks, chairs, credenzas, modular work stations, filing systems, etc.). In addition, the company produces and distributes state-of-the-art computer furniture and a specialized line of institutional furniture for the hospitality, health care, and educational markets. The company was founded over 50 years ago, and its stock (which trades under the symbol UVRS) has been listed on the NYSE since the late 1970s. Universal would be considered a *mid-cap stock,* with total market capitalization of around $2 or $3 billion. The company experienced rapid growth in the 1990s, as it expanded its product line, but because of its institutional division, was not as hard hit as others in the 2000–2002 bear market. Looking ahead, the general consensus is that the company should benefit nicely from the strong economic environment now in place. Everything about the economy and the industry looks good for the stock, so our investor decides to take a close look at Universal Office Furnishings.

H O T L I N K S

From the main page of the MSN site, go to [Investor], [Markets], [Top 10 Lists], [Industries] to find the 10 best-performing and 10 worst-performing industries. Go to:

moneycentral.msn.com

I N   R E V I E W

CONCEPTS

7.9 What is *industry analysis,* and why is it important?

7.10 Identify and briefly discuss several aspects of an industry that are important to its behavior and operating characteristics. Note especially how economic issues fit into industry analysis.

7.11 What are the four stages of an industry's growth cycle? Which of these stages offers the biggest payoff to investors? Which stage is most influenced by forces in the economy?

Fundamental Analysis

fundamental analysis
the in-depth study of the financial condition and operating results of a firm.

Fundamental analysis is the study of the financial affairs of a business for the purpose of better understanding the nature and operating characteristics of the company that issued the common stock. In this part of the chapter, we will deal with several aspects of fundamental analysis. We will examine the general concept of fundamental analysis, and introduce several types of financial statements that provide the raw material for this type of analysis. We will then describe some key financial ratios that are widely used in company analysis, and will conclude with an interpretation of those financial ratios. It's important to understand that this represents the more traditional approach to security analysis. It's commonly used to evaluate both growth- and value-oriented stocks, as well as income shares, turn-arounds, and other situations where investors rely on financial statements and other databases to at least partially form a decision.

The Concept

Fundamental analysis rests on the belief that *the value of a stock is influenced by the performance of the company that issued the stock.* If a company's prospects look strong, the market price of its stock is likely to reflect that and be bid up. However, the value of a security depends not only on the return it promises but also on the amount of its risk exposure. Fundamental analysis captures these dimensions (risk and return) and incorporates them into the valuation process. It begins with a historical analysis of the financial strength of a firm: the so-called *company analysis* phase. Using the insights obtained, along with economic and industry analyses, an investor can then formulate expectations about the future growth and profitability of a company.

In the historical (or company analysis) phase, the investor studies the financial statements of the firm to learn its strengths and weaknesses, identify any underlying trends and developments, evaluate operating efficiencies, and gain a general understanding of the nature and operating characteristics of the firm. The following points are of particular interest:

1. The competitive position of the company.
2. Its composition and growth in sales.
3. Profit margins and the dynamics of company earnings.
4. The composition and liquidity of corporate resources (the company's asset mix).
5. The company's capital structure (its financing mix).

The historical phase is in many respects the most demanding and the most time-consuming. Most investors, however, have neither the time nor the inclination to conduct such an extensive study, so they rely on published reports for the background material. Fortunately, individual investors have a variety of sources to choose from. These include the reports and recommendations of major brokerage houses, the popular financial media, and financial subscription services like S&P and *Value Line,* not to mention a whole array of computer-based software and online financial sources, such as Business Week Online, Morningstar.com, Quicken, MSN.Money, Wall Street on Demand, CNNMoney.com, and SmartMoney.com. These are all valuable sources of information, and the paragraphs that follow are not meant to replace them. Nevertheless to be an intelligent investor, you should have at least a basic understanding of financial reports and financial statement analysis. One of the lessons that came out of the recent market meltdown is that you can't always rely on others to do the work for you. The responsibility of being an informed investor rests with you, for it is you, ultimately, who will be making your own judgments about a company and its stock.

Financial Statements

Financial statements are a vital part of company analysis, because they enable investors to develop an opinion about the operating results and financial condition of a firm. Three types of financial statements are used in company analysis: the balance sheet, the income statement, and the statement of cash flows. The first two statements are essential to carrying out basic financial analysis, as they contain the data needed to compute many of the financial

CORE EARNINGS—Disenchanted with some of the things that companies were including and excluding from their earnings reports, Standard & Poor's decided to do something about it. In particular, it now takes the *reported earnings* of publicly traded companies and adjusts them to show the firm's **core earnings** from operations. Among other things, core earnings:

- Treat employee stock options as an expense.
- Exclude gains from pension plans.
- Cut out inappropriate extraordinary expenses.

These adjusted core earnings (which S&P started reporting in 2002) will eliminate many questionable accounting transactions and, in so doing, give investors a more accurate picture of company profits. Now if reported company earnings don't agree with S&P core earnings, you'll know why. By all means, if you have to chose between one or the other, chose the S&P core earnings number.

Source: "Standard & Poor's Eyes Corporate Earnings," *Kiplinger's Retirement Report,* August 2002, p. 6.

balance sheet
a financial summary of a firm's assets, liabilities, and shareholders' equity at a single point in time.

income statement
a financial summary of the operating results of a firm covering a specified period of time, usually a year.

statement of cash flows
a financial summary of a firm's cash flow and other events that caused changes in the company's cash position.

ratios. The third statement—the statement of cash flows—is also a key financial report; it is used primarily to assess the cash/liquidity position of the firm. Company statements are prepared on a quarterly basis (these are *abbreviated* statements, compiled for each 3-month period of operation) and again at the end of each calendar year or *fiscal year* (a 12-month period the company has defined as its operating year, which may or may not end on December 31). Annual financial statements must be fully verified by independent certified public accountants (CPAs). They then must be filed with the U.S. Securities and Exchange Commission, and distributed on a timely basis to all stockholders in the form of annual reports. By themselves, corporate financial statements are a most important source of information to the investor. When used with financial ratios and in conjunction with fundamental analysis, they become even more powerful. But as the *Investing in Action* box on page 304 suggests, to get the most from financial ratios, you must have a good understanding of the uses and limitations of the financial statements themselves.

The Balance Sheet The **balance sheet** is a statement of the company's assets, liabilities, and stockholders' equity. The *assets* represent the resources of the company (the things the company owns). The *liabilities* are its debts. *Equity* is the amount of capital the stockholders have invested in the firm. A balance sheet may be thought of as a summary of the firm's assets balanced against its debt and ownership positions *at a single point in time* (on the last day of the calendar or fiscal year, or at the end of the quarter). To balance, the total assets must equal the total amount of liabilities and equity.

A typical balance sheet is illustrated in Table 7.4. It shows the comparative 2003–2004 figures for Universal Office Furnishings, the firm our investor is analyzing. Note that although the Universal name is fictitious, the financial statements are not. *They are the actual financial statements of a real company.* Some of the entries have been slightly modified for pedagogical purposes, but these tables accurately depict what real financial statements look like and how they're used in financial statement analysis.

The Income Statement The **income statement** provides a financial summary of the operating results of the firm. It shows the amount of revenues generated over a period of time, the costs and expenses incurred over the same period, and the company's profits. (Profits are calculated by subtracting all costs and expenses, including taxes, from revenues.) Unlike the balance sheet, the income statement covers activities that have occurred over the course of time, or for a given operating period. Typically, this period extends no longer than a fiscal or calendar year. Table 7.5 (on page 302) shows the income statements for Universal Office Furnishings for 2003 and 2004. Note that these annual statements cover operations for the 12-month period ending on December 31, which corresponds to the date of the balance sheet. The income statement indicates how successful the firm has been in using the assets listed on the balance sheet. That is, management's success in operating the firm is reflected in the profit or loss the company generates during the year.

The Statement of Cash Flows The **statement of cash flows** provides a summary of the firm's cash flow and other events that caused changes in its cash position. A relatively new report, first required in 1988, it is also one of the most useful, because it shows how the company is doing in generating cash.

TABLE 7.4	Corporate Balance Sheet

Universal Office Furnishings, Inc.
Comparative Balance Sheet
December 31
($ in millions)

	2004	2003
Assets		
Current assets		
Cash and equivalents	$ 95.8	$ 80.0
Receivables	227.2	192.4
Inventories	103.7	107.5
Other current assets	73.6	45.2
Total current assets	500.3	425.1
Noncurrent assets		
Property, plant, & equipment, gross	771.2	696.6
Accumulated depreciation	(372.5)	(379.9)
Property, plant, & equipment, net	398.7	316.7
Other noncurrent assets	42.2	19.7
Total noncurrent assets	440.9	336.4
Total assets	**$941.2**	**$761.5**
Liabilities and Stockholders' Equity		
Current liabilities		
Accounts payable	$114.2	$ 82.4
Short-term debt	174.3	79.3
Other current liabilities	85.5	89.6
Total current liabilities	374.0	251.3
Noncurrent liabilities		
Long-term debt	177.8	190.9
Other noncurrent liabilities	94.9	110.2
Total noncurrent liabilities	272.7	301.1
Total Liabilities	**$646.7**	**$552.4**
Stockholders' equity		
Common shares	92.6	137.6
Retained earnings	201.9	71.5
Total equity	294.5	209.1
Total Liabilities and Stockholders' Equity	**$941.2**	**$761.5**

The fact is, a company's reported earnings may bear little resemblance to its cash flow. Whereas profits are simply the difference between revenues and the accounting costs that have been charged against them, *cash flow is the amount of money a company actually takes in as a result of doing business.*

Table 7.6 (on page 303) presents the 2003–2004 statement of cash flows for Universal Office Furnishings. This report brings together items from *both* the balance sheet and the income statement to show how the company obtained its cash and how it used this valuable liquid resource. The statement is broken into three parts. The most important part is the first one, labeled "Cash from Operations." It captures the *net cash flow from operations*—the line highlighted on the statement. This is what is often meant by the term *cash*

TABLE 7.5   Corporate Income Statement

Universal Office Furnishings, Inc.
Income Statements
Fiscal Year Ended December 31
($ in millions)

	2004	2003
Net sales	$1,938.0	$1,766.2
Cost of goods sold	1,128.5	1,034.5
Gross operating profit	$ 809.5	$ 731.7
Selling, administrative, and other operating expenses	497.7	445.3
Depreciation & amortization	77.1	62.1
Other income, net	0.5	12.9
Earnings before interest & taxes	$235.2	$237.2
Interest expense	13.4	7.3
Earnings before taxes	$221.8	$229.9
Income taxes	82.1	88.1
Net profit after taxes	**$139.7**	**$141.8**
Dividends paid per share	$0.15	$0.13
Earnings per share (EPS)	$2.26	$2.17
Number of common shares outstanding (in millions)	61.8	65.3

ratio analysis
the study of the relationships between financial statement accounts.

flow, as it represents the amount of cash generated by the company and available for investment and financing activities.

Note that Universal's 2004 cash flow from operations was over $200 million, down a bit from the year before. As it turned out, this gave the company more than enough for its investing activities ($150.9 million) and its financing activities ($35.4 million), so its actual cash position (see the line near the bottom of the statement, labeled "Net increase (decrease) in cash") increased by some $15.8 million. That result was a big improvement over the year before, when the firm's cash position fell by more than $35 million. A high (and preferably increasing) cash flow means the company has enough money to pay dividends, service debt, and finance growth. In addition, you'd like to see the firm's cash position increase over time because of the positive impact that has on the company's liquidity and its ability to meet operating needs in a prompt and timely fashion.

Financial Ratios

To see what accounting statements really have to say about the financial condition and operating results of a firm, you have to turn to *financial ratios.* Such ratios are useful because they provide a different perspective on the financial affairs of the firm—particularly with regard to the balance sheet and income statement—and thus *expand the information content of the company's financial statements.* Simply stated, **ratio analysis** is the study of the relationships between various financial statement accounts. Each measure relates one item on the balance sheet (or income statement) to another, or, as is more often the

TABLE 7.6   Statement of Cash Flows

Universal Office Furnishings, Inc.
Statements of Cash Flows
Fiscal Year Ended December 31
($ in millions)

	2004	2003
Cash from Operations		
Net earnings	$139.7	$141.8
Depreciation and amortization	77.1	62.1
Other noncash charges	5.2	16.7
Increase (decrease) in current assets	(41.7)	14.1
Increase (decrease) in current liabilities	21.8	(29.1)
Net cash flow from operations	$202.1	$205.6
Cash from Investing Activities		
Acquisitions of property, plant, and equipment—net	(150.9)	(90.6)
Net cash flow from investing activities	($150.9)	($90.6)
Cash from Financing Activities		
Proceeds from long-term borrowing	749.8	79.1
Reduction in long-term debt, including current maturities and early retirements	(728.7)	(211.1)
Net repurchase of capital stock	(47.2)	(9.8)
Payment of dividends on common stock	(9.3)	(8.5)
Net cash flow from financing activities	($35.4)	$150.3
Net increase (decrease) in cash	$15.8	($35.3)
Cash and equivalents at beginning of period	$80.0	$115.3
Cash and equivalents at end of period	$95.8	$80.0

case, a balance sheet account to an operating (income statement) element. In this way, the investor looks not so much at the absolute size of the financial statement accounts, but rather at what it indicates about the liquidity, activity, or profitability of the firm.

What Ratios Have to Offer The most significant contribution of financial ratios is that they enable an investor to assess the firm's past and present financial condition and operating results. The mechanics of ratio analysis are actually quite simple: Selected information is obtained from annual financial statements and used to compute a set of ratios, which are then compared to historical and/or industry standards to evaluate the financial condition and operating results of the company. When historical standards are used, the company's ratios are compared and studied from one year to the next. Industry standards, in contrast, involve comparison of a particular company's ratios to those of other companies in the same line of business.

Remember, the reason we're doing all this is *to develop information about the past that can be used to get a handle on the future*. It's only from an understanding of a company's past performance that you can forecast its future with some degree of accuracy. For example, even if sales have been expanding rapidly

INVESTING IN ACTION

THE TEN COMMANDMENTS OF FINANCIAL STATEMENT ANALYSIS

Individuals must pass a test before obtaining a driver's license, but investors don't need to pass any type of test before trying to use financial statements as part of their investment analyses. Yet analyzing financial statements requires at least as much knowledge and skill as driving an automobile. Perhaps each financial statement should contain a warning to potential users, similar to those found on many products. As a starter, the warning might include these ten commandments:

1. **Thou shalt not use financial statements in isolation.** Instead, use them with other available information, such as data on economy-wide conditions and industry-wide conditions.

2. **Thou shalt not use financial statements as the only source of firm-specific information.** There are many other sources of information about the company. Consider, for example, financial periodicals, analysts' reports, and, of course, the Internet.

3. **Thou shalt not avoid reading footnotes, which are an integral part of financial statements.** Financial statements cannot be reasonably analyzed without reading and understanding the footnotes.

4. **Thou shalt not focus on a single number. Financial statements are not designed to be reduced to a single number.** Net income is not intended to be the number that summarizes all the information relevant to an investment decision. A user must analyze growth and leverage, among other factors, as well as profitability.

5. **Thou shalt not overlook the implications of what is read.** It is not sufficient simply to know that a company is a high-growth or highly leveraged firm; one must also know that such characteristics typically imply higher risk as well.

6. **Thou shalt not ignore events subsequent to the financial statements.** Financial state-ments are not forecasts of the future; rather, they report the financial condition of the company as of year-end. They do not capture the effects of events that occur after year-end. They thus become increasingly out of date as the year progresses.

7. **Thou shalt not overlook the limitations of financial statements.** Financial statements report only a specified set of events, not all events or all possible financial effects of a single event. Financial statements do not generally represent estimates of the market values of the reported assets and liabilities, nor do they reflect changes in the market values of those assets and liabilities.

8. **Thou shalt not use financial statements without adequate knowledge.** Investors should be sufficiently competent to read, understand, and analyze financial statements.

9. **Thou shalt not shun professional help.** If unwilling or unable to attain adequate knowledge, the investor should defer to someone who does have this ability, such as a financial analyst or a professional money manager.

10. **Thou shalt not take unnecessary risks.** If unwilling or unable to obtain professional help, the investor should undertake investments where investment risk is minimal or where analysis of financial statements is not an issue.

CRITICAL THINKING QUESTIONS Which of the "Ten Commandments" listed do you feel is most important? Explain. Why is it important to read footnotes carefully when analyzing a company's financial statements?

over the past few years, you must carefully assess the reasons for the growth before naively assuming that past growth-rate trends will continue into the future. Such insights are obtained from financial ratios and financial statement analysis.

Financial ratios can be divided into five groups: (1) liquidity, (2) activity, (3) leverage, (4) profitability, and (5) common stock, or market, measures. Using the 2004 figures from the Universal financial statements (Tables 7.4 and 7.5), we will now identify and briefly discuss some of the more widely used measures in each of these five categories.

liquidity measures
financial ratios concerned with a firm's ability to meet its day-to-day operating expenses and satisfy its short-term obligations as they come due.

Measuring Liquidity Liquidity is concerned with the firm's ability to meet its day-to-day operating expenses and satisfy its short-term obligations as they come due. Of major concern is whether a company has adequate cash and other liquid assets on hand to service its debt and operating needs in a prompt and timely fashion. A general overview of a company's liquidity can be obtained from two simple measures: current ratio and net working capital. *Generally speaking, you'd like to see high or rising measures with both of these ratios.*

Current Ratio One of the most commonly cited of all financial ratios, the *current ratio* is computed as follows:

Equation 7.1

$$\text{Current ratio} = \frac{\text{Current assets}}{\text{Current liabilities}}$$

In 2004, Universal Office Furnishings (UVRS) had a current ratio of

$$\text{Current ratio for Universal} = \frac{\$500.3}{\$374.0} = \underline{\underline{1.34}}$$

This figure indicates that UVRS had $1.34 in short-term resources to service every dollar of current debt. That's a fairly good number and, by most standards today, would suggest that the company is carrying an adequate level of liquid assets.

Net Working Capital Though technically not a ratio, *net working capital* is often viewed as such. Actually, net working capital is an absolute measure of liquidity and indicates the dollar amount of equity in the working capital position of the firm. It is the difference between current assets and current liabilities. For 2004, the net working capital position for UVRS amounted to

Equation 7.2

$$\text{Net working capital} = \text{Current assets} - \text{Current liabilities}$$

$$\text{For Universal} = \$500.3 - \$374.0 = \underline{\$126.3 \text{ million}}$$

A net working capital figure that exceeds $125,000,000 is indeed substantial (especially for a firm this size) and serves to reinforce our contention that the liquidity position of this firm is good—so long as it is not made up of slow-moving, obsolete inventories and/or past-due accounts receivable.

activity ratios
financial ratios that are used to measure how well a firm is managing its assets.

Activity Ratios Measuring general liquidity is only the beginning of the analysis. We must also assess the composition and underlying liquidity of key current assets, and evaluate how effectively the company is managing these assets. Activity ratios compare company sales to various asset categories in order to measure how well the company is utilizing its assets. Three of the most widely used activity ratios deal with accounts receivable, inventory, and total assets. *Here again, you'd like to see high or rising measures with all three of these ratios.*

Accounts Receivable Turnover A glance at most financial statements will reveal that the asset side of the balance sheet is dominated by just a few accounts that make up 80% to 90%, or even more, of total resources. Certainly, this is the case with Universal Office Furnishings, where, as you can see in Table 7.4, three entries (accounts receivable, inventory, and net long-term assets) accounted for nearly 80% of total assets in 2004. Like Universal, most firms invest a significant amount of capital in accounts receivable, and for this reason they are viewed as a crucial corporate resource. *Accounts receivable turnover* is a measure of how these resources are being managed. It is computed as follows:

Equation 7.3

$$\text{Accounts receivable turnover} = \frac{\text{Annual sales}}{\text{Accounts receivable}}$$

$$\text{For Universal} = \frac{\$1,938.0}{\$227.2} = \underline{8.53}$$

In essence, this turnover figure indicates the kind of return (in the form of sales) the company is getting from its investment in accounts receivable. Other things being equal, the higher the turnover figure, the more favorable it is. In 2004, UVRS was turning its receivables about 8½ times a year. That excellent turnover rate suggests a very strong credit and collection policy. It also means that each dollar invested in receivables was supporting, or generating, $8.53 in sales.

Inventory Turnover Another important corporate resource—and one that requires a considerable amount of management attention—is inventory. Control of inventory is important to the well-being of a company and is commonly assessed with the *inventory turnover* measure:

Equation 7.4

$$\text{Inventory turnover} = \frac{\text{Annual sales}}{\text{Inventory}}$$

$$\text{For Universal} = \frac{\$1,938.0}{\$103.7} = \underline{18.69}$$

Again, the more sales the company can get out of its inventory, the better the return on this vital resource. In 2004, Universal was doing an outstanding job of getting the most from its inventory. A turnover of almost 19 times a year means that the firm is holding inventory for less than a month—actually, for about 20 days (365/18.69 = 19.5). That's the kind of performance you like to see. For the higher the turnover figure, the less time an item spends in inventory and the better the return the company is able to earn from funds tied up in inventory. (Note that, rather than sales, some analysts prefer to use *cost of goods sold* in the numerator of Equation 7.4, on the premise that the inventory account on the balance sheet is more directly related to cost of goods sold from the income statement. Because cost of goods sold is less than sales, using it will, of course, lead to a lower inventory turnover figure—for UVRS in 2004: $1,128.5/$103.7 = 10.88$, versus 18.69 when sales is used. Regardless of whether you use sales (which we'll continue to do in this chapter) or cost of goods sold, for analytical purposes you'd still use the measure in the same way.)

Total Asset Turnover *Total asset turnover* indicates how efficiently assets are being used to support sales. It is calculated as follows:

Equation 7.5

$$\text{Total asset turnover} = \frac{\text{Annual sales}}{\text{Total assets}}$$

$$\text{For Universal} = \frac{\$1,938.0}{\$941.2.7} = \underline{\underline{2.06}}$$

Note in this case that UVRS is generating more than $2.00 in revenues from every dollar invested in assets. This is a fairly high number and is important because it has a direct bearing on corporate profitability. The principle at work here is much like the return to an individual investor: Earning $100 from a $1,000 investment is far more desirable than earning the same amount from a $2,000 investment. A high total asset turnover figure suggests that corporate resources are being well managed and that the firm is able to realize a high level of sales (and, ultimately, profits) from its asset investments.

leverage measures
financial ratios that measure the amount of debt being used to support operations and the ability of the firm to service its debt.

Leverage Measures Leverage looks at the firm's financial structure, and indicates the amount of debt being used to support the resources and operations of the company. The amount of indebtedness within the financial structure and the ability of the firm to service its debt are major concerns in this phase of the analysis. There are two widely used leverage ratios. The first, the debt-equity ratio, measures the *amount of debt* being used by the company. The second, times interest earned, assesses how well the company can *service its debt*.

Debt-Equity Ratio The *debt-equity ratio* measures the relative amount of funds provided by lenders and owners. It is computed as follows:

Equation 7.6

$$\text{Debt-equity ratio} = \frac{\text{Long-term debt}}{\text{Stockholder's equity}}$$

$$\text{For Universal} = \frac{\$177.8}{\$294.5} = \underline{\underline{0.60}}$$

Because highly leveraged firms (those that use large amounts of debt) run an increased risk of defaulting on their loans, this ratio is particularly helpful in assessing a stock's risk exposure. The 2004 debt-equity ratio for UVRS is reasonably low (at 60%) and shows that most of the company's capital comes from its owners. Stated another way, there was only 60 cents worth of debt in the capital structure for every dollar of equity. Unlike the other measures we've looked at so far, a *low or declining* debt-equity ratio is preferable, as that would suggest the firm has a more reasonable debt load and, therefore, less exposure to financial risk.

Times Interest Earned   *Times interest earned* is a so-called coverage ratio. It measures the ability of the firm to meet its fixed interest payments and is calculated as follows:

Equation 7.7

$$\text{Times interest earned} = \frac{\text{Earnings before interest and taxes}}{\text{Interest expense}}$$

$$\text{For Universal} = \frac{\$253.2}{\$13.4} = \underline{\underline{17.55}}$$

The ability of the company to meet its interest payments (which, with bonds, are fixed contractual obligations) in a timely and orderly fashion is an important consideration in evaluating risk exposure. Universal's times interest earned ratio indicates that the firm has about $17.50 available to cover every dollar of interest expense. That's an outstanding coverage ratio—way above average! As a rule, a ratio 8 to 9 times earnings is considered strong, so a ratio that exceeds 17 is definitely up there. To put this number in perspective, there's usually little concern until times interest earned drops to something less than 2 or 3 times earnings. Clearly, low or declining measures definitely are *not* what you want to find here.

It's recently become popular to use an alternative earnings figure in the numerator for the times interest earned ratio. In particular, some analysts are adding back depreciation and amortization expenses to earnings, and are using what is known as "*earnings before interest, taxes, depreciation, and amortization* (EBITDA). Their argument is that because depreciation and amortization are both noncash expenditures (i.e., they're little more than bookkeeping entries), they should be added back to earnings to provide a more realistic "cash-based" figure. While that may be true, EBITDA figures invariably end up putting performance in a far more favorable light—which many argue is the principal motivation behind their use. In fact, EBITDA often results in *much higher* earnings figures and, as a result, tends to sharply increase ratios such as times interest earned. For example, in the case of UVRS, adding depreciation and amortization (2004: $77.1 million) to EBIT (2004: $235.2 million) results in a coverage ratio of $312.3/$13.4 = *23.31*—versus *17.5* when this ratio is computed in the conventional way (with EBIT).

profitability measures
financial ratios that measure a firm's returns by relating profits to sales, assets, or equity.

Measuring Profitability   **Profitability** is a relative measure of success. Each of the various profitability measures relates the returns (profits) of a company to its sales, assets, or equity. There are three widely used profitability measures: net profit margin, return on assets, and return on equity. Clearly, the more profitable the company, the better—thus, *higher or increasing measures of profitability are what you'd like to see.*

Net Profit Margin This is the "bottom line" of operations. *Net profit margin* indicates the rate of profit being earned from sales and other revenues. It is computed as follows:

Equation 7.8

$$\text{Net profit margin} = \frac{\text{Net profit after taxes}}{\text{Total revenues}}$$

$$\text{For Universal} = \frac{\$139.7}{\$1,938.0} = \underline{\underline{7.2\%}}$$

The net profit margin looks at profits as a percentage of sales (and other revenues). Because it moves with costs, it also reveals the type of control management has over the cost structure of the firm. Note that UVRS had a net profit margin of 7.2% in 2004. That is, the company's return on sales was better than 7 cents on the dollar. That may be about average for the large U.S. companies, but as we shall see, that's well above average for firms in the business equipment industry.

Return on Assets As a profitability measure, *return on assets (ROA)* looks at the amount of resources needed to support operations. Return on assets reveals management's effectiveness in generating profits from the assets it has available, and is perhaps *the single most important measure of return*. ROA is computed as follows:

Equation 7.9

$$\text{ROA} = \frac{\text{Net profit after taxes}}{\text{Total assets}}$$

$$\text{For Universal} = \frac{\$139.7}{\$941.2} = \underline{\underline{14.8\%}}$$

In the case of Universal Office Furnishings, the company earned almost 15% on its asset investments in 2004. That is a very healthy return, and, indeed, is well above average. As a rule, you'd like to see a company maintain as high an ROA as possible. The higher the ROA, the more profitable the company.

Return on Equity A measure of the overall profitability of the firm, *return on equity (ROE)* is closely followed by investors because of its direct link to the profits, growth, and dividends of the company. Return on equity—or return on investment (ROI), as it's sometimes called—measures the return to the firm's stockholders by relating profits to shareholder equity:

Equation 7.10

$$\text{ROE} = \frac{\text{Net profit after taxes}}{\text{Stockholder's equity}}$$

$$\text{For Universal} = \frac{\$139.7}{\$294.5} = \underline{\underline{47.4\%}}$$

ROE shows the annual payoff to investors, which in the case of UVRS amounts to nearly 48 cents for every dollar of equity. That, too, is an outstanding measure of performance and suggests that the company is doing what it has to do to keep its shareholders happy. Generally speaking, look out for a falling ROE, as it could mean trouble later on.

Breaking Down ROA and ROE Both ROA and ROE are important measures of corporate profitability. But to get the most from these two measures, we have to break them down into their component parts. ROA, for example, is made up of two key components: the firm's net profit margin and its total asset turnover. Thus, rather than using Equation 7.9 to find ROA, we can use the following expanded format:

Equation 7.11

$$\text{ROA} = \text{Net profit margin} \times \text{Total asset turnover}$$

Using the net profit margin and total asset turnover figures that we computed earlier (Equations 7.8 and 7.5, respectively), we can find Universal's 2004 ROA.

$$\text{ROA} = 7.2\% \times 2.06 = \underline{14.8\%}$$

Note that we end up with the same figure as that found with Equation 7.9. So why would you want to use the expanded version of ROA? *The major reason is that it shows you what's driving company profits.* As an investor, you want to know if ROA is moving up (or down) because of improvement (or deterioration) in the company's profit margin and/or its total asset turnover. Ideally, you'd like to see ROA moving up (or staying high) because the company's doing a good job in managing *both* its profits and its assets.

Going from ROA to ROE Just as ROA can be broken into its component parts, so too can the return on equity (ROE) measure. Actually, ROE is nothing more than an extension of ROA. It brings the company's financing decisions into the assessment of profitability. That is, the expanded ROE measure indicates the extent to which financial leverage (or "trading on the equity") can increase return to stockholders. The use of debt in the capital structure, in effect, means that ROE *will always be greater than ROA.* The question is how much greater. Rather than using the abbreviated version of ROE in Equation 7.10, we can compute ROE as follows:

Equation 7.12

$$\text{ROE} = \text{ROA} \times \text{Equity multiplier}$$

where

$$\text{Equity multiplier} = \frac{\text{Total assets}}{\text{Total stockholders' equity}}$$

To find ROE according to Equation 7.12, we first have to find the equity multiplier.

$$\text{Equity multiplier for Universal} = \frac{\$941.2}{\$294.5} = 3.20$$

Now we can find the 2004 ROE for Universal as follows:

$$\text{ROE} = 14.8 \times 3.20 = \underline{\underline{47.3\%}}$$

Here we can see that the use of debt (the equity multiplier) has magnified—in this case, tripled—returns to stockholders. (Note that small rounding errors account for the difference between the number computed here, 47.3%, and the one computed earlier, 47.4%, when we used Equation 7.10.)

An Expanded ROE Equation Alternatively, we can expand Equation 7.12 still further by breaking ROA *into its component parts.* In this case, we could compute ROE as

Equation 7.13

$$\text{ROE} = \text{ROA} \times \text{Equity multiplier}$$

$$= (\text{Net profit margin} \times \text{Total asset turnover}) \times \text{Equity multiplier}$$

For Universal $= 7.2\% \times 2.06 \times 3.20 = \underline{\underline{47.4\%}}$

This expanded version of ROE is especially helpful, because it enables investors to assess the company's profitability in terms of three key components: net profit margin, total asset turnover, and financial leverage. In this way, you can determine whether ROE is moving up simply because the firm is employing more debt, which isn't necessarily beneficial, or because of the way the firm is managing its assets and operations, which certainly does have positive long-term implications. To stockholders, ROE is a critical measure of performance (and thus merits careful attention) because of the impact it has on growth and earnings—both of which, as we'll see in Chapter 8, play vital roles in the stock valuation process.

common stock (market) ratios
financial ratios that convert key information about a firm to a per-share basis.

Common Stock Ratios Finally, there are a number of **common stock,** or so-called **market ratios,** that convert key bits of information about the company to a per-share basis. They tell the investor exactly what portion of total profits, dividends, and equity is allocated to each share of stock. Popular common stock ratios include earnings per share, price/earnings ratio, dividends per share, dividend yield, payout ratio, and book value per share. We examined two of these measures (earnings per share and dividend yield) in Chapter 6. Let's look now at the other four.

Price/Earnings Ratio This measure, an extension of the earnings per share ratio, is used to determine how the market is pricing the company's common stock. The price/earnings (P/E) ratio relates the company's earnings per share (EPS) to the market price of its stock.

Equation 7.14

$$\text{P/E} = \frac{\text{Market price of common stock}}{\text{EPS}}$$

To compute the P/E ratio, it is necessary to first know the stock's EPS. Using the earnings per share equation from the previous chapter, we see that the EPS for UVRS in 2004 was

$$\text{EPS} = \frac{\text{Net profit after taxes} - \text{Preferred dividends}}{\text{Number of common shares outstanding}}$$

$$\text{For Universal} = \frac{\$139.7 - \$0}{61.8} = \underline{\underline{\$2.26}}$$

In this case, the company's profits of \$139.7 million translate into earnings of \$2.26 for *each share* of outstanding common stock. Given this EPS figure and the stock's current market price (assume it is currently trading at \$41.50), we can use Equation 7.14 to determine the P/E ratio for Universal.

$$\text{P/E} = \frac{\$41.50}{\$2.26} = \underline{\underline{18.4}}$$

In effect, the stock is currently selling at a multiple of about 18 times its 2004 earnings.

Price/earnings multiples are widely quoted in the financial press and are an essential part of many stock valuation models. Other things being equal, you'd like to find stocks with *rising P/E ratios,* because higher P/E multiples usually translate into higher future stock prices and better returns to stockholders. But even though you'd like to see them going up, you also want to *watch out for P/E ratios that become too high* (relative either to the market or to what the stock has done in the past). When this multiple gets too high, it may be a signal that the stock is becoming overvalued (and may be due for a fall).

One way to assess the P/E ratio is to compare it to the company's rate of growth in earnings. The market has developed a measure of this comparison called the **PEG ratio.** Basically, it looks at the latest P/E relative to the 3- to 5-year rate of growth in earnings. (The earnings growth rate can be all historical—the last 3 to 5 years—or perhaps part historical and part forecasted.) The PEG ratio is computed as

PEG ratio
a financial ratio that relates a stock's price/earnings multiple to the company's rate of growth in earnings.

Equation 7.15

$$\text{PEG ratio} = \frac{\text{Stock's P/E ratio}}{\text{3- to 5-year growth rate in earnings}}$$

As we saw earlier, Universal Office Furnishings had a P/E ratio of 18.4 times earnings in 2004. If corporate earnings for the past 5 years had been growing at an average annual rate of, say, 15%, then its PEG ratio would be

$$\text{For Universal} = \frac{18.4}{15.0} = \underline{\underline{1.21}}$$

A PEG ratio this close to 1.0 is certainly reasonable. It suggests that the company's P/E is not out of line with the earnings growth of the firm. In fact, the idea is to *look for stocks that have PEG ratios that are equal to or less than 1.* In contrast, a high PEG means the stock's P/E has outpaced its growth in earnings and, if anything, the stock is probably "fully valued." Some investors, in fact, won't even look at stocks if their PEGs are too high—say, more than 1.5 or 2.0. At the minimum, PEG is probably something you would want to look at, because it certainly is not unreasonable to expect some correlation between a stock's P/E and its rate of growth in earnings.

Dividends per Share The principle here is the same as for EPS: to translate total common dividends paid by the company into a per-share figure. (*Note:* If it is not on the income statement, the amount of dividends paid to common stockholders can usually be found on the statement of cash flows—Table 7.6.) Dividends per share is measured as follows:

Equation 7.16

$$\text{Dividends per share} = \frac{\text{Annual dividends paid to common stock}}{\text{Number of common shares outstanding}}$$

$$\text{For Universal} = \frac{\$9.3}{61.8} = \underline{\$0.15}$$

For fiscal 2004, Universal paid out dividends of $0.15 per share—at a quarterly rate of about 3¾ cents per share.

As we saw in the preceding chapter, we can relate dividends per share to the market price of the stock to determine its *dividend yield:* i.e., $0.15 ÷ $41.50 = 0.4%. Clearly, you won't find Universal Office Furnishings within the income sector of the market. It pays very little in annual dividends and has a dividend yield of less than ½ of 1%.

Payout Ratio Another important dividend measure is the dividend payout ratio. It indicates how much of its earnings a company pays out to stockholders in the form of dividends. Well-managed companies try to maintain target payout ratios. If earnings are going up over time, so will the company's dividends. The payout ratio is calculated as follows:

Equation 7.17

$$\text{Payout ratio} = \frac{\text{Dividends per share}}{\text{Earnings per share}}$$

$$\text{For Universal} = \frac{\$0.15}{\$2.26} = \underline{0.07}$$

For Universal in 2004, dividends accounted for about 7% of earnings. Traditionally, most companies that paid dividends tended to pay out somewhere between 40% and 60% of earnings. By that standard, Universal's payout, like its dividend yield, is quite low. But that's not necessarily bad, as it indicates that the company is retaining most of its earnings to, at least in part, internally finance the firm's rapid growth. Although low dividend payout ratios are certainly not a cause for concern, *high payout ratios may be.* In particular, once the payout ratio reaches 70% to 80% of earnings, extra care should be taken. A payout ratio that high is often an indication that the company may not be able to maintain its current level of dividends. That generally means that dividends will have to be cut back to more reasonable levels. And if there's one thing the market doesn't like, it's cuts in dividends.

Book Value per Share The last common stock ratio is book value per share, a measure that deals with stockholders' equity. Actually, book value is simply another term for equity (or net worth). It represents the difference between total assets and total liabilities. Note that in this case we're defining equity as *common stockholders' equity,* which would *exclude* preferred stock. That is, *common stockholders' equity = total equity − preferred stocks.* (Universal has no preferred outstanding, so its total equity equals its common stockholders' equity.) Book value per share is computed as follows:

Equation 7.18

$$\text{Book value per share} = \frac{\text{Common stockholders' equity}}{\text{Number of common shares outstanding}}$$

$$\text{For Universal} = \frac{\$294.5}{61.8} = \underline{\$4.76}$$

Presumably, a stock should sell for *more* than its book value (as Universal does). If not, it could be an indication that something is seriously wrong with the company's outlook and profitability.

A convenient way to relate the book value of a company to the market price of its stock is to compute the price-to-book-value ratio.

Equation 7.19

$$\text{Price-to-book-value} = \frac{\text{Market price of common stock}}{\text{Book value per share}}$$

$$\text{For Universal} = \frac{\$41.50}{\$4.76} = \underline{8.72}$$

Widely used by investors, this ratio shows how aggressively the stock is being priced. Most stocks have a price-to-book-value ratio of more than 1.0—which simply indicates that the stock is selling for more than its book value. In fact, in strong bull markets, it's not uncommon to find stocks trading at four or five times their book values, or even more. Universal's price-to-book ratio of 8.7 times is definitely on the high side. That is something that you'll want to closely evaluate. It may indicate that the stock is already fully priced, or perhaps even overpriced. Or it could result from nothing more than a relatively low owners' equity ratio.

Interpreting the Numbers

Rather than compute all the financial ratios themselves, most investors rely on published reports for such information. Many large brokerage houses and a variety of financial services firms publish such reports. An example is given in Figure 7.1. These reports provide a good deal of vital information in a convenient and easy-to-read format. Best of all, they relieve investors of the chore of computing the financial ratios themselves. (Similar information is also available from a number of online services, as well as from various software providers.) Even so, you, as an investor, must be able to evaluate this published information. To do so, you need not only a basic understanding of financial ratios but also some standard of performance, or benchmark, against which you can assess trends in company performance.

Basically, two types of performance standards are used in financial statement analysis: historical and industry. With *historical standards*, various financial ratios and measures are run on the company for a period of 3 to 5 years (or longer). You would use these to assess developing trends in the company's operations and financial condition. That is, are they improving or deteriorating, and where do the company's strengths and weaknesses lie? In contrast,

---

INVESTOR FACTS

THE CASH-REALIZATION RATIO—Want to keep an eye out for signs that earnings are being propped up by financial shenanigans? Then try comparing the cash flow statement with the income statement. That can be done with the **cash-realization ratio**, which shows how much of a company's net income is being converted into cash. Simply divide *cash flow from operations* (from the cash flow statement) by *net income* (from the income statement), preferably using average figures over a 2- to 4-year period. Generally speaking, companies with the highest cash-realization ratios have the highest quality of earnings. Ideally, companies should have cash-realization ratios of at least 1.0, indicating that net income and cash flow from operations are equal. Higher ratios indicate that the company is generating more in cash flow than it is in income— *a very healthy sign*. A ratio of less than 1.0 means that the company is generating less in cash flow than it is in earnings, which can eventually spell trouble for stockholders.

FIGURE 7.1   **An Example of a Published Report with Financial Statistics**
This and similar reports are widely available to investors and play an important part in the security analysis process.
(*Source:* Standard & Poor's *Stock Reports,* July 12, 2003.)

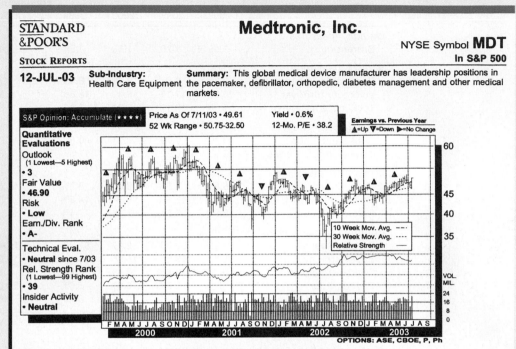

STANDARD &POOR'S

STOCK REPORTS

Medtronic, Inc.

NYSE Symbol **MDT**

In S&P 500

12-JUL-03   **Sub-Industry:** Health Care Equipment   **Summary:** This global medical device manufacturer has leadership positions in the pacemaker, defibrillator, orthopedic, diabetes management and other medical markets.

S&P Opinion: Accumulate (★★★★)   Price As Of 7/11/03 • 49.61   52 Wk Range • 50.75-32.50   Yield • 0.6%   12-Mo. P/E • 38.2

Earnings vs. Previous Year
▲=Up ▼=Down ▶=No Change

Quantitative Evaluations

Outlook (1 Lowest—5 Highest)
• **3**

Fair Value
• **46.90**

Risk
• **Low**

Earn./Div. Rank
• **A-**

Technical Eval.
• **Neutral** since 7/03

Rel. Strength Rank (1 Lowest—99 Highest)
• **39**

Insider Activity
• **Neutral**

10 Week Mov. Avg. -- --
30 Week Mov. Avg. - - - -
Relative Strength —

VOL. MIL.

OPTIONS: ASE, CBOE, P, Ph

Overview - 22-MAY-03

S&P estimates that FY 04 (Apr.) sales growth will approximate 18%, as strong performance for defibrillators, pacemakers, spinal surgery, neurostimulation and peripheral vascular devices, along with favorable foreign currency fluctuations, more than offset expected erosion in the cardiac stent markets and some reduced growth within the diabetes area. At present exchange rates, we believe foreign currency could add about $220 million to FY 04 revenues. Gross margins should widen, on new product launches and favorable currency, but we anticipate that R&D spending and SG&A costs will consume 10% and 32% of sales, respectively. EPS comparisons may benefit from a lower tax rate; we see FY 04 operating EPS growing 15%, to $1.62. Our Standard & Poor's Core Earnings per share estimate for FY 04 is $1.45. Looking into FY 05, we have established an operating EPS forecast of $1.87.

Valuation - 22-MAY-03

Following the company's FY 03 fourth quarter earnings release, MDT noted that earnings in FY 04 would likely approximate $1.61, below earlier guidance of $1.64. Although the company continues to experience strong demand across most product categories, we believe the more conservative guidance reflects concerns about the chance for a stronger dollar relative to the Euro, difficult comparisons in the cardiac rhythm management business, the expectation of a sharp decline in vascular, a slowdown in diabetes, and higher spending on corporate infrastructure. We have lowered our FY 04 EPS estimate to $1.62, from $1.67, but feel that there remains upside to our forecast should the U.S. dollar show further weakness or pacemaker sales continue to accelerate. At a recent P/E of about 30 times our FY 04 EPS forecast, the stock is priced at a slight premium to its medical device peers. However, we believe this premium is justified by the company's broad product base and long term record of consistent earnings growth in a highly competitive industry.

Key Stock Statistics

S&P EPS Est. 2004	1.62	Tang. Bk. Value/Share	1.93
P/E on S&P Est. 2004	30.6	Beta	0.63
S&P EPS Est. 2005	1.84	Shareholders	48,500
Dividend Rate/Share	0.29	Market cap. (B)	$ 60.5
Shs. outstg. (M)	1219.5	Inst. holdings	70%
Avg. daily vol. (M)	3.549		

Value of $10,000 invested 5 years ago: $ 14,555

Fiscal Year Ending Apr. 30

	2003	2002	2001	2000	1999	1998
Revenues (Million $)						
1Q	1,714	1,456	1,310	1,105	991.7	646.3
2Q	1,891	1,571	1,361	1,161	984.5	642.1
3Q	1,913	1,592	1,362	1,259	1,039	631.4
4Q	2,148	1,792	1,518	1,432	1,119	685.0
Yr.	7,665	6,411	5,552	5,015	4,134	2,605
Earnings Per Share ($)						
1Q	0.31	0.25	0.24	0.21	0.20	0.15
2Q	0.25	0.05	0.26	0.22	0.10	0.15
3Q	0.35	0.26	0.25	0.22	-0.03	0.01
4Q	0.40	0.25	0.29	0.25	0.13	0.17
Yr.	1.30	0.80	0.85	0.90	0.40	0.48

Next earnings report expected: late August

Dividend Data (Dividends have been paid since 1977.)

Amount ($)	Date Decl.	Ex-Div. Date	Stock of Record	Payment Date
0.063	Aug. 29	Oct. 02	Oct. 04	Oct. 25 '02
0.063	Oct. 24	Dec. 31	Jan. 03	Jan. 24 '03
0.063	Jan. 23	Apr. 02	Apr. 04	Apr. 25 '03
0.073	Jun. 26	Jul. 01	Jul. 03	Jul. 25 '03

For important regulatory information, go to www.standardandpoors.com, "Regulatory Disclosures."

The McGraw-Hill Companies

TABLE 7.7   **Comparative Historical and Industry Ratios**

	Historical Figures for Universal Office Furnishings				Industry Averages for the Office Equipment Industry in 2004
	2001	2002	2003	2004	
Liquidity measures					
Current ratio	1.55	1.29	1.69	1.34	1.45
Activity measures					
Receivables turnover	9.22	8.87	9.18	8.53	5.70
Inventory turnover	15.25	17.17	16.43	18.69	7.80
Total asset turnover	1.96	2.12	2.32	2.06	0.85
Leverage measures					
Debt-equity ratio	0.70	0.79	0.91	0.60	1.58
Times interest earned	15.37	26.22	32.49	17.55	5.60
Profitability measures					
Net profit margin	6.6%	7.5%	8.0%	7.2%	4.6%
Return on assets	9.8%	16.4%	18.6%	14.8%	3.9%
Return on equity	25.9%	55.5%	67.8%	47.4%	17.3%
Common stock measures					
Earnings per share	$1.92	$2.00	$2.17	$2.26	N/A
Price/earnings ratio	16.2	13.9	15.8	18.4	16.2
Dividend yield	0.3%	0.4%	0.4%	0.4%	1.1%
Payout ratio	5.2%	5.5%	6.0%	6.6%	24.8%
Price-to-book-value ratio	7.73	10.73	10.71	8.72	3.54

industry standards enable you to compare the financial ratios of the company with comparable firms or with the average results for the industry as a whole. Here, we focus on determining the relative strength of the firm with respect to its competitors. Using Universal Office Furnishings, we'll see how to use both of these standards of performance to evaluate and interpret financial ratios.

Using Historical and Industry Standards Look at Table 7.7. It provides a summary of historical data and average industry figures (for the latest year) for most of the ratios we have discussed. By carefully evaluating these ratios, we should be able to draw some basic conclusions about the financial condition, operating results, and general financial health of the company. By comparing the financial ratios contained in Table 7.7, we can make the following observations about UVRS:

1. Universal's *liquidity position* is a bit below average. But this doesn't seem to be a source of major concern, especially when you consider its receivables and inventory positions. That is, based on its respective turnover ratios (see item 2 below), both of these current assets seem to be very well controlled, which could explain the relatively low current ratio of this company. The current ratio is a bit below average, not because the firm has a lot of current liabilities, but because it is doing such a good job in controlling current assets.
2. Universal's *activity measures* are all way above average. This company consistently has very high turnover measures, which in turn make significant contributions not only to the firm's liquidity position but also to its profitability! Clearly, the company has been able to get a lot more from its assets than the industry as a whole.

TABLE 7.8   **Comparative Financial Statistics: Universal Office Furnishings and Its Major Competitors (All figures are for year-end 2004 or for the 5-year period ended in 2004; $ in millions)**

Financial Measure	Universal Office Furnishings	Cascade Industries	Colwyn Furniture	High Design, Inc.
Total assets	$ 941.2	$ 906.7	$342.7	$3,037.6
Long-term debt	$ 177.8	$ 124.2	$ 73.9	$ 257.8
Stockholders' equity	$ 294.5	$ 501.3	$183.9	$1,562.2
Stockholders' equity as a % of total assets	31.3%	55.3%	53.7%	51.4%
Total revenues	$1,938.0	$1,789.3	$642.2	$3,316.1
Net earnings	$ 139.7	$ 87.4	$ 38.5	$ 184.2
Net profit margin	7.2%	4.9%	6.0%	5.5%
5-year growth rates in:				
Total assets	14.36%	19.44%	17.25%	17.73%
Total revenues	18.84%	17.76%	15.91%	15.84%
EPS	56.75%	38.90%	21.10%	24.66%
Dividends	1.48%	11.12%	N/A	12.02%
Total asset turnover	2.06×	1.97×	1.88×	1.09×
Debt-equity ratio	0.60	0.43	1.46	0.17
Times interest earned	17.55×	13.38×	8.35×	14.36×
ROA	14.8%	9.5%	6.7%	6.7%
ROE	47.4%	18.8%	21.8%	13.0%
P/E ratio	18.4×	14.4×	13.3×	12.4×
PEG ratio	1.21	2.42	1.98	1.09
Payout ratio	6.6%	26.2%	N/A	32.4%
Dividend yield	0.4%	1.8%	N/A	2.6%
Price-to-book-value ratio	8.72	2.71	2.93	1.59

3. The *leverage position* of Universal Office Furnishings seems well controlled. The company tends to use a lot less debt in its financial structure than the average firm in the office equipment industry. The payoff for this judicious use of debt comes in the form of a coverage ratio that's well above average.

4. The *profitability picture* for Universal is equally attractive. The profit margin, return on assets, and ROE are all well above the industry norms. Clearly, the company is doing an outstanding job in managing its profits and is getting as much as it can from its sales, assets, and equity.

In summary, our analysis shows that this firm is very well managed and highly profitable. The results of this are reflected in *common stock ratios* that are consistently equal or superior to industry averages. Universal does not pay out a lot in dividends, but that's only because it's using those valuable resources to finance its growth and to reward its investors with consistently high ROEs.

Looking at the Competition In addition to analyzing a company historically and relative to the average performance of the industry, it's useful to evaluate the firm relative to two or three of its major competitors. A lot can be gained from seeing how a company stacks up against its competitors and by determining whether it is, in fact, well positioned to take advantage of unfolding developments. Table 7.8 offers an array of comparative financial statistics for Universal and three of its major competitors. One is about the same size

ETHICS IN INVESTING

COOKING THE BOOKS: WHAT WERE THEY THINKING?

The scandals involving fraudulent accounting practices at Enron, WorldCom, Adelphia, Xerox, Global Crossing, and Tyco have resulted in widespread public outrage. It appears that creative and un- ethical accounting practices kept real costs and debts off the books of these companies and inflated their stock prices. When the reality finally caught up with the fantasy, tens of thousands of investors and employees lost their life savings; at the same time, many of the corporate executives who were responsible for the fraud reaped huge financial rewards. For example, cooking the books at Enron cost investors almost $67 billion, while the implosion of WorldCom wiped out $175 billion of share-holder value, the biggest corporate bankruptcy in U.S. history.

Just two months after the Enron debacle, Global Crossing sought Chapter 11 protection from its creditors after the SEC started an official inquiry into the collapse and subpoenaed documents relating to widespread claims that the company had used "creative accounting" to inflate its earnings. The investigation also implicated accounting firm Arthur Andersen, which had been the auditor for both Global Crossing and Enron. When Global Crossing filed for bankruptcy in January 2002, it listed $22.4 billion in assets and $12.3 billion in debt. However, much

of its value appeared to result from less than ethical accounting practices approved by Arthur Andersen. Since the company went public in 1998, however, its founder and chairman Gary Winnick had profited handsomely, selling $734 million worth of Global Crossing stock.

Another telecom giant, Qwest Communications, was under investigation by the SEC for its accounting practices when it disclosed on July 28, 2002, that it had incorrectly accounted for more than $1 billion of revenue since 1999. Qwest had booked hundreds of millions of dollars of revenue at the end of its quarterly reporting period that should have been delayed until the next quarter. Qwest actually has $26 billion in debt, and like many other telecommunication companies, faces intense pressure to meet quarterly revenue and profit targets.

At WorldCom, internal audits revealed that $3.8 billion in operating expenses had been fraudulently disguised as capital expenditures over five quarters dating back to January 2001. The stock that had peaked around $65 currently trades at 2 cents on the OTC pink sheets. Arthur Andersen was again implicated as the corporate auditor in this scandal.

Xerox, a leading office machine supplier, had to restate $6.4 billion of revenues dating back to 1997. It reached agreement with the SEC over

continued on next page

(Cascade Industries), one is much smaller (Colwyn Furniture), and one is much larger (High Design, Inc.). (This type of firm-specific data can generally be obtained from industry surveys similar to those put out by S&P and others—or, again, from the Internet or from various software providers.)

As the data in Table 7.8 show, Universal can hold its own against other leading producers in the industry. Indeed, in virtually every category, Universal's numbers are about equal or superior to those of its three major competitors. It may not be the biggest (or the smallest), but it outperforms them all in profit margins and growth rates (in revenues and earnings). Equally important, it has the highest asset turnover, ROE, and price/earnings ratio. Tables 7.7 and 7.8 clearly show that Universal Office Furnishings is a solid, up-and-coming business that's been able to make a name for itself in a highly competitive industry. The company has done well in the past and appears to be well managed today. Our major concern at this point (and the topic of discussion in Chapter 8) is whether Universal can continue to produce above-average returns to investors.

ETHICS IN INVESTING

continued from previous page

the way it booked the long-term leases of copiers as revenues but the figures were three times larger than investors expected. The stock lost more than 90% of its value between summer 1999 and January 2001. However, there is some hope at Xerox, as the company has avoided filing for bankruptcy and the stock has enjoyed a modest rebound since its troubles began.

At Adelphia Communications, the 77-year-old company founder, John Rigas, his two sons, and two other former executives were arrested and charged with "looting Adelphia on a massive scale." The company filed for Chapter 11 protection from creditors in summer 2002, and Rigas and his sons are awaiting criminal trials expected to begin in 2004. Rigas had employed Adelphia as his family's personal bank, using corporate assets in "off-balance-sheet" personal loans exceeding $2 billion (more than $3 billion total for his entire family). At the same time, Adelphia has defaulted on its own obligations of $44.7 million interest and dividend payments. The stock's value has plummeted to less than 40 cents (down from a peak of $87 in May 1999) and has been delisted from Nasdaq. While Adelphia was relatively small compared to the other scandal-ridden firms, Rigas's plundering of his company has surpassed any corporate greed records.

Many analysts and accountants readily admit that accounting standards are almost incapable of dealing with complex merger deals and complicated corporate structures. Bankers often structure financial products that companies allow to exploit these weaknesses so as to enhance executive bonuses and to create fictitious shareholder value without increasing company's business expenses. Among the common accounting tricks used in the recent corporate scandals, the following appear to be the most popular: capitalizing operating expenses on the balance sheet (WorldCom), recognizing fictitious or premature revenues (Xerox, Qwest), creating off-balance-sheet liabilities (Enron), using off-balance-sheet derivative contracts transactions and company stock to hedge risk (Enron), and writing off goodwill as extraordinary loss rather than amortizing it over time (AOL Time Warner) so as to manipulate future earnings growth.

CRITICAL THINKING QUESTION One of the steps to strengthen corporate reporting is to separate internal and external audits of the company by requiring that an external auditor not be permitted to provide internal audits to the same client. Will this regulation be able to eliminate conflict of interest? Discuss.

One assumption that we made in our discussion of ratio analysis is that the accounting statements we're using are good. Unfortunately, as the *Ethics* box above explains, that hasn't always been the case.

IN REVIEW

CONCEPTS

7.12 What is *fundamental analysis?* Does the performance of a company have any bearing on the value of its stock? Explain.

7.13 Why do investors bother to look at the historical performance of a company when future behavior is what really counts? Explain.

7.14 What is *ratio analysis?* Describe the contribution of ratio analysis to the study of a company's financial condition and operating results.

7.15 Contrast historical standards of performance with industry standards. Briefly note the role of each in analyzing the financial condition and operating results of a company.

Summary

| LG 1 | **Discuss the security analysis process, including its goals and functions.** Success in buying common stocks is largely a matter of careful security selection and investment timing. Security analysis helps the investor make the selection decision by gauging the intrinsic value (underlying worth) of a stock. |

| LG 2 | **Understand the purpose and contributions of economic analysis.** Economic analysis evaluates the general state of the economy and its potential effects on security returns. Its purpose is to characterize the future economic environment the investor is likely to face, and to set the tone for the security analysis process. |

| LG 3 | **Describe industry analysis and note how it is used.** In industry analysis, the investor focuses on the activities of one or more industries. Especially important are how the competitive position of a particular industry stacks up against others and which companies within an industry hold special promise. |

| LG 4 | **Demonstrate a basic appreciation of fundamental analysis and why it is used.** Fundamental analysis looks closely at the financial and operating characteristics of the company—at its competitive position, its sales and profit margins, its asset mix, its capital structure, and, eventually, its future prospects. A key aspect of this analytical process is company analysis, which involves an in-depth study of the financial condition and operating results of the company. |

| LG 5 | **Calculate a variety of financial ratios and describe how financial statement analysis is used to gauge the financial vitality of a company.** The company's balance sheet, income statement, and statement of cash flows are all used in company analysis. An essential part of this analysis is financial ratios, which expand the perspective and information content of financial statements. There are five broad categories of financial ratios—liquidity, activity, leverage, profitability, and market (common stock) ratios. All involve the study of relationships between financial statement accounts. |

| LG 6 | **Use various financial measures to assess a company's performance, and explain how the insights derived form the basic input for the valuation process.** To evaluate financial ratios properly, it is necessary to base the analysis on historical and industry standards of performance. Historical standards are used to assess developing trends in the company. Industry benchmarks enable the investor to see how the firm stacks up against its competitors. Together, they provide insight into how well the company is situated to take advantage of unfolding market conditions and opportunities. |

Putting Your Investment Know-How to the Test

1. A firm has a ROE of 6% and a total debt/equity ratio of 0.5. Its ROA is
   a. 4%.
   b. 6%.
   c. 7.5%.
   d. 12%.

2. All of the following ratios include net income in their computations *except:*
   a. Total asset turnover.
   b. Profit margin.
   c. Return on equity.
   d. Return on assets.

3. Which one of the following would best explain a situation where the ratio of "net income to total equity" for a firm is higher than the industry average, while the ratio of "net income to total assets" is lower than the industry average?
   a. Net profit margin is higher than the industry average.
   b. Debt ratio is higher than the industry average.

c. Asset turnover is higher than the industry average.

d. Equity multiplier must be lower than the industry average.

4. If a firm's ratio of "total liabilities to total assets" is higher than the industry average while its ratio of "long-term debt to stockholders' equity" is lower than the industry average, it would most likely indicate that the firm

a. Has more current liabilities than the industry average.

b. Has more leased assets than the industry average.

c. Will be less profitable than the industry average.

d. Has more current assets than the industry average.

5. Which of the following is true about cash flow from financing?

a. It is an indication of the types of financing that the management supports.

b. Analysts use it as an indication of the quality of earnings.

c. It offers an insight into the financing habits of a company.

d. It provides information about all of the above.

6. Which of the following is *not* part of industry analysis?

a. Industry structure.   b. Degree of unionization.

c. Rate of industry growth.   d. Rate of inflation.

7. Which of the following statements about measures of relative value is *false?*

a. Price/sales (P/S) ratio is defined as the market value of the company divided by its sales.

b. Companies with low price/book value (P/BV) ratios tend to outperform high P/BV ratio firms on a risk-adjusted basis.

c. P/BV and price/cash flow (P/CF) ratios should be used in conjunction with price/earnings (P/E) ratios in fundamental analysis.

d. A major benefit to relative valuation methods such as P/BV and P/S is the ability to utilize them in comparing firms from different industries.

8. The price/earnings ratio is expected to be higher when

a. The ROE is higher.

b. The ROE is lower.

c. The price/book ratio is lower.

d. The dividend payout ratio is higher.

Use the following data to answer Questions 9 and 10.

Net income	$100
Depreciation	25
Goodwill amortization	20
Decrease in accounts receivable	10
Increase in inventory	20
Purchase of a new truck	30
Increase in accounts payable	15
Sale of common stock	45
Issuance of bonds	25
Purchase of machine	50

9. Cash flow from operating activities is

a. $125.   b. $135.

c. $150.   d. $180.

10. Cash flow from financing activities is

a. $25.   b. $45.

c. $70.   d. $85.

Answers: 1. a; 2. a; 3. b; 4. a; 5. d; 6. d; 7. d; 8. b; 9. c; 10. c

Discussion Questions

Q7.1   Economic analysis is generally viewed as an integral part of the "top-down" approach to security analysis. In this context, identify each of the following and note how each would probably behave in a strong economy.
   a. Fiscal policy
   b. Interest rates
   c. Industrial production
   d. Retail sales
   e. Producer prices

LG 1   LG 2

Q7.2   As an investor, what kind(s) of economic information would you look for if you were thinking about investing in the following?
   a. An airline stock
   b. A cyclical stock
   c. An electrical utility stock
   d. A building materials stock
   e. An aerospace firm, with heavy exposure in the defense industry

LG 5

Q7.3   Match the specific ratios in the left-hand column with the category in the right-hand column to which it belongs.
   a. Inventory turnover
   b. Debt-equity ratio
   c. Current ratio
   d. Net profit margin
   e. Return on assets
   f. Total asset turnover
   g. Price/earnings ratio
   h. Times interest earned
   i. Price-to-book-value ratio
   j. Payout ratio

   1. Profitability ratios
   2. Activity ratios
   3. Liquidity ratios
   4. Leverage ratios
   5. Common stock ratios

Problems

LG 5

P7.1   Assume you are given the following abbreviated financial statements.

	($ in millions)
Current assets	$150.0
Fixed and other assets	200.0
Total assets	$350.0
Current liabilities	$100.0
Long-term debt	50.0
Stockholders' equity	200.0
	$350.0
Common shares outstanding	10 million shares
Total revenues	$500.0
Total operating costs and expenses	435.0
Interest expense	10.0
Income taxes	20.0
Net profits	$ 35.0
Dividends paid to common stockholders	$ 10.0

On the basis of this information, calculate as many liquidity, activity, leverage, profitability, and common stock measures as you can. (*Note:* Assume the current market price of the common stock is $75 per share.)

 P7.2 BOOKV has $550,000,000 in total assets, no preferred stock, and total liabilities of $400,000,000. There are 300,000,000 shares of common stock outstanding. What is the book value per share?

 P7.3 BOOKV has $550,000,000 in total assets, no preferred stock, and total liabilities of $400,000,000. There are 300,000,000 shares of common stock outstanding. The stock is selling for $5.50 per share. What is the price-to-book ratio?

P7.4 The Amherst Company has net profits of $10 million, sales of $150 million, and 2.5 million shares of common stock outstanding. The company has total assets of $75 million and total stockholders' equity of $45 million. It pays $1 per share in common dividends, and the stock trades at $20 per share. Given this information, determine the following:
   a. Amherst's EPS.
   b. Amherst's book value per share and price-to-book-value ratio.
   c. The firm's P/E ratio.
   d. The company's net profit margin.
   e. The stock's dividend payout ratio and its dividend yield.
   f. The stock's PEG ratio, given that the company's earnings have been growing at an average annual rate of 7.5%.

P7.5 ZAPIT common stock is selling at a P/E ratio of 15 times trailing earnings. The stock price is $25. What were the earnings per share?

P7.6 PEGCOR has a P/E ratio of 15. Earnings per share are $2.00, and the expected EPS 5 years from today are $3.22. Calculate the PEG ratio. (Refer to Chapter 4 if necessary.)

P7.7 Highgate Computer Company produces $2 million in profits from $28 million in sales. It has total assets of $15 million.
   a. Calculate Highgate's total asset turnover and its net profit margin.
   b. Find the company's ROA, ROE, and book value per share, given that it has a total net worth of $6 million and 500,000 shares of common stock outstanding.

P7.8 The following data have been gathered from the financial statements of HiFly Corporation:

	2003	2004
Operating profit	$550,000,000	$600,000.000
Interest expense	200,000,000	250,000,000
Taxes	126,000,000	126,000,000
Net profit	224,000,000	224,000,000

Calculate the times interest earned ratios for 2003 and 2004. Is the company more or less able to meet its interest payments in 2004 when measured this way?

P7.9 Financial Learning Systems has 2.5 million shares of common stock outstanding and 100,000 shares of preferred stock. (The preferred pays annual cash dividends of $5 a share, and the common pays annual cash dividends of 25 cents a share.) Last year, the company generated net profits (after taxes) of $6,850,000. The company's balance sheet shows total assets of $78 million, total liabilities of $32 million, and $5 million in preferred stock. The firm's common stock is currently trading in the market at $45 a share.

   a. Given the preceding information, find the EPS, P/E ratio, and book value per share.

   b. What will happen to the price of the stock if EPS *rises* to $3.75 and the P/E ratio stays where it is? What will happen if EPS *drops* to $1.50 and the P/E ratio doesn't change?

   c. What will happen to the price of the stock if EPS rises to $3.75 and the P/E ratio jumps to 25 times earnings?

   d. What will happen if *both* EPS and the P/E ratio *drop*—to $1.50 and 10 times earnings, respectively?

   e. Comment on the effect that EPS and the P/E ratio have on the market price of the stock.

 LG 5

P7.10 The Buffalo Manufacturing Company has total assets of $10 million, an asset turnover of 2.0 times, and a net profit margin of 15%.

   a. What is Buffalo's return on assets?

   b. Find Buffalo's ROE, given that 40% of the assets are financed with stockholders' equity.

 LG 5

P7.11 Find the EPS, P/E ratio, and dividend yield of a company that has 5 million shares of common stock outstanding (the shares trade in the market at $25), earns 10% after taxes on annual sales of $150 million, and has a dividend payout ratio of 35%. At what rate would the company's net earnings be growing if the stock had a PEG ratio of 2.0?

LG 5

P7.12 FigureitOut Corporation has a net profit margin of 8% and a total asset turnover of 2 times. What is the company's return on assets?

LG 5

P7.13 FigureitOut Corporation has a net profit margin of 8%, a total asset turnover of 2 times, total assets of $1 billion, and total equity of $500 million. What is the company's return on equity?

LG 5

P7.14 FigureitOut Corporation has a net profit margin of 8%, a total asset turnover of 2 times, total assets of $1 billion, and total equity of $500 million. What were the company's sales and net profit?

LG 5

P7.15 Using the resources available at your campus or public library (or on the Internet), select any common stock you like and determine as many of the profitability, activity, liquidity, leverage, and market ratios as you can. Compute the ratios for the latest available fiscal year. (*Note:* Show your work for all calculations.)

LG 4 **LG 5** **LG 6**

P7.16 Listed below are six pairs of stocks. Pick *one of these pairs* and then, using the resources available at your campus or public library (or on the Internet), comparatively analyze the two stocks. Which is fundamentally stronger and holds more promise for the future? Compute (or obtain) as many ratios as you see fit. As part of your analysis, obtain the latest S&P and/or *Value Line* reports on both stocks, and use them for added insights about the firms and their stocks.

   a. Wal-Mart versus Target

   b. Sara Lee versus Campbell Soup

   c. IBM versus Intel

   d. Tupperware versus Ball Corporation

   e. Liz Claiborne versus Quicksilver

   f. General Dynamics versus Boeing

LG 4   LG 5   LG 6

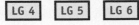

P7.17 Listed here are the 2003 and 2004 financial statements for Otago Bay Marine Motors, a major manufacturer of top-of-the-line outboard motors.

Otago Bay Marine Motors
Balance Sheets ($ in thousands)

	As of December 31,	
	2004	2003
Assets		
Current assets		
Cash and cash equivalents	$ 56,203	$ 88,942
Accounts receivable, net of allowances	20,656	12,889
Inventories	29,294	24,845
Prepaid expenses	5,761	6,536
Total current assets	111,914	133,212
Property, plant, and equipment, at cost	137,273	85,024
Less: Accumulated depreciation and amortization	(50,574)	(44,767)
Net fixed assets	86,699	40,257
Other assets	105,327	51,001
Total assets	$303,940	$224,470
Liabilities and Shareholders' Equity		
Current liabilities		
Notes and accounts payable	$ 28,860	$ 4,927
Dividends payable	1,026	791
Accrued liabilities	20,976	16,780
Total current liabilities	50,862	22,498
Noncurrent liabilities		
Long-term debt	40,735	20,268
Shareholders' equity		
Common stock	7,315	7,103
Capital in excess of par value	111,108	86,162
Retained earnings	93,920	88,439
Total shareholders' equity	212,343	181,704
Total liabilities and equity	$303,940	$224,470
Average number of common shares outstanding	10,848,000	10,848,000

Otago Bay Marine Motors Income Statements ($ in thousands)

	For the Year Ended December 31,	
	2004	2003
Net sales	$259,593	$245,424
Cost of goods sold	133,978	127,123
Gross profit margin	125,615	118,301
Operating expenses:	72,098	70,368
Earnings from operations	53,517	47,933
Other income (expense), net	4,193	3,989
Earnings before income taxes	57,710	51,922
Provision for income taxes	22,268	19,890
Net earnings	$ 35,442	$ 32,032
Cash dividends ($0.35 and $0.27 per share)	$ 3,769	$ 2,947
Average price per share of common stock (in the fourth quarter of the year)	$74.25	$80.75

a. On the basis of the information provided, calculate the following financial ratios for 2003 and 2004.

	Otago Bay Marine Motors		Industry Averages (for 2004)
	2003	2004	
Current ratio			2.36
Total asset turnover			1.27
Debt-equity ratio			10.00
Net profit margin			9.30
ROA			15.87
ROE			19.21
EPS			1.59
P/E ratio			19.87
Dividend yield			.44
Payout ratio			.26
Price-to-book-value			6.65

b. Considering the financial ratios you computed, along with the industry averages, how would you characterize the financial condition of Otago Bay Marine Motors? Explain.

LG 5   LG 6

P7.18 The following summary financial statistics were obtained from the 2000 Otago Bay Marine Motors (OBMM) annual report.

	2000 ($ in millions)
Net sales	$179.3
Total assets	$136.3
Net earnings	$ 20.2
Shareholders' equity	$109.6

a. Use the profit margin and asset turnover to compute the 2000 ROA for OBMM. Now introduce the equity multiplier to find ROE.

b. Use the summary financial information from the 2004 OBMM financial statements (see Problem 7.17) to compute the 2004 ROA and ROE. Use the same procedures to calculate these measures as you did in part **a**.

c. On the basis of your calculations, describe how *each* of the three components (profit margin, asset turnover, and leverage) contributed to the change in OBMM's ROA and ROE between 2000 and 2004. Which component(s) contributed the most to the change in ROA? Which contributed the most to the change in ROE?

d. Generally speaking, do you think that these changes are fundamentally healthy for the company?

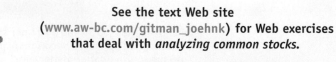

**See the text Web site
(www.aw-bc.com/gitman_joehnk) for Web exercises
that deal with *analyzing common stocks*.**

Case Problem 7.1 — *Some Financial Ratios Are Real Eye-Openers*

LG 5   LG 6

Jack Arnold is a resident of Lubbock, Texas, where he is a prosperous rancher and businessman. He has also built up a sizable portfolio of common stock, which, he believes, is due to the fact that he thoroughly evaluates each stock he invests in. As Jack says, "Y'all can't be too careful about these things! Anytime I'm fixin' to invest in a stock, you can bet I'm gonna learn as much as I can about the company." Jack prefers to compute his own ratios even though he could easily obtain analytical reports from his broker at no cost. (In fact, Billy Bob Smith, his broker, has been volunteering such services for years.)

Recently, Jack has been keeping an eye on a small chemical stock. This firm, South Plains Chemical Company, is big in the fertilizer business—which is something Jack knows a lot about. Not long ago, he received a copy of the firm's latest financial statements (summarized here) and decided to take a closer look at the company.

South Plains Chemical Company Balance Sheet
($ Thousands)

Cash	$ 1,250		
Accounts receivable	8,000	Current liabilities	$10,000
Inventory	12,000	Long-term debt	8,000
Current assets	21,250	Stockholders' equity	12,000
Fixed and other assets	8,750	Total liabilities and	
Total assets	$30,000	stockholders' equity	$30,000

Income Statement
($ Thousands)

Sales	$50,000
Cost of goods sold	25,000
Operating expenses	15,000
Operating profit	10,000
Interest expense	2,500
Taxes	2,500
Net profit	$5,000
Dividends paid to common stockholders ($ in thousands)	$1,250
Number of common shares outstanding	5 million
Recent market price of the common stock	$25

Questions

a. Compute the following ratios, using the South Plains Chemical Company figures.

	Latest Industry Averages		Latest Industry Averages
Liquidity		*Profitability*	
a. Net working capital	N/A	h. Net profit margin	8.5%
b. Current ratio	1.95	i. Return on assets	22.5%
Activity		j. ROE	32.2%
c. Receivables turnover	5.95	*Common Stock Ratios*	
d. Inventory turnover	4.50	k. Earnings per share	$2.00
e. Total asset turnover	2.65	l. Price/earnings ratio	20.0
Leverage		m. Dividends per share	$1.00
f. Debt-equity ratio	0.45	n. Dividend yield	2.5%
g. Times interest earned	6.75	o. Payout ratio	50.0%
		p. Book value per share	$6.25
		q. Price-to-book-value ratio	6.4

b. Compare the company ratios you prepared to the industry figures given in part **a**. What are the company's strengths? What are its weaknesses?

c. What is your overall assessment of South Plains Chemical? Do you think Jack should continue with his evaluation of the stock? Explain.

Case Problem 7.2

LG 2   LG 3   LG 5

Doris Looks at an Auto Issue

Doris Wise is a young career woman. She lives in Phoenix, Arizona, where she owns and operates a highly successful modeling agency. Doris manages her modest but rapidly growing investment portfolio, made up mostly of high-grade common stocks. Because she's young and single and has no pressing family requirements, Doris has invested primarily in stocks that offer the potential for attractive capital gains. Her broker recently recommended an auto company stock and sent her some literature and analytical reports to study. One report, prepared by the brokerage house she deals with, provided an up-to-date look at the economy, an extensive study of the auto industry, and an equally extensive review of several auto companies (including the one her broker recommended). She feels strongly about the merits of security analysis and believes it is important to spend time studying a stock before making an investment decision.

Questions

a. Doris tries to stay informed about the economy on a regular basis. At the present time, most economists agree that the economy, now well into the third year of a recovery, is healthy, with industrial activity remaining strong. What other information about the economy do you think Doris would find helpful in evaluating an auto stock? Prepare a list—and be specific. Which three items of economic information (from your list) do you feel are most important? Explain.

b. In relation to a study of the auto industry, briefly note the importance of each of the following.
1. Auto imports
2. The United Auto Workers union
3. Interest rates
4. The price of a gallon of gas

c. A variety of financial ratios and measures are provided about one of the auto companies and its stock. These are incomplete, however, so some additional information will have to be computed. Specifically, we know the following:

Net profit margin	15%
Total assets	$25 billion
Earnings per share	$3.00
Total asset turnover	1.5
Net working capital	$3.4 billion
Payout ratio	40%
Current liabilities	$5 billion
Price/earnings ratio	12.5

Given this information, calculate the following:
1. Sales.
2. Net profits after taxes.
3. Current ratio.
4. Market price of the stock.
5. Dividend yield.

Excel with Spreadsheets

You have been asked to analyze the financial statements of the Dayton Corporation for the two years ending 2002 and 2003.

	A	B	C	D	E
1	**Dayton Corporation**				
2	**Financial Data**				
3		2003	2002		
4	Net Sales	47,715	40,363		
5	Cost of Sales	27,842	21,485		
6	SG&A Expenses	8,090	7,708		
7	Depreciation Expense	628	555		
8	Interest Expense	754	792		
9	Tax Expense	3,120	3,002		
10	Cash & equivalents	2,144	2,536		
11	Receivables	5,215	5,017		
12	Inventory	3,579	3,021		
13	Other current assets	2,022	2,777		
14	Plant & Equipment	18,956	16,707		
15	Accumulated Depreciation	5,853	5,225		
16	Intangible assets	7,746	7,374		
17	Other non-current assets	10,465	7,700		
18	Payables	5,108	4,361		
19	Short-term notes payable	4,066	3,319		
20	Other Current Liabilities	2,369	2,029		
21	Long-term Debt	4,798	3,600		
22	Other non-current liabilities	4,837	5,020		
23	Common Stock	6,776	6,746		
24	Retained Earnings	16,050	14,832		
25	Common shares outstanding	2,300	2,300		
26	Current market price of stock	$45	$45		

Questions

a. Create a comparative balance sheet for the years 2003 and 2002, similar to the spreadsheet for Table 7.4 which can be viewed at www.aw-bc.com/gitman_joehnk.
b. Create a comparative income statement for the years 2003 and 2002, similar to the spreadsheet for Table 7.5 which can be viewed at www.aw-bc.com/gitman_joehnk.
c. Create a spreadsheet to calculate the listed financial ratios for both 2003 and 2002, similar to the spreadsheet for Table 7.7 which can be viewed at www.aw-bc.com/gitman_joehnk.

Ratios	2003	2002
Current ratio		
Quick ratio		
Accounts receivable turnover		
Inventory turnover		
Total asset turnover		
Debt-equity ratio		
Times interest earned		
Net profit margin		
Return on equity (ROE)		
Earnings per share		
Price/earnings ratio		
Book value per share		
Price-to-book-value		

Investing can be fun but it also takes a fair amount of work to determine the intrinsic value of your investments. As Burton Malkiel states in his book *A Random Walk Down Wall Street*, "It is the definition of the time period for the investment return and the predictability of the returns that often distinguish an investment from a speculation. An excellent analogy from the first *Superman* movie comes to mind. When the evil Luthor bought land in Arizona with the idea that California would soon slide into the ocean, thereby quickly producing far more valuable beach-front property, he was speculating. Had he bought such land as a long-term holding after examining migration patterns, housing–construction trends, and the availability of water supplies, he would probably be regarded as investing." Are you investing or speculating?

Ratio analysis utilizes data from financial statements, thereby permitting an investor to synthesize the information and determine whether a stock should be included in his or her portfolio. For example, are the firm's earnings coming from growth rather than selling assets or taking on more liability? A frequently quoted ratio is the PEG ratio, which compares the P/E ratio to the company's growth in earnings. Other informative market ratios are book value, which is a measure of stockholders' equity, and payout ratio, which indicates how much of a firm's earnings is paid out in dividends. This information can then be used to make buy and sell decisions.

Exercises

1. Go to www.esignal.com to get a quote on one of your stocks. Select "Fundamentals" and "Market Guide" from the side menu bar. Observe the financial data for the firm, such as earnings per share (EPS), declared dividends, market cap, and book value. Refer to your text if you are not familiar with any of these ratios.

2. The OTIS stock simulator calculates book value for your portfolio (account equity) so as to estimate your return on equity (profit or loss). Sign on to OTIS and click on "positions" to view gains or losses from your stocks. Evaluate stocks that have been losing value.

3. Find the PEG ratios for the investments in your portfolio by going to a financial Web site and viewing stock quotes. Are the ratios in an acceptable range?

4. Create a third Excel worksheet and list all dividend-bearing stocks. Create three columns with the following headings: Dividends, Earnings per Share, and Payout Ratio. Record the data on dividends and earnings per share for each stock. Program the formula for the payout ratio in the third column. Payout ratios should not be higher than 70% to 80%. Review the payout ratios to see if any fall outside the acceptable range.

Wwhat drives a stock's value? Many factors come into play, from positive industry trends to favorable earnings reports to company developments such as new products. Take Krispy Kreme Doughnuts, for example, whose many customers buy more than 5 million Krispy Kreme doughnuts every day in the company's 292 stores in 37 states, Canada, and Australia. Or maybe you were lucky enough to recognize a promising growth stock and gobble up shares soon after the company went public in April 2000 at $21 per share (which, after adjusting for *two* 2-for-1 stock splits, was more like $5.25 a share). The company's timing was particularly good: Investors were looking for an alternative to dot-com high fliers, and the company's popular brand and product appealed to many different types of consumers.

Krispy Kreme's strong fundamentals continue to please investors: low debt to equity ratio, excellent liquidity, rising revenues and net income, and rapid growth as it expands beyond its southeastern U.S. roots. In early 2004, the stock price was hovering around $36 and had a 52-week high close to $50.

Yet some analysts consider the stock overvalued. For the quarter ending July 31, 2003, its 12-month trailing price/earnings (P/E) ratio was almost 60, and the 12-month forward P/E was about 35. "This is a stock that people will always say is too expensive," says John Glass, a CIBC restaurant analyst. Glass estimates that on a 2004 P/E basis, its price is comparable to peers like Starbucks (P/E = 30). Krispy Kreme's earnings per share are growing faster, though—about 25% per year. Even so, Standard & Poor's analysts, using a discounted cash flow model and annual revenue growth of at least 20% for five years, downgraded the stock to "avoid." They thought the stock was trading at a price that reflected a 20% premium to its intrinsic value.

What do all of these numbers mean in terms of the value of Krispy Kreme's stock? This chapter explains how to determine a stock's intrinsic value by using dividend valuation, dividend and earnings, price/earnings, and other models.

Sources: "Krispy Kreme Announces Strong Fourth Quarter and Fiscal Year 2003 Results," *PRNewswire-FirstCall*, March 18, 2003, downloaded from www.krispykreme.com; Andy Serwer, "The Hole Story," *Fortune*, July 7, 2003, pp. 53–62; David Shook and Scott Livengood, "His Doughnut Stores Are His 'Children'," *Business Week Online*, December 9, 2002, downloaded from www.business.com; and "S&P Cuts Krispy Kreme to Avoid," *Business Week Online*, July 6, 2003, downloaded from www.businessweek.com.

LEARNING GOALS

After studying this chapter, you should be able to:

LG 1 Explain the role that a company's future plays in the stock valuation process.

LG 2 Develop a forecast of a stock's expected cash flow, starting with corporate sales and earnings, and then moving to expected dividends and share price.

LG 3 Discuss the concepts of intrinsic value and required rates of return, and note how they are used.

LG 4 Determine the underlying value of a stock using the zero-growth, constant-growth and variable-growth dividend valuation models.

LG 5 Use other types of present-value–based models to derive the value of a stock, as well as alternative price-relative procedures.

LG 6 Gain a basic appreciation of the procedures used to value different types of stocks, from traditional dividend-paying shares to more growth-oriented stocks.

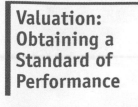

Valuation: Obtaining a Standard of Performance

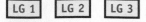

stock valuation
the process by which the underlying value of a stock is established on the basis of its forecasted risk and return performance.

Obtaining a standard of performance that can be used to judge the investment merits of a share of stock is the underlying purpose of **stock valuation**. A stock's intrinsic value provides such a standard, as it indicates the future risk and return performance of a security. The question of whether and to what extent a stock is under- or overvalued is resolved by comparing its current market price to its intrinsic value. At any given point in time, the price of a share of common stock depends on investor expectations about the future behavior of the security. If the outlook for the company and its stock is good, the price will probably be bid up. If conditions deteriorate, the price of the stock will probably go down. Let's look now at the single most important issue in the stock valuation process: *the future*.

Valuing a Company and Its Future

Thus far, we have examined several aspects of security analysis: economic and industry analysis, and the historical (company) phase of fundamental analysis. It should be clear, however, that it's *not the past* that's important but *the future*. The primary reason for looking at past performance is to gain insight about the future direction of the firm and its profitability. Granted, past performance provides no guarantees about future returns, but it can give us a good idea of a company's strengths and weaknesses. For example, it can tell us how well the company's products have done in the marketplace, how the company's fiscal health shapes up, and how management tends to respond to difficult situations. In short, the past can reveal how well the company is positioned to take advantage of the things that may occur in the future.

Because *the value of a stock is a function of its future returns*, the investor's task is to use available historical data to project key financial variables into the future. In this way, you can assess the future prospects of the company and the expected returns from its stock. We are especially interested in dividends and price behavior.

Forecasted Sales and Profits The key to our forecast is, of course, the future behavior of the *company* and the most important aspects to consider in this regard are the outlook for sales and the trend in the net profit margin. One way to develop a sales forecast is to assume that the company will continue to perform as it has in the past and simply extend the historical trend. For example, if a firm's sales have been growing at a rate of 10% per year, then assume they will continue at that rate. Of course, if there is some evidence about the economy, industry, or company that suggests a faster or slower rate of growth, the forecast should be adjusted accordingly. More often than not, this "naive" approach will be about as effective as more complex techniques.

Once the sales forecast has been generated, we can shift our attention to the net profit margin. We want to know what kind of return on sales to expect. A naive estimate can be obtained by simply using the average profit margin that has prevailed for the past few years. Again, it should be adjusted to account for any unusual industry or company developments. For most individual investors, valuable insight about future revenues and earnings can be obtained from industry or company reports put out by brokerage houses, advisory services (e.g., *Value Line*), the financial media (e.g., *Forbes*),

H O T

For help researching a company, try MSN Money Central. Enter a stock symbol and see earnings forecasts for the company.

moneycentral.msn.com/investor/
invsub/analyst/earnest.asp

and from various investor Web sites. Or, as the *Investing in Action* box on page 334 explains, you might even want to take a look at so-called "whisper forecasts" as a way to get a handle on earnings estimates.

Given a satisfactory sales forecast and estimate of the future net profit margin, we can combine these two pieces of information to arrive at future earnings.

Equation 8.1

$$\frac{\text{Future after-tax}}{\text{earnings in year } t} = \frac{\text{Estimated sales}}{\text{for year } t} \times \frac{\text{Net profit margin}}{\text{expected in year } t}$$

The *year t* notation in this equation simply denotes a given calendar or fiscal year in the future. It can be next year, the year after that, or any other year in which we are interested. Let's say that in the year just completed, a company reported sales of $100 million, we estimate that revenues will grow at an 8% annual rate, and the net profit margin should be about 6%. Thus, estimated sales next year will equal $108 million ($100 million × 1.08). And, with a 6% profit margin, we should expect to see earnings next year of

$$\frac{\text{Future after-tax}}{\text{earnings next year}} = \$108 \text{ million} \times 0.06 = \underline{\$6.5 \text{ million}}$$

Using this same process, we would then estimate sales and earnings *for other years* in our forecast period.

Forecasted Dividends and Prices At this point we have an idea of the future earnings performance of the company. We are now ready to evaluate the effects of this performance on returns to common stock investors. Given a corporate earnings forecast, we need three additional pieces of information:

- An estimate of future dividend payout ratios.
- The number of common shares that will be outstanding over the forecast period.
- A future price/earnings (P/E) ratio.

For the first two pieces of information, unless we have evidence to the contrary, we can simply project the firm's recent experience into the future. Payout ratios are usually fairly stable, so there is little risk in using a recent average figure. (Or, if a company follows a fixed-dividend policy, we could use the latest dividend rate in our forecast.) It is also generally safe to assume that the number of common shares outstanding will hold at the latest level or perhaps change at some moderate rate of increase (or decrease) that's reflective of the recent past.

Getting a Handle on the P/E Ratio The only really thorny issue in this process is coming up with an estimate of the future P/E ratio—a figure that has considerable bearing on the stock's future price behavior. Generally speaking, the P/E ratio is a function of several variables, including:

1. The growth rate in earnings.
2. The general state of the market.
3. The amount of debt in a company's capital structure.

INVESTING IN ACTION

I'VE GOT A SECRET: WHISPER FORECASTS

As a fiscal quarter ends, investors rush to compare companies' actual reported earnings with the consensus (average) security analyst estimates published by firms such as First Call, Zacks, and I/B/E/S. If companies' results fall below the analysts' predictions by even a penny or two, the firms' stock prices can tumble 30% or more in one day. In fact, *Kiplinger's* magazine considers this comparison practice to be perhaps the most important factor driving share price performance over the short term, and it affects longer-term performance as well.

Now investors have another set of earnings predictions to follow. "Whisper forecasts" are unofficial earnings estimates that circulate among traders and investors—rumors as opposed to "official" analyst estimates. Whisper numbers tend to be higher than analyst forecasts, and some believe that they are the analysts' *real* earnings estimates.

Whisper numbers are now available on the Internet. The data come from varied sources: discussions with stockbrokers, financial analysts, investor relations departments, and investors themselves. Whisper Number (www.whispernumber.com), the first of the specialized Web sites, combines information from investor forums with polling and daily computer searches of hundreds of thousands of sources. Other Web sites dedicated to these unofficial earnings reports include Earnings Whispers (www.earningswhispers.com) and the Whisper Number (www.thewhispernumber.com)—each of which claims to have the "real" whisper numbers. Most require registration to access basic features and charge for premium content.

How valid are whisper earnings estimates? Whisper Numbers claims that about 74% of the time, a company that beats the whisper number will see its stock rise within 5 days after the earnings announcement, and vice versa. This proved true in the case of Oracle, whose stock price dropped more than 5.5% after announcing earnings of $0.08 per share—on target with analysts' forecasts but below the Earnings Whispers number of $0.09 per share.

A formal study by three professors at Purdue and Indiana Universities compared average whisper forecasts and First Call consensus analyst estimates for 127 mostly high-tech firms from January 1995 to May 1997. They found whisper forecasts to be more accurate and to provide more information than analysts' forecasts. Because whisper forecasts are distributed widely, part of this information is reflected in stock prices before the actual earnings reports come out. Proponents of whisper forecasts claim that they also counteract the tendency for analysts to have a pessimistic bias, which derives from corporate pressure to keep estimates low so that positive earnings surprises are more common than disappointments. During the 2000–2002 market downturn, however, whisper numbers proved less accurate than analysts' forecasts.

Not everyone believes in whisper forecasts. Some in the industry criticize them as being rumors, unsubstantiated speculation, and idle gossip, gleaned from unknown sources who have no accountability. Many observers also question the ethics of the practice. After all, company insiders or short sellers could plant high numbers to manipulate prices. For this reason, investors should not use whisper forecasts except in conjunction with other securities analysis techniques and tools.

CRITICAL THINKING QUESTIONS What are *whisper forecasts* and how can investors use them? How accurate are whisper forecasts? Explain.

Sources: Mark Bagnoli, Messod Daniel Beneish, and Susan G. Watts, "Earnings Expectations: How Important are the Whispers?" *AAII Journal*, June 2000, pp. 11–14; Lynnette Khalfani, "Psst! Get the Scoop on Whisper Numbers," *Wall Street Journal*, January 12, 2001, p. C1; "Oracle Falls After Missing Whisper," *Earnings Whispers*, September 12, 2003, downloaded from www.earningswhispers.com; Manual Schiffros, "The Earnings Game," *Kiplinger's*, April 2000, pp. 60–62; and Whisper Number Web site, www.whispernumber.com, accessed September 17, 2003.

4. The current and projected rate of inflation.
5. The level of dividends.

As a rule, higher P/E ratios can be expected with higher rates of growth in earnings, an optimistic market outlook, and lower debt levels (less debt means less financial risk).

The link between the inflation rate and P/E multiples, however, is a bit more complex. Generally speaking, as inflation rates rise, so do bond interest rates. This, in turn, causes required returns on stocks to rise (so stock returns will remain competitive with bond returns) and higher required returns on stocks mean lower stock prices and lower P/E multiples. On the other hand, declining inflation (and interest) rates normally have positive effects on the economy and business conditions, and that translates into higher P/E ratios and stock prices. We can also argue that a high P/E ratio should be expected with high dividend payouts. In practice, however, most companies with high P/E ratios have *low dividend payouts*. The reason: Earnings growth tends to be more valuable than dividends, especially in companies with high rates of return on equity.

A Relative Price/Earnings Multiple A useful starting point for evaluating the P/E ratio is the *average market multiple*, which is simply the average P/E ratio of all the stocks in a given market index, like the S&P 500 or the DJIA. The average market multiple indicates the general state of the market. It gives us an idea of how aggressively the market, in general, is pricing stocks. Other things being equal, the higher the P/E ratio, the more optimistic the market—*unless, of course, the economy is in a slump, in which case a high P/E could simply be the result of lower earnings.* Table 8.1 lists S&P price/earnings multiples for the past 30 years. It shows that market multiples tend to move over a fairly wide range.

TABLE 8.1   Average Market P/E Multiples 1974–2003

Year	Market Multiples (Average S&P P/E Ratio)	Year	Market Multiples (Average S&P P/E Ratio)
1974	7.3	1989	15.1
1975	11.7	1990	15.5
1976	11.0	1991	26.2
1977	8.8	1992	22.8
1978	8.3	1993	21.3
1979	7.4	1994	17.0
1980	9.1	1995	17.4
1981	8.1	1996	20.7
1982	10.2	1997	23.9
1983	12.4	1998	32.3
1984	10.0	1999	33.4
1985	13.7	2000	26.4
1986	16.3	2001	46.5
1987	15.1	2002	31.9
1988	12.2	2003	23.0

Source: Average year-end multiples derived from various sources, including Standard & Poor's *Index of 500 Stocks* and its *Statistical Service—Security Price Index Record*. Listed P/Es are all year-end (December) figures, except 2003, which is as of end of the second quarter.

relative P/E multiple
a measure of how a stock's P/E behaves relative to the average market multiple.

With the market multiple as a benchmark, you can evaluate a stock's P/E performance relative to the market. That is, you can calculate a **relative P/E multiple** by dividing a stock's P/E by a market multiple. For example, if a stock currently has a P/E of 35 and the market multiple for the S&P 500 is, say, 25, the stock's relative P/E is 35/25 = 1.40. Looking at the relative P/E, you can quickly get a feel for how aggressively the stock has been priced in the market and what kind of relative P/E is normal for the stock. Other things being equal, a high relative P/E is desirable. The higher this measure, the higher the stock will be priced in the market. But watch out for the downside: High relative P/E multiples can also mean lots of price volatility. (Similarly, we can use average *industry* multiples to get a feel for the kind of P/E multiples that are standard for a given industry. We can then use that information, along with market multiples, to assess or project the P/E for a particular stock.)

Now we can generate a forecast of what the stock's *future* P/E will be over the anticipated *investment horizon* (the period of time over which we expect to hold the stock). For example, with the existing P/E multiple as a base, an *increase* might be justified if you believe the *market multiple* will increase (as the market tone becomes more bullish), and the *relative P/E* is likely to remain at its current level, or may even increase.

Estimating Earnings per Share So far we've been able to come up with an estimate for the dividend payout ratio, the number of shares outstanding, and the price/earnings multiple. We're now ready to forecast the stock's future earnings per share (EPS), which can be done as follows:

Equation 8.2

$$\text{Estimated EPS in year } t = \frac{\text{Future after-tax earnings in year } t}{\text{Number of shares of common stock outstanding in year } t}$$

Earnings per share is a critical part of the valuation process, for once you have EPS, you can combine it with (1) the dividend payout ratio to obtain (future) dividends per share, and (2) the price/earnings multiple to project the (future) price of the stock.

Equation 8.2 simply converts aggregate or total corporate earnings to a per-share basis, by relating company (forecasted) profits to the expected number of shares outstanding. Though this approach works quite effectively, some investors would rather bypass the projection of aggregate sales and earnings and instead *concentrate on earnings from a per-share basis right from the start*. That can be done by looking at the major forces that drive earnings per share: ROE and book value. Quite simply, by employing these two variables, we can define earnings per share as follows:

Equation 8.3

$$\text{EPS} = \text{ROE} \times \text{Book value per share}$$

This formula will produce the same results as the standard EPS equation shown first in Chapter 6 (Equation 6.1) and then again in Chapter 7. The major advantage of this form of the equation is that it allows you to assess the extent to which EPS is influenced by the company's book value and (especially) its ROE. As we saw in the previous chapter, ROE is a key financial measure, because it captures the amount of success the firm is having in managing its assets, operations, and capital structure. And as we see here, ROE not only is important in defining overall corporate profitability but also plays a crucial role in defining a stock's EPS.

To produce an estimated EPS using Equation 8.3, you would go directly to the two basic components of the formula and try to get a handle on their future behavior. In particular, what kind of growth is expected in the firm's book value per share, and what's likely to happen to the company's ROE? In the vast majority of cases, ROE is really the driving force, so it's important to produce a good estimate of that variable. Investors often do that by breaking ROE into its component parts—margin, turnover, and the equity multiplier (see Equation 7.13 in Chapter 7).

Once you have projected ROE and book value per share, you can plug these figures into Equation 8.3 to produce estimated EPS. The bottom line is that, one way or another (using the approach reflected in Equation 8.2 or that in Equation 8.3), you have to arrive at a forecasted EPS number that you are comfortable with. When that's been done, it's a pretty simple matter to use the forecasted payout ratio to estimate dividends per share:

Equation 8.4

$$\frac{\text{Estimated dividends}}{\text{per share in year } t} = \frac{\text{Estimated EPS}}{\text{for year } t} \times \frac{\text{Estimated}}{\text{payout ratio}}$$

The last item is the future price of the stock, which can be determined as

Equation 8.5

$$\frac{\text{Estimated share price}}{\text{at end of year } t} = \frac{\text{Estimated EPS}}{\text{in year } t} \times \frac{\text{Estimated P/E}}{\text{ratio}}$$

Pulling It All Together We've seen the various components that go into our estimates of future dividends and share prices. Now, to see how they all fit together, let's continue with the example we started above. Using the aggregate sales and earnings approach, if the company had 2 million shares of common stock outstanding and that number was expected to hold in the future, then given the estimated earnings of $6.5 million that we computed earlier, the firm should generate earnings per share (EPS) next year of

$$\frac{\text{Estimated EPS}}{\text{next year}} = \frac{\$6.5 \text{ million}}{2 \text{ million}} = \underline{\underline{\$3.25}}$$

This result, of course, would be equivalent to the firm having a projected ROE of, say, 15% and an estimated book value per share of $21.67. According to Equation 8.3, those conditions would also produce an estimated EPS of $3.25 (i.e., $0.15 \times \$21.67$). Using this EPS figure, along with an estimated payout ratio of 40%, we see that dividends per share next year should equal

$$\frac{\text{Estimated dividends}}{\text{per share next year}} = \$3.25 \times .40 = \underline{\underline{\$1.30}}$$

If the firm adheres to a *fixed-dividend policy*, this estimate may have to be adjusted to reflect the level of dividends being paid. For example, if the company has been paying annual dividends at the rate of $1.25 per share *and is expected to continue doing so for the near future*, then you would adjust estimated dividends accordingly (i.e., use $1.25/share). Finally, if it has been estimated that the stock should sell at 17.5 times earnings, then a share of stock in this company should be trading at a price of about $56.90 by the *end* of next year.

$$\begin{matrix}\text{Estimated share price} \\ \text{at the end of next year}\end{matrix} = \$3.25 \times 17.5 = \underline{\$56.88}$$

Actually, we are interested in the price of the stock at the end of our anticipated investment horizon. Thus the $56.90 figure would be appropriate if we had a 1-year horizon. However, if we had a 3-year holding period, we would have to extend the EPS figure for 2 more years and repeat our calculations with the new data. As we shall see, *the estimated share price is important because it has embedded in it the capital gains portion of the stock's total return.*

Developing an Estimate of Future Behavior

Using information obtained from Universal Office Furnishings (UVRS), we can illustrate the forecasting procedures we discussed above. Recall from Chapter 7 that an assessment of the economy and the office equipment industry was positive and that the company's operating results and financial condition looked strong, both historically and relative to industry standards. Because everything looks favorable for Universal, we decide to take a look at the future prospects of the company and its stock. Assume we have chosen a 3-year investment horizon, because we believe (from earlier studies of economic and industry factors) that the economy and the market for office equipment stocks will start running out of steam near the end of 2007 or early 2008. (Some investors prefer to use 1-year investment horizons, because they believe that trying to forecast out any further involves too many uncertainties. We use a 3-year investment horizon here primarily for illustration—and because we feel comfortable forecasting the numbers out that far. Should that not be the case, then by all means use a shorter investment horizon.)

Table 8.2 provides selected historical financial data for the company. They cover a 5-year period (ending with the latest fiscal year) and will provide the basis for much of our forecast. The data reveal that, with one or two exceptions, the company has performed at a fairly steady pace and has been able to maintain a very attractive rate of growth. Our economic analysis suggests that the economy is about to pick up, and our research (from Chapter 7) indicates that the industry and company are well situated to take advantage of the upswing. Therefore, we conclude that the rate of growth in sales should pick up dramatically from the abnormally low level of 2004, attaining a growth rate of over 20% in 2005—more in line with the firm's 5-year average. After a modest amount of pent-up demand is worked off, the rate of growth in sales should drop to about 19% in 2006 and to 15% in 2007.

The essential elements of the financial forecast for 2005–2007 are provided in Table 8.3 (on page 340). Highlights of the key assumptions and the reasoning behind them are as follows:

- *Net profit margin.* Various published industry and company reports suggest a comfortable improvement in earnings, so we decide to use a

TABLE 8.2	Selected Historical Financial Data, Universal Office Furnishings				
	2000	2001	2002	2003	2004
Total assets (millions)	$554.2	$694.9	$755.6	$761.5	$941.2
Total asset turnover	1.72×	1.85×	1.98×	2.32×	2.06×
Net sales (millions)	$953.2	$1,283.9	$1,495.9	$1,766.2	$1,938.0
Annual rate of growth in sales*	11.5%	34.7%	16.5%	18.1%	9.7%
Net profit margin	4.2%	3.6%	5.0%	8.0%	7.2%
Payout ratio	6.8%	5.6%	5.8%	6.0%	6.6%
Price/earnings ratio	13.5×	21.7×	14.9×	15.7×	18.4×
Number of common shares outstanding (millions)	77.7	78.0	72.8	65.3	61.8

*Annual rate of growth in sales = Change in sales from one year to the next ÷ Level of sales in the base (or earliest) years. For 2001, the annual rate of growth in sales equaled 34.7% = (2001 sales − 2000 sales)/2000 sales = ($1,283.9 − $953.2)/$953.2 = 0.3467.

profit margin of 8.0% in 2005 (up a bit from the latest margin of 7.2% recorded in 2004). We're projecting even better profit margins (8.5%) in 2006 and 2007, as some cost improvements start to take hold.

- *Common shares outstanding.* We believe the company will continue to pursue its share buyback program, but at a substantially lower pace than in the 2001–2004 period. From a current level of 61.8 million shares, we project that the number of shares outstanding will drop to 61.5 million in 2005, to 60.5 million in 2006, and to 59.5 million in 2007.

- *Payout ratio.* We assume that the dividend payout ratio will hold at a steady 6% of earnings, as it has for most of the recent past.

- *P/E ratio.* Primarily on the basis of expectations for improved growth in revenues and earnings, we are projecting a P/E multiple that will rise from its present level of 18½ times earnings to roughly 20 times earnings in 2005. Although this is a fairly conservative increase in the P/E, when it is coupled with the hefty growth in EPS, the net effect will be a big jump in the projected price of Universal stock.

Table 8.3 also shows the sequence involved in arriving at forecasted dividends and price behavior:

1. The company dimensions of the forecast are handled first. These include sales and revenue estimates, net profit margins, net earnings, and the number of shares of common stock outstanding. Note that after-tax earnings are derived according to the procedure described earlier in this chapter.
2. Next we estimate earnings per share, following the procedures established earlier.
3. The bottom line of the forecast is, of course, the returns in the form of dividends and capital gains expected from a share of Universal stock, given that the assumptions about net sales, profit margins, earnings per share and so forth hold up. We see in Table 8.3 that dividends should go up to 28 cents a share, which is a big jump from where it is now (15 cents/share). Even so, with annual dividends of a little over a quarter

TABLE 8.3   **Summary Forecast Statistics, Universal Office Furnishings**

	Latest Actual Figures (Fiscal 2004)	Average for the Past 5 Years (2000–2004)	Forecasted Figures		
			2005	2006	2007
Annual rate of growth in sales	9.7%	18.1%	22%	19%	15%
Net sales (millions)	$1,938.0	N/A*	$2,364.4**	$2,813.6**	$3,235.6**
× Net profit margin	7.2%	5.6%	8.0%	8.5%	8.5%
= Net after-tax earnings (millions)	$139.7	N/A	$189.2	$239.2	$275.0
÷ Common shares outstanding (millions)	61.2	71.1	61.5	60.5	59.0
= Earnings per share	$ 2.26	N/A	$ 3.08	$ 3.95	$ 4.66
× Payout ratio	6.6%	6.2%	6.0%	6.0%	6.0%
= Dividends per share	$ 0.15	$ 0.08	$ 0.18	$ 0.24	$ 0.28
Earnings per share	$ 2.26	N/A	$ 3.08	$ 3.95	$ 4.66
× P/E ratio	18.4	16.8	20	19	20
= Share price at year end	$ 41.58	N/A	$ 61.60	$ 75.00	$ 93.20

*N/A: Not applicable.

**Forecasted sales figures: Sales from *preceding* year × Growth rate in sales = Growth in sales; then Growth in sales + Sales from preceding year = Forecast sales for the year. For example, for 2005: $1,938.0 × 0.22 = $426.4 + $1938.0 = $2,364.4.

a share, it's clear that dividends still won't account for much of the stock's return. In fact, the dividend yield in 2007 is projected to *fall* to just 3/10 of 1%. Clearly, the returns from this stock are going to come from capital gains, not dividends. That's obvious when you look at year-end share prices, which are expected to more than double over the next 3 years. That is, if our projections are valid, the price of a share of stock should rise from around $41.50 to over $93.00 by year-end 2007.

We now have an idea of what the future cash flows of the investment are likely to be. We can now establish an intrinsic value for Universal Office Furnishings stock.

The Valuation Process

valuation
process by which an investor uses risk and return concepts to determine the value of a security.

Valuation is a process by which an investor determines the worth of a security using the risk and return concepts introduced in Chapter 5. This process can be applied to any asset that produces a stream of cash flow—a share of stock, a bond, a piece of real estate, or an oil well. To establish the value of an asset, the investor must determine certain key inputs, including the amount of future cash flows, the timing of these cash flows, and the rate of return required on the investment.

In terms of common stock, the essence of valuation is to determine what the stock *ought to be worth*, given estimated returns to stockholders (future dividends and price behavior) and the amount of potential risk exposure. Toward this end, we employ various types of stock valuation models, the end product of which represents the elusive intrinsic value we have been seeking. That is, the stock valuation models determine either an *expected rate of return* or

H O T

For a valuation example, see
www.stocksense.com/valuation.html

TARGET PRICES—A **target price** is the price an analyst expects a stock to reach within a certain period of time (usually a year). Target prices are normally based on an analyst's forecast of a company's sales, earnings, and other criteria, some of which are highly subjective. One common practice is to assume that a stock deserves to trade at a certain price/earnings multiple—say, on par with the average P/E multiples of similar stocks—and arrive at a target price by multiplying that P/E ratio by an estimate of what the EPS will be one year from now. Use these prices with care, however, because analysts will often raise their targets simply because a stock has reached the targeted price much sooner than expected.

required rate of return
the return necessary to compensate an investor for the risk involved in an investment.

the *intrinsic worth of a share of stock*, which in effect represents the stock's "justified price." In this way, we obtain a standard of performance, based on future stock behavior, that can be used to judge the investment merits of a particular security.

Either of two conditions would make us consider a stock a worthwhile investment candidate: (1) if the computed rate of return equals or exceeds the yield we feel is warranted, or (2) if the justified price (intrinsic worth) is equal to or greater than the current market price. Note especially that a security is considered acceptable even if its yield simply *equals* the required rate of return or if its intrinsic value simply *equals* the current market price of the stock. There is nothing irrational about such behavior. In either case, the security meets your minimum standards to the extent that it is giving you the rate of return you wanted.

Remember this, however, about the valuation process: Even though valuation plays an important part in the investment process, there is *absolutely no assurance* that the actual outcome will be even remotely similar to the forecasted behavior. The stock is still subject to economic, industry, company, and market risks, any one of which could negate *all* your assumptions about the future. Security analysis and stock valuation models are used not to guarantee success but to *help you better understand the return and risk dimensions of a proposed transaction*.

Required Rate of Return One of the key ingredients in the stock valuation process is the **required rate of return**. Generally speaking, the amount of return required by an investor should be related to the level of risk that must be assumed to generate that return. In essence, the required return establishes a level of compensation compatible with the amount of risk involved. Such a standard helps you determine whether the expected return on a stock (or any other security) is satisfactory. Because you don't know for sure what the cash flow of an investment will be, you should expect to earn a rate of return that reflects this uncertainty. Thus the greater the perceived risk, the more you should expect to earn. As we saw in Chapter 5, this is basically the notion behind the *capital asset pricing model* (CAPM).

Recall that using the CAPM, we define a stock's required return as

Equation 8.6

$$\frac{\text{Required}}{\text{rate of return}} = \frac{\text{Risk-free}}{\text{rate}} + \left[\frac{\text{Stock's}}{\text{beta}} \times \left(\frac{\text{Market}}{\text{return}} - \frac{\text{Risk-free}}{\text{rate}} \right) \right]$$

The required inputs for this equation are readily available: You can obtain a stock's beta from *Value Line* or S&P's *Stock Reports* (or from any one of many Internet sites, such as **Quicken.com, MSN MoneyCentral,** or **Morningstar.com**). The risk-free rate is basically the average return on Treasury bills for the past year or so. And a good proxy for the market return is the average stock return over the past 10 to 15 years (like the data reported in Table 6.1). This average return may, of course, have to be adjusted up or down a bit based on what you expect the market to do over the next year or so.

In the CAPM, the risk of a stock is captured by its beta. For that reason, the required return on a stock increases (or decreases) with increases (or decreases) in its beta. As an illustration of the CAPM at work, consider Universal's stock, which we'll assume has a beta of 1.30. Given that the risk-free rate is 5.5% and the expected market return is, say, 15%, this stock would have a required return of

$$\text{Required return} = 5.5\% + [1.30 \times (15.0\% - 5.5\%)] = \underline{17.85\%}$$

This return—let's round it to 18%—can now be used in a stock valuation model to assess the investment merits of a share of stock.

As an alternative, or perhaps even in conjunction with the CAPM, you could take a more subjective approach to finding the required return. For example, if your assessment of the historical performance of the company had uncovered some volatility in sales and earnings, you could conclude that the stock is subject to a good deal of business risk. Also important is market risk, as measured by a stock's beta. A valuable reference point in arriving at a measure of risk is the rate of return available on less risky but competitive investment vehicles. For example, you could *use the rate of return on long-term Treasury bonds or high-grade corporate issues* as a starting point in defining your desired rate of return. That is, starting with yields on long-term bonds, you could adjust those returns for the levels of business and market risk to which you believe the common stock is exposed.

To see how these elements make up the desired rate of return, let's go back to Universal Office Furnishings. Assume that it is now early 2005 and rates on high-grade corporate bonds are hovering around 9%. Given that our analysis thus far has indicated that the office equipment industry in general and Universal in particular are subject to a "fair" amount of business risk, we would want to adjust that figure upward—probably by around 2 or 3 points. In addition, with its beta of 1.30, we can conclude that the stock carries a good deal of market risk. Thus we should increase our base rate of return even more—say, by another 4 or 5 points. That is, starting from a base (high-grade corporate bond) rate of 9%, we tack on, say, 3% for the company's added business risk and another 4½ or 5% for the stock's market risk. Adding these up, we find that an appropriate required rate of return for Universal's common stock is around 17% or 17½%. This figure is reasonably close to what we would obtain with CAPM using a beta of 1.30, a risk-free rate of 5.5%, and an expected market return of 15% (as in Equation 8.6). The fact that the two numbers are close shouldn't be surprising. If they're carefully (and honestly) done, the CAPM and the subjective approach should yield similar results. Whichever procedure you use, the required rate of return stipulates the minimum return you should expect to receive from an investment. To accept anything less means you'll fail to be fully compensated for the risk you must assume.

IN REVIEW

CONCEPTS

8.1 What is the purpose of stock valuation? What role does *intrinsic value* play in the stock valuation process?

8.2 Are the expected future earnings of the firm important in determining a stock's investment suitability? Discuss how these and other future estimates fit into the stock valuation framework.

8.3 Can the growth prospects of a company affect its price/earnings multiple? Explain. How about the amount of debt a firm uses? Are there any other variables that affect the level of a firm's P/E ratio?

8.4 What is the *market multiple*, and how can it help in evaluating a stock's P/E ratio? Is a stock's *relative P/E* the same thing as the market multiple? Explain.

8.5 In the stock valuation framework, how can you tell whether a particular security is a worthwhile investment candidate? What roles does the required rate of return play in this process? Would you invest in a stock if all you could earn was a rate of return that equaled your required return? Explain.

Stock Valuation Models

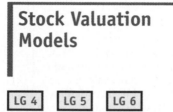

HOT

More often than not, investors tend to be either value investors or growth investors. An *Investing in Action* box at the book's home page discusses the differences.

www.aw-bc.com/gitman_joehnk

Take a look at the market and you'll discover that investors employ a number of different types of stock valuation models. Though they may all be aimed at a security's future cash benefits, their approaches to valuation are nonetheless considerably different. Take, for example, those investors who search for value in a company's financials—by keying in on such factors as book value, debt load, return on equity, and cash flow. These so-called *value investors* rely as much on historical performance as on earnings projections to identify undervalued stock. Then there are the *growth investors*, who concentrate primarily on growth in earnings. To them, though past growth is important, the real key lies in projected earnings—that is, in finding companies that are going to produce big earnings, along with big price/earnings multiples, in the future.

There are still other stock valuation models being used in this market—models that employ such variables as dividend yield, abnormally low P/E multiples, relative price performance over time, and even company size or market caps as key elements in the decision-making process. For purposes of our discussion here, we'll focus on several stock valuation models that derive value from the fundamental performance of the company and its stock. We'll look first at stocks that pay dividends and at a procedure known as the dividend valuation model. From there, we'll look at several valuation procedures that can be used with companies that pay little or nothing in dividends (the more growth-oriented companies). Finally, we'll move on to procedures that set the price of a stock based on how it behaves relative to earnings, cash flow, sales, or book value. The stock valuation procedures that we'll examine in this chapter are the same as those used by many professional security analysts. Or they were at least until the late 1990s, when, as discussed in the *Ethics* box on page 344, some analysts began to rely less on the numbers and more on the hype.

The Dividend Valuation Model

In the valuation process, the intrinsic value of any investment equals the *present value of its expected cash benefits*. For common stock, this amounts to the cash dividends received each year plus the future sale price of the stock. One way to view the cash flow benefits from common stock is to assume that the dividends will be received over an infinite time horizon—an assumption that is appropriate so long as the firm is considered a "going concern." Seen from this perspective, *the value of a share of stock is equal to the present value of all the future dividends it is expected to provide over an infinite time horizon.*

⚖ ETHICS IN INVESTING

STOCK ANALYSTS: DON'T ALWAYS BELIEVE THE HYPE

Buy, Sell, or Hold? This is probably the most important decision to make for investors. Unfortunately, many investors learned the hard way that buy and sell recommendations from analysts do not always mean "buy" or "sell" and on many occasions may even mean exactly the opposite.

It is interesting to note, that as the market peaked in the spring of 2000, 72% of stocks were still rated either buy or strong buy, while less than 1% were rated sell. Even when corporate earnings begun to crumble in 2001 and the economy started turning south, analysts were still quite optimistic about market direction, with 66% of stocks rated a buy and only 1.4% rated sell. As some giant corporate names such as Enron, WorldCom, and Global Crossing began to collapse amid allegations of fraud, some star Wall Street analysts still maintained a rosy outlook on each of them until just a few weeks before they filed for bankruptcy.

Take the Internet guru Mary Meeker of Morgan Stanley, for example. As the tech bubble began to deflate, she continued to recommend stocks for Priceline, Amazon, and Yahoo even as their prices were falling 80–90%. In 2001, Jack Grubman of Solomon Smith Barney maintained a $70 target for Global Crossing, while its stock was on the way to zero. He did the same a year later for WorldCom just weeks before the latter filed for Chapter 11. Recently, another star tech analyst, Henry Blodget, has been accused of privately deriding stocks he has publicly touted. Grubman and Blodget, who are facing civil and criminal probes, may be banished from the securities industry for life and face steep fines.

Why were these all-star analysts wrong so often? Conflict of interest is one explanation. Although they were paid to pick stocks, they were also very handsomely rewarded for generating investment banking business from the companies they covered. While being paid to do in-depth stock research, analysts were often pressured to make positive comments to please current or prospective investment banking clients. Some of them (Grubman) were close friends with CEOs of companies they covered (WorldCom). Such facts explain why these analysts had a vested interest to use the sell recommendation so sparingly.

Analyst hype has become a real problem for Wall Street and Main Street alike. That is why the securities industry has taken steps to correct the problem. The Fair Disclosure rule mandated by the SEC requires that all company information be released to the public rather than quietly disseminated to analysts. Some brokerages even ban analysts from owning stocks they cover. The SEC is also considering separating research from investment banking so that the analyst's job is to research stock rather than solicit potential clients.

Is analyst advice only worth the paper it's printed on? Not necessarily, as long as investors learn how to evaluate research reports and read between the lines. To start with, investors should probably lower analyst ratings by one notch. Given the analyst buy bias, a strong buy should be interpreted as a buy, a buy as a hold, and a hold or neutral as a recommendation to sell. Moreover, negative ratings should carry more weight than positive ones. While buy recommendations on average do not assure superior market performance, stock downgrades and those rare sell recommendations may signal problems down the road. Market data show that analysts often tend to be right when they turn negative on the stock. Investors should also pay attention to downward revisions of earnings estimates; it usually means that bad news often may get worse as changing business conditions may spread beyond individual companies. Often analyst's strengths are in spotting structural trends facing entire industries and problems facing company management. And when in doubt, investors should do their own homework and exercise common sense.

CRITICAL THINKING QUESTION Do you agree with the regulation forbidding analysts to own stock of the companies they cover?

Although a stockholder can earn capital gains in addition to dividends by selling a stock for more than he or she paid for it, from a strictly theoretical point of view, what is really being sold is the right to all remaining future dividends. Thus, just as the *current* value of a share of stock is a function of future dividends, the *future* price of the stock is also a function of future dividends. In this framework, the *future* price of the stock will rise or fall as the outlook for dividends (and the required rate of return) changes. This approach, which holds that the value of a share of stock is a function of its future dividends, is known as the **dividend valuation model (DVM)**.

dividend valuation model (DVM)
a model that values a share of stock on the basis of the future dividend stream it is expected to produce; its three versions are zero-growth, constant-growth, and variable-growth.

There are three versions of the dividend valuation model, each based on different assumptions about the future rate of growth in dividends: (1) *The zero-growth model* assumes that dividends will not grow over time. (2) *The constant-growth model*, which is the basic version of the dividend valuation model, assumes that dividends will grow by a fixed/constant rate over time. (3) *The variable-growth model* assumes that the rate of growth in dividends will vary over time. In one form or another, the DVM is widely used in practice to value many of the larger, more mature companies—and is, in fact, the centerpiece of the "Equity Investments" portion of the Level-I CFA program.

Zero Growth The simplest way to picture the dividend valuation model is to assume the stock has a fixed stream of dividends. In other words, dividends stay the same year in and year out, and they're expected to do so in the future. Under such conditions, the value of a zero-growth stock is simply *the capitalized value of its annual dividends*. To find the capitalized value, just divide annual dividends by the required rate of return, which in effect acts as the capitalization rate. That is,

H O T

See the dividend valuation model at
www.stocksense.com/valuation.html

Equation 8.7

$$\text{Value of a share of stock} = \frac{\text{Annual dividends}}{\text{required rate of return}}$$

For example, if a stock paid a (constant) dividend of $3 a share and you wanted to earn 10% on your investment, the value of the stock would be $30 a share ($3/0.10 = $30).

As you can see, the only cash flow variable that's used in this model is the fixed annual dividend. Given that the annual dividend on this stock never changes, does that mean the price of the stock never changes? Absolutely not! For as the capitalization rate—that is, the required rate of return—changes, so will the price of the stock. Thus, if the capitalization rate goes up to, say, 15%, the price of the stock will fall to $20 ($3/0.15). Although this may be a very simplified view of the valuation model, it's actually not as far-fetched as it may appear. As we'll see in Chapter 12, this is basically the procedure used to price *preferred stocks* in the marketplace.

Constant Growth The zero-growth model is a good beginning, but it does not take into account a growing stream of dividends, which is more likely to be the case in the real world. The standard and more widely recognized version of the dividend valuation model assumes that dividends will grow over time at a specified rate. In this version, the value of a share of stock is still considered to be a function of its future dividends, but such dividends are expected to grow forever (to infinity) at a constant rate of growth, *g*. Accordingly, the value of a share of stock can be found as follows:

Equation 8.8

$$\text{Value of a share of stock} = \frac{\text{Next year's dividends}}{\text{Required rate of return} - \text{Constant rate of growth in dividends}}$$

Equation 8.8a

$$V = \frac{D_1}{k - g}$$

where

D_1 = annual dividends expected to be paid *next* year (the first year in the forecast period)

k = the capitalization rate, or discount rate (which defines the required rate of return on the investment)

g = the annual rate of growth in dividends, which is expected to hold constant to infinity

This model succinctly captures the essence of stock valuation: *Increase* the cash flow (through *D* or *g*) and/or *decrease* the required rate of return (*k*), and the value of the stock will *increase*. Also note that in the DVM, *k defines* the *total return* to the stockholder and *g represents the expected capital gains* on the investments. We know that, in practice, there are potentially two components that make up the total return to a stockholder: dividends and capital gains. As it turns out, the returns from both dividends and capital gains are captured in the DVM. That is, because *k* represents total returns and *g* defines the amount of capital gains embedded in *k*, it follows that if you subtract *g* from *k (k − g)*, you'll have the expected dividend yield on the stock. Thus the expected total return on a stock (*k*) equals the returns from capital gains (*g*) plus the returns from dividends (*k − g*).

The constant-growth DVM should not be used with just any stock. Rather, *it is best suited to the valuation of mature, dividend-paying companies* that hold established market positions. These are companies with strong track records that have reached the "mature" stage of growth. This means that you're probably dealing with large-cap (or perhaps even some mature mid-cap) companies that have demonstrated an ability to generate steady—though perhaps not spectacular—rates of growth year in and year out. The growth rates *may not be identical* from year to year, but they tend to move within such a small range that they are seldom far off the average rate. These are companies that have established dividend policies and fairly predictable growth rates in earnings and dividends. In addition to its use in valuing mature, dividend-paying companies, the constant-growth DVM is also widely used to *value the market as a whole*. That is, using something like the DJIA or the S&P 500, analysts will often employ the DVM to determine the expected return on the market for the coming year—in other words, they'll use it to find the R_m in the capital asset pricing model (CAPM).

Applying the Constant-Growth DVM To use the constant-growth DVM, all that's required is some basic information about the stock's *current* level of dividends and the expected rate of growth in dividends, g. One popular and fairly simply way to find the dividend growth rate is to look at the *historical* behavior of dividends. If they are growing at a relatively constant rate, you could assume that they'll continue to grow at (or near) that average rate in the future. You can get historical dividend data in a company's annual report, from various online Internet sources, or from publications like *Value Line.* Given this stream of dividends, you can use basic present-value arithmetic to find the average rate of growth. Here's how: Take the level of dividends, say, 10 years ago and the level that's being paid today. Presumably, dividends today will be (much) higher than they were 10 years ago, so, using your calculator, find the present value discount rate that equates the (higher) dividend today to the level paid 10 years earlier. When you find that, you've found the growth rate, because in this case, the *discount rate is the average rate of growth in dividends.* (See Chapter 5 for a detailed discussion of how to use present value to find growth rates.)

Once you've determined the dividend growth rate, g, you can find next year's dividend, D_1, as $D_0 \times (1 + g)$, where D_0 equals the actual (current) level of dividends. Let's say that in the latest year Amalgamated Anything paid $2.50 a share in dividends. If you expect these dividends to grow at the rate of 6% a year, you can find next year's dividends as follows: $D_1 = D_0 (1 + g)$ = \$2.50 (1 + 0.06) = \$2.50 (1.06) = \$2.65. The only other information you need is the capitalization rate, or required rate of return, k. (Note that k must be greater than g for the constant-growth model to be mathematically operative.)

To see this dividend valuation model at work, consider a stock that currently pays an annual dividend of $1.75 a share. Let's say that by using the present-value approach described above, you find that dividends are growing at a rate of 8% a year, and you expect they will continue to do so into the future. In addition, you feel that because of the risks involved, the investment should carry a required rate of return of 12%. Given this information, you can use Equation 8.8 to price the stock. That is, given $D_0 = \$1.75$, $g = 0.08$, and $k = 0.12$, it follows that

$$\frac{\text{Value of a}}{\text{share of stock}} = \frac{D_0(1 + g)}{k - g} = \frac{\$1.75(1.08)}{0.12 - 0.08} = \frac{\$1.89}{0.04} = \underline{\$47.25}$$

Thus, if you want to earn a 12% return on this investment—made up of 8% in capital gains (g), plus 4% in dividend yield (i.e., \$1.89/\$47.25 = 0.04)—then according to the constant-growth dividend valuation model, you should pay no more than $47.25 a share for this stock.

With this version of the DVM, *the price of the stock will increase over time* so long as k and g don't change. In fact, as we noted earlier, the growth rate (g) defines the amount of (expected) capital gains embedded in the future price of the stock. So, if $g = 8\%$, then we can expect the future price of the stock to go up around 8% per year. This will occur because the cash flow from the investment will increase as dividends grow. To see how this happens, let's carry our example a little further. Recall that $D_0 = \$1.75$, $g = 8\%$, and $k = 12\%$. On the basis of this information, we found the current value of the stock to be $47.25. Now look what happens to the price of this stock if k and g don't change:

Year	Dividend	Stock Price*
(Current year) 0	$1.75	$47.25
1	1.89	51.00
2	2.04	55.00
3	2.20	59.50
4	2.38	64.25
5	2.57	69.50

*As determined by the dividend valuation model, given $g = 0.08$, $k = 0.12$, and D_0 = dividend level for any given year.

As the table shows, the price of the stock should rise from $47.25 today to around $69.50 in five years—as expected, that works out to an 8% growth rate. Just as we can use this version of the DVM to value a stock today, so too can we find the expected price of the stock *in the future* by using the same valuation model. To do this, we simply redefine the appropriate level of dividends. For example, to find the price of the stock in year 3, we use the expected dividend in the third year, $2.20, and increase it by the factor $(1 + g)$. Thus the stock price in year $3 = D_3 \times (1 + g)/(k - g) = \$2.20 \times (1 + 0.08)/(0.12 - 0.08) = \$2.38/0.04 = \$59.50$. Of course, if future expectations about k or g do change, the *future price* of the stock will change accordingly. Should that occur, an investor could use the new information to decide whether to continue to hold the stock.

Variable Growth Although the constant-growth dividend valuation model is an improvement over the zero-growth model, it still has some shortcomings. The most obvious is the fact that it does not allow for changes in expected growth rates. To overcome this problem, we can use a form of the DVM that allows for *variable rates of growth* over time. Essentially, the *variable-growth dividend valuation model* derives, in two stages, a value based on future dividends and the future price of the stock (which price is a function of all future dividends). The variable-growth version of the model finds the value of a share of stock as follows:

Equation 8.9

$$\text{Value of a share of stock} = \text{Present value of future dividends during the initial variable-growth period} + \text{Present value of the price of the stock at the end of the variable-growth period}$$

Equation 8.9a

$$V = (D_1 \times PVIF_1) + (D_2 \times PVIF_2) + \cdots$$
$$+ (D_v \times PVIF_v) + \left(\frac{D_v(1 + g)}{k - g} \times PVIF_v\right)$$

where

D_1, D_2, etc. = future annual dividends

$PVIF_t$ = present value interest factor, as specified by the required rate of return for a given year t (Table A.3 in the appendix)

v = number of years in the initial variable-growth period

Note that the last element in this equation is the standard constant-growth dividend valuation model, which is used to find the price of the stock at the end of the initial variable-growth period.

This form of the DVM is appropriate for companies that are expected to experience rapid or variable rates of growth for a period of time—perhaps for the first 3 to 5 years—and then settle down to a constant (average) growth rate thereafter. This, in fact, is the growth pattern of many companies, so the model has considerable application in practice. (It also overcomes one of the operational shortcomings of the constant-growth DVM in that k does not always have to be greater than g. That is, *during the variable-growth period*, the rate of growth, g, can be greater than the required rate of return, k, and the model will still be fully operational.)

Finding the value of a stock using Equation 8.9 is actually a lot easier than it looks. All you need do is follow these steps:

1. Estimate annual dividends during the initial variable-growth period and then specify the constant rate, g, at which dividends will grow after the initial period.
2. Find the present value of the dividends expected during the initial variable-growth period.
3. Using the constant-growth DVM, find the price of the stock at the end of the initial growth period.
4. Find the present value of the price of the stock (as determined in step 3). Note that the price of the stock is discounted at the same *PVIF* as the last dividend payment in the initial growth period, because the stock is being priced (per step 3) at the end of this initial period.
5. Add the two present-value components (from steps 2 and 4) to find the value of a stock.

Applying the Variable-Growth DVM To see how this works, let's apply the variable-growth model to one of our favorite companies: Sweatmore Industries. Let's assume that dividends will grow at a variable rate for the first 3 years (2004, 2005, and 2006). After that, the annual rate of growth in dividends is expected to settle down to 8% and stay there for the foreseeable future. Starting with the latest (2003) annual dividend of $2.21 a share, we estimate that Sweatmore's dividends should grow by 20% next year (in 2004), by 16% in 2005, and then by 13% in 2006 before dropping to an 8% rate. Using these (initial) growth rates, we therefore project that dividends in 2004 will amount to $2.65 a share ($2.21 × 1.20), and will rise to $3.08 ($2.65 × 1.16) in 2005 and to $3.48 ($3.08 × 1.13) in 2006. In addition, given Sweatmore's risk profile, we feel that the investment should produce a minimum (required) rate of return (k) of at least 14%. We now have all the input we need and are ready to put a value on Sweatmore Industries. Table 8.4 (on page 350) shows the variable-growth DVM in action. The value of Sweatmore stock, according to the variable-growth DVM, is just under $49.25 a share. In essence, that's the maximum price you should be willing to pay for the stock if you want to earn a 14% rate of return.

Defining the Expected Growth Rate Mechanically, application of the DVM is really quite simple. It relies on just three key pieces of information: future dividends, future growth in dividends, and a required rate of return. But this

EXCEL with
SPREADSHEETS

TABLE 8.4 Using the Variable-Growth DVM to Value Sweatmore Stock

Step

1. Projected annual dividends:

2004	$2.65
2005	3.08
2006	3.48

Estimated annual rate of growth in dividends, g, for 2007 and beyond: 8%

2. Present value of dividends, using a required rate of return, k, of 14%, during the initial variable-growth period:

Year	Dividends	×	PVIF (k = 14%)	=	Present Value
2004	$2.65		0.877		$2.32
2005	3.08		0.769		2.37
2006	3.48		0.675		2.35
				Total	$7.04 (to step 5)

3. Price of the stock at the end of the initial growth period:

$$P_{2006} = \frac{D_{2007}}{k - g} = \frac{D_{2006} \times (1 + g)}{k - g} = \frac{\$3.48 \times (1.08)}{0.14 - 0.08} = \frac{\$3.75}{0.06} = \underline{\$62.50}$$

4. Discount the price of the stock (as computed above) back to its present value, at k = 14%:

$$PV(P_{2006}) = \$62.50 \times PVIF_{14\%,\ 3\ yr} = \$62.50 \times 0.675 = \underline{\$42.19} \text{ (to step 5)}$$

5. Add the present value of the initial dividend stream (step 2) to the present value of the price of the stock at the end of the initial growth period (step 4):

Value of Sweatmore stock = $7.04 + $42.19 = $49.23

model is not without its difficulties, and certainly one of the most difficult (and most important) aspects of the DVM is *specifying the appropriate growth rate, g, over an extended period of time.* Whether you are using the constant-growth or the variable-growth version of the dividend valuation model, the growth rate, g, is a crucial element in the DVM and has an enormous impact on the value derived from the model. Indeed, the DVM is *very sensitive* to the growth rate being used, because that rate affects both the model's numerator and its denominator. As a result, in practice analysts spend a good deal of time trying to come up with a growth rate, g, that they feel is appropriate for a given company and its stock.

As we saw earlier in this chapter, we can define the growth rate from a strictly historical perspective (by using present value to find the past rate of growth) and then use it (or something close) in the DVM. That technique might work fine with the constant-growth model, but it has some obvious shortcomings with the variable-growth DVM. One procedure widely used in practice is to define the growth rate, g, as follows:

Equation 8.10

$$g = \text{ROE} \times \text{The firm's retention rate, } rr$$

where

$$rr = 1 - \text{Dividend payout ratio}$$

Both variables in Equation 8.10 (ROE and *rr*) are *directly related to the firm's rate of growth*, and both play key roles in defining a firm's future growth. The *retention rate* represents the percentage of the firm's profits that is plowed back into the company. Thus, if the firm pays out 35% of its earnings in dividends (i.e., it has a dividend payout ratio of 35%), then it has a retention rate of 65%: $rr = 1 - 0.35 = 0.65$. The retention rate, in effect, indicates the amount of capital that is flowing into the company to finance its growth. Other things being equal, the more money being retained in the company, the higher the rate of growth. The other component of Equation 8.10 is the familiar return on equity. Clearly, the more the company can earn on its retained capital, the higher the growth rate.

Let's look at some numbers to see how this actually works. For example, if a company retained, on average, about 80% of its earnings and generated an ROE of around 15%, you'd expect it to have a growth rate of around 12%:

$$g = \text{ROE} \times rr = 0.15 \times 0.80 = \underline{12\%}$$

Actually, the growth rate will probably be a bit more than 12%, because Equation 8.10 ignores financial leverage, which in itself will magnify growth. But at least the equation gives you a good idea what to expect. Or it can serve as a starting point in assessing past and future growth. That is, you can use Equation 8.10 to compute expected growth and then assess the two key components of the formula (ROE and *rr*) to see whether they're likely to undergo major changes in the future. If so, then what impact is the change in ROE and/or *rr* likely to have on the growth rate, *g*? The idea is to take the time to study the forces (ROE and *rr*) that drive the growth rate, because the DVM itself is so sensitive to the rate of growth being used. Employ a growth rate that's too high and you'll end up with an intrinsic value that's way too high also. The downside to that, of course, is that you may end up buying a stock that you really shouldn't.

Some Alternatives to the DVM

The variable-growth approach to stock valuation is fairly compatible with the way most people invest. That is, unlike the underlying assumptions in the standard dividend valuation model (which employs an infinite investment horizon), most investors have a holding period that seldom exceeds 5 to 7 years. Under such circumstances, *the relevant cash flows are future dividends and the future selling price of the stock.*

There are some alternatives to the DVM that use such cash flow streams to value stock. One is the so-called *dividends-and-earnings approach*, which in many respects is similar to the variable-growth DVM. Another is the *P/E approach*, which builds the stock valuation process around the stock's price/earnings ratio. One of the major advantages of these procedures is that *they don't rely on dividends as the key input.* Accordingly, they can be used with stocks that are more growth-oriented and pay little or nothing in dividends. It is very difficult, if not impossible, to apply the DVM to stocks that pay little or nothing in dividends. That's not a problem with the dividend-and-earnings approach or the P/E approach. Let's now take a closer look at both of these, as well as a technique that arrives at the expected return on the stock (in percentage terms) rather than a (dollar-based) "justified price."

A Dividends-and-Earnings Approach As we saw earlier, the value of a share of stock is a function of the amount and timing of future cash flows and the level of risk that must be taken on to generate that return. A stock valuation model has been developed that conveniently captures the essential elements of expected risk and return and does so in a present-value context. The model is as follows:

Equation 8.11

$$\text{Present value of a share of stock} = \text{Present value of future dividends} + \text{Present value of the price of the stock at the date of sale}$$

Equation 8.11a

$$V = (D_1 \times PVIF_1) + (D_2 \times PVIF_2) + \cdots$$
$$+ (D_N \times PVIF_N) + (SP_N \times PVIF_N)$$

where

D_t = future annual dividend in year t

$PVIF_t$ = present-value interest factor, specified at the required rate of return (Table A.3 in the appendix near the end of the book)

SP_N = estimated share price of the stock at date of sale, year N

N = number of years in the investment horizon

**dividends-and-earnings
(D&E) approach**
stock valuation approach that
uses projected dividends, EPS,
and P/E multiples to value a
share of stock.

This is the so-called **dividends-and-earnings (D&E) approach** to valuation. Note its similarities to the variable-growth DVM: It's also present-value–based, and its value is also derived from future dividends and the expected future price of the stock. The big difference between the two procedures revolves around the role that dividends play in determining the future price of the stock. That is, the D&E approach doesn't rely on dividends as the principal player in the valuation process. Therefore, it works just as well with companies that pay little or nothing in dividends as with stocks that pay out a lot in dividends. And along that line, whereas the variable-growth DVM relies on future dividends to price the stock, the D&E approach employs projected earnings per share and estimated P/E multiples. These are the same two variables that drive the price of the stock in the market. Thus, the D&E approach is far more flexible than the DVM and is easier to understand and apply. Using the D&E valuation approach, we focus on projecting future dividends and share price behavior over a defined, finite investment horizon, much as we did for Universal Office Furnishings in Table 8.3.

Especially important in the D&E approach is finding a viable P/E multiple that can be used to project the future price of the stock. This is a critical part of this valuation process, because of the major role that capital gains (and therefore the estimated price of the stock at its date of sale) play in defining the level of security returns. Using market or industry P/E ratios as benchmarks, you should try to establish a multiple that you feel the stock will trade at in the future. Like the growth rate, g, in the DVM, the P/E multiple is the single most important (and most difficult) variable to project in the D&E approach. Using this input, along with estimated future dividends, this present-value–based model generates a *justified price* based on estimated returns. This intrinsic value represents the price you should be willing to pay for the stock, given its expected dividend and price behavior, and assuming you want to generate a return that is equal to or greater than your required rate of return.

To see how this procedure works, consider once again the case of Universal Office Furnishings. Let's return to our original 3-year investment horizon. Given the forecasted annual dividends and share price from Table 8.3, along with a required rate of return of 18% (as computed earlier using Equation 8.6), we can see that the value of Universal's stock is

$$
\begin{aligned}
\frac{\text{Present value of a share}}{\text{of Universal stock}} &= \frac{(\$0.18 \times 0.847) + (\$0.24 \times 0.718) + (\$0.28 \times 0.609)}{+ (\$93.20 \times 0.609)} \\
&= \$0.15 + \$0.17 + 0.17 + \$56.76 \\
&= \underline{\$57.25}
\end{aligned}
$$

According to the D&E approach, Universal's stock should be valued at about $57 a share. That assumes, of course, that our projections hold up—particularly with regard to our forecasted EPS and P/E multiple in 2007. For example, if the P/E drops from 20 to 17 times earnings, then the value of a share of stock will drop to less than $50 (to around $48.75/share). Given that we have confidence in our projections, the present-value figure computed here means that we would realize our (18%) desired rate of return so long as we can buy the stock at no more than $57 a share. Because UVRS is currently trading at (around) $41.50, we can conclude that the stock at present is an *attractive investment vehicle*. That is, because we can buy the stock at *less* than its computed intrinsic value, we'll be able to earn our required rate of return, *and then some*. By most standards, Universal would be considered a highly risky investment, if for no other reason than the fact that *nearly all the return is derived from capital gains*. Indeed, dividends alone account for less than 1% of the value of the stock. That is, only 49 cents of the $57.25 comes from dividends! Clearly, if we're wrong about EPS or the P/E multiple, the future price of the stock (in 2007) could be way off the mark, and so, too, would our projected return.

Finding the Value of Non–Dividend-Paying Stocks

What about *finding the value of a stock that doesn't pay any dividends*—and isn't expected to do so for the foreseeable future? That's not a problem with the D&E approach. Using Equation 8.11, simply set all dividends to zero, so the computed value of the stock would come solely from its projected future price. In other words, the value of the stock will equal the present value of its price at the end of the holding period. Consider, for example, an investor who's looking at a stock that pays no dividends; she estimates that at the end of a 2-year holding period, this stock should be trading at around $70 a share. Using a 15% required rate of return, this stock would have a present value of $70 × *PVIF* (for 2 years and 15%) = $70 × 0.756 = $52.92. This value is, of course, the intrinsic value, or justified price of the stock. So long as it's trading for around $53 or less, it should be considered a worthwhile investment candidate. (*Note:* Rather than using interest tables, you can just as easily *use a hand-held calculator to find the value of this stock*. Here's what you do: Input **N** as 2, **I/Y** as 15, and **FV** as –70.00; then compute **PV**, which turns out to be *52.93*.)

Determining Expected Return Sometimes investors find it more convenient to deal in terms of expected return than a dollar-based justified price. This is no problem, nor is it necessary to sacrifice the present-value dimension of the stock valuation model to achieve such an end. That's because expected return can be found by using the (present-value–based) *internal rate of return (IRR)* procedure first introduced in Chapter 5. This approach to stock valuation uses forecasted dividend and price behavior, along with the *current market price*, to arrive at the fully compounded rate of return you can expect to earn from a given investment.

To see how a stock's expected return is computed, let's look once again at Universal Office Furnishings. Using 2005–2007 data from Table 8.3, along with the stock's current price of $41.58, we can determine Universal's expected return. To do so, we find the discount rate that equates the future stream of benefits (i.e., the future annual dividends and future price of the stock) to the stock's current market price. In other words, find the discount rate that produces a present value of future benefits equal to the price of the stock, and you have the IRR, or expected return on that stock.

Here's how it works: Using the Universal example, we know that the stock is expected to pay per-share dividends of $0.18, $0.24, and $0.28 over the next 3 years. At the end of that time, we hope to sell the stock for $93.20. Given that the stock is currently trading at $41.58, we're looking for the discount rate that will produce a present value (of the future annual dividends and stock price) equal to $41.58. That is,

$$(\$0.18 \times PVIF_1) + (\$0.24 \times PVIF_2) \\ + (\$0.28 \times PVIF_3) + (\$93.20 \times PVIF_3) = \$41.58$$

We need to solve for the discount rate (the present-value interest factors) in this equation. Through a process of "hit and miss" (and with the help of a personal computer or hand-held calculator), you'll find that with an interest factor of 31.3%, the present value of the future cash benefits from this investment will equal exactly $41.58. That, of course, is our expected return. Thus Universal can be expected to earn a fully compounded annual return of about 31%, assuming that the stock can be bought at $41.58, is held for 3 years (during which time investors receive indicated annual dividends), and then is sold for $93.20 at the end of the 3-year period. When compared to its 18% *required rate of return*, the 31.3% *expected return* makes Universal look like a very attractive investment candidate. [It's even easier to determine the return on stocks that don't pay dividends. Just *find the discount rate that equates the projected future price of the stock to its current share price.* For example, if Universal didn't pay dividends, then all we'd have to do is find the discount rate (*PVIF*) that equates the projected share price of $93.20 3 years from now to the stock's current price of $41.58. Using a hand-held calculator, we arrive at an expected rate of return of 30.9%: Input **PV** as –41.58, **FV** as 93.20, and **N** as 3; then compute **I/Y**, which turns out to be 30.87. Given the return of 31.3% with dividends versus the 30.9% return without dividends, the cash flow from dividends clearly doesn't play much of a role in defining the potential return on this stock.]

The Price/Earnings (P/E) Approach One of the problems with the stock valuation procedures we've looked at above is that they are fairly mechanical. They involve a good deal of "number crunching." Although such an approach

price/earnings (P/E) approach stock valuation approach that tries to find the P/E ratio that's most appropriate for the stock; this ratio, along with estimated EPS, is then used to determine a reasonable stock price.

is fine with some stocks, it doesn't work well with others. Fortunately, there is a more intuitive approach. That alternative is the **price/earnings (or P/E) approach** to stock valuation.

The P/E approach is a favorite of professional security analysts and is widely used in practice. It's relatively simple to use, because it's based on the standard P/E formula first introduced in Chapter 7 (Equation 7.14). There we showed that a stock's P/E ratio is equal to its market price divided by the stock's EPS. Using this equation and solving for the market price of the stock, we have

Equation 8.12

$$\text{Stock price} = \text{EPS} \times \text{P/E ratio}$$

Equation 8.12 basically captures the P/E approach to stock valuation. That is, given an *estimated* EPS figure, *you decide on a P/E ratio that you feel is appropriate for the stock. Then you use it in Equation 8.12 to see what kind of price you come up with and how that compares to the stock's current price.*

Actually, this approach is no different from what's used in the market every day. Look at the stock quotes in the *Wall Street Journal*. They include the stock's P/E ratio and show what investors are willing to pay for one dollar of earnings. Essentially, the *Journal* relates the company's earnings per share for the *last* 12 months (known as *trailing earnings*) to the latest price of the stock. In practice, however, investors buy stocks not for their past earnings but for their *expected future earnings*. Thus, in Equation 8.12, it's customary to use *forecasted EPS for next year*—that is, to use projected earnings one year out.

The first thing you have to do to implement the P/E approach is to come up with an expected EPS figure for next year. In the early part of this chapter, we saw how this might be done (see, for instance, Equation 8.3). Given the forecasted EPS, the next task is to evaluate the variables that drive the P/E ratio. Most of that assessment is intuitive. For example, you might want to look at the stock's expected rate of growth in earnings, any potential major changes in the firm's capital structure or dividends, and any other factors such as relative market or industry P/E multiples that might affect the stock's multiple. You could use such inputs to come up with a base P/E ratio, and then adjust that base, as necessary, to account for the perceived state of the market and/or anticipated changes in the rate of inflation.

Along with estimated EPS, we now have the P/E ratio we need to compute (via Equation 8.12) the price at which the stock should be trading. Take, for example, a stock that's currently trading at $37.80. One year from now, it's estimated that this stock should have an EPS of $2.25 a share. If you feel that the stock should be trading at a P/E ratio of 20 times projected earnings, then it should be valued at $45 a share (i.e., $2.25 × 20). By comparing this targeted price to the current market price of the stock, we can decide whether the stock is a good buy. In this case, we would consider the stock undervalued and therefore a good buy, since the computed price of the stock ($45) is more than its market price (of $37.80). While this is the principal application of the P/E approach, you'll find that *a variation of this procedure* is also used with the D&E and IRR approaches. That is, by using estimated figures for *both* EPS and the P/E multiple, an investor can come up with *the share price that's expected to prevail at the end of a given investment horizon.* Throw in any dividends that may be received, discount that cash flow (of dividends and future share price) back to the present, and you have either the *justified price*, as in the D&E approach, or the *expected rate of return*, as in the IRR approach.

Other Price-Relative Procedures

In addition to the P/E approach, there are several other price-relative procedures that are used by investors. These include:

- The price-to-cash-flow (P/CF) ratio
- The price-to-sales (P/S) ratio
- The price-to-book-value (P/BV) ratio

Like the P/E multiple, these procedures assess the value of a stock by relating share price to cash flow, sales, or book value. Let's now look at each of these in turn to see how they're used in stock valuation.

A Price-to-Cash-Flow (P/CF) Procedure This measure has long been popular with investors, because cash flow is felt to provide a more accurate picture of a company's earning power than net earnings. When used in stock valuation, the procedure is almost identical to the P/E approach. That is, a P/CF ratio is combined with a *projected* cash flow per share to arrive at what the stock should be trading for. Although it is quite straightforward, this procedure nonetheless has one problem—defining the appropriate cash flow measure. While some investors use *cash flow from operations*, as obtained from the statement of cash flows, others use *free cash flow*. But the one measure that seems to be the most popular with professional analysts is EBITDA (*earnings before interest, taxes, depreciation, and amortization*), which we'll use here. EBITDA represents "cash earnings" to the extent that the major noncash expenditures (depreciation and amortization) are added back to operating earnings (EBIT).

The price-to-cash-flow (P/CF) ratio is computed as follows:

Equation 8.13

$$\text{P/CF ratio} = \frac{\text{Market price of common stock}}{\text{Cash flow per share}}$$

where cash flow per share = EBITDA ÷ number of common shares outstanding. To use the P/CF procedure *to assess the current market price of a stock*, you first have to come up with a forecasted cash flow per share 1 year out, then define an appropriate P/CF multiple to use. For most firms, it is very likely that the cash flow (EBITDA) figure will be larger than net earnings available to stockholders and, as a result, *the cash flow multiple will probably be lower than the P/E multiple*—which some would argue is all too often the principal motivation for using the P/CF ratio (to end up with a lower, more respectable multiple). In any event, once an appropriate P/CF multiple is determined, simply multiply it by the expected cash flow per share 1 year from now to find the price at which the stock should be trading. That is, the computed price of a share of stock = cash flow per share × P/CF ratio.

To illustrate, assume a company currently is generating an EBITDA of $325 million, and that's expected to increase by some 12.5% to around $365 million ($325 million × 1.125) over the course of the next 12 months. On a per-share basis, let's say that translates into a *projected* cash flow per share of nearly $6.50. Now, if we feel this stock should be trading at about 8 times its projected cash flow per share, then it should be valued at around $52 a share. Thus, if it is currently trading in the market at $45.50 (or at 7 times its projected cash flow per share), we can conclude, once again, that the stock is undervalued and, therefore, should be considered a viable investment candidate.

Price-to-Sales (P/S) and Price-to-Book-Value (P/BV) Ratios Some companies, like new-technology and Internet firms, don't have much, if anything, in the way of earnings, or if they do have earnings, they're either unreliable or very erratic and therefore highly unpredictable. In these cases, valuation procedures based on earnings (and even cash flows) aren't much help. So investors turn to other procedures—those based on sales or book value, for example. While companies may not have much in the way of profits, they certainly have sales and, ideally, some book value. (As noted in Chapter 7, *book value* is simply another term for equity, or net worth.)

Both the price-to-sales (P/S) and price-to-book-value (P/BV) ratios are used exactly like the P/E and P/CF procedures. Recall that we defined the P/BV ratio in Equation 7.19 as follows:

$$\text{P/BV ratio} = \frac{\text{Market price of common stock}}{\text{Book value per share}}$$

We can define the P/S ratio in a similar fashion:

Equation 8.14

$$\text{P/S ratio} = \frac{\text{Market price of common stock}}{\text{Sales per share}}$$

where sales per share = net annual sales (or revenues) ÷ number of common shares outstanding.

Generally speaking, the lower the P/S ratio, the better. In fact, many investors look for stocks with P/S ratios of 2.0 or less, as these securities are felt to offer the most potential for future price appreciation. Especially attractive are very low P/S multiples of 1.0 or less. Think about it: With a P/S ratio of, say, 0.9, you can buy $1 in sales for only 90 cents! So long as the company isn't a basket case, such low P/S multiples may well be worth pursuing. Keep in mind, however, that while the emphasis may be on low multiples, *high P/S ratios aren't necessarily bad*. To determine if a high multiple—more than 3.0 or 4.0, for example—is justified, look at the company's net profit margin. Companies that can consistently generate high net profit margins often have high P/S ratios. There's a valuation rule to remember: *High profit margins should go hand-in-hand with high P/S multiples*. That makes sense, too, because a company with a high profit margin brings more of its sales down to the bottom line in the form of profits.

You'd also expect the price-to-book-value measure to be low, but probably not as low as the P/S ratio. Indeed, unless the market becomes grossly overvalued (think about what happened in 1999 or 2000), most stocks are likely to trade at multiples of less than 3 to 5 times their book values. And in this case, unlike with the P/S multiple, there's usually little justification for abnormally high price-to-book-value ratios—except perhaps for firms that have abnormally *low* levels of equity in their capital structures. Other than that, high P/BV multiples are almost always caused by "excess exuberance." As a rule, when stocks start trading at 7 or 8 times their book values, or more, it's a sure sign that they are becoming overvalued.

IN REVIEW

8.6 Briefly describe the *dividend valuation model* and the three versions of this model. Explain how CAPM fits into the *variable-growth DVM*.

8.7 What is the difference between the variable-growth dividend valuation model and the *dividends-and-earnings approach* to stock valuation? Which procedure would work better if you were trying to value a growth stock that pays little or no dividends? Explain.

8.8 How would you go about finding the *expected return* on a stock? Note how such information would be used in the stock selection process.

8.9 Briefly describe the *P/E approach* to stock valuation and note how this approach differs from the variable-growth DVM. Describe the *P/CF approach* and note how it is used in the stock valuation process. Compare the P/CF approach to the P/E approach, noting their relative strengths and weaknesses.

8.10 Briefly describe the *price/sales* ratio, and explain how it is used to value stocks. Why not just use the P/E multiple? How does the P/S ratio differ from the *P/BV measure?*

Summary

LG 1 **Explain the role that a company's future plays in the stock valuation process.** The final phase of security analysis involves an assessment of the investment merits of a specific company and its stock. The focus here is on formulating expectations about the company's prospects and the risk and return behavior of the stock. In particular, we would want some idea of the stock's future earnings, dividends, and share prices, because that's ultimately the basis of our return.

LG 2 **Develop a forecast of a stock's expected cash flow, starting with corporate sales and earnings, and then moving to expected dividends and share price.** Because the value of a share of stock is a function of its future returns, investors must try to formulate expectations about what they feel the future holds for the company and its stock. That's usually done by looking first at the company's projected sales and earnings, and then translating those data into forecasted dividends and share prices. Such insight is vital to the stock valuation process, as these variables define an investment's future cash flow and, therefore, investor returns.

LG 3 **Discuss the concepts of intrinsic value and required rates of return, and note how they are used.** Information such as projected sales, forecasted earnings, and estimated dividends are important in establishing intrinsic value. This is a measure, based on expected return and risk exposure, of what the stock ought to be worth. A key element is the investor's required rate of return, which is used to define the amount of return that should be earned given the stock's perceived exposure to risk. The more risk in the investment, the more return one should require.

LG 4 **Determine the underlying value of a stock using the zero-growth, constant-growth, and variable-growth dividend valuation models.** The dividend valuation model (DVM) derives the value of a share of stock from the stock's future growth in dividends. There are three versions of the DVM: zero-growth, which assumes that dividends are fixed and won't change in the future; constant-growth, which assumes that dividends will grow at a constant rate into the future; and variable-growth, which assumes that dividends will initially grow at varying (or abnormally high) rates, before eventually settling down to a constant rate of growth.

LG 5 **Use other types of present-value–based models to derive the value of a stock, as well as alternative price-relative procedures.** The DVM works well with some types of stocks, but not so well with others. As a result, investors may turn to other types of stock-valuation approaches, including the D&E and IRR approaches, as well as certain price-relative procedures, like the P/E, P/CF, P/S, and P/BV methods. For example, the dividends-and-earnings approach uses a finite investment horizon to derive a present-value–based "justified price." Alternatively, rather than using a dollar-based justified price, investors can determine the expected return on a stock (via IRR) by finding the discount rate that equates the stock's future cash flows to its current market price. Several other price-relative procedures exist as well, such as the price/earnings approach, which uses projected EPS and the stock's P/E ratio to determine whether a stock is fairly valued.

LG 6 **Gain a basic appreciation of the procedures used to value different types of stock, from traditional dividend-paying shares to more growth-oriented stocks.** All sorts of stock valuation models are used in the market; this chapter examined nine of the more widely used procedures. One thing that becomes readily apparent in stock evaluation is that one approach definitely does not fit all situations. Some approaches (like the DVM) work well with mature, dividend-paying companies; others (like the D&E, IRR, P/E, and P/CF approaches) are more suited to growth-oriented firms, which may or may not pay dividends. Other price-relative procedures (like P/S and P/BV) are often used to value companies that have little or nothing in earnings, or whose earnings records are highly sporadic.

Putting Your Investment Know-How to the Test

1. ABC Corporation has an expected ROE of 15%. What will be its dividend growth rate if its dividend payout rate is 30%?
   a. 4.5%   b. 10.5%
   c. 15.0%   d. 30.0%

2. An analyst gathered the following information about a common stock:

Annual dividend per share	$2.10
Risk-free rate	7%
Risk premium for this stock	4%

   If the annual dividend is expected to remain at $2.10, the value of the stock is *closest* to
   a. $19.09.   b. $30.00.
   c. $52.50.   d. $70.00.

3. The constant-growth dividend discount model will *not* produce a finite value for a stock if the dividend growth rate is
   a. Above its historical average.
   b. Below its historical average.
   c. Above the required rate of return on the stock.
   d. Below the required rate of return on the stock.

4. Two companies are identical except for substantially different dividend payout ratios. After several years, the company with the lower dividend payout ratio is *most likely* to have

   a. Lower stock price.
   b. Higher debt/equity ratio.
   c. Less rapid growth of earnings per share.
   d. More rapid growth of earnings per share.

5. Assume that at the end of the next year, Company A will pay $2.00 dividend per share, an increase from the current dividend of $1.50 per share. After that, the dividend is expected to increase at a constant rate of 5%. If you require a 12% return on the stock, what is the value of the stock?

   a. $28.57   b. $28.79
   c. $30.00   d. $31.78

   Use the following data to answer Questions 6 and 7

   Beachballs, Inc., expects abnormally high earnings for the next 3 years due to the forecast of unusually hot summers. After the 3-year period, their growth will level off to its normal rate of 6%. Dividends and earnings are expected to grow at 20% for years 1 and 2, and 15% in year 3. The last dividend paid was $1.00.

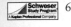

6. If Sarah Paulsen requires a 10% return on Beachballs, Inc., the price she is willing to pay for the stock is *closest* to

   a. $26.45.   b. $36.50.
   c. $37.75.   d. $50.00.

7. If Sarah is planning on selling Beachballs, Inc., after one year, the price will be *closest* to

   a. $28.45.   b. $36.50.
   c. $38.86.   d. $41.88.

8. XYZ Corp. has expected earnings of $5 per share for next year. The firm's ROE is 15% and its earning retention ratio is 40%. If the firm's capitalization rate is 10%, what is the value of the stock?

   a. $20   b. $25
   c. $50   d. $75

9. An analyst gathered the following data about the company:

   A historical earning retention rate of 60% that is projected to continue into the future.
   A sustainable return on equity of 10%.
   A beta of 1.0.
   The nominal risk-free rate is 5%.
   The expected market return is 10%.

   If next year's earnings is $2 per share, what value would be placed on this stock?

   a. $20.00.   b. $22.50.
   c. $30.50.   d. $35.45.

10. A stock is not expected to pay dividends until 3 years from now. The dividend is then expected to be $2.00 per share, the dividend payout ratio is expected to be 40%, and the return on equity is expected to be 15%. If the required rate of return is 12%, the value of the stock today is *closest* to

   a. $27.   b. $33.
   c. $53.   d. $67.

Answers: 1. b; 2. a; 3. c; 4. d; 5. a; 6. b; 7. c; 8. d; 9. a; 10. c

Discussion Questions

Q8.1 Using the resources available at your campus or public library, select a company from *Value Line* that would be of interest to you. (*Hint*: Pick a company that's been publicly traded for at least 10 to 15 years, and avoid public utilities, banks and other financial institutions.) Obtain a copy of the latest *Value Line* report on your chosen company. Using the historical and forecasted data reported in *Value Line*, along with one of the valuation techniques described in this chapter, calculate the maximum (i.e., justified) price you'd be willing to pay for this stock. Use the CAPM to find the required rate of return on your stock. (For this problem, use a market rate of return of 12%, and for the risk-free rate, use the latest 3-month Treasury bill rate.)

    a. How does the justified price you computed compare to the latest market price of the stock?

    b. Would you consider this stock to be a worthwhile investment candidate? Explain.

Q8.2 In this chapter, we examined nine different stock valuation procedures:

- Zero-growth DVM
- Constant-growth DVM
- Variable-growth DVM
- Dividends-and-earnings (D&E) approach
- Expected return (IRR) approach
- P/E approach
- Price-to-cash-flow ratio
- Price-to-sales ratio
- Price-to-book-value ratio

    a. Which one (or more) of these procedures would be most appropriate when trying to put a value on:

      1. A growth stock that pays little or nothing in dividends?

      2. The S&P 500?

      3. A relatively new company that has only a brief history of earnings?

      4. A large, mature, dividend-paying company?

      5. A preferred stock that pays a fixed dividend?

      6. A company that has a large amount of depreciation and amortization?

    b. Of the nine procedures listed above, which *three* do you think are the best? Explain.

    c. If you had to choose just *one* procedure to use in practice, which would it be? Explain. (*Note*: Confine your selection to the list above.)

Q8.3 Explain the role that the future plays in the stock valuation process. Why not just base the valuation on historical information? Explain how the intrinsic value of a stock is related to its required rate of return. Illustrate what happens to the value of a stock when the required rate of return increases.

Problems

P8.1 An investor estimates that next year's sales for New World Products should amount to about $75 million. The company has 2.5 million shares outstanding, generates a net profit margin of about 5%, and has a payout ratio of 50%. All figures are expected to hold for next year. Given this information, compute the following.

    a. Estimated net earnings for next year.

    b. Next year's dividends per share.

    c. The expected price of the stock (assuming the P/E ratio is 24.5 times earnings).

    d. The expected holding period return (latest stock price: $25 per share).

LG 2 **P8.2** GrowthCo had sales of $55 million in 2000, and is expected to have sales of $83,650,000 for 2003. The company's net profit margin was 5% in 2000, and is expected to increase to 8% by 2003. Estimate the company's net profit for 2003.

LG 2 **P8.3** Goodstuff Corporation has total equity of $500 million and 100 million shares outstanding. Its ROE is 15%. Calculate the company's EPS.

LG 2 **P8.4** Goodstuff Corporation has total equity of $500 million and 100 million shares outstanding. Its ROE is 15%. The dividend payout ratio is 33.3%. Calculate the company's dividends per share (round to the nearest penny).

LG 2 **P8.5** HighTeck has a ROE of 15%. Its earnings per share are $2.00, and its dividends per share are $0.20. Estimate HighTeck's growth rate.

LG 2 **P8.6** Last year InDebt Company paid $75 million of interest expense, and its average rate of interest for the year was 10%. The company's ROE is 15%, and it pays no dividends. Estimate next year's interest expense assuming that interest rates will fall by 25% and the company keeps a constant equity multiplier of 20%.

 LG 3 **P8.7** Charlene Lewis is thinking about buying some shares of Education, Inc., at $50 per share. She expects the price of the stock to rise to $75 over the next 3 years. During that time she also expects to receive annual dividends of $5 per share.
  a. What is the intrinsic worth of this stock, given a 10% required rate of return?
  b. What is its expected return?

 LG 4 **P8.8** Amalgamated Aircraft Parts, Inc., is expected to pay a dividend of $1.50 in the coming year. The required rate of return is 16%, and dividends are expected to grow at 7% per year. Using the dividend valuation model, find the intrinsic value of the company's common shares.

 **LG 4** **P8.9** Eddy is considering a stock purchase. The stock pays constant annual dividends of $2.00 per share, and is currently trading at $20. Eddy's required rate of return for this stock is 12%. Should he buy this stock?

 LG 4 **P8.10** Shelly is interested in the common stock of GreatDeal Corporation. It has paid annual dividends of $2.00, $2.24, and $2.51 over the past 3 years. Shelly has a required rate of return of 14% for this security. What is the most she should be willing to pay for this stock?

 LG 5 **P8.11** Assume you've generated the following information about the stock of Bufford's Burger Barns: The company's latest dividends of $4 a share are expected to grow to $4.32 next year, to $4.67 the year after that, and to $5.04 in year 3. In addition, the price of the stock is expected to rise to $77.75 in 3 years.
  a. Use the dividends-and-earnings model and a required return of 15% to find the value of the stock.
  b. Use the IRR procedure to find the stock's expected return.
  c. Given that dividends are expected to grow indefinitely at 8%, use a 15% required rate of return and the dividend valuation model to find the value of the stock.
  d. Assume dividends in year 3 actually amount to $5.04, the dividend growth rate stays at 8%, and the required rate of return stays at 15%. Use the dividend valuation model to find the price of the stock at the end of year 3. [*Hint:* In this case, the value of the stock will depend on dividends in year 4, which equal $D_3 \times (1 + g)$.] Do you note any similarity between your answer here and the forecasted price of the stock ($77.75) given in the problem? Explain.

LG 6　P8.12　Let's assume that you're thinking about buying stock in West Coast Electronics. So far in your analysis, you've uncovered the following information: The stock pays annual dividends of $2.50 a share (and that's not expected to change within the next few years—*nor are any of the other variables*). It trades at a P/E of 18 times earnings and has a beta of 1.15. In addition, you plan on using a risk-free rate of 7% in the CAPM, along with a market return of 14%. You would like to hold the stock for 3 years, at the end of which time you think EPS will peak at about $7 a share. Given that the stock currently trades at $70, use the IRR approach to find this security's expected return. Now use the present-value (dividends-and-earnings) model to put a price on this stock. Does this look like a good investment to you? Explain.

LG 6　P8.13　The price of Consolidated Everything is now $75. The company pays no dividends. Ms. Bossard expects the price 3 years from now to be $100 per share. Should Ms. B. buy Consolidated E. if she desires a 10% rate of return? Explain.

LG 5　P8.14　This year, Shoreline Light and Gas (SLL&G) paid its stockholders an annual dividend of $3 a share. A major brokerage firm recently put out a report on SLL&G stating that, in its opinion, the company's annual dividends should grow at the rate of 10% per year for each of the next 5 years and then level off and grow at the rate of 6% a year thereafter.

　　　a. Use the variable-growth DVM and a required rate of return of 12% to find the maximum price you should be willing to pay for this stock.

　　　b. Redo the SLL&G problem in part **a**, this time assuming that after year 5, dividends stop growing altogether (for year 6 and beyond, $g = 0$). Use all the other information given to find the stock's intrinsic value.

　　　c. Contrast your two answers and comment on your findings. How important is growth to this valuation model?

LG 5　P8.15　Assume there are three companies that in the past year paid exactly the same annual dividend of $2.25 a share. In addition, the future annual rate of growth in dividends for each of the three companies has been estimated as follows:

Buggies-Are-Us	Steady Freddie, Inc.	Gang Buster Group	
$g = 0$	$g = 6\%$	Year 1	$2.53
(i.e., dividends	(for the	2	$2.85
are expected	foreseeable	3	$3.20
to remain at	future)	4	$3.60
$2.25/share)		Year 5 and beyond: $g = 6\%$	

Assume also that as the result of a strange set of circumstances, these three companies all have the same required rate of return ($k = 10\%$).

　　　a. Use the appropriate DVM to value each of these companies.

　　　b. Comment briefly on the comparative values of these three companies. What is the major cause of the differences among these three valuations?

LG 6　P8.16　New Millenium Company's stock sells at a P/E ratio of 21 times earnings. It is expected to pay dividends of $2 per share in each of the next 5 years and to generate an EPS of $5 in year 5. Using the dividends-and-earnings model and a 12% discount rate, compute the stock's justified price.

LG 6　P8.17　A particular company currently has sales of $250 million; sales are expected to grow by 20% next year (year 1). For the year after next (year 2), the growth rate in sales is expected to equal 10%. Over each of the next 2 years, the company is expected to have a net profit margin of 8% and a payout ratio of 50%, and to maintain the common stock outstanding at 15 million shares. The stock always trades at a P/E of 15 times earnings, and the investor has a required rate of return of 20%. Given this information:

a. Find the stock's intrinsic value (its justified price).

b. Use the IRR approach to determine the stock's expected return, given that it is currently trading at $15 per share.

c. Find the holding period returns for this stock for year 1 and for year 2.

P8.18 Assume a major investment service has just given Oasis Electronics its highest investment rating, along with a strong buy recommendation. As a result, you decide to take a look for yourself and to place a value on the company's stock. Here's what you find: This year, Oasis paid its stockholders an annual dividend of $3 a share, but because of its high rate of growth in earnings, it dividends are expected to grow at the rate of 12% a year for the next 4 years and then to level out at 9% a year. So far, you've learned that the stock has a beta of 1.80, the risk-free rate of return is 6%, and the expected return on the market is 11%. Using the CAPM to find the required rate of return, put a value on this stock.

P8.19 Consolidated Software doesn't currently pay any dividends but is expected to start doing so in 4 years. That is, Consolidated will go 3 more years without paying any dividends, and then is expected to pay its first dividend (of $3 per share) in the fourth year. Once the company starts paying dividends, it's expected to continue to do so. The company is expected to have a dividend payout ratio of 40% and to maintain a return on equity of 20%. Based on the DVM, and given a required rate of return of 15%, what is the maximum price you should be willing to pay for this stock today?

P8.20 Assume you obtain the following information about a certain company:

Total assests	$50,000,000
Total equity	$25,000,000
Net income	$3,750,000
EPS	$5.00 per share
Dividend payout ratio	40%
Required return	12%

Use the constant-growth DVM to place a value on this company's stock.

P8.21 You're thinking about buying some stock in Affiliated Computer Corporation and want to use the P/E approach to value the shares. You've estimated that next year's earnings should come in at about $4.00 a share. In addition, although the stock normally trades at a relative P/E of 1.15 times the market, you believe that the relative P/E will rise to 1.25, whereas the market P/E should be around 18½ times earnings. Given this information, what is the maximum price you should be willing to pay for this stock? If you buy this stock today at $87.50, what rate of return will you earn over the next 12 months if the price of the stock rises to $110.00 by the end of the year? (Assume that the stock doesn't pay any dividends.)

P8.22 AviBank Plastics generated an EPS of $2.75 over the last 12 months. The company's earnings are expected to grow by 25% next year, and because there will be no significant change in the number of shares outstanding, EPS should grow at about the same rate. You feel the stock should trade at a P/E of around 30 times earnings. Use the P/E approach to set a value on this stock.

P8.23 Newco is a young company that has yet to make a profit. You are trying to place a value on the stock, but it pays no dividends and you cannot calculate a P/E ratio. You decide to look at other stocks in the same industry as Newco to see if there is a way that makes sense to value this company, because you believe it will become a strong competitor. You find the following information:

	Per-Share Data			
	Newco	Adolescentco	Middle-Ageco	Oldco
Sales	10	200	800	800
Profit	−10	10	60	80
Book Value	−2	2	5	8
Market Value	?	20	80	75

Estimate a market value for Newco. Discuss how your estimate could change if Newco was expected to grow much faster than the other companies.

P8.24 World Wide Web Wares (4W, for short) is an online retailer of small kitchen appliances and utensils. The firm has been around for a few years and has created a nice market niche for itself. In fact, it actually turned a profit last year, albeit a fairly small one. After doing some basic research on the company, you've decided to take a closer look. You plan to use the price/sales ratio to value the stock, and you have collected P/S multiples on the following Internet retailer stocks:

Company	P/S Multiples
Amazing.com	4.5
Really Cooking.com	4.1
Fixtures & Appliances Online	3.8

Find the *average P/S ratio* for these three firms. Given that 4W is expected to generate $40 million in sales next year, and will have 10 million shares of stock outstanding, use the average P/S ratio you computed above to put a value on 4W's stock.

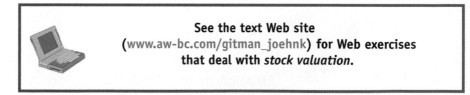

See the text Web site
(www.aw-bc.com/gitman_joehnk) **for Web exercises**
that deal with *stock valuation*.

Case Problem 8.1   *Chris Looks for a Way to Invest His Newfound Wealth*

Chris Norton is a young Hollywood writer who is well on his way to television superstardom. After writing several successful television specials, he was recently named the head writer for one of TV's top-rated sitcoms. Chris fully realizes that his business is a fickle one and, on the advice of his dad and manager, has decided to set up an investment program. Chris will earn about a half-million dollars this year. Because of his age, income level, and desire to get as big a bang as possible from his investment dollars, he has decided to invest in speculative, high-growth stocks.

Chris is currently working with a respected Beverly Hills broker and is in the process of building up a diversified portfolio of speculative stocks. The broker recently sent him information on a hot new issue. She advised Chris to study the numbers and, if he likes them, to buy as many as 1,000 shares of the stock. Among other things, corporate sales for the next 3 years have been forecasted as follows:

Year	Sales (in millions)
1	$22.5
2	35.0
3	50.0

The firm has 2.5 million shares of common stock outstanding. They are currently being traded at $70 a share and pay no dividends. The company has a net profit rate of 20%, and its stock has been trading at a P/E of around 40 times earnings. All these operating characteristics are expected to hold in the future.

Questions

a. Looking first at the stock:
   1. Compute the company's net profits and EPS for each of the next 3 years.
   2. Compute the price of the stock 3 years from now.
   3. Assuming that all expectations hold up and that Chris buys the stock at $70, determine his expected return on this investment.
   4. What risks is he facing by buying this stock? Be specific.
   5. Should he consider the stock a worthwhile investment candidate? Explain.

b. Looking at Chris's investment program in general:
   1. What do you think of his investment program? What do you see as its strengths and weaknesses?
   2. Are there any suggestions you would make?
   3. Do you think Chris should consider adding foreign stocks to his portfolio? Explain.

Case Problem 8.2 | *An Analysis of a High-Flying Stock*

LG 2 | **LG 6**

Glenn Wilt is a recent university graduate and a security analyst with the Kansas City brokerage firm of Lippman, Brickbats, and Shaft. Wilt has been following one of the hottest issues on Wall Street, C&I Medical Suppliies, a company that has turned in an outstanding performance lately and, even more important, has exhibited excellent growth potential. It has 5 million shares outstanding and pays a nominal annual dividend of 5 cents per share. Wilt has decided to take a closer look at C&I to see whether it still has any investment play left. Assume the company's sales for the past 5 years have been as follows:

Year	Sales (in millions)
2000	$10.0
2001	12.5
2002	16.2
2003	22.0
2004	28.5

Wilt is concerned with the future prospects of the company, not its past. As a result, he pores over the numbers and generates the following estimates of future performance:

Expected net profit margin	12%
Estimated annual dividends per share	5¢
Number of common shares outstanding	No change
P/E ratio at the end of 2005	35
P/E ratio at the end of 2006	50

Questions

a. Determine the average annual rate of growth in sales over the past 5 years. (Assume sales in 1999 amounted to $7.5 million.)
   1. Use this average growth rate to forecast revenues for next year (2005) and the year after that (2006).
   2. Now determine the company's net earnings and EPS for each of the next 2 years (2005 and 2006).
   3. Finally, determine the expected future price of the stock at the end of this 2-year period.

b. Because of several intrinsic and market factors, Wilt feels that 25% is a viable figure to use for a desired rate of return.
   1. Using the 25% rate of return and the forecasted figures you came up with in question **a,** compute the stock's justified price.
   2. If C&I is currently trading at $32.50 per share, should Wilt consider the stock a worthwhile investment candidate? Explain.

Excel with Spreadsheets

Fundamental to the valuation process is the determination of the intrinsic value of a security where an investor calculates the present value of the expected future cash benefits of the investment. Specifically, in the case of common stock, these future cash flows are defined by expected future dividend payments and future potential price appreciation. A simple but useful way to view stock value is that it is equal to the present value of all expected future dividends it may provide over an infinite time horizon.

Based on this latter concept, the dividend valuation model (DVM) has evolved. It can take on any one of three versions—the zero-growth model, the constant-growth model, and the variable-growth model.

Create a spreadsheet that applies the variable-growth model to predict the intrinsic value of the Rhyhorn Company common stock. Assume that dividends will grow at a variable rate for the next three years (2004, 2005, and 2006). After that, the annual rate of growth in dividends is expected to be 7% and stay there for the foreseeable future. Starting with the latest (2003) annual dividend of $2.00 per share, Rhyhorn's earnings and dividends are estimated to grow by 18% in 2004, by 14% in 2005, and by 9% in 2006 before dropping to a 7% rate. Given the risk profile of the firm, assume a minimum required rate of return of at least 12%. The spreadsheet for Table 8.4, which you can view on www.aw-bc.com/gitman_joehnk, is a good reference for solving this problem.

Questions

a. Calculate the projected annual dividends over the years 2004, 2005, and 2006.

b. Determine the present value of dividends during the initial variable-growth period.

c. What do you believe the price of Rhyhorn stock will be at the end of the initial growth period (2006)?

d. Having determined the expected future price of Rhyhorn stock in **c**, discount the price of the stock back to its present value.

e. Determine the total intrinsic value of Rhyhorn stock based on your calculations above.

TRADING ONLINE WITH OTIS

A fundamental analyst does not follow the crowd but rather looks to determine a stock's intrinsic value by studying financial statements and then making predictions as to the future earnings stream. An opposing idea is the efficient market hypothesis, which suggests that stocks are fairly priced and researching financial data is of little value in predicting the future. Instead, this hypothesis claims that unexpected news or investor expectations move tomorrow's prices. A proponent of this view was John Maynard Keynes, a famous economist whose theories you have probably encountered in your economics courses. Keynes would not get out of bed in the morning until he made his investment decisions. He basically took a psychological approach to investing by trying to determine investment sentiment and then making his portfolio decisions accordingly. He was apparently successful at following the crowds—his investments made him wealthy. This is a risky way to play the market.

Day trading probably falls under the rubric of following the crowds. Since the average day trader is not successful, this practice underlines the risk involved. Let's try your luck at day trading.

Exercises

1. Prior to the opening of the stock market visit www.whisper.com or one of the other whisper sites (see the *Investing in Action* box on page 334 in your text). After viewing stock information and economic news, select several stocks you expect to rise in price. Also, consider stocks you think will be declining in price as candidates to sell short.

2. Log on to OTIS and batch load the stocks you would like to buy. Then short those stocks whose prices you expect to fall. To make it worth your while, you should buy a large number of shares so you can capitalize on small price movements.

3. Spend several hours watching the prices of the stocks you selected and looking for news relating to the stocks traded. If the stock is going in the wrong direction, do not wait to sell—take your losses and move on. Sell when you calculate profits over and above your buying and selling costs. Select possible replacement stocks by going to whisper sites or any other financial Web site, such as www.esignal.com, to look for upgrades and downgrades, news, earnings reports, or any other information to help you select stocks to purchase.

4. Determine your profits from buying and selling during the day. Did you make any money?

CHAPTER 9

MARKET PRICE BEHAVIOR

LEARNING GOALS

After studying this chapter, you should be able to:

LG 1 Discuss the purpose of technical analysis and explain why the performance of the market is important to stock valuation.

LG 2 Describe some of the approaches to technical analysis, including, among others, the Dow theory, moving averages, charting, and various indicators of the technical condition of the market.

LG 3 Compute and use technical trading rules for individual stocks and the market as a whole.

LG 4 Explain the idea of random walks and efficient markets, and note the challenges these theories hold for the stock valuation process.

LG 5 Describe the weak, semi-strong, and strong versions of the efficient market hypothesis, and explain what market anomalies are.

LG 6 Demonstrate a basic appreciation for how psychological factors can affect investors' decisions, and how behavioral finance presents a challenge to the concept of market efficiency.

Using an online stock screener, you've identified two pharmaceutical companies as possible investments. Forest Laboratories develops, produces, and markets brand-name and generic drugs. Teva Pharmaceuticals, an Israeli company whose ADRs trade on the Nasdaq, is the world's largest manufacturer of generic drugs. Each company has solid fundamentals, good growth and return, and trades around $57 per share. How do you choose between them?

One answer lies in technical analysis, which looks at the impact of market forces such as supply and demand on stock price and tries to predict shifts in the market's direction. You pull charts for each company at StockCharts.com to see a picture—literally—of the historical stock price movements for a specific time period. The basic charts also show the 50- and 200-day moving averages (average price of the stock over the time period), and daily trading volume for the stock. The moving averages smooth out short-term price fluctuations to help you identify trends that occur over a longer time horizon.

Currently, Forest Labs is trading well above its 50- and 200-day moving averages, both about $51. Teva is above its 200-day moving average ($52.80) but is trading at close to its 50-day moving average ($57.78). Forest's chart thus gives a stronger buy signal, as does its general upward price trend. The only weak spot is its low volume, which could make it difficult for the stock to break out to a new high.

Next, you evaluate other technical indicators, such as the relative strength index, the advance-decline line, and short interest ratio. You buy Forest Labs now but monitor Teva to see if its chart signals a buy in the future.

Does the preceding discussion leave you confused? Read on to learn how to use technical indicators to identify candidates for your stock portfolio, as well as when to buy and sell those stocks. You'll also discover the differences between proponents of the efficient market hypotheses, who believe it is not possible to consistently outperform the market, and behavioral finance advocates, who take a psychological view of investor reactions.

Sources: Jonah Keri, "How to Use Moving Averages Wisely," *Investor's Business Daily*, January 8, 2002, downloaded from www.investor.com; Morningstar Stock Screener, http://screen.morningstar.com, December 8, 2003; Forest Laboratories and Teva Pharmaceuticals stock charts, Stockcharts.com, downloaded December 10, 2003, from www.stockcharts.com; Susan Scherreik, "Trading Volume Counts, Too," *Business Week*, February 17, 2003, p. 88–89; Steven B. Achelis, "Technical Analysis from A to Z," *Equis.com*, downloaded December 4, 2003, from www.equis.com/Education/TAAZ.

Technical Analysis

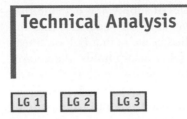

technical analysis
the study of the various forces at work in the marketplace and their effect on stock prices.

How many times have you turned on the TV or radio and in the course of the day's news heard a reporter say, "The market was up 47 points today" or "The market remained sluggish in a day of light trading"? Such comments reflect the importance of the stock market itself in determining the price behavior of common stocks. In fact, some experts believe that studying the market should be the major, if not the only, ingredient in the stock selection process. Contrary to our discussion (about fundamental analysis) in the previous chapter, these experts argue that much of what is done in security analysis is useless because it is the *market* that matters, not individual companies. Others argue that studying the stock market is only *one element* in the security analysis process and is useful in helping the investor time decisions.

Analyzing the various forces at work in the stock market is known as **technical analysis.** For some investors, it's another piece of information to use when deciding whether to buy, hold, or sell a stock. For others, it's the *only* input they use in their investment decisions. And for still others, technical analysis, like fundamental analysis, is regarded as a big waste of time. Here we will assume that market analysis does have some role to play in the investment decision process, and as such, we will examine the major principles of *technical analysis*, as well as some of the techniques used to assess market behavior. Following that, we'll look at the *efficient market hypothesis* and the questions it raises not only for technical analysis, but for the whole security analysis process. Finally, we'll discuss *behavioral finance* and the challenges it poses to the concept of market efficiency.

Principles of Market Analysis

Analyzing market behavior dates back to the 1800s, when there was no such thing as industry or company analysis. Detailed financial information simply was not made available to stockholders, let alone the general public. There were no industry figures, balance sheets, or income statements to study, no sales forecasts to make, and no EPS data or P/E multiples. About the only thing investors could study was the market itself. Some investors used detailed charts in an attempt to monitor what large market operators were doing. These charts were intended to show when major buyers were moving into or out of particular stocks and to provide information that could be used to make profitable buy-and-sell decisions. The charts centered on stock price movements. It was believed that these movements produced certain "formations" that indicated when the time was right to buy or sell a particular stock. The same principle is still applied today: Technical analysts argue that internal market factors, such as trading volume and price movements, often reveal the market's future direction long before it is evident in financial statistics.

If the behavior of stock prices were completely independent of market movements, market studies and technical analysis would be useless. But we have ample evidence that stock prices do, in fact, tend to move with the market. For example, studies of stock betas have shown that as a rule, anywhere from 20% to 50% of the price behavior of a stock can be traced to market forces. When the market is bullish, stock prices in general can be expected to behave accordingly. When the market turns bearish, you can safely expect most issues to be affected by the "downdraft."

Stock prices, in essence, react to various forces of supply and demand that are at work in the market. After all, it's the *demand* for securities and the *supply* of funds in the market that determine whether we're in a bull or a bear market. So long as a given supply-and-demand relationship holds, the market will remain strong (or weak). When the balance begins to shift, however, future prices can be expected to change as the market itself changes. Thus, more than anything else, technical analysis is intended to monitor the pulse of the supply-and-demand forces in the market and to detect any shifts in this important relationship.

Using Technical Analysis

Investors have a wide range of choices with respect to technical analysis. They can use the charts and complex ratios of the technical analysts. Or they can, more informally, use technical analysis just to get a general sense of the market. In the latter case, market behavior itself is not as important as the implications such behavior can have for the price performance of a particular stock. Thus technical analysis might be used in conjunction with fundamental analysis to determine when to add a particular stock to one's portfolio. Some investors and professional money managers, in fact, look at the technical side of a stock *before* doing any fundamental analysis. If the stock is found to be technically sound, then they'll look at its fundamentals; if not, they'll look for another stock. For these investors, the concerns of technical analysis are still the same: *Do the technical factors indicate that this might be a good stock to buy*?

Most investors rely on published sources, such as those put out by brokerage firms—or, now, widely available on the Internet—to obtain necessary technical insights. Such information provides the investor with a convenient and low-cost way of staying abreast of the market. Certainly, trying to determine the right (or best) time to get into the market is a principal objective of technical analysis—and one of the major pastimes of many investors.

Some technical analysis sites that help with research are the following:

www.dailystocks.com
cbs.marketwatch.com
www.stockcharts.com
www.technitrader.com
my.zacks.com

Measuring the Market

If assessing the market is a worthwhile endeavor, then we need some sort of tool or measure to do it. Charts are popular with many investors because they provide a visual summary of the behavior of the market and the price movements of individual stocks (we'll examine charting in more detail later in this chapter). As an alternative or supplement to *charting*, some investors prefer to study various *market statistics*. They might look at the market as a whole, or track certain technical conditions that exist within the market itself, such as the volume of trading, the amount of short selling, or the buy/sell patterns of small investors (i.e., odd-lot transactions). Let's now examine some of these approaches to technical analysis. Later, we'll look at some ratios and formulas that are used to measure—that is, quantify—various technical conditions in the market.

At the Bloomberg site shown below, click on charts. At cbs.marketwatch.com, choose [Investor Tools]; then [Stocks]. View upgrades, downgrades, and today's Hot Stocks.

www.bloomberg.com
cbs.marketwatch.com

The Big Picture

Technical analysis addresses those factors in the marketplace that can (or may) have an effect on the price movements of stocks in general. The idea is to try and get a handle on the general condition (or "tone") of the market, and to gain some insights into where the market may be headed over the course of the next few months. One way to do that is to look at *the overall behavior of the market*. Several approaches try to do just that, including (1) the Dow theory, (2) trading actions, and (3) the confidence index.

The Dow Theory The **Dow theory** is based on the idea that the market's performance can be described by the long-term price trend in the overall market. Named after Charles H. Dow, one of the founders of Dow Jones, this approach is supposed to signal the end of both bull and bear markets. Note that the theory does not indicate when a reversal will occur; rather, it is strictly an after-the-fact verification of what has already happened. It concentrates on the long-term trend in market behavior (known as the *primary trend*) and largely ignores day-to-day fluctuations or secondary movements. The Dow Jones industrial *and* transportation averages are used to assess the position of the market. Once a primary trend in the Dow Jones industrial average has been established, the market tends to move in that direction until the trend is canceled out by both the industrial and transportation averages. Known as *confirmation*, this crucial part of the Dow theory occurs when secondary movements in the industrial average are confirmed by secondary movements in the transportation average. When confirmation occurs, the market has changed from bull to bear, or vice versa, and a new primary trend is established. The key elements of the Dow theory are captured in Figure 9.1 (on page 374). Observe that in this case, the bull market comes to an end at the point of confirmation—when *both* the industrial and transportation averages are dropping. The biggest drawbacks of the Dow theory are that it is an after-the-fact measure with *no* predictive power, and that the investor really does not know at any given point whether an existing primary trend has a long way to go or is just about to end.

Trading Action This approach to technical analysis concentrates on minor trading characteristics in the market. Daily trading activity over long periods of time (sometimes extending back a half-century or more) is examined in detail to determine whether certain characteristics occur with a high degree of frequency. The results of such statistical analysis are a series of trading rules, some of which may seem a bit bizarre. Some examples: If the year starts out strong (that is, if January is a good month for the market), the chances are that the whole year will be good; if the party in power wins the presidential election, it is also going to be a good year for the market; and it is best to buy air conditioning stocks in October and sell the following March (this buy-and-sell strategy was found to be significantly more profitable over the long haul than buy-and-hold). A most unusual but *highly successful* market adage holds that if a team from the National Football Conference (or one that was originally in the NFL, like Indianapolis or Pittsburgh) wins the Super Bowl, the market's in for a good year. Don't laugh. For whatever the reason—which no one seems to know—it's been correct for 31 of the last 37 Super Bowls, including 2003, when the NFC's Tampa Bay Buccaneers beat the AFC's Oakland Raiders in Super Bowl XXVII. And—you guessed it—the market ended on the plus side for the first time in

Dow theory
a technical approach based on the idea that the market's performance can be described by the long-term price trend in the DJIA, as confirmed by the Dow transportation average.

The Dow Theory in Operation
Secondary movements (the sharp, short fluctuations in the Dow Jones industrial and transportation lines) are largely unimportant to the Dow theory. However, the primary trend in the DJIA, which is seen to remain on the upswing until a reversal is confirmed by the transportation average, is of key importance.

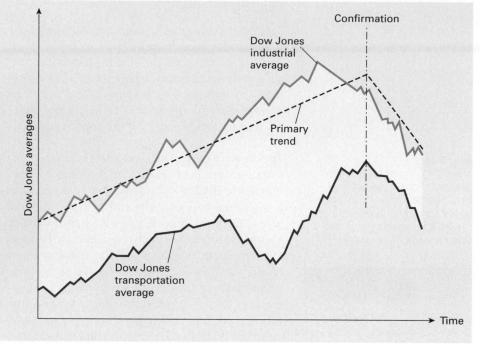

confidence index
a ratio of the average yield on high-grade corporate bonds to the average yield on low-grade corporate bonds; a technical indicator based on the theory that market trends usually appear in the bond market before they do in the stock market.

4 years. Clearly, the trading action approach is based on the simple assumption that the market moves in cycles and that these cycles have a tendency to repeat themselves. As a result, the contention seems to be that whatever has happened repeatedly in the past will probably reoccur in the future.

Confidence Index Another measure that attempts to capture the tone of the market is the **confidence index,** which deals not with the stock market, but rather with *bond* returns. Computed and published weekly in *Barron's* (see "Market Laboratory—Bonds"), the confidence index is a ratio that reflects *the spread* between the average yield on high-grade corporate bonds relative to the average yield on low-grade corporate bonds. The theory is that the trend of "smart money" is usually revealed in the bond market before it shows up in the stock market. Although low-rated bonds provide higher yields than high-grade issues, the logic is that the *spread in yields* between these two types of obligations will change over time as the amount of optimism or pessimism in the market outlook changes. Thus, a sustained rise in the confidence index (which occurs when the bond yield spread narrows) suggests an increase in investor confidence and a stronger stock market; a drop in the index portends a softer tone.

Technical Conditions Within the Market

Another way to assess the market is to keep track of the variables that drive its behavior—things like the volume of trading, short sales, and odd-lot trading. Clearly, if these kinds of variables do, in fact, influence market prices, then it would be in an investor's best interest to keep tabs on them, at least informally. Let's look at four of these market forces: (1) market volume, (2) breadth of the market, (3) short interest, and (4) odd-lot trading.

Market Volume Market volume is an obvious reflection of the amount of investor interest. Volume is a function of the supply of and demand for stock, and it indicates underlying market strengths and weaknesses. As a rule, the market is considered *strong* when volume goes up in a rising market or drops off during market declines. It is considered *weak* when volume rises during a decline or drops during rallies. For instance, the market would be considered strong if the Dow Jones Industrial Average went up by, say, 108 points while market volume was heavy. Investor eagerness to buy or sell is felt to be captured by market volume figures. The financial press regularly publishes volume data, so investors can easily watch this important technical indicator. An example of this and other vital market information is shown in Figure 9.2 (on page 376).

Breadth of the Market Each trading day, some stocks go up in price and others go down. In market terminology, some stocks *advance* and others *decline*. Breadth-of-the-market deals with these advances and declines. The idea is actually quite simple: So long as the number of stocks that advance in price on a given day exceeds the number that decline, the market is considered strong. The extent of that strength depends on the spread between the number of advances and declines. For example, if the spread narrows so that the number of declines starts to approach the number of advances, market strength is said to be deteriorating. Similarly, the market is considered weak when the number of declines repeatedly exceeds the number of advances. The principle behind this indicator is that the number of advances and declines reflects the underlying sentiment of investors. When the mood is optimistic, for example, look for advances to outnumber declines. Again, data on advances and declines are published daily in the financial press.

short interest
the number of stocks sold short in the market at any given time; a technical indicator believed to indicate future market demand.

Short Interest When investors anticipate a market decline, they sometimes sell a stock short. That is, they sell borrowed stock. The number of stocks sold short in the market at any given point in time is known as the **short interest**. The more stocks that are sold short, the higher the short interest. Because all short sales must eventually be "covered" (the borrowed shares must be returned), a short sale in effect ensures *future demand for the stock*. Thus, the market is viewed optimistically when the level of short interest becomes relatively high by historical standards. The logic is that as shares are bought back to cover outstanding short sales, the additional demand will push stock prices up. The amount of short interest on the NYSE, the AMEX, and Nasdaq's National Market is published monthly in the *Wall Street Journal* and *Barron's*. Figure 9.3 (on page 377) shows the type of information that's available.

Keeping track of the level of short interest can indicate future market demand, but it can also reveal *present* market optimism or pessimism. Short selling is usually done by knowledgeable investors, and a significant buildup or decline in the level of short interest is thought to reveal the sentiment of sophisticated investors about the current state of the market or a company. For example, a significant shift upward in short interest is believed to indicate pessimism concerning the *current* state of the market, even though it may signal optimism with regard to *future* levels of demand.

Odd-Lot Trading A rather cynical saying on Wall Street suggests that the best thing to do is just the opposite of whatever the small investor is doing. The

FIGURE 9.2

Some Market Statistics

Individual investors can obtain all sorts of technical information at little or no cost from brokerage houses, investment services, the popular financial media, or the Internet. Here, for example, is a sample of information from the *Wall Street Journal*. Note that a variety of information about market volume, new highs and lows, number of advancing and declining stocks, and the most actively traded issues is available from this one source. (*Source: Wall Street Journal*, August 11, 2003.)

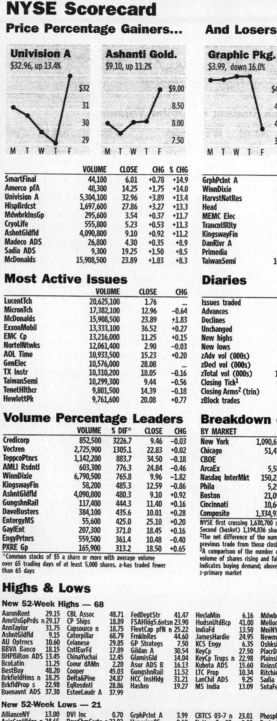

FIGURE 9.3 Short Interest on the Nasdaq

The amount of short selling in the market is closely watched by many investment professionals and individual investors. The summary report shown here provides an overview of the extent to which stocks are being shorted in the Nasdaq market. In addition to summary statistics, this monthly report lists all stocks that have been sold short and the number of shares shorted. (*Source: Wall Street Journal*, August 8, 2003. Copyright 2003 by Dow Jones & Co., Inc. Reproduced with permission of Dow Jones & Co., Inc. in textbook format via Copyright Clearance Center.)

NASDAQ SHORT-SELLING HIGHLIGHTS

LARGEST SHORT POSITIONS

RANK		JUL 15	JUN 13	CHANGE
1	Cisco Systems	107,613,696	111,798,504	-4,184,808
2	Microsoft Corp	102,722,196	100,614,132	2,108,064
3	Intel Corp	88,419,284	94,853,056	-6,433,772
4	Sirius Satellite	77,572,580	79,109,307	-1,536,727
5	Nextel Comm	76,453,541	76,531,944	-78,403
6	InterActiveCorp	61,869,451	55,240,711	6,628,740
7	Level 3 Communicat	50,614,328	42,553,733	8,060,595
8	Juniper Networks	48,644,355	45,871,541	2,772,814
9	Amazon.com	43,682,431	45,277,580	-1,595,149
10	Oracle Corp	43,272,694	48,370,961	-5,098,267
11	Applied Materials	43,243,332	41,877,502	1,365,830
12	Dell Inc s	42,356,977	44,586,606	-2,229,629
13	XM Satellite Radio	41,457,583	38,322,820	3,134,763
14	ADC Telecommun	38,714,739	28,083,250	10,631,489
15	Comcast Corp A	37,919,499	46,003,929	-8,084,430
16	Charter Comm A	33,765,949	36,227,358	-2,461,409
17	Amgen Inc	32,340,794	28,279,774	4,061,020
18	Yahoo! Inc	30,924,158	27,213,286	3,710,872
19	Sun Microsystems	29,977,271	33,120,664	-3,143,393
20	Comcast Corp A Spl	27,218,316	25,573,255	1,645,061
21	WebMD Corp	26,125,338	19,016,286	7,109,052
22	Qualcomm Inc	25,371,831	25,574,382	-202,551
23	Network Appliance	24,751,564	26,106,074	-1,354,510
24	Skyworks Solutions	23,951,817	26,823,507	-2,871,690
25	Andrew Corp	23,688,984	23,063,711	625,273
26	Cree Inc	23,181,646	21,897,915	1,283,731
27	RF Micro Devices	22,445,748	15,309,593	7,136,155
28	Ciena Corp	21,780,616	19,623,124	2,157,492
29	PeopleSoft Inc	21,488,559	14,026,087	7,462,472
30	Broadcom Corp A	20,809,605	18,576,307	2,233,298

LARGEST CHANGES

RANK		JUL 15	JUN 13	CHANGE
INCREASES (in shares)				
1	ADC Telecommun	38,714,739	28,083,250	10,631,489
2	ASML Hldg N.V.	17,275,639	7,368,472	9,907,167
3	Level 3 Communicat	50,614,328	42,553,733	8,060,595
4	PeopleSoft Inc	21,488,559	14,026,087	7,462,472
5	RF Micro Devices	22,445,748	15,309,593	7,136,155
6	WebMD Corp	26,125,338	19,016,286	7,109,052
7	InterActiveCorp	61,869,451	55,240,711	6,628,740
8	chinadotcom	6,466,515	336,349	6,130,166
9	Kmart Holding Corp	6,805,018	1,328,888	5,476,130
10	Alkermes Inc	19,983,292	15,106,221	4,877,071
11	Redback Networks	14,808,760	10,103,046	4,705,714
12	Durect Corp	4,300,529	107,797	4,192,732
13	Handspring Inc	8,262,533	4,157,361	4,105,172
14	Amgen Inc	32,340,794	28,279,774	4,061,020
15	J.D. Edwards & Co	6,716,093	2,923,572	3,792,521
16	Yahoo! Inc	30,924,158	27,213,286	3,710,872
17	Sonus Networks	8,581,329	5,068,133	3,513,196
18	Starbucks Corp	15,594,020	12,268,552	3,325,468
19	Lattice Semiconduc	5,658,861	2,484,826	3,174,035
20	XM Satellite Radio	41,457,583	38,322,820	3,134,763
DECREASES (in shares)				
1	Comcast Corp A	37,919,499	46,003,929	-8,084,430
2	Intel Corp	88,419,284	94,853,056	-6,433,772
3	Veritas Software	15,365,348	21,747,757	-6,382,409
4	Novellus Systems	13,752,502	19,333,283	-5,580,781
5	Oracle Corp	43,272,694	48,370,961	-5,098,267
6	KLA-Tencor Corp	17,951,684	22,651,821	-4,700,137
7	Cisco Systems	107,613,696	111,798,504	-4,184,808
8	Ericsson (LM) ADS	16,392,592	20,512,563	-4,119,971
9	Manugistics Group	8,500,102	11,802,238	-3,302,136
10	Fifth Third Bncp	6,966,110	10,262,731	-3,296,621
11	Legato Systems	4,757,777	8,033,416	-3,275,639
12	Sun Microsystems	29,977,271	33,120,664	-3,143,393
13	Earthlink Inc	12,094,234	15,084,018	-2,989,784
14	Skyworks Solutions	23,951,817	26,823,507	-2,871,690
15	Andrx Group	3,939,691	6,778,388	-2,838,697
16	Take-Two Sftwr	8,147,250	10,811,306	-2,664,056
17	InterMune Inc	2,576,335	5,172,186	-2,595,851
18	Charter Comm A	33,765,949	36,227,358	-2,461,409
19	Atmel Corp	6,736,985	9,181,508	-2,444,523
20	Roslyn Bancorp	3,860,566	6,275,893	-2,415,327
21	Sepracor Inc	6,601,506	9,009,672	-2,408,166
22	Electronic Arts	5,893,383	8,270,061	-2,376,678
23	Symantec Corp	12,982,844	15,356,704	-2,373,860
24	Dell Inc s	42,356,977	44,586,606	-2,229,629
25	Foundry Network	10,117,210	12,254,600	-2,137,390

Nasdaq Short Interest
Billions of shares

(Chart showing values 4.7, 4.4, 4.1, 3.8 over months J A S O N D J F M A M J J, 2002–2003)

Short Interest Ratio

Short Interest Ratio (2.7) is the number of trading days at average daily volume required to cover total short interest position.

(Chart showing values 3.0, 2.5, 2.0, 1.5 over months J A S O N D J F M A M J J, 2002–2003)

LARGEST SHORT INTEREST RATIOS

The short interest ratio is the number of days it would take to cover the short interest if trading continued at the average daily volume for the month.

RANK		JUL 15 SHORT INT	AVG DLY VOL-a	DAYS TO COVER
1	ML Mitts S&P MTSP	951,149	6,512	146
2	Creo Inc	1,289,384	10,682	121
3	1-800 Contacts	1,389,610	23,635	59
4	Zix Corp	6,310,633	155,293	41
5	AEterna Labs	1,884,024	47,337	40
6	ML SRtn Sel10 DWTN n	317,606	8,377	38
7	Neose Technolog	1,758,143	47,953	37
8	Renaissance Learng	2,746,192	75,323	36
9	Neoforma Inc	2,246,510	73,503	31
10	Universal Display	2,022,306	66,330	30
11	Conceptus Inc	10,595,452	371,699	29
12	Learning Tree Int'l	1,272,983	45,134	28
13	Qiagen N.V.	5,865,183	210,335	28
14	ZymoGenetics Inc	1,964,084	70,565	28
15	Insight Comm A	7,353,550	261,805	28
16	ScanSource Inc	3,175,649	117,440	27
17	LML Payment Sys	1,090,737	40,444	27
18	ParkerVision Inc	1,346,923	52,675	26
19	Optimal Robotics	1,086,265	41,989	26
20	Medis Technol	929,551	36,112	26

Issues that split in the latest month are excluded.

The largest percentage increase and decrease sections are limited to issues with previously established short positions in both months.

LARGEST % INCREASES

RANK		JUL 15	JUN 13	%
1	ML Mitts S&P MTSP	951,149	50	1,902,198.0
2	Crosswave Comm ADS	184,990	137	134,929.2
3	Internet Initiativ	1,228,465	3,247	37,733.8
4	Naspers Ltd ADS	142,421	1,246	11,330.3
5	Tegal Corp	272,068	2,552	10,561.0
6	Durect Corp	4,300,529	107,797	3,889.5
7	Aclara BioSciences	160,687	4,096	3,823.0
8	Gigamedia Ltd	195,784	5,417	3,514.3
9	EuroWeb Int'l	244,304	6,881	3,450.4
10	Warnaco Group	842,231	26,287	3,104.0
11	Innovo Group	308,188	9,981	2,987.7
12	Petroleum Devlpmt	251,029	9,850	2,448.5
13	Star Scientific	206,460	8,559	2,312.2
14	chinadotcom	6,466,515	336,349	1,822.6
15	Cache Inc	685,226	41,845	1,537.5
16	Big 5 Sporting Gds	172,177	12,590	1,267.6
17	GTC Biotherapeut	343,008	26,489	1,194.9
18	SM&A	325,509	27,851	1,068.8
19	Indevus Pharmas	2,095,891	182,167	1,050.5
20	Digitas Inc	816,612	71,485	1,042.4
21	Aastrom Bioscience	3,046,928	276,314	1,002.7
22	Qiao Xing Universl	800,862	75,351	962.8
23	Net Servicos Comm	851,456	82,581	931.1
24	White Elect Design	824,195	80,415	924.9
25	Network Engines	570,369	62,287	815.7
26	Ceradyne Inc	580,635	64,496	800.3
27	West Bancorp Inc	211,413	24,785	753.0
28	Accred Home Lendrs	748,469	89,206	739.0
29	eCollege.com	341,354	41,245	727.6
30	DOV Pharma	188,893	23,289	711.1
31	Epicor Software	964,085	119,513	706.7
32	Mesa Air Group	2,591,205	341,600	658.5
33	Komag Inc	661,122	91,339	623.8
34	Discovery Labs	1,957,226	285,384	585.8
35	ActivCard Corp	1,105,196	164,574	571.5

LARGEST % DECREASES

RANK		JUL 15	JUN 13	%
1	Bank United Ltg rt	5,584	176,263	-96.8
2	dELiA*s Corp A	30,018	730,875	-95.9
3	Cardiac Science	56,172	1,176,991	-95.2
4	GoAmerica Inc	45,187	930,744	-95.1
5	Santos Ltd ADS	13,951	159,796	-91.3
6	Roanoke Elec Steel	24,014	189,150	-87.3
7	Prime Medical Svc	38,303	232,744	-83.5
8	Lifecore Biomed	59,837	327,226	-81.7
9	Ladish Co	48,950	266,297	-81.6
10	Methode Elec A	83,226	439,966	-81.1
11	Johnson Outdoors	40,329	208,816	-80.7
12	Witness Systems	103,534	500,771	-79.3
13	Trikon Technolog	85,888	411,501	-79.1
14	Nu Horizons Electr	72,483	331,739	-78.2
15	Harvard Bioscienc	36,279	160,945	-77.5
16	Hall Kinion & Assc	80,982	357,899	-77.4
17	Discovery Partners	72,324	303,108	-76.1
18	ArQule Inc	143,717	601,860	-76.1
19	Ceres Group Inc	111,275	463,508	-76.0
20	Vical Inc	141,452	587,090	-75.9
21	Covansys Corp	80,691	334,151	-75.9
22	Zomax Inc	59,064	242,243	-75.6
23	Paradyne Networks	128,801	483,547	-73.4
24	Perry Ellis Int'l	148,012	531,260	-72.1
25	Quaker Fabric	61,717	219,703	-71.9
26	Summit America TV	445,985	1,525,165	-70.8
27	Exploration Co DE	142,675	469,705	-69.6
28	Flow Int'l Corp	81,691	268,331	-69.6
29	Methanex Corp	169,407	554,813	-69.5
30	Nymox Pharmaceut	117,530	376,534	-68.8
31	August Technology	140,261	447,819	-68.7
32	EVCI Career Collg	129,001	403,953	-68.1
33	Monterey Pasta	195,796	611,867	-68.0
34	Sangamo Bioscienc	104,681	326,968	-68.0
35	Applied Molecular	170,948	515,770	-66.9

theory of contrary opinion
a technical indicator that uses the amount and type of odd-lot trading as an indicator of the current state of the market and pending changes.

reasoning behind this is that as a group, small investors are notoriously wrong in their timing of investment decisions: The investing public usually does not come into the market in force until after a bull market has pretty much run its course, and it does not get out until late in a bear market. Although its validity is debatable, this is the premise behind a widely followed technical indicator and is the basis for the **theory of contrary opinion**. This theory uses the amount and type of odd-lot trading as an indicator of the current state of the market and pending changes.

Because many individual investors deal in transactions of less than 100 shares, their combined sentiments are supposedly captured in odd-lot figures. The idea is to see what odd-lot investors are doing "on balance." So long as there is little or no difference in the spread between the volume of odd-lot purchases and sales, the theory of contrary opinion holds that the market will probably continue pretty much along its current line (either up or down). When the balance of odd-lot purchases and sales begins to change dramatically, it may be a signal that a bull or bear market is about to end. For example, if the amount of odd-lot purchases starts to exceed odd-lot sales by an ever widening margin, it may suggest that speculation on the part of small investors is starting to get out of control—an ominous signal that the final stages of a bull market may be at hand.

Trading Rules and Measures

Market technicians—analysts who believe it is chiefly (or solely) supply and demand that drives stock prices—like to use a variety of mathematical equations and measures to assess the underlying condition of the market. These analysts often use computers to produce the measures, plotting them on a daily basis, and then use those measure as indicators of when to get into or out of the market or a particular stock. In essence, *they develop trading rules based on these market measures*. Technical analysts almost always use several of these market measures, rather than just one (or two), because one measure rarely works the same way for all stocks. Moreover, they generally look for *confirmation* of one measure by *another*—in other words, market analysts like to see three or four of these ratios and measures all pointing in the same direction.

There are no "magic" numbers associated with these indicators. Some analysts may consider 20% and 80% to be "critical" levels for an indicator; others may use 40% and 60% for the same indicator. Market technicians often determine the critical levels by using a process known as "backtesting," which involves using historical price data to generate buy and sell signals. That is, they compute the profits generated from a series of trading rules and then try to find the indicators that generate the greatest amount of profits. Those measures then become the buy and sell signals for the various market indicators they employ. It's all very mechanical.

Although literally dozens of these market measures and trading rules exist, we'll confine our discussion here to some of the more popular and widely used technical indicators, including: (1) advance-decline lines; (2) new highs and lows; (3) the arms index; (4) the mutual fund cash ratio; (5) on balance volume; and (6) the investment newsletter sentiment index. In addition to these, the *Investing in Action* box on page 380 describes yet another popular market measure, the *relative strength index (RSI)*.

INVESTOR FACTS

INDICATORS CAN BE KEY—
Before you turn to charts to get price and volume data for a particular stock, take the pulse of the overall market by looking at indicators in different categories. Here are a few more to add to your analytical tool box:

• **Interest rates:** Looking at the financial futures market can help you get a sense of where interest rates are heading, because financial institutions often buy forward contracts to lock in their borrowing rates.

• **Capital goods back orders:** Tracked by the Department of Commerce, an increase in this indicator means that companies are ordering goods, which means they anticipate growth.

• **Volatility:** When the Nasdaq Volatility Index (VXZ) and the Market Volatility Index (VIX) are low, a drop in the market may be ahead.

Sources: Julia Boorstin, "Making Sense of the Mixed Signals," *Fortune,* June 16, 2003, pp. 48–49; and Susan Scherreik, "Reading Interest-Rate Tea Leaves, *Business Week,* August 11, 2003, p. 100.

Advance-Decline Line Each trading day, the NYSE, AMEX, and Nasdaq publish statistics on how many of their stocks closed higher on the day (i.e., *advanced* in price) and how many closed lower (*declined* in price). The *advance-decline line*, or *A/D line*, is simply the difference between these two numbers. That is, to calculate it, you take the number of stocks that have risen in price and subtract the number that have declined, usually for the previous day. For example, if 1,000 issues advanced on a day when 450 issues declined, the day's *net number* would be 550 (i.e., 1,000 − 450). If 450 advanced and 1,000 declined, the net number would be −550 (450 − 1,000). *Each day's net number is then added to (or subtracted from) the running total, and the result is plotted on a graph.* If the graph is rising, then the advancing issues are dominating the declining issues and the market is considered strong. When declining issues start to dominate, then the graph will turn down as the market begins to soften. Technicians use the A/D line as a signal for when to buy or sell stocks.

New Highs–New Lows This measure is similar to the advance-decline line, but looks at price movements over a longer period of time. A stock is defined as reaching a "new high" if its current price is at the highest level it has been over the past year (sometimes referred to as the "52-week high"). Conversely, a stock makes a "new low" if its current price is at the lowest level it has been over the past year. The *new highs–new lows (NH-NL) indicator* is computed as the number of stocks reaching new 52-week highs minus the number reaching new lows. Thus you end up with a *net number*, which can be either positive (when new highs dominate) or negative (when new lows exceed new highs), just like with the advance-decline line. To smooth out the daily fluctuations, *the net number is often added to (or subtracted from) a 10-day moving average, and then plotted on a graph.* As you might have guessed, a graph that's increasing over time indicates a strong market, where new highs are dominating, whereas a declining graph indicates a weak market, where new lows are more common than new highs. Technicians following a momentum-based strategy will buy stocks when new highs dominate and sell them when there are more new lows than new highs. Alternatively, they might use the indicator to rotate money into stocks when the market looks strong, and to rotate money out of stocks and into cash or bonds when the market looks weak.

The Arms Index This indicator, also known as the TRIN, for "trading index," builds on the advance-decline line by considering *the volume* in advancing and declining stocks in addition to *the number of stocks* rising or falling in price. The formula is

$$\text{TRIN} = \frac{\text{Number of up stocks}}{\text{Number of down stocks}} \div \frac{\text{Volume in up stocks}}{\text{Volume in down stocks}}$$

As an example, suppose we are analyzing the S&P 500. Assume that on a given day, 300 of these stocks rose in price and 200 fell in price. Also assume that the total trading volume in the rising ("up") stocks was 400 million shares, and the total trading volume in the falling ("down") stocks was 800 million shares. The value of the TRIN for the day would be

$$\text{TRIN} = \frac{300}{200} \div \frac{400 \text{ million}}{800 \text{ million}} = 3.0$$

INVESTING IN ACTION

FINDING STRONG STOCKS CAN BE A RELATIVE PROPOSITION

One of the most widely used technical indicators is the *relative strength index (RSI)*, an internal index measuring a security's price relative to itself over time. The RSI indicates a security's momentum, and it gives the best results when used by active investors for short trading periods. It also helps to identify market extremes and points of divergence, signaling that a security is approaching its price top or bottom and may reverse its price trend. (Note: Another type of RSI shows how a security's or index's price movement performs *against a broad market measure* like the DJIA or S&P 500.)

The RSI is the ratio of the average price change on up days to the average price change on down days during the same period. The index formula is

$$RSI = 100 - \left[100 \Big/ \left(1 + \frac{\text{Average price change on up days}}{\text{Average price change on down days}} \right) \right]$$

The RSI can cover various periods of time (days, weeks, or months). The most common RSIs at technical analysis Web sites are 9-, 14-, and 25-period RSIs.

The RSI ranges between 0 and 100, with most RSIs falling between 30 and 70. Generally, RSI values above 70 or 80 indicate an *overbought* condition (more and stronger buying than fundamentals justify). This may signal that a reversal of the upward price trend is possible. RSI values below 30 indicate a possible *oversold* condition (more selling than fundamentals might indicate) and a possible reversal of the downward trend. When the RSI crosses these points, it signals a possible trend reversal. The wider 80–20 range is often used with the 9-day RSI, which tends to be more volatile than longer period RSIs. In bull markets 80 may be a better upper indicator than 70, whereas in bear markets, 20 is a more accurate lower level.

Different sectors and industries have varying RSI threshold levels. By watching the RSI over the long term (1 year or more), you can determine the historical RSI trading level and the turning points for a particular stock. Also, the entrance of the RSI into the extreme levels does not mean you should buy or sell—but it does tell you to watch for that possibility.

continued on next page

Alternatively, suppose the volume in up stocks was 700 million shares, and that in down stocks was 300 million. The value of the TRIN would then be

$$TRIN = \frac{300}{200} \div \frac{700 \text{ million}}{300 \text{ million}} = 0.64$$

Higher TRIN values are interpreted as being bad for the market, because even though more stocks rose than fell, the trading volume in the falling stocks was much greater. The underlying idea is that a strong market is characterized by more stocks rising in price than falling, *along with greater volume in the rising stocks than in the falling ones*, as in the second example.

Mutual Fund Cash Ratio This indicator looks at the cash position of mutual funds as an indicator of future market performance. The mutual fund cash

INVESTING IN ACTION

continued from previous page

How can you use the RSI in your own trading? Here are three possible strategies using extremes:

- Buy when the RSI moves above 70 and sell if it falls below 30. However, the trend may have further to run and you may trade too soon.
- Sell when the RSI crosses below 70 and buy when it moves above 30—a popular strategy when using 9-day RSIs. However, this strategy has the opposite drawback to the strategy above: You could enter a trade after the trend reversal occurs.
- Sell when an above-70 RSI begins to turn down or buy when a below-30 RSI turns upward. This also has some pitfalls, because the RSI tends to move to extremes during periods of strong price trends and may give false signals.

Another way to use RSIs is to compare price charts and RSIs. Most of the time both move in the same direction. According to Edward Nicoski, a technical strategist at U.S. Bancorp Piper Jaffrey, ideally the stock should hit a new high in both price and relative strength. If this doesn't happen, it can indicate that investors in the stock are losing interest. Hence a divergence between RSI and a price chart can be a strong predictor of a changing trend.

Like other technical indicators, the RSI has limitations. It should not be used alone but, rather, works best in combination with other tools such as charting, moving averages and trendlines. Among the Web sites that offer RSI as a charting option are BigCharts (**www.bigcharts.com**), MetaStock Online (**www.metastock.com**), and StockCharts (**www.stockcharts.com**).

CRITICAL THINKING QUESTIONS Explain how the relative strength index can help investors identify changing price trends. Then go to Stockcharts.com and pull up charts for Federal Express (FDX) and UPS (UPS). What does the RSI tell you about these stocks?

Sources: Steven B. Achelis, "Relative Strength Index," *Technical Analysis from A to Z*, downloaded December 12, 2003, from **www.equis.com/Education/TAAZ**; Susan Scherreik, "Put New Muscle in Your Portfolio," *Business Week*, May 5, 2003, pp. 100–101; and Wayne A. Thorp, "Measuring Internal Strength: Wilder's Indicator," *AAII Journal*, May 2000, pp. 28–32.

---

ratio (MFCR) measures the percentage of mutual fund assets that are held in cash, and is computed as follows:

$$\text{MFCR} = \text{Mutual fund cash position} \div \text{Total assets under management}$$

The assumption is that the higher the MFCR, the stronger the market. Indeed, the ratio is considered very bullish when it moves to abnormally high levels (i.e., when mutual fund cash exceeds 10% to 12% of total assets), and bearish when the ratio drops to very low levels (e.g., less than 5% of assets). The logic goes as follows: When fund managers hold a lot of cash—and the MFCR is high—that's good news for the market, because they will eventually have to invest that cash, buying stocks and causing prices to rise. If fund managers hold very little cash, investors might be concerned for two reasons. First, there is less demand for stocks if most of the cash is already invested. Second, if the market takes a downturn, investors might want to withdraw their money. Fund managers will then have to sell some of their stocks to accommodate these redemptions, putting additional downward pressure on prices.

On Balance Volume Technical analysts usually consider *stock prices* to be the key measure of market activity. However, they also consider *trading volume* as a secondary indicator. *On balance volume (OBV)* is a momentum indicator that relates volume to price change. It uses trading volume in addition to price and *tracks trading volume as a running total*. In this way, OBV indicates whether volume is flowing into or out of a security. When the security closes higher than its previous close, all the day's volume is considered up-volume, all of which is *added to the running total*. In contrast, when a stock closes lower, all the day's volume is considered down-volume, which is then *subtracted from the running total*. The OBV indicator is used to *confirm* price trends. According to this measure, you want to see a lot of volume when a stock's price is rising, because that would suggest that the stock will go even higher. On the other hand, if prices are rising but OBV is falling, technical analysts would describe the situation as a *divergence* and interpret it as a sign of possible weakness.

When analyzing OBV, it is the direction or trend that is important, not the actual value. To begin the computation of OBV, you can start with an arbitrary number, such as 50,000. Suppose you are calculating the OBV for a stock that closed yesterday at a price of $50 per share, and you start with an OBV value of 50,000. Assume that the stock trades 80,000 shares today and closes at $49. Because the stock declined in price, we would subtract the full 80,000 shares from the previous balance (our starting point of 50,000), so now the OBV is 50,000 − 80,000 = **−30.000**. (Note that the OBV is simply the *trading volume running total*.) If the stock trades 120,000 shares on the following day and closes up at $52 per share, we would then *add* all of those 120,000 shares to the previous day's OBV: −30,000 + 120,000 = **+90,000**. This process would continue day after day. The normal procedure is to plot these daily OBVs on a graph. As long as the graph is moving up, it's bullish; when the graph starts moving down, it's bearish.

Investment Newsletter Sentiment Index This index is published by *Investors Intelligence*, a firm that tracks popular newsletters across the country. It measures the percentage of investment newsletter authors who are bullish or bearish on stocks. The index becomes more bullish as the newsletter writers become more bullish; it turns bearish when the letter writers do. The logic behind this indicator is that, on average, the newsletter writers just can't seem to get it right. Thus the index tends to become very bullish when the market's about to peak and—you guessed it—the index tends to be most bearish when the market's pretty much bottomed out. For this reason, the index is considered a *contrary indicator* because you're probably *better off doing just the opposite of what these so-called market experts tell you to do*. The most common trigger point with this index seems to be 60%. That is, when more than 60% of the newsletter writers are bullish, you'd be well advised to start thinking about selling some of your stocks. Just the opposite course of action would seem appropriate when more than 60% of these writers are bearish: That would probably be a good time to start thinking about getting back in the market. Technicians often use the terms *overbought* and *oversold* with indicators such as this one. An *overbought* market is usually considered to be overvalued due to excessive buying (speculation) on the part of investors. Conversely, an *oversold* market is usually considered to be undervalued, due to excessive pessimism and selling by investors.

Charting

charting
the activity of charting price behavior and other market information and then using the patterns these charts form to make investment decisions.

Charting is perhaps the best-known activity of the technical analyst. Indeed, these analysts will use various types of charts to plot the behavior of everything from the Dow Jones Industrial Average and share price movements of individual stocks to moving averages (see below) and advance-decline lines. In fact, as noted above, just about every type of technical indicator is charted in one form or another. Figure 9.4 shows a typical stock chart. In this case, the price behavior of Medtronic, Inc., has been plotted, along with a variety of supplementary technical information about the stock.

Charts are popular because they provide a visual summary of activity over time. Perhaps more important (in the eyes of technicians, at least), they contain valuable information about developing trends and the future behavior of the

FIGURE 9.4   A Stock Chart

This chart for Medtronic, Inc., contains information about the daily price behavior of the stock, along with the stock's relative strength, its moving average, its trading volume, and several other pieces of supplementary data. (*Source*: Chart courtesy of Stockcharts.com. *Note*: Visit this Web site's glossary for expanded definitions.)

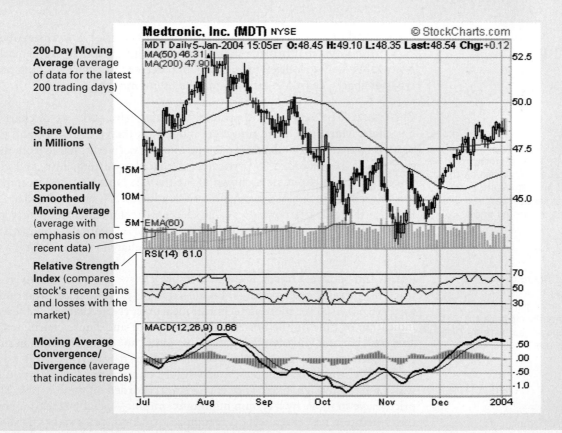

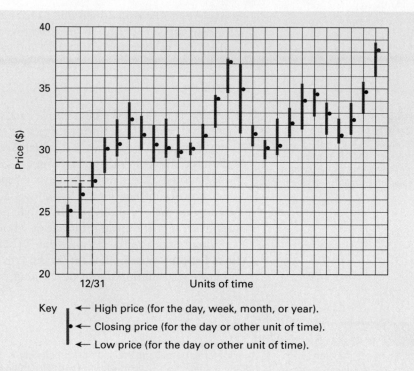

A Bar Chart

Bar charts are widely used to track stock prices, market averages, and numerous other technical measures.

Key
← High price (for the day, week, month, or year).
← Closing price (for the day or other unit of time).
← Low price (for the day or other unit of time).

market and/or individual stocks. Chartists believe price patterns evolve into *chart formations* that provide signals about the future course of the market or a stock. We will now briefly review the practice of charting, including popular types of charts, chart formations, and the use of moving averages.

Bar Charts The simplest and probably most widely used type of chart is the **bar chart.** Market or share prices are plotted on the vertical axis, and time is plotted on the horizontal axis. This type of chart derives its name from the fact that prices are recorded as vertical bars that depict high, low, and closing prices. A typical bar chart is shown in Figure 9.5. Note that on December 31, this particular stock had a high price of 29, a low of 27, and it closed at 27.50. Because these charts contain a time element, technicians frequently plot a variety of other pertinent information on them. For example, volume is often put at the base of bar charts (see the Medtronic chart in Figure 9.4).

bar chart
the simplest kind of chart, on which share price is plotted on the vertical axis and time on the horizontal axis; stock prices are recorded as vertical bars showing high, low, and closing prices.

point-and-figure charts
charts used to keep track of emerging price patterns by plotting significant price changes with X's and O's but with no time dimension used.

Point-and-Figure Charts **Point-and-figure charts** are used strictly to keep track of emerging price patterns. Because there is no time dimension on them, they are *not* used for plotting technical measures. (Note that while there is no indication of time on the horizontal axis of point-and-figure charts, technical analysts/chartists will often keep track of significant dates or points in time by placing letters or numbers directly on the body of the chart itself.) In addition to their treatment of time, point-and-figure charts are unique in two other ways. First, only *significant* price changes are recorded on these charts. That is, prices have to move by a certain minimum amount—usually at least a point or two—before a new price level is recognized. Second, price *reversals* show up

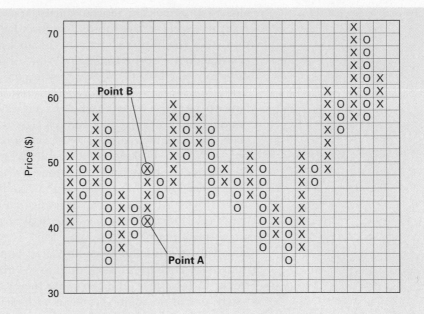

FIGURE 9.6

A Point-and-Figure Chart

Point-and-Figure charts are unusual because they have no time dimension. Rather, a column of *X*'s is used to reflect a general upward drift in prices, and a column of *O*'s is used when prices are drifting downward.

only after a predetermined change in direction occurs. Normally, only closing prices are charted, though some point-and-figure charts use all price changes during the day. An X is used to denote an increase in price, an O a decrease.

Figure 9.6 shows a common point-and-figure chart. In this case, the chart employs a 2-point box: That is, the stock must move by a minimum of 2 points before any changes are recorded. The chart can cover a span of 1 year or less if the stock is highly active. Or it can cover a number of years if the stock is not very active. As a rule, low-priced stocks are charted with 1-point boxes, moderately priced shares with increments of 2 to 3 points, and high-priced securities with 3- to 5-point boxes.

Here is how point-and-figure charts work: Suppose we are at point A on the chart in Figure 9.6. The stock has been hovering around this $40–$41 mark for some time. Assume, however, that it just closed at $42.25. Now, because the minimum 2-point movement has been met, the chartist would place an X in the box immediately *above* point A. The chartist would remain with this new box as long as the price moved (up or down) within the 2-point range of 42 to 44. Although the chartist follows *daily* prices, a new entry is made on the chart only after the price has changed by a certain minimum amount and moved into a new 2-point box. We see that from point A, the price generally moved up over time to nearly $50 a share. At that point (indicated as point B on the chart), things began to change as a reversal set in. That is, the price of the stock began to drift downward and in time moved out of the $48–$50 box. This reversal prompts the chartist to change columns and symbols, by moving one column to the right and recording the new price level with an O in the $46–$48 box. The chartist will continue to use O's as long as the stock continues to close on a generally lower note.

Chart Formations A chart by itself tells you little more than where the market or a stock has been. But to chartists, those price patterns yield formations that, along with things like resistance lines, support levels, and breakouts, tell them what to expect in the future. Chartists believe that history repeats itself, so they study the historical reactions of stocks (or the market) to various formations, and they devise trading rules based on these observations. It makes no difference to chartists whether they are following the market or an individual stock. *It is the formation that matters*, not the issue being plotted. If you know how to interpret charts (which is no easy task), you can see formations building and recognize buy and sell signals. These chart formations are often given exotic names, such as *head and shoulders*, *falling wedge*, *scallop and saucer*, *ascending triangle*, and *island reversal*, to name just a few.

Figure 9.7 shows four formations. The patterns form "support levels" and "resistance lines" that, when combined with the basic formations, yield buy and sell signals. Panel A is an example of a *buy* signal that occurs when prices break out above a resistance line in a particular pattern. In contrast, when prices break out below a support level, as they do at the end of the formation in panel B, a *sell* signal is said to occur. Supposedly, a sell signal means everything is in place for a major drop in the market (or in the price of a share of stock). A buy signal indicates that the opposite is about to occur. Unfortunately, one of the major problems with charting is that the formations rarely appear as neatly and cleanly as those in Figure 9.7. Rather, identifying and interpreting them often demands considerable imagination.

FIGURE 9.7

Some Popular Chart Formations

To chartists, each of these formations has meaning about the future course of events.

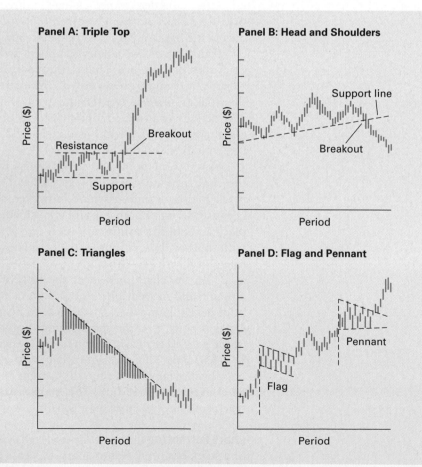

Moving Averages One problem with daily price charts is that they may contain a lot of often meaningless short-term price swings that do little more than mask the overall trend in prices. As a result, technical analysts will often use moving averages as a way to not only eliminate those minor blips, but also highlight underlying trends. A **moving average (MA)** is a mathematical procedure that records the average value of a series of prices, or other observations, over time. Because they incorporate a stream of these average values, MAs will basically smooth out a data series and make it easier to spot trends. The moving average is one of the oldest and most popular technical indicators and can, in fact, be used not only with share prices, but also with market indexes and even other technical measures.

Moving averages are computed over periods ranging from 10 to 200 days—meaning that from 10 to 200 data points are used in each calculation. For example, a series of 15 data points is used in a 15-day moving average. Actually, the length of the time period is important because it has a bearing on how the MA will behave. Shorter periods (10 to 30 days) are more sensitive and tend to more closely track actual daily behavior, whereas longer periods (say 100 to 200 days) are smoother and do a much better job of picking up the major trends. Several types of moving averages exist, with the most common (and the one we'll use here) being the *simple average*, which gives equal weight to each observation. In contrast, there are other procedures that give more weight to the most recent data points (which is done with the "exponential" and "weighted" averages) or apply more weight to the middle of the time period (e.g., "triangular" averages).

Using closing share prices as the basis of discussion, the simple moving average is calculated by adding up the closing prices over a given time period (e.g., 10 days), and then dividing this total by the length of the time period. Thus *the simple moving average is nothing more than the arithmetic mean*. To illustrate, consider the following stream of closing share prices:

> **moving average (MA)** a mathematical procedure that computes and records the average values of a series of prices, or other data, over time; results in a stream of average values that will act to smooth out a series of data.

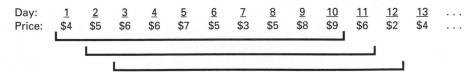

Day:	1	2	3	4	5	6	7	8	9	10	11	12	13	...
Price:	$4	$5	$6	$6	$7	$5	$3	$5	$8	$9	$6	$2	$4	...

Using a 10-day moving average, we'll add up the closing prices for days 1 through 10 ($4 + $5 + ... + $8 + $9 = $58) and then divide this total by 10 ($58/10 = $5.8). Thus the average closing price for this 10-day period was $5.80. The next day, the process is repeated once again for days 2 through 11; that turns out to be $60/10 = $6.00. This procedure is repeated each day, so that over time we have a series of these individual averages that, when linked together, form a *moving average line*. This line is then plotted on a chart, either by itself or along with other market information.

Figure 9.8 (on page 388) shows a 100-day moving average (the bold blue line) plotted against the daily closing prices for Medtronic, Inc. In contrast to the actual closing prices, the moving average provides a much smoother line, without all the short-term fluctuations, and clearly reveals the general trend in prices for this stock. Technicians will often use charts like the one in Figure 9.8 to help them make buy and sell decisions about a stock. Specifically, if the security's price starts moving above the moving average, then that situation should be read as a good time to buy, because prices should be drifting up (see

FIGURE 9.8   **A 100-Day Moving Average Line**

Moving average lines are often plotted along with the actual daily (or weekly) closing prices for a stock. They're also widely used with market indexes, such as the S&P 500, and a variety of technical indicators, including the advance-decline line.

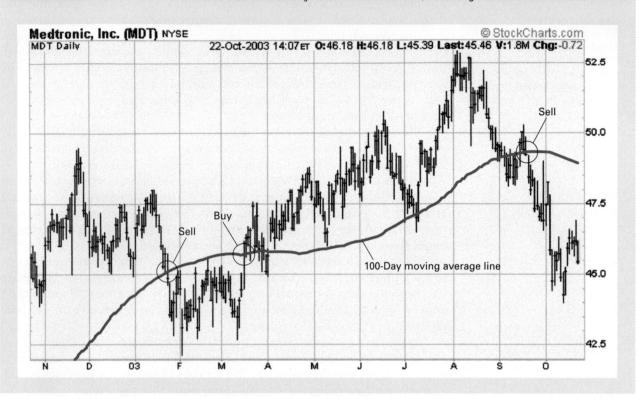

the buy signal on the chart). In contrast, a sell signal occurs when the security's price moves below the moving average line (see the two sell signals). Such a trading rule is not intended to get you in at the exact bottom or out at the exact top. Instead, it's meant to keep you in line with the security's price trend by buying shortly after the price hits the bottom and selling shortly after it reaches the top. And as seen in the figure, it does a fairly good job of that.

IN REVIEW

CONCEPTS

9.1 What is the purpose of *technical analysis*? Explain how and why it is used by technicians; note how it can be helpful in timing investment decisions.

9.2 Can the market really have a measurable effect on the price behavior of individual securities? Explain.

9.3 What is the *Dow theory*, and how is it used to analyze the market? Describe the *confidence index*, and note the feature that makes it unique.

9.4 Briefly describe each of the following, and explain how it is used in technical analysis:
a. Breadth of the market.
b. Short interest.
c. Odd-lot trading.

9.5 Briefly describe each of the following, and note how it is computed and how it is used by technicians:
   a. Advance-decline lines.
   b. Arms index.
   c. On balance volume.
   d Relative strength index.
   e. Moving averages.

9.6 What is a stock chart? What kind of information can be put on charts, and what is the purpose of charting?
   a. What is the difference between a bar chart and a point-and-figure chart?
   b. What are chart formations, and why are they important?

Random Walks and Efficient Markets

random walk hypothesis
the theory that stock price movements are unpredictable, so there's no way to know where prices are headed.

If a drunk were abandoned in an open field at night, where would you begin to search for him the next morning? The answer, of course, is the spot where the drunk was left the night before, because there's no way to predict where he will go. To some analysts, stock prices seem to wander about in a similar fashion. Observations of such erratic movements have led to a body of evidence called the **random walk hypothesis.** Its followers believe that price movements are unpredictable and therefore security analysis will not help to predict future market behavior. This hypothesis sharply contradicts the entire concept of technical analysis and, in fact, has serious implications for much of what we've discussed in this and the last two chapters.

A Brief Historical Overview

To describe stock prices as a random walk suggests that price movements cannot be expected to follow any type of pattern. Or, put another way, price movements are independent of one another. To find a theory for such behavior, researchers developed the concept of efficient markers. As we discussed briefly in Chapter 7, the basic idea behind an efficient market is that the market price of securities always fully reflects available information. This means that it would be difficult, if not impossible, to consistently outperform the market by picking "undervalued" stocks.

Random Walks The first evidence of random price movements dates back to the early 1900s. During that period, statisticians noticed that commodity prices seemed to follow a "fair game" pattern. That is, prices seemed to move up and down randomly, giving no advantage to any particular trading strategy. Although a few studies on the subject appeared in the 1930s, thorough examination of the randomness in stock prices did not begin until 1959. From that point on, particularly through the decade of the 1960s, the random walk issue was one of the most keenly debated topics in stock market literature. The development of high-speed computers has helped researchers compile convincing evidence that stock prices do, in fact, come very close to a random walk.

Efficient Markets Given the extensive random walk evidence, market researchers were faced with another question: What sort of market would produce prices that seem to fluctuate randomly? Such behavior could be the result

efficient market
a market in which securities reflect all possible information quickly and accurately.

of investors who are irrational and make investment decisions on whim. However, it has been argued much more convincingly that investors are not irrational. Rather, random price movements are evidence of highly efficient markets.

An **efficient market** is one in which security prices fully reflect all possible information. The concept holds that investors quickly incorporate all available information into their decisions about the price at which they are willing to buy or sell. At any point in time, then, the current price of a security incorporates all information. Additionally, the current price reflects not only past information, such as might be found in company reports and financial publications, but also information about events that have been announced but haven't yet occurred, like a forthcoming dividend payment. Even *predictions* about future information become embedded in current share prices—which, of course, happens all the time as investors actively forecast important events and incorporate those forecasts into their estimates. Because of keen competition among investors, when new information becomes known, the price of the security adjusts quickly. This adjustment is not always perfect. Sometimes it is too large and at other times too small. On average, however, it balances out and is correct. The new price, in effect, is set after investors have fully assessed the new information.

Why Should Markets Be Efficient?

Active markets, such as the New York Stock Exchange, are efficient because they are made up of many rational, highly competitive investors who react quickly and objectively to new information. Investors, searching for market profits, compete vigorously for new information and do extremely thorough analyses. The **efficient market hypothesis (EMH)**, which is the basic theory describing the behavior of such a market, has several tenets:

efficient markets hypothesis (EMH)
basic theory of the behavior of efficient markets, in which there are a large number of knowledgeable investors who react quickly to new information, causing securities prices to adjust quickly and accurately.

1. There are many knowledgeable investors actively analyzing, valuing, and trading any particular security. No one of these individual traders alone can affect the price of any security.
2. Information is widely available to all investors at approximately the same time, and this information is practically "free," or nearly so.
3. Information on events, such as labor strikes, industrial accidents, and changes in product demand, tends to emerge randomly.
4. Investors react quickly and accurately to new information, causing prices to adjust quickly and, on average, accurately.

For the most part, the securities markets do, in fact, exhibit these characteristics.

Levels of Market Efficiency

The efficient market hypothesis is concerned with *information*—not only the type and source of information, but also the quality and speed with which it is disseminated among investors. It is convenient to discuss the EMH in three cumulative categories or forms: past prices only; past prices *plus* all other public data; and past prices and public data *plus* private information. Together, these three ways of looking at information flows in the market represent three forms of the EMH: the weak, semi-strong, and strong forms.

weak form (EMH)
form of the EMH holding that past data on stock prices are of no use in predicting future prices.

Weak Form

The **weak form of the EMH** holds that past data on stock prices are of no use in predicting future price changes. If prices follow a random walk, price changes over time are random. Today's price change is unrelated to yesterday's or to that of any other day, just as each step by a drunk is unrelated to previous steps. If new information arrives randomly, then prices will change randomly.

A number of people have asserted that it is possible to profit from "runs" in a stock's price. They contend that when a stock's price starts moving up, it will continue to move up for a period of time, developing momentum. If you can spot a run, then, on the basis of past prices alone, you can develop a trading strategy that will produce a profit. The results from much careful research suggest that momentum in stock prices does exist, and if investors quickly trade at the beginning of the run, large profits can be made. But there's a problem: In addition to spotting a run (no easy task), an investor would have to make numerous trades; so when commissions are factored in, the person most likely to make a profit is the broker. Many other trading rules have been tested to determine whether profits can be made by examining past price movements, and there is very little, if any, evidence that a trading rule *based solely on past price data* can outperform a simple buy-and-hold strategy.

semi-strong form (EMH)
form of the EMH holding that abnormally large profits cannot be consistently earned using publicly available information.

Semi-strong Form

The **semi-strong form of the EMH** holds that abnormally large profits cannot be consistently earned using publicly available information. This information includes not only past price and volume data but also data such as corporate earnings, dividends, inflation, and stock splits. The semi-strong information set includes all of the information publicly considered in the weak form, *as well as all other information publicly available.* Tests of the semi-strong form of the EMH are basically concerned with the speed at which information is disseminated to investors. Research results generally support the position that stock prices adjust rapidly to new information and therefore support the semi-strong form of the EMH.

Most tests of semi-strong efficiency have examined how a stock price changes in response to an economic or financial event. A famous study involved stock splits. A stock split does not change the value of a company, so the value of the stock should not be affected by a stock split. The research indicated that there are sharp increases in the price of a stock *before* a stock split, but the changes after the split are random. Investors, therefore, cannot gain by purchasing stocks on or after the announcement of a split. To earn abnormal profits they would have to purchase before the split is announced. By the time of the announcement, the market has already incorporated into the price any favorable information associated with the split.

Other studies have examined the effects of major events on stock prices. The overwhelming evidence indicates that stock prices react within minutes, if not seconds, to any important new information. Certainly, by the time an investor reads about the event in the newspaper, the stock price has almost completely adjusted to the news. Even hearing about the event on the radio or television usually allows too little time to complete the transaction in time to make an abnormal profit.

strong form (EMH)
form of the EMH that holds that there is no information, public or private, that allows investors to earn abnormal profits consistently.

Strong Form

The **strong form of the EMH** holds that there is no information, public or private, that allows investors to consistently earn abnormal profits. It states that stock prices immediately adjust to any information, even if it isn't available to every investor. This extreme form of the EMH has not received universal support.

One type of private information is the kind obtained by corporate insiders, such as officers or directors of a corporation. They have access to valuable information about major strategic and tactical decisions the company makes. They also have detailed information about the financial state of the firm that may not be available to other shareholders. Corporate insiders may legally trade shares of stock in their company, if they report the transactions to the Securities and Exchange commission (SEC) each month. This information is then made public, usually within several weeks. It should not be surprising to learn that most studies of corporate insiders find that they can earn abnormally large profits when they sell their company stock. This, of course, is contrary to what you'd expect to find if the strong form of the EMH were true.

Other market participants occasionally have inside—nonpublic—information that they obtained *illegally*. With this information, they can gain an unfair advantage that permits them to earn an excess return. Clearly, those who trade securities on the basis of illegal inside information have an unfair advantage. Empirical research has confirmed that those with such inside information do indeed have an opportunity to earn an excess return—but there might be an awfully high price attached, such as spending time in prison, if they're caught.

Market Anomalies

market anomalies
irregularities or deviations from the normal behavior in an efficient market.

Despite considerable evidence in support of the EMH, there still exist some curious and as yet unexplained empirical results. In effect, some of the empirical studies have produced results that differed from what might be expected in a truly efficient market. These deviations from the norm are referred to as **market anomalies,** and they represent behavior that contradicts the EMH. Most of these anomalies, by the way, grew out of studies that were testing the semi-strong version of the EMH. Keep in mind that these are *empirical anomalies* and should not be viewed as trading rules that will enable you to consistently outperform the market. Rather, they are areas that have yet to be fully explained—and may exist only because of the capability of computers to search through millions of pieces of data in search of interesting correlations and associations.

Calendar Effects One widely cited anomaly is the so-called *calendar effect*, which holds that stock returns may be closely tied to the time of the year or the time of the week. That is, certain months or days of the week may produce better investment results than others. For example, the *January effect* shows a seasonality in the stock market, with a tendency for small-stock prices to go up during the month of January. Some explanations offer a tax-based reason for the phenomenon, but a completely satisfactory explanation has yet to be offered. The *weekend effect* is the result of evidence that stock returns, on average, are negative from the close of trading on Fridays until the close of trading on Mondays. The ability to consistently earn abnormal returns from using trading rules based on these results is still very questionable.

Small-Firm Effect Another anomaly is the *small-firm effect*, or size effect, which states that the size of the firm has a bearing on the level of stock returns. Indeed, several studies have shown that small firms earn higher returns than large firms, even after adjusting for risk and other considerations. Whether this is an invalidation of the EMH or a problem with misspecification of the mathematical models remains to be seen.

Earnings Announcements Another market anomaly has to do with how stock prices react to *earnings announcements*. Obviously, earnings announcements contain important information that should, and does, affect stock prices. However, much of the information has already been anticipated by the market, and so—if EMH is correct—prices should only react to the "surprise" portion of the announcement. Studies have shown, in fact, that a substantial amount of the price adjustment does occur prior to the actual announcement, but there is also a surprisingly large adjustment for some time after the announcement. In an efficient market, the prices should adjust quickly to any surprises in the earnings announcement. The fact that it takes several days (or even weeks) to fully adjust remains something of a mystery. Additionally, there is some documentation that abnormally large profits can consistently be obtained by buying stocks after unusually good *quarterly* earnings reports, and selling stocks after unusually bad *quarterly* earnings reports. This suggests that the majority of market investors don't bother to read and evaluate quarterly reports, but instead only concentrate on annual reports.

P/E Effect According to the *P/E effect*, the best way to make money in the market is to stick with stocks that have relatively low P/E ratios. The P/E multiple is widely followed in the market and widely used in the stock valuation process. Studies have shown that, on average, low P/E stocks outperform high P/E stocks, even after adjusting for risk and other factors. The reason has not been determined, but it appears that the results have endured over a long period. Since the P/E ratio is public information, it should be fully reflected in the current price, and purchasing low P/E stocks should not produce larger profits, if the markets are even reasonably efficient.

Possible Implications

The concept of an efficient market holds serious implications for investors. In particular, it could have considerable bearing on traditional security analysis and stock valuation procedures. Some, in fact, contend that investors should spend less time analyzing securities and more time on such matters as reducing taxes and transaction costs, eliminating unnecessary risk, and constructing a widely diversified portfolio. Make no mistake about it: *Even in an efficient market, all sorts of return opportunities are available.* But to proponents of efficient markets, the only way to increase returns is to invest in a portfolio of higher-risk securities.

Implications for Technical Analysis The most serious challenge the EMH evidence presents is to technical analysis. If price fluctuations are purely random, charts of past prices are unlikely to produce significant trading profits. In a highly efficient market, shifts in supply and demand occur so rapidly that technical indicators simply measure after-the-fact events, with no implications for the future. But if markets are less than perfectly efficient, information may be absorbed slowly, producing gradual shifts in supply and demand conditions—and profit opportunities for those who recognize the shifts early. Although the great bulk of evidence supports a random walk, many investors follow a technical approach because they believe it improves their investment results.

Implications for Fundamental Analysis Many strict fundamental analysts were at first pleased by the random walk attack on technical analysis. Further development of the efficient market concept, however, was not so well received: In an efficient market, it's argued, prices react so quickly to new information that not even security analysis will enable investors to realize consistently superior returns. Because of the extreme competition among investors, security prices are seldom far above or below their justified levels, and fundamental analysis thus loses much of its value. The problem is not that fundamental analysis is poorly done. On the contrary, it is done all too well! As a consequence, many investors, competing so vigorously for profit opportunities, simply eliminate the opportunities before other investors can capitalize on them.

So Who Is Right?

Some type of fundamental analysis probably has a role in the stock selection process, for even in an efficient market, there is no question that stock prices reflect a company's profit performance. Some companies are fundamentally strong and others fundamentally weak, and investors must be able to distinguish between the two. Thus some time can profitably be spent in evaluating a company and its stock to determine, not if it is undervalued, but whether it is fundamentally strong. The level of investor return, however, is more than a function of the fundamental condition of the company; it is also related to risk exposure. Fundamental analysis can help assess risk exposure and identify securities that possess risk commensurate with the return they offer.

The extent to which the markets are efficient is still subject to considerable debate. At present, there seems to be a growing consensus that although the markets may not be *perfectly* efficient, they are at least reasonably efficient.

In the final analysis, the individual investor must decide on the merits of fundamental and technical analysis. Certainly, a large segment of the investing public believes in security analysis, even in a market that may be efficient. What is more, the principles of stock valuation—that promised return should be commensurate with exposure to risk—are valid in any type of market setting.

IN REVIEW

CONCEPTS

9.7 What is the *random walk hypothesis*, and how does it apply to stocks? What is an *efficient market?* How can a market be efficient if its prices behave in a random fashion?

9.8 Explain why it is difficult, if not impossible, to consistently outperform an efficient market.
   a. Does this mean that high rates of return are not available in the stock market?
   b. How can an investor earn a high rate of return in an efficient market?

9.9 What are *market anomalies* and how do they come about? Do they support or refute the EMH? Briefly describe each of the following:
a. The January effect.
b. The P/E effect.
c. The size effect.

9.10 What are the implications of random walks and efficient markets for technical analysis? For fundamental analysis? Do random walks and efficient markets mean that technical analysis and fundamental analysis are useless? Explain.

Behavioral Finance: A Challenge to the Efficient Market Hypothesis

LG 6

For more than 30 years, the efficient market hypothesis (EMH) has been an influential force in financial markets. The notion that asset prices fully reflect all available information is supported by a large body of academic research. In practitioner circles, supporters of market efficiency include John Bogle of Vanguard, who helped pioneer the development of a special type of mutual fund known as an *index* fund. Managers of index funds don't try to pick individual stocks or bonds, because they assume that the market is efficient. They recognize that any time and energy spent researching individual securities will merely serve to increase the fund's expenses, which will drag down investors' returns. Indexing has become so popular that the Vanguard 500 Index Fund, which is designed to mirror the performance of the S&P 500, was the largest mutual fund in the United States in late 2003.

Although considerable evidence supports the concept of market efficiency, an increasing number of academic studies have begun to cast doubt on the notion that the EMH is as "true" as originally believed. This research documents various anomalies—deviations from accepted rules—in stock returns. A number of academics and practitioners have also recognized that emotions and other subjective factors play a role in investment decisions. This focus on investor behavior has resulted in a significant body of research, which is collectively referred to as *behavioral finance;* the authors of these studies are known as *behaviorists.* One notable event that acknowledged the importance of this field was the awarding of the 2002 Nobel Prize in economics to Daniel Kahneman, whose work integrated insights from psychology and economics. In addition to academic studies, some professional money managers incorporate concepts from behavioral finance into their construction and management of portfolios. To appreciate the ongoing debate between behaviorists and supporters of the EMH, it is necessary to understand the psychological factors that can affect investor behavior and the resulting effects on stock prices. The *Investing in Action* box on pages 396–397 details more about the opposing views of EMH and behavioral finance.

Investor Behavior and Security Prices

Researchers in behavioral finance believe that investors' decisions are affected by a number of beliefs and preferences. They also believe that the resulting biases will cause investors to overreact to certain types of financial information and underreact to others. We will now take a look at some of the behavioral factors that might influence the actions of investors.

INVESTING IN ACTION

SHOWDOWN AT THE EMH CORRAL

Investors, get ready for the big showdown! In one corner, the famous Fama—Eugene, that is—University of Chicago professor and coauthor of the efficient market hypothesis (EMH). According to the EMH, investors are rational, the markets are always right, and relevant new information is immediately reflected in stock prices. As a result, most investors can't beat the market and should invest in index funds that try to match the performance of major indexes.

In the opposing corner, representing the behavioral finance camp: Nobel Prize winner Daniel Kahneman of Princeton. He and his colleagues—including Yale University professor Robert Shiller (author of the 2000 bestseller *Irrational Exuberance*), and Richard Thaler from the University of Chicago— believe that investors aren't rational at all. Greed, fear, and other emotions motivate investors. "The efficient market theory tells you that prices more or less reflect the value of the company" says Lakonishok. He points to the Internet and media telecom bubbles as evidence that they do not. "How can you explain in a rational way valuations that made absolutely no sense?" he says.

Adds Robert Shiller, "[the emotional state of investors was] no doubt one of the most important factors causing the bull market" that peaked in early 2000—and its collapse.

In fact, both EMH and behavioral finance played a role in the tech bubble and its collapse. Proponents of EMH believed that, since markets were rational, rocketing stock prices were in line with their soaring expectations. Perhaps they first bought stocks in blue chip companies. As these investments prospered, they bought established technology companies like Microsoft and Oracle. Buoyed by their continued success, they gravitated to the cutting edge dot-coms. But as behaviorists will tell you, many investors then let their emotions overrule rational analysis. They became overconfident in their ability to pick winners, succumbed to "get-evenitis" and held on to losing stocks, hoping the prices would once again rise to former levels, ignored risks, and reacted too slowly to unexpected news. These more emotional influences, say the behaviorists, challenge the validity of EMH.

Which strategy, then, should investors follow? A recent study by three business professors, published in the *Economic Review* of the

continued on next page

Overconfidence Investors tend to be overconfident in their judgment, which frequently leads them to *underestimate* the level of risk in an investment. This underestimation of risk becomes even more important as the length of the investment horizon increases. In addition, overconfidence can cause financial analysts and money managers to make predictions that are too bold, giving investors a false sense of security. Highly overconfident investors typically make one of the biggest mistakes of all—they trade too much. Frequent trading leads to large transaction costs, which erode investment returns.

Biased Self-Attribution People tend to take credit for their successes ("buying that great stock was a smart move on my part") and blame others for their failures ("buying that lousy stock was my broker's fault"). This propensity obviously distorts reality and can lead to faulty investment decisions, as investors will tend to place more value on information that supports their preexisting beliefs and often disregard contradictory views.

INVESTING IN ACTION

continued from previous page

Federal Reserve bank of Atlanta, examined whether today's investors behave rationally or irrationally when they make investment decisions. Their report likens the rational investor who follows the EMH to Star Trek's very logical Mr. Spock, who is challenged by the emotional investor, in the person of Captain Kirk. Their findings indicate that both reason and emotion can work together to benefit investors. Rational investors fully analyze each situation but can get too caught up in the details, losing the forest for the trees. Emotional investors, on the other hand, listen to their gut instincts, which helps them focus on broader issues. However, even the most rational investor can't totally eliminate emotion—and shouldn't. The authors conclude, "While some argue that in certain situations, emotion may 'get in the way' and lead to suboptimal decision-making, we believe that emotion is an important aspect of the human condition that can actually enhance decision-making."

Interestingly, experts on both sides offer similar advice to investors. Princeton's Burton Malkiel, author of *A Random Walk Down Wall Street*, recommends acting as though markets are efficient, even if the EMH isn't always right. Build well-diversified portfolios with low expenses, using index funds, he says. Although behavioral theory says that investors can beat the market, Richard Thaler cautions that individual investors probably don't have the skills to do so—and neither do many active mutual fund managers. He, too, encourages individual investors to buy index funds and accept average market returns. In the end, both camps are winners.

CRITICAL THINKING QUESTION Would you consider yourself a rational or an emotional investor, and why? Describe how you would apply both EMH and behavioral concepts in developing your own investment strategy.

Sources: Lucy F. Ackert, Bryan K. Church, and Richard Deaves, "Emotion and Financial Markets," *Economic Review*, Federal Reserve Bank of Atlanta, Second Quarter 2003, pp. 33–41; Justin Fox, "Is the Market Rational?" *Fortune*, December 9, 2002, pp. 117–126; Chern Yeh Kwok, "Beating the Market Isn't for the Likes of Individual Investors," *St. Louis Post-Dispatch*, July 6, 2003, p. C.1; Seth Lubove, "Analyze This," *Forbes*, November 11, 2002, p. 162+; and Tom Walker, "Be Like Kirk, not Like Spock, on Wall Street," *Houston Chronicle*, August 11, 2003, pg. Business-1.

Loss Aversion Most individuals dislike losses much more than they like gains—in other words, we love it when we buy a stock and it goes up, but we really hate it when we buy a stock and it goes down! As a result of this *loss aversion*, many investors avoid selling their losing stocks, but instead hang on to them and hope that they will bounce back. This behavior often proves to be quite costly.

Representativeness This term encompasses a number of errors that people make when thinking about probabilities of events occurring. Two of the most common mistakes are the tendency to draw strong conclusions from small samples and to underestimate the effects of random chance. For example, investors may assume that a portfolio manager who has "beat the market" for each of the last three years will continue to do so. But they overlook two important facts. First, three years is a relatively short time period, especially compared to a typical investment horizon. Second, there are literally thousands

INVESTOR FACTS

FROM THEORY TO PRACTICE—
In addition to their academic responsibilities, EMH coauthor Eugene Fama and behaviorist Joseph Lakonishok are also money managers who practice what they preach. Fama is a director of Dimensional Fund Advisors (DFA), and Lakonishok is a partner at LSV Management. Even though the EMH suggests that no one can beat the market over the long term, most of DFA's funds have outperformed the indexes applicable to their asset categories. DFA's Large Cap Value fund (DFLVX) has outperformed its multi-cap value peers and the S&P 500 over various time horizons. LSV's Value Equity Fund, formed in 1999, has done even better—but not by much, as the following comparison indicates:

	Year-to-date (12/12/03)	1Yr	3Yr
LSVEX	29.21%	28.29%	7.95%
DFLVX	28.79	27.22	6.13
S&P 500	24.20	21.30	-6.40

Sources: Seth Lubove, "Analyze This," *Forbes*, November 11, 2002, p. 162+; Fund Snapshots, *Wall Street Journal Online;* online.wsj.com, downloaded December 13, 2003.

of managers running mutual funds and other investment portfolios. Even if their results are driven purely by random chance, a number of managers will display good performance over three consecutive years.

Narrow Framing Many people tend to analyze a situation in isolation, while ignoring the larger context. A common example in investment analysis is the propensity to analyze the attractiveness of a particular stock without considering the effect of this stock on an investor's existing portfolio. For example, an investor may get excited about the prospects for a hot new technology stock, but if the portfolio is already heavily invested in tech stocks, adding this new one may not be the right decision.

Belief Perseverance People typically ignore information that conflicts with their existing beliefs. If they believe a stock is good and purchase it, for example, they later tend to discount any signals of trouble. In many cases, they even avoid gathering new information, for fear it will contradict their initial opinion. It would be better to view each stock owned as a "new" stock when periodically reviewing a portfolio, and to ask whether the information available at that time would cause the investor to buy or sell the stock.

Behavioral Finance at Work in the Markets

Now that we have some understanding of the psychological factors that can affect financial decisions, let's examine some of the evidence. Specifically, we will discuss how behavioral finance can affect stock return predictability, investor behavior, and analyst behavior.

Stock Return Predictability If investors systematically underreact or overreact to some financial news, we may be able to detect certain patterns in stock returns over time. Predictability in stock prices can be measured by looking at the correlation of stock returns in a given period with those in a later period. Studies have found evidence of negative correlation over 3- to 5-year periods, suggesting it may be profitable to buy portfolios of stocks that have performed poorly in the past, as their values are likely to rise in the future. If investors extrapolate the past bad news for these firms well into the future, the stocks will become undervalued, and that is precisely when they should be purchased. Other studies find evidence of momentum in stock returns over 6- to 12-month time horizons. In other words, stocks that have recently risen in price tend to continue to increase, and those that have fallen continue to decline. Behaviorists have shown that this momentum can be driven by patterns of underreaction and overreaction.

Additional evidence of predictability in returns can be gleaned from a comparison of growth and value stocks. Growth stocks typically have high price-earnings and price-book ratios, whereas value stocks tend to have lower ratios. Evidence suggests that value stocks tend to outperform growth stocks, and behaviorists suggest that growth stocks perform poorly due to investors' excessive optimism about their future prospects.

Investor Behavior Studies of the behavior of individual investors reveal the important role played by psychology. One strong result relates to overconfidence: Investors who believe they have superior information tend to trade more, but earn lower returns due to the higher transaction costs they incur. In addition, investors tend to exhibit loss aversion and, therefore, sell stocks that have recently risen in price instead of those that have declined. Representativeness plays a big role in mutual fund investing, because investors tend to direct more money to funds that have recently experienced good performance.

If investors make decisions based on emotional factors rather than underlying economic fundamentals, their actions increase the risk of investing, even for professionals. One of the main forces in the markets necessary to support the EMH is arbitrage—the ability to exploit any errors in security prices. Irrational behavior by investors increases the risk of arbitrage and makes it less attractive, which in turn reduces market efficiency.

Analyst Behavior Because much of the information used by investors is generated via financial analysts, we need to understand how behavioral finance can bias analysts' forecasts of stock prices and earnings. Some evidence supports the idea of "herding" behavior by analysts, as they collectively tend to issue similar recommendations or earnings forecasts for stocks.

Analysts have also come under fire for being too optimistic—that is, for too frequently issuing buy recommendations and too rarely suggesting that investors sell stocks. Studies find that analysts' favorite stocks, those with the highest growth forecasts, typically earn lower returns than stocks with the least rosy growth forecasts.

Implications for Security Analysis

Our discussion of the psychological factors that affect financial decisions suggests that behavioral finance can play an important role in investing. So far, we have covered some of the main stock selection techniques using fundamental and technical analysis. We now turn our attention to implications of behavioral financial for security analysis.

Fundamental analysis of stocks frequently involves forecasts of dividends and earnings growth rates, as well as the analysis of price multiples like P/E ratios. If we construct such forecasts or use the forecasts constructed by financial analysts, we should be careful to avoid excessive optimism. An easy solution to this problem is to rework our analysis with more conservative forecast estimates to see whether our investment decision changes. In addition, we should recognize the potential for error in our forecasts. Significant errors may be especially likely to occur if we are working with limited data, as is usually the case with relatively new companies without long financial histories.

Stock valuation using multiples such as the P/E ratio involves comparing the multiple for a given stock with the average multiple for a group of stocks (often referred to as *comparable firms*, or simply *comparables*). If the stock is for a company in a large, well-established industry such as banking, our list of comparables will probably include many firms. On the other hand, when we analyze a stock in a newer, more specific industry such as optical networking, we will usually have at most a handful of firms to use as comparables. In these more specialized cases, the average price multiple for a small number of firms may be practically meaningless. One solution to this problem is to define the list of comparables more broadly. If we feel that most investors are too optimistic regarding the prospects for firms in this industry, we may want to adjust the average multiple downward to account for the excessive optimism.

Technical analysis of stocks uses the methods discussed earlier in this chapter. In some cases, our view of behavioral finance may indicate which method we should use. For instance, if we believe in momentum in stock returns, we may want to use a trend-following method such as moving averages to generate buy and sell signals. If we believe in overreaction, we may prefer to rely on overbought or oversold indicators such as the relative strength index (RSI).

Your Behavior as an Investor: It Does Matter

In light of all the possible biases in judgment and errors in decision making, you might be tempted to "throw in the towel" and avoid investing in stocks altogether. After all, Treasury bills and money market funds are nice and safe, and conservative investing avoids all of the pitfalls (other than the low returns). In fact, just the opposite is true: You may be making one of the biggest mistakes of all—choosing an incorrect asset allocation. One of the most important things you must do as an investor is to choose the asset allocation (the mix of stocks, bonds, and other investments) that is right for you, based on your investment time horizon, level of risk tolerance, and other relevant factors. Table 9.1 lists some other steps that you can take to improve your investment returns.

What lessons should we take away from our discussion of behavioral finance? Perhaps the greatest lesson is to recognize that we are human, so we will inevitably make mistakes or have occasional errors in judgment. The

TABLE 9.1   Using Behavioral Finance to Improve Investment Results

Studies have documented a number of behavioral factors that appear to influence investors' decisions and adversely affect their returns. By following some simple guidelines, you can avoid making mistakes and improve your portfolio's performance. A little common sense goes a long way in the financial markets!

- **Don't hesitate to sell a losing stock.** If you buy a stock at $20 and its price drops to $10, ask yourself whether you would buy that same stock if you came into the market today with $10 in cash. If the answer is yes, then hang onto it. If not, sell the stock and buy something else.

- **Don't chase performance.** The evidence suggests that there are no "hot hands" in investment management. Don't buy last year's hottest mutual fund if it doesn't make sense for you. Always keep your personal investment objectives and constraints in mind.

- **Be humble and open-minded.** Many investment professionals, some of whom are extremely well paid, are frequently wrong in their predictions. Indeed, that is the very nature of forecasting. Admit your mistakes and don't be afraid to take corrective action.

- **Review the performance of your investments on a periodic basis.** Remember the old saying, "Out of sight, out of mind." Don't be afraid to face the music and to make changes as your situation changes. Nothing runs on "auto-pilot" forever—including investment portfolios.

- **Don't trade too much.** Investment returns are uncertain, but transaction costs are guaranteed. Considerable evidence indicates that investors who trade frequently perform poorly.

better we understand how our behavior can influence our investment decisions, the easier it will be to avoid mistakes. In fact, we may even be able to profit from the mistakes of others. For example, if we feel that most investors overreact to bad news and sell stocks too soon, that may represent a great buying opportunity.

IN REVIEW

CONCEPTS

9.11 How can behavioral finance have any bearing on investor returns? Do supporters of behavioral finance believe in efficient markets? Explain.

9.12 Briefly explain how behavioral finance can affect each of the following:
  a. The predictability of stock returns.
  b. Investor behavior.
  c. Analyst behavior.

9.13 Considering how behavioral factors can affect investment decisions, list four steps that investors might take to improve their investment returns.

Summary

LG 1 **Discuss the purpose of technical analysis and explain why the performance of the market is important to stock valuation.** Technical analysis represents another phase of the stock valuation process. It deals with the behavior of the stock market itself and the various economic forces at work in the marketplace. Technical analysis is used as a way to assess the condition of the market and to determine whether it's a good time to be buying or selling stocks. Some investors try to keep tabs on the markets in an informal way, while others use complex mathematical formulas and rules to guide them in their buy and sell decisions.

LG 2 **Describe some of the approaches to technical analysis, including, among others, the Dow theory, moving averages, charting, and various indicators of the technical condition of the market.** Market analysts look at those factors in the marketplace that can affect the price behavior of stocks in general. This analysis can be done by assessing the overall condition of the market (as the Dow theory does), by informally or formally studying various internal market statistics (e.g., short interest or advance-decline lines), or by charting various aspects of the market (including the use of moving averages).

LG 3 **Compute and use technical trading rules for individual stocks and the market as a whole.** Technical analysts use a number of mathematical equations and measures to gauge the direction of the market, including advance-decline lines, new highs and lows, the arms index, the mutual fund cash ratio, on balance volume, and the investment newsletter sentiment index. They test different indicators using historical price data in an attempt to find those that generate profitable trading strategies, which then are developed into trading rules used to guide buy and sell decisions.

LG 4 **Explain the idea of random walks and efficient markets, and note the challenges these theories hold for the stock valuation process.** In recent years, both technical and fundamental analyses have been seriously challenged by the random walk and efficient market hypotheses. Indeed, considerable evidence indicates that stock prices do move in a random fashion. The efficient market hypothesis attempts to explain why prices behave randomly. The idea behind an efficient market is that available information is always fully reflected in the prices of securities, so investors should *not* expect to out-perform the market consistently.

LG 5 Describe the weak, semi-strong, and strong versions of the efficient market hypothesis, and explain what market anomalies are. The weak form of the EMH holds that all *market* information is fully embedded in the price of a stock, and therefore technical analysis is really a waste of time (as it cannot be used to consistently outperform the market). The semi-strong version states that all *public* information (market and other-wise) is embedded in the price of a stock. Furthermore, this information flows to the market in a random fashion and is quickly digested by the market participants; as a consequence, the use of such information (as in fundamental analysis) will be of little value in helping investors generate excess returns with any degree of consistency. The strong form holds that there is no information, *public or private*, that allows investors to consistently earn abnormal returns. While much empirical evidence supports the EMH, some studies have uncovered evidence that does *not* support it; the latter data constitute *market anomalies*.

LG 6 Demonstrate a basic appreciation for how psychological factors can affect investors' decisions, and how behavioral finance presents a challenge to the concept of market efficiency. A number of factors, such as overconfidence, loss aversion, representative-ness, and belief perseverance, can lead to incorrect investment decisions. If investors are not as rational as the efficient market hypothesis assumes, the resulting biases may lead to some level of predictability in stock returns. Any overreaction, underreaction, or other systematic predictability in financial markets represents a violation of market efficiency.

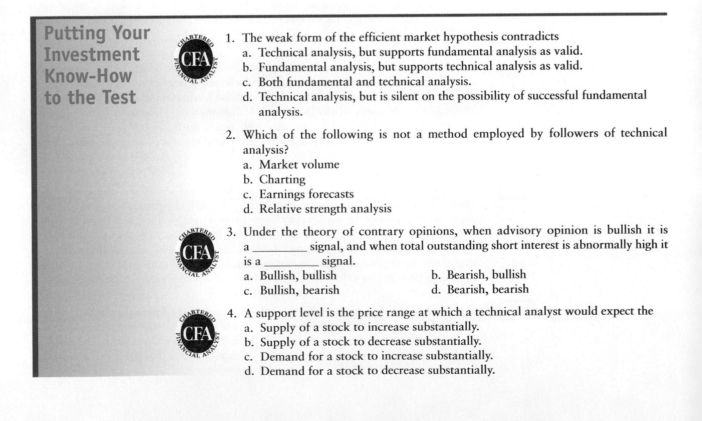

Putting Your Investment Know-How to the Test

1. The weak form of the efficient market hypothesis contradicts
   a. Technical analysis, but supports fundamental analysis as valid.
   b. Fundamental analysis, but supports technical analysis as valid.
   c. Both fundamental and technical analysis.
   d. Technical analysis, but is silent on the possibility of successful fundamental analysis.

2. Which of the following is not a method employed by followers of technical analysis?
   a. Market volume
   b. Charting
   c. Earnings forecasts
   d. Relative strength analysis

3. Under the theory of contrary opinions, when advisory opinion is bullish it is a _____ signal, and when total outstanding short interest is abnormally high it is a _____ signal.
   a. Bullish, bullish   b. Bearish, bullish
   c. Bullish, bearish   d. Bearish, bearish

4. A support level is the price range at which a technical analyst would expect the
   a. Supply of a stock to increase substantially.
   b. Supply of a stock to decrease substantially.
   c. Demand for a stock to increase substantially.
   d. Demand for a stock to decrease substantially.

5. Which one of the following would provide evidence *against* the semi-strong form of the efficient market theory?
   a. About 50% of pension funds outperform the market in any year.
   b. All investors have learned to exploit signals about future performance.
   c. Trend analysis is worthless in determining stock prices.
   d. Low P/E stocks tend to have positive abnormal returns over the long run.

6. The term "random walk" is used in investments to refer to
   a. Stock price changes that are random but predictable.
   b. Stock prices that respond slowly to both old and new information.
   c. Stock price changes that are random and unpredictable.
   d. Stock price changes that follow the pattern of past price changes.

7. Which of the following is *not* a perceived advantage of technical analysis?
   a. Technicians do not rely on getting information first.
   b. Technical analysts depend heavily on accounting information.
   c. Technical investors invest after the new equilibrium is under way.
   d. Technical investors need to know when to buy, not why investors are buying.

8. When technical analysts say a stock has a good relative strength, they mean the
   a. Ratio of the price of the stock to a market index has trended upward.
   b. Recent trading volume in the stock has exceeded the normal volume.
   c. Total return on the stock has exceeded the total return on other stocks in the same industry.
   d. Stock has performed well compared to other stocks in the same risk category.

9. A basic assumption of technical analysis in contrast to fundamental analysis is that
   a. Financial statements provide information crucial in valuing the stock.
   b. A stock's market price will approach its intrinsic value over time.
   c. Aggregate demand for and aggregate supply of goods and services are key determinants of stock value.
   d. Security prices move in patterns, which repeat over long periods.

10. A company announces an unexpectedly large cash dividend to its shareholders. In an efficient market *without* information leakage, the most likely expectation is
    a. An abnormal price change at the announcement.
    b. An abnormal price increase before the announcement.
    c. An abnormal price decrease after the announcement.
    d. No abnormal price change before or after the announcement.

Answers: 1. d; 2. c; 3. b; 4. c; 5. d; 6. c; 7. b; 8. a; 9. d; 10. a

---

Discussion Questions

LG 1

Q9.1 Briefly describe how technical analysis is used as part of the stock valuation process. What role does it play in an investor's decision to buy or sell a stock?

LG 2   LG 3

Q9.2 Describe each of the following approaches to technical analysis and note how it would be used by investors.
   a. Confidence index   **b.** Arms index
   c. Trading action   **d.** Odd-lot trading
   e. Charting   **f.** Moving averages
   g. On balance volume

Which of these approaches is likely to involve some type of mathematical equation or ratio?

Q9.3 Briefly define each of the following, and note the conditions that would suggest the market is technically strong
  a. Breadth of the market
  b. Short interest
  c. Relative strength index (RSI)
  d. Theory of contrary opinion
  e. Head and shoulders

LG 4 **LG 5** **Q9.4** Much has been written and said about the concept of an *efficient market.* It's probably safe to say that some of your classmates believe the markets are efficient and others believe they are not. Have a debate to see whether you can resolve this issue (at least among you and your classmates). Pick a side, either for or against efficient markets, and then develop your "ammunition." Be prepared to discuss these three aspects:
  a. What is an efficient market? Do such markets really exist?
  b. Are stock prices always (or nearly always) correctly set in the market? If so, does that mean little opportunity exists to find undervalued stocks?
  c. Can you cite any reasons to use fundamental and/or technical analysis in your stock selection process? If not, how would you go about selecting stocks?

LG 6 **Q9.5** Briefly define each of the following terms, and describe how it can affect investors' decisions:
  a. Loss aversion
  b. Representativeness
  c. Narrow framing
  d. Overconfidence
  e. Biased self-attribution

LG 6 **Q9.6** Describe how optimism may lead to biases in stock valuation using the discounted cash flow method. Discuss how scenario analysis may be used as a way to correct for these biases.

Problems

 P9.1 Compute the arms index for the S&P 500 over the following 3 days:

Day	Number of Stocks **Rising** in Price	Number of Stocks **Falling** in Price	Volume for Stocks **Rising** in Price	Volume for Stocks **Falling** in Price
1	350	150	850 million shares	420 million shares
2	275	225	450 million shares	725 million shares
3	260	240	850 million shares	420 million shares

Which of the 3 days would be considered the most bullish? Explain why.

 P9.2 Listed below is the percentage of investment newsletter writers who were expressing a bullish opinion for stocks for the first 6 months of a recent year:

Month	Percent Bullish
January	10%
February	35%
March	45%
April	60%
May	80%
June	55%

If a technical analyst were relying on these data, in which month would he or she have been most likely to buy stocks? When would the analyst have been most likely to sell stocks? Explain.

LG 3 **P9.3** Compute the level of on balance volume (OBV) for the following 3-day period for a stock, if the beginning level of OBV is 50,000 and the stock closed yesterday at $25:

Day	Closing Price	Trading Volume
1	$27	70,000 shares
2	$26	45,000 shares
3	$29	120,000 shares

Does the movement in OBV appear to confirm the rising trend in prices? Explain.

LG 3 **P9.4** Below are figures representing the number of stock making new highs and new lows for each month over a 6-month period:

Month	New Highs	New Lows
July	117	22
August	95	34
September	84	41
October	64	79
November	53	98
December	19	101

Would a technical analyst consider the trend to be bullish or bearish over this period? Explain.

LG 3 **P9.5** You hear a market analyst on television say that the advance/decline ratio for the session was 1.2. What does that mean?

LG 3 **P9.6** At the end of a trading day you find that, on the NYSE, 2,200 stocks advanced, and 1,000 stocks declined. What is the value of the advance-decline line for that day?

LG 3 **P9.7** You are given the following information:

Day	New Highs	New Lows
1 (yesterday)	117	22
2	95	34
3	84	41
4	64	79
5	53	98
6	19	101
7	19	105
8	18	110
9	19	90
10	22	88

a. Calculate the 10-day moving average NH-NL indicator.
b. If there are 120 new highs and 20 new lows today, what is the new 10-day moving average NH-NL indicator?

P9.8 You have collected the following NH-NL indicator data:

Day	NH-NL Indicator
1 (yesterday)	100
2	95
3	61
4	43
5	−15
6	−45
7	−82
8	−86
9	−92
10	−71

If you are a technician following a momentum-based strategy, are you buying or selling today?

 P9.9 You are presented with the following data

Week	Mutual Fund Cash Position	Mutual Fund Total Assets
Most recent	$281,478,000.00	$2,345,650,000.00
2	258,500,000.00	2,350,000,000.00
3	234,800,000.00	2,348,000,000.00
4	211,950,000.00	2,355,000,000.00
5	188,480,000.00	2,356,000,000.00

Calculate the MFCR for each week. Based on the result, are you bullish or bearish?

 P9.10 You find the closing prices for a stock you own. You want to use a 10-day moving average to monitor the stock. Calculate the 10-day moving average for days 11 through 20. Based on the data in the table below, are there any signals you should act on? Explain.

Day	Closing Price	Day	Closing Price
1	$25.25	11	$30.00
2	26.00	12	30.00
3	27.00	13	31.00
4	28.00	14	31.50
5	27.00	15	31.00
6	28.00	16	32.00
7	27.50	17	29.00
8	29.00	18	29.00
9	27.00	19	28.00
10	28.00	20	27.00

See the text Web site
(**www.aw-bc.com/gitman_joehnk**) **for Web exercises**
that deal with *market price behavior.*

Case Problem 9.1

LG 2   LG 3

Rhett Runs Some Technical Measures on a Stock

Rhett Weaver is an active stock trader and avid market technician. He got into technical analysis about 10 years ago, and although he now uses the Internet for much of his analytical work, he still enjoys running some of the numbers and doing some of the charting himself. Rhett likes to describe himself as a "serious stock trader" who relies on technical analysis for some—but certainly not all—of the information he uses to make an investment decision; unlike some market technicians, he does not totally ignore a stock's fundamentals! Right now he's got his eye on a stock that he's been tracking for the past 3 or 4 months.

The stock is Nautilus Navigation, a mid-sized high-tech company that's been around for a number of years and has actually demonstrated an ability to generate profits year-in and year-out. The problem is that the earnings are a bit erratic, tending to bounce up and down from year to year, which causes the price of the stock to be a bit erratic as well. And that's exactly why Rhett likes the stock—as a trader, the volatile prices enable him to move in and out of the stock over relatively short (3- to 6-month) periods of time.

Rhett has already determined that the stock has "decent" fundamentals, so he doesn't have to worry about its basic soundness. Hence, he can concentrate on the technical side of the stock. In particular, he wants to run some technical measures on the market price behavior of the security. Accordingly, he's obtained recent closing prices on the stock, which are shown in the table below:

Recent Price Behavior: Nautilus Navigation

14 (8/15/04)	18.55	20	17.50
14.25	17.50	20.21	18.55
14.79	17.50	20.25	19.80
15.50	17.25	20.16	19.50
16	17	20	19.25
16	16.75	20.25	20
16.50	16.50	20.50	20.90
17	16.55	20.80	21.
17.25	16.15	20	21.75
17.20	16.80	20	22.50
18	17.15	20.25	23.25
18 (9/30/04)	17.22	20	24
18.55	17.31 (10/31/04)	19.45	24.25
18.65	17.77	19.20	24.15
18.80	18.23	18.25 (11/30/04)	24.75
19	19.22	17.50	25
19.10	20.51	16.75	25.50
18.92	20.15	17	25.55 (12/31/04)

Nautilus shares are actively traded on the Nasdaq National Market and enjoy considerable market interest.

Questions

a. Use the closing share prices in the table above to compute the stock's relative strength index (RSI) for (1) the 20-day period from 9/30/04 to 10/31/04; and (2) the 22-day period from 11/30/04 to 12/31/04. [*Hint*: Use a simple (unweighted) average to compute the numerator (average price change on up days) and the denominator (average price change on down days) of the RSI formula shown in the *Investing in Action* box on page 380.]

1. Contrast the two RSI measures you computed. Is the index getting bigger or smaller, and is that good or bad?
2. Is the latest RSI measure giving a buy or a sell signal? Explain.

b. Based on the above closing share prices, prepare a moving average line covering the period shown in the table; use a 10-day time frame to calculate the individual average values.

Note: Click on *"Moving Averages"* at the Gitman and Joehnk Web site (www.aw-bc.com/gitman_joehnk) for a price chart and a 10-day moving average line for Nautilus Navigation.

1. Plot the daily closing prices for nautilus from 8/15/04 through 12/31/04 on a graph/chart.
2. On the same graph/chart, plot a moving average line using the individual average values computed earlier. Identify any buy or sell signals.
3. As of 12/31/04, was the moving average line giving a buy, hold, or sell signal? Explain. How does that result compare to what you found with the RSI in part **a**? Explain.

c. Prepare a point-and-figure chart of the closing prices for Nautilus Navigation (use a 1-point system, in which each box is worth $1). Discuss how this and similar charts are used by technical analysts.

d. Based on the technical measures and charts you've prepared, what course of action would you recommend that Rhett take with regard to Nautilus Navigation? Explain.

Case Problem 9.2 — *Deb Takes Measure of the Market*

LG 2   LG 3

Several months ago, Deb Forrester received a substantial sum of money from the estate of her late aunt. Deb initially placed the money in a savings account because she was not sure what to do with it. Since then, however, she has taken a course in investments from a highly respected professor at the local university. The textbook for the course was, in fact, this one, and they just completed Chapter 9. Excited about what she has learned in class, Deb has decided that she definitely wants to invest in stocks. But before she does, she wants to use her newfound knowledge in technical analysis to determine whether now would be a good time to enter the market.

Deb has decided to use all five of the following measures to help her determine if now is, indeed, a good time to start putting money into the stock market:

• Dow theory

• Advance-decline line

• New highs-new lows (NH-NL) indicator *(Assume the current 10-day moving average is zero and the last 10 periods were each zero.)*

• Arms index

• Mutual fund cash ratio

Deb goes to the Internet and, after considerable effort, is able to put together the table of data shown on the next page.

Questions

a. Based on the data presented in the table, calculate a value (where appropriate) for periods 1 through 5, for each of the five measures listed above. (*Hint:* There are no values to compute for the Dow theory; just plot the averages.) Chart your results, where applicable.

	Period 1	Period 2	Period 3	Period 4	Period 5
Dow Industrial Average	8,300	7,250	8,000	9,000	9,400
Dow Transportation Average	2,375	2,000	2,000	2,850	3,250
New highs	68	85	85	120	200
New lows	75	60	80	75	20
Volume up	600,000,000	836,254,123	275,637,497	875,365,980	1,159,534,297
Volume down	600,000,000	263,745,877	824,362,503	424,634,020	313,365,599
Mutual fund cash (trillions of dollars)	$0.31	$0.32	$0.47	$0.61	$0.74
Total assets managed (trillions of dollars)	$6.94	$6.40	$6.78	$6.73	$7.42
Advancing issues (NYSE)	1,120	1,278	1,270	1,916	1,929
Declining issues (NYSE)	2,130	1,972	1,980	1,334	1,321

b. Discuss each measure individually and note what it indicates for the market, as it now stands. Taken collectively, what do these five measures indicate about the current state of the market? According to these measures, is this a good time for Deb to consider getting into the market, or should she wait a while? Explain.

c. Comment on the time periods used in the table, which are not defined here. What if they were relatively long intervals of time? What if they were relatively short? Explain how the length of the time periods can affect the measures.

Excel with Spreadsheets

Technical analysis looks at the demand and supply for securities based on trading volumes and price studies. Charting is a common method used to identify and project price trends in a security. A well-known technical indicator is the Bollinger Band. It creates two bands, one above and one below, the price performance of a stock. The upper band is a resistance level and represents the level above which the stock is unlikely to rise. The bottom forms a support level and shows the price which a stock is unlikely to fall below.

According to technicians, if you see a significant "break" in the upper band, the expectation is that the stock price will fall in the immediate future. A "break" in the lower band signals that the security is about to rise in value. Either of these occurrences will dictate a unique investment strategy.

Replicate the following technical analysis for Amazon.Com (AMZN)

- Go to www.moneycentral.msn.com
- Symbol(s): **AMZN**
- In the left-hand column, click on "Charts". You need to update to MSN Money Deluxe if you have not already done so.
- If download was required, fill in the Symbol box with "AMZN"
- A one-year chart appears by default
- Click on "Analysis"
- Click on "Price Indicators"
- Choose "Bollinger Bands"

- The price performance graph for Amazon stock with an upper and lower red Bollinger band should appear.
- Make sure that the graph covers, at a minimum, the months of June through December 2003.

Questions

a.   On approximately July 7, 2003, what happened to the upper band (resistance level) of Amazon Stock?

b.   During the following nine days, how did the price of the stock behave?

c.   Is this in line with what a technician would predict?

d.   What strategy would a technician have undertaken on the seventh of July?

e.   On approximately November 18, 2003, what happened to the lower band (support level) of Amazon stock?

f.   During the following ten days, how did the price of the stock behave?

g.   Is this in line with what a technician would predict?

h.   What strategy would a technician have undertaken on the eighteenth of November?

TRADING ONLINE WITH OTIS

TRADING ONLINE WITH OTIS

Analyzing securities is as much an art as a science. Fundamental analysts study financial statements to assess the value of a stock. Technical analysts believe that fundamentals have already been incorporated into a stock and that it is the forces of supply and demand that play a major role in the direction of the stock. The art of charting price trends to determine buying and selling opportunities is their mainstay.

Exercises

1. Students can view some of the numerous types of charts that technical analysts watch to obtain information about a stock or the direction of the market. Choose a stock from your OTIS portfolio to analyze. After choosing the stock click on performance to see the market value of the stock. Now let's use some technical analysis to consider whether you would sell, hold, or purchase more shares of the stock by going to www.bigcharts.com.

   a. Click on quick chart and see if you can identify a positive or negative trend (recall positive trendlines are determined by high points and negative trendlines by low points—you can view trendlines on www.stockcharts.com under chart school).

   b. Click on interactive chart and select indicators. Then go to "moving averages" and request one simple moving average (SMA) and place a 50 in the box next to the bar to obtain a 50-day moving average. Try to identify past buying and selling points (when the SMA crosses the price line from above it is a sell signal and when the SMA crosses from below it is a buy signal). What is the SMA presently indicating?

   c. Redraw the chart with the relative strength indicator (RSI). The RSI compares recent gains to losses and uses a value between 1 and 100 to determine if the stock is overbought or oversold (see pages 380–381). Assess the RSI for your stock and see if it is in an overbought or oversold range.

2. Log on to www.stockcharts.com and go to "chart school." Click on point and figure charts to obtain a more comprehensive understanding of how these charts are used. Return to the home page and click on point and figure charts. Obtain a point and figure chart for your stock and print it out. Examine the chart to identify trends, points of resistance or support, and breakouts. What does this chart signal for the future?

3. Evaluate your investments based on performance, fundamental, and technical analysis. Re-position your portfolio by making the appropriate trades on the OTIS stock simulator.

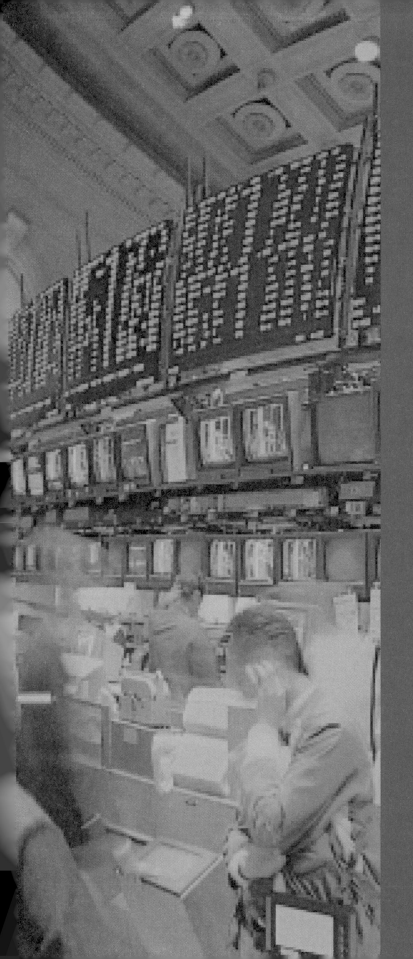

PART FOUR

INVESTING IN FIXED-INCOME SECURITIES

CHAPTER 10

FIXED-INCOME SECURITIES

How do you get to be a highly regarded passenger airline in less than 3 years—and profitable in 1? If you are JetBlue Airlines, you begin with lots of start-up funding to become the best-capitalized new airline in history. Then, you fly only new Airbus A320 aircraft, luxuriously outfitted with all-leather seats and up to 24 channels of DirecTV programming for every customer. Add low fares, focus on the highest-quality customer service, and you have the ingredients for success. By fall 2003, just 3½ years after its February 2000 inaugural flight, JetBlue was serving 23 airports nationwide and adding new cites and flights as demand for its services continued to grow.

JetBlue has more than 47 Airbuses in service and more on order, as well as orders for smaller Embraer 190 aircraft to be delivered starting in 2005. Acquiring and maintaining this airline fleet is expensive; the company's annual capital expenditures in recent years have been in the range of $450 million to $540 million. Making these and future capital expenditures for aircraft and facilities is critical to JetBlue's continued success.

Like most companies in capital-intensive industries, JetBlue funds its growth by using a combination of equity (it went public in April 2002) and long-term debt. Its June 30, 2003, balance sheet showed $758.30 million in long-term debt, up from about $291 million on December 31, 2001. The company's overall financial strength makes it possible to issue long-term debt at competitive rates. For example, its floating-rate equipment notes due through 2014 carried a 3.5% weighted average rate. As of June 30, 2003, JetBlue's long-term debt to equity ratio was 1.58, compared to the industry average of about 2.15, and its interest coverage was 6.44 times—a healthy cushion.

Before you invest in any fixed-income debt securities, whether issued by JetBlue or any other company, you'll want to consider credit quality, interest rates, maturity, and other factors. Chapters 10 and 11 will provide the background you need to make wise choices in the bond market.

Sources: "JetBlue Airways to Accelerate Fleet Growth with Two Additional Airbus Orders in 2003," Company Press Release, February 10, 2003, downloaded from www.jetblue.com; material at JetBlue Web site, www.jetblue.com; and "JetBlue Airways Corp., finance.yahoo.com.

Why Invest in Bonds?

LG 1

bonds
negotiable, publicly traded long-term debt securities, whereby the issuer agrees to pay a fixed amount of interest over a specified period of time and to repay a fixed amount of principal at maturity.

In contrast to stocks, *bonds are liabilities*—they are nothing more than publicly traded IOUs where the bondholders are actually *lending money* to the issuer. Technically, **bonds** can be described as negotiable, publicly traded, long-term debt securities. They are issued in various denominations, by a variety of borrowing organizations, including the U.S. Treasury, agencies of the U.S. government, state and local governments, and corporations. Bonds are often referred to as *fixed-income securities* because the debt-service obligations of the issuers are fixed. That is, the issuing organization agrees to pay a fixed amount of interest periodically and to repay a fixed amount of principal at maturity.

Like many other types of investment vehicles, bonds provide investors with two kinds of income: (1) They provide a generous amount of current income, and (2) given the right market environment, they can also be used to generate substantial amounts of capital gains. The current income, of course, is derived from the interest payments received over the life of the issue. Capital gains, in contrast, are earned whenever market interest rates fall. A basic trading rule in the bond market is that *interest rates and bond prices move in opposite directions*. When interest rates rise, bond prices fall. When rates drop, bond prices move up. Thus, it is possible to buy bonds at one price and to sell them later at a higher price. Of course, it is also possible to incur a capital loss, should market rates move against you. Taken together, the current income and capital gains earned from bonds can lead to attractive returns.

Bonds are also a versatile investment outlet. They can be used conservatively by those who seek high current income, or they can be used aggressively by those who go after capital gains. Although bonds have long been considered attractive investments for those seeking current income, it wasn't until the late 1960s and the advent of volatile interest rates that they also became recognized for their capital gains potential and as trading vehicles. Investors found that, given the relation of bond prices to interest rates, the number of profitable trading opportunities increased substantially as wider and more frequent swings in interest rates began to occur.

In addition, certain types of bonds can be used for tax shelter: Municipal obligations are perhaps the best known in this regard. But as we'll see later in this chapter, Treasury and certain federal agency issues also offer some tax advantages. Finally, because of the general high quality of many bond issues, they can also be used for the preservation and long-term accumulation of capital. For with quality issues, not only do investors have a high degree of assurance that they'll get their money back at maturity, but the stream of interest income is also highly dependable.

Putting Bond Market Performance in Perspective

The bond market is driven by interest rates. In fact, *the behavior of interest rates is the single most important force in the bond market*. Interest rates determine not only the amount of current income investors will receive but also the amount of capital gains (or losses) bondholders will incur. It's not surprising, therefore, that bond market participants follow interest rates closely and that bond market performance is often portrayed in terms of market interest rates.

FIGURE 10.1

The Behavior of Interest Rates Over Time—1961–2003

From an era of relative stability, bond interest rates rose dramatically and became highly volatile. The net result was that bond yields not only became competitive with the returns offered by other securities but also provided investors with attractive capital gains opportunities. (2003 yields through the second quarter, June 2003.)

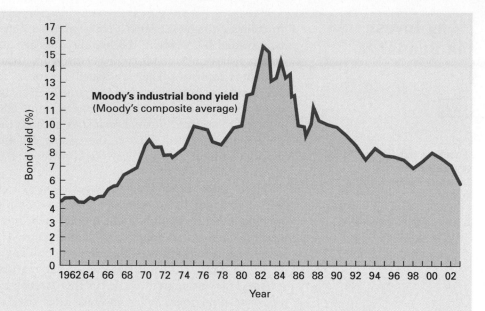

Figure 10.1 provides a look at bond interest rates over the 43-year period from 1961 through 2003. It shows that from a state of relative stability, interest rates rose steadily in the latter half of the 1960s. Over the course of the next 15 years, the rates paid on high-grade bonds nearly tripled. Indeed, interest rates rose from the 4% to 5% range in the early 1960s to over 16% by 1981. But then rates dropped sharply. By 1986 they were back to the single-digit range once again. Thus, after a protracted bear market, bonds abruptly reversed course, and the strongest bull market on record occurred from 1982 through early 1987. (The bond market is considered *bearish* when market interest rates are high or rising, *bullish* when rates are low or falling.) Even though interest rates did move back up for a short time in 1987–1988, they quickly retreated and by 2002–2003, had fallen to levels not seen in nearly 40 years (since the early 1960s). Indeed, by early 2003, long-term Treasury bonds were yielding *a little over 4%*.

Historical Returns As with stocks, *total returns* in the bond market are made up of both current income and capital gains (or losses). Tables 10.1 and 10.2 (on pages 417 and 418) provide an overview of (total) returns in the bond market—on an annual basis and for various investment horizons—over the 43-year period from 1961 through the second quarter of 2003. Take a look at Table 10.1, which lists *year-end market yields* and total *annual returns* for high-grade corporate bonds. Note how bond returns started to slip in 1965, as market yields began to climb. In fact, from 1965 to 1981, there were no fewer than 8 years when average returns were negative—which is highly unusual for the bond market. In contrast, look what happened over the 20-year period from 1982 through 2002, when rates were in a general state of decline: There were only 3 years of negative returns (in 1987, 1994, and 1999), whereas double-digit returns (of 10.7% to 43.8%) occurred in no fewer than 12 of the 20 years.

TABLE 10.1	Historical Annual Yields and Returns in the Bond Market, 1961–2003* (Yields and returns based on performance of high-grade corporate bonds)				
Year	Year-End Bond Yields*	Total Rates of Return**	Year	Year-End Bond Yields*	Total Rates of Return**
2003*	5.25%	10.61%	1981	14.98%	−0.96%
2002	6.48	11.95	1980	13.15	−2.62
2001	7.08	12.16	1979	10.87	−4.18
2000	7.62	9.18	1978	9.32	−0.07
1999	7.05	−5.76	1977	8.50	1.71
1998	6.53	9.16	1976	8.14	18.65
1997	7.16	13.46	1975	8.97	14.64
1996	7.43	2.20	1974	8.89	−3.06
1995	6.86	27.94	1973	7.79	1.14
1994	8.64	−5.76	1972	7.41	7.26
1993	7.31	13.64	1971	6.48	11.01
1992	8.34	9.34	1970	6.85	18.37
1991	8.58	20.98	1969	7.83	−8.09
1990	9.61	6.48	1968	6.62	2.57
1989	9.18	15.29	1967	6.30	−4.95
1988	9.81	10.49	1966	5.55	0.20
1987	10.33	−1.47	1965	4.79	−0.46
1986	9.02	18.71	1964	4.46	4.77
1985	10.63	27.99	1963	4.46	2.19
1984	12.05	16.39	1962	4.34	7.95
1983	12.76	4.70	1961	4.56	4.82
1982	11.55	43.80			

*Year-end bond yields are for Aa-rated corporate bonds; 2003 yields and returns through the second quarter (June) 2003.

**Total return figures are based on interest income as well as capital gains (or losses).

Sources: Annual yields derived from year-end Moody's and S&P bond yields on Aa- (AA-) rated corporate issues. Total return figures (for 1961–1985) from Ibbotson and Sinquefield, *Stocks, Bonds, Bills, and Inflation: Historical Returns.* Total returns for 1986 through the second quarter of 2003 obtained from *the Lehman Bros. Long-Term Corporate Bond* database.

Table 10.2 contains return performance over various holding periods of 5 to 43 years. These figures demonstrate the type of long-term returns possible from bonds and show that *average annual returns of around 8% to 10% on high-grade issues are not out of the question.* Although such performance may lag behind that of stocks (which it should, *over the long run,* in light of the reduced exposure to risk), it really isn't that bad, especially from the perspective of risk-adjusted rate of return. The big question facing bond investors, however, is what kind of returns will they be able to produce over the next 10 to 12 years? The 1980s and 1990s, through 2002–2003, were very good for bond investors. *But that market was driven by falling interest rates, which in turn produced hefty capital gains and outsize returns.* Whether market interest rates will (or even can) continue on that path is doubtful. Most market observers, in fact, caution against expecting abnormally high rates of return over the next decade or so.

Bonds Versus Stocks Although bonds definitely have their good points (low risk, high levels of current income, and desirable diversification properties), they also have a significant downside: their *comparative* returns. The fact is, *relative* to stocks, there's a big give-up in returns—which, of course, is the price you pay for the even bigger reduction in risk! But just because there's a deficit

TABLE 10.2   Holding Period Returns in the Bond Market: 1961–2003*

Holding Period	Average Annual Returns*	Cumulative Total Returns	Amount to Which a $10,000 Investment Will Grow Over the Holding Period
5(+) years: 1998–2003*	8.42%	55.98%	$15,598
5 years: 1993–97	9.70	58.88	15,888
10 years: 1993–2002	8.40	124.04	22,404
15 years: 1988–2002	9.72	301.98	40,198
25 years: 1978–2002	9.50	866.84	96,684
42(+) years: 1961–2003*	7.28	1,881.74	198,174
The 1990s: 1990–99	8.7%	130.2%	$23,020
The 1980s: 1980–89	13.0	240.2	34,022
The 1970s: 1970–79	6.2	83.1	18,305
The 1960s: 1960–69	1.7	18.1	11,809

*Average annual return figures are fully compounded returns and are based on interest income as well as capital gains (or losses). 2003 data through the second quarter (June).

Sources: Total return figures (1961–85) from Ibbotson and Sinquefield, *Stocks, Bonds, and Inflation: Historical Returns.* Total return data for 1986 through the second quarter of 2003 from *Lehman Bros. Long-Term Corporate Bond* series.

in long-term returns, doesn't mean that bonds are always the underachievers. Consider, for example, what's happened over the past 20 years or so: Starting in the 1980s, fixed-income securities held their own against stocks and continued to do so through the early 1990s, only to fall far behind for the rest of the decade. But then along came a nasty bear market in stocks (2000–2002) and the impact was nothing short of spectacular. The net result of all this can be seen in Figure 10.2, which tracks the comparative returns of stocks (via the S&P 500) and bonds (using the Lehman Bros. Long Bond Index) over the 1990s and through mid-2003. As can be seen, for the first half of the period, bonds held up very well, pretty much matching the returns in the stock market. But things started to change in 1995, as stock returns shot up, while bond returns began to level off. Thus, for the decade as a whole (1990–1999), bonds produced average annual returns of 8.7%, whereas stocks turned in average returns of 18.2%. That difference meant that a $10,000 investment in bonds would have led to a terminal value of some $23,000, compared to more than $53,000 for stocks.

That's a high opportunity cost to pay for holding bonds, and it prompted some market observers to question whether bonds should have *any place at all* in an investment portfolio. They reasoned that if interest rates had, in fact, bottomed out, then bonds wouldn't have much to offer, other than relatively low returns. But the market experts overlooked one tiny detail: It wasn't bonds that would prove to be the problem, it was stocks! As can be seen in Figure 10.2, the bear market had a devastating effect on stocks. So much so, in fact, that by mid-2003 the differential returns between stocks and bonds had all but evaporated. Indeed, over the period from January 1990 through June 2003, stocks outperformed bonds by only half a percentage point (10.2% versus 9.7%). The bottom line was a terminal value of slightly over $37,000 for stocks, compared to nearly $35,000 for bonds.

FIGURE 10.2 **Comparative Performance of Stocks and Bonds in the 1990s and Through Mid-2003**

This graph shows what happened to $10,000 invested in bonds over the 13½-year period from January 1990 to June 2003, versus the same amount invested in stocks. Clearly, while stocks held a commanding lead through early 2000, the ensuing bear market erased virtually all of that advantage. As a result, stocks and bonds ended the period at almost the same ending (or "terminal") values. (*Source: Morningstar Principia Pro for Mutual Funds, release date June 30, 2003.*)

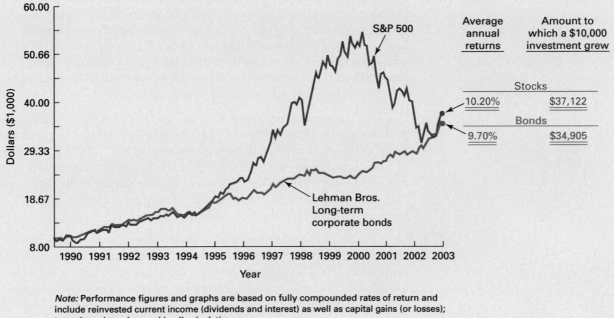

Note: Performance figures and graphs are based on fully compounded rates of return and include reinvested current income (dividends and interest) as well as capital gains (or losses); taxes have been ignored in all calculations.

Most investors would agree that's a very low price to pay for *the level of stability that bonds bring to a portfolio.* The fact is, bond returns are far more stable than stock returns, plus they possess *excellent portfolio diversification properties.* Thus, except for the most aggressive of investors, bonds have a lot to contribute from a portfolio perspective. Indeed, as a general rule, adding bonds to a portfolio will, *up to a point,* have a much greater impact on lowering risk than on return. Face it: you don't buy bonds for their high returns (except when you think interest rates are heading down). Rather, you buy them for their current income and/or for the stability they bring to your portfolio. And that's still true, even today.

Exposure to Risk

Like any other type of investment vehicle, fixed-income securities should be viewed in terms of their risk and return. Generally speaking, bonds are exposed to five major types of risks: interest rate risk, purchasing power risk, business/financial risk, liquidity risk, and call risk.

- **Interest Rate Risk.** Interest rate risk is the number one source of risk to fixed-income investors, *because it's the major cause of price volatility in* *the bond market.* For bonds, interest rate risk translates into market risk: The behavior of interest rates, in general, affects *all* bonds and cuts across *all* sectors of the market, even the U.S. Treasury market. When market interest rates rise, bond prices fall, and vice versa. And as interest rates become more volatile, so do bond prices.

- **Purchasing Power Risk.** Purchasing power risk accompanies inflation. During periods of mild inflation, bonds do pretty well, because their returns tend to outstrip inflation rates. Purchasing power risk really heats up, though, when inflation takes off, as it did in the late 1970s; when that happens, bond yields start to lag behind inflation rates. The reason: Even though market yields are rising with inflation, your return is locked in by the fixed coupon rate on your bond.

- **Business/Financial Risk.** This is basically the risk that the *issuer will default on interest and/or principal payments.* Also known as *credit risk*, business/financial risk has to do with the quality and financial integrity of the issuer. The stronger the issuer, the less business/financial risk there is to worry about. This risk doesn't even exist for some securities (e.g., U.S. Treasuries). For others, such as corporate and municipal bonds, it's a very important consideration.

- **Liquidity Risk.** Liquidity risk is the risk that a bond will be difficult to unload, at a reasonable price, if you want to sell it. In certain sectors of the market, this is a far bigger problem than investors realize. For even though the U.S. bond market is enormous, much of the activity occurs in the primary/new-issue market. Therefore, with the exception of the Treasury market and a good deal of the agency market, relatively little trading is done in the secondary markets, particularly with corporates and municipals. And where there's little trading, there's lots of liquidity risk. So, if liquidity is important to you, steer clear of thinly traded bonds.

- **Call Risk.** Call risk, or *prepayment risk*, is the risk that a bond will be "called" (retired) long before its scheduled maturity date. Issuers are often given the opportunity to prepay their bonds, and they do so by calling them in for prepayment. (We'll examine call features later in this chapter.) When issuers call their bonds, the bondholders end up getting cashed out of the deal and have to find another place for their investment funds—and there's the problem. Because bonds are nearly always called for prepayment after interest rates have taken a big fall, comparable investment vehicles just aren't available. Thus you have to replace a high-yielding bond with a much lower-yielding issue. From the bondholder's perspective, a called bond means not only a disruption in cash flow but also a sharply reduced rate of return.

The returns on bonds are, of course, related to risk—other things being equal, the more risk embedded in a bond, the greater the expected return. But with bonds, the amount and types of risks involved depends, in large part, on the type of bond (i.e., its issue characteristics). For example, as we'll see later in the chapter, there's more interest rate risk with a long bond than a short bond. In addition, it's sometimes difficult to compare the risk exposure of one bond to another, because the bonds typically have different issue characteristics. That is, one issue could have *more* interest rate and call risks, but *less* credit and liquidity risks than another issue. These different degrees of risk exposure often get buried in the net differential returns. We'll examine the various features that affect a bond's risk exposure, like maturity, coupon, call features, and agency ratings, as we work our way through this chapter.

IN REVIEW

CONCEPTS

10.1 What appeal do bonds hold for individual investors? Give several reasons why bonds make attractive investment outlets.

10.2 How would you describe the behavior of market interest rates and bond returns over the last 30–40 years? Do swings in market interest rates have any bearing on bond returns? Explain.

10.3 Identify and briefly describe the five types of risk to which bonds are exposed. What is the most important source of risk for bonds in general? Explain.

Essential Features of a Bond

A *bond* is a negotiable, long-term debt instrument that carries certain obligations (including the payment of interest and the repayment of principal) on the part of the issuer. Because bondholders are only lending money to the issuer, they are not entitled to any of the rights and privileges that go along with an ownership position. But bondholders, as well as bond issuers, do have a number of well-defined rights and privileges that together help define the essential features of a bond. We'll now take a look at some of these features. As you will see, when it comes to bonds, it's especially important to know what you're getting into, *for many seemingly insignificant features (like a bond's coupon or maturity) can have dramatic effects on its price behavior and investment return.* This is especially true in periods of low interest rates, because knowing what to buy and when to buy can mean the difference between earning a mediocre return and earning a highly competitive one.

Bond Interest and Principal

In the absence of any trading, a bond investor's return is limited to fixed interest and principal payments. That's because bonds involve *a fixed claim on the issuer's income* (as defined by the size of the periodic interest payments) and *a fixed claim on the assets of the issuer* (equal to the repayment of principal at maturity). As a rule, bonds pay interest every 6 months. There are exceptions, however; some issues carry interest payment intervals as short as a month, and a few as long as a year. The amount of interest due is a function of the **coupon**, which defines the annual interest income that will be paid by the issuer to the bondholder. For instance, a $1,000 bond with an 8% coupon pays $80 in interest annually—generally in the form of two $40 semiannual payments. The coupon return on a bond is often defined in terms of its **current yield**, which is a measure of the amount of annual interest income that a bond produces relative to its prevailing market price. It is found by dividing annual coupon income by the market price of the bond. For example, if an 8% bond

coupon
feature on a bond that defines the amount of annual interest income.

current yield
measure of the annual interest income a bond provides relative to its current market price.

is currently priced in the market at $875, then it would have a current yield of 9.14%: ($1,000 × .08)/$875 = $80/$875 = .0914. We'll look at this bond valuation measure in more detail in Chapter 11.

The **principal** amount of a bond, also known as an issue's *par value*, specifies the amount of capital that must be repaid at maturity. For example, there is $1,000 of principal in a $1,000 bond. Of course, debt securities regularly trade at market prices that differ from their principal (par) values. This occurs whenever an issue's coupon differs from the prevailing market rate of interest. That is, the price of the issue changes inversely with interest rates until its yield is compatible with the prevailing market yield. Such behavior explains why a 7% issue will carry a market price of only $825 in a 9% market. The drop in price from its par value of $1,000 is necessary to raise the yield on this bond from 7% to 9%. In essence, the new, higher yield is produced in part from annual coupons and in part from capital gains, as the price of the issue moves from $825 back to $1,000 at maturity.

Maturity Date

Unlike common stock, all debt securities have limited lives and will expire on a given date in the future, the issue's **maturity date.** Whereas interest payments are made semiannually over the life of the issue, principal is repaid only at maturity—or possibly before, in the case of callable issues. The maturity date on a bond is fixed (and never changes). It not only defines the life of a new issue but also denotes the amount of time remaining for older, outstanding bonds. Such a life span is known as an issue's *term to maturity*. For example, a new issue may come out as a 25-year bond, but 5 years later, it will have only 20 years remaining to maturity.

Two types of bonds can be distinguished on the basis of maturity: term and serial issues. A **term bond** has a single, fairly lengthy maturity date and is the most common type of issue. A **serial bond,** in contrast, has a series of different maturity dates, perhaps as many as 15 or 20, within a single issue. For example, a 20-year term bond issued in 2004 has a single maturity date of 2024, but that same issue as a serial bond might have 20 annual maturity dates that extend from 2004 through 2024. At each of these annual maturity dates, a certain portion of the issue would come due and be paid off. Maturity is also used to distinguish a *note* from a *bond*. That is, a debt security that's originally issued with a maturity of 2 to 10 years is known as a **note,** whereas a *bond* technically has an initial term to maturity of more than 10 years. In practice, notes are often issued with maturities of 5 to 7 years, whereas bonds normally carry maturities of 20 to 30 years or more.

Principles of Bond Price Behavior

The price of a bond is a function of its coupon, its maturity, and the movement of market interest rates. The relationship of bond prices to market interest rates is captured in Figure 10.3. Basically, the graph reinforces the *inverse relationship* that exists between bond prices and market rates: *Lower* rates lead to *higher* bond prices.

Figure 10.3 also shows the difference between premium and discount bonds. A **premium bond** is one that sells for more than its par value. A premium results whenever market interest rates drop below the bond's coupon rate.

principal
on a bond, the amount of capital that must be repaid at maturity.

maturity date
the date on which a bond matures and the principal must be repaid.

term bond
a bond that has a single, fairly lengthy maturity date.

serial bond
a bond that has a series of different maturity dates.

note
a debt security originally issued with a maturity of from 2 to 10 years.

premium bond
a bond with a market value in excess of par; occurs when interest rates drop below the coupon rate.

FIGURE 10.3 **The Price Behavior of a Bond**

A bond will sell at its par value so long as the prevailing market interest rate remains the same as the bond's coupon—in this case, 10%. However, when the market rates drop, bond prices move up. When rates rise, bond prices move down. As a bond approaches its maturity, the price of the issue moves toward its par value, regardless of the level of prevailing interest rates.

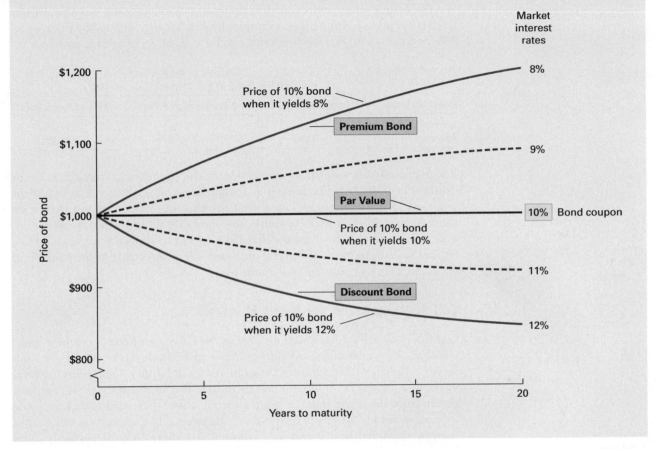

discount bond
a bond with a market value lower than par; occurs when market rates are greater than the coupon rate.

A **discount bond,** in contrast, sells for less than par. The discount is the result of market rates being greater than the issue's coupon rate. Thus, the 10% bond in Figure 10.3 trades at a premium when market rates are at 8%, but at a discount when rates are at 12%.

When a bond is first issued, it is usually sold to the public at a price that equals or is very close to its par value. Likewise, when the bond matures—some 15, 20, or 30 years later—it will once again be priced at its par value. What happens to the price of the bond in between is of considerable interest to most bond investors. And in this regard, we know that the extent to which bond prices move depends not only on the *direction* of change in interest rates but also on the *magnitude* of such change: The greater the moves in interest rates, the greater the swings in bond prices.

However, bond price volatility also varies according to an issue's coupon and maturity. That is, bonds with *lower coupons* and/or *longer maturities* have *lots of price volatility* and are more responsive to changes in market interest rates. (Note in Figure 10.3 that for a given change in interest rates—e.g., from 10% to 8%—the largest change in price occurs when the bond has the greatest number of years to maturity.) Therefore, if a *decline* in interest rates is anticipated, you should seek lower coupons and longer maturities (to maximize capital gains). When interest rates move *up*, you should do just the opposite: seek high coupons with short maturities. This choice will minimize price variation and act to preserve as much capital as possible.

Actually, of the two variables, the *maturity* of an issue has the greater impact on price volatility. For example, look what happens to the price of an 8% bond when market interest rates rise by 1, 2, or 3 percentage points:

	Change in the Price of an 8% Bond When Interest Rates Rise by:		
Bond Maturity	1 Percentage Point	2 Percentage Points	3 Percentage Points
5 years	−4.0%	−7.7%	−11.2%
25 years	−9.9%	−18.2%	−25.3%

For purposes of this illustration, we assume the changes in interest rate occur "instantaneously," so the maturities remain fixed, at 5 or 25 years. Given the computed price changes, it's clear that the shorter (5-year) bond offers a lot more price stability. Such behavior is universal with all fixed-income securities, and is very important. It means that if you want to reduce your exposure to capital loss or, more to the point, to lower the price volatility in your bond holdings, then just *shorten your maturities*.

Call Features—Let the Buyer Beware!

Consider the following situation: You've just made an investment in a high-yielding, 25-year bond. Now all you have to do is sit back and let the cash flow in, right? Well, perhaps. Certainly, that will happen for the first several years. But, if market interest rates drop, it's also likely that you'll receive a notice from the issuer that the bond is being *called*. This means that the issue is being retired before its maturity date. There's really nothing you can do but turn in the bond and invest your money elsewhere. It's all perfectly legal because every bond is issued with a **call feature**, which stipulates whether and under what conditions a bond can be called in for retirement prior to maturity.

call feature
feature that specifies whether and under what conditions the issuer can retire a bond prior to maturity.

Basically, there are three types of call features:

1. A bond can be *freely callable*, which means the issuer can prematurely retire the bond at any time.
2. A bond can be *noncallable*, which means the issuer is prohibited from retiring the bond prior to maturity.
3. The issue could carry a *deferred call*, which means the issue cannot be called until after a certain length of time has passed from the date of issue. In essence, the issue is noncallable during the deferment period and then becomes freely callable thereafter.

Obviously, in our illustration above, either the high-yielding bond was issued as freely callable or it became freely callable with the end of its call deferment period.

Call features are placed on bonds *for the benefit of the issuers*. They're used most often to replace an issue with one that carries a lower coupon, and the issuer benefits by the reduction in annual interest cost. Thus, when market interest rates undergo a sharp decline, bond issuers retire their high-yielding bonds (by calling them in) and replace them with lower-yielding obligations. *The net result is that the investor is left with a much lower rate of return than anticipated.*

In a half-hearted attempt to compensate investors who find their bonds called out from under them, a **call premium** is tacked onto a bond and paid to investors, along with the issue's par value, when the bond is called. The sum of the par value plus call premium represents the issue's **call price.** This is the amount the issuer must pay to retire the bond prematurely. As a general rule, call premiums usually equal about 8 to 12 months' interest at the earliest date of call and then become progressively smaller as the issue nears maturity. Using this rule, the initial call price of a 9% bond could be as high as $1,090, where $90 represents the call premium.

In addition to call features, some bonds may carry **refunding provisions.** These are much like call features except that they prohibit just one thing: the premature retirement of an issue from the proceeds of a lower-coupon bond. For example, a bond could come out as freely callable but *nonrefundable* for 5 years. In this case, the bond would probably be sold by brokers as a *deferred refunding issue,* with little or nothing said about its call feature. The distinction is important, however, as it means that a nonrefunding or deferred refunding issue *can still be called and prematurely retired for any reason other than refunding.* Thus, an investor could face a call on a high-yielding nonrefundable issue so long as the issuer has the cash to retire the bond prematurely.

Sinking Funds

Another provision that's important to investors is the **sinking fund,** which stipulates how a bond will be paid off over time. This provision applies only to term bonds, of course, because serial issues already have a predetermined method of repayment. Not all (term) bonds have sinking-fund requirements, but for those that do, a sinking fund specifies the annual repayment schedule that will be used to pay off the issue. It indicates how much principal will be retired each year. Sinking-fund requirements generally begin 1 to 5 years after the date of issue and continue annually thereafter until all or most of the issue is paid off. Any amount not repaid (which might equal 10% to 25% of the issue) would then be retired with a single "balloon" payment at maturity. Unlike a call or refunding provision, the issuer generally does not have to pay a call premium with sinking-fund calls. Instead, the bonds are normally called at par for sinking-fund purposes.

There's another difference between sinking-fund provisions and call or refunding features. That is, whereas a call or refunding provision gives the issuer the *right* to retire a bond prematurely, a sinking-fund provision *obligates* the issuer to pay off the bond systematically over time. The issuer has no choice. It must make sinking-fund payments in a prompt and timely fashion or run the risk of being in default.

Secured or Unsecured Debt

A single issuer may have a number of different bonds outstanding at any given point in time. In addition to coupon and maturity, one bond can be differentiated from another by the type of collateral behind the issue. Issues can be either junior or senior. **Senior bonds** are secured obligations, which are backed

call premium
the amount added to a bond's par value and paid to investors when a bond is retired prematurely.

call price
the price the issuer must pay to retire a bond prematurely; equal to par value plus the call premium.

refunding provisions
provisions that prohibit the premature retirement of an issue from the proceeds of a lower-coupon refunding bond.

sinking fund
a provision that stipulates the amount of principal that will be retired annually over the life of a bond.

senior bonds
secured debt obligations, backed by a legal claim on specific property of the issuer.

mortgage bonds
senior bonds secured by real estate.

collateral trust bonds
senior bonds backed by securities owned by the issuer but held in trust by a third party.

equipment trust certificates
senior bonds secured by specific pieces of equipment; popular with transportation companies such as airlines.

first and refunding bonds
bonds secured in part with both first and second mortgages.

junior bonds
debt obligations backed only by the promise of the issuer to pay interest and principal on a timely basis.

debenture
an unsecured (junior) bond.

subordinated debentures
unsecured bonds whose claim is secondary to other debentures.

income bonds
unsecured bonds requiring that interest be paid only after a specified amount of income is earned.

by a legal claim on some specific property of the issuer. Such issues would include **mortgage bonds,** which are secured by real estate; **collateral trust bonds,** which are backed by financial assets owned by the issuer but held in trust by a third party; **equipment trust certificates,** which are secured by specific pieces of equipment (e.g., boxcars and airplanes) and are popular with railroads and airlines; and **first and refunding bonds,** which are basically a combination of first mortgage and junior lien bonds (i.e., the bonds are secured in part by a first mortgage on some of the issuer's property and in part by second or third mortgages on other properties). (Note that first and refunding bonds are *less secure* than, and should *not* be confused with, straight first-mortgage bonds.)

Junior bonds, on the other hand, are backed only by the promise of the issuer to pay interest and principal on a timely basis. There are several classes of unsecured bonds, the most popular of which is known as a **debenture.** For example, a major company, like Hewlett-Packard, could issue, say, $500 million worth of 20-year debenture bonds. Being a debenture, the bond would be totally unsecured, meaning there is no collateral backing up the obligation, other than the good name of the issuer. In the final analysis, it's the quality of the issuer that matters. And for that reason, highly regarded firms have no trouble selling *billion-dollar issues*, and at highly competitive rates. It's done all the time.

Subordinated debentures can also be found in the market. These issues have a claim on income secondary to other debenture bonds. **Income bonds,** the most junior of all bonds, are unsecured debts requiring that interest be paid only after a certain amount of income is earned. With these bonds, there is no legally binding requirement to meet interest payments on a timely or regular basis so long as a specified amount of income has not been earned. These issues are similar in many respects to *revenue bonds* found in the municipal market.

IN REVIEW

CONCEPTS

10.4 Can issue characteristics (such as coupon and call features) affect the yield and price behavior of bonds? Explain.

10.5 What is the difference between a *call feature* and a *sinking-fund provision?* Briefly describe the three different types of call features. Can a bond be freely callable but nonrefundable?

10.6 What is the difference between a *premium bond* and a *discount bond?* What three attributes are most important in determining an issue's price volatility?

The Market for Debt Securities

LG 4   LG 5

Thus far, our discussion has dealt with basic bond features. We now shift attention to a review of the market in which these securities are traded. To begin with, the bond market is chiefly over-the-counter in nature, as listed bonds represent only a small portion of total outstanding obligations. In addition, this market is far more stable than the stock market. Indeed, although interest rates—and therefore bond prices—do move up and down over time, when bond price activity is measured on a daily basis, it is *remarkably stable.*

There are two other things that stand out about the bond market: It's big, and it has been growing rapidly. From a $250 billion market in 1950, it has grown to the point where, in 2002, the amount of bonds outstanding in this country exceeded *$17 trillion!* That makes the bond market about 75% bigger than the U.S. stock market.

Here's what the U.S. bond market looked like in 2002:

	Amount Outstanding ($ in trillions)
U.S. Treasury securities	$2.2
Agency securities	2.1
Municipal bonds	1.5
Corporate bonds	5.2
Mortgage-backed securities	2.9
Foreign issues and Eurodollar bonds	3.3
Total	$17.2

Source: "Size & Structure of the World Bond Market: 2002," Merrill Lynch.

The growth in this market has also been remarkable, as it has more than doubled in size since 1992. That translates into a compound rate of growth of nearly 9% a year. Domestic issues alone (*excluding* foreign issues and Eurodollar bonds) account for $13.9 trillion, or 81% of the total U.S. market. Let's now take a look at the various segments of the market.

Major Market Segments

There are bonds available in today's market to meet almost any investment objective and to suit just about any type of investor. As a matter of convenience, the bond market is normally separated into four major segments, according to type of issuer: Treasury, agency, municipal, and corporate. As we shall see, each sector has developed its own features, as well as its own trading characteristics.

Treasury Bonds "Treasuries" (or "governments," as they are sometimes called) are a dominant force in the fixed-income market. If not the most popular type of bond, they certainly are the best known. In addition to T-bills (a popular short-term debt security), the U.S. Treasury issues notes and bonds. It also issues *inflation-indexed securities*, which are the newest type of Treasury debt, introduced in January 1997. All Treasury obligations are of the highest quality because they are all backed by the "full faith and credit" of the U.S. government. This backing, along with their liquidity, makes them very popular with individual and institutional investors both here and abroad. Indeed, Treasury securities are traded in all the major markets of the world, from New York to London to Sydney and Tokyo.

Treasury notes are issued with maturities of 2, 3, 5, and 10 years, whereas **Treasury bonds** carry 20- and 30-year maturities. (Note that while the Treasury is authorized to issue these securities, *the last time it issued 20-year bonds was in January 1986 and the last 30-year bond was issued in August 2001.* Even so, many of these bonds are still outstanding and actively traded in the secondary market.) The Treasury issues its securities at regularly scheduled auctions, the results of which are widely reported by the financial media (see Figure 10.4 on page 428). The Treasury establishes the initial yields and coupons on the securities it issues in this auction process.

Treasury notes
U.S. Treasury debt securities that are issued with maturities of 2 to 10 years or less.

Treasury bonds
U.S. Treasury securities that are issued with 20- and 30-year maturities.

FIGURE 10.4	**The Reported Results of a Treasury Note Auction**

Treasury auctions are closely followed by the financial media; here, the results of a 3-year Treasury note auction are reported. These auctions are highly competitive. The number of bids submitted generally far exceeds the size of the issue, so the spread between the highest and lowest bids is quite small—sometimes as small at 2 basis points, or 2/100 of 1%. (*Source:* Department of the Treasury—Bureau of Public Debt, and *Wall Street Journal*, August 6, 2003.)

AUCTION RESULTS

Here are the results of yesterday's Treasury auction of 3-year notes. All bids are awarded at a single price at the market-clearing yield. Rates are determined by the difference between that price and the face value.

3-YEAR NOTES

Applications	$31,575,013,000 ⎤ The amount of bids submitted.
Accepted bids	$24,000,053,000 ⎤ Size of the issue—the dollar amount of accepted bids.
Bids at market-clearing yield accepted	65.84%
Accepted noncompetitively	$278,013,000 ⎤ The amount of noncompetitive bids submitted (and accepted).
" Foreign noncompetitively	$0
Auction price (Rate)	99.865 (2.422%) ⎤ The average price and yield (rate) on the issue.
Interest rate	2.375%
CUSIP number	912828BF6 ⎤ The coupon that the issue will carry, which is set after the auction.

The notes are dated August 15, 2003 and mature August 15, 2006.

All Treasury notes (and bonds) are sold in $1,000 denominations. Interest income from these securities is subject to normal federal income tax but *is exempt from state and local taxes*. The Treasury today issues only *noncallable* securities. The last time the U.S. Treasury issued callable debt was in 1984. Until then, most Treasury bonds carried long-term call deferments, under which the bonds became freely callable during the last 5 years of the issue's life. There are still some deferred-call Treasuries outstanding; they're easy to identify because the deferred-call features are a specific part of the bond listing system. For example, a 10% issue of 2005–2010 signifies that this Treasury bond has a maturity date of 2010 and a deferred-call feature that extends through 2005.

Inflation-Protection Securities As noted above, the newest form of Treasury security is the **Treasury inflation-indexed obligation.** Also known as **TIPS,** which stands for "Treasury inflation-protection securities," they are issued as notes (with 10-year maturities) and, until 2001, as bonds (with 30-year maturities). They offer investors the opportunity to stay ahead of inflation by periodically adjusting their returns for any inflation that has occurred. That is, if inflation is running at an annual rate of, say, 3%, then at the end of the year, the par (maturity) value of the bond will increase by 3%. (Actually, the adjustments to par value are done every 6 months.) Thus the par value of a

Treasury inflation-indexed obligations (TIPS)
a type of Treasury security that provides protection against inflation by adjusting investor returns for the annual rate of inflation.

INVESTING IN ACTION

SOME TIPS ON TIPS

Bondholders look at inflation like Superman looks at kryptonite. Superman weakens when faced with the dreaded substance and would die if exposed to it for long. Bondholders weaken when inflation heats up because it causes bond prices to buckle and fixed payments to lose their purchasing power. Some people have the mistaken impression that they can't lose money investing in Treasury bonds. But they can because bond prices fall in an inflationary environment. So that investors can buy its bonds without fearing inflation, in 1997 Uncle Sam created TIPS, Treasury inflation-protected securities.

Here's how TIPS work: The government issues a 10-year bond with a $1,000 face value that pays, say, 3% interest—and that rate stays fixed for the life of the issue. But if the consumer price index rises, so does the face amount of the bond. For example, because the CPI rose 2.4% in 2002, the new face amount was adjusted up to $1,000 × 1.024 = $1,024. Therefore, in 2003, the annual interest payment was $30.72 (3% of $1,024). When the TIPS mature in 10 years, the investor gets the inflation-adjusted face value at that time, which could be as much as $2,000 if inflation really takes off. A lot can change over a decade, but inflation looks pretty tame these days. As one professional investor puts it, buying TIPS now is like buying flood insurance during a drought. TIPS also protect you if deflation occurs. The bond's value will not fall below its initial face value (of $1,000).

Unlike the case with conventional fixed-income securities, the investor doesn't have to worry about the Treasury bond's value plummeting if inflation heats up. Take a look at what happens to a conventional Treasury bond if inflation begins to rise sharply. If the bond's coupon is, say, 5%, investors get 5% per year, or $50, no matter what happens to the level of prices. In 10 years, that $1,000 principal will certainly have less purchasing power than it does today. It might be able to buy just $700 worth of goods. In addition, rising inflation generally means rising interest rates. In the marketplace, conventional bond prices fall when interest rates

rise. Therefore, an investor who wishes to sell a conventional bond prior to maturity is likely to take a loss if interest rates are higher than when the bond was purchased.

TIPS protect investors from such erosion in bond prices. TIPS are not so great, however, if inflation stays dormant, because the investors are getting only 3% on their money. (In fact, the coupon for the July 2003 10 year TIPS was just 1⅞%, compared to 4.25% for a regular 10 year Treasury note issued in August 2003.)

There's one other downside to TIPS: taxes. Investors have to pay a tax on the increasing face value of their bonds—$34 in the first year in the foregoing example. That may not seem like much, but the government doesn't actually pay out the increase in the bond's face value until maturity. Thus you end up paying taxes on income you've earned but don't have in hand. For that reason, TIPS probably make the most sense for individual retirement accounts (IRAs) and other tax-deferred retirement accounts. You can buy TIPS directly from the U.S. Treasury using Treasury Direct or from a broker. Several mutual fund companies now offer funds that buy only TIPS.

TIPS are also a good idea for investors who want to allocate a portion of their assets to income-generating securities and don't want to worry that inflation will erode their value. But the tradeoff for that protection is significant: loss of about half the income.

CRITICAL THINKING QUESTIONS Why would investors be interested in TIPS? Why would the U.S. Treasury issue such a security? What are the advantages and disadvantages of this security from the investor's point of view?

Sources: Robert Barker, "A Bond Anybody Can Love," *Business Week*, June 19, 2000, p. 260; Iris L. Blasi and Frank Byrt, "TIPS Are Finally Getting Respect," The *Wall Street Journal*, July 11, 2002, p. D.9; James Grant, "An Inflation Tip," *Forbes*, October 30, 2000, p. 402; and "Treasury Inflation Protected Securities: What You Should Know," *InvestinginBonds.com*, downloaded from www.investinginbonds.com, accessed September 30, 2003.

$1,000 bond will grow to $1,030 at the end of the first year. If the 3% inflation rate continues for the second year, the par value will once again increase, this time from $1,030 to $1,061 ($1,030 × 1.03). Unfortunately, the coupons on these securities are set very low, because they're meant to provide investors with so-called *real (inflation-adjusted) returns.* Thus one of these bonds might carry a coupon of only 3.5% at a time when regular T-bonds are paying, say, 6.5% or 7%. But there's an advantage even to this: *Even though the coupon rates are fixed for the life of the issue, the actual size of the coupon payment will increase over time as the par value on the bond goes up.* For investors who are concerned about inflation protection, these securities may be just the ticket. But as the accompanying *Investing in Action* box on page 427 suggests, TIPS are a lot more complex than the traditional Treasury bond.

agency bonds
debt securities issued by various agencies and organizations of the U.S. government.

Agency Bonds **Agency bonds** are debt securities issued by various agencies and organizations of the U.S. government, such as the Federal Home Loan Bank, the Federal Farm Credit Systems, the Small Business Administration, the Student Loan Marketing Association, and the Federal National Mortgage Association. Though these securities are the closest things to Treasuries, they are not obligations of the U.S. Treasury and technically should not be considered the same as Treasury bonds. Even so, *they are very high-quality securities that have almost no risk of default.* In spite of the similar default risk exposure, however, these securities usually provide yields that are comfortably above the market rates for Treasuries. Thus they offer investors a way to increase returns with little or no real difference in risk.

There are basically two types of agency issues: government-sponsored and federal agencies. Although there are only six government-sponsored organizations, the number of federal agencies exceeds two dozen. To overcome some of the problems in the marketing of many relatively small federal agency securities, Congress established the Federal Financing Bank to consolidate the financing activities of all federal agencies. (As a rule, the generic term *agency* is used to denote both government-sponsored and federal agency obligations.)

Selected characteristics of some of the more popular agency bonds are presented in Table 10.3. As the list of issuers shows, most of the government agencies that exist today were created to support either agriculture or housing. Although agency issues are not direct liabilities of the U.S. government, a few of them actually do carry government guarantees and therefore represent the full faith and credit of the U.S. Treasury. But even those issues that do not carry such guarantees are highly regarded in the marketplace. Because they are all viewed as *moral obligations* of the U.S. government, it's highly unlikely that Congress would ever allow one of them to default. Also, like Treasury securities, agency issues are normally noncallable or carry lengthy call deferment features. One final point: Since 1986 *all new agency (and Treasury) securities* have been issued in *book entry form.* This means that no certificate of ownership is issued to the buyer of the bonds. Rather, the buyer receives a "confirmation" of the transaction, and his or her name is entered in a computerized logbook, where it remains as long as the security is owned.

H OT L I N E
To access a database of corporate, agency, and municipal bond offerings, go to
www.investinginbonds.com

municipal bonds
debt securities issued by states, counties, cities, and other political subdivisions; most of these bonds are tax-exempt (free of federal income tax on interest income).

Municipal Bonds **Municipal bonds** are the issues of states, counties, cities, and other political subdivisions (such as school districts and water and sewer districts). This is a $1.5 trillion market today, and it's the only segment of the

TABLE 10.3 Characteristics of Some Popular Agency Issues

Type of Issue	Minimum Denomination	Initial Maturity	Tax Status*		
			Federal	State	Local
Federal Farm Credit System	$ 1,000	13 months to 15 years	T	E	E
Federal Home Loan Bank	10,000	1 to 20 years	T	E	E
Federal Land Banks	1,000	1 to 10 years	T	E	E
Farmers Home Administration	25,000	1 to 25 years	T	T	T
Federal Housing Administration	50,000	1 to 40 years	T	T	T
Federal Home Loan Mortgage Corp.** ("Freddie Mac")	25,000	18 to 30 years	T	T	T
Federal National Mortgage Association** ("Fannie Mae")	25,000	1 to 30 years	T	T	T
Government National Mortgage Association** (GNMA—"Ginnie Mae")	25,000	12 to 40 years	T	T	T
Student Loan Marketing Association	10,000	3 to 10 years	T	E	E
Tennessee Valley Authority (TVA)	1,000	5 to 50 years	T	E	E
U.S. Postal Service	10,000	25 years	T	E	E
Federal Financing Corp.	1,000	1 to 20 years	T	E	E

*T = taxable; E = tax-exempt.
**Mortgage-backed securities.

HOT LINKS

For more information on municipal bonds, go to investinginbonds.com. Scroll down the left and click on [MuniBonds] under "Investors Guide".

www.investinginbonds.com/
muni_bond_prices.htm

general obligation bonds
municipal bonds backed by the full faith, credit, and taxing power of the issuer.

revenue bonds
municipal bonds that require payment of principal and interest only if sufficient revenue is generated by the issuer.

municipal bond guarantees
guarantees from a party other than the issuer that principal and interest payments will be made in a prompt and timely manner.

bond market where the individual investor plays a major role: About 40% of all municipal bonds are directly held by individuals (which excludes the 36% that are held by mutual funds). These bonds are often issued as *serial obligations*, which means that the issue is broken into a series of smaller bonds, each with its own maturity date and coupon.

Municipal bonds ("munis") are brought to the market as either general obligation or revenue bonds. **General obligation bonds** are backed by the full faith, credit, and taxing power of the issuer. **Revenue bonds**, in contrast, are serviced by the income generated from specific income-producing projects (e.g., toll roads). Although general obligations used to dominate the municipal market, the vast majority of munis today come out as revenue bonds (accounting for about 70% to 75% of the new-issue volume).

The distinction between a general obligation bond and a revenue bond is important for a bondholder, because the issuer of a revenue bond is obligated to pay principal and interest *only if a sufficient level of revenue is generated*. If the funds aren't there, the issuer does not have to make payment on the bond. General obligation bonds, however, are required to be serviced in a prompt and timely fashion irrespective of the level of tax income generated by the municipality. Obviously, revenue bonds involve a lot more risk than general obligations, and because of that, they provide higher yields. Regardless of the type, municipal bonds are customarily issued in $5,000 denominations.

A somewhat unusual aspect of municipal bonds is the widespread use of **municipal bond guarantees**. With these guarantees, a party other than the issuer assures the bondholder that principal and interest payments will be made in a prompt and timely manner. The third party, in essence, provides an additional source of collateral in the form of insurance, placed on the bond at the date of issue, that is nonrevocable over the life of the obligation. As a result of the guarantee, bond quality is improved. The three principal insurers are the Municipal Bond Investors Assurance Corporation (MBIA), the American Municipal Bond Assurance Corporation (AMBAC), and the Financial Guaranty Insurance Company (FGIC). These guarantors will normally insure any general obligation or revenue bond as long as it carries an S&P rating of triple-B or better. (We'll explore bond ratings later in this chapter.) Municipal bond insurance results in higher ratings (usually triple-A) and improved liquidity for these bonds, which are generally more actively traded in the secondary markets. Insured bonds are especially common in the revenue market, and insurance markedly boosts their attractiveness. Whereas an uninsured revenue bond lacks certainty of payment, a guaranteed issue is very much like a general obligation bond because the investor knows that principal and interest payments will be made on time.

Tax Advantages Without a doubt, the thing that makes municipal securities unique is the fact that, in most cases, their interest income is exempt from federal income taxes. That's why these issues are known as *tax-free*, or *tax-exempt*, bonds. Normally, the obligations are also exempt from state and local taxes *in the state in which they were issued*. For example, a California issue is free of California tax if the bondholder lives in California, but its interest income is subject to state tax if the investor resides in Arizona. Note that *capital gains on municipal bonds are not exempt from taxes*.

Individual investors are the biggest buyers of municipal bonds, and tax-free yield is certainly a major draw. Table 10.4 shows what a taxable bond would have to yield to equal the net yield of a tax-free bond. *It demonstrates how the yield attractiveness of municipals varies with an investor's income level*. Clearly, the higher the individual's tax bracket, the more attractive municipal bonds become. Generally speaking, an investor has to be in one of the higher federal tax brackets (28% to 35%) before municipal bonds offer yields that are competitive with fully taxable issues. This is so because municipal yields are (almost always) lower than those available from fully taxable issues (such as corporates). So, unless the tax effect is sufficient to raise the yield on a municipal to a figure that equals or surpasses taxable rates, it doesn't make much sense to buy municipal bonds.

Taxable Equivalent Yields We can determine the level of return a fully taxable bond would have to provide in order to match the after-tax return of a lower-yielding, tax-free issue by computing what is known as a municipal's **taxable equivalent yield**. Indeed, use of the taxable equivalent yield is standard convention in the market, as it facilitates comparing the return on a given municipal bond to any number of fully taxable issues. This measure can be calculated according to the following simple formula:

taxable equivalent yield
the return a fully taxable bond would have to provide to match the after-tax return of a lower-yielding, tax-free municipal bond.

Equation 10.1

$$\text{Taxable equivalent yield} = \frac{\text{Yield on municipal bond}}{1 - \text{Federal tax rate}}$$

For example, if a municipal offered a yield of 6.5%, then an individual in the 35% tax bracket would have to find a fully taxable bond with a yield of 10.0% (i.e., 6.5%/0.65 = 10.0%) to reap the same after-tax returns as the municipal.

Note, however, that Equation 10.1 considers *federal taxes only*. As a result, the computed taxable equivalent yield applies only to certain situations:

TABLE 10.4 Taxable Equivalent Yields for Various Tax-Exempt Returns

| Taxable Income* | | | Tax-Free Yield | | | | | |
Joint Returns ($000)	Individual Returns ($000)	Federal Tax Bracket	5%	6%	7%	8%	9%	10%
$0–$14.0	$0–$7.0	10%	5.55%	6.66%	7.77%	8.88%	10.00%	11.11%
$14.0–$56.8	$7.0–$28.4	15	5.88	7.06	8.24	9.41	10.59	11.76
$56.8–$114.6	$28.4–$68.8	25	6.67	8.00	9.33	10.67	12.00	13.33
$114.6–$174.7	$68.8–$143.5	28	6.94	8.33	9.72	11.11	12.50	13.89
$174.7–$311.9	$143.5–$311.9	33	7.46	8.96	10.45	11.94	13.43	14.92
$311.9 and above	$311.9 and above	35	7.69	9.23	10.77	12.31	13.85	15.38

*Taxable income and federal tax rates effective January 1, 2003.

(1) to states that have no state income tax, (2) to situations where the investor is looking at an out-of-state bond (which would be taxable by the investor's state of residence), or (3) where the investor is comparing a municipal bond to a Treasury (or agency) bond—in which case *both* the Treasury and the municipal bonds are free from state income tax. Under any of these conditions, the only tax that's relevant is federal income tax, so using Equation 10.1 is appropriate. But what if the investor is comparing an in-state bond to, say, a corporate bond? In this case, the in-state bond would be free from both federal and state taxes, but the corporate bond would not. As a result, Equation 10.1 could not be used. Instead, the investor should use a form of the equivalent yield formula that considers *both* federal and state income taxes:

Equation 10.2

$$\frac{\text{Taxable equivalent yield for}}{\text{both federal and state taxes}} = \frac{\text{Municipal bond yield}}{1 - \left[\frac{\text{Federal}}{\text{tax rate}} + \frac{\text{State}}{\text{tax rate}}\left(1 - \frac{\text{Federal}}{\text{tax rate}}\right)\right]}$$

When both federal and state taxes are included in the calculations, the net effect is to *increase* the taxable equivalent yield. Of course, the size of the increase depends on the level of state income taxes. In a high-tax state like California, for example, the impact can be substantial. Return to the 6.5% municipal bond introduced above. If a California resident in the maximum federal and state tax brackets (35% and 11%, respectively) were considering a corporate issue, she would have to get a yield of 11.25% on the corporate to match the 6.5% yield on the California bond:

$$\frac{\text{Taxable equivalent yield for}}{\text{both federal and state taxes}} = \frac{6.5}{1 - [0.35 + 0.11(1 - 0.35)]}$$

$$= \frac{6.5}{1 - [0.35 + 0.072]}$$

$$= \underline{11.25\%}$$

This yield compares to a taxable equivalent yield of 10.0% when only federal taxes were included in the calculation. That's a difference of more than one full percentage point—certainly *not* an insignificant amount.

Corporate Bonds Corporations are the major nongovernmental issuers of bonds. The market for corporate bonds is customarily subdivided into four segments: *industrials* (the most diverse of the groups), *public utilities* (the dominant group in terms of volume of new issues), *rail and transportation bonds*, and *financial issues* (e.g., banks, finance companies). Not only is there a full range of bond qualities available in the corporate market, but there is also a wide assortment of different types of bonds. These range from first-mortgage obligations to convertible bonds (which we'll examine in Chapter 12), debentures, subordinated debentures, senior subordinated issues, capital notes (a type of unsecured debt issued by banks and other financial institutions), and income bonds. Interest on corporate bonds is paid semiannually, and sinking funds are fairly common. The bonds usually come in $1,000 denominations and are issued on a term basis with a single maturity date. Maturities usually range from 25 to 40 years or more. Many corporates, especially the longer ones, carry call deferment provisions that prohibit prepayment for the first 5 to 10 years. Corporate issues are popular with individuals because of their relatively attractive yields.

Most corporates fit the general description above. One that does not is the *equipment trust certificate*, a security issued by railroads, airlines, and other transportation concerns. The proceeds from equipment trust certificates are used to purchase equipment (e.g., jumbo jets and railroad engines) that serves as the collateral for the issue. These bonds are usually issued in serial form and carry uniform annual installments throughout. They normally carry maturities that range from 1 year to a maximum of 15 to 17 years. An attractive feature of equipment trust certificates is that despite a near-perfect payment record that dates back to pre-Depression days, these issues generally offer above-average yields to investors.

Specialty Issues

In addition to the basic bond vehicles described above, investors can choose from a number of *specialty issues*—bonds that possess unusual issue characteristics. For the most part, these bonds have coupon or repayment provisions that are out of the ordinary. Most are issued by corporations, although they are being used increasingly by other issuers as well. Four of the most actively traded specialty issues today are zero-coupon bonds, mortgage-backed securities, asset-backed securities, and high-yield junk bonds. All four of these rank as some of the more popular bonds on Wall Street. Let's now take a closer look at each of these specialty issues.

zero-coupon bonds
bonds with no coupons that are sold at a deep discount from par value.

Zero-Coupon Bonds As the name implies, **zero-coupon bonds** have no coupons. Rather, these securities are sold at a deep discount from their par values and then increase in value over time at a compound rate of return so that at maturity, they are worth much more than their initial investment. Other things being equal, the cheaper the zero-coupon bond, the greater the return an investor can earn: For example, a bond with a 6% yield might cost $420, but one with a 10% yield might cost only $240.

Because they don't have coupons, these bonds do not pay interest semiannually. In fact, they pay *nothing* to the investor until the issue matures. As strange as it might seem, this feature is the main attraction of zero-coupon bonds. Because there are no interest payments, investors do not have to worry about reinvesting coupon income twice a year. Instead, the fully compounded rate of return on a zero-coupon bond is virtually guaranteed at the rate that existed when the issue was purchased. For example, in mid-2003, U.S. Treasury zero-coupon bonds with 10-year maturities were available at yields of around 4.8%. Thus, for around $600, you could buy a bond that would be worth $1,000 at maturity in 10 years. And that 4.8% yield is a fully compounded rate of return that's *locked in* for the life of the issue—or what's left of it (10 years in this case).

H O T

To read about Treasury strips, go to:

www.bondsonline.com/asp/treas/zeros.asp

The foregoing advantages notwithstanding, zeros do have some serious disadvantages. One is that if rates do move up over time, you won't be able to participate in the higher return (you'll have no coupon income to reinvest). In addition, zero-coupon bonds are subject to tremendous price volatility: If market rates climb, you'll experience a sizable capital loss as the prices of zero-coupons plunge. (Of course, if interest rates *drop*, you'll reap enormous capital gains if you hold long-term zeros. Indeed, such issues are unsurpassed in capital gains potential.) A final disadvantage is that the IRS has ruled that zero-coupon bondholders must report *interest as it is accrued*, even though no interest is actually received. For this reason, most fully taxable zero-coupon bonds should either be used in tax-sheltered investments, such as IRAs, or be held by minor children who are likely to be taxed at the lowest rate, if at all.

Treasury strips (strip-Ts)
zero-coupon bonds created from U.S. Treasury securities.

Zeros are issued by corporations, municipalities, and federal agencies. You can even buy U.S. Treasury notes and bonds in the form of zero-coupon securities. They're known as **Treasury strips,** or **strip-Ts,** for short. Actually, the Treasury does *not* issue zero-coupon bonds. Instead, it *allows government securities dealers to sell regular coupon-bearing notes and bonds in the form of zero-coupon securities*. Essentially, the coupons are stripped from the bond, repackaged, and then sold separately as zero-coupon bonds. For example, a 10-year Treasury note has 20 semiannual coupon payments, plus one principal payment. These 21 cash flows can be repackaged and sold as 21 different zero-coupon securities, with maturities that range from 6 months to 10 years. Because they sell at such large discounts, Treasury strips are often sold in minimum denominations (par values) of $10,000. But with their big discounts, you'll probably pay only about half that amount (or less) for $10,000 worth of 10-year strip-Ts. Because there's an active secondary market for Treasury strips, investors can get in and out of these securities with ease just about any time they want. Strip-Ts offer the maximum in issue quality, a wide array of different maturities, and an active secondary market—all of which explains why they are so popular.

mortgage-backed bond
a debt issue secured by a pool of home mortgages; issued primarily by federal agencies.

Mortgage-Backed Securities Simply put, a **mortgage-backed bond** is a debt issue that is secured by a pool of residential mortgages. An issuer, such as the Government National Mortgage Association (GNMA), puts together a pool of home mortgages and then issues securities in the amount of the total mortgage pool. These securities, also known as *pass-through securities* or *participation certificates*, are usually sold in minimum denominations of $25,000. Though their maturities can go out as far as 30 years, the average life is generally much shorter (perhaps as short as 8 to 10 years) because many of the mortgages are paid off early.

As an investor in one of these securities, you hold an undivided interest in the pool of mortgages. When a homeowner makes a monthly mortgage payment, that payment is essentially passed through to you, the bondholder, to pay off the mortgage-backed bond you hold. Although these securities come with normal coupons, *the interest is paid monthly rather than semiannually*. Actually, the monthly payments received by bondholders are, like mortgage payments, made up of both principal and interest. Because the principal portion of the payment represents return of capital, it is considered tax-free. The interest portion, however, is subject to ordinary state and federal income taxes.

Mortgage-backed securities are issued primarily by three federal agencies. Although there are some state and private issuers (mainly big banks and S&Ls), agency issues dominate the market and account for 90% to 95% of the activity. The major agency issuers of mortgage-backed securities (MBSs) are:

- *Government National Mortgage Association (GNMA).* Known as Ginnie Mae, it is the oldest and largest issuer of MBSs.

- *Federal Home Loan Mortgage Corporation (FHLMC).* Known as Freddie Mac, it was the first to issue pools containing conventional mortgages. Stock in FHLMC is publicly owned and traded on the NYSE.

- *Federal National Mortgage Association (FNMA).* Known as Fannie Mae, it's the newest agency player and the leader in marketing seasoned/older mortgages. Its stock is also publicly owned and traded on the NYSE.

One problem with mortgage-backed securities is that they *are self-liquidating investments;* that is, a portion of the monthly cash flow to the investor is repayment of principal. Thus, the investor is always receiving back part of the original investment capital, so at maturity there is *no* big principal payment. To counter this problem, a number of *mutual funds* were formed that invest in mortgage-backed securities *but* automatically reinvest the capital/principal portion of the cash flows. Mutual fund investors therefore receive only the interest from their investments and are thus able to preserve their capital.

Collateralized Mortgage Obligations Loan prepayments are another problem with mortgage-backed securities. In fact, it was in part an effort to defuse some of the prepayment uncertainty in standard mortgage-backed securities that led to the creation of **collateralized mortgage obligations (CMOs).** Normally, as pooled mortgages are prepaid, all bondholders receive a pro-rated share of the prepayments. The net effect is to sharply reduce the life of the bond. A CMO, in contrast, divides investors into classes (called "tranches," which is French for "slice"), depending on whether they want a short-, intermediate-, or long-term investment. Although interest is paid to all bondholders, all principal payments go first to the shortest tranche until it is fully retired. Then the next class in the sequence becomes the sole recipient of principal, and so on, until the last tranche is retired.

collateralized mortgage obligation (CMO)
mortgage-backed bond whose holders are divided into classes based on the length of investment desired; principal is channeled to investors in order of maturity, with short-term classes first.

Basically, CMOs are *derivative securities* created from traditional mortgage-backed bonds, which are placed in a trust. Participation in this trust is then sold to the investing public in the form of CMOs. The net effect of this transformation is that CMOs look and behave very much like any other bond:

They offer predictable interest payments and have (relatively) predictable maturities. However, although they carry the same triple-A ratings and implicit U.S. government backing as the mortgage-backed bonds that underlie them, CMOs represent a quantum leap in complexity. Some types of CMOs can be as simple and safe as Treasury bonds. But others can be far more volatile—and risky—than the standard MBSs they're made from. That's because when putting CMOs together, Wall Street performs the financial equivalent of gene splicing: Investment bankers isolate the interest and principal payments from the underlying MBSs and rechannel them to the different tranches. It's not issue quality or risk of default that's the problem here, but rather prepayment, or call, risk. All the bonds will be paid off; it's just a matter of when. Different types of CMO tranches have different levels of prepayment risk. The overall risk in a CMO cannot, of course, exceed that of the underlying mortgage-backed bonds, so in order for there to be some tranches with very little (or no) prepayment risk, others have to endure a lot more. The net effect is that while some CMO tranches are low in risk, others are loaded with it.

Asset-Backed Securities The creation of mortgage-backed securities and CMOs quickly led to the development of a new market technology—the process of **securitization**, whereby various lending vehicles are transformed into marketable securities, much like a mortgage-backed security. Investment bankers are now selling billions of dollars worth of pass-through securities, known as **asset-backed securities (ABS)**, which are backed by pools of auto loans, credit card bills, and home equity lines (three of the principal types of collateral), as well as computer leases, hospital receivables, small business loans, truck rentals, and even royalty fees. These securities, first introduced in the mid-1980s, are created when an investment banker bundles together some type of debt-linked asset (such as loans or receivables), and then sells investors—via asset-backed securities—the right to receive all or part of the future payments made on that debt. For example, GMAC, the financing arm of General Motors, is a regular issuer of collateralized *auto loan* securities. When it wants to get some of its car loans off its books, GMAC takes the monthly cash flow from a pool of auto loans and pledges them to a new issue of bonds, which are then sold to investors. In similar fashion, *credit card receivables* are regularly used as collateral for these bonds (indeed, they represent the biggest segment of the ABS market), as are *home equity loans*, the second-biggest type of ABS.

Investors are drawn to ABSs for a number of reasons. One is the relatively *high yields* they offer. Another is their *short maturities*, which often extend out no more than 3 to 5 years. A third is the *monthly, rather than semiannual, principal/interest payments* that accompany many of these securities. Also important to investors is their *high credit quality*. That's due to the fact that most of these deals are backed by generous credit protection. For example, the securities are often overcollateralized, which means that the pool of assets backing the bonds may be 25% to 50% larger than the bond issue itself. For whatever reason, the vast majority of ABSs receive the highest credit rating possible (triple-A) from the leading agencies.

Junk Bonds Junk bonds (or *high-yield bonds*, as they're also called) are highly speculative securities that have received low, sub-investment-grade ratings (typically Ba or B). These bonds are issued primarily by corporations and, also, by municipalities. Junk bonds often take the form of *subordinated debentures*,

securitization
the process of transforming lending vehicles such as mortgages into marketable securities.

asset-backed securities (ABS)
securities similar to mortgage-backed securities that are backed by a pool of bank loans, leases, and other assets.

junk bonds
high-risk securities that have low ratings but high yields.

INVESTING IN ACTION

AT LAST—BONDS FOR THE LITTLE GUY

Did the stock market's topsy-turvey performance over the past few years make you jittery about buying stocks? Perhaps you wanted to purchase bonds but didn't want to tie up your money for 20 years, or you would rather hold individual bonds instead of paying fees to a mutual fund. Now you have another option: *medium-term* or *direct access notes (DANs)*, original-issue corporate bonds designed for individual investors. Major companies such as Banc of America, Boeing, Diageo PLC, Dow Chemical, GE Capital, Household Finance, IBM, and UPS have all sold this new type of debt security through a network of more than 300 brokerage firms. Current offerings range in maturity from 18 months to 25 years.

These notes are sold at face value ($1,000), so you know the coupon and cost before you make a purchase. The broker buys the bonds from the issuer at a discount, so you don't pay a commission on your purchase. As with any fixed-income security, yields vary based on the issuers' credit ratings and maturity. New issues are offered every Monday. Because the $1,000 offering price is available for the entire first week, investors can take the time to consider which DANs are best suited for their portfolios. Many DANs pay interest monthly, rather than the more typical semiannual payments of traditional corporate bonds. This steady income stream makes them attractive to retired people. Another special feature is the "death put," or survivor's option. If you inherit a DAN, you can ask the issuing company to redeem the bond at its par value—regardless of its current price.

While DANs offer higher yields than Treasury notes, they have the same interest rate and credit risks as other bond investments:

- Rising interest rates will cause the price of the bond in the secondary market to drop.
- You must assess the company, or credit, risk—that is, the issuer's ability to repay both interest and principal.

DANs have a limited secondary market, which may make it difficult to sell the note before maturity. Most investors who buy DANs plan to hold them to maturity. Some of these notes also carry call provisions. Advantages of these securities include greater investor control and flexibility. You can choose the maturities, yields, and payment dates that are best for your needs. To get greater diversification, as you would with a bond fund, investors can buy several issues instead of just one DAN.

For more information about DANS, go to www.directnotes.com or www.internotes.com.

CRITICAL THINKING QUESTION Summarize the advantages and disadvantages of DANs. Would they be a good choice for your portfolio? Explain.

Sources: David McNaughton, "Some Bonds Entice Individuals," *Atlanta Journal and Constitution*, December 8, 2002, p. H6; Direct Access Notes, La Salle Broker Dealer Services, www.directnotes.com, accessed September 24, 2003; and Jeff D. Opdyke and Carrick Mollenkamp, "Corporate Bonds for the Little Guy," *The Wall Street Journal*, July 30, 2002, pp. D1, D2.

PIK-bond
a payment-in-kind junk bond that gives the issuer the right to make annual interest payments in new bonds rather than in cash.

which means the debt is unsecured and has a low claim on assets. These bonds are called "junk" because of their high risk of loss. The companies that issue them generally have excessive amounts of debt in their capital structures, and their ability to service that debt is subject to considerable doubt. Probably the most unusual type of junk bond is something called a **PIK-bond**. PIK stands for *payment in kind* and means that rather than paying the bond's coupon in cash, the issuer can make annual interest payments in the form of additional debt. This "financial printing press" usually goes on for 5 or 6 years, after which time the issuer is supposed to start making interest payments in real money.

Traditionally, the term *junk bond* was applied to issues of troubled companies, which might have been highly rated when first issued but slid to low ratings through corporate mismanagement, heavy competition, or other factors. That all changed during the 1980s, when the vast majority of junk bonds originated not with troubled companies but with a growing number of mature (fairly well-known) firms that used enormous amounts of debt to finance takeovers and buyouts. These companies would change overnight from investment-grade firms to junk as they piled on debt to finance a takeover—or the threat of one. (Wall Street refers to these firms as "fallen angels.")

Why would any rational investor be drawn to junk bonds? The answer is simple: They offer very high yields. Indeed, in a typical market, relative to investment-grade bonds, you can expect to pick up anywhere from 2.5 to 5 percentage points in added yield. For example, not long ago, investors were getting 11% or 12% yields on junk bonds, compared to 7% or 8% on investment-grade corporates. Obviously, *such yields are available only because of the correspondingly higher exposure to risk*. However, as we saw earlier in this chapter, there's more to bond returns than yield alone: The *returns* you actually end up with don't always correspond to the *yields* you went in with. Junk bonds are subject to a good deal of risk, and their prices are unstable. Indeed, unlike investment-grade bonds, whose prices are closely linked to the behavior of market interest rates, junk bonds tend to behave more like stocks. As a result, the returns you actually end up with are highly unpredictable. Accordingly, only investors who are thoroughly familiar with the risks involved, and who are comfortable with such risk exposure, should use these securities.

A Global View of the Bond Market

Globalization has hit the bond market, just as it has the stock market. Foreign bonds have caught on with U.S. investors because of their high yields and attractive returns. There are risks with foreign bonds, of course, but high risk of default is *not* one of them. Instead, the big risk with foreign bonds has to do with the impact that currency fluctuations can have on returns in U.S. dollars.

By mid-year 2003, the total value of the world bond market had reached some $33 trillion. The United States has the biggest debt market, accounting for about 52% of the total. Following the United States is *Euroland*, which accounts for about 20% of the market (principally in Germany, Italy, and France). Close behind is Japan at 16%, followed by the United Kingdom (at 3%) and Canada (at less than 2%). Together, these issuers account for slightly more than 90% of the world bond market. Worldwide, various forms of government bonds (e.g., Treasuries, agencies, and munis) dominate the market, accounting for about 55% of the total.

U.S.-Pay Versus Foreign-Pay Bonds There are several ways to invest in foreign bonds (*excluding* foreign bond mutual funds, which we'll examine in Chapter 13). From the perspective of a U.S. investor, foreign bonds can be divided into two broad categories on the basis of the currency in which the bond is denominated: *U.S.-pay* (or dollar-denominated) bonds and *foreign-pay* (or non-dollar-denominated) bonds. All the cash flows—including purchase price, maturity value, and coupon income—from dollar-denominated foreign bonds are in U.S. dollars, whereas the cash flows from nondollar bonds are designated in a foreign currency, such as the euro, British pound, or Swiss franc.

Yankee bonds
bonds issued by foreign governments or corporations but denominated in dollars and registered with the SEC.

Eurodollar bonds
foreign bonds denominated in dollars but not registered with the SEC, thus restricting sales of new issues.

Dollar-Denominated Bonds   Dollar-denominated foreign bonds are of two types: Yankee bonds and Eurodollar bonds. **Yankee bonds** are issued by foreign governments or corporations or by so-called supernational agencies, like the World Bank and the InterAmerican Bank. These bonds are issued and traded in the United States; they're registered with the SEC, and all transactions are in U.S. dollars. Buying a Yankee bond is really no different from buying any other U.S. bond: These bonds are traded on U.S. exchanges and the OTC market, and *because everything is in dollars, there's no currency exchange risk to deal with.* The bonds are generally very high in quality (which is not surprising, given the quality of the issuers) and offer highly competitive yields to investors.

Eurodollar bonds, in contrast, are issued and traded outside the United States. They are denominated in U.S. dollars, but they are not registered with the SEC, which means underwriters are legally prohibited from selling new issues to the U.S. public. (Only "seasoned" Eurodollar issues can be sold in this country.) The Eurodollar market today is dominated by foreign-based investors (though that is changing) and is primarily aimed at institutional investors.

Foreign-Pay Bonds   From the standpoint of U.S. investors, foreign-pay international bonds encompass all those issues denominated in a currency other than dollars. These bonds are issued and traded overseas and are not registered with the SEC. Examples are German government bonds, which are payable in euros; Japanese bonds, issued in yen; and so forth. When investors speak of *foreign bonds*, it's this segment of the market that most of them are thinking of.

Foreign-pay bonds are subject to changes in currency exchange rates, which can dramatically affect total returns to U.S. investors. The returns on foreign-pay bonds are a function of three things: (1) the level of coupon (interest) income earned on the bonds; (2) the change in market interest rates, which determine the level of capital gains (or losses); and (3) the behavior of currency exchange rates. The first two variables are the same as those that drive bond returns in this country and are, of course, just as important to foreign bonds as they are to domestic bonds. Thus, if you're investing overseas, you still want to know what the yields are today and where they're headed. *It's really the third variable that separates the return behavior of dollar-denominated from foreign-pay bonds.*

We can assess returns from foreign-pay bonds by employing the same (modified) holding period return formula first introduced in our discussion of foreign stock returns. (See Equation 6.6 in Chapter 6.) For example, assume a U.S. investor purchased a Swedish government bond, in large part because of the attractive 7½% coupon it carried. If the bond was bought at par and market rates fell over the course of the year, the security itself would have provided a return in excess of 7½% (because the decline in rates would provide some capital gains). However, if the Swedish krona (SEK) fell relative to the dollar, the total return (in U.S. dollars) could have actually ended up at a lot less than 7½%, depending on what happened to the U.S. $/SEK exchange rate. To find out exactly how this investment turned out, you could use Equation 6.6, and make a few (very minor) modifications to it (e.g., use interest income in place of dividends received). Like foreign stocks, *foreign-pay bonds can pay off from both the behavior of the security and the behavior of the currency*. That combination, in many cases, means superior returns to U.S.

investors. Knowledgeable investors find these bonds attractive not only because of their competitive returns but also because of *the positive diversification effects they have on bond portfolios.*

IN REVIEW

CONCEPTS

10.7 Briefly describe each of the following types of bonds: (a) *Treasury bonds*, (b) *agency issues*, (c) *municipal securities*, and (d) *corporate bonds*. Note some of the major advantages and disadvantages of each.

10.8 Briefly define each of the following and note how they might be used by fixed-income investors: (a) *zero-coupon bonds*, (b) *CMOs*, (c) *junk bonds*, and (d) *Yankee bonds*.

10.9 What are the special tax features of (a) *Treasury securities*, (b) *agency issues*, and (c) *municipal bonds?*

10.10 Describe an *asset-backed security* (ABS) and identify some of the different forms of collateral used with these issues. Briefly note how an ABS differs from a MBS. What is the central idea behind securitization?

10.11 Identify the six or seven biggest bond markets in the world. How important is the U.S. bond market relative to the rest of the world?

10.12 What's the difference between dollar-denominated and non-dollar-denominated (foreign-pay) bonds? Briefly describe the two major types of U.S.-pay bonds. Can currency exchange rates affect the total return of U.S.-pay bonds? Of foreign-pay bonds? Explain.

Trading Bonds

LG 6

In large part as a result of the perceived safety and stability of bonds, many individual investors view bond investing as a relatively simple process. Such thinking, however, can often lead to unsatisfactory results, even losses. The fact is that not all bonds are alike, and picking the right security for the time is just as important for bond investors as it is for stock investors. Indeed, success in the bond market demands a thorough understanding not only of the different types of bonds but also of the many technical factors that drive bond yields, prices, and returns—things like call features, refunding provisions, and the impact that coupon and maturity can have on bond price volatility. Also, because bond ratings are so important to a smooth-running bond market, investors should become thoroughly familiar with them. Let's now take a look at these ratings and at the quotation system used for bonds.

Bond Ratings

bond ratings
letter grades that designate investment quality and are assigned to a bond issue by rating agencies.

Bond ratings are like grades: A letter grade that designates investment quality is assigned to an issue on the basis of extensive, professionally conducted financial analysis. They denote the amount of *credit risk* embedded in a bond and are widely used by fixed-income investors. Indeed, these ratings are an important part of the municipal and corporate bond markets, where issues are regularly evaluated and rated by one or more of the rating agencies. Even some agency issues, like the Tennessee Valley Authority (TVA), are rated, though they always receive ratings that confirm the obvious—that the issues are prime grade. The two largest and best-known rating agencies are Moody's and Standard & Poor's; another lesser known but still important bond-rating agency is Fitch Investors Service.

How Ratings Work Every time a large new issue comes to the market, it is analyzed by a staff of professional bond analysts to determine default risk exposure and investment quality. (A fee, usually ranging from $1,000 to $15,000 and paid by the issuer or the underwriter of the securities, is charged for rating each bond.) The rating agency thoroughly studies the financial records of the issuing organization and assesses its future prospects. Although the specifics of the actual credit analysis conducted by the rating agencies change with each issue, several major factors enter into most bond ratings. With a corporate issue, for example, these factors include an analysis of the issue's indenture provisions, an in-depth study of the firm's earning power (including the stability of its earnings), a look at the company's liquidity and how it is managed, a study of the company's relative debt burden, and an in-depth exploration of its coverage ratios to determine how well it can service both existing debt and any new bonds that are being contemplated or proposed. As you might expect, the firm's financial strength and stability are very important in determining the appropriate bond rating. Although, there is far more to setting a rating than cranking out a few financial ratios, the fact is a strong relationship exists between the operating results and financial condition of the firm and the rating its bonds receive. Generally, higher ratings are associated with more profitable companies that rely *less* on debt as a form of financing, are more liquid, have stronger cash flows, and have no trouble servicing their debt in a prompt and timely fashion.

Table 10.5 lists the various ratings assigned to bonds by the two major services. In addition to the standard rating categories noted in the table, Moody's uses numerical modifiers (1, 2, or 3) on bonds rated double-A to B, while S&P uses plus (+) or minus (−) signs on the same rating classes to show relative standing within a major rating category. For example, A+ (or A1) means a strong, high A rating, whereas A− (or A3) indicates that the issue is on the low end of the A rating scale. Except for slight variations in designations (Aaa versus AAA), the meanings and interpretations are basically the same.

Note that the top four ratings (Aaa through Baa, or AAA through BBB) designate *investment-grade* bonds. Such ratings are highly coveted by issuers, as they indicate financially strong, well-run companies. The next two ratings (Ba/B or BB/B) are reserved for junk bonds. These ratings mean that although *the principal and interest payments on the bonds are still being met in a timely fashion*, the risk of default is relatively high. The issuers of these bonds generally lack the financial strength that backs investment-grade issues. (Sometimes the Caa1/CCC1 category is counted as part of the junk category, although technically the C rating class is meant to designate bonds that are already in default or getting very close to it.) Most of the time, Moody's and S&P assign identical ratings. Sometimes, however, an issue carries two different ratings. These **split ratings** are viewed simply as "shading" the quality of an issue one way or another. For example, an issue might be rated Aa by Moody's but A or A+ by S&P.

Also, just because a bond is given a certain rating at the time of issue doesn't mean it will keep that rating for the rest of its life. Ratings change as

BETTING ON AN UPGRADE—"You say *potayto* and I say *potahto*," as the old song goes. It turns out that some corporate bonds appear to be of investment-grade quality to one credit rating agency but look like junk to another. Such bonds—which are given a low *investment-grade* rating by one agency and a lower *junk bond* rating by another—are known as *crossover bonds*, and they are proving to be popular with investors. For one thing, they usually pay higher interest rates than a purely investment-grade bond, because one rating agency thinks the credit risk is greater. But they also offer investors the opportunity for capital appreciation. The reason: Often, the rating agency that called the bond junk eventually upgrades its credit rating, making the bond more valuable.

split ratings
different ratings given to a bond issue by the two major rating agencies.

TABLE 10.5   **Bond Ratings**

Moody's	S&P	Definition
Aaa	AAA	*High-grade investment bonds.* The highest rating assigned, denoting extremely strong capacity to pay principal and interest. Often called "gilt-edge" securities.
Aa	AA	*High-grade investment bonds.* High quality by all standards but rated lower primarily because the margins of protection are not quite as strong.
A	A	*Medium-grade investment bonds.* Many favorable investment attributes, but elements may be present that suggest susceptibility to adverse economic changes.
Baa	BBB	*Medium-grade investment bonds.* Adequate capacity to pay principal and interest but possibly lacking certain protective elements against adverse economic conditions.
Ba	BB	*Speculative issues.* Only moderate protection of principal and interest in varied economic times. (This is one of the ratings carried by junk bonds.)
B	B	*Speculative issues.* Generally lacking desirable characteristics of investment bonds. Assurance of principal and interest may be small; this is another junk-bond rating.
Caa	CCC	*Default.* Poor-quality issues that may be in default or in danger of default.
Ca	CC	*Default.* Highly speculative issues, often in default or possessing other market shortcomings.
C		*Default.* These issues may be regarded as extremely poor in investment quality.
	C	*Default.* Rating given to income bonds on which no interest is paid.
	D	*Default.* Issues actually in default, with principal or interest in arrears.

Source: Moody's *Bond Record* and Standard & Poor's *Bond Guide.*

HOT LINKS

For further explanation of Moody's bond ratings, go to:

www.bondpickers.com/?cmd=ratings

the financial condition of the issuer changes. In fact, all rated issues are reviewed on a regular basis to ensure that the assigned rating is still valid. Many issues do carry a single rating to maturity, but it is not uncommon for ratings to be revised up or down. As you might expect, the market responds to rating revisions by adjusting bond yields accordingly. For example, an upward revision (e.g., from A to AA) causes the market yield on the bond to drop, as a reflection of the bond's improved quality. One final point: Although it may appear that the firm is receiving the rating, it is actually the *issue* that receives it. As a result, a firm's different issues can have different ratings. The senior securities, for example, might carry one rating and the junior issues another, lower rating.

What Ratings Mean Investors pay close attention to agency ratings, because ratings can affect not only potential market behavior but comparative market yields as well. Specifically, *the higher the rating, the lower the yield*, other things being equal. For example, whereas an A-rated bond might offer a 7.5% yield, a comparable triple-A issue would probably yield something like 7%. Furthermore, investment-grade securities are far more interest-sensitive and tend to exhibit more uniform price behavior than junk bonds and other lower-rated issues. Perhaps most important, *bond ratings serve to relieve individual investors of the drudgery of evaluating the investment quality of an issue on their own.* Large institutional investors often have their own staff of credit analysts who independently assess the creditworthiness of various corporate and municipal issuers; individual investors, in contrast, have little if anything to gain from conducting their own credit analysis. After all, credit analysis is time-consuming and costly, and it demands a good deal more expertise than the average individual investor possesses. Most important, the ratings are closely adhered to by a large segment of the bond investment community, in large part because it has been shown that *the rating agencies do a remarkably good job of assessing bond quality*. Thus individual investors can depend on assigned agency ratings as a viable measure of the creditworthiness of the issuer and an issue's risk of default. A word of caution is in order, however: Bear in mind that bond ratings are intended to measure only an issue's *default risk*, which has no bearing whatsoever on an issue's exposure to *market risk*. Thus, if interest rates increase, even the highest-quality issues go down in price, subjecting investors to capital loss and market risk.

Reading the Quotes

One thing you quickly learn in the bond market is that transactions are not always as easy to conduct as they may seem. In the first place, many bonds have relatively "thin" markets. Indeed, some issues may trade only five or ten bonds a week, and many have no secondary market at all. There are, of course, numerous high-volume issues, but even so, you should pay particularly close attention to an issue's trading volume—especially if you're looking for lots of price action and need prompt order executions. In addition, it's not always easy to obtain current information on bond prices. That's because most bonds trade in over-the-counter markets rather than on centralized exchanges; and except for Treasury securities, the financial pages provide little information on general market activity and even less on particular securities. Indeed, daily price quotes are widely available on only a few of the thousands of publicly traded corporate and municipal bonds. Finally, investors often have to look to both brokers and bankers to complete transactions. Most brokerage houses tend to confine their activities to new issues and to secondary market transactions of listed Treasury obligations, agency issues, and corporate bonds. Commercial banks, in contrast, are still the major dealers in municipal bonds and are active in Treasury and agency securities as well.

Except for municipal issues (which are usually quoted in terms of the yield they offer), bonds are quoted on the basis of their dollar prices. Such quotes are always interpreted as a *percent of par*. Thus, a quote of 97 does not mean $97.00 but, instead, means that the issue is trading at 97% of the par value of the obligation. In the bond market, it's assumed that we're dealing with bonds that have par values of $1,000—or some multiple thereof. Accordingly, a quote of 97 translates into a dollar price of $970. (With bond quotes, 1 point = $10.) As you can see in Figures 10.5 and 10.6 (on pages 445 and 447), one quotation system is used for corporate bonds and another for governments. (Treasuries and agencies are quoted the same.)

Corporate Bond Quotes To understand the system used with corporate bonds, take a look at Figure 10.5. These quotes appeared in the *Wall Street Journal* on August 1, 2003, and represent trades that occurred the day before, on Thursday, July 31. Looking at the highlighted Sara Lee quote, we can see that the name of the issuer is followed parenthetically by the company's ticker symbol (in this case, SLE). The next two items are self-explanatory: This particular issue carries a coupon of 3.875% and will mature on June 15, 2013

H O T

Two great sites for getting bond quotes, as well as a lot of other information about bonds, are:

www.bondsonline.com
www.investinginbonds.com

FIGURE 10.5 Price Quotations for Corporate Notes and Bonds

Like most fixed-income securities, corporate notes and bonds are quoted as a percentage of their par values. Listed here are *Wall Street Journal* quotes for the 40 most actively traded (fixed-rate) corporate bonds; the *Journal* doesn't devote any space to thinly traded issues for the simple reason that there are just too many of them (literally hundreds of NYSE-listed bonds, for example, trade just 5 or 10 bonds a day). These quotes are for transactions that took place either on listed markets (like the NYSE) or, more likely, in the OTC market. (*Source: Wall Street Journal*, August 1, 2003.)

Corporate Bonds

Thursday, July 31, 2003

Forty most active fixed-coupon corporate bonds

COMPANY (TICKER)	COUPON	MATURITY	LAST PRICE	LAST YIELD	EST SPREAD	UST	EST $ VOL (000's)
General Motors (GM)	8.375	Jul 15, 2033	93.455	9.008	365	30	340,425
Bank of America (BAC)	3.250	Aug 15, 2008	96.625	3.997	78	5	194,555
Bank of America (BAC)	4.750	Aug 15, 2013	95.398	5.348	94	10	146,190
General Motors (GM)	7.125	Jul 15, 2013	97.628	7.465	305	10	146,096
General Electric (GE)	5.000	Feb 01, 2013	98.037	5.265	85	10	144,634
Comcast Cable Communications Holdings (CMCSA)	8.375	Mar 15, 2013	118.129	5.878	147	10	135,940
General Motors (GM)	8.250	Jul 15, 2023	95.410	8.738	335	30	117,653
Ford Motor Credit (F)	7.250	Oct 25, 2011	98.903	7.428	301	10	117,617
Goldman Sachs Group (GS)	4.750	Jul 15, 2013	93.669	5.588	119	10	111,659
Citigroup (C)	3.500	Feb 01, 2008	98.772	3.800	58	5	104,746
DaimlerChrysler North America Holding (DCX)	4.050	Jun 04, 2008	96.129	4.960	168	5	99,620
Morgan Stanley (MWD)	5.300	Mar 01, 2013	97.882	5.588	118	10	93,529
Wal-Mart Stores (WMT)	4.550	May 01, 2013	96.497	5.008	54	10	88,205
Sara Lee (SLE)	3.875	Jun 15, 2013	90.546	5.106	63	10	85,019	← Sara Lee Issue (note)
American Express (AXP)	4.875	Jul 15, 2013	97.153	5.246	83	10	83,560
General Electric Capital (GE)	3.500	May 01, 2008	98.251	3.907	62	5	82,391
General Motors Acceptance (GMAC)	8.000	Nov 01, 2031	92.482	8.718	336	30	81,937
Comcast Holdings (CMCSA)	5.300	Jan 15, 2014	95.530	5.875	147	10	80,008
Household Finance (HSBC)	4.750	Jul 15, 2013	93.210	5.652	123	10	77,682
Ford Motor Credit (F)	7.375	Oct 28, 2009	102.108	6.949	373	5	74,962
General Dynamics (GD)	4.250	May 15, 2013	93.395	5.116	71	10	71,113
Household Finance (HSBC)	6.500	Jan 24, 2006	108.740	2.811	53	3	70,691
Sprint Capital (FON)	8.750	Mar 15, 2032	109.755	7.885	254	30	67,855
General Electric Capital (GE)	5.450	Jan 15, 2013	100.252	5.415	90	10	65,319
Citigroup (C)	5.625	Aug 27, 2012	102.275	5.305	80	10	64,782
DaimlerChrysler North America Holding (DCX)	8.500	Jan 18, 2031	110.332	7.598	225	30	62,075
Bank of America (BAC)	4.875	Jan 15, 2013	96.507	5.351	93	10	60,155
Lehman Brothers Holdings (LEH)	6.625	Jan 18, 2012	109.515	5.218	68	10	59,943
AT&T Wireless Services (AWE)	8.125	May 01, 2012	114.634	5.951	155	10	57,225
Wells Fargo (WFC)	6.625	Jul 15, 2004	104.919	1.364	n.a.	n.a.	54,683
Citigroup (C)	6.000	Feb 21, 2012	106.012	5.122	69	10	54,483
Tenet Healthcare (THC)	7.375	Feb 01, 2013	94.500	8.221	372	10	51,310
Ford Motor Credit (F)	6.875	Feb 01, 2006	105.095	4.682	245	3	51,085
General Motors Acceptance (GMAC)	4.500	Jul 15, 2006	100.270	4.399	219	3	50,093
Bank of America (BAC)	7.400	Jan 15, 2011	114.869	4.984	50	10	50,048
Washington Mutual Bank (WM)	6.875	Jun 15, 2011	111.644	5.060	64	10	49,328

(thus, it has 10 years to maturity). Next is the "last price" at which the issue traded on July 31; in other words, the last trade for the day was made at 90.546% of par. Unless you're a big-time investor, this is probably *not* the price you'd pay to buy the bond, as these prices are for minimum *trades of $1 million or more*. Buy in smaller lots and a "dealer spread" will be tacked on, meaning you'll buy at a higher price or sell at a lower price than the one quoted here.

Following the last price is the "last yield" (of 5.106%), which represents the bond's closing *yield-to-maturity* (a fully compounded measure of return that captures both current income and capital gains or losses, and which will be examined in detail in the next chapter). Note that this issue is trading at a *discount* (its price of 90.546 is less than par), because the market yield on the bond (5.106%) is more than its coupon (3.875%). The next two columns ("Est. Spread" and "UST") show the spread (or differential) between the yield on the Sara Lee bond and a comparable U.S. Treasury security. The spread is measured in "basis points," where 1 basis point = 1/100 of 1%; in other words, there are 100 basis points in a percentage point. Note in Figure 10.5 that SLE's last yield was 63 basis points higher than a comparable 10-year Treasury; the 10 in the "UST" column indicates that a 10-year Treasury is used as the benchmark issue in the yield spread measure. Finally, as can be seen in the last column, some $85 million worth of these SLE bonds changed hands on July 31, 2003.

Government Bond Quotes In contrast to corporates (and munis), U.S. government bonds (Treasuries as well as agency issues) are listed in thirty-secondths of a point. With government bonds, the figures to the right of the colon (:) indicate the number of thirty-seconds in the fractional bid or ask price. For example, look at the ask price of the highlighted 9.25% Treasury issue in Figure 10.6: It is being quoted at 141:08 (ask). Translated, that means the bond is being quoted at $141\frac{8}{32}$, or 141.25% of par. Thus, if you wanted to buy, say, $15,000 worth of this issue, you would have to pay $21,187.50 (i.e., $15,000 × 1.4125). Here again, these quotes are for minimum trades of $1 million or more, so the amount you'd actually pay would likely be more than that after dealer spreads and other transaction costs are tacked on. Also note that this bond is trading at a very big premium (of some 41% *above* its par value). This, of course, would be due to the fact that market interest rates have fallen well below the bond's coupon—in this case, the bond's yield is about half the coupon.

As can be seen in Figure 10.6, the quotes on Treasury (and agency) securities include not only the coupon (see the "Rate" column), but also the month and year of maturity. In addition, note that the securities are quoted in bid/ask terms. The bid price signifies what the bond dealers are willing to pay for the securities (which is how much you can sell them for), whereas the ask price is what the dealers will sell the issues for (or what you'd have to pay to buy them). Again, keep in mind that these bid/ask prices ignore dealer spreads/transaction costs. When these costs are factored in, you'll end up getting *less* than the quoted price when you sell and paying *more* than the quoted price when you buy. Finally, the last two columns in the quotes include the change ("CHG") in the ask price and the yield-to-maturity on the issue, based on the latest ask price ("ASK YLD").

Quotes on Zero-Coupon Bonds Also included in Figure 10.6 are quotes for some zero-coupon bonds. You'll find these listed under the heading "U.S. Treasury Strips." As we discussed earlier in this chapter, these securities are created by "stripping" the coupons from their bond issues and selling them separately from the principal. Thus the principal and interest *cash flows* can be sold on their own. (Look at the quotes: A *ci* behind the maturity date means the issue is made up of coupon/interest cash flow, whereas an *np* or *bp* means it is made up of principal from a note or bond.) The prices of most zeros are quite low compared to regular coupon bonds. For example, note the highlighted strip-T of February 2010. This issue is trading at an ask price of $76\frac{31}{32}$, or at less than $770 for each $1,000 in par value. The same issue in coupon form is the highlighted 6½% U.S. Treasury note of February 2010, which is trading at an ask price of just under 115½. Thus, the strip-T version is selling

FIGURE 10.6 Price Quotes for U.S. Treasury Securities

Listed here are *Wall Street Journal* quotes for some coupon-bearing and zero-coupon Treasury securities. Note that Treasuries are quoted in fractions of thirty-seconds of a point, rather than in decimals (like corporate bonds). You can also see here that both coupon and maturity play vital roles in the quotation system. For example, look at the Treasury quotes (the one on the left) and you'll find no less than five issues that mature in 2007, yet these bonds have five different (ask) prices. The reason: five different coupons. If you look back at Figure 10.5, you'll find the same thing with corporates. (*Source: Wall Street Journal*, August 1, 2003.)

TREASURIES

RATE	MATURITY MO/YR	BID	ASKED	CHG	ASK YLD
5.625	Feb 06n	108:27	108:28	-10	2.02
9.375	Feb 06	118:02	118:03	-12	2.03
2.000	May 06n	99:15	99:16	-9	2.19
4.625	May 06n	106:17	106:18	-10	2.18
6.875	May 06n	112:17	112:18	-10	2.20
7.000	Jul 06n	113:10	113:11	-10	2.30
6.500	Oct 06n	112:12	112:13	-10	2.45
3.500	Nov 06n	103:03	103:04	-10	2.50
6.625	May 07n	113:27	113:28	-10	2.74
4.375	May 07n	105:23	105:24	-11	2.76
3.250	Aug 07n	101:10	101:11	-10	2.89
6.125	Aug 07n	112:10	112:11	-10	2.87
3.000	Nov 07n	99:29	99:30	-11	3.01
3.625	Jan 08i	109:14	109:15	-10	1.42
3.000	Feb 08n	99:13	99:14	-12	3.13
6.500	Feb 10n	115:13	115:14	-22	3.81
11.750	Feb 10	115:07	115:08	-9	1.67
10.000	May 10	114:11	114:12	-10	1.78
5.750	Aug 10n	110:28	110:29	-24	3.96
12.750	Nov 10	123:26	123:27	-11	2.02
5.000	Feb 11n	105:25	105:26	-26	4.09
13.875	May 11	131:03	131:04	-16	2.28
5.000	Aug 11n	105:11	105:12	-28	4.20
14.000	Nov 11	136:15	136:16	-12	2.38
12.000	Aug 13	140:06	140:07	-17	3.27
13.250	May 14	150:25	150:26	-20	3.48
12.500	Aug 14	148:02	148:03	-25	3.57
11.750	Nov 14	144:26	144:27	-27	3.69
11.250	Feb 15	158:11	158:12	-55	4.65
10.625	Aug 15	153:21	153:22	-56	4.72
9.875	Nov 15	146:29	146:30	-54	4.78
9.250	Feb 16	141:07	141:08	-52	4.83
7.250	May 16	122:02	122:03	-49	4.90
7.500	Nov 16	124:11	124:12	-53	4.97
8.750	May 17	137:08	137:09	-55	4.98
8.875	Aug 17	138:22	138:23	-56	5.00
9.125	May 18	140:22	140:23	-87	5.15
9.000	Nov 18	140:18	140:19	-74	5.13
8.875	Feb 19	139:13	139:14	-73	5.15
8.125	Aug 19	131:10	131:11	-73	5.22
8.500	Feb 20	135:29	135:30	-75	5.23
8.750	May 20	138:30	138:31	-75	5.23
8.750	Aug 20	139:01	139:02	-75	5.25
7.875	Feb 21	129:03	129:04	-74	5.30
8.125	May 21	132:06	132:07	-76	5.30
8.125	Aug 21	132:06	132:07	-77	5.32
8.000	Nov 21	130:28	130:29	-76	5.33
7.250	Aug 22	122:00	122:01	-74	5.39
7.625	Nov 22	126:23	126:24	-76	5.38
7.125	Feb 23	120:21	120:22	-73	5.40
6.250	Aug 23	109:29	109:30	-69	5.43
7.500	Nov 24	126:01	126:02	-78	5.42
7.625	Feb 25	127:24	127:25	-79	5.42
6.875	Aug 25	118:06	118:07	-73	5.44
6.000	Feb 26	106:29	106:30	-68	5.46

← U.S. Treasury note (6.500 Feb 10n)
← U.S. Treasury bond (9.250 Feb 16)

U.S. TREASURY STRIPS

MATURITY	TYPE	BID	ASKED	CHG	ASK YLD
Feb 06	bp	94:26	94:28	-10	2.10
Feb 06	np	94:28	94:29	-10	2.08
May 06	ci	93:30	93:31	-11	2.25
May 06	np	93:27	93:28	-11	2.28
Jul 06	ci	94:07	94:09	-12	2.01
Jul 06	np	93:08	93:10	-12	2.36
Aug 06	ci	93:04	93:06	-12	2.35
Oct 06	np	92:05	92:07	-11	2.55
Nov 06	ci	91:31	92:01	-13	2.55
Nov 06	np	91:27	91:29	-16	2.59
Feb 07	ci	90:20	90:22	-12	2.79
Feb 07	np	90:27	90:29	-12	2.72
May 07	ci	89:20	89:22	-13	2.90
May 07	np	89:24	89:26	-13	2.87
Aug 07	np	88:24	88:26	-13	2.96
Aug 07	ci	88:23	88:25	-14	2.97
Aug 07	np	88:20	88:23	-13	2.99
Nov 07	ci	87:29	87:31	-14	3.02
Nov 07	np	87:20	87:22	-14	3.09
Feb 08	ci	86:16	86:18	-15	3.21
Feb 08	np	86:14	86:17	-14	3.22
May 08	ci	85:09	85:12	-15	3.34
May 08	np	85:06	85:09	-15	3.36
Aug 08	ci	84:18	84:21	-16	3.34
Nov 08	ci	83:08	83:10	-16	3.48
Nov 08	np	82:31	83:02	-16	3.55
Feb 09	ci	81:15	81:18	-23	3.72
May 09	ci	80:09	80:12	-23	3.82
May 09	np	80:21	80:24	-24	3.73
Aug 09	ci	79:17	79:20	-24	3.82
Aug 09	np	79:10	79:13	-24	3.86
Nov 09	ci	78:29	79:00	-25	3.79
Nov 09	bp	77:17	77:20	-25	4.08
Feb 10	ci	76:17	76:20	-27	4.12
Feb 10	np	76:28	76:31	-27	4.05
May 10	ci	75:15	75:18	-27	4.18
Aug 10	ci	74:18	74:22	-28	4.20
Aug 10	np	74:18	74:22	-28	4.20
Nov 10	ci	73:28	74:00	-29	4.18
Feb 11	ci	72:02	72:06	-29	4.38
Feb 11	np	72:13	72:17	-29	4.31

Stripped (zero-coupon) Treasury → (Feb 10 np)

at about two-thirds the price of the comparable coupon-bearing security. Keep in mind that these quotes occurred at a time when market yields were at near-40-year lows. As a result, the market prices are abnormally high. Several years ago, in early 2000, when market yields were more like 6% or 7%, this same February 2010 strip-T was trading at something closer to $525.

I N   R E V I E W

10.13   What are *bond ratings,* and how can they affect investor returns? What are *split ratings?*

10.14   From the perspective of an individual investor, what good are bond ratings? Do bond ratings indicate the amount of market risk embedded in a bond? Explain.

10.15   Bonds are said to be quoted "as a percent of par." What does that mean? What is 1 point worth in the bond market?

10.16   Why should an aggressive bond trader be concerned with the trading volume of a particular issue?

Summary

LG 1   **Explain the basic investment attributes of bonds and their use as investment vehicles.** Bonds are publicly traded debt securities that provide investors with two basic sources of return: (1) current income and (2) capital gains. Current income is derived from the coupon (interest) payments received over the life of the issue. Capital gains can be earned whenever market interest rates fall. In addition to their yields and returns, bonds can be used to shelter income from taxes and for the preservation and long-term accumulation of capital. Just as important, the diversification properties of bonds are such that they can greatly enhance portfolio stability.

LG 2   **Describe the essential features of a bond and distinguish among different types of call, refunding, and sinking-fund provisions.** All bonds carry some type of coupon, which specifies the annual rate of interest to be paid by the issuer. Bonds also have predetermined maturity dates: Term bonds carry a single maturity date, and serial bonds have a series of maturity dates. Every bond is issued with some type of call feature, be it freely callable, noncallable, or deferred callable. Call features spell out whether an issue can be prematurely retired and, if so, when. Some bonds (temporarily) prohibit the issuer from paying off one bond with the proceeds from another by including a refunding provision. Others are issued with sinking-fund provisions, which specify how a bond is to be paid off over time.

LG 3   **Describe the relationship between bond prices and yields, and explain why some bonds are more volatile than others.** The price behavior of a bond depends on the issue's coupon and maturity and on the movement in market interest rates. When interest rates go down, bond prices go up, and vice versa. However, the extent to which bond prices move up or down depends on the coupon and maturity of an issue. Bonds with lower coupons and/or longer maturities generate larger price swings.

LG 4   **Identify the different types of bonds and the kinds of investment objectives these securities can fulfill.** The bond market is divided into four major segments: Treasuries, agencies, municipals, and corporates. Treasury bonds are issued by the U.S. Treasury and are virtually default-free. Agency bonds are issued by various political subdivisions of the U.S. government and make up an increasingly important segment of the bond market. Municipal bonds are issued by state and local governments in the form of either general obligation or revenue bonds. Corporate bonds make up the major non-government sector of the market and are backed by the assets and profitability of the issuing companies. Generally speaking, Treasuries are attractive because of their high quality, agencies and corporates because of the added returns they provide, and munis because of the tax shelter they offer.

LG 5 **Discuss the global nature of the bond market and the difference between dollar-denominated and non-dollar-denominated foreign bonds.** There's growing investor interest in foreign bonds, particularly foreign-pay securities, because of their highly competitive yields and returns. Foreign-pay bonds cover all those issues that are denominated in some currency other than U.S. dollars. These bonds have an added source of return: currency exchange rates. In addition, there are dollar-denominated foreign bonds—Yankee bonds and Eurodollar bonds. These have no currency exchange risk because they are issued in U.S. dollars.

LG 6 **Describe the role that bond ratings play in the market and the quotation system used with various types of bonds.** Municipal and corporate issues are regularly rated for bond quality by independent rating agencies. A rating of Aaa indicates an impeccable record. Lower ratings, such as A or Baa, indicate more risk. As with all investments, the returns required of lower-quality instruments generally are higher than those required of high-quality bonds. The bond market also has its own quotation system, wherein bonds are quoted as a percent of par.

Putting Your Investment Know-How to the Test

1. Which of the following statements regarding interest rates is *false?*
   a. The longer the maturity of the bond, the higher the interest rate risk.
   b. There is an inverse relationship between bond prices and interest rates.
   c. The higher the coupon rate on the bond, the higher the interest rate risk.
   d. Bond prices fall less when interest rates rise than they rise when interest rates fall.

2. Which of the following Standard and Poor's bond ratings would be considered junk grade?
   a. A rating
   b. BBB rating
   c. BB rating
   d. All of the above

3. All else being equal, which one of the following bonds will sell for the lowest price (or highest yield)?
   a. Callable subordinated debentures
   b. Noncallable senior bonds
   c. Callable mortgage bonds
   d. Noncallable debentures

4. The refunding provision of an indenture allows bonds to be retired *unless*
   a. They are replaced with a new issue having a lower interest cost.
   b. The remaining time to maturity is less than 5 years.
   c. The stated time period in the indenture has not passed.
   d. The stated time period in the indenture has passed.

5. To a taxpayer in the 34% tax bracket, a municipal bond available at a price of 100 and a coupon rate of 10% has a taxable equivalent yield of
   a. 6.6%.   b. 10.0%.
   c. 13.4%.   d. 15.2%.

6. A collateral trust bond is
   a. Unsecured.
   b. Secured by other securities held outside the firm.
   c. Secured by real estate owned by the firm.
   d. Secured by the equipment owned by the firm.

7. A revenue bond is distinguished from a general obligation bond in that revenue bonds
   a. Are issued by counties, special districts, cities, towns and state-controlled authorities, whereas general obligation bonds are only issued by the states themselves.
   b. Are typically secured by limited taxing power, whereas general obligation bonds are secured by unlimited taxing power.
   c. Are issued to finance projects and are secured by the revenues of the project being financed.
   d. Have first claim to any revenue increase of the tax authority issuing the bonds.

8. Bonds that are issued in the currency of one country but sold in other national markets are called
   a. Eurodollar bonds.   b. Samurai bonds.
   c. Yankee bonds.   d. Foreign-pay bonds.

9. The dollar value of a U.S. Treasury bond quoted at 92.24 is
   a. $92.24.   b. $922.40.
   c. $927.50.   d. None of the above.

10. What is true about the U.S. agency bonds?
    a. They are backed by the "full faith and credit" of the U.S. government.
    b. Their interest is exempt from federal and state taxes.
    c. All else constant, they provide higher yields than U.S. Treasury bonds.
    d. All of the above.

Answers: 1. c; 2. b; 3. a; 4. a; 5. d; 6. b; 7. c; 8. d; 9. c; 10. c

---

Discussion Questions

LG 1

Q10.1 Using the bond returns in Tables 10.1 and 10.2 as a basis of discussion:
  a. Compare the returns during the 1970s to those produced in the 1980s. How do you explain the differences?
  b. How did the bond market do in the 1990s? How does the performance in this decade compare to that in the 1980s? Explain.
  c. What do you think would be a fair rate of return to expect from bonds in the future? Explain.

LG 1

Q10.2 Use the data in Tables 6.1 and 6.2 (for stocks) and Tables 10.1 and 10.2 (for bonds) to compare returns for stocks and bonds during the '70s, '80s, and '90s.
  a. Using both annual and holding-period returns, how would you describe the comparative performance of these two markets over each of the three decades? Which market was more volatile? How did the return performance of bonds compare to stocks over the 3½-year period from 2000 through mid-2003?
  b. In view of these comparative returns, develop an argument for why investors *should* hold bonds. Can you think of any reason(s) why investors should *not* hold bonds? What are they?
  c. Assume that you're out of school and hold a promising, well-paying job. How much of your portfolio (in percentage terms) would you, personally, want to hold in bonds? Explain. What role do you see bonds playing in your own portfolio, particularly as you go farther and farther into the future?

LG 4

Q10.3 Identify and briefly describe each of the following types of bonds.
  a. Agency bonds   **b.** Municipal bonds
  c. Zero-coupon bonds   **d.** Junk bonds
  e. Foreign bonds   **f.** Collateralized mortgage obligations (CMOs)

What type of investor do you think would be most attracted to each?

Q10.4 "Treasury securities are guaranteed by the U.S. government. Therefore, there is no risk in the ownership of such bonds." Briefly discuss the wisdom (or folly) of this statement.

Q10.5 Select the security in the left-hand column that best fits the investor desire described in the right-hand column.

a. 5-year Treasury note.	1. Lock in a high coupon yield.
b. A bond with a low coupon and a long maturity.	2. Accumulate capital over a long period of time.
c. Yankee bond.	3. Generate a monthly income.
d. Insured revenue bond.	4. Avoid a lot of price volatility.
e. Long-term Treasury strips.	5. Generate tax-free income.
f. Noncallable bond.	6. Invest in a foreign bond.
g. CMO.	7. Go for the highest yield available.
h. Junk bond.	8. Invest in a pool of credit-card receivables.
i. ABS.	9. Go for maximum price appreciation.

Q10.6 Using the quotes in Figures 10.5 and 10.6, answer the following questions.
a. What's the dollar (bid) price of the November 10 Treasury strip bond, and when does it mature?
b. What's the yield on the November 10 Treasury strip issue?
c. Which is higher priced: Sprint Capital 8.75% bond of 2032 or the 8.75% U.S. Treasury of August 20? (Use the ask price with the Treasury issue.) Both bonds carry the same coupons; so why don't they sell for about the same price?
d. What's the dollar (ask) price of the 14% U.S. Treasury of November 11? Why is that issue priced so high?
e. Which bond was more actively traded, GE 5% of 2013 or the GMAC 8% of 2031?
f. Which of the following bonds has the highest yield-to-maturity: the Citigroup 3½% of 2008, the 13¼% U.S. Treasury of May 14, or the February 9 strip-T? Which one would produce the most dollar amount of annual interest income (per $1,000 par bond)?

Problems

P10.1 A 6%, 15-year bond has 3 years remaining on a deferred call feature (the call premium is equal to 1 year's interest). The bond is currently priced in the market at $850. What is the issue's current yield?

P10.2 A 12%, 20-year bond is currently trading at $1,250. What is the current yield?

P10.3 Charlie buys a 10% corporate bond with a current yield of 6%. How much did he pay for the bond?

P10.4 An investor is in the 28% tax bracket and lives in a state with no income tax. He is trying to decide which of two bonds to purchase. One is a 7½% corporate bond that is selling at par. The other is a municipal bond with a 5¼% coupon that is also selling at par. If all other features of these two bonds are comparable, which should the investor select? Why? Would your answer change if this were an *in-state* municipal bond and the investor lived in a place with high state income taxes? Explain.

P10.5 An investor lives in a state where her tax rate on interest income is 8%. She is in the 33% federal tax bracket. She owns a 7% corporate bond trading at par. What is her after-tax current yield on this bond?

LG 4

P10.6 Sara Jordan is a wealthy investor who's looking for a tax shelter. Sara is in the maximum (35%) federal tax bracket and lives in a state with a very high state income tax. (She pays the maximum of 11½% in state income tax.) Sara is currently looking at two municipal bonds, both of which are selling at par. One is a double-A-rated *in-state* bond that carries a coupon of 6⅜%. The other is a double-A-rated *out-of-state* bond that carries a 7⅛% coupon. Her broker has informed her that comparable fully taxable corporate bonds are currently available with yields of 9¾%. Alternatively, long Treasuries are now available at yields of 9%. She has $100,000 to invest, and because all the bonds are high-quality issues, she wants to select the one that will give her maximum after-tax returns.

a. Which one of the four bonds should she buy?
b. Rank the four bonds (from best to worst) in terms of their taxable equivalent yields.

LG 4

P10.7 Rob is looking for a fixed-income investment. He is considering two bond issues:

a. A Treasury with a yield of 5%.
b. An in-state municipal bond with a yield of 4%.

Rob is in the 33% federal tax bracket and the 8% state tax bracket. Which bond would provide Rob with a higher tax-adjusted yield?

LG 6

P10.8 Which of the following three bonds offers the highest current yield?

a. A 9½%, 20-year bond quoted at 97¾.
b. A 16%, 15-year bond quoted at 164⅝.
c. A 5¼%, 18-year bond quoted at 54.

LG 6

P10.9 Assume that an investor pays $850 for a long-term bond that carries a 7½% coupon. Over the course of the next 12 months, interest rates drop sharply. As a result, the investor sells the bond at a price of $962.50.

a. Find the current yield that existed on this bond at the beginning of the year. What was it by the end of the 1-year holding period?
b. Determine the holding period return on this investment. (See Chapter 5 for the HPR formula.)

LG 3

P10.10 Charlie buys a 10% corporate bond with a current yield of 6%. When he sells the bond 1 year later, the current yield on the bond is 7%. How much did Charlie make on this investment?

LG 1

P10.11 In early January 1998, an investor purchased $30,000 worth of some Baa-rated corporate bonds. The bonds carried a coupon of 8⅞% and mature in 2015. The investor paid 94⅛ when she bought the bonds. Over the 5-year period from 1998 through 2002, the bonds were priced in the market as follows:

	Quoted Prices		
Year	Beginning of the Year	End of the Year	Year-End Bond Yields
1998	94⅛	100⅝	8.82%
1999	100⅝	102	8.70
2000	102	104⅝	8.48
2001	104⅝	110¼	8.05
2002	110¼	121⅛	7.33

Coupon payments were made on schedule throughout the 5-year period.
a. Find the annual holding period returns for 1998 through 2002. (See Chapter 5 for the HPR formula.)
b. Use the return information in Table 10.1 to evaluate the investment performance of this bond. How do you think it stacks up against the market? Explain.

LG 4 P10.12 Richie purchased a 13% zero-coupon bond with a 15-year maturity and a $20,000 par value 15 years ago. The bond matures tomorrow. How much will Richie receive in total from this investment, assuming all payments are made on these bonds as expected?

LG 4 P10.13 Archie purchased an interest-bearing security last year, planning to hold it until maturity. He received interest payments, and, to his surprise, a sizable amount of the principal was paid back in the first year. This happened again in year 2. What type of security did Archie purchase?

 LG 5 P10.14 Letticia Garcia, an aggressive bond investor, is currently thinking about investing in a foreign (non-dollar-denominated) government bond. In particular, she's looking at a Swiss government bond that matures in 15 years and carries a 9½% coupon. The bond has a par value of 10,000 Swiss francs (CHF) and is currently trading at 110 (i.e., at 110% of par).

Letticia plans to hold the bond for a period of 1 year, at which time she thinks it will be trading at 117½—she's anticipating a sharp decline in Swiss interest rates, which explains why she expects bond prices to move up. The current exchange rate is 1.58 CHF/U.S. $, but she expects that to fall to 1.25 CHF/U.S. $. Use the foreign investment return formula introduced in Chapter 6 (Equation 6.6) to answer the questions below.
a. Ignoring the currency effect, find the bond's total return (in its local currency).
b. Now find the total return on this bond in *U.S. dollars*. Did currency exchange rates affect the return in any way? Do you think this bond would make a good investment? Explain.

LG 6 P10.15 Red Electrica Espana SA (E.REE) is refinancing its bank loans by issuing Eurobonds to investors. You are considering buying $10,000 of these bonds, which will yield 6%. You are also looking at a U.S. bond with similar risk that will yield 5%. You expect that interest rates will not change over the next year, after which you will sell the bonds you purchase.
a. How much will you make on each bond if you buy it, hold it for 1 year, and then sell it for $10,000 (or the Eurodollar equivalent)?
b. Assume the dollar/euro exchange rate goes from 1.11 to 0.98. How much will this currency change affect the proceeds from the Eurobond? (Assume you receive annual interest at the same time you sell the Eurobond.)

**See the text Web site
(www.aw-bc.com/gitman_joehnk) for Web exercises
that deal with *fixed-income securities*.**

Case Problem 10.1   *Max and Heather Develop a Bond Investment Program*

LG 4   LG 6

Max and Heather Peters, along with their two teenage sons, Terry and Thomas, live in Portland, Oregon. Max is a sales rep for a major medical firm, and Heather is a personnel officer at a local bank. Together, they earn an annual income of around $100,000. Max has just learned that his recently departed rich uncle has named him in his will to the tune of some $250,000 after taxes. Needless to say, the family is elated. Max intends to spend $50,000 of his inheritance on a number of long-overdue family items (like some badly needed remodeling of their kitchen and family room, the down payment on a new Porsche Boxster, and braces to correct Tom's overbite). Max wants to invest the remaining $200,000 in various types of fixed-income securities.

Max and Heather have no unusual income requirements or health problems. Their only investment objectives are that they want to achieve some capital appreciation and they want to keep their funds fully invested for a period of at least 20 years. They would rather not have to rely on their investments as a source of current income but want to maintain some liquidity in their portfolio just in case.

Questions

a. Describe the type of *bond investment program* you think the Peters family should follow. In answering this question, give appropriate consideration to both return and risk factors.

b. List several different types of bonds that you would recommend for their portfolio, and briefly indicate why you would recommend each.

c. Using a recent issue of the *Wall Street Journal* or *Barron's*, construct a $200,000 bond portfolio for the Peters family. *Use real securities* and select any bonds (or notes) you like, given the following ground rules:
   1. The portfolio must include at least one Treasury, one agency, and one corporate bond; also, in total, the portfolio must hold at least 5, but no more than 8 bonds or notes.
   2. No more than 5% of the portfolio can be in short-term U.S. Treasury bills (but note that if you hold a T-bill, that limits your selections to just 7 other notes/bonds).

Security Issuer-Coupon-Maturity	Latest Quoted Price	Number of Bonds Purchased	Amount Invested	Annual Coupon Income	Current Yield
Example: U.S. Treas - 8½%-'15	96⁸⁄₃₂	25	$ 24,062	$ 2,125	8.83%
1.					
2.					
3.					
4.					
5.					
6.					
7.					
8.					
Totals	—		$200.000	$	%

3. Ignore all transaction costs (i.e., invest the full $200,000) and assume all securities have par values of $1,000 (though they can be trading in the market at something other than par).

4. Use the latest available quotes to determine how many bonds/notes/bills you can buy.

d. Prepare a schedule listing all the securities in your recommended portfolio. *Use a form like the one shown on the previous page*, and include the information it calls for on each security in the portfolio.

e. *In one brief paragraph*, note the key investment attributes of your recommended portfolio and the investment objectives you hope to achieve with it.

Case Problem 10.2 *The Case of the Missing Bond Ratings*

LG 6

While a lot goes into a bond rating, it's probably safe to say that there's nothing more important in determining a bond's rating than the underlying financial condition and operating results of the company issuing the bond. Just as financial ratios can be used in the analysis of common stocks, they can also be used in the analysis of bonds—a process we refer to as *credit analysis*. In credit analysis, attention is directed toward the basic liquidity and profitability of the firm, the extent to which the firm employs debt, and the ability of the firm to service its debt.

The following financial ratios are often helpful in carrying out such analysis: (1) current ratio, (2) quick ratio, (3) net profit margin, (4) return on total capital, (5) long-term debt to total capital, (6) owners' equity ratio, (7) pretax interest coverage, and (8) cash flow to total debt. The first two ratios measure the liquidity of the firm, the next two its profitability, the following two the debt load, and the final two the ability of the firm to service its debt load. (For ratio 5, the *lower* the ratio, the better. For all the others, the *higher* the ratio, the better.) The following table lists each of these ratios for six different companies.

A Table of Financial Ratios
(All ratios are real and pertain to real companies)

Financial Ratio	Company 1	Company 2	Company 3	Company 4	Company 5	Company 6
1. Current ratio	1.13 ×	1.39 ×	1.78 ×	1.32 ×	1.03 ×	1.41 ×
2. Quick ratio	0.48 ×	0.84 ×	0.93 ×	0.33 ×	0.50 ×	0.75 ×
3. Net profit margin	4.6%	12.9%	14.5%	2.8%	5.9%	10.0%
4. Return on total capital	15.0%	25.9%	29.4%	11.5%	16.8%	28.4%
5. Long-term debt to total capital	63.3%	52.7%	23.9%	97.0%	88.6%	42.1%
6. Owners' equity ratio	18.6%	18.9%	44.1%	1.5%	5.1%	21.2%
7. Pretax interest coverage	2.3 ×	4.5 ×	8.9 ×	1.7 ×	2.4 ×	6.4 ×
8. Cash flow to total debt	34.7%	48.8%	71.2%	20.4%	30.2%	42.7%

Notes: Ratio (2)—Whereas the current ratio relates current assets to current liabilities, the quick ratio considers only the most liquid current assets (cash, short-term securities, and accounts receivable) and relates them to current liabilities.
Ratio (4)—Relates pretax profit to the total capital structure (long-term debt + equity) of the firm.
Ratio (6)—Shows the amount of stockholders' equity used to finance the firm (stockholders' equity ÷ total assets).
Ratio (8)—Looks at the amount of corporate cash flow (from net profits + depreciation) relative to the total (current + long-term) debt of the firm
The other four ratios are as described in Chapter 6.

Questions

a.   Three of these companies have bonds that carry investment-grade ratings. The other three companies carry junk-bond ratings. Judging by the information in the table, which three companies have the investment-grade bonds and which three have the junk bonds? Briefly explain your selections.

b.   One of these six companies is a AAA-rated firm and one is B-rated. Identify those two companies. Briefly explain your selection.

c.   Of the remaining four companies, one carries a AA rating, one carries an A rating, and two are BB-rated. Which companies are they?

Excel with Spreadsheets

The cash flow components of bond investments is made up of the annual interest payments and the future redemption value or its par value. Just like other time-value-of-money considerations, the bond cash flows are discounted back in order to determine their present value.

In comparing bonds to stocks, many investors look at the respective returns. The total returns in the bond market are made up of both current income and capital gains. Bond investment analysis should include the determination of the current yield as well as a specific holding period return.

On January 13, 2004, you gather the following information on three corporate bonds issued by the General Motors Acceptance Corp (GMA). Remember that corporate bonds are quoted as a percent of their par value. Assume the par value of each bond to be $1,000. These debentures are quoted in eighths of a point. **Create a spreadsheet** that will model and answer the following three bond investment problems.

Bonds	Current Yield	Volume	Close
GMA 5.3 07	?	25	105 ⅞
GMA 6.65s 14	?	45	103
GMA 7.4 16	?	37	104 ⅝

Questions

a.   Calculate the current yields for these three GMA corporate debentures.
b.   Calculate the holding period returns under the following three scenarios:
   1.   Purchased the 5.3 bonds for 990 on January 13, 2003.
   2.   Purchased the 6.65s for 988 on January 13, 2003.
   3.   Purchased the 7.4 bonds for 985 on January 13, 2001.
c.   As of January 13, 2004, GMA common stock had a close price of $26.20. The price of GMA stock in January 2001 was $25.25. The stock paid a 2002 dividend of $.46, a 2003 dividend of $.46, and a 2004 dividend of $.46.
   1.   Calculate the current (January 13, 2004) dividend yield for this security.
   2.   Assuming you purchased the stock in January 2001, what is the holding period return as of January 2004?

I f you live in San Diego County, Phoenix, or New Orleans and you watch cable television, you may be one of Cox Communications' 6.5 million customers. The fourth largest cable television provider in the United States, Cox provides an array of other communications and entertainment services, including local and long distance digital telephone service, high-speed Internet access, and commercial voice and data services. In addition, Cox invests in cable programming networks such as the Discovery Channel.

Keeping up with the latest telecommunications technology is expensive. Cox must build and upgrade its extensive networks to carry an increasing volume of voice and data transmissions. In 2002 alone, Cox spent almost $2 billion to enhance its broadband network in anticipation of offering its customers new services and as part of its additional investments in cable programming, technology and telecommunications companies. Long-term debt is an essential component of Cox's capital structure; as of September 30, 2003, the company had $6.9 billion of long-term debt on its books, giving it a long-term debt-to-equity ratio of 0.72. In November 2000, Standard & Poor's Corporation downgraded Cox bonds one notch from BBB+ to BBB, the next to lowest investment grade rating. The lower rating meant that it would cost Cox more to issue future debt, such as its September 2003 $750 million issue of 5-year, $3\frac{7}{8}$% and 12-year, $5\frac{1}{2}$% subordinated notes.

As we'll see in this chapter, many factors determine a bond's price, including the credit quality and the general level of interest rates. Investors must evaluate these factors when deciding whether the market value of a bond will provide the return they need.

Sources: "Cox Communications, Inc. Announces Debt Offering," *Business Wire*, September 17, 2002, downloaded from www.cox.com; and material at Cox Communications Web site, www.cox.com.

LEARNING GOALS

After studying this chapter, you should be able to:

LG 1 Explain the behavior of market interest rates, and identify the forces that cause interest rates to move.

LG 2 Describe the term structure of interest rates, and note how these so-called yield curves can be used by investors.

LG 3 Understand how bonds are valued in the marketplace.

LG 4 Describe the various measures of yield and return, and explain how these standards of performance are used in bond valuation.

LG 5 Understand the basic concept of duration, how it can be measured, and its use in the management of bond portfolios.

LG 6 Discuss various bond investment strategies and the different ways these securities can be used by investors.

The Behavior of Market Interest Rates

LG 1   LG 2

Equation 11.1

$$r_i = r^* + IP + RP$$

You will recall from Chapter 4 that rational investors try to earn a return that fully compensates them for risk. In the case of bondholders, that required return (r_i) has three components: the real rate of return (r^*), an expected inflation premium (IP), and a risk premium (RP). Thus the required return on a bond can be expressed by the following equation:

The real rate of return and inflation premium are external economic factors, and *together they equal the risk-free rate (R_F)*. Now, to find the required return, we need to consider the unique features and properties of the bond issue itself; we can do this by adding the bond's risk premium to the risk-free rate. A bond's risk premium (RP) will take into account key issue and issuer characteristics, including such variables as the type of bond, the issue's term-to-maturity, its call features, and bond rating. Together, the three components in Equation 11.1 (r^*, IP, and RP) drive the required return on a bond. Recall in the previous chapter that we identified *five types of risks* to which bonds are exposed. As it turns out, all five of these risks are embedded in a bond's required rate of return. That is, the bond's risk premium (RP) addresses, among other things, the business and financial (credit) risk characteristics of an issue, along with its liquidity and call risks, whereas the risk-free rate (R_f) takes into account interest rate and purchasing power risks.

Viewed from the perspective of the market as a whole, it is these investor returns in the aggregate that go into (i.e., define) prevailing market interest rates. And because these interest rates have a significant bearing on bond prices and yields, they are closely monitored by investors. For example, the more conservative investors watch interest rates because one of their major objectives is to lock in high yields. Aggressive traders also have a stake in interest rates because their investment programs are often built on the capital gains opportunities that accompany major swings in rates.

Keeping Tabs on Market Interest Rates

Just as there is no single bond market but a series of different market sectors, so too there is no single interest rate that applies to all segments of the market. Rather, each segment has its own, unique level of interest rates. Granted, the various rates do tend to drift in the same direction over time and follow the same general pattern of behavior. But it's also common for **yield spreads** (interest rate differentials) to exist among the various market sectors. Some of the more important market yields and yield spreads are as follows:

yield spreads
differences in interest rates that exist among various sectors of the market.

- Municipal bonds usually carry the lowest market rates because of their tax-exempt feature. As a rule, their market yields are about 20% to 30% lower than corporates. (There are occasionally exceptions to this rule and we recently saw one of them—in 2003, some Treasury yields were actually lower than the yields on comparable munies!) In the taxable sector, Treasuries have the lowest yields (because they have the least risk), followed by agencies and then corporates, which provide the highest returns.

- Issues that normally carry bond ratings (e.g., municipals or corporates) generally display the same behavior: The lower the rating, the higher the yield.

- There is generally a direct relationship between the coupon an issue carries and its yield. Discount (low-coupon) bonds yield the least, and premium (high-coupon) bonds yield the most.

- In the municipal sector, revenue bonds yield more than general obligation bonds.

- Bonds that are freely callable generally provide the highest returns, at least at date of issue. These are followed by deferred call obligations and then by noncallable bonds, which yield the least.

- As a rule, bonds with long maturities tend to yield more than short issues. However, this rule does not always hold; sometimes, as in 2002, short-term yields equal or exceed the yields on long-term bonds.

The preceding list can be used as a general guide to the higher-yielding segments of the market. For example, income-oriented municipal bond investors might do well to consider certain high-quality revenue bonds as a way to increase yields; and investors who like to stick to high-quality issues might select agency bonds, rather than Treasuries, for the same reason.

As an investor, you should pay close attention to interest rates and yield spreads, and try to stay abreast not only of the current state of the market but also of the *future direction in market rates*. For example, if you are a conservative (income-oriented) investor and think that rates have just about peaked, that should be a clue to try to lock in the prevailing high yields with some form of call protection. (For example, buy bonds, like Treasuries or double-A-rated utilities, that are noncallable or still have lengthy call deferments.) In contrast, if you're an aggressive bond trader who thinks rates have peaked (and are about to drop), that should be a signal to buy bonds that offer maximum price appreciation potential (low-coupon bonds that still have a long time before they mature.) Clearly, in either case, *the future direction of interest rates is important*!

But how do you formulate such expectations? Unless you have considerable training in economics, you will probably have to rely on various published sources. Fortunately, a wealth of such information is available. Your broker is an excellent source for such reports, as are investor services like Moody's and Standard & Poor's; and, of course, there are numerous online sources. Finally, there are widely circulated business and financial publications (like the *Wall Street Journal*, *Forbes*, *Business Week*, and *Fortune*, to name a few) that regularly address the current state and future direction of market interest rates. One of the best sources is illustrated in Figure 11.1 (on page 460). Predicting the direction of interest rates is not easy. However, by taking the time to read some of these publications and reports regularly and carefully, you, too, can keep track of the behavior of interest rates and at least get a handle on what experts predict is likely to occur in the near future—say, over the next 6 to 12 months, perhaps even longer.

FIGURE 11.1   **A Popular Source of Information About Interest Rates and the Credit Markets**

The "Credit Markets" column, which appears every day in the *Wall Street Journal*, provides a capsule view of the current conditions and future prospects in the bond market. Note that on this particular day, a good deal of the article was devoted to the unusually large calendar of new Treasury issues coming to the market. (*Source: Wall Street Journal*, August 8, 2003. Copyright 2003 by Dow Jones & Co., Inc. Reproduced with permission of Dow Jones & Co., Inc. in textbook format via Copyright Clearance Center.)

CREDIT MARKETS

U.S. Sale of 10-Year Notes Is Hailed

Investors, Traders Fix Eyes On Fed's Tuesday Meeting; Market Sentiment Improves

By AGNES T. CRANE
Dow Jones Newswires

NEW YORK—A well-received sale of $18 billion of 10-year notes capped what many hailed as the successful placement of $60 billion of new government securities this week, despite a horrendous start to the Treasury Department's record quarterly refunding auction.

In the last leg of the three-part refunding package, the government awarded the new 10-year notes at a yield of 4.37%, largely in line with where they traded in the gray market in the minutes leading up to the sale.

The bid-to-cover ratio, a gauge of demand, was 2, the highest level since May 2002, but in line with the average of the past 10 auctions. At a time of ballooning federal budget deficits, the cost for the government, however, was greater since awarded yields overall were substantially higher than the record lows in May.

Yield Comparisons
Based on Merrill Lynch Bond Indexes, priced as of midafternoon Eastern time.

	8/7	8/6	52-WEEK HIGH	52-WEEK LOW
Corp. Govt. Master	3.72%	3.77%	4.43%	2.81%
Treasury				
1-10 yr	2.33	2.36	2.73	1.57
10+ yr	5.00	5.04	5.20	3.86
Agencies				
1-10 yr	2.74	2.82	3.17	1.77
10+ yr	5.48	5.52	5.72	4.24
Corporate				
1-10 yr High Quality	3.47	3.51	4.34	2.47
Medium Quality	4.30	4.34	6.21	3.38
10+ yr High Quality	6.01	6.04	6.60	4.79
Medium Quality	6.62	6.65	7.76	5.36
Yankee bonds (1)	4.10	4.15	5.22	3.21
Current-coupon mortgages (2)				
GNMA 6.50% (3)	5.40	5.51	5.78	3.70
FNMA 6.50%	5.43	5.58	6.11	3.99
FHLMC 6.50%	5.49	5.62	6.16	4.10
High-yield corporates	9.42	9.39	13.96	8.46
Tax-Exempt Bonds				
7-12 yr G.O. (AA)	3.95	4.02	4.13	2.82
12-22 yr G.O. (AA)	4.81	4.87	4.97	3.79
22+ yr revenue (A)	5.21	5.25	5.32	4.32

Note: High quality rated AAA-AA; medium quality A-BBB/Baa; high yield, BB/Ba-C.
(1) Dollar-denominated, SEC-registered bonds of foreign issuers sold in the U.S. (2) Reflects the 52-week high and low of mortgage-backed securities indexes rather than the individual securities shown. (3) Government guaranteed.

was 4.206%. The 30-year bond's price was up 14/32 point at 102 10/32 to yield 5.216%, down from 5.246% Wednesday.

The 10-year note sale may have fallen short compared with the five-year note auction, which benefited from a surge of domestic and foreign interest that pushed the bid-to-cover ratio to 2.48, but it shined brightly next to the three-year note sale.

Corporate Bonds

Lockheed Martin plans a 30-year, $850 million convertible note offering featuring an unusual floating-rate feature that implies it is hoping for steady short-term rates, analysts said.

With the recent widening of U.S. Treasury yields, a floating-rate coupon means Lockheed is taking the interest-rate risk of the issue, which is atypical for an industrial conglomerate whose income streams aren't heavily tied to variable rates.

Late Wednesday, Lockheed Martin said the notes would include a coupon that ranges from 0.45 to 0.90 percentage point below the three-month London interbank offered rate, and a conversion premium of 52.5% to 57.5%. By midday yesterday, the coupon had been narrowed to 0.20 to 0.30 percentage point under the Libor rate, according to a fund manager.

—Mara Lemos

AUCTION RESULTS

Here are the results of the Treasury auction of 10-year notes. All bids are awarded at a single price at the market-clearing yield. Rates are determined by the difference between that price and the face value.

Applications	$35,975,558,000
Accepted bids	$18,000,002,000
Bids at market-clearing yield accepted	82.62%
Accepted noncompetitively	$239,733,000
" foreign noncompetitively	$0
Auction price (rate)	99.036 (4.370%)
Interest rate	4 1/4%
Cusip number	912828BH2

The notes are dated Aug. 15, 2003, and mature Aug. 15, 2013.

What Causes Rates to Move?

Although interest rates are a complex economic issue, we do know that certain forces are especially important in influencing their general behavior. Serious bond investors should make it a point to become familiar with the major determinants of interest rates and try to monitor those variables, at least informally.

FIGURE 11.2

FIGURE 11.2

The Impact of Inflation on the Behavior of Interest Rates

The behavior of interest rates has always been closely tied to the movements in the rate of inflation. What changed in the early 1980s, however, was the spread between inflation and interest rates. Whereas a spread of roughly 3 points was common in the past, it has held at about 5 to 6 percentage points since 1982.

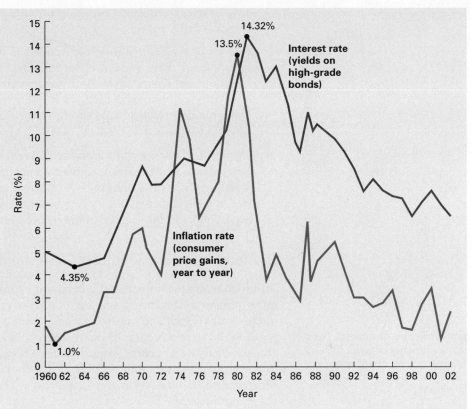

And in that regard, perhaps no variable is more important than *inflation*. Changes in the inflation rate (or even expectations about its future course) have a direct and pronounced effect on market interest rates. Clearly, if inflation is expected to slow down, then market interest rates should fall as well. To gain an appreciation of the extent to which interest rates are linked to inflation, take a look at Figure 11.2. Note that as inflation drifts up, so do interest rates. On the other hand, a drop in inflation is matched by a similar decline in interest rates.

In addition to inflation, there are at least five other important economic variables that can significantly affect the level of interest rates:

- *Changes in the money supply.* An increase in the money supply pushes rates down (as it makes more funds available for loans), and vice versa. This is true only up to a point, however. If the growth in the money supply becomes excessive, it can lead to inflation, which, of course, means higher interest rates.

- *The size of the federal budget deficit.* When the U.S. Treasury has to borrow large amounts to cover the budget deficit, the increased demand for funds exerts an upward pressure on interest rates. That's why bond market participants become so concerned when the budget deficit gets bigger and bigger—*other things being equal*, that means more upward pressure on market interest rates.

- *The level of economic activity.* Businesses need more capital when the economy expands. This need increases the demand for funds, and rates tend to rise. During a recession, economic activity contracts, and rates typically fall.

- *Policies of the Federal Reserve.* Actions of the Federal Reserve to control inflation also have a major effect on market interest rates. For example, when the Fed wants to slow real (or perceived) inflation, it usually does so by driving up interest rates, as it did several times in 1999–2000. Unfortunately, such actions can have the nasty side effect of slowing down business activity as well.

- *The level of interest rates in major foreign markets.* Today, investors look beyond national borders for investment opportunities. If rates in major foreign markets rise, that puts pressure on rates in the United States to rise as well; if they don't, foreign investors may be tempted to dump their dollars to buy higher-yielding foreign securities.

The Term Structure of Interest Rates and Yield Curves

term structure of interest rates
the relationship between the interest rate or rate of return (yield) on a bond and its time to maturity.

yield curve
a graph that represents the relationship between a bond's term to maturity and its yield at a given point in time.

Although many factors affect the behavior of market interest rates, one of the most popular and widely studied is *bond maturity*. The relationship between interest rates (yield) and time to maturity for any class of similar-risk securities is called the **term structure of interest rates.** This relationship can be depicted graphically by a **yield curve,** which relates a bond's *term* to maturity to its *yield* to maturity at a given point in time. A particular yield curve exists for only a short period of time. As market conditions change, so do the yield curve's shape and location.

Types of Yield Curves Two different types of yield curves are illustrated in Figure 11.3. By far, the most common type is curve 1, the *upward-sloping* curve. It indicates that yields tend to increase with longer maturities. That's because the longer a bond has to go to maturity, the greater the potential for price volatility and the risk of loss. Investors, therefore, require higher risk premiums to induce them to buy the longer, riskier bonds. Occasionally, the yield curve becomes *inverted*, or downward sloping, as shown in curve 2, which occurs when short-term rates are higher than long-term rates. This curve generally results from actions by the Federal Reserve to curtail inflation by driving short-term interest rates way up. In addition to these, there are two other types of yield curves that appear from time to time: the *flat* yield curve, when rates for short- and long-term debt are essentially the same, and the *humped* yield curve, when intermediate-term rates are the highest.

Plotting Your Own Curves Yield curves are constructed by plotting the yields for a group of bonds that are similar in all respects but maturity. Treasury securities (bills, notes, and bonds) are typically used to construct yield curves. There are several reasons for this: Their yields are easily found in financial publications, they have no risk of default, and they are homogeneous with regard to quality and other issue characteristics. Investors can also construct yield curves for other classes of debt securities, such as A-rated municipal bonds, Aa-rated corporate bonds, or even certificates of deposit.

Figure 11.4 (on page 464) shows the yield curves for Treasury securities on two dates, July 10, 2000, and July 29, 2003. To draw these curves, you

H O T

For the latest information on the U.S. economy and bonds, go to the SmartMoney Web site at:

www.smartmoney.com/bonds

FIGURE 11.3

Two Types of Yield Curves

A yield curve relates term-to-maturity to yield-to-maturity at a given point in time. Although yield curves come in many shapes and forms, the most common is the *upward-sloping curve*. It shows that investor returns (yields) increase with longer maturities.

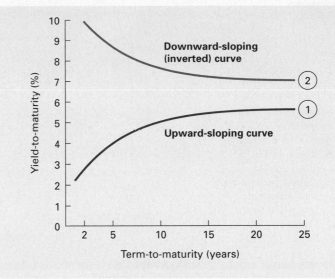

need Treasury quotes from the *Wall Street Journal*. (Note that actual quoted yields for curve 2 are provided in the boxed information right below the graph.) Given the required quotes, select the yields for the Treasury bills, notes, and bonds maturing in approximately 3 months, 6 months, and 1, 2, 5, 10, 20, and 30 (actually 28) years. The yields used for this curve are highlighted in Figure 11.4. (You could include more points, but they would not have much effect on the general shape of the curve.) Next, plot the points on a graph whose horizontal (*x*) axis represents time to maturity in years and whose vertical (*y*) axis represents yield to maturity. Connect the points to create the curves shown in Figure 11.4. You'll notice that while curve 1 is downward sloping, it still ended with a higher yield than curve 2, which is upward sloping. The reason: Curve 2 reflects the 40-year lows that existed in market yields in 2003.

Explanations of the Term Structure of Interest Rates As we noted earlier, the shape of the yield curve can change over time. Three commonly cited theories—the expectations hypothesis, the liquidity preference theory, and the market segmentation theory—explain more fully the reasons for the general shape of the yield curve.

expectations hypothesis
theory that the shape of the yield curve reflects investor expectations of future interest rates.

Expectations Hypothesis The **expectations hypothesis** suggests that the yield curve reflects investor expectations about the future behavior of interest rates. This theory argues that the relationship between rates today and rates expected in the future is due primarily to investor expectations about inflation. If investors anticipate higher rates of inflation in the future, they will require higher long-term interest rates today, and vice versa. To see how this explanation can be applied in practice, consider the behavior of U.S. Treasury securities.

Because Treasury securities are considered essentially risk-free, only two components determine their yield: the real rate of interest and inflation expectations. Since the real rate is the same for all maturities, it follows that variations in yields are caused by differing inflation expectations associated with

FIGURE 11.4

Yield Curves on U.S. Treasury Issues

Here we see two yield curves constructed from actual market data (quotes). Note the different shapes of the two curves: Curve 1 has a slight downward slope (i.e., the 30-year yield is actually less than T-bill rates), while curve 2 has a normal upward slope. Even so, curve 2 remained well below curve 1 because of the historically low yields that existed in 2003. (*Source: Wall Street Journal*, July 29, 2003.)

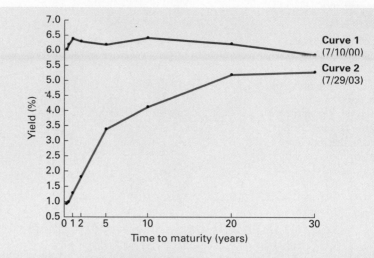

Yield Data for Curve 2
Treasury Issues—Bills, Notes, and Bonds
Tuesday, July 29, 2003

Treasury Bills

MATURITY	DAYS TO MAT	BID	ASKED	CHG	ASK YLD
Jul 31 03	1	0.95	0.94	0.03	0.95
Aug 07 03	8	0.98	0.97	0.07	0.98
Aug 14 03	15	0.89	0.88	0.01	0.89
Aug 21 03	22	0.94	0.93	...	0.94
Aug 28 03	29	0.94	0.93	0.03	0.94
Sep 04 03	36	0.93	0.92	0.04	0.93
Sep 11 03	43	0.92	0.91	0.02	0.92
Sep 18 03	50	0.90	0.89	0.03	0.90
Sep 25 03	57	0.91	0.90	0.02	0.91
Oct 02 03	64	0.92	0.91	0.01	0.92
Oct 09 03 (3 Month →)	71	0.94	0.93	0.03	0.94
Oct 16 03	78	0.94	0.93	0.02	0.94
Oct 23 03	85	0.96	0.95	0.02	0.97
Oct 30 03	92	0.96	0.95	0.01	0.97
Nov 06 03	99	0.96	0.95	0.02	0.97
Nov 13 03	106	0.96	0.95	0.02	0.97
Nov 20 03	113	0.96	0.95	...	0.97
Nov 28 03	121	0.97	0.96	0.01	0.98
Dec 04 03	127	0.98	0.97	0.01	0.99
Dec 11 03	134	0.97	0.96	0.01	0.98
Dec 18 03	141	0.97	0.96	...	0.98
Dec 26 03	149	0.98	0.97	0.01	0.99
Jan 02 04 (6 Month →)	156	0.99	0.98	0.01	1.00
Jan 08 04	162	0.98	0.97	...	0.99
Jan 15 04	169	0.98	0.97	...	0.99
Jan 22 04	176	0.98	0.97	...	0.99
Jan 29 04	183	0.99	0.98	...	1.00

Government Bonds & Notes

RATE	MATURITY MO/YR	BID	ASKED	CHG	ASK YLD
3.875	Jul 03n	100:00	100:00	-1	0.12
5.250	Aug 03n	100:05	100:06	-1	0.64
5.750	Aug 03n	100:06	100:07	...	0.78
3.625	Mar 04n	101:22	101:23	-1	1.04
3.375	Apr 04n	101:22	101:23	-1	1.05
5.250	May 04n	103:08	103:09	-1	1.06
7.250	May 04n	104:26	104:27	-1	1.08
12.375	May 04	108:27	108:28	-2	1.10
3.250	May 04n	101:24	101:25	-1	1.08
2.875	Jun 04n	101:19	101:20	...	1.09
2.250	Jul 04n	101:02	101:03	-1	1.13
2.125	Aug 04n	101:00	101:01	-1	1.15
6.000	Aug 04n	105:00	105:00	-2	1.15
7.250	Aug 04n	106:09	106:10	-1	1.15
13.750	Aug 04	113:00	113:01	-2	1.14
1.875	Sep 04n	100:24	100:25	-1	1.20
2.125	Oct 04n	101:01	101:02	-1	1.25
5.875 (1 Year →)	Nov 04n	105:26	105:27	-2	1.29
7.875	Nov 04n	108:12	108:13	-1	1.30
11.625	Nov 04	113:04	113:05	-4	1.32
2.000	Nov 04n	100:28	100:29	-1	1.31
1.750	Dec 04n	100:17	100:18	-1	1.35
1.625	Jan 05n	100:10	100:11	-1	1.39
7.500	Feb 05n	109:07	109:08	-3	1.42
1.500	Feb 05n	100:02	100:03	-2	1.44
1.625	Mar 05n	100:07	100:08	-2	1.47
1.625	Apr 05n	100:04	100:05	-3	1.52
6.500	May 05n	108:23	108:24	-4	1.53
6.750	May 05n	109:05	109:06	-3	1.53
12.000	May 05	118:21	118:22	-4	1.41
1.250	May 05n	99:13	99:14	-3	1.55
1.125	Jun 05n	99:03	99:04	-2	1.59
1.500	Jul 05n	99:21	99:22	-3	1.66
6.500	Aug 05n	109:21	109:22	-4	1.65
10.750	Aug 05	118:03	118:04	-6	1.68
5.750 (2 Year →)	Nov 05n	108:24	108:25	-5	1.82
5.875	Nov 05n	109:01	109:02	-5	1.81
5.625	Feb 06n	109:01	109:02	-6	1.96
9.375	Feb 06	118:10	118:11	-6	1.94
2.000	May 06n	99:20	99:21	-5	2.13
5.500	Feb 08n	110:06	110:07	-13	3.07
2.625	May 08n	97:10	97:11	-12	3.23
5.625	May 08n	110:21	110:22	-13	3.20
8.375	Aug 08	100:10	100:11	-1	0.23
4.750 (5 Year →)	Nov 08n	106:15	106:16	-15	3.39
8.750	Nov 08	102:05	102:06	-1	1.20
3.875	Jan 09i	111:03	111:04	-16	1.73
5.500	May 09n	110:10	110:11	-15	3.51
9.125	May 09	106:05	106:06	-2	1.24
6.000	Aug 09n	112:25	112:26	-16	3.62
10.375	Nov 09	111:13	111:14	-4	1.41
4.250	Jan 10i	113:28	113:29	-20	1.95
6.500	Feb 10n	115:23	115:24	-17	3.76

Government Bonds & Notes (cont.)

RATE	MATURITY MO/YR	BID	ASKED	CHG	ASK YLD
11.750	Feb 10	115:14	115:15	-5	1.57
10.000	May 10	114:18	114:19	-4	1.69
5.750	Aug 10n	111:09	111:10	-17	3.90
12.750	Nov 10	124:01	124:02	-7	1.97
3.500	Jan 11i	109:24	109:25	-19	2.08
5.000 (10 Year →)	Feb 11n	106:08	106:09	-17	4.02
13.875	May 11	131:10	131:11	-10	2.23
5.000	Aug 11n	105:28	105:29	-18	4.13
14.000	Nov 11	136:13	136:14	-15	2.42
3.375	Jan 12i	108:29	108:30	-16	2.21
8.750	Aug 20	140:15	140:16	-39	5.15
7.875	Feb 21	130:18	130:19	-38	5.19
8.125 (20 Year →)	May 21	133:21	133:22	-38	5.20
8.125	Aug 21	133:24	133:25	-37	5.21
8.000	Nov 21	132:12	132:13	-37	5.23
7.250	Aug 22	123:18	123:19	-35	5.27
7.625	Nov 22	128:08	128:09	-39	5.27
7.125	Feb 23	122:05	122:06	-37	5.29
6.250	Aug 23	111:10	111:11	-33	5.32
7.500	Nov 24	127:20	127:21	-38	5.31
7.625	Feb 25	129:12	129:13	-38	5.32
6.875	Aug 25	119:23	119:24	-35	5.34
6.000	Feb 26	108:09	108:10	-33	5.36
6.750	Aug 26	118:08	118:09	-37	5.36
6.500	Nov 26	115:02	115:03	-32	5.36
6.625	Feb 27	116:25	116:26	-32	5.36
6.375	Aug 27	113:12	113:13	-35	5.37
6.125	Nov 27	110:00	110:01	-34	5.38
3.625	Apr 28i	112:14	112:15	-43	2.91
5.500	Aug 28	101:12	101:13	-32	5.40
5.250	Nov 28	98:00	98:01	-31	5.39
5.250	Feb 29	98:01	98:02	-30	5.39
3.875	Apr 29i	117:09	117:10	-49	2.91
6.125	Aug 29	110:06	110:07	-34	5.39
6.250	May 30	112:12	112:13	-34	5.37
5.375 (30 Year → i.e., 28)	Feb 31	101:04	101:05	-32	5.29

different maturities. This hypothesis can be illustrated using the July 10, 2000, yields for four of the Treasury maturities in Figure 11.4. If we assume that the real rate of interest is 3%, then the inflation expectation during the period to maturity is as shown in column 3 of the following table.

Maturity	(1) July 10, 2000 Yield	(2) Real Rate of Interest	(3) Inflation Expectation [(1) − (2)]
3 months	6.04%	3.00%	3.04%
1 year	6.40	3.00	3.40
5 years	6.20	3.00	3.20
10 years	6.43	3.00	3.43

According to the expectations hypothesis, the numbers in column 3 would suggest that in early July 2000, investors didn't foresee much of a problem with inflation. As a result, the yield curve (in Figure 11.4) was a lot flatter in 2000 than it was in 2003.

Generally, under the expectations hypothesis, an increasing inflation expectation results in an upward-sloping yield curve, a decreasing inflation expectation results in a downward-sloping yield curve, and a stable inflation expectation results in a relatively flat yield curve. Although, as we'll see below, other theories do exist, the observed strong relationship between inflation and interest rates lends considerable credence to this widely accepted theory.

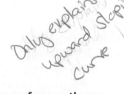
Only explains upward sloping curve

Liquidity Preference Theory More often than not, yield curves have an upward slope, as in 2003. One explanation for the frequency of upward-sloping yield curves is the **liquidity preference theory.** This theory states that, intuitively, long-term bond rates should be higher than short-term rates because of the added risks involved with the longer maturities. In other words, because of the risk differential (real or perceived) between long- and short-term debt securities, rational investors will prefer the less risky, short-term obligations *unless they can be motivated, via higher interest rates, to invest in the longer bonds.*

Actually, there are a number of reasons why rational investors should prefer short-term securities. To begin with, they are more liquid (more easily converted to cash) and less sensitive to changing market rates, which means there is less risk of loss of principal. For a given change in market rates, the prices of longer-term bonds will show considerably more movement than the prices of short-term bonds. Simply put, uncertainty increases over time, and investors therefore require a premium to invest in long maturities. In addition, just as investors tend to require a premium for tying up funds for longer periods, borrowers will also pay a premium in order to obtain long-term funds. Borrowers thus assure themselves that funds will be available, and they avoid having to roll over short-term debt at unknown and possibly unfavorable rates. All of these preferences and market forces explain why higher rates of interest should be associated with longer maturities and why it's perfectly rational to expect upward-sloping yield curves.

Market Segmentation Theory Another often-cited theory, the **market segmentation theory,** suggests that the market for debt is segmented on the basis

liquidity preference theory
theory that investors tend to prefer the greater liquidity of short-term securities and therefore require a premium to invest in long-term securities.

market segmentation theory
theory that the market for debt is segmented on the basis of maturity, that supply and demand within each segment determine the prevailing interest rate, and that the slope of the yield curve depends on the relationship between the prevailing rates in each segment.

of the maturity preferences of different types of financial institutions and investors. According to this theory, the yield curve changes as the supply and demand for funds within each maturity segment determine its prevailing interest rate. The equilibrium between the financial institutions that supply the funds for short-term maturities (e.g., banks) and the borrowers of those short-term funds (e.g., businesses with seasonal loan requirements) establishes interest rates in the short-term markets. Similarly, the equilibrium between suppliers and demanders in such long-term markets as life insurance and real estate determines the prevailing long-term interest rates.

The shape of the yield curve can be either upward or downward sloping, as determined by the general relationship between rates in each market segment. When supply outstrips demand for short-term loans, short-term rates are relatively low. If, at the same time, the demand for long-term loans is higher than the available supply of funds, then long-term rates will move up. Thus, low rates in the short-term segment and high rates in the long-term segment cause an upward-sloping yield curve, and vice versa.

Which Theory Is Right? It is clear *that all three theories* of the term structure have merit in explaining the shape of the yield curve. From them, we can conclude that at any time, the slope of the yield curve is affected by (1) inflationary expectations, (2) liquidity preferences, and (3) the supply and demand conditions in the short- and long-term market segments. Upward-sloping yield curves result from higher inflation expectations, lender preferences for shorter-maturity loans, and greater supply of short- rather than of long-term loans relative to the respective demand in each market segment. The opposite behavior, of course, results in a flat or downward-sloping yield curve. At any point in time, the interaction of these forces determines the prevailing slope of the yield curve.

Using the Yield Curve in Investment Decisions   Bond investors often use yield curves in making investment decisions. As noted earlier, yield curves change in accordance with market conditions. Analyzing the changes in yield curves over time provides investors with information about future interest rate movements and how they can affect price behavior and comparative returns. For example, if the yield curve begins to rise sharply, it usually means that inflation is starting to heat up or is expected to do so in the near future. In that case, investors can expect that interest rates, too, will rise. Under these conditions, most seasoned bond investors will turn to short or intermediate (3 to 5 years) maturities, which provide reasonable returns and at the same time minimize exposure to capital loss when interest rates go up (and bond prices fall). A downward-sloping yield curve, though unusual, generally results from actions of the Federal Reserve to reduce inflation. As suggested by the expectations hypothesis, this would signal that rates have peaked and are about to fall.

Another factor to consider is the difference in yields on different maturities—the "steepness" of the curve. For example, a steep yield curve is one where long-term rates are *much higher* than short-term rates. This shape is often seen as an indication that long-term rates may be near their peak and are about to fall, thereby narrowing the spread between long and short rates. Steep yield curves are generally viewed as a bullish sign. For aggressive bond investors, they could be the signal to start moving into long-term securities. Flatter yield curves, on the other hand, sharply reduce the incentive for going long-term. For example, look at yield curve 1 in Figure 11.4. Note that the difference in yield between the 5- and 20-year maturities is quite small. (In fact, it's almost nonexistent, as it amounts to *only 3 basis points*, or ³⁄₁₀₀ of 1%.) As a result, there's not much incentive to go long-term. Under these conditions, investors would be well advised to just stick with the 5- to 10-year maturities, which will generate about the same yield as long bonds but without the risks. You'll also notice that in July 2000, the 30-year bonds had even lower yields. A lot of this was due to a "scarcity effect" as the Treasury began to sharply curtail the supply of long bonds. In other words, because there was more demand than supply, rates fell.

IN REVIEW

CONCEPTS

11.1 Is there a single market rate of interest applicable to all segments of the bond market, or are there a series of market yields? Explain and note the investment implications of such a market environment.

11.2 Explain why interest rates are important to both conservative and aggressive bond investors. What causes interest rates to move, and how can you monitor such movements?

11.3 What is the *term structure of interest rates*, and how is it related to the *yield curve*? What information is required to plot a yield curve? Describe an upward-sloping yield curve and explain what it has to say about the behavior of interest rates. Do the same for a flat yield curve.

11.4 How might you, as a bond investor, use information about the term structure of interest rates and yield curves when making investment decisions?

The Pricing of Bonds

LG 3

If there's one common denominator in the bond market, it's the way bonds are priced. No matter who the issuer is, what kind of bond it is, or whether it's fully taxable or tax-free, all bonds are priced pretty much the same. In particular, all bonds (including *notes* with maturities of more than 1 year) are priced according to the *present value of their future cash flow* streams. Indeed, once the prevailing or expected market yield is known, the whole process becomes rather mechanical.

Bond prices are driven by market yields. That's because in the marketplace, the *appropriate yield at which the bond should sell is determined first*, and then that yield is used to find the price (or market value) of the bond. The appropriate yield on a bond is a function of certain market and economic forces (e.g., the risk-free rate of return and inflation), as well as key issue and issuer characteristics (e.g., years to maturity and the bond rating). Together, these forces combine to form the *required rate of return*, which is the rate of return the investor would like to earn in order to justify an investment in a given fixed-income security. In the bond market, required return is market driven and is generally considered to be the issue's market yield. That is, the required return defines the yield at which the bond should be trading and serves as the *discount rate* in the bond valuation process.

Basically, bond investors are entitled to two distinct types of cash flows: (1) the periodic receipt of coupon income over the life of the bond, and (2) the recovery of principal (or par value) at the end of the bond's life. Thus, in valuing a bond, you're dealing with an *annuity* of coupon payments plus a large *single cash flow*, as represented by the recovery of principal at maturity. These cash flows, along with the required rate of return on the investment, are then used in a present-value-based bond valuation model to find the dollar price of a bond. We'll demonstrate the bond valuation process in two ways. First, we'll use *annual compounding*—that is, because of its computational simplicity, we'll assume we're dealing with coupons that are paid once a year. Second, we'll examine bond valuation under conditions of *semiannual compounding*, which is more like the way most bonds actually pay their coupons.

We'll use present-value interest factors to define and illustrate the various bond price and yield measures. But all these calculations can be done just as easily (in fact, more easily) on a good hand-held calculator. Even so, before you revert to the regular use of one of these calculators (see the *Calculator Use* sections for keystroke guidelines), we strongly encourage you to work through the bond valuation model at least once or twice, using the procedures outlined below. Doing so will help you gain a thorough understanding of what's embedded in a bond price or yield measure.

Annual Compounding

Along with a table of present-value interest factors (see Appendix A, Tables A.3 and A.4), the following information is needed to value a bond: (1) the size of the annual coupon payment, (2) the bond's par value, and (3) the number of years remaining to maturity. The prevailing market yield (or an estimate of future market rates) is then used as the discount rate to compute the price of a bond, as follows:

Equation 11.2

$$\text{Bond price} = \frac{\text{Present value of the annuity}}{\text{of annual interest income}} + \frac{\text{Present value of the}}{\text{bond's par value}}$$

Equation 11.2a

$$BP = (I \times PVIFA) + (PV \times PVIF)$$

where

I = amount of annual interest income

$PVIFA$ = present-value interest factor for an *annuity* (Appendix A, Table A.4)

PV = par value of the bond, which is assumed to be $1,000

$PVIF$ = present-value interest factor for a *single cash flow* (Appendix A, Table A.3)

To illustrate the bond price formula in action, consider a 20-year, 9½% bond that is being priced to yield 10%. From this we know the bond pays an annual coupon of 9½% (or $95), has 20 years left to maturity, and should be priced to provide a market yield of 10%. As we saw in Chapter 4, the maturity and market yield information is used to find the appropriate present-value interest factors (in Appendix A, Tables A.3 and A.4). Given these interest factors, we can now use Equation 11.2 to find the price of our bond.

$$\begin{aligned}
\text{Bond price} \ =& \ (\$95 \times \textit{PVIFA} \text{ for 10\% and 20 years}) \ + \\
& \ (\$1{,}000 \times \textit{PVIF} \text{ for 10\% and 20 years}) \\
\\
=& \ (\$95 \times 8.514) + (\$1{,}000 \times .149) = \underline{\$957.83}
\end{aligned}$$

Note that because this is a coupon-bearing bond, we have an annuity of coupon payments of $95 a year for 20 years, plus a single cash flow of $1,000 that occurs at the end of year 20. Thus, in bond valuation, we find the present value of the coupon annuity and then add that amount to the present value of the recovery of principal at maturity. In this particular case, you should be willing to pay about $958 for this bond, so long as you're satisfied with earning 10% on your money.

CALCULATOR USE For *annual compounding*, to price a 20-year, 9½% bond to yield 10%, use the keystrokes shown in the margin, where:

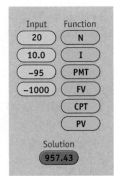

Input	Function
20	N
10.0	I
−95	PMT
−1000	FV
	CPT
	PV

Solution
957.43

N = number of years to maturity,

I = yield on the bond (what the bond is being priced to yield),

PMT = stream of annual coupon payments,

FV = par value of the bond, and

PV = computed price of the bond.

Semiannual Compounding

Although using annual compounding, as we did above, simplifies the valuation process a bit, it's not the way bonds are actually valued in the marketplace. In practice, most (domestic) bonds pay interest every 6 months, so semiannual compounding is used in valuing bonds. Fortunately, it's relatively easy to go from annual to semiannual compounding: All you need do is cut the annual coupon payment in half, and make two minor modifications to the present-value interest factors. Given these changes, finding the price of a bond under conditions of semiannual compounding is much like pricing a bond using annual compounding. That is,

Equation 11.3

$$\text{Bond price (with semi-} \atop \text{annual compounding)} = \text{Present value of an annuity} \atop \text{of \textit{semiannual} coupon payments} + \text{Present value of the} \atop \text{bond's par value}$$

Equation 11.3a

$$BP = (I/2 \times PVIFA^*) + (PV \times PVIF^*)$$

where

$PVIFA^*$ = present-value interest factor for an annuity, with required return and years-to-maturity adjusted for *semiannual compounding* (Appendix A, Table A.4)

$PVIF^*$ = present-value interest factor for a single cash flow, with required return and years-to-maturity adjusted for *semiannual compounding* (Appendix A, Table A.3)

I, PV = as described above

Note that in Equation 11.3, we adjusted the present-value interest factors (both *PVIFA* and *PVIF*) to accommodate semiannual compounding. By simply *cutting the required return in half and doubling the number of years to maturity*, we are, in effect, dealing with a semiannual measure of return and using the number of 6-month periods to maturity (rather than *years*). For example, in our bond illustration above, we wanted to price a 20-year bond to yield 10%. With semiannual compounding, we would be dealing with a semiannual return of 10%/2 = 5%, and with 20 × 2 = 40 semiannual periods to maturity. Thus we'd find the present-value interest factors for 5% and 40 periods from Table A.4 (for *PVIFA**) and from Table A.3 (for *PVIF**). Note that we adjust *the present-value interest factor* for the $1,000 par value, because that too will be subject to semiannual compounding, even though the cash flow will still be received in one lump sum.

To see how this all fits together, consider once again the 20-year, 9½% bond. This time assume it's being priced to yield 10%, *compounded semiannually*. Using Equation 11.3, you'd have:

$$
\begin{aligned}
\text{Bond price (with semi-annual compounding)} &= (\$95/2 \times PVIFA^* \text{ for 5\% and 40 periods}) \\
&\quad + (\$1,000 \times PVIF^* \text{ for 5\% and 40 periods}) \\[2mm]
&= (\$47.50 \times 17.159) + (\$1,000 \times .142) = \underline{\$957.02}
\end{aligned}
$$

The price of the bond in this case ($957.02) is slightly less than the price we obtained with annual compounding ($957.83). Clearly, it doesn't make much difference whether we use annual or semiannual compounding, though the differences do tend to increase a bit with lower coupons and shorter maturities.

CALCULATOR USE For *semiannual compounding*, to price a 20-year, 9½% bond to yield 10%, use the keystrokes shown in the margin, where:

N = number of 6-month periods to maturity (20 × 2 = 40),

I = yield on the bond, adjusted for semiannual compounding (10/2 = 5.0),

PMT = stream of semiannual coupon payments (95.00/2 = 47.50), and

FV *and* PV = remain the same.

Note that the price of the bond is a bit higher here due to rounding (i.e., we get $957.10 with the calculator versus $957.02 with the tables).

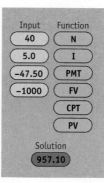

Input	Function
40	N
5.0	I
−47.50	PMT
−1000	FV
	CPT
	PV

Solution
957.10

IN REVIEW

CONCEPTS

11.5 Explain how market yield affects the price of a bond. Could you price a bond without knowing its market yield? Explain.

11.6 Why are bonds generally priced using semiannual compounding? Does it make much difference if you use annual compounding?

Measures of Yield and Return

LG 4

As surprising as it may seem, in the bond market, investment decisions are made more on the basis of a bond's yield than its dollar price. Not only does yield affect the price at which a bond trades, but it also serves as an important measure of return. To use yield as a measure of return, we *simply reverse the bond valuation process* described above and solve for yield rather than price. Actually, there are three widely used measures of yield: current yield, yield-to-maturity, and yield-to-call. We'll look at all three of them here, along with a concept known as *expected return*, which measures the expected (or actual) rate of return earned over a specific holding period.

Current Yield

current yield
return measure that indicates the amount of current income a bond provides relative to its market price.

Current yield is the simplest of all bond return measures, but it also has the most limited application. This measure looks at just one source of return: *a bond's interest income*. In particular, it indicates the amount of current income a bond provides relative to its prevailing market price. It is calculated as follows:

Equation 11.4

$$\text{Current yield} = \frac{\text{Annual interest}}{\text{Current market price of the bond}}$$

For example, an 8% bond would pay $80 per year in interest for every $1,000 of principal. However, if the bond were currently priced at $800, it would have a current yield of 10% ($80/$800 = 0.10). Current yield is a measure of a bond's annual coupon income, so it would be of interest primarily to investors seeking high levels of current income.

Yield-to-Maturity

yield-to-maturity (YTM)
the fully compounded rate of return earned by an investor over the life of a bond, including interest income and price appreciation.

promised yield
yield-to-maturity.

Yield-to-maturity (YTM) is the most important and widely used bond valuation measure. It evaluates both interest income and price appreciation and considers total cash flow received over the life of an issue. Also known as **promised yield**, YTM shows the fully compounded rate of return earned by an investor, *given that the bond is held to maturity and all principal and interest payments are made in a prompt and timely fashion*. In addition, because YTM is a present-value-based measure of return, it's assumed that *all the coupons will be reinvested, for the remaining life of the issue, at an interest rate equal to the bond's yield-to-maturity*. This "reinvestment assumption" plays a vital role in YTM, and will be discussed in more detail later in this chapter (see "Yield Properties"). Yield-to-maturity is used not only to gauge the return on a single issue but also to track the behavior of the market in general. In other words, market interest rates are basically a reflection of the average promised yields that exist in a given segment of the market. Promised yield provides valuable insight into an issue's investment merits and is used to assess the attractiveness of alternative investment vehicles. Other things being equal, the higher the promised yield of an issue, the more attractive it is.

Although there are a couple of ways to compute promised yield, the best and most accurate procedure is one that is derived directly from the bond valuation model described above. That is, assuming annual compounding, you can use Equation 11.2 to measure the YTM on a bond. The difference is that now, instead of trying to determine the price of the bond, *we know its price and are trying to find the discount rate that will equate the present value of the bond's cash flow (coupon and principal payments) to its current market price.* This procedure may sound familiar: It's just like the *internal rate of return* measure described in Chapter 4. Indeed, we're basically looking for the internal rate of return on a bond. When we find that, we have the bond's yield-to-maturity.

Unfortunately, unless you have a hand-held calculator or computer software that will do the calculations for you, finding yield-to-maturity is a matter of trial and error. Let's say we want to find the yield-to-maturity on a 7½% ($1,000 par value) bond that has 15 years remaining to maturity and is currently trading in the market at $809.50. From Equation 11.2, we know that

$$\text{Bond price} = (I \times PVIFA) + (PV \times PVIF)$$

As it now stands, we know the current market price of the bond ($809.50), the amount of annual interest/coupon income (7½% = $75), the par value of the bond ($1,000), and the number of years to maturity (15). To compute yield-to-maturity, we need to find the discount rate (in the present-value interest factors) that produces a bond price of $809.50.

Here's what we have so far:

$$\text{Bond price} = (I \times PVIFA) + (PV \times PVIF)$$

$$\$809.50 = (\$75 \times PVIFA \text{ for 15 years and a discount rate of ?\%)}$$
$$+ (\$1,000 \times PVIF \text{ for 15 years and a discount rate of ?\%)}$$

Right now we know only one thing about the yield on this bond—it has to be more than 7½%. (Why? Because this is a discount bond, so the yield-to-maturity must exceed the coupon rate.) Through trial and error, we might start with a discount rate of, say, 8% or 9% (or any number above the bond's coupon). Sooner or later, we'll move to a discount rate of 10%. And look what happens at that point: Using Equation 11.2 to price this bond at a discount rate of 10%, we see that

$$\text{Bond price} = (\$75 \times PVIFA \text{ for 15 years and 10\%)}$$
$$+ (\$1,000 \times PVIFA \text{ for 15 years and 10\%)}$$

$$= (\$75 \times 7.606) + (\$1,000 \times 0.239)$$

$$= \underline{\$809.45}$$

The computed price of $809.45 is reasonably close to the bond's current market price of $809.50. As a result, the 10% rate represents the yield-to-maturity on this bond. That is, 10% is the discount rate that leads to a *computed bond price that's equal (or very close) to the bond's current market price.* In this case, if you were to pay $809.50 for the bond and hold it to maturity, you would expect to earn a yield of 10.0%. Now there's no doubt that promised yield is an important measure of performance. However, as discussed in the *Investing in Action* box on pages 474–475, this measure tells only part of the story.

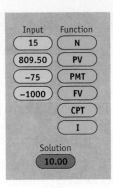

Input	Function
15	N
809.50	PV
−75	PMT
−1000	FV
	CPT
	I

Solution
10.00

CALCULATOR USE For *annual compounding*, to find the YTM of a 15-year, 7½% bond that is currently priced in the market at $809.50, use the keystrokes shown in the margin. The present value (*PV*) key represents the current market price of the bond, and all other keystrokes are as defined earlier.

Using Semiannual Compounding Given some fairly simple modifications, it's also possible to find yield-to-maturity using semiannual compounding. To do so, we cut the annual coupon in half, double the number of years (periods) to maturity, and use the bond valuation model in Equation 11.3. Returning to our 7½%, 15-year bond, let's see what happens when we try a discount rate of 10%. In this case, with semiannual compounding, we'd use a discount rate of 5% (10% ÷ 2); using this discount rate and 30 six-month periods to maturity (15 × 2) to specify the present-value interest factor, we have

$$\text{Bond price} = (\$75/2 \times \textit{PVIFA*} \text{ for 5\% and 30 periods})$$
$$+ (\$1{,}000 \times \textit{PVIFA} \text{ for 5\% and 30 periods})$$

$$= (\$37.50 \times 15.373) + (\$1{,}000 \times 0.231) = \underline{\$807.49}$$

As you can see, a semiannual discount rate of 5% results in a computed bond value that's a bit short of our target price of $809.50. Given the inverse relationship between price and yield, it follows that if we need a higher price, we'll have to try a lower yield (discount rate). Therefore, we know the semiannual yield on this bond has to be something less than 5%. Through interpolation, we find that a semiannual discount rate of (around) 4.97% gives us a computed bond value that's very close to $809.50.

At this point, because we're dealing with semiannual cash flows, to be technically accurate we should find the bond's "effective" annual yield. However, that's not the way it's done in practice. Rather, *market convention is to simply state the annual yield as twice the semiannual yield.* This practice produces what the market refers to as the **bond-equivalent yield**. Returning to the bond-yield problem we started above, we know that the issue has a semiannual yield of 4.97%. According to the bond-equivalent yield convention, all we have to do now is *double the solving rate in order to obtain the annual rate of return on this bond.* Doing this gives us a yield-to-maturity (or promised yield) of 4.97% × 2 = 9.94%. This is the annual rate of return we'll earn on the bond if we hold it to maturity.

bond-equivalent yield
the annual yield on a bond, calculated as twice the semiannual yield.

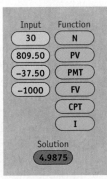

Input	Function
30	N
809.50	PV
−37.50	PMT
−1000	FV
	CPT
	I

Solution
4.9875

CALCULATOR USE For *semiannual compounding,* to find the YTM of a 15-year, 7½% bond that is currently priced in the market at $809.50, use the keystrokes shown here. As before, the *PV* key is the current market price of the bond, and all other keystrokes are as defined earlier. Remember that to find the bond-equivalent yield, you have to double the computed value of *I*. That is, 4.9875% × 2 = 9.975%.

Yield Properties Actually, in addition to holding the bond to maturity, there are a couple of other critical assumptions embedded in any yield-to-maturity figure. The promised yield measure—whether computed with annual or semiannual compounding—is based on present-value concepts and therefore contains important *reinvestment assumptions.* That is, the yield-to-maturity figure itself is the *minimum required reinvestment rate the investor must subsequently*

INVESTING IN ACTION

THERE'S MORE TO BOND RETURNS THAN YIELD ALONE

When individuals choose bond investments, they usually focus on yields, in the belief that higher yields generate better returns. But yields and returns are two different things, and investors who blindly chase higher yields can end up regretting it.

The fact is that yield is only part of the story: It tells you what you can expect going into an investment, not what you'll actually end up earning on the deal. Indeed, yield is often a poor proxy for return, and confusing the two can be damaging to your wealth!

Total return for fixed-income investments is made up of not only the initial yield but also (1) interest on reinvested interest and (2) price change. Only in the case of short-term investments, such as 1-year CDs or 6-month Treasury bills, is yield a good gauge of return. For long-term bonds and bonds purchased at prices far above or below face value, other factors often dwarf yield in determining returns. That's true even when the bonds are of triple-A quality.

For instance, interest on interest easily becomes the biggest factor in returns for buy-and-hold investors in long-term bonds, especially if interest rates rise during the life of the bond. If you bought a 30-year Treasury bond yielding 6.0% today and interest rates subsequently rose so that your average reinvestment rate was 8.0% over the life of the bond, more

than 75% of your total return at maturity would come from income on reinvested interest. On the other hand, although interest on interest dominates bond returns for long holding periods, price change dominates return for short-term investors. In either case, *future interest rate changes are the major concern for investors who want to safeguard their total returns.*

The starting yield on a bond becomes a bigger boon or burden to investors the longer the bond's maturity—which makes total returns on longer-term bonds much more sensitive to interest rate swings. For instance, from 1950 to 1980, long-term Treasury bonds actually had lower total returns than money market funds, despite their persistently higher yields. In the 1980s and 1990s, by contrast, a steady decline in interest rates meant long-term bonds put on a much better showing than yields would have indicated. Rising bond prices, caused by falling market rates, pushed total returns on Treasury bonds up to an average of 12.6% a year, beating T-bill returns by 3.7 percentage points.

In 2002, the third consecutive year that bond returns rose, rising prices were again the biggest component of bond returns. Yields fell as the Fed cut interest rates and inflation stayed low. Yields on the benchmark 10% Treasury note fell sharply; after starting the year at about 5% and reaching 5.4%, the yield hit a 44 year low of 3.57

continued on next page

earn on each of the interim coupon receipts in order to generate a return equal to or greater than the promised yield. In essence, the calculated yield-to-maturity figure is the return "promised" only so long as the issuer meets all interest and principal obligations on a timely basis and the investor reinvests all coupon income (from the date of receipt to maturity) at an average rate equal to or greater than the computed promised yield. In our example above, the investor would have to reinvest (to maturity) each of the coupons received over the next 15 years at a rate of about 10%. *Failure to do so would result in a realized yield of less than the 10% promised.* In fact, if the worst did occur and the investor made no attempt to reinvest any of the coupons, he or she would earn a realized yield over the 15-year investment horizon of just over 6½%—far short of the 10% promised return. Thus, unless it's a zero-coupon bond, a significant portion of a bond's total return over time is derived from the *reinvestment of coupons.*

INVESTING IN ACTION

continued from previous page

on October 9, 2002. However, principal values (prices) rose, so that total returns on these 10 year notes was 14.82%, and Treasury securities with maturities greater than 10 years returned 16.77% (versus only 4.21% and 4.26%, respectively, in 2001). Shorter-term Treasury notes also did well; total return for 5 to 7 year notes was almost 13%.

The only bond sector to post losses was high-yield corporate bonds, with returns of –1.89%. As the scandals involving Enron, Tyco, WorldCom and others rocked the corporate sector, the value of those companies' bonds plummeted. WorldCom, for example, fell in price from $75 to less than $25. Even investment-grade corporates felt the pressure from the scandals, as total returns fell slightly to 10.17% from 10.70% in 2001.

Yields remained low through fall 2003: 4.30% for 10-year Treasury notes and 4.87% for the Dow Jones Corporate Bond Index on October 9, 2003.

Of course, no one really knows where interest rates will go—and trying to predict them can prove to be a fruitless exercise. But investors can get a handle on the risks they face in the short run by considering how total returns on different investments might react to interest rate changes over, say, the next 12 months. For example, if interest rates were to fall 1 percentage point over the next 12 months, a typical portfolio of long-term bonds (with lives of more than 10 years) would generate an estimated total return of about 13%. But if interest rates were to rise by 1 percentage point, the total return would shrink to about 1%, making a money market fund return look good by comparison. Looking at the problem this way tells the investor how much rates would have to rise before the returns on long-term bonds were reduced to the level of, say, bank CDs or some other short-term benchmark. Clearly, the farther rates have to rise, the more cushion you have and the more secure your investments.

The old adage "You can't judge a book by its cover" certainly does apply to the bond market: Just because a bond promises a yield of *x* percent doesn't mean that's the return you'll actually end up with.

CRITICAL THINKING QUESTIONS Is there any difference between a bond's yield and its return? If so, which of these measures is more important? Explain.

Sources: Aaron Lucchetti, "The Bond Market Slams on the Brakes," *Wall Street Journal*, August 4, 2003, pp. C1, C11; "Markets Diary," *Wall Street Journal*, October 10, 2003, p. C1; and Gregory Zuckerman, "Investors Seek Safety Amid Corporate Scandals, Stock's Decline," *Wall Street Journal*, January 2, 2003, p. R4.

This reinvestment assumption was first introduced in Chapter 4, when we discussed the role that "interest on interest" plays in measuring investment returns (see pp. 157–159). As noted, when using present-value-based measures of return, such as YTM, there are actually three components of return: (1) coupon/interest income; (2) capital gains (or losses); and (3) interest on interest. Whereas current income and capital gains make up the profits from an investment, interest on interest is a measure of what you do with those profits. In the context of yield-to-maturity, the computed YTM defines the required, or minimum, reinvestment rate. Put your investment profits (i.e., coupon income) to work at this rate and you'll earn a rate of return equal to YTM. And this applies to any coupon-bearing bond—so long as there's an annual or semiannual flow of coupon income, the reinvestment of that income and interest on interest are matters that you must deal with. Also, keep in mind that the bigger the coupon and/or the longer the maturity, the more important the reinvestment assumption. Indeed, for many long-term, high-coupon bond investments, interest on interest by itself can account for well over half the cash flow.

Finding the Yield on a Zero The same promised-yield procedures described above (Equation 11.2 with annual compounding or Equation 11.3 with semi-annual compounding) can also be used to find the yield-to-maturity on a zero-coupon bond. The only difference is that the coupon portion of the equation can be ignored because it will, of course, equal zero. All you have to do to find the promised yield on a zero is to divide the current market price of the bond by $1,000 (the bond's par value) and then look for the computed interest factor in the present-value Table A.3 (in Appendix A).

To illustrate, consider a 15-year zero-coupon issue that can be purchased today for $315. Dividing this amount by the bond's par value of $1,000, we obtain an interest factor of $315/$1,000 = 0.315. Now, using annual compounding, look in Table A.3 (the table of present-value interest factors for single cash flows). Go down the first column to year 15 and then look across that row until you find an interest factor that equals (or is very close to) 0.315. Once you've found the factor, look up the column to the "Interest Rate" heading and you've got the promised yield of the issue. Using this approach, we see that the bond in our example has a promised yield of 8%. Had we been using semiannual compounding, we'd do exactly the same thing, except we'd go down to "year 30" and start the process there.

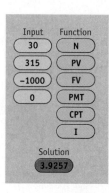

Input	Function
30	N
315	PV
−1000	FV
0	PMT
	CPT
	I

Solution
3.9257

CALCULATOR USE For *semiannual compounding*, to find the YTM of a 15-year, 7½% bond that is currently priced in the market at $315, use the keystrokes shown in the margin. *PV* is the current market price of the bond, and all other keystrokes are as defined earlier. To find the bond-equivalent yield, double the computed value of *I*. That is, 3.9257% × 2 = 7.85%.

Yield-to-Call

Bonds can be either noncallable or callable. Recall from Chapter 10 that a *non-callable bond* prohibits the issuer from calling the bond in for retirement prior to maturity. Because such issues will remain outstanding to maturity, they can all be valued by using the standard *yield-to-maturity* measure. In contrast, a *callable bond* gives the issuer the right to retire the bond prematurely, so the issue may or may not remain outstanding to maturity. As a result, YTM may not always be the appropriate measure of value. Instead, we must consider the impact of the bond being called away prior to maturity. A common way to do that is to use a measure known as **yield-to-call** (YTC), which shows the yield on a bond if the issue remains outstanding *not* to maturity, but rather until its first (or some other specified) call date.

yield-to-call (YTC)
the yield on a bond if it remains outstanding only until a specified call date.

Yield-to-call is commonly used with bonds that carry *deferred-call provisions*. Remember that such issues start out as noncallable bonds and then, after a call deferment period (of 5 to 10 years), become freely callable. Under these conditions, *YTC would measure the expected yield on a deferred-call bond assuming that the issue is retired at the end of the call deferment period* (that is, when the bond first becomes freely callable). We can find YTC by making two simple modifications to the standard YTM equation (Equation 11.2 or 11.3). First, we define the length of the investment horizon (N) as *the number of years to the first call date*, not the number of years to maturity. Second, instead of using the bond's par value ($1,000), we *use the bond's call price* (which is stipulated in the indenture and is nearly always greater than the bond's par value).

For example, assume you want to find yield-to-call on a 20-year, 10½% deferred-call bond that is currently trading in the market at $1,204, but has 5 years to go to first call (that is, before it becomes freely callable), at which time it can be called in at a price of $1,085. Thus, rather than using the bond's maturity of 20 years in the valuation equation (Equation 11.2 or 11.3), we use the number of years to first call (5 years), and rather than the bond's par value, $1,000, we use the issue's call price, $1,085. Note, however, we still use the bond's coupon (10½%) and its current market price ($1,204). Thus, for annual compounding, here's what we'd have:

Equation 11.5

$$\text{Bond price} = (I \times PVIFA) + (CP \times PVIF)$$

$$\$1,204.00 = (\$105 \times PVIFA \text{ for 5 years and a discount rate of ?\%})$$
$$+ (\$1,085 \times PVIF \text{ for 5 years and a discount rate of ?\%})$$

In Equation 11.5, *CP* equals the call price on the issue, and the present-value interest factors (for both *PVIFA* and *PVIF*) are for the number of years to first call date, not the term to maturity.

Through trial and error, we finally hit upon a discount rate of 7%. At that point, the present value of the future cash flows (coupons over the next 5 years, plus call price) will exactly (or very nearly) equal the bond's current market price of $1,204. That is,

$$\text{Bond price} = (\$105 \times PVIFA_{5 \text{ years, } 7\%}) + (\$1,085 \times PVIF_{5 \text{ years, } 7\%})$$

$$= (\$105 \times 4,100) + (\$1,085 \times 0.713)$$
$$= \$430.50 + \$773.61 = \underline{\$1,204.11}$$

Thus *the YTC on this bond is 7%*. In contrast, the bond's YTM is 8.36%. In practice, bond investors normally compute *both* YTM and YTC for deferred-call bonds that are *trading at a premium*. They do this to find which of the two yields is lower; market convention is to *use the lower, more conservative measure of yield (YTM or YTC) as the appropriate indicator of value*. As a result, the premium bond in our example would be valued relative to its yield-to-call. The assumption is that because interest rates have dropped so much (the bond is trading 2 percentage points below its coupon), it will be called in the first chance the issuer gets. However, the situation is totally different when this or any bond trades at a discount. Why? Because YTM on any *discount bond*, whether callable or not, *will always be less* than YTC. Thus YTC is a totally irrelevant measure for discount bonds—it's used only with premium bonds.

CALCULATOR USE For *annual compounding*, to find the YTC of a 20-year, 10½% bond that is currently trading at $1,204 but can be called in 5 years at a call price of $1,085, use the keystrokes shown in the margin. In this computation, N is the number of years to first call date, and FV represents the bond's call price. All other keystrokes are as defined earlier.

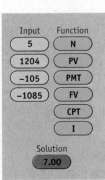

Expected Return

Rather than just buying and holding bonds, some investors prefer to actively trade in and out of these securities over fairly short investment horizons. As a result, yield-to-maturity and yield-to-call have relatively little meaning, other than as indicators of the rate of return used to price the bond. These investors obviously need an alternative measure of return that can be used to assess the investment appeal of those bonds they intend to trade in and out of. Such an alternative measure is **expected return**. It indicates the rate of return an investor can expect to earn by holding a bond over a period of time that's less than the life of the issue. (Expected return is also known as **realized yield,** because it shows the return an investor would realize by trading in and out of bonds over short holding periods.)

Expected return lacks the precision of yield-to-maturity (and YTC), because the major cash flow variables are largely the product of investor estimates. In particular, going into the investment, both the length of the holding period and the future selling price of the bond are pure estimates and therefore subject to uncertainty. Even so, we can use pretty much the same procedure to find realized yield as we did to find promised yield. That is, with some simple modifications to the standard bond-pricing formula, we can use the following equation to find the expected return on a bond.

expected return
the rate of return an investor can expect to earn by holding a bond over a period of time that's less than the life of the issue.

realized yield
expected return.

Equation 11.6

$$\text{Bond price} = \begin{array}{c}\text{Present value of the bond's}\\\text{annual interest income}\\\text{over the holding period}\end{array} + \begin{array}{c}\text{Present value of the bond's}\\\text{future price at the}\\\text{end of the holding period}\end{array}$$

Equation 11.6a

$$BP = (I \times PVIFA) + (FV \times PVIF)$$

where the present-value interest factors (for both *PVIFA* and *PVIF*) are for the length of the expected holding period only, not for the term to maturity, and *FV* is the expected future price of the bond.

Note that in this case, the *expected future price* of the bond is used in place of the par value ($1,000), and *the length of the holding period* is used in place of the term to maturity. As indicated above, we must determine the *future price* of the bond when computing expected realized yield; this is done by using the standard bond price formula, as described earlier. The most difficult part of deriving a reliable future price is, of course, coming up with future market interest rates that you feel will exist when the bond is sold. By evaluating current and expected market interest rate conditions, *the investor estimates a promised yield that the issue is expected to carry at the date of sale and then uses that yield to calculate the bond's future price.*

To illustrate, take one more look at our 7½%, 15-year bond. This time, let's assume that you feel the price of the bond, which is now trading at a discount, will rise sharply as interest rates fall over the next few years. In particular, assume the bond is currently priced at $810 (to yield 10%) and that you anticipate holding the bond for 3 years. Over that time, you expect market rates to drop, so the price of the bond should rise to around $960 by the end of the 3-year holding period. (Actually, we found the future price of the bond—$960—by assuming interest rates would fall to 8% in year 3. We then used the standard bond price formula—in this case Equation 11.2—to find the value of a 7½%, 12-year obligation, which is how many years to maturity a

15-year bond will have at the end of a 3-year holding period.) Thus, we are assuming that you will buy the bond today at a market price of $810 and sell it 3 years later—after interest rates have declined to 8%—at a price of $960. Given these assumptions, the expected return (realized yield) on this bond is 14.6%, which is the discount rate in the following equation that will produce a current market price of $810.

$$\text{Bond price} = (\$75 \times PVIFA \text{ for 3 years and } 14.6\%)$$
$$+ (\$960 \times PVIF \text{ for 3 years and } 14.6\%)$$

$$= (\$75 \times 2.301) + (\$960 \times 0.664) = \underline{\$810.02}$$

The better-than-14½% return on this investment is fairly substantial, but keep in mind that this is only a measure of *expected return*. It is, of course, subject to variation if things do not turn out as anticipated, particularly with regard to the market yield expected at the end of the holding period. (*Note*: This illustration uses annual compounding, but you could just as easily have used *semiannual compounding*, which, everything else being the same, would have resulted in an expected yield of 14.4% rather than the 14.6% found with annual compounding. Also, if the anticipated horizon is 1 year or less, you would want to use the simple *holding period return (HPR)* measure described in Chapter 4.)

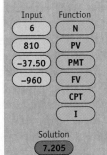

Input	Function
6	N
810	PV
−37.50	PMT
−960	FV
	CPT
	I

Solution
7.205

CALCULATOR USE For *semiannual compounding*, to find the expected return on a 7½% bond that is currently priced in the market at $810 but is expected to rise to $960 within a 3-year holding period, use the keystrokes shown in the margin. In this computation, *PV* is the current price of the bond, and *FV* is the expected price of the bond at the end of the (3-year) holding period. All other keystrokes are as defined earlier. To find the bond-equivalent yield, double the computed value of *I*: 7.205% × 2 = 14.41%.

Valuing a Bond

Depending on investor objectives, the value of a bond can be determined by either its promised yield or its expected return. Conservative, income-oriented investors employ *promised yield* (YTM or YTC) to value bonds. Coupon income over extended periods of time is their principal objective, and promised yield provides a viable measure of return—assuming, of course, the reinvestment assumptions embedded in the yield measure are reasonable. More aggressive bond traders, on the other hand, use *expected return* to value bonds. The capital gains that can be earned by buying and selling bonds over relatively short holding periods is their chief concern, and expected return is more important to them than the promised yield at the time the bond is purchased.

In either case, promised or expected yield provides a *measure of return* that can be used to determine the relative attractiveness of fixed-income securities. But to do so, we must evaluate the measure of return in light of the *risk* involved in the investment. Bonds are no different from stocks in that the amount of return (promised or expected) should be sufficient to cover the

H O T L I N K S

To answer questions such as "What is my yield to maturity?", "What is my yield to call?", and "How will rate changes affect my bond's current value?" you can use the bond calculators at:

**www.financenter.com/
consumertools/calculators**

investor's exposure to risk. Thus, the greater the amount of perceived risk, the greater the return the bond should generate. If the bond meets this hurdle, it could then be compared to other potential investments. If you find it difficult to do better in a risk–return sense, then the bond under evaluation should be given serious consideration as an investment outlet.

IN REVIEW

CONCEPTS

11.7 What's the difference between *current yield* and *yield-to-maturity?* Between *promised yield* and *realized yield?* How does *YTC* differ from *YTM?*

11.8 Briefly describe the term *bond-equivalent yield.* Is there any difference between promised yield and bond-equivalent yield? Explain.

11.9 Why is the reinvestment of interest income so important to bond investors?

Duration and Immunization

LG 5

One of the problems with yield-to-maturity (YTM) is that it assumes you can reinvest the bond's periodic coupon payments at the same rate over time. But if you reinvest this interest income at a lower rate (or if you spend it), your real return will be much lower than that indicated by YTM. The assumption that interest rates will remain constant is a key weakness of YTM. Another flaw is that YTM assumes the issuer will make all payments on time and won't call the bonds before maturity, as often happens when interest rates drop. For bonds that are not held to maturity, prices will reflect prevailing interest rates, which are likely to differ from YTM. If rates have moved up since a bond was purchased, the bond will sell at a discount. If interest rates have dropped, it will sell at a premium.

The problem with yield-to-maturity, then, is that it fails to take into account the effects of reinvestment risk and price (or market) risk. To see how reinvestment and price risks behave relative to one another, consider a situation in which market interest rates have undergone a sharp decline. Under such conditions, bond prices will, of course, rise; as such, you might be tempted to cash out your holdings and take some gains (i.e., do a little "profit taking"). Indeed, selling before maturity is the only way to take advantage of falling interest rates, because a bond will pay its par value at maturity, regardless of prevailing interest rates. That's the good news about falling rates, but there is a downside: When interest rates fall, so do the opportunities to invest at high rates. Therefore, although you gain on the price side, you lose on the reinvestment side. Even if you don't sell out, you are faced with increased reinvestment risk, because in order to earn the YTM promised on your bonds, you have to be able to reinvest each coupon payment at the same YTM rate. Obviously, as rates fall, you'll find it increasingly difficult to reinvest the stream of coupon payments at or above the YTM rate. When market rates rise, just the opposite happens: The price of the bond falls, but your reinvestment opportunities improve.

What is needed is a measure of performance that overcomes these deficiencies and takes into account both price and reinvestment risks. Such a yardstick is provided by something called **duration**. It captures in a single measure the extent to which the price of a bond will react to different interest rate environments. Because duration gauges the price volatility of a bond, it gives you a better idea of how likely you are to earn the return (YTM) you expect. That in turn will help you tailor your holdings to your expectations of interest rate movements.

duration
a measure of bond price volatility, which captures both price and reinvestment risks and which is used to indicate how a bond will react in different interest rate environments.

The Concept of Duration

The concept of duration was first developed in 1938 by actuary Frederick Macaulay to help insurance companies match their cash inflows with payments. When applied to bonds, duration recognizes that the amount and frequency of interest payments, yield-to-maturity, and term to maturity all affect the "time dimension" of a bond. Term to maturity is important because it influences how much a bond's price will rise or fall as interest rates change. In general, when rates move, bonds with longer maturities fluctuate more than shorter-term issues. On the other hand, while the amount of price risk embedded in a bond is related to the issue's term to maturity, the amount of reinvestment risk is directly related to the size of a bond's coupon: Bonds that pay high coupons have greater reinvestment risk simply because there's more to reinvest.

As it turns out, both price and reinvestment risk are related in one way or another to interest rates, and therein lies the conflict. For *any* change in interest rates (whether up or down) will cause price risk and reinvestment risk to push and pull bonds in opposite directions. An increase in rates will produce a drop in price but will lessen reinvestment risk by making it easier to reinvest coupon payments at or above the YTM rate. Declining rates, in contrast, will boost prices but increase reinvestment risk. At some point in time, these two forces should exactly offset each other. *That point in time is a bond's duration.*

In general, bond duration possesses the following properties:

- Higher coupons result in shorter durations.
- Longer maturities mean longer durations.
- Higher yields (YTMs) lead to shorter durations.

A bond's coupon, maturity, and yield interact to produce the issue's measure of duration. Knowing a bond's duration is helpful because it captures the underlying price volatility of a bond. That is, since *a bond's duration and volatility are directly related, it follows that the shorter the duration, the less volatility in bond prices—and vice versa, of course.*

Measuring Duration

Duration is a measure of the effective, as opposed to actual, maturity of a fixed-income security. As we will see, only those bonds promising a single payment to be received at maturity (zero-coupon bonds) have durations equal to their actual years to maturity. For all other bonds, *duration measures are always less than their actual maturities*.

Although a bond's term to maturity is a useful concept, it falls short of being a reliable measure of a bond's effective life, because it does not consider all of the bond's cash flows or the time value of money. Duration is a far superior measure of the effective timing of a bond's cash flows, as it explicitly considers both the time value of money and the bond's coupon and principal payments. Duration may be thought of as the *weighted-average life of a bond*, where the weights are the relative future cash flows of the bond, all of which are discounted to their present values. Mathematically, we can find the duration of a bond as follows:

Equation 11.7

$$\text{Duration} = \sum_{t=1}^{T}\left[\frac{PV(C_t)}{P_{\text{bond}}} \times t\right]$$

where

$PV(C_t)$ = present value of a future coupon or principal payment

P_{bond} = current market price of the bond

t = year in which the cash flow (coupon or principal) payment is received

T = remaining life of the bond, in years

The duration measure obtained from Equation 11.7 is commonly referred to as *Macaulay duration*—named after the actuary who developed the concept.

Although duration often is computed using semiannual compounding, Equation 11.7 uses *annual coupons and annual compounding* in order to keep the ensuing discussion and calculations as simple as possible. But even so, the formula looks more formidable than it really is. If you follow the basic steps noted below, you'll find that duration is not tough to calculate. Here are the steps involved:

Step 1. Find the present value of each annual coupon or principal payment [$PV(C_t)$]. *Use the prevailing YTM on the bond as the discount rate.*

Step 2. Divide this present value by the current market price of the bond (P_{bond}).

Step 3. Multiply this relative value by the year in which the cash flow is to be received (t).

Step 4. Repeat Steps 1 through 3 for each year in the life of the bond, and then *add up* the values computed in Step 3.

Duration for a Single Bond   Table 11.1 illustrates the four-step procedure for calculating the duration of a 7½%, 15-year bond priced (at $957) to yield 8%. Note that this particular 15-year bond has a duration of less than 9½ years (9.36 years, to be exact). Here's how we found that value: Along with the current market price of the bond ($957), the first three columns of Table 11.1 provide the basic input data: Column (1) is the year (t) of the cash flow. Column (2) is the amount of the annual cash flows (from coupons and principal).

EXCEL with
SPREADSHEETS

TABLE 11.1 Duration Calculation for a 7½%, 15-Year Bond Priced to Yield 8%

(1)	(2)	(3)	(4)	(5)	(6)
Year (t)	Annual Cash Flow (C_t)	PVIF (at 8%)	Present Value of Annual Cash Flows [$PV(C_t)$] (2) × (3)	$PV(C_t)$ Divided by Current Market Price of the Bond* (4) ÷ $957	Time-Weighted Relative Cash Flow (1) × (5)
1	$ 75	.926	$69.45	.0726	.0726
2	75	.857	64.27	.0672	.1343
3	75	.794	59.55	.0622	.1867
4	75	.735	55.12	.0576	.2304
5	75	.681	51.08	.0534	.2668
6	75	.630	47.25	.0494	.2962
7	75	.583	43.72	.0457	.3198
8	75	.540	40.50	.0423	.3386
9	75	.500	37.50	.0392	.3527
10	75	.463	34.72	.0363	.3628
11	75	.429	32.18	.0336	.3698
12	75	.397	29.78	.0311	.3734
13	75	.368	27.60	.0288	.3749
14	75	.340	25.50	.0266	.3730
15	1,075	.315	338.62	.3538	5.3076
					Duration: 9.36 yr

*If this bond is priced to yield 8%, it will be quoted in the market at $957.

DIFFERENT BONDS, SAME DURATIONS—Sometimes, you really can't judge a book—or a bond, for that matter—by its cover. Here are three bonds that, on the surface, appear to be totally different:

- An 8-year, zero-coupon bond priced to yield 6%.
- A 12-year, 8½% bond that trades at a yield of 8%.
- An 18-year, 10½% bond priced to yield 13%.

Although these three bonds have different coupons and different maturities, they have one thing in common: They all have *identical durations* of 8 years. Thus, if interest rates went up or down by 50 to 100 basis points, the market prices of these bonds would all behave pretty much the same!

Column (3) lists the appropriate present-value interest factors, given an 8% discount rate (which is equal to the prevailing YTM on the bond).

The first thing we do (Step 1) is find the present value of each of the annual cash flows (column 4). Then (Step 2) we divide each of these present values by the current market price of the bond (column 5). Multiplying the relative cash flows from column (5) by the year (*t*) in which the cash flow occurs (Step 3) results in a time-weighted value for each of the annual cash flow streams (column 6). Adding up all the values in column (6) (Step 4) yields the duration of the bond. As you can see, the duration of this bond is a lot less than its maturity—a condition that would exist with any coupon-bearing bond. In addition, keep in mind *that the duration on any bond will change over time* as YTM and term to maturity change. For example, the duration on this 7½%, 15-year bond will fall as the bond nears maturity and/or as the market yield (YTM) on the bond increases.

Duration for a Portfolio of Bonds The concept of duration is not applied merely to single securities. It can also be applied to whole portfolios of fixed-income securities. The duration of an entire portfolio is fairly easy to calculate. All we need are the durations of the individual securities in the portfolio and their weights (i.e., the proportion that each security contributes to the overall value of the portfolio). Given this, *the duration of a portfolio is simply the weighted average of the durations of the individual securities in the portfolio.* Actually, this weighted-average approach provides only an *approximate measure of duration.* But it is a reasonably close approximation and, as such, is widely used in practice—so we'll use it, too.

To see how duration is measured using this approach, consider the following five-bond portfolio:

Bond	Amount Invested*	Weight	×	Bond Duration	=	Portfolio Duration
Government bonds	$ 270,000	0.15		6.25		0.9375
Aaa corporates	180,000	0.10		8.90		0.8900
Aa utilities	450,000	0.25		10.61		2.6525
Agency issues	360,000	0.20		11.03		2.2060
Baa industrials	$ 540.000	0.30		12.55		3.7650
	$1,800.000	1.00				10.4510

*Amount invested = Current market price × Par value of the bonds. That is, if the government bonds are quoted at 90 and the investor holds $300,000 in these bonds, then 0.90 × $300,000 = $270,000.

In this case, the $1.8 million bond *portfolio* has an average duration of approximately 10.5 years. Obviously, if you want to change the duration of the portfolio, you can do so by (1) changing the asset mix of the portfolio (shift the weight of the portfolio to longer- or shorter-duration bonds, as desired) and/or (2) adding new bonds to the portfolio with the desired duration characteristics. As we will see below, this approach is often used in a bond portfolio strategy known as *bond immunization*.

Bond Duration and Price Volatility

A bond's price volatility is, in part, a function of its term to maturity and, in part, a function of its coupon yield. Unfortunately, there is no exact relationship between bond maturities and bond price volatilities with respect to interest rate changes. There is, however, a fairly close relationship between bond duration and price volatility—at least, so long as the market doesn't experience wide swings in yield. Duration can be used as a viable predictor of price volatility *only so long as the yield swings are relatively small* (no more than 50 to 100 basis points, or so). That's because whereas duration is a straight-line relationship, the price-yield relationship of a bond is convex in nature. That is, when bond yields change, bond prices actually move in a curved (convex) manner rather than in a straight line, as depicted by duration. Thus, when the market (or bond) undergoes a *big change* in yield, duration will *understate* the appreciation in price when rates fall and *overstate* the price decline when rates rise. Assuming that's not the case (i.e., that we're dealing with relatively small changes in market yield), then multiplying a bond's duration value by −1 results in its price elasticity with respect to interest rate changes. By calculating a bond's duration, we can obtain a fairly accurate measure of how much its price will change relative to a given (reasonably small) change in market interest rates.

The mathematical link between bond price and interest rate changes involves the concept of *modified duration*. To find modified duration, we simply take the (Macaulay) duration for a bond (as found from Equation 11.7) and adjust it for the bond's yield to maturity.

Equation 11.8

$$\text{Modified duration} = \frac{(\text{Macaulay})\text{Duration in years}}{1 + \text{Yield to maturity}}$$

Thus the modified duration for the 15-year bond discussed above is

$$\text{Modified duration} = \frac{9.36}{1 + 0.08} = \underline{\underline{8.67}}$$

Note that here we use the bond's computed (Macaulay) duration of 9.36 years and the same YTM we used to compute duration in Equation 11.7; in this case, the bond was priced to yield 8%, so we use a yield-to-maturity of 8%.

To determine, in percentage terms, how much the price of this bond would change as market interest rates increased from, say, 8% to 8½%, we multiply the modified duration value calculated above first by −1 (because of the inverse relationship between bond prices and interest rates) and then by the change in the level of the market interest rates. That is,

Equation 11.9

$$\begin{array}{l}\text{Percent change} \\ \text{in bond price}\end{array} = -1 \times \text{Modified duration} \times \text{Change in interest rates}$$

$$= -1 \times 8.67 \times 0.5\% = -\underline{\underline{4.33}}$$

Thus a 50-basis-point (or ½ of 1%) increase in market interest rates will lead to an almost 4½% drop in the price of this 15-year bond. Such information is useful to bond investors seeking—or trying to avoid—price volatility.

Uses of Bond Duration Measures

Bond investors have learned to use duration analysis in many ways. For example, as we saw above, you can use modified duration to measure the potential price volatility of a particular issue. Another, perhaps more important use of duration is in the *structuring of bond portfolios*. That is, if you thought that interest rates were about to increase, you could reduce the overall duration of the portfolio by selling higher-duration bonds and buying shorter-duration bonds. Such a strategy would prove profitable, because shorter-duration bonds do not decline in value to the same degree as longer-duration bonds. On the other hand, if you felt that interest rates were about to decline, the opposite strategy would be appropriate.

Although active, short-term investors frequently use duration analysis in their day-to-day operations, longer-term investors also employ it in planning their investment decisions. Indeed, a strategy known as *bond portfolio immunization* represents one of the most important uses of duration.

Bond Immunization Some investors hold portfolios of bonds not for the purpose of "beating the market," but rather to *accumulate a specified level of wealth by the end of a given investment horizon*. For these investors, bond portfolio immunization often proves to be of great value. Immunization allows you to derive a specified rate of return from bond investments over a given investment interval *regardless of what happens to market interest rates over the course of the holding period*. In essence, you are able to "immunize" your portfolio from the effects of changes in market interest rates over a given investment horizon.

To understand how and why bond portfolio immunization is possible, you need to understand that changes in market interest rates lead to two distinct and opposite changes in bond valuation: The first effect is known as the *price effect*. It results in portfolio valuation changes when interest rates change before the end of the desired investment horizon. This is true because interest rate decreases lead to bond price increases, and vice versa. The second effect is known as the *reinvestment effect*. It arises because the YTM calculation assumes that all coupon payments will be reinvested at the YTM rate that existed when the bond was purchased. If interest rates increase, however, the coupons may be reinvested at a higher rate, leading to increases in investor wealth. Of course, the opposite is true when interest rates decrease. Thus, whereas an increase in rates has a negative effect on a bond's price, it has a positive effect on the reinvestment of coupons. Therefore, when interest rate changes do occur, the price and reinvestment effects work against each other from the standpoint of the investor's wealth.

When do these counteracting effects offset each other and leave the investor's position unchanged? You guessed it: when the average duration of the portfolio just equals the investment horizon. This should not come as much of a surprise, because such a property is already embedded in the duration measure itself. And, if it applies to a single bond, it should also apply to the *weighted-average duration of a bond portfolio*. When such a condition (of offsetting price and reinvestment effects) exists, *a bond portfolio is said to be immunized*. More specifically, your wealth position is immunized from the effects of interest rate changes *when the weighted-average duration of the bond portfolio exactly equals your desired investment horizon*. Table 11.2 provides an example of bond immunization using a 10-year, 8% coupon bond with a duration of 8 years. Here, we assume the investor's desired investment horizon is also 8 years in length.

The example in Table 11.2 assumes that you originally purchased the 8% coupon bond at par. It further assumes that market interest rates for bonds of this quality drop from 8% to 6% at the end of the fifth year. Because you had an investment horizon of exactly 8 years and desire to lock in an interest rate return of exactly 8%, it follows that you expect to have a terminal value of $1,850.90 [i.e., $1,000 invested at 8% for 8 years = $1,000 \times (1.08)^8 = $1,850.90], regardless of interest rate changes in the interim. As can be seen from the results in Table 11.2, the immunization strategy netted you a total of $1,850.31—just 59 cents short of your desired goal. Note that in this case, although reinvestment opportunities declined in years 5, 6, and 7 (when market interest rates dropped to 6%), that same lower rate led to a higher market price for the bond. That higher price, in turn, provided enough capital gains to offset the loss in reinvested income. This remarkable result clearly demonstrates the power of bond immunization and the versatility of bond duration. And note that even though the table uses a single bond for purposes of illustration, the same results can be obtained from a bond *portfolio* that is maintained at the *proper weighted-average duration*.

Although bond immunization is a powerful investment tool, it is clearly *not* a passive investment strategy. Maintaining a fully immunized portfolio (of more than one bond) requires *continual portfolio rebalancing*. Indeed, every time interest rates change, the duration of a portfolio changes. Because effective immunization requires that the portfolio have a duration value equal in length to the *remaining investment horizon*, the composition of the portfolio must be rebalanced each time interest rates change.

TABLE 11.2   **Bond Immunization**

Year	Cash Flow from Bond							Terminal Value of Reinvested Cash Flow
1	$80	$\times$	$(1.08)^4$	$\times$	$(1.06)^3$		$=$	$ 129.63
2	80	$\times$	$(1.08)^3$	$\times$	$(1.06)^3$		$=$	120.03
3	80	$\times$	$(1.08)^2$	$\times$	$(1.06)^3$		$=$	111.14
4	80	$\times$	(1.08)	$\times$	$(1.06)^3$		$=$	102.90
5	80	$\times$	$(1.06)^3$				$=$	95.28
6	80	$\times$	$(1.06)^2$				$=$	89.89
7	80	$\times$	(1.06)				$=$	84.80
8	80						$=$	80.00
8	$1,036.64*							1,036.64
					Total			$1,850.31
					Investor's required wealth at 8%			$1,850.90
					Difference			$ .59

*The bond could be sold at a market price of $l,036.64, which is the value of an 8% bond with 2 years to maturity that is priced to yield 6%.

Note: Bond interest coupons are assumed to be paid at year-end. Therefore, there are 4 years of reinvestment at 8% and 3 years at 6% for the first year's $80 coupon.

Further, even in the absence of interest rate changes, a bond's duration declines more slowly than its term to maturity. This, of course, means that the mere passage of time will dictate changes in portfolio composition. Such changes will ensure that the duration of the portfolio continues to match the remaining time in the investment horizon. In summary, portfolio immunization strategies can be extremely effective, but it is important to realize that immunization is not a passive strategy and is not without potential problems, the most notable of which are associated with portfolio rebalancing.

IN REVIEW

CONCEPTS

11.10 What does the term *duration* mean to bond investors, and how does the duration of a bond differ from its maturity? What is *modified duration*, and how is it used?

11.11 Describe the process of *bond portfolio immunization*, and explain why an investor would want to immunize a portfolio. Would you consider portfolio immunization a passive investment strategy comparable to, say, a buy-and-hold approach? Explain.

Bond Investment Strategies

LG 6

Generally, bond investors tend to follow one of three kinds of investment programs. First, there are those who live off the income: the conservative, quality-conscious, income-oriented investors who seek to maximize current income. Then there are the speculators (bond traders), who have a considerably different investment objective: to maximize capital gains, often within a short time span. This investment approach requires considerable expertise, because

INVESTING IN ACTION

GETTING STARTED IN BOND INVESTING

As returns on equity investments fell during the 2000–2003 bear market, many investors shifted their funds into fixed-income securities in an attempt to preserve capital and stabilize their portfolios. If you want to join them and add bonds to your portfolio, you'll need to answer some basic questions before you start. Do you want a taxable or tax-exempt security? The answer will depend on your tax bracket and whether you are buying the securities for a tax-advantaged account like your 401(k) retirement account. The next question is a bit harder: Should you buy individual bonds or a bond mutual fund? Recent research has analyzed the risks and rewards of each alternative.

Individual bonds offer certain advantages. You know the interest rate you will earn and how much you will get back when the bond matures. Such instruments are less costly to purchase than mutual funds, which carry ongoing fees. Individual bonds may suit your needs if you need a fixed level of income or are planning for a specific goal or date for which you need funds. In that case zero-coupon bonds are a good choice, because you buy them at a discount and get the par value at maturity. While they offer modest returns, their risk is correspondingly low.

With individual bonds, you have control over your portfolio of fixed-income investments.

However, investing in bonds is not always simple. For one thing, it can be difficult to ferret out information. Credit research is more challenging for corporate and municipal bonds than for stocks. You also need to understand a bond's features, such as call options. And inflation can erode the buying power of the income stream you will receive over the bond's life. Schwab research indicates that to have a well-diversified portfolio of corporate bonds you'd need at least $50,000; if you prefer municipal bonds, you'd need twice that amount. If you don't have that much to invest, bond funds may be a wiser choice.

With a bond fund, you let a professional manager deal with these issues. Monitoring your portfolio is easier. But be sure to analyze total returns, not just yields. Unlike with individual bonds, however, you have no guarantee of a fixed interest rate. Bond fund returns are governed by market interest rate trends, so you can't predict the value of your fund shares in the future. They are also more vulnerable to market fluctuations because the manager is buying and selling securities; investors could lose their

continued on next page

it is based almost entirely on estimates of the future course of interest rates. Finally, there are the serious long-term investors, whose objective is to maximize *total return*—from both current income and capital gains—over fairly long holding periods.

In order to achieve the objectives of any one of these three programs, you need to adopt a strategy that is compatible with your goals. Professional money managers use a variety of techniques to manage the multimillion (or multibillion)-dollar bond portfolios under their direction. These range from passive approaches, to semiactive strategies, to active, fully managed strategies using interest rate forecasting and yield spread analysis. Most of these strategies are fairly complex and require substantial computer support. Even so, we can look briefly at some of the more basic strategies to gain an appreciation of the different ways in which fixed-income securities can be used to reach different investment objectives. Before doing that, however, you

HOT

Another bond portfolio strategy is called a *barbell*. For information on that approach, see the *Investing in Action* box at:

www.aw-bc.com/gitman_joehnk

INVESTING IN ACTION

continued from previous page

principal with a bond fund, whereas they would not if they held a bond of a good credit quality to maturity. And, of course, you should factor in expenses: The lower your fund's expenses, the higher your return. Look for funds with an expense ratio of 80 basis points or lower.

Some factors are important whether you choose individual bonds or bond funds. Both react to interest rate changes. The duration of the bond or the fund tells you just how sensitive it is to interest rates. The duration of a bond mutual fund is the average of the durations of the bonds in its portfolio. The duration of a money market fund would be close to zero; that of a short-term fund would be 1 to 3 years; that of a medium-term fund would be 4 to 6 years and that of a long-term fund would be 7 to 10 years. If interest rates increase by one point, a long-term fund with a duration of 12 years would fall about 12%. As you might expect, longer-term bonds and bond funds are the most sensitive to interest rate fluctuations. At the Morningstar site (www.morningstar.com) you can find taxable and tax-exempt bond funds categorized by their potential interest rate sensitivity based on their duration over the past few years: ultrashort, short, intermediate, and long.

Don't forget about credit risk, or the possibility that the issuer will default on its obligations. If you are seeking minimal risk, stick with Treasury securities, GNMA mortgages, and securities issued by government-sponsored enterprises or bond funds that invest most of their assets in these securities. If you can tolerate a bit more credit risk, consider investment-grade (BBB or better) corporate bonds or funds that invest only in comparably rated bonds. High-yield, or junk, bonds and funds are, of course, the riskiest.

CRITICAL THINKING QUESTIONS What are some of the advantages and disadvantages of buying bonds directly? What are the advantages and disadvantages of buying bond funds?

Sources: Scott Berry, "Tips for Choosing a Bond Fund," *Morningstar.com*, October 9, 2002, downloaded from news.morningstar.com/news; Chris Kelsch, "How Risky Is Your Bond Fund?" *Morningstar.com*, March 24, 2000, downloaded from news.morningstar.com/news; Peter Di Teresa, "Should You Buy Bonds or Bond Funds?" *Morningstar.com*, August 24, 2000, downloaded from news.morningstar.com/news; and "With Troubles in the Bond Market, Fixed-Income Investments Can't Be Ignored," *PR Newswire*, August 21, 2003.

might want to take a look at the *Investing in Action* box above, which offers some guidelines for getting started in bonds and introduces another way to invest in bonds—via mutual funds (a topic we discuss in detail in Chapter 13).

Passive Strategies

The bond immunization strategies we discussed above are considered to be primarily *passive* in nature, to the extent that investors using these tools typically are *not* attempting to beat the market. Rather, these investors immunize their portfolios in an effort to lock in specified rates of return (or terminal values) that they deem acceptable, given the risks involved. Generally speaking, passive investment strategies are characterized by a lack of input regarding investor expectations of changes in interest rate and/or bond price. Further, these strategies typically do not generate significant transaction costs. A *buy-and-*

HOT

Thornburg Investment Management has an informative article about laddering at:

www.thornburginvestments.com/ research/articles/laddering-1101.asp *hold* strategy is perhaps the most passive of all investment strategies: All that is required is that the investor replace bonds that have deteriorating credit ratings, have matured, or have been called. Although buy-and-hold investors restrict their ability to earn above-average returns, they also minimize the losses that transaction costs represent.

One popular approach that is a bit more active than buy-and-hold is the use of so-called **bond ladders.** In this strategy, equal amounts are invested in a *series* of bonds with staggered maturities. Here's how a bond ladder works: Suppose you want to confine your investing to fixed-income securities with maturities of 10 years or less. Given that maturity constraint, you could set up a ladder by investing (roughly) equal amounts in, say, 3-, 5-, 7-, and 10-year issues. Then, when the 3-year issue matures, the money from it (along with any new capital) would be put into a new 10-year note. The process would continue rolling over like this so that eventually you would hold a full ladder of staggered 10-year notes. By rolling into new 10-year issues every 2 or 3 years, you can do a kind of dollar-cost averaging and thereby lessen the impact of swings in market rates. Actually, the laddered approach is a safe, simple, and almost automatic way of investing for the long haul. Indeed, once the ladder is set up, it should be followed in a fairly routine manner. A key ingredient of this or any other passive strategy is, of course, the use of high-quality investment vehicles that possess attractive features, maturities, and yields.

Trading on Forecasted Interest Rate Behavior

In contrast, a highly risky approach to bond investing is the *forecasted interest rate* approach. Here, the investor seeks attractive capital gains when interest rates are expected to decline and preservation of capital when an increase in interest rates is anticipated. It's risky because it relies on the imperfect forecast of future interest rates. The idea is to increase the return on a bond portfolio by making strategic moves in anticipation of interest rate changes. Such a strategy is essentially *market timing*. An unusual feature of this tactic is that most of the trading is done with *investment-grade securities*, because a high degree of interest rate sensitivity is required to capture the maximum amount of price behavior.

Once interest rate expectations have been specified, this strategy rests largely on technical matters. For example, when a decline in rates is anticipated, aggressive bond investors often seek to lengthen the maturity (or duration) of their bonds (or bond portfolios). The reason: Longer-term bonds rise more in price than shorter-term issues. At the same time, investors look for low-coupon and/or moderately discounted bonds, which will add to duration and increase the amount of potential price volatility. These interest swings are usually short-lived, so bond traders try to earn as much as possible in as short a time as possible. (Margin trading—the use of borrowed money to buy bonds—is also used as a way of magnifying returns when rate declines are expected.) When rates start to level off and move up, these investors begin to shift their money out of long, discounted bonds and into high-yielding issues with short maturities. In other words, they do a complete reversal. During those periods when bond prices are dropping, investors are more concerned about preservation of capital, so they take steps to protect their money from capital losses. Thus, they tend to use such short-term obligations as Treasury bills, money funds, short-term (2–5 year) notes, or even variable-rate notes.

bond ladders
an investment strategy wherein equal amounts of money are invested in a series of bonds with staggered maturities.

Bond Swaps

bond swap
an investment strategy wherein an investor simultaneously liquidates one bond holding and buys a different issue to take its place.

In a **bond swap,** an investor simultaneously liquidates one position and buys a different issue to take its place. Swaps can be executed to increase current yield or yield-to-maturity, to take advantage of shifts in interest rates, to improve the quality of a portfolio, or for tax purposes. Although some swaps are highly sophisticated, most are fairly simple transactions. They go by a variety of colorful names, such as "profit takeout," "substitution swap," and "tax swap," but they are all used for one basic reason: *to seek portfolio improvement.* We will briefly review two types of bond swaps that are fairly simple and hold considerable appeal: the yield pickup swap and the tax swap.

yield pickup swap
replacement of a low-coupon bond for a comparable higher-coupon bond in order to realize an increase in current yield and yield-to-maturity.

In a **yield pickup swap,** an investor switches out of a low-coupon bond into a comparable higher-coupon issue in order to realize an instantaneous pickup of current yield and yield-to-maturity. For example, you would be executing a yield pickup swap if you sold 20-year, A-rated, 6½% bonds (which were yielding 8% at the time) and replaced them with an equal amount of 20-year, A-rated, 7% bonds that were priced to yield 8½%. By executing the swap, you would improve your current yield (your coupon income would increase from $65 a year to $70 a year) as well as your yield-to-maturity (from 8% to 8½%). Basically, such swap opportunities arise because of the *yield spreads* that normally exist between, say, industrial and public utility bonds. The mechanics are fairly simple, and you can execute such swaps simply by watching for swap candidates and/or asking your broker to do so. In fact, the only thing you have to be careful of is that transaction costs do not eat up all the profits.

tax swap
replacement of a bond that has a capital loss for a similar security; used to offset a gain generated in another part of an investor's portfolio.

The other type of swap that's popular with many investors is the **tax swap,** which is also relatively simple and involves few risks. The technique can be used whenever an investor has a substantial tax liability that has come about as a result of selling some security holdings at a profit. The objective is to execute a swap so that the tax liability accompanying the capital gains can be *eliminated or substantially reduced.* This is done by selling an issue that has undergone a capital *loss* and replacing it with a comparable obligation. For example, assume that you had $10,000 worth of corporate bonds that you sold (in the current year) for $15,000, resulting in a capital gain of $5,000. You can eliminate the tax liability accompanying the capital gain by selling securities that have *capital losses of $5,000.* Let's assume you find you hold a 20-year, 4¾% municipal bond that (strictly by coincidence, of course) has undergone a $5,000 drop in value. Thus you have the required tax shield in your portfolio. All you have to do is find a viable swap candidate. Suppose you find a comparable 20-year, 5% municipal issue currently trading at about the same price as the issue being sold. By selling the 4¾s and simultaneously buying a comparable amount of the 5s, you will not only increase your tax-free yields (from 4¾% to 5%) but also eliminate the capital gains tax liability. The only precaution is that *identical issues cannot be used* in such swap transactions. The IRS would consider that a "wash sale" and disallow the loss. Moreover, the capital loss must occur in the same taxable year as the capital gain. This limitation explains why the technique is so popular with knowledgeable investors, particularly at year-end, when tax loss sales and tax swaps multiply as investors hurry to establish capital losses.

HOTLINKS

For details on IRS regulations regarding wash sales, go to the books' Web site and click on Chapter 17. Go to the section on Tax-Favored Income, and then go to discussions of Strategies that Trade Current Income for Capital Gains and Tax Swaps.

www.aw-bc.com/gitman_joehnk

IN REVIEW

CONCEPTS

11.12 Briefly describe a *bond ladder*, and note how and why an investor would use this investment strategy. What is a *tax swap*, and why would it be used?

11.13 What strategy would you expect an aggressive bond investor (someone who's looking for capital gains) to employ?

11.14 Why is interest sensitivity important to bond speculators? Does the need for interest sensitivity explain why active bond traders tend to use high-grade issues? Explain.

Summary

LG 1 **Explain the behavior of market interest rates, and identify the forces that cause interest rates to move.** The behavior of interest rates is the single most important force in the bond market. It determines not only the amount of current income an investor will receive but also the investor's capital gains (or losses). Changes in market interest rates can have a dramatic impact on the total returns obtained from bonds over time.

LG 2 **Describe the term structure of interest rates, and note how these yield curves can be used by investors.** Many forces drive the behavior of interest rates over time, including inflation, the cost and availability of funds, and the level of interest rates in major foreign markets. One particularly important force is the term structure of interest rates, which relates yield-to-maturity to term-to-maturity.

LG 3 **Understand how bonds are valued in the marketplace.** Bonds are valued (priced) in the marketplace on the basis of their required rates of return (or market yields). The whole process of pricing a bond begins with the yield it should provide. Once that piece of information is known (or estimated), a standard, present-value-based model is used to find the dollar price of a bond.

LG 4 **Describe the various measures of yield and return, and explain how these standards of performance are used in bond valuation.** Four types of yields are important to investors: current yield, promised yield, yield-to-call, and expected yield (or return). Promised yield (yield-to-maturity) is the most widely used bond valuation measure. It captures both the current income and the price appreciation of an issue. The same can be said of yield-to-call, which assumes the bond will be outstanding only until its first call date. Expected return, in contrast, is a valuation measure that's used by aggressive bond traders to show the total return that can be earned from trading in and out of a bond long before it matures.

LG 5 **Understand the basic concept of duration, how it can be measured, and its use in the management of bond portfolios.** Bond duration is an important concept in bond valuation. Duration takes into account the effects of both reinvestment and price (or market) risks. It captures, in a single measure, the extent to which the price of a bond will react to different interest rate environments. Equally important, duration can be used to immunize whole bond portfolios from the often devastating forces of changing market interest rates.

LG 6 **Discuss various bond investment strategies and the different ways these securities can be used by investors.** As investment vehicles, bonds can be used as a source of income, as a way to seek capital gains by speculating on the movement in interest rates, or as a way to earn attractive long-term returns. To achieve these objectives, investors often employ one or more of the following strategies: passive strategies such as buy-and-hold, bond ladders, and portfolio immunization; bond trading based on forecasted interest rate behavior; and bond swaps.

Putting Your Investment Know-How to the Test

1. According to the liquidity preference theory of the term structure of interest rates, which of the following should an investor generally expect?
   a. A higher yield on short-term bonds than on long-term bonds.
   b. A higher yield on long-term bonds than on short-term bonds.
   c. The same yield on both long-term and short-term bonds.
   d. None of the above.

2. A bond will sell at the premium when
   a. Its coupon rate exceeds its current yield and its current yield exceeds its yield to maturity.
   b. Its coupon rate is less than its current yield and its current yield exceeds its yield to maturity.
   c. Its coupon rate exceeds its current yield but is less than its yield to maturity.
   d. Its coupon rate is less than its current yield and its current yield is less than its yield to maturity.

3. Consider a 5-year bond with a 10% coupon that has a present yield-to-maturity of 8%. If interest rates remain constant, one year from now the price of this bond will be
   a. Higher.
   b. Lower.
   c. The same.
   d. Cannot be determined.

4. Zello Corporation's $1,000 par-value bond sells for $960, matures in 5 years, and has a 7% coupon rate paid semiannually. What is the bond's yield to maturity?
   a. 7.0%   b. 7.3%
   c. 8.0%   d. 8.1%

5. A bond with a 12% coupon, 10 years to maturity, and selling at 88 has a yield-to-maturity of
   a. More than 14%.
   b. Between 13% and 14%.
   c. Between 12% and 13%.
   d. Less than 12%.

6. Zello Corporation's $1,000 par value bond sells for $960, matures in 5 years, and has a 7% coupon rate paid semiannually. What is the bond's current yield?
   a. 7.0%   b. 7.3%
   c. 8.0%   d. 8.1%

7. Using semiannual compounding, a 15-year, zero-coupon bond that has a par value of $1,000 and a required return of 8% would be priced at
   a. $308.   b. $315.
   c. $464.   d. $555.

8. Which bond has the longest duration?
   a. 8-year maturity, 6% coupon.
   b. 8-year maturity, 11% coupon.
   c. 15-year maturity, 6% coupon.
   d. 15-year maturity, 11% coupon.

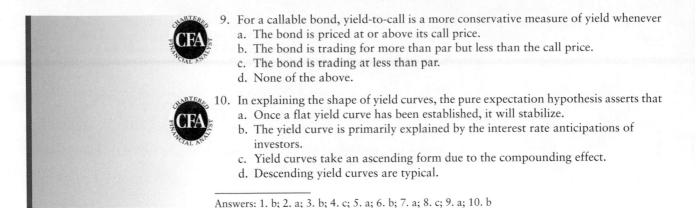

9. For a callable bond, yield-to-call is a more conservative measure of yield whenever
   a. The bond is priced at or above its call price.
   b. The bond is trading for more than par but less than the call price.
   c. The bond is trading at less than par.
   d. None of the above.

10. In explaining the shape of yield curves, the pure expectation hypothesis asserts that
    a. Once a flat yield curve has been established, it will stabilize.
    b. The yield curve is primarily explained by the interest rate anticipations of investors.
    c. Yield curves take an ascending form due to the compounding effect.
    d. Descending yield curves are typical.

Answers: 1. b; 2. a; 3. b; 4. c; 5. a; 6. b; 7. a; 8. c; 9. a; 10. b

Discussion Questions

LG 1 **Q11.1** Briefly describe each of the following theories of the term structure of interest rates.
   a. Expectations hypothesis.
   b. Liquidity preference theory.
   c. Market segmentation theory.

According to these theories, what conditions would result in a downward-sloping yield curve? What conditions would result in an upward-sloping yield curve? Which theory do *you* think is most valid, and why?

LG 2 **Q11.2** Using a recent copy of the *Wall Street Journal* or *Barron's*, find the bond yields for Treasury securities with the following maturities: 3 months, 6 months, 1 year, 3 years, 5 years, 10 years, 15 years, and 20 years. Construct a yield curve based on these reported yields, putting term-to-maturity on the horizontal (x) axis and yield-to-maturity on the vertical (y) axis. Briefly discuss the general shape of your yield curve. What conclusions might you draw about future interest rate movements from this yield curve?

LG 5 **Q11.3** Briefly explain what will happen to a bond's duration measure if each of the following events occur.
   a. The yield-to-maturity on the bond falls from 8½% to 8%.
   b. The bond gets 1 year closer to its maturity.
   c. Market interest rates go from 8% to 9%.
   d. The bond's *modified* duration falls by half a year.

LG 6 **Q11.4** Assume that an investor comes to you looking for advice. She has $200,000 to invest and wants to put it all into bonds.
   a. If she considers herself a fairly aggressive investor who is willing to take the risks necessary to generate the big returns, what kind of investment strategy (or strategies) would you suggest? Be specific.
   b. What kind of investment strategies would you recommend if your client were a very conservative investor who could not tolerate market losses?
   c. What kind of investor do you think is most likely to use:
       (1) An immunized bond portfolio?
       (2) A yield pickup swap?
       (3) A bond ladder?
       (4) A long-term zero-coupon bond when interest rates fall?

LG 4   LG 5

Q11.5 Using the resources available at your campus or public library (or on the Internet), select any six bonds you like, consisting of *two* Treasury bonds, *two* corporate bonds, and *two* agency issues. Determine the latest current yield and promised yield for each. (For promised yield, use annual compounding.) In addition, find the duration and modified duration for each bond.

    a. Assuming that you put an equal amount of money into each of the six bonds you selected, find the duration for this six-bond portfolio.

    b. What would happen to your bond portfolio if market interest rates fell by 100 basis points?

    c. Assuming that you have $100,000 to invest, use at least four of these bonds to develop a bond portfolio that emphasizes either the potential for capital gains or the preservation of capital. Briefly explain your logic.

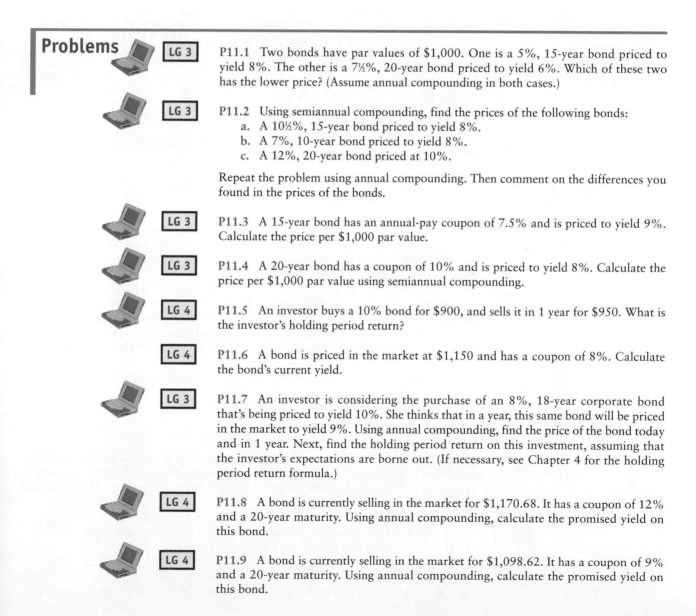

Problems

LG 3

P11.1 Two bonds have par values of $1,000. One is a 5%, 15-year bond priced to yield 8%. The other is a 7½%, 20-year bond priced to yield 6%. Which of these two has the lower price? (Assume annual compounding in both cases.)

LG 3

P11.2 Using semiannual compounding, find the prices of the following bonds:
    a. A 10½%, 15-year bond priced to yield 8%.
    b. A 7%, 10-year bond priced to yield 8%.
    c. A 12%, 20-year bond priced at 10%.

Repeat the problem using annual compounding. Then comment on the differences you found in the prices of the bonds.

LG 3

P11.3 A 15-year bond has an annual-pay coupon of 7.5% and is priced to yield 9%. Calculate the price per $1,000 par value.

LG 3

P11.4 A 20-year bond has a coupon of 10% and is priced to yield 8%. Calculate the price per $1,000 par value using semiannual compounding.

LG 4

P11.5 An investor buys a 10% bond for $900, and sells it in 1 year for $950. What is the investor's holding period return?

LG 4

P11.6 A bond is priced in the market at $1,150 and has a coupon of 8%. Calculate the bond's current yield.

LG 3

P11.7 An investor is considering the purchase of an 8%, 18-year corporate bond that's being priced to yield 10%. She thinks that in a year, this same bond will be priced in the market to yield 9%. Using annual compounding, find the price of the bond today and in 1 year. Next, find the holding period return on this investment, assuming that the investor's expectations are borne out. (If necessary, see Chapter 4 for the holding period return formula.)

LG 4

P11.8 A bond is currently selling in the market for $1,170.68. It has a coupon of 12% and a 20-year maturity. Using annual compounding, calculate the promised yield on this bond.

LG 4

P11.9 A bond is currently selling in the market for $1,098.62. It has a coupon of 9% and a 20-year maturity. Using annual compounding, calculate the promised yield on this bond.

LG 4 **P11.10** Compute the current yield of a 10%, 25-year bond that is currently priced in the market at $1,200. Use annual compounding to find the promised yield on this bond. Repeat the promised yield calculation, but this time use semiannual compounding to find yield-to-maturity.

LG 4 **P11.11** A 10%, 25-year bond has a par value of $1,000 and a call price of $1,075. (The bond's first call date is in 5 years.) Coupon payments are made semiannually (so use semiannual compounding where appropriate).
  a. Find the current yield, YTM, and YTC on this issue, given that it is currently being priced in the market at $1,200. Which of these three yields is the highest? Which is the lowest? Which yield would you use to value this bond? Explain.
  b. Repeat the three calculations above, given that the bond is being priced at $850. Now which yield is the highest? Which is the lowest? Which yield would you use to value this bond? Explain.

LG 4 **P11.12** Assume that an investor is looking at two bonds: Bond A is a 20-year, 9% (semiannual pay) bond that is priced to yield 10½%. Bond B is a 20-year, 8% (annual pay) bond that is priced to yield 7½%. Both bonds carry 5-year call deferments and call prices (in 5 years) of $1,050.
  a. Which bond has the higher current yield?
  b. Which bond has the higher YTM?
  c. Which bond has the higher YTC?

LG 4 **P11.13** A zero-coupon bond that matures in 15 years is currently selling for $209 per $1,000 par value. What is the promised yield?

LG 4 **P11.14** A zero-coupon ($1,000 par value) bond that matures in 10 years has a promised yield of 9%. What is the bond's price?

LG 4 **P11.15** A 25-year, zero-coupon bond was recently being quoted at 11.625. Find the current yield *and* the promised yield of this issue, given that the bond has a par value of $1,000. Using semiannual compounding, determine how much an investor would have to pay for this bond if it were priced to yield 12%.

LG 4 **P11.16** Assume that an investor pays $800 for a long-term bond that carries an 8% coupon. In 3 years, he hopes to sell the issue for $950. If his expectations come true, what realized yield will this investor earn? (Use annual compounding.) What would the holding period return be if he were able to sell the bond (at $950) after only 9 months?

LG 4 **P11.17** Using annual compounding, find the yield-to-maturity for each of the following bonds.
  a. A 9½%, 20-year bond priced at $957.43.
  b. A 16%, 15-year bond priced at $1,684.76.
  c. A 5½%, 18-year bond priced at $510.65.

Now assume that each of the above three bonds is callable as follows: Bond **a** is callable in 7 years at a call price of $1,095; bond **b** is callable in 5 years at $1,250; and bond **c** is callable in 3 years at $1,050. Use annual compounding to find the yield-to-call for each bond.

LG 5 **P11.18** A bond has a Macaulay duration equal to 9.5 and a yield to maturity of 7.5%. What is the modified duration of this bond?

LG 5 **P11.19** A bond has a Macaulay duration of 8.62 and is priced to yield 8%. If interest rates go up so that the yield goes to 8.5%, what will be the percentage change in the price of the bond?

LG 5 P11.20 A bond has a Macaulay duration of 8.62 and is priced to yield 8%. If interest rates go down so that the yield goes to 7.5%, what will be the percentage change in the price of the bond?

 LG 5 P11.21 Find the Macaulay duration and the modified duration of a 20-year, 10% corporate bond priced to yield 8%. According to the modified duration of this bond, how much of a price change would this bond incur if market yields rose to 9%? Using annual compounding, calculate the price of this bond in 1 year if rates do rise to 9%. How does this price change compare to that predicted by the modified duration? Explain the difference.

 **LG 5** P11.22 Which *one* of the following bonds would you select if you thought market interest rates were going to fall by 50 basis points over the next 6 months?
    a. A bond with a Macaulay duration of 8.46 years that's currently being priced to yield 7½%.
    b. A bond with a Macaulay duration of 9.30 years that's priced to yield 10%.
    c. A bond with a Macaulay duration of 8.75 years that's priced to yield 5¾%.

LG 5 **LG 6** P11.23 Mary Richards is an aggressive bond trader who likes to speculate on interest rate swings. Market interest rates are currently at 9%, but she expects them to fall to 7% within a year. As a result, Mary is thinking about buying either a 25-year, zero-coupon bond or a 20-year, 7½% bond. (Both bonds have $1,000 par values and carry the same agency rating.) Assuming that Mary wants to maximize capital gains, which of the two issues should she select? What if she wants to maximize the total return (interest income and capital gains) from her investment? Why did one issue provide better capital gains than the other? Based on the duration of each bond, which one should be more price volatile?

LG 5 **LG 6** P11.24 Elliot Karlin is a 35-year-old bank executive who has just inherited a large sum of money. Having spent several years in the bank's investments department, he's well aware of the concept of duration and decides to apply it to his bond portfolio. In particular, Elliot intends to use $1 million of his inheritance to purchase four U.S. Treasury bonds:
    1. An 8½%, 13-year bond that's priced at $1,045 to yield 7.47%.
    2. A 7⅞%, 15-year bond that's priced at $1,020 to yield 7.60%.
    3. A 20-year stripped Treasury that's priced at $202 to yield 8.22%.
    4. A 24-year, 7½% bond that's priced at $955 to yield 7.90%.
  a. Find the duration and the modified duration of each bond.
  b. Find the duration of the whole bond portfolio if Elliot puts $250,000 into each of the four U.S. Treasury bonds.
  c. Find the duration of the portfolio if Elliot puts $360,000 each into bonds 1 and 3 and $140,000 each into bonds 2 and 4.
  d. Which portfolio—**b** or **c**—should Elliot select if he thinks rates are about to head up and he wants to avoid as much price volatility as possible? Explain. From which portfolio does he stand to make more in annual interest income? Which portfolio would you recommend, and why?

See the text Web site (www.aw-bc.com/gitman_joehnk) for Web exercises that deal with *bond valuation*.

Case Problem 11.1

LG 3   LG 4   LG 6

The Bond Investment Decisions of Kelley and Erin Coates

Kelley and Erin Coates live in the Boston area, where Kelley has a successful orthodontics practice. Kelley and Erin have built up a sizable investment portfolio and have always had a major portion of their investments in fixed-income securities. They adhere to a fairly aggressive investment posture and actively go after both attractive current income and substantial capital gains. Assume that it is now 2005 and Erin is currently evaluating two investment decisions: One involves an addition to their portfolio, the other a revision to it.

The Coates' first investment decision involves a short-term trading opportunity. In particular, Erin has a chance to buy a 7½%, 25-year bond that is currently priced at $852 to yield 9%; she feels that in 2 years the promised yield of the issue should drop to 8%.

The second is a bond swap. The Coates hold some Beta Corporation 7%, 2020 bonds that are currently priced at $785. They want to improve both current income and yield-to-maturity, and are considering one of three issues as a possible swap candidate: (a) Dental Floss, Inc., 7½%, 2020, currently priced at $780; (b) Root Canal Products of America, 6½%, 2018, selling at $885; and (c) Kansas City Dental Insurance, 8%, 2022, priced at $950. All of the swap candidates are of comparable quality and have comparable issue characteristics.

Questions

a. Regarding the short-term trading opportunity:
   1. What basic trading principle is involved in this situation?
   2. If Erin's expectations are correct, what will the price of this bond be in 2 years?
   3. What is the expected return on this investment?
   4. Should this investment be made? Why?

b. Regarding the bond swap opportunity:
   1. Compute the current yield and the promised yield (use semiannual compounding) for the bond the Coates currently hold and for each of the three swap candidates.
   2. Do any of the three swap candidates provide better current income and/or current yield than the Beta Corporation bonds the Coates now hold? If so, which one(s)?
   3. Do you see any reason why Erin should switch from her present bond holding into one of the other three issues? If so, which swap candidate would be the best choice? Why?

Case Problem 11.2

LG 4   LG 5   LG 6

Grace Decides to Immunize Her Portfolio

Grace Hesketh is the owner of an extremely successful dress boutique in downtown Chicago. Although high fashion is Grace's first love, she's also interested in investments, particularly bonds and other fixed-income securities. She actively manages her own investments and over time has built up a substantial portfolio of securities. She's well versed on the latest investment techniques and is not afraid to apply those procedures to her own investments.

Grace has been playing with the idea of trying to immunize a big chunk of her bond portfolio. She'd like to cash out this part of her portfolio in 7 years and use the proceeds to buy a vacation home in her home state of Oregon. To do this, she intends to use the $200,000 she now has invested in the following four corporate bonds (she currently has $50,000 invested in each one).

1. A 12-year, 7½% bond that's currently priced at $895.
2. A 10-year, zero-coupon bond priced at $405.
3. A 10-year, 10% bond priced at $1,080.
4. A 15-year, 9¼% bond priced at $980.
   (*Note:* These are all noncallable, investment-grade, nonconvertible/straight bonds.)

Questions

a. Given the information provided, find the current yield and the promised yield for each bond in the portfolio. (Use annual compounding.)

b. Calculate the Macaulay and modified durations of each bond in the portfolio, and indicate how the price of each bond would change if interest rates were to rise by 75 basis points. How would the price change if interest rates were to fall by 75 basis points?

c. Find the duration of the current four-bond portfolio. Given the 7-year target that Grace has, would you consider this to be an immunized portfolio? Explain.

d. How could you lengthen or shorten the duration of this portfolio? What's the shortest portfolio duration you can achieve? What's the longest?

e. Using one or more of the four bonds described above, is it possible to come up with a $200,000 bond portfolio that will exhibit the duration characteristics Grace is looking for? Explain.

f. Using one or more of the four bonds, put together a $200,000 immunized portfolio for Grace. Because this portfolio will now be immunized, will Grace be able to treat it as a buy-and-hold portfolio—one she can put away and forget about? Explain.

Excel with Spreadsheets

All bonds are priced according to the present value of their future cash flow streams. The key components of bond valuation are par value, coupon interest rate, term to maturity, and market yield. It is market yield that drives bond prices. In the market for bonds, the appropriate yield at which the bond should sell is determined first, and then that yield is used to find the market value of the bond. The market yield can also be referred to as the required rate of return. It implies that this is the rate of return that a rational investor requires before he or she will invest in a given fixed-income security.

Create a spreadsheet to model and answer the following bond valuation questions.

Questions

a. One of the bond issues outstanding by the AT&T Corporation has an annual-pay coupon of 5.625% plus a par value of $1,000.00 at maturity. This bond has a remaining maturity of 3 years. The required rate of return on securities of similar-risk grade is 6.76%. What is the value of this corporate bond today?

b. What is the current yield for the AT&T bond?

c. In the case of the AT&T bond issue from question **a**, if the coupon interest payment is compounded on a semiannual basis, what would be the value of this security today?

d. How would the price of the AT&T bond react to changing market interest rates? To find out, determine how the price of the issue reacts to changes in the bond's yield-to-maturity (YTM). Find the value of the security when the YTM is (1) 5.625%, (2) 8.0%, and (3) 4.5%. Label your findings as being a premium, par, or discount bond; comment on your findings.

e. The Tommy Hilfiger Company has a bond issue outstanding with the following characteristics: par of $1,000.00, a semiannual-pay coupon of 6.5%, remaining maturity of 2 years, and a current price of $878.74. What is the bond's yield-to-maturity (YTM)?

CHAPTER 12

PREFERRED STOCKS AND CONVERTIBLE SECURITIES

What do Alltel (telecommunications), Citigroup (financial institution), Virginia Electric and Power (utility), Six Flags (theme parks), HRPT Properties Trust (real estate), and NeoRx (biotechnology) share in common? Though their industries and market capitalizations vary widely, all of these companies issue preferred stock. This investment category is enjoying renewed popularity in the face of volatile common stock prices, historically low bond yields, and money market funds with return rates of less than 1%. Investors looking for income-producing securities were attracted to preferred yields that could reach 10% and averaged 7.1% in mid-December 2003, compared to about 6% for high-quality log-term corporate bonds.

Many individual investors are taking a hard look at the role that preferred stock can play in their portfolios. Preferred stock is generally issued with a $25 par value, as opposed to $1,000 for most corporate bonds, placing these equities well within the reach of the average investor. In fact, individual investors are major buyers of preferreds, which contributes to these stocks' price stability.

In addition to the traditional preferred stocks that pay fixed dividends, you can buy other forms such as adjustable-rate preferreds, trust preferreds (which pay interest rather than dividends), and convertible preferreds that can be turned into common stock. This wide range of options makes buying preferred stock more difficult than you might think. Two Web sites that offer quotes and other information worth checking out are Preferred Stock Online (**www.preferredstockonline.com**) and QuantumOnline.com (**www.quantumonline.com**). In this chapter, you'll learn about preferred stock and other hybrid investments, such as convertible securities, and the advantages they offer investors.

Sources: Jeffrey R. Kosnett and Courtney McGrath, "Aim High," *Kiplinger's Personal Finance Magazine*, February 2003, p. 38; David Landis, "Juicy Yields from Quirky Stocks," *Kiplinger's Personal Finance Magazine*, November 1, 2003; pp. 58, 60; and Jeff D. Opdyke and Tom Herman, "Wall Street Pushes Preferred Stock; Tax Cut Spurs Interest in Dividend-Rich Shares, But Many Don't Qualify for New Low Rate," *The Wall Street Journal*, August 19, 2003, p. D1.

LEARNING GOALS

After studying this chapter, you should be able to:

LG 1 Describe the basic features of preferred stock, including sources of value and exposure to risk.

LG 2 Discuss the rights and claims of preferred stockholders, and note some of the popular issue characteristics that are often found with these securities.

LG 3 Understand the various measures of investment worth, and identify several investment strategies that can be used with preferred stocks.

LG 4 Identify the fundamental characteristics of convertible securities, and explain the nature of the underlying conversion privilege.

LG 5 Describe the advantages and disadvantages of investing in convertible securities, including their risk and return attributes.

LG 6 Measure the value of a convertible security, and explain how these securities can be used to meet different investment objectives.

Preferred Stocks

LG 1   LG 2

preferred stock
a stock that has a prior claim
(ahead of common) on the
income and assets of the
issuing firm.

What would you think of a stock that promised to pay you a fixed annual dividend for life—nothing more, nothing less? If you're an income-oriented investor, the offer might sound pretty good. But where would you find such an investment? Right on the NYSE or AMEX, where hundreds of these securities trade every day, in the form of *preferred stock*—a type of security that looks like a stock but doesn't behave like one. In the first two sections of this chapter we will look at preferred stock as an investment vehicle. In the third and fourth sections we will turn our attention to *convertible securities*. These are securities originally issued as bonds (or preferred stock) that later can be converted into shares of the issuing firm's common stock. Both of these investment vehicles—preferred stock and convertibles—are forms of *fixed-income* corporate securities. As you'll see in the chapter, both are also *hybrid securities,* meaning they contain elements of both debt and equity.

Preferred stocks carry fixed dividends that are paid quarterly and are expressed either in dollar terms or as a percentage of the stock's par (or stated) value. They are used by companies that need money but don't want to raise debt to get it; in effect, they are widely viewed by issuers as an alternative to debt. Companies like to issue preferreds because they don't count as common stock (and, therefore, don't affect EPS). However, being a form of equity, they don't count as debt, either—and therefore don't add to the company's debt load. There are today nearly a thousand OTC and listed preferred stocks outstanding. Many of them are issued by public utilities, although the number of industrial, financial, and insurance issues is rapidly increasing.

Preferred Stocks as Investment Vehicles

Preferred stocks are available in a wide range of quality ratings, from investment-grade to highly speculative. Table 12.1 provides a representative sample of some actively traded preferred stocks. It shows the types of annual dividends and dividend yields that these securities were providing in August 2003.

Advantages and Disadvantages Without a doubt, the number one reason that investors are attracted to preferred stocks is the current income they provide. Take another look at Table 12.1—note the *very attractive dividend yields* these securities offer. Such returns compare favorably to those available on other fixed-income securities and dividend-paying common stocks, and they explain in large part why income-oriented investors are so attracted to these investment vehicles. Another reason for investing in these securities is the level of safety they offer investors. That is, despite a few well-publicized incidents, *high-grade* preferred stocks have an excellent record of meeting dividend payments in a timely manner—certainly an important consideration to income-oriented investors. A final advantage is the low unit cost ($25 to $50 per share) of many of the issues, which gives even small investors the opportunity to actively participate in preferreds.

While preferreds do, indeed, pay hefty dividends, most of them unfortunately *do not qualify for the new preferential tax rate* (of 15% or less). The

TABLE 12.1	A Sample of Some High-Yielding Preferred Stock		
Issuer	Annual Dividend	Market Price	Dividend Yield
AT&T	$2.06	$25.38	8.1%
Alabama Power	1.46	24.95	5.9
Bank One	2.13	27.70	7.7
Citigroup	3.12	52.20	6.0
Cleveland Electric	2.25	26.65	8.4
Disney	1.75	25.70	6.8
El Paso Energy	2.38	30.00	7.9
Host Marriott	2.50	22.20	11.3
Nova Chemical	2.26	24.95	9.1
Public Storage Co.	2.44	27.43	8.9

Note: All of these issues are straight (nonconvertible) preferred stocks traded on the NYSE.
All the information that appears in this table was obtained in August 2003.
Source: Wall Street Journal, August 11, 2003.

reason: During the 1990s, Wall Street created a new type of preferred stock, so-called *trust preferreds*, that actually qualified as debt for tax purposes—meaning the dividends paid by the issuer could be treated as a tax-deductible expense. As a result, what was initially intended as a big windfall for the issuer has turned into a *big disadvantage* for investors. Right now, it's estimated that about two-thirds of all outstanding preferred stocks don't qualify for the new tax treatment, though that's expected to change as the more traditional preferred stocks (which pay dividends from after-tax profits) start making a comeback. Until then, let the buyer beware!

Another drawback of preferred stocks is their susceptibility to inflation and high interest rates. That is, like many other fixed-income securities, preferred stock values go down when rates go up. Thus, these securities simply have not proved to be satisfactory long-term hedges against inflation. Still another disadvantage is that preferred dividends may be suspended, or "passed," if the earnings of the corporate issuer drop off. Unlike the coupon payments on a bond, dividends on preferreds have no legal backing, and failure to pay them does not lead to default. Preferreds also lack substantial capital gains potential. Although it is possible to enjoy fairly attractive capital gains from preferred stocks when interest rates decline dramatically, these amounts generally do not match the price performance of common stocks.

 Sources of Value With the exception of convertible preferreds, the value of high-grade preferred stocks is a function of the dividend yields they provide. More specifically, the value (or market price) of a preferred stock is closely related to prevailing market rates: As the general level of interest rates moves up, so do the yields on preferreds, and their prices decline accordingly. When interest rates drift downward, so do the yields on preferreds, as their prices rise. Just like bond prices, therefore, *the price behavior of a high-grade preferred stock is inversely related to market interest rates*. Moreover, its price is directly linked to the issue's level of income. That is, other things being equal, the higher the dividend payment, the higher the market price of an issue. Thus, the price of a preferred stock can be defined as follows:

Equation 12.1

$$\text{Price of a preferred stock} = \frac{\text{Annual dividend income}}{\text{Prevailing market yield}}$$

This equation is simply a variation of the standard dividend yield formula, but here we solve for the price of the issue. (You might also detect a similarity between this formula and *the zero-growth dividend valuation model* introduced in Chapter 8—see Equation 8.7.) The equation shown here (12.1) is used to price preferred stocks and to compute the future price of a preferred, given an estimate of expected market yields. For example, a $2.50 preferred stock (meaning the stock pays a dividend of $2.50 per year) would be priced at $20.83 if the prevailing market yield were 12%:

$$\text{Price} = \frac{\$2.50}{0.12} = \underline{\underline{\$20.83}}$$

Note that as market yield decreases, you get higher preferred stock prices, thus giving you the inverse relationship between price and yield.

The yield that a preferred stock offers (and therefore its market value) is a function of not only market interest rates but also the issue's credit quality: *The lower the quality of a preferred, the higher its yield.* Such behavior is, of course, compatible with the risk-return tradeoffs that usually exist in the marketplace. Fortunately, preferred stocks are rated, much like bonds, by Moody's and Standard & Poor's. Finally, the value of a preferred is also affected by issue characteristics such as call features and sinking-fund provisions. For example, freely callable preferreds normally provide higher yields than noncallable issues because of their greater call risk. Quality and issue features, however, have only slight effects on price behavior over time, and they certainly do not compare in importance with the movement of market yields.

Risk Exposure Preferred stock investors are exposed to both business and interest rate risks. *Business risk* is important with preferreds, because these securities are a form of equity ownership and, as such, lack many of the legal protections of bonds. Annual operating costs and corporate financial strength, therefore, are of concern to preferred stockholders. Preferred stock ratings (discussed later in the chapter) can be used to assess the amount of business risk embedded in an issue. Higher-quality/higher-rated issues are believed to possess less business risk.

Because of the fixed-income nature of these securities and the way they're valued in the market, *interest rate risk* is also important to preferred stockholders. That is, when market interest rates move up, the value of these securities (like that of bonds) falls. Indeed, such risk exposure can be very damaging if interest rates move against you in a big way.

Market Transactions Preferred stocks are subject to the same transaction costs (brokerage fees and transfer taxes) as shares of common stock. In addition, preferred stock investors use the same types of orders (market, limit, and stop-loss) and operate under the same margin requirements. And in some newspapers, even the quotes for preferred stocks are commingled with those of common. However, as can be seen in Figure 12.1, the *Wall Street Journal* has a separate listing for preferred stock quotes, which includes the name of the

FIGURE 12.1

Published Quotes for Preferred Stock

In publications like the *Wall Street Journal*, preferred stock quotes are listed separately from common stocks. Many companies have more than one issue of preferred outstanding, in which case, each issue is identified alphabetically, such as pfF, pfG, etc. (*Source: Wall Street Journal, August 11, 2003.*)

PREFERRED STOCK LISTINGS				
STOCK	DIV	YLD	CLOSE	CHG
CinnBell pfB	3.38	9.0	37.70	0.22
Citlgroup pfF	3.18	6.0	53	−0.50
Citigroup pfG	3.11	6.0	52.25	0.15
Citigroup pfH	3.12	6.0	52.20	0.20
Citigroup pfM	2.93	5.8	50.64	−0.01
Citigroup pfS	1.50	6.1	24.46	0.12
Citigroup pfV	1.78	6.8	26.24	0.19
Citigroup pfW	1.75	6.9	25.37	0.14
Citigroup pfX	1.72	6.7	25.62	0.13
Citigroup pfZ	1.74	6.8	25.72	0.21
CtznUtil Tr	2.50	5.0	5.0	...
ClevelandElec	2.25	8.4	26.65	0.05
ClvdElec pfL	7.00	7.0	100.50	0.50
ColonlProppfD	.51p	...	25.84	0.29
ColonlProppfC	2.31	8.5	27.19	0.14
ComcastHldg	1.43	4.9	29	...
ComercaCappfZ	1.90	7.3	26.14	0.18
ComrclRlty pf	2.25	8.4	26.69	0.39
ConAgraCappfB	1.25	5.0	24.85	−0.01

Citigroup's preferred stocks

stock, the amount of annual dividends, the dividend yield, closing price, and change in price.

Also, note that a single company can have any number of preferred stock issues outstanding, each with its own annual dividend. Certainly, that's the case with the Citigroup preferreds. The quotes in Figure 12.1 show, for example, that there are nine issues of preferred stock listed for Citigroup. Actually, the company may have even more preferred issues outstanding, but if those issues did not trade on the day of the quotes, they would not be listed. Citigroup's preferreds pay annual dividends of anywhere from $1.50 to $3.18 per share. (Note that, generally speaking, the higher the annual dividend, the higher the price of the stock.) At quoted market prices, these preferreds were providing current yields of 5.8% to 6.9%. Observe also the relatively low unit cost of the stock. With very few exceptions, preferred stocks usually trade at around $25 to $50 a share.

Issue Characteristics

Preferred stocks possess features that not only distinguish them from other types of securities but also help differentiate one preferred from another. For example, preferred stocks may be issued as convertible or nonconvertible, although the majority fall into the nonconvertible category. A convertible preferred has a **conversion feature** that allows the holder to convert the preferred stock into a specified number of shares of the issuing company's common stock. Because convertible preferreds are, for all intents and purposes, very much like

conversion feature
allows the holder of a convertible preferred to convert to a specified number of shares of the issuing company's common stock.

convertible bonds, we will discuss them later in the chapter. At this point, we'll concentrate on *nonconvertible issues*, although many of the features we are about to discuss apply equally to convertible preferreds. In addition to convertibility, investors should be aware of several other important features of preferred stocks; they include the rights of preferred stockholders and the special provisions (such as those pertaining to passed dividends or call features) that are built into preferred stock issues.

Rights of Preferred Stockholders   The contractual agreement of a preferred stock specifies the rights and privileges of preferred stockholders. The most important of these deal with the level of annual dividends, the claim on income, voting rights, and the claim on assets. The issuing company agrees that it will pay preferred stockholders a (minimum) fixed level of quarterly dividends and that such payments *will take priority over common stock dividends*. The only condition is that the firm generate income sufficient to meet the preferred dividend requirements. However, the firm is not legally bound to pay dividends. Of course, it cannot pass dividends on preferred stock and then pay dividends on common stock. To do so would violate the preferreds' prior claim on income.

adjustable-rate (floating-rate) preferreds
preferred stock whose dividends are adjusted periodically in line with yields on certain Treasury issues.

Although most preferred stocks are issued with dividend rates that remain fixed for the life of the issue, in the early 1980s some preferreds began to appear with floating dividend rates. Known as **adjustable-rate** (or **floating-rate) preferreds**, these issues adjust their dividends periodically in line with yields on specific Treasury issues, although minimum and maximum dividend rates are usually established as a safeguard for investors and issuers.

Even though they hold an ownership position in the firm, preferred stockholders normally have no voting rights. However, if conditions deteriorate to the point where the firm needs to pass one or more consecutive quarterly dividends, preferred shareholders are usually given the right to elect a certain number of corporate directors so that their views can be represented. And if liquidation becomes necessary, the holders of preferreds are given a prior claim on assets. These preferred claims, limited to the par or stated value of the stock, must be satisfied before the claims of the common stockholders. Of course, this obligation does not always mean that the full par or stated value of the preferred will be recovered, because the claims of senior securities (like bonds) must be met first. That is, all bonds (including convertible bonds) have a higher claim on assets (and income) than preferred stock, whereas preferreds have a higher claim than common stock. Thus preferred shareholders have a claim that's somewhere between that of bondholders and common stockholders.

preference (prior preferred) stock
a type of preferred stock that has seniority over other preferred stock in its right to receive dividends and in its claim on assets.

Finally, when a company has more than one issue of preferred stock outstanding, it sometimes issues **preference** (or **prior preferred) stock**. Essentially, this stock has seniority over other preferred stock in its right to receive dividends and in its claim on assets in the event of liquidation. Therefore, preference stocks should be viewed as *senior preferreds*. They're usually easy to pick out in the financial pages because they use the letters *pr* instead of *pf* in their quotes.

Preferred Stock Provisions   There are three preferred stock provisions that investors should be well aware of *before* making an investment in a preferred security. Especially important is the obligation of the issuer in case any divi-

cumulative provision
a provision requiring that any preferred dividends that have been passed must be paid in full before dividends can be restored to common stockholders.

in arrears
having outstanding unfulfilled preferred dividend obligations.

noncumulative provision
a provision found on some preferred stocks excusing the issuing firm from having to make up any passed dividends.

INVESTOR FACTS

HOW TO HIDE FROM RISING RATES—One of the biggest fears of fixed-income investors (including preferred stock investors) is rising interest rates. To hedge against rising rates, investors often turn to *adjustable-rate preferreds*, whose cash dividends are adjusted quarterly to reflect market conditions. The dividends on adjustable preferreds usually have a floor and a ceiling, but that still leaves plenty of room to move up or down with market rates. When rates move up, rather than the price of the issue going down, the dividend payment goes up instead. Bottom line: There's far less price volatility with adjustables than with fixed-rate preferreds.

dends are missed. In addition, you should determine whether the stock has a call feature and/or a sinking fund provision. Let's start by looking at how passed dividends are handled, which depends on whether the preferred stock is issued on a cumulative or a noncumulative basis.

Fortunately for investors, most preferred stocks are issued on a **cumulative** basis. This means that any preferred dividends that have been passed *must be made up in full* before dividends can be paid to common stockholders. Any outstanding unfulfilled preferred dividend obligations are said to be **in arrears,** and so long as dividends on preferred stock remain in arrears, a corporation may not make dividend payments on common shares. Assume, for example, that a firm normally pays a $1 quarterly dividend on its preferred stock but has missed the dividend for three quarters in a row. In this case, the firm has preferred dividends in arrears of $3 a share. It must meet these past dividends, along with the next quarterly dividend, before it can pay dividends to common shareholders. The firm could fulfill this obligation by paying, say, $2 per share to the preferred stockholders at the next quarterly dividend date and $3 per share at the following one (with the $3 covering the remaining $2 in arrears and the current $1 quarterly payment). If the preferred stock had carried a **noncumulative provision,** the issuing company would have been under no obligation to make up any of the passed dividends. Of course, the firm could not make dividend payments on common stock either. But it could resume such payments simply by meeting the next quarterly preferred dividend. Other things being equal, a cumulative preferred stock should be more highly valued than an issue without such a provision. That is, the cumulative feature should increase the price (and in so doing, lower the yield) of these issues.

Since the early 1970s, it has become increasingly popular to issue preferred stocks with call features. Today, a large number of preferreds carry this provision, which gives the firm the right to call the preferred for retirement. Callable preferreds are usually issued on a *deferred-call basis,* which means they cannot be retired for a certain number of years after the date of issue. After the deferral period, usually 5 to 7 years, the preferreds become freely callable. Of course, such issues are then susceptible to call if the market rate for preferreds declines dramatically. This explains why the yields on freely callable preferreds should be higher than those on noncallable issues. As with bonds, the call price of a preferred is made up of the par value of the issue and a call premium that may amount to as much as one year's dividends.

Another preferred stock feature that has become popular is the *sinking-fund provision.* This provision specifies how all or a part of an issue will be paid off—amortized—over time. Sinking-fund preferreds actually have *implied* maturity dates. They are used by firms to reduce the cost of financing, because sinking-fund issues generally have *lower* yields than nonsinking-fund preferreds. A typical sinking-fund preferred might require the firm to retire half the issue over a 10-year period by retiring, say, 5% of the issue each year. Unfortunately, the investor has no control over which shares are called for sinking-fund purposes. Sinking-fund provisions not withstanding, many preferred issues today actually have *explicit* maturity dates. These began to appear in the 1990s, when, as noted earlier, Wall Street started creating trust preferred stocks that qualified as debt for tax purposes. So, as is customary with bonds, preferred stocks also started coming out with maturity dates, most of which were very lengthy—often 30 to 50 years.

IN REVIEW

CONCEPTS

12.1 Define a *preferred stock*. What types of prior claims do preferred shareholders enjoy? How do *trust preferreds* differ from traditional preferreds?

12.2 In what ways is a preferred stock like equity? In what ways is it like a bond?

12.3 What are the advantages and the disadvantages of investing in preferreds?

12.4 Distinguish a *cumulative* preferred from a *callable* preferred. Do cumulative dividend provisions and call features affect the investment merits of preferred issues? Explain.

Valuing and Investing in Preferreds

LG 3

As we just saw, although preferred stocks may be a form of equity, they behave in the market more like a bond than a stock. Therefore, it seems logical that *preferreds should be valued much like bonds,* with market interest rates and investment quality playing key roles. Similarly, when it comes to investing in preferreds, you would expect interest rates (either the level of market interest rates or the movements therein) to play key roles in preferred stock investment strategies. In fact, that's exactly what you find: The two most widely used preferred stock strategies involve either going after high levels of current income or seeking capital gains when market rates are falling.

Putting a Value on Preferreds

Evaluating the investment suitability of preferreds involves assessing comparative return opportunities. Let's look now at some of the return measures that are important to preferred stockholders, and then at the role that agency ratings play in the valuation process.

Dividend Yield: A Key Measure of Value Dividend yield is critical to determining the price and return behavior of most preferred stocks. It is computed according to the following simple formula:

Equation 12.2

$$\text{Dividend yield} = \frac{\text{Annual dividend income}}{\text{Current market price of the preferred stock}}$$

dividend yield
a measure of the amount of return earned on annual dividends.

Dividend yield is a measure of the amount of return earned on annual dividends, and is the basis upon which comparative preferred investment opportunities are evaluated. (It is basically the same as the *dividend yield* used in Chapter 7 with common stocks and is comparable to the *current yield* measure used with bonds, as described in Chapter 11.)

Here's how dividend yield works: Suppose an 8% preferred stock has a par value of $25 and is currently trading at a price of $27.50 per share. For preferreds whose dividends are denoted as a percentage of par (or stated) value, the dollar value of the annual dividend is found by multiplying the dividend rate (in this case, 8%) by the par value ($25). Thus, the annual dividend on this stock is $0.08 \times \$25 = \$2$. Therefore, the dividend yield in this example is

$$\text{Dividend yield} = \frac{\$2}{\$27.50} = \underline{7.27\%}$$

As you can see, at $27.50 a share, this preferred is yielding about 7.3% to investors. If the price of this preferred moves down (to say, $21 a share), the dividend yield increases (in this case, to about 9½%). In practice, we would expect investors to compute or have available a current dividend yield measure for each preferred under consideration and then to make a choice by comparing the yields on the alternative preferreds—along with, of course, the risk and issue characteristics of each.

H O T

For preferred stock terms, visit:

www.briefing.com/FreeServices/
Education/edu_Preferred_Stock.htm

Expected Return Whereas long-term investors may consider dividend yield a key factor, that's not necessarily the case with the short-term traders. Instead, these traders generally focus on anticipated price behavior and the expected return from buying and selling an issue over a short period of time. Thus *the expected future price of a preferred* is important to short-term traders. Expected price can be found by first forecasting future market interest rates and then using that information to determine expected future price. To illustrate, suppose a preferred stock pays $3 in dividends and its yield is expected to decline to 6% within the next 3 years. If such market rates prevail, then 3 years from now, the issue will have a market price of $50 (using Equation 12.1, annual dividend ÷ yield = $3 ÷ 0.06 = $50). This forecasted price, along with the current market price and level of annual dividends, would then be used in either the expected return or holding period return formula to assess the return potential of the investment.

To continue with our example, if the stock were currently priced at $28 a share, it would have an *expected return* (over the 3-year investment horizon) of a very attractive 30.3%. This can be found by using *the IRR approach* we first introduced in Chapter 4 and then applied (as a measure of expected return) to common stocks in Chapter 8 and to bonds in Chapter 11. Basically, you'd want to find the discount rate, in the present-value-based yield formula, that equates the expected future cash flows from this preferred to its current market price of $28 a share. (The preferred's cash flows are the $50 price in 3 years, plus the annual dividends of $3 a share over each of the next 3 years.) As it turns out, that discount rate equals 30.3%; at that rate, the present value of the future cash flows amounts to $28 a share. (As an aside, *this problem can readily be solved with a financial calculator* by letting $N = 3$, $PV = 28$, $PMT = -3$, $FV = -50$ and then solve for I. Try it. You should end up with a value (return) of 30.34.)

You now have a measure of the relative attractiveness of this preferred stock. Of course, other things (like risk) being equal, the higher the expected return, the more appealing the investment. (Note that if the above performance had occurred over a period of 6 months, rather than 3 years, you would use the *holding period return* measure to assess the potential return of this preferred. See Chapter 4 for details.)

book value (net asset value)
a measure of the amount of debt-free assets supporting each share of preferred stock.

Book Value The **book value** (or **net asset value**) of a preferred stock is a measure of the amount of debt-free assets supporting each share of preferred stock. In this regard, note that it's the *total book value of the firm* that's of concern here, not just the amount of preferred equity listed on the balance sheet. That's because, relative to common equity, preferred shareholders have a prior claim on all the net assets of the firm. Thus, book value per share is found by subtracting all the liabilities of the firm from its total assets and dividing the difference by the number of preferred shares outstanding. This measure, in essence, reflects the quality of an issue with regard to the preferred's *claim on assets*. Obviously, a preferred with a book value of $150 per share enjoys generous asset support and more than adequately secures a par value of, say, $25 a share. Net asset value is most relevant when it is used relative to an issue's par (or stated) value. Other things being equal, *the quality of an issue improves as the margin by which book value exceeds par value increases.*

fixed charge coverage
a measure of how well a firm is able to cover its preferred stock dividends.

Fixed Charge Coverage Fixed charge coverage is a measure of how well a firm is able to cover its preferred dividends. Here attention is centered on the firm's ability to service preferred dividends and live up to the preferred's preferential *claim on income*. As such, fixed charge coverage is important in determining the quality of a preferred stock. Fixed charge coverage is computed as follows:

Equation 12.3

$$\text{Fixed charge coverage} = \frac{\text{Earnings before interest and taxes (EBIT)}}{\text{Interest expense} + \dfrac{\text{Preferred dividends}}{0.65}}$$

Note in this equation that preferred dividends are adjusted by a factor of 0.65. This adjustment is used with "traditional" preferred stocks and takes into account the fact that *a company pays dividends from the earnings that are left after taxes*. The adjustment factor (0.65) implies a corporate tax rate of 35%, which is a reasonable rate to use for our purposes here. By making the indicated adjustment, you essentially place preferred dividends on the same basis as interest paid on bonds, which is a tax-deductible expense. *Normally, the higher the fixed charge coverage, the greater the margin of safety.* A ratio of 1.0 means the company is generating just enough earnings to meet its preferred dividend payments—not a very healthy situation. A coverage ratio of 0.7 suggests the potential for some real problems, whereas a coverage of, say, 7.0 indicates that preferred dividends are fairly secure.

As noted with the common stock interest coverage ratio (see the times interest earned measure in Chapter 7, Equation 7.7), fixed charge coverage is often computed with EBITDA in the numerator, rather than EBIT. Since earnings before interest, taxes, depreciation, and amortization will normally be more than EBIT, use of EBITDA will result in a higher coverage ratio—something that should be taken into consideration when assessing this measure. Also, if you're dealing with one of the newer debt-like preferreds, then you can *drop the adjustment factor (0.65) in the denominator*, because preferred dividends are treated just like interest expense in these cases. Doing so will, of course, lead to a higher fixed-charge coverage—the denominator will be smaller, so other things being equal, the fixed-charge coverage ratio will be higher.

Agency Ratings Standard & Poor's has long rated the investment quality of preferred stocks, and since 1973, so has Moody's. S&P uses basically the same rating system as it does for bonds; Moody's uses a slightly different system. For both agencies, the greater the likelihood that the issuer will be able to pay dividends promptly, the higher the rating. Much like bonds, the top four ratings designate *investment-grade* (high-quality) preferreds. Although preferreds come in a full range of agency ratings, most tend to fall in the medium-grade categories (a and baa), or lower. Generally speaking, higher agency ratings reduce the market yield of an issue and increase its interest sensitivity. Agency ratings not only eliminate much of the need for fundamental analysis, but also help investors get a handle on the yield and potential price behavior of an issue.

Investment Strategies

There are several investment strategies that preferred stockholders can follow. Each is useful in meeting a different investment objective, and each offers a different level of return and exposure to risk.

Looking for Yields This strategy represents perhaps the most popular use of preferred stocks and is ideally suited for serious long-term investors. *High current income* is the objective, and the procedure basically involves seeking out those preferreds with the most attractive yields. While yield is necessarily a key variable, consideration is also given to such features as the quality of the issue, whether the dividends are cumulative, the existence of any call or sinking-fund provisions, and, of course, whether the dividend qualifies for the new preferential tax rate.

Certainty of income and safety are important in this strategy, because yields are attractive only as long as dividends are paid. Some investors never buy anything but the highest-quality preferreds. Others sacrifice quality in return for higher yields when the economy is strong and use higher-quality issues only during periods of economic distress. Whenever you leave one of the top four agency ratings, you should recognize the speculative position you are assuming. This is especially so with preferreds, since their dividends lack legal enforcement.

Like common shares, most preferreds pay dividends on a quarterly basis. Even so, some special breeds of preferred stocks offer not only attractive yields but also monthly income. One of these is a type of hybrid security known as a **monthly income preferred stock** (**MIPS**, for short). However, as the *Investing in Action* box on pages 512 and 513 explains, although these securities do offer attractive yields, they are a very unusual type of investment vehicle. As such, you should learn as much as you can about these, and other specialty, securities before investing in them.

monthly income preferred stock (MIPS)
a type of preferred stock that offers attractive tax provisions to the issuers, and attractive monthly returns to investors.

Trading on Interest Rate Swings Rather than assuming a "safe" buy-and-hold position, the investor who trades on movements in interest rates adopts an aggressive short-term trading posture. This is done for one major reason: *capital gains.* Of course, although a high level of return is possible with this approach, it comes with higher risk exposure. Because preferreds are fixed-income securities, the market behavior of *investment-grade issues* is closely linked to movements in interest rates. If market interest rates are expected to decline substantially, attractive capital gains opportunities may be realized from preferred stocks. Indeed, this is precisely what happened in the mid-1980s, and again in the early 1990s (1991 through 1993) and in 2000–2003, when market

INVESTING IN ACTION

MIPS: THERE'S MORE TO THEM THAN HIGHER YIELDS AND MONTHLY INCOME

In 1993 Goldman Sachs & Co., a leading investment banking firm, invented *monthly income preferred stock*, or *MIPS*, which looks like a win–win arrangement: Everyone seems to benefit. The issuer gets a tax deduction. The investor gets high *monthly* income, as well as the upside potential inherent in a stock. Here's how they work: XYZ Corporation creates a new entity called a limited-life company (LLC) that sells MIPS to the public and lends the proceeds to the parent corporation. The parent pays interest to the LLC on the loan, which in turn is paid to MIPS holders in the form of monthly dividends.

From the issuer's point of view, MIPS are attractive because the payments are tax deductible, even though MIPS are not considered straight debt and thus do not raise the corporation's debt ratio. That's good, because credit rating agencies don't like to see debt ratios rise. MIPS are typically listed on the New York Stock Exchange, like many preferred stocks. Issuers have included such household names as Aetna, GTE, and Corning. From the investor's point of view, MIPS offer higher yields than certificates of deposit and money market funds.

They also provide higher yields than corporate bonds and conventional preferred stock. And the payments are made monthly, whereas bonds pay interest every 6 months and stocks pay dividends quarterly.

The yield on conventional preferred stock tends to be driven down by corporate investors, who can deduct up to 70% of the dividend payments from their corporate income tax. Individual investors don't get that tax break, so conventional preferreds haven't been marketed heavily to individuals. But MIPS have gotten their attention.

Not everyone thinks MIPS are great. The first drawback is that despite the term *preferred* in their name, MIPS are quite low on the issuing corporation's list of obligations. If an issuer gets into financial trouble, MIPS holders have to stand toward the end of the repayment line. The second drawback is lack of call protection. If interest rates fall, the issuer can redeem the securities at par without paying a penalty. That leaves the investor stuck with cash to reinvest at lower rates. The third drawback has to do with your taxes. Corporations set up partnerships to

continued on next page

interest rates dropped sharply. During such periods, it's not uncommon to find preferreds generating *annual* returns of 20% to 30%, or more.

As is probably clear by now, this strategy is identical to that used by bond investors. In fact, many of the same principles used with bonds apply to preferred stocks. For example, it is important to select high-grade preferred stocks, because interest sensitivity is a key ingredient of this strategy. Moreover, margin trading is often used to magnify short-term holding period returns. A basic difference is that the very high leverage rates of bonds are not available with preferreds, because they fall under the same, less generous margin requirements as common stocks. The investment selection process is simplified somewhat as well, because neither maturity nor the size of the annual preferred dividend (which is equivalent to a bond's coupon) has any effect on the *rate of price volatility*. That is, a $2 preferred will appreciate just as much (in percentage terms) as an $8 preferred for a given change in market yields.

Speculating on Turnarounds This speculative investment strategy can prove profitable if you're nimble enough to catch a trading opportunity before every-

INVESTING IN ACTION

continued from previous page

issue these securities, which means that you get a K-1 instead of a Form 1099 at the end of the year. In contrast to 1099s, which are sent out at the end of January, most K-1s aren't sent out until mid-March. And they're a more complicated document. That means you'll spend more time on your taxes—or your accountant will, which means a higher bill to you. Indeed, a high accounting fee could even wipe out the higher yields that MIPS offer. And, if these dividends are actually interest payments, then they won't qualify for the new preferential tax rates!

Don't like MIPS? Then look at QUIPS, PRIDES, and PINES—some of the other types of hybrid specialty preferreds. *Quarterly Income Preferred Securities*, or *QUIPS*, are structured like MIPS but pay cumulative quarterly distributions. *PRIDES, Preferred Redeemable Increased Dividend Equity Securities*, were developed by Merrill Lynch. They are similar to convertible securities and are sold in units that comprise an interest-bearing security, which provides stable cash flow, and a contract obligating the investor to purchase an underlying security at maturity. For example, in December 2001, Cinergy, Inc., sold 5 million units of Income PRIDES. Each unit included a $50 preferred trust security and a

stock purchase contract. Holders received a 9.5% cash payment, paid quarterly, and were required to buy stock at a price within a range specified at the time of the unit purchase. *PINES, Public Income Notes*, are unsecured, unsubordinated debentures sold in small share amounts, such as $25. They trade on the stock exchanges but also pay fixed quarterly interest payments. Because they pay a fixed interest amount yet are traded on stock exchanges, PINES represent a hybrid between bonds and preferred stocks. SBC Communications, Inc., has a 7% PINES issue that trades on the NYSE, for example. In the 12-month period ending November 24, 2003, these shares traded between $25.21 and $27.68.

CRITICAL THINKING QUESTIONS Why might investors be interested in buying MIPS? Do these securities have any noteworthy features? Are there any unusual risks associated with them? Explain.

Sources: Cinergy, Inc., 2001 Annual Report, downloaded from www.cinergy.com; *Explanation of Security Acronyms*, QuantumOnline.com, downloaded from www.quantumonline.com/SecurityAcronyms.htm, accessed November 24, 2003; and *Investopedia.com*, www.investopedia.com, accessed November 24, 2003.

one else does. The idea is to find preferred stocks whose dividends have gone into arrears and whose rating has tumbled to one of the speculative categories. The price of the issue, of course, would be depressed to reflect the corporate problems of the issuer. There is more to this strategy, however, than simply finding a speculative-grade preferred stock. The difficult part is to uncover a speculative issue whose fortunes, for one reason or another, *are about to undergo a substantial turnaround*. This strategy requires a good deal of fundamental analysis and is, in many respects, akin to investing in speculative common stock.

In essence, the investor is betting that the firm will undergo a turnaround and will once again be able to service its preferred dividend obligations in a prompt and timely fashion. Such a bet obviously involves a fair amount of risk. Unfortunately, although the rewards from this kind of high-risk investing can be substantial, they are somewhat limited. For example, if a turnaround candidate is expected to recover to a single-a rating, then its capital gains potential would likely be limited to the approximate price level of other a-rated preferreds. This condition is depicted in Figure 12.2 (on page 514). As

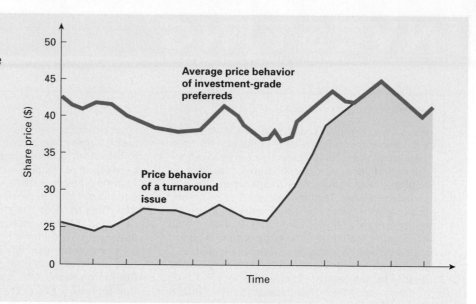

FIGURE 12.2

Price Pattern of a Hypothetical Preferred Turnaround Candidate

Although a turnaround issue seeks the price level of other preferreds of comparable quality and dividend payout, this level also acts as a type of price cap and clearly limits capital appreciation.

the figure shows, although price performance may be somewhat limited, it is still substantial and can readily amount to holding period returns of 50% or more. But in view of the substantial risks involved, such returns are certainly not out of line.

Investing in Convertible Preferreds The investor following this strategy uses the conversion feature to go after speculative opportunities and the chance for attractive returns. The use of *convertible preferreds* is based on their link to the company's common stock and on the belief that they will provide generous price appreciation. Convertibles will be reviewed in detail below, but at this point, suffice it to say that as the price of the underlying common stock appreciates, so does the market price of a convertible preferred. This strategy can offer handsome returns, but remember that investors who employ it are actually speculating on the common stock dimension of the security. Therefore, it is the equity position of the issue that should be subjected to scrutiny. The idea is to look for equity situations that hold considerable promise for appreciation, and then, rather than buying the common stock of the firm, purchase its convertible preferred instead.

IN REVIEW

CONCEPTS

12.5 Describe how high-grade preferred stocks are priced in the market. What role does dividend yield play in the valuation of preferred stocks? Could you use the zero-growth dividend valuation model to value a preferred stock? Explain.

12.6 Discuss why dividend yield is critical in evaluating the investment merits of high-grade preferred stocks during periods when market yields are expected to decline.

12.7 Identify several investment uses of preferred stocks. Would preferreds be suitable for both conservative and aggressive investors? Explain.

Convertible Securities

convertible securities
fixed-income obligations that have a feature permitting the holder to convert the security into a specified number of shares of the issuing company's common stock.

equity kicker
another name for the conversion feature, giving the holder of a convertible security a deferred claim on the issuer's common stock.

H O T

For a brief review of convertible securities see:

www.convertbond.com/tutor/
ConvertibleTypes.asp

deferred equity
securities issued in one form and later redeemed or converted into shares of common stock.

Convertible securities, more commonly known simply as *convertibles,* represent still another type of fixed-income security. Usually issued as debenture notes or bonds (or, as noted above, even as preferred stocks), these securities are subsequently convertible into shares of the issuing firm's common stock. Although they possess the features and performance characteristics of both fixed-income and equity securities, convertibles should be viewed primarily *as a form of equity.* That's because most investors commit their capital to such obligations not for the yields they provide but, rather, for the potential price performance of the stock side of the issue. In fact, it is always a good idea *to determine whether a corporation has convertible issues outstanding whenever you are considering a common stock investment.* In some circumstances, the convertible may be a better investment than the firm's common stock.

Convertibles as Investment Outlets

Convertible securities are popular with investors because of their **equity kicker**—that is, the right of the investor to convert his or her bonds into the company's common stock. Because of this feature, the market price of a convertible has a tendency to behave very much like the price of its underlying common stock. Convertibles are used by all types of companies and are issued either as convertible *bonds* (by far the most common type) or as convertible *preferreds.* Companies like to issue convertibles principally because *they enable firms to raise equity capital at fairly attractive prices.* That is, when a company issues stock in the normal way (by selling more shares in the company), it does so by setting a price on the stock that's *below* prevailing market prices. For example, it might be able to get $25 for a stock that's currently priced in the market at, say, $30 a share. In contrast, when it issues the stock indirectly through a convertible issue, a firm can set a price that's *above* the prevailing market—for example, it might be able to get $35 for the same stock. As a result, the company can raise the *same amount of money* by issuing a lot less stock through a convertible than by selling it directly in the market. Thus, companies issue convertibles *not* as a way of raising debt capital but as a way of raising equity. Because they are supposed to be converted eventually into shares of the issuing company's common stock, convertibles are usually viewed as a form of **deferred equity.**

Not surprisingly, whenever the stock market is strong, convertibles tend to perform well. When the market softens, so does interest in convertibles. Convertible bonds and convertible preferreds are both linked to the equity position of the firm, so they are usually considered interchangeable for investment purposes. Except for a few peculiarities (e.g., the fact that preferreds pay dividends rather than interest and do so on a quarterly basis rather than semi-annually), convertible bonds and convertible preferreds are evaluated in much the same way. Because of their similarities, the discussion that follows will be couched largely in terms of bonds, but the information and implications apply equally well to convertible preferreds.

Convertible Notes and Bonds Convertible bonds are usually issued as debentures (long-term, unsecured corporate debt), but they carry the provision that within a stipulated time period, *the bond may be converted into a certain*

H O T

For information on how to hedge your bets with convertible bonds, see:

moneycentral.msn.com/articles/invest/strat/3295.asp

forced conversion
the calling in of convertible bonds by the issuing firm.

conversion privilege
the conditions and specific nature of the conversion feature on convertible securities.

conversion period
the time period during which a convertible issue can be converted.

number of shares of the issuing company's common stock. (Convertible *notes* are just like convertible bonds except that the debt portion of the security carries a shorter maturity—usually of 5 to 10 years. Other than the life of the debt, there is no real difference between the two types of issues: They're both unsecured debt obligations, and they're usually subordinated to other forms of debt. Most important, they're both convertible into common stock on pretty much the same terms. Thus, for our purposes here, we'll use the terms interchangeably.)

Generally speaking, there is little or no cash involved at the time of conversion. You merely trade in the convertible bond (or note) for a stipulated number of shares of common stock. For example, assume that a certain convertible security recently came to the market, and it carried the provision that each $1,000 note could be converted into shares of the issuing company's stock at $62.55 a share. Thus, *regardless of what happens to the market price of the stock,* the convertible investor can redeem each note for 15.98 shares of the company's stock ($1,000 ÷ $62.55 = 15.98 shares). So, if the company's stock is trading in the market at, say, $125 a share at the time of conversion, then the investor would have just converted a $1,000 debt obligation into $1,997.50 worth of stock (15.98 × $125 = $1,997.50). Not surprisingly, this conversion privilege comes at a price: *the low coupon (or dividend) that convertibles usually carry.* That is, when new convertible issues come to the market, their coupons are normally just a fraction of those on comparable straight (nonconvertible) bonds. Indeed, the more attractive the conversion feature, the lower the coupon.

Actually, while it's the *bondholder* who has the right to convert the bond at any time, more often than not, the issuing firm initiates conversion by calling the bonds—a practice known as **forced conversion.** To provide the corporation with the flexibility to retire the debt and force conversion, most convertibles come out as freely callable issues, or they carry very short call deferment periods. To force conversion, the corporation would call for the retirement of the bond and give the bondholder one of two options: either convert the bond into common stock, or redeem it for cash at the stipulated call price (which, in the case of convertibles, contains very little call premium). So long as the convertible is called when the market value of the stock exceeds the call price of the bond (which is almost always the case), seasoned investors would never choose the second option. Instead, they would opt to convert the bond, as the firm wants them to. Then they can hold the stocks if they want to, or they can sell their new shares in the market (and end up with more cash than they would have received by taking the call price). After the conversion is complete, the bonds no longer exist; instead, there is additional common stock in their place.

Conversion Privilege The key element of any convertible is its **conversion privilege,** which stipulates the conditions and specific nature of the conversion feature. To begin with, it states exactly when the debenture can be converted. With some issues, there may be an initial waiting period of 6 months to perhaps 2 years after the date of issue, during which time the security cannot be converted. The **conversion period** then begins, and the issue can be converted at any time. The conversion period typically extends for the remaining life of the debenture, but in some instances, it may exist for only a certain number of

HOT

A good glossary of convertibles can be found at:

www.convertbond.com/tutor/Glossary.asp

conversion ratio
the number of shares of common stock into which a convertible issue can be converted.

conversion price
the stated price per share at which common stock will be delivered to the investor in exchange for a convertible issue.

HOT

Excellent PowerPoint slides on convertibles are available from:

www.duke.edu/~maug/teaching/ acf/ACFSyllabus.html

PERC (preferred equity redemption cumulative stock)
preferred securities that carry potentially restrictive conversion privileges in exchange for attractive dividend returns.

years. This is done to give the issuing firm more control over its capital structure. If the issue has not been converted by the end of its conversion period, it reverts to a straight-debt issue with no conversion privileges.

From the investor's point of view, the most important piece of information is the *conversion price* or the *conversion ratio*. These terms are used interchangeably and specify, either directly or indirectly, the number of shares of stock into which the bond can be converted. **Conversion ratio** denotes the number of common shares into which the bond can be converted. **Conversion price** indicates the stated value per share at which the common stock will be delivered to the investor in exchange for the bond. When you stop to think about these two measures, it becomes clear that a given conversion ratio implies a certain conversion price, and vice versa. For example, a $1,000 convertible bond might stipulate a conversion ratio of 20, which means that the bond can be converted into 20 shares of common stock. This same privilege could also be stated in terms of a conversion price: The $1,000 bond may be used to acquire the stock at a "price" of $50 per share. Here, the conversion ratio of 20 signifies a conversion price of $50. (One basic difference between a convertible debenture and a convertible preferred relates to conversion ratio: The conversion ratio of a debenture generally deals with large multiples of common stock, such as 15, 20, or 30 shares. In contrast, the conversion ratio of a preferred is generally very small, often less than 1 share of common and seldom more than 3 or 4 shares.)

The conversion ratio is generally fixed over the conversion period, although some convertibles are issued with variable ratios/prices. In such cases, the conversion ratio decreases (while the conversion price increases) over the life of the conversion period, to reflect the supposedly higher value of the equity. The conversion ratio is also normally adjusted for stock splits and significant stock dividends, to maintain the conversion rights of the investor. As a result, if a firm declares, say, a 2-for-1 stock split, the conversion ratio of any of its outstanding convertible issues also doubles. And when the conversion ratio includes a fraction, such as 33½ shares of common, the conversion privilege specifies how any fractional shares are to be handled. Usually, the investor can either put up the additional funds necessary to purchase another full share of stock at the conversion price or receive the cash equivalent of the fractional share (at the conversion price). Table 12.2 (on page 518) lists some basic features for a number of actively traded convertible bonds and preferreds, and reveals a variety of conversion privileges and issue characteristics.

PERCs and LYONs Wall Street is notorious for taking a basic investment product and turning it into a new investment vehicle. Certainly that's the case with two very special types of convertible securities, known as PERCs and LYONs. These securities have certain features and characteristics that separate them from the rest of the pack of convertibles. The acronym **PERC** stands for **preferred equity redemption cumulative stock.** It is a type of *convertible preferred* that offers not only an equity kicker but an attractive dividend yield to boot. There is a catch, however: A cap is placed on the capital appreciation potential of these securities. A regular convertible stipulates (or implies) a certain number of shares of stock into which the security can be converted, regardless of the market value of the stock. A PERC, on the other hand, stipulates a

TABLE 12.2 Convertible Preferred Stocks and Bonds

Convertible Preferreds	S&P Rating	Market Price/ Convertibles	Yield*	Conversion Ratio	Conversion Premium	Payback Period
Cummins, Inc. $3.50 pfd	BB	$46.13	7.59%	1.05	44.8%	6.4 years
Ford Motor $3.25 pfd	BBB−	48.93	6.64	2.82	36.1	6.1
Host Marriott $3.38 pfd	B	40.31	8.37	3.25	19.2	1.9
International Paper $2.63 pfd	BB+	47.19	5.56	0.93	23.9	5.4
Rouse Co. $3.00 pfd	BB+	46.28	6.48	1.31	13.1	5.6
Sinclair Broadcast Group $3.00 pfd	B−	37.00	8.11	2.19	36.8	3.3
Union Pacific Corp. $3.13 pfd	BB	50.25	6.22	0.73	19.0	3.1
Washington Mutual $2.69 pfd	BBB−	49.44	5.44	1.21	22.5	6.3
Convertible Bonds/Notes						
Barnes & Noble $5.25%—2009	B+	$977.50	5.7%	30.76	41.2%	5.4 years
Briggs & Stratton 5.00%—2006	BBB−	991.25	5.3	20.18	36.4	11.0
Community Health 4.25%—2008	B−	1,018.75	3.9	29.85	36.5	6.4
First Data Corp. 2.00%—2008	A+	1,098.75	0.2	24.42	30.9	14.4
GAP Inc. 5.75%—2009	BB+	1,108.75	3.9	62.03	30.7	5.0
JC Penney 5.00%—2008	BB+	917.50	6.7	35.09	38.9	8.0
Pepsico 2.00%—2007	AA+	941.25	3.3	17.17	28.3	21.4
United Parcel Service 1.75%—2007	AAA	1,028.75	1.2	14.15	18.2	23.5

*Yield-to-maturity for convertible bonds; current yield for convertible preferreds; all prices and yields as of July 2003.

Source: Morgan Stanley Dean Witter, *ConvertBond.com.*

certain *dollar amount of the underlying common stock that will be received on the stipulated maturity date of the PERC.* Such a conversion privilege sets a cap on the amount of capital gains you can earn. For example, a conversion price of $50 a share defines the most you can receive. If the underlying stock is trading at $50 or less on the maturity date of the PERC, you receive one share of stock. But if it's trading at more than $50 a share, you'll receive less than a full share of stock. Thus, if the stock is at $75, you'll receive two-thirds of a share, or $50 worth of stock. This is the price you pay to have both the equity kicker and an attractive dividend yield. In essence, in return for the relatively high dividend yield, you have to be willing to accept limits on the equity kicker. As an investor, you have to decide which is more important to you: full participation in the equity kicker or an attractive dividend yield.

LYON (liquid yield option note)
a zero-coupon bond that carries both a conversion feature and a put option.

The acronym **LYON** stands for **liquid yield option note.** Basically, a LYON is a *zero-coupon bond* that carries both *a conversion feature* and *a put option.* These bonds are convertible, at a fixed conversion ratio, for the life of the issue. Thus, they offer the built-in increase in value over time that accompanies any zero-coupon bond (as it moves toward its par value at maturity), plus full participation in the equity side of the issue via the equity kicker. Unlike with a PERC, there's no current income with a LYON (because it is a zero-coupon bond), but there's no limit on capital gains either. In addition, the option feature enables you to "put" the bonds back to the issuer (at specified values). That is, *the put option gives bondholders the right to redeem their bonds periodically at prespecified prices.* Thus you know you can get out of these securities, at set prices, if things move against you. Although LYONs may appear to provide the best of all worlds, they do have some negatives. True, LYONs provide downside protection (via the put option feature) and full participation in the equity kicker. But being zero-coupon bonds, they don't generate current income. And you have to watch out for the put option: Depending on the type of put option, the payout doesn't have to be in cash—it can be in stocks or bonds/notes. One other thing: Because the conversion ratio on the LYON is fixed, while the underlying value of the zero-coupon bond keeps increasing (as it moves to maturity), *the conversion price on the stock increases over time.* Thus the market price of the stock had better go up by more than the bond's rate of appreciation or you'll never be able to convert your LYON.

Sources of Value

Because convertibles—even PERCs and LYONs—are fixed-income securities linked to the equity position of the firm, they are normally valued in terms of *both the stock and the bond dimensions* of the issue. In fact, it is ultimately both of these dimensions that give the convertible its value. This, of course, explains why it is so important to analyze the underlying common stock *and* to formulate interest rate expectations when considering convertibles as an investment outlet. Let's look first at the stock dimension.

Convertible securities trade much like common stock whenever the market price of the stock starts getting close to (or exceeds) the stated conversion price. (In effect, they will derive their value from the underlying common stock.) This means that whenever a convertible trades near its par value ($1,000) or above, it will exhibit price behavior that closely matches that of the underlying common stock: If the stock goes up in price, so does the convertible, and vice versa. In fact, the absolute price change of the convertible will exceed that of the common because of the conversion ratio, which will define the convertible's rate of change in price. For example, if a convertible carries a conversion ratio of, say, 20, then for every point the common stock goes up (or down) in price, the price of the convertible will move *in the same direction* by roughly that same multiple (in this case, 20). In essence, whenever a convertible trades as a stock, its market price will approximate a multiple of the share price of the common, with the size of the multiple being defined by the conversion ratio.

When the price of the common is depressed, so that its trading price is well below the conversion price, the convertible loses its tie to the underlying common stock and begins to trade as a bond. When that happens, the convertible becomes linked to prevailing bond yields, and investors focus their attention on *market rates of interest.* However, because of the equity kicker and their relatively low agency ratings, *convertibles generally do not possess high interest rate sensitivity.* Gaining more than a rough idea of what the prevailing yield of a convertible obligation ought to be is often difficult. For example, if the issue is rated Baa and the market rate for this quality range is 9%, then the convertible should be priced to yield *something around 9%,* plus or minus perhaps half a percentage point. The bond feature will also establish a *price floor* for the convertible, which tends to parallel interest rates and is independent of the behavior of common share prices. This bond floor is especially important with so-called busted convertibles. Basically, a convertible bond is considered to be "busted" when the market price of the underlying common stock falls so

INVESTING IN ACTION

BUSTED CONVERTIBLES—DOWN BUT NOT OUT

Investors typically choose convertible bonds to take advantage of the upside potential that the equity kicker provides. For this reason, convertibles are popular in rising equity markets, when their prices move like those of stocks rather than bonds. At the same time, their semiannual interest payments make them less risky than owning common stock—even though the coupon rate will be lower than the return for a comparable straight bond because of the conversion privilege.

But what happens when stock prices take a nose dive, as they did from 2000 through 2002? If the convertible's stock price falls far enough below the conversion price so that the right to convert becomes irrelevant, you have a "busted convertible." In 2001, for example, approximately 40% of all convertible bonds were classified as being members of this category. Some experienced investors, however, eagerly bought these securities.

Why would anyone buy busted convertibles? Despite the strange name, these securities offer investors some attractive returns. Because the share price was so low, the convertibles acted more like bonds than stock and traded based on yield and credit rating. In fact, some issues yielded more than 15%!

Let's look at an example showing how the numbers work. In January 1999, Amazon.com issued 10-year convertibles with a 4.75% coupon and priced at 100% of par ($1,000)—a good deal for the young company, because the prime rate on bank borrowings for top credits was 8%. Investors were lured by the right to convert each bond into 12.8 shares of stock in this rising Internet upstart. The stock was selling for $61.50, giving each convertible bond a value of $787 (12.8 × $61.50) and a conversion premium of 27% ($1,000 par value ÷ $787). As Amazon's shares doubled in price, the convertible's price rose to 153% of par. When the dot-com bubble burst, however, the price of Amazon's stock plunged. In early 2001, the stock traded at around $15.50, while the convertible was valued at just $198 (12.8 × $15.50). With the bond priced at 37.50, the conversion premium was 89% (375 ÷ 198), meaning that Amazon's shares

needed to increase by 89% to bring the convertible in line with the share price. Clearly, Amazon's high conversion premium qualified it for busted-convertible status, and the issue was trading like a bond. (One expert uses a 45% or higher conversion premium as the benchmark to define busted convertibles.) At such a deep discount, the current yield on the 4.75% coupon jumped to 12.6%, and the yield to maturity, including capital gains, was even higher. While this example is several years old, it demonstrates why investors were willing to buy busted convertibles.

As attractive as the yields may be given the right market circumstances, busted convertibles represent a risky investment and are difficult for individual investors to analyze and purchase. Listings of busted convertibles are hard to find, you'll pay high fees to buy these instruments, and many of the issuing companies are rated below investment grade, increasing the risk even further. Mutual funds that specialize in convertible bonds offer another option that is more accessible—and safer—for individual investors. Calamos, Pioneer, and Greenspring are several of the fund families that took advantage of busted convertibles. In spring 2001, 80% of the Calamos High Yield fund consisted of busted convertibles (although this would not be the case in 2003, when stock prices rebounded). This fund's total return was almost 10% for the 3-year period ending December 31, 2002, compared with a return of −14.6% for the S&P 500. Clearly, busted convertibles took investors in this fund for a good ride.

CRITICAL THINKING QUESTIONS What is a busted convertible bond, and why would an investor consider buying this type of bond? What are the risks of these securities?

Sources: "Fund Snapshot: Calamos High Yield Fund," *The Wall Street Journal Online*, downloaded December 15, 2003, from online.wsj.com; Janice Revell, "Busted Convertibles May Be Worth a Spin," *Fortune*, April 16, 2001, p. 398; Eric J. Savitz, "Fund of Information: Fixing on Busted Convertibles," *Barron's*, March 11, 2002, p. F3; and Paul Sturm, "Free Stock Options," *Smart Money*, March 2001, pp. 63–64.

low that there's very little chance the convertible will ever be converted or trade as a stock again. While that may be bad news for the issuer, it also means, as more fully explained in the *Investing in Action* box, that some potentially very attractive return opportunities exist for more aggressive investors.

Advantages and Disadvantages of Investing in Convertibles

The major advantage of a convertible issue is that it reduces downside risk (via the issue's bond value or price floor) and at the same time provides upward price potential comparable to that of the firm's common stock. This two-sided feature is critical with convertibles and is impossible to match with straight common stock or straight debt. Another benefit is that the current income from bond interest normally exceeds the income from the dividends that would be paid with a *comparable investment* in the underlying common stock.

For example, let's say you had the choice of investing $1,000 in a new 4% convertible or investing the same amount in the company's common stock, currently trading at $42.50 a share. (As is customary with *new* convertibles, the stock price will be a bit *below* the bond's conversion price—of $50 a share.) Under these circumstances, you could buy *one* convertible or 23½ *shares* of common stock ($1,000/$42.50 = 23.5). If the stock paid $1.00 a share in annual dividends, a $1,000 investment in the stock would yield $23.50 a year in dividends. In contrast, you could collect substantially more by putting the same amount into the company's convertible bond, where you would receive $40.00 a year in interest income. Thus, it is possible with convertibles to reap the advantages of common stock (in the form of potential upward price appreciation) and yet generate improved current income.

On the negative side, buying the convertible instead of directly owning the underlying common stock means you have to give up some potential profits. Consider the example in the preceding paragraph: Put $1,000 directly into the common stock and you can buy 23½ shares; put the same $1,000 into the company's convertible bond and you end up with a claim on only 20 shares of stock. Thus the convertible bond investor is left with a *shortfall* of 3½ shares of stock—which represents potential price appreciation you will never enjoy. In effect, it's a *give-up* you have to absorb in exchange for the convertible's higher current income and safety. Looked at from another angle, this is basically what **conversion premium** is all about. That is, unless the market price of the stock exceeds the conversion price by a wide margin, a convertible almost always trades at a price that is above its true value. The amount of this excess price is conversion premium, which has the unfortunate side effect of diluting the price appreciation potential of a convertible. One other disadvantage of owning convertibles is that any investor who truly wants to hold bonds can almost certainly find better current and promised yields from straight-debt obligations.

So then, if improved returns are normally available from the direct investment in either straight debt and/or straight equity, why buy convertibles? The answer is simple: Convertibles provide a great way to achieve attractive risk-return tradeoffs. In particular, by combining the characteristics of both stocks and bonds into one security, convertibles offer some risk protection and, at the same time, considerable—though perhaps not maximum—upward price potential. Thus, although the return may not be the most in absolute terms, neither is the risk.

HOT LINKS

Find three basic ways to invest with convertibles at:

moneycentral.msn.com/articles/
invest/strat/3295.asp

conversion premium
the amount by which the market price of a convertible exceeds its conversion value.

Executing Trades

Convertible bonds are subject to the same brokerage fees and transfer taxes as straight corporate debt, while convertible preferreds trade at the same costs as straight preferreds and common stock. Any market or limit order that can be used with bonds or stocks can also be used with convertibles.

Convertible notes and bonds normally are *not* quoted in the *Wall Street Journal* (occasionally they'll show up if they're one of the 40 most actively traded bonds), so you'll have to go to another source—*Barron's*, for example. (If you're an avid investor in convertible securities, you might want to look at *Investor's Business Daily*, which lists "Convertible Bonds & Securities" separately; in addition to coupons, maturities, and yields, these quotes include conversion ratios, S&P ratings, and conversion premiums.) With the *Barron's* quotes, any convertible notes and bonds that traded in the preceding week are listed along with other corporate bonds. They are distinguished from straight-debt issues by the letters *cv* in the "Cur Yld" column, as illustrated in Figure 12.3 (see, for example, the 4¼% Nortel convertible notes of 2008). While no high-priced issues are included in these quotes, it's not uncommon for some convertibles to trade at fairly high prices—at 125% to 150% of par, or more, for instance. It'll happen whenever the underlying common stock trades at prices that are *well above the issue's conversion price.*

FIGURE 12.3

Listed Quotes for Convertible Bonds

Convertible bonds (there are four in this figure) are listed along with other corporate issues and are identified by the letters *cv* in the "Cur Yld" column. Except for this distinguishing feature, they are quoted like any other corporate bond. (*Source: Barrons,* August 11, 2003.)

52-Weeks High	52-Weeks Low	Name and Coupon	Cur Yld	Sales $1,000	Weekly High	Weekly Low	Weekly Last	Net Chg
119⅛	112⅛	GEICap 7⅞06	6.9	15	115¼	114⅜	114⅜	− ⅝
105⅜	91	GMA 6⅛08	6.0	23	102⅝	101¼	102¼	+ ⅝
100⅛	85¾	GMA dc6s11	6.2	27	97¾	96½	96½	...
105¼	99⅝	JCPL 7½23	7.3	20	103½	102⅛	102½	− ½
99⅜	60	KCS En 8⅞06	9.1	55	99⅜	95	97⅜	+ 1⅜
112	100	KerrM 5¼10	cv	10	102⅛	102⅛		...
123½	116¼	Lilly 8⅜06	7.1	20	117⅛	117⅛	117⅛	− ⅛
95½	83¾	Loews 3⅛07	cv	33	93⅝	93⅝	93⅝	+ ½
96⅞	35⅛	Lucent 7¼06	7.8	170	93⅛	92¾	92¾	− ¼
104½	29⅞	Lucent 5½08	6.8	60	83½	81	81	− 1⅜
74⅜	28	Lucent 6½28	10.4	40	64	62½	62½	− 4½
76	25¾	Lucent 6.45s29	10.1	182	64	63	64	− 2
109⅜	88⅝	MBNA 8.28s26	8.1	34	102⅜	100½	102⅜	+ ⅞
102¼	98⅜	MPac 4¼05	4.2	1	100⅝	100⅝	100⅝	+ ⅜
70¼	58¼	MPac 5s45f	...	3	64	64	64	− 4
107⅝	101⅝	NRurU 5¾08	5.4	25	106	106	106	+ ¼
108¼	96	NRurU 5.7s10	5.4	5	105⅝	105⅝	105⅝	− 2⅝
111½	100	NatwFS 8s27	7.4	20	108¾	108½	108½	+ ⅜
104	92¼	NETelTel 6⅞23	6.7	15	102¼	102¼	102¼	− ¾
109⅞	90	NYTel 6.70s23	6.6	60	101⅛	101⅛	101⅛	− ⅝
103⅛	90⅛	NYTel 7s25	6.9	34	102	102	102	...
112⅛	91¼	NYTel 7s33	6.9	78	101⅛	101	101	− 1
88½	38	Nortel 4¼08	cv	5	82⅛	82⅛	82⅛	− 3⅞
98	81¼	PG&E 7.8s25	8.1	10	95¾	95¾	95¾	− 2
101½	82½	ParkerD 5½04	cv	295	97¾	96 37/128	96½	− 1⅛
108½	99¾	Penney 8s10	...	105	101	99¾		...
112¾	99	PhilIP 7⅛28	6.8	52	105⅛	104	104⅝	− ½

Nortel Convertible Notes

Convertible preferreds, in contrast, normally are listed with other preferreds, but carry no distinguishing notations. As a result, you must turn to some other source to find out whether a preferred is convertible. The national business newspaper, *Investor's Business Daily,* provides a separate list of preferred stocks traded on the NYSE, AMEX, and Nasdaq and uses boldface type to highlight the convertible issues.

IN REVIEW

CONCEPTS

12.8 What is a *convertible debenture?* How does a *convertible bond* differ from a *convertible preferred?*

12.9 Identify the *equity kicker* of a convertible security and explain how it affects the value and price behavior of convertibles.

12.10 Explain why it is necessary to examine both the bond and stock properties of a convertible debenture when determining its investment appeal.

12.11 What are the investment attributes of convertible debentures? What are the disadvantages of such investment vehicles?

Valuing and Investing in Convertibles

LG 6

Basically, investing in convertibles can take two different forms: Either you use convertibles as a type of deferred equity investment, in which case you're looking at the stock side of the security, or you use convertibles as a high-yield, fixed-income investment, where it's the bond value that's important. Regardless of which approach you follow, to get the most from your investment program, you need a good understanding of the normal price and investment behavioral characteristics of convertibles. Of course, you also have to know how to value a convertible. So let's now take a look at the valuation concepts used with convertible bonds. Later we'll look at a couple of convertible bond investment strategies.

Measuring the Value of a Convertible

In order to evaluate the investment merits of convertible securities, you must consider both the bond and the stock dimensions of the issue. Fundamental security analysis of the equity position is, of course, especially important in light of the key role the equity kicker plays in defining the price behavior of a convertible. In contrast, market yields and agency ratings are widely used in evaluating the bond side of the issue. But there's more: *In addition to analyzing the bond and stock dimensions of the issue, it is essential to evaluate the conversion feature itself.* The two critical areas in this regard are conversion value and investment value. These measures have a vital bearing on a convertible's price behavior and therefore can have a dramatic effect on an issue's holding period return.

conversion value
an indication of what a convertible issue would trade for if it were priced to sell on the basis of its stock value.

Conversion Value In essence, **conversion value** indicates what a convertible issue would trade for if it were priced to sell on the basis of its stock value. Conversion value is easy to find:

Equation 12.4

$$\text{Conversion value} = \text{Conversion ratio} \times \text{Current market price of the stock}$$

For example, a convertible that carries a conversion ratio of 20 would have a conversion value of $1,200 if the firm's stock traded at a current market price of $60 per share (20 × $60 = $1,200).

Sometimes an alternative measure is used, in which case the **conversion equivalent**, also known as **conversion parity**, may be computed. The conversion equivalent indicates the price at which the common stock would have to sell in order to make the convertible security worth its present market price. Conversion equivalent is calculated as follows:

conversion equivalent (conversion parity)
the price at which the common stock would have to sell in order to make the convertible security worth its present market price.

Equation 12.5

$$\text{Conversion equivalent} = \frac{\text{Current market price of the convertible bond}}{\text{Conversion ratio}}$$

Thus, if a convertible were trading at $1,400 and had a conversion ratio of 20, the conversion equivalent of the common stock would be $70 per share ($1,400 ÷ 20 = $70). In effect, you would expect the current market price of the common stock in this example to be at or near $70 per share in order to support a convertible trading at $1,400.

Conversion Premium Unfortunately, convertible issues *seldom* trade precisely at their conversion values. Rather, as noted earlier, they usually trade at a conversion premium. The absolute size of an issue's conversion premium is found by taking the difference between the convertible's market price and its conversion value (per Equation 12.4). To place the premium on a relative basis, simply divide the dollar amount of the conversion premium by the issue's conversion value. That is,

Equation 12.6

$$\text{Conversion premium (in \$)} = \frac{\text{Current market price}}{\text{of the convertible bond}} - \frac{\text{Conversion}}{\text{value}}$$

where conversion value is found according to Equation 12.4. Then

Equation 12.7

$$\text{Conversion premium (in \%)} = \frac{\text{Conversion premium (in \$)}}{\text{Conversion value}}$$

To illustrate, if a convertible trades at $1,400 and its conversion value equals $1,200, it has a conversion premium of $200 ($1,400 − $1,200 = $200). In relation to what the convertible should be trading at, this $200 differential would amount to a conversion premium of 16.7% ($200/$1,200 = 0.167). Conversion premiums are common in the market and can often amount to as much as 30% to 40% (or more) of an issue's true conversion value. (Due to a variety of market factors, the average conversion premium in June 2003 was a hefty 60%, as compared to an average premium of just 15% in early 2000. What's a typical premium? Probably somewhere in between these two values.)

Investors are willing to pay a premium primarily because of the added current income a convertible provides relative to the underlying common stock. An investor can recover this premium through the added current income the convertible provides, or by selling the issue at a premium equal to or greater than that which existed at the time of purchase. Unfortunately, the latter source of recovery is tough to come by, because conversion premiums tend to fade away as the price of the convertible goes up. That means that if a convertible is purchased for its potential price appreciation (which most are), then the investor must accept the fact that all or a major portion of the price premium is very likely to disappear as the convertible appreciates over time and moves closer to its true conversion value. Thus, if an investor hopes to recover any conversion premium, it will probably have to come from the added current income that the convertible provides.

Payback Period The size of the conversion premium can obviously have a major impact on investor return. So, when picking convertibles, one of the major questions you should ask is whether the premium is justified. One way to assess conversion premium is to compute the issue's **payback period,** a measure of the length of time it will take for the buyer to recover the conversion premium from the *extra* interest income earned on the convertible. Because this added income is a principal reason for the conversion premium, it makes sense to use it to assess the premium. The payback period can be found as follows:

payback period
the length of time it takes for the buyer of a convertible to recover the conversion premium from the extra current income earned on the convertible.

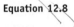

Equation 12.8

$$\text{Payback period} = \frac{\text{Conversion premium (in \$)}}{\begin{array}{c}\text{Annual interest} \\ \text{income from the} \\ \text{convertible bond}\end{array} - \begin{array}{c}\text{Annual dividend} \\ \text{income from the} \\ \text{underlying common stock}\end{array}}$$

In this equation, annual dividends are found by multiplying the stock's latest annual dividends per share by the bond's conversion ratio.

For example, in the foregoing illustration, the bond had a conversion premium of $200. Now let's say this bond (which carries a conversion ratio of 20) has an 8½% coupon, and the underlying stock paid dividends this past year of 50 cents a share. Given this information, we can use Equation 12.8 to find the payback period.

$$\begin{aligned}\text{Payback period} &= \frac{\$200}{\$85 - (20 \times \$0.50)} \\[2mm] &= \frac{\$200}{\$85 - (\$10.00)} = \underline{\underline{2.7 \text{ years}}}\end{aligned}$$

In essence, the investor in this case will recover the premium in 2.7 years (a fairly decent payback period). As a rule, everything else being equal, *the shorter the payback period, the better.* Also, watch out for excessively high premiums (of 50% or more); you may have real difficulty ever recovering such astronomical premiums. Indeed, to avoid such premiums, most experts recommend that you look for convertibles that have payback periods of around 5 to 7 years, or less. As a point of reference, the average payback period was (a very high) 7.4 years in June 2003, versus a more typical 3.3 years in early 2000. Be careful when using this measure, however: Some convertibles will have *very high payback periods simply because they carry very low coupons* (of 1% to 2%, or less). Take another look at Table 12.2. In addition to basic issue characteristics, Table 12.2 shows the conversion premium and payback period for each issue listed. Note especially the last two convertibles in the table: Pepsico and United Parcel Service. Both have relatively low conversion premiums, but very high payback periods. The reason: Both carry very low coupons, of 2.00% and 1.75%, respectively. Clearly, in order to get the most from these investments, you would be well advised to take the time to fully evaluate a bond's conversion premium (and its payback period) before investing.

investment value
the price at which a convertible would trade if it were nonconvertible and priced at or near the prevailing market yields of comparable nonconvertible issues.

Investment Value The price floor of a convertible is defined by its bond properties and is the focus of the investment value measure. It's the point within the valuation process where attention centers on current and expected market interest rates. **Investment value** is the price at which the bond would trade if it were nonconvertible and if it were priced at or near the prevailing market yields of comparable nonconvertible bonds.

The same bond price formulas given in Chapter 11 (see, for example, Equations 11.2 or 11.3) are used to compute investment value. Because the coupon and maturity are known, the only additional piece of information needed is the market yield-to-maturity of comparably rated issues. For example, if comparable nonconvertible bonds were trading at 9% yields and if a particular 20-year convertible carried a 6% coupon, its investment value would be roughly $725. (See if you can find the investment value of this convertible using a hand-held calculator; *Hint:* Input $N = 20$, $I/Y = 9$, $PMT = -60$, and $FV = -1,000$; then compute PV. Did you come up with a little over $726?) This figure indicates how far the convertible will have to fall before it hits its price floor and begins trading as a straight-debt instrument. Other things being equal, the greater the distance between the current market price of a convertible and its investment value, the farther the issue can fall in price and, as a result, the greater the downside risk exposure.

An Overview of Price and Investment Behavior

As noted earlier in this chapter, the price behavior of a convertible security is influenced by both the equity and the fixed-income elements of the obligation. The variables that play key roles in defining the market value of a typical convertible therefore include (1) the potential price behavior of the underlying common stock and (2) expectations regarding the pattern of future market yields and interest rates.

The typical price behavior of a convertible issue is depicted in Figure 12.4. In the top panel are the three market elements of a convertible bond: the bond value (or price floor), the stock (conversion) value, and the actual market price of the convertible. The figure reveals the customary relationship among these three elements and shows that conversion premium is a common occurrence. Note especially that the conversion premium tends to diminish as the price of the stock increases.

The top panel of Figure 12.4 is somewhat simplified because of the steady price floor (which unrealistically assumes no variation in market interest rates) and the steady upswing in the stock's value. The lower panel of the figure relaxes these conditions, although for simplicity we ignore conversion pre-

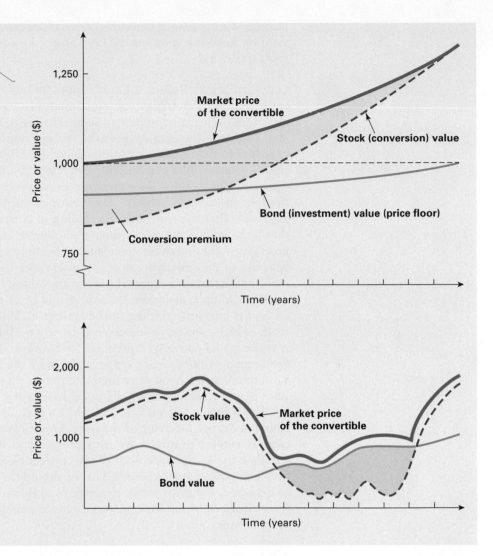

FIGURE 12.4

Typical Price Behavior of a Convertible Bond

The price behavior of a convertible security is tied to either the stock or the bond dimension of the issue. When the price of the underlying stock is up, the convertible trades much like the stock; when the price of the stock falls, the bond value acts as a price floor for the convertible.

mium. The figure illustrates that the market value of a convertible approximates the price behavior of the underlying stock *so long as stock value is greater than bond value.* When the stock value drops below the bond value floor, as it does in the shaded area of the lower panel, the market value of the convertible becomes linked to the bond portion of the obligation, and it continues to move as a debt security until the price of the underlying stock picks up again and approaches or equals this price floor.

Investment Strategies

Investors can use convertibles to generate attractive returns from either the stock or the bond side of the issue. For stock investors, convertibles can serve as a form of deferred equity, where the investor is more focused on capital gains than on current income. This, of course, represents a fairly aggressive use of convertibles. But for the more conservative investor, who is looking for current income as a key source of return, convertibles can also serve as a form of high-yielding fixed-income security. Let's now take a look at both of these investment strategies.

Convertibles as Deferred Equity Investments Convertible securities (even zero-coupon convertibles) are purchased most often because of their equity attributes. Using convertibles as an alternative to common stock, you may be able to match (or even exceed) the return from the common, but with less exposure to risk. Also, convertibles generally offer better current income than stocks. Convertibles can be profitably used as alternative equity investments whenever you feel that *the underlying stock offers desired capital gains opportunities*. In order to achieve maximum price appreciation, you would want assurance that the convertible is trading in concert with its stock value and that it does not have an inordinate amount of conversion premium. If these necessary conditions exist, then you can begin to focus on the potential market behavior of the underlying stock. To assess such behavior you need to evaluate both the current and expected conversion values.

For example, assume a 7% convertible bond carries a conversion ratio of 25 and is currently trading in the market at $900. In addition, assume the stock (which pays no dividends) is currently trading at $32, so the convertible is trading at a conversion premium of $100, or 12.5%. The formulation of future interest rates also comes into play with this trading strategy, as you will want to assess the bond price floor and the extent of downward risk exposure. That is, using the approach discussed in Chapter 11, you would try to get a handle on future interest rates, which can then be used to determine the possible bond price behavior of the issue. Generally speaking, a drop in interest rates is viewed positively by convertible bond investors, as such behavior signals a rise in the price floor of the convertible issue and therefore a reduction in downside risk exposure. That is, should the common stock not perform as expected, the price of the convertible could still go up as the (bond) price floor rises—or at the least, it would reduce any drop in the price of the convertible issue.

A Measure of Expected Return More important than the bond price floor is the anticipated behavior of the common stock and the conversion premium. To continue our example, assume that you expect the price of the stock to rise to $60 per share within the next 2 years. A conversion ratio of 25 would yield a future conversion value of $1,500. If an expected conversion premium of 6% to 7% (or about $100) is added on, it means the market price of the convertible should rise to about $1,600 by the end of the 2-year investment horizon.

The expected future price of the convertible, along with its annual coupon payment and current market price, can then be used to determine the issue's expected return. That is, using the internal rate of return (IRR) procedure, you want to find the discount rate that equates the annual coupon payments ($70 a year) over the next 2 years, plus the expected future price of the convertible ($1,600), to the current market price ($900) of the issue. Putting all this into a formula (see Equation 11.2), you end up with something like this:

$$\$900 = (\$70 \times PVIFA_{2\,yr,\,?\%}) \times (\$1,600 \times PVIFA_{2\,yr,\,?\%})$$

Using annual compounding to solve this equation (see the calculator solutions below), you'll find that the present-value discount rate that equates the future cash flow of the convertible to its current price is 40.2%—which is, of course, the expected return on this investment. (You can, of course, easily solve this problem using a hand-held calculator—see the calculator keystrokes below.)

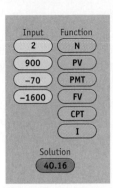

Input	Function
2	N
900	PV
−70	PMT
−1600	FV
	CPT
	I

Solution
40.16

CALCULATOR USE For *annual compounding,* to find the expected return on a 7% convertible bond that is currently trading at $900 but is expected to be trading at $1,600 in 2 years, use the keystrokes shown in the margin where N = length of the holding period (2 years), PV = current market price of the convertible, PMT = annual coupon payments, and FV = expected (future) price of the convertible in 2 years.

Some Important Considerations Although this 40.2% rate of return may indeed appear attractive, you should be sure of several points before committing capital to this security. In particular, you should be certain that this approach is, in fact, superior to a direct investment in the issuer's common stock (at least from a risk-return point of view). You also should determine that there is no better rate of return (with commensurate risk exposure) available from some other investment vehicle. To the extent that these conditions are met, investing in a convertible may be a suitable course of action, especially if (1) the price of the underlying common stock is under strong upward pressure, (2) bond interest rates are falling sharply, and (3) there is little or no conversion premium in the price of the convertible. The first condition means that conversion value should move up, leading to appreciation in the price of the convertible. The second means that the bond value (price floor) should also move up, thereby reducing exposure to risk. And the third means that you should be able to capture all or most of the price appreciation of the underlying common stock rather than losing a chunk of it to the inevitable drop in conversion premium. Although it would be nice if all three of these attributes were available from a single security, very rarely is that the case. Thus investors normally have to settle for only one or two of these features and then assess the effect of the missing condition(s) on potential returns.

Convertibles as High-Yield Fixed-Income Investments Another common use of convertibles is to buy them for the attractive fixed-income returns they offer. The key element in this strategy is the issue's bond dimension. Some convertible securities provide current yields and yields-to-maturity that are highly competitive with straight-debt obligations. Investors should make certain, however, that the high yields are not a function of low (speculative) ratings. Normally, investors using this strategy would seek discount issues, particularly those trading close to their bond price floors. Otherwise, the issue would be trading at a premium price, which would certainly involve a yield give-up, and perhaps a substantial one. Most investors who use this strategy view convertibles as ideal for locking in high rates of return. They are not widely used for speculating on interest rates, however, because even investment-grade convertibles often lack the needed interest sensitivity (because of the equity kicker). Yet for those who use convertibles to seek high, safe yields, the equity kicker can provide an added source of return if the underlying stock does indeed take off. You then have a bond that offers a handsome rate of return and an equity kicker to boot.

IN REVIEW

12.12 What is the difference between *conversion parity* and *conversion value*? How would you describe the *payback period* on a convertible? What is the *investment value* of a convertible, and what does it reveal?

12.13 Discuss the alternative investment uses of convertible debentures. What are the three major attributes that investors should look for when using convertibles as deferred equity investments?

Summary

LG 1 **Describe the basic features of preferred stock, including sources of value and exposure to risk.** Preferred stocks are hybrid securities that combine features of both debt and equity. Preferred stocks are considered senior to common: They have a higher claim on the income and assets of the issuing company. Among other things, this means that preferred dividends have to be paid before the company can pay dividends to its common stockholders. As investment vehicles, preferreds provide attractive dividend yields. When interest rates decline, they can produce capital gains as well.

LG 2 **Discuss the rights and claims of preferred stockholders, and note some of the popular issue characteristics that are often found with these securities.** Preferreds are considered less risky than common stock because their shareholders enjoy a senior position with regard to dividend payments and asset claims. The most important feature of a preferred stock is its preferential claim on dividends. Investors should also be aware of several other preferred stock provisions, including: the obligations of the issuer in case any dividends are missed (whether the stock is cumulative or noncumulative), whether it is callable, and whether it carries sinking-fund provisions. Also important is whether the preferred's dividends qualify for the new preferential tax rate—most do not.

LG 3 **Understand the various measures of investment worth, and identify several investment strategies that can be used with preferred stocks.** Except for convertible preferreds, the value of a preferred is generally linked to the dividend yield it provides to investors. Indeed, the price behavior of a preferred stock is inversely related to market interest rates. The principal reason for holding preferreds is their yield. But they can also be held for capital gains purposes by investors willing to trade on interest rates or on turnaround situations.

LG 4 **Identify the fundamental characteristics of convertible securities, and explain the nature of the underlying conversion privilege.** Convertible securities are initially issued as bonds (or preferreds), but can subsequently be converted into shares of common stock. These securities offer investors a stream of fixed income (in the form of annual coupon payments), plus an equity kicker (in the form of a conversion feature).

LG 5 **Describe the advantages and disadvantages of investing in convertible securities, including their risk and return attributes.** Convertibles provide a combination of both good upside potential (from the equity feature) and good downside protection (through the fixed-income characteristics). This risk-return tradeoff, combined with the relatively high current income of convertibles, is unmatched by any other type of security.

LG 6 Measure the value of a convertible security, and explain how these securities can be used to meet different investment objectives. The value of a convertible depends largely on the price behavior of the underlying common stock. This is captured in the security's conversion value, which represents the convertible's worth if it were converted into common stock. Investors use convertible securities primarily as a form of deferred equity, where the investment is a way to capture the capital gains potential of the underlying common stock. Convertibles can also be used as high-yielding fixed-income investments. In this case, the investor principally goes after the higher current income of the bond (and the equity kicker is viewed as little more than a pleasant by-product).

Putting Your Investment Know-How to the Test

1. Preferred stock is similar to a debt instrument because
   a. It gives the holder voting power in electing the firm's board.
   b. It promises to pay its holder a fixed stream of income.
   c. The dividend expense is tax deductible for a firm.
   d. None of the above.

2. A firm's preferred stock often sells at yields below its bonds because
   a. Preferred stock generally carries a higher agency rating.
   b. Owners of preferred stock have a prior claim on the firm's earnings.
   c. Owners of preferred stock have a prior claim on a firm's assets in the event of liquidation.
   d. Corporations owning stock may exclude from income taxes most of the dividend income they receive.

3. A convertible bond has a par value of $1,000 but its current market price is $900. The current price of the issuing company's stock is $17.50. If the conversion ratio is 40 shares, what is the bond's conversion premium?
   a. $100   b. $200
   c. $300   d. $700

4. A firm that fails to pay dividends on its preferred stock is said to be
   a. Insolvent.   b. In arrears.
   c. Illiquid.   d. Nonconvertible.

5. Preferred stocks resemble equities because they
   a. Promise to pay a fixed stream of income each year.
   b. Have a contractual obligation to pay the dividend.
   c. Represent asset ownership in a company.
   d. Offer voting power in electing the firm's management.

6. A convertible bond has a par value of $1,000 but sells for $960, while its market conversion value is $900. The market price for the issuing company stock is $30. What is the conversion ratio?
   a. 30 shares   b. 32 shares
   c. 40 shares   d. 60 shares

7. Zello Corporation's $1,000 par-value convertible bond sells for $960, matures in 5 years, and has an 8% coupon rate paid annually. Zello's stock trades at $20 and pays $1 in annual dividends; the conversion ratio is 40 shares. What is Zello's payback period?
   a. 2 years
   b. 3 years
   c. 4 years
   d. There is not enough information to calculate the payback period.

8. ABC Corporation's $1,000 par-value convertible bond sells for $950. ABC's stock trades at $25 and pays $1 in annual dividends; the conversion ratio is 35 shares. If the payback period is 3 years, what is ABC's annual coupon rate?

   a. 3%   b. 4%

   c. 5%   d. 6%

9. The time period during which a convertible bond can be converted is called

   a. A payback period.   b. A conversion period.

   c. Conversion privilege.   d. Coupon deferment.

10. The fixed-charge coverage on a preferred stock is

   a. Equal to the company's par value.

   b. The company's debt-free assets per preferred share.

   c. The company's annual dividend per share of preferred stock.

   d. None of the above.

Answers: 1. b; 2. d; 3. b; 4. b; 5. c; 6. a; 7. c; 8. c; 9. b; 10. d

Discussion Questions

Q12.1 Briefly describe each of the following, and note how each differs from a conventional preferred stock.

   a. Convertible preferreds

   b. Floating-rate preferreds

   c. Prior preferred stocks

   d. Trust preferreds

As an investor, why would you choose a *convertible preferred* over a straight preferred? Why would you choose a *floating-rate preferred* over a (fixed-rate) preferred? Finally, instead of investing in a conventional preferred, why not just invest in a common stock?

LG 2

Q12.2 Is it possible for a firm to pass (miss) dividends on preferred stocks, even if it earns enough to pay them? Explain. What usually happens when a company passes a dividend on a cumulative preferred stock? Are common stock dividends affected in any way?

Q12.3 Why do companies like to issue convertible securities—what's in it for them? What about preferred stocks—why do companies like to issue them?

Q12.4 Describe *PERCs* and *LYONs*, noting especially the unusual features and characteristics of each. How does each differ from conventional convertibles? Are there any similarities between these securities and conventional convertibles? Explain. What kind of investor might be attracted to a PERC? To a LYON?

Q12.5 Using the resources available at your campus or public library, or on the Internet, find the information requested below.

   a. Select any two *convertible debentures* (notes or bonds) and determine the conversion ratio, conversion parity, conversion value, conversion premium, and payback period for each.

   b. Select any two *convertible preferreds* and determine the conversion ratio, conversion parity, conversion value, conversion premium, and payback period for each.

   c. In what way(s) are the two convertible bonds and the two convertible preferreds you selected similar to one another? Are there any differences? Explain.

Problems

LG 3

P12.1 An adjustable-rate preferred is currently selling at a dividend yield of 9%. Assume that the dividend rate on the stock is adjusted once a year and that it is currently paying an annual dividend of $5.40 a share. Because of major changes that have occurred in the market, it's anticipated that annual dividends will drop to $4.50 a share on the next dividend adjustment date, which is just around the corner. What will the new dividend yield on this issue be if its market price does not change? What will the new market price on the issue be if the stock's dividend yield holds at 9%? What will it be if the yield drops to 7%?

P12.2 The Bullorbear Company has 500,000 shares of $2 preferred stock outstanding. It generates an EBIT of $40 million and has annual interest payments of $2 million. Given this information, determine the fixed charge coverage of the preferred stock—assume the dividends qualify for the preferential tax rate. Given the firm also has $5.5 million in depreciation and amortization, use EBITDA to find the fixed charge coverage of this preferred.

P12.3 The Bullorbear Company has 500,000 shares of $2 *trust* preferred stock outstanding. The firm generates an EBIT of $40 million and has annual interest payments of $2 million. Given this information, determine the fixed charge coverage on these trust preferred stocks.

P12.4 You purchased 100 shares of a $2.00 preferred stock 1 year and 1 day ago for $25 per share. You sold the stock today for $30 per share. Assuming you are in a 25% tax bracket, calculate your after-tax holding period return:
   a. Assuming the dividends are treated as dividends for tax purposes.
   b. Assuming the dividends are treated as interest income for tax purposes.

P12.5 Assume that you are evaluating several investments, including the stock of a mature company that pays annual dividends of $2 and is currently trading at $25. Another investment is a *trust* preferred stock that pays $2.40 in annual dividends and is also trading at $25. Given that you do not expect the price of either stock to change, which investment will provide a higher dollar return if you are in a 33% tax bracket?

P12.6 Select one of the preferred stocks listed in Table 12.1—assume the dividends qualify for the preferential tax rate. Using the resources available at your campus or public library, or on the Internet, determine the following.
   a. The stock's latest market price.
   b. Its dividend yield.
   c. Its fixed charge coverage.
   d. Its book value per share.
   e. Its stated par value.

Comment briefly on the issue's yield and the quality of its claim on income and assets.

P12.7 Sara-J Co. has a preferred stock outstanding that pays annual dividends of $3.50 a share. At what price would this stock be trading if market yields were 7½%? Use one of the dividend valuation models (from Chapter 8) to price this stock, assuming you have a 7½% required rate of return. Are there any similarities between the two prices? Explain.

P12.8 Charlene Weaver likes to speculate with preferred stock by trading on movements in market interest rates. Right now, she believes the market is poised for a big drop in rates. Accordingly, she is thinking seriously about investing in a certain preferred stock that pays $7 in annual dividends and is currently trading at $75 a share.

What rate of return will she realize on this investment if the market yield on the preferred drops to 6½% within 2 years? What if the drop in rates takes place in 1 year?

LG 6 **P12.9** A certain convertible bond has a conversion ratio of 21. The current market price of the underlying common stock is $40. What is the bond's conversion equivalent?

LG 6 **P12.10** You are considering investing $850 in Whichway Corporation. You can buy common stock at $25 per share; this stock pays no dividends. You can also buy a convertible bond that is currently trading at $850 and has a conversion ratio of 30. It pays $50 per year in interest. Given you expect the price of the stock to rise to $35 per share in 1 year, which instrument should you purchase?

LG 6 **P12.11** A certain 6% annual pay convertible bond (maturing in 20 years) is convertible at the holder's option into 20 shares of common stock. The bond is currently trading at $800. The stock (which pays 75¢ a share in annual dividends) is currently priced in the market at $35 a share.
   a. What is the current yield of the convertible bond?
   b. What is the conversion price?
   c. What is the conversion ratio?
   d. What is the conversion value of this issue? What is its conversion parity?
   e. What is the conversion premium, in dollars and as a percentage?
   f. What is the bond's payback period?
   g. What is the yield-to-maturity of the convertible bond?
   h. If comparably rated nonconvertible bonds sell to yield 8%, what is the investment value of the convertible?

LG 6 **P12.12** An 8% convertible bond carries a par value of $1,000 and a conversion ratio of 20. Assume that an investor has $5,000 to invest and that the convertible sells at a price of $1,000 (which includes a 25% conversion premium). How much total income (coupon plus capital gains) will this investment offer if, over the course of the next 12 months, the price of the stock moves to $75 per share and the convertible trades at a price that includes a conversion premium of 10%? What is the holding period return on this investment? Finally, given the information in the problem, determine what the underlying common stock is currently selling for.

LG 6 **P12.13** Assume you just paid $1,200 for a convertible bond that carries a 7½% coupon and has 15 years to maturity. The bond can be converted into 24 shares of stock, which are now trading at $50 a share. Find the bond investment value of this issue, given that comparable nonconvertible bonds are currently selling to yield 9%.

LG 6 **P12.14** Find the conversion value of a *convertible preferred stock* that carries a conversion ratio of 1.8, given that the market price of the underlying common stock is $40 a share. Would there be any conversion premium if the convertible preferred were selling at $90 a share? If so, how much (in dollar and percentage terms)? Also, explain the concept of conversion parity, and then find the conversion parity of this issue, given that the preferred trades at $90 per share.

See the text Web site (www.aw-bc.com/gitman_joehnk) for Web exercises that deal with *preferred stocks and convertible securities*.

Case Problem 12.1 · Penni Shows a Preference for Preferreds

LG 1   LG 2

Kathleen "Penni" Jock is a young career woman who has built up a substantial investment portfolio. Most of her holdings are preferred stocks—a situation she does not
want to change. Penni is now considering the purchase of $4,800 worth of LaRamie
Corporation's $5 preferred, which is currently trading at $48 a share. Penni's stockbroker, Mr. Michaels, has told her that he feels the market yield on preferreds like
LaRamie should drop to 7% within the next 3 years and that these preferreds would
make a sound investment. Instead of buying the LaRamie preferred, Penni could choose
an alternative investment (with comparable risk exposure) that she is confident can
produce earnings of about 10% over each of the next 3 years.

Questions

a.   If preferred yields behave as Penni's stockbroker thinks they will, what will be the
price of the LaRamie $5 preferred in 3 years?

b.   What return will this investment offer over the 3-year holding period if all the
expectations about it come true (particularly with regard to the price it is supposed to
reach)? How much profit (in dollars) will Penni make from her investment?

c.   Would you recommend that she buy the LaRamie preferred? Why?

d.   What are the investment merits of this transaction? What are its risks?

Case Problem 12.2 · Dave and Marlene Consider Convertibles

LG 5   LG 6

Dave and Marlene Jenkins live in Hayward, California, where she manages a bridal
shop and he runs an industrial supply firm. Their annual income is usually in the
middle to upper nineties; they have no children and maintain a "comfortable" lifestyle.
Recently, they came into some money and are eager to invest it in a high-yielding fixed-
income security. Though they are not aggressive investors, they like to maximize the
return on every investment dollar they have. For this reason, they like the high yields
and added equity kicker of convertible bonds and are now looking at such an issue as a
way to invest their recent windfall. In particular, Dave and Marlene have their eye on
the convertible debentures of MedTech, Inc. They have heard that the price of the stock
is on the way up, and after some in-depth analysis of their own, feel the company's
prospects are indeed bright. They've also looked at market interest rates, and on the
basis of economic reports obtained from their broker, they expect interest rates to
decline sharply.

The details on the convertible they're looking at are as follows: It's a 20-year,
$1,000 par value issue that carries a 7½% annual-pay coupon and is at present trading
at $800. The issue is convertible into 15 shares of stock. The stock, which pays no div-
idends, was recently quoted at $49.50 per share.

Questions

a.   Ignoring conversion premium, find the price of the convertible if the stock goes up
to $66.67 per share in 2 years. What if it goes up to $75 per share? To $100 per share?
Repeat the computations, assuming that the convertible will trade at a 5% conversion
premium.

b.   Find the promised yield of the convertible. (*Hint:* Use annual compounding and the same approach that we used with straight bonds in Chapter 11.)

1.   Now find the bond value of the convertible if, within 2 years, interest rates drop to 8%. (*Remember:* In 2 years, the security will have only 18 years remaining to maturity.) What if interest rates drop to 6%?

2.   What implication does the drop in interest rates hold as far as the investment appeal of the convertible is concerned?

c.   Given expected future stock prices and interest rate levels (as stated above), find the minimum and maximum expected yield that this investment offers over the 2-year holding period. (Assume a zero conversion premium in both cases.)

1.   What is the worst return Dave and Marlene can expect over their 2-year holding period if the price of the stock drops to $40 per share and interest rates drop to 9%?

2.   What if the price of the stock drops to $40 and interest rates rise to 11%?

d.   Should Dave and Marlene invest in the MedTech convertibles? Discuss the pros and cons of the investment.

Excel with Spreadsheets

Preferred stock is a unique type of equity and is referred to as a hybrid security—it has characteristics of both bonds and common stock. In practice, preferred stocks are valued more like bonds, with market interest rates and investment quality playing major roles. For those investors interested in preferred stock investing, it is likely that interest rates play a key role in their investment strategies. The two main strategies involve either seeking high levels of dividend income or taking advantage of falling market interest rates resulting in capital gains.

Create a spreadsheet to model and answer the following questions related to preferred stock investments.

Questions

a.   The Scully Corporation issued preferred stock with a stated dividend of 8% of par. Preferred stock of this type currently yields 7% with a par value of $75. Assume that the firm has 800,000 shares of the preferred outstanding at this time and that the dividends (which qualify for the preferential tax rates) are paid annually. Reviewing its income statement, the EBIT is $85 million and it has annual interest payments of $3 million. The firm is in the 30% federal tax bracket.

1.   What is the value of Scully's preferred stock?
2.   What is the fixed charge coverage of Scully preferred stock?

b.   A group of speculators are interested in the Scully preferred stock as the current market interest rates are quite volatile. These speculators hope to gain from the potential movement in market rates. The group believes that the future course of rates will follow a downward trend, which should translate into an increase in their equity value.

1.   Given the information about Scully preferred and your valuation calculations from problem **a,** what will be the realized holding period return on this investment if the market yield on the preferred drops to 5% after 1 year?
2.   What will be the realized holding period return on this investment if the market yield on the preferred rises to 8% after 1 year?

TRADING ONLINE WITH OTIS

Common stock shareholders may receive income from dividends, but this income is not guaranteed. Preferred shareholders, on the other hand, are guaranteed a yield, usually in the form of a fixed dividend payment. Nevertheless, there are some risks involved in owning preferreds. For example, preferred stocks often have a limited life, are usually callable, and are subject to interest rate risk. Interest rate risk is a major problem for fixed-income securities, because inflation may erode the purchasing power of the fixed payments. Despite the existence of interest rate risk, a well-balanced portfolio should include a broad mix of securities, such as stocks, bonds, preferred stocks, foreign investments, and some cash for buying opportunities.

Exercises

1. Determine the current yields on preferred stocks by looking in the *Wall Street Journal*. Are these yields higher than you are receiving on your common stock dividends?

2. Log on to OTIS to view the interest received on your cash holdings by going to "History." Then go to "Analytics" and select "Overnight Interest Rates" to see the rates you have been receiving (you can also go to the help screen and click on "Account Value" to see how the rates are determined). Are the daily interest rates you are receiving higher than the inflation rate?

PART FIVE

PORTFOLIO MANAGEMENT

CHAPTER 13
MUTUAL FUNDS: PROFESSIONALLY MANAGED PORTFOLIOS

CHAPTER 14
MANAGING YOUR OWN PORTFOLIO

CHAPTER 13

MUTUAL FUNDS: PROFESSIONALLY MANAGED PORTFOLIOS

LEARNING GOALS

After studying this chapter, you should be able to:

LG 1 Describe the basic features of mutual funds, and note what they have to offer as investment vehicles.

LG 2 Distinguish between open- and closed-end funds, as well as other types of professionally managed investment companies, and discuss the various types of fund loads, fees, and charges.

LG 3 Discuss the types of funds available and the variety of investment objectives these funds seek to fulfill.

LG 4 Discuss the investor services offered by mutual funds and how these services can fit into an investment program.

LG 5 Gain an appreciation of the investor uses of mutual funds, along with the variables to consider when assessing and selecting funds for investment purposes.

LG 6 Identify the sources of return and compute the rate of return earned on a mutual fund investment.

B ack in 1976, John Bogle, founder of the Vanguard Group, had a radical idea: create a mutual fund that would hold only stock in the Standard & Poor's 500 stock index of large companies. Unlike many other mutual funds, the Vanguard 500 Index fund wouldn't try to outperform the equities market, but rather would strive to keep pace with the returns offered by the S&P 500 index. Instead of constantly buying and selling a diversified portfolio of equities, Vanguard would limit itself to the small number of trades necessary to mirror changes in the S&P index. Investors would be rewarded with an unimaginative portfolio that Bogle promised would offer consistent returns and low operating costs.

Flash forward to today. The Vanguard 500 Index fund is the largest mutual fund in the world, with net assets exceeding $84 billion. Just as Bogle predicted, the fund's emphasis on limited stock turnover has kept its operating expenses low. For every $1,000 an investor places in the fund, Vanguard extracts just $1.80 per year for operating costs, compared with a mutual fund industry average of $15 annually per $1,000 invested. Even more impressive to investors seeking steady, long-term growth, the Vanguard 500 Index fund has offered predictable returns, averaging 9.10% per year since 1992, just below the 9.18% average annual return of the S&P 500 index itself.

If the Vanguard 500 Index fund's investment strategy doesn't appeal to you, you can choose from more than 8,300 mutual funds sold by Vanguard and other mutual fund firms in the United States. Your choices range from funds that track other market indexes to funds focusing on companies in a particular industry sector—for instance, pharmaceutical companies—to emerging markets funds that invest in stocks in developing economies. Other options include funds that buy and sell a broad range of stocks, bonds, and even shares in other mutual funds in an attempt to maximize investor profits. Before choosing a mutual fund, however, it's important to understand how such funds are managed and the factors affecting their performance. As you'll learn in this chapter, with this information under your belt, mutual funds can help you reach your investment goals.

Sources: Geoffrey Colvin, "The Pressure Is On at Vanguard," *Fortune*, December 8, 2003, p. 58; Robert Frick, "The New Spin on Indexing," *Kiplinger's Personal Finance Magazine*, March 1, 2003, pp. 34–38; Michael Maiello and James M. Clash, "Beating the Broad Market," *Forbes*, February 3, 2003, p. 80; and Jody Yen, "Risky Business," *Forbes*, February 3, 2003, p. 94.

The Mutual Fund Phenomenon

mutual fund
an investment company that invests its shareholders' money in a diversified portfolio of securities.

Questions of which stock or bond to select, when to buy, and when to sell have plagued investors for as long as there have been organized securities markets. Such concerns lie at the very heart of the mutual fund concept and in large part explain the growth that mutual funds have experienced. Many investors lack the time, know-how, or commitment to manage their own portfolios, so they turn to professional money managers and simply let them decide which securities to buy and when to sell. More often than not, when investors look for professional help, they look to mutual funds.

Basically, a **mutual fund** is a type of financial services organization that receives money from its shareholders and then invests those funds on their behalf in a diversified portfolio of securities. Thus, when investors buy shares in a mutual fund, they actually become *part owners of a widely diversified portfolio of securities*. In an abstract sense, a mutual fund can be thought of as the *financial product* sold to the public by an investment company. That is, the investment company builds and manages a portfolio of securities and sells ownership interests—shares of stock—in that portfolio through a vehicle known as a mutual fund.

Recall from Chapter 5 that portfolio management deals with both asset allocation and security selection decisions. By investing in mutual funds, investors delegate some, if not all, of the *security selection decisions* to professional money managers. As a result, they can concentrate on key asset allocation decisions—which, of course, play a vital role in determining long-term portfolio returns. Indeed, it's for this reason that *many investors consider mutual funds to be the ultimate asset allocation vehicle*. For with mutual funds, all investors have to do is decide where they want to invest—in large-cap stocks, for example, or in technology stocks, high-yield bonds, the S&P 500 index, or international securities—and then let the professional money managers at the mutual funds do the rest (i.e., decide which securities to buy and sell, and when).

Mutual funds have been a part of the investment landscape for over 75 years. The first one (MFS) was started in Boston in 1924 and is still in business today. By 1940 the number of mutual funds had grown to 68, and by 1980 there were 564 of them. But that was only the beginning: The next 20 years saw unprecedented growth in the mutual fund industry, as assets under management grew from less than $100 billion in 1980 to some $6.4 *trillion* in 2002. Indeed, by 2002, *there were nearly 8,300 publicly traded mutual funds*. (Actually, counting duplicate and multiple fund offerings from the same portfolio, there were more like *15,000 funds available*.) To put that number in perspective, *there are more mutual funds in existence today than there are stocks listed on the New York and American exchanges combined*. The mutual fund industry has grown so much, in fact, that it is now *the largest financial intermediary* in this country—even ahead of banks.

An Overview of Mutual Funds

Mutual funds are big business in the United States and, indeed, all over the world. As the year 2003 began, an estimated 95 million individuals in 54 million U.S. households owned mutual funds. That's nearly half of all U.S. households! Table 13.1 (on page 542) provides some additional statistics about mutual funds in this country and abroad. Clearly, mutual funds appeal to a lot

TABLE 13.1   Some Mutual Fund Statistics

I. Total Number of U.S. Shareholder Accounts (in millions)

	1990*	2002*
Stock funds	22.2	164.4
Bond funds	13.6	25.6
Money market funds	23.0	45.5
Other funds	3.2	15.5
Total	62.0	251.0

II. Total Number of Funds

	1990*	2002*
Stock funds	1,099	4,756
Bond funds	1,046	2,036
Money market funds	741	989
Other funds	193	475
Total—U.S. funds	3,079	8,256
Number of funds in other countries**	N/A	44,870
Total—worldwide	N/A	53,126

III. Total Net Assets Under Management (in billions of dollars)

	1990*	2002*
Stock funds	$239.5	$2,667.1
Bond funds	291.3	1,125.1
Money market funds	498.3	2,272.0
Other funds	31.1	327.4
Total—U.S. funds	$1,065.2	$ 6,391.6
Net assets under mgmt. in other countries**	N/A	$ 4,828.6
Total—worldwide	N/A	$11,220.2

IV. Composition of Mutual Fund Ownership in the United States (relative to total mutual fund assets)

	1990*	2002*
Owned by U.S. households		
in dollars	$790 billion	$4.7 trillion
% of total	74.0%	74.0%
Owned by institutions		
in dollars	$275 billion	$1.7 trillion
% of total	26.0%	26.0%

Notes: *All data are for year-end 1990 and 2002.

**Totals for 38 countries, the major ones being Canada, France, Germany, United Kingdom, Japan, Italy, Korea, Spain, Ireland, and Luxembourg..

Source: 2003 Mutual Fund Fact Book, Investment Company Institute, 2003; obtained from www.ici.org.

of investors—investors from all walks of life and all income levels. They range from inexperienced to highly experienced investors who all share a common view: Each has decided, for one reason or another, to turn over at least a part of his or her investment management activities to professionals.

Pooled Diversification As noted above, an investment in a mutual fund really represents *an ownership position in a professionally managed portfolio of securities.* To appreciate the extent of such diversification, take a look at

FIGURE 13.1 **A Partial List of Portfolio Holdings**

This exhibit represents just *two pages* of security holdings for this particular fund. The total list of holdings goes on for 21 pages and includes stocks in hundreds of different companies. Certainly, this is far more diversification than most individual investors could ever hope to achieve. (*Source: Fidelity Contrafund,* June 30, 2003.)

Investments (Unaudited) – continued

Common Stocks – continued

	Shares	Value (Note 1) (000s)
INDUSTRIALS – continued		
Electrical Equipment – 0.1%		
American Power Conversion Corp.	1,128,200	$ 17,589
Cooper Industries Ltd. Class A	139,400	5,757
Rockwell Automation, Inc.	235,500	5,614
		28,960
Industrial Conglomerates – 3.4%		
3M Co.	7,623,490	983,278
Tomkins PLC	2,966,800	11,147
Tyco International Ltd.	1,783,100	33,843
		1,028,268
Machinery – 1.3%		
CUNO, Inc. (a)	4,000	144
Danaher Corp.	3,489,420	237,455
Dionex Corp. (a)	53,400	2,123
Donaldson Co., Inc.	513,000	22,803
ESCO Technologies, Inc. (a)	204,900	9,016
PACCAR, Inc.	1,643,430	111,030
Pall Corp.	327,900	7,378
Wabash National Corp. (a)	604,400	8,480
		398,429
Marine – 0.0%		
CP Ships Ltd.	140,900	2,347
Road & Rail – 0.3%		
Canadian National Railway Co.	306,120	14,781
Canadian Pacific Railway Ltd.	218,350	4,910
Heartland Express, Inc. (a)	1,494,231	33,247
Knight Transportation, Inc. (a)	682,550	16,995
Landstar System, Inc. (a)	294,074	18,483
Norfolk Southern Corp.	7,900	152
P.A.M. Transportation Services, Inc. (a)	78,600	1,974
		90,542
Trading Companies & Distributors – 0.0%		
Fastenal Co.	59,488	2,019
MSC Industrial Direct Co., Inc. Class A (a)	131,900	2,361
		4,380
TOTAL INDUSTRIALS		3,906,170

See accompanying notes which are an integral part of the financial statements.

Semiannual Report   16

Common Stocks – continued

	Shares	Value (Note 1) (000s)
INFORMATION TECHNOLOGY – 10.1%		
Communications Equipment – 1.0%		
Adtran, Inc. (a)	230,072	$ 11,800
Avocent Corp. (a)	742,633	22,227
Cisco Systems, Inc. (a)	78,700	1,314
Comverse Technology, Inc. (a)	1,631,400	24,520
NetScreen Technologies, Inc. (a)	2,659,200	59,965
Nokia Corp. sponsored ADR	7,900	130
QUALCOMM, Inc.	411,300	14,704
SafeNet, Inc. (a)	38,400	1,074
Scientific-Atlanta, Inc.	2,746,100	65,467
Sycamore Networks, Inc. (a)	3,739,300	14,322
Telefonaktiebolaget LM Ericsson ADR (a)	4,117,391	43,768
UTStarcom, Inc. (a)	835,300	29,712
		289,003
Computers & Peripherals – 1.0%		
Apple Computer, Inc. (a)	2,012,500	38,479
ATI Technologies, Inc. (a)	939,500	9,341
Avid Technology, Inc. (a)	234,900	8,238
Cray, Inc. (a)	486,500	3,843
Dell Computer Corp. (a)	1,129,300	36,092
Electronics for Imaging, Inc. (a)	744,721	15,110
Hutchinson Technology, Inc. (a)	133,700	4,397
Lexmark International, Inc. Class A (a)	260,100	18,407
Logitech International SA (Reg.) (a)	200,592	7,541
SanDisk Corp. (a)	79,100	3,192
Seagate Technology	4,351,300	76,800
Storage Technology Corp. (a)	383,700	9,876
Western Digital Corp. (a)	7,267,500	74,855
		306,171
Electronic Equipment & Instruments – 0.6%		
CDW Corp. (a)	39,200	1,795
Flextronics International Ltd. (a)	2,079,500	21,606
Flir Systems, Inc. (a)(c)	2,911,200	87,773
Lexar Media, Inc. (a)	474,300	4,525
National Instruments Corp. (a)	82,995	3,136
Roper Industries, Inc.	46,300	1,722
Symbol Technologies, Inc.	4,194,100	54,565
Thermo Electron Corp. (a)	336,800	7,080
Waters Corp. (a)	318,000	9,263
		191,465

See accompanying notes which are an integral part of the financial statements.

17   Semiannual Report

Figure 13.1. It provides a partial list of the securities held in the portfolio of a major mutual fund. (The exhibit shows just two pages out of a 21-page list of security holdings.) Note that in June 2003, this fund owned anywhere from 4,000 shares of CUNO, Inc., to more than 7.6 *million* shares of 3M Company. Furthermore, note that within each industry segment, the fund diversified its holdings across a number of different stocks. Clearly, this is far more diversification than most investors could ever attain. Yet each investor who owns shares in this fund is, in effect, a part owner of this diversified portfolio.

Of course, not all funds are as big or as widely diversified as the one depicted in Figure 13.1. But whatever the size of the fund, as the securities held by it move up and down in price, the market value of the mutual fund shares moves accordingly. And when dividend and interest payments are received by the fund, they too are passed on to the mutual fund shareholders and distributed

pooled diversification
a process whereby investors buy into a diversified portfolio of securities for the collective benefit of the individual investors.

WHO OWNS THE FUNDS, AND WHY?—Mutual funds are one of the most popular investments in the United States, with about 95 million individuals in nearly half of all households owning one or more funds. The average mutual fund shareholder is 45 years old, married, college educated, and employed, with $69,000 of household income, $74,400 in mutual fund assets, and $199,000 in total financial assets. Almost 90% own equity mutual funds, and about half own money market funds.

Almost all mutual fund investors consider their holdings to be long-term savings, with retirement and education being their primary investment objectives. The top four reasons they select mutual funds are professional management, investment diversification, potential for high returns, and ease of making investment.

Source: 2003 Mutual Fund Fact Book (Washington, DC: Investment Company Institute, May 2000), downloaded from www.ici.org.

management fee
a fee levied annually for professional mutual fund services provided; paid regardless of the performance of the portfolio.

on the basis of prorated ownership. Thus, if you own 1,000 shares in a mutual fund and that represents 1% of all shares outstanding, you will receive 1% of the dividends paid by the fund. And when a security held by the fund is sold for a profit, the capital gain is also passed on to fund shareholders on a prorated basis. The whole mutual fund idea, in fact, rests on the concept of **pooled diversification**. This process works very much like health insurance, whereby individuals pool their resources for the collective benefit of all the contributors.

Attractions and Drawbacks of Mutual Fund Ownership The attractions of mutual fund ownership are numerous. One of the most important is *diversification*. It benefits fund shareholders by spreading out holdings over a wide variety of industries and companies, thus reducing risk. Another appeal of mutual funds is *full-time professional management,* which relieves investors of many of the day-to-day management and record-keeping chores. What's more, the fund is probably able to offer better investment expertise than individual investors can provide. Still another advantage is that most mutual fund investments can be started with a *modest capital outlay*. Sometimes no minimum investment is required, and after the initial investment additional shares can usually be purchased in small amounts. The *services that mutual funds offer* also make them appealing to many investors: These include automatic reinvestment of dividends, withdrawal plans, and exchange privileges. Finally, mutual funds offer *convenience*. They are relatively easy to acquire; the funds handle the paperwork and record keeping; their prices are widely quoted; and it is possible to deal in fractional shares.

There are, of course, some major drawbacks to mutual fund ownership. One of the biggest disadvantages is that mutual funds in general can be costly and involve *substantial transaction costs*. Many funds carry sizable commission fees ("load charges"). In addition, a **management fee** is levied annually for the professional services provided. It is deducted right off the top, regardless of whether the fund has had a good or a bad year. And, in spite of all the professional management and advice, it seems that *mutual fund performance* over the long haul is at best about equal to what you would expect from the market as a whole. There are some notable exceptions, of course, but most funds do little more than keep up with the market. And in many cases, they don't even do that.

Figure 13.2 shows the investment performance for 12 different types of equity (or equity-oriented) funds over the 10½-year period from January 1993 through mid-2003. The reported returns are average, fully compounded annual rates of return. They assume that all dividends and capital gains distributions are reinvested into additional shares of stock. Note that when compared to the S&P 500, only four fund categories outperformed the market, whereas several fell far short. The message is clear: *Consistently beating the market is no easy task,* even for professional money managers. Although a handful of funds have given investors above-average and even spectacular rates of return, most mutual funds simply do not meet those levels of performance. This is not to say that the long-term returns from mutual funds are substandard or that they fail to equal what you could achieve by putting your money in, say, a savings account or some other risk-free investment outlet. Quite the contrary: The long-term returns from mutual funds have been substantial (and perhaps even better than what a lot of

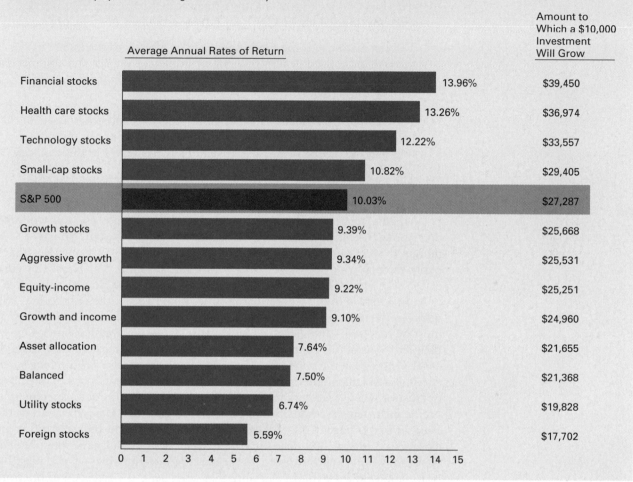

FIGURE 13.2   **The Comparative Performance of Mutual Funds Versus the Market**

Even with the services of professional money managers, it's tough to outperform the market. In this case, the average performance of 8 out of the 12 fund categories failed to meet the market's standard of return (for the period from January 1993 to mid-2003). (*Source: Morningstar*, June 2003.)

Average Annual Rates of Return

Amount to Which a $10,000 Investment Will Grow

	Average Annual Rates of Return	Amount to Which a $10,000 Investment Will Grow
Financial stocks	13.96%	$39,450
Health care stocks	13.26%	$36,974
Technology stocks	12.22%	$33,557
Small-cap stocks	10.82%	$29,405
S&P 500	10.03%	$27,287
Growth stocks	9.39%	$25,668
Aggressive growth	9.34%	$25,531
Equity-income	9.22%	$25,251
Growth and income	9.10%	$24,960
Asset allocation	7.64%	$21,655
Balanced	7.50%	$21,368
Utility stocks	6.74%	$19,828
Foreign stocks	5.59%	$17,702

0 1 2 3 4 5 6 7 8 9 10 11 12 13 14 15

individual investors could have achieved on their own), but most of these returns can be traced to strong market conditions and/or to the reinvestment of dividends and capital gains.

How Mutual Funds Are Organized and Run   Although it's tempting to think of a mutual fund as a single large entity, that view is not really accurate. Various functions—investing, record keeping, safekeeping, and others—are split among two or more companies. To begin with, there's the fund itself, which is organized as a separate corporation or trust and is *owned by the shareholders*, not by the firm that runs it. In addition, there are several other major players:

- The *management company* runs the fund's daily operations. Management companies are the firms we know as Fidelity, Vanguard, T. Rowe Price, American Century, and Dreyfus. They are the ones that create the funds in the first place. Usually, the management firm also serves as investment adviser.

- The *investment adviser* buys and sells stocks or bonds and otherwise oversees the portfolio. Usually, three parties participate in this phase of the operation: (1) *the money manager,* who actually runs the portfolio and makes the buy and sell decisions; (2) *securities analysts,* who analyze securities and look for viable investment candidates; and (3) *traders,* who buy and sell big blocks of securities at the best possible price.

- The *distributor* sells the fund shares, either directly to the public or through authorized dealers (like major brokerage houses and commercial banks). When you request a prospectus and sales literature, you deal with the distributor.

- The *custodian* physically safeguards the securities and other assets of the fund, without taking a role in the investment decisions. To discourage foul play, an independent party (usually a bank) serves in this capacity.

- The *transfer agent* keeps track of purchase and redemption requests from shareholders and maintains other shareholder records.

All this separation of duties is designed to protect the mutual fund investor/shareholder. Obviously, as a mutual fund investor, you will lose money if your fund's stock or bond holdings go down in value. But that's really the only risk of loss you face with a mutual fund. The chance of your ever losing *money from a mutual fund collapse* is almost nonexistent. Here's why: In addition to the separation of duties noted above, the only formal link between the mutual fund and the company that manages it is a contract that must be renewed—and approved by shareholders—on a regular basis. One of the provisions of this contract is that the fund's assets—stocks, bonds, cash, or other securities in the portfolio—can *never be in the hands of the management company.* As still another safeguard, each fund must have a board of directors, or trustees, who are elected by shareholders and are charged with keeping tabs on the management company and renewing its contract. Unfortunately, as the *Ethics* box on pages 548–549 explains, the mutual fund industry did come close to a crisis in 2003, when it was revealed that a handful of fund families were allowing some big investors to execute questionable—if not illegal—transactions in their funds. But note that even here, *the integrity of the fund portfolios was never at risk;* rather, the scandal revolved around some highly questionable trades that took place in the funds.

Mutual Fund Regulations We discussed securities regulations in Chapter 2, but it might be helpful to review some of the major regulatory provisions that apply to mutual funds. To begin with, the *Securities Act of 1933* requires the filing of full information about a mutual fund with the SEC. This act also requires the fund to provide potential investors with a fund profile or current prospectus. This document discloses the fund's management, its investment policies and objectives, and other essential data. In addition, the purchase and sale of mutual fund shares are subject to the antifraud provisions of the *Securities Exchange Act of 1934,* while the *Investment Advisers Act of 1940* regulates the activities of the investment advisers that work for mutual funds. Most importantly, to qualify for investment company status, a fund must comply with the provisions of the *Investment Company Act of 1940.* That comprehensive piece of legislation provides the foundation for the regulation of the mutual fund industry and, among other things, establishes standards of income distribution, fee structures, and diversification of assets.

From a tax perspective, a mutual fund can be treated as an essentially tax-exempt organization (and thereby avoid the double taxation of dividends and income) so long as it qualifies under *Subchapter M* of the Internal Revenue Code of 1954. Briefly, to operate as a regulated investment company and enjoy the attendant tax benefits, a fund must annually distribute to its shareholders all of its realized capital gains and at least 90% of its interest and dividend income. That way, the fund will pay *no* taxes on any of its earnings, whether they're derived from current income or capital gains.

Open- or Closed-End Funds

Although investing in mutual funds has been made as simple as possible, investors nevertheless should have a clear understanding of what they're getting into. For starters, it's essential that you be aware of the different organizational structures, particularly with regard to open- and closed-end funds, as well as a type of fund that combines the characteristics of both open- and closed-end funds, the so-called exchange-traded fund.

open-end investment company
a type of investment company in which investors buy shares from, and sell them back to, the mutual fund itself, with no limit on the number of shares the fund can issue.

Open-End Investment Companies The term *mutual fund* is commonly used to describe an open-end investment company. In an **open-end investment company**, investors buy their shares from, and sell them back to, the mutual fund itself. When an investor buys shares in an open-end fund, the fund issues new shares of stock and fills the purchase order with those new shares. There is no limit, other than investor demand, to the number of shares the fund can issue. (Occasionally, funds *temporarily* close themselves to new investors—they won't open any new accounts—in an attempt to keep fund growth in check.) All open-end mutual funds stand behind their shares and buy them back when investors decide to sell. There is never any trading between individuals.

H O T

American Association of Individual Investors glossary of mutual fund terms is at:

www.aaii.com/mfunds/glossary/

Open-end mutual funds are the dominant type of investment company and account for well over 95% of the assets under management. All the statistics cited above, including those in Table 13.1, pertain to these types of funds. Many of these funds are very large and hold *billions* of dollars' worth of securities. Indeed, in 2003, the typical stock or bond fund held an average portfolio of some $550 million, and there were nearly 600 billion-dollar funds.

Both buy and sell transactions in (open-end) mutual funds are carried out at prices based on the current market value of all the securities held in the fund's portfolio. (Technically, this would also include the book value of any other assets, such as cash and receivables from securities transactions, that the fund might hold at the time, though for all practical purposes, these other assets generally account for only a tiny fraction of the fund's total portfolio.) Known as

net asset value (NAV)
the underlying value of a share of stock in a particular mutual fund.

the fund's **net asset value (NAV)**, this current market value is calculated at least once a day and represents the underlying value of a share of stock in a particular mutual fund. NAV is found by taking the total market value of all assets held by the fund, less any liabilities, and dividing this amount by the number of fund shares outstanding. For example, if the market value of all the assets held by the XYZ mutual fund on a given day equaled $10 million, and if XYZ on

⚖ ETHICS IN INVESTING

WHEN MUTUAL FUNDS BEHAVE BADLY

For the nearly 95 million Americans who own them, mutual funds were once considered a relatively safe place to invest money. That remained true until September 2003, when New York Attorney General Eliot Spitzer shook the mutual fund industry with allegations of illegal after-hours trading, special deals for large institutional investors, market timing in flagrant violation of funds' written policies, and an array of other abuses. These violations could be costing long-term fund investors billions of dollars.

Executives and portfolio managers from several industry giants, including Putnam Investments, Alliance Capital, Strong Capital, PBHG, Nations Funds, Wachovia/Prudential, and Fred Alger Management, have either resigned or now face civil and criminal charges. Several other big names in the securities industry, such as Charles Schwab, American Express, Morgan Stanley, Bank One, and Janus Capital, are either under investigation by the SEC and the New York State Attorney General's office or have decided to settle the charges of improper behavior.

Many mutual fund abuses stem from *market timing,* a practice in which short-term traders seek to exploit differences between hours of operations of various global markets. For example, when the U.S. market rallies on strong economic news, short-term traders buy shares of

U.S.-based international funds with large Asian holdings just before the close of the market at 4 PM EST. Prices of these funds, often calculated between 4 and 6 PM, reflect current prices of the U.S. securities but previous-day prices of Asian-based stocks, which typically close around 2 AM. When the next-day Tokyo and other Asian markets rally following Wall Street's lead, the market timer sells shares of Asian holdings at the higher price, pocketing the profits. Most funds strictly prohibit this kind of activity, yet exceptions have been made for large institutional investors who may trade millions of dollars' worth of fund shares.

Under federal law, investors can purchase or sell shares of a mutual fund at today's price as long as the fund receives the order before 4 PM EST. Mutual fund shares bought or sold after 4 PM are priced at the next day's closing net asset value. Yet many institutional investors in the past were able to profit by placing a late order after the market close when news came out that was likely to move stocks higher or lower the next day. The investor could use this information to purchase or sell shares at the 4 PM closing price. According to regulators, this practice resembles betting on a winning horse after the horse race is over. Although *late trading* is illegal, many mutual funds did not enforce that rule for some of their privileged clients.

continued on next page

that particular day had 500,000 shares outstanding, the fund's net asset value per share would be $20 ($10,000,000 ÷ 500,000). This figure, as we will see, is then used to derive the price at which the fund shares are bought and sold.

Closed-End Investment Companies Although the term *mutual fund* is supposed to be used only with open-end funds, it is also commonly used to refer to closed-end investment companies. **Closed-end investment companies** operate with a fixed number of shares outstanding, and do not regularly issue new shares of stock. In effect, they have a capital structure like that of any other corporation, except that the corporation's business happens to be investing in marketable securities. Shares in closed-end investment companies, like those of any other common stock, are actively traded in the secondary market. But

closed-end investment companies
a type of investment company that operates with a fixed number of shares outstanding.

ETHICS IN INVESTING

continued from previous page

Another form of abuse involved the use of index funds for *ultra-fast computer trading* when powerful computer programs detected minuscule differences (measured in fractions of a percentage point) between the prices of index futures and underlying indexes. If the price of an index future exceeded the value of the underlying stock index, the investor could sell short an index future and simultaneously purchase the corresponding index fund. When both the index and the index future converged in price, the investor would close out the short position and sell the index fund, locking in the difference in price as profit. For an institutional investor able to commit more than $100 million on each transaction, this arbitrage activity repeated several times in a week might result in substantial profits earned almost on a risk-free basis as index and index futures prices converged each day at the market close.

The abuses did not stop there. The National Association of Securities Dealers and the SEC cracked down on widespread abuses in mutual fund sales practices that overcharged investors on sales charges, or loads. NASD estimates that at least $86 million is owed to investors for 2001 and 2002. Also, several funds closed to new investors charged their existing shareholders millions of dollars in marketing and sales fees. Some fund managers—like Gary Pilgrim of

PBHG Funds, for example—not only tolerated market timing and other trading abuses but also handsomely profited from them by investing millions of dollars of their own money in the market timing schemes.

Although people's savings invested in the funds were never at stake, investors suffered losses because *these abuses resulted in higher fund expenses and trading costs as well as sub-par returns resulting from the funds' higher than necessary cash positions needed to accommodate frequent purchases and redemptions by professional traders.* These costs were borne not by the fund or its management that permitted these practices, but rather by the fund's long-term investors. However, many funds that settled with the regulators promised to reimburse the existing stockholders for losses resulting from overcharging fees or trading abuses.

CRITICAL THINKING QUESTION The SEC has proposed several regulations intended to curb mutual trading abuses. They include strict enforcement of trading hours and the imposition of 2% redemption fees if a fund is sold in less than 90 days after the purchase. Do you think this will eliminate trading abuses?

unlike open-end funds, *all trading in closed-end funds is done between investors in the open market.* The fund itself plays no role in either buy or sell transactions. Once the shares are issued, the fund is out of the picture. By far, most closed-end investment companies are traded on the New York Stock Exchange, a few are traded on the American Exchange, and occasionally some are traded in the OTC market or on some other exchange. Even so, while these shares are traded (on the NYSE, AMEX, or Nasdaq) like any other stock, their quotes are listed separately—in the *Wall Street Journal* at least. Figure 13.3 (on page 550) shows the quotes for a small sample of closed-end funds listed on the NYSE, including Gabelli Equity Trust (one of the bigger closed-end investment companies). These quotes are grouped by the exchange on which the funds are traded, and include little more than share prices and dividends.

FIGURE 13.3

Stock Quotations for Closed-End Investment Companies

The quotes for closed-end investment companies are listed separately from other common stocks. As can be seen, they provide only a minimal amount of information, including the fund's abbreviated name and symbol, the latest annual dividend, the latest closing price, and the net change in price. (*Source: Wall Street Journal*, November 18, 2003.)

CLOSED-END FUNDS

STOCK (SYM)	DIV	LAST	NET CHG
FstFnlFd **FF**	2.96e	18.20	−0.35
FstIsrael **ISL**	.35e	11.15	−0.03
FlrtyClayPfdSec **FFC** n	2.07	26.33	0.03
FlrtyPfd Income **PFD**	1.10a	17.34	0.69
FlrtyPfdIncomOp **PFO**	.88a	13.31	0.11
FlrtyClayTotRet **FLC** n	.16p	25.71	0.11
FltngRteIncoFd **FRA** n		20.19	0.19
FtDearborn **FTD**	.80	14.79	−0.04
40/86StrInco **CFD**	.94e	10.90	−0.01
FraGrthFd **FRF**		7.18	−0.19
FrnklnMulti **FMI**	.42	7.15	−0.06
FrnklnUnvlTr **FT**	.36	5.53	...
GabelliConv **GCV**	.80	10.22	0.03
GabelliConv pfB n	.78e	25.02	−0.23
GabelliTr **GAB**	.56a	7.68	−0.04
GabelliTr pfB	1.80	26.95	...
GabelliTr pfD n		24.97	0.04
GabelliMlti **GGT**		8.39	−0.09
GabelMlti pfB n	.73e	25.30	0.06
GabelliUtilTr **GUT**	.72a	9.01	−0.07
GenAmInv **GAM**	.86e	28.22	−0.37
GermanyFd **GER**	e	6.91	−0.07
NewGrmnyFd **GF**	.00e	6.67	−0.13
GlblHiInco **GHI**	1.83e	17.44	0.14

Gabelli → Equity Trust **(GAB)**

A closed-end fund is, in many respects, both a common stock and an investment company. As the original form of investment company, closed-end funds have enjoyed a long history that dates back to nineteenth-century England and Scotland. In the United States, closed-end funds were actively traded during the 1920s bull market, when they far outnumbered their open-end relatives. During that freewheeling era, however, they were highly leveraged and consequently were hit hard during the Crash of 1929, earning a bad reputation with investors. They remained something of an oddity for decades afterward. It wasn't until the bull market that began in the early 1980s that closed-end funds came back into fashion.

Many of the investment advisers that today run closed-end funds (like Nuveen, MFS, Eaton Vance, Dreyfus, PIMCO, and Franklin-Templeton) also manage open-end funds, often with similar investment objectives. They offer both closed- and open-end funds because they are really *two different investment products*. For although it may not appear so at first glance, there are some major differences between these two types of funds. To begin with, closed-end funds have a fixed amount of capital to work with. Therefore, they don't have to be concerned about keeping cash on hand (or readily available) to meet redemptions. Equally important, because there is no pressure on portfolio managers to cash in these securities at inopportune times, they can be more aggressive in their investment styles by investing in obscure yet attractive securities that may not be actively traded. And, of course, because they don't have new money flowing in all the time, portfolio managers don't have to worry about finding new investments. Instead, they can concentrate on a set portfolio of securities.

Of course, this also puts added pressures on the money managers, since their investment styles and fund portfolios are closely monitored and judged by the market. That is, the share prices of closed-end companies are determined not only by their net asset values but also by general supply and demand conditions in the market. As a result, depending on the market outlook and investor expectations, closed-end companies generally trade at a discount or premium to NAV. (They almost never trade at net asset value.) Share price discounts and premiums can at times become quite large. In fact, it's not unusual for such spreads to amount to as much as 25% to 30% of net asset value (occasionally more) depending on market judgments and expectations. (We'll discuss closed-end funds in more detail later in this chapter.)

Exchange-Traded Funds

exchange-traded fund (ETF)
an open-end mutual fund that trades as a listed security on a stock exchange.

Combine some of the operating characteristics of an open-end fund with some of the trading characteristics of a closed-end fund, and what you'll end up with is something called an *exchange-traded fund*. These securities are being promoted as the newest product to hit the fund world, but they're really a recreation of a product that's been around since the early 1990s. Technically, an **exchange-traded fund (ETF)** is a type of open-end mutual fund that trades as a listed security on one of the stock exchanges (mostly the AMEX). Actually, all ETFs thus far (mid-year 2003) have been structured as *index funds* set up to match the performance of a certain segment of the market. They do this by owning all, or a representative sample, of the stocks in a targeted market segment or index. (We'll examine traditional index funds in more detail later in this chapter.) Thus, ETFs offer the professional money management of traditional mutual funds *and* the liquidity of an exchange-traded stock.

Even though these securities are like closed-end funds in that ETFs are traded on listed exchanges, *they are in reality open-end mutual funds,* where the number of shares outstanding can be increased or decreased in response to market demand. That is, although ETFs can be bought or sold like any stock on a listed exchange, *the ETF distributor can also create new shares or redeem old shares.* This is done through a special type of security known as a *payment-in-kind creation unit.* (Without getting into all the messy details, these units are created by exchange specialists, or so-called "authorized participants", who deposit with a trustee a portfolio, or market basket, of stocks that track an index. The authorized participant then receives from the trustee new ETF shares, on the index, to be sold in the open market. To redeem shares, the authorized participant simply turns in ETF shares in exchange for the underlying stocks.) This is all done to ensure an efficient and orderly market, and to prevent the fund shares from trading at (much of) a discount or premium, thereby avoiding one of the pitfalls of closed-end funds. Individual investors, of course, are *not* involved in the creation of these fund shares (that's handled by big institutional investors). Instead, they buy and sell ETFs in the secondary market by placing orders with their brokers, as they would normally do with any stock.

H O T

Which are the most active index shares—Nasdaq 100 index shares, SPDRs, Midcap SPDRs, or Diamonds? To find out, visit:

amex.com

By mid-2002, there were more than 100 ETFs listed on the American Stock Exchange, and all but a handful of them were based on some domestic or international stock market index. The biggest and oldest (started in 1993) are based on the S&P 500 and are known as *spiders*. In addition to spiders, there are *diamonds* (which are based on the DJIA) and *qubes* (based on the Nasdaq 100 and so-named because of their QQQ ticker symbol). There also are ETFs based on 39 international markets (from Australia and Canada to Germany, Japan, and the United Kingdom), and 8 that are based on bond measures. Just about every major U.S. index, in fact, has its own ETF. So do a lot of minor indexes (some of which were created by the distributors) that cover very specialized (and sometimes fairly small) segments of the market.

The net asset values of ETFs are set at a fraction of the underlying index value at any given time. For example, if the S&P 500 index stands at, say, 1064.46, the EFT on that index will trade at around 106.50 (that is, at about 1/10 of the index). Likewise, the ETF on the Dow is set at 1/100 of the DJIA. (Thus, when the DJIA is at say, 10449.30, the EFT will trade at around 104.50). At year-end 2002, the market value of all outstanding ETFs amounted to more than $100 billion, though just two of them, the S&P 500 spiders and Nasdaq qubes, accounted for nearly 60% of that total.

ETFs combine many of the advantages of closed-end funds with those of traditional (open-end) index funds. As with closed-end funds, you can buy and sell ETFs at *any time of the day* by placing an order through your broker (and paying a standard commission, just as you would with any other stock). In contrast, you *cannot* trade a traditional open-end fund on an intraday basis; all buy and sell orders for those funds are filled at the end of the trading day, at closing prices. What's more, because ETFs are passively managed, they offer all the advantages of any index fund: low cost, low portfolio turnover, and low taxes. In fact, the fund's tax liability is kept very low, because ETFs rarely distribute any capital gains to shareholders. Thus, you could hold one of these things for decades and never pay a dime in capital gains taxes (at least not until you sell the shares). The *Investing in Action* box on pages 554–555 provides some additional information about ETFs—information that might help you decide whether they are right for you.

Some Important Considerations

When you buy or sell shares in a *closed-end* investment company (or in *ETFs,* for that matter), you pay a commission, just as you would with any other listed or OTC stock. This is not the case with open-end mutual funds, however, as the cost of investing in an open-end fund depends on the types of fees and load charges that the fund levies on its investors.

Load and No-Load Funds The *load charge* on an open-end fund is the commission the investor pays when buying shares in a fund. Generally speaking, the term **load fund** is used to describe a mutual fund that charges a commission when shares are bought. (Such charges are also known as *front-end loads.*) In a **no-load fund** no sales charges are levied. Load charges can be fairly substantial and can amount to as much as 8½% of the *purchase price* of the shares. However, very few funds charge the maximum. Instead, many funds charge commissions of only 2% or 3%. Such funds are known as **low-load funds.**

load fund
a mutual fund that charges a commission when shares are bought; also known as a *front-end load fund*.

no-load fund
a mutual fund that does not charge a commission when shares are bought.

low-load fund
a mutual fund that charges a small commission (2% to 3%) when shares are bought.

Although there may be little or no difference in the performance of load and no-load funds, *the cost savings with no-load funds tend to give investors a head start in achieving superior rates of return.* Unfortunately, the true no-load fund is becoming harder to find, as more and more no-loads are becoming *12(b)-1 funds.* While these funds do not directly charge commissions at the time of purchase, they *annually* assess what are known as 12(b)-1 charges to make up for any lost commissions. (These charges are more fully described below.) Overall, less than 30% of the funds sold today are pure no-loads; the rest charge some type of load or fee.

Occasionally, a fund will have a **back-end load,** which means commissions are levied when shares are sold. These loads may amount to as much as 7¼% of the value of the shares sold, although back-end loads tend to decline over time and usually disappear altogether after 5 or 6 years from date of purchase. The stated purpose of back-end loads is to enhance fund stability by discouraging investors from trading in and out of the funds over short investment horizons. In addition, a substantial (and growing) number of funds charge something called a **12(b)-1 fee** that's assessed annually for as long as you own the fund. Known appropriately as *hidden loads,* these fees are designed to help funds (particularly the no-loads) cover their distribution and marketing costs. They can amount to as much as 1% per year of assets under management. In good markets and bad, these fees are paid right off the top, and that can take its toll. Consider, for instance, $10,000 invested in a fund that charges a 1% 12(b)-1 fee. That translates into a charge of $100 per year—certainly not an insignificant amount of money.

The latest trend in mutual fund fees is the so-called *multiple-class sales charge.* You'll find such arrangements at firms like Dreyfus, Merrill Lynch, MFS, Evergreen, Franklin/Templeton, Scudder, and Putnam. The mutual fund simply issues different classes of stocks on the same portfolio of securities, with each class having a different fee structure. For example, class A shares might have normal front-end loads; class B shares might have no front-end loads but substantial back-end loads along with maximum annual 12(b)-1 fees; and class C shares might carry only 12(b)-1 fees of up to 1% per year. In other words, you "choose your own poison."

To try to bring some semblance of order to fund charges and fees, in 1992 the SEC instituted a series of caps on mutual fund fees. Under the 1992 rules, a mutual fund cannot charge more than 8½% in *total sales charges and fees,* including front- and back-end loads as well as 12(b)-1 fees. Thus, if a fund charges a 5% front-end load and a 1% 12(b)-1 fee, it can charge a maximum of only 2½% in back-end load charges without violating the 8½% cap. In addition, the SEC set a 1% cap on annual 12(b)-1 fees and, perhaps more significantly, stated that true no-load funds cannot charge more than 0.25% in annual 12(b)-1 fees. If they do, they have to drop the no-load label in their sales and promotional material.

Other Fees and Costs Another cost of owning mutual funds is the *management fee.* This is the compensation paid to the professional managers who administer the fund's portfolio. It must be paid regardless of whether a fund is load or no-load, and whether it is an open- or closed-end fund, or an exchange-traded fund. Unlike load charges, which are one-time costs, management fees and 12(b)-1 charges, if imposed, are levied annually. They are paid

back-end load
a commission charged on the *sale* of shares in a mutual fund.

12(b)-1 fee
a fee levied annually by many mutual funds to cover management and other operating costs; amounts to as much as 1% of the average net assets.

INVESTOR FACTS

THE ABC's OF FUND FEES— A shares, B shares, C shares— what's an investor to do? Here's a guide to use in deciding which type of mutual fund share is best for you.

1. **A shares:** Usually involve modest front-end load charges and perhaps a small 12(b)-1 fee (typically 0.25%). *These shares usually make the most sense for long-term investors.*
2. **B shares:** Normally have substantial back-end loads for a period of up to 6 years, plus maximum 12(b)-1 fees of 1% per year. The lack of a front-end load make them look attractive to investors, but the fact is *most investors should steer clear of them— they are a bad deal!*
3. **C shares:** Usually a small back-end load if you sell within a year, plus a 12(b)-1 fee of up to 1%. *These shares are normally a better deal than B shares.*

Bottom line: If you're a long-term investor, go for the A shares; if not, go for the C shares.

INVESTING IN ACTION

ADDING ETFS TO YOUR INVESTMENT PORTFOLIO

Want to buy some diamonds? Or maybe spiders or qubes are more your style. These exchange-traded funds (ETFs) are similar to index mutual funds but trade like stocks. Each share represents a basket of securities that closely tracks one specific index. Investors can choose from about 120 different types of ETFs that trade on the American Stock Exchange. They include diamonds, a basket of the Dow Jones Industrial Average stocks; spiders (SPDRS), S&P 500 Depository Receipts; qubes (QQQs), a basket of Nasdaq 100 Index stocks; and even bond ETFs, that track the Lehman Brothers and other bond indexes. New ETFs are introduced regularly; two recent offerings targeted Treasury Inflation-Protected Securities and the 50 highest dividend-yielding stocks in the Dow averages.

Because ETFs trade on the stock market, it's easy to buy and sell them through a brokerage account during the entire day—not just after the markets close, as with mutual funds. ETFs also have extremely low costs because they have no research or management fees and minimal back-office costs. "Basically, a computer manages the ETF fund rather than some $5 million-a-year portfolio manager," says Jeff Seely, chief executive officer of the Seattle online brokerage ShareBuilder Securities Corporation. For exam-

ple, annual expenses for SPDRS are just 0.11%, well below the 1.4% fee charged by the average actively managed mutual fund. Another benefit comes from their tax status. Because they are not actively managed, ETFs have minimal turn-over and generate little or no taxable income and capital gains distributions. Investors do not incur a tax liability until they sell the ETF at a profit.

Performance has been attractive as well, helped by ETFs' low expense ratios. ETFs that track broad stock indexes, such as the S&P 500, the DJIA, or the Wilshire 5000, have generally achieved higher returns than about 75% of actively managed funds.

ETFs do have some drawbacks, however. While fees are low, investors incur brokerage commissions when they trade ETFs, as well as a small bid/ask spread. Frequent trades can quickly wipe out any profits. ETFs do not offer dividend reinvestment or monthly investment programs. And, whereas traditional mutual funds can reinvest dividends and capital gains immediately to continuously compound their gains, ETFs can reinvest the cash only monthly or quarterly.

Despite the downside, ETFs provide investors with a quick way to get exposure to a market

continued on next page

regardless of the fund's performance. In addition, there are the administrative costs of operating the fund. These are fairly modest and represent the normal cost of doing business (e.g., the commissions paid when the fund buys and sells securities). The various fees that funds charge generally range from less than 0.5% to as much as 3% or 4% of average assets under management. Total expense ratios bear watching, because high expenses take their toll on performance. As a point of reference, in 2003, domestic stock funds had average expense ratios of around 1.50%, foreign stock funds of around 1.90%, stock index funds of around 0.70%, and domestic bond funds of around 1.10%. In addition to these management fees, some funds may charge an *exchange fee*, assessed whenever an investor transfers money from one fund to another within the same fund family, and/or an *annual maintenance fee*, to help defer the costs of providing service to low-balance accounts.

A final cost of mutual funds is the taxes paid on securities transactions. To avoid double taxation, nearly all mutual funds operate as *regulated investment*

INVESTING IN ACTION

continued from previous page

segment. They offer diversification and precise market tracking, and they appeal to both active traders and long-term investors. It's easy to add a specific equity component based on one of the following factors:

- **Style:** Choose an ETF that tracks a growth or value index such as the S&P 400 Mid Cap Barra Growth or the S&P 600 Small Cap Value.
- **Size:** Market capitalization is another ETF segmentation strategy. You will find ETFs that track small-, mid-, and large-cap companies, using the S&P, Dow, Nasdaq, and Russell indexes.
- **Sector:** Many ETFs, including Barclays' iShares and Merrill Lynch's HOLDRS, target specific industries or sectors such as biotechnology, real estate investment trusts, pharmaceuticals, telecommunications, health care, energy, noncyclical companies, and subsectors of the Internet industry. They offer exposure to a small part of an industry that mutual funds may not cover, yet broader coverage than an investor would gain by buying several individual stocks.
- **Region:** ETFs make it easy to achieve geographical diversification, whether for just one country or an entire region, without the high loads and fees imposed by most foreign

stock funds. Examples include Barclays' iShares, such as the Webs (World Equity Benchmark shares) that track the Morgan Stanley Capital International (MSCI) indexes for 20 countries, and regional ETFs that track the S&P Europe 350 and Global 100 and MSCI European Monetary Union. However, international index funds are a less costly way to get broad exposure.

Investors can track ETF total returns and compare them to the returns for traditional mutual funds in similar sectors at Morningstar.com (www.morningstar.com) and with the *Wall Street Journal*'s monthly Mutual Fund Report.

CRITICAL THINKING QUESTIONS What are four ways of structuring exchange-traded funds? What investment advantages do ETFs offer?

Sources: Jeff Brown, "Exchange-Traded Funds Can Be Gentle Alternative to Mutual Funds," *Philadelphia Enquirer*, December 9, 2003, downloaded from www.infotrac.com; Bill Deener, "Exchange-Traded Funds Remain Worth a Look for Investors," *Dallas Morning News*, December 1, 2003, downloaded from www.infotrac.com; Christopher J. Traulsen, "Four New ETFs on Tap," *Morningstar.com*, August 28, 2003, downloaded from www.morningstar.com; and "What Are iShares," *iShares*, www.ishares.com, downloaded December 10, 2003.

---

companies. This means that all (or nearly all) of the dividend and interest income is passed on to the investor, as are any capital gains realized when securities are sold. The mutual fund therefore passes the tax liability on to its shareholders. This holds true whether such distributions are reinvested in the company (in the form of additional mutual fund shares) or paid out in cash. Mutual funds annually provide each stockholder with a summary report on the amount of dividends and capital gains received and the amount of taxable income earned by the fund shareholder.

Keeping Track of Fund Fees and Loads Critics of the mutual fund industry have come down hard on the proliferation of fund fees and charges. Some argue that the different charges and fees are meant to do one thing: Confuse the investor. A lot of funds were going to great lengths (lowering a cost here, tacking on a fee there, hiding a charge somewhere else) to make themselves look like something they weren't. The funds were following the letter of the law, and were fully disclosing all their expenses and fees. The trouble was that the funds were able to hide all but the most conspicuous charges in "legalese."

Fortunately, steps have been taken to bring fund fees and loads out into the open.

For one thing, fund charges are more widely reported now than they were in past. Most notably, today you can find detailed information about the types and amounts of fees and charges on just about any mutual fund by accessing a variety of Web sites, such as www.quicken.com/investments/mutualfunds, www.kiplinger.com/investing/funds/, or www.morningstar.com/Funds/. Figure 13.4 provides excerpts from one of these sites and shows the kind of information that's readily available, at no charge, on the Web.

Alternatively, you can use the mutual fund quotes that appear daily in most major, large-city newspapers or in the *Wall Street Journal*. For example, look at the *Wall Street Journal* quotations in Figure 13.5 (on page 558). Note the use of the letters *r, p,* and *t* behind the name of the fund. An *r* behind a fund's name means that the fund charges some type of redemption fee, or back-end load, when you sell your shares. This is the case, for example, with the Fidelity Aggressive Growth Fund. A *p* in the quotes means that the fund levies a 12(b)-1 fee, which you'll have to pay, for example, if you invest in the Diversified Equity Growth Fund. Finally, a *t* indicates funds that charge both redemption fees and 12(b)-1 fees. Note, for example, that the Cohen & Steers Equity Income Fund is one such fund.

The quotations, of course, tell you only the *kinds* of fees charged by the funds. They do not tell you *how much* is charged. To get the specifics on the amount charged, you'll have to turn to other sources. Furthermore, these published quotes (which are fairly representative of what you'd find in other major newspapers) *tell you nothing about the front-end loads,* if any, charged by the funds. Refer once again to the quotes in Figure 13.5, and compare the Dodge & Cox Balanced and FPA Paramount Funds. They look alike, don't they? But they're not. For even though neither of them charges redemption or 12(b)-1 fees, only one of them is a no-load fund. Dodge & Cox does not charge a front-end load, and is in fact a no-load fund. The FPA fund, in contrast, comes with a hefty 5¼% front-end load. As a point of interest, the other three funds highlighted in Figure 13.5—Cohen & Steers Equity Income, Diversified Equity Growth, and Fidelity Aggressive Growth—don't charge front-end loads either, but you'd never know that from the quotes. (It should be noted that the *Wall Street Journal* also publishes a *Monthly Mutual Fund Review* on the first or second Monday of each month. Among other things, it provides some specifics on front-end loads and annual expense charges, including 12(b)-1 fees.)

In addition to the public sources noted above, the mutual funds themselves are required by the SEC to fully disclose all of their fees and expenses in a standardized, easy-to-understand format. Every fund profile or prospectus must contain, up front, a fairly detailed *fee table,* much like the one illustrated in Table 13.2 (on page 559). This table has three parts. The first specifies *all shareholder transaction costs*. In effect, this tells you what it's going to cost to buy and sell shares in the mutual fund. The next section lists the *annual operating expenses* of the fund. Showing these expenses as a percentage of average net assets, the fund must break out management fees, 12(b)-1 fees, and any

FIGURE 13.4   Fund Fees and Charges on the Web

The Internet has become the motherlode of information on just about any topic imaginable, including mutual fund fees and charges. Here's an example of information taken from the Morningstar Web site. These excerpts show, among other things, all the fees and expenses levied by each fund. The two funds in the exhibit provide a stark contrast in fees and expenses. The A shares for the PF Putnam Equity Income fund carry both a high (5½%) front-end load and a ½% 12(b)-1 fee, along with a substantial total management fee/expense ratio (of 1.90%). The Vanguard Small Cap Index fund, on the other hand, provides a vivid example of a truly low-cost fund: no loads or fees and a *very low* total management fee/expense ratio (of 0.27%). (*Source:* **www.morningstar.com/fund/fees**, November 18, 2003. © 2003 Morningstar, Inc. Used with permission.)

M⊙RNINGSTAR.com

PF Putnam Equity Income A(PFAEX)

Fees and Expenses

Maximum Sales Fees %		Total Cost Projections	Cost per $10,000
Initial	**5.50**	3-Year	**$1114**
Deferred	**None**	5-Year	$
Redemption	**None**	10-Year	$

Maximum Fees %		Actual Fees %	
Administrative	0.00	12b-1	**0.50**
Management	0.95	Management	**0.95**
12b-1	0.50	Total Expense Ratio (03-31-03)	**1.90**
		(Category Average)	1.40

Vanguard Small Cap Index (NAESX)

Fees and Expenses

Maximum Sales Fees %		Total Cost Projections	Cost per $10,000
Initial	**None**	3-Year	**$87**
Deferred	**None**	5-Year	$152
Redemption	**None**	10-Year	$343

Maximum Fees %		Actual Fees %	
Administrative	0.00	12b-1	**0.00**
Management	0.24	Management	**0.24**
12b-1	0.00	Total Expense Ratio (12-31-02)	**0.27**
		(Category Average)	1.57

other expenses. The third section provides a rundown of *the total cost over time* of buying, selling, and owning the fund. This part of the table contains both transaction and operating expenses and shows what the total costs would be over hypothetical 1-, 3-, 5-, and 10-year holding periods. To ensure consistency and comparability, the funds must follow a rigid set of guidelines when constructing the illustrative costs.

FIGURE 13.5

Mutual Fund Quotes

Open-end mutual funds are listed separately from other securities. They have their own quotation system, an example of which, from the *Wall Street Journal,* is shown here. Note that these securities are quoted in dollars and cents and that the quotes include not only the fund's NAV but year-to-date (YTD) and 3-year returns as well. Also included is an indication of whether the fund charges redemption and/or 12(b)-1 fees. (*Source: Wall Street Journal,* November 18, 2003.)

Mutual Fund Quotations

FUND	NAV	NET CHG	YTD %RET	3-YR %RET
Citizens Funds				
CitCGSt p	17.80	−0.15	18.7	−13.5
CitEmGrSt	12.39	−0.13	27.3	−18.5
CitGblSt	14.47	−0.17	13.4	−15.8
Clipper	84.50	−0.45	11.6	8.4
Cohen & Steers				
EqIncA p	14.14	−0.02	29.5	19.6
EqIncB t	13.73	−0.02	28.8	18.8
EqIncC t	13.73	−0.02	28.8	18.8
InstlRlty	37.44	−0.09	32.5	16.0
RltyShrs	55.47	−0.14	32.6	15.8
Colo Bonds	9.32	...	5.7	6.7
Diversified Funds				
AggrEq p	11.16	−0.13	24.4	−16.3
Balance p	13.12	−0.06	12.3	−2.1
CoreBond p	12.82	0.02	3.7	7.3
EqGrow p	17.14	−0.11	20.7	−12.0
Gro&Inc p	16.51	−0.10	16.1	−13.4
HiQual p	11.80	0.01	1.5	5.5
HiYldBd p	9.38	0.01	23.1	9.5
InLHorSA	10.74	−0.05	15.5	−1.8
IntGvt p	11.35	0.01	0.8	5.6
IntHorSA	10.77	−0.04	12.2	0.7
IntlEq p	12.30	−0.23	22.3	−6.7
LgHorSA	9.00	−0.07	18.1	−5.9
SpecEq p	22.65	−0.30	37.6	1.2
StHorSA	11.01	0.01	5.5	5.5
StkIdx p	8.15	−0.05	19.8	−7.8
Val&Inc p	20.87	−0.13	17.0	0.6
Dodge & Cox				
Balanced	69.99	−0.43	17.6	10.2
Income	12.95	0.03	5.1	9.6
Intl Stk	21.50	−0.46	36.0	NS
Stock	106.41	−0.99	22.5	9.2
FFTW Funds				
LtdDur	10.05	0.01	2.2	5.8
US Sht	9.44x	...	1.3	2.7
WWFxdIn	9.90	0.01	8.8	10.0
FMI CommonStock	21.20	−0.09	17.8	13.1
FMI FocusFd	31.60	−0.32	37.6	2.5
FPA Funds				
Capit	35.25	−0.61	31.2	20.3
FPACres	20.96	−0.14	20.9	21.5
NwInc	11.26	−0.01	6.9	8.6
Parmt	11.82	−0.13	39.1	16.7
Peren	27.80	−0.25	36.2	16.7
Fidelity Invest				
A Mgr	15.24	−0.04	12.5	−0.4
AggrGr r	14.24	−0.17	27.3	−29.1
AggrInt	13.93	−0.30	29.8	0.3
AMgrAggr	9.64	−0.13	39.1	−8.9
AMgrGr	13.82	−0.07	15.5	−3.4
AMgrIn	12.01	−0.03	12.6	4.6
Balanc	15.99	−0.10	21.8	4.9
BluCh	37.62	−0.24	18.2	−11.6
Canad r	25.28	−0.12	39.5	8.6
CapAp	22.79	−0.32	40.9	0.3
ChinaReg	14.96	−0.21	37.8	1.3

NAV: The price you get when you *sell* shares, or what you pay when you *buy* no-load funds.

Cohen & Steers Equity Income: A fund with both a redemption fee and a 12(b)-1 fee (t).

Diversified Equity Growth: A fund with a 12(b)-1 fee (p).

Dodge & Cox Blanced: A true no-load fund (no front-end, back-end, or 12(b)-1 fees).

FPA Paramount: A fund with a 5¼% front-end load, but no redemption or 12(b)-1 fees.

Fidelity Aggressive Growth: A fund with a redemption fee (r).

TABLE 13.2	Mutual Fund Fee Table (Required by Federal Law)

The following table describes the fees and expenses that are incurred when you buy, hold, or sell shares of the fund.

Shareholder Fees (paid by the investor directly)

Maximum sales charge (load) on purchases (as a % of offering price)	3%
Sales charge (load) on reinvested distributions	None
Deferred sales charge (load) on redemptions	None
Exchange fees	None
Annual account maintenance fee (for accounts under $2,500)	$12.00

Annual fund operating expenses (paid from fund assets)

Management fee	0.45%
Distribution and service (12b-1) fee	None
Other expenses	0.20%
Total annual fund operating expenses	**0.65%**

Example

This example is intended to help an investor compare the cost of investing in different funds. The example assumes a $10,000 investment in the fund for one, three, five, and ten years and then a redemption of all fund shares at the end of those periods. The example also assumes that an investment returns 5 percent each year and that the fund's operating expenses remain the same. Although actual costs may be higher or lower, based on these assumptions an investor's costs would be:

1 year	$364
3 years	$502
5 years	$651
10 years	$1,086

Other Types of Investment Companies

In addition to open-end, closed-end, and exchange-traded funds, there are four other types of investment companies: (1) unit investment trusts, (2) real estate investment trusts, (3) annuities, and (4) hedge funds. Unit investment trusts, annuities, and hedge funds are similar to mutual funds to the extent that they, too, invest primarily in marketable securities, such as stocks and bonds. Real estate investment trusts, in contrast, invest primarily in various types of real estate–related investments, like mortgages. We'll look at unit investment trusts and hedge funds in this section. The other two types of investment companies are discussed in detail at the book's Web site.

HOT

For a detailed discussion of two other types of investment companies—real estate investment trusts and annuities—see our Web site, at:

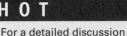
www.aw-bc.com/gitman_joehnk

unit investment trust (UIT)
a type of investment vehicle whereby the trust sponsors put together a fixed/unmanaged portfolio of securities and then sell ownership units in the portfolio to individual investors.

Unit Investment Trusts A **unit investment trust (UIT)** represents little more than an interest in an *unmanaged* pool of investments. UITs are like mutual funds to the extent that they involve a portfolio of securities. But that's where the similarity ends. Once a portfolio of securities is put together, it is simply held in safekeeping for investors under conditions set down in a trust agreement. Traditionally, these portfolios were made up of various types of *fixed-income securities,* with long-term municipal bonds being the most popular type of investment vehicle. There is no trading in the portfolios, so the returns, or yields, are fixed and fairly predictable—at least for the short term. Not surprisingly, these unit investment trusts appeal mainly to income-oriented investors looking for a safe, steady stream of income.

At year-end 1990, taxable and tax-free bond trusts accounted for about 95% of total UIT assets outstanding. About this time, however, brokerage firms began aggressively marketing a new type of investment product—the *stock-oriented UIT*. These new equity trusts caught on quickly and by year-end 1999, accounted for about 65% of the $90 billion UIT market. But then the 2000–2002 bear market hit. Not surprisingly, these products quickly fell out of favor. Indeed, by 2002, equity trusts outstanding fell to $14.6 billion and represented just 40% of the total market—which by then had also fallen, to only $36 billion. Except for the shorter terms (1 to 5 years for equity trusts versus 15 to 30 years for fixed-income products), these trusts are no different from the traditional bond-oriented UITs: Once the portfolios are put together, they usually remain untouched for the life of the trust.

Various sponsoring brokerage houses put together these pools of securities and then sell units of the pool to investors. (Each unit is like a share in a mutual fund.) For example, a brokerage house might put together a pool of corporate securities that amounts to, say, $100 million. The sponsoring firm would then sell units in this pool to the investing public at anywhere from $250 (for many equity trusts) to $1,000 per unit (common for fixed-income products). The sponsoring organization does little more than routine record-keeping. It services the investments by collecting coupons or dividends and distributing the income (often on a monthly basis) to the holders of the trust units.

Hedge Funds First of all, in spite of the name similarities, it is important to understand that hedge funds are *not* mutual funds. They are totally different types of investment products! **Hedge funds** are set up as private entities, usually in the form of *limited partnerships* and, as such, are *largely unregulated*. The *general partner* runs the fund and directly participates in the fund's profits—often taking an "incentive fee" of 10–20% of the profits, in addition to a base fee of 1–2% of assets under management. The *limited partners are the investors* and consist mainly of institutions, such as pension funds, endowments, and private banks, as well as high-income individual investors. Because hedge funds are unregulated, they can be sold only to "accredited investors," meaning the individual investor must have a net worth in excess of $1 million and/or an annual income (from qualified sources) of at least $200,000 to $300,000. Many hedge funds are, by choice, even more restrictive and limit their investors to only *very*-high-net-worth individuals; in addition, some hedge funds limit the number of investors they'll let in (often to no more than 100 investors).

These practices, of course, stand in stark contrast to the way mutual funds perform. That is, while hedge funds are largely unregulated, mutual funds are very highly regulated and monitored. In addition, individuals don't need to qualify or be accredited to invest in mutual funds. Although some mutual funds do have minimum investments of $50,000 to $100,000 or more, they are the exception rather than the rule. Not so with hedge funds—many of them have minimum investments that can run into the millions of dollars! Also, mutual fund performance is open for all to see, whereas hedge funds simply don't divulge such information, at least not to the general public. Indeed, mutual funds are required by law to provide certain periodic and standardized pricing and valuation information to investors, as well as the general public, while hedge funds are totally free from such requirements. Try to get a

hedge fund
a type of unregulated investment vehicle that invests money for a very select group of institutional and high-net-worth individual investors; the investment objectives usually are to not only preserve capital, but also deliver positive returns in all market conditions.

price quote or a public report on a hedge fund and you're likely to run into a brick wall—that world (of hedge funds) is very secretive and about as *non-transparent* as you can get.

Hedge funds and mutual funds are similar in one respect, however: Both are pooled investment vehicles that accept investors' money and invest those funds on a collective basis. Put another way, *both sell shares (or participation) in a professionally managed portfolio of securities.* Most hedge funds structure their portfolios so as to reduce volatility and risk, while trying to preserve capital (i.e., "hedge" against market downturns) and still deliver positive returns under different market conditions. They do so by taking often very complex market positions that involve both long and short positions, the use of various arbitrage strategies (to lock in profits), as well as the use of options, futures, and other derivative securities. Indeed, hedge funds will invest in almost any opportunity in almost any market so long as impressive gains are believed to be available at reasonable levels of risk. Thus, these funds are anything but low-risk, fairly stable investment vehicles. In 2002, it was *estimated* (because hedge funds are largely unregulated, no accurate records are available) that there were approximately 4,200 hedge funds in existence, which in total had about $550 billion under management.

IN REVIEW

CONCEPTS

13.1 What is a *mutual fund?* Discuss the mutual fund concept, including the importance of diversification and professional management.

13.2 What are the attractions and drawbacks of mutual fund ownership?

13.3 Briefly describe how a mutual fund is organized. Who are the key players in a typical mutual fund organization?

13.4 Define each of the following:
   a. Open-end investment companies
   b. Closed-end investment companies
   c. Exchange-traded funds
   d. Unit investment trusts
   e. Hedge funds

13.5 What is the difference between a *load fund* and a *no-load fund?* What are the advantages of each type? What is a 12(b)-1 fund? Can such a fund operate as a no-load fund?

13.6 Describe a *back-end load,* a *low load,* and a *hidden load.* How can you tell what kind of fees and charges a fund has?

Types of Funds and Services

LG 3   LG 4

Some mutual funds specialize in stocks, others in bonds. Some have maximum capital gains as an investment objective, some high current income. Some funds appeal to speculators, others are of interest primarily to income-oriented investors. Every fund has a particular investment objective, and each fund is expected to do its best to conform to its stated investment policy and objective. Categorizing funds according to their investment policies and objectives is a common practice in the mutual fund industry. The categories indicate similarities in how the funds manage their money, and also their risk and return characteristics. Some of the more popular types of mutual funds are growth, aggressive growth, value, equity-income, balanced, growth-and-income, bond, money market, index, sector, socially responsible, asset allocation, and international funds.

Of course, it's possible to define fund categories based on something other than stated investment objectives. For example, Morningstar, the industry's leading research and reporting service, has developed *a classification system based on a fund's portfolio position*. Essentially, the firm carefully evaluates the make-up of a fund's portfolio to determine where its security holdings are concentrated. It then uses that information to classify funds on the basis of investment style (growth, value, or blend), market segment (small-, mid-, or large-cap), or other factors. Such information has been found to be especially useful in helping *mutual fund investors make informed asset allocation decisions* when structuring or rebalancing their own portfolios. That benefit notwithstanding, let's stick with the investment-objective classification system noted above, and examine the various types of mutual funds to see what they are and how they operate.

Types of Mutual Funds

growth fund
a mutual fund whose primary goals are capital gains and long-term growth.

Growth Funds The objective of a **growth fund** is simple: capital appreciation. Long-term growth and capital gains are the primary goals. Growth funds invest principally in well-established, large- or mid-cap companies that have above-average growth potential. They may offer little (if anything) in the way of dividends and current income. Because of the uncertain nature of their investment income, growth funds may involve a fair amount of risk exposure. They are usually viewed as long-term investment vehicles most suitable for the more aggressive investor who wants to build up capital and has little interest in current income.

aggressive growth fund
a highly speculative mutual fund that seeks large profits from capital gains.

Aggressive Growth Funds Aggressive growth funds are the so-called performance funds that tend to increase in popularity when markets heat up. **Aggressive growth funds** are highly speculative investment vehicles that seek large profits from capital gains. Most are fairly small (60% of these funds have assets under management of less than $50 million), and their portfolios consist mainly of "high-flying" common stocks. These funds often buy stocks of small, unseasoned companies, stocks with relatively high price/earnings multiples, and common stocks whose prices are highly volatile. They seem to be especially fond of turnaround situations and may even use leverage in their portfolios (i.e., buy stocks on margin); they also use options fairly aggressively, various hedging techniques, and perhaps even short selling. These techniques are designed, of course, to yield big returns. But aggressive funds are also highly speculative and are among the most volatile of all mutual funds. When the markets are good, aggressive growth funds do well; conversely, when the markets are bad, these funds often experience substantial losses.

value fund
a mutual fund that seeks stocks that are undervalued in the market by investing in shares that have low P/E multiples, high dividend yields, and promising futures.

Value Funds **Value funds** confine their investing to stocks considered to be *undervalued* by the market. That is, the funds look for stocks that are fundamentally sound but have yet to be discovered. These funds hold stocks as much for their underlying intrinsic value as for their *growth potential*. In stark

HOT LINKS

For more information on fund objectives, go to the sites below and read the sections on investment strategy.

www.fool.com/school/mutualfunds/
basic/read.htm
www.wachovia.com/misc/0,,133,00.html
www.axaonline.com/rs/3p/sp/5058.html

contrast to growth funds, value funds look for stocks with relatively low price/earnings ratios, high dividend yields, and moderate amounts of financial leverage. They prefer undiscovered companies that offer the potential for growth, rather than those that are already experiencing rapid growth.

Value investing is not easy. It involves extensive evaluation of corporate financial statements and any other documents that will help fund managers uncover value (investment opportunities) *before the rest of the market does* (that's the key to the low P/Es). And the approach seems to work. For even though value investing is generally regarded as *less risky* than growth investing (lower P/Es, higher dividend yields, and fundamentally stronger companies all translate into reduced risk exposure), the long-term return to investors in value funds is competitive with that from growth funds and even aggressive growth funds. Thus, value funds are often viewed as a viable investment alternative for relatively conservative investors who are looking for the attractive returns that common stocks have to offer, yet want to keep share price volatility and investment risk in check.

equity-income fund
a mutual fund that emphasizes current income and capital preservation and invests primarily in high-yielding common stocks.

Equity-Income Funds Equity-income funds emphasize current income by investing primarily in high-yielding common stocks. Capital preservation is also important, and so are capital gains, although capital appreciation is not a primary objective of equity-income funds. These funds invest heavily in high-grade common stocks, some convertible securities and preferred stocks, and occasionally even junk bonds or certain types of high-grade foreign bonds. As far as their stock holdings are concerned, they lean heavily toward blue chips (including perhaps even "baby blues"), public utilities, and financial shares. They like securities that generate hefty dividend yields but also consider potential price appreciation over the longer haul. In general, because of their emphasis on dividends and current income, these funds tend to hold higher-quality securities that are subject to less price volatility than the market as a whole. They're generally viewed as a fairly low-risk way of investing in stocks.

balanced fund
a mutual fund whose objective is to generate a balanced return of both current income and long-term capital gains.

Balanced Funds Balanced funds tend to hold a balanced portfolio of both stocks and bonds for the purpose of generating a well-balanced return of both current income and long-term capital gains. In many respects, they're much like equity-income funds, but balanced funds usually put more into fixed-income securities; generally, they keep at least 25% to 50% of their portfolios in bonds. The bonds are used principally to provide current income, and stocks are selected mainly for their long-term growth potential.

The funds can, of course, shift the emphasis in their security holdings one way or the other. Clearly, the more the fund leans toward fixed-income securities, the more income-oriented it will be. For the most part, balanced funds tend to confine their investing to high-grade securities, including growth-oriented blue-chip stocks, high-quality income shares, and high-yielding investment-grade bonds. Balanced funds are usually considered a relatively safe form of investing, in which you can earn a competitive rate of return without having to endure a lot of price volatility. (*Note:* Equity-income funds and the more income-oriented balanced funds, as well as certain types of bond funds, are sometimes all lumped together and referred to as *income funds*, because of their emphasis on generating high levels of current income.)

growth-and-income fund
a mutual fund that seeks both long-term growth and current income, with primary emphasis on capital gains.

Growth-and-Income Funds **Growth-and-income funds** also seek a balanced return made up of both current income and long-term capital gains, but they place a greater emphasis on growth of capital. Unlike balanced funds, growth-and-income funds put most of their money into equities. In fact, it's not unusual for these funds to have 80% to 90% of their capital in common stocks. They tend to confine most of their investing to quality issues, so growth-oriented blue-chip stocks appear in their portfolios, along with a fair amount of high-quality income stocks. Part of the appeal of these funds is the fairly substantial returns many have generated over the long haul. Of course, these funds involve a fair amount of risk, if for no other reason than the emphasis they place on stocks and capital gains. Thus growth-and-income funds are most suitable for those investors who can tolerate the risk and price volatility.

bond fund
a mutual fund that invests in various kinds and grades of bonds, with income as the primary objective.

Bond Funds As the name implies, **bond funds** invest exclusively in various types and grades of bonds—from Treasury and agency bonds to corporates and municipals. Income is the primary investment objective, although capital gains are not ignored. There are three important advantages to buying shares in bond funds rather than investing directly in bonds. First, the bond funds are generally more liquid than direct investments in bonds. Second, they offer a cost-effective way of achieving a high degree of diversification in an otherwise expensive investment vehicle. (Most bonds carry minimum denominations of $1,000 to $5,000.) Third, bond funds will automatically reinvest interest and other income, thereby allowing the investor to earn fully compounded rates of return.

Bond funds are generally considered to be a fairly conservative form of investment. But they are not without risk; that's because *the prices of the bonds held in the fund's portfolio fluctuate with changing interest rates.* Many bond funds are managed pretty conservatively, but a growing number are becoming increasingly aggressive. In fact, a lot of the growth that bond funds have experienced recently can be attributed to this more active investment posture. Some of that growth, however, can also be traced to the 2000–2002 bear market in stocks. During that time investors drew a lot of their money out of stocks and put it into safer and higher-yielding bonds. Indeed, from year-end 1999 to year-end 2002, the amount of assets under management in bond funds grew from some $800 billion (or 12% of total mutual fund assets) to more than $1.1 trillion (nearly 18% of total assets).

In today's market, investors can find everything from high-grade government bond funds to highly speculative funds that invest in nothing but junk bonds or even in highly volatile derivative securities. Here's a list of the different types of domestic bond funds available to investors:

- *Government bond funds,* which invest in U.S. Treasury and agency securities.

- *Mortgage-backed bond funds,* which put their money into various types of mortgage-backed securities of the U.S. government (e.g., GNMA issues). These funds appeal to investors for several reasons: (1) They provide diversification. (2) They are an affordable way to get into mortgage-backed securities. (3) They allow investors (if they so choose) to reinvest the principal portion of the monthly cash flow, thereby enabling them to preserve rather than consume their capital.

- *High-grade corporate bond funds,* which invest chiefly in investment-grade securities rated triple-B or better.

- *High-yield corporate bond funds,* which are risky investments that buy junk bonds for the yields they offer.

- *Convertible bond funds,* which invest primarily in securities (domestic and possibly foreign) that can be converted or exchanged into common stocks. These funds offer investors some of the price stability of bonds, along with the capital appreciation potential of stocks.

- *Municipal bond funds,* which invest in tax-exempt securities and are suitable for investors who seek tax-free income. Like their corporate counterparts, municipal funds can be packaged as either high-grade or high-yield funds. A special type of municipal bond fund is the so-called *single-state fund,* which invests in the municipal issues of only one state, thus producing (for residents of that state) interest income that is *fully exempt* from both federal and state taxes (and possibly even local/city taxes as well).

- *Intermediate-term bond funds,* which invest in bonds with maturities of 7 to 10 years or less and offer not only attractive yields but relatively low price volatility as well. Shorter (2- to 5-year) funds are also available; these shorter-term funds are often used as substitutes for money market investments by investors looking for higher returns on their money, especially when short-term rates are way down.

Clearly, no matter what you're looking for in a fixed-income security, you're likely to find a bond fund that fits the bill. The number and variety of such funds have skyrocketed in the past 15 years or so, and by mid-2003, there were over 2,000 publicly traded bond funds that together had more than $1.1 *trillion* worth of bonds under management.

money market mutual fund (money fund)
a mutual fund that pools the capital of investors and uses it to invest in short-term money market instruments.

Money Market Funds The first **money market mutual fund,** or **money fund** for short, was set up in November 1972 with just $100,000 in total assets. It was a new idea that applied the mutual fund concept to the buying and selling of short-term money market instruments—bank certificates of deposit, U.S. Treasury bills, and the like. For the first time, investors with modest amounts of capital were given access to the high-yielding money market, where many instruments require minimum investments of $100,000 or more. The idea caught on quickly, and the growth in money funds was nothing short of phenomenal. That growth temporarily peaked in 1982, when the introduction of money market deposit accounts by banks and S&Ls caused money fund assets to level off and eventually decline. It didn't take long for the industry to recover, however, and by mid-2003, there were some 1,000 money funds that together held nearly $2.3 trillion in assets.

There are several different kinds of money market mutual funds:

- *General-purpose money funds,* which invest in any and all types of money market investment vehicles, from Treasury bills and bank CDs to corporate commercial paper. The vast majority of money funds are of this type. They invest their money wherever they can find attractive short-term yields.

- *Government securities money funds,* which were established as a way to meet investor concerns for safety. They effectively eliminate any risk of default by confining their investments to Treasury bills and other short-term securities of the U.S. government, or its agencies.

- *Tax-exempt money funds*, which limit their investing to very short (30- to 90-day) tax-exempt municipal securities. Because their income is free from federal income taxes, they appeal predominantly to investors in high tax brackets. The yields on these funds are about 20% to 30% below the returns on other types of money funds, so you need to be in a high enough tax bracket to produce a competitive after-tax return. Some tax-exempt funds confine their investing to the securities of a single state so that residents of high-tax states can enjoy income that's free from both federal and state taxes.

Just about every major brokerage firm has at least four or five money funds of its own, and hundreds more are sold by independent fund distributors. Most require minimum investments of $1,000 (although $2,500 to $5,000 minimums are not uncommon). Because the maximum average maturity of their holdings cannot exceed 90 days, money funds are highly liquid investment vehicles. They're also very low in risk and virtually immune to capital loss, because at least 95% of the fund's assets must be invested in top-rated/prime-grade securities. On the other hand, since the fund's interest income tends to follow general interest rate conditions, the returns to shareholders are subject to the ups and downs of market interest rates. Even so, the yields on money funds are highly competitive with those of other short-term securities. And with the check-writing privileges they offer, money funds are just as liquid as checking or savings accounts. They are viewed by many investors as a convenient, safe, and (reasonably) profitable way to accumulate capital and temporarily store idle funds.

Index Funds "If you can't beat 'em, join 'em." That saying pretty much describes the idea behind index funds. Essentially, an **index fund** is a type of mutual fund that buys and holds a portfolio of stocks (or bonds) equivalent to those in a market index like the S&P 500. An index fund that's trying to match the S&P 500, for example, would hold the same 500 stocks that are held in that index, in exactly (or very nearly) the same proportions. Rather than trying to beat the market, as most actively managed funds do, *index funds simply try to match the market*. That is, they seek to match the performance of the index on which the fund is based. They do this through low-cost investment management. In fact, in most cases, the whole portfolio is run almost entirely by a computer that matches the fund's holdings with those of the targeted index.

The approach of index funds is strictly buy-and-hold. Indeed, about the only time an index-fund portfolio changes is when the targeted market index alters its "market basket" of securities. (Occasionally an index will drop a few securities and replace them with new ones.) A pleasant by-product of this buy-and-hold approach is that the funds have extremely low portfolio turnover rates and, therefore, very little in *realized* capital gains. As a result, aside from a modest amount of dividend income, these funds produce very little taxable income from year to year, which leads many high-income investors to view them as a type of tax-sheltered investment.

In addition to their tax shelter, these funds provide something else: By simply trying to match the market, index funds actually produce *highly competitive returns*. It's very tough to outperform the market, whether you are a professional money manager or a seasoned individual investor. Index funds readily acknowledge this fact and don't even try to outperform the market;

index fund
a mutual fund that buys and holds a portfolio of stocks (or bonds) equivalent to those in a specific market index.

instead, all they try to do is match market returns. Surprisingly, the net result of this strategy, combined with *a very low cost structure,* is that most index funds outperform the vast majority of all other types of stock funds. Historical data show that only about 20% to 25% of stock funds outperform the market. Because an index fund pretty much matches the market, these funds tend to produce better returns than 75% to 80% of competing stock funds. Granted, every now and then the fully managed stock funds will have a year (or two) when they outperform index funds. But these are the exception rather than the rule, especially when you look at multi-year returns, covering periods of 3 to 5 years or more—indeed, over most multi-year periods, the vast majority of fully managed stock funds just can't keep up with index funds.

Besides the S&P 500, which is the most popular index, a number of other market indexes are used, including the S&P Midcap 400, the Russell 2000 Small Stock, and the Wilshire 5000 indexes, as well as value-stock indexes, growth-stock indexes, international-stock indexes, and even bond indexes. When picking index funds, be sure to avoid high-cost funds, as such fees significantly *reduce* the chance that the fund will be able to match the market. Also, avoid index funds that use gimmicks as a way to "enhance" yields: That is, rather than follow the index, these funds will "tilt" their portfolios in an attempt to outperform the market. Your best bet is to buy a *true* index fund (one that has no added "bells and whistles"), and a low-cost one at that.

sector fund
a mutual fund that restricts its investments to a particular segment of the market.

Sector Funds One of the hottest products on Wall Street is the so-called **sector fund**, a mutual fund that restricts its investments to a particular sector (or segment) of the market. These funds concentrate their investment holdings in one or more industries that make up the sector being aimed at. For example, a health care sector fund would focus on such industries as drug companies, hospital management firms, medical suppliers, and biotech concerns. The portfolio of a sector fund would consist of promising growth stocks from these particular industries. Among the more popular sector funds are those that concentrate their investments in technology, financial services, leisure and entertainment, real estate (REITs), natural resources, electronics, chemicals, computers, telecommunications, utilities, and, of course, health care—all the "glamour" industries.

The overriding investment objective of a sector fund is *capital gains.* A sector fund is similar to a growth fund in many respects and should be considered speculative. The sector fund concept is based on the belief that the really attractive returns come from small segments of the market. So rather than diversifying your portfolio across the market, put your money where the action is! It's an interesting notion that may warrant consideration by investors willing to take on the added risks that often accompany these funds.

socially responsible fund
a mutual fund that actively and directly incorporates ethics and morality into the investment decision.

Socially Responsible Funds For some, investing is far more than just cranking out financial ratios and calculating investment results. To these investors, the security selection process doesn't end with bottom lines, P/E ratios, growth rates, and betas. Rather, it also includes the *active, explicit consideration of moral, ethical, and environmental issues.* The idea is that social concerns should play just as big a role in investment decisions as do profits and other financial matters. Not surprisingly, a number of funds cater to such investors: Known as **socially responsible funds,** they actively and directly incorporate ethics and morality into the investment decision. Their investment decisions, in effect, revolve around *both* morality and profitability.

Socially responsible funds consider only certain companies for inclusion in their portfolios. If a company doesn't meet the fund's moral, ethical, or environmental tests, fund managers simply won't consider buying the stock, no matter how good the bottom line looks. Generally speaking, these funds refrain from investing in companies that derive revenues from tobacco, alcohol, gambling, or weapons, or that operate nuclear power plants. In addition, the funds tend to favor firms that produce "responsible" products or services, that have strong employee relations and positive environmental records, and that are socially responsive to the communities in which they operate. Although these screens might seem to eliminate a lot of stocks from consideration, these funds (most of which are fairly small) still find plenty of securities to choose from. As far as performance is concerned, the general perception is that there's a price to pay, in the form of lower average returns, for socially responsible investing. For example, in late 2003, year-to-date returns on 149 socially responsible funds averaged slightly less than 14.0%, whereas domestic stock funds in general turned in year-to-date returns of 20.6%. Such comparative performance should come as no surprise, however, for whenever you add more investment hurdles, you're likely to reduce return potential. But to those who truly believe in socially responsible investing, the sacrifice apparently is worth it.

Asset Allocation Funds   Studies have shown that the most important decision an investor can make is where to allocate his or her investment assets. As we saw in Chapter 5, *asset allocation* involves deciding how you're going to divide up your investments among different types of securities. For example, what portion of your money do you want to devote to money market securities, what portion to stocks, and what portion to bonds? Asset allocation deals in broad terms (types of securities) and does not address individual security selection. Strange as it may seem, asset allocation has been found to be a far more important determinant of total portfolio returns than individual security selection.

Because many individual investors have a tough time making asset allocation decisions, the mutual fund industry has created a product to do the job for them. Known as **asset allocation funds**, these funds spread investors' money across different types of markets. That is, whereas most mutual funds concentrate on one type of investment—whether stocks, bonds, or money market securities—asset allocation funds put money into all these markets. Many of them also include foreign securities in the asset allocation scheme. Some even include inflation-resistant investments, such as gold or real estate. By mid-year 2003, there were nearly 200 asset allocation funds in existence. All were designed for people who want to hire fund managers not only to select individual securities but also to allocate money among the various markets.

Here's how a typical asset allocation fund works. The money manager establishes a desired allocation mix, which might look something like this: 50% of the portfolio goes to U.S. stocks, 30% to bonds, 10% to foreign securities, and 10% to money market securities. Securities are then purchased for the fund in these proportions, and the overall portfolio maintains the desired mix. Actually, each segment of the fund is managed almost as a separate portfolio. Thus securities within, say, the stock portion are bought, sold, and held as the market dictates.

What really separates asset allocation funds from the rest of the pack is that *as market conditions change over time, the asset allocation mix changes*

asset allocation fund
a mutual fund that spreads investors' money across stocks, bonds, money market securities, and possibly other asset classes.

as well. For example, if the U.S. stock market starts to soften, funds will be moved out of stocks to some other area. As a result, the stock portion of the portfolio might drop to, say, 35%, and the foreign securities portion might increase to 25%. Of course, there's no assurance that the money manager will make the right moves at the right time, but the expectation is that he or she will. (It's interesting to note that *balanced funds* are really a form of asset allocation fund, except that they tend to follow a *fixed-mix* approach to asset allocation. That is, the fund may put, say, 60% of the portfolio into stocks and 40% into bonds, and then pretty much stick to that mix, no matter what the markets are doing.)

Asset allocation funds are supposed to provide investors with one-stop shopping. That is, rather than buying a couple of stock funds, a couple of bond funds, and so on, you find an asset allocation fund that fits your needs and invest in it. The success of these funds rests not only on how well the money manager picks securities but also on how well he or she times the market and moves capital among different segments of the market.

international fund
a mutual fund that does all or most of its investing in foreign securities.

International Funds In their search for higher yields and better returns, U.S. investors have shown a growing interest in foreign securities. Sensing an opportunity, the mutual fund industry has been quick to respond with a proliferation of so-called **international funds**—a type of mutual fund that does all or most of its investing in foreign securities. Just compare the number of international funds that are around today with those in existence a few years ago: In 1985 there were only about 40 of these funds; by 2003, the number had grown to more than 750. The fact is that a lot of people would like to invest in foreign securities but simply don't have the experience or know-how to do so. International funds may be just the vehicle for such investors, *provided they have at least a basic appreciation of international economics*. Because these funds deal with the international economy, balance-of-trade positions, and currency valuations, investors should have a fundamental understanding of what these issues are and how they can affect fund returns.

Technically, the term *international fund* describes a type of fund that invests *exclusively in foreign securities*. Such funds often confine their activities to specific geographic regions (e.g., Mexico, Australia, Europe, or the Pacific Rim). In contrast, *global funds* invest not only in foreign securities but also in U.S. companies—usually multinational firms. As a rule, global funds provide more diversity and, with access to both foreign and domestic markets, can go wherever the action is.

Regardless of whether they're global or international (we'll use the term *international* to apply to both), you'll find just about any type of fund you could possibly want in the international sector. There are international stock funds, international bond funds, even international money market funds. There are aggressive growth funds, balanced funds, long-term growth funds, high-grade bond funds, and so forth. There are funds that confine their investing to large, established markets (like Japan, Germany, and Australia) and others that stick to the more exotic (and risky) emerging markets (such as Thailand, Mexico, Chile, and even former Communist countries like Poland). No matter what your investment philosophy or objective, you're likely to find what you're looking for in the international area.

Basically, these funds attempt to take advantage of international economic developments in two ways: (1) by capitalizing on changing market conditions and (2) by positioning themselves to benefit from devaluation of the dollar. They can make money either from rising share prices in a foreign market or, perhaps just as important, from a falling dollar (which in itself produces capital gains for U.S. investors in international funds). Many of these funds, however, attempt to protect their investors from currency exchange risks by using various types of *hedging strategies*. That is, by using foreign currency options and futures, or some other type of derivative product (some of which are discussed in Chapters 15 and 16), the fund tries to eliminate (or reduce) the effects of fluctuating currency exchange rates. Some funds, in fact, do this on a permanent basis: In essence, these funds try to hedge away exchange risk so that they can concentrate on the higher returns offered by the foreign securities themselves. Others use currency hedges only occasionally, when they feel there's a real chance of a substantial swing in currency values. But even with currency hedging, international funds are still considered fairly high-risk investments and should be used only by investors who understand and are able to tolerate such risks.

Investor Services

Ask most investors why they buy a particular mutual fund and they'll probably tell you that the fund provides the kind of income and return they're looking for. Now, no one would question the importance of return in the investment decision, but there are some other important reasons for investing in mutual funds, not the least of which are the valuable services they provide. Some of the most sought-after *mutual fund services* are automatic investment and reinvestment plans, regular income programs, conversion and phone-switching privileges, and retirement programs.

Automatic Investment Plans   It takes money to make money. For an investor, that means being able to accumulate the capital to put into the market. Unfortunately, that's not always easy. But mutual funds have come up with a program that makes savings and capital accumulation as painless as possible. The program is the **automatic investment plan.** This service allows fund shareholders to automatically funnel fixed amounts of money *from their paychecks or bank accounts* into a mutual fund. It's much like a payroll deduction plan.

> **automatic investment plan**
> a mutual fund service that allows shareholders to automatically send fixed amounts of money from their paychecks or bank accounts into the fund.

This fund service has become very popular, because it enables shareholders to invest on a regular basis without having to think about it. Just about every fund group offers some kind of automatic investment plan for virtually all of its stock and bond funds. To enroll, you simply fill out a form authorizing the fund to siphon a set amount (usually a minimum of $25 to $100 per period) from your bank account or paycheck at regular intervals, such as monthly or quarterly. Once enrolled, you'll be buying more shares every month or quarter (most funds deal in fractional shares). Of course, if it's a load fund, you'll still have to pay normal sales charges on your periodic investments. To remain diversified, you can divide your money among as many funds (within a given fund family) as you like. Finally, you can get out of the program at any time, without penalty, by simply calling the fund. Although convenience is perhaps the chief advantage of automatic investment plans, they also make solid investment sense: One of the best ways of building up a sizable amount of capital is to *add funds to your investment program system-*

atically over time. The importance of making regular contributions to your investment portfolio cannot be overstated; it ranks right up there with compound interest.

Automatic Reinvestment Plans An automatic reinvestment plan is another of the real draws of mutual funds and is offered by just about every open-end fund. Whereas automatic investment plans deal with money the shareholder is putting into a fund, automatic *re*investment plans deal with the dividends the funds pay to their shareholders. Much like the dividend reinvestment plans we looked at with stocks (in Chapter 6), the **automatic reinvestment plans** of mutual funds enable you to keep your capital fully employed. Through this service, dividend and/or capital gains income is automatically used to buy additional shares in the fund (most funds deal in fractional shares). Such purchases are often commission-free. Keep in mind, however, that even though you may reinvest all dividends and capital gains distributions, the IRS still treats them as cash receipts and taxes them as investment income in the year in which they were received.

Automatic reinvestment plans are especially attractive because they enable you to earn fully compounded rates of return. That is, by plowing back profits, you can essentially put them to work in generating even more earnings. Indeed, the effects of these plans on total accumulated capital over the long run can be substantial. Figure 13.6 (on page 572) shows the long-term impact of one such plan. (These are the actual performance numbers for a *real* mutual fund, Vanguard Health Care.) In the illustration, we assume the investor starts out with $10,000 and, except for the reinvestment of dividends and capital gains, *adds no new capital over time*. Even so, note that the initial investment of $10,000 grew to $145,000 over a 15-year period (which amounts to a compounded rate of return of almost 20%). Of course, not all periods will match this performance, nor will all mutual funds be able to perform as well, even in strong markets. The point is that as long as care is taken in selecting an appropriate fund, *attractive benefits can be derived from the systematic accumulation of capital offered by automatic reinvestment plans*.

Regular Income Although automatic investment and reinvestment plans are great for the long-term investor, what about the investor who's looking for a steady stream of income? Once again, mutual funds have a service to meet this need. Called a **systematic withdrawal plan**, it's offered by most open-end funds. Once enrolled in one of these plans, an investor automatically receives a predetermined amount of money every month or quarter. Most funds require a minimum investment of $5,000 or more to participate. The size of the minimum payment must normally be $50 or more per period (with no limit on the maximum). The funds will pay out the monthly or quarterly income first from dividends and realized capital gains. If this source proves to be inadequate and the shareholder so authorizes, the fund can then tap the principal or original paid-in capital to meet the required periodic payments.

Conversion Privileges and Phone Switching Sometimes investors find it necessary to switch out of one fund and into another. For example, an investor's objectives or the investment climate itself may have changed. **Conversion** (or **exchange**) **privileges** were devised to meet such needs conveniently and economically. Investment management companies that offer a

automatic reinvestment plan
a mutual fund service that enables shareholders to automatically buy additional shares in the fund through the reinvestment of dividends and capital gains income.

systematic withdrawal plan
a mutual fund service that enables shareholders to automatically receive a predetermined amount of money every month or quarter.

conversion (exchange) privilege
feature of a mutual fund that allows shareholders to move money from one fund to another, within the same family of funds.

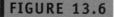

FIGURE 13.6   **The Effects of Reinvesting Income**

Reinvesting dividends or capital gains can have a tremendous impact on one's investment position. This graph shows the results of a hypothetical investor who initially invested $10,000 in Vanguard Health Care and, for a period of 15 years, reinvested all dividends and capital gains distributions in additional fund shares. (No adjustment has been made for any income taxes payable by the shareholder, which is appropriate so long as the fund was held in an IRA or Keogh account.) (*Source: Morningstar Principia for Mutual Funds*, June 30, 2003.)

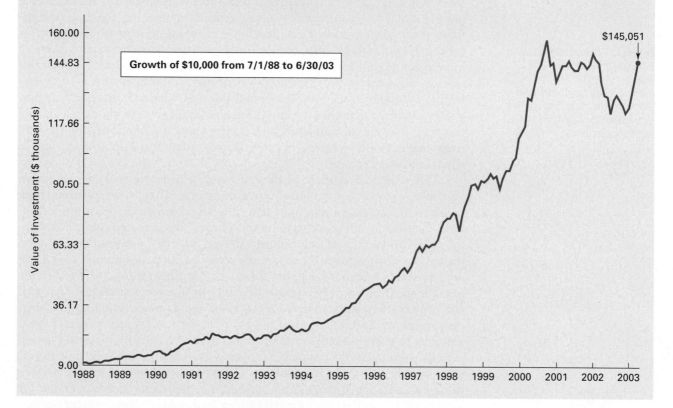

fund families
different kinds of mutual funds offered by a single investment management company.

number of different funds—known as **fund families**—often provide conversion privileges. These enable shareholders to move easily from one fund to another. With *phone switching* you simply pick up the phone to move money among funds. The only constraint is that the switches must be confined to the same *family* of funds. For example, you can switch from a Dreyfus growth fund to a Dreyfus money fund, or any other fund managed by Dreyfus.

With some fund families, the alternatives open to investors seem almost without limit. Indeed, some of the larger families offer literally hundreds of funds. Fidelity has over 300 different funds in its family: from high-performance stock funds to bond funds, tax-exempt funds, a couple of dozen sector funds, and a couple of dozen money funds. More than 400 fund families are in operation today. The two biggest—Fidelity and Vanguard—each has more than *half-a-trillion dollars* in assets under management, and that *excludes* their money market funds. Other big fund families include American Funds ($400 billion under management), Franklin/Templeton ($175 billion), Putnam ($150 billion), and PIMCO ($140 billion). Each of these, and all the other fund families, provide low-cost conversion/phone-switching privileges. Some even provide these privileges for free, although most have limits on the number of times such switches can occur each year.

Conversion privileges are usually considered beneficial for shareholders, as they allow investors to meet their ever-changing long-term goals. They also permit investors to manage their mutual fund holdings more aggressively by allowing them to move in and out of funds as the investment environment changes. Unfortunately, there is one major drawback: For tax purposes, the exchange of shares from one fund to another is regarded as a sale transaction followed by a subsequent purchase of a new security. As a result, if any capital gains exist at the time of the exchange, the investor is liable for the taxes on that profit, even though the holdings were not truly "liquidated."

Retirement Programs As a result of government legislation, self-employed individuals are permitted to divert a portion of their pretax income into self-directed retirement plans. And all working Americans, whether or not they are self-employed, are allowed to establish individual retirement arrangements (IRAs). Indeed, with legislation passed in 1997, *qualified investors* can now choose between deductible and nondeductible (Roth) IRAs. Even those who make too much to qualify for one of these programs can set up special non- deductible IRAs. Today all mutual funds provide a special service that allows individuals to set up tax-deferred retirement programs as either IRA or Keogh accounts—or, through their place of employment, to participate in a tax-sheltered retirement plan, such as a 401(k). The funds set up the plans and handle all the administrative details so that the shareholder can easily take full advantage of available tax savings.

H O T

You can obtain details on the various IRA programs, as well as other tax-sheltered retirement plans at the book's Web site. Click on the Web chapter titled "Tax-Advantaged Investments" and then on "Tax Deferred Retirement Programs." To access our Web site, go to:

www.aw-bc.com/gitman_joehnk

IN REVIEW

CONCEPTS

13.7 Briefly describe each of the following types of mutual funds:
a. Aggressive growth funds
b. Equity-income funds
c. Growth-and-income funds
d. Bond funds
e. Sector funds
f. Socially responsible funds

13.8 What is an *asset allocation fund,* and how does it differ from other types of mutual funds?

13.9 If growth, income, and capital preservation are the primary objectives of mutual funds, why do we bother to categorize funds by type? Do you think such classifications are helpful in the fund selection process? Explain.

13.10 What are *fund families?* What advantages do fund families offer investors? Are there any disadvantages?

13.11 Briefly describe some of the investor services provided by mutual funds. What are *automatic reinvestment plans,* and how do they differ from *automatic investment plans?* What is phone switching, and why would an investor want to use this service?

Investing in Mutual Funds

Suppose you are confronted with the following situation: You have money to invest and are trying to select the right place to put it. You obviously want to pick a security that meets your idea of acceptable risk and will generate an attractive rate of return. The problem is that you have to make the selection from a list of nearly 8,300 securities. Sound like a "mission impossible"? Well that's basically what you're up against when trying to select a suitable mutual fund. However, if you approach the problem systematically, it may not be so formidable a task. First, it might be helpful to examine more closely the various investor uses of mutual funds. With this background, we can then look at the selection process and at several measures of return that can be used to assess performance. As we will see, it is possible to whittle down the list of alternatives by matching your investment needs with the investment objectives of the funds.

Investor Uses of Mutual Funds

Mutual funds can be used in a variety of ways. For instance, performance funds can serve as a vehicle for capital appreciation, whereas bond funds can provide current income. Regardless of the kind of income a mutual fund provides, investors tend to use these securities for one of three reasons: (1) as a way to accumulate wealth, (2) as a storehouse of value, or (3) as a speculative vehicle for achieving high rates of return.

Accumulation of Wealth Accumulation of wealth is probably the most common reason for using mutual funds. Basically, the investor uses mutual funds over the long haul to build up investment capital. Depending on investor goals, a modest amount of risk may be acceptable, but usually preservation of capital and capital stability are considered important. The whole idea is to form a "partnership" with the mutual fund in building up as big a pool of capital as possible: *You provide the capital by systematically investing and reinvesting in the fund, and the fund provides the return by doing its best to invest your resources wisely.*

Storehouse of Value Investors also use mutual funds as a storehouse of value. The idea is to find a place where investment capital can be fairly secure and relatively free from deterioration yet still generate a relatively attractive rate of return. Short- and intermediate-term bond funds are logical choices for such purposes, and so are money funds. Capital preservation and income over the long term are very important to some investors. Others might seek storage of value only for the short term, using, for example, money funds as a place to "sit it out" until a more attractive opportunity comes along.

Speculation and Short-Term Trading Although speculation is becoming more common, it is still not widely used by mutual fund investors. The reason, of course, is that most mutual funds are long-term in nature and thus not meant to be used as aggressive trading vehicles. However, a growing number of funds (e.g., sector funds) now cater to speculators. Some investors have found that mutual funds are, in fact, attractive outlets for speculation and short-term trading.

One way to do this is to trade in and out of funds aggressively as the investment climate changes. Load charges can be avoided (or reduced) by dealing in

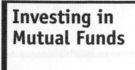

families of funds offering low-cost conversion privileges and/or by dealing only in no-load funds. Other investors might choose to invest in funds for the long run but still seek high rates of return by investing in aggressive mutual funds. A number of funds follow very aggressive trading strategies, which may appeal to investors willing to accept substantial risk exposure. These are usually the fairly specialized, smaller funds. Examples are sophisticated enhanced-yield funds, leverage funds, option funds, emerging-market funds, small-cap aggressive growth funds, and sector funds. In essence, investors in such funds are simply applying the basic mutual fund concept to their investment needs by letting professional money managers handle their accounts in a way they would like to see them handled: *aggressively.*

The Selection Process

When it comes to mutual funds, there is one question every investor has to answer right up front: Why invest in a mutual fund to begin with—why not just go it alone by buying individual stocks and bonds directly? For beginning investors and investors with little capital, the answer is simple: With mutual funds, investors are able to achieve far more diversification than they could ever get on their own, and they get the help of professional money managers at a very reasonable cost. For more seasoned investors, the answers are probably a bit more involved. Certainly, diversification and professional money management come into play, but there are other reasons as well. The competitive returns offered by mutual funds are a factor with many investors, as are the services they provide. Many seasoned investors simply have decided they can get better returns over the long haul by carefully selecting mutual funds than by investing on their own. As a result, they put all or a big chunk of their money into funds. Some of these investors use part of their capital to buy and sell individual securities on their own and use the rest *to buy mutual funds that invest in areas they don't fully understand or don't feel well informed about.* For example, they'll use mutual funds to get into foreign markets, to buy mortgage-backed securities, to buy junk bonds (where diversification is so very important), or to buy value funds (because that's such a tricky and time-consuming way to invest).

Once you have decided to use mutual funds, you have to decide which fund(s) to buy. In many respects, the selection process is critical in determining how much success you will have with mutual funds. It means putting into action all you know about funds, in order to gain as much return as possible from an acceptable level of risk. The selection process begins with an assessment of your own investment needs, which sets the tone of the investment program. Obviously, what you want to do is select from those 8,300 or so funds the one or two (or six or eight) that will best meet your total investment needs.

Objectives and Motives for Using Funds Selecting the right investment means finding those funds that are most suitable to your investment needs. The place to start is with your own investment objectives. In other words, why do you want to invest in a mutual fund, and what are you looking for in a fund? Obviously, an attractive rate of return would be desirable, but there is also the matter of a tolerable amount of risk exposure. Probably, when you look at your own risk temperament in relation to the various types of mutual funds available, you will discover that certain types of funds are more appealing to

KNOWING WHERE TO LOOK IS HALF THE BATTLE—If mutual fund prospectuses seemed daunting in the past, you might want to give them another try. The fund industry, in response to new SEC rules, now prepares more readable, streamlined prospectuses and offers fund profiles, briefer documents that provide key information in a tidy 2 to 6 pages. Here are some guidelines to help sort through the material:

Expenses: This critical section lists all fees and their amounts.

Investment Objectives: Here you will find a description of the fund's investment style and perhaps some information on the types of securities it will buy.

Long-Term Total Returns: Are they consistent or volatile? If they are missing from the prospectus, be wary: They might be low.

Management: Look at the fund manager's biography. How long has he or she managed the fund?

you than others. For instance, aggressive growth or sector funds are usually *not* attractive to individuals who wish to avoid high exposure to risk.

Another important factor in the selection process is the intended use of the mutual fund. That is, do you want to invest in mutual funds as a means of accumulating wealth, as a storehouse of value, or to speculate for high rates of return? This information puts into clearer focus the question of exactly what you are trying to do with your investment dollars. Finally, there is the matter of the types of services provided by the fund. If you are particularly interested in certain services, you should be sure to look for them in the funds you select. Having assessed what you are looking for in a fund, you are ready to look at what the funds have to offer.

What the Funds Offer Just as each individual has a set of investment needs, each fund has its own *investment objective,* its own *manner of operation,* and its own *range of services.* These three parameters are useful in helping you to assess investment alternatives. But where do you find such information? One obvious place is the fund's *profile,* or its prospectus, which supplies information on investment objectives, portfolio composition, management, and past performance. Publications such as the *Wall Street Journal, Barron's, Money, Fortune,* and *Forbes* also offer useful information about mutual funds. These sources provide a wealth of operating and performance statistics in a convenient and easy-to-read format. For instance, each year *Forbes* rates a couple thousand mutual funds, and every quarter *Barron's* publishes an extensive mutual fund performance report.

A number of reporting services also provide background information and assessments on funds. Among the best in this category are *Morningstar Mutual Funds* (a sample of which is shown in Figure 13.7), Wiesenberger's *Investment Companies* (an annual publication with quarterly updates), and *Value Line Mutual Fund Survey* (which produces a mutual fund report similar to its stock report). In addition, all sorts of performance statistics are available on disks and on the Internet for easy use on home computers. For example, quarterly or annually updated software is available, at very low cost, from Morningstar or from the American Association of Individual Investors (AAII). Using sources like these, investors can obtain information on such things as investment objectives, load charges and annual expense rates, summary portfolio analyses, services offered, historical statistics, and reviews of past performance.

Whittling Down the Alternatives At this point, fund selection becomes a process of elimination. A large number of funds can be eliminated from consideration simply because they fail to meet stated needs. Some funds may be too risky; others may be unsuitable as a storehouse of value. Thus, rather than trying to evaluate 8,300 different funds, you can narrow down the list to two or three *types* of funds that best match your investment needs. From here, you can whittle down the list a bit more by introducing other constraints. For example, because of cost considerations, you may want to deal only in no-load or low-load funds (more on this topic below). Or you may be seeking certain services that are important to your investment goals.

Now we introduce the final (but certainly not the least important) element in the selection process: the *fund's investment performance.* Useful information includes (1) how the fund has performed over the past 5 to 7 years, (2) the type of return it has generated in good markets as well as bad, (3) the level and

FIGURE 13.7 Some Relevant Information About Specific Mutual Funds

Investors who want in-depth information about the operating characteristics, investment holdings, and market behavior of specific mutual funds, such as the Clipper Fund profiled here, can usually find what they're looking for in publications like *Morningstar Mutual Funds* or, as shown here, from computer-based information sources like *Morningstar's Principia*. (*Source:* Morningstar, Inc., *Principia,* release date: June 30, 2003.)

Data through May 31, 2003 For internal and/or client reporting purposes only.

Clipper

	Ticker	Load	NAV	Yield	Total Assets	Mstar Category
	CFIMX	None	$79.63	1.3%	$4,659 mil	Large Value

Manager Strategy

This fund's management searches for established companies with dominant franchises but only buys ones trading at discounts of at least 30% to its estimates of intrinsic value. Management uses discounted cash-flow analysis to estimate a company's worth but uses the sale price of comparable companies if the latter value is more conservative. The managers also look for factors such as insiders who are buying company stock and share-repurchase programs. The fund is concentrated, holding just 20 to 30 names. It eschews pricey sectors such as technology, and it will sit on big bond or cash stakes if the managers can't find stocks cheap enough and financially strong enough to meet their criteria.

Historical Profile

Return High
Risk Below Avg
Rating ★★★★ Highest

76% 59% 72% 74% 66% 70% 92% 89%

Investment Style
Equity
Stock %

Portfolio Manager(s)

James H. Gipson. Since 02-84.
Michael C. Sandler. Since 02-84.
Bruce Veaco. Since 01-86.
Peter Quinn. Since 08-87.
Kelly Sucoka. Since 04-02.

	1992	1993	1994	1995	1996	1997	1998	1999	2000	2001	2002	05-03	History
	51.74	50.05	46.09	60.74	67.57	76.86	75.37	65.28	79.25	83.53	75.73	79.63	NAV
	15.90	11.26	-2.51	45.22	19.43	30.44	19.20	-2.02	37.40	10.26	-5.51	5.15	Total Return %
	8.28	1.20	-3.82	7.68	-3.51	-2.91	-9.38	-23.06	46.50	22.14	16.58	-5.19	+/-S&P 500
	2.09	-6.86	-0.52	6.87	-2.14	-4.74	3.56	-9.38	30.39	15.85	10.01	-5.04	+/-Russ 1000 VI
	1.99	1.46	1.41	1.64	1.37	2.01	2.26	2.98	2.86	1.36	1.29	0.00	Income Return %
	13.91	9.80	-3.92	43.58	18.06	28.43	16.94	-5.00	34.54	8.90	-6.80	5.15	Capital Return %
	12	68	75	1	56	24	9	83	1	3	1	97	Total Rtn % Rank Cat
	0.95	0.75	0.71	0.76	0.83	1.36	1.63	2.25	1.87	1.08	1.08	0.00	Income $
	3.02	6.73	2.00	5.42	4.27	9.83	12.86	6.16	8.38	2.75	2.11	0.00	Capital Gains $
	1.12	1.11	1.11	1.11	1.08	1.08	1.06	1.10	1.09	1.08	1.07	—	Expense Ratio %
	2.02	1.41	1.41	1.39	1.32	1.84	2.13	2.54	2.88	1.72	1.65	—	Income Ratio %
	46	64	45	31	24	31	65	63	46	23	48	—	Turnover Rate %
	210	240	247	404	543	824	1,234	961	1,366	2,685	5,002	4,659	Net Assets $mil

Performance 05-31-03

	1st Qtr	2nd Qtr	3rd Qtr	4th Qtr	Total
1999	-3.34	7.37	-4.31	-1.34	-2.02
2000	-3.03	5.55	16.20	15.54	37.40
2001	1.03	3.02	-2.52	8.67	10.26
2002	5.71	-6.22	-12.34	8.73	-5.51
2003	-10.17				

Trailing	Total Return%	-/- S&P 500	-/- Russ 1000 VI	%Rank All Cat	Growth of $10,000
3 Mo	15.24	0.21	-0.79	30 46	11,524
6 Mo	2.03	-1.84	-3.39	86 89	10,203
1 Yr	-6.93	1.13	0.92	54 13	9,307
3 Yr Avg	13.15	24.00	15.29	3 1	14,488
5 Yr Avg	10.67	11.74	9.60	2 1	16,599
10 Yr Avg	15.46	5.53	4.68	1 1	42,088
15 Yr Avg	15.26	3.61	3.31	2 2	84,139

Tax Analysis	Tax-Adj Rtn%	%Rank Cat	Tax-Cost Rat	%Rank Cat
3 Yr Avg	10.97	1	1.93	81
5 Yr Avg	7.61	1	2.76	90
10 Yr Avg	12.29	2	2.75	80

Potential Capital Gain Exposure: 0% of assets

Rating and Risk

Time Period	Load-Adj Return %	Morningstar Rtn vs Cat	Morningstar Risk vs Cat	Morningstar Risk-Adj Rating
1 Yr	-6.93			
3 Yr	13.15	High	Avg	★★★★★
5 Yr	10.67	High	-Avg	★★★★★
10 Yr	15.46	High	-Avg	★★★★★
Incept	15.75			

Other Measures	Standard Index S&P 500	Best Fit Index Russ 1000 VI
Alpha	18.6	14.6
Beta	0.52	0.80
R-Squared	38	70
Standard Deviation	17.81	
Mean	13.15	
Sharpe Ratio	0.58	

Portfolio Analysis 03-31-03

Share change since 12-02 Total Stocks:32	Sector	PE	YTD Ret%	% Assets
⊕ Freddie Mac	Financial	7.8	-14.82	8.73
⊕ Tyco Intl	Ind Mtrls	—	10.94	8.16
⊕ Electronic Data Sys	Business	9.6	23.46	6.71
⊕ Fannie Mae	Financial	16.3	6.85	5.44
⊕ Altria Group	Goods	7.9	11.74	5.03
⊕ Tenet Healthcare	Health	9.0	-26.77	4.15
⊕ American Express	Financial	20.7	19.45	4.03
⊕ El Paso	Energy	—	17.95	3.37
⊕ Equity Residential Prope	Financial	35.8	7.45	3.35
⊕ UST, Inc.	Goods	—	10.00	2.94
⊕ Wyeth	Health	13.2	28.07	2.71
⊕ Pfizer	Health	21.1	16.83	2.54
AOL Time Warner	Media	—	18.63	2.43
⊕ McDonald's	Consumer	24.3	39.12	2.40
⊕ Sara Lee	Goods	11.8	-14.64	2.36
⊕ Kraft Foods	Goods	16.5	-15.81	2.33
⊕ Safeway	Consumer	15.7	-15.28	2.17
⊕ CVS	Consumer	14.9	6.32	2.14
⊕ Merrill Lynch	Financial	16.5	21.49	2.09
⊕ Kroger	Consumer	10.3	2.91	1.93

Current Investment Style

Value Blnd Growth — Large Mid Small

	Market Cap %
Giant	26.7
Large	52.9
Mid	20.4
Small	0.0
Micro	0.0
Median $mil:	26,579

Value Measures		Rel S&P 500
Price/Earnings	9.8	0.6
Price/Book	1.4	0.6
Price/Sales	0.7	0.5
Price/Cash Flow	0.8	0.1
Dividend Yield %	3.1	1.8

Growth Measures	%	Rel S&P 500
Long-Term Erngs	15.9	1.2
Book Value	7.1	1.1
Sales	8.3	3.3
Cash Flow	27.8	4.2
Historical Erngs	13.2	1.2

Profitability	%	Rel S&P 500
Return on Equity	16.8	1.1
Return on Assets	8.2	1.2
Net Margin	8.5	0.9

Sector Weightings	% of Stocks	Rel S&P 500	3 Year High Low	
Info	2.7	0.1	—	
Software	0.0	0.0	0	0
Hardware	0.0	0.0	0	0
Media	2.7	0.8	3	0
Telecom	0.0	0.0	0	0
Service	68.4	1.5	—	
Health	12.4	1.0	12	0
Consumer	11.4	1.4	17	11
Business	11.5	2.8	17	11
Financial	33.1	1.6	39	33
Mfg	28.9	0.9	—	
Goods	14.6	1.3	24	11
Ind Mtrls	10.5	0.9	12	6
Energy	3.8	0.6	4	0
Utilities	0.0	0.0	0	0

Composition		
● Cash	7.7	
● Stocks	88.8	
● Bonds	2.3	
● Other	1.1	
Foreign	9.2	(% of Stock)

Morningstar's Take by Christopher Traulsen 06-15-03

Clipper Fund's current malaise comes with the territory.

This fund is up just 6.6% for the year to date through June 13, 2003, and it trails 99% of all large-value funds for the period. A lack of technology exposure has hurt. But by far the bigger issue has been stock-specific problems. One of the biggest is Freddie Mac, the fund's top holding as of March 31. Freddie is mired in scandal. Earnings are to be restated, a criminal probe is under way, and top executives have been shown the door. The stock is down 14%.

The managers' response to the Freddie debacle is telling. They didn't panic and sell. Instead, they held and tried to analyze the real risks of the situation. When all is said and done, they decided there's more smoke than fire here and think any earnings restatements should be in an upward direction. Such a measured response is typical; the team's value approach often leads it to buy controversial names. Tenet Healthcare, El Paso, and

Tyco were all purchases in 2002. Such companies limit the fund's price risk but expose it to substantial business risk. The latter is magnified by the fund's concentrated portfolio.

Fortunately, the managers here have proved themselves strong stock-pickers over time. They've built one of the finest long-term records in the mutual fund world, largely by using sell-offs to build positions in cheap companies. The fund is also a good diversifier, with a low R-squared relative to the S&P 500. Investors should note, however, that although the fund has been less volatile than its typical peer, its concentration and patience with struggling companies make it ill-suited for those with short time horizons.

This fund's minimum for taxable accounts has increased to $25,000 from $5,000. Those who don't want to put that much here could go with PBHG Clipper Focus instead, which has much lower minimums. Its portfolio is nearly the same as this fund's, but it is kept fully invested.

Address:	9601 Wilshire Boulevard Suite 828 Beverly Hills, CA 90210 800-776-5033	Minimum Purchase:	$25000	Add: $1000	IRA: $3000
		Min Auto Inv Plan:	$25000	Add: $150	
		Sales Fees:	No-load		
Web Address:	www.clipperfund.com	Management Fee:	1.00%		
Inception:	02-29-84	Actual Fees:	Mgt:1.00%	Dist: —	
Advisor:	Pacific Financial Research, Inc.	Expense Projections:	3Yr:$350	5Yr:$606	10Yr:$1340
Subadvisor:	None	Income Distrib:	Annually		
NTF Plans:	Fidelity Retail-NTF, CommonWealth NTF	Total Cost (relative to category):	Below Avg		

MORNINGSTAR® Mutual Funds

stability of dividend and capital gains distributions, and (4) the amount of volatility/risk in the fund's return. Note that the dividend and capital gains distribution is an important indication not only of how much current income the fund distributes annually but also of the fund's *tax efficiency*. As a rule, funds that have low dividends and low asset turnover expose their shareholders to less taxes and therefore have higher tax-efficiency ratings. And while you're looking at performance, it probably wouldn't hurt to check out the fund's *fee structure*. Be on guard for funds that charge abnormally high management fees; they can really hurt returns over time. Another important consideration is *how well a particular fund fits into your portfolio*. If you're trying to follow a certain asset allocation strategy, then be sure to take that into account when you're thinking about adding a fund (or two) to your portfolio. You can easily do so by using the fund categories developed by Morningstar (for example, look in the upper-right corner of Figure 13.7 and you'll find the "Mstar Category" for Clipper—it's a large-cap value fund).

Note that in this decision process, considerable weight is given to *past performance*. As a rule, the past is given little or no attention in the investment decision. After all, it's the future that matters. Although the *future performance* of a mutual fund is still the variable that holds the key to success, investors should look carefully at past investment results to see how successful the fund's investment managers have been. In essence, the success of a mutual fund rests in large part on the *investment skills of the fund managers*. Therefore, look for consistently good performance, in up as well as down markets, over *extended* periods of time (5 years or more). Most important, check whether the same key people are still running the fund. Although past success is certainly no guarantee of future performance, a strong team of money managers can have a significant bearing on the level of fund returns.

Stick with No-Loads or Low-Loads There's a long-standing "debate" in the mutual fund industry regarding load funds and no-load funds. Do load funds add value? If not, then why pay the load charges? As it turns out, empirical results generally do not support the idea that load funds provide added value. Load fund returns, in general, don't seem to be any better than the returns from no-load funds. In fact, in many cases, the funds with abnormally high loads and 12(b)-1 charges often produce returns that are far less than what you can get from no-load funds. In addition, because of compounding, the differential returns tend to widen with longer holding periods. But that should come as no surprise, because big load charges and/or 12(b)-1 fees reduce your investable capital—and therefore the amount of money you have working for you. In fact, the only way a load fund can overcome this handicap is to produce *superior returns*, which is no easy thing to do, year in and year out. Granted, a handful of load funds have produced very attractive returns over extended periods of time, but they are the exception rather than the rule.

Obviously, it's in your best interest to pay close attention to load charges (and other fees). As a rule, to maximize returns, you should *seriously consider sticking to no-load funds or to low-loads* (funds that have total load charges, including 12(b)-1 fees, of 3% or less). At the very minimum, you should consider a more expensive load fund *only* if it has a much better performance record (and offers more return potential) than a less expensive fund. There may well be times when the higher costs are justified. But far more often than not, you're better off trying to minimize load charges. That shouldn't be difficult to do, however, because there are literally thousands of no-load and low-load funds to choose from. And they come in all types and sizes. What's more, most of the top-performing funds are found in the universe of no-loads or low-loads. So why would you even want to look anywhere else?

Investing in Closed-End Funds

The assets of closed-end funds (CEFs) represent only a fraction of the $6.4 trillion invested in open-end funds. Indeed, by year-end 2002, there were only about 560 CEFs, which together held total assets of some $155 billion (less than 2% of the amount held by open-end funds). Like open-end funds, CEFs come in a variety of types and styles, including funds that specialize in municipal bonds, taxable bonds, various types of equity securities, and international securities, as well as regional and single-country funds. Both taxable and tax-free bonds dominate the CEF universe, and account for nearly 80% of assets under management. In fact, municipal bonds alone account for about 56% of CEF assets. In addition to bonds and the domestic equity market, many closed-end funds target foreign stock markets. For example, regional funds focus on a group of countries within a broad geographic area, such as Europe or Latin America. In contrast, *single-country funds* target either *emerging markets* (such as Brazil, China, the Czech Republic, India, Indonesia, Mexico, the Philippines, and Turkey) or *developed markets* (such as France, Germany, Japan, and the United Kingdom).

Some Key Differences Between Closed-End and Open-End Funds Because closed-end funds trade like stocks, you must deal with a broker to buy or sell shares, and the usual brokerage commissions apply. Open-end funds, in contrast, are bought from and sold to the fund operators themselves. Another important difference between open- and closed-end funds is their liquidity. You can buy and sell relatively large dollar amounts of an open-end mutual fund at its net asset value (NAV) without worrying about affecting the price. However, a relatively large buy or sell order for a CEF could easily bump its price up or down. Thus, the greater liquidity of open-end funds gives them a distinct advantage. Like open-end funds, most CEFs offer dividend reinvestment plans, but in many cases, that's about it. CEFs simply don't provide the full range of services that mutual fund investors are accustomed to.

All things considered, probably the most important difference is the way these funds are priced in the marketplace. This is important because it *directly affects* investor costs and returns. That is, whereas open-end funds can be bought and sold at NAV (plus any front-end load or minus any redemption charge), CEFs *have two values*—a market value (or stock price) and a NAV. The two are rarely the same, because CEFs typically trade at either a premium or a discount. A *premium* occurs when a fund trades for more than its NAV; a *discount* occurs when it trades for less. As a rule, CEFs trade at discounts. Indeed, at mid-year 2003, the typical CEF traded at an average *discount of around 5% to 10%*. In addition to normal competitive pressures in the marketplace, other factors that can lead to discounts (or premiums) include the fund's *relative performance*, its annual payout or yield, the *name recognition* of the fund's manager, a significant amount of *illiquid* holdings in the fund's portfolio, and/or a substantial amount of *unrealized* appreciation sitting in the fund's portfolio. Premiums (+) and discounts (−), along with NAVs and

FIGURE 13.8

Selected Performance on CEFs

As can be seen here, the market prices of closed-end funds often exceed or fall short of the fund's NAV. *Premiums* occur when the fund's (closing) price is greater than its NAV; *discounts* occur when the fund's NAV is greater than its closing price. To find the "PREM/DISC" as reported in the quotes, simply divide the fund's quoted "CLOSE" by its quoted "NAV," and then subtract 1. (*Source: The Wall Street Journal*, November 18, 2003.)

Gabelli → Equity Trust (GAB)

CLOSED-END FUNDS

STOCK (SYM)	EXCH	NAV	CLOSE	NET CHG	VOL 100s	PREM /DISC	DIV	52 WK TTL RET
General Equity Funds								
AdamsExp **ADX**	N	14.24	12.66	0.00	732	−11.1	1.30	17.8
AllncAll **AMO**	N	14.31	15.15	−0.09	36	5.9	1.32	18.9
BlueChipVal **BLU**	N	5.36	6.03	−0.14	432	12.5	.49	37.4
BoulderGro **BIF** h	N	6.53	5.44	0.00	84	−16.7	.07	8.0
BouldrTotR **BTF**	N	17.34	14.39	0.08	30	−17.0	.03	17.8
CntlSec **CET**	A	23.10	20.21	−0.13	40	−12.5	2.55	22.1
CornstnStrat **CLM**	A	6.59	8.46	−0.03	248	28.4	1.04	66.0
CornrstnTtlRtn Fd **CRF**	A	13.33	16.73	0.27	304	25.5	2.11	64.4
Equus II **EQS**	N	12.49	8.60	0.06	505	−31.1	.72	30.7
GabelliTr **GAB**	N	7.46	7.72	0.02	1649	3.5	.56	17.9
GenAmInv **GAM**	N	31.83	28.59	−0.05	345	−10.2	.86	16.0
LibtyASE **USA**	N	8.55	9.42	−0.01	2073	10.2	.97	41.6
LibtyASG **ASG**	N	6.32	6.60	−0.08	402	4.4	.72	36.7
RoyceFocus **FUND**	O	9.12	8.39	−0.08	z28085	−8.0	.09	62.1
RycMcroCap **OTCM**	O	13.01	12.90	0.00	z36055	−0.8	.94	64.3
RoyceValTr **RVT**	N	16.66	16.87	−0.22	1020	1.3	1.31	30.0
S&P 500 Fd **PEFX**	N	9.64	8.69	0.08	z24426	−9.9	.01	3.9
SlBrosFd **SBF**	N	13.22	11.35	−0.07	755	−14.1	.11	21.0
SourceCap **SOR**	N	56.85	59.53	−0.16	21	4.7	3.50	16.0
TriContl **TY**	N	18.48	15.75	−0.13	818	−14.8	.19	13.7
ZweigFd **ZF**	N	5.50	4.72	0.00	5546	−14.2	.50	−0.6

Note: "EXCH" = Exchange fund is traded on: N = NYSE; A = AMEX; O = OTC.

52-week total returns are reported weekly (on Mondays) in the *Wall Street Journal*, an example of which appears in Figure 13.8.

The premium or discount on CEFs is calculated as follows:

Equation 13.1

$$\text{Premium (or discount)} = (\text{Share price} - \text{NAV})/\text{NAV}$$

Suppose Fund A has a NAV of $10. If its share price is $8, it will sell at a 20% discount. That is,

$$\text{Premium (or discount)} = (\$8 - \$10)/\$10$$

$$= \$2/\$10 = .20 = \underline{-20\%}$$

Because this value is negative, the fund is trading at a *discount* (or below its NAV). On the other hand, if this same fund were priced at $12 per share, it would be trading at a *premium* of 20%—that is, ($12 − $10)/$10 = $2/$10 = 0.20. Because the value is positive, the fund is trading at a premium (above its NAV).

What to Look for in a Closed-End Fund If you know what to look for and your timing and selection are good, you may find that some *deeply discounted CEFs* provide a great way to earn attractive returns. For example, if a fund trades at a 20% discount, you pay only 80 cents for each dollar's worth of assets. If you can buy a fund at an abnormally wide discount (say, more than 10% to 15%) and then sell it when the discount narrows or turns to a premium, you can enhance your overall return. In fact, even if the discount does not narrow, your return will be improved, because the yield on your investment is higher than it would be with an otherwise equivalent open-end fund. The reason: You're investing less money. Here's a simple example. Suppose a CEF trades at $8, a 20% discount from its NAV of $10. If the fund distributed $1 in dividends for the year, it would yield 12.5% ($1 divided by its $8 price). However, if it was a no-load, open-end fund, it would be trading at its higher NAV and therefore would yield only 10% ($1 divided by its $10 NAV). Thus, when investing in CEFs, pay special attention to the size of the premium and discount. In particular, keep your eyes open for funds trading at deep discounts, because that feature alone can enhance potential returns.

For the most part, except for the premium or discount, a CEF should be analyzed just like any other mutual fund. That is, check out the fund's expense ratio, portfolio turnover rate, past performance, cash position, and so on. In addition, study the history of the discount. Information on closed-end funds can be found in such publications as *Morningstar Closed-End Funds* and *Value Line Investment Survey*. Also, keep in mind that with CEFs, you probably won't get a prospectus (as you might with an open-end fund), because they do not continuously offer new shares to investors.

One final point to keep in mind when developing a closed-end fund investment program: Stay clear of new issues (IPOs) of closed-end funds and funds that sell at steep *premiums*. Never buy new CEFs when they are brought to the market as IPOs. Why? Because IPOs are always brought to the market at *hefty premiums*. You therefore face the almost inevitable risk of losing money as the shares fall to a discount within a month or two. This drop in price occurs because the IPO funds have to be offered at a premium just to cover the amount of the underwriting spread. You also want to avoid funds that are trading at premiums—especially at steep premiums—such as volatile single-country portfolios. That too can lead to built-in losses when, if sentiment sours, these premiums quickly turn into discounts.

Measuring Performance

As in any investment decision, return performance is a major dimension in the mutual fund selection process. The level of dividends paid by the fund, its capital gains, and its growth in capital are all important aspects of return. Such return information enables you to judge the investment behavior of a fund and to appraise its performance in relation to other funds and investment vehicles. Here, we will look at different measures that mutual fund investors use to assess return. Also, because risk is so important in defining the investment behavior of a fund, we will examine mutual fund risk as well.

Sources of Return An open-end mutual fund has three potential sources of return: (1) dividend income, (2) capital gains distribution, and (3) change in the price (or net asset value) of the fund. Depending on the type of fund, some mutual funds derive more income from one source than another. For example, we would normally expect income-oriented funds to have much higher dividend income than capital gains distributions.

TABLE 13.3   A Report of Mutual Fund Income and Capital Changes
(For a share outstanding throughout the year)

	2004	2003	2002
1. **Net asset value, beginning of period**	**$24.47**	**$27.03**	**$24.26**
2. **Income from investment operations**:			
3. Net investment income	$0.60	$0.66	$0.50
4. Net gains on securities (realized and unrealized)	6.37	(1.74)	3.79
5. Total from investment operations	6.97	(1.08)	4.29
6. **Less distributions**:			
7. Dividends from net investment income	($0.55)	($0.64)	($0.50)
8. Distributions from realized gains	(1.75)	(.84)	(1.02)
9. Total distributions	(2.30)	(1.48)	(1.52)
10. **Net asset value, end of period**	$29.14	$24.47	$27.03
11. **Total return**	28.48%	(4.00%)	17.68%
12. **Ratios/supplemental data**			
13. Net assets, end of period ($000)	$307,951	$153,378	$108,904
14. Ratio of expenses to average net assets	1.04%	0.85%	0.94%
15. Ratio of net investment income to average net assets	1.47%	2.56%	2.39%
16. Portfolio turnover rate*	85%	144%	74%

Portfolio turnover rate relates the number of shares bought and sold by the fund to the total number of shares held in the fund's portfolio. A high turnover rate (in excess of 100%) means the fund has been doing a lot of trading.

dividend income
income derived from the dividend and interest income earned on the security holdings of a mutual fund.

capital gains distributions
payments made to mutual fund shareholders that come from the profits that a fund makes from the sale of its securities.

Open-end mutual funds regularly publish reports that recap investment performance. One such report is the *Summary of Income and Capital Changes,* an example of which is provided in Table 13.3. This statement is found in the fund's profile or prospectus, and gives a brief overview of the fund's investment activity, including expense ratios and portfolio turnover rates. Of interest to us here is the top part of the report (which runs from "net asset value, beginning of period" to "net asset value, end of period"—lines 1 to 10). This part reveals the amount of dividend income and capital gains distributed to the shareholders, along with any change in the fund's net asset value.

Dividend income (see line 7 of Table 13.3) is derived from the dividend and interest income earned on the security holdings of the mutual fund. It is paid out of the *net investment income* that's left after all operating expenses have been met. When the fund receives dividend or interest payments, it passes these on to shareholders in the form of dividend payments. The fund accumulates all of the current income it has received for the period and then pays it out on a prorated basis. Thus, if a fund earned, say, $2 million in dividends and interest in a given year and if that fund had 1 million shares outstanding, each share would receive an annual dividend payment of $2. Keep in mind that because the mutual fund itself is tax exempt, any taxes due on dividend earnings are payable by the individual investor. For funds that are not held in tax-deferred accounts, like IRAs or 401(k)s, the amount of taxes due on dividends will depend on the source of such dividends. That is, *if these distributions are derived from dividends earned on the fund's common stock holdings, then they are subject to a preferential tax rate of 15%, or less.* However, if these distributions are derived from interest earnings on bonds, dividends from REITs, or dividends from most types of preferred stocks, then such dividends *do not qualify for the preferential tax treatment,* but instead are taxed as ordinary income.

Capital gains distributions (see line 8) work on the same principle, except that these payments are derived from the *capital gains actually earned* by the fund. It works like this: Suppose the fund bought some stock a year ago for $50 and sold that stock in the current period for $75 per share. Clearly, the fund has achieved capital gains of $25 per share. If it held 50,000 shares of this stock, it would have realized a total capital gain of $1,250,000 ($25 × 50,000 = $1,250,000). Given that the fund has 1 million shares outstanding, each share is entitled to $1.25 in the form of a capital gains distribution. (From a tax perspective, if the capital gains are long-term in nature, then they qualify for the preferential tax rate of 15%, or less; if not, then they're treated as ordinary income.) Note that these (capital gains) distributions apply only to *realized* capital gains (that is, the security holdings were actually sold and the capital gains actually earned).

unrealized capital gains (paper profits)
a capital gain made only "on paper"—that is, not realized until the fund's holdings are sold.

Unrealized capital gains (or **paper profits**) are what make up the third and final element of a mutual fund's return. When the fund's holdings go up or down in price, the net asset value of the fund moves accordingly. Suppose an investor buys into a fund at $10 per share and sometime later the fund is quoted at $12.50. The difference of $2.50 per share is the unrealized capital gains. It represents the profit that shareholders would receive (and are entitled to) if the fund were to sell its holdings. (Actually, as Table 13.3 shows, some of the change in net asset value can also be made up of undistributed income.)

The return on *closed-end* investment companies is derived from the same three sources as that of open-end funds and from a *fourth source* as well: changes in price discounts or premiums. But because the discount or premium is already embedded in the share price of a fund, it follows that, for a closed-end fund, the third element of return—change in share price—is made up not only of change in net asset value but also of change in price discount or premium.

What About Future Performance? There's no doubt that a statement like the one in Table 13.3 provides a convenient recap of a fund's past behavior. Looking at past performance is useful, but it doesn't tell you what the future will be. Ideally, you want an indication of what the same three elements of return—dividend income, capital gains distribution, and change in NAV—*will be*. But it's extremely difficult—if not impossible—to get a firm grip on what the future holds in dividends, capital gains, and NAV. This is because a mutual fund's future performance is directly linked to the *future make-up of the securities in its portfolio,* something that is next to impossible to get a clear reading on. It's not like evaluating the expected performance of a share of stock, in which case you're keying in on one company. With mutual funds, investment performance depends on the behavior of many different stocks and bonds.

Where, then, do you look for insight into future performance? Most market observers suggest that the first place to look is the market itself. In particular, try to get a fix on the future direction of *the market as a whole*. This is important because the behavior of a well-diversified mutual fund tends to reflect the general tone of the market. Thus, if the feeling is that the market is going to be drifting up, so should the investment performance of mutual funds. Also spend some time evaluating the *track records* of mutual funds in which you are interested. Past performance has a lot to say about the investment skills of the fund's money managers. In essence, look for funds that you think will be able to capture the best of what the future market environment holds.

Measures of Return A simple but effective measure of performance is to describe mutual fund return in terms of the three major sources noted above: dividends earned, capital gains distributions received, and change in price. When dealing with investment horizons of 1 year or less, we can easily convert these fund payoffs into a return figure by using the standard holding period return (HPR) formula. The computations necessary are illustrated below using the 2004 figures from Table 13.3. Referring to the exhibit, we can see that in 2004, this hypothetical no-load, open-end fund paid 55 cents per share in dividends and another $1.75 in capital gains distributions. It had a price at the beginning of the year of $24.47 that rose to $29.14 by the end of the year. Thus, summarizing this investment performance, we have

Price (NAV) at the *beginning* of the year (line 1)	$24.47
Price (NAV) at the *end* of the year (line 10)	29.14
Net increase	$ 4.67
Return for the year:	
Dividends received (line 7)	$ 0.55
Capital gains distributions (line 8)	1.75
Net increase in price (NAV)	4.67
Total return	$ 6.97
Holding period return (HPR)	**28.48%**
(Total return/beginning price)	

This HPR measure (which is shown in Table 13.3 as "Total Return" on line 11) not only captures all the important elements of mutual fund return but also provides a handy indication of yield. Note that the fund had a total dollar return of $6.97. On the basis of a beginning investment of $24.47 (the initial share price of the fund), the fund produced an annual return of nearly 28.5%.

HPR with Reinvested Dividends and Capital Gains Many mutual fund investors have their dividends and/or capital gains distributions reinvested in the fund. How, then, do you obtain a measure of return when you receive your (dividend/capital gains) payout in additional shares of stock rather than cash? With slight modifications, you can continue to use holding period return. The only difference is that you have to keep track of the number of shares acquired through reinvestment. To illustrate, let's continue with the example above and assume that you initially bought 200 shares in the mutual fund. Assume also that you were able to acquire shares through the fund's reinvestment program at an average price of $26.50 a share. Thus, the $460 in dividends and capital gains distributions [($.55 + $1.75) × 200] provided you with another 17.36 shares in the fund ($460/$26.50). Holding period return under these circumstances would relate the market value of the stock holdings at the beginning of the period with the holdings at the end:

Equation 13.2

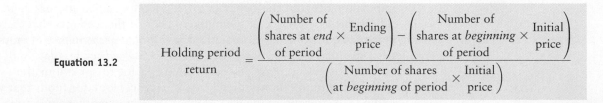

$$\text{Holding period return} = \frac{\left(\begin{array}{c}\text{Number of}\\ \text{shares at } end\\ \text{of period}\end{array} \times \begin{array}{c}\text{Ending}\\ \text{price}\end{array}\right) - \left(\begin{array}{c}\text{Number of}\\ \text{shares at } beginning\\ \text{of period}\end{array} \times \begin{array}{c}\text{Initial}\\ \text{price}\end{array}\right)}{\left(\begin{array}{c}\text{Number of shares}\\ \text{at } beginning \text{ of period}\end{array} \times \begin{array}{c}\text{Initial}\\ \text{price}\end{array}\right)}$$

Thus, the holding period return on this investment would be

$$\text{Holding period return} = \frac{(217.36 \times \$29.14) - (200 \times \$24.47)}{(200 \times \$24.47)}$$

$$= \frac{(\$6,333.87) - (\$4,894.00)}{(\$4,894.00)} = \underline{29.4\%}$$

This holding period return, like the preceding one, provides a rate-of-return measure that can now be used to compare the performance of this fund to those of other funds and investment vehicles.

Measuring Long-Term Returns Rather than using 1-year holding periods, it is sometimes necessary to assess the performance of mutual funds over extended periods of time. In these cases, it would be inappropriate to employ holding period return as a measure of performance, because it ignores the time value of money. Instead, when faced with multiple-year investment horizons, we can use the present-value-based *internal rate of return* (IRR) procedure to determine the fund's average annual compound rate of return. To illustrate, refer once again to Table 13.3. Assume that this time we want to find the annual rate of return over the full 3-year period (2002 through 2004). In this case, we see that the mutual fund had the following annual dividends and capital gains distributions:

	2004	2003	2002
Annual dividends paid	$ .55	$ .64	$ .50
Annual capital gains distributed	$1.75	$ .84	$1.02
Total distributions	$2.30	$1.48	$1.52

Now, given that the fund had a price of $24.26 at the beginning of the period (1/1/02) and was trading at $29.14 at the end of 2004 (3 years later), we have the following time line of cash flows:

Initial Cash Flow	Subsequent Cash Flows		
	Year 1	Year 2	Year 3
$24.26 (Beginning Price)	$1.52 (Distributions)	$1.48 (Distributions)	$2.30 + $29.14 (Distributions + Ending Price)

The idea is to find the discount rate that will equate the annual dividends/capital gains distributions *and* the ending price in year 3 to the beginning (2002) price of the fund ($24.26).

Using standard present-value calculations, we find that the mutual fund in Table 13.3 provided its investors with an annual rate of return of 13.1% over the 3-year period from 2002 through 2004. That is, at 13.1%, the present value of the cash flows in years 1, 2, and 3 equals the beginning price of the fund ($24.26). Such information helps us assess fund performance and compare the return performance of one fund to other funds and investment vehicles. According to SEC regulations, if mutual funds report historical return behavior, they must do so in a standardized format that employs fully compounded, total-return figures similar to those obtained from the above present value-based measure of return. The funds are not required to report such information, but if they do cite performance in their promotional material, they must follow a full-disclosure manner of presentation that takes into account not only dividends and capital gains distributions but also any increases or decreases in the fund's NAV that have occurred over the preceding 1-, 3-, 5-, and 10-year periods.

Returns on Closed-End Funds   The returns of CEFs have traditionally been reported on the basis of their NAVs. That is, *price premiums and discounts were ignored when computing return measures.* It is, however, becoming increasingly common to see return performance expressed in terms of *actual market prices,* a practice that captures the impact of changing market premiums or discounts on holding period returns. As you might expect, the greater the premiums or discounts and the greater the changes in these values over time, the greater their impact on reported returns. It's not at all uncommon for CEFs to have different market-based and NAV-based holding period returns. When NAVs are used, you find the returns on CEFs in exactly the same way as you do the returns on open-end funds. In contrast, when market values (i.e., actual market prices) are used to measure return, all you need do *is substitute the market price of the fund* (with its embedded premium or discount) *for the corresponding NAV in the holding period or internal rate of return* measures. Some CEF investors like to run *both* NAV-based and market-based measures of return to see how changing premiums (or discounts) have added to or hurt the returns on their mutual fund holdings. Even so, as a rule, NAV-based return numbers are generally viewed as the preferred measures of performance. Because fund managers often have little or no control over changes in premiums or discounts, NAV-based measures are felt to give a truer picture of the performance of the fund itself.

The Matter of Risk   Because most mutual funds are so diversified, their investors are largely immune to the business and financial risks normally present with individual securities. Even with extensive diversification, however, the investment behavior of most funds is still exposed to a considerable amount of *market risk.* In fact, because mutual fund portfolios are so well diversified, they often tend to perform very much like the market—or some segment of the market that's being targeted by the fund. Although a few funds, like gold funds, tend to be defensive (countercyclical), market risk is still an important behavioral ingredient for most types of mutual funds, both open- and closed-end. Investors should be aware of the effect the general market has on the investment performance of a mutual fund. For example, if the market is trending downward and you anticipate that trend to continue, it might be best to place any new investment capital into something like a money fund until the market reverses itself. At that time, you can make a more long-term commitment.

Another important risk consideration revolves around *the management practices of the fund itself.* If the portfolio is managed conservatively, the risk of a loss in capital is likely to be much less than that for aggressively managed funds. Obviously, the more speculative the investment goals of the fund, the greater the risk of instability in the net asset value. But, a conservatively managed portfolio does not necessarily eliminate all price volatility. The securities in the portfolio are still subject to inflation, interest rate, and general market risks. However, these risks are generally reduced or minimized as the investment objectives and portfolio management practices of the funds become more conservative.

IN REVIEW

CONCEPTS

13.12 How important is the general behavior of the market in affecting the price performance of mutual funds? Explain. Why is a fund's past performance important to the mutual fund selection process? Does the future behavior of the market matter in the selection process? Explain.

13.13 What is the major/dominant type of closed-end fund? What is the difference between regional funds and single-country funds? How do CEFs differ from open-end funds?

13.14 Identify three potential sources of return to mutual fund investors and briefly discuss how each could affect total return to shareholders. Explain how the discount or premium of a closed-end fund can also be treated as a return to investors.

13.15 Discuss the various types of risk to which mutual fund shareholders are exposed. What is the major risk exposure of mutual funds? Are all funds subject to the same level of risk? Explain.

Summary

LG 1 **Describe the basic features of mutual funds, and note what they have to offer as investment vehicles.** Mutual fund shares represent ownership in a diversified, professionally managed portfolio of securities. Many investors who lack the time, know-how, or commitment to manage their own money turn to mutual funds. Mutual funds shareholders benefit from a level of diversification and investment performance they might otherwise find difficult to achieve. In addition, they can establish an investment program with a limited amount of capital and obtain a variety of investor services not available elsewhere.

LG 2 **Distinguish between open- and closed-end mutual funds, as well as other types of professionally managed investment companies, and discuss the various types of fund loads, fees, and charges.** Open-end funds have no limit on the number of shares they may issue. Closed-end funds have a fixed number of shares outstanding and trade in the secondary markets like any other share of common stock. Exchange-traded funds possess characteristics of both open-end and closed-end funds. Other types of investment companies are unit investment trusts, hedge funds (a type of private, unregulated investment vehicle available to institutional and high-net-worth individual investors), REITs (which invest primarily in various types of real estate products), and variable annuities. Mutual fund investors face an array of loads, fees, and charges, including front-end loads, back-end loads, annual 12(b)-1 charges, and annual management fees. Some of these costs are one-time charges (e.g., front-end loads). Others are paid annually [e.g., 12(b)-1 and management fees]. Investors should understand fund costs, which can be a real drag on fund performance and return.

LG 3   **Discuss the types of funds available and the variety of investment objectives these funds seek to fulfill.** Each fund has an established investment objective that determines its investment policy and identifies it as a certain type of fund. Some of the more popular types of funds are growth funds, aggressive growth funds, value funds, equity income funds, balanced funds, growth-and-income funds, asset allocation funds, index funds, bond funds, money funds, sector funds, socially responsible funds, and international funds. The different categories of funds have different risk-return characteristics.

LG 4   **Discuss the investor services offered by mutual funds and how these services can fit into an investment program.** Mutual funds also offer special services, such as automatic investment and reinvestment plans, systematic withdrawal programs, low-cost conversion and phone-switching privileges, and retirement programs.

LG 5   **Gain an appreciation of the investor uses of mutual funds, along with the variables to consider when assessing and selecting funds for investment purposes.** Mutual funds can be used to accumulate wealth, as a storehouse of value, or as a vehicle for speculation and short-term trading. The fund selection process generally starts by assessing the investor's needs and wants. The next step is to consider what the funds have to offer, particularly with regard to investment objectives, risk exposure, and investor services. The investor then narrows down the alternatives by aligning his or her needs with the types of funds available and, from this short list of funds, applies the final selection tests: fund performance and cost.

LG 6   **Identify the sources of return and compute the rate of return earned on a mutual fund investment.** The payoff from investing in a mutual fund includes dividend income, distribution of realized capital gains, growth in capital (unrealized capital gains), and—for closed-end funds—the change in premium or discount. Various measures of return recognize these elements and provide simple yet effective ways of gauging the annual rate of return from a mutual fund. Risk is also important to mutual fund investors. A fund's extensive diversification may protect investors from business and financial risks. But considerable market risk still remains because most funds tend to perform much like the market, or like that segment of the market in which they specialize.

Putting Your Investment Know-How to the Test

1. A charge on the sale of shares in mutual fund is called a
   a. Front-end load.
   b. Back-end load.
   c. 12(b)-1 charge.
   d. Management fee.

2. Which of the following investment companies invests in a portfolio that is fixed for the life of the fund?
   a. A mutual fund
   b. A money market fund
   c. A unit investment trust
   d. An asset allocation fund

3. The structure of an investment company is *least likely* to be characterized by
   a. A corporate form of organization.
   b. Investment of a pool of funds from many investors in a portfolio of investments.

    c. An annual management fee ranging from 3% to 5% of the total value of the fund.

    d. A board of directors who hires a separate investment management company to manage the portfolio of securities and to handle other administrative duties.

4. The net asset value (NAV) of a mutual fund is defined as the
    a. Book value of assets divided by the number of shares outstanding.
    b. Book value of assets minus liabilities divided by the number of shares outstanding.
    c. Market value of assets divided by the number of shares outstanding.
    d. Market value of assets minus liabilities divided by the number of shares outstanding.

5. Consider a no-load mutual fund with $200 million in assets, $20 million in debt, and 20 million shares at the beginning of the year; and $300 million in assets, $25 million in debt, and 25 million shares at the end of the year. During the year investors receive combined dividends and capital gains distributions of $0.70 per share. What is the annual rate of return on this fund?
    a. 22.2%   b. 25.0%
    c. 28.7%   d. 30.0%

6. The ZYX fund is a closed-end fund with assets currently worth $300 million. It has liabilities of $15 million and 10 million shares outstanding. If the shares sell for $31, what is its percentage premium (or discount) to its net asset value (NAV)?
    a. 8.8% premium
    b. 3.3% premium
    c. 8.8% discount
    d. 3.3% discount

7. Sector funds concentrate their investment portfolios in
    a. Government securities.
    b. Bonds of a particular maturity.
    c. Securities issued by firms in a particular industry.
    d. Municipal bonds from certain geographic areas.

8. Mutual funds whose goal is to generate both current income and long-term capital appreciation by holding a portfolio of stocks and bonds in relatively stable proportions are called
    a. Growth-and-income funds.
    b. Balanced funds.
    c. Index funds.
    d. Equity-income funds.

9. The ABC Fund sells class A shares with a front-end load of 6% and class B shares with a 1% 12(b)-1 annual fee and a 1% redemption charge voided after 10 years. If you plan to sell the fund after 8 years, which shares offer a better choice?
    a. Class A.
    b. Class B.
    c. There is no difference between the two.
    d. Not enough information is given to calculate the returns.

10. Which of the following is *not* an exchange-traded fund?
    a. Diamond   b. Qube
    c. Cobra   d. Spider

Answers: 1. a; 2. c; 3. c; 4. b; 5. d; 6. a; 7. c; 8. b; 9. a; 10. c

Discussion Questions

LG 1
LG 2

Q13.1 Contrast *mutual fund ownership* with *direct investment in stocks and bonds*. Assume your class is going to debate the merits of investing through mutual funds versus investing directly in stocks and bonds. Develop some arguments on each side of this debate and be prepared to discuss them in class. If you had to choose one side to be on, which would it be? Why?

LG 2

Q13.2 Based on the mutual fund quotes in Figure 13.5, answer the questions listed below for each of the following five funds:
 (1) Clipper Fund (Clipper).
 (2) Diversified High Yield Bonds (HiYldBd).
 (3) Fidelity Canada (Canad).
 (4) Cohen & Steers Equity Income/C shares (EqIncC).
 (5) FMI Focus Fund (FMI Focusfd).

Based on the information reported in Figure 13.5:
 a. How much would you receive for each fund if you were selling them?
 b. Which of the five listed funds have 12(b)-1 fees?
 c. Which funds have redemption fees?
 d. Do any of the funds have both 12(b)-1 and redemption fees?
 e. Can you tell whether any of the funds are no-loads?
 f. Which fund has the highest front-end load?
 g. Which fund has the highest year-to-date return? Which has the lowest?

LG 3

Q13.3 For each pair of funds listed below, select the one that is likely to be the *less* risky. Briefly explain your answer.
 a. Growth versus growth-and-income funds.
 b. Equity-income versus high-grade corporate bond funds.
 c. Balanced versus sector funds.
 d. Global versus value funds.
 e. Intermediate-term bonds versus high-yield municipal bond funds.

LG 2 **LG 3**

Q13.4 Describe an ETF and explain how these funds combine the characteristics of both open-end and close-end funds. Consider the Vanguard family of funds. Which of its funds most closely resembles a "spider" (SPDR)? In what respects are the Vanguard fund (that you selected) and spiders the same? How are they different? If you could invest in only one of them, which would it be? Explain.

LG 2 **LG 6**

Q13.5 In the absence of any load charges, open-end mutual funds are priced at (or very close to) their net asset values, whereas closed-end funds rarely trade at their NAVs. Explain why one type of fund would normally trade at its NAV while the other type (CEFs) usually does not. What are price premiums and discounts, and in what segment of the mutual fund market will you usually find them? Look in a recent edition of the *Wall Street Journal* (*Hint:* pick one that comes out on Mondays), and find five funds that trade at a discount and five funds that trade at a premium. List all 10 of them, including the sizes of their respective discounts and premiums. What's the biggest price discount you could find? How about the biggest price premium? What would cause a fund to trade at a discount? At a premium?

LG 3 **LG 5**

Q13.6 Imagine that you've just inherited $20,000. Now you're faced with the "problem" of how to spend it. You could make a down payment on a condo, or you could buy that sports car you've always wanted. Or you could build a mutual fund portfolio. After some soul-searching, you decide to build a $20,000 mutual fund portfolio. Using actual mutual funds and actual quoted prices, come up with a plan to invest as much of the $20,000 as you can in a portfolio of mutual funds. (In addition to one or more open-end funds, include at least one CEF *or* one ETF.) Be specific! Briefly describe your planned portfolio, including the investment objectives you are trying to achieve.

Problems

LG 6

P13.1 A year ago, an investor bought 200 shares of a mutual fund at $8.50 per share. Over the past year, the fund has paid dividends of 90 cents per share and had a capital gains distribution of 75 cents per share.

    a. Find the investor's holding period return, given that this no-load fund now has a net asset value of $9.10.

    b. Find the holding period return, assuming all the dividends and capital gains distributions are reinvested into additional shares of the fund at an average price of $8.75 per share.

LG 6

P13.2 A year ago, the Really Big Growth Fund was being quoted at a NAV of $21.50 and an offer price of $23.35. Today it's being quoted at $23.04 (NAV) and $25.04 (offer). What is the holding period return on this load fund, given that it was purchased a year ago and that its dividends and capital gains distributions over the year have totaled $1.05 per share? (*Hint:* You, as an investor, buy fund shares at the offer price and sell at the NAV.)

LG 6

P13.3 The All-State Mutual Fund has the following 5-year record of performance.

	2003	2002	2001	2000	1999
Net investment income	$ 0.98	$ 0.85	$ 0.84	$ 0.75	$ 0.64
Dividends from net investment income	(0.95)	(0.85)	(0.85)	(0.75)	(0.60)
Net realized and unrealized gains (or losses) on security transactions	4.22	5.08	(2.18)	2.65	(1.05)
Distributions from realized gains	(1.05)	(1.00)	—	(1.00)	—
Net increase (decrease) in NAV	$ 3.20	$ 4.08	($ 2.19)	$ 1.65	($ 1.01)
NAV at beginning of year	12.53	8.45	10.64	.99	10.00
NAV at end of year	$15.73	$12.53	$ 8.45	$10.64	$ 8.99

Find this no-load fund's 5-year (1999–2003) average annual compound rate of return. Also find its 3-year (2001–2003) average annual compound rate of return. If an investor bought the fund in 1999 at $10.00 a share and sold it 5 years later (in 2003) at $15.73, how much total profit per share would she have made over the 5-year holding period?

LG 6

P13.4 You've uncovered the following per-share information about a certain mutual fund.

	2002	2003	2004
Ending share prices:			
Offer	$46.20	$64.68	$61.78
NAV	43.20	60.47	57.75
Dividend income	2.10	2.84	2.61
Capital gains distribution	1.83	6.26	4.32
Beginning share prices:			
Offer	55.00	46.20	64.68
NAV	51.42	43.20	60.47

On the basis of this information, find the fund's holding period return for 2002, 2003, and 2004. (In all three cases, assume you buy the fund at the beginning of the year and sell it at the end of each year.) In addition, find the fund's average annual compound rate of return over the 3-year period, 2002–2004. What would the 2003 holding period return have been if the investor had initially bought 500 shares of stock and reinvested both dividends and capital gains distributions into additional shares of the fund at an average price of $52.50 per share?

 **LG 2** **LG 6**   **P13.5** Listed is the 10-year, per-share performance record of Larry, Moe, & Curly's Growth Fund, as obtained from the fund's May 30, 2004, prospectus.

					Years Ended March 31					
	2004	**2003**	**2002**	**2001**	**2000**	**1999**	**1998**	**1997**	**1996**	**1995**
1. **Net asset value, beginning of period**	$58.60	$52.92	$44.10	$59.85	$55.34	$37.69	$35.21	$34.25	$19.68	$29.82
2. **Income from investment operations:**										
3. Net investment income	$1.39	$1.35	$1.09	$0.63	$0.42	$ 0.49	$ 0.79	$0.37	$ 0.33	$0.38
4. Net gains on securities (realized and unrealized)	8.10	9.39	8.63	(6.64)	11.39	19.59	5.75	2.73	15.80	(0.02)
5. Total from investment operations	9.49	10.74	9.72	(6.01)	11.81	20.08	6.54	3.10	16.13	0.36
6. **Less distributions:**										
7. Dividends from net investment income	($0.83)	($1.24)	($0.90)	($0.72)	($0.46)	($0.65)	($0.37)	($0.26)	($0.33)	($0.58)
8. Distributions from realized gains	(2.42)	(3.82)	—	(9.02)	(6.84)	(1.78)	(3.69)	(1.88)	(1.23)	(9.92)
9. Total distributions	(3.25)	(5.06)	(0.90)	(9.74)	(7.30)	(2.43)	(4.06)	(2.14)	(1.56)	(10.50)
10. **Net asset value, end of period**	$64.84	$58.60	$52.92	$44.10	$59.85	$55.34	$37.69	$35.21	$34.25	$19.68

Use this information to find LM&C's holding period return in 2004 and 2001. Also find the fund's rate of return over the 5-year period 2000–2004, and the 10-year period 1995–2004. Finally, rework the four return figures assuming the LM&C fund has a front-end load charge of 3% (of NAV). Comment on the impact of load charges on the return behavior of mutual funds.

 **LG 3** **LG 6**   **P13.6** Using the resources available at your campus or public library (or those available on the Internet), select five mutual funds—a growth fund, an equity-income fund, an international (stock) fund, an index fund, and a high-yield corporate bond fund—that you feel would make good investments. Briefly explain why you selected these funds. List the funds' holding period returns for the past year and their annual compound rates of return for the past 3 years. (Use a schedule like the one in Table 13.3 to show relevant performance figures.)

 LG 6   **P13.7** One year ago, Super Star Closed-End Fund had a NAV of $10.40 and was selling at an 18% discount. Today its NAV is $11.69 and it is priced at a 4% premium. During the year, Super Star paid dividends of 40 cents and had a capital gains distribution of 95 cents. On the basis of the above information, calculate each of the following.

    a. Super Star's NAV-based holding period return for the year.

    b. Super Star's market-based holding period return for the year. Did the market premium/discount hurt or add value to the investor's return? Explain.

    c. Repeat the market-based holding period return calculation, except this time assume the fund started the year at an 18% *premium* and ended it at a 4% *discount*. (Assume the beginning and ending NAVs remain at $10.40 and $11.69, respectively.) Is there any change in this measure of return? Why?

LG 6   **P13.8** The Well Managed Closed-End Fund turned in the following performance for the year 2004.

	Beginning of the Year	End of the Year
NAV	$7.50	$9.25
Market price of the fund shares	$7.75	$9.00
Dividends paid over the year	—	$1.20
Capital gains distributed over the year	—	$0.90

    a. Based on this information, what was the NAV-based HPR for the WMCEF in 2004?

    b. Find the percentage (%) premium or discount at which the fund was trading at the beginning of the year and at the end of the year.

    c. What was the market-based HPR for the fund in 2004? Did the market premium or discount add to or hurt the holding period return on this CEF? Explain.

LG 6   **P13.9** Three years ago, you invested in the Future Investco Mutual Fund by purchasing 1,000 shares of the fund at a net asset value of $20.00 per share. Because you did not need the income, you elected to reinvest all dividends and gains distributions. Today, you sell your 1,100 shares in this fund for $22.91 per share. What is the compounded rate of return on this investment over the three-year period?

LG 6   **P13.10** Refer to Problem 13.9 above. If there were a 3% load on this fund, assuming you purchased the same number of shares, what would your rate of return be?

LG 6   **P.13.11** You invested in the no-load OhYes Mutual Fund one year ago by purchasing 1,000 shares of the fund at the net asset value of $25.00 per share. The fund distributed dividends of $1.50 and capital gains of $2.00. Today, the NAV is $26. What was your holding period return?

LG 6   **P13.12** Refer to Problem 13.11 above. If OhYes was a load fund with a 2% front end load, what would be the HPR?

LG 6   **P13.13** Refer to Figure 13.8. You purchased shares of AdamsExp (**ADX**) at the end of the day quoted. The fund pays the same dividend this year as that quoted, and at the end of the year the fund is quoted as having a NAV of $15.00 and a close of $14.50. What is your holding period return?

LG 6   **P13.14** Refer to Problem 13.13 above. Now assume that you hold your shares of AdamsExp for three years. Each year you receive the same dividend, and at the end of year three, the fund has a NAV of $15.00 and a close of $15.68. What is the compound annual rate of return for the three-year period?

LG 6   **P13.15** You are considering the purchase of shares of a closed end mutual fund. The NAV is equal to $22.50 and the latest close is $20.00. Is this fund trading at a premium or a discount? How big is the premium or discount?

LG 6   **P13.16** You purchased 1,000 shares of MutualMagic one year ago for $20.00 per share. During the year, you received $2.00 in dividends, half of which were from dividends on stock the fund held and half of which was from interest earned on bonds in the fund portfolio. Assuming your federal marginal tax rate is 25%, how much will you owe in federal taxes on the distributions you received this year (your answer should be in dollars).

> See the text Web site
> (www.aw-bc.com/gitman_joehnk) **for Web exercises**
> **that deal with** *mutual funds.*

Case Problem 13.1 *Reverend Robin Ponders Mutual Funds*

Reverend Robin is the minister of a church in the San Antonio area. He is married, has one young child, and earns a "modest income." Because religious organizations are not notorious for their generous retirement programs, the reverend has decided he should do some investing on his own. He would like to set up a program that enables him to supplement the church's retirement program and at the same time provide some funds for his child's college education (which is still some 12 years away). He is not out to break any investment records but wants some backup to provide for the long-run needs of his family.

Although he has a modest income, Reverend Robin believes that with careful planning, he can probably invest about $250 a quarter (and, with luck, increase this amount over time). He currently has about $15,000 in a savings account that he would be willing to use to begin this program. In view of his investment objectives, he is not interested in taking a lot of risk. Because his knowledge of investments extends to savings accounts, Series EE savings bonds, and a little bit about mutual funds, he approaches you for some investment advice.

Questions

a. In light of Reverend Robin's long-term investment goals, do you think mutual funds are an appropriate investment vehicle for him?

b. Do you think he should use his $15,000 savings to start a mutual fund investment program?

c. What type of mutual fund investment program would you set up for the reverend? Include in your answer some discussion of the types of funds you would consider, the investment objectives you would set, and any investment services (e.g., withdrawal plans) you would seek. Would taxes be an important consideration in your investment advice? Explain.

Case Problem 13.2 *Tom Yee Seeks the Good Life*

Tom Yee is a widower who recently retired after a long career with a major Midwestern manufacturer. Beginning as a skilled craftsman, he worked his way up to the level of shop supervisor over a period of more than 30 years with the firm. Tom receives Social Security benefits and a generous company pension. Together, these two sources amount to over $4,500 per month (part of which is tax-free). The Yees had no children, so he lives alone. Tom owns a two-bedroom rental house that is next to his home, and the rental income from it covers the mortgage payments for both the rental house and his house.

Over the years, Tom and his late wife, Camille, always tried to put a little money aside each month. The results have been nothing short of phenomenal. The value of Tom's liquid investments (all held in bank CDs and passbook savings accounts) runs well into the six figures. Up to now, Tom has just let his money grow and has not used any of his savings to supplement his Social Security, pension, and rental income. But things are about to change. Tom has decided, "What the heck, it's time I start living the good life!" Tom wants to travel and, in effect, start reaping the benefits of his labors. He has therefore decided to move $100,000 from one of his savings accounts to one or two high-yielding mutual funds. He would like to receive $1,000–$1,500 a month from the fund(s) for as long as possible, because he plans to be around for a long time.

Questions

a. Given Tom's financial resources and investment objectives, what kinds of mutual funds do you think he should consider?

b. What factors in Tom's situation should be taken into consideration in the fund selection process? How might these affect Tom's course of action?

c. What types of services do you think he should look for in a mutual fund?

d. Assume Tom invests in a mutual fund that earns about 10% annually from dividend income and capital gains. Given that Tom wants to receive $1,000 to $1,500 a month from his mutual fund, what would be the size of his investment account 5 years from now? How large would the account be if the fund earned 15% on average and everything else remained the same? How important is the fund's rate of return to Tom's investment situation? Explain.

Excel with Spreadsheets

In the Wall Street Journal, open-ended mutual funds are listed separately from other securities. They have their own quotation system where two primary data variables are the net asset value (NAV) and the year-to-date returns. The NAV represents the price you get when you sell shares, or what you pay when you buy no-load funds.

Create a spreadsheet model similar to the spreadsheet for Table 13.3, which you can view at www.aw-bc.com/gitman_joehnk, to analyze the following three years of data relating to the MoMoney Mutual Fund. It should report the amount of dividend income and capital gains distributed to the shareholders, along with any other changes in the fund's net asset value.

A	B	C	D	E
1	**2003**	**2002**	**2001**	
2 NAV, beginning of period	$ 35.24	$ 37.50	$ 36.25	
3 Net investment income	$ 0.65	$ 0.75	$ 0.60	
4 Net gains on securities	$ 5.25	$ 4.75	$ (3.75)	
5 Dividends from net investment income	$ 0.61	$ 0.57	$ 0.52	
6 Distributions from realized gains	$ 1.75	$ 2.01	$ 1.55	

Questions

a. What is the total income from the investment operations?
b. What are the total distributions from the investment operations?
c. Calculate the net asset value for MoMoney Fund as of the end of the years 2002, 2001, and 2000.
d. Calculate the holding period returns for each of the years 2003, 2002, and 2001.

CHAPTER 14

MANAGING YOUR OWN PORTFOLIO

LEARNING GOALS

After studying this chapter, you should be able to:

LG 1 Construct portfolios with asset allocations and risk-return profiles consistent with the investor's objectives.

LG 2 Discuss the data and indexes needed to measure and compare investment performance.

LG 3 Understand the techniques used to measure income, capital gains, and total portfolio return.

LG 4 Use the Sharpe, Treynor, and Jensen measures to compare a portfolio's return with a risk-adjusted, market-adjusted rate of return, and discuss portfolio revision.

LG 5 Describe the role and logic of dollar-cost averaging, constant-dollar plans, constant-ratio plans, and variable-ratio plans.

LG 6 Explain the role of limit and stop-loss orders in investment timing, warehousing liquidity, and timing investment sales.

He's known as the "Oracle of Omaha" for his stock-picking prowess. As chairman of Berkshire Hathaway Inc., Warren Buffet has multiplied his investors' money by a factor of 4,000 since taking over the company in 1966. The Omaha-based corporation's 40 subsidiaries include insurance (the largest sector), apparel, building products, financial services, food and gourmet retailers, flight services, home furnishings, and jewelry retailers. In addition to operating these companies, Berkshire Hathaway is a public investment company with major holdings in more than 500 companies. Its list of investments reads like a veritable who's who of American business: American Express, Coca-Cola, Disney, Gillette, McDonald's, Wells Fargo, and many others.

Owning a piece of this diversified company will cost you a pretty penny. In January 2004, the A shares were trading at roughly $89,300 per share, up 47 percent since February 2003—remarkable performance for a company of this size. (Only have a few thousand to spend? You can buy B shares, which trade for one-thirtieth of the A shares' value, or about $2,965.) From 1966 to 2003, Berkshire Hathaway's book value per share has grown from $19 to more than $46,750.

What's the secret to Buffet's success? His long-term investing horizon and patience are legendary—and traits that are often in short supply on Wall Street. His claim to fame has been his ability to buy businesses at prices far below what he calls their "intrinsic" value, which includes such intangibles as quality of management and the power of superior brand names. Buffet waits until a desired investment reaches his target price (perceived value) and won't buy until then. "We measure our success by the long-term progress of the companies rather than by the month-to-month movements of their stocks," he says.

As you'll see in this chapter, which introduces the basics of portfolio management, investing is a process of analysis, followed by action, followed by still more analysis. You may not be the next Warren Buffet (or maybe you will!), but understanding his techniques for building and evaluating your own portfolio will put you on the right track.

Sources: Berkshire Hathaway corporate Web site, www.berkshirehathaway.com, accessed December 22, 2003; Mathew Emmert, "Warren, Show Me the Money," *Motley Fool*, December 15, 2003, downloaded from www.fool.com; and "The Smart Money 30," *Smart Money*, December 2003, p. 84.

Portfolio Planning in Action

LG 1

We begin this chapter by analyzing four portfolios that have been developed by individual investors to meet four different investment objectives. The principles and ideas discussed throughout this book are applied to these four situations.

In each of these analyses, the objectives and the portfolios are real, although the investors' and securities' names are fictitious. When possible, asset allocation weights are given. The specific reasons why a stock or bond is included in the portfolio are also given. As a useful exercise, you might want to consider each situation and develop your own recommendations using current investment information. The *Investing in Action* box on page 598 emphasizes the importance of keeping good records of transactions as your portfolio grows over time.

The four cases have different risk-return profiles because the investors for whom the portfolios are designed have different incomes and lifestyles. Each portfolio relies heavily on the *traditional approach* (see Chapter 5), with the following exceptions: First, the number of securities in each portfolio is *below the normal number* the traditional portfolio manager would be likely to recommend. In line with *modern portfolio theory (MPT)* (see Chapter 5), it is assumed that the proper interindustry diversification can be achieved with the careful selection of 8 to 12 securities in a $100,000 portfolio. A traditionalist might recommend more. Second, beta (see Chapter 5) is utilized to quantify risk in the all-equity portfolios. Thus these examples blend elements of MPT with the traditional approach to portfolio management.

Dara Yasakawa: Woman Wonder

At age 28, Dara Yasakawa has done well for herself. She has built a $300,000 investment portfolio. It consists of investment real estate in Honolulu, Hawaii, with a current market value of $240,000, and $60,000 in short-term securities. Her current asset allocation is therefore 80% real estate ($240,000 ÷ $300,000) and 20% short-term securities ($60,000 ÷ $300,000). Dara is currently employed as the controller of Kamehameha Management, a real estate management firm in Honolulu. She is a CPA, and her income from salary and property rentals is $90,000 per year. This puts her in a 35% marginal income tax bracket (federal and Hawaii state income tax combined). Dara is single and relatively debt-free.

Dara Yasakawa has decided to diversify her portfolio, to reduce her risk exposure and increase her overall investment return. Most of her net worth consists of rental condominiums in Honolulu. The Hawaii real estate market is somewhat unpredictable, and Dara wishes to lessen her risk exposure in that market. She asked her investment adviser, Marjorie Wong, to help her diversify into common stock. Marjorie recommended selling one of Dara's properties for $60,000 and selling $15,000 of her short-term securities to obtain $75,000 to invest in common stock. The resulting asset allocation would be 60% real estate ($180,000 ÷ $300,000), 25% common stock ($75,000 ÷ $300,000), and 15% short-term securities ($45,000 ÷ $300,000). Because of her relatively young age and her strong future earning capacity, Dara can bear the risks of a speculative investment program. Her portfolio of stocks will emphasize issues that have a strong price appreciation potential.

Dara Yasakawa's common stock portfolio is presented in Table 14.1 (on page 599). It consists of eight stocks, all of which have above-average risk-

INVESTOR FACTS

A LITTLE GOES A LONG WAY—
Too much diversification can be as bad as too little. According to a recent study by *Dow Theory Forecasts* analyst David Wright, five to nine funds investing in domestic and international stocks and bonds are all you need. Putting together five conservative stock funds, he created a portfolio with a 15 percent standard deviation. Adding a high-yield bond fund shaved it to 14 percent, and a municipal bond fund trimmed it to 12 percent. But adding another large-stock fund pushed the standard deviation up to 13 percent. "More is not always better," Wright says. Florida money manager Harold Evensky agrees. He advises his clients to reduce costs and boost returns by buying fewer, cheaper funds. This results in tax savings, easier rebalancing, and lower expense ratios.

Sources: Jean Sherman Chatzky, "Do You Own Too Many Funds?" *Money*, July 2003, p. 132; and Chet Currie, "Temper Diversification to Avoid Diminishing Returns," *The Dallas Morning News*, July 9, 2000, p. 11H.

INVESTING IN ACTION

TAMING THE PORTFOLIO MONSTER

As your portfolio grows in number and type of investments, it's easy to become overwhelmed and confused by the paperwork you accumulate. Before long, you might lose control of your investments or lose track of important details, such as why you bought that stock in the first place. "People tend to build portfolios the way they pick up seashells on the beach," says Roger Gibson, author of *Asset Allocation: Balancing Financial Risk*. As a result, many investors don't know whether the parts of their portfolio make sense when taken together.

How do you get an overall view of your portfolio? A good place to start is by doing a thorough housecleaning of your financial assets. That means sorting through stacks of paper: mutual fund "welcome" kits, prospectuses, annual and quarterly reports, brokerage firm and mutual fund statements. Take all the paperwork from each brokerage firm and mutual fund and put it in one pile, organized by date, with the most recent mailing on top. You can throw out items you no longer need, such as welcome kits, old annual reports, and monthly or quarterly statements whose information is included in the annual statement. Then file each set of documents in an individual file folder.

Next list all of your assets categorized by asset categories. Across the top, make columns for cash, domestic bonds, international bonds, domestic stocks, international stocks, real estate, and so on. Use the rows for the source, such

as ABC mutual fund or XYZ brokerage firm. If one investment falls into two or more categories, such as a 401(k) retirement plan with both bond and stock investments, then divide it accordingly. Add up all of your assets by category, and calculate the percentage of your portfolio for each asset category.

You may discover that you have many small, similar investments that can be consolidated to simplify your portfolio while still achieving your objectives. For example, do you really need three stockbrokers, or can you combine your accounts at one firm? The same goes for mutual funds. You may want to concentrate on one or two large fund families with many fund choices. Consolidating brokerage firms and mutual funds will certainly cut down on the blizzard of paperwork.

Having organized records also will be a major benefit at tax time. Your records will provide you with the necessary details about securities you sold during the year—such as the purchase and sale dates, the number of shares you bought or sold, and the purchase and sale prices. But most important, having neat files and summary tables will make it easy for you to make informed investment decisions that fit your life circumstances.

CRITICAL THINKING QUESTION Evaluate the system described above for keeping track of your portfolio records. How might this system help you consolidate your portfolio?

---

return potential. The betas of the issues range from 1.13 to 2.31. The portfolio's beta (calculated using Equation 5.4 from Chapter 5) is approximately 1.59, indicating an above-average risk exposure. The portfolio is diversified across industry lines, with a fairly wide mix of securities. All are selected for their above-average price appreciation potential. Altuna Airlines, an interisland carrier in Hawaii, was chosen because of the expected increase in the number of visitors to Hawaii. Betta Computer is a fast-growing personal computer manufacturer. Easy Work Inc. is a growing retailer that services the do-it-yourself home improvement market. Gomez Industries is a rapidly expanding glass manufacturer and photo processor. Hercules is a growing brewer. Jama Motor, based in Japan, provides a measure of international diversification for the portfolio. eChowNow is an expanding Internet-based home grocery oper-

TABLE 14.1 Dara Yasakawa's Common Stock Portfolio

Objective: Speculative Growth (High Risk, Potential for High Return)

Number of Shares	Company	Dividend per Share	Dividend Income	Price per Share	Total Cost (including commission)	Beta	Dividend Yield
1,200	Altuna Airlines	$ —	$ —	$ 7	$ 8,480	1.75	—%
300	Betta Computer	—	—	30	9,090	1.87	—
400	Easy Work Inc.	—	—	25	10,090	1.59	—
300	Gomez Industries	0.36	108	30	9,090	1.19	1.2
300	Hercules Brewing	0.80	240	32	9,700	1.27	2.5
300	Jama Motor ADR	0.35	105	33	10,000	1.13	1.1
500	eChowNow	—	—	20	10,100	1.79	—
1,300	Ranch Petroleum	—	—	6	7,880	2.31	—
	Total		$453		$74,430		0.6%

Portfolio beta = 1.59

ation based in California. Ranch Petroleum is a small oil company with refining and oil-production interests.

Most of these securities are not "household names." Rather, they are firms with exciting growth potential. Given the portfolio's beta, Dara's holdings should fluctuate in value at a rate approximately 1.6 times greater than the stock market as a whole. The dividend yield on the portfolio is a relatively low 0.6%. Most of the return Dara anticipates from this portfolio is in the form of price appreciation. She plans to hold the stocks for at least 3 to 5 years to realize this anticipated appreciation. Given Dara Yasakawa's relatively high marginal income tax bracket, it seems preferable for her to defer taxes and earn returns in the form of capital gains.

Bob and Gail Weiss: Lottery Winners

Bob Weiss, a professor of political science at the University of West Bay City in Michigan, and his wife, Gail, are lucky people. Professor Weiss bought a $1 Michigan State Lottery ticket and won $300,000! After paying income taxes on the prize and spending a small amount for personal needs, Bob and Gail had $210,000 left. Because of their philosophy of saving any windfalls and not spending accumulated capital on day-to-day living expenses, they chose to invest these funds. (In contrast, many lottery winners simply blow their winnings on fast living.)

Bob Weiss is 37 years of age and has a secure teaching position. His salary is approximately $80,000 per year. In addition, he earns approximately $20,000 per year from book publishing royalties and some consulting work. Bob Weiss's tax bracket (federal and state) is approximately 33%. His life insurance protection of approximately $120,000 is provided by the university. Gail Weiss is a librarian. She currently is at home with their two young children and is not expected to be a source of steady income for another several years.

The Weiss family owns (free and clear) their home in Bay City. In addition, they have about $40,000 in a money market mutual fund. Therefore, their asset allocation prior to the lottery windfall was 100% money funds ($40,000 ÷ $40,000). They have no outstanding debts.

TABLE 14.2	Bob and Gail Weiss's Common Stock Portfolio						
Objective: Long-Term Growth (Average Risk, Moderate Dividends)							
Number of Shares	Company	Dividend per Share	Dividend Income	Price per Share	Total Cost (including commission)	Beta	Dividend Yield
1,000	Bancorp West, Inc.	$1.20	$ 1,200	$22	$ 22,200	0.86	5.4%
600	BST Inc.	2.80	1,680	40	24,200	1.00	6.9
1,000	Florida Southcoast Banks	1.20	1,200	23	23,200	0.84	5.2
1,000	Kings	1.60	1,600	25	25,300	0.88	6.3
500	Light Newspapers	0.92	460	46	23,200	1.12	2.0
600	Miller Foods	1.88	1,128	37	22,400	1.07	5.0
800	State Oil of California	1.00	800	27	21,800	1.30	3.7
600	Vornox	2.28	1,368	40	24,200	1.04	5.7
600	Woodstock	1.30	780	36	21,880	1.32	3.6%
	Total		$10,216		$208,300		4.9%

Portfolio beta = 1.04

The Weisses asked their investment adviser, Gene Bowles, to develop an investment portfolio for them. Together, they decided on the following strategy: First, Bob and Gail tend to be somewhat risk-averse; they do not wish to bear inordinate amounts of risk of loss. In addition, the Weisses indicated they would welcome some increase in spendable income. Given these facts, Gene Bowles suggested the portfolio presented in Table 14.2. With this portfolio their asset allocation would become about 84% common stock ($210,000 ÷ $250,000) and 16% money funds ($40,000 ÷ $250,000).

The emphasis in the portfolio is long-term growth at an average risk level, with a moderate dividend return. The portfolio consists of nine issues. This appears to be sufficient diversification. The portfolio's beta is 1.04, indicating a level of nondiversifiable risk about equal to the stock market as a whole. The portfolio's dividend yield is about 4.9%, which approximates the average dividend return for the entire stock market. The betas of individual securities in the portfolio vary somewhat. However, the portfolio's overall risk is moderate.

The Weiss portfolio consists of stocks from a wide range of U.S. businesses. All the companies have above-average growth potential. None is engaged in high-risk businesses that could face technological obsolescence or heavy foreign competition. Two banking stocks are included: Bancorp West, Inc., and Florida Southcoast Banks. The former is a well-managed bank holding company that owns the largest bank in California. The latter is a growing bank holding company located on the south coast of Florida. Both regions are experiencing rapid economic growth and population increases. BST Inc. appears to be well positioned in the growing communications industry. Kings is a food processor with a solid future. Light Newspapers is a large chain with many Sunbelt papers. Miller Foods is expanding as well, helped by its 2004 acquisition of Denton Companies, a superbly managed supermarket chain. The portfolio has two natural resource stocks, State Oil of California and Woodstock. These companies are well positioned in their respective industries. Vornox is a major drug firm that should benefit from America's aging demographic mix. All of the stocks in the Weisses' portfolio are securities of well-managed companies. With this portfolio, the Weisses will have potential price appreciation coupled with a steady dividend income.

Julio and Gina Vitello: Retirees

Having just sold their family business and liquidated their real estate investment property, Julio and Gina Vitello are eager to begin their retirement. At age 60, both have worked hard for 35 years building the successful business they recently sold. In addition, they have made some successful real estate investments over the years. The sale of their business and real estate holdings has netted them $600,000 after taxes. They wish to invest these funds and have asked their investment adviser, Jane Tuttle, to develop a portfolio for them.

Relevant financial information about the Vitellos is as follows: They own their home free and clear and have a $300,000 bond portfolio that yields yearly income of $30,000. In addition, they have $100,000 in short-term securities that they wish to hold as a ready cash reserve. Their most recent asset allocation is therefore 60% business and real estate investments ($600,000 ÷ $1,000,000), 30% bonds ($300,000 ÷ $1,000,000), and 10% short-term securities ($100,000 ÷ $1,000,000). Julio has a $200,000 whole-life insurance policy on his life, with Gina the designated beneficiary.

Now that they are retired, neither of the Vitellos plans to seek employment. They do have a small pension plan that will begin paying an income of $30,000 per year in 5 years. However, their main source of income will be their investment portfolio. During their last few working years, their combined yearly income was approximately $85,000. Their standard of living is comfortable, and they do not wish to change their lifestyle significantly. They do not plan to spend any of their investment capital on living expenses, because they want to keep their estate intact for their two children. Thus the Vitellos' basic investment objective is current income with some capital appreciation potential.

The Vitellos do not wish to reinvest in real estate, but rather have asked Jane Tuttle to develop a $600,000 securities portfolio for them. (They will leave their $300,000 bond portfolio and $100,000 in short-term securities undisturbed.) Their resulting asset allocation would shift to 60% common stock, 30% bonds, and 10% short-term securities. The portfolio Jane developed for the Vitellos is shown in Table 14.3 (on page 602).

The Vitello's portfolio contains nine stocks with approximately $65,000 invested in each issue. The emphasis is on quality, with low-risk/high-yield issues, and diversification. The portfolio's beta is approximately 0.80—a risk level that is below that of the general stock market. It is expected that a large portion of the portfolio's total return (dividends plus price appreciation) will be in the form of dividend income. The portfolio has a current dividend yield of approximately 8.7%, an above-average dividend yield. Dividend income totals over $52,000. That amount, added to the bond income and the short-term securities' interest, will provide the Vitellos with a gross income of about $85,000. The Vitellos' after-tax income will equal their working years' income, so they will not have to alter their lifestyle.

Four public utility stocks are included in the Vitellos' portfolio. Utility stocks are often suitable for low-risk, current-income-oriented portfolios. High-quality electric and natural gas concerns tend to have moderate growth in earnings and dividends. The four issues in the portfolio—Findly Power and Light, Gulf Gas and Electric, Public Power Company, and Southwest Utilities—have growing service areas and records of increases in profits and dividends. The stocks of two large U.S. companies, Energon and Smith, Roberts & Company,

TABLE 14.3	Julio and Gina Vitello's Common Stock Portfolio

Objective: Current Income (Low Risk, High Yield)

Number of Shares	Company	Dividend per Share	Dividend Income	Price per Share	Total Cost (including commission)	Beta	Dividend Yield
3,000	Alaska Bancorp, Inc.	$1.20	$ 3,600	$22	$ 66,600	0.86	5.4%
2,000	Dallas National Corporation	2.40	4,800	30	60,600	0.81	7.9
2,500	Energon	3.00	7,500	27	68,100	1.01	11.0
2,000	Findly Power and Light	3.36	6,720	32	64,600	0.63	10.4
2,000	Geoco	2.80	5,600	35	70,700	1.13	7.9
2,500	Gulf Gas and Electric	3.00	7,500	28	70,700	0.53	10.6
4,000	Public Power Company	1.76	7,040	16	64,600	0.72	10.9
2,500	Smith, Roberts & Company	1.36	3,400	27	68,100	0.92	5.0
3,000	Southwest Utilities	2.04	6,120	21	63,600	0.60	9.6
	Total		$52,280		$597,600		8.7%

Portfolio beta = 0.80

are included in the portfolio. Energon is a large U.S. energy company that offers a high dividend yield. Smith, Roberts is one of the largest retailers, and the company is now diversifying into information services. Two bank holding company stocks were also selected: Alaska Bancorp and Dallas National. Alaska Bancorp offers a top-quality vehicle to participate in Alaska's growth. Dallas National was selected because of its above-average dividend yield and because the firm is well positioned in the strong Dallas market. Additionally, the company has raised its dividend several times in recent years, and future dividend increases are expected. Geoco is a large company with chemical and other diversified operations. All the issues in the Vitellos' portfolio are well-known, relatively large corporations. Stability, low risk, and a relatively high dividend yield with some potential for increased share values characterize the stocks in this portfolio.

For a very different picture of investing for retirement, see the *Ethics* box on page 603.

Lucille Hatch: Widow

Most retirees have less money to invest than the Vitellos in the preceding example. Lucille Hatch, age 70, was recently widowed. Between the estate of her late husband, her personal assets, and their jointly owned assets, she has approximately $485,000 in liquid assets. All of it is in savings and money market accounts (short-term investments). Her current asset allocation is therefore 100% short-term investments. Lucille owns her home free and clear. Other than the interest on her savings, her income consists of $900 per month from Social Security. Unfortunately, her husband's employer did not have a pension plan. She has turned to her investment adviser, Charles Puckett, to discuss strategy and develop an investment policy.

Between Social Security and interest earned on her short-term investments, Lucille Hatch's current income is approximately $35,000 annually. She wishes to increase that income, if possible, while only minimally raising her risk exposure. Charles Puckett recommended the investment portfolio

⚖ ETHICS IN INVESTING

RETIREMENT AT ENRON

The first signs of trouble at Enron appeared in the summer of 2001, when Jeffrey Skilling unexpectedly resigned as the CEO. He was replaced by the company founder and former CEO Ken Lay. Lay assured Enron employees that the company had a bright future and said that they should step up and buy more company stock that, according to Lay, was undervalued.

What Lay did not tell his employees was that he and many other Enron executives were ready to dump millions of Enron shares. To make the situation worse, when insiders were selling their stock at will, the company prohibited its workers from selling stock held in voluntary retirement plans while the share price plunged. Many Enron employees—especially those who kept most of their retirement funds in Enron stock—lost everything when Enron declared bankruptcy in December 2001. Their fate was shared by employees at Global Crossing, K-mart, WorldCom, and other companies who had put too many of their retirement eggs in the company stock basket.

The company took extraordinary steps to prevent employees from making transactions with their 401(k) plan assets. These actions were later scrutinized by the U.S. Congress and the Labor Department. "Enron's employees have gotten the short end of the stick in the sudden collapse of this company, and we are committed to doing everything we can to help them," Labor Secretary Elaine Chao said in a statement.

More troubling was the news that despite the bankruptcy proceedings and massive layoffs of Enron workers—many of whom lost their entire retirement savings—the company paid $55 million in bonuses and incentives to a small group of employees. At the same time Linda Lay, the wife of the ex-CEO, stated in a TV interview that the couple had not been spared by Enron's collapse and was struggling to avoid personal bankruptcy. What the Lays did *not* reveal was that one year before Enron's collapse they had shifted millions of dollars of personal assets and bought variable annuities that guaranteed the couple an annual income of about $900,000 beginning in 2007. Under the current Texas law, annuity income is totally protected from creditors and potential lawsuits.

CRITICAL THINKING QUESTION Since the Enron scandal, Congress has been contemplating legislation that would require employees to diversify their retirement plans and prohibit them from investing all of their money in one company's stock. Would you support such legislation?

---

presented in Table 14.4 (on page 604). The portfolio's objective is to maximize current income while keeping risk at a low level. All of the money is invested in fixed-income securities. Approximately $415,000 goes to high-quality corporate bonds, and the balance ($70,000) is retained in short-term investments to provide a substantial contingency reserve. The resulting asset allocation is about 86% bonds ($415,000 ÷ $485,000) and 14% short-term investments ($70,000 ÷ $485,000). Investing in the bond portfolio will increase Lucille Hatch's yearly income from approximately $35,000 to about $48,700 ($10,800 Social Security, $3,500 earnings on short-term investments, and $34,400 bond interest). This puts her in a 30% marginal tax bracket (federal and state tax combined). Taxable corporate bonds were recommended over tax-free municipal bonds because her after-tax rate of return would be greater with the former.

TABLE 14.4 **Lucille Hatch's Bond Portfolio**

Objective: Maximize Current Income (Minimal Risk)

Par Value	Issue	Standard & Poor's Bond Rating	Interest Income	Quoted Price	Total Cost	Yield to Maturity	Current Yield
$70,000	Boise Northern 8.875% due 2026	A	$ 6,212.50	100	$ 70,000	8.875%	8.875%
70,000	Dalston Company 7.500% due 2010	A	5,250.00	98	68,600	8.000	7.650
70,000	Maryland-Pacific 6.700% due 2008	A	4,690.00	97	67,900	7.860	6.900
70,000	Pacific Utilities 8.875% due 2034	AA	6,212.50	100	70,000	8.875	8.875
70,000	Trans-States Telephone 8.700% due 2040	A	6,090.00	97	67,900	8.980	8.970
70,000	Urban Life 8.500% due 2011	AA	5,950.00	100	70,600	8.500	8.500
	Total		$34,405.00		$414,400	8.515%	8.300%

Turning to the portfolio, we see that there are six corporate bond issues that cost about $70,000 each. Each issuer is a high-quality company with a low risk of default. Lucille's portfolio is diversified in several ways: First, it contains a mix of utility, industrial, railroad, and financial issues. The two utility bond issues are Pacific Utilities and Trans-States Telephone. Both companies are large and financially secure. The two industrial concerns, Dalston and Maryland-Pacific, are large as well. Boise Northern is a financially solid railroad, and Urban Life is a large, secure insurance company. A second added measure of diversification is attained by staggering the bonds' maturities. They mature in six different years: 2008, 2010, 2011, 2026, 2034, and 2040. The shorter-term bonds will provide ready cash when they mature, and they generally will fluctuate less in price than the longer-term bonds. The portfolio has been diversified to keep the risk of loss low. By switching funds out of her short-term investments into bonds, Lucille Hatch was able to increase her current income substantially while experiencing only a small increase in risk.

IN REVIEW

CONCEPTS

14.1 Describe and contrast the expected portfolios for each of the following investors:
a. A retired investor in need of income.
b. A high-income, financially secure investor.
c. A young investor with a secure job and no dependents.

Evaluating the Performance of Individual Investments

LG 2

Imagine that one of your most important personal goals is to have accumulated $20,000 of savings 3 years from now in order to make the down payment on your first house. You project that the desired house will cost $100,000 and that the $20,000 will be sufficient to make a 15% down payment and pay the associated closing costs. Your calculations indicate that this goal can be achieved by investing existing savings plus an additional $200 per month over the next 3 years in a vehicle earning 12% per year. Projections of your earnings over the 3-year period indicate that you should just be able to set aside the needed $200 per month. You consult with an investment adviser, Cliff Orbit, who leads you to believe that under his management, the 12% return can be achieved.

It seems simple: Give Cliff your existing savings, send him $200 each month over the next 36 months, and at the end of that period, you will have the $20,000 needed to purchase the house. Unfortunately, there are many uncertainties involved. What if you don't set aside $200 each month? What if Cliff fails to earn the needed 12% annual return? What if in 3 years the desired house costs more than $100,000? Clearly, you must do more than simply devise what appears to be a feasible plan for achieving a future goal. Rarely is an investor guaranteed that planned investment and portfolio outcomes will actually occur. Although the four portfolios developed in the prior section are consistent with the investors' goals, there is no guarantee that their actual outcomes will be as forecast. Therefore, it is important to assess periodically your progress toward achieving your investment goals.

As actual outcomes occur, you must compare them to the *planned* outcomes and make any necessary alterations in your plans—or in your goals. Knowing how to measure investment performance is therefore crucial. Here we will emphasize measures suitable for analyzing investment performance. We begin with sources of data.

Obtaining Needed Data

The first step in analyzing investment returns is gathering data that reflect the actual performance of each investment. As pointed out in Chapter 3, many sources of investment information are available, both online and in print. The *Wall Street Journal* and Yahoo.com, for example, contain numerous items of information useful in assessing the performance of securities. The same type of information that is used to *make* an investment decision is used to *evaluate* the performance of investments. Two key areas to stay informed about are (1) returns on owned investments and (2) economic and market activity.

Return Data The basic ingredient in analyzing investment returns is current market information, such as daily price quotations for stocks and bonds. Investors often maintain logs that contain the cost of each investment, as well as dividends, interest, and other sources of income received. By regularly recording price and return data, you can create an ongoing record of price fluctuations and cumulative returns. You should also monitor corporate earnings and dividends, which will affect a company's stock price. The two sources of investment return—current income and capital gains—must of course be combined to determine total return. Combining return components using the techniques presented in Chapter 4 will be illustrated for some popular investment vehicles later in this chapter.

Economic and Market Activity Changes in the economy and market will affect returns—both the level of current income and the market value of an investment vehicle. The astute investor keeps abreast of international, national, and local economic and market developments. By following economic and market changes, you should be able to assess their potential impact on returns. As economic and market conditions change, you must be prepared to make revisions in the portfolio. In essence, being a knowledgeable investor will improve your chances of generating a profit (or avoiding a loss).

Indexes of Investment Performance

In measuring investment performance, it is often worthwhile to compare your returns with broad-based market measures. Indexes useful for the analysis of common stock include the Dow Jones Industrial Average (DJIA), the Standard & Poor's 500 Stock Composite Index (S&P 500), and the Nasdaq Composite Index. (Detailed discussions of these averages and indexes can be found in Chapter 3.) Although the DJIA is widely cited by the news media, it is *not* considered the most appropriate comparative gauge of stock price movement, because of its narrow coverage. If your portfolio is composed of a broad range of common stocks, the S&P 500 index is probably a more appropriate tool.

A number of indicators are also available for assessing the general behavior of the bond markets. These indicators consider either bond price behavior or bond yield. The Dow Jones Corporate Bond Index, based on the closing prices of 32 industrial, 32 financial, and 32 utility/telecom bonds, is a popular measure of bond price behavior. It reflects the mathematical average of the closing prices of the bonds. Also available are bond yield data. These reflect the rate of return one would earn on a bond purchased today and held to maturity. Popular sources of these data include the *Wall Street Journal*, *Barron's*, Standard & Poor's, Mergent, Yahoo.com, and the Federal Reserve. Indexes of bond price and bond yield performance can be obtained for specific types of bonds (industrial, utility, and municipal), as well as on a composite basis. In addition, indexes reported in terms of *total returns* are available for both stocks and bonds. They combine dividend/interest income with price behavior (capital gain or loss) to reflect total return.

The Lipper indexes are frequently used to assess the general behavior of mutual funds. They are available for various types of equity and bond funds. Unfortunately, for most other types of funds, no widely published index or average is available. A few other indexes cover listed options and futures.

Measuring the Performance of Investment Vehicles

Reliable techniques for consistently measuring the performance of each investment vehicle are needed to monitor an investment portfolio. In particular, the holding period return (HPR) measure, first presented in Chapter 4, can be used to determine *actual* return performance. Investment holdings need to be evaluated periodically over time—at least once a year. HPR is an excellent way to assess actual return behavior, because it captures *total return* performance. It is most appropriate for holding or assessment periods of 1 year or less. Total return, in this context, includes the periodic cash income from the investment as well as price appreciation (or loss), whether realized or unrealized. The calculation of returns for periods of more than a year should be made using yield (internal rate of return), because it recognizes the time value of money. Yield can be calculated using the techniques described in Chapter 4 (pages 155–159). Because the following discussions center on the annual assessment of return, HPR will be used as the measure of return.

The formula for HPR, presented in Chapter 4 (Equation 4.8) and applied throughout this chapter, is restated in Equation 14.1:

Equation 14.1
$$\text{Holding period return} = \frac{\underset{\text{during period}}{\text{Current income}} + \underset{\text{during period}}{\text{Capital gain (or loss)}}}{\text{Beginning investment value}}$$

Equation 14.1a
$$\text{HPR} = \frac{C + CG}{V_0}$$

where

Equation 14.2
$$\underset{\text{during period}}{\text{Capital gain (or loss)}} = \underset{\text{investment value}}{\text{Ending}} - \underset{\text{investment value}}{\text{Beginning}}$$

Equation 14.2a
$$CG = V_n - V_0$$

Stocks and Bonds There are several measures of investment return for stocks and bonds. *Dividend yield,* discussed in Chapter 6, measures the current yearly dividend return earned from a stock investment. It is calculated by dividing a stock's yearly cash dividend by its price. The *current yield* and *yield-to-maturity* (promised yield) for bonds, analyzed in Chapter 11, capture various components of return but do not reflect actual total return. The *holding period return* method *measures the total return (income plus change in value) actually earned on an investment over a given investment period.* We will use HPR, with a holding period of approximately 1 year, in the illustrations that follow.

Stocks The HPR for common and preferred stocks includes both cash dividends received and any price change in the security during the period of ownership. Table 14.5 (on page 608) illustrates the HPR calculation as applied to the actual performance of a common stock. Assume you purchased 1,000 shares of Dallas National Corporation in May 2004 at a cost of $27,312 (including commissions). After holding the stock for just over 1 year, you sold the stock, reaping proceeds of $32,040. You also received $2,000 in cash dividends during the period of ownership and realized a $4,728 capital gain on the sale. Thus the calculated HPR is 24.63%.

This HPR was calculated without consideration for income taxes paid on the dividends and capital gain. Because many investors are concerned with both pretax and after-tax rates of return, it is useful to calculate an after-tax HPR. We assume, for simplicity in this example, that you are in the 30% ordinary tax bracket (federal and state combined). We also assume that, for federal

---

TABLE 14.5 Calculation of Pretax HPR on a Common Stock

Security: Dallas National Corporation common stock
Date of purchase: May 1, 2004
Purchase cost: $27,312
Date of sale: May 7, 2005
Sale proceeds: $32,040
Dividends received (May 2004 to May 2005): $2,000

$$\text{Holding period return} = \frac{\$2,000 + (\$32,040 - \$27,312)}{\$27,312}$$

$$= +\underline{\$24.63\%}$$

---

and state tax purposes, dividends and capital gains for holding periods of more than 12 months are taxed at a 15% rate. Thus both your dividend and capital gain income is taxed at a 15% rate. Income taxes reduce the after-tax dividend income to $1,700 [(1 − 0.15) × $2,000] and the after-tax capital gain to $4,019 [(1 − 0.15) × ($32,040 − $27,312)]. The after-tax HPR is therefore 20.94% [($1,700 + $4,019) ÷ $27,312], a reduction of 3.69 percentage points. It should be clear that both pretax HPR and after-tax HPR are useful gauges of return.

Bonds The HPR for a bond investment is similar to that for stocks. The calculation holds for both straight debt and convertible issues. It includes the two components of a bond investor's return: interest income and capital gain or loss. Calculation of the HPR on a bond investment is illustrated in Table 14.6. Assume you purchased Phoenix Brewing Company bonds for $10,000, held them for just over 1 year, and then realized $9,704 at their sale. In addition, you earned $1,000 in interest during the period of ownership. The HPR of this investment is 7.04%. The HPR is lower than the bond's current yield of 10% ($1,000 interest ÷ $10,000 purchase price) because the bonds were sold at a capital loss. Assuming a 30% ordinary tax bracket and a 15% capital gains tax rate (because the bond has been held more than 12 months), the after-tax HPR is 4.48%: {[(1 − 0.30) × $1,000] + [(1 − 0.15) × ($9,704 − $10,000)]} ÷ $10,000. This is about 2.6% less than the pretax HPR.

Mutual Funds The two basic components of return from a mutual fund investment are dividend income (including any capital gains distribution) and change in value. The basic HPR equation for mutual funds is identical to that

---

TABLE 14.6 Calculation of Pretax HPR on a Bond

Security: Phoenix Brewing Company 10% bonds
Date of purchase: June 2, 2004
Purchase cost: $10,000
Date of sale: June 5, 2005
Sale proceeds: $9,704
Interest earned (June 2004 to June 2005): $1,000

$$\text{Holding period return} = \frac{\$1,000 + (\$9,704 - \$10,000)}{\$10,000}$$

$$= +\underline{\$7.04\%}$$

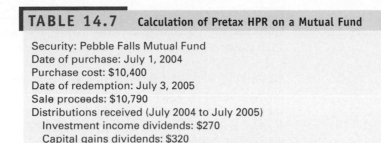

TABLE 14.7 Calculation of Pretax HPR on a Mutual Fund

Security: Pebble Falls Mutual Fund
Date of purchase: July 1, 2004
Purchase cost: $10,400
Date of redemption: July 3, 2005
Sale proceeds: $10,790
Distributions received (July 2004 to July 2005)
    Investment income dividends: $270
    Capital gains dividends: $320

$$\text{Holding period return} = \frac{(\$270 + \$320) + (\$10,790 - \$10,400)}{\$10,400}$$

$$= +\underline{\$9.42\%}$$

for stocks. Table 14.7 presents a holding period return calculation for a no-load mutual fund. Assume you purchased 1,000 shares of the fund in July 2004 at a NAV of $10.40 per share. Because it is a no-load fund, no commission was charged, so your cost was $10,400. During the 1-year period of ownership, the Pebble Falls Mutual Fund distributed investment income dividends totaling $270 and capital gains dividends of $320. You redeemed (sold) this fund at a NAV of $10.79 per share, thereby realizing $10,790. As seen in Table 14.7, the pretax holding period return on this investment is 9.42%. Assuming a 30% ordinary tax bracket and a 15% dividend and capital gains tax rate (because the fund has been held for more than 12 months), the after-tax HPR for the fund is 8.01%: {[(1 − 0.15) × ($270 + $320)] + [(1 − 0.15) × ($10,790 − $10,400)]} ÷ $10,400. This is about 1.4% below the pretax return.

Options and Futures The only source of return on options and futures is capital gains. To calculate a holding period return for an investment in a call option, for instance, the basic HPR formula is used, but current income is set equal to zero. If you purchased a call on 100 shares of ecommerce.com for $325 and sold the contract for $385 after holding it for just over 12 months, the pretax holding period return would be 18.46%. This is simply sales proceeds ($385) minus cost ($325) divided by cost. Assuming the 15% capital gains tax rate applies, the after-tax HPR would be 15.69%, which is the after-tax gain of $51 [(1 − 0.15) × $60] divided by cost ($325). The HPRs of futures are calculated in a similar fashion. Because the return is in the form of capital gains only, the HPR analysis can be applied to any investment on a pretax or an after-tax basis. (The same basic procedure is used for securities that are sold short.)

Comparing Performance to Investment Goals

After computing an HPR (or yield) on an investment, you should compare it to your investment goal. Keeping track of an investment's performance will help you decide which investments you should continue to hold and which you might want to sell. Clearly, an investment would be a candidate for sale under

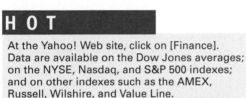

the following conditions: (1) The investment failed to perform up to expectations and no real change in performance is anticipated. (2) It has met the original investment objective. (3) Better investment outlets are currently available.

Balancing Risk and Return In this book, we have frequently discussed the basic tradeoff between investment risk and return. The relationship is fundamentally as follows: To earn more return, you must take more risk. In analyzing an investment, the key question is, "Am I getting the proper return for the amount of investment risk I am taking?"

Nongovernment security investments are by nature riskier than U.S. government bonds or insured money market deposit accounts. This implies that *a rational investor should invest in these riskier vehicles only when the expected rate of return is well in excess of what could have been earned from a low-risk investment.* Thus one benchmark against which to compare investment returns is the rate of return on low-risk investments. If one's risky investments are outperforming low-risk investments, they are obtaining extra return for taking extra risk. If they are not outperforming low-risk investments, you should carefully reexamine your investment strategy.

Isolating Problem Investments A *problem investment* is one that has not lived up to expectations. It may be a loss situation or an investment that has provided a return less than you expected. Many investors try to forget about problem investments, hoping the problem will go away or the investment will turn itself around. This is obviously a mistake. Problem investments require immediate attention, not neglect. In studying a problem investment, the key question is, "Should I take my loss and get out, or should I hang on and hope it turns around?"

It is best to analyze each investment in a portfolio periodically. For each, two questions should be considered. First, has it performed in a manner that could reasonably be expected? Second, if you didn't currently own it, would you buy it today? If the answers to both are negative, then the investment probably should be sold. A negative answer to one of the questions qualifies the investment for the "problem list." It should then be watched closely. In general, maintaining a portfolio of investments requires constant attention and analysis to ensure the best chance of satisfactory returns. Problem investments need special attention and work.

IN REVIEW

CONCEPTS

14.2 Why is it important to continuously manage and control your portfolio?

14.3 What role does current market information play in analyzing investment returns? How do changes in economic and market activity affect investment returns? Explain.

14.4 Which indexes can you use to compare your investment performance to general market returns? Briefly explain each of these indexes.

14.5 What are indicators of bond market behavior, and how are they different from stock market indicators? Name three sources of bond yield data.

14.6 Briefly discuss *holding period return (HPR)* and *yield* as measures of investment return. Are they equivalent? Explain.

14.7 Distinguish between the types of dividend distributions that mutual funds make. Are these dividends the only source of return for a mutual fund investor? Explain.

14.8 Under what three conditions would an investment holding be a candidate for sale? What must be true about the expected return on a risky investment, when compared with the return on a low-risk investment, to cause a rational investor to acquire the risky investment? Explain.

14.9 What is a *problem investment?* What two questions should one consider when analyzing each investment in a portfolio?

Assessing Portfolio Performance

active portfolio management building a portfolio using traditional and modern approaches and managing and controlling it to achieve its objectives; a worthwhile activity that can result in superior returns.

A portfolio can be either passively or actively built and managed. A *passive portfolio* results from buying and holding a well-diversified portfolio over the given investment horizon. An *active portfolio* is built using the traditional and modern approaches presented in Chapter 5 and is managed and controlled to achieve its stated objectives. Passive portfolios may at times outperform equally risky active portfolios. But evidence suggests that **active portfolio management** can result in superior returns. Many of the ideas presented in this text are consistent with the belief that active portfolio management will improve your chance of earning superior returns.

Once a portfolio is built, the first step in active portfolio management is to assess performance on a regular basis and use that information to revise the portfolio. Calculating the portfolio return can be tricky. The procedures used to assess portfolio performance are based on many of the concepts presented earlier in this chapter. Here we will demonstrate how to assess portfolio performance, using a hypothetical securities portfolio over a 1-year holding period. We will examine each of three measures that can be used to compare a portfolio's return with a risk-adjusted, market-adjusted rate of return.

Measuring Portfolio Return

Table 14.8 (on page 612) presents the investment portfolio, as of January 1, 2005, of Bob Hathaway. He is a 50-year-old widower, whose children are married. His income is $60,000 per year. His primary investment objective is long-term growth with a moderate dividend return. He selects stocks with two criteria in mind: quality and growth potential. On January 1, 2005, his portfolio consisted of 10 issues, all of good quality. Hathaway has been fortunate in his selection process: He has approximately $74,000 in unrealized price appreciation in his portfolio. During 2005, he decided to make a change in the portfolio. On May 7 he sold 1,000 shares of Dallas National Corporation for $32,040. Hathaway's holding period return for that issue was discussed earlier in this chapter (see Table 14.5). Using proceeds from the Dallas National sale, he acquired an additional 1,000 shares of Florida Southcoast Banks on May 10, because he liked the prospects for the Florida bank. Florida Southcoast is based in one of the fastest-growing counties in the country.

Measuring the Amount Invested Every investor would be well advised to list his or her holdings periodically, as is done in Table 14.8. The table shows

TABLE 14.8 Bob Hathaway's Portfolio (January 1, 2005)

Number of Shares	Company	Date Acquired	Total Cost (including commission)	Cost per Share	Current Price per Share	Current Value
1,000	Bancorp West, Inc.	1/16/03	$ 21,610	$21.61	$30	$ 30,000
1,000	Dallas National Corporation	5/01/04	27,312	27.31	29	29,000
1,000	Dator Companies, Inc.	4/13/99	13,704	13.70	27	27,000
500	Excelsior Industries	8/16/02	40,571	81.14	54	27,000
1,000	Florida Southcoast Banks	12/16/02	17,460	17.46	30	30,000
1,000	Maryland-Pacific	9/27/02	22,540	22.54	26	26,000
1,000	Moronson	2/27/02	19,100	19.10	47	47,000
500	Northwest Mining and Mfg.	4/17/03	25,504	51.00	62	31,000
1,000	Rawland Petroleum	3/12/03	24,903	24.90	30	30,000
1,000	Vornox	4/16/03	37,120	37.12	47	47,000
	Total		$249,824			$324,000

number of shares, acquisition date, cost, and current value for each issue. These data aid in continually formulating strategy decisions. The cost data, for example, are used to determine the amount invested. Hathaway's portfolio does not utilize the leverage of a margin account. Were leverage present, all return calculations would be based on the investor's *equity* in the account. (Recall from Chapter 2 that an investor's equity in a margin account equals the total value of all the securities in the account minus any margin debt.)

To measure Hathaway's return on his invested capital, we need to calculate the 1-year holding period return. His invested capital as of January 1, 2005, is $324,000. No new additions of capital were made in the portfolio during 2005, although he sold one stock, Dallas National, and used the proceeds to buy another, Florida Southcoast Banks.

Measuring Income There are two sources of return from a portfolio of common stocks: income and capital gains. Current income is realized from dividends or, for bonds, is earned in the form of interest. Investors must report taxable dividends and interest on federal and state income tax returns. Companies are required to furnish income reports (Form 1099-DIV for dividends and Form 1099-INT for interest) to stockholders and bondholders. Many investors maintain logs to keep track of dividend and interest income as it is received.

Table 14.9 lists Hathaway's dividends for 2005. He received two quarterly dividends of 45 cents per share before he sold the Dallas National stock. He also received two 32-cent-per-share quarterly dividends on the additional Florida Southcoast Banks shares he acquired. His total dividend income for 2005 was $10,935.

Measuring Capital Gains Table 14.10 shows the unrealized gains in value for each of the issues in the Hathaway portfolio. The January 1, 2005, and December 31, 2005, values are listed for each issue except the additional shares of Florida Southcoast Banks. The amounts listed for Florida Southcoast Banks reflect the fact that 1,000 additional shares of the stock were acquired

TABLE 14.9   Dividend Income on Hathaway's Portfolio (Calendar year 2005)

Number of Shares	Company	Annual Dividend per Share	Dividends Received
1,000	Bancorp West, Inc.	$1.20	$ 1,200
1,000	Dallas National Corporation*	1.80	900
1,000	Dator Companies, Inc.	1.12	1,120
500	Excelsior Industries	2.00	1,000
2,000	Florida Southcoast Banks**	1.28	1,920
1,000	Maryland-Pacific	1.10	1,100
1,000	Moronson	—	—
500	Northwest Mining and Mfg.	2.05	1,025
1,000	Rawland Petroleum	1.20	1,200
1,000	Vornox	1.47	1,470
	Total		$10,935

*Sold May 7, 2005.
**1,000 shares acquired on May 10, 2005.

on May 10, 2005, at a cost of $32,040. Hathaway's current holdings had beginning-of-the-year values of $327,040 (including the additional Florida Southcoast Banks shares at the date of purchase) and are worth $356,000 at year-end.

During 2005, the portfolio increased in value by 8.9%, or $28,960, in unrealized capital gains. In addition, Hathaway realized a capital gain in 2005 by selling his Dallas National holding. From January 1, 2005, until its sale on May 7, 2005, the Dallas National holding rose in value from $29,000 to

TABLE 14.10   Unrealized Gains in Value of Hathaway's Portfolio (January 1, 2005, to December 31, 2005)

Number of Shares	Company	Market Value (1/1/05)	Market Price (12/31/05)	Market Value (12/31/05)	Unrealized Gain (Loss)	Percentage Change
1,000	Bancorp West, Inc.	$ 30,000	$27	$ 27,000	($ 3,000)	−10.0%
1,000	Dator Companies, Inc.	27,000	36	36,000	9,000	+33.3
500	Excelsior Industries	27,000	66	33,000	6,000	+22.2
2,000	Florida Southcoast Banks*	62,040	35	70,000	7,960	+12.8
1,000	Maryland-Pacific	26,000	26	26,000	—	—
1,000	Moronson	47,000	55	55,000	8,000	+17.0
500	Northwest Mining and Mfg.	31,000	60	30,000	(1,000)	− 3.2
1,000	Rawland Petroleum	30,000	36	36,000	6,000	+20.0
1,000	Vornox	47,000	43	43,000	(4,000)	− 8.5
	Total	$327,040**		$356,000	$28,960	+ 8.9%

*1,000 additional shares acquired on May 10, 2005, at a cost of $32,040. The value listed is the cost plus the market value of the previously owned shares as of January 1, 2005.

**This total includes the $324,000 market value of the portfolio on January 1, 2005 (from Table 14.8) plus the $3,040 *realized* gain on the sale of the Dallas National Corporation stock on May 7, 2005. The inclusion of the realized gain in this total is necessary to calculate the *unrealized* gain on the portfolio during 2005.

$32,040. This was the only sale in 2005, so the total *realized* gain was $3,040. During 2005, the portfolio had both a realized gain of $3,040 and an unrealized gain of $28,960. The total gain in value equals the sum of the two: $32,000. Put another way, no capital was added to or withdrawn from the portfolio over the year. Therefore, the total capital gain is simply the difference between the year-end market value (of $356,000, from Table 14.10) and the value on January 1 (of $324,000, from Table 14.8). This, of course, amounts to $32,000. Of that amount, for tax purposes, only $3,040 is considered realized.

Measuring the Portfolio's Holding Period Return We use the holding period return (HPR) to measure the total return on the Hathaway portfolio during 2005. The basic 1-year HPR formula for portfolios is

Equation 14.3

$$\text{Holding period return for a portfolio} = \frac{\text{Dividends and interest received} + \text{Realized gain} + \text{Unrealized gain}}{\text{Initial equity investment} + \left(\text{New funds} \times \frac{\text{Number of months in portfolio}}{12}\right) - \left(\text{Withdrawn funds} \times \frac{\text{Number of months withdrawn from portfolio}}{12}\right)}$$

Equation 14.3a

$$\text{HPR}_p = \frac{C + RG + UG}{E_0 + \left(NF \times \dfrac{ip}{12}\right) - \left(WF \times \dfrac{wp}{12}\right)}$$

This formula includes both the realized gains (income plus capital gains) and the unrealized yearly gains of the portfolio. Portfolio additions and deletions are time-weighted for the number of months they are in the portfolio.

Table 14.10 lays out in detail the portfolio's change in value: All the issues that are in the portfolio as of December 31, 2005, are listed, and the unrealized gain during the year is calculated. The beginning and year-end values are included for comparison purposes. The crux of the analysis is the HPR calculation for the year, presented in Table 14.11. All the elements of a portfolio's return are included. Dividends total $10,935 (from Table 14.9). The realized gain of $3,040 represents the increment in value of the Dallas National holding from January 1, 2005, until its sale. During 2005 the portfolio had a $28,960 unrealized gain (from Table 14.10). There were no additions of new funds, and no funds were withdrawn. Utilizing Equation 14.3 for HPR, we find that the portfolio had a total return of 13.25% in 2005.

Comparison of Return with Overall Market Measures

Bob Hathaway can compare the HPR figure for his portfolio with market measures such as stock indexes. This comparison will show how Hathaway's portfolio is doing in relation to the stock market as a whole. The S&P 500 Stock Composite Index and the Nasdaq Composite Index are acceptable indexes for this type of analysis. They are broadly based and so can be said to represent the stock market as a whole. Assume that during 2005, the return on the S&P 500 index was +10.75% (including both dividends and capital gains). The return from Hathaway's portfolio was +13.25%, which compares very

TABLE 14.11 Holding Period Return Calculation on Hathaway's Portfolio (January 1, 2005, to December 31, 2005, holding period)

Data

Portfolio value (1/1/05):	$324,000
Portfolio value (12/31/05):	$356,000
Realized appreciation (1/1/05 to 5/7/05 when Dallas National Corporation was sold):	$3,040
Unrealized appreciation (1/1/05 to 12/31/05):	$28,960
Dividends received:	$10,935
New funds invested or withdrawn:	None

Portfolio HPR Calculation

$$HPR_p = \frac{\$10,935 + \$3,040 + \$28,960}{\$324,000}$$

$$= +\underline{13.25\%}$$

favorably with the broadly based index. The Hathaway portfolio performed about 23% better than the broad indicator of stock market return.

Such a comparison factors out general market movements, but *it fails to consider risk.* Clearly, a raw return figure, such as this +13.25%, requires further analysis. A number of risk-adjusted, market-adjusted rate-of-return measures are available for use in assessing portfolio performance. Here we'll discuss three of the most popular—Sharpe's measure, Treynor's measure, and Jensen's measure—and demonstrate their application to Hathaway's portfolio.

Sharpe's Measure Sharpe's measure of portfolio performance, developed by William F. Sharpe, compares the risk premium on a portfolio to the portfolio's standard deviation of return. The risk premium on a portfolio is the total portfolio return minus the risk-free rate. Sharpe's measure can be expressed as the following formula:

Sharpe's measure
a measure of portfolio performance that measures the *risk premium per unit of total risk,* which is measured by the portfolio standard deviation of return.

Equation 14.4

$$\text{Sharp's measure} = \frac{\text{Total portfolio return} - \text{Risk-free rate}}{\text{Portfolio standard deviation of return}}$$

Equation 14.4a

$$SM = \frac{r_p - R_F}{s_p}$$

This measure allows the investor to assess the *risk premium per unit of total risk,* which is measured by the portfolio standard deviation of return.

Assume the risk-free rate, R_F, is 7.50% and the standard deviation of return on Hathaway's portfolio, s_p, is 16%. The total portfolio return, r_p, which is the HPR for Hathaway's portfolio calculated in Table 14.11, is 13.25%. Substituting those values into Equation 14.4, we get Sharpe's measure, *SM.*

$$SM = \frac{13.25\% - 7.50\%}{16\%} = \frac{5.75\%}{16\%} = \underline{0.36}$$

Sharpe's measure is meaningful when compared either to other portfolios or to the market. In general, the higher the value of Sharpe's measure, the better—the higher the risk premium per unit of risk. If we assume that the market return, r_m, is currently 10.75% and the standard deviation of return for the market portfolio, s_{p_m}, is 11.25%, Sharpe's measure for the market, SM_m, is

$$SM_m = \frac{10.75\% - 7.50\%}{11.25\%} = \frac{3.25\%}{11.25\%} = \underline{\underline{0.29}}$$

Because Sharpe's measure of 0.36 for Hathaway's portfolio is greater than the measure of 0.29 for the market portfolio, Hathaway's portfolio exhibits superior performance. Its risk premium per unit of risk is above that of the market. Had Sharpe's measure for Hathaway's portfolio been below that of the market (below 0.29), the portfolio's performance would be considered inferior to the market performance.

Treynor's measure
a measure of portfolio performance that measures the *risk premium per unit of nondiversifiable risk,* which is measured by the portfolio beta.

Treynor's Measure Jack L. Treynor developed a portfolio performance measure similar to Sharpe's measure. **Treynor's measure** uses the portfolio beta to measure the portfolio's risk. Treynor therefore focuses only on *nondiversifiable risk,* assuming that the portfolio has been built in a manner that diversifies away all diversifiable risk. (In contrast, Sharpe focuses on *total risk.*) Treynor's measure is calculated as shown in Equation 14.5.

Equation 14.5

$$\text{Treynor's measure} = \frac{\text{Total portfolio return} - \text{Risk-free rate}}{\text{Portfolio beta}}$$

Equation 14.5a

$$TM = \frac{r_p - R_F}{b_p}$$

This measure gives the *risk premium per unit of nondiversifiable risk,* which is measured by the portfolio beta.

Using the data for the Hathaway portfolio presented earlier and assuming that the beta for Hathaway's portfolio, b_p, is 1.20, we can substitute into Equation 14.5 to get Treynor's measure, TM, for Hathaway's portfolio.

$$TM = \frac{13.25\% - 7.50\%}{1.20} = \frac{5.75\%}{1.20} = \underline{\underline{4.79\%}}$$

H O T

A good discussion of the Sharpe, Treynor, and Jenson measures of performance can be found at:

**www.cbe.wwu.edu/Hall/MBA542/
evaluation-of-portfolio-performa.htm**

Treynor's measure, like Sharpe's measure, is useful when compared either to other portfolios or to the market. Generally, the higher the value of Treynor's measure, the better—the greater the risk premium per unit of nondiversifiable risk. Again assuming that the market return, r_m, is 10.75%, and recognizing that, by definition, the beta for the market portfolio, b_{p_m}, is 1.00, we can use Equation 14.5 to find Treynor's measure for the market, TM_m.

$$TM_m = \frac{10.75\% - 7.50\%}{1.00} = \frac{3.25\%}{1.00} = \underline{3.25\%}$$

The fact that Treynor's measure of 4.79% for Hathaway's portfolio is greater than the market portfolio measure of 3.25% indicates that Hathaway's portfolio exhibits superior performance. Its risk premium per unit of nondiversifiable risk is above that of the market. Conversely, had Treynor's measure for Hathaway's portfolio been below that of the market (below 3.25%), the portfolio's performance would be viewed as inferior to that of the market.

Jensen's measure (Jensen's alpha)
a measure of portfolio performance that uses the portfolio beta and CAPM to calculate its *excess return,* which may be positive, zero, or negative.

Jensen's Measure (Jensen's Alpha) Michael C. Jensen developed a portfolio performance measure that seems quite different from the measures of Sharpe and Treynor yet is theoretically consistent with Treynor's measure. **Jensen's measure,** also called **Jensen's alpha,** is based on the *capital asset pricing model (CAPM),* which was developed in Chapter 5 (see Equation 5.3). It calculates the portfolio's *excess return.* Excess return is the amount by which the portfolio's actual return deviates from its required return, which is determined using its beta and CAPM. The value of the excess return may be positive, zero, or negative. Like Treynor's measure, Jensen's measure focuses only on the *nondiversifiable,* or *relevant, risk* by using beta and CAPM. It assumes that the portfolio has been adequately diversified. Jensen's measure is calculated as shown in Equation 14.6.

Equation 14.6

Jensen's measure = (Total portfolio return − Risk-free rate) − [Portfolio beta × (Market return − Risk-free rate)]

Equation 14.6a

$$JM = (r_p - R_F) - [b_p \times (r_m - R_F)]$$

Jensen's measure indicates the difference between the portfolio's actual return and its required return. Positive values are preferred. They indicate that the portfolio earned a return in excess of its risk-adjusted, market-adjusted required return. A value of zero indicates that the portfolio earned *exactly* its required return. Negative values indicate the portfolio failed to earn its required return.

Using the data for Hathaway's portfolio presented earlier, we can substitute into Equation 14.6 to get Jensen's measure, *JM,* for Hathaway's portfolio.

$$JM = (13.25\% - 7.50\%) - [1.20 \times (10.75\% - 7.50\%)]$$

$$= 5.75\% - (1.20 \times 3.25\%) = 5.75\% - 3.90\% = \underline{1.85\%}$$

The 1.85% value for Jensen's measure indicates that Hathaway's portfolio earned an *excess return* 1.85 percentage points above its required return, given its nondiversifiable risk as measured by beta. Clearly, Hathaway's portfolio has outperformed the market on a risk-adjusted basis.

Note that unlike the Sharpe and Treynor measures, Jensen's measure, through its use of CAPM, automatically adjusts for the market return. Therefore, there is no need to make a separate market comparison. In general, the higher the value of Jensen's measure, the better the portfolio has performed.

TIME TO REVISE YOUR PORTFOLIO?—Over time, you will need to review your portfolio to ensure that it reflects the right risk-return characteristics for your goals and needs. Here are four good reasons to perform this task:

- A major life event—marriage, birth of a child, job loss, illness, loss of a spouse, a child's finishing college—changes your investment objectives.
- The proportion of one asset class increases or decreases substantially.
- You expect to reach a specific goal within 2 years.
- The percentage in an asset class varies from your original allocation by 10% or more.

portfolio revision
the process of selling certain issues in a portfolio and purchasing new ones to replace them.

Only those portfolios with positive Jensen measures have outperformed the market on a risk-adjusted basis. Because of its computational simplicity, its reliance only on nondiversifiable risk, and its inclusion of both risk and market adjustments, Jensen's measure (alpha) tends to be preferred over those of Sharpe and Treynor for assessing portfolio performance.

Portfolio Revision

In the Hathaway portfolio we have been discussing, one transaction occurred during 2005. The reason for this transaction was that Hathaway believed the Florida Southcoast Banks stock had more return potential than the Dallas National stock. You should periodically analyze your portfolio with one basic question in mind: "Does this portfolio continue to meet my needs?" In other words, does the portfolio contain those issues that are best suited to your risk-return needs? Investors who systematically study the issues in their portfolios will occasionally find a need to sell certain issues and purchase new securities to replace them. This process is commonly called **portfolio revision.** As the economy evolves, certain industries and stocks become either less or more attractive as investments. In today's stock market, timeliness is the essence of profitability.

Given the dynamics of the investment world, periodic reallocation and rebalancing of the portfolio are a necessity. Many circumstances require such changes. As we demonstrated earlier in this chapter, as an investor nears retirement, the portfolio's emphasis normally evolves from a strategy that stresses growth/capital appreciation to one that seeks to preserve capital. Changing a portfolio's emphasis normally occurs as an evolutionary process rather than an overnight switch. Individual issues in the portfolio often change in risk-return characteristics. As this occurs, you would be wise to eliminate those issues that do not meet your objectives. In addition, the need for diversification is constant. As issues rise or fall in value, their diversification effect may be lessened. Thus portfolio revision may be needed to maintain diversification in the portfolio.

IN REVIEW

CONCEPTS

14.10 What is *active portfolio management?* Will it result in superior returns? Explain.

14.11 Describe the steps involved in measuring portfolio return. Explain the role of the portfolio's HPR in this process, and explain why one must differentiate between realized and unrealized gains.

14.12 Why is comparing a portfolio's return to the return on a broad market index generally inadequate? Explain.

14.13 Briefly describe each of the following return measures available for assessing portfolio performance, and explain how they are used.
   a. Sharpe's measure.
   b. Treynor's measure.
   c. Jensen's measure (Jensen's alpha).

14.14 Why is Jensen's measure (alpha) generally preferred over the measures of Sharpe and Treynor for assessing portfolio performance? Explain.

14.15 Explain the role of *portfolio revision* in the process of managing a portfolio.

Timing Transactions

The essence of timing is to "buy low and sell high." This is the dream of all investors. Although there is no tried-and-true way to achieve such a goal, there are several methods you can utilize to time purchases and sales. First, there are formula plans, which we discuss next. Investors can also use limit and stop-loss orders as a timing aid, can follow procedures for warehousing liquidity, and can take into consideration other aspects of timing when selling their investments.

Formula Plans

formula plans
mechanical methods of portfolio management that try to take advantage of price changes that result from cyclical price movements.

Formula plans are mechanical methods of portfolio management that try to take advantage of price changes that result from cyclical price movements. Formula plans are not set up to provide unusually high returns. Rather, they are conservative strategies employed by investors who do not wish to bear a high level of risk. Four popular formula plans are discussed here: dollar-cost averaging, the constant-dollar plan, the constant-ratio plan, and the variable-ratio plan.

Dollar-Cost Averaging **Dollar-cost averaging** is a formula plan in which a fixed dollar amount is invested in a security at fixed time intervals. In this passive buy-and-hold strategy, the periodic dollar investment is held constant. To make the plan work, you must have the discipline to invest on a regular basis. The goal of a dollar-cost averaging program is growth in the value of the security to which the funds are allocated. The price of the investment security will probably fluctuate over time. If the price declines, more shares are purchased per period. Conversely, if the price rises, fewer shares are purchased per period.

dollar-cost averaging
a formula plan for timing investment transactions, in which a fixed dollar amount is invested in a security at fixed time intervals.

Look at the example of dollar-cost averaging in Table 14.12 (on page 620). The table shows investment of $500 per month in the Wolverine Mutual Fund, a growth-oriented, no-load mutual fund. Assume that during 1 year's time, you have placed $6,000 in the mutual fund shares. (Because this is a no-load fund, shares are purchased at net asset value, NAV.) You made purchases at NAVs ranging from a low of $24.16 to a high of $30.19. At year-end, the value of your holdings in the fund was slightly less than $6,900. Dollar-cost averaging is a passive strategy; other formula plans are more active.

constant-dollar plan
a formula plan for timing investment transactions, in which the investor establishes a target dollar amount for the speculative portion of the portfolio and establishes trigger points at which funds are transferred to or from the conservative portion as needed to maintain the target dollar amount.

Constant-Dollar Plan A **constant-dollar plan** consists of a portfolio that is divided into two parts, speculative and conservative. The speculative portion consists of securities that have high promise of capital gains. The conservative portion consists of low-risk investments such as bonds or a money market account. The target dollar amount for the speculative portion is constant. The investor establishes trigger points (upward or downward movement in the speculative portion) at which funds are removed from or added to that portion. The constant-dollar plan basically skims off profits from the speculative portion of the portfolio if it rises a certain percentage or amount in value and adds these funds to the conservative portion of the portfolio. If the speculative portion of the portfolio declines by a specific percentage or amount, funds are added to it from the conservative portion.

Assume that you have established the constant-dollar plan shown in Table 14.13 (on page 621). The beginning $20,000 portfolio consists of $10,000 invested in a high-beta, no-load mutual fund and $10,000 deposited in a money market account. You have decided to rebalance the portfolio every time

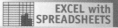

TABLE 14.12 **Dollar-Cost Averaging**
($500 per month, Wolverine Mutual Fund shares)

Transactions

Month	Net Asset Value (NAV) Month-End	Number of Shares Purchased
January	$26.00	19.23
February	27.46	18.21
March	27.02	18.50
April	24.19	20.67
May	26.99	18.53
June	25.63	19.51
July	24.70	20.24
August	24.16	20.70
September	25.27	19.79
October	26.15	19.12
November	29.60	16.89
December	30.19	16.56

Annual Summary

Total investment: $6,000.00
Total number of shares purchased: 227.95
Average cost per share: $26.32
Year-end portfolio value: $6,881.81

constant-ratio plan
a formula plan for timing
investment transactions, in
which a desired fixed ratio of
the speculative portion to the
conservative portion of the
portfolio is established; when
the actual ratio differs by a
predetermined amount from the
desired ratio, transactions are
made to rebalance the portfolio
to achieve the desired ratio.

the speculative portion is worth $2,000 more or $2,000 less than its initial value of $10,000. If the speculative portion of the portfolio equals or exceeds $12,000, you sell sufficient shares of the fund to bring its value down to $10,000. The proceeds from the sale are added to the conservative portion. If the speculative portion declines in value to $8,000 or less, you use funds from the conservative portion to purchase sufficient shares to raise the value of the speculative portion to $10,000.

Two portfolio-rebalancing actions are taken in the time sequence illustrated in Table 14.13. Initially, $10,000 was allocated to each portion of the portfolio. When the mutual fund's net asset value (NAV) rose to $12.00, the speculative portion was worth $12,000. At that point you sold 166.67 shares valued at $2,000, and added the proceeds to the money market account. Later, the mutual fund's NAV declined to $9.50 per share, causing the value of the speculative portion to drop below $8,000. This change triggered the purchase of sufficient shares to raise the value of the speculative portion to $10,000. Over the long run, if the speculative investment of the constant-dollar plan rises in value, the conservative component of the portfolio will increase in dollar value as profits are transferred into it.

Constant-Ratio Plan The **constant-ratio plan** is similar to the constant-dollar plan except that it establishes a desired fixed *ratio* of the speculative portion to the conservative portion of the portfolio. When the actual ratio of the two differs by a predetermined amount from the desired ratio, rebalancing occurs. At that point, transactions are made to bring the actual ratio back to the desired ratio. If you use the constant-ratio plan, you must decide on the appropriate apportionment of the portfolio between speculative and conserva-

TABLE 14.13 Constant-Dollar Plan

Mutual Fund NAV	Value of Speculative Portion	Value of Conservative Portion	Total Portfolio Value	Transactions	Number of Shares in Speculative Portion
$10.00	$10,000.00	$10,000.00	$20,000.00		1,000
11.00	11,000.00	10,000.00	21,000.00		1,000
12.00	12,000.00	10,000.00	22,000.00		1,000
› 12.00	10,000.00	12,000.00	22,000.00	Sold 166.67 shares	833.33
11.00	9,166.63	12,000.00	21,166.63		833.33
9.50	7,916.64	12,000.00	19,916.64		833.33
→ 9.50	10,000.00	9,916.64	19,916.64	Purchased 219.30 shares	1,052.63
10.00	10,526.30	9,916.64	20,442.94		1,052.63

tive investments. You must also choose the ratio trigger point at which transactions occur.

To see how this works, assume that the constant-ratio plan illustrated in Table 14.14 is yours. The initial portfolio value is $20,000. You have decided to allocate 50% of the portfolio to the speculative, high-beta mutual fund and 50% to a money market account. You will rebalance the portfolio when the ratio of the speculative portion to the conservative portion is greater than or equal to 1.20 or less than or equal to 0.80. A sequence of changes in net asset value (NAV) is listed in Table 14.14. Initially, $10,000 is allocated to each portion of the portfolio. When the fund NAV reaches $12, the 1.20 ratio triggers the sale of 83.33 shares. Then the portfolio is back to its desired 50:50 ratio. Later, the fund NAV declines to $9, lowering the value of the speculative portion to $8,250. The ratio of the speculative portion to the conservative portion is then 0.75, which is below the 0.80 trigger point. You purchase 152.78 shares to bring the desired ratio back up to the 50:50 level.

The long-run expectation under a constant-ratio plan is that the speculative securities will rise in value. When this occurs, the investor will sell securities to reapportion the portfolio and increase the value of the conservative portion. This philosophy is similar to the constant-dollar plan, except that a ratio is utilized as a trigger point.

TABLE 14.14 Constant-Ratio Plan

Mutual Fund NAV	Value of Speculative Portion	Value of Conservative Portion	Total Portfolio Value	Ratio of Speculative Portion to Conservative Portion	Transactions	Number of Shares in Speculative Portion
$10.00	$10,000.00	$10,000.00	$20,000.00	1.000		1,000
11.00	11,000.00	10,000.00	21,000.00	1.100		1,000
12.00	12,000.00	10,000.00	22,000.00	1.200		1,000
→ 12.00	11,000.00	11,000.00	22,000.00	1.000	Sold 83.33 shares	916.67
11.00	10,083.00	11,000.00	21,083.00	0.917		916.67
10.00	9,166.70	11,000.00	20,166.70	0.833		916.67
9.00	8,250.00	11,000.00	19,250.00	0.750		916.67
→ 9.00	9,625.00	9,625.00	19,250.00	1.000	Purchased 152.78 shares	1,069.44
10.00	10,694.40	9,625.00	20,319.40	1.110		1,069.44

variable-ratio plan
a formula plan for timing investment transactions, in which the ratio of the speculative portion to the total portfolio value varies depending on the movement in value of the speculative securities; when the ratio rises or falls by a predetermined amount, the amount committed to the speculative portion of the portfolio is reduced or increased, respectively.

Variable-Ratio Plan The **variable-ratio plan** is the most aggressive of these four fairly passive formula plans. It attempts to turn stock market movements to the investor's advantage by timing the market. That is, it tries to "buy low and sell high." The ratio of the speculative portion to the total portfolio value varies depending on the movement in value of the speculative securities. When the ratio rises a certain predetermined amount, the amount committed to the speculative portion of the portfolio is reduced. Conversely, if the value of the speculative portion declines so that it drops significantly in proportion to the total portfolio value, the amount committed to the speculative portion of the portfolio is increased.

When implementing the variable-ratio plan, you have several decisions to make. First, you must determine the initial allocation between the speculative and conservative portions of the portfolio. Next, you must choose trigger points to initiate buy or sell activity. These points are a function of the ratio between the value of the speculative portion and the value of the total portfolio. Finally, you must set adjustments in that ratio at each trigger point.

Assume that you use the variable-ratio plan shown in Table 14.15. Initially, you divide the portfolio equally between the speculative and the conservative portions. The speculative portion consists of a high-beta (around 2.0) mutual fund. The conservative portion is a money market account. You decide that when the speculative portion reaches 60% of the total portfolio, you will reduce its proportion to 45%. If the speculative portion of the portfolio drops to 40% of the total portfolio, then you will raise its proportion to 55%. The logic behind this strategy is an attempt to time the cyclical movements in the mutual fund's value. When the fund moves up in value, profits are taken, and the proportion invested in the no-risk money market account is increased. When the fund declines markedly in value, the proportion of capital committed to it is increased.

A sequence of transactions is depicted in Table 14.15. When the fund net asset value (NAV) climbs to $15, the 60% ratio trigger point is reached, and you sell 250 shares of the fund. The proceeds are placed in the money market account, which causes the speculative portion then to represent 45% of the value of the portfolio. Later the fund NAV declines to $10, causing the speculative portion of the portfolio to drop to 35%. This triggers a portfolio rebalancing, and you purchase 418.75 shares, moving the speculative portion to 55%. When the fund NAV then moves to $12, the total portfolio is worth in

TABLE 14.15 Variable-Ratio Plan

Mutual Fund NAV	Value of Speculative Portion	Value of Conservative Portion	Total Portfolio Value	Ratio of Speculative Portion to Total Portfolio Value	Transactions	Number of Shares in Speculative Portion
$10.00	$10,000.00	$10,000.00	$20,000.00	0.50		1,000
15.00	15,000.00	10,000.00	25,000.00	0.60		1,000
→ 15.00	11,250.00	13,750.00	25,000.00	0.45	Sold 250 shares	750
10.00	7,500.00	13,750.00	21,250.00	0.35		750
→ 10.00	11,687.50	9,562.50	21,250.00	0.55	Purchased 418.75 shares	1,168.75
12.00	14,025.00	9,562.50	23,587.50	0.59		1,168.75

excess of $23,500. In comparison, had the initial investment of $20,000 been allocated equally and had no rebalancing been done between the mutual fund and the money market account, the total portfolio value at this time would have been only $22,000 ($12 × 1,000 = $12,000 in the speculative portion plus $10,000 in the money market account).

Using Limit and Stop-Loss Orders

In Chapter 3 we discussed the market order, the limit order, and the stop-loss order. (See pages 109–111 to review these types of orders.) Here we will see how the limit and stop-loss orders can be employed to rebalance a portfolio. These types of security orders, if properly used, can increase return by lowering transaction costs.

Limit Orders There are many ways investors can use limit orders when securities are bought or sold. For instance, if you have decided to add a stock to the portfolio, a limit order to buy will ensure that you buy only at the desired purchase price or below. A limit *good-'til-canceled (GTC)* order to buy instructs the broker to buy stock until the entire order is filled. The primary risk in using limit instead of market orders is that the order may not be executed. For example, if you placed a GTC order to buy 100 shares of State Oil of California at $27 per share and the stock never traded at $27 per share or less, the order would never be executed. Thus you must weigh the need for immediate execution (market order) against the possibility of a better price with a limit order.

Limit orders, of course, can increase your return if they enable you to buy a security at a lower cost or sell it at a higher price. During a typical trading day, a stock will fluctuate up and down over a normal trading range. For example, suppose the common shares of Jama Motor traded 10 times in the following sequence: 36.00, 35.88, 35.75, 35.94, 35.50, 35.63, 35.82, 36.00, 36.13, 36.00. A market order to sell could have been executed at somewhere between 35.50 (the low) and 36.13 (the high). A limit order to sell at 36.00 would have been executed at 36.00. Thus 50 cents per share might have been gained by using a limit order.

Stop-Loss Orders Stop-loss orders can be used to limit the downside loss exposure of an investment. For example, assume you purchase 500 shares of Easy Work at 26.00 and have set a specific goal to sell the stock if it reaches 32.00 or drops to 23.00. To implement this goal, you would enter a GTC stop order to sell with a price limit of 32.00 and another stop order at a price of 23.00. If the issue trades at 23.00 or less, the stop-loss order becomes a market order, and the broker sells the stock at the best price available. Or, if the issue trades at 32.00 or higher, the broker will sell the stock. In the first situation, you are trying to reduce your losses; in the second, you are attempting to protect a profit.

whipsawing
the situation where a stock temporarily drops in price and then bounces back upward.

The principal risk in using stop-loss orders is **whipsawing**—a situation where a stock temporarily drops in price and then bounces back upward. If Easy Work dropped to 23.00, then 22.57, and then rallied back to 26.00, you would have been sold out at a price between 23.00 and 22.57. For this reason, limit orders, including stop-loss orders, require careful analysis before they are placed. You must consider the stock's probable fluctuations as well as the need to purchase or sell the stock when choosing among market, limit, and stop-loss orders.

Warehousing Liquidity

Investing in risky stocks or in options or futures offers probable returns in excess of those available with money market deposit accounts or bonds. However, stocks and options and futures are risky investments. One recommendation for an efficient portfolio is to keep a portion of it in a low-risk, highly liquid investment to protect against total loss. The low-risk asset acts as a buffer against possible investment adversity. A second reason for maintaining funds in a low-risk asset is the possibility of future opportunities. When opportunity strikes, an investor who has extra cash available will be able to take advantage of the situation. If you have set aside funds in a highly liquid investment, you need not disturb the existing portfolio.

There are two primary media for warehousing liquidity: money market deposit accounts at financial institutions and money market mutual funds. The money market accounts at savings institutions provide relatively easy access to funds and furnish returns competitive with (but somewhat lower than) money market mutual funds. Over time, the products offered by financial institutions are expected to become more competitive with those offered by mutual funds and stock brokerage firms.

Timing Investment Sales

Knowing when to sell a stock is as important as deciding which stock to buy. Periodically, you should review your portfolio and consider possible sales and new purchases. Here we discuss two issues relevant to the sale decision: tax consequences and achieving investment goals.

Tax Consequences Taxes affect nearly all investment actions. All investors can and should understand certain basics. The treatment of capital losses is important: *A maximum of $3,000 of losses in excess of capital gains can be written off against other income in any one year.* If you have a loss position in an investment and have concluded that it would be wise to sell it, the best time to sell is when a capital gain is available against which the loss can be applied. Clearly, one should carefully consider the tax consequences of investment sales prior to taking action.

Achieving Investment Goals Every investor would enjoy buying an investment at its lowest price and selling it at its top price. At a more realistic level, an investment should be sold when it no longer meets the needs of the portfolio's owner. In particular, if an investment has become either more or less risky than is desired, or if it has not met its return objective, it should be sold. The tax consequences mentioned above help to determine the appropriate time to sell. However, *taxes are not the foremost consideration in a sale decision.* The dual concepts of risk and return should be the overriding concerns.

For some tips on knowing when and what to sell, see the *Investing in Action* box on our Web site:

www.aw-bc.com/gitman_joehnk

Each investment should be examined periodically in light of its return performance and relative risk. You should sell any investment that no longer belongs in the portfolio and should buy vehicles that are more suitable. Finally, you should not hold out for every nickel of profit. Very often, those who hold out for the top price watch the value of their holdings plummet. If an investment looks ripe to sell, sell it, take the profit, reinvest it in an appropriate vehicle, and enjoy your good fortune.

IN REVIEW

CONCEPTS

14.16 Explain the role that *formula plans* can play in the timing of security transactions. Describe the logic underlying the use of these plans.

14.17 Briefly describe each of the following plans and differentiate among them.
a. Dollar-cost averaging. b. Constant-dollar plan.
c. Constant-ratio plan. d. Variable-ratio plan.

14.18 Describe how a limit order can be used when securities are bought or sold. How can a stop-loss order be used to reduce losses? To protect profit?

14.19 Give two reasons why an investor might want to maintain funds in a low-risk, highly liquid investment.

14.20 Describe the two items an investor should consider before reaching a decision to sell an investment vehicle.

Summary

Construct portfolios with asset allocations and risk-return profiles consistent with the investor's objectives. An investor's objectives determine the asset allocations and risk-return profile for his or her portfolio. A single investor who wants to build wealth quickly will tend to allocate funds to more risky assets that have high growth potential. A retired couple who need income to meet their living expenses will allocate funds to conservative, low-risk investment vehicles that provide periodic income in the form of dividends or interest.

LG 2

Discuss the data and indexes needed to measure and compare investment performance. To analyze the performance of individual investments, the investor must gather current market information and stay abreast of international, national, and local economic and market developments. Indexes of investment performance such as the Dow Jones Industrial Average (DJIA) and bond market indicators are available for use in assessing market behavior. The performance of individual investment vehicles can be measured on both a pretax and an after-tax basis by using the holding period return (HPR). HPR measures the total return (income plus change in value) actually earned on the investment during the investment period. HPR can be compared to investment goals to assess whether the proper return is being earned for the risk involved and to isolate any problem investments.

LG 3

Understand the techniques used to measure income, capital gains, and total portfolio return. To measure portfolio return, the investor must estimate the amount invested, the income earned, and any capital gains (both realized and unrealized) over the relevant current time period. Using these values, the investor can calculate the portfolio's holding period return (HPR) by dividing the total returns by the amount of investment during the period. Comparison of the portfolio's HPR to overall market measures can provide some insight with regard to the portfolio's performance relative to the market.

LG 4 **Use the Sharpe, Treynor, and Jensen measures to compare a portfolio's return with a risk-adjusted, market-adjusted rate of return, and discuss portfolio revision.** A risk-adjusted, market-adjusted evaluation of a portfolio's return can be made using Sharpe's measure, Treynor's measure, or Jensen's measure. Sharpe's and Treynor's measures find the risk premium per unit of risk, which can be compared with similar market measures to assess the portfolio's performance. Jensen's measure, which is theoretically consistent with Treynor's measure, calculates the portfolio's excess return using beta and CAPM. Because it is relatively easy to calculate and directly makes both risk and market adjustments, Jensen's measure tends to be preferred. Portfolio revision—selling certain issues and purchasing new ones to replace them—should take place when returns are unacceptable or when the portfolio fails to meet the investor's objectives.

LG 5 **Describe the role and logic of dollar-cost averaging, constant-dollar plans, constant-ratio plans, and variable-ratio plans.** Formula plans are used to time purchase and sale decisions to take advantage of price changes that result from cyclical price movements. The four commonly used formula plans are dollar-cost averaging, the constant-dollar plan, the constant-ratio plan, and the variable-ratio plan. All of them have certain decision rules or triggers that signal a purchase and/or sale action.

LG 6 **Explain the role of limit and stop-loss orders in investment timing, warehousing liquidity, and timing investment sales.** Limit and stop-loss orders can be used to trigger the rebalancing of a portfolio to contribute to improved portfolio returns. Low-risk, highly liquid investment vehicles such as money market deposit accounts and money market mutual funds can warehouse liquidity. Such liquidity can protect against total loss and allow the investor to seize quickly any attractive opportunities that occur. Investment sales should be timed to obtain maximum tax benefits (or minimum tax consequences) and to contribute to the achievement of the investor's goals.

Putting Your Investment Know-How to the Test

1. An individual investor's investment objectives should be expressed in terms of
   a. Risk and return.
   b. Capital market expectations.
   c. Liquidity needs and time horizon.
   d. Tax factors and regulatory constraints.

2. The process of asset allocation deals with allocating funds between:
   a. Individual stocks.
   b. Various categories of assets such as stocks, bonds, and real estate.
   c. Long- and short-term investments.
   d. Consumption of savings.

3. A portfolio has beta of 0.9 and an expected return of 10%. The risk-free rate is 7% and the market is expected to yield 11%. According to Treynor's measure of risk, this portfolio is
   a. Outperforming the market.
   b. Underperforming the market.
   c. Providing market performance.
   d. The portfolio performance cannot be determined from the information given.

4. An analyst gathers the following data:

> Expected return rate on the market = 15%
> Risk-free rate = 8%
> Expected rate of return on portfolio X = 17%
> Portfolio X beta = 1.25

Using Jensen's portfolio performance measure, portfolio X on a risk-adjusted basis
a. Outperforms the market by 0.25%.
b. Outperforms the market by 2%.
c. Provides the same return as the market.
d. Underperforms the market by 1.6%.

5. Portfolios X and Y are both well diversified. The risk-free rate is 8%. The return for the market is 16%.

Portfolio	Expected Return	Beta
X	16%	1.00
Y	12%	0.25

Using the Jensen's portfolio performance measure, which of the following statements about Portfolio X and Portfolio Y is true on a risk-adjusted basis?
a. Portfolio X underperforms, Portfolio Y provides the same return as the market.
b. Portfolio X provides the same return as the market, Portfolio Y outperforms it.
c. Portfolio X underperforms, Portfolio Y outperforms the market.
d. Portfolio X provides the same return as the market, Portfolio Y underperforms it.

6. Which of the following formula plans of portfolio management does *not* involve market timing decisions?
a. Dollar-cost averaging
b. Constant-dollar plan
c. Constant-ratio plan
d. Variable-ratio plan

7. Which of the following statements *best* reflects the importance of the asset allocation decision to the investment process? The asset allocation decision:
a. Helps the investor decide on realistic investment goals.
b. Identifies the specific securities to include in a portfolio.
c. Determines most of the portfolio's returns and volatility over time.
d. Creates a standard by which to establish an appropriate investment horizon.

8. The holding period return on a stock is equal to
a. The dividend yield plus risk premium.
b. The dividend amount over the period plus the current yield.
c. The capital gain over the period plus the dividend yield.
d. The capital gain over the period plus the dividend amount.

9. Portfolio A has a return of 20% and a standard deviation of 25%. The risk-free rate is 10%. What is Sharpe's measure of portfolio performance?
a. 0.40   b. 0.50   c. 0.75   d. 0.80

10. Bob Smith purchased 1,000 shares of ZXZ Corporation at $40 per share. During the year he collected $1 per share in dividends. On the last day of the year, he sold 400 shares at $50. Assuming no transaction costs, Bob has to report the following for tax purposes:
a. $6,000 in unrealized gains, $4,000 in realized gains, and $1,000 in dividend income.
b. $10,000 in capital gains and $1,000 in dividend income.
c. $4,000 in capital gains and $400 in dividend income.
d. $4,000 in capital gains and $1,000 in dividend income.

Answers: 1. a; 2. b; 3. b; 4. a; 5. b; 6. a; 7. c; 8. c; 9. a; 10. d

Discussion Questions

| LG 2 |

Q14.1 Choose an established local (or nearby) company whose stock is listed and actively traded on a major exchange. Find the stock's closing price at the end of each of the preceding 6 years and the amount of dividends paid in each of the preceding 5 years. Also, obtain the value of the Dow Jones Industrial Average (DJIA) at the end of each of the preceding 6 years.

    a. Use Equation 14.1 to calculate the pretax holding period return (HPR) on the stock for each of the preceding 5 years.

    b. Study the international, national, and local economic and market developments that occurred during the preceding 5 years.

    c. Compare the stock's returns to the DJIA for each year over the 5-year period of concern.

    d. Discuss the stock's returns in light of the economic and market developments noted in part **b** and the behavior of the DJIA as noted in part **c** over the 5 preceding years. How well did the stock perform in light of these factors?

| LG 2 |

Q14.2 Assume that you are in the 35% ordinary tax bracket (federal and state combined) and that dividends and capital gains for holding periods of more than 12 months are taxed at a 15% rate. Select a major stock, bond, and mutual fund in which you are interested in investing. For each of them, gather data for each of the past 3 years on the annual dividends or interest paid and the capital gain (or loss) that would have resulted had they been purchased at the start of each year and sold at the end of each year. For the mutual fund, be sure to separate any dividends paid into investment income dividends and capital gains dividends.

    a. For each of the three investment vehicles, calculate the pretax and after-tax HPR for each of the 3 years.

    b. Use your annual HPR findings in part **a** to calculate the average after-tax HPR for each of the investment vehicles over the 3-year period.

    c. Compare the average returns found in part **b** for each of the investment vehicles. Discuss the relative risks in view of these returns and the characteristics of each vehicle.

| LG 3 |

Q14.3 Choose six actively traded stocks for inclusion in your investment portfolio. Assume the portfolio was created 3 years earlier by purchasing 200 shares of each of the six stocks. Find the acquisition price of each stock, the annual dividend paid by each stock, and the year-end prices for the 3 calendar years. Record for each stock its total cost, cost per share, current price per share, and total current value at the end of each of the 3 calendar years.

    a. For each of the 3 years, find the amount invested in the portfolio.

    b. For each of the 3 years, measure the annual income from the portfolio.

    c. For each of the 3 years, determine the unrealized capital gains from the portfolio.

    d. For each of the 3 years, calculate the portfolio's HPR, using the values in parts **a, b,** and **c.**

    e. Use your findings in part **d** to calculate the average HPR for the portfolio over the 3-year period. Discuss your finding.

| LG 4 |

Q14.4 Find five actively traded stocks and record their prices at the start and the end of the most recent calendar year. Also, find the amount of dividends paid on each stock during that year and each stock's beta at the end of the year. Assume that the five stocks were held during the year in an equal-dollar-weighted portfolio (20% in each stock) created at the start of the year. Also find the current risk-free rate, R_F, and the market return, r_m, for the given year. Assume that the standard deviation for the portfolio of the five stocks is 14.25% and that the standard deviation for the market portfolio is 10.80%.

a. Use the formula presented in Chapter 5 (Equation 5.1) to find the portfolio return, r_p, for the year under consideration.

b. Calculate Sharpe's measure for both the portfolio and the market. Compare and discuss these values. On the basis of this measure, is the portfolio's performance inferior or superior? Explain.

c. Calculate Treynor's measure for both the portfolio and the market. Compare and discuss these values. On the basis of this measure, is the portfolio's performance inferior or superior? Explain.

d. Calculate Jensen's measure (Jensen's alpha) for the portfolio. Discuss its value. On the basis of this measure, is the portfolio's performance inferior or superior? Explain.

e. Compare, contrast, and discuss your analysis using the three measures in parts **b, c,** and **d.** Evaluate the portfolio.

LG 5 Q14.5 Choose a high-growth mutual fund and a money market mutual fund. Find and record their closing net asset values (NAVs) at the end of each *week* for the immediate past year. Assume that you wish to invest $10,400.

a. Assume you use dollar-cost averaging to buy shares in both the high-growth and the money market funds by purchasing $100 of each of them at the end of each week—a total investment of $10,400 (52 weeks × $200/week). How many shares would you have purchased in each fund by year-end? What are the total number of shares, the average cost per share, and the year-end portfolio value of each fund? Total the year-end fund values and compare them to the total that would have resulted from investing $5,200 in each fund at the end of the first week.

b. Assume you use a constant-dollar plan with 50% invested in the high-growth fund (speculative portion) and 50% invested in the money market fund (conservative portion). If the portfolio is rebalanced every time the speculative portion is worth $500 more or $500 less than its initial value of $5,200, what would be the total portfolio value and the number of shares in the speculative portion at year-end?

c. Assume that, as in part **b,** you initially invest 50% in the speculative portion and 50% in the conservative portion. But in this case you use a constant-ratio plan under which rebalancing to the 50:50 mix occurs whenever the ratio of the speculative to the conservative portion is greater than or equal to 1.25 or less than or equal to 0.75. What would be the total portfolio value and the number of shares in the speculative portion at year-end?

d. Compare and contrast the year-end values of the total portfolio under each of the plans in parts **a, b,** and **c.** Which plan would have been best in light of these findings? Explain.

Problems

LG 1 P14.1 Refer to the table below:

	Fund A	Fund B
Beta	1.8	1.1
Investor A	20%	80%
Investor B	80%	20%

As between Investor A and Investor B, which is more likely to represent a retired couple? Why?

LG 1 P14.2 Portfolio A and Portfolio B had the same holding period return last year. Most of the returns from Portfolio A came from dividends, while most of the returns from Portfolio B came from capital gains. Which portfolio is owned by a single working person making a high salary, and which is owned by a retired couple? Why?

LG 2 P14.3 Mark Smith purchased 100 shares of Tomco Corporation in December 2004, at a total cost of $1,762. He held the shares for 15 months and then sold them, netting $2,500. During the period he held the stock, the company paid him $200 in cash dividends. How much, if any, was the capital gain realized upon the sale of stock? Calculate Mark's pretax HPR.

LG 2 P14.4 Joe Smart purchased 1,000 shares of a speculative stock on January 2 for $2.00 per share. On July 1, he sold them for $9.50 per share. He uses an online broker that charges him $10 per trade. What was Mr. Smart's annualized HPR on this investment?

LG 2 P14.5 Jill Clark invested $25,000 in the bonds of Industrial Aromatics, Inc. She held them for 13 months, at the end of which she sold them for $26,746. During the period of ownership she received $2,000 interest. Calculate the pretax and after-tax HPR on Jill's investment. Assume that she is in the 31% ordinary tax bracket (federal and state combined) and pays a 15% capital gains rate on dividends and on capital gains for holding periods longer than 12 months.

LG 2 P14.6 Charlotte Smidt bought 2,000 shares of the balanced no-load LaJolla Fund exactly 1 year and 2 days ago for a NAV of $8.60 per share. During the year, the fund distributed investment income dividends of 32 cents per share and capital gains dividends of 38 cents per share. At the end of the year, Charlotte, who is in the 35% ordinary tax bracket (federal and state combined) and pays a 15% capital gains rate on dividends and on capital gains for holding periods longer than 12 months, realized $8.75 per share on the sale of all 2,000 shares. Calculate Charlotte's pretax and after-tax HPR on this transaction.

LG 2 P14.7 Marilyn Gore, who is in a 33% ordinary tax bracket (federal and state combined) and pays a 15% capital gains rate on dividends and capital gains for holding periods longer than 12 months, purchased 10 options contracts for a total cost of $4,000 just over 1 year ago. Marilyn netted $4,700 upon the sale of the 10 contracts today. What are Marilyn's pretax and after-tax HPRs on this transaction?

LG 3 P14.8 Mom and Pop had a portfolio of long-term bonds that they purchased many years ago. The bonds pay 12% interest annually, and the face value is $100,000. If Mom and Pop are in the 25% tax bracket, what is their annual after tax HPR on this investment (assume it trades at par)?

LG 3 P14.9 On January 1, 2005, Simon Love's portfolio of 15 common stocks, completely equity-financed, had a market value of $264,000. At the end of May 2005, Simon sold one of the stocks, which had a beginning-of-year value of $26,300, for $31,500. He did not reinvest those or any other funds in the portfolio during the year. He received total dividends from stocks in his portfolio of $12,500 during the year. On December 31, 2005, Simon's portfolio had a market value of $250,000. Find the HPR on Simon's portfolio during the year ended December 31, 2005. (Measure the amount of withdrawn funds at their beginning-of-year value.)

LG 4 P14.10 Congratulations! Your portfolio returned 11% last year, 2% better than the market return of 9%. Your portfolio had a standard deviation of earnings equal to 18%, and the risk free rate is equal to 6%. Calculate Sharpe's Measure for your portfolio. If the market's Sharpe's Measure is .3, did you do better or worse than the market from a risk/return perspective?

P14.11 Niki Malone's portfolio earned a return of 11.8% during the year just ended. The portfolio's standard deviation of return was 14.1%. The risk-free rate is currently 6.2%. During the year, the return on the market portfolio was 9.0% and its standard deviation was 9.4%.

   a. Calculate Sharpe's measure for Niki Malone's portfolio for the year just ended.

   b. Compare the performance of Niki's portfolio found in part **a** to that of Hector Smith's portfolio, which has a Sharpe's measure of 0.43. Which portfolio performed better? Why?

   c. Calculate Sharpe's measure for the market portfolio for the year just ended.

   d. Use your findings in parts **a** and **c** to discuss the performance of Niki's portfolio relative to the market during the year just ended.

P14.12 Your portfolio has a beta equal to 1.3. It returned 12% last year. The market returned 10%, and the risk free rate is 6%. Calculate Treynor's Measure for your portfolio and the market. Did you earn a better return than the market given the risk you took?

P14.13 During the year just ended, Anna Schultz's portfolio, which has a beta of 0.90, earned a return of 8.6%. The risk-free rate is currently 7.3%, and the return on the market portfolio during the year just ended was 9.2%.

   a. Calculate Treynor's measure for Anna's portfolio for the year just ended.

   b. Compare the performance of Anna's portfolio found in part **a** to that of Stacey Quant's portfolio, which has a Treynor's measure of 1.25%. Which portfolio performed better? Explain.

   c. Calculate Treynor's measure for the market portfolio for the year just ended.

   d. Use your findings in parts **a** and **c** to discuss the performance of Anna's portfolio relative to the market during the year just ended.

P14.14 Your portfolio returned 13% last year, with a beta equal to 1.5. The market return was 10%, and the risk free rate 6%. Did you earn more or less than the required rate of return on your portfolio (use Jensen's Measure)?

P14.15 Chee Chew's portfolio has a beta of 1.3 and earned a return of 12.9% during the year just ended. The risk-free rate is currently 7.8%. The return on the market portfolio during the year just ended was 11.0%.

   a. Calculate Jensen's measure (Jensen's alpha) for Chee's portfolio for the year just ended.

   b. Compare the performance of Chee's portfolio found in part **a** to that of Carri Uhl's portfolio, which has a Jensen's measure of −0.24. Which portfolio performed better? Explain.

   c. Use your findings in part **a** to discuss the performance of Chee's portfolio during the period just ended.

P14.16 The risk-free rate is currently 8.1%. Use the data in the accompanying table for the Fio family's portfolio and the market portfolio during the year just ended to answer the questions that follow.

Data Item	Fios' Portfolio	Market Portfolio
Rate of return	12.8%	11.2%
Standard deviation of return	13.5%	9.6%
Beta	1.10	1.00

   a. Calculate Sharpe's measure for the portfolio and the market. Compare the two measures, and assess the performance of the Fios' portfolio during the year just ended.

    b. Calculate Treynor's measure for the portfolio and the market. Compare the two, and assess the performance of the Fios' portfolio during the year just ended.

    c. Calculate Jensen's measure (Jensen's alpha). Use it to assess the performance of the Fios' portfolio during the year just ended.

    d. On the basis of your findings in parts **a, b,** and **c,** assess the performance of the Fios' portfolio during the year just ended.

LG 5

P14.17 Over the past 2 years, Jonas Cone has used a dollar-cost averaging formula to purchase $300 worth of FCI common stock each month. The price per share paid each month over the 2 years is given in the following table. Assume that Jonas paid no brokerage commissions on these transactions.

	Price per Share of FCI			Price per Share of FCI	
Month	Year 1	Year 2	Month	Year 1	Year 2
January	11.63	11.38	July	12.38	12.75
February	11.50	11.75	August	12.50	13.00
March	11.50	12.00	September	12.25	13.25
April	11.00	12.00	October	12.50	13.00
May	11.75	12.13	November	11.85	13.38
June	12.00	12.50	December	11.50	13.50

    a. How much was Jonas's total investment over the 2-year period?

    b. How many shares did Jonas purchase over the 2-year period?

    c. Use your findings in parts **a** and **b** to calculate Jonas's average cost per share of FCI.

    d. What was the value of Jonas's holdings in FCI at the end of the second year?

LG 5

P14.18 Refer to the table below:

		MM Mutual		
Time Period	Stock Price	Shares	Fund NAV	Shares
1	$20.00	1,000	$20.00	1,000
2	$25.00		$21.00	

Assume you are using a constant dollar plan with a re-balancing trigger of $1,500. The stock price represents your speculative portfolio and the MM mutual fund represents your conservative portfolio. What action, if any, should you take in time period 2? Be specific.

LG 5

P14.19 Refer to Problem 14.18 above. Now assume you are using a constant-ratio plan with a rebalance trigger of speculative-to-conservative of 1.25. What action, if any, should you take in time period 2? Be specific.

LG 5

P14.20 Refer to the table below:

		MM Mutual		
Time Period	Stock Price	Shares	Fund NAV	Shares
1	$20.00	1,000	$20.00	1,000
2	$30.00	1,000	$19.00	1,000

Assume you are using a variable-ratio plan. You have decided that when the speculative portfolio reaches 60% of the total, you will reduce its proportion to 45%. What action, if any, should you take in time period 2? Be specific.

See the text Web site
(www.aw-bc.com/gitman_joehnk) **for Web exercises**
that deal with *managing your own portfolio.*

Case Problem 14.1   *Assessing the Stalchecks' Portfolio Performance*

LG 2   **LG 3**   **LG 4**

Mary and Nick Stalcheck have an investment portfolio containing four vehicles. It was developed to provide them with a balance between current income and capital appreciation. Rather than acquire mutual fund shares or diversify within a given class of investment vehicle, they developed their portfolio with the idea of diversifying across various types of vehicles. The portfolio currently contains common stock, industrial bonds, mutual fund shares, and options. They acquired each of these vehicles during the past 3 years, and they plan to invest in other vehicles sometime in the future.

Currently, the Stalchecks are interested in measuring the return on their investment and assessing how well they have done relative to the market. They hope that the return earned over the past calendar year is in excess of what they would have earned by investing in a portfolio consisting of the S&P 500 Stock Composite Index. Their research has indicated that the risk-free rate was 7.2% and that the (before-tax) return on the S&P 500 portfolio was 10.1% during the past year. With the aid of a friend, they have been able to estimate the beta of their portfolio, which was 1.20. In their analysis, they have planned to ignore taxes, because they feel their earnings have been adequately sheltered. Because they did not make any portfolio transactions during the past year, all of the Stalchecks' investments have been held more than 12 months and they would have to consider only unrealized capital gains, if any. To make the necessary calculations, the Stalchecks have gathered the following information on each of the four vehicles in their portfolio.

Common stock. They own 400 shares of KJ Enterprises common stock. KJ is a diversified manufacturer of metal pipe and is known for its unbroken stream of dividends. Over the past few years, it has entered new markets and, as a result, has offered moderate capital appreciation potential. Its share price has risen from 17.25 at the start of the last calendar year to 18.75 at the end of the year. During the year, quarterly cash dividends of 20, 20, 25, and 25 cents were paid.

Industrial bonds. The Stalchecks own eight Cal Industries bonds. The bonds have a $1,000 par value, have a 9.250% coupon, and are due in 2015. They are A-rated by Moody's. The bond was quoted at 97.000 at the beginning of the year and ended the calendar year at 96.375%.

Mutual fund. The Stalchecks hold 500 shares in the Holt Fund, a balanced, no-load mutual fund. The dividend distributions on the fund during the year consisted of 60 cents in investment income and 50 cents in capital gains. The fund's NAV at the beginning of the calendar year was $19.45, and it ended the year at $20.02.

Options. The Stalchecks own 100 options contracts on the stock of a company they follow. The value of these contracts totaled $26,000 at the beginning of the calendar year. At year-end the total value of the options contracts was $29,000.

Questions

a. Calculate the holding period return on a before-tax basis for each of these four investment vehicles.

b. Assuming that the Stalchecks' ordinary income is currently being taxed at a combined (federal and state) tax rate of 38%, and that they would pay a 15% capital gains tax on dividends and capital gains for holding periods longer than 12 months, determine the after-tax HPR for each of their four investment vehicles.

c. Recognizing that all gains on the Stalchecks' investments were unrealized, calculate the before-tax portfolio HPR for their four-vehicle portfolio during the past calendar year. Evaluate this return relative to its current income and capital gain components.

d. Use the HPR calculated in question **c** to compute Jensen's measure (Jensen's alpha). Use that measure to analyze the performance of the Stalchecks' portfolio on a risk-adjusted, market-adjusted basis. Comment on your finding. Is it reasonable to use Jensen's measure to evaluate a four-vehicle portfolio? Why or why not?

e. On the basis of your analysis in questions **a, c,** and **d,** what, if any, recommendations might you offer the Stalchecks relative to the revision of their portfolio? Explain your recommendations.

Case Problem 14.2 *Evaluating Formula Plans: Charles Spurge's Approach*

LG 5

Charles Spurge, a mathematician with Ansco Petroleum Company, wishes to develop a rational basis for timing his portfolio transactions. He currently holds a security portfolio with a market value of nearly $100,000, divided equally between a very conservative, low-beta common stock, ConCam United, and a highly speculative, high-beta stock, Fleck Enterprises. On the basis of his reading of the investments literature, Charles does not believe it is necessary to diversify one's portfolio across 8 to 15 securities. His own feeling, based on his independent mathematical analysis, is that one can achieve the same results by holding a two-security portfolio in which one security is very conservative and the other is highly speculative. His feelings on this point will not be altered. He plans to continue to hold such a two-security portfolio until he finds that his theory does not work. During the past couple of years, he has earned a rate of return in excess of the risk-adjusted, market-adjusted rate expected on such a portfolio.

Charles's current interest centers on possibly developing his own formula plan for timing portfolio transactions. The current stage of his analysis focuses on the evaluation of four commonly used formula plans in order to isolate the desirable features of each. The four plans being considered are (1) dollar-cost averaging, (2) the constant-dollar plan, (3) the constant-ratio plan, and (4) the variable-ratio plan. Charles's analysis of the plans will involve the use of two types of data. Dollar-cost averaging is a passive buy-and-hold strategy in which the periodic investment is held constant. The other plans are more active in that they involve periodic purchases and sales within the portfolio. Thus, differing data are needed to evaluate the plans.

For evaluating the dollar-cost averaging plan, Charles decided he would assume an investment of $500 at the end of each 45-day period. He chose to use 45-day time intervals to achieve certain brokerage fee savings that would be available by making larger transactions. The $500 per 45 days totaled $4,000 for the year and equaled the total amount Charles invested during the past year. (*Note:* For convenience, the returns earned on the portions of the $4,000 that remain uninvested during the year are ignored.) In evaluating this plan, he would assume that half ($250) was invested in the conservative stock (ConCam United) and the other half in the speculative stock (Fleck Enterprises). The share prices for each of the stocks at the end of the eight 45-day periods when purchases were to be made are given in the accompanying table.

	Price per Share	
Period	ConCam	Fleck
1	22.13	22.13
2	21.88	24.50
3	21.88	25.38
4	22.00	28.50
5	22.25	21.88
6	22.13	19.25
7	22.00	21.50
8	22.25	23.63

To evaluate the three other plans, Charles decided to begin with a $4,000 portfolio evenly split between the two stocks. He chose to use $4,000, because that amount would correspond to the total amount invested in the two stocks over one year using dollar-cost averaging. He planned to use the same eight points in time given earlier to assess the portfolio and make transfers within it if required. For each of the three plans evaluated using these data, he established the following triggering points.

Constant-dollar plan. Each time the speculative portion of the portfolio is worth 13% more or less than its initial value of $2,000, the portfolio is rebalanced to bring the speculative portion back to its initial $2,000 value.

Constant-ratio plan. Each time the ratio of the value of the speculative portion of the portfolio to the value of the conservative portion is (1) greater than or equal to 1.15 or (2) less than or equal to 0.84, the portfolio is rebalanced through sale or purchase, respectively, to bring the ratio back to its initial value of 1.0.

Variable-ratio plan. Each time the value of the speculative portion of the portfolio rises above 54% of the total value of the portfolio, its proportion is reduced to 46%. Each time the value of the speculative portion of the portfolio drops below 38% of the total value of the portfolio, its proportion is raised to 50%.

Questions

a. Under the dollar-cost averaging plan, determine the total number of shares purchased, the average cost per share, and the year-end portfolio value expressed both in dollars and as a percentage of the amount invested for (1) the conservative stock, (2) the speculative stock, and (3) the total portfolio.

b. Using the constant-dollar plan, determine the year-end portfolio value expressed both in dollars and as a percentage of the amount initially invested for (1) the conservative portion, (2) the speculative portion, and (3) the total portfolio.

c. Repeat question **b** for the constant-ratio plan. Be sure to answer all parts.

d. Repeat question **b** for the variable-ratio plan. Be sure to answer all parts.

e. Compare and contrast your results from questions **a** through **d**. You may want to summarize them in tabular form. Which plan would appear to have been most beneficial in timing Charles's portfolio activities during the past year? Explain.

Excel with Spreadsheets

While most people believe that it is not possible to consistently time the market, there are several plans that allow investors to time purchases and sales of securities. These are referred to as formula plans—mechanical methods of managing a portfolio that attempt to take advantage of cyclical price movements. The objective is to mitigate the level of risk facing the investor.

One such formula plan is dollar-cost averaging. Here, a fixed dollar amount is invested in a security at fixed intervals. One objective is to increase the value of the security of interest over time. If prices decline, more shares are purchased; when market prices increase, fewer shares are purchased per period. The essence is that an investor is more likely not to buy overvalued securities.

Over the past 12 months, March 2005 through February 2006, Mrs. Paddock has used the dollar-cost averaging formula to purchase $1,000 worth of Neo common stock each month. The monthly price per share paid over the 12-month period is given below. Assume that Mrs. Paddock paid no brokerage commissions on these transactions.

Create a spreadsheet model similar to the spreadsheet for Table 14.12, which you can view at www.aw-bc.com/gitman_joehnk, to analyze the following investment situation through dollar-cost averaging.

2005	March	$14.30
	April	16.18
	May	18.37
	June	16.25
	July	14.33
	August	15.14
	September	15.93
	October	19.36
	November	23.25
	December	18.86
2006	January	22.08
	February	22.01

Questions

a. What is the total investment over the period from March 2005 through February 2006?
b. What is the total number of Neo shares purchased over the 12-month period?
c. What is the average cost per share?
d. What is the year-end (February 2006) portfolio value?
e. What is the profit or loss as of the end of February 2006?
f. What is the return on the portfolio after the 12-month period?

TRADING ONLINE WITH OTIS

Each investment should be examined periodically in light of its return performance and relative risk. You should sell any investment that no longer belongs in the portfolio and should buy vehicles that are more suitable. Finally, you should not hold out for every nickel of profit. Very often, those who hold out for the top price watch the value of their holdings plummet. If an investment looks ripe to sell, sell it, take the profit, reinvest it in an appropriate vehicle, and enjoy your good fortune.

It is time to assess your investments in terms of their return performance. This can be achieved by observing your performance return on the OTIS Stock Simulator.

Exercises

1. Compare the performance of each stock in your portfolio to that of the S&P 500 as a whole.

2. Research those stocks that are not performing well by reviewing stock ratings, P/E ratios, earnings reports, and operating efficiency ratings. Compare the statistics for each stock to its industry as a whole. Sell investments with poor fundamentals, being careful not to let emotions play a role in your decision making.

3. Buy replacement stocks using a disciplined approach. Use a stock screener to select a stock. Examine the fundamentals and recent headlines in the stock summary page, then use technical analysis to determine when to buy the stock

4. At the end of the semester you will want to measure the value of the portfolio, using the formula on page 305, to calculate your return on equity (ROE). Compare your ROE to that of the S&P 500 to determine whether you beat the market.

PART SIX

DERIVATIVE SECURITIES

CHAPTER 15
OPTIONS: PUTS,
CALLS, AND
WARRANTS

CHAPTER 16
COMMODITIES
AND FINANCIAL
FUTURES

639

CHAPTER 15

OPTIONS: PUTS, CALLS, AND WARRANTS

Put, call, strike price, naked option, in-the-money option, market index option—these terms are all part of the confusing, mysterious world of options. And from what you have heard about options, you may wonder why you even need to know about them! Options can indeed be speculative instruments that can lead to losses for even the most experienced investor. Many options investors use them to speculate on near-term stock price changes.

Options can also can play a role in the conservative investor's portfolio. They are versatile investments, a form of insurance that allows you to hedge risk. For example, you can protect stock holdings from a decline in market price, increase income against current stock holdings, prepare to buy a stock at a lower price, position yourself for a big market move even when you don't know which way prices will go, and benefit from a rising stock price without buying the actual stock.

When might options work to your advantage? Suppose you are going to buy a car in two months and plan to sell stock to pay for it. You could sell your stock now and hold the fund. But if the stock price is currently down and you think it will come back by the time you need the funds, you can use options to lock in the current price and still have the opportunity to participate in the upside. Assume you own 200 shares of Amazon.com. Currently the stock is trading at about $50 but has been as high as $61 in the past 52 weeks. You can buy a put option at $50 that expires in four months, at a cost of $4 a share, or $800 ($4 × 200 shares). If the stock drops below $50, the put locks in your right to sell at $50. If the price rises, you will not exercise your option. Once the price rises above the $4 a share you paid for your insurance, or $54, you make a profit. "It puts a floor under your wealth," says Lee Reid, head of retail options at A.G. Edwards.

This is just one example of how you can use options with stocks in your portfolio. In the following chapter you will learn about the essential characteristics of options and how they can be used effectively in your investment program.

Sources: Learning Center, Chicago Board Options Exchange, accessed December 23, 2003, www.cboe.com/education/learningcenter; Daniel Kadlec, "Know Your Options," *Time*, June 26, 2000, p. 80.

Put and Call Options

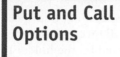

option
a security that gives the holder the right to buy or sell a certain amount of an underlying financial asset at a specified price for a specified period of time.

HOT LINKS

For a more extensive discussion of rights, including their basic characteristics and investment attributes, see this textbook's Web site at

www.aw-bc.com/gitman_joehnk

When investors buy shares of common or preferred stock, they become the registered owners of those securities and are entitled to all the rights and privileges of ownership. Investors who acquire bonds or convertible issues are also entitled to the benefits of ownership. Stocks, bonds, and convertibles are all examples of *financial assets.* They represent financial claims on the issuing organization. In contrast, investors who buy options acquire nothing more than the right to subsequently buy or sell other, related securities. That is, an **option** gives the holder the right to buy or sell a certain amount of an underlying asset (such as common stocks) at a specified price over a specified period of time. Options are *contractual instruments,* whereby two parties enter into a contract to give something of value to the other. The option *buyer* has the right to buy or sell an underlying asset for a given period of time, at a price that was fixed at the time of the contract. The option *seller* stands ready to buy or sell the underlying asset according to the terms of the contract, for which the seller has been paid a certain amount of money.

We'll look at two basic kinds of options in this chapter: (1) puts and calls and (2) warrants. Another kind of option is the *stock right.* Rights are like short-term call options that originate when corporations raise money by issuing new shares of common stocks (see Chapter 6 for a discussion of *rights offerings*). Essentially, the rights enable stockholders to buy shares of the new issue at a specified price for a specified, fairly short period of time. Because their life span is so short—usually no more than a few weeks—stock rights hold very little investment appeal for the average individual investor. Puts and calls, on the other hand, enjoy considerable popularity as attractive trading vehicles, and so, to a lesser extent, do warrants. These securities are a bit unusual, however, and their use requires special investor know-how.

Basic Features and Behavioral Characteristics

One of the market phenomena of the 1970s was the remarkable performance and investment popularity of stock options, particularly puts and calls on common stock. By the early 1980s, the interest in options spilled over to other kinds of financial assets. Today, investors can trade puts and calls on:

- Common stock
- Stock indexes
- Exchange-traded funds
- Foreign currencies
- Debt instruments
- Commodities and financial futures

As we will see, although the underlying financial assets may vary, the basic features and behavioral characteristics of these securities are pretty much the same. Regardless of the type, much of the popularity of options stems from the fact that *investors can buy a lot of price action with a limited amount of capital, while nearly always enjoying limited exposure to risk.*

put
a negotiable instrument that enables the holder to sell the underlying security at a specified price over a set period of time.

call
a negotiable instrument that gives the holder the right to buy securities at a stated price within a certain time period.

derivative securities
securities, such as puts, calls, and other options, that derive their value from the price behavior of an underlying real or financial asset.

leverage
the ability to obtain a given equity position at a reduced capital investment, thereby magnifying returns.

option maker (writer)
the individual or institution that writes/creates put and call options.

A Negotiable Contract Puts and calls are negotiable instruments, issued in bearer form, that allow the holder to buy or sell a specified amount of a specified security at a specified price. For example, a put or a call on common stock covers 100 shares of stock in a specific company. A **put** enables the holder to sell the underlying security at the specified price (known as the *exercise* or *strike price*) over a set period of time. A **call,** in contrast, gives the holder the right to buy the securities at the stated (strike) price within a certain time period. As with any option, there are no voting rights, no privileges of ownership, and no interest or dividend income. Instead, *puts and calls possess value to the extent that they allow the holder to participate in the price behavior of the underlying financial asset.*

Because puts and calls derive their value from the price behavior of some other real or financial asset, they are known as **derivative securities.** Rights and warrants, as well as futures contracts (which we'll study in Chapter 16), are also derivative securities. The fact is that many different types of derivative securities are available. Although certain segments of this market are for big institutional investors only, there's still ample room for the individual investor. Many of these securities—especially those listed on exchanges—are readily available to, and are actively traded by, individuals as well as institutions.

One of the key features of puts and calls (and of many other types of derivative securities) is the very attractive **leverage** opportunities they offer investors. Such opportunities exist because of the low prices these options carry relative to the market prices of the underlying financial assets. And what's more, the lower cost in no way affects the payoff or capital appreciation potential of your investment! To illustrate, consider a call on a common stock that gives the holder the right to buy 100 shares of a $50 stock at a (strike) price of $45 a share. The stock, of course, would be priced at $50. But the call would trade at an effective price of only $5 a share (or the difference between the market price of the common and the price at which it can be purchased, as specified on the call). Because a single stock option always involves 100 shares of stock, the actual cost of our $5 call would be $500. Even so, for $500 you get (just about) all the capital gains potential of a $5,000 investment—or at least that part of the capital gains that occurs over the life of the call option.

Maker Versus Buyer Puts and calls are a unique type of security because they are *not* issued by the organizations that issue the underlying stock or financial asset. Instead, puts and calls *are created by investors.* It works like this: Suppose you want to sell to another investor the right to buy 100 shares of common stock. You could do this by "writing a call." The individual (or institution) writing the option is known as the **option maker** or **writer.** As the option writer, you sell the option in the market and so are entitled to receive the price paid for the put or call (less modest commissions and other transaction costs). The put or call option is now a full-fledged financial asset and trades in the open market much like any other security.

Puts and calls are both written (sold) and purchased through securities brokers and dealers. In fact, they're just as easy to buy and sell as common stocks; a simple phone call, or a few mouse clicks, is all it takes. The writer stands behind the option, because it is the *writer* who must buy or deliver the stocks or other financial assets according to the terms of the option. (*Note:* The writers of puts and calls *have a legally binding obligation* to stand behind the terms of the contracts they have written. The buyer can just walk away from the deal if it turns sour; the writer cannot.) Puts and calls are written for a variety of reasons, most of which we will explore below. At this point, suffice it to say that writing options can be a viable investment strategy and can be a profitable course of action because, more often than not, *options expire worthless.*

How Puts and Calls Work Taking the *buyer's* point of view, let's now briefly examine how puts and calls work and how they derive their value. To understand the mechanics of puts and calls, it is best to look at their profit-making potential. For example, using stock options as a basis of discussion, consider a stock currently priced at $50 a share. Assume you can buy a call on the stock for $500, which enables you to purchase 100 shares of the stock at a fixed price of $50 each. A rise in the price of the underlying security (in this case, common stock) is what you, as an investor, hope for. What is the profit potential from this transaction if the price of the stock does indeed move up to, say, $75 by the expiration date on the call?

The answer is that you will earn $25 ($75 − $50) on each of the 100 shares of stock in the call—in other words, you'll earn a total gross profit of $2,500 from your $500 investment. This is so because you have the right to buy 100 shares of the stock, from the option writer, at a price of $50 each, and then immediately turn around and sell them in the market for $75 a share. You could have made the same ($2,500) profit by investing directly in the common stock. But because you would have had to invest $5,000 (100 shares × $50 per share), your rate of return would have been much lower. Obviously, there is considerable difference between the return potential of common stocks and calls. It is this difference that attracts investors and speculators to calls whenever the price outlook for the underlying financial asset is positive. Such differential returns, of course, are the direct result of *leverage,* which rests on the principle of reducing the level of capital required in a given investment position *without materially affecting the dollar amount of the payoff or capital appreciation from that investment.* (Note that although our illustration is couched in terms of common stock, this same valuation principle applies to any of the other financial assets that may underlie call options, such as market indexes, foreign currencies, and futures contracts.)

A similar situation can be worked out for puts. Assume that for the same $50 stock you could pay $500 and buy a put to *sell* 100 shares of the stock at a strike price of $50 each. As the buyer of a put, you want the price of the stock to *drop.* Assume that your expectations are correct and the price of the stock does indeed drop, to $25 a share. Here again, you realize a gross profit of $25 for each of the 100 shares in the put. Such profit is available by going to the market and buying 100 shares of the stock at a price of $25 a share and then immediately selling them to the writer of the put at a price of $50 per share.

Fortunately, put and call investors do *not* have to exercise their options and make simultaneous buy and sell transactions in order to receive their profit. That's because *the options themselves have value and therefore can be traded in the secondary market.* In fact, the value of both puts and calls is directly linked to the market price of the underlying financial asset. That is, the *value of a call* increases as the market price of the underlying security *rises.* The *value of a put* increases as the price of the security *declines.* Thus *investors can get their money out of options by selling them in the open market,* just as with any other security.

INVESTOR FACTS

AMERICAN OR EUROPEAN OPTIONS?—Put and call options can be issued in either *American* or *European* form. Actually, this has absolutely nothing to do with where the options are traded, but rather with when they can be exercised. An **American** option can be exercised on any business day that the option is traded; a **European** option can be exercised only on the day of expiration. For all practical purposes, most investors couldn't care less whether an option is American or European. The reason: Just because an option can't be exercised prior to expiration doesn't mean you have to hold it to maturity. Any option— American or European—can be sold at any time, on or before its expiration.

Advantages and Disadvantages The major advantage of investing in puts and calls is the leverage they offer. This feature also carries the advantage of limiting the investor's exposure to risk, because only a set amount of money (the purchase price of the option) can be lost. Also appealing is the fact that puts and calls can be used profitably when the price of the underlying security goes up *or* down.

A major disadvantage of puts and calls is that the holder enjoys neither interest or dividend income nor any other ownership benefits. Moreover, because the instruments have limited lives, the investor has a limited time frame in which to capture desired price behavior. Another disadvantage is that puts and calls themselves are a bit unusual, and many of their trading strategies are complex. Thus investors must possess special knowledge and must fully understand the subtleties of this trading vehicle.

Options Markets

Although the concept of options can be traced back to the writings of Aristotle, options trading in the United States did not begin until the late 1700s. And even then, up to the early 1970s, this market remained fairly small, largely unorganized, and the almost private domain of a handful of specialists and traders. All of this changed, however, on April 26, 1973, when a new securities market was created with the opening of the Chicago Board Options Exchange (CBOE).

Conventional Options Prior to the creation of the CBOE, put and call options trading was conducted in the over-the-counter market through a handful of specialized dealers. Investors who wished to purchase puts and calls contacted their own brokers, who contacted the options dealers. The dealers would find individuals (or institutions) willing to write the options. If the buyer wished to exercise an option, he or she did so with the writer and no one else—a system that largely prohibited any secondary trading. On the other hand, there were virtually no limits to what could be written, so long as the buyer was willing to pay the price. Put and call options were written on New York and American exchange stocks, as well as on regional and over-the-counter securities, for as short a time as 30 days and for as long as a year. Over-the-counter options, known today as **conventional options**, were initially hit hard by the CBOE. However, the conventional (OTC) market has bounced back and is today every bit as big as the listed market, though it is used almost exclusively by institutional investors. Accordingly, our attention in this chapter will focus on listed markets, like the CBOE, where individual investors do most of their options trading.

Listed Options The creation of the CBOE signaled the birth of so-called **listed options**, a term that describes put and call options traded on organized exchanges rather than over the counter. The CBOE launched trading in calls on just 16 firms. From these rather humble beginnings, there evolved in a relatively short time a large and active market for listed options. Today, trading in listed options is done in both puts and calls and takes place on five exchanges, the largest of which is the CBOE. Options are also traded on the AMEX, the Philadelphia Exchange, the Pacific Stock Exchange, and the

H O T

Some questions and answers by investors regarding options, along with a good glossary on options, are available at:

www.cboe.com/LearnCenter

conventional options
put and call options sold over the counter.

listed options
put and call options listed and traded on organized securities exchanges, such as the CBOE.

International Securities Exchange. (The newest participant in this market, the ISE was launched in May 2000 and is the first fully electronic U.S. options exchange.) In total, *put and call options are now traded on over 2,300 different stocks*. (Actually, around 4,000 options were listed on all five exchanges in early 2003, as many of the more actively traded options are listed on more than one exchange.) Although many of the options are written on large, well-known NYSE companies, the list also includes a number of AMEX and OTC/Nasdaq stocks, both large and small, and in both the "old-economy" and the "new-economy" (high-tech) sectors of the market. Indeed, many of the most actively traded options today are those written on high-tech stocks. In addition to stocks, listed options are available on stock indexes, exchange-traded funds, debt securities, foreign currencies, and even commodities and financial futures.

Listed options not only provided a convenient market for the trading of puts and calls, but also standardized expiration dates and exercise prices. The listed options exchanges created a clearinghouse organization that eliminated direct ties between buyers and writers of options and reduced the cost of executing put and call transactions. They also developed an active secondary market, with wide distribution of price information. As a result, it is now as easy to trade a listed option as a listed stock.

Stock Options

The advent of the CBOE and the other listed option exchanges had a quick and dramatic impact on the trading volume of puts and calls. In fact, the level of activity in listed stock options grew so rapidly that it took only 8 years for the annual volume of contracts traded to pass the 100 million mark. Today well over 750 million listed options contracts are traded each year, most of which are stock options. Indeed, of the 780 million contracts traded in 2002, *more than 90% (or 708 million contracts) were stock options*. During that year, the volume of contracts traded was divided among the five options exchanges as follows:

	Total Number of Contracts Traded (millions)	Percentage of the Total
CBOE	267.6	34.3%
AMEX	186.1	23.8
ISE	152.4	19.5
Philadelphia Exchange	89.0	11.4
Pacific Exchange	85.4	11.0
Total	**780.5**	**100.0%**

The CBOE, AMEX, and ISE account for about *75% of all stock options trading*, while the CBOE alone handles *over 91% of all index options trading*.

The continued expansion of listed options exchanges has unquestionably added a new dimension to investing. In order to avoid serious (and possibly expensive) mistakes with these securities, however, you must fully understand their basic features. In the sections that follow, we will look closely at the investment attributes of stock options and trading strategies that can be used with them. Later, we'll explore stock-index (and ETF) options and then briefly look

strike price
the stated price at which you can buy a security with a call or sell a security with a put.

expiration date
the date at which an option expires.

at other types of puts and calls, including interest rate and currency options, and long-term options. (Futures options will be taken up in Chapter 16, after we study futures contracts.)

Stock Option Provisions Because of their low unit cost, stock options (or *equity options,* as they're also called) are very popular with individual investors. Except for the underlying financial asset, they are like any other type of put or call, subject to the same kinds of contract provisions and market forces. As far as stock options are concerned, there are two provisions that are especially important: (1) the price—known as the *strike price*—at which the stock can be bought or sold, and (2) the amount of time remaining until expiration. As we'll see below, both the strike price and the time remaining to expiration have a significant bearing on the valuation and pricing of options.

Strike Price The **strike price** represents the price contract between the buyer of the option and the writer. For a call, the strike price specifies the price at which each of the 100 shares of stock can be bought. For a put, it represents the price at which the stock can be sold to the writer. With conventional (OTC) options, there are no constraints on the strike price. With listed options, however, strike prices are *standardized:* Stocks selling for less than $25 per share carry strike prices that are set in 2½ dollar increments ($7.50, $10.00, $12.50, $15, and so on.). The increment jumps to $5 for stocks selling between $25 and $200 per share. For stocks that trade at more than $200 a share, the strike price is set in $10 increments. Of course, the strike price is adjusted for substantial stock dividends and stock splits.

Expiration Date The **expiration date** is also an important provision, because it specifies the life of the option, just as the maturity date indicates the life of a bond. The expiration date, in effect, specifies the length of the contract between the holder and the writer of the option. Thus, if you hold a 6-month call on Sears with a strike price of, say, $40, that option gives you the right to buy 100 shares of Sears common stock at $40 per share at any time over the next 6 months. *No matter what happens to the market price of the stock*, you can use your call option to buy 100 shares of Sears at $40 a share. If the price of the stock moves up, you stand to make money. If it goes down, you'll be out the cost of the option.

Expiration dates for options in the conventional market can fall on any working day of the month. In contrast, expiration dates are standardized in the *listed* options market. The exchanges initially created three expiration cycles for all listed options. Each issue is assigned to one of these three cycles. One cycle is January, April, July, and October. Another is February, May, August, and November. The third is March, June, September, and December. The exchanges still use the same three expiration cycles, but they've been altered so that investors are always able to trade in the two nearest (current and following) months, plus the next two closest months in the option's regular expiration cycle. For reasons that are pretty obvious, this is sometimes referred to as a *two-plus-two* schedule.

Take, for example, the January cycle. The following options are available in January: January, February, April, and July. These represent the two current months (January and February) and the next two months in the cycle (April

FIGURE 15.1 Quotations for Listed Stock Options

The quotes for puts and calls are listed side by side. In addition to the closing price of the option, the latest price of the underlying security is shown, along with the strike price on the option. (*Source: Wall Street Journal*, August 15, 2003.)

Call option quotes

Put option quotes

Number of August 2003 BEA puts traded (with a strike price of 12.50)

Strike price on the option

Month of expiration (October 2003)

Name of company

Market price of the underlying common stock

Price of a January 2004 call (that carries a strike price of 15)

Quotes for an **ETF option** (Dow Diamonds)

Number of January 2004 ETrade calls traded (with a strike price of 7.50)

Price of a September 2003 GE put (that carries a strike price of 30)

OPTION/STRIKE		EXP	-CALL-		-PUT-	
			VOL	LAST	VOL	LAST
Altria	40	Aug	5563	0.30	6120	0.55
39.85	40	Sep	5124	1.60	678	2.20
39.85	42.50	Aug	4265	0.05	115	2.80
39.85	42.50	Sep	13177	0.65	239	4 ·
AndrxCp	20	Sep	3166	0.45	...	...
AutoNatn	17.50	Aug	10273	0.65	...	...
18.10	17.50	Sep	10270	1	33	0.40
BEA Sys	12.50	Aug	9639	0.35	4794	0.25
Broadcom	20	Aug	3157	1.50	915	0.05
21.26	20	Sep	5230	2.35	5418	0.90
21.26	22.50	Sep	3136	1.05	478	2.05
ChevrnTex	60	Sep	7368	13.90	...	...
72.82	65	Sep	24151	9.20	56	0.10
72.82	70	Aug	18679	4	60	0.05
72.82	70	Sep	4238	4.10	191	0.40
Cisco	15	Oct	144	3	5184	0.20
17.79	15	Jan	275	3.50	5395	0.60
17.79	17.50	Aug	9214	0.30	4356	0.05
Citigrp	45	Aug	5564	0.30	1655	0.10
CocaCola	45	Aug	10094	0.15	806	0.20
45.01	50	Feb	8238	0.80	...	...
Comcst sp	32.50	Oct	4489	0.60	...	...
DJIA Diam	90	Aug	5384	3.30	250	0.05
93.33	91	Aug	5816	2.30	1067	0.05
93.33	92	Aug	3934	1.35	1922	0.05
93.33	93	Aug	3255	0.50	1983	0.20
DellInc	30	Aug	3490	1.60	6126	0.10
32.34	32.50	Aug	20594	0.15	1679	1.20
32.34	32.50	Sep	7396	0.70	650	1.70
Documnt	20	Oct	3510	0.70	...	...
ETrade	7.50	Jan	10403	1.75	18	0.70
17.34	10	Oct	5583	0.35	13	1.70
17.34	10	Jan	5233	0.65	5	2.10
EMC	11	Aug	3183	0.25	892	0.10
EdisInt	15	Aug	16612	2.50	...	...
17.32	15	Sep	7350	2.90	3531	0.35
17.32	17.50	Aug	4435	0.30	120	0.20
17.32	17.50	Sep	5426	1	181	1.10
ExxonMob	37.50	Oct	4174	0.80	420	1.35
FordM	10	Dec	8062	1.25	103	0.65
Gen El	27.50	Aug	3235	1.05	10	0.05
28.78	30	Sep	10969	0.30	1079	1.85

and July). In February, the available contracts would be February, March, April, and July. The expiration dates continue rolling over in this way during the course of the year. Given the month of expiration, the actual day of expiration is always the same: the Saturday following the third Friday of each expiration month. Thus, for all practical purposes, *listed options always expire on the third Friday of the month of expiration.*

Put and Call Transactions Option traders are subject to commission and transaction costs whenever they buy or sell an option, or whenever an option is written. The writing of puts and calls is subject to normal transaction costs because these costs effectively represent remuneration to the broker or dealer for *selling* the option.

Listed options have their own marketplace and quotation system. Finding the price (or *premium*, as it's called) of a listed stock option is fairly easy, as the options quotations in Figure 15.1 (on page 647) indicate. Note that quotes are provided for calls and puts separately. For each option, quotes are listed for various combinations of strike prices and expiration dates. Because there are so many options and a substantial number of them are rarely traded, financial publications like the *Wall Street Journal* list quotes only for the most actively traded options. Also, the quotes listed are only for the options that actually traded on the day in question. For example, in Figure 15.1, there may be many other options available on Cisco, but only the ones that actually traded (on Thursday, August 14, 2003) are listed.

The quotes are standardized: The name of the company and the closing price of the underlying stock are listed first; note that Cisco stock closed at $17.79. The strike price is listed next, followed by the expiration date (or month in which the option expires). Then the volume and closing prices of the call (and/or put) options are quoted relative to their strike prices and expiration dates. For example, a January (2004) Cisco *call* with a strike price of $15 was quoted at 3.50 (which translates into a dollar price of $350 because stock options trade in 100-share lots). In contrast, a January (2004) Cisco *put* with the same strike price ($15) was quoted at 0.60 (or just $60 for each 100-share put option).

IN REVIEW

CONCEPTS

15.1 Describe *put* and *call* options. Are they issued like other corporate securities? Explain.

15.2 What are *listed options*, and how do they differ from *conventional options?*

15.3 What are the main investment attractions of put and call options? What are the risks?

15.4 What is a *stock option?* What is the difference between a stock option and a *derivative security?* Describe a derivative security and give several examples.

15.5 What is a *strike price?* How does it differ from the market price of the stock? Do both puts and calls have strike prices? Explain.

15.6 Why do put and call options have expiration dates? Is there a market for options that have passed their expiration dates? Explain.

Options Pricing and Trading

The value of a put or call depends to a large extent on the market behavior of the financial asset that underlies the option. Getting a firm grip on the current and expected future value of a put or call is extremely important to options traders and investors. Thus, to get the most from any options trading program, it is imperative that you understand how options are priced in the market. *Continuing to use stock options as a basis of discussion,* let's look now at the basic principles of options valuation and pricing. We'll start with a brief review of how profits are derived from puts and calls. Then we'll take a look at several ways in which investors can use these options.

The Profit Potential from Puts and Calls

Although the quoted market price of a put or call is affected by such factors as time to expiration, stock volatility, and market interest rates, by far the most important variable is the *price behavior of the underlying common stock.* This is the variable that drives any significant moves in the price of the option and that determines the option's profit (return) potential. Thus, when the underlying stock *moves up in price, calls do well.* When the price of the underlying stock *drops, puts do well.* Such performance also explains why it's important to get a good handle on the expected future price behavior of a stock *before* buying or selling (writing) an option.

The typical price behavior of an option is illustrated graphically in Figure 15.2 (on page 650). The diagram on the left depicts a call, the one on the right a put. The *call* diagram is constructed assuming you pay $500 for a call that carries a strike price of $50. With the call, the diagram shows what happens to the value of the option when the price of the stock increases. Observe that a call does not gain in value until the price of the stock *advances past the stated exercise price* ($50). Also, because it costs $500 to buy the call, the stock has to move up another 5 points (from $50 to $55) in order for you to recover the premium and thereby reach a break-even point. So long as the stock continues to rise in price, everything from there on out is profit. Once the premium is recouped, the profit from the call position is limited only by the extent to which the stock price increases over the remaining life of the contract.

The value of a put is also derived from the price of the underlying stock, except that their respective market prices move in opposite directions. The *put* diagram in Figure 15.2 assumes you can buy a put for $500 and obtain the right to sell the underlying stock at $50 a share. It shows that the value of the put remains constant until the market price of the corresponding stock *drops to the exercise price* ($50) on the put. Then, as the price of the stock continues to fall, the value of the option increases. Again, note that because the put cost $500, you don't start making money on the investment until the price of the stock drops below the break-even point of $45 a share. Beyond that point, the profit from the put is defined by the extent to which the price of the underlying stock continues to fall over the remaining life of the option.

Fundamental Value

As we have seen, the intrinsic value of a put or call depends ultimately on the exercise price stated on the option, as well as on the prevailing market price of

FIGURE 15.2   **The Valuation Properties of Put and Call Options**

The value of a put or call reflects the price behavior of its underlying common stock (or other financial asset). The cost of the option has been recovered when the option passes its break-even point. After that, the profit potential of a put or call is limited only by the price behavior of the underlying asset and by the length of time to the expiration of the option.

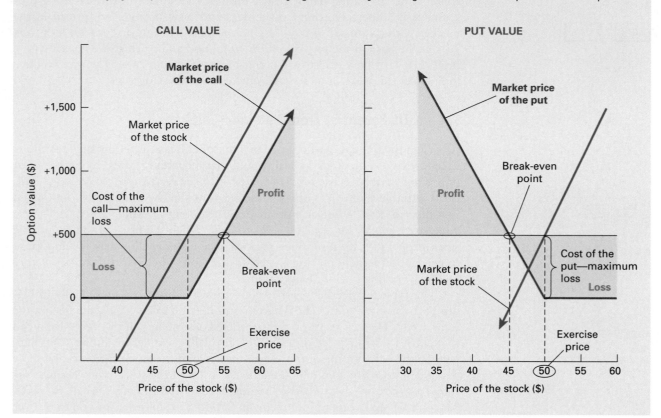

the underlying common stock. More specifically, the *fundamental value of a call* is determined according to the following simple formula:

Equation 15.1

$$\text{Fundamental value of a call} = \left(\begin{array}{c}\text{Market price of} \\ \text{underlying} \\ \text{common stock,} \\ \text{or other} \\ \text{financial asset}\end{array} - \begin{array}{c}\text{Strike price} \\ \text{on} \\ \text{the call}\end{array}\right) \times 100$$

$$V = (MP - SPC) \times 100$$

In other words, the fundamental value of a call is nothing more than the difference between market price and strike price. As implied in Equation 15.1, a call has an intrinsic value whenever the market price of the underlying financial asset exceeds the strike price stipulated on the call. A simple illustration will show that a call carrying a strike price of $50 on a stock currently trading at $60 has an intrinsic (fundamental) value of $1,000: ($60 − $50) × 100 = $10 × 100 = $1,000.

A put, on the other hand, cannot be valued in the same way, because puts and calls allow the holder to do different things. To find the *fundamental value of a put*, we must change the order of the equation a bit:

Equation 15.2

$$\text{Fundamental value of a put} = \left(\begin{array}{c} \text{Strike price} \\ \text{on} \\ \text{the put} \end{array} - \begin{array}{c} \text{Market price of} \\ \text{underlying} \\ \text{common stock,} \\ \text{or other} \\ \text{financial asset} \end{array} \right) \times 100$$

$$V = (SPP - MP) \times 100$$

In this case, a put has value so long as the market price of the underlying stock (or financial asset) is less than the strike price stipulated on the put.

H O T

Options calculators are available at:

**www.cboe.com/tradtool/optioncalculator.asp
(Java calculator)**

in-the-money
a call option with a strike price less than the market price of the underlying security; a put option whose strike price is greater than the market price of the underlying security.

out-of-the-money
a call option with no real value because the strike price exceeds the market price of the stock; a put option whose market price exceeds the strike price.

option premium
the quoted price the investor pays to buy a listed put or call option.

H O T

Visit this site to see the most actively traded options:

www.cboe.com/MktData/MostActives.asp

In-the-Money/Out-of-the-Money When written, options do not necessarily have to carry strike prices at the prevailing market prices of the underlying common stocks. Also, as an option subsequently trades on listed exchanges, the price of the option will move in response to moves in the price of the underlying common stock. When a call has a strike price that is less than the market price of the underlying common stock, it has a positive intrinsic value and is known as an **in-the-money** option. A major portion of the option price in this case is based on (or derived from) the fundamental value of the call. When the strike price exceeds the market price of the stock, the call has no "real" value, in which case it is known as an **out-of-the-money** option. Because the option has no intrinsic value, its price is made up solely of investment premium.

As you might expect, the situation is reversed for put options. That is, a put is considered in-the-money when its strike price is greater than the market price of the stock. It's considered out-of-the-money when the market price of the stock exceeds the strike price. These terms are much more than exotic names given to options. As we will see, they characterize the investment behavior of options and can affect return and risk.

Option Prices and Premiums Put and call values, as found according to Equations 15.1 and 15.2, denote what an option should be worth, *in the absence of any time premium*. In fact, options rarely trade at their fundamental (intrinsic) values. Instead, they almost always trade at prices that exceed their intrinsic values, especially for options that still have a long time to run. That is, puts and calls nearly always trade at premium prices. The term **option premium** is used to describe the market price of listed put and call options. Technically, the option premium is the (quoted) price the buyer pays for the *right* to buy or sell a certain amount of the underlying financial asset at a specified price for a specified period of time. The option seller, on the other hand, receives the premium and gets to keep it whether or not the option is exercised. To the seller, the option premium represents compensation for agreeing to fulfill certain *obligations* of the contract.

As we'll see below, the term *premium* is also used to denote the extent to which the market price of an option exceeds its fundamental or intrinsic value. Thus, to avoid confusion and keep matters as simple as possible, we'll use the word *price* in the usual way: to describe the amount it takes to buy an option in the market.

What Drives Options Prices?

Option prices can be reduced to two separate components. The first is the *fundamental* (or *intrinsic*) value of the option, which is driven by the current market price of the underlying financial asset. As we saw in Equations 15.1 and 15.2, the greater the difference between the market price of the underlying asset and the strike price on the option, the greater the fundamental value of the put or call. The second component of an option price is customarily referred to as the **time premium**. It represents, in effect, the excess value embedded in the option price. That is, time premium is *the amount by which the option price exceeds the option's fundamental value.* Table 15.1 lists some quoted prices for an actively traded call option. These quoted prices (panel A) are then separated into fundamental value (panel B) and time premium (panel C). Note that three strike prices are used—$65, $70, and $75. Relative to the market price of the stock ($71.75), one strike price ($65) is well below market; this is an in-the-money call. One ($70) is fairly near the market. The third ($75) is well above the market; this is an out-of-the-money call. Note the considerable difference in the makeup of the options prices as we move from an in-the-money call to an out-of-the-money call.

Panel B in the table lists the fundamental values of the call options, as determined by Equation 15.1. For example, note that although the March 65 call (the call with the March expiration date and $65 strike price) is trading at 7.75, its intrinsic value is only 6.75. The intrinsic value (of 6.75) represents, in effect, the extent to which the option is trading in-the-money. But observe that

time premium
the amount by which the option price exceeds the option's fundamental value.

TABLE 15.1 — Option Price Components for an Actively Traded Call Option

Price	Strike Price	Expiration Months		
		February	March	June
Panel A: Quoted Options Prices				
71.75	65	—	7.75	9.75
71.75	70	2.25	3.88	6.75
71.75	75	0.19	1.50	3.88
Panel B: Underlying Fundamental Values				
71.75	65	—	6.75	6.75
71.75	70	1.75	1.75	1.75
71.75	75	neg.	neg.	neg.
Panel C: Time Premiums				
71.75	65	—	1.00	3.00
71.75	70	0.50	2.12	5.00
71.75	75	0.19	1.50	3.88

Note: neg. indicates that options have negative fundamental values.

although most of the price of the March 65 call is made up of fundamental value, not all of it is. Now look at the calls with the $75 strike price. None of these has any fundamental value; they're all out-of-the-money, and, as such, their prices are made up solely of time premium. Basically, the value of these options is determined entirely by the *belief* that the price of the underlying stock could rise to over $75 a share before the options expire.

Panel C shows the amount of *time premium* embedded in the call prices. Such a premium represents the difference between the *quoted call price* (panel A) and the call's *fundamental value* (panel B). It shows that the price of (just about) every traded option contains at least some premium. Indeed, unless the options are about to expire, you'd expect them to be trading at a premium. Also, note that with all three strike prices, *the longer the time to expiration, the greater the size of the premium.*

As you might expect, *time to expiration* is an important element in explaining the size of the price premium in panel C. However, a couple of other variables also have a bearing on the behavior of this premium. One is the *price volatility of the underlying common stock*. Other things being equal, the more volatile the stock is, the more it enhances the speculative appeal of the option—and therefore the bigger the time premium is. In addition, the size of the premium is *directly related to the level of interest rates*. That is, the amount of premium embedded in a call option generally increases along with interest rates. Less important variables include the dividend yield on the underlying common stock, the trading volume of the option, and the exchanges on which the option is listed. For the most part, therefore, four major forces drive the price of an option. They are, in descending order of importance, (1) the price behavior of the underlying financial asset, (2) the amount of time remaining to expiration, (3) the amount of price volatility in the underlying financial asset, and (4) the general level of interest rates.

Option-Pricing Models Some fairly sophisticated option-pricing models have been developed, notably by Myron Scholes and the late Fisher Black, to value options. Many active options traders use these formulas to identify and trade over- and undervalued options. Not surprisingly, these models are based on the same variables we identified above. For example, the five parameters used in the Black-Scholes option-pricing model are (1) the risk-free rate of interest, (2) the price volatility of the underlying stock, (3) the current price of the underlying stock, (4) the strike price of the option, and (5) the option's time to expiration.

HOT

A more detailed discussion of the Black-Scholes option-pricing model, including the basic equations used in the model, can be found on the book's Web site, at:

www.aw-bc.com/gitman_joehnk

Trading Strategies

For the most part, stock options can be used in three different kinds of trading strategies: (1) buying puts and calls for speculation, (2) hedging with puts and calls, and (3) option writing and spreading.

Buying for Speculation

Buying for speculation is the simplest and most straightforward use of puts and calls. Basically, it is just like buying stock ("buy low, sell high") and, in fact, represents an alternative to investing in stock. For example, if you feel the market price of a particular stock is going to move up, one way to capture that price appreciation is to buy a call on the stock. In contrast, if you feel the stock is about to drop in price, a put could convert that price decline into a profitable situation. In essence, investors buy options rather than stock whenever the options are likely to yield a greater return. The principle here, of course, is to get the biggest return from your investment dollar. Puts and calls often meet this objective because of the added leverage they offer. Furthermore, options offer *valuable downside protection:* The most you can lose is the cost of the option, which is always less than the cost of the underlying stock. Thus, by using options as a vehicle for speculation, you can put a cap on losses and still get almost as much profit potential as with the underlying stock.

Speculating with Calls To illustrate the essentials of speculating with options, imagine that you have uncovered a stock you feel will move up in price over the next 6 months. What would happen if you were to buy a call on this stock rather than investing directly in the firm's common? To find out, let's see what the numbers show. The price of the stock is now $49, and you anticipate that within 6 months, it will rise to about $65. You need to determine the expected return associated with each of your investment alternatives. Because (most) options have relatively short lives, and because we're dealing in this case with an investment horizon of only 6 months, holding period return can be used to measure yield (see Chapter 4). Thus, if your expectations about the stock are correct, it should go up by $16 a share and, in so doing, provide you with a 33% holding period return [($65 − $49)/$49 = $16/$49 = 0.33].

But there are also some listed options available on this stock. Let's see how they would do. For illustrative purposes, we will use two 6-month calls that carry a $40 and a $50 strike price, respectively. Table 15.2 compares the

EXCEL with
SPREADSHEETS

TABLE 15.2	Speculating with Call Options		
	100 Shares of Underlying Common Stock	6-Month Call Options on the Stock	
		$40 Strike Price	$50 Strike Price
Today			
Market value of stock (at $49/share)	$4,900		
Market price of calls*		$1,100	$ 400
6 Months Later			
Expected value of stock (at $65/share)	$6,500		
Expected price of calls*		$2,500	$1,500
Profit	$1,600	$1,400	$1,100
Holding Period Return**	**33%**	**127%**	**275%**

*The price of the calls was computed according to Equation 15.1. It includes some investment premium in the purchase price but none in the expected sales price.

**Holding period return (HPR) = (Ending price of the stock or option − Beginning price of the stock or option)/Beginning price of the stock or option.

behavior of these two calls with the behavior of the underlying common stock. Clearly, from a holding period return perspective, either call option represents a superior investment to buying the stock itself. The dollar amount of profit may be a bit more with the stock, but note that the size of the required investment ($4,900) is a lot more too, so that alternative has the lowest HPR.

Observe that one of the calls is an in-the-money option (the one with the $40 strike price). The other is out-of-the-money. The difference in returns generated by these calls is rather typical. That is, investors are usually able to generate much better rates of return with lower-priced (out-of-the-money) options and also enjoy less exposure to loss. Of course, a major drawback of out-of-the-money options is that their price is made up solely of investment premium—a sunk cost that will be lost if the stock does not move in price.

Speculating with Puts To see how you can speculate in puts, consider the following situation. You're looking at a stock that's now priced at $51, but you anticipate a drop in price to about $35 per share within the next 6 months. If that occurs, you could sell the stock short and make a profit of $16 per share. (See Chapter 2 for a discussion of short selling.) Alternatively, you can purchase an out-of-the-money put (with a strike price of $50) for, say, $300. Again, if the price of the underlying stock does indeed drop, you will make money with the put. The profit and rate of return on the put are summarized below, along with the comparative returns from short selling the stock.

Comparative Performance Given Price of Stock Moves from $51 to $35/Share Over a 6-Month Period:	Buy 1 Put ($50 strike price)	Short Sell 100 Shares of Stock
Purchase price (today)	$300	
Selling price (6 months later)	1,500*	
Short sell (today)		$5,100
Cover (6 months later)		3,500
Profit	$1,200	$1,600
Holding period return	400%	63%**

*The price of the put was computed according to Equation 15.2 and does not include any investment premium.
**Assumes the short sale was made with a required margin deposit of 50%.

Once again, in terms of holding period return, the stock option is the superior investment vehicle by a wide margin.

Of course, not all option investments perform as well as the ones in our examples. Success with this strategy rests on picking the right underlying common stock. Thus *security analysis and proper stock selection are critical dimensions of this technique*. It is a highly risky investment strategy, but it may be well suited for the more speculatively inclined investor.

Hedging: Modifying Risks

hedge
a combination of two or more securities into a single investment position for the purpose of reducing or eliminating risk.

A **hedge** is simply a combination of two or more securities into a single investment position for the purpose of reducing risk. Let's say you hold a stock and want to reduce the amount of downside risk in this investment—you can do that by setting up a hedge. In essence, you're using the hedge as a way to *modify your exposure to risk*; to be more specific, you're trying to change not only the

TABLE 15.3 Limiting Capital Loss with a Put Hedge

		Stock	Put*
Today			
Purchase price of the stock		$25	
Purchase price of the put			$1.50
Sometime Later			
A. Price of common goes *up* to:		**$50**	
Value of put			$ 0
Profit:			
100 shares of stock ($50 − $25)	$2,500		
Less: Cost of put	− 150		
	Profit: $2,350		
B. Price of common goes *down* to:		**$10**	
Value of put**			$15
Profit:			
100 shares of stock (loss: $10 − $25)	−$1,500		
Value of put (profit)	+ 1,500		
Less: Cost of put	− 150		
	Loss: $ 150		

*The put is purchased simultaneously and carries a strike price of $25.
**See Equation 15.2.

chance of loss, but also the *amount lost*, if the worst does occur. A simple hedge might involve nothing more than buying stock and simultaneously buying a put on that same stock. Or it might consist of selling some stock short and then buying a call. There are many types of hedges, some of which are very simple and others very sophisticated. They are all used for the same basic reason: to earn or protect a profit without exposing the investor to excessive loss.

An options hedge may be appropriate if you have generated a profit from an earlier common stock investment and wish to protect that profit. Or it may be appropriate if you are about to enter into a common stock investment and wish to protect your money by limiting potential capital loss. If you hold a stock that has gone up in price, the purchase of a put would provide the type of downside protection you need; the purchase of a call, in contrast, would provide protection to a short seller of common stock. Thus option hedging always involves two transactions: (1) the initial common stock position (long or short) and (2) the simultaneous or subsequent purchase of the option.

Protective Puts: Limiting Capital Loss Let's examine a simple options hedge in which a put is used to limit your exposure to capital loss. Assume that you want to buy 100 shares of stock. Being a bit apprehensive about the stock's outlook, you decide to use an option hedge to protect your capital against loss. Therefore, you simultaneously (1) buy the stock and (2) buy a put on the stock (which fully covers the 100 shares owned). This type of hedge is known as a *protective put*. Preferably, the put would be a low-priced option with a strike price at or near the current market price of the stock. Suppose you purchase the common at $25 and pay $150 for a put with a $25 strike

EXCEL with SPREADSHEETS

TABLE 15.4 Protecting Profits with a Put Hedge

	Stock	3-Month Put with a $75 Strike Price
Purchase price of the stock	$ 35	
Today		
Market price of the stock	$ 75	
Market price of the put		$2.50
3 Months Later		
A. Price of common goes *up* to:	$100	
Value of put		$ 0
Profit:		
100 shares of stock ($100 − $35)	$6,500	
Less: Cost of put	− 250	
Profit:	$6,250	
B. Price of common goes *down* to:	$ 50	
Value of put*		$25
Profit:		
100 shares of stock ($50 − $35)	$1,500	
Value of put (profit)	2,500	
Less: Cost of put	− 250	
Profit:	$3,750	

*See Equation 15.2.

price. Now, no matter what happens to the price of the stock over the life of the put, *you can lose no more than $150.* At the same time, *there's no limit on the gains.* If the stock does not move, you will be out the cost of a put. If it drops in price, then whatever is lost on the stock will be made up with the put. The bottom line? The most you can lose is the cost of the put ($150, in this case). However, if the price of the stock goes up (as hoped), the put becomes useless, and you will earn the capital gains on the stock (less the cost of the put, of course).

The essentials of this option hedge are shown in Table 15.3. The $150 paid for the put is sunk cost. That's lost no matter what happens to the price of the stock. In effect, it is the price paid for the hedge. Moreover, this hedge is good only for the life of the put. When this put expires, you will have to replace it with another put or forget about hedging your capital.

Protective Puts: Protecting Profits The other basic use of an option hedge involves entering into the options position *after* a profit has been made on the underlying stock. This could be done because of investment uncertainty or for tax purposes (to carry over a profit to the next taxable year). For example, if you bought 100 shares of a stock at $35 and it moved to $75, there would be a profit of $40 per share to protect. You could protect the profit with an option hedge by buying a put. Assume you buy a 3-month put with a $75 strike price at a cost of $250. Now, regardless of what happens to the stock over the life of the put, you are guaranteed a minimum profit of $3,750 (the

$4,000 profit in the stock made so far, less the $250 cost of the put). This can be seen in Table 15.4 (on page 657). Note that if the price of the stock should fall, the worst that can happen is a guaranteed minimum profit of $3,750. And there is still *no limit on how much profit can be made.* As long as the stock continues to go up, you will reap the benefits. (But watch out: *The cost of this kind of insurance can become very expensive just when its needed the most*—that is, when market prices are falling. Under such circumstances, it's not uncommon to find put options trading at price premiums of 20% to 30%, or more, above their prevailing fundamental values. Essentially, that means the price of the stock position you're trying to protect has to fall 20% to 30% before the protection even starts to kick in! Clearly, as long as high option price premiums prevail, the hedging strategies described above are a lot less attractive. They still may prove to be helpful, but only for very wide swings in value—those that occur over fairly short periods of time, as defined by the life of the put option.)

One final point: Although the preceding discussion pertained to put hedges, it should be clear that call hedges can also be set up to limit the loss or protect a profit on a short sale. For example, when a stock is sold short, a call can be purchased to protect the short seller against a rise in the price of the stock—with the same basic results as outlined above.

Enhancing Returns: Options Writing and Spreading

The advent of listed options has led to many intriguing options-trading strategies. Yet, despite the appeal of these techniques, there is one important point that all the experts agree on: *Such specialized trading strategies should be left to experienced investors who fully understand their subtleties.* Our goal at this point is not to master these specialized strategies but to explain in general terms what they are and how they operate. There are two types of specialized options strategies: (1) writing options and (2) spreading options.

Writing Options Generally, investors write options because they believe the price of the underlying stock is going to move in their favor. That is, it is not going to rise as much as the buyer of a call expects, nor will it fall as much as the buyer of a put hopes. *More often than not, the option writer is right;* he or she makes money far more often than the buyer of the put or call. Such favorable odds explain, in part, the underlying economic motivation for writing put and call options. Options writing represents an investment transaction to the writers: They receive the full option premium (less normal transaction costs) in exchange for agreeing to live up to the terms of the option.

naked options
options written on securities not owned by the writer.

Naked Options Investors can write options in one of two ways. One is to write **naked options,** which involves writing options on stock not owned by the writer. You simply write the put or call, collect the option premium, and hope the price of the underlying stock does not move against you. If successful, naked writing can be highly profitable because of the modest amount of capital required. Remember, though: The amount of return to the writer is always limited to the amount of option premium received. On the other hand, there is really *no limit to loss exposure.* That's the catch: The price of the underlying stock can rise or fall by just about any amount over the life of the option and can deal a real blow to the writer of the naked put or call.

Covered Options The amount of risk exposure is a lot less for those who write **covered options**. That's because, in this case, the options are written against stocks the investor (writer) already owns or has a position in. For example, you could write a call against stock you own or write a put against stock you have short sold. In this way, you can use the long or short position to meet the terms of the option. Such a strategy is a fairly conservative way to generate attractive rates of return. The object is to write a slightly *out-of-the-money* option, pocket the option premium, and hope the price of the underlying stock will move up or down to (but not exceed) the option's strike price. In effect, you are adding option premium to the other usual sources of return (dividends and/or capital gains). But there's more: While the option premium adds to the return, it also reduces risk. It can be used to cushion a loss if the price of the stock moves against the investor.

There is a hitch to all this, of course: *The amount of return the covered option investor can realize is limited.* For once the price of the underlying common stock exceeds the strike price on the option, the option becomes valuable. When that happens, *you start to lose money on the options*. From this point on, for every dollar you make on the stock position, you lose an equal amount on the option position. That's a major risk of writing covered call options—if the price of the underlying stock takes off, you'll miss out on the added profits.

To illustrate the ins and outs of *covered call writing*, let's assume you own 100 shares of PFP, Inc.—an actively traded, high-yielding common stock. The stock is currently trading at $73.50 and pays *quarterly* dividends of $1 a share. You decide to write a 3-month call on PFP, giving the buyer the right to take the stock off your hands at $80 a share. Such options are trading in the market at 2.50, so you receive $250 for writing the call. You fully intend to hold on to the stock, so you'd like to see the price of PFP stock rise to no more than 80 by the expiration date on the call. If that happens, the call option will expire worthless. As a result, not only will you earn the dividends and capital gains on the stock, but you also get to pocket the $250 you received when you wrote the call. Basically, *you've just added $250 to the quarterly return on your stock*.

Table 15.5 (on page 661) summarizes the profit and loss characteristics of this covered call position. Note that the maximum profit on this transaction occurs *when the market price of the stock equals the strike price on the call*. If the price of the stock keeps going up, you miss out on the added profits. Even so, the $1,000 profit that's earned at a stock price of 80 or above translates into a (3-month) holding period return of a very respectable 13.6% ($1,000/$7,350). That represents an *annualized* return of nearly 55%! With this kind of return potential, it's not difficult to see why covered call writing is so popular. Moreover, as *situation D* in the table illustrates, covered call writing adds a little cushion to losses: The price of the stock has to drop more than 2½ points (which is what you received when you wrote/sold the call) before you start losing money.

Besides covered calls and protective puts, there are many different ways of combining options with other types of securities to achieve a given investment

covered options
options written against stock owned (or short sold) by the writer.

CREATE YOUR OWN CONVERTIBLES—What can you do when you want to buy a company's convertible bond but it doesn't offer one? You can design your own (synthetic) convertible by combining interest-bearing securities and call options. One popular method is the 90/10 strategy. You place 10% of your money into call options, and the 90% goes in an interest-bearing security such as a money market instrument that is held until the option expires. The options provide leverage and give you the right to buy shares in the company (just like a convertible); the money market security limits risk. Your downside loss exposure is the amount of the call premium less the interest you earn on the money market investments.

Source: Witold Sames, "Up, Down, or Sideways," *Bloomberg Personal,* October 1997, p. 30; and Avital Louria Hahn, "Market Laps Up Synthetic Convert; MSDW, AIG Cleanup," *Investment Dealers' Digest,* May 15, 2000, downloaded from www.findarticles.com.

option spreading
combining two or more options with different strike prices and/or expiration dates into a single transaction.

option straddle
the simultaneous purchase (or sale) of a put and a call on the same underlying common stock (or financial asset).

objective. Probably none is more unusual than the creation of so-called *synthetic securities.* A case in point: Say you want to buy a convertible bond on a certain company, but that company doesn't have any convertibles outstanding. That's really not a big problem. You can create your own customized convertible by combining a straight (nonconvertible) bond with a listed call option on your targeted company.

Spreading Options **Option spreading** is nothing more than the combination of two or more options into a single transaction. You could create an options spread, for example, by simultaneously buying and writing options on the same underlying stock. These would not be identical options. They would differ with respect to strike price and/or expiration date. Spreads are a very popular use of listed options, and they account for a substantial amount of the trading activity on the listed options exchanges. These spreads go by a variety of exotic names, such as *bull spreads, bear spreads, money spreads, vertical spreads,* and *butterfly spreads.* Each spread is different and each is constructed to meet a certain type of investment goal.

Consider, for example, a *vertical spread.* It would be set up by *buying* a call at one strike price and then *writing* a call (on the same stock and for the same expiration date) at a higher strike price. For instance, you could buy a February call on XYZ at a strike price of, say, 30 and simultaneously sell (write) a February call on XYZ at a strike price of 35. Strange as it may sound, such a position would generate a hefty return if the price of the underlying stock went up by just a few points. Other spreads are used to profit from a falling market. Still others try to make money when the price of the underlying stock moves either up *or* down.

Whatever the objective, most spreads are created to take advantage of differences in prevailing option prices and premiums. The payoff from spreading is usually substantial, but *so is the risk.* In fact, some spreads that seem to involve almost no risk may end up with devastating results if the market and the difference between option premiums move against the investor. The *Investing in Action* box on page 662 explains how and when to use several types of spread strategies.

Option Straddles A variation on this theme involves an **option straddle**. This is the simultaneous purchase (or sale) of *both* a put *and* a call on the same underlying common stock. Unlike spreads, straddles normally involve the same strike price and expiration date. Here, the object is to earn a profit from *either* a big or a small swing in the price of the underlying common stock. For example, in a *long straddle*, you *buy* an equal number of puts and calls. You make money in the long straddle when the underlying stock undergoes a big change in price—either up or down. If the price of the stock shoots way up, you make money on the call side of the straddle but are out the cost of the puts. If the price of the stock plummets, you make money on the puts, but the calls are useless. In either case, so long as you make more money on one side than the cost of the options for the other side, you're ahead of the game. In a similar fashion, in a *short straddle,* you *sell/write* an equal number of puts and calls. You make money in this position when the price of the underlying stock goes nowhere. In effect, you get to keep all or most of the option premiums you collected when you wrote the options.

EXCEL with
SPREADSHEETS

TABLE 15.5 **Covered Call Writing**

	Stock	3-Month Call with an $80 Strike Price
Current market price of the stock	$73.50	
Current market price of the call		$ 2.50
3 Months Later		
A. Price of the stock is *unchanged*:	**$73.50**	
Value of the call		$ 0
Profit:		
Quarterly dividends received	$ 100	
Proceeds from sale of call	250	
Total profit: $ 350		
B. Price of the stock goes *up* to:	**$80** ←	Price Where Maximum Profit Occurs
Value of the call		$ 0
Profit:		
Quarterly dividends received	$ 100	
Proceeds from sale of call	250	
Capital gains on stock ($80 − $73.50)	650	
Total profit: $1,000		
C. Price of the stock goes *up* to:	**$90**	
Value of the call*		$10
Profit:		
Quarterly dividends received	$ 100	
Proceeds from sale of call	250	
Capital gains on stock ($90 − $73.50)	1,650	
Less: Loss on call	(1,000)	
Net profit: $1,000		
D. Price of the stock *drops* to:	**$71**	Break-Even Price
Value of the call*		$ 0
Profit:		
Capital loss on stock ($71 − $73.50)	($ 250)	} $0 profit or loss
Proceeds from sale of call	250	
Quarterly dividends	100	
Net profit: $ 100		

*See Equation 15.1.

Except for obvious structural differences, the principles that underlie the creation of straddles are much like those for spreads. The object is to combine options that will enable you to capture the benefits of certain types of stock price behavior. But keep in mind that if the prices of the underlying stock and/or the option premiums do not behave in the anticipated manner, you lose. *Spreads and straddles are extremely tricky and should be used only by knowledgeable investors.*

HOT

For a more thorough discussion of synthetic convertibles, click on "Customized Convertibles" on the book's Web site:

www.aw-bc.com/gitman_joehnk

INVESTING IN ACTION

THE CALL OF THE BULL AND BEAR SPREADS

As you've learned in this chapter, options are tools that do, in fact, increase your investment options. They offer flexibility, risk management, and the chance to profit from market movements without actually buying a particular stock. Once you've mastered the basics of single puts and calls, you may want to move on to more advanced strategies such as spreads that combine two or more options into a single transaction.

Let's first consider *bull spreads*, vertical spreads designed to profit from a moderately bullish market. With a *bull call spread*, you would *buy* a call option with a lower strike price and at the same time *write* a call option on the same stock at a higher strike price. For example, suppose in late December, 2003, after fighting the crowds at Target's (TGT) post-holiday sales, you feel pretty confident that the retailer's stock will rise above its current trading level of about $37.50. To implement a bull call spread you'd purchase the TGT April 37.50 call at $2.70 and sell the TGT April 42.50 call at $0.90. The net cost of this bull call spread is $1.80 ($2.70 − $0.90). If the stock is trading above $42.50 at the April expiration, when both options are in the money, your profit would equal the difference between the strike prices less your net cost to set up the spread: ($42.50 − $37.50) − $1.80 = $5 − $1.80 = $3.20 per share, or $320 for the spread. (If you were very bullish on Target, a regular call would probably bring you higher profits.)

This spread hedges your positions in two ways. You offset the call premium for the lower strike price with the premium you get from selling the higher strike price premium, reducing the cost of the long call and the chance you'll lose the whole premium. In addition, the long call limits the risk on the sale of higher strike price call. So both your upside potential profit and your potential loss are limited, with the greatest loss if the underlying stock price falls below the lower strike price. To break even on the above transaction, Target shares would have to reach $39.30—the strike price of the purchased call plus the net cost of the spread: $37.50 + $1.80 = $39.30.

What if you think a certain stock will fall over the next few months, and the market looks stable or somewhat bearish? In this case, you'd want to set up a *bear call spread*. This involves buying a higher strike call and selling a lower strike call for the same expiration dates. Because Eastman Kodak's stock seemed stuck at around $25 in late 2003, and you think it will suffer still more, you purchase EK April $25 calls for $1.65 and sell EK April $22.50 calls for $3.30. Your maximum profit is $1.65 per share, the difference between the two option premiums. To break even you'd have to sell the shares for $24.15, the sum of the lower strike price and your net cost: $22.50 + $1.65 = $24.15. If the underlying EK stock goes above $24.15, you lose money on the spread. Like the bull call spread, this spread acts as a double hedge.

Before you embark on any spread strategies, be sure you have a thorough understanding of options trading techniques. Once you do, however, you will have a valuable tool that can help you profit from market movements and provide a safety net for your portfolio.

CRITICAL THINKING QUESTIONS What are option spreads, and how can they help investors? When would you use a bull call spread, and why? A bear call spread?

Sources: Delayed Market Quotes, *Chicago Board Options Exchange*, downloaded December 27, 2003, from www.cboe.com; Richard Croft, "Credit Spreads or Debit Spreads: Is One Approach More Attractive than the Other?" *National Post* (Canada), April 15, 2003, p. IN3; Richard Croft, "Entering Option Trades: And a Look at the Exotic Butterfly Spread," *National Post* (Canada), January 14, 2003, p. IN3; Richard Croft, "Find Safety in Bear Call Spreads, *National Post* (Canada), September 30, 2003, p. IN3; "Strategies," Options Clearing Corporation Learning Center, downloaded December 23, 2003, from www.optionsclearing.com; "Options Strategies," OptionsCentral.com, downloaded December 22, 2003, from www.optionscentral.com; and "Options Strategies," Optionetics.com, downloaded December 22, 2003, from www.optionetics.com.

IN REVIEW

15.7 Briefly explain how you would make money on (a) a call option and (b) a put option. Do you have to exercise the option to capture the profit? Explain.

15.8 How do you find the intrinsic (fundamental) value of a call? Of a put? Does an *out-of-the-money option* have intrinsic value? Explain.

15.9 Name at least four variables that affect the price behavior of listed options, and briefly explain how each affects prices. How important are fundamental (intrinsic) value and time value to in-the-money options? To out-of-the-money options?

15.10 Describe at least three different ways in which investors can use stock options.

15.11 What's the most that can be made from writing calls? Why would an investor want to write *covered calls?* Can you reduce the risk on the underlying common stock by writing covered calls? Explain.

15.12 What is a *synthetic security?* Give an example of a synthetic security.

Stock-Index and Other Types of Options

LG 5

Imagine being able to buy or sell a major stock market index like the S&P 500—and at a reasonable cost. Think of what you could do: If you felt the market was heading up, you could invest in a security that tracks the price behavior of the S&P 500 index and make money when the market goes up. No longer would you have to go through the process of selecting specific stocks that you hope will capture the market's performance. Rather, you could play the *market as a whole.* Well, that's exactly what you can do with *stock-index options*—puts and calls that are written on major stock market indexes. Index options have been around since 1983 and have become immensely popular with both individual and institutional investors. Let's now take a closer look at these popular and often highly profitable investment vehicles.

Stock-Index Options: Contract Provisions

stock-index option
a put or call option written on a specific stock market index, such as the S&P 500.

Basically, a **stock-index option** is a put or call written on a specific stock market index. The underlying security in this case is the specific market index. Thus, when the market index moves in one direction or another, the value of the index option moves accordingly. Because there are no stocks or other financial assets backing these options, settlement is defined in terms of cash. Specifically, the cash value of an *index option* is equal to 100 times the published market index that underlies the option. For example, if the S&P 500 is at 1,200, then the value of an S&P 500 index option will be $100 \times 1,200 =$ $120,000. If the underlying index moves up or down in the market, so will the cash value of the option. [*Note:* Options on exchange-traded funds (ETFs) are very similar to index options and will be discussed below. For now, our attention will focus solely on index options.]

In mid-2003, put and call options were available on more than 80 market measures of performance. These included options on just about every major

U.S. stock market index or average (such as the Dow Jones Industrial Average, the S&P 500, the Russell 2000, and the Nasdaq 100), options on a handful of foreign markets (e.g., Mexico, Japan, and the EAFE), and options on different segments of the market (pharmaceuticals, oil services, semiconductors, bank, and utility indexes). Many of these options, however, are very thinly traded and really don't amount to much of a market. As of mid-2003, four indexes dominated the stock-index options market, accounting for the vast majority of trading activity:

- The S&P 500 Index (SPX)
- The S&P 100 Index (DEX)
- The Dow Jones Industrial Average (DJX)
- The Nasdaq 100 Index (NDX)

The S&P 500 Index is a widely used index that captures the market behavior of large-cap stocks. The S&P 100 Index is another large-cap index composed of 100 stocks, drawn from the S&P 500, that have actively traded stock options. The most popular index of all is the DJIA. Trading in this measure of the blue-chip segment of the market began in October 1997. Within a matter of weeks, it became one of the most actively traded index options. The Nasdaq 100 index tracks the behavior of the 100 largest (non-financial) stocks on the Nasdaq and is composed of mostly large, high-tech companies (such as Intel and Cisco). Options on the S&P 500 (SPX) and the DJIA (DJX) are, by far, the most popular instruments—indeed, there's more trading in these two contracts than in all the other index options combined. Though all five of the options exchanges deal in index options, the CBOE dominates the market, accounting for more than 90% of all trades.

Both puts and calls are available on index options. They are valued and have issue characteristics like any other put or call. That is, a put lets a holder profit from a drop in the market. (When the underlying market index goes down, the value of a put goes up.) A call enables the holder to profit from a market that's going up. Also, as seen in Figure 15.3, these options even have a quotation system that is very similar to that used for puts and calls on stocks. (Actually, there is one small difference between the *Wall Street Journal* quotes for stock options and those for index options: The closing value for the underlying index is not listed with the rest of the quote. Instead, these values are listed separately in a table that accompanies the quotes.)

Putting a Value on Stock-Index Options As is true of equity options, the market price of index options is a function of the difference between the strike price on the option (stated in terms of the underlying index) and the latest published stock market index. To illustrate, consider the highly popular S&P 100 Index traded on the CBOE. As the index option quotes in Figure 15.3 reveal, this index recently closed at 495.29. (See the "Current values for the underlying indexes" at the bottom of the exhibit.) At the same time, there was an October call on this index that carried a strike price of 490. A stock-index *call* will have a value so long as the underlying index exceeds the index strike price (just the opposite for puts). Hence, the intrinsic value of this call would be 495.29 − 490 = 5.29. However, as the quotes in Figure 15.3 show, this call

FIGURE 15.3

Quotations on Index Options

The quotation system used with index options is a lot like that used with stock options: Strike prices and expiration dates are shown along with closing option prices. The biggest differences are that put (p) and call (c) quotes are mixed together, and the closing values for the underlying indexes are shown separately. (*Source: Wall Street Journal,* August 13, 2003.)

CHICAGO

STRIKE	VOL	LAST	NET CHG	OPEN INT
DJ INDUS AVG(DJX)				
Aug 89 c	20	3.80	...	1,274
Aug 90 c	4,415	3	...	15,443
Aug 90 p	50	0.05	...	9,258
Oct 90 p	42	1.80	...	4,105
Sep 91 c	4,214	3.20	...	22,163
Sep 91 p	396	1.10	...	23,908
Aug 92 c	9,085	1.10	...	19,852
Aug 92 p	1,551	0.05	...	14,585
Sep 92 c	4,429	2.55	...	35,758
Sep 92 p	2,035	1.75	...	28,929
Oct 92 c	6	3.20	...	3,158
Oct 92 p	273	2.50	...	3,427
Aug 93 c	11,794	0.30	...	8,080
Aug 93 p	10,280	0.20	...	8,870
Sep 93 c	9,687	1.90	...	5,780
Sep 93 p	10,436	2.10	...	2,187
Aug 94 c	1,412	0.05	...	11,087
Aug 94 p	205	1.10	...	4,894
Sep 94 c	2,409	1.50	...	9,024
Sep 94 p	58	2.50	...	1,524
Oct 94 c	3	2.25	...	5,284
Oct 94 p	4	3.40	...	1,231
Sep 95 c	1,450	1.10	...	6,440
Sep 95 p	60	3.10	...	366
Sep 96 c	651	0.80	...	15,115
Oct 96 c	6	1.35	...	2,061
Sep 98 c	35	0.35	...	7,143
Oct 98 c	302	0.85	...	6,926
Aug 100 p	2	6.90	...	267
Sep 100 c	10	0.10	...	3,845
Sep 100 p	2	7.40	...	507
Call Vol........6,314		Open Int..465,250		
Put Vol. 13,678		Open Int..687,784		

S & P 100(OEX)

STRIKE	VOL	LAST	NET CHG	OPEN INT
Sep 320 p	10	0.05	-0.05	614
Nov 380 p	1	1.20	...	427
Sep 400 p	1	0.25	...	1,947
Oct 400 p	83	1	-0.15	735
Nov 400 p	410	2.15	-0.10	65
Sep 410 p	2	0.20	-0.20	900
Oct 410 p	1	1.40	-0.05	14
Sep 420 p	146	0.50	...	2,962
Oct 420 p	1	1.75	0.20	356
Sep 430 p	78	0.80	-0.05	1,941
Oct 430 p	18	2.50	0.35	237
Sep 440 p	271	1.15	0.10	3,982
Oct 440 p	50	3	-0.30	201
Nov 440 p	50	5.60	-1.90	115
Nov 480	1	13.50	-1.50	8
Aug 485 c	298	10.80	-5.00	1,829
Aug 485 p	3,261	0.50	0.05	6,279
Sep 485 c	20	21.20	...	323
Sep 485 p	193	7.60	1.20	1,086
Aug 490 c	2,414	7.30	-3.30	6,970
Aug 490 p	8,401	1	0.05	9,563
Sep 490 c	177	15.30	-2.20	2,765
Sep 490 p	416	9.20	1.00	5,960
Oct 490 c	6	20	-1.40	902
Oct 490 p	24	15.20	2.20	333
Aug 495 c	6,703	3.50	-2.90	6,633
Aug 495 p	7,422	2.60	0.70	6,867
Aug 500 c	11,425	1.25	-2.15	11,075
Aug 500 p	4,861	5.50	1.60	7,264
Sep 500 c	1,057	9.70	-1.80	5,847
Sep 500 p	380	15.20	3.00	3,390
Oct 500 c	963	13.70	-1.30	979
Oct 500 p	11	17.50	1.00	699
Nov 500 c	50	18.90	0.90	634
Nov 500 p	15	24	1.00	631
Aug 505 c	4,959	0.35	-0.95	7,539
Aug 505 p	426	9.50	2.50	1,666
Sep 505 c	72	6.90	-1.70	238
Sep 505 p	9	16.90	1.90	143

Name of index → DJ INDUS AVG(DJX)

Open interest: Number of contracts outstanding on this one (Sept-92-call) option

Month of expiration → Oct

c: Call option → Sep 94 c

p: Put option → Oct 94 p

Strike price → 485

Price of a September call option with a strike price of 490

Current values for the underlying indexes
DJIA: 92.72
S&P 100: 495.29

was actually trading at 20—nearly 15 points *above* the call's underlying fundamental value. This difference, of course, was the *time premium*.

If the S&P 100 Index in our example were to go up to, say, 525 by late October (the expiration date on the call), this option would be quoted at 525 − 490 = 35. Because index options (like equity options) are valued in multiples of $100, this contract would be worth $3,500. Thus, if you had purchased this option when it was trading at 20, it would have cost you $2,000 ($20 × $100) and, in less than 2 months, would have generated a profit of $3,500 − $2,000 = $1,500. That translates into a holding period return of a whopping 75% ($1,500/$2,000).

Full Value Versus Fractional Value Most broad-based index options use the full market value of the underlying index for purposes of options trading and valuation. But that's not the case with two of the Dow Jones measures. In particular, the option on the *Dow Jones Industrial Average is based on 1% (1/100) of the actual Industrial Average, and the Dow Transportation Average option is based on 10% (1/10) of the actual average.* For example, if the DJIA is at 9,272, the index option would be valued at 1% of that amount, or 92.72. Thus, the cash value of this option is not $100 times the underlying DJIA but $100 times 1% of the DJIA, *which equals the Dow Jones Industrial Average itself*: $100 × 92.72 = $9,272. Fortunately, the option strike prices are also based on the same 1% of the Dow, so there is really no effect on option valuation: What matters is the difference between the strike price on the option and (1% of) the DJIA. For instance, note in Figure 15.3 that the DJIA option index closed at 92.72 (at the time, the actual Dow was at 9,272). Note also that there was a September call option available on this index with a strike price of 91—it was trading at 3.20 (or $320). Using Equation 15.1, you can see that this in-the-money option had an intrinsic value of 92.72 − 91 = 1.72. The difference between the option's market value (3.20) and its intrinsic value (1.72) is, of course, the time premium.

Investment Uses

Although index options, like equity options, can be used in spreads, straddles, or even covered calls, they are perhaps used most often for speculating or for hedging. When used as a speculative vehicle, index options give investors an opportunity to play the market as a whole, with a relatively small amount of capital. Like any other put or call, *index options provide attractive leverage opportunities and at the same time limit exposure to loss to the price paid for the option.*

Index Options as Hedging Vehicles Index options are equally effective as *hedging vehicles*. In fact, hedging is a major use of index options and accounts for a good deal of the trading in these securities. To see how these options can be used for hedging, consider an investor who holds a diversified portfolio of common stocks. One way to protect the portfolio against an adverse market is to buy puts on one of the market indexes. If you hold a portfolio of, say, a dozen different stocks and you think the market is heading down, you can protect your capital by selling all of your stocks. However, that could become expensive, especially if you plan to get back into the market after it drops, and it could lead to a good deal of unnecessary taxes. Fortunately, there is a way to "have your cake and eat it too," and that is to hedge your stock portfolio with a stock index put. In this way, if the market does go down, you'll make money on your puts, which can then be used to buy more stocks at the lower, "bargain" prices. On the other hand, if the market continues to go up, you'll be out *only the cost of the puts*. That amount could well be recovered from the increased value of your stock holdings. The principles of hedging with stock-index options are exactly the same as those for hedging with equity options. The only difference is that with stock-index options, you're trying to protect a *whole portfolio of stocks* rather than *individual* stocks.

Like hedging with individual equity options, the cost of protecting your portfolio with index options can become very expensive (with price premiums of 20% to 30%, or more) when markets are falling and the need for this type of portfolio insurance is the greatest. That, of course, will have an impact on the effectiveness of this strategy. Also, the amount of profit you make or the protection you obtain depends in large part on how closely the behavior of your stock portfolio is matched by the behavior of the stock-index option you employ. *There is no guarantee that the two will behave in the same way.* You should therefore select an index option that closely reflects the nature of the stocks in your portfolio. If, for example, you hold a number of small-cap stocks, you might be well advised to select something like the Russell 2000 index option as the hedging vehicle. If you hold mostly blue chips, you might choose the DJIA index option. You probably can't get dollar-for-dollar portfolio protection, but you should try to get as close a match as possible. This and other considerations are discussed in the *Investing in Action* box on page 668, which deals with the use of index options in portfolio hedging.

A Word of Caution Given their effectiveness for either speculating in or hedging the entire market, it's little wonder that index options have become so popular with investors. But a word of caution is in order: Although trading index options appears simple and seems to provide high rates of return, these vehicles involve *high risk* and are subject to considerable price volatility. They should not be used by amateurs. True, there's only so much you can lose with these options. The trouble is that it's very easy to lose that amount. Attractive profits are indeed available from these securities. But they're not investments you can buy and then forget about until just before they expire. With the wide market swings that are so common today, *these securities must be closely monitored on a daily basis.*

Other Types of Options

Options on stocks and stock indexes account for most of the market activity in listed options. But put and call options can also be obtained on exchange-traded funds (ETFs), debt instruments, and foreign currencies. You can also buy puts and calls with extended expiration dates; these options are known as *LEAPS.* Let's now take a brief look at these other kinds of options, starting with options on ETFs.

Options on Exchange-Traded Funds In addition to various market indexes, put and call options are also available on 50 or so *exchange-traded funds*

INVESTING IN ACTION

USING INDEX OPTIONS TO PROTECT A WHOLE PORTFOLIO

When the stock market heads down, investors begin to worry about protecting the value of their portfolios. But simply liquidating their stock holdings and putting the proceeds into a money market fund is too drastic a step for most people. Not only would they incur substantial brokerage commissions and capital gains taxes, but they would also lose out if the market rallies. A far less drastic—and less costly—way for investors to shield their portfolios from the possibility of a sustained sell-off is to buy "insurance" in the form of stock-index put options.

These options offer a simple method of insuring the value of an entire portfolio with a single trade. That can be especially helpful because many issues in an investor's portfolio may not have individual put options traded on them. Such portfolio protection is similar to any other kind of insurance. The more protection investors want and the less risk they are willing to bear, the more the insurance costs. For example, suppose an investor wants to hedge a $125,000 stock portfolio and, after examining the characteristics of the major stock indexes, concludes that the S&P 100 best matches the portfolio. With the S&P 100 Index standing at, say, 675 in February, the market value of the S&P 100 Index would be $67,500. So the investor would buy two puts to approximate the $125,000 portfolio value.

The investor might buy two May 660 puts that expire in 3 months (i.e., in June) with a strike price of 660 and a price of about 23. To turn that into dollars, an investor multiplies by 100; the puts would cost $2,300 each—$4,600 for both—or 3.7% of the $125,000 portfolio. If the market retreats about 15% from current levels, bringing the S&P 100 down to about 574, each May 660 put would be worth a minimum of 86 points (660 − 574), or $8,600. After paying their cost, the investor would have a profit on the puts of $12,600 ($8,600 − $2,300 = $6,300 × 2), offsetting a substantial portion of the $18,750 the portfolio would have lost in a 15% decline.

By purchasing puts with strike prices that are 15 points below the current level of the S&P Index, the investor effectively insures the portfolio against any losses that occur *after* the market has fallen 15 points, or 2.2%, to 660. An investor willing to bear more market risk could reduce the insurance cost even further by purchasing puts with even lower strike prices. On the other hand, to be fully insured, an investor might have bought puts with a higher strike price, but that would have raised the cost of the insurance. May 670 puts, for instance, would have cost about 27, or $2,700 each. Harrison Roth, an options strategist, says the basic question for investors is, "Do you want to hedge against any and all declines, or do you simply want protection against catastrophic moves?" He believes most investors are in the second camp.

Even with relatively low-cost puts such as the May 660s, the cost of put option hedges can add up if the insurance goes unused. Buying 3-month puts like these four times a year would cost the equivalent of almost 15% of a $125,000 portfolio. One way to reduce the cost is to sell the put options before they expire. Put options lose most of their value in the final few weeks before their expiration if they have strike prices below the current price of the underlying securities. For this reason, some market advisers recommend that investors hold their options for only a month, sell them, and then buy the next month out. This strategy recovers most of the options' value, significantly reducing the cost to hedge, even after the higher commissions.

CRITICAL THINKING QUESTION Explain how index options can be used by investors to hedge or protect a whole portfolio of stocks.

(ETFs). As more fully explained in Chapter 13, ETFs are like mutual funds that have been structured to track the performance of a wide range of market indexes—in other words, *ETFs are a type of index fund*. They trade like shares of common stock on listed exchanges, primarily the AMEX, and cover everything from broad market measures, such as the DJIA, the S&P 500, and the Nasdaq 100, to market sectors like energy, financials, health care, and semiconductors.

There's clearly a good deal of overlap in the markets and market segments covered by index options and ETF options. In fact, these two options contracts share many similarities. In addition to their similar market coverage, they perform very much the same in the market, are valued the same, and are used for many of the same reasons (particularly for speculation and as hedging vehicles). All of which should come as no surprise: After all, an ETF option is written on an underlying *index fund* (for example, one that tracks the S&P 500) just like an index option is written on the same underlying *market index* (the S&P 500). Both do pretty much the same thing—either directly or indirectly track the performance of a market measure—so of course they should behave in the same way.

The only real difference is that options on ETFs are operationally like stock options in that each put or call option covers 100 shares of the underlying exchange-traded fund, rather than $100 of the underlying market index, as is the case with index options. But even that's not a big deal, because in the end both trade at 100 times the underlying index (or ETF). (One minor point: Because they're treated operationally like equity options, ETF options are quoted along with stock options, rather than being listed with index options. Take another look at Figure 15.1—notice the Dow Diamond ETF options listed among the stock options.) Thus, while operationally ETF options may be closer to stock options, they function more like index options and, as such, are viewed in the market as viable alternatives to index options. These contracts have definitely caught the fancy of investors, especially those that track the major market indexes. In fact, two of these contracts (the Nasdaq 100 ETF and the Dow Diamond ETF) were among the five most actively traded index and ETF options in 2003.

interest rate options
put and call options written on fixed-income (debt) securities.

Interest Rate Options Puts and calls on fixed-income (debt) securities are known as **interest rate options**. At the present time, interest rate options are only written on U.S. Treasury securities. There are four maturities used: 30-year T-bonds, 10-year and 5-year T-notes, and short-term (13-week) T-bills. These options are a bit unusual because they are *yield-based* rather than price-based. This means they track the yield behavior (rather than the price behavior) of the underlying Treasury security. Other types of options (equity and index options) are set up so that they react to movements in the price (or value) of the underlying asset. Interest rate options, in contrast, are set up to react to *the yield of the underlying Treasury security*. Thus, when yields rise, the value of a call goes up. When yields fall, puts go up in value. In effect, because bond prices and yields move in opposite directions, the value of an interest rate call option goes up at the very time that the price (or value) of the underlying debt security is going down. (The opposite is true for puts.) This unusual behavioral characteristic may help explain why the market for interest rate options remains very small. Most professional investors simply don't care for interest rate options. Instead, they prefer to use interest rate futures contracts or options on these futures contracts (both of which will be examined in Chapter 16).

currency options
put and call options
written on foreign currencies.

Currency Options Foreign exchange options, or just **currency options** as they're more commonly called, provide a way for investors to speculate on foreign exchange rates or to hedge foreign currency or foreign security holdings. Currency options are available on the currencies of most of the countries with which the United States has strong trading ties. These options are traded on the Philadelphia Exchange and include the following currencies:

- British pound
- Canadian dollar
- Swiss franc
- Japanese yen
- Australian dollar
- Euro

Note that in addition to pounds, francs, and yen, there are also options available on the *euro,* the currency unit used within the European Economic Community. Puts and calls on euros and other foreign currencies give the holders the right to sell or buy large amounts of the specified currency.

However, in contrast to the standardized contracts used with stock and stock-index options, the specific unit of trading in this market varies with the particular underlying currency. The details are spelled out in Table 15.6. Currency options are traded in full or fractional cents per unit of the underlying currency, relative to the amount of foreign currency involved. Thus, if a put or call on the British pound were quoted at, say, 6.40 (which is read as "6.4 cents"), it would be valued at $2,000, because 31,250 British pounds underlie this option (that is, 31,250 × 0.064 = $2,000).

The value of a currency option is linked to the exchange rate between the U.S. dollar and the underlying foreign currency. For example, if the Canadian dollar becomes stronger *relative to the U.S. dollar,* causing the exchange rate to go up, the price of a *call* option on the Canadian dollar will increase, and the price of a *put* will decline. [*Note:* Some cross-currency options are available in the market, but such options/trading techniques are beyond the scope of this book. Here, we will focus solely on foreign currency options (or futures) linked to U.S. dollars.]

To understand how you can make money with currency options, consider a situation in which an investor wants to speculate on exchange rates. The strike

H O T

This site contains links to foreign currency options, FLEX options, and many others:

www.phlx.com/products/index.html

TABLE 15.6	Foreign Currency Option Contracts on the Philadelphia Exchange		
Underlying Currency*	Size of Contracts	Underlying Currency*	Size of Contracts
British pound	31,250 pounds	Canadian dollar	50,000 dollars
Swiss franc	62,500 francs	Japanese yen	6,250,000 yen
Euro	62,500 Euros	Australian dollar	50,000 dollars

*The British pound, Swiss franc, euro, Canadian dollar, and Australian dollar are all quoted in full cents. The Japanese yen is quoted in hundredths of a cent.

price of a currency option is stated in terms of *exchange rates*. Thus a strike price of 150 implies that each unit of the foreign currency (such as one British pound) is worth 150 cents, or $1.50, in U.S. money. If you held a 150 call on this foreign currency, you would make money if *the foreign currency strengthened relative to the U.S. dollar* so that the exchange rate rose—say, to 155. In contrast, if you held a 150 put, you would profit from a decline in the exchange rate—say, to 145. Success in forecasting movements in foreign exchange rates is obviously essential to a profitable foreign currency options program.

LEAPS They look like regular puts and calls, and they behave pretty much like regular puts and calls, but they're not regular puts and calls. They're different. We're talking about **LEAPS,** which are puts and calls with lengthy expiration dates. Basically, LEAPS are long-term options. Whereas standard options have maturities of 8 months or less, LEAPS have expiration dates that extend out as far as 3 years. Known formally as *Long-term Equity AnticiPation Securities,* they are listed on all five of the major options exchanges. LEAPS are available on several hundred stocks and more than two dozen stock indexes and ETFs.

Aside from their time frame, LEAPS work like any other equity or index option. For example, a single (equity) LEAPS contract gives the holder the right to buy or sell 100 shares of stock at a predetermined price on or before the specified expiration date. LEAPS give investors more time to be right about their bets on the direction of a stock or stock index, and they give hedgers more time to protect their positions. But there's a price for this extra time: You can expect to pay a lot more for a LEAPS than you would for a regular (short-term) option. For example, in mid-2003, a 2-month call on Citigroup (with a strike price of 45) was trading at 0.90. The same call with a 1½-year expiration date was trading at 5.10. The difference should come as no surprise. LEAPS, being nothing more than long-term options, are loaded with *time premium.* And as we saw earlier in this chapter, other things being equal, *the more time an option has to expiration, the higher the quoted price.*

LEAPS
long-term options.

I N   R E V I E W

CONCEPTS

15.13 Briefly describe the differences and similarities between *stock-index options* and *stock options.* Do the same for *foreign currency options* and stock options.

15.14 Identify and briefly discuss two different ways to use stock-index options. Do the same for foreign currency options.

15.15 Why would an investor want to use index options to hedge a portfolio of common stock? Could the same objective be obtained using *options on ETFs?* If the investor thinks the market is in for a fall, why not just sell the stock?

15.16 What are *LEAPS?* Why would an investor want to use a LEAPS option rather than a regular listed option?

Warrants

LG 6

warrant
a long-lived option that gives the holder the right to buy stock in a company at a price specified on the warrant.

A **warrant** is a long-term option that gives the holder the right to buy a certain number of shares of stock in a certain company for a given period of time. Like most options, warrants are found in the corporate sector of the market. Occasionally, warrants can be used to purchase preferred stock or even bonds, but common stock is the leading redemption vehicle.

General Attributes

Of the various types of options, warrants normally have the longest lives, with maturities that extend out 5, 10, or even 20 years or more. Some warrants have no maturity date at all. Warrants have no voting rights, pay no dividends, and have no claim on the assets of the company. What they do offer is a chance to participate indirectly in the market behavior of the issuing firm's common stock and, in so doing, to generate capital gains. Warrants are perhaps most closely related to *call LEAPS* (long-term *call* options), although there are some important differences. First, whereas call LEAPS cover 100 shares of stock, a warrant usually covers just one or two shares of the underlying stock (or some fraction thereof). The second big difference involves the issuer of the instruments: Whereas warrants are issued by the same company that issues the underlying stock, LEAPS can be written by anybody or any institution.

Warrants are usually created as "sweeteners" to bond issues. To make a bond more attractive, the issuing company sometimes attaches warrants, giving the holder *the right to purchase a stipulated number of shares at a stipulated price anytime within a stipulated period.* A single warrant usually allows the holder to buy one full share of stock. (Some involve more than one share per warrant and a few involve fractional shares.) The life of a warrant is specified by its *expiration date.* The stock purchase price stipulated on the warrant is known as the *exercise price.* Because warrants are a type of equity issue, they can be margined at the same rate as common stock. They are purchased through brokers and are subject to transaction costs similar to those for common stock.

Advantages and Disadvantages

Warrants offer investors several advantages. One is their tendency to exhibit price behavior much like the common stock to which they are linked—just what you'd expect from a call option. Warrants, therefore, provide the investor with an alternative way of achieving capital gains from an equity issue. That is, instead of buying the stock, you can purchase warrants on the stock. Indeed, such a tactic may be even more rewarding than investing directly in the stock. Another advantage is the relatively low unit cost and the attractive leverage potential that accompanies it. That is, you can use warrants to obtain a given equity position at a substantially reduced capital investment. And in so doing, you can *magnify returns,* because the warrant provides roughly the same capital appreciation potential as the more costly common stock. A final advantage of warrants is that their low unit cost leads to reduced downside risk exposure. In essence, the lower unit cost simply means there is less to lose if the investment goes sour. For example, a $50 stock can drop to $25 if the market falls. But there is no way that the same company's $10 warrants can drop by the same amount.

However, warrants do have some *disadvantages*. For one thing, warrants pay no dividends. This means that investors sacrifice current income. Second, because these issues usually carry an expiration date, there is only a certain period of time during which you can capture the price behavior sought. Although this may not be much of a problem with long-term warrants, it can be a burden for those issues with fairly short lives (of 1 to 2 years, or less).

Putting a Value on Warrants

A warrant, like any option, is a type of *derivative security*—that is, the value of a warrant is directly linked to the price behavior of the underlying common stock. Thus, under the right conditions, when the stock goes up (or down) in price, the warrants will, too. Actually, warrants possess value whenever the market price of the underlying common exceeds the exercise price on the warrant. This so-called *fundamental value* is determined as follows:

Equation 15.3   Fundamental value of a warrent $= (M - E) \times N$

where

$M =$ prevailing market price of the common stock

$E =$ exercise price stipulated on the warrant

$N =$ number of shares of stock that can be acquired with one warrant (If one warrant entitles the holder to buy one share of stock, $N = 1$. If two warrants are necessary to buy one share of stock, $N = 0.5$, and so on.)

The fundamental value calculated by the formula represents what the market value of a warrant *should be,* given the input data. As an example, consider a warrant that carries an exercise price of $40 per share and enables the holder to purchase one share of stock per warrant. If the common stock has a current market price of $50 a share, then the warrants should be valued at $10 each:

Fundamental value of a warrent $= (\$50 - \$40) \times 1 = (\$10) \times 1 = \underline{\$10}$

Obviously, the greater the spread between the market and exercise prices, the greater the fundamental value of a warrant. *So long as the market price of the stock equals or exceeds the exercise price of the warrant,* and the redemption provision carries a 1-to-1 ratio (one share of common stock can be bought with each warrant), the value of a warrant will be closely linked to the price behavior of the common stock.

Premium Prices Equation 15.3 indicates how warrants should be valued, but they seldom are priced exactly that way in the marketplace. Instead, the market price of a warrant usually *exceeds* its fundamental value. This happens when warrants with negative values trade at prices greater than zero. It also occurs when warrants with positive fundamental values trade at even higher market prices (e.g., when a warrant that's valued at $10 trades at $15). This discrepancy is known as **warrant premium**. As a rule, the amount of premium

warrant premium
the difference between the true value of a warrant and its market price.

FIGURE 15.4

The Normal Price Behavior of Warrant Premiums

Observe that as the price of the underlying common stock increases, the amount of premium in the market price of the warrant tends to decrease—though it never totally disappears.

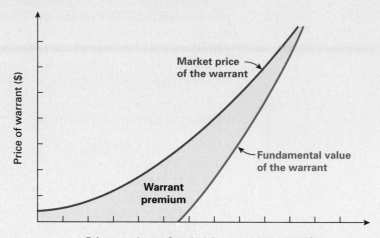

embedded in the market price of a warrant is directly related to the option's time to expiration and the volatility of the underlying common stock. On the other hand, the amount of premium does tend to diminish as the underlying (fundamental) value of a warrant increases. This can be seen in Figure 15.4, which shows the typical behavior of warrant premiums.

The premium on a warrant is easy to measure: Just take the difference between the value of a warrant (as computed with Equation 15.3) and its market price. For instance, a warrant has $5 in premium if it has a value of $10 but is trading at $15. The amount of premium can also be expressed on a relative (percentage) basis by dividing the dollar premium by the warrant's fundamental value. For example, there is a 50% premium embedded in the price of that $15 warrant (the dollar premium ÷ the fundamental value of the warrant = $5 ÷ $10 = 0.50). Premiums on warrants can at times become fairly substantial. Indeed, premiums of 20% to 30% or more are not at all uncommon.

Trading Strategies

Because their attraction to investors rests primarily with the capital gains opportunities they provide, warrants are used chiefly as alternatives to common stock investments. Let's now look at some warrant-trading strategies and the basic ways in which these securities can be profitably employed by investors.

The Basic Price Behavior of Warrants Because warrants carry relatively low unit costs, they possess much greater *price volatility* and the potential for generating substantially higher *rates of return* than a direct investment in the underlying common stock. Consider the following illustration, which involves the common shares and warrants of the same company. Assume the price of the common is now $50 per share. The warrant, which carries a one-to-one redemption provision, has a $40 exercise price. (We will ignore premium in this illustration.) Observe what happens when the price of the stock increases by $10.

	Common Stock	Warrant
Issue price *before* increase	$50	$10
Increase in price of common	$10	—
Issue price *after* increase	$60	$20
Increase in market value	$10	$10
Holding period return	**20%**	**100%**
(increase in value/beginning issue price)		

The warrant provides a rate of return five times greater than the common stock. The reason is, of course, that the two issues move parallel to one another, though the warrant carries a much lower unit cost.

As in our illustration above, the holding period return formula is used to assess the payoff when the investment horizon is 1 year or less. In contrast, the standard expected return (IRR) measure is used when the investment horizon amounts to more than a year. For example, in the illustration above, if we felt the warrant should go from a price of $10 to $20 over a 3-year period of time, it would have an expected return of around 26%. Note that in this case, because we can ignore dividends, all we need do is find the discount rate that equates the price of $20 in 3 years to the warrant's current market price of $10. This is pretty much like finding the yield on a zero-coupon bond. That is, because there are no dividends on warrants, the returns are based solely on the capital gains produced by the investment.

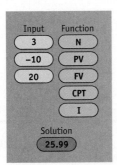

CALCULATOR USE For *annual compounding,* to find the expected return (IRR) on a warrant that goes from a price of $10 to $20 in a 3-year period of time, use the keystrokes shown in the margin. In this computation, *N* is the number of years in the investment horizon, *PV* is the current market price of the warrant, and *FV* is the expected market price of the warrant (in 3 years).

Trading with Warrants Warrant trading generally follows one of two approaches: (1) The leverage embedded in warrants is used to magnify dollar returns, or (2) their low unit cost is used to reduce the amount of invested capital and limit losses. The first approach is the more aggressive. The second has considerable merit as a conservative strategy.

Our comparative illustration above (where the price of the stock goes from $50 to $60 a share) can be used to demonstrate the first technique, which seeks to magnify returns. If you want to make a $5,000 equity investment and if price appreciation is the main objective, you would be better off committing such a sum to the warrants. The reason is that a $5,000 investment in the common stock will buy 100 shares of stock ($5,000 ÷ $50 = 100 shares), which will generate only $1,000 in capital gains ($10 profits per share × 100 shares). That same $5,000 invested in the lower-priced warrants will buy 500 warrants ($5,000 ÷ $10 = 500 warrants). This will result in $5,000 in profits ($10 in profits per warrant × 500 warrants). The common stock provides a 20% HPR, whereas the warrants yield 100%. The biggest risk in this investment is the potential loss exposure. If the price of the stock decreases by $10, the warrant investment is virtually wiped out. (Actually, the warrant will probably retain some value greater than zero, but not much.) In contrast, the price of the stock drops to "only" $40, and as a stockholder, you will still have $4,000 in capital left.

One way to limit this exposure to loss is to follow the second, more conservative trading approach: You buy only enough warrants to realize the level of capital gains available from the common stock. Again, in our illustration above, because we are dealing with options that carry one-to-one redemption provisions, you would need to acquire only 100 warrants to obtain the same price behavior as that of 100 shares of stock. Thus, rather than buying $5,000 worth of stock, you would purchase only $1,000 worth of the warrants to realize the same capital gains. If the stock performs as expected, you will realize a 100% return by generating the same amount of capital gains as the stock ($1,000). But this will be done with substantially less capital, so the yield with the warrants will be greater *and* the loss exposure will be less. In this case, if the price of the stock drops by 10 points, the most the warrant holder can lose is $1,000. If the price of the stock drops by *more* than $10 a share, the warrant holder still will lose no more than $1,000, whereas the stockholder can lose a lot more.

IN REVIEW

CONCEPTS

15.17 What is a *warrant* and what is its chief attraction? Describe the leverage features of a warrant and note why leverage is so attractive to investors.

15.18 What factors are important in determining the investment appeal of warrants? Why is the price of the warrant itself so important in the investment decision?

Summary

LG 1 **Discuss the basic nature of options in general and puts and calls in particular, and understand how these investment vehicles work.** An option gives the holder the right to buy or sell a certain amount of some real or financial asset at a set price for a set period of time. Puts and calls are by far the most widely used type of option. These derivative securities offer attractive value and considerable leverage potential. A put enables the holder to *sell* a certain amount of a specified security at a specified price over a specified time period. A call gives the holder the right to *buy* the security at a specified price over a specified period of time.

LG 2 **Describe the options market and note key options provisions, including strike prices and expiration dates.** The options market is made up of conventional (OTC) options and listed options. OTC options are used predominantly by institutional investors. Listed options are traded on organized exchanges such as the CBOE and the AMEX. The creation of listed options exchanges led to the use of standardized options features and opened the way for widespread use of options by individual investors. Among the provisions stipulated on options are the strike price (the stipulated price at which the underlying asset can be bought or sold) and the expiration date (the date when the contract expires).

LG 3 **Explain how put and call options are valued and the forces that drive options prices in the marketplace.** The value of a call is measured as the market price of the underlying security less the strike price designated on the call. The value of a put is its strike price less the market price of the security. The value of an option is driven by the current market price of the underlying asset. Most puts and calls sell at premium prices. The size of the premium depends on the length of the option contract (the so-called time premium), the speculative appeal and amount of price volatility in the underlying financial asset, and the general level of interest rates.

LG 4 **Describe the profit potential of puts and calls, and note some popular put and call investment strategies.** Investors who hold puts make money when the value of the underlying asset goes down over time. In contrast, call investors make money when the underlying asset moves up in price. Aggressive investors will use puts and calls either for speculation or in highly specialized writing and spreading programs. Conservative investors are attracted to puts and calls because of their low unit costs and the limited risk they offer in absolute dollar terms. Conservative investors often use options in covered call writing programs or to form hedge positions in combination with other securities.

LG 5 **Describe market index options, puts and calls on foreign currencies, and LEAPS, and show how these securities can be used by investors.** Standardized put and call options are available on stock-market indexes, like the S&P 500 (in the form of index options or ETF options), and on a number of foreign currencies (currency options). Also available are LEAPS, which are listed options that carry lengthy expiration dates. Although these securities can be used just like stock options, the index and currency options tend to be used primarily for speculation or to develop hedge positions.

LG 6 **Discuss the investment characteristics of stock warrants, and describe the trading strategies that can be used to gain maximum benefits from this investment vehicle.** A warrant is similar to a call option, but its maturity is much longer. Usually attached to bond issues as "sweeteners," warrants allow the holder to purchase common stock at a set exercise price on or before a stipulated expiration date. Trading in warrants is done primarily as a substitute for common stock investing and is based on the magnified capital gains that warrants offer. The value of a warrant changes directly with, and by approximately the same amount as, the underlying common stock. Because a warrant's unit cost is often much lower than that of the common stock, the same dollar change in price produces a much larger percentage yield.

Putting Your Investment Know-How to the Test

1. A call is "in-the-money" when
   a. The stock price is above the exercise price.
   b. The stock price is below the exercise price.
   c. The stock price and the exercise price are equal.
   d. There is not enough information to tell.

2. Which of the following statements describing options is *false?*
   a. A put option gives its holder the right to sell an asset for a specified price on or before the option's expiration date.
   b. A call option will be exercised only if the market value of the underlying asset is more than the exercise price.
   c. A put option's profit increases when the value of the underlying asset increases.
   d. A put option will be exercised only if the market value of the underlying asset is less than the exercise price.

3. A put on Stock X with a strike price of $40 is priced at $2.00 per share, while a call with a strike price of $40 is priced at $3.50. What is the maximum per-share

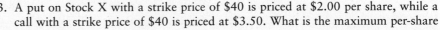

loss for the *writer* of the put and the maximum per share *gain* for the *writer* of the uncovered call?

	Maximum Loss to Put Writer	Maximum Gain to Call Writer
a.	$38.00	$ 3.50
b.	$38.00	$36.50
c.	$40.00	$ 3.50
d.	$40.00	$40.00

4. An investor buys two calls and one put on ABC stock, all with a strike price of $45. The calls cost $5 each, and the put costs $4. If the investor closes the position when ABC is priced at $55, the investor's *per-share* gain or loss is
   a. $4 loss.   b. $6 gain.
   c. $10 gain.   d. $20 gain.

5. An American option is more valuable than a European option on the same dividend-paying stock with the same terms because the
   a. European option contract is not adjusted for stock splits and stock dividends.
   b. American option can be exercised from the date of purchase until expiration, but the European option can be exercised only at expiration.
   c. European option does not conform to the Black-Scholes model and is often mispriced.
   d. American options are traded on U.S. exchanges, which offer much more volume and liquidity.

6. The current price of an asset is 100. An out-of-the-money American put option with an exercise price of 90 is purchased along with the asset. If the break-even point for this hedge is at an asset price of $114 at expiration, then the value of the American put at the time of purchase must have been
   a. $0.   b. $4.
   c. $10.   d. $14.

7. The current price of an asset is 75. A 3-month, at-the-money American call option on the asset has a current value of 5. At what value of the asset will a covered call writer break even at expiration?
   a. $70   b. $75
   c. $80   d. $85

8. An investor buys a call option with a $25 exercise price priced at $4 and writes a call option with a $40 exercise price priced at $2.50. If the price of the stock increases to $50 at expiration and the options are exercised on the expiration date, the net profit at expiration (ignoring transaction costs) is
   a. $8.50.   b. $13.50.
   c. $16.50.   d. $23.50.

9. If a stock is selling for $25, the exercise price of a put option on that stock is $20, and the time to expiration of the option is 90 days, the minimum and maximum prices for the put today are
   a. $0 and $5.   b. $0 and $20.
   c. $5 and $20.   d. $5 and $25.

10. An investor buys a stock for $40 per share and simultaneously sells a call option on the stock with an exercise price of $42 for a premium of $3 per share. Ignoring dividends and transactions cost, what is the *maximum* profit that the writer of this covered call can earn if the position is held to expiration?
   a. $2   b. $3
   c. $5   d. $8

Answers: 1. a; 2. c; 3. a; 4. b; 5. b; 6. d; 7. a; 8. b; 9. b; 10. c

Discussion Questions

LG 2

Q15.1 Using the stock or index option quotations in Figures 15.1 and 15.3, respectively, find the option premium, the time premium, and the stock or index break-even point for the following puts and calls.

a. The September ChevronTexaco *call* with the $65 strike price.
b. The January E*Trade *put* with the $10 strike price.
c. The August Dow Diamond ETF *call* with the $90 strike price.
d. The August S&P 100 *call* with the 485 strike price.
e. The August DJIA *put* with the 100 strike price.

LG 3

LG 3 **Q15.2** Prepare a schedule similar to the one in Table 15.1 for the September and October S&P 100 *calls* listed in Figure 15.3. (Use the ones with the strike prices of 490 and 500.) Do the same for the September and October *puts* (using the same two strike prices). Briefly explain your findings.

LG 5

Q15.3 Assume you hold a well-balanced portfolio of common stocks. Under what conditions might you want to use a stock-index (or ETF) option to hedge the portfolio?

a. Briefly explain how such options could be used to hedge a portfolio against a drop in the market.
b. Discuss what happens if the market does, in fact, go down.
c. What happens if the market goes up instead?

LG 3 **LG 4**

Q15.4 Using the resources available at your campus or public library (or on the Internet), complete each of the following tasks. (*Note:* Show your work for all calculations.)

a. Find an *in-the-money call* that has 2 or 3 months to expiration. (Select an *equity option* that is at least $2 or $3 in the money.) What's the fundamental value of this option, and how much premium is it carrying? Using the current market price of the underlying stock (the one listed with the option), determine what kind of dollar and percentage return the option would generate if the underlying stock goes up 10%. How about if the stock goes down 10%?
b. Repeat part **a**, but this time use an *in-the-money put*. (Choose an equity option that's at least $2 or $3 in the money and has 2 or 3 months to expiration.) Answer the same questions as above.
c. Repeat once more the exercise in part **a**, but this time use an *out-of-the-money call*. (Select an equity option, at least $2 or $3 out of the money with 2 or 3 months to expiration.) Answer the same questions.
d. Compare the valuation properties and performance characteristics of in-the-money calls and out-of-the-money calls [from parts **a** and **c**]. Note some of the advantages and disadvantages of each.

Problems

LG 3

P15.1 Cisco stock is selling for $19. Call options with an $18 exercise price are priced at $2.50. What is the fundamental value of the option, and what is the time premium?

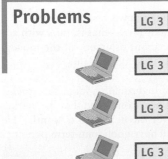

LG 3

P15.2 Gillet is trading at $31.11. Call options with a strike price of $35 are priced at $0.30. What is the fundamental value of the option, and what is the time premium?

LG 3

P15.3 PALM is trading at $26. Put options with a strike price of $35 are priced at $10.50. What is the fundamental value of the option, and what is the time premium?

LG 3

P15.4 PALM is trading at $26. Put options with a strike price of $17.50 are priced at $0.85. What is the fundamental value of the option, and what is the time premium?

P15.5 A 6-month call on a certain common stock carries a strike price of $60. It can be purchased at a cost of $600. Assume that the underlying stock rises to $75 per share by the expiration date of the option. How much profit would this option generate over the 6-month holding period? Using HPR, what is its rate of return?

LG 4 **LG 5** **P15.6** You believe that oil prices will be rising more than expected, and that rising prices will result in lower earnings for industrial companies that use a lot of petroleum-related products in their operations. You also believe that the effects on this sector will be magnified because consumer demand will fall as oil prices rise. You locate an exchange traded fund, XLB, that represents a basket of industrial companies. You don't want to short the ETF because you don't have enough margin in your account. XLB is currently trading at $23. You decide to buy a put option (for 100 shares) with a strike price of $24, priced at $1.20. It turns out that you are correct. At expiration, XLB is trading at $20. Calculate your profit.

XLB: Materials—$23.00

	Calls			Puts	
Strike	Expiration	Price	Strike	Expiration	Price
$20	November	$0.25	$20	November	$1.55
$24	November	$0.25	$24	November	$1.20

LG 4 **LG 5** **P15.7** Refer to the table for XLB in Problem 15.6. What happens if you are wrong and the price of XLB increases to $25 on the expiration date?

 **LG 5** **P15.8** Dorothy Lasnicka does a lot of investing in the stock market and is a frequent user of stock-index options. She is convinced that the market is about to undergo a broad retreat and has decided to buy a put on the S&P 100 Index. The put carries a strike price of 890 and is quoted in the financial press at 4.50. Although the S&P Index of 100 stocks is currently at 886.45, Dorothy thinks it will drop to 865 by the expiration date on the option. How much profit will she make, and what will be her holding period return if she is right? How much will she lose if the S&P 100 goes up (rather than down) by 25 points and reaches 915 by the date of expiration?

LG 3 **LG 4** **P15.9** Bill Weeks holds 600 shares of Lubbock Gas and Light. He bought the stock several years ago at 48.50, and the shares are now trading at 75. Bill is concerned that the market is beginning to soften. He doesn't want to sell the stock, but he would like to be able to protect the profit he's made. He decides to hedge his position by buying 6 puts on Lubbock G&L. The 3-month puts carry a strike price of 75 and are currently trading at 2.50.

a. How much profit or loss will Bill make on this deal if the price of Lubbock G&L does indeed drop, to $60 a share, by the expiration date on the puts?

b. How would he do if the stock kept going up in price and reached $90 a share by the expiration date?

c. What do you see as the major advantages of using puts as hedge vehicles?

d. Would Bill have been better off using in-the-money puts—that is, puts with an $85 strike price that are trading at 10.50? How about using out-of-the-money puts—say, those with a $70 strike price, trading at 1.00? Explain.

LG 4 **LG 5** **P15.10** P. F. Chang holds a well-diversified portfolio of high-quality, large-cap stocks. The current value of Chang's portfolio is $535,000, but he is concerned that the market is heading for a big fall (perhaps as much as 20%) over the next 3 to 6 months. He doesn't want to sell all his stocks because he feels they all have good long-term potential and should perform nicely once stock prices have bottomed out. As a result, he's thinking about using index options to hedge his portfolio. Assume that the S&P 500 currently stands at 1,070 and among the many put options available on this index are two that have caught his eye: (1) a 6-month put with a strike price of 1,050 that's trading at 26, and (2) a 6-month put with a strike price of 990 that's quoted at 4.50.

    a. How many S&P 500 puts would Chang have to buy to protect his $535,000 stock portfolio? How much would it cost him to buy the necessary number of 1,050 puts? How much would it cost to buy the 990 puts?

    b. Now, considering the performance of both the put options and the Chang portfolio, determine how much *net* profit (or loss) Chang will earn from each of these put hedges if both the market (as measured by the S&P 500) and the Chang portfolio fall by 15% over the next 6 months. What if the market and the Chang portfolio fall by only 5%? What if they go up by 10%?

    c. Do you think Chang should set up the put hedge and, if so, using which put option? Explain.

    d. Finally, assume that the DJIA is currently at 10,950 and that a 6-month put option on the Dow is available with a strike price of 108, and is currently trading at 2.50. How many of these puts would Chang have to buy to protect his portfolio, and what would they cost? Would Chang be better off with the Dow options or the S&P 1,050 puts? Briefly explain.

P15.11 Angelo Martino just purchased 500 shares of AT&E at 61.50, and he has decided to write covered calls against these stocks. Accordingly, he sells 5 AT&E calls at their current market price of 5.75. The calls have 3 months to expiration and carry a strike price of 65. The stock pays a quarterly dividend of 80 cents a share (the next dividend to be paid in about a month).

    a. Determine the total profit and holding period return Angelo will generate if the stock rises to $65 a share by the expiration date on the calls.

    b. What happens to Angelo's profit (and return) if the price of the stock rises to more than $65 a share?

    c. Does this covered call position offer any protection (or cushion) against a drop in the price of the stock? Explain.

P15.12 Bob owns stock in a retailer that he believes is highly undervalued. Bob expects that the stock will increase in value nicely over the long term. He is concerned, however, that the entire retail industry may fall out of favor with investors as some larger companies report falling sales. There are no options traded on his stock, but Bob would like to hedge against his fears about retail. He locates a symbol RTH, which is a Retail HOLDRS (go to www.amex.com and look this symbol up). Can Bob hedge against the risk he is concerned with by using RTH? Using options?

P15.13 Here's your chance to try your hand at setting up an index-option *straddle*. Use the quotes for the DJIA index options listed in Figure 15.3. Assume that the market, as measured by the DJIA, stands at 9,300 and you decide to set up a *long straddle* on the Dow by buying 100 September 93 calls and an equal number of September 93 puts. (Ignore transaction costs.)

    a. What will it cost you to set up the straddle, and how much profit (or loss) do you stand to make if the market falls by 750 points by the expiration dates on the options? What if it goes up by 750 points by expiration? What if it stays at 9,300?

    b. Repeat part **a**, but this time assume that you set up a *short straddle* by selling/writing 100 September 93 puts and calls.

    c. What do you think of the use of option straddles as an investment strategy? What are the risks, and what are the rewards?

LG 6   P15.14 Assume that 1 warrant gives the holder the right to buy 2½ shares of stock at an exercise price of $40.

    a. What is the value of this warrant if the current market price of the stock is $44? At what premium (in dollars and as a percentage) would the warrants be trading if they were quoted in the market at a price of $12.50?

    b. Rework this problem given that 1 warrant gives the holder the right to buy just 1 share of stock at the stipulated exercise price. In this case, assume that the warrants are currently trading in the market at a price of $5 each.

LG 6   P15.15 A particular warrant carries an exercise price of $20. Assume it takes 3 of these warrants to buy 1 share of stock. At what price would the warrant be trading if it sold at a 20% premium and the market price of the stock was $35 per share? What holding period return will an investor make if he or she buys these warrants (at a 20% premium) when the stock is trading at $35 and sells them sometime later, when the stock is at $48.50 and the premium on the warrants has dropped to 15%?

See the text Web site
(**www.aw-bc.com/gitman_joehnk**) **for Web exercises that deal with *options*.**

Case Problem 15.1   *The Franciscos' Investment Options*

LG 3   **LG 4**   **LG 6**

Hector Francisco is a successful businessman in Atlanta. The box-manufacturing firm he and his wife, Judy, founded several years ago has prospered. Because he is self-employed, Hector is building his own retirement fund. So far, he has accumulated a substantial sum in his investment account, mostly by following an aggressive investment posture. He does this because, as he puts it, "In this business, you never know when the bottom's gonna fall out." Hector has been following the stock of Rembrandt Paper Products (RPP), and after conducting extensive analysis, he feels the stock is about ready to move. Specifically, he believes that within the next 6 months, RPP could go to about $80 per share, from its current level of $57.50. The stock pays annual dividends of $2.40 per share. Hector figures he would receive two quarterly dividend payments over his 6-month investment horizon.

In studying the company, Hector has learned that it has some warrants outstanding. They mature in 8 years and carry an exercise price of $45. Also, the company has 6-month call options (with $50 and $60 strike prices) listed on the CBOE. Each warrant is good for 1 share of stock, and they are currently trading at $15. The CBOE calls are quoted at $8 for the options with $50 strike prices and at $5 for the $60 options.

Questions

a. How many alternative investment vehicles does Hector have if he wants to invest in RPP for no more than 6 months? What if he has a 2-year investment horizon?

b. Using a 6-month holding period and assuming the stock does indeed rise to $80 over this time frame:
1. Find the market price of the warrants at the end of the holding period, given that they then trade at a premium of 10%.
2. Find the value of both calls, given that at the end of the holding period neither contains any investment premium.
3. Determine the holding period return for each of the four investment alternatives open to Hector Francisco.

c. Which course of action would you recommend if Hector simply wants to maximize profit? Would your answer change if other factors (e.g., comparative risk exposure) were considered along with return? Explain.

Case Problem 15.2   *Fred's Quandary: To Hedge or Not to Hedge*

LG 3   LG 4

A little more than 10 months ago, Fred Weaver, a mortgage banker in Phoenix, bought 300 shares of stock at $40 per share. Since then, the price of the stock has risen to $75 per share. It is now near the end of the year, and the market is starting to weaken. Fred feels there is still plenty of play left in the stock but is afraid the tone of the market will be detrimental to his position. His wife, Denise, is taking an adult education course on the stock market and has just learned about put and call hedges. She suggests that he use puts to hedge his position. Fred is intrigued by the idea, which he discusses with his broker, who advises him that the needed puts are indeed available on his stock. Specifically, he can buy 3-month puts, with $75 strike prices, at a cost of $550 each (quoted at 5.50).

Questions

a. Given the circumstances surrounding Fred's current investment position, what benefits could be derived from using the puts as a hedge device? What would be the major drawback?

b. What will Fred's minimum profit be if he buys three puts at the indicated option price? How much would he make if he did not hedge but instead sold his stock immediately at a price of $75 per share?

c. Assuming Fred uses three puts to hedge his position, indicate the amount of profit he will generate if the stock moves to $100 by the expiration date of the puts. What if the stock drops to $50 per share?

d. Should Fred use the puts as a hedge? Explain. Under what conditions would you urge him *not* to use the puts as a hedge?

Excel with Spreadsheets

One of the positive attributes of investing in options is the profit potential from the puts or calls. The quoted market price of the option is influenced by the time to expiration, stock volatility, market interest rates, and the behavior of the price of the underlying common stock. The latter variable tends to drive the price movement in options and impacts its potential for profitable returns.

Create a spreadsheet model, similar to that presented below, in order to calculate the profits and/or losses from investing in the option described.

	A	B	C	D	E	F	G	H	I	J
1										
2						Long		100		3-Month Call Option
3						Position		Shares of		on the Stock
4						No		Underlying		Strike Price
5						Option		Common Stock		$$$
6										
7	Today									
8										
9	Market value of stock			$$		$$		$$		
10	Call Strike Price			$$						
11	Call option premium			$$						
12										
13										
14	Scenario One: 3 Months Later									
15	Expected market value of stock			$$		$$		$$		
16	Stock value @ strike price			$$						$$
17	Call premium			$$						$$
18	Breakeven Point			$$						$$
19										
20	Profit (Loss)					$$		$$		

John has been following the stock market very closely over the past 18 months and has a strong belief that future stock prices will be significantly higher. He has two alternatives that he can follow. The first is to use a long-term strategy—purchase the stock today and sell it sometime in the future at a possibly higher price. The other alternative is to buy a three-month call option. The relevant information needed to analyze the two alternatives is presented below:

Current stock price = $49.00
Desires to buy one round lot = 100 shares
3-month call option has a strike price of $51 and a call premium of $2.00

Questions:

a. In scenario 1, if the stock price 3 months from now is $58,
  1. What is the long-position profit or loss?
  2. What is the break-even point of the call option?
  3. Is the option in or out of the money?
  4. What is the option profit or loss?
b. In scenario 2, if the stock price 3 months from now is $42,
  1. What is the long-position profit or loss?
  2. What is the break-even point of the call option?
  3. Is the option in or out of the money?
  4. What is the option profit or loss?

I f Peter Smith told you to buy futures, would you
think he was a hack fortune teller trying to sell you
a reading, or that he'd made a grammatical error?
As strange as it may sound, you heard Smith correctly.
You can indeed "buy futures" for many different commodities or
financial instruments. Essentially, a future is a contract to buy
or sell a certain amount of an item—for example, agricultural
products or foreign currencies—at a set price for delivery on a
specific future date.

Smith's firm, Columbia Futures Group, specializes in selling
futures to individual investors, who make up about 85% of his
clients. "People today still don't understand how to invest in
commodities," said Smith, who co-founded Columbia in 1990.
"Obviously, educating your client base is a real challenge."

In general, commodities price movements mirror inflation
and exhibit a negative correlation with stocks and bonds. This
proved true in 2002, for example. As economies around the world
recovered and corporations needed more raw materials, their
commodities markets posted sizable gains. Investors who bought
platinum and gold that year earned returns of 21.5% and 24.8%,
respectively, versus −23.4% for the S&P 500. In addition, the
weakening U.S. dollar made dollar denominated commodities less
expensive in foreign markets, boosting exports.

Investors who want the diversification effects of futures
without buying individual commodity contracts can go the mutual
fund route. The Oppenheimer Real Asset Fund and the newer
Pimco Commodity Real Return Strategy Fund invest in broad
baskets of energy and agricultural products, metals, and livestock.
Oppenheimer's fund returned 20% in 2003, just under the S&P
500's 24.1%, but over 3 years returned 3.7% compared to −3.2%
for the S&P 500. PIMCO's fund, launched in June 2002, turned in
a banner performance in its first calendar year: 27.8% return.

Before buying either fund, investing in individual commodities,
or trading financial futures, however, you should understand how
these specialized and often high-risk investments work. This
chapter will introduce you to the world of commodities and
illustrates how to use futures contracts as a tool to minimize risk.

Sources: Pallavi Gogoi, "Back to the Futures," *Business Week,* July 14, 2003, p. 92; Jeff
Meisner, "A Future in Futures," *Puget Sound Business Journal,* May 9, 2003, p. 29; and Anne
Kates Smith, "Hard Assets, Hardly Tame," *Kiplinger's Personal Finance,* June 2003, p. 49.

CHAPTER 16

COMMODITIES AND FINANCIAL FUTURES

LEARNING GOALS

After studying this chapter, you should
be able to:

LG 1 Describe the essential features of a
futures contract and explain how the futures
market operates.

LG 2 Explain the role that hedgers and
speculators play in the futures market,
including how profits are made and lost.

LG 3 Describe the commodities segment
of the futures market and the basic
characteristics of these investment vehicles.

LG 4 Discuss the trading strategies
investors can use with commodities, and
explain how investment returns are measured.

LG 5 Explain the difference between a
physical commodity and a financial future,
and discuss the growing role of financial
futures in the market today.

LG 6 Discuss the trading techniques that
can be used with financial futures, and
note how these securities can be used in
conjunction with other investment vehicles.

The Futures Market

LG 1   LG 2

"Psst, hey buddy. Wanna buy some copper? How about some coffee, or pork bellies, or propane? Maybe the Japanese yen or Swiss franc strikes your fancy?" Sound a bit unusual? Perhaps, but these items have one thing in common: They all represent real investment vehicles. This is the more exotic side of investing—the market for commodities and financial futures—and it often involves a considerable amount of speculation. In fact, the risks are enormous. But with a little luck, the payoffs can be phenomenal, too. Even more important than luck is the need for patience and know-how. Indeed, *these are specialized investment products that require specialized investor skills.*

The amount of futures trading in the United States has mushroomed over the past two or three decades. An increasing number of investors have turned to futures trading as a way to earn attractive, highly competitive rates of return. But it's *not* the traditional commodities contracts that have drawn many of these investors; rather, it's the new investment vehicles that are being offered. Indeed, a major reason behind the growth in the volume of futures trading has been the *number and variety of futures contracts now available for trading.* Today, markets exist for the traditional primary commodities, such as grains and metals, as well as for processed commodities, crude oil and gasoline, electricity, foreign currencies, money market securities, U.S. and foreign debt securities, Eurodollar securities, and common stocks. You can even buy listed put and call *options* on just about any actively traded futures contract. All these commodities and financial assets are traded in what is known as the *futures market.*

Market Structure

cash market
a market where a product or commodity changes hands in exchange for a cash price paid when the transaction is completed.

futures market
the organized market for the trading of futures contracts.

When a bushel of wheat is sold, the transaction takes place in the **cash market.** The bushel changes hands in exchange for the cash price paid to the seller. The transaction occurs at that point in time and for all practical purposes is completed then and there. Most traditional securities are traded in this type of market. However, a bushel of wheat can also be sold in the **futures market,** the organized market for the trading of futures contracts. In this market, the seller would not actually deliver the wheat until some mutually agreed-upon date in the future. As a result, the transaction would not be completed for some time: The seller would receive partial payment for the bushel of wheat at the time the agreement was entered into and the balance on delivery. The buyer, in turn, would own a highly liquid futures contract that could be held (and presented for delivery of the bushel of wheat) or traded in the futures market. No matter what the buyer does with the contract, as long as it is outstanding, the seller has a *legally binding obligation to make delivery* of the stated quantity of wheat on a specified date in the future. The buyer/holder has a similar *obligation to take delivery* of the underlying commodity.

H O T   L I N K S

For information on more than 70 exchanges around the world and details on the futures and options contracts they trade, see:

www.numa.com/ref/exchange.htm

futures contract
a commitment to deliver a certain amount of some specified item at some specified date in the future.

delivery month
the time when a commodity must be delivered; defines the life of a futures contract.

Futures Contracts A **futures contract** is a commitment to deliver a certain amount of a specified item at a specified date at an agreed-upon price. Each market establishes its own contract specifications. These include not only the quantity and quality of the item but also the delivery procedure and delivery month. The **delivery month** on a futures contract is much like the expiration date on put and call options. It specifies when the commodity or item must be

DRIVING THE DESK—Across the farm belt, rural women are organizing commodity clubs to plot hedging strategies on futures exchanges. As the U.S. government phases out crop subsidies, growers are looking for ways to get more income from their crops. One way to do that is to stop selling crops at harvest prices, usually the year's lowest, and instead use the futures market to lock in higher prices. The number of farmers using futures is growing quickly. Because many farm wives handle the family's bookkeeping, they are the ones attending futures trading seminars, subscribing to trading-advisory services, and accessing market information on the Internet. Besides, adds one farm wife, "Getting a farmer to do paperwork is like nailing butter to a wall. . . . So I drive the desk."

delivered and thus defines the life of the contract. For example, the Chicago Board of Trade specifies that each of its soybean contracts will involve 5,000 bushels of USDA No. 2 yellow soybeans; delivery months are January, March, May, July, August, September, and November. In addition, futures contracts have *their own trading hours*. Unlike listed stocks and bonds, which begin and end trading at the same time, normal trading hours for commodities and financial futures vary widely. For example, oats trade from 9:30 A.M. to 1:15 P.M. (Central); silver, from 7:25 A.M. to 1:25 P.M.; live cattle, from 9:05 A.M. to 1:00 P.M.; U.S. Treasury bonds, from 7:20 A.M. to 2:00 P.M.; and S&P 500 stock-index contracts, from 8:30 A.M. to 3:15 P.M. It sounds a bit confusing, but it seems to work.

Table 16.1 lists a cross section of 12 different commodities and financial futures. (*Note*: The market value of a single contract, as reported in Table 16.1, is found by multiplying the size of the contract by the latest quoted price of the underling commodity. For example, there are 37,500 pounds of coffee in a single contract, so if coffee's trading at 60¢ a pound, then the market value of one contract is 37,500 × $0.60 = $22,500.) As you can see, the typical futures contract covers a large quantity of the underlying product or financial instrument. However, although the value of a single contract is normally quite large, the actual amount of investor capital required to deal in these vehicles is relatively small, because *all trading in this market is done on a margin basis*.

Options Versus Futures Contracts In many respects, futures contracts are closely related to the call options we studied in Chapter 15. For example, both involve the future delivery of an item at an agreed-upon price, and both are derivative securities. But there is a *significant difference* between a futures contract and an options contract. To begin with, a futures contract *obligates* a person to buy or sell a specified amount of a given commodity on or before a stated date—unless the contract is canceled or liquidated before it expires. In contrast, an option gives the holder the *right* to buy or sell a specific amount of a real or financial asset at a specific price over a specified period of time. In addition, whereas *price* (strike price) is one of the specified variables on a call

TABLE 16.1	Futures Contract Dimensions	
Contract	Size of a Contract*	Recent Market Value of a Single Contract**
Corn	5,000 bu	$ 11,350
Wheat	5,000 bu	18,300
Live cattle	40,000 lb	32,000
Pork bellies	40,000 lb	33,200
Coffee	37,500 lb	22,500
Cotton	50,000 lb	27,500
Gold	100 troy oz	36,500
Copper	25,000 lb	20,000
Japanese yen	12.5 million yen	100,000
Treasury bills	$1 million	99,300
Treasury bonds	$100,000	106,200
S&P 500 Stock Index	$250 times the index	250,000

*The size of some contracts may vary by exchange.
**Contract values are representative of those that existed at mid-year 2003.

option, it is *not* stated anywhere on a futures contract. Instead, the price on a futures contract is established through trading on the floor of a commodities exchange. This means that *the delivery price is set at whatever price the contract sells for*. So, if you bought a contract 3 months ago at $2.50 a bushel, then that's the price you'll pay to take delivery of the underlying product, even if the contract trades at, say, $3.00 a bushel at its date of expiration (i.e., delivery date). Equally important, the risk of loss with an option is limited to the price paid for it. A futures contract has *no such limit on exposure to loss*. Finally, while options contracts have an explicit up-front cost (in the form of an option premium), futures contracts do not. Granted, the purchase of a futures contract does involve a margin deposit, but that's nothing more than a refundable *security deposit*, not a sunk cost (like an option premium).

Major Exchanges Futures contracts in this country got their start in the agricultural segment of the economy over 150 years ago, when individuals who produced, owned, and/or processed foodstuffs sought a way to protect themselves against adverse price movements. Later, futures contracts came to be traded by individuals who were not necessarily connected with agriculture, but who wanted to make money with commodities by speculating on their price swings.

The first organized commodities exchange in this country was the Chicago Board of Trade, which opened its doors in 1848. Over time, additional markets opened. At one time there were more than a dozen U.S. exchanges that dealt in listed futures contracts. Since then, this market has gone through a period of consolidation and as a result, there are now just eight commodities exchanges left in operation in this country. The Chicago Board of Trade (CBT) is the largest and most active U.S. exchange. The CBT is followed in size by the Chicago Mercantile Exchange (CME), and the New York Mercantile Exchange (NYMerc). Together, these three exchanges account for about 80% to 90% of all the trading conducted on American futures exchanges.

Most exchanges deal in a number of different commodities or financial assets, and many commodities and financial futures are traded on more than one exchange. Although the exchanges are highly efficient and annual volume has surpassed the trillion-dollar mark, most futures trading is still conducted by **open outcry auction**: Actual trading on the floors of these exchanges is conducted through a series of shouts, body motions, and hand signals, as shown in Figure 16.1.

Trading in the Futures Market

Basically, the futures market contains two types of traders: hedgers and speculators. The market could not exist and operate efficiently without either one. The **hedgers** are commodities producers and processors who use futures contracts as a way to protect their interests in the underlying commodity or financial instrument. For example, if a rancher thinks the price of cattle will drop in the near future, he will hedge his position by selling a futures contract on cattle in the hope of locking in as high a price as possible for his herd. In effect, the hedgers provide the underlying strength of the futures market and represent the very reason for its existence. (Today, hedgers also include financial institu-

---

H O T

Visit the Chicago Board of Trade at the site below. Check out [Knowledge Center] for Glossary of Terms, Contract Specs, Educational Programs, and FAQs (frequently asked questions).

www.cbot.com

open outcry auction
in futures trading, an auction in which trading is done through a series of shouts, body motions, and hand signals.

hedgers
producers and processors who use futures contracts to protect their interest in an underlying commodity or financial instrument.

FIGURE 16.1

The Auction Market at Work on the Floor of the Chicago Board of Trade

Traders employ a system of open outcry and hand signals to indicate whether they wish to buy or sell and the price at which they wish to do so. Fingers held *vertically* indicate the number of contracts a trader wants to buy or sell. Fingers held *horizontally* indicate the fraction of a cent above or below the last traded full-cent price at which the trader will buy or sell. (*Source:* Copyright © 2003 Board of Trade of the City of Chicago, Inc. All Rights Reserved. Used with permission.)

tions and corporate money managers.) *Speculators*, in contrast, give the market liquidity. They are the ones who trade futures contracts simply to earn a profit on expected swings in the price of a futures contract. They are the investors who have no inherent interest in any aspect of the commodity or financial future other than the price action and potential capital gains it can produce.

Trading Mechanics Once futures contracts are created, they can readily be traded in the market. Like common stocks, futures contracts are bought and sold through local brokerage offices, or on one of the many Internet sites. Except for setting up a special commodities trading account, there is really no difference between trading futures and dealing in stocks or bonds. The same types of orders are used, and the use of margin is the standard way of trading futures. Any investor can buy or sell any contract, with any delivery month, at any time, so long as it is currently being traded on one of the exchanges.

Buying a contract is referred to as taking a *long position*. Selling one is termed taking a *short position*. It is exactly like going long or short with stocks and has the same connotation: The investor who is long wants the price to rise, and the short seller wants it to drop. Both long and short positions can be liquidated simply by executing an offsetting transaction. The short seller, for example, would cover his or her position by buying an equal amount of the contract. In general, only about 1% of all futures contracts are settled by delivery. The rest are offset prior to the delivery month. All trades are subject to normal transaction costs, which include **round-trip commissions** of about $60 to $90 for each contract traded. (A round-trip commission includes the commission costs on both ends of the transaction—to buy and sell a contract.) The exact size of the commission depends on the number and type of contracts being traded.

round-trip commissions
the commission costs on both ends (buying and selling) of a futures transaction.

Margin Trading Buying on margin means putting up only a fraction of the total price in cash. Margin, in effect, is the *amount of equity* that goes into the deal. Margin trading plays a crucial role in futures transactions because *all futures contracts are traded on a margin basis*. The margin required usually ranges from about 2% to 10% of the value of the contract. This is very low when compared to the margin required for stocks and most other types of securities. Furthermore, there is *no borrowing* required on the part of the investor to finance the balance of the contract. The margin, or **margin deposit**, as it is called with futures, represents security to cover any loss in the market value of the contract that may result from adverse price movements. It exists simply as a way to guarantee fulfillment of the contract. The margin deposit is not a partial payment for the commodity or financial instrument, nor is it in any way related to the value of the product or item underlying the contract.

margin deposit
amount deposited with a broker to cover any loss in the market value of a futures contract that may result from adverse price movements.

The size of the required margin deposit is specified as a dollar amount. It varies according to the type of contract (i.e., the amount of price volatility in the underlying commodity or financial asset). In some cases, it also varies according to the exchange on which the commodity is traded. Table 16.2 gives the margin requirements for the same 12 commodities and financial instruments listed in Table 16.1 on page 687. Compared to the size and value of the futures contracts, margin requirements are very low. The **initial deposit** noted in Table 16.2 is the amount of investor capital that must be deposited with the broker when the transaction is initiated and represents the amount of money required to make a given investment.

initial deposit
the amount of investor capital that must be deposited with a broker at the time of a commodity transaction.

After the investment is made, the market value of a contract will, of course, rise and fall as the quoted price of the underlying commodity or financial instrument goes up or down. Such market behavior will cause the amount of margin on deposit to change. To be sure that an adequate margin is always on hand, investors are required to meet a second type of margin requirement, the **maintenance deposit**. This deposit, which is slightly less than the initial deposit, establishes the minimum amount of margin that must be kept in the account at all times. For instance, if the initial deposit on a commodity is $1,000 per contract, its maintenance margin might be $750. So long as the market value of the contract does not fall by more than $250 (the difference between the contract's

maintenance deposit
the minimum amount of margin that must be kept in a margin account at all times.

TABLE 16.2	Margin Requirements for a Sample of Commodities and Financial Futures	
	Initial Margin Deposit	Maintenance Margin Deposit
Corn	$ 550	$ 400
Wheat	900	650
Live cattle	800	600
Pork bellies	1,620	1,200
Coffee	1,680	1,200
Cotton	1,400	1,000
Gold	2,025	1,500
Copper	1,350	1,000
Japanese yen	1,900	1,400
Treasury bills	400	300
Treasury bonds	3,000	2,250
S&P 500 Stock Index	17,800	14,250

Note: These margin requirements were specified by a major full-service brokerage firm in mid-2003. They may equal or exceed the minimums established by the various exchanges. They are meant to be typical of the ongoing requirements that customers are expected to live up to. Depending on the volatility of the market, exchange-minimum margin requirements are changed frequently. Thus the requirements in this table are also subject to change on short notice.

initial and maintenance margins), the investor has no problem. But if the market moves against the investor and the value of the contract drops by more than the allowed amount, the investor will receive a *margin call*. He or she must then immediately deposit enough cash to bring the position back to the initial margin level.

mark-to-the-market
a daily check of an investor's margin position, determined at the end of each session, at which time the broker debits or credits the account as needed.

An investor's margin position is checked daily via a procedure known as **mark-to-the-market.** That is, the gain or loss in a contract's value is determined at the end of each session. At that time the broker debits or credits the trader's account accordingly. In a falling market, an investor may receive a number of margin calls and be required to make additional margin payments. Failure to do so will mean that the broker has no choice but to close out the position—that is, to sell the contract.

IN REVIEW

CONCEPTS

16.1 What is a *futures contract?* Briefly explain how it is used as an investment vehicle.

16.2 Discuss the difference between a *cash market* and a *futures market.*

16.3 What is the major source of return to commodities speculators? How important is current income from dividends and interest?

16.4 Why are both hedgers and speculators important to the efficient operation of a futures market?

16.5 Explain how margin trading is conducted in the futures market.
   a. What is the difference between an *initial deposit* and a *maintenance deposit?*
   b. Are investors ever required to put up additional margin? If so, when?

Commodities

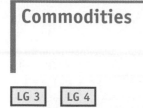
Physical commodities like grains, metals, wood, and meat make up a major portion of the futures market. They have been actively traded in this country for well over a century. The material that follows focuses on *commodities trading*. We begin with a review of the basic characteristics and investment merits of these vehicles.

Basic Characteristics

Various types of physical commodities are found on nearly all of the U.S. futures exchanges. (In fact, several of them deal only in commodities.) The market for commodity contracts is divided into four major segments: grains and oilseeds, livestock and meat, metals and petroleum, and food and fiber. Such segmentation does not affect trading mechanics and procedures. It merely provides a convenient way of categorizing commodities into groups based on similar underlying characteristics. Table 16.3 shows the diversity of the commodities market and the variety of contracts available. Although the list changes yearly, the table indicates that investors had nearly three dozen different commodities to choose from in 2003. And a number of these (e.g., soybeans, wheat, and sugar) are available in several different forms or grades. Actually, Table 16.3 lists only *some of the more actively traded commodities. Not included* are dozens of commodities (such as butter, cheese, boneless beef, and others) that are not widely traded but still make up a part of this market.

A Commodities Contract Every commodity (whether actively or thinly traded) has certain specifications that spell out in detail the amounts and quality of the product being traded. Figure 16.2 (on page 694) is an excerpt from the "Futures Prices" section of the *Wall Street Journal* and shows the contract and quotation system used with commodities. Each commodity quote is made up of the same five parts, and all prices are quoted in an identical fashion. In particular, the quote for each commodities contract specifies: (1) the product; (2) the exchange on which the contract is traded; (3) the size of the contract (in bushels, pound, tons, etc.); (4) the method of valuing the contract, or pricing unit (e.g., cents per pound or dollars per ton); and (5) the delivery month. Using a corn contract as an illustration, we can see each of these parts in the following illustration:

KEY
① the product
② the exchange
③ the size of the contract
④ the pricing unit
⑤ the delivery months

	Open	High	Low	Settle	Change	Lifetime High	Lifetime Low	Open Interest
① ② ③ ④ Corn (CBT)—5,000 bu.; cents per bu.								
May	253½	253¾	252¼	252½	−1¾	286½	230½	42,796
July	258	258	256½	256¾	−1¾	288	233	60,477
Sept.	260	260½	259	259	−1½	263	236	7,760
Dec.	263½	264	262½	263	−1¼	267¼	244	41,638
Mar. 04	271¾	272	270½	271	−1¼	276	254¾	11,098
May	277¼	278	276¼	277	−1	281	273¼	1,326

⑤ (to the left of Sept.)

The quotation system used for commodities is based on the size of the contract and the pricing unit. The financial media generally report the open, high,

TABLE 16.3	Major Classes of Commodities	
Grains and Oilseeds	*Metals and Petroleum*	
Corn	Electricity	
Oats	Copper	
Soybeans	Gold	
Soybean meal	Platinum	
Soybean oil	Silver	
Wheat	Palladium	
Barley	Gasoline	
Canola	Heating oil	
Flaxseed	Crude oil	
Rice	Natural gas	
Livestock and Meat	*Food and Fiber*	
Cattle—live	Cocoa	
Cattle—feeder	Coffee	
Hogs	Milk	
Pork bellies	Orange juice	
	Sugar	
	Cotton	
	Lumber	

settle price
the closing price (last price of the day) for commodities and financial futures.

open interest
the number of contracts currently outstanding on a commodity or financial future.

low, and closing prices for each delivery month. With commodities, the last price of the day, or the closing price, is known as the **settle price**. Also reported, at least by the *Wall Street Journal,* is the amount of **open interest** in each contract—that is, the number of contracts currently outstanding. Note in the illustration on page 692 that the settle price for May corn was 252½. Since the pricing system is cents per bushel, this means that the contract was being traded at $2.52½ per bushel and the market value of the contract was $12,625. (Each contract involves 5,000 bushels of corn and each bushel is worth $2.52½; thus 5,000 × $2.525 = $12,625.)

Price Behavior Commodity prices react to a unique set of economic, political, and international pressures—as well as to the weather. The explanation of *why* commodity prices change is beyond the scope of this book. But it should be clear that they do move up and down just like any other investment vehicle, which is precisely what speculators want. Because we are dealing in such large trading units (5,000 bushels of this or 40,000 pounds of that), even a modest price change can have an enormous impact on the market value of a contract, and therefore on investor returns or losses. For example, if the price of corn goes up or down by just 20 cents per bushel, the value of a *single contract* will change by $1,000. A corn contract can be bought with a $550 initial margin deposit, so it is easy to see the effect this kind of price behavior can have on investor return.

But do commodity prices really move all that much? Judge for yourself: The price change columns in Figure 16.2 show some excellent examples of sizable price changes that occur from one day to the next. Note, for example, that March 2004 corn fell $200 (5,000 bushels × $0.04 = $200), November soybeans rose $125, September Kansas City wheat fell $275, and September heating oil went up a whopping $1,285. Keep in mind that these are *daily*

FIGURE 16.2 Quotations on Actively Traded Commodity Futures Contracts

These quotes reveal at a glance key information about the various commodities, including the latest high, low, and closing ("settle") prices, as well as the lifetime high and low prices for each contract. (*Source: Wall Street Journal,* August 22, 2003.)

Thursday, August 21, 2003

Grain and Oilseed Futures

	OPEN	HIGH	LOW	SETTLE	CHG	LIFETIME HIGH	LIFETIME LOW	OPEN INT
Corn (CBT)-5,000 bu.; cents per bu.								
Sept	226.50	230.25	222.50	224.50	−2.25	276.00	204.50	72,688
Dec	236.25	239.25	230.50	232.50	−3.75	269.00	209.50	220,578
Mr04	243.00	246.00	237.25	239.25	−4.00	264.00	219.00	48,823
May	249.00	249.25	240.75	242.25	−4.75	260.25	225.00	11,965
July	249.75	250.00	241.25	242.75	−5.00	264.50	229.25	12,418
Sept	244.00	244.00	237.00	238.00	−3.50	254.00	231.00	1,850
Dec	244.00	244.00	239.75	241.00	−2.00	260.00	232.50	7,145
Est vol 27,163; vol Wed 70,907; open int 376,264, −2,321.								
Oats (CBT)-5,000 bu.; cents per bu.								
Sept	140.75	141.50	139.50	140.00	.25	175.00	123.50	870
Dec	144.00	145.00	143.00	143.25	.25	163.50	124.50	4,317
Mr04	149.25	150.00	148.00	148.00	−.50	153.75	131.00	394
Est vol 1,052; vol Wed 356; open int 5,597, +26.								
Soybeans (CBT)-5,000 bu.; cents per bu.								
Sept	578.00	591.00	576.50	578.50	2.00	620.00	466.00	11,229
Nov	578.75	590.00	575.00	579.25	2.50	590.00	484.00	128,121
Ja04	580.00	592.00	578.00	582.75	3.00	592.00	507.00	16,879
Mar	581.00	587.50	575.00	578.50	1.25	590.00	508.00	16,387
May	577.00	579.75	569.00	572.50	.75	586.00	515.50	19,812
Aug	574.00	574.00	566.00	567.00	−.50	574.00	521.00	220
Nov	555.00	557.50	551.00	551.75	−2.25	558.00	483.00	1,732
Est vol 67,831; vol Wed 80,275; open int 200,028, +3,241.								
Soybean Meal (CBT)-100 tons; $ per ton.								
Sept	190.70	192.00	187.20	189.60	3.10	195.00	148.00	22,497
Oct	182.60	185.80	180.50	183.00	2.20	186.50	148.10	18,904
Dec	181.80	185.80	179.80	182.20	1.40	185.80	148.00	70,362
Ja04	184.00	185.30	180.30	181.60	.90	185.30	151.00	9,537
Mar	183.50	184.80	180.20	182.00	1.00	185.00	152.50	10,866
May	182.50	183.40	178.70	180.00	...	183.50	153.00	10,384
July	183.00	183.50	179.00	180.00	−.50	184.50	152.50	5,472
Aug	182.00	182.00	178.00	178.00	−.60	183.00	154.00	1,494
Sept	180.50	180.50	177.00	177.00	−1.00	181.50	154.00	2,119
Est vol 32,949; vol Wed 43,839; open int 152,994, +3,064.								
Soybean Oil (CBT)-60,000 lbs.; cents per lb.								
Sept	20.15	20.36	19.98	20.06	.07	23.55	19.20	21,061
Oct	20.19	20.36	19.98	20.08	.07	23.15	18.95	27,227
Dec	20.03	20.36	19.91	20.09	.12	22.88	18.88	66,069
Ja04	20.09	20.29	19.92	20.06	.12	22.77	18.92	9,598
Mar	19.95	20.13	19.80	20.00	.15	22.50	19.00	10,695
July	19.70	19.75	19.50	19.50	.05	21.50	19.01	7,037
Est vol 24,541; vol Wed 31,965; open int 155,735, +786.								
Wheat (CBT)-5,000 bu.; cents per bu.								
Sept	366.75	372.50	360.50	363.00	−3.00	387.00	285.00	24,840
Dec	378.00	385.00	373.50	376.00	−2.75	399.00	291.00	82,272
Mr04	385.50	392.00	381.75	384.25	−2.75	405.00	301.50	12,729
July	338.00	340.00	336.25	337.50	−.50	346.00	298.00	2,301
Dec	345.00	345.00	345.00	345.00	−1.00	351.00	330.00	45
Est vol 34,796; vol Wed 32,739; open int 122,801, −758.								
Wheat (KC)-5,000 bu.; cents per bu.								
Sept	376.00	376.00	364.00	365.75	−5.50	405.00	300.75	19,002
Dec	386.50	386.50	374.00	376.75	−5.00	408.00	309.00	48,193
Mr04	387.00	388.00	377.00	379.50	−3.50	408.00	314.00	5,834
May	371.00	371.00	364.50	365.50	−3.50	381.00	315.00	766
Est vol 15,647; vol Wed 10,556; open int 74,980, −1,383.								
Wheat (MPLS)-5,000 bu.; cents per bu.								
Sept	389.00	391.00	380.00	384.25	−2.75	422.00	318.00	8,836
Dec	394.00	396.00	385.50	389.25	−2.75	425.00	325.50	17,154
Mr04	398.00	400.00	390.00	393.75	−2.50	420.00	344.00	2,715
Sept	366.00	366.00	364.00	366.00	2.00	375.00	354.00	121
Est vol 5,989; vol Wed 6,595; open int 28,937, +453.								

Petroleum Futures

	OPEN	HIGH	LOW	SETTLE	CHG	LIFETIME HIGH	LIFETIME LOW	OPEN INT
Crude Oil, Light Sweet (NYM)-1,000 bbls.; $ per bbl.								
Oct	31.00	32.40	31.00	31.88	0.84	32.63	20.55	173,606
Nov	30.77	32.05	30.75	31.61	0.86	32.05	20.70	53,928
Dec	30.20	31.35	30.16	31.01	0.83	31.70	15.92	69,199
Ja04	29.69	30.62	29.64	30.41	0.74	30.62	20.35	26,187
Feb	29.21	29.90	29.21	29.85	0.65	29.99	20.35	12,401
Mar	28.76	29.25	28.72	29.32	0.57	29.44	20.35	15,953
Apr	28.35	28.82	28.35	28.81	0.50	28.92	20.35	15,782
May	27.95	28.20	27.95	28.36	0.45	28.39	20.35	8,932
June	27.63	28.00	27.63	27.95	0.36	28.01	20.53	18,970
July	27.30	27.53	27.30	27.62	0.31	27.70	20.86	7,142
Aug	27.01	27.19	27.01	27.32	0.26	27.19	20.84	4,840
Sept	26.87	26.87	26.86	27.05	0.22	27.45	20.82	9,994
Oct	26.63	26.65	26.63	26.79	0.19	26.65	23.75	4,967
Nov	26.40	26.40	26.40	26.53	0.15	26.40	24.75	5,214
Dec	26.20	26.25	26.15	26.31	0.13	26.47	16.35	22,193
Dc05	24.45	24.45	24.45	24.83	−0.04	24.80	17.00	9,991
Dc06	24.95	24.95	24.95	24.71	−0.01	24.95	19.10	9,958
Est vol 219,621; vol Wed 185,654; open int 522,675, −4,000.								
Heating Oil No. 2 (NYM)-42,000 gal.; $ per gal.								
Sept	.8025	.8500	.8025	.8330	.0306	.8620	.6215	29,112
Oct	.8155	.8590	.8155	.8427	.0291	.8680	.6290	42,058
Nov	.8255	.8650	.8247	.8502	.0281	.8700	.6450	13,928
Dec	.8336	.8710	.8335	.8562	.0271	.8725	.6500	20,926
Ja04	.8460	.8615	.8460	.8582	.0256	.8730	.6540	9,985
Feb	.8350	.8525	.8350	.8457	.0226	.8580	.6500	8,214
Mar	.8090	.8250	.8090	.8142	.0191	.8250	.6370	4,996
Apr	.7780	.7895	.7780	.7817	.0156	.7900	.6275	4,207
May	.7510	.7620	.7510	.7507	.0126	.7620	.6140	1,399
June	.7325	.7350	.7325	.7337	.0101	.7420	.6354	3,209
July	.7290	.7290	.7290	.7282	.0081	.7345	.6415	745
Est vol 49,084; vol Wed 35,860; open int 145,546, +384.								
Gasoline-NY Unleaded (NYM)-42,000 gal.; $ per gal.								
Sept	1.0040	1.1220	1.0040	1.0993	.0957	1.1220	.6900	31,701
Oct	.9121	.9660	.9121	.9497	.0376	.9660	.6815	52,174
Nov	.8580	.8830	.8580	.8757	.0206	.8830	.6600	8,885
Dec	.8250	.8425	.8250	.8377	.0166	.8425	.6750	7,605
Ap04	.8700	.8775	.8700	.8757	.0131	.8775	.7975	1,818
Est vol 74,464; vol Wed 56,988; open int 106,628, +3,637.								
Natural Gas (NYM)-10,000 MMBtu.; $ per MMBtu								
Sept	5.120	5.340	5.040	5.275	.156	6.680	2.880	39,509
Oct	5.154	5.370	5.070	5.305	.155	6.700	2.910	48,781
Nov	5.385	5.535	5.300	5.490	.115	6.750	3.050	26,555
Dec	5.603	5.750	5.550	5.695	.092	6.880	3.250	25,197
Ja04	5.730	5.860	5.670	5.810	.084	6.945	3.300	22,284
Feb	5.645	5.780	5.610	5.720	.067	6.760	3.260	17,001
Mar	5.535	5.650	5.480	5.595	.052	6.490	3.150	15,782
Apr	5.005	5.115	5.000	5.065	.012	5.515	2.970	15,039
May	4.960	5.010	4.900	4.975	.015	5.305	3.030	11,740
June	n.a.	5.010	4.940	4.975	.025	5.240	3.010	11,237
July	4.940	5.000	4.930	4.965	.025	5.250	3.040	8,319
Aug	4.930	5.010	4.930	4.965	.025	5.230	3.120	8,390
Sept	4.910	4.970	4.910	4.930	.015	5.640	3.100	6,017
Oct	4.925	4.935	4.920	4.947	.012	5.190	3.100	6,381
Nov	5.060	5.103	5.060	5.112	.009	5.380	3.270	6,655
Dec	5.260	5.270	5.260	5.282	.009	5.543	3.460	8,937
Ja05	5.350	5.350	5.350	5.372	−.001	5.650	3.520	7,481
Mar	5.135	5.135	5.135	5.135	−.016	5.425	3.640	6,751
May	4.678	4.678	4.678	4.655	−.023	4.930	3.500	3,646
June	4.630	4.660	4.630	4.635	−.023	4.890	3.530	3,404
Est vol 87,200; vol Wed 64,310; open int 351,371, −488.								

price swings that occurred on *single* contracts. These are sizable changes, even by themselves. But when you look at them relative to the (very small) original investment required (sometimes as low as $550), they quickly add up to serious returns (or losses)! And they occur not because of the volatility of the underlying prices but because of the sheer magnitude of the commodities contracts themselves.

Clearly, this kind of price behavior is one of the magnets that draws investors to commodities. The exchanges recognize the volatile nature of commodities contracts and try to put lids on price fluctuations by imposing daily price limits and maximum daily price ranges. (Similar limits are also put on some financial futures.) The **daily price limit** restricts the interday change in the price of the underlying commodity. For example, the price of corn can change by no more than 10 cents per bushel from one day to the next. The daily limit on copper is 3 cents per pound. Such limits, however, still leave plenty of room to turn a quick profit. For example, the daily limits on corn and copper translate into per-day changes of $500 for one corn contract and $750 for a copper contract. The **maximum daily price range,** in contrast, limits the amount the price can change *during* the day and is usually equal to twice the daily limit restrictions. For example, the daily price limit on corn is 10 cents per bushel and its maximum daily range is 20 cents per bushel.

daily price limit
restriction on the day-to-day change in the price of an underlying commodity.

maximum daily price range
the amount a commodity price can change during the day; usually equal to twice the daily price limit.

Return on Invested Capital Futures contracts have only one source of return: the capital gains that can be earned when prices move in a favorable direction. There is no current income of any kind. The volatile price behavior of futures contracts is one reason why high returns are possible; the other is leverage. That is, because all futures trading is done on margin, it takes only a small amount of money to control a large investment position—and to participate in the price swings that accompany futures contracts. Of course, the use of leverage also means that it is possible for an investment to be wiped out with just one or two bad days.

Investment return on a commodities contract can be measured by calculating **return on invested capital.** This is simply a variation of the standard holding period return formula, where return is based on the *amount of money actually invested in the contract,* rather than on the value of the contract itself. It is used because of the generous amount of leverage (margin) used in commodities trading. The return on invested capital for a commodities position can be determined according to the following simple formula:

return on invested capital
return to investors based on the amount of money actually invested in a security, rather than the value of the contract itself.

Equation 16.1

$$\text{Return on invested capital} = \frac{\begin{array}{c}\text{Selling price of} \\ \text{commodity contract}\end{array} - \begin{array}{c}\text{Purchase price of} \\ \text{commodity contract}\end{array}}{\text{Amount of margin deposit}}$$

Equation 16.1 can be used for both long and short transactions. To see how it works, assume you just bought two September corn contracts at 280 ($2.80 per bushel) by depositing the required initial margin of $1,100 ($550 for each contract). Your investment amounts to only $1,100, but you control 10,000 bushels of corn worth $28,000 at the time of purchase. Now, assume that September corn has just closed at 294, so you decide to sell out and take your profit. Your return on invested capital is

$$\text{Return on invested capital} = \frac{\$29,400 - \$28,000}{\$1,100}$$

$$= \frac{\$1,400}{\$1,100} = \underline{\underline{127.3\%}}$$

Clearly, this high rate of return was due not only to an increase in the price of the commodity but also (and perhaps more crucially) to the fact that you were using very low margin. (The initial margin in this particular transaction equaled less than 5% of the underlying value of the contract.)

Trading Commodities

Investing in commodities takes one of three forms. The first, *speculating*, involves using commodities as a way to generate capital gains. In essence, speculators try to capitalize on the wide price swings that are characteristic of so many commodities. As explained in the accompanying *Ethics in Investing* box, this is basically what Enron was doing—until things started turning nasty. While volatile price movements may appeal to speculators, they frighten many other investors. As a result, some of these more cautious investors turn to *spreading*, the second form of commodities investing. Futures investors use this trading technique as a way to capture some of the benefits of volatile commodities prices but without all the exposure to loss.

HOT

You can study the behavior of commodity prices in a chart at:

www.barchart.com/

Finally, commodities futures can be used as *hedging* vehicles. A hedge in the commodities market is more of a technical strategy that is used almost exclusively by producers and processors to protect a position in a product or commodity. For example, a producer or grower would use a commodity hedge to obtain as *high a price* as possible for the goods he or she sells. The processor or manufacturer who uses the commodity would use a hedge for the opposite reason: to obtain the goods at as *low a price* as possible. A successful hedge, in effect, means added income to producers or lower costs to processors.

Let's now look briefly at the two trading strategies that are most used by individual investors—speculating and spreading—to gain a better understanding of how commodities can be used as investment vehicles.

Speculating Speculators are in the market for one reason: They hope to capitalize on swings in commodity prices by going long or short. To see why a speculator would go long when prices are expected to rise, assume you buy a March silver contract at 595½ (i.e., $5.95½ an ounce) by depositing the required initial margin of $1,250. One silver contract involves 5,000 troy ounces, so it has a market value of $29,775. If silver goes up, you make money. Assume that it does and that by February (1 month before the contract expires), the price of the contract rises to 614. You then liquidate the contract and make a profit of 18½ cents per ounce (614 − 595½). That means a $925 profit from an investment of just $1,250—which translates into a return on invested capital of 74.0%.

HOT

At the Chicago Board of Trade Web site, go to [Knowledge Center], [FAQ], and answer the question "What is hedging and speculating?"

www.cbot.com

⚖ ETHICS IN INVESTING

TRADING ENERGY FUTURES AT ENRON

Before it was known for its financial problems, Enron had become famous as a business pioneer, blazing new trails in the market for trading risk. Long known as a traditional utility firm in the business of operating pipelines and shipping natural gas, Enron ended up getting 90 percent of its revenues from trading derivatives. In the 1980s, when the price of natural gas was deregulated, Enron decided to transform itself by exploiting new opportunities in the commodities business. As a result of deregulation, the price of natural gas could go down and up, exposing producers and consumers to risk against which new hedge instruments had to be offered. Although natural gas futures were trading at the New York Mercantile Exchange at the time, traditional exchanges, such as NYMEX, could offer only a limited hedge that did not take into account regional discrepancies in gas prices. Enron was able to fill this void by agreeing to deliver natural gas to any location in the United States at any time.

In addition to trading natural gas and other energy contracts, in the late 1990s Enron began trading weather derivatives for which no underlying commodities existed—only bets on the weather. With weather derivatives transactions worth an estimated $3.5 billion in the United States alone, Enron was considering creating a similar weather market in Europe. Its products became ever more complicated and even more bizarre—a temperature-linked bond, for example. The 5-year, $105 million issue (called weather-indexed return securities, or WINRS) was tied to the value of portfolios of heating and cooling degree-day options at several U.S. cities at expiration and was offered to investors in October 1999.

With the development of more derivative products and thanks to its near-monopoly position, Enron's trading business was initially highly profitable. According to company data, by September 2001 the firm's Internet-based trading exchange, EnronOnline, was processing about 4,000 transactions per day worldwide, with an average deal size of about $500,000. The value of online transaction activity conducted through EnronOnline was expected to reach approximately $510 billion—a healthy increase from the $101 billion in transactions during 2000. At that time, the company offered more than 1,800 different contracts for 16 commodity-product categories, ranging from oil and natural gas to weather derivatives, broadband services, and emissions allocations. And unlike traditional commodity and futures exchanges and brokers, Enron's online commodity and derivative business was not subject to federal regulations.

However, Enron eventually lost its unique position as the energy business started to become more crowded. When other firms entered the online commodity business, such as Enron's Houston neighbor and rival El Paso Energy, and Wall Street firms like Goldman Sachs and Morgan Stanley, they started competing by charging less for commissions and exploiting the same regional price discrepancies that had been Enron's bread and butter. As a result, Enron's trading operation became less profitable. To find new markets and products, the company expanded into other areas such as water, foreign power sources, telecommunications, and broadband services. It lost billions of dollars on each of those investments. And the farther it moved away from its core business of supplying gas, the more money Enron lost.

The company sought to hide those losses by entering into all sorts of risky and bizarre financial contracts. When financial institutions began to realize that Enron was essentially a shell game, they withdrew their credit. At that point, despite rosy assurances from its founder and CEO Ken Lay just months before bankruptcy proceedings, Enron went into a death spiral.

CRITICAL THINKING QUESTIONS Could the Enron debacle have been prevented? If so, what actions should have been taken by auditors, regulators, and lawmakers?

Of course, instead of rising, the price of silver could have dropped by 18½ cents per ounce. In this case, you would have lost most of your original investment ($1,250 − $925 leaves only $325, out of which would have to come a round-trip commission of $60 or $70). But the drop in price would be just what a *short seller* is after. Here's why: You sell "short" the March silver at 595½ and buy it back sometime later at 577. Clearly, the difference between the selling price and the purchase price is the same 18½ cents. But in this case it is *profit,* because the selling price exceeds the purchase price. (See Chapter 2 for a review of short selling.)

Spreading Instead of attempting to speculate on the price behavior of a futures contract, you might choose to follow the more conservative tactic of *spreading.* Much like spreading with put and call options, the idea is to combine two or more different contracts into one position that offers the potential for a modest amount of profit but restricts your exposure to loss. One very important reason for spreading in the commodities market is that, unlike options, *there is no limit to the amount of loss that can occur with a futures contract.* You set up a spread by buying one contract and simultaneously selling another. Although one side of the transaction will lead to a loss, you hope that the profit earned from the other side will more than offset the loss, and that the net result will be at least a modest amount of profit. And if you're wrong, the spread will serve to limit (but not eliminate) any losses.

Here is a simple example of how a spread might work: Suppose you buy contract A at 533½ and at the same time short sell contract B for 575½. Sometime later, you close out your interest in contract A by selling it at 542, and you simultaneously cover your short position in B by purchasing a contract at 579. Although you made a profit of 8½ points (542 − 533½) on the long position, contract A, you lost 3½ points (575½ − 579) on the contract you shorted, B. The net effect, however, is a profit of 5 points. If you were dealing in cents per pound, those 5 points would mean a profit of $250 on a 5,000-pound contract. All sorts of commodity spreads can be set up for almost any type of investment situation. Most of them, however, are highly sophisticated and require specialized skills.

IN REVIEW

CONCEPTS

16.6 List and briefly define the five essential parts of a commodities contract. Which parts have a direct bearing on the price behavior of the contract?

16.7 Briefly define each of the following:
a. Settle price.
b. Daily price limit.
c. Open interest.
d. Maximum daily price range.
e. Delivery month.

16.8 What is the one source of return on futures contracts? What measure is used to calculate the return on a commodities contract?

16.9 Note several approaches to investing in commodities and explain the investment objectives of each.

Financial Futures

LG 5   LG 6

financial futures
a type of futures contract in which the underlying "commodity" is a financial asset, such as debt securities, foreign currencies, or common stocks.

Another dimension of the futures market is **financial futures,** a segment of the market in which futures contracts are traded on a variety of financial instruments. Actually, financial futures are an extension of the commodities concept. They were created for much the same reason as commodities futures, they are traded in the same market, their prices behave a lot like commodities, and they have similar investment merits. But financial futures are unique because of the underlying assets. Let's now look more closely at financial futures and see how investors can use them.

The Financial Futures Market

Though relatively young, the financial futures market is the dominant type of futures contract. Indeed, the level of trading in financial futures far surpasses that of traditional commodities. Much of the interest in financial futures is due to hedgers and big institutional investors who use these contracts as portfolio management tools. But individual investors can also find plenty of opportunities here. For example, financial futures offer yet another way to speculate on the behavior of interest rates. And they can also be used to speculate in the stock market. They even offer a convenient way to speculate in the highly specialized foreign currency markets.

The financial futures market was established in response to the economic turmoil the United States experienced during the 1970s. The dollar had become unstable on the world market and was causing serious problems for multinational firms. Closer to home, interest rates had become highly volatile, which caused severe difficulties for corporate treasurers, financial institutions, and money managers in general. All of these parties needed a way to protect themselves from the wide fluctuations in the value of the dollar and interest rates. Thus a market for financial futures was born. Hedging provided the economic rationale for the market in financial futures. But speculators were quick to join in, as they found the price volatility of these instruments attractive and at times highly profitable.

At present, most of the financial futures trading in this country occurs on just two exchanges—the Chicago Board of Trade and the Chicago Mercantile Exchange. Financial futures also are traded on several foreign exchanges, the most noteworthy of which is the London International Financial Futures Exchange. The three basic types of financial futures include foreign currencies, debt securities, and stock indexes.

currency futures
futures contracts on foreign currencies, traded much like commodities.

Foreign Currencies, Interest Rates, and Stock Indexes The financial futures market started rather inconspicuously in May 1972, with the listing of a handful of foreign currency contracts. Known as **currency futures,** they have become a major hedging vehicle as international trade has mushroomed. Most of the currency trading today is conducted in the following seven foreign currencies:

- British pound
- Swiss franc
- Mexican peso
- Euro
- Canadian dollar
- Japanese yen
- Australian dollar

interest rate futures
futures contracts on debt securities.

stock-index futures
futures contracts written on broad-based measures of stock market performance (e.g., the S&P 500 Stock Index), allowing investors to participate in the general movements of the stock market.

single-stock futures contract
a new type of futures contract where the underlying asset is 100 shares of common stock in a specific publicly traded company, like Intel, Starbucks, or Wal-Mart; think of them as the futures market version of stock options.

All of these currencies are issued by countries with which the United States has strong international trade and exchange ties.

In October 1975, the first futures contract on debt securities, or **interest rate futures,** as they are more commonly known, was established when trading started in GNMA pass-through certificates (a special type of mortgage-backed bond issued by an agency of the U.S. government). In time, other issues were added and today, trading is carried out in a variety of U.S. and foreign debt securities and interest rates, including:

- U.S. Treasury bills
- U.S. Treasury notes
- U.S. Treasury bonds
- U.S. agency notes
- Municipal bonds (via a muni bond index)
- Various 30-day interest rate contracts (e.g., 30-day Federal Funds)
- Interest rate swaps
- 90-day Euromarket deposits (e.g., Eurodollar deposits, Euroyen deposits)
- Various foreign government bonds (e.g., bonds issued by the British, German, and Canadian governments)

Interest rate futures were immediately successful, and their popularity continues to grow.

In February 1982, still another type of trading vehicle was introduced: the stock-index futures contract. **Stock-index futures,** as they are called, are contracts pegged to broad-based measures of stock market performance. Today, trading is done in most of the (major) U.S. stock indexes, including:

- The Dow Jones Industrial Average
- The S&P 500 Index
- The S&P MidCap 400 Index
- The NYSE Composite Index
- The Nasdaq 100 Index
- The Russell 2000 Index

In addition to these (and other) U.S. indexes, investors can trade stock-index futures contracts based on the London, Tokyo, Paris, Sydney, Berlin, Zurich, and Toronto stock exchanges. Stock-index futures, which are similar to the stock-index options we discussed in Chapter 15, allow investors to participate in the general movements of the entire stock market. The newest innovation in the financial futures market came into being in December 2000, when federal legislation was changed to allow the trading of **single-stock futures contracts.** Now investors can buy and sell futures contracts that are written on 100-share lots of a given common stock. While the jury's still out on their popularity, the nearby *Investing in Action* box provides a brief description of these instruments and how they can be used by investors.

INVESTING IN ACTION

ARE SINGLE STOCK FUTURES IN *YOUR* FUTURE?

Several years ago, a new type of investment—single stock futures (SSF)—began trading on a newly created contracts exchange called OneChicago, which is owned by the Chicago Board of Trade, the Chicago Mercantile Exchange, and the Chicago Board Options Exchange. Within a few years of their introduction, SSF's average trading volume was in excess of 150 million shares.

A type of futures contract, a single stock future is a promise to buy or sell 100-share lots of an individual stock or exchange traded fund (ETF) on a certain day in the future at an agreed-upon price. Over 100 of the biggest and most well-known companies, such as General Motors, Schlumberger, and others, offer SSFs. Because SSFs are both a stock and a futures contract, they have two levels of federal regulation, with the Commodity Futures Trading Commission and the Securities and Exchange Commission jointly overseeing the exchanges' operations.

SSFs have a minimum price fluctuation or "tick" of one cent per share or $1 per contract. Thus, each $1 move in the price of the SSF stock equates to a $100 move in the futures contract. For example, if you bought one Home Depot SSF contract at $48 and then offset the position by selling the same contract at $51, you would have realized a $300 profit on your contract.

Individual investors can use SSFs to own shares of individual companies at a lower cost than if they purchased the stock outright. The cost of getting in is lower, as are the transactions costs. The margin requirement for SSFs is significantly lower than for regular stock trades (20 percent rather than 50 percent), which allows an investor to control shares at a lower cost. Investors also save on interest charges, because none are assessed when buying or selling a stock on margin in an SSF.

Depending on an investor's risk profile, he or she could use SSFs to speculate outright on an anticipated increase or decrease in the price of a stock. While SSFs are highly leveraged investments and thus carry substantial risk, a smart investor can make more on the futures version of a stock than by buying the stock itself.

In addition to buying and selling futures contracts on one specific company stock, an investor can trade in Narrow-Based Indices (NBI), which is a form of futures contract. An NBI groups stocks in a concentrated area of the equities market such as airlines, banks and investment banking, biotech, energy, oil services, pharmaceuticals, software, and retail. Each group includes five to nine companies in a specific industry sector. With NBIs, investors can take a long or short position in a concentrated area without incurring multiple transactions costs.

CRITICAL THINKING QUESTIONS For what type of person and for what reasons might investing in single-stock futures be better than trading stocks? Should someone who trades single-stock futures exclude stocks from his or her portfolio?

Sources: "Single Stock Futures Contract Specs," last updated June 19, 2003, downloaded from www.onechicago.com; Patrick Lafferty, "In My Opinion. Will Single Stock Futures Attract Investors?" September 19, 2002, downloaded from www.forbes.com; and Mark Skertic, "OneChicago to Shift its Aim to Stock Pros," *Chicago Tribune*, December 5, 2003, downloaded from www.chicagotribune.com.

Stock index futures (and other futures contracts) are a type of *derivative security*. Like options, they derive their value from the price behavior of the assets that underlie them. In the case of stock-index futures, they are supposed to reflect the general performance of the stock market as a whole, or various segments of the market. Thus, when the market for large-cap stocks, as measured by the S&P 500, goes up, the value of an S&P 500 futures contract should go up as well. Accordingly, investors can use stock-index futures as a way to buy or sell the market—or reasonable proxies thereof—and thereby participate in broad market moves.

Contract Specifications In principle, financial futures contracts are like commodities contracts. They control large sums of the underlying financial instrument and are issued with a variety of delivery months. All this can be seen in Figure 16.3, which lists quotes for several foreign currency, interest rate, and stock-index futures contracts. Looking first at currency futures, we see that the contracts entitle the holders to a certain position in a specified foreign currency. In effect, the owner of a currency future holds a claim on a certain amount of foreign money. The precise amount ranges from 62,500 British pounds to 12.5 million Japanese yen. Similarly, holders of interest rate futures have a claim on a certain amount of the underlying debt security. This claim is also quite large. It amounts to $100,000 worth of Treasury notes and bonds, $1 million worth of Treasury bills, and $5 million in 30-day Federal Funds contracts.

Stock-index futures, however, are a bit different because the seller of one of these contracts is *not* obligated to deliver the *underlying stocks* at the expiration date. Instead, ultimate delivery is in the form of *cash*. (This is fortunate, as it would indeed be a task to make delivery of the 2,000 small-cap stocks that are in the Russell 2000 Index or the 500 issues in the S&P Index.) Basically, the amount of underlying cash is set at a certain multiple of the value of the underlying stock index. For example:

Index	*Multiple*
DJIA	$10 × index
S&P 500	$250 × index
Nasdaq 100	$100 × index
S&P 400	$500 × index
NYSE Composite	$500 × index
Russell 2000	$500 × index

Thus, if the S&P 500 stood at 1,075, then the amount of cash underlying a single S&P 500 stock-index futures contract would be $250 × 1,075 = $268,750. Again, the amount is substantial. In terms of delivery months, the lives of financial futures contracts run from about 12 months or less for most stock-index and currency futures to about 8 years or less for interest rate instruments.

Prices and Profits We have described three basic types of financial futures. Not surprisingly, the price of each type of contract is quoted somewhat differently.

- *Foreign currency futures*. All currency futures are quoted in dollars or cents per unit of the underlying foreign currency (e.g., dollars per British pound or cents per Japanese yen). Thus, according to the closing ("settle") prices in Figure 16.3, one September British pound contract was worth $99,537.50 (62,500 pounds × 1.5926). At the same time,

FIGURE 16.3

Quotations on Selected Actively Traded Financial Futures

The trading exchange, size of the trading unit, pricing unit, and delivery months are all vital pieces of information included as part of the quotation system used with financial futures. (*Source: Wall Street Journal,* August 21, 2003.)

Currency Futures

	OPEN	HIGH	LOW	SETTLE	CHG	LIFETIME HIGH	LOW	OPEN INT
Japanese Yen (CME)-¥12,500,000; $ per ¥								
Sept	.8451	.8496	.8426	.8477	.0022	.8815	.8220	96,626
Dec	.8471	.8517	.8454	.8501	.0022	.8915	.8318	21,336
Est vol 19,360; vol Tue 31,110; open int 118,044, +2,616.								
Canadian Dollar (CME)-CAD 100,000; $ per CAD								
Sept	.7155	.7169	.7091	.7119	-.0025	.7470	.6185	53,902
Dec	.7122	.7136	.7065	.7090	-.0025	.7432	.6160	4,387
Mr04	.7085	.7095	.7040	.7065	-.0025	.7395	.6150	1,984
Est vol 10,477; vol Tue 13,331; open int 61,784, -2,610.								
British Pound (CME)-£62,500; $ per £								
Sept	1.5850	1.5946	1.5832	1.5926	.0070	1.6800	1.5100	46,791
Dec	1.5746	1.5840	1.5742	1.5824	.0070	1.6690	1.5000	1,045
Est vol 5,887; vol Tue 6,808; open int 47,837, -49.								
Swiss Franc (CME)-CHF 125,000; $ per CHF								
Sept	.7209	.7226	.7178	.7211	.0002	.7842	.6270	54,609
Dec	.7208	.7239	.7197	.7226	.0002	.7835	.6773	1,078
Est vol 9,231; vol Tue 18,195; open int 55,803, +2,307.								

Interest Rate Futures

	OPEN	HIGH	LOW	SETTLE	CHG	LIFETIME HIGH	LOW	OPEN INT
Treasury Bonds (CBT)-$100,000; pts 32nds of 100%								
Sept	107-10	107-28	106-07	106-22	-21	123-03	103-27	482,825
Dec	106-00	106-15	104-28	105-10	-21	121-18	102-14	46,713
Est vol 248,282; vol Tue 280,143; open int 529,972, +1,836.								
Treasury Notes (CBT)-$100,000; pts 32nds of 100%								
Sept	112-01	12-125	11-025	111-12	-20.0	120-14	09-195	894,930
Dec	110-05	10-205	109-11	109-20	-21.0	19-015	107-16	180,603
Est vol 664,529; vol Tue 138,840; open int 1,075,534, +4,516.								
10 Yr. Agency Notes (CBT)-$100,000; pts 32nds of 100%								
Sept	107-29	107-29	107-14	107-21	-21.0	117-06	104-01	3,981
Est vol 32; vol Tue 28; open int 3,981, +24.								
5 Yr. Treasury Notes (CBT)-$100,000; pts 32nds of 100%								
Sept	112-04	12-105	111-17	11-245	-10.5	117-01	10-205	800,655
Est vol 288,898; vol Tue 279,655; open int 839,628, -21,709.								
30 Day Federal Funds (CBT)-$5,000,000; 100 - daily avg.								
Sept	98.995	99.000	98.995	99.000	...	99.220	98.210	46,230
Oct	99.00	99.00	99.00	99.00	...	99.23	98.70	36,185
Nov	99.00	99.00	99.00	99.00	-.01	99.05	98.48	27,412
Dec	98.99	99.00	98.95	98.99	-.01	99.23	98.40	21,469
Ja04	98.98	98.99	98.98	98.98	...	99.24	98.66	38,618
Feb	98.92	98.92	98.91	98.92	-.01	99.22	98.70	30,029
Apr	98.76	98.77	98.76	98.78	-.01	99.17	98.62	12,222
Est vol 15,141; vol Tue 14,106; open int 335,608, +617.								

Index Futures

	OPEN	HIGH	LOW	SETTLE	CHG	LIFETIME HIGH	LOW	OPEN INT
DJ Industrial Average (CBT)-$10 x index								
Sept	9402	9420	9356	9390	-32	9435	7460	41,609
Dec	9370	9390	9330	9357	-32	11490	7675	2,823
Est vol 8,818; vol Tue 19,118; open int 44,457, +676.								
Idx prl: Hi 9423.26; Lo 9364.03; Close 9397.51, -31.39.								
S&P 500 Index (CME)-$250 x index								
Sept	100170	100320	99580	99900	-390	121490	77200	550,998
Dec	99550	100150	99450	99730	-390	122650	77400	58,244
Est vol 43,475; vol Tue 52,717; open int 611,615, +4,343.								
Idx prl: Hi 1003.54; Lo 996.62; Close 1000.30, -2.05.								
S&P Midcap 400 (CME)-$500 x index								
Sept	505.50	508.75	504.00	507.50	...	508.75	377.75	13,286
Est vol 600; vol Tue 568; open int 13,286, +45.								
Idx prl: Hi 508.41; Lo 504.29; Close 507.79, +.41.								
Nasdaq 100 (CME)-$100 x index								
Sept	129900	130900	128900	129950	-300	132000	95250	84,678
Dec	130300	130750	130300	130150	-300	130750	102950	593
Est vol 10,453; vol Tue 14,019; open int 85,272, -355.								
Idx prl: Hi 1307.45; Lo 1288.75; Close 1299.73, +.04.								

a December Japanese yen contract was valued at $106,262.50 (because a quote of 0.8501 cent per yen equals less than a penny per yen, we have 12,500,000 yen × $0.008501).

- *Interest rate futures.* Except for the quotes on Treasury bills and other short-term securities, interest rate futures contracts are priced as a percentage of the par value of the underlying debt instrument (e.g., Treasury notes or bonds). Because these instruments are quoted in increments of 1/32 of 1%, a quote of 107–21 for the settle price of the September 10-year agency note (in Figure 16.3) translates into 107–21/32, which converts to a quote of 107.6563% of par. Apply this rate to the $100,000 par value of the underlying security, and we see that this contract is worth $107,656.30 ($100,000 × 1.076563). *The pricing mechanism for T-bills and other short-term interest rate contracts is discussed at the book's Web site*—see the nearby HotLinks for details.

- *Stock-index futures.* Stock-index futures are quoted in terms of the actual underlying index. But, as noted above, they carry a face value of anywhere from $10 to $500 times the index. Thus, according to the settle price in Figure 16.3, the December S&P 500 contract would be worth $249,325, because the value of this particular contract is equal to $250 times the (settle) price of the index (997.30 × $250). On the other hand, the value of the September DJIA contract is 9390 × $10 = $93,900.

The value of an interest rate futures contract responds to interest rates exactly as the debt instrument that underlies the contract. That is, when interest rates go up, the value of an interest rate futures contract goes down, and vice versa. The quote system used for interest rate as well as currency and stock-index futures is set up to reflect the *market value of the contract* itself. Thus, when the price or quote of a financial futures contract increases (for example, when interest rates fall or a stock-index goes up), then the investor who is long makes money. In contrast, when the price decreases, the short seller makes money.

H O T

For information on the pricing of futures on Treasury bills and other short-term securities, visit the book's Web site at:

www.aw-bc.com/gitman_joehnk

Price behavior is the only source of return to speculators. Even though stocks and debt securities are involved in some financial futures, such contracts have no claim on the dividend and interest income of the underlying issues. Even so, huge profits (or losses) are possible with financial futures because of the equally large size of the contracts. For instance, if the price of Swiss francs goes up by just 2 cents against the dollar, the investor is ahead $2,500. Likewise, a 3-point drop in the NYSE Composite Index means a $1,500 loss to an investor (3 × $500). When related to the relatively small initial margin deposit required to make transactions in the financial futures markets, such price activity can mean very high rates of return—or very high risk of a total wipeout.

Trading Techniques

Like commodities, financial futures can be used for hedging, spreading, and speculating. Multinational companies and firms that are active in international trade might consider *hedging* with currency or Euromarket futures. Various financial institutions and corporate money managers often use interest rate futures for hedging purposes. In either case, the objective is the same: to lock in the best monetary exchange or interest rate possible. In addition, individual investors and portfolio managers often hedge with stock-index futures as a way to protect their security holdings against temporary market declines. Financial futures can also be used for *spreading*. This tactic is popular with investors who simultaneously buy and sell combinations of two or more contracts to form a desired investment position. Finally, financial futures are widely used for *speculation*.

Although investors can employ any one of the three trading strategies noted above, we will focus primarily on the use of financial futures by speculators and hedgers. We will first examine speculating in currency and interest rate futures. Then we'll look at how these contracts can be used to hedge investments in stocks, bonds, and foreign securities.

Speculating in Financial Futures Speculators are especially interested in financial futures because of the size of the contracts. For instance, in mid-2003, Canadian dollar contracts were worth over $71,000, Treasury notes and bonds were going for around $110,000, and 30-day federal funds contracts were being quoted at more than $4.9 million each. With contracts of this size, it obviously doesn't take much movement in the underlying asset to produce big price swings—and therefore big profits.

Currency and interest rate futures are popular with investors, and can be used for just about any speculative purpose. For example, if you expect the dollar to be devalued relative to the euro, you could buy euro currency futures, because the contracts should go up in value. Or, if you anticipate a rise in interest rates, you might "go short" (sell) interest rate futures, because they should go down in value. Because margin is used and financial futures have the same source of return as commodities (price appreciation), return on invested capital (Equation 16.1) is also used to measure the profitability of these contracts.

 Going Long a Foreign Currency Contract Suppose you believe that the Swiss franc (CHF) is about to appreciate in value relative to the dollar. You decide to go long (buy) three September CHF contracts at 0.7055—i.e., at a quote of just over 70 cents a franc. Each contract would be worth $88,187.50 (125,000 CHF × 0.7055), so the total underlying value of the three contracts would be $264,562.50. Even so, given an initial margin requirement of, say, $2,500 per contract, you would have to deposit only $7,500 to acquire this position. Now, if Swiss francs move up just a few pennies, say, from 0.7055 to 0.75 (75 cents a franc), the value of the three contracts will rise to $281,250, and in a matter of months, you will have made a profit of $16,687.50. Using Equation 16.1 for return on invested capital, we find that such a profit translates into an unbelievable 222% rate of return. Of course, an even smaller fractional change in the other direction would have wiped out this investment, so it should be clear that these *high returns are not without equally high risk.*

Going Short an Interest Rate Contract Let's assume that you're anticipating a sharp rise in long-term rates. A rise in rates translates into a drop in the value of interest rate futures. So you decide to short sell two June T-bond contracts at 115-00, which means that the contracts are trading at 115% of par. Thus the two contracts are worth $230,000 ($100,000 × 1.15 × 2). The amount of money required to make the investment is only $6,000 (the initial margin deposit is $3,000 per contract). Assume that interest rates do, in fact, move up. As a result, the price on Treasury bond contracts drops to 106-16 (or 106½). Under such circumstances, you would buy back the two June T-bond contracts (in order to cover the short position) and in the process make a profit of $17,000. (You originally sold the two contracts at $230,000 and bought them back sometime later at $213,000. As with any investment, such a difference between what you pay for a security and what you sell it for is profit.) In this case, the return on invested capital amounts to 283%. Again, however, this kind of return is due in no small part to the *enormous risk of loss* you assumed.

Trading Stock-Index Futures Most investors use stock-index futures for speculation or hedging. (Stock-index futures are similar to the *index options* introduced in Chapter 15. Therefore, much of the discussion that follows also applies to index options.) Whether speculating or hedging, the key to success is *predicting the future course of the stock market*. Because you are "buying the market" with stock-index futures, it is important to get a handle on the future direction of the market via technical analysis (as discussed in Chapter 9) or some other technique. Once you have a feel for the market's direction, you can formulate a stock-index futures trading or hedging strategy. For example, if you feel that the market is headed up, you would want to go long (buy stock-index futures). In contrast, if your analysis suggests a sharp drop in equity values, you could make money by going short (selling stock-index futures).

Assume, for instance, that you believe the market is undervalued and a move up is imminent. You can try to identify one or a handful of stocks that should go up with the market (and assume the stock selection risks that go along with this approach). Or you can buy an S&P 500 stock-index futures contract currently trading at, say, 1,074.45. To execute this speculative transaction, you would need to deposit an initial margin of $17,800. Now, if the market does rise so that the S&P 500 Index moves to, say, 1,122.85 by the expiration of the futures contract, you earn a profit of $12,100—that is, $(1,122.85 - 1,074.45) \times \$250 = \$12,100$. Given the $17,800 investment, your return on invested capital would amount to a hefty 68%. Of course, keep in mind that if the market drops by some 90 points (or less than 6 percent), the investment will be a *total loss*.

Hedging with Stock-Index Futures Stock-index futures also make excellent hedging vehicles. They provide investors with a highly effective way of protecting stock holdings in a declining market. Although this tactic is not perfect, it does enable investors to obtain desired protection against a decline in market value without disturbing their equity holdings. Here's how a so-called *short hedge* would work: Assume that you hold a total of 2,000 shares of stock in a dozen different companies and that the market value of this portfolio is around $235,000. If you think the market is about to undergo a temporary sharp decline, you can do one of two things: sell all of your shares or buy puts on each of the stocks. Clearly, these alternatives are cumbersome and/or costly and therefore undesirable for protecting a widely diversified portfolio. The desired results could also be achieved, however, by *short selling stock-index futures*. (Basically the same protection can be obtained in this hedging situation by turning to options and buying *stock-index puts*.)

Suppose for purposes of our illustration that you short sell one NYSE stock-index futures contract at 468.75. Such a contract would provide a close match to the current value of your portfolio (it would be valued at 468.75 × $500 = $234,375), and yet the stock-index futures contract would require an initial margin deposit of only $3,500. (Margin deposits are lower for hedgers than for speculators.) Now, if the NYSE Composite Index drops to 448.00, you will make a profit from the short-sale of some $10,000. That is, because the index fell 20.75 points (468.75 − 448.00), the total profit will be $10,375 (20.75 × $500). Ignoring taxes, this profit can then be added to the portfolio (additional shares of stock can be purchased at their new lower prices). The net result will be a new portfolio position that will approximate the one that existed prior to the decline in the market.

How well the "before" and "after" portfolio positions match will depend on how far the portfolio dropped in value. If the average price dropped about $5 per share in our example, the positions will closely match. But this does not always happen. The price of some stocks will change more than others, so the amount of protection provided by this type of short hedge depends on how sensitive the stock portfolio is to movements in the market. Thus, the types of stocks that are held in the portfolio are an important consideration in structuring a stock-index short hedge.

A key to success with this kind of hedging is to make sure that the characteristics of the hedging vehicle (the futures contract) closely match those of the portfolio (or security position) being protected. Thus, if the portfolio is made up mostly (or exclusively) of large-cap stocks, use something like the S&P 500 Stock Index futures contract as the hedging vehicle. If the portfolio is mostly blue-chip stocks, use the DJIA contract. And if the portfolio holds mostly tech stocks, consider the Nasdaq 100 Index contract. Again, the point is to pick a hedging vehicle that closely reflects the types of securities you want to protect. For the investor who keeps that caveat in mind, hedging with stock-index futures can be a low-cost yet effective way of obtaining protection against loss in a declining stock market.

Hedging Other Securities Just as stock-index futures can be used to hedge stock portfolios, *interest rate futures* can be used to hedge bond portfolios. Or, *foreign currency futures* can be used with foreign securities as a way to protect against foreign exchange risk. *Let's consider an interest rate hedge:* If you held a substantial portfolio of bonds, the last thing you would want to see is a big jump in interest rates, which could cause a sharp decline in the value of your portfolio. Assume you hold around $300,000 worth of Treasury and agency issues, with an average (approximate) maturity of about 18 years. If you believe that market rates are headed up, you can hedge your bond portfolio by short selling three U.S. Treasury bond futures contracts. (Each T-bond futures contract is worth about $100,000, so it would take three of them to cover a $300,000 portfolio.) Now, if rates do head up, the portfolio will be protected against loss. As we noted with stocks above, the exact amount of protection will depend on how well the T-bond futures contracts parallel the price behavior of your particular bond portfolio.

There is, of course, a downside: *If market interest rates go down, rather than up, you will miss out on potential profits as long as the short hedge position remains in place.* This is so because the profits being made in the portfolio will be offset by losses from the futures contracts. Actually, this will occur with any type of portfolio (stocks, bonds, or anything else) that's tied to an offsetting short hedge, because when you create the short hedge you essentially lock in a position at that point. Although you don't lose anything when the market falls, you also don't make anything when the market goes up. In either case, the profits you make from one position are offset by losses from the other.

Hedging Foreign Currency Exposure   Now let's see how futures contracts can be used to hedge foreign exchange risk. Let's assume that you have just purchased $200,000 worth of British government 1-year notes. (You did this because higher yields were available on the British notes than on comparable U.S. Treasury securities.) Because these notes are denominated in pounds, this investment is subject to loss if currency exchange rates move against you (i.e., if the value of the dollar rises relative to the pound). If all you wanted was the higher yield offered by the British note, you could eliminate most of the currency exchange risk by setting up a currency hedge. Here's how: Let's say that at the current exchange rate, one U.S. dollar will "buy" 0.60 pound. This means that pounds are worth about $1.65 (i.e., $1.00/0.60£ = $1.65). Now, if currency contracts on British pounds were trading at around $1.65 a pound, you would have to *sell* two contracts to protect the $200,000 investment. Each contract covers 62,500 pounds, so if they're being quoted at 1.65, then each contract is worth $1.65 × 62,500 = $103,125.

Assume that 1 year later, the value of the dollar has increased, relative to the pound, so that one U.S. dollar will now "buy" 0.65 pound. Under such conditions, a British pound futures contract would be quoted at around 1.54 (i.e., $1.00/.065£ = $1.54). At this price, each futures contract would be worth $96,250 (62,500 × $1.54). Each contract, in effect, would be worth $6,875 less than it was a year ago. But because the contract was sold short when the hedge was set up, you will make a profit of $6,875 per contract—for a total profit of $13,750 on the two contracts. Unfortunately, that's not *net profit,* because this profit will offset the loss you will incur on the British note investment. In very simple terms, when you sent $200,000 overseas to buy the British notes, the money was worth about £121,000. However, when you brought the money back a year later, those 121,000 pounds purchased only about 186,500 U.S. dollars. Thus, you are out some $13,500 on your original investment. Were it not for the currency hedge, you'd be out the full $13,500, and the return on this investment would be a lot lower. But the hedge covered the loss (plus a little extra to boot), and the net effect was that you were able to enjoy the added yield of the British note without having to worry about any potential loss from currency exchange rates.

Financial Futures and the Individual Investor

Like commodities, financial futures can play an important role in your portfolio so long as three factors apply: (1) You thoroughly understand these investment vehicles. (2) You clearly recognize the tremendous risk exposure of these vehicles. And (3) you are fully prepared (financially and emotionally) to absorb some losses. Financial futures are highly volatile securities that have enormous potential for profit and for loss. For instance, in the year 2003, during a 6-month period of time, the December S&P 500 futures contract fluctuated in price from a low of 774.0 to a high of 1,226.5. This range of over 450 points for a single contract translates into a *potential* profit—or loss—of some $113,000, and all from an initial investment of only $17,800. Investment diversification is obviously essential as a means of reducing the potentially devastating impact of price volatility. Financial futures are exotic investment vehicles, but if properly used, they can provide generous returns.

H O T

For information on commodity trading, pools, and advisers, visit the CFTC page at:

www.cftc.gov/opa/brochures/opafutures.htm

Options on Futures

The evolution that began with listed stock options and financial futures spread, over time, to interest rate options and stock-index futures. Eventually, it led to the merger of options and futures and to the creation of the ultimate leverage vehicle: *options on futures contracts*. **Futures options,** as they are called, represent listed puts and calls on actively traded futures contracts. In essence, they give the holders the right to buy (with calls) or sell (with puts) a single standardized futures contract for a specific period of time at a specified strike price. Table 16.4 lists many of the actively traded futures options available in 2003. Such options are available on both commodities and financial futures. For the most part, these puts and calls cover the same amount of assets as the underlying futures contracts—for example, 112,000 pounds of sugar, 100 ounces of gold, 62,500 British pounds, or $100,000 in Treasury bonds. Thus, they also involve the same amount of price activity as is normally found with commodities and financial futures.

futures options
options that give the holders the right to buy or sell a single standardized futures contract for a specified period of time at a specified strike price.

Futures options have the same standardized strike prices, expiration dates, and quotation system as other listed options. Depending on the strike price on the option and the market value of the underlying futures contract, these options can also be in the money or out of the money. Futures options are valued like other puts and calls—by the difference between the option's strike price and the market price of the underlying futures contract (see Chapter 15).

TABLE 16.4   **Futures Options: Puts and Calls on Futures Contracts**

Commodities			
Corn	Pork bellies	Sugar	Gold
Soybeans	Lean hogs	Wheat	Silver
Soybean meal	Feeder cattle	Oats	Crude oil
Soybean oil	Orange juice	Rice	Natural gas
Cotton	Cocoa	Platinum	Heating oil
Live cattle	Coffee	Copper	Gasoline

Financial Futures	
British pound	Treasury notes
Euro	Treasury bonds
Swiss franc	Agency notes
Japanese yen	Muni bond index
Canadian dollar	German government bonds
Mexican peso	NYSE Composite Index
U.S. dollar index	S&P 500 Stock Index
Eurodollar deposits	Dow Jones Industrial Average
Treasury bills	Nasdaq 100 Index

Moreover, they can also be used like any other listed option—for speculating or hedging, in options writing programs, or for spreading. The biggest difference between a futures option and a futures contract is that *the option limits the loss exposure* to the price of the option. The most you can lose is the price paid for the put or call option. With the futures contract, there is no real limit to the amount of loss an investor can incur.

At the Web site of the Chicago Mercantile Exchange, go to [Educational Resources], [CME Education Center], [Online Interactive Features], [Web Instant Lessons], and read the Web Instant Lesson 12, "Options on Futures."

www.cme.com

To see how futures options work, assume that you want to trade some gold contracts. You believe that the price of gold will increase over the next 4 or 5 months, from its present level of $285 an ounce to around $330 an ounce. You can buy a futures contract at 288.10 by depositing the required initial margin of $2,025. Alternatively, you can buy a futures call option with a $280 strike price that is currently being quoted at 10.90. (Because the underlying futures contract covers 100 ounces of gold, the total cost of this option would be $10.90 × 100 = $1,090.) The call is an in-the-money option, because the market price of gold exceeds the exercise price on the option. The figures below summarize what happens to both investments if the price of gold increases by $45 an ounce by the expiration date and also what happens if the price of gold drops by $45 an ounce.

	Futures Contract		Futures Option	
	Dollar Profit (or Loss)	Return on Invested Capital	Dollar Profit (or Loss)	Return on Invested Capital
If price of gold *increases* by $45 an ounce	$4,190	206.9%	$3,910	358.7%
If price of gold *decreases* by $45 an ounce	($4,810)	—	($1,090)	—

Clearly, the futures option provides not only a competitive rate of return (in this case, it's a lot higher), but also a reduced exposure to loss. Futures options offer interesting investment opportunities. But as always, *they should be used only by knowledgeable commodities and financial futures investors.*

IN REVIEW

CONCEPTS

16.10 What is the difference between physical *commodities* and *financial futures?* What are their similarities?

16.11 Describe a *currency future* and contrast it with an *interest rate future.* What is a *stock-index future,* and how can it be used by investors?

16.12 Discuss how stock-index futures can be used for speculation and for hedging. What advantages are there to speculating with stock-index futures rather than specific issues of common stock?

16.13 What are *futures options?* Explain how they can be used by speculators. Why would an investor want to use an option on an interest rate futures contract rather than the futures contract itself?

Summary

LG 1   **Describe the essential features of a futures contract, and explain how the futures market operates.** Commodities and financial futures are traded in futures markets. Today, there are eight U.S. exchanges that deal in futures contracts, which are commitments to make (or take) delivery of a certain amount of some real or financial asset at a specified date in the future.

LG 2   **Explain the role that hedgers and speculators play in the futures market, including how profits are made and lost.** Futures contracts control large amounts of the underlying commodity or financial instrument. They can produce wide price swings and very attractive rates of return (or very unattractive losses). Such returns (or losses) are further magnified because all trading in the futures market is done on margin. A speculator's profit is derived directly from the wide price fluctuations that occur in the market. Hedgers derive their profit from the protection they gain against adverse price movements.

LG 3   **Describe the commodities segment of the futures market and the basic characteristics of these investment vehicles.** Commodities such as grains, metals, and meat make up the traditional (commodities) segment of the futures market. A large portion of this market is concentrated in the agricultural segment of our economy. There's also a very active market for various metals and petroleum products. As the prices of commodities go up and down in the market, the respective futures contracts behave in much the same way. Thus, if the price of corn goes up, the value of corn futures contracts rises as well.

LG 4   **Discuss the trading strategies that investors can use with commodities, and explain how investment returns are measured.** The trading strategies used with commodities contracts are speculating, spreading, and hedging. Regardless of whether investors are in a long or a short position, they have only one source of return from commodities and financial futures: appreciation (or depreciation) in the price of the contract. Rate of return on invested capital is used to assess the actual or potential profitability of a futures transaction.

LG 5   **Explain the difference between a physical commodity and a financial future, and discuss the growing role of financial futures in the market today.** Whereas commodities deal with physical assets, financial futures deal with financial assets, such as stocks, bonds, and currencies. Though the nature of the underlying assets differs, both are traded in the same place: the futures market. Financial futures are the newcomers, but the volume of trading in financial futures now far exceeds that of commodities.

LG 6   **Discuss the trading techniques that can be used with financial futures, and note how these securities can be used in conjunction with other investment vehicles.** There are three major types of financial futures: currency futures, interest rate futures, and stock-index futures. (There are also single-stock financial futures, but the jury's still out on them.) The first type deals in different kinds of foreign currencies. Interest rate futures involve various types of short- and long-term debt instruments. Stock-index futures are pegged to broad movements in the stock market, as measured by such indexes as the S&P 500 and the NYSE Composite Index. These securities can be used for speculating, spreading, or hedging. They hold a special appeal to investors who use them to hedge other security positions. For example, interest rate futures contracts are used to protect bond portfolios against a big jump in market interest rates. Likewise, currency futures are used to hedge the foreign currency exposure that accompanies investments in foreign securities.

Putting Your Investment Know-How to the Test

1. On the maturity date, stock index futures contracts require delivery of
   a. Common stock.
   b. Common stock plus accrued dividends.
   c. Treasury bills.
   d. Cash.

2. In futures trading, the minimum level to which an equity position may fall before requiring additional margin is the
   a. Initial margin.
   b. Variation margin.
   c. Cash flow margin.
   d. Maintenance margin.

3. Most futures contracts are closed through
   a. Delivery.
   b. Arbitrage.
   c. Reversing trades.
   d. Exchange-for-physicals.

4. An investor who takes a long position in a futures contract of one maturity and a short position in a contract of a different maturity but on the same commodity is engaging in
   a. An arbitrage.
   b. A cross position.
   c. A spread position.
   d. A swap.

5. Which of the following statements regarding the margin on a futures contract is *false*?
   a. An investor may withdraw the excess margin in the account if it is above the initial margin.
   b. The gains and losses from the futures position are added and subtracted each day from the margin account.
   c. If the investor's margin falls below the maintenance margin level, the investor must make a deposit and bring it back to the initial margin level.
   d. The variation margin is the amount that is added to or subtracted from the margin account each day as the value of the futures contract changes.

6. Sarah Jones buys one contract of May corn at $2.50 per bushel. The contract size is 5,000 bushels. The initial margin requirement was $2,000 and the maintenance margin level is 75% of the initial margin. At what price will Sarah receive a margin call?
   a. $2.00
   b. $2.30
   c. $2.40
   d. $2.60

7. An investor who wants to take advantage of an expected fall in interest rates should
   a. Buy S&P 500 index futures.
   b. Sell Treasury bond futures.
   c. Take a long position in Treasury bond futures.
   d. Buy gold futures options.

8. On January 1, Ken Jones sold one April S&P 500 index futures contract at a price of 500. If the April futures price is 480 on February 1, what would Ken's profit be when he closes his position?
   a. $5,000
   b. $10,000
   c. $15,000
   d. $20,000

9. If the S&P 500 index futures contract is overpriced relative to the spot (actual) S&P 500 index, a money manager should
   a. Buy all the stocks in the S&P 500 and write put options on the S&P.
   b. Sell all the stock in the S&P 500 and buy call options on the S&P 500 index.
   c. Sell S&P 500 index futures and buy all the stocks in the S&P 500.
   d. Sell short all the stock in the S&P 500 and buy S&P 500 index futures.

10. Which of the following are *not* financial futures contracts?
    a. Dow Jones Industrial Average.
    b. New York Stock Exchange Composite index.
    c. S&P 500 index.
    d. Nasdaq Composite index.

Answers: 1. d; 2. d; 3. c; 4. c; 5. d; 6. c; 7. c; 8. b; 9. c; 10. d

Discussion Questions

LG 1

Q16.1 Three of the biggest U.S. commodities exchanges—the CBT, CME, and NYMerc—were identified in this chapter. Other U.S. exchanges and several foreign commodities exchanges are also closely followed in the United States. Obtain a recent copy of the *Wall Street Journal* and look in the "Futures Prices" section of the paper for the futures quotes. As noted in this chapter, futures quotes include the name of the exchange on which a particular contract is traded.
   a. Using these quotes, how many more U.S. *commodities exchanges* can you identify? List them.
   b. Are quotes from *foreign exchanges* listed in the *Wall Street Journal?* If so, list them, too.
   c. For each U.S. and foreign exchange you found in parts **a** and **b**, give an example of one or two contracts traded on that exchange. For example: CBT—Chicago Board of Trade: oats and Treasury bonds.

LG 3 **LG 5**

Q16.2 Using settle prices from Figures 16.2 and 16.3, find the value of the following commodities and financial futures contracts.
   a. October soybean oil.
   b. May 2004 corn.
   c. September heating oil.
   d. December British pounds.
   e. September Treasury notes.
   f. September S&P 500 Index.

LG 4 **LG 6**

Q16.3 Listed below are a variety of futures transactions. On the basis of the information provided, indicate how much profit or loss you would make in each of the transactions. (*Hint:* You might want to refer to Figures 16.2 and 16.3 for the size of the contract, pricing unit, and so on.)
   a. You buy three yen contracts at a quote of 1.0180 and sell them a few months later at 1.0365.
   b. The price of wheat goes up 60 cents a bushel, and you hold three contracts.
   c. You short sell two crude oil contracts at $28.75 a barrel, and the price of crude oil drops to $24.10 a barrel.
   d. You recently purchased a Swiss franc contract at 0.7272, and 6 weeks later the contract is trading at 0.685.
   e. You short sell S&P 500 contracts when the index is at 996.55 and cover when the index moves to 971.95.
   f. You short three corn contracts at $2.34 a bushel, and the price of corn goes to $2.49½ a bushel.

Problems

LG 3

LG 4

P16.1 Jeff Rink considers himself a shrewd commodities investor. Not long ago he bought one July cotton contract at 54 cents a pound, and he recently sold it at 58 cents a pound. How much profit did he make? What was his return on invested capital if he had to put up a $1,500 initial deposit?

LG 3   LG 4

P16.2 You just heard a news story about mad cow disease in a neighboring country, and you believe that feeder cattle prices will rise dramatically in the next few months as buyers of cattle shift to U.S. suppliers. Of course, someone else believes that prices will fall in the next few months because people will be afraid to eat beef. You go to the CME and find out that feeder cattle futures for delivery in April are currently quoted at 88.8. The contract size is 50,000 lb. What is the market value of one contract?

LG 3   LG 4

P16.3 You decide to act on your hunches about feeder cattle, so you purchase four contracts for April delivery at 88.8. You are required to put down 10%. How much equity/capital did you need to make this transaction?

LG 3   LG 4

P16.4 As it turns out, you were correct when you purchased four contracts for feeder cattle at 88.8, and the spot price of cattle is 101.2 on the delivery date given in your contracts. How much money did you make? What was your return on invested capital?

LG 4

P16.5 Julie McCain is a regular commodities speculator. She is currently considering a short position in July oats, which are now trading at 148. Her analysis suggests that July oats should be trading at about 140 in a couple of months. Assuming that her expectations hold up, what kind of return on invested capital will she make if she shorts three July oats contracts (each contract covers 5,000 bushels of oats) by depositing an initial margin of $500 per contract?

LG 5   LG 6

P16.6 You were just notified that you will receive $100,000 in two months from the estate of a deceased relative. You want to invest this money in safe, interest-bearing instruments, so you decide to purchase 5-year Treasury notes. You believe, however, that interest rates are headed down, and you will have to pay a lot more in 2 months than you would today for 5-year Treasury notes. You decide to look into futures, and find a quote of 111–08.5 for 5-year Treasuries deliverable in two months. What does the quote mean in terms of price, and how many contracts will you need to buy? How much money will you need to buy the contract, and how much will you need to settle the contract?

LG 5   LG 6

P16.7 Mark Seby is thinking about doing some speculating in interest rates. He thinks rates will fall and, in response, the price of Treasury bond futures should move from 92–15, their present quote, to a level of about 98. Given a required margin deposit of $3,000 per contract, what would Mark's return on invested capital be if prices behave as he expects?

LG 5   LG 6

P16.8 Annie Ryan has been an avid stock market investor for years. She manages her portfolio fairly aggressively and likes to short sell whenever the opportunity presents itself. Recently, she has become fascinated with stock-index futures, especially the idea of being able to play the market as a whole. Annie thinks the market is headed down, and she decides to short sell some NYSE Composite stock-index futures. Assume she shorts three contracts at 787.95 and has to make a margin deposit of $16,000 for each contract. How much profit will she make, and what will her return on invested capital be if the market does indeed drop so that the NYSE contracts are trading at 765.00 by the time they expire?

LG 6 **P16.9** A wealthy investor holds $500,000 worth of U.S. Treasury bonds. These bonds are currently being quoted at 105% of par. The investor is concerned, however, that rates are headed up over the next 6 months, and he would like to do something to protect this bond portfolio. His broker advises him to set up a hedge using T-bond futures contracts. Assume these contracts are now trading at 111–06.

a. Briefly describe how the investor would set up this hedge. Would he go long or short? How many contracts would he need?

b. It's now 6 months later, and rates have indeed gone up. The investor's Treasury bonds are now being quoted at $93^1/_2$, and the T-bond futures contracts used in the hedge are now trading at 98–00. Show what has happened to the value of the bond portfolio and the profit (or loss) made on the futures hedge.

c. Was this a successful hedge? Explain.

LG 6 **P16.10** Not long ago, Vanessa Woods sold her company for several million dollars (after taxes). She took some of that money and put it into the stock market. Today, Vanessa's portfolio of blue-chip stocks is worth $3.8 million. Vanessa wants to keep her portfolio intact, but she's concerned about a developing weakness in the market for blue chips. She decides, therefore, to hedge her position with 6-month futures contracts on the Dow Jones Industrial Average (DJIA), which are currently trading at 10,960.

a. Why would she choose to hedge her portfolio with the DJIA rather than the S&P 500?

b. Given that Vanessa wants to cover the full $3.8 million in her portfolio, describe how she would go about setting up this hedge.

c. If each contract required a margin deposit of $5,000, how much money would she need to set up this hedge?

d. Assume that over the next 6 months stock prices do fall, and the value of Vanessa's portfolio drops to $3.3 million. If DJIA futures contracts are trading at 9,400, how much will she make (or lose) on the futures hedge? Is it enough to offset the loss in her portfolio? That is, what is her net profit or loss on the hedge?

e. Will she now get her margin deposit back, or is that a "sunk cost"—gone forever?

LG 5 **LG 6** **P16.11** A quote for a futures contract for British pounds is 1.6683. The contract size for British pounds is 62,500. What is the dollar equivalent of this contract?

LG 5 **P16.12** You have purchased a futures contract for euros. The contract is for 125,000 euros, and the quote was 1.1636. On the delivery date, the exchange quote is 1.1050. Assuming you took delivery of the euros, how many dollars would you have after converting back to dollars? What is your profit or loss (before commissions)?

LG 4 **P16.13** An American currency speculator feels strongly that the value of the Canadian dollar is going to fall relative to the U.S. dollar over the short run. If he wants to profit from these expectations, what kind of position (long or short) should he take in Canadian dollar futures contracts? How much money would he make from each contract if Canadian dollar futures contracts moved from an initial quote of 0.6775 to an ending quote of 0.6250?

LG 6 **P16.14** With regard to futures options, how much profit would an investor make if she bought a call option on gold at 7.20 when gold was trading at $482 an ounce, given that the price of gold went up to $525 an ounce by the expiration date on the call? (*Note:* Assume the call carried a strike price of 480.)

**See the text Web site
(www.aw-bc.com/gitman_joehnk) for Web exercises
that deal with *commodities and financial futures*.**

Case Problem 16.1   *T. J.'s Fast-Track Investments: Interest Rate Futures*

T. J. Patrick is a young, successful industrial designer in Portland, Oregon, who enjoys the excitement of commodities speculation. T. J. has been dabbling in commodities since he was a teenager—he was introduced to this market by his dad, who is a grain buyer for one of the leading food processors. T. J. recognizes the enormous risks involved in commodities speculating but feels that because he's young, he can afford to take a few chances. As a principal in a thriving industrial design firm, T. J. earns more than $100,000 a year. He follows a well-disciplined investment program and annually adds $15,000 to $20,000 to his portfolio.

Recently, T. J. has started playing with financial futures—interest rate futures, to be exact. He admits he is no expert in interest rates, but he likes the price action these investment vehicles offer. This all started several months ago, when T. J. met Vinnie Banano, a broker who specializes in financial futures, at a party. T. J. liked what Vinnie had to say (mostly how you couldn't go wrong with interest-rate futures) and soon set up a trading account with Vinnie's firm, Banano's of Portland.

The other day, Vinnie called T. J. and suggested he get into 5-year Treasury note futures. He reasoned that with the Fed pushing up interest rates so aggressively, the short to intermediate sectors of the term structure would probably respond the most—with the biggest jump in yields. Accordingly, Vinnie recommended that T. J. short sell some 5-year T-note contracts. In particular, Vinnie thinks that rates on these T-notes should go up by a full point (moving from about 5½% to around 6½%), and that T. J. should short four contracts. This would be a $4,000 investment, because each contract requires an initial margin deposit of $1,000.

Questions

a. Assume T-note futures are now being quoted at 103–16.
   1. Determine the current underlying value of this T-note futures contract.
   2. What would this futures contract be quoted at if Vinnie is right and the yield does go up by 1 percentage point, to 6½%, on the date of expiration? (*Hint:* It'll be quoted at the same price as its underlying security, which in this case is *assumed to be a 5-year, 6% semiannual-pay U.S. Treasury note*. If necessary, refer back to Chapter 11 and review the material on pricing semiannual-pay bonds.)

b. How much profit will T. J. make if he shorts four contracts at 103–16 and then covers when 5-year T-note contracts are quoted at 98–00? Also, calculate the return on invested capital from this transaction.

c. What happens if rates go down? For example, how much will T. J. make if the yield on T-note futures goes down by just ¾ of 1%, in which case these contracts would be trading at 105–8?

d. What risks do you see in the recommended short-sale transaction? What is your assessment of T. J.'s new interest in financial futures? How do you think it compares to his established commodities investment program?

Case Problem 16.2   *Jim and Polly Pernelli Try Hedging with Stock-Index Futures*

LG 5   **LG 6**

Jim Pernelli and his wife, Polly, live in Augusta, Georgia. Like many young couples, the Pernellis are a two-income family. Jim and Polly are both college graduates and hold high-paying jobs. Jim has been an avid investor in the stock market for a number of years and over time has built up a portfolio that is currently worth nearly $275,000. The Pernellis' portfolio is well diversified, although it is heavily weighted in high-quality, mid-cap growth stocks. The Pernellis reinvest all dividends and regularly add investment capital to their portfolio. Up to now, they have avoided short selling and do only a modest amount of margin trading.

Their portfolio has undergone a substantial amount of capital appreciation in the last 18 months or so, and Jim is eager to protect the profit they have earned. And that's the problem: Jim feels the market has pretty much run its course and is about to enter a period of decline. He has studied the market and economic news very carefully and does not believe the retreat will cover an especially long period of time. He feels fairly certain, however, that most, if not all, of the stocks in his portfolio will be adversely affected by these market conditions—though some will drop more in price than others.

Jim has been following stock-index futures for some time and believes he knows the ins and outs of these securities pretty well. After careful deliberation, Jim and Polly decide to use stock-index futures—in particular, the S&P MidCap 400 futures contract—as a way to protect (hedge) their portfolio of common stocks.

Questions

a. Explain why the Pernellis would want to use stock-index futures to hedge their stock portfolio, and how they would go about setting up such a hedge. Be specific.
   1. What alternatives do Jim and Polly have to protect the capital value of their portfolio?
   2. What are the benefits and risks of using stock-index futures as hedging vehicles?

b. Assume that S&P MidCap 400 futures contracts are currently being quoted at 525.60. How many contracts would the Pernellis have to buy (or sell) to set up the hedge?
   1. Say the value of the Pernelli portfolio dropped 12% over the course of the market retreat. To what price must the stock-index futures contract move in order to cover that loss?
   2. Given that a $12,500 margin deposit is required to buy or sell a single S&P 400 futures contract, what would be the Pernellis' return on invested capital if the price of the futures contract changed by the amount computed in part **b1**, above?

c. Assume that the value of the Pernelli portfolio declined by $52,000, while the price of an S&P 400 futures contract moved from 525.60 to 447.60. (Assume that Jim and Polly short sold one futures contract to set up the hedge.)
   1. Add the profit from the hedge transaction to the new (depreciated) value of the stock portfolio. How does this amount compare to the $275,000 portfolio that existed just before the market started its retreat?

2. Why did the stock-index futures hedge fail to give complete protection to the Pernelli portfolio? Is it possible to obtain *perfect* (dollar-for-dollar) protection from these types of hedges? Explain.

d.   What if, instead of hedging with futures contracts, the Pernellis decide to set up the hedge by using *futures options?* Fortunately, such options are available on the S&P MidCap 400 Index. These futures options, like their underlying futures contracts, are also valued/priced at $500 times the underlying S&P 400 Index. Now, suppose a put on the S&P MidCap 400 futures contract (with a strike price of 525) is currently quoted at 5.80, and a comparable call is quoted at 2.35. Use the same portfolio and futures price conditions as set out in part **c** to determine how well the portfolio would be protected if these futures *options* were used as the hedge vehicle. (*Hint:* Add the net profit from the hedge to the new depreciated value of the stock portfolio.) What are the advantages and disadvantages of using futures options, rather than the stock-index futures contract itself, to hedge a stock portfolio?

Excel with Spreadsheets

One of the unique features of futures contracts is that they have only one source of return—the capital gains that can accrue when price movements have an upward bias. Remember that there are no current cash flows associated with this financial asset. These instruments are known for their volatility due to swings in prices and the use of leverage upon purchase. With futures trading done on margin, small amounts of capital are needed to control relatively large investment positions.

Assume that you are interested in investing in commodity futures—specifically, Oats Futures Contracts. Refer to Figure 16.2, *Quotations on Actively Traded Commodity Futures Contracts.* Find the section that reads **"OATS (CBT) 5000 bu.; cents per bushel."** Suppose you had purchased five December oats contracts at the settle price of 143.25. The required amount of investor capital to be deposited with a broker at the time of the initial transaction is 5.35% of a contract's value. Create a spreadsheet to model and answer the following questions concerning the investment in futures contracts.

Questions

a.   What is the total amount of your initial deposit for the five contracts?
b.   What is the total amount of bushels of oats that you control?
c.   What is the purchase price of the oats commodity contracts you control according to the December settlement date?
d.   Assume that the December oats actually settles at 143.25; you decide to sell and take your profit. What is the selling price of the oats commodity contracts?
e.   Calculate the return on invested capital earned on this transaction (remember that the return is based on the amount of funds actually invested in the contract, rather than on the value of the contract itself).

APPENDIX A

FINANCIAL TABLES

TABLE A.1
**FUTURE-VALUE
INTEREST FACTORS FOR
ONE DOLLAR, *FVIF***

TABLE A.2
**FUTURE-VALUE
INTEREST FACTORS FOR
A ONE-DOLLAR ANNUITY,
*FVIFA***

TABLE A.3
**PRESENT-VALUE
INTEREST FACTORS FOR
ONE DOLLAR, *PVIF***

TABLE A.4
**PRESENT-VALUE
INTEREST FACTORS FOR
A ONE-DOLLAR ANNUITY,
*PVIFA***

TABLE A.1   Future-Value Interest Factors for One Dollar, *FVIF*

Period	1%	2%	3%	4%	5%	6%	7%	8%	9%	10%	11%	12%	13%	14%	15%	16%	17%	18%	19%	20%
1	1.010	1.020	1.030	1.040	1.050	1.060	1.070	1.080	1.090	1.100	1.110	1.120	1.130	1.140	1.150	1.160	1.170	1.180	1.190	1.200
2	1.020	1.040	1.061	1.082	1.102	1.124	1.145	1.166	1.188	1.210	1.232	1.254	1.277	1.300	1.322	1.346	1.369	1.392	1.416	1.440
3	1.030	1.061	1.093	1.125	1.158	1.191	1.225	1.260	1.295	1.331	1.368	1.405	1.443	1.482	1.521	1.561	1.602	1.643	1.685	1.728
4	1.041	1.082	1.126	1.170	1.216	1.262	1.311	1.360	1.412	1.464	1.518	1.574	1.630	1.689	1.749	1.811	1.874	1.939	2.005	2.074
5	1.051	1.104	1.159	1.217	1.276	1.338	1.403	1.469	1.539	1.611	1.685	1.762	1.842	1.925	2.011	2.100	2.192	2.288	2.386	2.488
6	1.062	1.126	1.194	1.265	1.340	1.419	1.501	1.587	1.677	1.772	1.870	1.974	2.082	2.195	2.313	2.436	2.565	2.700	2.840	2.986
7	1.072	1.149	1.230	1.316	1.407	1.504	1.606	1.714	1.828	1.949	2.076	2.211	2.353	2.502	2.660	2.826	3.001	3.185	3.379	3.583
8	1.083	1.172	1.267	1.369	1.477	1.594	1.718	1.851	1.993	2.144	2.305	2.476	2.658	2.853	3.059	3.278	3.511	3.759	4.021	4.300
9	1.094	1.195	1.305	1.423	1.551	1.689	1.838	1.999	2.172	2.358	2.558	2.773	3.004	3.252	3.518	3.803	4.108	4.435	4.785	5.160
10	1.105	1.219	1.344	1.480	1.629	1.791	1.967	2.159	2.367	2.594	2.839	3.106	3.395	3.707	4.046	4.411	4.807	5.234	5.695	6.192
11	1.116	1.243	1.384	1.539	1.710	1.898	2.105	2.332	2.580	2.853	3.152	3.479	3.836	4.226	4.652	5.117	5.624	6.176	6.777	7.430
12	1.127	1.268	1.426	1.601	1.796	2.012	2.252	2.518	2.813	3.138	3.498	3.896	4.334	4.818	5.350	5.936	6.580	7.288	8.064	8.916
13	1.138	1.294	1.469	1.665	1.886	2.133	2.410	2.720	3.066	3.452	3.883	4.363	4.898	5.492	6.153	6.886	7.699	8.599	9.596	10.699
14	1.149	1.319	1.513	1.732	1.980	2.261	2.579	2.937	3.342	3.797	4.310	4.887	5.535	6.261	7.076	7.987	9.007	10.147	11.420	12.839
15	1.161	1.346	1.558	1.801	2.079	2.397	2.759	3.172	3.642	4.177	4.785	5.474	6.254	7.138	8.137	9.265	10.539	11.974	13.589	15.407
16	1.173	1.373	1.605	1.873	2.183	2.540	2.952	3.426	3.970	4.595	5.311	6.130	7.067	8.137	9.358	10.748	12.330	14.129	16.171	18.488
17	1.184	1.400	1.653	1.948	2.292	2.693	3.159	3.700	4.328	5.054	5.895	6.866	7.986	9.276	10.761	12.468	14.426	16.672	19.244	22.186
18	1.196	1.428	1.702	2.026	2.407	2.854	3.380	3.996	4.717	5.560	6.543	7.690	9.024	10.575	12.375	14.462	16.879	19.673	22.900	26.623
19	1.208	1.457	1.753	2.107	2.527	3.026	3.616	4.316	5.142	6.116	7.263	8.613	10.197	12.055	14.232	16.776	19.748	23.214	27.251	31.948
20	1.220	1.486	1.806	2.191	2.653	3.207	3.870	4.661	5.604	6.727	8.062	9.646	11.523	13.743	16.366	19.461	23.105	27.393	32.429	38.337
21	1.232	1.516	1.860	2.279	2.786	3.399	4.140	5.034	6.109	7.400	8.949	10.804	13.021	15.667	18.821	22.574	27.033	32.323	38.591	46.005
22	1.245	1.546	1.916	2.370	2.925	3.603	4.430	5.436	6.658	8.140	9.933	12.100	14.713	17.861	21.644	26.186	31.629	38.141	45.923	55.205
23	1.257	1.577	1.974	2.465	3.071	3.820	4.740	5.871	7.258	8.954	11.026	13.552	16.626	20.361	24.891	30.376	37.005	45.007	54.648	66.247
24	1.270	1.608	2.033	2.563	3.225	4.049	5.072	6.341	7.911	9.850	12.239	15.178	18.788	23.212	28.625	35.236	43.296	53.108	65.031	79.496
25	1.282	1.641	2.094	2.666	3.386	4.292	5.427	6.848	8.623	10.834	13.585	17.000	21.230	26.461	32.918	40.874	50.656	62.667	77.387	95.395
30	1.348	1.811	2.427	3.243	4.322	5.743	7.612	10.062	13.267	17.449	22.892	29.960	39.115	50.949	66.210	85.849	111.061	143.367	184.672	237.373
35	1.417	2.000	2.814	3.946	5.516	7.686	10.676	14.785	20.413	28.102	38.574	52.799	72.066	98.097	133.172	180.311	243.495	327.988	440.691	590.657
40	1.489	2.208	3.262	4.801	7.040	10.285	14.974	21.724	31.408	45.258	64.999	93.049	132.776	188.876	267.856	378.715	533.846	750.353	1051.642	1469.740
45	1.565	2.438	3.781	5.841	8.985	13.764	21.002	31.920	48.325	72.888	109.527	163.985	244.629	363.662	538.752	795.429	1170.425	1716.619	2509.583	3657.176
50	1.645	2.691	4.384	7.106	11.467	18.419	29.456	46.900	74.354	117.386	184.559	288.996	450.711	700.197	1083.619	1670.669	2566.080	3927.189	5988.730	9100.191

Using the Calculator to Compute the Future Value of a Single Amount

Before you begin, clear the memory, ensure that you are in the *end mode* and that your calculator is set for *one payment per year*, and set the number of decimal places that you want (usually two for dollar-related accuracy).

Sample Problem

You place $800 in a savings account at 6% compounded annually. What is your account balance at the end of 5 years?

Hewlett-Packard HP 12C, 17 BII, and 19 BII[a]

Input	Function
800	PV
5	N
6	I%YR
	FV

Solution
1070.58 [b]

---

[a] For the 12C, you would use the **n** key instead of the **N** key, and the **i** key instead of the **I%YR** key.

[b] The minus sign that precedes the output should be ignored.

TABLE A.1 (Continued)

Period	21%	22%	23%	24%	25%	26%	27%	28%	29%	30%	31%	32%	33%	34%	35%	40%	45%	50%
1	1.210	1.220	1.230	1.240	1.250	1.260	1.270	1.280	1.290	1.300	1.310	1.320	1.330	1.340	1.350	1.400	1.450	1.500
2	1.464	1.488	1.513	1.538	1.562	1.588	1.613	1.638	1.664	1.690	1.716	1.742	1.769	1.796	1.822	1.960	2.102	2.250
3	1.772	1.816	1.861	1.907	1.953	2.000	2.048	2.097	2.147	2.197	2.248	2.300	2.353	2.406	2.460	2.744	3.049	3.375
4	2.144	2.215	2.289	2.364	2.441	2.520	2.601	2.684	2.769	2.856	2.945	3.036	3.129	3.224	3.321	3.842	4.421	5.063
5	2.594	2.703	2.815	2.932	3.052	3.176	3.304	3.436	3.572	3.713	3.858	4.007	4.162	4.320	4.484	5.378	6.410	7.594
6	3.138	3.297	3.463	3.635	3.815	4.001	4.196	4.398	4.608	4.827	5.054	5.290	5.535	5.789	6.053	7.530	9.294	11.391
7	3.797	4.023	4.259	4.508	4.768	5.042	5.329	5.629	5.945	6.275	6.621	6.983	7.361	7.758	8.172	10.541	13.476	17.086
8	4.595	4.908	5.239	5.589	5.960	6.353	6.767	7.206	7.669	8.157	8.673	9.217	9.791	10.395	11.032	14.758	19.541	25.629
9	5.560	5.987	6.444	6.931	7.451	8.004	8.595	9.223	9.893	10.604	11.362	12.166	13.022	13.930	14.894	20.661	28.334	38.443
10	6.727	7.305	7.926	8.594	9.313	10.086	10.915	11.806	12.761	13.786	14.884	16.060	17.319	18.666	20.106	28.925	41.085	57.665
11	8.140	8.912	9.749	10.657	11.642	12.708	13.862	15.112	16.462	17.921	19.498	21.199	23.034	25.012	27.144	40.495	59.573	86.498
12	9.850	10.872	11.991	13.215	14.552	16.012	17.605	19.343	21.236	23.298	25.542	27.982	30.635	33.516	36.644	56.694	86.380	129.746
13	11.918	13.264	14.749	16.386	18.190	20.175	22.359	24.759	27.395	30.287	33.460	36.937	40.745	44.912	49.469	79.371	125.251	194.620
14	14.421	16.182	18.141	20.319	22.737	25.420	28.395	31.691	35.339	39.373	43.832	48.756	54.190	60.181	66.784	111.119	181.614	291.929
15	17.449	19.742	22.314	25.195	28.422	32.030	36.062	40.565	45.587	51.185	57.420	64.358	72.073	80.643	90.158	155.567	263.341	437.894
16	21.113	24.085	27.446	31.242	35.527	40.357	45.799	51.923	58.808	66.541	75.220	84.953	95.857	108.061	121.713	217.793	381.844	656.841
17	25.547	29.384	33.758	38.740	44.409	50.850	58.165	66.461	75.862	86.503	98.539	112.138	127.490	144.802	164.312	304.911	553.674	985.261
18	30.912	35.848	41.523	48.038	55.511	64.071	73.869	85.070	97.862	112.454	129.086	148.022	169.561	194.035	221.822	426.875	802.826	1477.892
19	37.404	43.735	51.073	59.567	69.389	80.730	93.813	108.890	126.242	146.190	169.102	195.389	225.517	260.006	299.459	597.625	1164.098	2216.838
20	45.258	53.357	62.820	73.863	86.736	101.720	119.143	139.379	162.852	190.047	221.523	257.913	299.937	348.408	404.270	836.674	1687.942	3325.257
21	54.762	65.095	77.268	91.591	108.420	128.167	151.312	178.405	210.079	247.061	290.196	340.446	398.916	466.867	545.764	1171.343	2447.515	4987.883
22	66.262	79.416	95.040	113.572	135.525	161.490	192.165	228.358	271.002	321.178	380.156	449.388	530.558	625.601	736.781	1639.878	3548.896	7481.824
23	80.178	96.887	116.899	140.829	169.407	203.477	244.050	292.298	349.592	417.531	498.004	593.192	705.642	838.305	994.653	2295.829	5145.898	11222.738
24	97.015	118.203	143.786	174.628	211.758	256.381	309.943	374.141	450.974	542.791	652.385	783.013	938.504	1123.328	1342.781	3214.158	7461.547	16834.109
25	117.388	144.207	176.857	216.539	264.698	323.040	393.628	478.901	581.756	705.627	854.623	1033.577	1248.210	1505.258	1812.754	4499.816	10819.242	25251.164
30	304.471	389.748	497.904	634.810	807.793	1025.904	1300.477	1645.488	2078.208	2619.936	3297.081	4142.008	5194.516	6503.285	8128.426	24201.043	69348.375	191751.000
35	789.716	1053.370	1401.749	1861.020	2465.189	3258.053	4296.547	5653.840	7423.988	9727.598	12719.918	16598.906	21617.363	28096.695	36448.051	130158.687	*	*
40	2048.309	2846.941	3946.340	5455.797	7523.156	10346.879	14195.051	19426.418	26520.723	36117.754	49072.621	66519.313	89962.188	121388.437	163433.875	700022.688	*	*
45	5312.758	7694.418	11110.121	15994.316	22958.844	32859.457	46897.973	66748.500	94739.937	134102.187	*	*	*	*	*	*	*	*
50	13779.844	20795.680	31278.301	46889.207	70064.812	104354.562	154942.687	229345.875	338440.000	497910.125	*	*	*	*	*	*	*	*

*Not shown because of space limitations.

Texas Instruments BA-35, BAII, BAII Plus[c]

Input	Function
800	PV
5	N
6	%i
	CPT
	FV

Solution
1070.58[d]

---

[c] For the Texas Instruments BAII, you would use the **2nd** key instead of the **CPT** key; for the Texas Instruments BAII Plus, you would use the **I/Y** key instead of the **%i** key.
[d] If a minus sign precedes the output, it should be ignored.

TABLE A.2 Future-Value Interest Factors for a One-Dollar Annuity, *FVIFA*

Period	1%	2%	3%	4%	5%	6%	7%	8%	9%	10%	11%	12%	13%	14%	15%	16%	17%	18%	19%	20%
1	1.000	1.000	1.000	1.000	1.000	1.000	1.000	1.000	1.000	1.000	1.000	1.000	1.000	1.000	1.000	1.000	1.000	1.000	1.000	1.000
2	2.010	2.020	2.030	2.040	2.050	2.060	2.070	2.080	2.090	2.100	2.110	2.120	2.130	2.140	2.150	2.160	2.170	2.180	2.190	2.200
3	3.030	3.060	3.091	3.122	3.152	3.184	3.215	3.246	3.278	3.310	3.342	3.374	3.407	3.440	3.472	3.506	3.539	3.572	3.606	3.640
4	4.060	4.122	4.184	4.246	4.310	4.375	4.440	4.506	4.573	4.641	4.710	4.779	4.850	4.921	4.993	5.066	5.141	5.215	5.291	5.368
5	5.101	5.204	5.309	5.416	5.526	5.637	5.751	5.867	5.985	6.105	6.228	6.353	6.480	6.610	6.742	6.877	7.014	7.154	7.297	7.442
6	6.152	6.308	6.468	6.633	6.802	6.975	7.153	7.336	7.523	7.716	7.913	8.115	8.323	8.535	8.754	8.977	9.207	9.442	9.683	9.930
7	7.214	7.434	7.662	7.898	8.142	8.394	8.654	8.923	9.200	9.487	9.783	10.089	10.405	10.730	11.067	11.414	11.772	12.141	12.523	12.916
8	8.286	8.583	8.892	9.214	9.549	9.897	10.260	10.637	11.028	11.436	11.859	12.300	12.757	13.233	13.727	14.240	14.773	15.327	15.902	16.499
9	9.368	9.755	10.159	10.583	11.027	11.491	11.978	12.488	13.021	13.579	14.164	14.776	15.416	16.085	16.786	17.518	18.285	19.086	19.923	20.799
10	10.462	10.950	11.464	12.006	12.578	13.181	13.816	14.487	15.193	15.937	16.722	17.549	18.420	19.337	20.304	21.321	22.393	23.521	24.709	25.959
11	11.567	12.169	12.808	13.486	14.207	14.972	15.784	16.645	17.560	18.531	19.561	20.655	21.814	23.044	24.349	25.733	27.200	28.755	30.403	32.150
12	12.682	13.412	14.192	15.026	15.917	16.870	17.888	18.977	20.141	21.384	22.713	24.133	25.650	27.271	29.001	30.850	32.824	34.931	37.180	39.580
13	13.809	14.680	15.618	16.627	17.713	18.882	20.141	21.495	22.953	24.523	26.211	28.029	29.984	32.088	34.352	36.786	39.404	42.218	45.244	48.496
14	14.947	15.974	17.086	18.292	19.598	21.015	22.550	24.215	26.019	27.975	30.095	32.392	34.882	37.581	40.504	43.672	47.102	50.818	54.841	59.196
15	16.097	17.293	18.599	20.023	21.578	23.276	25.129	27.152	29.361	31.772	34.405	37.280	40.417	43.842	47.580	51.659	56.109	60.965	66.260	72.035
16	17.258	18.639	20.157	21.824	23.657	25.672	27.888	30.324	33.003	35.949	39.190	42.753	46.671	50.980	55.717	60.925	66.648	72.938	79.850	87.442
17	18.430	20.012	21.761	23.697	25.840	28.213	30.840	33.750	36.973	40.544	44.500	48.883	53.738	59.117	65.075	71.673	78.978	87.067	96.021	105.930
18	19.614	21.412	23.414	25.645	28.132	30.905	33.999	37.450	41.301	45.599	50.396	55.749	61.724	68.393	75.836	84.140	93.404	103.739	115.265	128.116
19	20.811	22.840	25.117	27.671	30.539	33.760	37.379	41.446	46.018	51.158	56.939	63.439	70.748	78.968	88.211	98.603	110.283	123.412	138.165	154.739
20	22.019	24.297	26.870	29.778	33.066	36.785	40.995	45.762	51.159	57.274	64.202	72.052	80.946	91.024	102.443	115.379	130.031	146.626	165.417	186.687
21	23.239	25.783	28.676	31.969	35.719	39.992	44.865	50.422	56.764	64.002	72.264	81.698	92.468	104.767	118.809	134.840	153.136	174.019	197.846	225.024
22	24.471	27.299	30.536	34.248	38.505	43.392	49.005	55.456	62.872	71.402	81.213	92.502	105.489	120.434	137.630	157.414	180.169	206.342	236.436	271.028
23	25.716	28.845	32.452	36.618	41.430	46.995	53.435	60.893	69.531	79.542	91.147	104.602	120.203	138.295	159.274	183.600	211.798	244.483	282.359	326.234
24	26.973	30.421	34.426	39.082	44.501	50.815	58.176	66.764	76.789	88.496	102.173	118.154	136.829	158.656	184.166	213.976	248.803	289.490	337.007	392.480
25	28.243	32.030	36.459	41.645	47.726	54.864	63.248	73.105	84.699	98.346	114.412	133.333	155.616	181.867	212.790	249.212	292.099	342.598	402.038	471.976
30	34.784	40.567	47.575	56.084	66.438	79.057	94.459	113.282	136.305	164.491	199.018	241.330	293.192	356.778	434.738	530.306	647.423	790.932	966.698	1181.865
35	41.659	49.994	60.461	73.651	90.318	111.432	138.234	172.314	215.705	271.018	341.583	431.658	546.663	693.552	881.152	1120.699	1426.448	1816.607	2314.173	2948.294
40	48.885	60.401	75.400	95.024	120.797	154.758	199.630	259.052	337.872	442.580	581.812	767.080	1013.667	1341.979	1779.048	2360.724	3134.412	4163.094	5529.711	7343.715
45	56.479	71.891	92.718	121.027	159.695	212.737	285.741	386.497	525.840	718.881	986.613	1358.208	1874.086	2590.464	3585.031	4965.191	6879.008	9531.258	13203.105	18280.914
50	64.461	84.577	112.794	152.664	209.341	290.325	406.516	573.756	815.051	1163.865	1668.723	2399.975	3459.344	4994.301	7217.488	10435.449	15088.805	21812.273	31514.492	45496.094

Using the Calculator to Compute the Future Value of an Annuity

Before you begin, clear the memory, ensure that you are in the *end mode* and that your calculator is set for *one payment per year*, and set the number of decimal places that you want (usually two for dollar-related accuracy).

Sample Problem

You want to know what the future value will be at the end of 5 years if you place five end-of-year deposits of $1,000 in an account paying 7% annually. What is your account balance at the end of 5 years?

Hewlett-Packard HP 12C, 17 BII, and 19 BII[a]

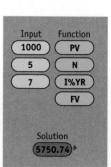

Input	Function
1000	PV
5	N
7	I%YR
	FV

Solution
5750.74[b]

---

[a] For the 12C, you would use the **n** key instead of the **N** key, and the **i** key instead of the **I%YR** key.

[b] The minus sign that precedes the output should be ignored.

TABLE A.2 *(Continued)*

Period	21%	22%	23%	24%	25%	26%	27%	28%	29%	30%	31%	32%	33%	34%	35%	40%	45%	50%
1	1.000	1.000	1.000	1.000	1.000	1.000	1.000	1.000	1.000	1.000	1.000	1.000	1.000	1.000	1.000	1.000	1.000	1.000
2	2.210	2.220	2.230	2.240	2.250	2.260	2.270	2.280	2.290	2.300	2.310	2.320	2.330	2.340	2.350	2.400	2.450	2.500
3	3.674	3.708	3.743	3.778	3.813	3.848	3.883	3.918	3.954	3.990	4.026	4.062	4.099	4.136	4.172	4.360	4.552	4.750
4	5.446	5.524	5.604	5.684	5.766	5.848	5.931	6.016	6.101	6.187	6.274	6.362	6.452	6.542	6.633	7.104	7.601	8.125
5	7.589	7.740	7.893	8.048	8.207	8.368	8.533	8.700	8.870	9.043	9.219	9.398	9.581	9.766	9.954	10.946	12.022	13.188
6	10.183	10.442	10.708	10.980	11.259	11.544	11.837	12.136	12.442	12.756	13.077	13.406	13.742	14.086	14.438	16.324	18.431	20.781
7	13.321	13.740	14.171	14.615	15.073	15.546	16.032	16.534	17.051	17.583	18.131	18.696	19.277	19.876	20.492	23.853	27.725	32.172
8	17.119	17.762	18.430	19.123	19.842	20.588	21.361	22.163	22.995	23.858	24.752	25.678	26.638	27.633	28.664	34.395	41.202	49.258
9	21.714	22.670	23.669	24.712	25.802	26.940	28.129	29.369	30.664	32.015	33.425	34.895	36.429	38.028	39.696	49.152	60.743	74.887
10	27.274	28.657	30.113	31.643	33.253	34.945	36.723	38.592	40.556	42.619	44.786	47.062	49.451	51.958	54.590	69.813	89.077	113.330
11	34.001	35.962	38.039	40.238	42.566	45.030	47.639	50.398	53.318	56.405	59.670	63.121	66.769	70.624	74.696	98.739	130.161	170.995
12	42.141	44.873	47.787	50.895	54.208	57.738	61.501	65.510	69.780	74.326	79.167	84.320	89.803	95.636	101.840	139.234	189.734	257.493
13	51.991	55.745	59.778	64.109	68.760	73.750	79.106	84.853	91.016	97.624	104.709	112.302	120.438	129.152	138.484	195.928	276.114	387.239
14	63.909	69.009	74.528	80.496	86.949	93.925	101.465	109.611	118.411	127.912	138.169	149.239	161.183	174.063	187.953	275.299	401.365	581.858
15	78.330	85.191	92.669	100.815	109.687	119.346	129.860	141.302	153.750	167.285	182.001	197.996	215.373	234.245	254.737	386.418	582.980	873.788
16	95.779	104.933	114.983	126.010	138.109	151.375	165.922	181.867	199.337	218.470	239.421	262.354	287.446	314.888	344.895	541.985	846.321	1311.681
17	116.892	129.019	142.428	157.252	173.636	191.733	211.721	233.790	258.145	285.011	314.642	347.307	383.303	422.949	466.608	759.778	1228.165	1968.522
18	142.439	158.403	176.187	195.993	218.045	242.583	269.885	300.250	334.006	371.514	413.180	459.445	510.792	567.751	630.920	1064.689	1781.838	2953.783
19	173.351	194.251	217.710	244.031	273.556	306.654	343.754	385.321	431.868	483.968	542.266	607.467	680.354	761.786	852.741	1491.563	2584.665	4431.672
20	210.755	237.986	268.783	303.598	342.945	387.384	437.568	494.210	558.110	630.157	711.368	802.856	905.870	1021.792	1152.200	2089.188	3748.763	6648.508
21	256.013	291.343	331.603	377.461	429.681	489.104	556.710	633.589	720.962	820.204	932.891	1060.769	1205.807	1370.201	1556.470	2925.862	5436.703	9973.762
22	310.775	356.438	408.871	469.052	538.101	617.270	708.022	811.993	931.040	1067.265	1223.087	1401.215	1604.724	1837.068	2102.234	4097.203	7884.215	14961.645
23	377.038	435.854	503.911	582.624	673.626	778.760	900.187	1040.351	1202.042	1388.443	1603.243	1850.603	2135.282	2462.669	2839.014	5737.078	11433.109	22443.469
24	457.215	532.741	620.810	723.453	843.032	982.237	1144.237	1332.649	1551.634	1805.975	2101.247	2443.795	2840.924	3300.974	3833.667	8032.906	16579.008	33666.207
25	554.230	650.944	764.596	898.082	1054.791	1238.617	1454.180	1706.790	2002.608	2348.765	2753.631	3226.808	3779.428	4424.301	5176.445	11247.062	24040.555	50500.316
30	1445.111	1767.044	2160.459	2640.881	3227.172	3941.953	4812.891	5873.172	7162.785	8729.805	10632.543	12940.672	15737.945	19124.434	23221.258	60500.207	154105.313	383500.000
35	3755.814	4783.520	6090.227	7750.094	9856.746	12527.160	15909.480	20188.742	25596.512	32422.090	41028.887	51868.563	65504.199	82634.625	104134.500	325394.688	*	*
40	9749.141	12936.141	17153.691	22728.367	30088.621	39791.957	52570.707	69376.562	91447.375	120389.375	*	*	*	*	*	*	*	*
45	25294.223	34970.230	48300.660	66638.937	91831.312	126378.937	173692.875	238384.312	326686.375	447005.062	*	*	*	*	*	*	*	*

*Not shown because of space limitations.

Texas Instruments BA-35, BAII, BAII Plus[c]

Input	Function
1000	PMT
5	N
7	%i
	CPT
	FV

Solution
5750.74 [d]

[c] For the Texas Instruments BAII, you would use the **2nd** key instead of the **CPT** key; for the Texas Instruments BAII Plus, you would use the **I/Y** key instead of the **%i** key.
[d] If a minus sign precedes the output, it should be ignored.

TABLE A.3   Present-Value Interest Factors for One Dollar, *PVIF*

Period	1%	2%	3%	4%	5%	6%	7%	8%	9%	10%	11%	12%	13%	14%	15%	16%	17%	18%	19%	20%
1	.990	.980	.971	.962	.952	.943	.935	.926	.917	.909	.901	.893	.885	.877	.870	.862	.855	.847	.840	.833
2	.980	.961	.943	.925	.907	.890	.873	.857	.842	.826	.812	.797	.783	.769	.756	.743	.731	.718	.706	.694
3	.971	.942	.915	.889	.864	.840	.816	.794	.772	.751	.731	.712	.693	.675	.658	.641	.624	.609	.593	.579
4	.961	.924	.888	.855	.823	.792	.763	.735	.708	.683	.659	.636	.613	.592	.572	.552	.534	.516	.499	.482
5	.951	.906	.863	.822	.784	.747	.713	.681	.650	.621	.593	.567	.543	.519	.497	.476	.456	.437	.419	.402
6	.942	.888	.837	.790	.746	.705	.666	.630	.596	.564	.535	.507	.480	.456	.432	.410	.390	.370	.352	.335
7	.933	.871	.813	.760	.711	.665	.623	.583	.547	.513	.482	.452	.425	.400	.376	.354	.333	.314	.296	.279
8	.923	.853	.789	.731	.677	.627	.582	.540	.502	.467	.434	.404	.376	.351	.327	.305	.285	.266	.249	.233
9	.914	.837	.766	.703	.645	.592	.544	.500	.460	.424	.391	.361	.333	.308	.284	.263	.243	.225	.209	.194
10	.905	.820	.744	.676	.614	.558	.508	.463	.422	.386	.352	.322	.295	.270	.247	.227	.208	.191	.176	.162
11	.896	.804	.722	.650	.585	.527	.475	.429	.388	.350	.317	.287	.261	.237	.215	.195	.178	.162	.148	.135
12	.887	.789	.701	.625	.557	.497	.444	.397	.356	.319	.286	.257	.231	.208	.187	.168	.152	.137	.124	.112
13	.879	.773	.681	.601	.530	.469	.415	.368	.326	.290	.258	.229	.204	.182	.163	.145	.130	.116	.104	.093
14	.870	.758	.661	.577	.505	.442	.388	.340	.299	.263	.232	.205	.181	.160	.141	.125	.111	.099	.088	.078
15	.861	.743	.642	.555	.481	.417	.362	.315	.275	.239	.209	.183	.160	.140	.123	.108	.095	.084	.074	.065
16	.853	.728	.623	.534	.458	.394	.339	.292	.252	.218	.188	.163	.141	.123	.107	.093	.081	.071	.062	.054
17	.844	.714	.605	.513	.436	.371	.317	.270	.231	.198	.170	.146	.125	.108	.093	.080	.069	.060	.052	.045
18	.836	.700	.587	.494	.416	.350	.296	.250	.212	.180	.153	.130	.111	.095	.081	.069	.059	.051	.044	.038
19	.828	.686	.570	.475	.396	.331	.277	.232	.194	.164	.138	.116	.098	.083	.070	.060	.051	.043	.037	.031
20	.820	.673	.554	.456	.377	.312	.258	.215	.178	.149	.124	.104	.087	.073	.061	.051	.043	.037	.031	.026
21	.811	.660	.538	.439	.359	.294	.242	.199	.164	.135	.112	.093	.077	.064	.053	.044	.037	.031	.026	.022
22	.803	.647	.522	.422	.342	.278	.226	.184	.150	.123	.101	.083	.068	.056	.046	.038	.032	.026	.022	.018
23	.795	.634	.507	.406	.326	.262	.211	.170	.138	.112	.091	.074	.060	.049	.040	.033	.027	.022	.018	.015
24	.788	.622	.492	.390	.310	.247	.197	.158	.126	.102	.082	.066	.053	.043	.035	.028	.023	.019	.015	.013
25	.780	.610	.478	.375	.295	.233	.184	.146	.116	.092	.074	.059	.047	.038	.030	.024	.020	.016	.013	.010
30	.742	.552	.412	.308	.231	.174	.131	.099	.075	.057	.044	.033	.026	.020	.015	.012	.009	.007	.005	.004
35	.706	.500	.355	.253	.181	.130	.094	.068	.049	.036	.026	.019	.014	.010	.008	.006	.004	.003	.002	.002
40	.672	.453	.307	.208	.142	.097	.067	.046	.032	.022	.015	.011	.008	.005	.004	.003	.002	.001	.001	.001
45	.639	.410	.264	.171	.111	.073	.048	.031	.021	.014	.009	.006	.004	.003	.002	.001	.001	.001	*	*
50	.608	.372	.228	.141	.087	.054	.034	.021	.013	.009	.005	.003	.002	.001	.001	.001	*	*	*	*

*PVIF is zero to three decimal places.

Using the Calculator to Compute the Present Value of a Single Amount

Before you begin, clear the memory, ensure that you are in the *end mode* and that your calculator is set for *one payment per year*, and set the number of decimal places that you want (usually two for dollar-related accuracy).

Sample Problem

You want to know the present value of $1,700 to be received at the end of 8 years, assuming an 8% discount rate.

Hewlett-Packard HP 12C, 17 BII, and 19 BII[a]

Input	Function
1700	FV
5	N
8	I%YR
	PV

Solution
918.46 [b]

---

[a] For the 12C, you would use the **n** key instead of the **N** key, and the **i** key instead of the **I%YR** key.

[b] The minus sign that precedes the output should be ignored.

TABLE A.3 (Continued)

Period	21%	22%	23%	24%	25%	26%	27%	28%	29%	30%	31%	32%	33%	34%	35%	40%	45%	50%
1	.826	.820	.813	.806	.800	.794	.787	.781	.775	.769	.763	.758	.752	.746	.741	.714	.690	.667
2	.683	.672	.661	.650	.640	.630	.620	.610	.601	.592	.583	.574	.565	.557	.549	.510	.476	.444
3	.564	.551	.537	.524	.512	.500	.488	.477	.466	.455	.445	.435	.425	.416	.406	.364	.328	.296
4	.467	.451	.437	.423	.410	.397	.384	.373	.361	.350	.340	.329	.320	.310	.301	.260	.226	.198
5	.386	.370	.355	.341	.328	.315	.303	.291	.280	.269	.259	.250	.240	.231	.223	.186	.156	.132
6	.319	.303	.289	.275	.262	.250	.238	.227	.217	.207	.198	.189	.181	.173	.165	.133	.108	.088
7	.263	.249	.235	.222	.210	.198	.188	.178	.168	.159	.151	.143	.136	.129	.122	.095	.074	.059
8	.218	.204	.191	.179	.168	.157	.148	.139	.130	.123	.115	.108	.102	.096	.091	.068	.051	.039
9	.180	.167	.155	.144	.134	.125	.116	.108	.101	.094	.088	.082	.077	.072	.067	.048	.035	.026
10	.149	.137	.126	.116	.107	.099	.092	.085	.078	.073	.067	.062	.058	.054	.050	.035	.024	.017
11	.123	.112	.103	.094	.086	.079	.072	.066	.061	.056	.051	.047	.043	.040	.037	.025	.017	.012
12	.102	.092	.083	.076	.069	.062	.057	.052	.047	.043	.039	.036	.033	.030	.027	.018	.012	.008
13	.084	.075	.068	.061	.055	.050	.045	.040	.037	.033	.030	.027	.025	.022	.020	.013	.008	.005
14	.069	.062	.055	.049	.044	.039	.035	.032	.028	.025	.023	.021	.018	.017	.015	.009	.006	.003
15	.057	.051	.045	.040	.035	.031	.028	.025	.022	.020	.017	.016	.014	.012	.011	.006	.004	.002
16	.047	.042	.036	.032	.028	.025	.022	.019	.017	.015	.013	.012	.010	.009	.008	.005	.003	.002
17	.039	.034	.030	.026	.023	.020	.017	.015	.013	.012	.010	.009	.008	.007	.006	.003	.002	.001
18	.032	.028	.024	.021	.018	.016	.014	.012	.010	.009	.008	.007	.006	.005	.005	.002	.001	.001
19	.027	.023	.020	.017	.014	.012	.011	.009	.008	.007	.006	.005	.004	.004	.003	.002	.001	*
20	.022	.019	.016	.014	.012	.010	.008	.007	.006	.005	.005	.004	.003	.003	.002	.001	.001	*
21	.018	.015	.013	.011	.009	.008	.007	.006	.005	.004	.003	.003	.003	.002	.002	.001	*	*
22	.015	.013	.011	.009	.007	.006	.005	.004	.004	.003	.003	.002	.002	.002	.001	.001	*	*
23	.012	.010	.009	.007	.006	.005	.004	.003	.003	.002	.002	.002	.001	.001	.001	*	*	*
24	.010	.008	.007	.006	.005	.004	.003	.003	.002	.002	.002	.001	.001	.001	.001	*	*	*
25	.009	.007	.006	.005	.004	.003	.003	.002	.002	.001	.001	.001	.001	.001	.001	*	*	*
30	.003	.003	.002	.002	.001	.001	.001	.001	*	*	*	*	*	*	*	*	*	*
35	.001	.001	.001	.001	*	*	*	*	*	*	*	*	*	*	*	*	*	*
40	*	*	*	*	*	*	*	*	*	*	*	*	*	*	*	*	*	*
45	*	*	*	*	*	*	*	*	*	*	*	*	*	*	*	*	*	*
50	*	*	*	*	*	*	*	*	*	*	*	*	*	*	*	*	*	*

*PVIF is zero to three decimal places.

Texas Instruments BA-35, BAII, BAII Plus[c]

Input	Function
1700	FV
8	N
8	%i
	CPT
	PV

Solution
918.46 [d]

---

[c] For the Texas Instruments BAII, you would use the **2nd** key instead of the **CPT** key; for the Texas Instruments BAII Plus, you would use the **I/Y** key instead of the **%i** key.

[d] If a minus sign precedes the output, it should be ignored.

TABLE A.4   Present-Value Interest Factors for a One-Dollar Annuity, *PVIFA*

Period	1%	2%	3%	4%	5%	6%	7%	8%	9%	10%	11%	12%	13%	14%	15%	16%	17%	18%	19%	20%
1	.990	.980	.971	.962	.952	.943	.935	.926	.917	.909	.901	.893	.885	.877	.870	.862	.855	.847	.840	.833
2	1.970	1.942	1.913	1.886	1.859	1.833	1.808	1.783	1.759	1.736	1.713	1.690	1.668	1.647	1.626	1.605	1.585	1.566	1.547	1.528
3	2.941	2.884	2.829	2.775	2.723	2.673	2.624	2.577	2.531	2.487	2.444	2.402	2.361	2.322	2.283	2.246	2.210	2.174	2.140	2.106
4	3.902	3.808	3.717	3.630	3.546	3.465	3.387	3.312	3.240	3.170	3.102	3.037	2.974	2.914	2.855	2.798	2.743	2.690	2.639	2.589
5	4.853	4.713	4.580	4.452	4.329	4.212	4.100	3.993	3.890	3.791	3.696	3.605	3.517	3.433	3.352	3.274	3.199	3.127	3.058	2.991
6	5.795	5.601	5.417	5.242	5.076	4.917	4.767	4.623	4.486	4.355	4.231	4.111	3.998	3.889	3.784	3.685	3.589	3.498	3.410	3.326
7	6.728	6.472	6.230	6.002	5.786	5.582	5.389	5.206	5.033	4.868	4.712	4.564	4.423	4.288	4.160	4.039	3.922	3.812	3.706	3.605
8	7.652	7.326	7.020	6.733	6.463	6.210	5.971	5.747	5.535	5.335	5.146	4.968	4.799	4.639	4.487	4.344	4.207	4.078	3.954	3.837
9	8.566	8.162	7.786	7.435	7.108	6.802	6.515	6.247	5.995	5.759	5.537	5.328	5.132	4.946	4.772	4.607	4.451	4.303	4.163	4.031
10	9.471	8.983	8.530	8.111	7.722	7.360	7.024	6.710	6.418	6.145	5.889	5.650	5.426	5.216	5.019	4.833	4.659	4.494	4.339	4.192
11	10.368	9.787	9.253	8.760	8.306	7.887	7.499	7.139	6.805	6.495	6.207	5.938	5.687	5.453	5.234	5.029	4.836	4.656	4.486	4.327
12	11.255	10.575	9.954	9.385	8.863	8.384	7.943	7.536	7.161	6.814	6.492	6.194	5.918	5.660	5.421	5.197	4.988	4.793	4.611	4.439
13	12.134	11.348	10.635	9.986	9.394	8.853	8.358	7.904	7.487	7.013	6.750	6.424	6.122	5.842	5.583	5.342	5.118	4.910	4.715	4.533
14	13.004	12.106	11.296	10.563	9.899	9.295	8.745	8.244	7.786	7.367	6.982	6.628	6.302	6.002	5.724	5.468	5.229	5.008	4.802	4.611
15	13.865	12.849	11.938	11.118	10.380	9.712	9.108	8.560	8.061	7.606	7.191	6.811	6.462	6.142	5.847	5.575	5.324	5.092	4.876	4.675
16	14.718	13.578	12.561	11.652	10.838	10.106	9.447	8.851	8.313	7.824	7.379	6.974	6.604	6.265	5.954	5.668	5.405	5.162	4.938	4.730
17	15.562	14.292	13.166	12.166	11.274	10.477	9.763	9.122	8.544	8.022	7.549	7.120	6.729	6.373	6.047	5.749	5.475	5.222	4.990	4.775
18	16.398	14.992	13.754	12.659	11.690	10.828	10.059	9.372	8.756	8.201	7.702	7.250	6.840	6.467	6.128	5.818	5.534	5.273	5.033	4.812
19	17.226	15.679	14.324	13.134	12.085	11.158	10.336	9.604	8.950	8.365	7.839	7.366	6.938	6.550	6.198	5.877	5.584	5.316	5.070	4.843
20	18.046	16.352	14.878	13.590	12.462	11.470	10.594	9.818	9.129	8.514	7.963	7.469	7.025	6.623	6.259	5.929	5.628	5.353	5.101	4.870
21	18.857	17.011	15.415	14.029	12.821	11.764	10.836	10.017	9.292	8.649	8.075	7.562	7.102	6.687	6.312	5.973	5.665	5.384	5.127	4.891
22	19.661	17.658	15.937	14.451	13.163	12.042	11.061	10.201	9.442	8.772	8.176	7.645	7.170	6.743	6.359	6.011	5.696	5.410	5.149	4.909
23	20.456	18.292	16.444	14.857	13.489	12.303	11.272	10.371	9.580	8.883	8.266	7.718	7.230	6.792	6.399	6.044	5.723	5.432	5.167	4.925
24	21.244	18.914	16.936	15.247	13.799	12.550	11.469	10.529	9.707	8.985	8.348	7.784	7.283	6.835	6.434	6.073	5.746	5.451	5.182	4.937
25	22.023	19.524	17.413	15.622	14.094	12.783	11.654	10.675	9.823	9.077	8.422	7.843	7.330	6.873	6.464	6.097	5.766	5.467	5.195	4.948
30	25.808	22.396	19.601	17.292	15.373	13.765	12.409	11.258	10.274	9.427	8.694	8.055	7.496	7.003	6.566	6.177	5.829	5.517	5.235	4.979
35	29.409	24.999	21.487	18.665	16.374	14.498	12.948	11.655	10.567	9.644	8.855	8.176	7.586	7.070	6.617	6.215	5.858	5.539	5.251	4.992
40	32.835	27.356	23.115	19.793	17.159	15.046	13.332	11.925	10.757	9.779	8.951	8.244	7.634	7.105	6.642	6.233	5.871	5.548	5.258	4.997
45	36.095	29.490	24.519	20.720	17.774	15.456	13.606	12.108	10.881	9.863	9.008	8.283	7.661	7.123	6.654	6.242	5.877	5.552	5.261	4.999
50	39.196	31.424	25.730	21.482	18.256	15.762	13.801	12.233	10.962	9.915	9.042	8.304	7.675	7.133	6.661	6.246	5.880	5.554	5.262	4.999

Using the Calculator to Compute the Present Value of an Annuity

Before you begin, clear the memory, ensure that you are in the *end mode* and that your calculator is set for *one payment per year*, and set the number of decimal places that you want (usually two for dollar-related accuracy).

Sample Problem

You want to know what the present value of an annuity of $700 per year received at the end of each year for 5 years will be, given a discount rate of 8%.

Hewlett-Packard HP 12C, 17 BII, and 19 BII[a]

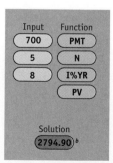

Input	Function
700	PMT
5	N
8	I%YR
	PV

Solution
2794.90[b]

---

[a] For the 12C, you would use the **n** key instead of the **N** key, and the **i** key instead of the **I%YR** key.

[b] The minus sign that precedes the output should be ignored.

TABLE A.4 (Continued)

Period	21%	22%	23%	24%	25%	26%	27%	28%	29%	30%	31%	32%	33%	34%	35%	40%	45%	50%
1	.826	.820	.813	.806	.800	.794	.787	.781	.775	.769	.763	.758	.752	.746	.741	.714	.690	.667
2	1.509	1.492	1.474	1.457	1.440	1.424	1.407	1.392	1.376	1.361	1.346	1.331	1.317	1.303	1.289	1.224	1.165	1.111
3	2.074	2.042	2.011	1.981	1.952	1.923	1.896	1.868	1.842	1.816	1.791	1.766	1.742	1.719	1.696	1.589	1.493	1.407
4	2.540	2.494	2.448	2.404	2.362	2.320	2.280	2.241	2.203	2.166	2.130	2.096	2.062	2.029	1.997	1.849	1.720	1.605
5	2.926	2.864	2.803	2.745	2.689	2.635	2.583	2.532	2.483	2.436	2.390	2.345	2.302	2.260	2.220	2.035	1.876	1.737
6	3.245	3.167	3.092	3.020	2.951	2.885	2.821	2.759	2.700	2.643	2.588	2.534	2.483	2.433	2.385	2.168	1.983	1.824
7	3.508	3.416	3.327	3.242	3.161	3.083	3.009	2.937	2.808	2.002	2.730	2.677	2.619	2.662	2.508	2.263	2.057	1.883
8	3.726	3.619	3.518	3.421	3.329	3.241	3.156	3.076	2.999	2.925	2.854	2.786	2.721	2.658	2.598	2.331	2.109	1.922
9	3.905	3.786	3.673	3.566	3.463	3.366	3.273	3.184	3.100	3.019	2.942	2.868	2.798	2.730	2.665	2.379	2.144	1.948
10	4.054	3.923	3.799	3.682	3.570	3.465	3.364	3.269	3.178	3.092	3.009	2.930	2.855	2.784	2.715	2.414	2.168	1.965
11	4.177	4.035	3.902	3.776	3.656	3.544	3.437	3.335	3.239	3.147	3.060	2.978	2.899	2.824	2.752	2.438	2.185	1.977
12	4.278	4.127	3.985	3.851	3.725	3.606	3.493	3.387	3.286	3.190	3.100	3.013	2.931	2.853	2.779	2.456	2.196	1.985
13	4.362	4.203	4.053	3.912	3.780	3.656	3.538	3.427	3.322	3.223	3.129	3.040	2.956	2.876	2.799	2.469	2.204	1.990
14	4.432	4.265	4.108	3.962	3.824	3.695	3.573	3.459	3.351	3.249	3.152	3.061	2.974	2.892	2.814	2.478	2.210	1.993
15	4.489	4.315	4.153	4.001	3.859	3.726	3.601	3.483	3.373	3.268	3.170	3.076	2.988	2.905	2.825	2.484	2.214	1.995
16	4.536	4.357	4.189	4.033	3.887	3.751	3.623	3.503	3.390	3.283	3.183	3.088	2.999	2.914	2.834	2.489	2.216	1.997
17	4.576	4.391	4.219	4.059	3.910	3.771	3.640	3.518	3.403	3.295	3.193	3.097	3.007	2.921	2.840	2.492	2.218	1.998
18	4.608	4.419	4.243	4.080	3.928	3.786	3.654	3.529	3.413	3.304	3.201	3.104	3.012	2.926	2.844	2.494	2.219	1.999
19	4.635	4.442	4.263	4.097	3.942	3.799	3.664	3.539	3.421	3.311	3.207	3.109	3.017	2.930	2.848	2.496	2.220	1.999
20	4.657	4.460	4.279	4.110	3.954	3.808	3.673	3.546	3.427	3.316	3.211	3.113	3.020	2.933	2.850	2.497	2.221	1.999
21	4.675	4.476	4.292	4.121	3.963	3.816	3.679	3.551	3.432	3.320	3.215	3.116	3.023	2.935	2.852	2.498	2.221	2.000
22	4.690	4.488	4.302	4.130	3.970	3.822	3.684	3.556	3.436	3.323	3.217	3.118	3.025	2.936	2.853	2.498	2.222	2.000
23	4.703	4.499	4.311	4.137	3.976	3.827	3.689	3.559	3.438	3.325	3.219	3.120	3.026	2.938	2.854	2.499	2.222	2.000
24	4.713	4.507	4.318	4.143	3.981	3.831	3.692	3.562	3.441	3.327	3.221	3.121	3.027	2.939	2.855	2.499	2.222	2.000
25	4.721	4.514	4.323	4.147	3.985	3.834	3.694	3.564	3.442	3.329	3.222	3.122	3.028	2.939	2.856	2.499	2.222	2.000
30	4.746	4.534	4.339	4.160	3.995	3.842	3.701	3.569	3.447	3.332	3.225	3.124	3.030	2.941	2.857	2.500	2.222	2.000
35	4.756	4.541	4.345	4.164	3.998	3.845	3.703	3.571	3.448	3.333	3.226	3.125	3.030	2.941	2.857	2.500	2.222	2.000
40	4.760	4.544	4.347	4.166	3.999	3.846	3.703	3.571	3.448	3.333	3.226	3.125	3.030	2.941	2.857	2.500	2.222	2.000
45	4.761	4.545	4.347	4.166	4.000	3.846	3.704	3.571	3.448	3.333	3.226	3.125	3.030	2.941	2.857	2.500	2.222	2.000
50	4.762	4.545	4.348	4.167	4.000	3.846	3.704	3.571	3.448	3.333	3.226	3.125	3.030	2.941	2.857	2.500	2.222	2.000

Texas Instruments BA-35, BAII, BAII Plus[c]

Input	Function
700	PMT
5	N
8	%i
	CPT
	FV

Solution
2794.90 [d]

[c] For the Texas Instruments BAII, you would use the **2nd** key instead of the **CPT** key; for the Texas Instruments BAII Plus, you would use the **I/Y** key instead of the **%i** key.

[d] If a minus sign precedes the output, it should be ignored.

INDEX